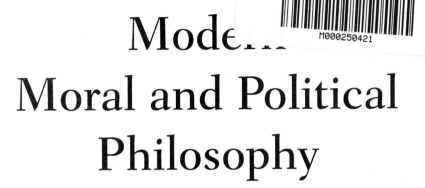

Modern Moral and Political Philosophy

Robert C. Cummins

University of California, Davis

Thomas D. Christiano

University of Arizona

Mayfield Publishing Company

Mountain View, California

London • Toronto

This book is dedicated to the memory of Niccolò Machiavelli,
who, tortured for his lifelong devotion to the Republic of Florence,
would not submit or bear false witness to save himself.
He must be the most widely misunderstood figure
in the history of political philosophy.

Copyright © 1999 by Mayfield Publishing Company

Library of Congress Cataloging-in-Publication Data

Cummins, Robert, 1944–
    Modern moral and political philosophy / Robert C. Cummins, Thomas
D. Christiano.
        p.   cm.
    Includes bibliographical references.
    ISBN 0-7674-0283-9 (alk. paper)
    1. Political science—Philosophy. 2. Ethics. I. Christiano,
Thomas. II. Title.
JA71.C85   1998
320'.01—dc21   98-8247
                                                                CIP

Manufactured in the United States of America
10 9 8 7 6 5 4 3 2 1

Mayfield Publishing Company
1280 Villa Street
Mountain View, CA 94041

Sponsoring editor, Ken King; *production editors,* Linda Ward and Lynn Rabin-Bauer; *copy editor,* Anne Montague; *design and art manager,* Jean Mailander; *text and cover designer,* Joan Greenfield; *photo researcher,* Brian Pecko; *manufacturing manager,* Randy Hurst. The text was set in 9.5/12 Century Book by TBH Typecast, Inc., and printed on 45# Glatfelter Restorecote by Malloy Lithographing, Inc.

Cover: *Sala delle Prospective* by Baldassare Peruzzi, fresco, 1518–19, Villa Farnesina, Rome.
© Scala/Art Resource, NY.

Contents

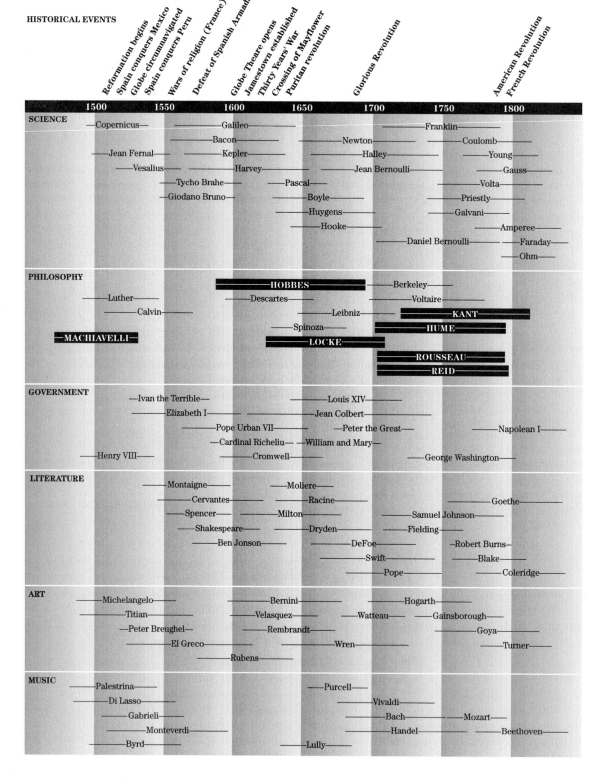

HISTORICAL EVENTS

Reformation begins
Spain conquers Mexico
Globe circumnavigated
Spain conquers Peru
Wars of religion (France)
Defeat of Spanish Armada
Globe Theare opens
Jamestown established
Thirty Years' War
Crossing of Mayflower
Puritan revolution
Glorious Revolution
American Revolution
French Revolution

1500   1550   1600   1650   1700   1750   1800

SCIENCE

—Copernicus—
————Galileo————
————Franklin————
————Bacon————
————Newton————
————Coulomb————
—Jean Fernal—
—Kepler—
————Halley————
————Young————
—Vesalius—
————Harvey————
————Jean Bernoulli————
————Gauss————
—Tycho Brahe—
————Pascal————
————Volta————
—Giodano Bruno—
————Boyle————
————Priestly————
————Huygens————
————Galvani————
————Hooke————
————Amperee————
————Daniel Bernoulli————
————Faraday————
————Ohm————

PHILOSOPHY

————HOBBES————
————Berkeley————
————Descartes————
————Voltaire————
—Luther——
—Calvin——
————Leibniz————
———KANT———
—MACHIAVELLI—
————Spinoza————
———HUME———
————LOCKE————
———ROUSSEAU———
———REID———

GOVERNMENT

—Ivan the Terrible—
————Louis XIV————
—Elizabeth I—
————Jean Colbert————
—Pope Urban VII—
————Peter the Great————
————Napolean I————
—Cardinal Richeliu——William and Mary—
—Henry VIII—
————Cromwell————
————George Washington————

LITERATURE

—Montaigne—
————Moliere————
—Cervantes—
————Racine————
————Goethe————
—Spencer—
————Milton————
————Samuel Johnson————
—Shakespeare—
————Dryden————
————Fielding————
—Ben Jonson—
————DeFoe————
—Robert Burns—
————Swift————
————Blake————
————Pope————
————Coleridge————

ART

—Michelangelo—
————Bernini————
————Hogarth————
—Titian—
————Velasquez————
————Watteau————
————Gainsborough————
—Peter Breughel—
————Rembrandt————
————Goya————
—El Greco—
————Wren————
————Turner————
————Rubens————

MUSIC

—Palestrina—
————Purcell————
—Di Lasso—
————Vivaldi————
—Gabrieli—
————Bach————
————Mozart————
—Monteverdi—
————Handel————
————Beethoven————
—Byrd—
————Lully————

Preface

THE EARLY MODERN PERIOD IN WESTERN EUROPE PRODUCED AN UNPRECEDENTED flowering of science, philosophy, and art. For moral and political thought, the early modern period is seminal. It experienced the European discovery of the new world, calling into question the universality of Western values. It saw the traumatic breakup of the Christian Church in the West, requiring people to learn how to deal with fundamental disagreements. It saw the rise of the modern nation state with its immense power and uncertain legitimacy. All the authors represented in this book after Machiavelli were deeply concerned to find an adequate ground for moral and political theorizing in the light of these revolutionary changes. The authors represented in this book—Machiavelli, Hobbes, Locke, Hume, Reid, Rousseau, and Kant—constitute, along with Plato and Aristotle, the core of Western moral and political philosophy, and hence of many courses in philosophy and political science. Yet there has been no single text that pulls this material together into one volume. This left instructors with the unwelcome prospect of ordering several books, a costly business, and risky too, since, all too often, one or more of the books didn't show up on time.

Included in this volume are the central texts of the period. We have endeavored to keep editing to a minimum, preferring complete texts whenever possible. Only in the case of Hobbes' Leviathan have we omitted chapters, and these we think few would regard as essential to the development of the main argument. In keeping with the needs of an undergraduate course, scholarly apparatus is absent in the interest of readability, but, of course, the author's original footnotes have been retained. Each author is introduced with a brief biography (an autobiography in Hume's case) and some notes on the text designed to introduce the student to the central themes. We have not attempted to provide extended interpretations; those belong in the academic journals. Unless otherwise noted, all translations are our own.

ACKNOWLEDGMENTS

We thank Frank Romer of the Classics Department, Julia Annas of the Philosophy Department, and Dan Russell, graduate student in Philosophy at the University of Arizona for help in translating or locating translations of some of the Greek and Latin quotes in the texts. We also thank Ann Montague for her patient and careful copyediting of the text. Linda Ward at Mayfield faithfully shepherded the manuscript through the various stages of the process of production, taking last-minute changes easily in stride. Finally, Ken King, aside from being a helpful and patient editor, helped us locate a more modern and readable text of Hobbes's Leviathan. Moreover, he must be one of the last editors in academic publishing who can offer a contract over the phone in response to a fifteen-minute pitch.

Some Suggested Syllabi

MODERN MORAL PHILOSOPHY

    Machiavelli, *The Prince*, chapters 7, 8, 15–18

    Hobbes, *Leviathan*, all selections through chapter 17

    Hume, *Treatise of Human Nature*, book III, part I; part II, sections 1–6; part III

    Rousseau, *Discourse on Inequality*

    Reid, *Essays on the Active Powers of Man*, essay III, part III; essay V

    Kant, *Foundations of the Metaphysics of Morals*

POLITICAL PHILOSOPHY (emphasizing the problem of reconciling individual interest with the common good)

    Machiavelli, *The Prince*

    Hobbes, *Leviathan*, all selections

    Locke, *Second Treatise on Civil Government*

    Hume, *Treatise of Human Nature*, book III, part II, sections 1–11

    Rousseau, *Discourse on Inequality* and *The Social Contract*

POLITICAL PHILOSOPHY (emphasizing issues of social contract theory)

    Hobbes, *Leviathan*, all selections

    Locke, *Second Treatise on Civil Government* and *Letter Concerning Toleration*

    Hume, *Treatise of Human Nature*, book III, part II, sections 1–11; "Of the Original Contract"

    Reid, *Essays on the Active Powers*, essay V, chapters 1, 3, 5, 6

    Rousseau, *Discourse on Inequality* and *The Social Contract*

    Kant, "Metaphysical First Principles"

MODERN MORAL AND POLITICAL PHILOSOPHY

    Machiavelli, *The Prince*, chapters 7, 8, 15–18

    Hobbes, *Leviathan*, selections through chapter 19

    Locke, *Second Treatise on Civil Government*, chapters 1–11, 18–19

    Rousseau, *The Social Contract*, books I, II, IV chapters 1–3, 8

    Hume, *Treatise of Human Nature*, book III, part I; part II, sections 1–6; part III, sections 1, 6

    Reid, *Essays on the Active Powers*, essay III, part III, chapters 1, 2, 5; essay V, chapters 4, 5, 7

    Kant, *Foundations of the Metaphysics of Morals*

Niccolò Machiavelli

MORE, PERHAPS, THAN IN THE CASE OF ANY OTHER PHILOSOPHER, MACHIAVELLI'S life story, his career, and his writings are inseparable from the political history of his state (though Hobbes comes to mind as well). To tell Machiavelli's story is to tell the story of Florence, the republic he served.

In 1469, the same year that Lorenzo "the Magnificent" de' Medici came to power, Machiavelli was born on May 3 in Florence into a family with a long history of public service. His father was a lawyer employed by the state. Though Machiavelli complains of having been poor, the family seems to have been well enough off to afford a country house in addition to their house in town. Though little is known about his childhood, he apparently enjoyed an affectionate and secure upbringing. His homelife, however, stood in stark contrast to the troubles that plagued Florence throughout Machiavelli's life, troubles that shaped Machiavelli's career and his thought. When he was nine, the Pazzi family, with the pope's support, plotted to kill Lorenzo de' Medici and his brother Giuliano. They assassinated Giuliano, but not Lorenzo. An enraged, or perhaps frightened, populace rallied to Lorenzo and went on a bloody rampage against the Pazzi and their supporters. The carnage, and the papal intrigue that caused it, made a deep impression on the young Machiavelli.

Machiavelli's education was typical for a young Florentine gentleman of the time, consisting mainly of the ancient Roman and Greek authors. Examples and lessons from those authors dominated all of his thinking and writing, as it did with most of his Italian contemporaries, whose model of learning was less the discovery of new knowledge than the rediscovery of lost wisdom. Unlike many of his contemporaries, however, Machiavelli always took his reading with a grain of salt, maintaining a sardonic, tongue-in-cheek attitude throughout what we will see was a very trying career in public service.

In 1492 Lorenzo de' Medici died and was succeeded by his son Piero, who was then only twenty-one and far too inexperienced to deal with the complexities of the delicate political and military situation that was Florence, surrounded as it was by hostile papal lands to the south and east, and Milan to the north. Piero foolishly supported the king of Naples in his dispute with Milan and the French. When the French inevitably marched through Florence in 1494 on their way to Naples, Pisa, an important Florentine possession, revolted, and the Florentines took the opportunity to drive out the Medici. The result was a religious republic headed by the Dominican friar Savonarola (infamous for the bonfires of the vanities, a wholesale destruction of art and literature) and governed by a Grand Council of 1,000 and a Small Council of 80, an arrangement that lasted just eighteen years. Machiavelli seems to have approved of Savonarola's attack on Florentine "moral corruption," but he didn't care for his religious and political policies. The French held on to Naples less than two years, and Florence found itself now allied to a humiliated France opposed by the pope, Naples, Venice, and Spain.

Machiavelli may have gained some reputation by predicting both disasters in succession. In any case, when Savonarola was burned at the stake in 1498, Machiavelli was nominated by the Small Council, and elected by the Grand Council, to the important posts of secretary to the second chancery of the republic, and as secretary to the Ten, a committee responsible for diplomatic and military affairs. He was, in a sense, a hired technocrat, whose job was to raise taxes, prepare defenses, and to predict the wars and the ever shifting alliances that controlled the fate of his city. (Machiavelli was always an employee of the state, never a politician in his own right. One plausible theory is that his father was illegitimate, which would have barred Machiavelli from elected office.) Almost immediately, a fiasco occurred that confirmed Machiavelli's lifelong distrust of the then universal practice of relying exclusively on mercenaries for military matters. Paolo Vitelli was hired to recapture Pisa. He breached the walls, and victory seemed certain, when suddenly he withdrew, allowing Pisa to repair the walls. At the urging of the Ten, Vitelli was executed, but the damage was done.

Florence once again sought help from France, where Louis XII had just become king, succeeding Charles VIII, and was anxious to erase the humiliation his predecessor had suffered in Italy. Louis lent French and Swiss mercenaries to Florence for the recapture of Pisa, but the scheme ended in disaster when the soldiers mutinied. The result of this double catastrophe in Pisa was Machiavelli's first major diplomatic mission to Paris. There he seems to have impressed the prime minister, Cardinal d'Amboise, for, after Machiavelli's return, the French took Machiavelli's advice and intervened to curb Cesare Borgia's scheme to gobble up Florentine land as part of his French-supported conquest of neighboring Romagna.

Gratifying as this personal success was, the outcome was less than could be desired. Cesare Borgia, though supported by the French, was mainly dependent on the pope, Alexander VI, who happened to be his father. Machiavelli rightly predicted that in view of the pope's advancing age, Borgia would have to press quickly to secure his holdings, for he could hardly count on another Borgia pope. Cesare only appeared to stay out of Florentine affairs. Using various agents, including Vitelli's brother Vitellozzo, he induced the communes of Arezzo and Valdichiana to revolt against Florence. As a second to Bishop Soberini, Machiavelli was sent to sound out Cesare, to talk him out of his anti-Florentine activities, or at least to buy time. Perhaps Pope Alexander would die, or, even more hopeful, a conspiracy of Cesare's own commanders incited by Florence would succeed in bringing him down. Cesare appeared to back off, but it was a ruse. He lured the rebellious commanders to a meeting, where he had them strangled. Machiavelli returned both impressed and frightened by Cesare Borgia.

In the event, the crisis was resolved, as Machiavelli predicted it might be, by the pope's death in 1503. Machiavelli went to Rome for the election of Julius II, who impressed Machiavelli even more by outmaneuvering Cesare Borgia and ultimately destroying him. This, however, left a power vacuum in Romagna, which led to threats from Venice and the Spanish. That crisis, in 1504, sent Machiavelli to Paris again. A delicate balance of power was worked out, and Florence narrowly escaped foreign invasion. The incident was celebrated by Machiavelli's poem the *Decannale*, commemorating ten years of republican survival in Florence. At the end of the poem, however, Machiavelli predicted more trouble (a safe prediction, as the reader must realize by now), and, radically, urging the formation of a citizen militia to replace the traditional reliance on mercenaries.

By this time, Machiavelli was a seasoned diplomat and political spin doctor with a considerable reputation. His confidence, however, seems to have been seriously undermined by an incident that occurred in 1506. Julius II marched unarmed into rebellious Perugia, and, rather than losing his life as Machiavelli predicted, returned to Rome with the keys to the city. While this had no immediate impact on Florence, the incident had a profound effect on Machiavelli, who struggled to rationalize the whole affair in various ways for the rest of his life. It is worth keeping in mind that Machiavelli evidently thought of Julius's success in Perugia as a kind of counterexample to his political theories.

Machiavelli finally persuaded the city to allow him to implement his radical plan to form a citizen militia, and in 1509 he seemed vindicated when the new 10,000-man militia finally recovered Pisa. His success was short-lived, however. In the face of rising Venetian power, the pope united with France and Spain to subdue them. Venice collapsed, but saved itself by sowing dissension among its precariously allied enemies. The resulting break between Pope Julius II and France was a disaster for Florence, for Florence was dependent on and equal to neither. Rather than try to pick the winner, Machiavelli undertook two missions to Paris to try to repair the break. It didn't work, however, and in 1512 the French were driven out of Italy by an alliance between the pope and the Spanish. Spanish troops smashed Machiavelli's beloved militia, and the Medici were returned to power in Florence, effectively ending the republic.

Machiavelli was dismissed from office, of course. But worse followed. A failed conspiracy against the Medici had used Machiavelli's name to round up support; whether it was with Machiavelli's knowledge is not known. An order for Machiavelli's arrest was issued, and Machiavelli turned himself in, knowing he would be tortured by *strappado:* being hung by the wrists and periodically dropped several feet until the rope snapped tight again. Nearly everyone subjected to this treatment confessed whether they were guilty or not, even knowing that confession was generally followed by execution. Machiavelli endured six drops in three days, but never confessed. The torturers were not convinced, but Machiavelli was released from jail on the condition that he not leave the environs of Florence. During this forced retirement, Machiavelli wrote the *Discourses on the First Ten Books of Livy*, a discussion of the republican form of government. He also began his most famous work, *The Prince*.

The following year, Machiavelli was pardoned as part of a general amnesty proclaimed to celebrate the election of Giovanni de' Medici, brother to the ruler of Florence, to the papacy. There followed a frustrating period of failed attempts to reenter public life under a regime that profoundly mistrusted Machiavelli's republican past and sympathies. Some have suggested that *The Prince* was written partly to demonstrate that Machiavelli had something to offer the Medici as well. *The Prince* is couched as advice to a new hereditary ruler, an outsider put in control of a new state. The pope was certainly looking about for a state suitable for his brother Giuliano, something he eventually found in Umbria. In any case, Machiavelli finally did secure a job as historian of Florence. He completed his history in 1525 and traveled to Rome to present it to Giulio de' Medici, by then Pope Clement VII. He died two years later on June 20, 1527.

NOTES ON THE TEXT

The Prince was revolutionary in Machiavelli's own day and has remained a profound challenge to moral and political philosophy since. Machiavelli meant it essentially as a kind of book of advice to rulers. Primarily he intended it for new princes who desired to conquer and then hold on to new acquisitions. Many such books were published in Italy in the fifteenth century, and books of advice to rulers had been prominent in the ancient world. They espoused honesty, fidelity, generosity, humaneness, and justice as among the most useful attributes of a ruler and criticized debauchery and sexual license as sure to be his downfall. They also tended to play down the role of armed force in politics on the grounds that a virtuous ruler would be loved by his subjects. Machiavelli rarely discusses morality except to reject moralism entirely in favor of a more apparently realistic approach. He counsels honesty when it is useful but notes that dishonesty is often necessary to maintain power. He recommends the breaking of promises and the most hideous of murders as a prince's means to achieve his ends. The most praised person in *The Prince* is Cesare Borgia, whose exploits are described in gory detail in chapter 7.

Machiavelli condones evil not for its own sake but only as a means to the achievement of political power and ultimately the glory and honor, which are the main aims he ascribes to those who pretend to rulership. Machiavelli's endorsement of evil means must also be understood against the background of his pessimistic view of human nature. He sees human beings as essentially duplicitous, self-absorbed, slaves to intense and unruly passions, fickle, gullible, and amoral. In such a dog-eat-dog world one cannot achieve any of the ends one desires without heeding the advice offered in *The Prince*.

The advice consists in counsels of prudence. Machiavelli does not consider being guided by one's self-interest to be an easy achievement. What is quite striking about Machiavelli's discussion is the complexity of emotions that he attributes to people and the important part these play in his political theory. The prince must avoid being tempted by flattery or deceived by other aspirants to power. He must be able to act cruelly and unjustly when circumstances require. He must be devoted to the study and cultivation of the arts of warfare. The prince must be prepared for constant changes in fortunes. He must be flexible and willing to alter his plans. Princes must avoid the pitfalls of rigidity, irresoluteness, lack of spirit, and vulnerability to bad luck. (Princes generally fail to adhere to these difficult demands and thereby fail to achieve their aims; so *The Prince* ends on a note of pessimism.)

The prince must rule with an eye to fostering fear and love in his subjects and avoiding their hatred and contempt. Fear is to be trusted more than love, however, because it is a more stable and effective motivation. Hence, the prince must have a good army: a good army is the foundation of good laws. Machiavelli makes detailed recommendations about the organization of the army.

Hatred and contempt can be avoided in large part by simulation and dissimulation. The prince must be harsh with his resistant subjects all at once and then desist in order to instill fear but not inspire hatred. In an interesting passage, Machiavelli endorses the action of Cesare Borgia, whose henchman murdered a number of persons in Romagna. While these actions brought about peace and order to Romagna, they also inspired a growing hatred of Borgia. In order to stem this hatred, Borgia had his henchman executed and publicly dismembered to the satisfaction of his subjects. The prince can rely on the fact that people do not know how power is organized and they are overawed by his majesty. He must also engage in bold and novel projects in order to impress his subjects. Finally, Machiavelli repeatedly insists that the most effective ways of avoiding the hatred and contempt of his subjects is to desist from taking their property and violating their womenfolk. This is the one point where Machiavelli seems to agree with the traditional endorsement of morality.

It should be noted that though Machiavelli's advice shows the prince the road to personal glory and is disdainful of moral constraints, he also thinks that a prince who follows his advice will bring about the benefits of peace and order for nearly all his subjects. Machiavelli often repeats his contention that princes who try to be just or humane end up bringing about far greater disasters for their subjects.

The order of discussion in *The Prince* is roughly as follows.

Chapters 1–3 classify the different kinds of states and delimit the object of Machiavelli's concern. Chapters 4–11 identify the different ways one can come to power and the vicissitudes of rulership under these different circumstances. They also announce many of the main themes of the book. Chapters 12–14 discuss the importance of armies to political power and how they should be organized. Chapters 15–18 discuss Machiavelli's revolutionary views about morality in politics. Chapters 19–21 discuss the all-important task of maintaining the respect of the population. Chapters 22–23 discuss the topic of what kind of advisers the prince should choose and how to deal with his advisers. Chapters 24–25 discuss the role of luck in human affairs and how to handle it. Chapter 26 concludes with an analysis of the prospects for change in sixteenth-century Italy.

The Prince

Niccolò Machiavelli to Lorenzo the Magnificent, Son of Piero di Medici

It is customary for those who wish to gain the favour of a prince to endeavour to do so by offering him gifts of those things which they hold most precious, or in which they know him to take especial delight. In this way princes are often presented with horses, arms, cloth of gold, gems, and such-like ornaments worthy of their grandeur. In my desire, however, to offer to Your Highness some humble testimony of my devotion, I have been unable to find among my possessions anything which I hold so dear or esteem so highly as that knowledge of the deeds of great men which I have acquired through a long experience of modern events and a constant study of the past.

With the utmost diligence I have long pondered and scrutinised the actions of the great, and now I offer the results to Your Highness within the compass of a small volume: and although I deem this work unworthy of Your Highness's acceptance, yet my confidence in your humanity assures me that you will receive it with favour, knowing that it is not in my power to offer you a greater gift than that of enabling you to understand in a very short time all those things which I have learnt at the cost of privation and danger in the course of many years. I have not sought to adorn my work with long phrases or high-sounding words or any of those superficial attractions and ornaments with which many writers seek to embellish their material, as I desire no honour for my work but such as the novelty and gravity of its subject may justly deserve. Nor will it, I trust, be deemed presumptuous on the part of a man of humble and obscure condition to attempt to discuss and direct the government of princes; for in the same way that landscape painters station themselves in the valleys in order to draw mountains or high ground, and ascend an eminence in order to get a good view of the plains, so it is necessary to be a prince to know thoroughly the nature of the people, and one of the populace to know the nature of princes.

May I trust, therefore, that Your Highness will accept this little gift in the spirit in which it is offered; and if Your Highness will deign to peruse it, you will recognise in it my ardent desire that you may attain to that grandeur which fortune and your own merits presage for you.

And should Your Highness gaze down from the summit of your lofty position towards this humble spot, you will recognise the great and unmerited sufferings inflicted on me by a cruel fate.

Chapter I
*The Various Kinds of Government
and the Ways by Which They Are Established*

All states and dominions which hold or have held sway over mankind are either republics or monarchies. Monarchies are either hereditary, in which the rulers have been for many years of the same family, or else they are of recent foundation. The newly founded ones are either entirely new, as was Milan to Francesco Sforza, or else they are, as it were, new members grafted on to the hereditary possessions of the prince that annexes them, as is the kingdom of Naples to the King of Spain. The dominions thus acquired have either been previously accustomed to the rule of another prince, or else have been free states, and they are annexed either by force of arms of the prince himself, or of others, or else fall to him by good fortune or special ability.

Chapter II
Of Hereditary Monarchies

I will not here speak of republics, having already treated of them fully in another place. I will deal only with monarchies, and will discuss how the various kinds described above can be governed and maintained. In the first place, the difficulty of maintaining hereditary states accustomed to a reigning family is far less than in new monarchies; for it is sufficient not to transgress ancestral usages, and to adapt one's self to unforeseen circumstances; in this way such a prince, if of ordinary assiduity, will always be able to maintain his position, unless some very exceptional and excessive force deprives him of it; and even if he be thus deprived, on the slightest mischance happening to the new occupier, he will be able to regain it.

We have in Italy the example of the Duke of Ferrara, who was able to withstand the assaults of the Venetians in 1484 and of Pope Julius in 1510, for no other reason than because of the antiquity of his family in that dominion. Inasmuch as the legitimate prince has less cause and less necessity to give offence, it is only natural that he should be more loved; and, if no extraordinary vices make him hated, it is only reasonable for his subjects to be naturally attached to him, the memories and causes of innovations being forgotten in the long period over which his rule has extended; whereas one change always leaves the way prepared for the introduction of another.

Chapter III
Of Mixed Monarchies

But it is in the new monarchy that difficulties really exist. First, if it is not entirely new, but a member, as it were, of a mixed state, its disorders spring at first from a natural difficulty which exists in all new dominions, because men change masters willingly, hoping to better themselves; and this belief makes them take arms against their rulers, in which they are deceived, as experience later proves that they have gone from bad to worse. This is the result of another very natural cause, which is the inevitable harm inflicted on those over whom the prince obtains dominion, both by his soldiers and by an infinite number of other injuries caused by his occupation.

Thus you find enemies in all those whom you have injured by occupying that dominion, and you cannot maintain the friendship of those who have helped you to obtain this possession, as you will not be able to fulfill their expectations, nor can you use strong measures with them, being under an obligation to them; for which reason, however strong your armies may be, you will always need the favour of the inhabitants to take possession of a province. It was from these causes that Louis XII of France, though able to occupy Milan without trouble, immediately lost it, and the forces of Ludovico alone were sufficient to take it from him the first time, for the inhabitants who had willingly opened their gates to him, finding themselves deluded in the hopes they had cherished and not obtaining those benefits they had anticipated, could not bear the vexatious rule of their new prince.

It is indeed true that, after reconquering rebel territories, they are not so easily lost again, for the ruler is now, by the fact of the rebellion, less averse to secure his position by punishing offenders, unmasking suspects, and strengthening himself in weak places. So that although the mere appearance of such a person as Duke Ludovico on the frontier was sufficient to cause France to lose Milan the first time, to make her lose her grip of it the second time was only possible when all the world was against her, and after her armies had been defeated and driven out of Italy; which was the result of the causes above mentioned. Nevertheless it was taken from her both the first and the second time. The general causes of the first loss have been already discussed; it remains now to be seen what were the causes of the second loss and by what means France could have avoided it, or what measures might have been taken by another ruler in that position which were not taken by the King of France. Be it observed, therefore, that those states which on annexation are united to a previously existing state may or may not be of the same nationality and language. If they are, it is very easy to hold them, especially if they are not accustomed to freedom; and to possess them securely it suffices that the family of the princes which formerly governed them be extinct. For the rest, their old condition not being disturbed, and there being no dissimilarity of customs, the people settle down quietly under their new rulers, as is seen in the case of Burgundy, Brittany, Gascony, and Normandy, which have been so long united to France; and although there may be some slight differences of language, the customs of the people are nevertheless similar, and they can get along well together. Whoever obtains possession of such territories and wishes to retain them must bear in mind two things: the one, that the blood of their old rulers be extinct; the other, to make no alteration either in their laws or in their taxes; in this way they will in a very short space of time become united with their old possessions and form one state.

But when dominions are acquired in a province differing in language, laws, and customs, the difficulties to be overcome are great, and it requires good fortune as well as great industry to retain them; one of the best and most certain means of doing so would be for the new ruler to take up his residence there. This would render possession more secure and durable, and it is what the Turk has done in Greece. In spite of all the other measures taken by him to hold that state, it would not have been possible to retain it had he not gone to live there. Being on the spot, disorders can be seen as they arise and can quickly be remedied, but living at a distance, they are only heard of when they get beyond remedy. Besides which, the province is not despoiled by your officials, the subjects being able to obtain satisfaction by direct recourse to their prince; and wishing to be loyal they have more reason to love him, and should they be otherwise inclined they will have greater cause to fear him. Any external Power who wishes to assail that state will be less disposed to do so; so that as long as he resides there he will be very hard to dispossess.

The other and better remedy is to plant colonies in one or two of those places which form, as it were, the keys of the land, for it is necessary either to do this or to maintain a large force of armed men. The colonies will cost the prince little; with little or no expense on his part, he can send and maintain them; he only injures those whose lands and houses are taken to give to the new inhabitants, and these form but a small proportion of the state, and those who are injured, remaining poor and scattered, can never do any harm to him, and all the others are, on the one hand, not injured and therefore easily pacified; and, on the other, are fearful of offending lest they should be treated like those who have been dispossessed. To conclude, these colonies cost nothing, are more faithful, and give less offence; and the injured parties, being poor and scattered, are unable to do mischief, as I have shown. For it must be noted that men must either be caressed or else annihilated; they will revenge themselves for small injuries, but cannot do so for great ones; the injury therefore that we do to a man must be such that we need not fear his vengeance. But by maintaining a garrison instead of colonists, one will spend much more, and consume all the revenues of that state in guarding it, so that the acquisition will result in a loss, besides giving much greater offence, since it injures every one in that state with the quartering of the army on it; which being an inconvenience felt by all, every one becomes an enemy, and these are enemies which can do mischief, as, though beaten, they remain in their own homes. In every way, therefore, a garrison is as useless as colonies are useful.

Further, the ruler of a foreign province as described should make himself the leader and defender of his less powerful neighbours, and endeavour to weaken the stronger ones, and take care that they are not invaded by some foreigner not less powerful than himself. And it will be always the case that he will be invited to intervene at the request of those who are discontented either through ambition or fear, as was seen when the Ætolians invited the Romans into Greece; and in whatever province they entered, it was always at the request of the inhabitants. And the rule is that when a powerful foreigner enters a province, all the less powerful inhabitants become his adherents, moved by the envy they bear to those ruling over them; so much so that with regard to these minor potentates he has no trouble whatever in winning them over, for they willingly join forces with the state that he has acquired. He has merely to be careful that they do not assume too much power and authority, and he can easily with his own forces and their favour put down those that are powerful and remain in everything arbiter of that province. And he who does not govern well in this way will soon lose what he has acquired, and while he holds it will meet with infinite difficulty and trouble.

The Romans in the provinces they took, always followed this policy; they established colonies, inveigled the less powerful without increasing their strength, put down the most powerful and did not allow foreign rulers to obtain influence in them. I will adduce the province of Greece as a sole example. They made friends with the Achæans and the Ætolians, the kingdom of Macedonia was cast down, and Antiochus driven out, nor did they allow the merits of the Achæans or the Ætolians to gain them any increase of territory, nor did the persuasions of Philip induce them to befriend him without reducing his influence, nor could the power of Antiochus make them consent to allow him to hold any state in that province.

For the Romans did in these cases what all wise princes should do, who consider not only present but also future discords and diligently guard against them; for being foreseen they can easily be remedied, but if one waits till they are at hand, the medicine is no longer in time, as the malady has become incurable; it happening with this as with those hectic fevers, as doctors say, which at their beginning are easy to cure but difficult to recognise, but in course of time when they have not at first been recognised and treated, become easy to recognise and difficult to cure. Thus it happens in matters of state; for knowing afar off (which it is only given to a prudent man to do) the evils that are brewing, they are easily cured. But when, for want of such knowledge, they are allowed to grow so that every one can recognise them, there is no longer any remedy to be found. Therefore, the Romans, observing disorders while yet remote, were always able to find a remedy, and never allowed them to increase in order to avoid a war; for they knew that war is not to be avoided, and can be deferred only to the advantage of the other side; they therefore declared war against Philip and Antiochus in Greece, so as not to have to fight them in Italy, though they might at the time have avoided either; this they did not choose to do, never caring to do that which is now every day to be heard in the mouths of our wise men, namely to enjoy the advantages of delay, but preferring to trust their own virtue and prudence; for time brings with it all things, and may produce indifferently either good or evil.

But let us return to France and examine whether she did any of these things; and I will speak not of Charles, but of Louis as the one whose proceedings can be better seen, as he held possession in Italy for a longer time; you will then see that he did the opposite of all those things which must be done to keep possession of a foreign state. King Louis was called into Italy by the ambition of the Venetians, who wished by his coming to gain half of Lombardy. I will not blame the king for coming nor for the part he took, because wishing to plant his foot in Italy, and not having friends in the country, on the contrary the conduct of King Charles having caused all doors to be closed to him, he was forced to accept what friendships he could find, and his schemes would have speedily been successful if he had made no mistakes in his other proceedings.

The king then, having acquired Lombardy, immediately won back the reputation lost by Charles. Genoa yielded, the Florentines became his friends, the Marquis of Mantua, the Dukes of Ferrara and Bentivogli, the Lady of Forlì, the Lords of Faenza, Pesaro, Rimini, Camerino, and Piombino, the inhabitants of Lucca, of Pisa, and of Siena, all approached him with offers of friendship. The Venetians might then have seen the effects of their temerity, how to gain a few cities in Lombardy they had made the king ruler over two-thirds of Italy.

Consider how little difficulty the king would have had in maintaining his reputation in Italy if he had observed the aforesaid rules, and kept a firm and sure hold over all those friends of his, who being many in number and weak, and fearful, one of the Church, another of the Venetians, were always obliged to hold fast to him, and by whose aid he could easily make sure of any who were still great. But he was hardly in Milan before he did exactly the opposite, by giving aid to Pope Alexander to occupy the Romagna. Nor did he perceive that, in taking this course, he weakened himself, by casting off his friends and those who had fled to his protection, and strengthened the Church by adding further temporal powers to the spiritual power, which gives it such authority. And having made the first mistake, he was obliged to follow it up, whilst, to put a stop to the ambition of Alexander and prevent him becoming ruler of Tuscany, he was forced to come to Italy. And not content with having increased the power of the Church and lost his friends, he, now coveting the kingdom of Naples, divided it with the King of Spain; and where he alone was the arbiter of Italy, he now brought in a companion, so that the ambitious of that province who were dissatisfied with him might have some one else to appeal to; and where he might have left in that kingdom a king tributary to himself, he dispossessed him in order to bring in another who was capable of driving him out.

The desire to acquire possessions is a very natural and ordinary thing, and when those men do it who can do so successfully, they are always praised and not blamed, but when they cannot and yet want to do so at all costs, they make a mistake deserving of great blame. If France, therefore, with her own forces could have taken Naples, she ought to have done so; if she could not, she ought not to have shared it. And if the partition of Lombardy with the Venetians is to be excused, as having been the means of allowing the French king to set foot in Italy, this other partition deserves blame, not having the excuse of necessity.

Louis had thus made these five mistakes: he had crushed the smaller Powers, increased the power in Italy of one potentate, brought into the land a very powerful foreigner, he had not come to live there himself, nor had he established any colonies. Still these mistakes, if he had lived, might not have injured him, had he not made the sixth, that of taking the state from the Venetians; for, if he had not strengthened the Church and brought the Spaniards into Italy, it would have been right and necessary to humble them; having once taken those measures, he ought never to have consented to their ruin; because, had the Venetians been strong, it would have kept the others from making attempts on Lombardy partly because the Venetians would not have consented to any measures by which they did not get it for themselves, and partly because the others would not have wanted to take it from France to give it to Venice, and would not have had the courage to attack both.

If any one urges that King Louis yielded Romagna to Alexander and the kingdom of Naples to Spain in order to avoid war, I reply, with the reasons already given, that one ought never to allow a disorder to take place in order to avoid war, for war is not thereby avoided, but only deferred to your disadvantage. And if others allege the promise given by the king to the pope to undertake that enterprise for him, in return for the dissolution of his marriage and for the cardinalship of Rohan, I reply with what I shall say later on about the faith of princes and how it is to be observed. Thus King Louis lost Lombardy through not observing any of those conditions which have been observed by others who have taken provinces and wished to retain them. Nor is this any miracle, but very reasonable and natural. I spoke of this matter with Cardinal Rohan at Nantes when Valentine, as Cesare Borgia, son of Pope Alexander, was commonly called, was occupying the Romagna, for on Cardinal Rohan saying to me that the Italians did not understand war, I replied that the French did not understand politics, for if they did they would never allow the Church to become so great. And experience shows us that the greatness in Italy of the Church and also of Spain have been caused by France, and her ruin has proceeded from them. From which may be drawn a general rule, which never or very rarely fails, that whoever is the cause of another becoming powerful is ruined himself; for that power is produced by him either through craft or force, and both of these are suspected by the one who has been raised to power.

Chapter IV
Why the Kingdom of Darius,
Occupied by Alexander, Did Not Rebel Against
the Successors of the Latter After His Death

Considering the difficulties there are in holding a newly acquired state, some may wonder how it came to pass that Alexander the Great became master of Asia in a few years, and had hardly occupied it when he died, from which it might be supposed that the whole state would have rebelled. However, his successors maintained themselves in possession, and had no further difficulties in doing so than those which arose among themselves from their own ambitions.

I reply that the kingdoms known to history have been governed in two ways: either by a prince and his servants, who, as ministers by his grace and permission, assist in governing the realm; or by a prince and by barons, who hold their positions not by favour of the ruler but by antiquity of blood. Such barons have states and subjects of their own, who recognise them as their lords, and are naturally attached to them. In those states which are governed by a prince and his servants, the prince possesses more authority, because there is no one in the state regarded as a superior other than himself, and if others are obeyed it is merely as ministers and officials of the prince, and no one regards them with any special affection.

Examples of these two kinds of government in our own time are those of the Turk and the King of France. All the Turkish monarchy is governed by one ruler, the others are his servants, and dividing his kingdom into "sangiacates," he sends to them various administrators, and changes or recalls them at his pleasure. But the King of France is surrounded by a large number of ancient nobles, recognised as such by their subjects, and loved by them; they have their prerogatives, of which the king cannot deprive them without danger to himself. Whoever now considers these two states will see that it would be difficult to acquire the state of the Turk; but having conquered it, it would be very easy to hold it. In many respects, on the other hand, it would be easier to conquer the kingdom of France, but there would be great difficulty in holding it.

The causes of the difficulty of occupying the Turkish kingdom are, that the invader could not be invited by princes of that kingdom, nor hope to facilitate his enterprise by the rebellion of those near the ruler's person, as will be evident from reasons given above. Because, being all slaves, and dependent, it will be more difficult to corrupt them, and even if they were corrupted, little effect could be hoped for as they would not be able to carry the people with them for the reasons mentioned. Therefore, whoever assaults the Turk must be prepared to meet his united forces, and must rely more on his own strength than on the disorders of others; but having once conquered him, and beaten him in battle so that he can no longer raise armies, nothing else is to be feared except the family of the prince, and if this be extinguished, there is no longer any one to be feared, others having no credit with the people; and as the victor before the victory could place no hope in them, so he need not fear them afterwards.

The contrary is the case in kingdoms governed like that of France, because it is easy to enter them by winning over some baron of the kingdom, there being always malcontents, and those desiring innovations. These can, for the reasons stated, open the way to you and facilitate victory; but afterwards, if you wish to keep possession, infinite difficulties arise, both from those who have aided you and from those you have oppressed. Nor is it sufficient to suppress the family of the prince, for there remain those nobles who will take the lead in new revolutions, and being neither able to content them nor exterminate them, you will lose the state whenever an occasion arises.

Now if you will consider what was the nature of the government of Darius you will find it similar to the kingdom of the Turk, and therefore Alexander had first to overthrow it completely and invade the territory, after which victory, Darius being dead, the state remained secure to Alexander, for the reasons discussed above. And his successors, had they remained united, might have enjoyed it in peace, nor did any tumults arise in the kingdom except those fomented by themselves. But it is impossible to possess with such ease countries constituted like France. Hence arose the frequent rebellions of Spain, France, and Greece against the Romans, owing to the numerous principalities which existed in those states; for, as long as the memory of these lasted, the Romans were always uncertain of their conquest; but when the memory of these principalities had been extinguished and with the power and duration of the empire, they became unchallenged masters. When the Romans fell out amongst themselves, any one of them could count on the support of that part of the province where he had established authority. The Romans alone were recognised as rulers there after the extinction of the old line of princes. Considering these things, therefore, let no one be surprised at the facility with which Alexander was able to hold Asia, and at the difficulties that others have had in holding conquered territories, like Pyrrhus and many others; as this was not caused by the greater or lesser ability of the conqueror, but depended on the dissimilarity of the conditions.

Chapter V
The Way to Govern Cities or Dominions That, Previous to Being Occupied, Lived Under Their Own Laws

When those states which have been acquired are accustomed to live at liberty under their own laws, there are three ways of holding them. The first is to despoil them; the second is to go and live there in person; the third is to allow them to live under their own laws, taking tribute of them, and creating within the country a government composed of a few who will keep it friendly to you. Because this government, being created by the prince, knows that it cannot exist without his friendship and protection, and will do all it can to keep them. What is more, a city used to liberty can be more easily held by means of its citizens than in any other way, if you wish to preserve it.

There is the example of the Spartans and the Romans. The Spartans held Athens and Thebes by creating within them a government of a few; nevertheless they lost them. The Romans, in order to hold Capua, Carthage, and Numantia, ravaged them, but did not lose them. They wanted to hold Greece in almost the same way as the Spartans held it, leaving it free and under its own laws, but they did not succeed; so that they were compelled to lay waste many cities in that province in order to keep it, because in truth there is no sure method of holding them except by despoiling them. And whoever becomes the ruler of a free city and does not destroy it, can expect to be destroyed by it, for it can always find a motive for rebellion in the name of liberty and of its ancient usages, which are forgotten neither by lapse of time nor by benefits received; and whatever one does or provides, so long as the inhabitants are not separated or dispersed, they do not forget that name and those usages, but appeal to them at once in every emergency, as did Pisa after being so many years held in servitude by the Florentines. But when cities or provinces have been accustomed to live under a prince, and the family of that prince is extinguished, being on the one hand used to obey, and on the other not having their old prince, they cannot unite in choosing one from among themselves, and they do not know how to live in freedom, so that they are slower to take arms, and a prince can win them over with greater facility and establish himself securely. But in republics there is greater life, greater hatred, and more desire for vengeance; they do not and cannot cast aside the memory of their ancient liberty, so that the surest way is either to lay them waste or reside in them.

Chapter VI
Of New Dominions Which Have Been Acquired by One's Own Arms and Ability

Let no one marvel if in speaking of new dominions both as to prince and state, I bring forward very exalted instances, for men walk almost always in the paths trodden by others, proceeding in their actions by imitation. Not being always able to follow others exactly, nor attain to the excellence of those he imitates, a prudent man should always follow in the path trodden by great men and imitate those who are most excellent, so that if he does not attain to their greatness, at any rate he will get some tinge of it. He will do as prudent archers, who when the place they wish to hit is too far off, knowing how far their bow will carry, aim at a spot much higher than the one they wish to hit, not in order to reach this height with their arrow, but by help of this high aim to hit the spot they wish to.

I say then that in new dominions, where there is a new prince, it is more or less easy to hold them according to the greater or lesser ability of him who acquires them. And as the fact of a private individual becoming a prince presupposes either great ability or good fortune, it would appear that either of these things would in part mitigate many difficulties. Nevertheless those who have been less beholden to good fortune have maintained themselves best. The matter is also facilitated by the prince being obliged to reside personally in his territory, having no others. But to come to those who have become princes through their own merits and not by fortune, I regard as the greatest Moses, Cyrus, Romulus, Theseus, and their like. And although one should not speak of Moses, he having merely carried out what was ordered him by God, still he deserves admiration, if only for that grace which made him worthy to speak with God. But regarding Cyrus and others who have acquired or founded kingdoms, they will all be found worthy of admiration; and if their particular actions and methods are examined they will not appear very different from those of Moses, although he had so great a Master. And in examining their life and deeds it will be seen that they owed nothing to fortune but the opportunity which gave them matter to be shaped into what form they thought fit; and without that opportunity their powers would have been wasted, and without their powers the opportunity would have come in vain.

It was thus necessary that Moses should find the people of Israel slaves in Egypt and oppressed by the Egyptians, so that they were disposed to follow him in order to escape from their servitude. It was necessary that Romulus should be unable to remain in Alba, and should have been exposed at his birth, in order that he might become King of Rome and founder of that nation. It was necessary that Cyrus should find the Persians discontented with the empire of the Medes, and the Medes weak and effeminate through long peace. Theseus could not have shown his abilities if he had not found the Athenians dispersed. These opportunities, therefore, gave these men their chance, and their own great qualities enabled them to profit by them, so as to ennoble their country and augment its fortunes.

Those who by the exercise of abilities such as these become princes, obtain their dominions with difficulty but retain them easily, and the difficulties which they have in acquiring their dominions arise in part from the new rules and regulations that they have to introduce in order to establish their position securely. It must be considered that there is nothing more difficult to carry out, nor more doubtful of success, nor more dangerous to handle, than to initiate a new order of things. For the reformer has enemies in all those who profit by the old order, and only lukewarm defenders in all those who would profit by the new order, this lukewarmness arising partly from fear of their adversaries, who have the laws in their favour; and partly from the incredulity of mankind, who do not truly believe in anything new until they have had actual experience of it. Thus it arises that on every opportunity for attacking the reformer, his opponents do so with the zeal of partisans, the others only defend him half-heartedly, so that between them he runs great danger. It is necessary, however, in order to investigate thoroughly this question, to examine whether these innovators are independent, or whether they depend upon others, that is to say, whether in order to carry out their designs they have to entreat or are able to compel. In the first case they invariably succeed ill, and accomplish nothing; but when they can depend on their own strength and are able to use force, they rarely fail. Thus it comes about that all armed prophets have conquered and unarmed ones failed; for besides what has been already said, the character of peoples varies, and it is easy to persuade them of a thing, but difficult to keep them in that persuasion. And so it is necessary to order things so that when they no longer believe, they can be made to believe by force. Moses, Cyrus, Theseus, and Romulus would not have been able to keep their constitutions observed for so long had they been disarmed, as happened in our own time with Fra Girolamo Savonarola, who failed entirely in his new rules when the multitude began to disbelieve in him, and he had no means of holding fast those who had believed nor of compelling the unbelievers to believe. Therefore such men as these have great difficulty in making their way, and all their dangers are met on the road and must be overcome by their own abilities; but when once they have overcome them and have begun to be held in veneration, and have suppressed those who envied them, they remain powerful and secure, honoured and happy.

To the high examples given I will add a lesser one, which, however, is in some measure comparable and will serve as an instance of all such cases, that of Hiero of Syracuse, who from a private individual became Prince of Syracuse without other aid from fortune beyond the opportunity; for the Syracusans, being oppressed, elected him as their captain, from which post he rose by ability to be prince; while still in private life his virtues were such that it was written of him, that he lacked nothing to reign but the kingdom. He abolished the old militia, raised a new one, abandoned his old friendships and formed others; and as he had thus friends and soldiers of his own choosing, he was able on this foundation to build securely, so that while he had great trouble in acquiring his position he had little in maintaining it.

Chapter VII
Of New Dominions Acquired
by the Power of Others or by Fortune

Those who rise from private citizens to be princes merely by fortune have little trouble in rising but very much in maintaining their position. They meet with no difficulties on the way as they fly over them, but all their difficulties arise when they are established. Such are they who are granted a state either for money or by favour of him who grants it, as happened to many in Greece, in the cities of Ionia and of the Hellespont, who were created princes by Darius in order to hold these places for his security and glory; such were also those emperors who from private citizens rose to power by bribing the army. Such as these depend absolutely on the good will and fortune of those who have raised them, both of which are extremely inconstant and unstable. They neither know how to, nor are in a position to, maintain their rank, for unless he be a man of great genius it is not likely that one who has always lived in a private position should know how to command, and they are unable to maintain themselves because they possess no forces friendly and faithful to them. Moreover, states quickly founded, like all other things of rapid beginnings and growth, cannot have deep roots and wide ramifications, so that the first storm destroys them, unless, as already said, the man who thus becomes a prince is of such great genius as to be able to take immediate steps for maintaining what fortune has thrown into his lap, and lay afterwards those foundations which others make before becoming princes.

With regard to these two methods of becoming a prince—by ability or by good fortune—I will here adduce two examples which have occurred within our memory, those of Francesco Sforza and Cesare Borgia. Francesco, by appropriate means and through great abilities, from citizen became Duke of Milan, and what he had attained after a thousand difficulties he maintained with little trouble. On the other hand, Cesare Borgia, commonly called Duke Valentine, acquired the state by the influence of his father and

lost it when that influence failed, and that although every measure was adopted by him and everything done that a prudent and capable man could do to establish himself firmly in a state that the arms and the favours of others had given him. For, as we have said, he who does not lay his foundations beforehand may by great abilities do so afterwards, although with great trouble to the architect and danger to the building. If, then, one considers the procedure of the duke, it will be seen how firm were the foundations he had laid to his future power, which I do not think it superfluous to examine, as I know of no better precepts for a new prince to follow than may be found in his actions, and if his measures were not successful, it was through no fault of his own but only by the most extraordinary malignity of fortune.

In wishing to aggrandise the duke his son, Alexander VI had to meet very great difficulties both present and future. In the first place, he saw no way of making him ruler of any state that was not a possession of the Church. He knew that the Duke of Milan and the Venetians would not consent in his attempt to take papal cities, because Faenza and Rimini were already under the protection of the Venetians. He saw, moreover, that the military forces of Italy, especially those which might have served him, were in the hands of those who would fear the greatness of the pope, and therefore he could not depend upon them, being all under the command of the Orsini and Colonna and their adherents. It was, therefore, necessary to disturb the existing condition and bring about disorders in the states of Italy in order to obtain secure mastery over a part of them; this was easy, for he found the Venetians, who, actuated by other motives, had invited the French into Italy, which he not only did not oppose, but facilitated by dissolving the first marriage of King Louis. The king came thus into Italy with the aid of the Venetians and the consent of Alexander, and had hardly arrived at Milan before the pope obtained troops from him for his enterprise in the Romagna, which was made possible for him thanks to the reputation of the king. The duke having thus obtained the Romagna and defeated the Colonna, was hindered by two things in maintaining it and proceeding further: the one, his forces, of which he doubted the fidelity; the other the will of France; that is to say, he feared lest the arms of the Orsini of which he had availed himself should fail him, and not only hinder him in obtaining more but take from him what he had already conquered, and he also feared that the king might do the same. He had evidence of this as regards the Orsini when, after taking Faenza, he assaulted Bologna and observed their backwardness in the assault. And as regards the king, he perceived his designs when, after taking the dukedom of Urbino, he attacked Tuscany, and the king made him desist from that enterprise. Whereupon the duke decided to depend no longer on the fortunes and arms of others. The first thing he did was to weaken the parties of the Orsini and Colonna in Rome by gaining all their adherents who were gentlemen and making them his own followers, by granting them large remuneration, and appointing them to commands and offices according to their rank, so that their attachment to their parties was extinguished in a few months, and entirely concentrated on the duke. After this he awaited an opportunity for crushing the chiefs of the Orsini, having already suppressed those of the Colonna family, and when the opportunity arrived he made good use of it, for the Orsini, seeing at length that the greatness of the duke and of the Church meant their own ruin, convoked a diet at Magione in the Perugino. Hence sprang the rebellion of Urbino and the tumults in Romagna and infinite dangers to the duke, who overcame them all with the help of the French; and having regained his reputation, neither trusting France nor other foreign forces, in order not to venture on their alliance, he had recourse to stratagem. He dissembled his aims so well that the Orsini made their peace with him, being represented by Signor Paulo, whose suspicions the duke disarmed with every courtesy, presenting him with robes, money, and horses, so that in their simplicity they were induced to come to Sinigaglia and fell into his hands. Having thus suppressed these leaders and made their partisans his friends, the duke had laid a very good foundation to his power, having all the Romagna with the duchy of Urbino, and having gained the favour of the inhabitants, who began to feel the benefit of his rule.

And as this part is worthy of note and of imitation by others, I will not omit mention of it. When he took the Romagna, it had previously been governed by weak rulers, who had rather despoiled their subjects than governed them, and given them more cause for disunion than for union, so that the province was a prey to robbery, assaults, and every kind of disorder. He, therefore, judged it necessary to give them a good government in order to make them peaceful and obe-

dient to his rule. For this purpose he appointed Messer Remirro de Orco, a cruel and able man, to whom he gave the fullest authority. This man, in a short time, was highly successful in rendering the country orderly and united, whereupon the duke, not deeming such excessive authority expedient, lest it should become hateful, appointed a civil court of justice in the centre of the province under an excellent president, to which each city appointed its own advocate. And as he knew that the harshness of the past had engendered some amount of hatred, in order to purge the minds of the people and to win them over completely, he resolved to show that if any cruelty had taken place it was not by his orders, but through the harsh disposition of his minister. And having found the opportunity, he had him cut in half and placed one morning in the public square at Cesena with a piece of wood and blood-stained knife by his side. The ferocity of this spectacle caused the people both satisfaction and amazement. But to return to where we left off.

The duke being now powerful and partly secured against present perils, being armed himself, and having in a great measure put down those neighbouring forces which might injure him, had now to get the respect of France, if he wished to proceed with his acquisitions, for he knew that the king, who had lately discovered his error, would not give him any help. He began therefore to seek fresh alliances and to vacillate with France on the occasion of the expedition that the French were undertaking towards the kingdom of Naples against the Spaniards, who were besieging Gaeta. His intention was to assure himself of them, which he would soon have succeeded in doing if Alexander had lived.

These were the measures taken by him with regard to the present. As to the future, he feared that a new successor to the states of the Church might not be friendly to him and might seek to deprive him of what Alexander had given him, and he sought to provide against this in four ways. First, by destroying all who were of the blood of those ruling families which he had despoiled, in order to deprive the pope of any opportunity. Secondly, by gaining the friendship of the Roman nobles, so that he might through them hold, as it were, the pope in check. Thirdly, by obtaining as great a hold on the College as he could. Fourthly, by acquiring such power before the pope died as to be able to resist alone the first onslaught.

Of these four things he had at the death of Alexander accomplished three, and the fourth he had almost accomplished. For of the dispossessed rulers he killed as many as he could lay hands on, and very few escaped; he had gained to his party the Roman nobles; and he had a great influence in the College. As to new possessions, he designed to become lord of Tuscany, and already possessed Perugia and Piombino, and had assumed the protectorate over Pisa; and as he had no longer to fear the French (for the French had been deprived of the kingdom of Naples by the Spaniards in such a way that both parties were obliged to buy his friendship) he seized Pisa. After this, Lucca and Siena at once yielded, partly through hate of the Florentines and partly through fear; the Florentines had no resources, so that, had he succeeded as he had done before, in the very year that Alexander died he would have gained such strength and renown as to be able to maintain himself without depending on the fortunes or strength of others, but solely by his own power and ability. But Alexander died five years after Cesare Borgia had first drawn his sword. He was left with only the state of Romagna firmly established, and all the other schemes in mid-air, between two very powerful and hostile armies, and suffering from a fatal illness. But the valour and ability of the duke were such, and he knew so well how to win over men or vanquish them, and so strong were the foundations that he had laid in this short time, that if he had not had those two armies upon him, or else had been in good health, he would have survived every difficulty. And that his foundations were good is seen from the fact that the Romagna waited for him more than a month; in Rome, although half dead, he remained secure, and although the Baglioni, Vitelli, and Orsini entered Rome they found no followers against him. He was able, if not to make pope whom he wished, at any rate to prevent a pope being created whom he did not wish. But if at the death of Alexander he had been well, everything would have been easy. And he told me on the day that Pope Julius II was elected, that he had thought of everything which might happen on the death of his father, and provided against everything, except that he had never thought that at his father's death he would be dying himself.

Reviewing thus all the actions of the duke, I find nothing to blame; on the contrary, I feel bound, as I have done, to hold him up as an example to be imitated by all who by fortune and with the arms of others have risen to power. For with his great courage and high ambition he could not have acted otherwise, and his designs were only frustrated by the short life of Alexander and his own illness. Whoever, therefore, deems it necessary in his new principality to secure himself against enemies, to gain friends, to conquer by force or fraud, to make himself beloved and feared by the people, followed and reverenced by the soldiers, to destroy those who can and may injure him, introduce innovations into old customs, to be severe and kind, magnanimous and liberal, suppress the old militia, create a new one, maintain the friendship of kings and princes in such a way that they are glad to benefit him and fear to injure him, such a one can find no better example than the actions of this man. The only thing he can be accused of is that in the creation of Julius II he made a bad choice; for, as has been said, not being able to choose his own pope, he could still prevent any one individual being made pope, and he ought never to have permitted any of those cardinals to be raised to the papacy whom he had injured, or who when pope would stand in fear of him. For men commit injuries either through fear or through hate. Those whom he had injured were, among others, San Pietro ad Vincula, Colonna, San Giorgio, and Ascanio. All the others, if elected to the pontificate, would have had to fear him except Rohan and the Spaniards; the latter through their relationship and obligations to him, the former from his great power, being related to the King of France. For these reasons the duke ought above all things to have created a Spaniard pope; and if unable, then he should have consented to Rohan being appointed and not San Pietro ad Vincula. And whoever thinks that in high personages new benefits cause old offences to be forgotten, makes a great mistake. The duke, therefore, erred in this choice, and it was the cause of his ultimate ruin.

Chapter VIII
Of Those Who Have Attained the Position of Prince by Villainy

But as there are still two ways of becoming prince which cannot be attributed entirely either to fortune or to ability, they must not be passed over, although one of them could be more fully discussed if we were treating of republics. These are when one becomes prince by some nefarious or villainous means, or when a private citizen becomes the prince of his country through the favour of his fellow-citizens. And in speaking of the former means, I will give two examples, one ancient, the other modern, without entering further into the merits of this method, as I judge them to be sufficient for any one obliged to imitate them.

Agathocles the Sicilian rose not only from private life but from the lowest and most abject position to be King of Syracuse. The son of a potter, he led a life of the utmost wickedness through all the stages of his fortune. Nevertheless his wickedness was accompanied by such vigour of mind and body that, having joined the militia, he rose through its ranks to be prætor of Syracuse. Having been appointed to this position, and having decided to become prince, and to hold with violence and without the support of others that which had been constitutionally granted him; and having imparted his design to Hamilcar the Carthaginian, who was fighting with his armies in Sicily, he called together one morning the people and senate of Syracuse, as if he had to deliberate on matters of importance to the republic, and at a given signal had all the senators and the richest men of the people killed by his soldiers. After their death he occupied and held rule over the city without any civil strife. And although he was twice beaten by the Carthaginians and ultimately besieged, he was able not only to defend the city, but leaving a portion of his forces for its defence, with the remainder he invaded Africa, and in a short time liberated Syracuse from the siege and brought the Carthaginians to great extremities, so that they were obliged to come to terms with him, and remain contented with the possession of Africa, leaving Sicily to Agathocles. Whoever considers, therefore, the actions and qualities of this man, will see few if any things which can be attributed to fortune; for, as above stated, it was not by the favour of any person, but through the grades of the militia, in which he had advanced with a thousand hardships and perils, that he arrived at the position of prince, which he afterwards maintained by so many courageous and perilous expedient. It cannot be called virtue to kill one's fellow-citizens, betray one's friends, be without faith, without pity, and without religion; by these methods one may indeed gain power, but not glory. For if the virtues of Agathocles in braving and overcoming perils, and his greatness of soul in supporting and surmounting obstacles be considered, one sees no reason for holding him inferior to any of the most renowned captains. Nevertheless his barbarous cruelty and inhumanity, together with his countless atrocities, do not permit of his being named among the most famous men. We cannot attribute to fortune or virtue that which he achieved without either.

In our own times, during the pontificate of Alexander VI, Oliverotto da Fermo had been left as a young fatherless boy under the care of his maternal uncle, Giovanni Fogliani, who brought him up, and sent him in early youth to soldier under Paolo Vitelli, in order that he might, trained in that hard school, obtain a good military position. On the death of Paolo he fought under his brother Vitellozzo, and in a very short time, being of great intelligence, and active in mind and body, he became one of the leaders of his troops. But deeming it servile to be under others, he resolved, with the help of some citizens of Fermo, who preferred servitude to the liberty of their country, and with the favour of the Vitelli, to occupy Fermo; he therefore wrote to Giovanni Fogliani, how, having been for many years away from home, he wished to come to see him and his city, and as far as possible to inspect his estates. And as he had only laboured to gain honour, in order that his fellow-citizens might see that he had not spent his time in vain, he wished to come honourably accompanied by one hundred horsemen, his friends and followers, and prayed him that he would be pleased to order that he should be received with honour by the citizens of Fermo, by which he would honour not only him, Oliverotto, but also himself, as he had been his pupil. Giovanni did not fail in any due courtesy towards his nephew; he caused him to be honourably received by the people of Fermo, and lodged him in his own houses. After waiting some days to arrange all that was necessary to his villainous projects, Oliverotto invited Giovanni Fogliani and all the principal men of Fermo to a grand banquet. After the dinner and the entertainments usual at such feasts, Oliverotto artfully introduced certain important matters of discussion, speaking of the greatness of Pope Alexander, and of his son Cesare, and of their enterprises. To which discourses Giovanni and others having replied, he all at once rose, saying that these matters should be spoken of in a more private place, and withdrew into a room where Giovanni and the other citizens followed him. They were no sooner seated than soldiers rushed out of hiding-places and killed Giovanni and all the others. After which massacre Oliverotto mounted his horse, rode through the town and besieged the chief magistrate in his palace, so that through fear they were obliged to obey him and form a government, of which he made himself prince. And all those being dead who, if discontented, could injure him, he fortified himself with new orders, civil and military, in such a way that within the year that he held the principality he was not only safe himself in the city of Fermo, but had become formidable to all his neighbours. And his overthrow would have been difficult, like that of Agathocles, if he had not allowed himself to be deceived by Cesare Borgia, when he captured the Orsini and Vitelli at Sinigaglia, as already related, where he also was taken, one year after the parricide he had committed, and strangled, together with Vitellozzo, who had been his teacher in ability and atrocity.

Some may wonder how it came about that Agathocles, and others like him, could, after infinite treachery and cruelty, live secure for many years in their country and defend themselves from external enemies without being conspired against by their subjects; although many others have, owing to their cruelty, been unable to maintain their position in times of peace, not to speak of the uncertain times of war. I believe this arises from the cruelties being exploited well or badly. Well committed may be called those (if it is permissible to use the word well of evil) which are perpetuated once for the need of securing one's self, and which afterwards are not persisted in, but are exchanged for measures as useful to the subjects as possible. Cruelties ill committed are those which, although at first few, increase rather than diminish with time. Those who follow the former method may remedy in some measure their condition, both with God and man; as did Agathocles. As to the others, it is impossible for them to maintain themselves.

Whence it is to be noted, that in taking a state the conqueror must arrange to commit all his cruelties at once, so as not to have to recur to them every day, and so as to be able, by not making fresh changes, to reassure people and win them over by benefiting them. Whoever acts otherwise, either through timidity or bad counsels, is always obliged to stand with knife in hand, and can never depend on his subjects, because they, owing to continually fresh injuries, are unable to depend upon him. For injuries should be done all together, so that being less tasted, they will give less offence. Benefits should be granted little by little, so that they may be better enjoyed. And above all, a prince must live with his subjects in such a way

that no accident of good or evil fortune can deflect him from his course; for necessity arising in adverse times, you are not in time with severity, and the good that you do does not profit, as it is judged to be forced upon you, and you will derive no benefit whatever from it.

Chapter IX
Of the Civic Principality

But we now come to the case where a citizen becomes prince not through crime or intolerable violence, but by the favour of his fellow-citizens, which may be called a civic principality. To attain this position depends not entirely on worth or entirely on fortune, but rather on cunning assisted by fortune. One attains it by help of popular favour or by the favour of the aristocracy. For in every city these two opposite parties are to be found, arising from the desire of the populace to avoid the oppression of the great, and the desire of the great to command and oppress the people. And from these two opposing interests arises in the city one of the three effects: either absolute government, liberty, or licence. The former is created either by the populace or the nobility, depending on the relative opportunities of the two parties; for when the nobility see that they are unable to resist the people, they unite in exalting one of their number and creating him prince, so as to be able to carry out their own designs under the shadow of his authority. The populace, on the other hand, when unable to resist the nobility, endeavour to exalt and create a prince in order to be protected by his authority. He who becomes prince by help of the nobility has greater difficulty in maintaining his power than he who is raised by the populace, for he is surrounded by those who think themselves his equals, and is thus unable to direct or command as he pleases. But one who is raised to leadership by popular favour finds himself alone and has no one, or very few, who are not ready to obey him. Besides which, it is impossible to satisfy the nobility by fair dealing and without inflicting injury on others, whereas it is very easy to satisfy the mass of the people in this way. For the aim of the people is more honest than that of the nobility, the latter desiring to oppress, and the former merely to avoid oppression. It must also be added that the prince can never insure himself against a hostile populace on account of their number, but he can against the hostility of the great, as they are but few. The worst that a prince has to expect from a hostile people is to be abandoned, but from hostile nobles he has to fear not only desertion but their active opposition, and as they are more far-seeing and more cunning, they are always in time to save themselves and take sides with the one whom they expect will conquer. The prince is, moreover, obliged to live always with the same people, but he can easily do without the same nobility, being able to make and unmake them at any time, and improve their position or deprive them of it as he pleases.

And to throw further light on this part of my argument, I would say, that the nobles are to be considered in two different manners; that is, they are either to be ruled so as to make them entirely dependent on your fortunes, or else not. Those that are thus bound to you and are not rapacious, must be honoured and loved; those who stand aloof must be considered in two ways, they either do this through pusillanimity and natural want of courage, and in this case you ought to make use of them, and especially such as are of good counsel, so that they may honour you in prosperity and in adversity you have not to fear them. But when they are not bound to you of set purpose and for ambitious ends, it is a sign that they think more of themselves than of you; and from such men the prince must guard himself and look upon them as secret enemies, who will help to ruin him when in adversity.

One, however, who becomes prince by favour of the populace, must maintain its friendship, which he will find easy, the people asking nothing but not to be oppressed. But one who against the people's wishes becomes prince by favour of the nobles, should above all endeavour to gain the favour of the people; this will be easy to him if he protects them. And as men, who receive good from whom they expected evil, feel under a greater obligation to their benefactor, so the populace will soon become even better disposed towards him than if he had become prince through their favour. The prince can win their favour in many ways, which vary according to circumstances, for which no certain rule can be given, and will therefore be passed over. I will only say, in conclusion, that it is necessary for a prince to possess the friendship of the people; otherwise he has no resource in times of adversity.

Nabis, prince of the Spartans, sustained a siege by the whole of Greece and a victorious Roman army, and defended his country against them and maintained his own position. It sufficed when the danger arose for him to make sure of a few, which would not have sufficed if the populace had been hostile to him. And let no one oppose my opinion in this by quoting the trite proverb, "He who builds on the people, builds on mud"; because that is true when a private citizen relies upon the people and persuades himself that they will liberate him if he is oppressed by enemies or by the magistrates; in this case he might often find himself deceived, as were in Rome the Gracchi and in Florence Messer Georgio Scali. But when it is a prince who founds himself on this basis, one who can command and is a man of courage, and does not get frightened in adversity, and does not neglect other preparations, and one who by his own valour and measures animates the mass of the people, he will not find himself deceived by them, and he will find that he has laid his foundations well.

Usually these principalities are in danger when the prince from the position of a civil ruler changes to an absolute one, for these princes either command themselves or by means of magistrates. In the latter case their position is weaker and more dangerous, for they are at the mercy of those citizens who are appointed magistrates, who can, especially in times of adversity, with great facility deprive them of their position, either by acting against them or by not obeying them. The prince is not in time, in such dangers, to assume absolute authority, for the citizens and subjects who are accustomed to take their orders from the magistrates are not ready in these emergencies to obey his, and he will always in difficult times lack men whom he can rely on. Such a prince cannot base himself on what he sees in quiet times, when the citizens have need of the state; for then every one is full of promises and each one is ready to die for him when death is far off; but in adversity, when the state has need of citizens, then he will find but few. And this experience is the more dangerous, in that it can only be had once. Therefore a wise prince will seek means by which his subjects will always and in every possible condition of things have need of his government, and then they will always be faithful to him.

Chapter X
How the Strength of All States Should Be Measured

In examining the character of these principalities it is necessary to consider another point, namely, whether the prince has such a position as to be able in case of need to maintain himself alone, or whether he has always need of the protection of others. The better to explain this I would say that I consider those capable of maintaining themselves alone who can, through abundance of men or money, put together a sufficient army, and hold the field against any one who assails them; and I consider to have need of others, those who cannot take the field against their enemies, but are obliged to take refuge within their walls and stand on the defensive. We have already discussed the former case and will speak of it in future as occasion arises. In the second case there is nothing to be said except to encourage such a prince to provision and fortify his own town, and not to trouble about the surrounding country. And whoever has strongly fortified his town and, as regards the government of his subjects, has proceeded as we have already described and will further relate, will be attacked with great reluctance, for men are always averse to enterprises in which they foresee difficulties, and it can never appear easy to attack one who has his town stoutly defended and is not hated by the people.

The cities of Germany are absolutely free, have little surrounding country, and obey the emperor when they choose, and they do not fear him or any other potentate that they have about them. They are fortified in such a manner that every one thinks that to reduce them would be tedious and difficult, for they all have the necessary moats and bastions, sufficient artillery, and always keep food, drink, and fuel for one year in the public storehouses. Beyond which, to keep the lower classes satisfied, and without loss to the commonwealth, they have always enough means to give them work for one year in these employments which form the nerve and life of the town, and in the industries by which the lower classes live. Military exercises are still held in high reputation, and many regulations are in force for maintaining them.

A prince, therefore, who possesses a strong city and does not make himself hated, cannot be assaulted; and if he were to be so, the assailant would be obliged to retire shamefully; for so many things change, that it is almost impossible for any one to maintain a siege for a year with his armies idle. And to those who urge that the people, having their possessions outside and seeing them burnt, will not have patience, and the long siege and self-interest will make them forget their prince, I reply that a powerful and courageous prince will always overcome those difficulties by now raising the hopes of his subjects that the evils will not last long, now impressing them with fear of the enemy's cruelty, now by dexterously assuring himself of those who appear too bold. Besides which, the enemy would naturally burn and ravage the country on first arriving and at the time when men's minds are still hot and eager to defend themselves, and therefore the prince has still less to fear, for after some time, when people have cooled down, the damage is done, the evil has been suffered, and there is no remedy, so that they are the more ready to unite with their prince, as it appears that he is under an obligation to them, their houses having been burnt and their possessions ruined in his defence.

It is the nature of men to be as much bound by the benefits that they confer as by those they receive. From which it follows that, everything considered, a prudent prince will not find it difficult to uphold the courage of his subjects both at the commencement and during a state of siege, if he possesses provisions and means to defend himself.

Chapter XI
Of Ecclesiastical Principalities

It now only remains to us to speak of ecclesiastical principalities, with regard to which the difficulties lie wholly before they are possessed. They are acquired either by ability or by fortune; but are maintained without either, for they are sustained by ancient religious customs, which are so powerful and of such quality that they keep their princes in power in whatever manner they proceed and live. These princes alone have states without defending them, have subjects without governing them, and their states, not being defended, are not taken from them; their subjects not being governed do not resent it, and neither think nor are capable of alienating themselves from them. Only these principalities, therefore, are secure and happy. But as they are upheld by higher causes, which the human mind cannot attain to, I will abstain from speaking of them; for being exalted and maintained by God, it would be the work of a presumptuous and foolish man to discuss them. However, I might be asked how it has come about that the Church has reached such great temporal power, when, previous to Alexander VI, the Italian potentates—and not merely the really powerful ones, but every lord or baron, however insignificant—held it in slight esteem as regards temporal power; whereas now it is dreaded by a king of France, whom it has been able to drive out of Italy, and has also been able to ruin the Venetians. Therefore, although this is well known, I do not think it superfluous to call it to mind.

Before Charles, King of France, came into Italy, this country was under the rule of the Pope, the Venetians, the King of Naples, the Duke of Milan, and the Florentines. These potentates had to have two chief cares: one, that no foreigner should enter Italy by force of arms, the other that none of the existing governments should extend its dominions. Those chiefly to be watched were the Pope and the Venetians. To keep back the Venetians required the alliance of all the others, as in the defence of Ferrara, and to keep down the Pope they made use of the Roman barons. These were divided into two factions, the Orsini and the Colonna, and as there was constant quarreling between them, and they were constantly under arms, before the eyes of the Pope, they kept the papacy weak and infirm. And although there arose now and then a resolute Pope like Sextus, yet his fortune or ability was never able to liberate him from these evils. The shortness of their life was the reason of this, for in the course of ten years which, as a general rule, a Pope lived, he had great difficulty in suppressing even one of the factions, and if, for example, a Pope had almost put down the Colonna, a new Pope would succeed who was hostile to the Orsini, which caused the Colonna to spring up again, and he was not in time to suppress them.

This caused the temporal power of the Pope to be of little esteem in Italy. Then arose Alexander VI who, of all the pontiffs who have ever reigned, best showed how a pope might prevail both by money and by force. With Duke Valentine as his instrument, and seizing the opportunity of the French invasion, he did all that I have previously described in speaking of the actions of the duke. And although his object was to aggrandise not the Church but the duke, what he did resulted in the aggrandisement of the Church, which after the death of the duke became the heir of his labours. Then came Pope Julius, who found the Church powerful, possessing all Romagna, all the Roman barons suppressed, and the factions destroyed by the severity of Alexander. He also found the way open for accumulating wealth in ways never used before the time of Alexander. These measures were not only followed by Julius, but increased; he resolved to gain Bologna, put down the Venetians, and drive the French from Italy, in all which enter-

prises he was successful. He merits the greater praise, as he did everything to increase the power of the Church and not of any private person. He also kept the Orsini and Colonna parties in the condition in which he found them, and although there were some leaders among them who might have made changes, there were two things that kept them steady: one, the greatness of the Church, which they dreaded; the other, the fact that they had no cardinals, who are the origin of the tumults among them. For these parties are never at rest when they have cardinals, for these stir up the parties both within Rome and outside, and the barons are forced to defend them. Thus from the ambitions of prelates arise the discords and tumults among the barons. His holiness, Pope Leo X, therefore, has found the pontificate in a very powerful condition, from which it is hoped that as those popes made it great by force of arms, so he through his goodness and infinite other virtues will make it both great and venerated.

Chapter XII
The Different Kinds of Militia and Mercenary Soldiers

Having now discussed fully the qualities of these principalities of which I proposed to treat, and partially considered the causes of their prosperity or failure, and having also showed the methods by which many have sought to obtain such states, it now remains for me to treat generally of the methods, both offensive and defensive, that can be used in each of them. We have said already how necessary it is for a prince to have his foundations good, otherwise he is certain to be ruined. The chief foundations of all states, whether new, old, or mixed, are good laws and good arms. And as there cannot be good laws where there are not good arms, and where there are good arms there must be good laws, I will not now discuss the laws, but will speak of the arms.

I say, therefore, that the arms by which a prince defends his possessions are either his own, or else mercenaries, or auxiliaries, or mixed. The mercenaries and auxiliaries are useless and dangerous, and if any one supports his state by the arms of mercenaries, he will never stand firm or sure, as they are disunited, ambitious, without discipline, faithless, bold amongst friends, cowardly amongst enemies, they have no fear of God, and keep no faith with men. Ruin is only deferred as long as the assault is postponed; in peace you are despoiled by them, and in war by the enemy. The cause of this is that they have no love or other motive to keep them in the field beyond a trifling wage, which is not enough to make them ready to die for you. They are quite willing to be your soldiers so long as you do not make war, but when war comes, it is either fly or decamp altogether. I ought to have little trouble in proving this, since the ruin of Italy is now caused by nothing else but through her having relied for many years on mercenary arms. These did indeed help certain individuals to power, and appeared courageous when matched against each other, but when the foreigner came they showed their worthlessness. Thus it came about that King Charles of France was allowed to take Italy without the slightest trouble, and those who said that it was owing to our sins, spoke the truth, but it was not the sins they meant but those that I have related. And as it was the sins of princes, they too have suffered the punishment.

I will explain more fully the defects of these arms. Mercenary captains are either very capable men or not; if they are, you cannot rely upon them, for they will always aspire to their own greatness, either by oppressing you, their master, or by oppressing others against your intentions; but if the captain is not an able man, he will generally ruin you. And if it is replied to this that whoever has armed forces will do the same, whether these are mercenary or not, I would reply that as armies are to be used either by a prince or by a republic, the prince must go in person to take the position of captain, and the republic must send its own citizens. If the man sent turns out incompetent, it must change him; and if capable, keep him by law from going beyond the proper limits. And it is seen by experience that only princes and armed republics make very great progress, whereas mercenary forces do nothing but harm, and also an armed republic submits less easily to the rule of one of its citizens than a republic armed by foreign forces.

Rome and Sparta were for many centuries well armed and free. The Swiss are well armed and enjoy great freedom. As an example of mercenary armies in antiquity there are the Carthaginians, who were oppressed by their mercenary soldiers, after the termination of the first war with the Romans, even while they still had their own citizens as captains. Philip of Macedon was made captain of their forces by the Thebans after the death of Epaminondas, and after gaining the victory he deprived them of liberty. The

Milanese, on the death of Duke Philip, hired Francesco Sforza against the Venetians, who having overcome the enemy at Caravaggio, allied himself with them to oppress the Milanese his own employers. The father of this Sforza, being a soldier in the service of Queen Giovanna of Naples, left her suddenly unarmed, by which she was compelled, in order not to lose the kingdom, to throw herself into the arms of the King of Aragon. And if the Venetians and Florentines have in times past increased their dominions by means of such forces, and their captains have not made themselves princes but have defended them, I reply that the Florentines in this case have been favoured by chance, for of the capable leaders whom they might have feared, some did not conquer, some met with opposition, and others directed their ambition elsewhere. The one who did not conquer was Sir John Hawkwood, whose fidelity could not be known as he was not victorious, but every one will admit that, had he conquered, the Florentines would have been at his mercy. Sforza had always the Bracceschi against him which served as a mutual check. Francesco directed his ambition towards Lombardy; Braccio against the Church and the kingdom of Naples.

But let us look at what occurred a short time ago. The Florentines appointed Paolo Vitelli their captain, a man of great prudence, who had risen from a private station to the highest reputation. If he had taken Pisa no one can deny that it was highly important for the Florentines to retain his friendship, because had he become the soldier of their enemies they would have had no means of opposing him; and if they had retained him they would have been obliged to obey him. As to the Venetians, if one considers the progress they made, it will be seen that they acted surely and gloriously so long as they made war with their own forces; that it was before they commenced their enterprises on land that they fought courageously with their own gentlemen and armed populace, but when they began to fight on land they abandoned this virtue, and began to follow the Italian custom. And at the commencement of their land conquests they had not much to fear from their captains, their territories not being very large, and their reputation being great, but as their possessions increased, as they did under Carmagnola, they had an example of their mistake. For seeing that he was very powerful, after he had defeated the Duke of Milan, and knowing, on the other hand, that he was but lukewarm in this war, they considered that they would not make any more conquests with him, and they neither would nor could dismiss him, for fear of losing what they had already gained. In order to make sure of him they were therefore obliged to execute him. They then had for captains Bartolommeo da Bergamo, Roberto da San Severino, Count di Pitigliano, and such like, from whom they had to fear loss instead of gain, as happened subsequently at Vailà, where in one day they lost what they had laboriously gained in eight hundred years; for with these forces, only slow and trifling acquisitions are made, but sudden and miraculous losses. And as I have cited these examples from Italy, which has now for many years been governed by mercenary forces, I will now deal more largely with them, so that having seen their origin and progress, they can be better remedied.

You must understand that in these latter times, as soon as the empire began to be repudiated in Italy and the pope to gain greater reputation in temporal matters, Italy was divided into many states; many of the principal cities took up arms against their nobles, who, favoured by the emperor, had held them in subjection, and the Church encouraged this in order to increase its temporal power. In many other cities one of the inhabitants became prince. Thus Italy having fallen almost entirely into the hands of the Church and a few republics, and the priests and other citizens not being accustomed to bear arms, they began to hire foreigners as soldiers. The first to bring into reputation this kind of militia was Alberigo da Como, a native of Romagna. Braccio and Sforza, who were in their day the arbiters of Italy, were, amongst others, trained by him. After these came all those others who up to the present day have commanded the armies of Italy, and the result of their prowess has been that Italy has been overrun by Charles, preyed on by Louis, tyrannized over by Ferrando, and insulted by the Swiss. The system adopted by them was, in the first place, to increase their own reputation by discrediting the infantry. They did this because, as they had no country and lived on their earnings, a few foot soldiers did not augment their reputation, and they could not maintain a large number and therefore they restricted themselves almost entirely to cavalry, by which with a smaller number they were well paid and honoured. They reduced things to such a state that in an army of 20,000 soldiers there were not 2,000 foot. They had also used every means to spare themselves

and the soldiers any hardship or fear by not killing each other in their encounters, but taking prisoners without expectation of ransom. They made no attacks on fortifications by night; and those in the fortifications did not attack the tents at night, they made no stockades or ditches round their camps, and did not take the field in winter. All these things were permitted by their military code, and adopted, as we have said, to avoid trouble and danger, so that they have reduced Italy to slavery and degradation.

Chapter XIII
Of Auxiliary, Mixed, and Native Troops

When one asks a powerful neighbour to come to aid and defend one with his forces, they are termed auxiliaries and are as useless as mercenaries. This was done in recent times by Julius, who seeing the wretched failure of his mercenary forces, in his Ferrara enterprise, had recourse to auxiliaries, and arranged with Ferrando, King of Spain, that he should help him with his armies. These forces may be good in themselves, but they are always dangerous for those who borrow them, for if they lose you are defeated, and if they conquer you remain their prisoner. And although ancient history is full of examples of this, I will not depart from the example of Pope Julius II, which is still fresh. Nothing could be less prudent than the course he adopted; for, wishing to take Ferrara, he put himself entirely into the power of a foreigner. But by good fortune there arose a third cause which prevented him reaping the effects of his bad policy; for when his auxiliaries were beaten at Ravenna, the Swiss rose up and drove back the victors, against all expectation of himself or others, so that he was not taken prisoner by the enemy which had fled, nor by his own auxiliaries, having conquered by other arms than theirs. The Florentines, being totally disarmed, hired 10,000 Frenchmen to attack Pisa, by which measure they ran greater risk than at any period of their struggles. The emperor of Constantinople, to oppose his neighbours, put 10,000 Turks into Greece, who after the war would not go away again, which was the beginning of the servitude of Greece to the infidels.

And one, therefore, who wishes not to conquer would do well to use these forces, which are much more dangerous than mercenaries, as with them ruin is complete, for they are all united, and owe obedience to others, whereas with mercenaries, when they have conquered, it requires more time and a good opportunity for them to injure you; as they do not form a single body and have been engaged and paid by you, therefore a third party that you have made leader cannot at once acquire enough authority to be able to injure you. In a word, the greatest danger with mercenaries lies in their cowardice and reluctance to fight, but with auxiliaries the danger lies in their courage.

A wise prince, therefore, always avoids these forces and has recourse to his own, and would prefer rather to lose with his own men than conquer with the forces of others, not deeming it a true victory which is gained by foreign arms. I never hesitate to cite the example of Cesare Borgia and his actions. This duke entered Romagna with auxiliary troops, leading forces composed entirely of French soldiers, and with these he took Imola and Forlì; but as they seemed unsafe, he had recourse to mercenaries as a less risky policy, and hired the Orsini and Vitelli. Afterwards finding these uncertain to handle, unfaithful, and dangerous, he suppressed them, and relied upon his own men. And the difference between these forces can be easily seen if one considers the difference between the reputation of the duke when he had only the French, when he had the Orsini and Vitelli, and when he had to rely on himself and his own soldiers. His reputation will be found to have constantly increased, and he was never so highly esteemed as when everyone saw that he was the sole master of his forces.

I do not wish to depart from recent Italian instances, but I cannot omit Hiero of Syracuse, whom I have already mentioned. This man being, as I said, made head of the army by the Syracusans, immediately recognised the uselessness of that militia which was organized like our Italian mercenary troops, and as he thought it unsafe either to retain them or dismiss them, he had them cut in pieces and thenceforward made war with his own arms and not those of others. I would also call to mind a symbolic tale from the Old Testament which well illustrates this point. When David offered to Saul to go and fight against the Philistine champion Goliath, Saul, to encourage him, armed him with his own arms, which when David had tried on, he refused saying, that with them he could not fight so well; he preferred, therefore, to face the enemy with his own sling and knife. In short, the arms of others either fail, overburden, or else impede you. Charles VII, father of King Louis XI, having through good fortune and bravery liberated France from the English, recognised this necessity of being armed with his own forces, and established in his kingdom a system of men-at-arms and infantry. Afterwards King Louis his son abolished the infantry and began to hire Swiss, which mistake being followed by others is, as may now be seen, a cause of danger to that kingdom. For by giving such reputation to the Swiss, France has disheartened all her own troops, the infantry having been abolished and the men-at-arms being obliged to foreigners for assistance; for being accustomed to fight with Swiss troops, they think they cannot conquer without them. Whence it comes that the French are insufficiently strong to oppose the Swiss, and without the aid of the Swiss they will not venture against others. The armies of the French are thus of a mixed kind, partly mercenary and partly her own; taken together they are much better than troops entirely composed of mercenaries or auxiliaries, but much inferior to national forces.

And let this example be sufficient, for the kingdom of France would be invincible if Charles's military organisation had been developed or maintained. But men with their lack of prudence initiate novelties and, finding the first taste good, do not notice the poison within, as I pointed out previously in regard to wasting fevers.

The prince, therefore, who fails to recognise troubles in his state as they arise, is not truly wise, and it is given to few to be thus. If we consider the first cause of the collapse of the Roman Empire we shall find it merely due to the hiring of Goth mercenaries, for from that time we find the Roman strength begin to weaken. All the advantages derived from the Empire fell to the Goths.

I conclude then by saying that no prince is secure without his own troops, on the contrary he is entirely dependent on fortune, having no trustworthy means of defence in time of trouble. It has always been held and proclaimed by wise men "quod nihil sit tam infirmum aut instabile quam fama potentiae non sua vi nixae." One's own troops are those composed either of subjects or of citizens or of one's own dependants; all others are mercenaries or auxiliaries. The way to organise one's own troops is easily learnt if the methods of the four princes mentioned above be studied, and if one considers how Philip, father of Alexander the Great, and many republics and sovereigns have organised theirs. With such examples as these there is no need to labour the point.

Chapter XIV
The Duties of a Prince with Regard to the Militia

A prince should therefore have no other aim or thought, nor take up any other thing for his study, but war and its organisation and discipline, for that is the only art that is necessary to one who commands, and it is of such virtue that it not only maintains those who are born princes, but often enables men of private fortune to attain to that rank. And one sees, on the other hand, that when princes think more of luxury than of arms, they lose their state. The chief cause of the loss of states, is the contempt of this art, and the way to acquire them is to be well versed in the same.

Francesco Sforza, through being well armed, became, from private status, Duke of Milan; his sons, through wishing to avoid the fatigue and hardship of war, from dukes became private persons. For among other evils caused by being disarmed, it renders you contemptible; which is one of those disgraceful things which a prince must guard against, as will be explained later. Because there is no comparison whatever between an armed and a disarmed man; it is not reasonable to suppose that one who is armed will obey willingly one who is unarmed; or that any unarmed man will remain safe among armed servants. For one being disdainful and the other suspicious, it is not possible for them to act well together. And therefore a prince who is ignorant of military matters, besides the other misfortunes already mentioned, cannot be esteemed by his soldiers, nor have confidence in them.

He ought, therefore, never to let his thoughts stray from the exercise of war; and in peace he ought to practise it more than in war, which he can do in two ways: by action and by study. As to action, he must, besides keeping his men well disciplined and exercised, engage continually in hunting, and thus accustom his body to hardships; and meanwhile learn the nature of the land, how steep the mountains are, how the valleys debouch, where the plains lie, and understand the nature of rivers and swamps. To all this he should devote great attention. This knowledge is useful in two ways. In the first place, one learns to know one's country, and can the better see how to defend it. Then by means of the knowledge and experience gained in one locality, one can easily understand any other that it may be necessary to observe; for the hills and valleys, plains and rivers of Tuscany, for instance, have a certain resemblance to those of other provinces, so that from a knowledge of the country in one province one can easily arrive at a knowledge of others. And that prince who is lacking in this skill is wanting in the first essentials of a leader; for it is this which teaches how to find the enemy, take up quarters, lead armies, plan battles, and lay siege to towns with advantage.

Philopœmen, prince of the Achaei, among other praises bestowed on him by writers, is lauded because in times of peace he thought of nothing but the methods of warfare, and when he was in the country with his friends, he often stopped and asked them: If the enemy were on that hill and we found ourselves here with our army, which of us would have the advantage? How could we safely approach him maintaining our order? If we wished to retire, what ought we to do? If they retired, how should we follow them? And he put before them as they went along all the contingencies that might happen to an army, heard their opinion, gave his own, fortifying it by argument; so that thanks to these constant reflections there could never happen any incident when actually leading his armies for which he was not prepared.

But as to exercise for the mind, the prince ought to read history and study the actions of eminent men, see how they acted in warfare, examine the causes of their victories and defeats in order to imitate the former and avoid the latter, and above all, do as some men have done in the past, who have imitated some one, who has been much praised and glorified, and have always kept his deeds and actions before them, as they say Alexander the Great imitated Achilles, Cæsar Alexander, and Scipio Cyrus. And whoever reads the life of Cyrus written by Xenophon will perceive in the life of Scipio how gloriously he imitated the former, and how, in chastity, affability, humanity, and liberality Scipio conformed to those qualities of Cyrus as described by Xenophon.

A wise prince should follow similar methods and never remain idle in peaceful times, but industriously make good use of them, so that when fortune changes she may find him prepared to resist her blows, and to prevail in adversity.

Chapter XV
Of the Things for Which Men, and Especially Princes, Are Praised or Blamed

It now remains to be seen what are the methods and rules for a prince as regards his subjects and friends. And as I know that many have written of this, I fear that my writing about it may be deemed presumptuous, differing as I do, especially in this matter, from the opinions of others. But my intention being to write something of use to those who understand, it appears to me more proper to go to the real truth of the matter than to its imagination; and many have imagined republics and principalities which have never been seen or known to exist in reality; for how we live is so far removed from how we ought to live, that he who abandons what is done for what ought to be done, will rather learn to bring about his own ruin than his preservation. A man who wishes to make a profession of goodness in everything must necessarily come to grief among so many who are not good. Therefore it is necessary for a prince, who wishes to maintain himself, to learn how not to be good, and to use this knowledge and not use it, according to the necessity of the case.

Leaving on one side, then, those things which concern only an imaginary prince, and speaking of those that are real, I state that all men, and especially princes, who are placed at a greater height, are reputed for certain qualities which bring them either praise or blame. Thus one is considered liberal, another *misero* or miserly (using a Tuscan term, seeing that *avaro* with us still means one who is rapaciously acquisitive and *misero* one who makes grudging use of his own); one a free giver, another rapacious; one cruel, another merciful; one a breaker of his word, another trustworthy; one effeminate and pusillanimous, another fierce and high-spirited; one humane, another haughty; one lascivious, another chaste; one frank, another astute; one hard, another easy; one serious, another frivolous; one religious, another an unbeliever, and so on. I know that every one will admit that it would be highly praiseworthy in a prince to possess all the above-named qualities that are reputed good, but as they cannot all be possessed or observed, human conditions not permitting of it, it is necessary that he should be prudent enough to avoid the scandal of those vices which would lose him the state, and guard himself if possible against those which will not lose it him, but if not able to, he can indulge them with less scruple. And yet he must not mind incurring the scandal of those vices, without which it would be difficult to save the state, for if one considers well, it will be found that some things which seem virtues would, if followed, lead to one's ruin, and some others which appear vices result in one's greater security and wellbeing.

Chapter XVI
Of Liberality and Niggardliness

Beginning now with the first qualities above named, I say that it would be well to be considered liberal; nevertheless liberality such as the world understands it will injure you, because if used virtuously and in the proper way, it will not be known, and you will incur the disgrace of the contrary vice. But one who wishes to obtain the reputation of liberality among men, must not omit every kind of sumptuous display, and to such an extent that a prince of this character will consume by such means all his resources, and will be at last compelled, if he wishes to maintain his name for liberality, to impose heavy taxes on his people, become extortionate, and do everything possible to obtain money. This will make his subjects begin to hate him, and he will be little esteemed being poor, so that having by this liberality injured many and benefited but few, he will feel the first little disturbance and be endangered by every peril. If he recognises this and wishes to change his system, he incurs at once the charge of niggardliness.

A prince, therefore, not being able to exercise this virtue of liberality without risk if it be known, must not, if he be prudent, object to be called miserly. In course of time he will be thought more liberal, when it is seen that by his parsimony his revenue is sufficient, that he can defend himself against those who make war on him, and undertake enterprises without burdening his people, so that he is really liberal to all those from whom he does not take, who are infinite in number, and niggardly to all to whom he does not give, who are few. In our times we have seen nothing great done except by those who have been esteemed niggardly; the others have all been ruined. Pope Julius II, although he had made use of a reputation for liberality in order to attain the papacy, did not seek to retain it afterwards, so that he might be able to wage war. The present King of France has carried on so many wars without imposing an extraordinary tax, because his extra expenses were covered by the parsimony he had so long practised. The present King of Spain, if he had been thought liberal, would not have engaged in and been successful in so many enterprises.

For these reasons a prince must care little for the reputation of being a miser, if he wishes to avoid robbing his subjects, if he wishes to be able to defend himself, to avoid becoming poor and contemptible, and not to be forced to become rapacious; this niggardliness is one of those vices which enable him to reign. If it is said that Cæsar attained the empire through liberality, and that many others have reached the highest positions through being liberal or being thought so, I would reply that you are either a prince already or else on the way to become one. In the first case, this liberality is harmful; in the second, it is certainly necessary to be considered liberal. Cæsar was one of those who wished to attain the mastery over Rome, but if after attaining it he had lived and had not moderated his expenses, he would have destroyed that empire. And should any one reply that there have been many princes, who have done great things with their armies, who have been thought extremely liberal, I would answer by saying that the prince may either spend his own wealth and that of his subjects or the wealth of others. In the first case he must be sparing, but for the rest he must not neglect to be very liberal. The liberality is very necessary to a prince who marches with his armies, and lives by plunder, sack, and ransom, and is dealing with the wealth of others, for without it he would not be followed by his soldiers. And you may be very generous indeed with what is not the property of yourself or your subjects, as were Cyrus, Cæsar, and Alexander; for spending the wealth of others will not diminish your reputation, but increase it, only spending your own resources will injure you. There is nothing which destroys itself so much as liberality, for by using it you lose the power of using it, and become either poor and despicable, or, to escape poverty, rapacious and hated. And of all things that a prince must guard against, the most important are being despicable or hated, and liberality will lead you to one or other of these conditions. It is, therefore, wiser to have the name of a miser, which produces disgrace without hatred, than to incur of necessity the name of being rapacious, which produces both disgrace and hatred.

Chapter XVII
Of Cruelty and Clemency, and Whether
It Is Better to Be Loved or Feared

Proceeding to the other qualities before named, I say that every prince must desire to be considered merciful and not cruel. He must, however, take care not to misuse this mercifulness. Cesare Borgia was considered cruel, but his cruelty had brought order to the Romagna, united it, and reduced it to peace and fealty. If this is considered well, it will be seen that he was really much more merciful than the Florentine people, who, to avoid the name of cruelty, allowed Pistoia to be destroyed. A prince, therefore, must not mind incurring the charge of cruelty for the purpose of keeping his subjects united and faithful; for, with a very few examples, he will be more merciful than those who, from excess of tenderness, allow disorders to arise, from whence spring bloodshed and rapine; for these as a rule injure the whole community, while the executions carried out by the prince injure only individuals. And of all princes, it is impossible for a new prince to escape the reputation of cruelty, new states being always full of dangers. Wherefore Virgil through the mouth of Dido says:

> Harsh necessity, and my new kingdom, force me to do such things and to guard my frontiers everywhere.

Nevertheless he must be cautious in believing and acting, and must not be afraid of his own shadow, and must proceed in a temperate manner with prudence and humanity, so that too much confidence does not render him incautious, and too much diffidence does not render him intolerant.

From this arises the question whether it is better to be loved more than feared, or feared more than loved. The reply is, that one ought to be both feared and loved, but as it is difficult for the two to go together, it is much safer to be feared than loved, if one of the two has to be wanting. For it may be said of men in general that they are ungrateful, voluble dissemblers, anxious to avoid danger, and covetous of gain; as long as you benefit them, they are entirely yours; they offer you their blood, their goods, their life, and their children, as I have before said, when the necessity is remote; but when it approaches, they revolt. And the prince who has relied solely on their words, without making other preparations, is ruined; for the friendship which is gained by purchase and not through grandeur and nobility of spirit is bought but not secured, and at a pinch is not to be expended in your service. And men have less scruple in offending one who makes himself loved than one who makes himself feared; for love is held by a chain of obligation which, men being selfish, is broken whenever it serves their purpose; but fear is maintained by a dread of punishment which never fails.

Still, a prince should make himself feared in such a way that if he does not gain love, he at any rate avoids hatred; for fear and the absence of hatred may well go together, and will be always attained by one who abstains from interfering with the property of his citizens and subjects or with their women. And when he is obliged to take the life of any one, let him do so when there is a proper justification and manifest reason for it; but above all he must abstain from taking the property of others, for men forget more easily the death of their father than the loss of their patrimony. Then also pretexts for seizing property are never wanting, and one who begins to live by rapine will always find some reason for taking the goods of others, whereas causes for taking life are rarer and more fleeting.

But when the prince is with his army and has a large number of soldiers under his control, then it is extremely necessary that he should not mind being thought cruel, for without this reputation he could not keep an army united or disposed to any duty. Among the noteworthy actions of Hannibal is numbered this, that although he had an enormous army, composed of men of all nations and fighting in foreign countries, there never arose any dissension either among them or against the prince, either in good fortune or in bad. This could not be due to anything but his inhuman cruelty, which together with his infinite other virtues, made him always venerated and terrible in the sight of his soldiers, and without it his other virtues would not have sufficed to produce that effect. Thoughtless writers admire on the one hand his actions, and on the other blame the principal cause of them.

And that it is true that his other virtues would not have sufficed may be seen from the case of Scipio (famous not only in regard to his own times, but all times of which memory remains), whose armies rebelled against him in Spain, which arose from nothing but his excessive kindness, which allowed more licence to the soldiers than was consonant with military discipline. He was reproached with this in the senate by Fabius Maximus, who called him a corrupter of the Roman militia. Locri having been destroyed by one of Scipio's officers was not revenged by him, nor was the insolence of that officer punished, simply by reason of his easy nature; so much so, that some one wishing to excuse him in the senate, said that there were many men who knew rather how not to err, than how to correct the errors of others. This disposition would in time have tarnished the fame and glory of Scipio had he persevered in it under the empire, but living under the rule of the senate this harmful quality was not only concealed but became a glory to him.

I conclude, therefore, with regard to being feared and loved, that men love at their own free will, but fear at the will of the prince, and that a wise prince must rely on what is in his power and not on what is in the power of others, and he must only contrive to avoid incurring hatred, as has been explained.

Chapter XVIII
In What Way Princes Must Keep Faith

How laudable it is for a prince to keep good faith and live with integrity, and not with astuteness, every one knows. Still the experience of our times shows those princes to have done great things who have had little regard for good faith, and have been able by astuteness to confuse men's brains, and who have ultimately overcome those who have made loyalty their foundation.

You must know, then, that there are two methods of fighting, the one by law, the other by force: the first method is that of men, the second of beasts; but as the first method is often insufficient, one must have recourse to the second. It is therefore necessary for a prince to know well how to use both the beast and the man. This was covertly taught to rulers by ancient writers, who relate how Achilles and many others of those ancient princes were given to Chiron the centaur to be brought up and educated under his discipline. The parable of this semi-animal, semi-human teacher is meant to indicate that a prince must know how to use both natures, and that the one without the other is not durable.

A prince being thus obliged to know well how to act as a beast must imitate the fox and the lion, for the lion cannot protect himself from traps, and the fox cannot defend himself from wolves. One must therefore be a fox to recognise traps, and a lion to frighten wolves. Those that wish to be only lions do not understand this. Therefore, a prudent ruler ought not to keep faith when by so doing it would be against his interest, and when the reasons which made him bind himself no longer exist. If men were all good, this precept would not be a good one; but as they are bad, and would not observe their faith with you, so you are not bound to keep faith with them. Nor have legitimate grounds ever failed a prince who wished to show colourable excuse for the non-fulfilment of his promise. Of this one could furnish an infinite number of modern examples, and show how many times peace has been broken, and how many promises rendered worthless, by the faithlessness of princes, and those that have been best able to imitate the fox have succeeded best. But it is necessary to be able to disguise this character well, and to be a great feigner and dissembler; and men are so simple and so ready to obey present necessities, that one who deceives will always find those who allow themselves to be deceived.

I will only mention one modern instance. Alexander VI did nothing else but deceive men, he thought of nothing else, and found the occasion for it; no man was ever more able to give assurances, or affirmed things with stronger oaths, and no man observed them less; however, he always succeeded in his deceptions, as he well knew this aspect of things.

It is not, therefore, necessary for a prince to have all the above-named qualities, but it is very necessary to seem to have them. I would even be bold to say that to possess them and always to observe them is dangerous, but to appear to possess them is useful. Thus it is well to seem merciful, faithful, humane, sincere, religious, and also to be so; but you must have the mind so disposed that when it is needful to be otherwise you may be able to change to the opposite qualities. And it must be understood that a prince, and especially a new prince, cannot observe all those things which are considered good in men, being often obliged, in order to maintain the state, to act against faith, against charity, against humanity, and against religion. And, therefore, he must have a mind disposed to adapt itself according to the wind, and as the variations of fortune dictate, and, as I said before, not

deviate from what is good, if possible, but be able to do evil if constrained.

A prince must take great care that nothing goes out of his mouth which is not full of the above-named five qualities, and, to see and hear him, he should seem to be all mercy, faith, integrity, humanity, and religion. And nothing is more necessary than to seem to have this last quality, for men in general judge more by the eyes than by the hands, for every one can see, but very few have to feel. Everybody sees what you appear to be, few feel what you are, and those few will not dare to oppose themselves to the many, who have the majesty of the state to defend them; and in the actions of men, and especially of princes, from which there is no appeal, the end justifies the means. Let a prince therefore aim at conquering and maintaining the state, and the means will always be judged honourable and praised by every one, for the vulgar [are] always taken by appearances and the issue of the event; and the world consists only of the vulgar, and the few who are not vulgar are isolated when the many have a rallying point in the prince. A certain prince of the present time, whom it is well not to name, never does anything but preach peace and good faith, but he is really a great enemy to both, and either of them, had he observed them, would have lost him state or reputation on many occasions.

Chapter XIX
That We Must Avoid Being Despised and Hated

But as I have now spoken of the most important of the qualities in question, I will now deal briefly and generally with the rest. The prince must, as already stated, avoid those things which will make him hated or despised; and whenever he succeeds in this, he will have done his part, and will find no danger in other vices. He will chiefly become hated, as I said, by being rapacious, and usurping the property and women of his subjects, which he must abstain from doing, and whenever one does not attack the property or honour of the generality of men, they will live contented; and one will only have to combat the ambition of a few, who can be easily held in check in many ways. He is rendered despicable by being thought changeable, frivolous, effeminate, timid, and irresolute; which a prince must guard against as a rock of danger, and so contrive that his actions show grandeur, spirit, gravity, and fortitude; and as to the government of his subjects, let his sentence be irrevocable, and let him adhere to his decisions so that no one may think of deceiving or cozening him.

The prince who creates such an opinion of himself gets a great reputation, and it is very difficult to conspire against one who has a great reputation, and he will not easily be attacked, so long as it is known that he is capable and reverenced by his subjects. For a prince must have two kinds of fear: one internal as regards his subjects, one external as regards foreign powers. From the latter he can defend himself with good arms and good friends, and he will always have good friends if he has good arms; and internal matters will always remain quiet, if they are not perturbed by conspiracy and there is no disturbance from without; and even if external powers sought to attack him, if he has ruled and lived as I have described, he will always, if he stands firm, be able to sustain every shock, as I have shown that Nabis the Spartan did. But with regard to the subjects, if not acted on from outside, it is still to be feared lest they conspire in secret, from which the prince may guard himself well by avoiding hatred and contempt, and keeping the people satisfied with him, which it is necessary to accomplish, as has been related at length. And one of the most potent remedies that a prince has against conspiracies, is that of not being hated by the mass of the people; for whoever conspires always believes that he will satisfy the people by the death of their prince; but if he thought to offend them by doing this, he would fear to engage in such an undertaking, for the difficulties that conspirators have to meet are infinite. Experience shows that there have been very many conspiracies, but few have turned out well, for whoever conspires cannot act alone, and cannot find companions except among those who are discontented; and as soon as you have disclosed your intention to a malcontent, you give him the means of satisfying himself, for by revealing it he can hope to secure everything he wants; to such an extent that seeing a certain gain by doing this, and seeing on the other hand only a doubtful one and full of danger, he must either be a rare friend to you or else a very bitter enemy to the prince if he keeps faith with you. And to express the matter in a few words, I say, that on the side of the conspirator there is nothing but fear, jealousy, suspicion, and dread of punishment which frightens him; and on the side of the prince there is the majesty of government, the laws, the protection of friends and of the state which guard him. When to these things is added the goodwill of the people, it is impossible that any one should have the temerity to conspire. For whereas generally a conspirator has to fear before the execution of his plot, in this case, having the people for an enemy, he must also fear after his crime is accomplished, and thus he is not able to hope for any refuge.

Numberless instances might be given of this, but I will content myself with one which took place within the memory of our fathers. Messer Annibale Bentivogli, Prince of Bologna, ancestor of the present Messer Annibale, was killed by the Canneschi, who conspired against him. He left no relations but Messer Giovanni, who was then an infant, but after the murder the people rose up and killed all the Canneschi. This arose from the popular goodwill that the house of Bentivogli enjoyed at that time, which was so great that, as there was nobody left after the death of Annibale who could govern the state, the Bolognese hearing that there was one of the Bentivogli family in Florence, who had till then been thought the son of a blacksmith, came to fetch him and gave him the government of the city, and it was governed by him until Messer Giovanni was old enough to assume the government.

I conclude, therefore, that a prince need trouble little about conspiracies when the people are well disposed, but when they are hostile and hold him in hatred, then he must fear everything and everybody. Well-ordered states and wise princes have studied diligently not to drive the nobles to desperation, and to satisfy the populace and keep it contented, for this is one of the most important matters that a prince has to deal with.

Among the kingdoms that are well ordered and governed in our time is France, and there we find numberless good institutions on which depend the liberty and security of the king; of these the chief is the parliament and its authority, because he who established that kingdom, knowing the ambition and insolence of the great nobles, deemed it necessary to have a bit in their mouths to check them. And knowing on the other hand the hatred of the mass of the people against the great, based on fear, and wishing to secure them, he did not wish to make this the special care of the king, to relieve him of the dissatisfaction that he might incur among the nobles by favouring the people, and among the people by favouring the nobles. He therefore established a third judge that, without direct charge of the king, kept in check the great and favoured the lesser people. Nor could any better or more prudent measure have been adopted, nor better precaution for the safety of the king and the kingdom. From which another notable rule can be drawn, that princes should let the carrying out of unpopular duties devolve on others, and bestow favours themselves. I conclude again by saying that a prince must esteem his nobles, but not make himself hated by the populace.

It may perhaps seem to some, that considering the life and death of many Roman emperors that they are instances contrary to my opinion, finding that some who always lived nobly and showed great strength of character, nevertheless lost the empire, or were killed by their subjects who conspired against them. Wishing to answer these objections, I will discuss the qualities of some emperors, showing the cause of their ruin not to be at variance with what I have stated, and I will also meanwhile consider the things to be noted by whoever reads the deeds of these times. I will content myself with taking all those emperors who succeeded to the empire from Marcus the philosopher to Maximinus: these were Marcus, Commodus his son, Pertinax, Julianus Severus, Antoninus, Caracalla his son, Macrinus, Heliogabalus, Alexander, and Maximinus. And the first thing to note is, that whereas other princes have only to contend against the ambition of the great and the insolence of the people, the Roman emperors had a third difficulty, that of having to support the cruelty and avarice of the soldiers, which was such that it was the cause of the ruin of many, it being hardly possible to satisfy both the soldiers and the people. For the people love tranquillity, and therefore like pacific princes, but the soldiers prefer a prince of military spirit, who is insolent, cruel, and rapacious. They wish him to exercise these qualities on the people so that they may get double pay and give vent to their avarice and cruelty. Thus it came about that those emperors who, by nature or art, had not such a reputation as could keep both parties in check, were invariably ruined, and the greater number of them who were raised to the empire being new men, knowing the difficulties of these two opposite dispositions, confined themselves to satisfying the soldiers, and thought little of injuring the people. This choice was necessary, princes not being able to avoid being hated by someone. They must first try not to be hated by the mass of the people; if they cannot accomplish this they must use every means to escape the hatred of the most powerful parties. And therefore these emperors, who being new men had need of

extraordinary favours, adhered to the soldiers rather than to the people; whether this, however, was of use to them or not, depended on whether the prince knew how to maintain his reputation with them. From these causes it resulted that Marcus, Pertinax, and Alexander, being all of modest life, lovers of justice, enemies of cruelty, humane and benign, all came to a sad end except Marcus. Marcus alone lived and died in honour, because he succeeded to the empire by hereditary right and did not owe it either to the soldiers or to the people; besides which, possessing many virtues which made him revered, he kept both parties in their place as long as he lived and was never either hated or despised. But Pertinax was created emperor against the will of the soldiers, who being accustomed to live licentiously under Commodus, could not put up with the honest life to which Pertinax wished to limit them, so that having made himself hated, and to this contempt being added because he was old, he was ruined at the very beginning of his administration.

Whence it may be seen that hatred is gained as much by good works as by evil, and therefore, as I said before, a prince who wishes to maintain the state is often forced to do evil, for when that party, whether populace, soldiery, or nobles, whichever it be that you consider necessary to you for keeping your position, is corrupt, you must follow its humour and satisfy it, and in that case good works will be inimical to you. But let us come to Alexander, who was of such goodness, that among other things for which he is praised, it is said that in the fourteen years that he reigned no one was put to death by him without a fair trial. Nevertheless, being considered effeminate, and a man who allowed himself to be ruled by his mother, and having thus fallen into contempt, the army conspired against him and killed him.

Considering, on the other hand, the qualities of Commodus, Severus, Antoninus, Caracalla, and Maximinus, you will find them extremely cruel and rapacious; to satisfy the soldiers there was no injury which they would not inflict on the people, and all except Severus ended badly. Severus, however, had such abilities that by maintaining the soldiers friendly to him, he was able to reign happily, although he oppressed the people, for his virtues made him so admirable in the sight both of the soldiers and the people that the latter were, in some degree, astonished and stupefied, while the former were respectful and contented.

As the deeds of this ruler were great and notable for a new prince, I will briefly show how well he could use the qualities of the fox and the lion, whose natures, as I said before, it is necessary for a prince to imitate. Knowing the sloth of the Emperor Julianus, Severus, who was leader of the army in Slavonia, persuaded the troops that it would be well to go to Rome to avenge the death of Pertinax, who had been slain by the Prætorian guard, and under this pretext, without revealing his aspirations to the throne, marched with his army to Rome and was in Italy before his departure was known. On his arrival in Rome the senate elected him emperor through fear, and killed Julianus. There remained after this beginning two difficulties to be faced by Severus before he could obtain the whole control of the empire: one in Asia, where Nigrinus, head of the Asiatic armies, had declared himself emperor; the other in the West from Albinus, who also aspired to the empire. And as he judged it dangerous to show himself hostile to both, he decided to attack Nigrinus and deceive Albinus, to whom he wrote that having been elected emperor by the senate he wished to share that dignity with him; he sent him the title of Cæsar and, by deliberation of the senate, he was declared his colleague; all of which was accepted as true by Albinus. But when Severus had defeated and killed Nigrinus, and pacified things in the East, he returned to Rome and charged Albinus in the senate with having, unmindful of the benefits received from him, traitorously sought to assassinate him, and stated that he was therefore obliged to go and punish his ingratitude. He then went to France to meet him, and there deprived him of both his position and his life.

Whoever examines in detail the actions of Severus, will find him to have been a very ferocious lion and an extremely astute fox, and will find him to have been feared and respected by all and not hated by the army; and will not be surprised that he, a new man, should have been able to hold so much power, since his great reputation defended him always from the hatred that his rapacity might have produced in the people. But Antoninus his son was also a man of great ability, and possessed qualities that rendered him admirable in the sight of the people and also made him popular with the soldiers, for he was a military man, capable of enduring the most extreme hardships, disdainful of delicate food, and every other luxury, which made him loved by all the armies. However, his ferocity and cruelty were so great and

unheard of, through his having, after executing many private individuals, caused a large part of the population of Rome and all that of Alexandria to be killed, that he became hated by all the world and began to be feared by those about him to such an extent that he was finally killed by a centurion in the midst of his army. Whence it is to be noted that this kind of death, which proceeds from the deliberate action of a determined man, cannot be avoided by princes, since any one who does not fear death himself can inflict it, but a prince need not fear much on this account, as such men are extremely rare. He must only guard against committing any grave injury to any one he makes use of, or has about him for his service, like Antoninus had done, having caused the death with contumely of the brother of that centurion, and also threatened him every day, although he still retained him in his bodyguard, which was a foolish and dangerous thing to do, as the fact proved.

But let us come to Commodus, who might easily have kept the empire, having succeeded to it by heredity, being the son of Marcus, and it would have sufficed for him to follow in the steps of his father to have satisfied both the people and the soldiers. But being of a cruel and bestial disposition, in order to be able to exercise his rapacity on the people, he sought to favour the soldiers and render them licentious; on the other hand, by not maintaining his dignity, by often descending into the theatre to fight with gladiators and committing other contemptible actions, little worthy of the imperial dignity, he became despicable in the eyes of the soldiers, and being hated on the one hand and despised on the other, he was conspired against and killed.

There remains to be described the character of Maximus. He was an extremely warlike man, and as the armies were annoyed with the effeminacy of Alexander, which we have already spoken of, he was elected emperor after the death of the latter. He did not enjoy it for long, as two things made him hated and despised: the one his base origin, as he had been a shepherd in Thrace, which was generally known and caused great disdain on all sides; the other, because he had at the commencement of his rule deferred going to Rome to take possession of the Imperial seat, and had obtained a reputation for great cruelty, having through his prefects in Rome and other parts of the empire committed many acts of cruelty. The whole world being thus moved by indignation for the baseness of his blood, and also by the hatred caused by fear of his ferocity, he was conspired against first by Africa and afterwards by the senate and all the people of Rome and Italy. His own army also joined them, for besieging Aquileia and finding it difficult to take, they became enraged at his cruelty, and seeing that he had so many enemies, they feared him less and put him to death.

I will not speak of Heliogabalus, of Macrinus, or Julianus, who being entirely contemptible were immediately suppressed, but I will come to the conclusion of this discourse by saying that the princes of our time have less difficulty than these in being obliged to satisfy in an extraordinary degree their soldiers in their states; for although they must have a certain consideration for them, yet any difficulty is soon settled, for none of these princes have armies that are inextricably bound up with the administration of the government and the rule of their provinces as were the armies of the Roman empire. If it was then necessary to satisfy the soldiers rather than the people, it was because the soldiers could do more than the people; now, it is more necessary for all princes, except the Turk and the Sultan, to satisfy the people than the soldiers, for the people can do more than the soldiers. I except the Turk, because he always keeps about him 12,000 infantry and 15,000 cavalry, on which depend the security and strength of his kingdom, and it is necessary for him to postpone every other consideration to keep them friendly. It is the same with the kingdom of the Sultan, which being entirely in the hands of the soldiers, he is bound to keep their friendship regardless of the people. And it is to be noted that this state of the Sultan is different from that of all other princes, being similar to the Christian pontificate, which cannot be called either a hereditary kingdom or a new one, for the sons of the dead prince are not his heirs, but he who is elected to position by those who have authority. And as this order is ancient it cannot be called a new kingdom, there being none of these difficulties which exist in new ones; as although the prince is new, the rules of that state are old and arranged to receive him as if he were their hereditary lord.

But returning to our matter, I say that whoever studies the preceding argument will see that either hatred or contempt were the causes of the ruin of the emperors named and will also observe how it came about that, some of them acting in one way and some in another, in both ways there were some who had a fortunate and others an unfortunate ending. As Perti-

nax and Alexander were both new rulers, it was useless and injurious for them to try and imitate Marcus, who was a hereditary prince; and similarly with Caracalla, Commodus, and Maximinus it was pernicious for them to imitate Severus, as they had not sufficient ability to follow in his footsteps. Thus a new prince cannot imitate the actions of Marcus, in his dominions, nor is it necessary for him to imitate those of Severus; but he must take from Severus those things that are necessary to found his state, and from Marcus those that are useful and glorious for conserving a state that is already established and secure.

Chapter XX
Whether Fortresses and Other Things Which Princes Often Contrive Are Useful or Injurious

Some princes, in order to hold their possessions securely, have disarmed their citizens, some others have kept their subject lands divided into parts, others have fomented enmities against themselves, others have endeavoured to win over those whom they suspected at the commencement of their rule: some have constructed fortresses, others have cast them down and destroyed them. And although one cannot pronounce a definite judgment as to these things without going into the particulars of the state to which such a deliberation is to be applied, still I will speak in such a general way as the matter will permit.

A new prince has never been known to disarm his subjects, on the contrary, when he has found them disarmed he has always armed them, for by arming them these arms become your own, those that you suspected become faithful and those that were faithful remain so, and from being merely subjects become your partisans. And since all the subjects cannot be armed, when you give the privilege of arms to some, you can deal more safely with the others; and this different treatment that they recognise renders your men more obliged to you. The others will excuse you, judging that those have necessarily greater merit who have greater danger and heavier duties. But when you disarm them, you commence to offend them and show that you distrust them either through cowardice or lack of confidence, and both of these opinions generate hatred against you. And as you cannot remain unarmed, you are obliged to resort to a mercenary militia, of which we have already stated the value; and even if it were good it cannot be sufficient in number to defend you against powerful enemies and suspected subjects. Therefore, as I have said, a new prince in a new dominion always has his subjects armed. History is full of such examples.

But when a prince acquires a new state as an addition to his old one, then it is necessary to disarm that state, except those who in acquiring it have sided with you; and even these one must, when time and opportunity serve, render weak and effeminate, and arrange things so that all the arms of the new state are in the hands of your soldiers who live near you in your old state.

Our forefathers and those who were esteemed wise used to say that it was necessary to hold Pistoia by means of factions and Pisa with fortresses, and for this purpose they fomented differences in some of their subject towns in order to possess them more easily. In those days when there was a balance of power in Italy, this was doubtless well done, but does not seem to me to be a good precept for the present time, for I do not believe that the divisions thus created ever do any good; on the contrary, it is certain that when the enemy approaches, the cities thus divided will be at once lost, for the weaker faction will always side with the enemy and the other will not be able to stand.

The Venetians, actuated, I believe, by the aforesaid motives, fomented the Guelf and Ghibelline factions in the cities subject to them, and although they never allowed them to come to bloodshed, they yet encouraged these differences among them, so that the citizens, being occupied in their own quarrels, might not act against them. This, however, did not avail them anything, as was seen when, after the defeat of Vailà, a part of those subjects immediately took courage and seized the whole state. Such methods, besides, argue weakness in a prince, for in a strong government such dissensions will never be permitted. They are profitable only in time of peace, as by such means it is easy to manage one's subjects, but when it comes to war, the fallacy of such a policy is at once shown.

Without doubt princes become great when they overcome difficulties and opposition, and therefore fortune, especially when it wants to render a new prince great, who has greater need of gaining a great reputation than a hereditary prince, raises up enemies and compels him to undertake wars against them, so that he may have cause to overcome them, and thus climb up higher by means of that ladder which his enemies have brought him. There are many who think therefore that a wise prince ought, when he has the chance, to foment astutely some enmity, so that by suppressing it he will augment his greatness.

Princes, and especially new ones, have found more faith and more usefulness in those men, whom at the beginning of their power they regarded with suspicion, than in those they at first confided in. Pandolfo Petrucci, Prince of Siena, governed his state more by those whom he suspected than by others. But of this we cannot speak at large, as it strays from the subject; I will merely say that these men who at the beginning of a new government were enemies, if they are of a kind to need support to maintain their position, can be very easily gained by the prince, and they are the more compelled to serve him faithfully as they know they must by their deeds cancel the bad opinion previously held of them, and thus the prince will always derive greater help from them than from those who, serving him with greater security, neglect his interests.

And as the matter requires it, I will not omit to remind a prince who has newly taken a state with the secret help of its inhabitants that he must consider well the motives that have induced those who have favoured him to do so, and if it is not natural affection for him, but only because they were not contented with the state as it was, he will have great trouble and difficulty in maintaining their friendship, because it will be impossible for him to content them. And on well examining the cause of this in the examples drawn from ancient and modern times it will be seen that it is much easier to gain the friendship of those men who were contented with the previous condition and were therefore at first enemies, than that those who not being contented, became his friends and helped him to occupy it.

It has been the custom of princes in order to be able to hold their state securely, to erect fortresses, as a bridle and bit to those who have designs against them, and in order to have a secure refuge against a sudden assault. I approve this method, because it was anciently used. Nevertheless, Messer Niccolò Vitelli has been seen in our own time to destroy two fortresses in Città di Castello in order to keep that state. Guid'Ubaldo, Duke of Urbino, on returning to his dominions from which he had been driven by Cesare Borgia, razed to their foundations all the fortresses of that province, and considered that without them it would be more difficult for him to lose the state again. The Bentivogli, in returning to Bologna, took similar measures. Therefore fortresses may or may not be useful according to the times; if they do good in one way, they do harm in another. The question may be discussed thus: a prince who fears his own people more than foreigners ought to build fortresses, but he who has greater fear of foreigners than of his own people ought to do without them. The castle of Milan built by Francesco Sforza has given and will give more trouble to the house of Sforza than any other disorder in that state. Therefore the best fortress is to be found in the love of the people, for although you may have fortresses they will not save you if you are hated by the people. When once the people have taken arms against you, there will never be lacking foreigners to assist them. In our times we do not see that they have profited any ruler, except the Countess of Forlì on the death of her consort Count Girolamo, for she was thus enabled to escape the popular rising and await help from Milan and recover the state; the circumstances being then such that no foreigner could assist the people. But afterwards they were of little use to her when Cesare Borgia attacked her and the people being hostile to her allied themselves with the foreigner. So that then and before it would have been safer for her not to have been hated by the people than to have had the fortresses. Having considered these things I would therefore praise the one who erects fortresses and the one who does not, and would blame any one who, trusting in them, recks little of being hated by his people.

Chapter XXI
How a Prince Must Act in Order To Gain Reputation

Nothing causes a prince to be so much esteemed as great enterprises and giving proof of prowess. We have in our own day Ferdinand, King of Aragon, the present King of Spain. He may almost be termed a new prince, because from a weak king he has become for fame and glory the first king in Christendom, and if you regard his actions you will find them all very great and some of them extraordinary. At the beginning of his reign he assailed Granada, and that enterprise was the foundation of his state. At first he did it at his leisure and without fear of being interfered with; he kept the minds of the barons of Castile occupied in this enterprise, so that thinking only of that war they did not think of making innovations, and he

thus acquired reputation and power over them without their being aware of it. He was able with the money of the Church and the people to maintain his armies, and by that long war to lay the foundations of his military power, which afterwards has made him famous. Besides this, to be able to undertake greater enterprises, and always under the pretext of religion, he had recourse to a pious cruelty, driving out the Moors from his kingdom and despoiling them. No more miserable or unusual example can be found. He also attacked Africa under the same pretext, undertook his Italian enterprise, and has lately attacked France; so that he has continually contrived great things, which have kept his subjects' minds uncertain and astonished, and occupied in watching their result. And these actions have arisen one out of the other, so that they have left no time for men to settle down and act against him.

It is also very profitable for a prince to give some outstanding example of his greatness in the internal administration, like those related of Messer Bernabò of Milan. When it happens that some one does something extraordinary, either good or evil, in civil life, he must find such means of rewarding or punishing him which will be much talked about. And above all a prince must endeavour in every action to obtain fame for being great and excellent.

A prince is further esteemed when he is a true friend or a true enemy, when, that is, he declares himself without reserve in favour of some one or against another. This policy is always more useful than remaining neutral. For if two neighbouring powers come to blows, they are either such that if one wins, you will have to fear the victor, or else not. In either of these two cases it will be better for you to declare yourself openly and make war, because in the first case if you do not declare yourself, you will fall a prey to the victor, to the pleasure and satisfaction of the one who has been defeated, and you will have no reason nor anything to defend you and nobody to receive you. For, whoever wins will not desire friends whom he suspects and who do not help him when in trouble, and whoever loses will not receive you as you did not take up arms to venture yourself in his cause.

Antiochus went to Greece, being sent by the Ætolians to expel the Romans. He sent orators to the Achaeians who were friends of the Romans to encourage them to remain neutral; on the other hand the Romans persuaded them to take up arms on their side. The matter was brought before the council of the Achaeians for deliberation, where the ambassador of Antiochus sought to persuade them to remain neutral, to which the Roman ambassador replied: "As to what is said that it is best and most useful for your state not to meddle in our war, nothing is further from the truth: for if you do not meddle in it you will become, without any favour or any reputation, the prize of the victor."

And it will always happen that the one who is not your friend will want you to remain neutral, and the one who is your friend will require you to declare yourself by taking arms. Irresolute princes, to avoid present dangers, usually follow the way of neutrality and are mostly ruined by it. But when the prince declares himself frankly in favour of one side, if the one to whom you adhere conquers, even if he is powerful and you remain at his discretion, he is under an obligation to you and friendship has been established, and men are never so dishonest as to oppress you with such a patent ingratitude. Moreover, victories are never so prosperous that the victor does not need to have some scruples, especially as to justice. But if your ally loses, you are sheltered by him, and so long as he can, he will assist you; you become the companion of a fortune which may rise again. In the second case, when those who fight are such that you have nothing to fear from the victor, it is still more prudent on your part to adhere to one; for you go to the ruin of one with the help of him who ought to save him if he were wise, and if he conquers he rests at your discretion, and it is impossible that he should not conquer with your help.

And here it should be noted that a prince ought never to make common cause with one more powerful than himself to injure another, unless necessity forces him to it, as before said; for if he wins you rest in his power, and princes must avoid as much as possible being under the will and pleasure of others. The Venetians united with France against the Duke of Milan, although they could have avoided that alliance, and from it resulted their own ruin. But when one cannot avoid it, as happened in the case of the Florentines when the Pope and Spain went with their armies to attack Lombardy, then the prince ought to join for the above reasons. Let no state believe that it can always follow a safe policy, rather let it think that all are doubtful. This is found in the nature of things, that one never tries to avoid one difficulty without running

into another, but prudence consists in being able to know the nature of the difficulties, and taking the least harmful as good.

A prince must also show himself a lover of merit, give preferment to the able, and honour those who excel in every art. Moreover he must encourage his citizens to follow their callings quietly, whether in commerce, or agriculture, or any other trade that men follow, so that this one shall not refrain from improving his possessions through fear that they may be taken from him, and that one from starting a trade for fear of taxes; but he should offer rewards to whoever does these things, and to whoever seeks in any way to improve his city or state. Besides this, he ought, at convenient seasons of the year, to keep the people occupied with festivals and shows; and as every city is divided either into guilds or into classes, he ought to pay attention to all these groups, mingle with them from time to time and give them an example of his humanity and munificence, always upholding, however, the majesty of his dignity, which must never be allowed to fail in anything whatever.

Chapter XXII
Of the Secretaries of Princes

The choice of a prince's ministers is a matter of no little importance; they are either good or not according to the prudence of the prince. The first impression that one gets of a ruler and of his brains is from seeing the men that he has about him. When they are competent and faithful one can always consider him wise, as he has been able to recognise their ability and keep them faithful. But when they are the reverse, one can always form an unfavourable opinion of him, because the first mistake that he makes is in making this choice.

There was nobody who knew Messer Antonio da Venafro as the minister of Pandolfo Petrucci, Prince of Siena, who did not consider Pandolfo to be a very prudent man, having him for his minister. There are three different kinds of brains, the one understands things unassisted, the other understands things when shown by others, the third understands neither alone nor with the explanations of others. The first kind is most excellent, the second also excellent, but the third useless. It is therefore evident that if Pandolfo was not of the first kind, he was at any rate of the second. For every time the prince has the judgment to know the good and evil that any one does or says, even if he has no originality of intellect, yet he can recognise the bad and good works of his minister and correct the one and encourage the other; and the minister cannot hope to deceive him and therefore remains good.

For a prince to be able to know a minister there is this method which never fails. When you see the minister think more of himself than of you, and in all his actions seek his own profit, such a man will never be a good minister, and you can never rely on him; for whoever has in hand the state of another must never think of himself but of the prince, and not mind anything but what relates to him. And, on the other hand, the prince, in order to retain his fidelity ought to think of his minister, honouring and enriching him, doing him kindnesses, and conferring on him honours and giving him responsible tasks, so that the great honours and riches bestowed on him cause him not to desire other honours and riches, and the offices he holds make him fearful of changes. When princes and their ministers stand in this relation to each other, they can rely the one upon the other; when it is otherwise, the result is always injurious either for one or the other of them.

Chapter XXIII
How Flatterers Must Be Shunned

I must not omit an important subject, and mention of a mistake which princes can with difficulty avoid, if they are not very prudent, or if they do not make a good choice. And this is with regard to flatterers, of which courts are full, because men take such pleasure in their own things and deceive themselves about them that they can with difficulty guard against this plague; and by wishing to guard against it they run the risk of becoming contemptible. Because there is no other way of guarding one's self against flattery than by letting men understand that they will not offend you by speaking the truth; but when every one can tell you the truth, you lose their respect. A prudent prince must therefore take a third course, by choosing for his council wise men, and giving these alone full liberty to speak the truth to him, but only of those things that he asks and of nothing else; but he must ask them about everything and hear their opinion, and afterwards deliberate by himself in his own way, and in these councils and with each of these men

comport himself so that every one may see that the more freely he speaks, the more he will be acceptable. Beyond these he should listen to no one, go about the matter deliberately, and be determined in his decisions. Whoever acts otherwise either acts precipitately through flattery or else changes often through the variety of opinions, from which it follows that he will be little esteemed.

I will give a modern instance of this. Pre' Luca, a follower of Maximilian, the present emperor, speaking of his majesty said that he never took counsel with anybody, and yet that he never did anything as he wished; this arose from his following the contrary method to the aforesaid. As the emperor is a secret man he does not communicate his designs to any one or take any advice, but as on putting them into effect they begin to be known and discovered, they begin to be opposed by those he has about him, and he is easily diverted from his purpose. Hence it comes to pass that what he does one day he undoes the next, no one ever understands what he wishes or intends to do, and no reliance is to be placed on his deliberations.

A prince, therefore, ought always to take counsel, but only when he wishes, not when others wish; on the contrary he ought to discourage absolutely attempts to advise him unless he asks it, but he ought to be a great asker, and a patient hearer of the truth about those things of which he has inquired; indeed, if he finds that any one has scruples in telling him the truth he should be angry. And since some think that a prince who gains the reputation of being prudent is so considered, not by his nature but by the good counsellors he has about him, they are undoubtedly deceived. It is an infallible rule that a prince who is not wise himself cannot be well advised, unless by chance he leaves himself entirely in the hands of one man who rules him in everything, and happens to be a very prudent man. In this case he may doubtless be well governed, but it would not last long, for that governor would in a short time deprive him of the state; but by taking counsel with many, a prince who is not wise will never have united councils and will not be able to bring them to unanimity for himself. The counsellors will all think of their own interests, and he will be unable either to correct or to understand them. And it cannot be otherwise, for men will always be false to you unless they are compelled by necessity to be true. Therefore it must be concluded that wise counsels, from whomever they come, must necessarily be due to the prudence of the prince, and not the prudence of the prince to the good counsels received.

Chapter XXIV
Why the Princes of Italy Have Lost Their States

The before-mentioned things, if prudently observed, make a new prince seem ancient, and render him at once more secure and firmer in the state than if he had been established there of old. For a new prince is much more observed in his actions than a hereditary one, and when these are recognised as virtuous, he wins over men more and they are more bound to him than if he were of the ancient blood. For men are much more taken by present than by past things, and when they find themselves well off in the present, they enjoy it and seek nothing more; on the contrary, they will do all they can to defend him, so long as the prince is not in other things deficient. And thus he will have the double glory of having founded a new realm and adorned it and fortified it with good laws, good arms, good friends, and good examples; as he will have double shame who is born a prince and through want of prudence has lost his throne.

And if one considers those rulers who have lost their position in Italy in our days, such as the King of Naples, the Duke of Milan, and others, one will find in them first a common defect as to their arms, for the reasons discussed at length, then we observe that some of them either had the people hostile to them, or that if the people were friendly they were not able to make sure of the nobility, for without these defects, states are not lost that have enough strength to be able to keep an army in the field. Philip of Macedon, not the father of Alexander the Great, but the one who was conquered by Titus Quintius, did not possess a great state compared to the greatness of Rome and Greece which assailed him, but being a military man and one who knew how to ingratiate himself with the people and make sure of the great, he was able to sustain the war against them for many years; and if at length he lost his power over some cities, he was still able to keep his kingdom.

Therefore, those of our princes who had held their possessions for many years must not accuse fortune for having lost them, but rather their own remissness; for having never in quiet times considered that things might change (as it is a common fault of men not to reckon on storms in fair weather) when adverse times came, they only thought of fleeing, instead of defending themselves; and hoped that the people, enraged by the insolence of the conquerors, would recall them. This measure, when others are wanting, is good; but it is very bad to have neglected the other remedies for that one, for nobody would desire to fall because he believed that he would then find some one to pick him up. This may or may not take place, and if it does, it does not afford you security, as you have not helped yourself but been helped like a coward. Only those defences are good, certain, and durable, which depend on yourself alone and your own ability.

Chapter XXV
How Much Fortune Can Do in Human Affairs and How It May Be Opposed

It is not unknown to me how many have been and are of opinion that worldly events are so governed by fortune and by God, that men cannot by their prudence change them, and that on the contrary there is no remedy whatever, and for this they may judge it to be useless to toil much about them, but let things be ruled by chance. This opinion has been more held in our day, from the great changes that have been seen, and are daily seen, beyond every human conjecture. When I think about them, at times I am partly inclined to share this opinion. Nevertheless, that our free-will may not be altogether extinguished, I think it may be true that fortune is the ruler of half our actions, but that she allows the other half or thereabouts to be governed by us. I would compare her to an impetuous river that, when turbulent, inundates the plains, casts down trees and buildings, removes earth from this side and places it on the other; every one flees before it, and everything yields to its fury without being able to oppose it; and yet though it is of such a kind, still when it is quiet, men can make provision against it by dykes and banks, so that when it rises it will either go into a canal or its rush will not be so wild and dangerous. So it is with fortune, which shows her power where no measures have been taken to resist her, and directs her fury where she knows that no dykes or barriers have been made to hold her. And if you regard Italy, which has been the seat of these changes, and who has given the impulse to them, you will see her to be a country without dykes or banks of any kind. If she had been protected by proper measures, like Germany, Spain, and France, this inundation would not have caused the great changes that it has, or would not have happened at all.

This must suffice as regards opposition to fortune in general. But limiting myself more to particular cases, I would point out how one sees a certain prince to-day fortunate and to-morrow ruined, without seeing that he has changed in character or otherwise. I believe this arises in the first place from the causes that we have already discussed at length; that is to say, because the prince who bases himself entirely on fortune is ruined when fortune changes. I also believe that he is happy whose mode of procedure accords with the needs of the times, and similarly he is unfortunate whose mode of procedure is opposed to the times. For one sees that men in those things which lead them to the aim that each one has in view, namely, glory and riches, proceed in various ways; one with circumspection, another with impetuosity, one by violence, another by cunning, one with patience, another with the reverse; and each by these diverse ways may arrive at his aim. One sees also two cautious men, one of whom succeeds in his designs, and the other not, and in the same way two men succeeded equally by different methods, one being cautious, the other impetuous, which arises only from the nature of the times, which does or does not conform to their method of procedure. From this it results, as I have said, that two men, acting differently, attain the same effect, and of two others acting in the same way, one attains his goal and not the other. On this depend also the changes in prosperity, for if it happens that time and circumstances are favourable to one who acts with caution and prudence he will be successful, but if time and circumstances change he will be ruined, because he does not change his mode of procedure. No man is found so prudent as to be able to adapt himself to this, either because he cannot deviate from that to which his nature disposes him, or else because having always prospered by walking in one path, he cannot persuade himself that it is well to leave it; and therefore the cautious man, when it is time to act suddenly, does not know how to do so and is consequently ruined; for if one could change one's nature with time and circumstances, fortune would never change.

Pope Julius II acted impetuously in everything he did and found the times and conditions so in conformity with that mode of procedure, that he always obtained a good result. Consider the first war that he made against Bologna while Messer Giovanni Bentivogli was still living. The Venetians were not pleased with it, neither was the King of Spain, France was conferring with him over the enterprise, notwithstanding which, owing to his fierce and impetuous disposition, he engaged personally in the expedition. This move caused both Spain and the Venetians to halt and hesitate, the latter through fear, the former through the desire to recover the entire kingdom of Naples. On the other hand, he engaged with him the King of France, because seeing him make this move and desiring his friendship in order to put down the Venetians, that king judged that he could not refuse him his troops without manifest injury. Thus Julius by his impetuous move achieved what no other pontiff with the utmost human prudence would have succeeded in doing, because, if he had waited till all arrangements had been made and everything settled before leaving Rome, as any other pontiff would have done, it would never have succeeded. For the King of France would have found a thousand excuses, and the others would have inspired him with a thousand fears. I will omit his other actions, which were all of this kind and which all succeeded well, and the shortness of his life did not suffer him to experience the contrary, for had times followed in which it was necessary to act with caution, his ruin would have resulted, for he would never have deviated from these methods to which his nature disposed him.

I conclude then that fortune varying and men remaining fixed in their ways, they are successful so long as these ways conform to circumstances, but when they are opposed then they are unsuccessful. I certainly think that it is better to be impetuous than cautious, for fortune is a woman, and it is necessary, if you wish to master her, to conquer her by force; and it can be seen that she lets herself be overcome by the bold rather than by those who proceed coldly. And therefore, like a woman, she is always a friend to the young, because they are less cautious, fiercer, and master her with greater audacity.

Chapter XXVI
Exhortation to Liberate Italy from the Barbarians

Having now considered all the things we have spoken of, and thought within myself whether at present the time was not propitious in Italy for a new prince, and if there was not a state of things which offered an opportunity to a prudent and capable man to introduce a new system that would do honour to himself and good to the mass of the people, it seems to me that so many things concur to favour a new ruler that I do not know of any time more fitting for such an enterprise. And if, as I said, it was necessary in order that the power of Moses should be displayed that the people of Israel should be slaves in Egypt, and to give scope for the greatness and courage of Cyrus that the Persians should be oppressed by the Medes, and to illustrate the pre-eminence of Theseus that the Athenians should be dispersed, so at the present time, in order that the might of an Italian genius might be recognised, it was necessary that Italy should be reduced to her present condition, and that she should be more enslaved than the Hebrews, more oppressed than the Persians, and more scattered than the Athenians: without a head, without order, beaten, despoiled, lacerated, and overrun, and that she should have suffered ruin of every kind.

And although before now a gleam of hope has appeared which gave hope that some individual might be appointed by God for her redemption, yet at the highest summit of his career he was thrown aside by fortune, so that now, almost lifeless, she awaits one who may heal her wounds and put a stop to the pillaging of Lombardy, to the rapacity and extortion in the Kingdom of Naples and in Tuscany, and cure her of those sores which have long been festering. Behold how she prays God to send some one to redeem her from this barbarous cruelty and insolence. Behold her ready and willing to follow any standard if only there be some one to raise it. There is nothing now she can hope for but that your illustrious house may place itself at the head of this redemption, being by its power and fortune so exalted, and being favoured by God and the Church, of which it is now the ruler. Nor will this be very difficult, if you call to mind the actions and lives of the men I have named. And although those men were rare and marvellous, they were nonetheless men, and each of them had less opportunity than the present, for their enterprise was not juster than this, nor easier, nor was God more their friend than He is yours. Here is a just cause; *iustum enim est bellum quibus necessarium, et pia arma ubi nulla nisi in armis spes est.* Here is the greatest willingness, nor can there be great difficulty where there is great willingness, provided that the measures are adopted of those whom I have set before you as examples. Besides this, unexampled wonders have been seen here performed by God, the

sea has been opened, a cloud has shown you the road, the rock has given forth water, manna has rained, and everything has contributed to your greatness, the remainder must be done by you. God will not do everything, in order not to deprive us of free-will and the portion of the glory that falls to our lot.

It is no marvel that none of the before-mentioned Italians have done that which it is to be hoped your illustrious house may do; and if in so many revolutions in Italy and so many warlike operations, it always seems as if military capacity were extinct, this is because the ancient methods were not good, and no one has arisen who knew how to discover new ones. Nothing does so much honour to a newly risen man than the new laws and measures which he introduces. These things, when they are well based and have greatness in them, render him revered and admired, and there is not lacking scope in Italy for the introduction of every kind of new organisation. Here there is great virtue in the members, if it were not wanting in the heads. Look how in duels and in contests of a few the Italians are superior in strength, dexterity, and intelligence. But when it comes to armies, they make a poor show; which proceeds entirely from the weakness of the leaders, for those that know are not obeyed and every one thinks that he knows, there being hitherto nobody who has raised himself so high both by valour and fortune as to make the others yield. Hence it comes about that for so long a time, in all the wars waged during the last twenty years, whenever there has been an entirely Italian army it has always been a failure, as witness first Taro, then Alexandria, Capua, Genoa, Vailà, Bologna, and Mestri.

If your illustrious house, therefore, wishes to follow those great men who redeemed their countries, it is before all things necessary, as the true foundation of every undertaking, to provide yourself with your own forces, for you cannot have more faithful, or truer and better soldiers. And although each one of them may be good, they will united become even better when they see themselves commanded by their prince, and honoured and favoured by him. It is therefore necessary to prepare such forces in order to be able with Italian prowess to defend the country from foreigners. And although both the Swiss and Spanish infantry are deemed terrible, nonetheless they each have their defects, so that a third method of array might not only oppose them, but be confident of overcoming them. For the Spaniards cannot sustain the attack of cavalry, and the Swiss have to fear infantry which meets them with resolution equal to their own. From which it has resulted, as will be seen by experience, that the Spaniards cannot sustain the attack of French cavalry, and the Swiss are overthrown by Spanish infantry. And although a complete example of the latter has not been seen, yet an instance was furnished in the battle of Ravenna, where the Spanish infantry attacked the German battalions, which are organised in the same way as the Swiss. The Spaniards, through their bodily agility and aided by their bucklers, had entered between and under their pikes and were in a position to attack them safely without the Germans being able to defend themselves; and if the cavalry had not charged them they would have utterly destroyed them. Knowing therefore the defects of both these kinds of infantry, a third kind can be created which can resist cavalry and need not fear infantry, and this will be done by the choice of arms and a new organisation. And these are the things which, when newly introduced, give reputation and grandeur to a new prince.

This opportunity must not, therefore, be allowed to pass, so that Italy may at length find her liberator. I cannot express the love with which he would be received in all those provinces which have suffered under these foreign invasions, with what thirst for vengeance, with what steadfast faith, with what love, with what grateful tears. What doors would be closed against him? What people would refuse him obedience? What envy could oppose him? What Italian would withhold allegiance? This barbarous domination stinks in the nostrils of every one. May your illustrious house therefore assume this task with that courage and those hopes which are inspired by a just cause, so that under its banner our fatherland may be raised up, and under its auspices be verified that saying of Petrarch:

Valour against fell wrath
Will take up arms; and be the combat quickly sped!
For, sure, the ancient worth,
That in Italians stirs the heart, is not yet dead.

Thomas Hobbes

HOBBES WAS BORN OUTSIDE OF MALMESBURY, ENGLAND, ON APRIL 5, 1588, A MONTH before the Spanish Armada set sail for English waters. Hobbes claimed years later that he was born prematurely as a result of his mother's fear of the impending invasion. Though some of the Hobbes family had done well in the cloth business, Hobbes's father was a troubled minister of the Church of England, curate of the poor parish of Broken-borough. In October 1602, Hobbes senior failed to appear for a visit of the archdeacon. Two months later he was taken to the archdeacon's court for failure to perform his duty. The following year, he was in the episcopal court for slandering the vicar of Fox-ley. He failed to show up for the public act of penitence the court prescribed. He was fined, and failed to pay. Finally, when he physically attacked the vicar in question, he was excommunicated. Since the altercation occurred on church grounds, the offense was serious, and the Reverend Hobbes disappeared into London.

By this time, young Thomas Hobbes (now fourteen) was already at Oxford, at Magdalen Hall, through the good offices of Robert Latimer, a Magdalen Hall graduate, who had taught Hobbes Latin and Greek to a high standard. In his autobiography, Hobbes claims that he had little use for the Aristotelian logic and physics, preferring to spend his time studying maps of the earth and stars. He also complained that geometry did not have the place it should have had in the curriculum. Though Hobbes was hardly an outstanding student, he must have had some attractive traits, because when he graduated in 1608 he was recommended by the Master of the College as tutor to the son of William Cavendish, a recently created baron and future earl of Devonshire. The patronage of the Cavendish family made Hobbes's career. At one stroke, he had access to a fine library, the opportunity to travel with his student, the young William, and entrée into the best society. Hobbes visited the Continent with William, as a companion as much as a tutor, for William was only a few years younger than Hobbes. They seem to have divided their time about equally between fast living and serious study. They both learned Italian in Venice, part of Cavendish's "homework" being a translation of Francis Bacon's *Essays* into Italian. Cavendish, an intellectual in his own right, published a rather elegant essay called *A Discourse Against Flatterie* in 1611. Probably the most important consequence of this trip to France and Italy was Hobbes's discovery that the bright young intellectuals of Europe shared his low opinion of Aristotelian Scholastic philosophy and science.

On returning to England, Hobbes served for a while as secretary to Francis Bacon, then lord chancellor, probably as a result of contact between Cavendish and Bacon in connection with the Italian translation of Bacon's work. This was one of those potentially fateful meetings between two great philosophers that seem to have borne no fruit whatever. Though Cavendish was much influenced by Bacon, Hobbes seems to have been totally untouched. Still, it was another notable contact in Hobbes's growing network of powerful acquaintances. That Hobbes was by now a trusted associate of Cavendish is evidenced by the fact that he was given a share in the Virginia Company by Cavendish as part of a scheme to increase the voting strength of his party in the company.

Though Cavendish was never really an active politician, he was twice a member of Parliament, and kept up a correspondence with Fulgenzio Micanzio, secretary to Paolo Sarpi, the political leader who was then steering Venice through its troubles with the pope. Hobbes translated Micanzio's letters and circulated them, an action that put Hobbes squarely in the anti-papal camp. One would have thought this would hardly endear him to an already unpopular Catholic monarch (Charles I), but the major issue of the day in England was Charles's wish to be recognized as an absolute sovereign, and Hobbes was on record as supporting Charles in this matter. Indeed, Hobbes seems to have translated Thucydides' *Peloponnesian Wars* into English with the intention of demonstrating how foolish it was to support popular rhetoric over the sovereign. The move was well-timed. His patron died about this time, probably from too much good living, and Hobbes dedicated the translation to him when it was published a year after William's death in 1628.

Hobbes's friend and patron was not a financial wizard. On his death, his wife Christian let Hobbes go as part of her retrenchment strategy and, perhaps, because she may have blamed Hobbes for William's style of life. If so, the blame was probably placed unfairly; though William was nominally Hobbes's pupil in the early years, William was an adult aristocrat by the time Hobbes met him. Hobbes was hardly in a position to control his young charge, let alone the earl he later became. In any case, Hobbes didn't suffer: he was taken as tutor to the son of Sir Gervase Clinton, a neighbor of one branch of the Cavendish family, and was again treated to the traditional trip to the Continent as part of his pupil's education. It was during this trip that Hobbes discovered Euclid, whose method of precise definition and deductive proof made a profound impression.

Back in England in 1630, Hobbes was again employed by the Cavendish family, this time as tutor to another William Cavendish, third earl of Devonshire. Hobbes's duties seem to have left him plenty of time for study and discussion with a couple of prominent intellectual groups. And once again, Hobbes took his charge on a continental tour in 1634. Having been commissioned by the earl of Newcastle to find a copy of Galileo's *Dialogues*, he met Galileo himself, who had been put under house arrest by the Inquisition in 1633. By this time, Hobbes had a strong interest in the mechanical philosophy, and he embraced Galileo's controversial principal of inertia. During this trip, he also met Mersenne, whose circle included Gassendi and Descartes. Gassendi became one of Hobbes's closest friends, but Hobbes and Descartes were enemies for life. All were working on the mechanical philosophy but, unlike Descartes, Hobbes was a staunch materialist, convinced that interaction between material bodies and an immaterial soul was impossible. In 1640–41, after Hobbes had returned to England, the two exchanged acrimonious letters concerning secondary qualities. They both agreed that perceptions of color and heat had no similarity to the mechanical causes of those perceptions in external objects. The dispute was about precedence. This tells us something about both men, and their feelings for each other, since both knew full well that Galileo had preceded both of them! Still, Descartes must have had some respect for Hobbes, since Mersenne arranged for Hobbes to be one of the six "objectors" in the edition he produced of Descartes's *Meditations* with objections and replies. Hobbes would hardly have been included if Descartes had considered him an idiot. Hobbes also tells us that he greatly respected Descartes's science; it was his dualistic metaphysics he rejected.

At this same time, politics overtook Hobbes. His pro-royalist stance, expressed in *The Elements of Law*, put him in the middle of a dispute between king and Parliament which ended in civil war and the Commonwealth being led by Cromwell. In 1640, after a debate in the Long Parliament in which he was attacked by anti-royalists, Hobbes, fearing for his safety, fled to the Continent, where he stayed until 1652. *De Cive*, intended as the third part of a comprehensive philosophy, was published in 1641. The first two parts, *De Corpore* and *De Homine*, were not published until much later (1655 and 1658 respectively), but Hobbes seems to have had the plan in his head and worked on them throughout the 1640s when he had the time. There were other claims on his time, however. In 1646, he was made an offer he couldn't refuse: tutor of mathematics to the exiled Prince Charles (later Charles II). He did, however, find time to write a popularized version of *De Cive*, titled *Leviathan*. It became his most famous work. Though written in France, it was published in England in 1651.

Hobbes was beginning to feel his age. He had developed a shaking in the hands, probably Parkinson's disease, which required him to do all his writing by dictation for the remainder of his life. Mersenne died, and Gassendi left Paris. Hobbes was already thinking of returning to England when he was barred from the French court as a result of the fierce anti-Catholic arguments in *Leviathan*. The clergy made an attempt to have him arrested. Commonwealth or no, Hobbes returned to England in 1652, where he took the Engagement Oath declaring loyalty to the new government. Although a defense of absolute sovereignty, *Leviathan* is certainly consistent with obeying the legitimate government, and even with the legitimacy of the Commonwealth. Ironically, Hobbes had more trouble after the restoration of the monarchy, when the work was periodically attacked as atheistic. His patrons—the Cavendish family and, up to a point, his ex-pupil, the king—proved too powerful, however, and these attacks never came to anything serious, though they surely would have had Hobbes been less well connected.

Hobbes remained in London the rest of his life, always surrounded by controversy. He continued his writing, including many vain attempts to square the circle, which may have contributed to his failure to be admitted to the Royal Society. It is probable, however, that the real reason he was kept out was the association of his name with atheism. Not that the Royal Society was a religious stronghold, but it could ill-afford the bad press Hobbes's election would have occasioned. He was revered on the Continent, where frequent reprintings of *De Cive* were read by a wide range of thinkers including Leibniz and Spinoza. Hobbes died at ninety-one on December 4, 1679, a week after suffering a stroke.

NOTES ON THE TEXT

Thomas Hobbes's *Leviathan* is similar in many respects to Machiavelli's *The Prince*. Hobbes views human beings as essentially driven by the passions for glory and honor as well as self-preservation. For Hobbes, one of the main purposes of political thinking is to show people the way to achieving their own individual well-being and to counsel them to stick to this despite their desires for glory and eminence. But Hobbes also had a very different ambition. He thinks it is possible to devise moral and political principles for the design of a stable commonwealth that will work for the advantage of all. Hobbes starts from a conception of human beings similar to, but more systematic and simpler than, that of Machiavelli and attempts to show how traditional principles of morality can be constructed from it as well as how rational political principles can be erected on its foundation.

While Hobbes is far more sanguine about demonstrating the rationality of being moral than Machiavelli is, he has a far darker view of the world, in which men fail to heed his moral and political principles. On the one hand, he thinks that a social world without powerful and stable political authority would be torn by constant fighting. Hobbes's thesis is that in a state of nature there would be a war of all against all. The basis of this idea is that people are self-interested, and to secure their futures they seek more and more power for themselves. This leads to constant conflicts of interest. But, Hobbes thinks, people are equal in their capacity to harm one another. For the sake of greater gain and glory, they are constantly seeking to take things from each other, and since people are equal, no one can be secure against attack from others. For Hobbes, the best defense is a good offense, and so it is prudent in the state of nature to be constantly on the attack. As a consequence, no one can trust anyone else, constant fighting breaks out, and life is "nasty, brutish, and short." This vision of the state of nature must be constantly kept in mind in reading *Leviathan*, since Hobbes thinks that departure from his principles always threatens a return to the state of war.

On the other hand, Hobbes thinks that this state of nature can be left behind. There are two components to his view. First, Hobbes attempts to show that individuals do, under certain circumstances, have reasons of self-interest to come together to live under rules with other individuals in peace. He also thinks he can persuade those who think otherwise that it is never rational to break faith with one's fellows once the arrangement has been set up. For Hobbes, this is the basis of natural law, and it is the essence of morality. Second, Hobbes thinks that no stable cooperative arrangement among human beings is possible without the existence of a powerful political institution called the sovereign. The basic idea for Hobbes is that the trust necessary for establishing long-term cooperation between self-interested persons cannot be maintained unless everyone knows that anyone who violates the rules of the arrangement will be punished by an all-powerful sovereign. This gives each person the incentive to go along with the arrangement and it gives each person the assurance that almost everyone else will go along with the arrangement. So the first thing that individuals in a state of nature must agree to is to submit to an all-powerful sovereign. One point to note here is that the sovereign is not party to the agreement. It has no duties to the people, but they have duties to it. The sovereign is the supreme political power of a society. There are no constitutional limits on it. For Hobbes, constitutional limits and duties would only require another sovereign to ensure that the limited sovereign is acting within the limits. Ultimately, people are ruled by other people, and not by laws. In Hobbes's view, the sovereign does not have to be an individual or a family. Hobbes allows that an aristocracy can be sovereign and even a democratic assembly can be sovereign as long as there are no checks to their power.

Hobbes spends the remainder of our readings in *Leviathan* spelling out the features of a commonwealth that are most conducive to peace and stability. In addition to his rejection of constitutional limitations on power, Hobbes argues that sovereignty ought not to be divided as it is in the United States, where political power is shared between Congress, the president, and the Supreme Court. He argues that divided sovereignty leads to conflict between the different powers and ultimately to a state of war (as it did between the king and the Parliament in the English Civil War). He argues that the best kind of sovereign is an absolute monarchy, although he does not think of his reasoning as conclusive here. He argues against natural rights of private property. Since the sovereign must be all-powerful, all rights must come from the sovereign and hence all rights may be withdrawn (except the right to defend one's life). He also argues against the rights to freedom of expression and assembly. For Hobbes, people are primarily interested in blowing their own horns and defeating their opponents in discussion. The consequence is that free discussion can only lead to more conflict. Finally, he reserves his strongest criticism for the idea that people have a right to rebel against the sovereign. The sovereign is the one and only guarantor of peace and stability in society. To do away with it is to risk a return to war in the state of nature.

Leviathan

or The Matter, Form and Power
of a Commonwealth, Ecclesiastical and Civil

PART I: *OF MAN*

Chapter I
Of Sense

Concerning the thoughts of man, I will consider them first singly, and afterwards in train, or dependence upon one another. Singly, they are every one a "representation" or "appearance" of some quality, or other accident of a body without us, which is commonly called an "object." Which object worketh on the eyes, ears, and other parts of a man's body; and by diversity of working, produceth diversity of appearances.

The original of them all, is that which we call "sense," for there is no conception in a man's mind, which hath not at first, totally or by parts, been begotten upon the organs of sense. The rest are derived from that original.

To know the natural cause of sense, is not very necessary to the business now in hand; and I have elsewhere written of the same at large. Nevertheless, to fill each part of my present method, I will briefly deliver the same in this place.

The cause of sense, is the external body, or object, which presseth the organ proper to each sense, either immediately, as in the taste and touch; or mediately, as in seeing, hearing, and smelling; which pressure, by the mediation of the nerves, and other strings and membranes of the body, continued inwards to the brain and heart, causeth there a resistance, or counter-pressure, or endeavour of the heart to deliver itself, which endeavour, because "outward," seemeth to be some matter without. And this "seeming," or "fancy," is that which men call "sense"; and consisteth, as to the eye, in a "light," or "colour figured"; to the ear, in a "sound"; to the nostril, in an "odour"; to the tongue and palate, in a "savour"; and to the rest of the body, in "heat," "cold," "hardness," "softness," and such other qualities as we discern by "feeling." All which qualities, called "sensible," are in the object, that causeth them, but so many several motions of the matter, by which it presseth our organs diversely.

Neither in us that are pressed, are they anything else, but divers motions; for motion produceth nothing but motion. But their appearance to us is fancy, the same waking, that dreaming. And as pressing, rubbing, or striking the eye, makes us fancy a light; and pressing the ear, produceth a din; so do the bodies also we see, or hear, produce the same by their strong, though unobserved action. For if those colours and sounds were in the bodies, or objects that cause them, they could not be severed from them, as by glasses, and in echoes by reflection, we see they are; where we know the thing we see is in one place, the appearance in another. And though at some certain distance the real and very object seem invested with the fancy it begets in us; yet still the object is one thing, the image or fancy is another. So that sense, in all cases, is nothing else but original fancy, is caused, as I have said, by the pressure, that is, by the motion, of external things upon our eyes, ears, and other organs thereunto ordained.

But the philosophy schools, through all the universities of Christendom, grounded upon certain texts of Aristotle, teach another doctrine, and say, for the cause of "vision," that the thing seen, sendeth forth on every side a "visible species," in English, a "visible show," "apparition," or "aspect," or "a being seen"; the receiving whereof into the eye, is "seeing." And for the cause of "hearing," that the thing heard, sendeth forth an "audible species," that is, an "audible aspect," or "audible being seen," which entering at the ear, maketh "hearing." Nay, for the cause of "understanding" also, they say the thing understood, sendeth forth an "intelligible species," that is, an "intelligible being seen," which, coming into the understanding, makes us understand. I say not this, as disproving the use of universities; but because I am to speak hereafter of their office in a commonwealth, I must let you see on all occasions by the way, what things would be amended in them; amongst which the frequency of insignificant speech is one.

Chapter II
Of Imagination

That when a thing lies still, unless somewhat else stir it, it will lie still for ever, is a truth that no man doubts of. But that when a thing is in motion, it will eternally be in motion, unless somewhat else stay it, though the reason be the same, namely, that nothing can change itself, is not so easily assented to. For men measure, not only other men, but all other things, by themselves; and because they find themselves subject after motion to pain, and lassitude, think everything else grows weary of motion, and seeks repose of its own accord; little considering, whether it be not some other motion, wherein that desire of rest they find in themselves, consisteth. From hence it is, that the schools say, heavy bodies fall downwards, out of an appetite to rest, and to conserve their nature in that place which is most proper for them; ascribing appetite, and knowledge of what is good for their conservation, which is more than man has, to things inanimate, absurdly.

When a body is once in motion, it moveth, unless something else hinder it, eternally; and whatsoever hindreth it, cannot in an instant, but in time, and by degrees, quite extinguish it; and, as we see in the water, though the wind cease, the waves give not over rolling for a long time after: so also it happeneth in that motion, which is made in the internal parts of a man, then, when he sees, dreams, &c. For after the object is removed, or the eye shut, we still retain an image of the thing seen, though more obscure than when we see it. And this is it, the Latins call "imagination," from the image made in seeing; and apply the same, though improperly, to all the other senses. But the Greeks call it "fancy"; which signifies "appearance," and is as proper to one sense, as to another. "Imagination," therefore, is nothing but "decaying sense"; and is found in men, and many other living creatures, as well sleeping, as waking.

The decay of sense in men waking, is not the decay of the motion made in sense; but an obscuring of it, in such manner as the light of the sun obscureth the light of the stars; which stars do no less exercise their virtue, by which they are visible, in the day than in the night. But because amongst many strokes, which our eyes, ears, and other organs receive from external bodies, the predominant only is sensible; therefore, the light of the sun being predominant, we are not affected with the action of the stars. And any object being removed from our eyes, though the impression it made in us remain, yet other objects more present succeeding, and working on us, the imagination of the past is obscured and made weak, as the voice of a man is in the noise of the day. From whence it followeth, that the longer the time is, after the sight or sense of any object, the weaker is the imagination. For the continual change of man's body destroys in time the parts which in sense were moved: so that distance of time, and of place, hath one and the same effect in us. For as at a great distance of place, that which we look at appears dim, and without distinction of the smaller parts; and as voices grow weak and inarticulate; so also, after great distance of time, our imagination of the past is weak; and we lose, for example, of cities we have seen, many particular streets, and of actions, many particular circumstances. This "decaying sense," when we would express the thing itself, I mean "fancy" itself, we call "imagination," as I said before: but when we would express the decay, and signify that the sense is fading, old, and past, it is called "memory." So that imagination and memory are but one thing, which for divers considerations hath divers names.

Much memory, or memory of many things, is called "experience." Again, imagination being only of those things which have been formerly perceived by sense, either all at once, or by parts at several times; the former, which is the imagining the whole object as it was presented to the sense, is "simple" imagination, as when one imagineth a man, or horse, which he hath seen before. The other is "compounded"; as when, from the sight of a man at one time, and of a horse at another, we conceive in our mind a Centaur. So when a man compoundeth the image of his own person with the image of the actions of another man, as when a man imagines himself a Hercules or an Alexander, which happeneth often to them that are much taken with reading of romances, it is a compound imagination, and properly but a fiction of the mind. There be also other imaginations that rise in men, though waking, from the great impression made in sense: as from gazing upon the sun, the impression leaves an image of the sun before our eyes a long time after; and from being long and vehemently attent upon geometrical figures, a man shall in the dark, though awake, have the images of lines and angles before his eyes; which kind of fancy hath no particular name, as being a thing that doth not commonly fall into men's discourse.

The imaginations of them that sleep are those we call "dreams." And these also, as also all other imaginations, have been before, either totally or by parcels, in the sense. And because in sense, the brain and nerves, which are the necessary organs of sense, are so benumbed in sleep as not easily to be moved by the action of external objects, there can happen in sleep no imagination, and therefore no dream, but what proceeds from the agitation of the inward parts

of man's body; which inward parts, for the connection they have with the brain, and other organs, when they be distempered, do keep the same in motion; whereby the imaginations there formerly made, appear as if a man were waking; saving that the organs of sense being now benumbed, so as there is no new object, which can master and obscure them with a more vigorous impression, a dream must needs be more clear, in this silence of sense, than our waking thoughts. And hence it cometh to pass, that it is a hard matter, and by many thought impossible, to distinguish exactly between sense and dreaming. For my part, when I consider that in dreams I do not often nor constantly think of the same persons, places, objects, and actions, that I do waking; nor remember so long a train of coherent thoughts, dreaming, as at other times; and because waking I often observe the absurdity of dreams, but never dream of the absurdities of my waking thoughts; I am well satisfied, that, being awake, I know I dream not, though when I dream I think myself awake.

And seeing dreams are caused by the distemper of some of the inward parts of the body, divers distempers must needs cause different dreams. And hence it is that lying cold breedeth dreams of fear, and raiseth the thought and image of some fearful object, the motion from the brain to the inner parts and from the inner parts to the brain being reciprocal; and that as anger causeth heat in some parts of the body when we are awake, so when we sleep the overheating of the same parts causeth anger, and raiseth up in the brain the imagination of an enemy. In the same manner, as natural kindness, when we are awake, causeth desire, and desire makes heat in certain other parts of the body; so also too much heat in those parts, while we sleep, raiseth in the brain an imagination of some kindness shown. In sum, our dreams are the reverse of our waking imaginations; the motion when we are awake beginning at one end, and when we dream at another.

The most difficult discerning of a man's dream, from his waking thoughts, is then, when by some accident we observe not that we have slept: which is easy to happen to a man full of fearful thoughts, and whose conscience is much troubled; and that sleepeth, without the circumstances of going to bed or putting off his clothes, as one that noddeth in a chair. For he that taketh pains, and industriously lays himself to sleep, in case any uncouth and exorbitant fancy come unto him, cannot easily think it other than a dream. We read of Marcus Brutus (one that had his life given him by Julius Cæsar, and was also his favourite, and notwithstanding murdered him), how at Philippi, the night before he gave battle to Augustus Cæsar, he saw a fearful apparition, which is commonly related by historians as a vision; but considering the circumstances, one may easily judge to have been but a short dream. For sitting in his tent, pensive and troubled with the horror of his rash act, it was not hard for him, slumbering in the cold, to dream of that which most affrighted him; which fear, as by degrees it made him wake, so also it must needs make the apparition by degrees to vanish; and having no assurance that he slept, he could have no cause to think it a dream, or anything but a vision. And this is no very rare accident; for even they that be perfectly awake, if they be timorous and superstitious, possessed with fearful tales, and alone in the dark, are subject to the like fancies, and believe they see spirits and dead men's ghosts walking in churchyards; whereas it is either their fancy only, or else the knavery of such persons as make use of such superstitious fear, to pass disguised in the night, to places they would not be known to haunt.

From this ignorance of how to distinguish dreams, and other strong fancies, from vision and sense, did arise the greatest part of the religion of the Gentiles in time past, that worshipped satyrs, fauns, nymphs, and the like; and now-a-days the opinion that rude people have of fairies, ghosts, and goblins, and of the power of witches. For as for witches, I think not that their witchcraft is any real power; but yet that they are justly punished, for the false belief they have that they can do such mischief, joined with their purpose to do it if they can; their trade being nearer to a new religion than to a craft or science. And for fairies, and walking ghosts, the opinion of them has, I think, been on purpose either taught or not confuted, to keep in credit the use of exorcism, of crosses, of holy water, and other such inventions of ghostly men. Nevertheless, there is no doubt but God can make unnatural apparitions; but that He does it so often, as men need to fear such things, more than they fear the stay or change of the course of nature, which He also can stay, and change, is no point of Christian faith. But evil men, under pretext that God can do any thing, are so bold as to say any thing when it serves their turn, though they think it untrue; it is the part of a wise man to believe them no farther than right reason makes that which they say appear credible. If this superstitious fear of spirits were taken away, and with it, prognostics from dreams, false prophecies, and many other things depending thereon, by which crafty ambitious persons abuse the simple people, men would be much more fitted than they are for civil obedience.

And this ought to be the work of the schools: but they rather nourish such doctrine. For, not knowing what imagination or the senses are, what they receive, they teach: some saying that imaginations rise of themselves, and have no cause; others that they rise most commonly from the will; and that good thoughts are blown (inspired) into a man by God, and evil thoughts by the devil; or that good thoughts are poured (infused) into a man by God, and evil ones by the devil. Some say the senses receive the species of things, and deliver them to the common sense; and the common sense delivers them over to the fancy, and the fancy to the memory, and the memory to the judgment, like handing of things from one to another, with many words making nothing understood.

The imagination that is raised in man, or any other creature indued with the faculty of imagining, by words, or other voluntary signs, is that we generally call "understanding"; and is common to man and beast. For a dog by custom will understand the call, or the rating of his master; and so will many other beasts. That understanding which is peculiar to man, is the understanding not only his will, but his conceptions and thoughts, by the sequel and contexture of the names of things into affirmations, negations, and other forms of speech; and of this kind of understanding I shall speak hereafter.

Chapter III
Of the Consequence or Train of Imaginations

By "consequence," or "train" of thoughts, I understand that succession of one thought to another, which is called, to distinguish it from discourse in words, "mental discourse."

When a man thinketh on anything whatsoever, his next thought after, is not altogether so casual as it seems to be. Not every thought to every thought succeeds indifferently. But as we have no imagination, whereof we have not formerly had sense, in whole, or in parts; so we have no transition from one imagination to another, whereof we never had the like before in our senses. The reason whereof is this. All fancies are motions within us, relics of those made in the sense: and those motions that immediately succeeded one another in the sense, continue also together after sense: insomuch as the former coming again to take place, and be predominant, the latter followeth, by coherence of the matter moved, in such manner, as water upon a plane table is drawn which way any one part of it is guided by the finger. But because in sense, to one and the same thing perceived, sometimes one thing, sometimes another succeedeth, it comes to pass in time, that in the imagining of anything, there is no certainty what we shall imagine next; only this is certain, it shall be something that succeeded the same before, at one time or another.

This train of thoughts, or mental discourse, is of two sorts. The first is "unguided," "without design," and inconstant; wherein there is no passionate thought, to govern and direct those that follow, to itself, as the end and scope of some desire, or other passion: in which case the thoughts are said to wander, and seem impertinent one to another, as in a dream. Such are commonly the thoughts of men, that are not only without company, but also without care of anything; though even then their thoughts are as busy as at other times, but without harmony; as the sound which a lute out of tune would yield to any man; or in tune, to one that could not play. And yet in this wild ranging of the mind, a man may oft-times perceive the way of it, and the dependence of one thought upon another. For in a discourse of our present civil war, what could seem more impertinent, than to ask, as one did, what was the value of a Roman penny? Yet the coherence to me was manifest enough. For the thought of the war, introduced the thought of the delivering up the king to his enemies; the thought of that, brought in the thought of the delivering up of Christ; and that again the thought of the thirty pence, which was the price of that treason; and thence easily followed that malicious question; and all this in a moment of time; for thought is quick.

The second is more constant; as being "regulated" by some desire, and design. For the impression made by such things as we desire, or fear, is strong, and permanent, or, if it cease for a time, of quick return: so strong it is sometimes, as to hinder and break our sleep. From desire, ariseth the thought of some means we have seen produce the like of that which we aim at; and from the thought of that, the thought of means to that mean; and so continually, till we come to some beginning within our own power. And

because the end, by the greatness of the impression, comes often to mind, in case our thoughts begin to wander, they are quickly again reduced into the way: which observed by one of the seven wise men, made him give men this precept, which is now worn out, *Respice finem;* that is to say, in all your actions, look often upon what you would have, as the thing that directs all your thoughts in the way to attain it.

The train of regulated thoughts is of two kinds; one, when of an effect imagined we seek the causes, or means that produce it: and this is common to man and beast. The other is, when imagining anything whatsoever, we seek all the possible effects, that can by it be produced; that is to say, we imagine what we can do with it, when we have it. Of which I have not at any time seen any sign, but in man only; for this is a curiosity hardly incident to the nature of any living creature that has no other passion but sensual, such as are hunger, thirst, lust, and anger. In sum, the discourse of the mind, when it is governed by design, is nothing but "seeking," or the faculty of invention, which the Latins called *sagacitas*, and *solertia;* a hunting out of the causes, of some effect, present or past; or of the effects, of some present or past cause. Sometimes a man seeks what he hath lost; and from that place, and time, wherein he misses it, his mind runs back, from place to place, and time to time, to find where, and when he had it; that is to say, to find some certain, and limited time and place, in which to begin a method of seeking. Again, from thence, his thoughts run over the same places and times, to find what action, or other occasion might make him lose it. This we call "remembrance," or calling to mind: the Latins call it "reminiscentia," as it were a "re-conning" of our former actions.

Sometimes a man knows a place determinate, within the compass whereof he is to seek; and then his thoughts run over all the parts thereof, in the same manner as one would sweep a room, to find a jewel; or as a spaniel ranges the field, till he finds a scent; or as a man should run over the alphabet, to start a rhyme.

Sometimes a man desires to know the event of an action; and then he thinketh of some like action past, and the events thereof one after another; supposing like events will follow like actions. As he that foresees what will become of a criminal, reckons what he has seen follow on the like crime before; having this order of thoughts, the crime, the officer, the prison, the judge, and the gallows. Which kind of thoughts is called "foresight," and "prudence," or "providence"; and sometimes "wisdom"; though such conjecture, through the difficulty of observing all circumstances, be very fallacious. But this is certain; by how much one man has more experience of things past, than another, by so much also he is more prudent, and his expectations the seldomer fail him. The "present" only has a being in nature; things "past" have a being in the memory only, but things to "come" have no being at all; the "future" being but a fiction of the mind, applying the sequels of actions past, to the actions that are present; which with most certainty is done by him that has most experience, but not with certainty enough. And though it be called prudence, when the event answereth our expectation; yet in its own nature, it is but presumption. For the foresight of things to come, which is providence, belongs only to him by whose will they are to come. From him only, and supernaturally, proceeds prophecy. The best prophet naturally is the best guesser; and the best guesser, he that is most versed and studied in the matters he guesses at: for he hath most "signs" to guess by.

A "sign" is the evident antecedent of the consequent; and contrarily, the consequent of the antecedent, when the like consequences have been observed before: and the oftener they have been observed, the less uncertain is the sign. And therefore he that has most experience in any kind of business, has most signs, whereby to guess at the future time; and consequently is the most prudent: and so much more prudent than he that is new in that kind of business, as not to be equalled by any advantage of natural and extemporary wit: though perhaps many young men think the contrary.

Nevertheless it is not prudence that distinguisheth man from beast. There be beasts, that at a year old observe more, and pursue that which is for their good, more prudently, than a child can do at ten.

As prudence is a "presumption" of the "future," contracted from the "experience" of time "past": so there is a presumption of things past taken from other things, not future, but past also. For he that hath seen by what courses and degrees a flourishing state hath first come into civil war, and then to ruin; upon the sight of the ruins of any other state, will guess, the like war, and the like courses have been there also. But this conjecture has the same uncertainty almost with the conjecture of the future; both being grounded only upon experience.

There is no other act of man's mind, that I can remember, naturally planted in him, so as to need no other thing, to the exercise of it, but to be born a man, and live with the use of his five senses. Those other faculties of which I shall speak by and by, and which seem proper to man only, are acquired and increased by study and industry; and of most men learned by instruction, and discipline; and proceed all from the invention of words, and speech. For besides sense, and thoughts, and the train of thoughts, the mind of man has no other motion; though by the help of speech, and method, the same faculties may be improved to such a height, as to distinguish men from all other living creatures.

Whatsoever we imagine is "finite." Therefore there is no idea, or conception of any thing we call "infinite." No man can have in his mind an image of infinite magnitude; nor conceive infinite swiftness, infinite time, or infinite force, or infinite power. When we say any thing is infinite, we signify only that we are not able to conceive the ends, and bounds of the things named; having no conception of the thing, but of our own inability. And therefore the name of God is used, not to make us conceive him, for he is incomprehensible; and his greatness, and power are unconceivable; but that we may honour him. Also because, whatsoever, as I said before, we conceive, has been perceived first by sense, either all at once, or by parts; a man can have no thought, representing any thing, not subject to sense. No man therefore can conceive any thing, but he must conceive it in some place; and indued with some determinate magnitude; and which may be divided into parts; nor that any thing is all in this place, and all in another place at the same time; nor that two, or more things can be in one, and the same place at once: for none of these things ever have, nor can be incident to sense; but are absurd speeches, taken upon credit, without any signification at all, from deceived philosophers, and deceived, or deceiving schoolmen.

• • •

Chapter VI
Of the Interior Beginnings of Voluntary Motions;
Commonly Called the Passions; and the
Speeches by Which They Are Expressed

There be in animals, two sorts of "motions" peculiar to them: one called "vital"; begun in generation, and continued without interruption through their whole life; such as are the "course" of the "blood," the "pulse," the "breathing," the "concoction, nutrition, excretion," &c., to which motions there needs no help of imagination: the other is "animal motion," otherwise called "voluntary motion"; as to "go," to "speak," to "move" any of our limbs, in such manner as is first fancied in our minds. That sense is motion in the organs and interior parts of man's body, caused by the action of the things we see, hear, &c.; and that fancy is but the relics of the same motion, remaining after sense, has been already seen in the first and second chapters. And because "going," "speaking," and the like voluntary motions, depend always upon a precedent thought of "whither," "which way," and "what"; it is evident, that the imagination is the first internal beginning of all voluntary motion. And although unstudied men do not conceive any motion at all to be there, where the thing moved is invisible; or the space it is moved in is, for the shortness of it, insensible; yet that doth not hinder, but that such motions are. For let a space be never so little, that which is moved over a greater space, whereof that little one is part, must first be moved over that. These small beginnings of motion, within the body of man, before they appear in walking, speaking, striking, and other visible actions, are commonly called "endeavour."

This endeavour, when it is toward something which causes it, is called "appetite," or "desire"; the latter being the general name; and the other oftentimes restrained to signify the desire of food, namely "hunger" and "thirst." And when the endeavour is fromward something, it is generally called "aversion." These words, "appetite" and "aversion," we have from the Latins; and they both of them signify the motions, one of approaching, the other of retiring. So also do the Greek words for the same, which are ὁρμὴ and ἀφορμὴ. For Nature itself does often press upon men those truths, which afterwards, when they look for somewhat beyond Nature, they stumble at. For the schools find in mere appetite to go, or move, no actual motion at all: but because some motion they must acknowledge, they call it metaphorical motion; which is but an absurd speech: for though words may be called metaphorical, bodies and motions cannot.

That which men desire, they are also said to "love": and to "hate" those things for which they have aversion. So that desire and love are the same thing; save that by desire, we always signify the absence of the object: by love most commonly the presence of the same. So also by aversion, we signify the absence; and by hate, the presence of the object.

Of appetites and aversions, some are born with men; as appetite of food, appetite of excretion, and exoneration, which may also and more properly be called aversions, from somewhat they feel in their bodies; and some other appetites, not many. The rest, which are appetites of particular things, proceed from experience, and trial of their effects upon themselves or other men. For of things we know not at all, or believe not to be, we can have no further desire than to taste and try. But aversion we have for things, not only which we know have hurt us, but also that we do not know whether they will hurt us, or not.

Those things which we neither desire, nor hate, we are said to "contemn"; "contempt" being nothing else but an immobility, or contumacy of the heart, in resisting the action of certain things; and proceeding from that the heart is already moved otherwise, by other more potent objects; or from want of experience of them.

And because the constitution of a man's body is in continual mutation, it is impossible that all the same things should always cause in him the same appetites and aversions: much less can all men consent, in the desire of almost any one and the same object.

But whatsoever is the object of any man's appetite or desire, that is it which he for his part calleth "good"; and the object of his hate and aversion, "evil": and of his contempt, "vile" and "inconsiderable." For these words of good, evil, and contemptible, are ever used with relation to the person that useth them: there being nothing simply and absolutely so; nor any common rule of good and evil, to be taken from the nature of the objects themselves; but from the person of the man, where there is no commonwealth; or, in a commonwealth, from the person that representeth it; or from an arbitrator or judge, whom men disagreeing shall by consent set up, and make his sentence the rule thereof.

The Latin tongue has two words, whose significations approach to those of good and evil; but are not precisely the same; and those are *pulchrum* and *turpe.* Whereof the former signifies that, which by some apparent signs promiseth good; and the latter, that which promiseth evil. But in our tongue we have not so general names to express them by. But for *pulchrum* we say in some things, "fair"; in others, "beautiful," or "handsome," or "gallant," or "honourable," or "comely," or "amiable"; and for *turpe,* "foul," "deformed," "ugly," "base," "nauseous," and the like, as the subject shall require; all which words, in their proper places, signify nothing else but the "mien," or countenance, that promiseth good and evil. So that of good there be three kinds; good in the promise, that is *pulchrum;* good in effect, as the end desired, which is called *jucundum,* "delightful"; and good as the means, which is called *utile,* "profitable"; and as many of evil: for "evil" in promise, is that they call *turpe;* evil in effect, and end, is *molestum,* "unpleasant," "troublesome"; and evil in the means, *inutile,* "unprofitable," "hurtful."

As, in sense, that which is really within us, is, as I have said before, only motion, caused by the action of external objects, but in apparence; to the sight, light and colour; to the ear, sound; to the nostril, odour, &c.: so, when the action of the same object is continued from the eyes, ears, and other organs to the heart, the real effect there is nothing but motion, or endeavour; which consisteth in appetite, or aversion, to or from the object moving. But the appearance, or sense of that motion, is that we either call "delight" or "trouble of mind."

This motion, which is called appetite, and for the appearance of it "delight," and "pleasure," seemeth to be a corroboration of vital motion, and a help thereunto; and therefore such things as caused delight, were not improperly called *jucunda, à juvando,* from helping or fortifying; and the contrary *molesta,* "offensive," from hindering, and troubling the motion vital.

"Pleasure" therefore, or "delight," is the apparence, or sense of good; and "molestation," or "displeasure," the apparence, or sense of evil. And consequently all appetite, desire, and love, is accompanied with some delight more or less; and all hatred and aversion, with more or less displeasure and offence.

Of pleasures or delights, some arise from the sense of an object present; and those may be called "pleasure of sense"; the word "sensual," as it is used by those only that condemn them, having no place till there be laws. Of this kind are all onerations and exonerations of the body; as also all that is pleasant, in the "sight," "hearing," "smell," "taste," or "touch." Others arise from the expectation, that proceeds from foresight of the end, or consequence of things; whether those things in the sense please or displease. And these are "pleasures of the mind" of him that draweth those consequences, and are generally called "joy." In the like manner, displeasures are some in the sense, and called "pain"; others, in the expectation of consequences, and are called "grief."

These simple passions called "appetite," "desire," "love," "aversion," "hate," "joy," and "grief," have their names for divers considerations diversified. As first, when they one succeed another, they are diversely called from the opinion men have of the likelihood of attaining what they desire. Secondly, from the object loved or hated. Thirdly, from the consideration of many of them together. Fourthly, from the alteration or succession itself.

For "appetite," with an opinion of attaining, is called "hope."

The same, without such opinion, "despair."

"Aversion," with opinion of "hurt" from the object, "fear."

The same, with hope of avoiding that hurt by resistence, "courage."

Sudden "courage," "anger."

Constant "hope," "confidence" of ourselves.

Constant "despair," "diffidence" of ourselves.

"Anger" for great hurt done to another, when we conceive the same to be done by injury, "indignation."

"Desire" of good to another, "benevolence," "good will," "charity." If to man generally, "good-nature."

"Desire" of riches, "covetousness"; a name used always in signification of blame; because men contending for them, are displeased with one another's attaining them; though the desire in itself, be to be blamed, or allowed, according to the means by which those riches are sought.

"Desire" of office, or precedence, "ambition": a name used also in the worse sense, for the reason before mentioned.

"Desire" of things that conduce but a little to our ends, and fear of things that are but of little hindrance, "pusillanimity."

"Contempt" of little helps and hindrances, "magnanimity."

"Magnanimity," in danger of death or wounds, "valour," "fortitude."

"Magnanimity" in the use of riches, "liberality."

"Pusillanimity" in the same, "wretchedness," "miserableness," or "parsimony"; as it is liked or disliked.

"Love" of persons for society, "kindness."

"Love" of persons for pleasing the sense only, "natural lust."

"Love" of the same, acquired from rumination, that is, imagination of pleasure past, "luxury."

"Love" of one singularly, with desire to be singularly beloved, "the passion of love." The same, with fear that the love is not mutual, "jealousy."

"Desire," by doing hurt to another, to make him condemn some fact of his own, "revengefulness."

"Desire" to know why, and how, "curiosity"; such as is in no living creature but "man": so that man is distinguished, not only by his reason, but also by this singular passion from other "animals"; in whom the appetite of food, and other pleasures of sense, by predominance, take away the care of knowing causes; which is a lust of the mind, that by a perseverance of delight in the continual and indefatigable generation of knowledge, exceedeth the short vehemence of any carnal pleasure.

"Fear" of power invisible, feigned by the mind, or imagined from tales publicly allowed, "religion"; not allowed, "superstition." And when the power imagined, is truly such as we imagine, "true religion."

"Fear," without the apprehension of why, or what, "panic terror," called so from the fables that make Pan the author of them; whereas in truth, there is always in him that so feareth, first, some apprehension of the cause, though the rest run away by example, every one supposing his fellow to know why. And therefore this passion happens to none but in a throng, or multitude of people.

"Joy," from apprehension of novelty, "admiration"; proper to man, because it excites the appetite of knowing the cause.

"Joy," arising from imagination of a man's own power and ability, is that exultation of the mind which is called "glorying": which if grounded upon the experience of his own former actions, is the same with "confidence": but if grounded on the flattery of others, or only supposed by himself, for delight in the consequences of it, is called "vain-glory": which name is properly given; because a well-grounded "confidence" begetteth attempt; whereas the supposing of power does not, and is therefore rightly called "vain."

"Grief," from opinion of want of power, is called "dejection" of mind.

The "vain-glory" which consisteth in the feigning or supposing of abilities in ourselves, which we know are not, is most incident to young men, and nourished by the histories or fictions of gallant persons; and is corrected oftentimes by age, and employment.

"Sudden glory," is the passion which maketh those "grimaces" called "laughter"; and is caused either by some sudden act of their own, that pleaseth them; or by the apprehension of some deformed thing in another, by comparison whereof they suddenly applaud themselves. And it is incident most to them, that are conscious of the fewest abilities in themselves; who are forced to keep themselves in their own favour, by observing the imperfections of other men. And therefore much laughter at the defects of others, is a sign of pusillanimity. For of great minds, one of the proper works is, to help and free others from scorn; and compare themselves only with the most able.

On the contrary, "sudden dejection," is the passion that causeth "weeping"; and is caused by such accidents, as suddenly take away some vehement hope, or some prop of their power: and they are most subject to it, that rely principally on helps external, such as are women and children. Therefore some weep for the loss of friends; others for their unkindness; others for the sudden stop made to their thoughts of revenge, by reconciliation. But in all cases, both laughter, and weeping, are sudden motions; custom taking them both away. For no man laughs at old jests; or weeps for an old calamity.

"Grief," for the discovery of some defect of ability, is "shame," or the passion that discovereth itself in "blushing": and consisteth in the apprehension of something dishonourable; and in young men is a sign of the love of good reputation, and commendable: in old men it is a sign of the same; but because it comes too late, not commendable.

The "contempt" of good reputation is called "impudence."

"Grief," for the calamity of another, is "pity"; and ariseth from the imagination that the like calamity may befall himself; and therefore is called also "compassion," and in the phrase of this present time a "fellow-feeling": and therefore for calamity arriving from great wickedness, the best men have the least pity; and for the same calamity, those hate pity, that think themselves least obnoxious to the same.

"Contempt," or little sense of the calamity of others, is that which men call "cruelty"; proceeding from security of their own fortune. For, that any man should take pleasure in other men's great harms, without other end of his own, I do not conceive it possible.

"Grief," for the success of a competitor in wealth, honour, or other good, if it be joined with endeavour to enforce our own abilities to equal or exceed him, is called "emulation"; but joined with endeavour to supplant, or hinder a competitor, "envy."

When in the mind of man, appetites, and aversions, hopes, and fears, concerning one and the same thing, arise alternately; and divers good and evil consequences of the doing, or omitting the thing propounded, come successively into our thoughts; so that sometimes we have an appetite to it; sometimes an aversion from it; sometimes hope to be able to do it; sometimes despair, or fear to attempt it; the whole sum of desires, aversions, hopes, and fears continued till the thing be either done, or thought impossible, is that we call "deliberation."

Therefore of things past, there is no "deliberation"; because manifestly impossible to be changed: nor of things known to be impossible, or thought so; because men know, or think, such deliberation vain. But of things impossible, which we think possible, we may deliberate; not knowing it is in vain. And it is called "deliberation"; because it is a putting an end to the "liberty" we had of doing or omitting according to our own appetite, or aversion.

This alternate succession of appetites, aversions, hopes, and fears, is no less in other living creatures than in man: and therefore beasts also deliberate.

Every "deliberation" is then said to "end," when that whereof they deliberate, is either done or thought impossible; because till then we retain the liberty of doing or omitting, according to our appetite, or aversion.

In "deliberation," the last appetite, or aversion, immediately adhering to the action, or to the omission thereof, is that we call the "will"; the act, not the faculty, of "willing." And beasts that have "deliberation," must necessarily also have "will." The definition of the "will," given commonly by the schools, that it is a "rational appetite," is not good. For if it were, then could there be no voluntary act against reason. For a "voluntary act" is that which proceedeth from the "will," and no other. But if instead of a rational appetite, we shall say an appetite resulting from a precedent deliberation, then the definition is the same that I have given here. Will, therefore, is the last appetite in deliberating. And though we say in common discourse, a man had a will once to do a thing, that nevertheless he forbore to do; yet that is properly but an inclination, which makes no action voluntary; because the action depends not of it, but of the last inclination or appetite. For if the intervenient appetites, make any action voluntary; then by the same reason, all intervenient aversions should make the same

action involuntary; and so one and the same action should be both voluntary and involuntary.

By this it is manifest, that not only actions that have their beginning from covetousness, ambition, lust, or other appetites to the thing propounded; but also those that have their beginning from aversion, or fear of those consequences that follow the omission, are "voluntary actions."

The forms of speech by which the passions are expressed, are partly the same, and partly different from those, by which we express our thoughts. And first, generally all passions may be expressed "indicatively"; as, "I love," "I fear," "I joy," "I deliberate," "I will," "I command": but some of them have particular expressions by themselves, which nevertheless are not affirmations, unless it be when they serve to make other inferences, besides that of the passion they proceed from. Deliberation is expressed "subjunctively"; which is a speech proper to signify suppositions, with their consequences: as, "if this be done, then this will follow"; and differs not from the language of reasoning, save that reasoning is in general words; but deliberation for the most part is of particulars. The language of desire, and aversion, is "imperative"; as, "do this," "forbear that"; which when the party is obliged to do, or forbear, is "command"; otherwise "prayer"; or else "counsel." The language of vainglory, of indignation, pity, and revengefulness, "optative": but of the desire to know, there is a peculiar expression, called "interrogative"; as, "what is it," "when shall it," "how is it done," and "why so?" Other language of the passions I find none: for cursing, swearing, reviling, and the like, do not signify as speech; but as the actions of a tongue accustomed.

These forms of speech, I say, are expressions, or voluntary significations of our passions: but certain signs they be not; because they may be used arbitrarily, whether they that use them have such passions or not. The best signs of passions present, are either in the countenance, motions of the body, actions, and ends, or aims, which we otherwise know the man to have.

And because in deliberation, the appetites, and aversions, are raised by foresight of the good and evil consequences, and sequels of the action whereof we deliberate; the good or evil effect thereof dependeth on the foresight of a long chain of consequences, of which very seldom any man is able to see to the end. But for so far as a man seeth, if the good in those consequences be greater than the evil, the whole chain is that which writers call "apparent," or "seeming good." And contrarily, when the evil exceedeth the good, the whole is "apparent," or "seeming evil": so that he who hath by experience, or reason, the greatest and surest prospect of consequences, deliberates best himself; and is able when he will, to give the best counsel unto others.

"Continual success" in obtaining those things which a man from time to time desireth, that is to say, continual prospering, is that men call "felicity"; I mean the felicity of this life. For there is no such thing as perpetual tranquility of mind, while we live here; because life itself is but motion, and can never be without desire, nor without fear, no more than without sense. What kind of felicity God hath ordained to them that devoutly honour Him, a man shall no sooner know, than enjoy; being joys, that now are as incomprehensible as the word of school-men "beatifical vision" is unintelligible.

The form of speech whereby men signify their opinion of the goodness of anything, is "praise." That whereby they signify the power and greatness of anything, is "magnifying." And that whereby they signify the opinion they have of a man's felicity is by the Greeks called μακαρισμός, for which we have no name in our tongue. And thus much is sufficient for the present purpose, to have been said of the "passions."

• • •

Chapter X
Of Power, Worth, Dignity, Honour, and Worthiness

The "power of a man," to take it universally, is his present means; to obtain some future apparent good: and is either "original" or "instrumental."

"Natural power," is the eminence of the faculties of body or mind; as extraordinary strength, form, prudence, arts, eloquence, liberality, nobility. "Instrumental" are those powers, which acquired by these, or by fortune, are means and instruments to acquire more: as riches, reputation, friends, and the secret working of God, which men call good luck. For the nature of power is in this point like to fame, increasing as it proceeds; or like the motion of heavy bodies, which the further they go, make still the more haste.

The greatest of human powers, is that which is compounded of the powers of most men, united by consent, in one person, natural or civil, that has the use of all their powers depending on his will; such as is the power of a commonwealth: or depending on the wills of each particular; such as is the power of a faction, or of divers factions leagued. Therefore to have servants, is power; to have friends, is power: for they are strengths united.

Also riches joined with liberality, is power; because it procureth friends, and servants; without liberality, not so; because in this case they defend not; but expose men to envy, as a prey.

Reputation of power, is power; because it draweth with it the adherence of those that need protection.

So is reputation of love of a man's country, called popularity, for the same reason.

Also, what quality soever maketh a man beloved, or feared of many; or the reputation of such quality, is power; because it is a means to have the assistance and service of many.

Good success is power: because it maketh reputation of wisdom, or good fortune; which makes men either fear him, or rely on him.

Affability of men already in power, is increase of power; because it gaineth love.

Reputation of prudence in the conduct of peace or war, is power; because to prudent men, we commit the government of ourselves, more willingly than to others.

Nobility is power, not in all places, but only in those commonwealths where it has privileges: for in such privileges, consisteth their power.

Eloquence is power, because it is seeming prudence.

Form is power; because being a promise of good, it recommendeth men to the favour of women and strangers.

The sciences are small power; because not eminent; and therefore, not acknowledged in any man; nor are at all, but in a few, and in them, but of a few things. For science is of that nature, as none can understand it to be, but such as in a good measure have attained it.

Arts of public use, as fortification, making of engines, and other instruments of war; because they confer to defence and victory, are power: and though the true mother of them be science, namely the mathematics; yet, because they are brought into the light by the hand of the artificer, they be esteemed, the midwife passing with the vulgar for the mother, as his issue.

The "value," or "worth" of a man, is as of all other things, his price; that is to say, so much as would be given for the use of his power: and therefore is not absolute; but a thing dependent on the need and judgment of another. An able conductor of soldiers, is of great price in time of war present, or imminent; but in peace not so. A learned and uncorrupt judge, is much worth in time of peace; but not so much in war. And as in other things, so in men, not the seller, but the buyer determines the price. For let a man, as most men do, rate themselves at the highest value they can; yet their true value is no more than it is esteemed by others.

The manifestation of the value we set on one another, is that which is commonly called honouring, and dishonouring. To value a man at a high rate, is to "honour" him; at a low rate, is to "dishonour" him. But high, and low, in this case, is to be understood by comparison to the rate that each man setteth on himself.

The public worth of a man, which is the value set on him by the commonwealth, is that which men commonly call "dignity." And this value of him by the commonwealth, is understood, by offices of command, judicature, public employment; or by names and titles, introduced for distinction of such value.

To pray to another, for aid of any kind, is "to honour"; because a sign we have an opinion he has power to help; and the more difficult the aid is, the more is the honour.

To obey, is to honour, because no man obeys them whom they think have no power to help, or hurt them. And consequently to disobey, is to "dishonour."

To give great gifts to a man, is to honour him; because it is buying of protection, and acknowledging of power. To give little gifts, is to dishonour; because it is but alms, and signifies an opinion of the need of small helps.

To be sedulous in promoting another's good, also to flatter, is to honour; as a sign we seek his protection or aid. To neglect, is to dishonour.

To give way or place to another, in any commodity, is to honour; being a confession of greater power. To arrogate, is to dishonour.

To show any sign of love, or fear of another, is to honour; for both to love, and to fear, is to value. To contemn, or less to love or fear than he expects, is to dishonour; for it is undervaluing.

To praise, magnify, or call happy, is to honour; because nothing but goodness, power, and felicity is valued. To revile, mock, or pity, is to dishonour.

To speak to another with consideration, to appear before him with decency, and humility, is to honour him; as signs of fear to offend. To speak to him rashly, to do anything before him obscenely, slovenly, impudently, is to dishonour.

To believe, to trust, to rely on another, is to honour him; sign of opinion of his virtue and power. To distrust, or not believe, is to dishonour.

To hearken to a man's counsel, or discourse, of what kind soever, is to honour; as a sign we think him wise, or eloquent, or witty. To sleep, or go forth, or talk the while, is to dishonour.

To do those things to another, which he takes for signs of honour, or which the law or custom makes so, is to honour; because in approving the honour done by others, he acknowledgeth the power which others acknowledge. To refuse to do them, is to dishonour.

To agree with in opinion, is to honour; as being a sign of approving his judgment and wisdom. To dissent, is dishonour, and an upbraiding of error; and if the dissent be in many things, of folly.

To imitate, is to honour; for it is vehemently to approve. To imitate one's enemy, is to dishonour.

To honour those another honours, is to honour him; as a sign of approbation of his judgment. To honour his enemies, is to dishonour him.

To employ in counsel, or in actions of difficulty, is to honour; as a sign of opinion of his wisdom, or other power. To deny employment in the same cases, to those that seek it, is to dishonour.

All these ways of honouring, are natural; and as well within as without commonwealths. But in commonwealths, where he, or they that have the supreme authority, can make whatsoever they please to stand for signs of honour, there be other honours.

A sovereign doth honour a subject, with whatsoever title, or office, or employment, or action, that he himself will have taken for a sign of his will to honour him.

The king of Persia honoured Mordecai, when he appointed he should be conducted through the streets in the king's garment, upon one of the king's horses, with a crown on his head, and a prince before him, proclaiming, "Thus shall it be done to him that the king will honour." And yet another king of Persia, or the same another time, to one that demanded for some great service, to wear one of the king's robes, gave him leave so to do; but with this addition, that he should wear it as the king's fool; and then it was dishonour. So that of civil honour, the fountain is in the person of the commonwealth, and dependeth on the will of the sovereign; and is therefore temporary, and called "civil honour"; such as magistracy, offices, titles; and in some places, coats and scutcheons painted: and men honour such as have them, as having so many signs of favour in the commonwealth; which favour is power.

"Honourable" is whatsoever possession, action, or quality, is an argument and sign of power.

And therefore to be honoured, loved, or feared of many, is honourable; as arguments of power. To be honoured of few or none, "dishonourable."

Dominion and victory is honourable; because acquired by power; and servitude, for need, or fear, is dishonourable.

Good fortune, if lasting, honourable; as a sign of the favour of God. Ill fortune, and losses, dishonourable. Riches are honourable; for they are power. Poverty, dishonourable. Magnanimity, liberality, hope, courage, confidence, are honourable; for they proceed from the conscience of power. Pusillanimity, parsimony, fear, diffidence, are dishonourable.

Timely resolution, or determination of what a man is to do, is honourable; as being the contempt of small difficulties and dangers. And irresolution, dishonourable; as a sign of too much valuing of little impediments, and little advantages: for when a man has weighed things as long as the time permits, and resolves not, the difference of weight is but little; and therefore if he resolve not, he overvalues little things, which is pusillanimity.

All actions and speeches that proceed, or seem to proceed, from much experience, science, discretion, or wit, are honourable; for all these are powers. Actions, or words that proceed from error, ignorance, or folly, dishonourable.

Gravity, as far forth as it seems to proceed from a mind employed on something else, is honourable; because employment is a sign of power. But if it seem to proceed from a purpose to appear grave, it is dishonourable. For the gravity of the former, is like the steadiness of a ship laden with merchandize; but of the latter, like the steadiness of a ship ballasted with sand, and other trash.

To be conspicuous, that is to say, to be known, for wealth, office, great actions, or any eminent good, is honourable; as a sign of the power for which he is conspicuous. On the contrary, obscurity is dishonourable.

To be descended from conspicuous parents, is honourable; because they the more easily attain the aids and friends of their ancestors. On the contrary, to be descended from obscure parentage, is dishonourable.

Actions proceeding from equity, joined with loss, are honourable; as signs of magnanimity: for magnanimity is a sign of power. On the contrary, craft, shifting, neglect of equity, is dishonourable.

Covetousness of great riches, and ambition of great honours, are honourable; as signs of power to obtain them. Covetousness, and ambition, of little gains or preferments, is dishonourable.

Nor does it alter the case of honour, whether an action, so it be great and difficult, and consequently a sign of much power, be just or unjust: for honour consisteth only in the opinion of power. Therefore the ancient heathen did not think they dishonoured, but greatly honoured the gods, when they introduced them in their poems, committing rapes, thefts, and other great but unjust, or unclean acts: insomuch as nothing is so much celebrated in Jupiter, as his adulteries; nor in Mercury, as his frauds and thefts: of whose praises, in a hymn of Homer, the greatest is this, that being born in the morning, he had invented music at noon, and before night, stolen away the cattle of Apollo from his herdsmen.

Also amongst men, till there were constituted great commonwealths, it was thought no dishonour to be a pirate, or a highway thief; but rather a lawful trade, not only amongst the Greeks, but also amongst all other nations, as is manifest by the histories of ancient time. And at this day, in this part of the world, private duels are and always will be honourable, though unlawful, till such time as there shall be honour ordained for them that refuse, and ignominy for them that make the challenge. For duels also are many times effects of courage; and the ground of courage is always strength or skill, which are power; though for the most part they be effects of rash speaking, and of the fear of dishonour, in one or both the combatants; who engaged by rashness, are driven into the lists to avoid disgrace.

Scutcheons, and coats of arms hereditary, where they have any eminent privileges, are honourable; otherwise not: for their power consisteth either in such privileges, or in riches, or some such thing as is equally honoured in other men. This kind of honour, commonly called gentry, hath been derived from the ancient Germans. For there never was any such thing known, where the German customs were unknown. Nor is it now anywhere in use, where the Germans have not inhabited. The ancient Greek commanders, when they went to war, had their shields painted with such devices as they pleased; insomuch that an unpainted buckler was a sign of poverty, and of a common soldier; but they transmitted not the inheritance of them. The Romans transmitted the marks of their families: but they were the images, not the devices of their ancestors. Amongst the people of Asia, Africa, and America, there is not, nor was ever, any such thing. The Germans only had that custom; from whom it has been derived into England, France, Spain, and Italy, when in great numbers they either aided the Romans, or made their own conquests in these western parts of the world.

For Germany, being anciently, as all other countries in their beginnings, divided amongst an infinite number of little lords, or masters of families, that continually had wars one with another; those masters, or lords, principally to the end they might, when they were covered with arms, be known by their followers; and partly for ornament, both painted their armour, or their scutcheon, or coat, with the picture of some beast, or other thing, and also put some eminent and visible mark upon the crest of their helmets. And this ornament both of the arms, and crest, descended by inheritance to their children; to the eldest pure, and to the rest with some note of diversity, such as the old master, that is to say in Dutch, the "Here-alt" thought fit. But when many such families, joined together, made a greater monarchy, this duty of the Herealt, to distinguish scutcheons, was made a private office apart. And the issue of these lords is the great and ancient gentry; which for the most part bear living creatures, noted for courage and rapine; or castles, battlements, belts, weapons, bars, palisades, and other notes of war; nothing being then in honour but virtue military. Afterwards, not only kings, but popular commonwealths, gave divers manners of scutcheons, to such as went forth to the war, or returned from it, for encouragement, or recompense to their service. All which, by an observing reader, may be found in such ancient histories, Greek and Latin, as make mention of the German nation and manners in their times.

Titles of "honour," such as are duke, count, marquis, and baron, are honourable; as signifying the value set upon them by the sovereign power of the commonwealth: which titles, were in old time titles of office and command, derived some from the Romans, some from the Germans and French: dukes, in Latin, "duces," being generals in war: counts, "comites," such as bear the general company out of friendship, and were left to govern and defend places conquered and pacified: marquises, "marchiones," were counts that governed the marches, or bounds of the empire. Which titles of duke, count, and marquis, came into the empire about the time of Constantine the Great, from the customs of the German "militia." But baron seems to have been a title of the Gauls, and signifies a great man; such as were the king's or prince's men, whom they employed in war about their persons; and seems to be derived from "vir," to "ber," and "bar," that signified the same in the language of the Gauls, that "vir" in Latin; and thence to "bero," and "baro," so that such men were called "berones," and after "barones"; and, in Spanish, "varones." But he that would know more particularly the original of titles of honour, may find it, as I have done this, in Mr. Selden's most excellent treatise of that subject. In process of time these offices of honour, by occasion of trouble, and for reasons of good and peaceable government, were turned into mere titles; serving, for the most part, to distinguish the precedence, place, and order of subjects in the commonwealth: and men were made dukes, counts, marquises, and barons of places, wherein they had neither possession nor command: and other titles also were devised to the same end.

"Worthiness," is a thing different from the worth or value of a man; and also from his merit, or desert, and consisteth in a particular power, or ability for that, whereof he is said to be worthy: which particular ability is usually named "fitness," or "aptitude."

For he is worthiest to be a commander, to be a judge, or to have any other charge, that is best fitted, with the qualities required to the well discharging of it; and worthiest of riches, that has the qualities most requisite for the well using of them: any of which qualities being absent, one may nevertheless be a worthy man, and valuable for something else. Again, a man may be worthy of riches, office, and employment, and nevertheless can plead no right to have it before another; and therefore cannot be said to merit or deserve it. For merit presupposeth a right, and that the thing deserved is due by promise: of which I shall say more hereafter, when I shall speak of contracts.

Chapter XI
Of the Difference of Manners

By manners I mean not here decency of behaviour; as how one should salute another, or how a man should wash his mouth, or pick his teeth before company, and such other points of the "small morals"; but those qualities of mankind that concern their living together in peace and unity. To which end we are to consider that the felicity of this life consisteth not in the repose of a mind satisfied. For there is no such *finis ultimus*, utmost aim, nor *summum bonum*, greatest good, as is spoken of in the books of the old moral philosophers. Nor can a man any more live, whose desires are at an end, than he whose senses and imaginations are at a stand. Felicity is a continual progress of the desire, from one object to another, the attaining of the former being still but the way to the latter. The cause whereof is that the object of man's desire is not to enjoy once only, and for one instant of time, but to assure for ever the way of his future desire. And therefore the voluntary actions and inclinations of all men, tend not only to the procuring, but also to the assuring of a contented life; and differ only in the way, which ariseth partly from the diversity of passions in divers men; and partly from the difference of the knowledge or opinion each one has of the causes which produce the effect desired.

So that in the first place, I put for a general inclination of all mankind, a perpetual and restless desire of power after power, that ceaseth only in death. And the cause of this is not always that a man hopes for a more intensive delight than he has already attained to, or that he cannot be content with a moderate power; but because he cannot assure the power and means to live well, which he hath present, without the acquisition of more. And from hence it is that kings, whose power is greatest, turn their endeavours to the assuring it at home by laws, or abroad by wars; and when that is done, there succeedeth a new desire; in some, of fame from new conquest; in others, of ease and sensual pleasure; in others, of admiration, or being flattered for excellence in some art, or other ability of the mind.

Competition of riches, honour, command, or other power, inclineth to contention, enmity, and war; because the way of one competitor, to the attaining of his desire, is to kill, subdue, supplant, or repel the other. Particularly, competition of praise, inclineth to a reverence of antiquity. For men contend with the living, not with the dead; to these ascribing more than due, that they may obscure the glory of the other.

Desire of ease, and sensual delight, disposeth men to obey a common power, because by such desires a man doth abandon the protection that might be hoped for from his own industry and labour. Fear of death, and wounds, disposeth to the same, and for the same reason. On the contrary, needy men, and hardy, not contented with their present condition, as also all men that are ambitious of military command, are inclined to continue the causes of war; and to stir up trouble and sedition, for there is no honour military but by war; nor any such hope to mend an ill game, as by causing a new shuffle.

Desire of knowledge, and arts of peace, inclineth men to obey a common power: for such desire, containeth a desire of leisure; and consequently protection from some other power than their own.

Desire of praise, disposeth to laudable actions, such as please them whose judgment they value; for of those men whom we contemn, we contemn also the praises. Desire of fame after death does the same. And though after death, there be no sense of the praise given us on earth, as being joys, that are either swallowed up in the unspeakable joys of Heaven, or extinguished in the extreme torments of hell: yet is not such fame vain; because men have a present delight therein, from the foresight of it, and of the benefit that may redound thereby to their posterity: which though they now see not, yet they imagine; and anything that is pleasure in the sense, the same also is pleasure in the imagination.

To have received from one, to whom we think ourselves equal, greater benefits than there is hope to requite, disposeth to counterfeit love; but really secret hatred; and puts a man into the estate of a desperate debtor, that in declining the sight of his creditor, tacitly wishes him there, where he might never see him more. For benefits oblige, and obligation is thraldom; and unrequitable obligation perpetual thraldom; which is to one's equal, hateful. But to have received benefits from one, whom we acknowledge for superior, inclines to love; because the obligation is no new depression: and cheerful acceptation, which men call "gratitude," is such an honour done to the obliger, as is taken generally for retribution. Also to receive benefits, though from an equal, or inferior, as long as there is hope of requital, disposeth to love: for in the intention of the receiver, the obligation is of aid and service mutual; from whence proceedeth an emulation of who shall exceed in benefiting; the most noble and profitable contention possible; wherein the victor is pleased with his victory, and the other revenged by confessing it.

To have done more hurt to a man, than he can or is willing to expiate, inclineth the doer to hate the sufferer. For he must expect revenge, or forgiveness; both which are hateful.

Fear of oppression, disposeth a man to anticipate, or to seek aid by society: for there is no other way by which a man can secure his life and liberty.

Men that distrust their own subtlety, are, in tumult and sedition, better disposed for victory, than they that suppose themselves wise, or crafty. For these love to consult, the other, fearing to be circumvented, to strike first. And in sedition, men being always in the precincts of battle, to hold together, and use all advantages of force, is a better stratagem, than any that can proceed from subtlety of wit.

Vain-glorious men, such as without being conscious to themselves of great sufficiency, delight in supposing themselves gallant men, are inclined only to ostentation; but not to attempt: because when danger or difficulty appears, they look for nothing but to have their insufficiency discovered.

Vain-glorious men, such as estimate their sufficiency by the flattery of other men, or the fortune of some precedent action, without assured ground of hope from the true knowledge of themselves, are inclined to rash engaging; and in the approach of danger, or difficulty, to retire if they can: because not seeing the way of safety, they will rather hazard their honour, which may be salved with an excuse; than their lives, for which no salve is sufficient.

Men that have a strong opinion of their own wisdom in matter of government, are disposed to ambition. Because without public employment in council or magistracy, the honour of their wisdom is lost. And therefore eloquent speakers are inclined to ambition; for eloquence seemeth wisdom, both to themselves and others.

Pusillanimity disposeth men to irresolution, and consequently to lose the occasions, and fittest opportunities of action. For after men have been in deliberation till the time of action approach, if it be not then manifest what is best to be done, it is a sign,

the difference of motives, the one way and the other, are not great: therefore not to resolve then, is to lose the occasion by weighing of trifles; which is pusillanimity.

Frugality, though in poor men a virtue, maketh a man unapt to achieve such actions as require the strength of many men at once: for it weakeneth their endeavour, which is to be nourished and kept in vigour by reward.

Eloquence, with flattery, disposeth men to confide in them that have it; because the former is seeming wisdom, the latter seeming kindness. Add to them military reputation, and it disposeth men to adhere, and subject themselves to those men that have them. The two former having given them caution against danger from him; the latter gives them caution against danger from others.

Want of science, that is, ignorance of causes, disposeth, or rather constraineth a man to rely on the advice and authority of others. For all men whom the truth concerns, if they rely not on their own, must rely on the opinion of some other, whom they think wiser than themselves, and see not why he should deceive them.

Ignorance of the signification of words, which is want of understanding, disposeth men to take on trust, not only the truth they know not; but also the errors; and which is more, the nonsense of them they trust: for neither error nor nonsense, can without a perfect understanding of words, be detected.

From the same it proceedeth, that men give different names to one and the same thing, from the difference of their own passions: as they that approve a private opinion, call it opinion; but they that mislike it, heresy: and yet heresy signifies no more than private opinion; but has only a greater tincture of choler.

From the same also it proceedeth, that men cannot distinguish, without study and great understanding, between one action of many men, and many actions of one multitude; as for example, between one action of all the senators of Rome in killing Cataline, and the many actions of a number of senators in killing Cæsar; and therefore are disposed to take for the action of the people, that which is a multitude of actions done by a multitude of men, led perhaps by the persuasion of one.

Ignorance of the causes, and original constitution of right, equity, law, and justice, disposeth a man to make custom and example the rule of his actions; in such manner, as to think that unjust which it hath been the custom to punish; and that just, of the impunity and approbation whereof they can produce an example, or, as the lawyers which only use this false measure of justice barbarously call it, a precedent; like little children, that have no other rule of good and evil manners, but the correction they receive from their parents and masters; save that children are constant to their rule, whereas, men are not so; because grown old, and stubborn, they appeal from custom to reason, and from reason to custom, as it serves their turn; receding from custom when their interest requires it, and setting themselves against reason, as oft as reason is against them: which is the cause, that the doctrine of right and wrong is perpetually disputed, both by the pen and the sword: whereas the doctrine of lines, and figures, is not so; because men care not, in that subject, what be truth, as a thing that crosses no man's ambition, profit, or lust. For I doubt not, but if it had been a thing contrary to any man's right of dominion, or to the interest of men that have dominion, "that the three angles of a triangle, should be equal to two angles of a square"; that doctrine should have been, if not disputed, yet by the burning of all books of geometry, suppressed, as far as he whom it concerned was able.

Ignorance of remote causes, disposeth men to attribute all events to the causes immediate, and instrumental; for these are all the causes they perceive. And hence it comes to pass, that in all places, men that are grieved with payments to the public, discharge their anger upon the publicans, that is to say, farmers, collectors, and other officers of the public revenue; and adhere to such as find fault with the public government; and thereby, when they have engaged themselves beyond hope of justification, fall also upon the supreme authority, for fear of punishment, or shame of receiving pardon.

Ignorance of natural causes, disposeth a man to credulity, so as to believe many times impossibilities: for such know nothing to the contrary, but that they may be true; being unable to detect the impossibility. And credulity, because men like to be hearkened unto in company, disposeth them to lying: so that ignorance itself without malice, is able to make a man both to believe lies, and tell them; and sometimes also to invent them.

Anxiety for the future time, disposeth men to inquire into the causes of things: because the knowledge of them maketh men the better able to order the present to their best advantage.

Curiosity, or love of the knowledge of causes, draws a man from the consideration of the effect, to seek the cause; and again, the cause of that cause; till of necessity he must come to this thought at last, that there is some cause, whereof there is no former cause, but is eternal; which is it men call God. So that it is impossible to make any profound inquiry into natural causes, without being inclined thereby to believe there is one God eternal; though they cannot have any idea of Him in their mind, answerable to His nature. For as a man that is born blind, hearing men talk of warming themselves by the fire, and being brought to warm himself by the same, may easily conceive, and assure himself, there is somewhat there, which men call "fire," and is the cause of the heat he feels; but cannot imagine what it is like; nor have an idea of it in his mind, such as they have that see it: so also by the visible things of this world, and their admirable order, a man may conceive there is a cause of them, which men call God; and yet not have an idea or image of Him in his mind.

And they that make little or no inquiry into the natural causes of things, yet from the fear that proceeds from the ignorance itself, of what it is that hath the power to do them much good or harm, are inclined to suppose, and feign unto themselves, several kinds of powers invisible; and to stand in awe of their own imaginations; and in time of distress to invoke them; as also in the time of an expected good success, to give them thanks; making the creatures of their own fancy, their gods. By which means it hath come to pass, that from the innumerable variety of fancy, men have created in the world innumerable sorts of gods. And this fear of things invisible, is the natural seed of that, which every one in himself calleth religion; and in them that worship, or fear that power otherwise than they do, superstition.

And this seed of religion, having been observed by many; some of those that have observed it, have been inclined thereby to nourish, dress, and form it into laws; and to add to it of their own invention, any opinion of the causes of future events, by which they thought they should be best able to govern others, and make unto themselves the greatest use of their powers.

Chapter XII
Of Religion

Seeing there are no signs, nor fruit of "religion," but in man only; there is no cause to doubt, but that the seed of "religion" is also only in man; and consisteth in some peculiar quality, or at least in some eminent degree thereof, not to be found in any other living creatures.

And first, it is peculiar to the nature of man, to be inquisitive into the causes of the events they see, some more, some less; but all men so much, as to be curious in the search of the causes of their own good and evil fortune.

Secondly, upon the sight of anything that hath a beginning, to think also it had a cause, which determined the same to begin, then when it did, rather than sooner or later.

Thirdly, whereas there is no other felicity of beasts, but the enjoying of their quotidian food, ease, and lusts; as having little or no foresight of the time to come, for want of observation, and memory of the order, consequence, and dependence of the things they see; man observeth how one event hath been produced by another; and remembereth in them antecedence and consequence; and when he cannot assure himself of the true causes of things, (for the causes of good and evil fortune for the most part are invisible,) he supposes causes of them, either such as his own fancy suggesteth, or trusteth the authority of other men, such as he thinks to be his friends, and wiser than himself.

The two first make anxiety. For being assured that there be causes of all things that have arrived hitherto, or shall arrive hereafter, it is impossible for a man, who continually endeavoureth to secure himself against the evil he fears, and procure the good he desireth, not to be in a perpetual solicitude of the time to come; so that every man, especially those that are over-provident, are in a state like to that of Prometheus. For as Prometheus, which, interpreted, is "the prudent man," was bound to the hill Caucasus, a place of large prospect, where an eagle feeding on his liver, devoured in the day, as much as was repaired in the night: so that man, which looks too far before him in the care of future time, hath his heart all the day long gnawed on by fear of death, poverty, or other calamity, and has no repose, nor pause of his anxiety, but in sleep.

This perpetual fear, always accompanying mankind in the ignorance of causes, as it were in the dark, must needs have for object something. And therefore when there is nothing to be seen, there is nothing to accuse, either of their good or evil fortune, but some "power," or agent "invisible," in which sense perhaps it was, that some of the old poets said, that the gods were at first created by human fear: which spoken of the gods, that is to say, of the many gods of the Gentiles, is very true. But the acknowledging of one God, eternal, infinite, and omnipotent, may more easily be derived, from the desire men have to know the causes of natural bodies, and their several virtues and operations, than from the fear of what was to befall them in time to come. For he that from any effect he seeth come to pass, should reason to the next and immediate cause thereof, and from thence to the cause of that cause, and plunge himself profoundly in the pursuit of causes, shall at last come to this, that there must be, as even the heathen philosophers confessed, one first mover; that is, a first and an eternal cause of all things, which is that which men mean by the name of God, and all this without thought of their fortune; the solicitude whereof both inclines to fear, and hinders them from the search of the causes of other things, and thereby gives occasion of feigning of as many gods as there be men that feign them.

And for the matter or substance of the invisible agents so fancied, they could not by natural cogitation fall upon any other conceit, but that it was the same with that of the soul of man; and that the soul of man was of the same substance with that which appeareth in a dream to one that sleepeth; or in a looking-glass, to one that is awake; which, men not knowing that such apparitions are nothing else but creatures of the fancy, think to be real and external substances, and therefore call them ghosts: as the Latins called them *imagines* and *umbræ*, and thought thĕm spirits, that is, thin aërial bodies, and those invisible agents which they feared to be like them, save that they appear and vanish when they please. But the opinion that such spirits were incorporeal, or immaterial, could never enter into the mind of any man by nature; because, though men may put together words of contradictory signification, as "spirit," and "incorporeal," yet they can never have the imagination of anything answering to them: and therefore, men that by their own meditation arrive to the acknowledgment of one infinite, omnipotent, and eternal God, chose rather to confess He is incomprehensible, and above their understanding, than to define His nature by "spirit incorporeal," and then confess their definition to be unintelligible; or, if they give Him such a title, it is not "dogmatically" with intention to make the divine nature understood; but "piously," to honour him with attributes, of significations as remote as they can from the grossness of bodies visible.

Then for the way by which they think these invisible agents wrought their effects; that is to say, what immediate causes they used, in bringing things to pass, men that know not what it is that we call "causing," that is, almost all men, have no other rule to guess by, but by observing and remembering what they have seen to precede the like effect at some other time, or times before, without seeing between the antecedent and subsequent event, any dependence or connection at all: and therefore from the like things past, they expect the like things to come; and hope for good or evil luck, superstitiously, from things that have no part at all in the causing of it: as the Athenians did for their war at Lepanto, demand another Phormio; the Pompeian faction for their war in Africa, another Scipio; and others have done in divers other occasions since. In like manner they attribute their fortune to a stander-by, to a lucky or unlucky place, to words spoken, especially if the name of God be amongst them; as charming and conjuring, the liturgy of witches; inasmuch as to believe, they have power to turn a stone into bread, bread into a man, or anything into anything.

Thirdly, for the worship which naturally men exhibit to powers invisible, it can be no other, but such expressions of their reverence, as they would use towards men; gifts, petitions, thanks, submission of body, considerate addresses, sober behaviour, premeditated words, swearing, that is, assuring one another of their promises, by invoking them. Beyond that reason suggesteth nothing; but leaves them either to rest there; or for further ceremonies, to rely on those they believe to be wiser than themselves.

Lastly, concerning how these invisible powers declare to men the things which shall hereafter come to pass, especially concerning their good or evil fortune in general, or good or ill success in any particular undertaking, men are naturally at a stand; save that using to conjecture of the time to come, by the time past, they are very apt, not only to take casual things, after one or two encounters, for prognostics of the like encounter ever after, but also to believe the like prognostics from other men, of whom they have once conceived a good opinion.

And in these four things, opinion of ghosts, ignorance of second causes, devotion towards what men fear, and taking of things casual for prognostics, consisteth the natural seed of "religion"; which by reason of the different fancies, judgments, and passions of several men, hath grown up into ceremonies so different, that those which are used by one man, are for the most part ridiculous to another.

For these seeds have received culture from two sorts of men. One sort have been they that have nourished and ordered them, according to their own invention. The other have done it, by God's commandment and direction: but both sorts have done it, with a purpose to make those men that relied on them, the more apt to obedience, laws, peace, charity, and civil society. So that the religion of the former sort is a part of human politics; and teacheth part of the duty which earthly kings require of their subjects. And the religion of the latter sort is divine politics; and containeth precepts to those that have yielded themselves subjects in the kingdom of God. Of the former sort were all the founders of commonwealths, and the lawgivers of the Gentiles: of the latter sort, were Abraham, Moses, and our blessed Saviour; by whom have been derived unto us the laws of the kingdom of God.

And for that part of religion, which consisteth in opinions concerning the nature of powers invisible, there is almost nothing that has a name, that has not been esteemed amongst the Gentiles, in one place or another, a god, or devil; or by their poets feigned to be inanimated, inhabited, or possessed by some spirit or other.

The unformed matter of the world, was a god by the name of Chaos.

The heaven, the ocean, the planets, the fire, the earth, the winds, were so many gods.

Men, women, a bird, a crocodile, a calf, a dog, a snake, an onion, a leek, were deified. Besides that, they filled almost all places with spirits called "demons"; the plains, with Pan and Panises, or Satyrs; the woods, with Fauns, and Nymphs; the sea, with Tritons, and other Nymphs; every river and fountain, with a ghost of his name, and with Nymphs; every house with its "Lares," or familiars; every man with his "Genius"; hell with ghosts, and spiritual officers, as Charon, Cerberus, and the Furies; and in the night-time, all places with "larvæ," "lemures," ghosts of men deceased, and a whole kingdom of fairies and bug-bears. They have also ascribed divinity, and built temples to mere accidents and qualities; such as are time, night, day, peace, concord, love, contention, virtue, honour, health, rust, fever, and the like; which when they prayed for, or against, they prayed to, as if there were ghosts of those names hanging over their heads, and letting fall, or withholding that good or evil, for or against which they prayed. They invoked also their own wit, by the name of Muses; their own ignorance, by the name of Fortune; their own lusts, by the name of Cupid; their own rage, by the name of Furies; their own privy members, by the name of Priapus; and attributed their pollutions to Incubi and Succubæ: insomuch as there was nothing, which a poet could introduce as a person in his poem, which they did not make either a "god," or a "devil."

The same authors of the religion of the Gentiles, observing the second ground for religion, which is men's ignorance of causes; and thereby their aptness to attribute their fortune to causes, on which there was no dependence at all apparent, took occasion to obtrude on their ignorance, instead of second causes, a kind of second and ministerial gods; ascribing the cause of fecundity, to Venus; the cause of arts, to Apollo; of subtlety and craft, to Mercury; of tempests and storms, to Æolus; and of other effects, to other gods; insomuch as there was amongst the heathen almost as great variety of gods as of business.

And to the worship, which naturally men conceived fit to be used towards their gods, namely, oblations, prayers, thanks, and the rest formerly named; the same legislators of the Gentiles have added their images, both in picture and sculpture; that the more ignorant sort, that is to say, the most part or generality of the people, thinking the gods for whose representation they were made, were really included, and as it were housed within them, might so much the more stand in fear of them: and endowed them with lands, and houses, and officers, and revenues, set apart from all other human uses; that is, consecrated, and made holy to those their idols; as caverns, groves, woods, mountains, and whole islands; and have attributed to them, not only the shapes, some of men, some of beasts, some of monsters; but also the faculties and passions of men and beasts: as sense, speech, sex, lust, generation, and this not only by mixing one with another, to propagate the kind of gods, but also by mixing with men and women, to beget mongrel gods, and but inmates of heaven, as Bacchus, Hercules, and others; besides anger, revenge, and other passions, of living creatures, and the actions proceeding from them, as fraud, theft, adultery, sodomy, and any vice that may be taken for an effect of power, or a cause of pleasure; and all such vices, as amongst men are taken to be against law, rather than against honour.

Lastly, to the prognostics of time to come; which are naturally but conjectures upon experience of time past; and supernaturally, divine revelation; the same authors of the religion of the Gentiles, partly upon pretended experience, partly upon pretended revelation, have added innumerable other superstitious ways of divination; and made men believe they should find their fortunes, sometimes in the ambiguous or senseless answers of the priests at Delphi, Delos, Ammon, and other famous oracles; which answers were made ambiguous by design, to own the event both ways; or absurd, by the intoxicating vapour of the place, which is very frequent in sulphurous caverns: sometimes in the leaves of the Sybils; of whose prophecies, like those perhaps of Nostradamus (for the fragments now extant seem to be the invention of later times), there were some books in reputation in the time of the Roman Republic: sometimes in the insignificant speeches of madmen, supposed to be possessed with a divine spirit, which possession they called enthusiasm; and these kinds of foretelling events were accounted theomancy, or prophecy: sometimes in the aspect of the stars at their nativity; which was called horoscopy, and esteemed a part of judiciary astrology: sometimes in their own hopes and fears, called thumomancy, or presage: sometimes in the prediction of witches, that pretended conference with the dead: which is called necromancy, conjuring, and witchcraft; and is but juggling and confederate knavery: sometimes in the casual flight or feeding of birds; called augury: sometimes in the entrails of a sacrificed beast; which was "aruspicina": sometimes in dreams; sometimes in croaking of ravens, or chattering of birds; sometimes in the lineaments of the face; which was called metoposcopy; or by palmistry in the lines of the hand; in casual words, called "omina": sometimes in monsters, or unusual accidents; as eclipses, comets, rare meteors, earthquakes, inundations, uncouth births, and the like, which they called "portenta," and "ostenta," because they thought them to portend or foreshow some great calamity to come; sometimes, in mere lottery, as cross and pile, counting holes in a sieve; dipping of verses in Homer, and Virgil; and innumerable other such vain conceits. So easy are men to be drawn to believe anything, from such men as have gotten credit with them; and can with gentleness and dexterity take hold of their fear and ignorance.

And therefore the first founders and legislators of commonwealths among the Gentiles, whose ends were only to keep the people in obedience and peace, have in all places taken care; first, to imprint in their minds a belief, that those precepts which they gave concerning religion, might not be thought to proceed from their own device, but from the dictates of some god, or other spirit; or else that they themselves were of a higher nature than mere mortals, that their laws might the more easily be received: so Numa Pompilius pretended to receive the ceremonies he instituted amongst the Romans, from the nymph Egeria: and the first king and founder of the kingdom of Peru, pretended himself and his wife to be the children of the Sun; and Mahomet, to set up his new religion, pretended to have conferences with the Holy Ghost, in form of a dove. Secondly, they have had a care to make it believed, that the same things were displeasing to the gods which were forbidden by the laws. Thirdly, to prescribe ceremonies, supplications, sacrifices, and festivals, by which they were to believe, the anger of the gods might be appeased; and that ill success in war, great contagions of sickness, earthquakes, and each man's private misery, came from the anger of the gods, and their anger from the neglect of their worship, or the forgetting or mistaking some point of the ceremonies required. And though amongst the ancient Romans, men were not forbidden to deny that which in the poets is written of the pains and pleasures after this life; which divers of great authority and gravity in that state have in their harangues openly derided; yet that belief was always more cherished than the contrary.

And by these, and such other institutions, they obtained in order to their end, which was the peace of the commonwealth, that the common people in their misfortunes, laying the fault on neglect, or error in their ceremonies, or on their own disobedience to the laws, were the less apt to mutiny against their governors; and being entertained with the pomp and pastime of festivals, and public games, made in honour of the gods, needed nothing else but bread to keep them from discontent, murmuring, and commotion against the state. And therefore the Romans, that had conquered the greatest part of the then known world, made no scruple of tolerating any religion whatsoever

in the city of Rome itself; unless it had something in it that could not consist with their civil government; nor do we read that any religion was there forbidden, but that of the Jews; who, being the peculiar kingdom of God, thought it unlawful to acknowledge subjection to any mortal king or state whatsoever. And thus you see how the religion of the Gentiles was part of their policy.

But where God Himself, by supernatural revelation, planted religion; there He also made to Himself a peculiar kingdom; and gave laws not only of behaviour towards Himself, but also towards one another; and thereby in the kingdom of God, the policy, and laws civil, are a part of religion; and therefore the distinction of temporal and spiritual domination, hath there no place. It is true that God is king of all the earth; yet may He be king of a peculiar and chosen nation. For there is no more incongruity therein, than that he that hath the general command of the whole army, should have withal a peculiar regiment, or company of his own. God is king of all the earth by His power; but of His chosen people He is king by covenant. But to speak more largely of the kingdom of God, both by nature and covenant, I have in the following discourse assigned another place (chapter xxxv).

From the propagation of religion, it is not hard to understand the causes of the resolution of the same into its first seeds, or principles; which are only an opinion of a deity, and powers invisible and supernatural; that can never be so abolished out of human nature, but that new religions may again be made to spring out of them, by the culture of such men as for such purpose are in reputation.

For seeing all formed religion, is founded at first upon the faith which a multitude hath in some one person, whom they believe not only to be a wise man, and to labour to procure their happiness, but also to be a holy man, to whom God Himself vouchsafeth to declare His will supernaturally; it followeth necessarily, when they that have the government of religion, shall come to have either the wisdom of those men, their sincerity, or their love suspected; or when they shall be unable to show any probable token of divine revelation; that the religion which they desire to uphold, must be suspected likewise; and, without the fear of the civil sword, contradicted and rejected.

That which taketh away the reputation of wisdom, in him that formeth a religion, or addeth to it when it is already formed, is the enjoining of a belief of contradictories; for both parts of a contradiction cannot possibly be true; and therefore to enjoin the belief of them, is an argument of ignorance; which detects the author in that; and discredits him in all things else he shall propound as from revelation supernatural; which revelation a man may indeed have of many things above, but of nothing against natural reason.

That which taketh away the reputation of sincerity, is the doing or saying of such things, as appear to be signs, that what they require other men to believe is not believed by themselves; all which doings or sayings are therefore called scandalous, because they be stumbling-blocks, that make men to fall in the way of religion; as injustice, cruelty, profaneness, avarice, and luxury. For who can believe that he that doth ordinarily such actions as proceed from any of these roots, believeth there is any such invisible power to be feared, as he affrighteth other men withal for lesser faults?

That which taketh away the reputation of love, is the being detected of private ends; as when the belief they require of others, conduceth, or seemeth to conduce to the acquiring of dominion, riches, dignity, or secure pleasure, to themselves only, or specially. For that which men reap benefit by to themselves, they are thought to do for their own sakes, and not for love of others.

Lastly, the testimony that men can render of divine calling, can be no other than the operation of miracles; or true prophecy, which also is a miracle; or extraordinary felicity. And therefore, to those points of religion, which have been received from them that did such miracles; those that are added by such as approve not their calling by some miracle, obtain no greater belief than what the custom and laws of the places, in which they be educated, have wrought into them. For as in natural things, men of judgment require natural signs and arguments; so in supernatural things, they require signs supernatural, which are miracles, before they consent inwardly, and from their hearts.

All which causes of the weakening of men's faith, do manifestly appear in the examples following. First, we have the example of the children of Israel; who when Moses, that had approved his calling to them by miracles, and by the happy conduct of them out of Egypt, was absent but forty days, revolted from the worship of the true God, recommended to them by him; and setting up (Exod. xxxiii. 1, 2) a golden calf for their god, relapsed into the idolatry of the Egyptians; from whom they had been so lately delivered. And again, after Moses, Aaron, Joshua, and that generation which had seen the great works of God in Israel (Judges ii. 11) were dead; another generation arose, and served Baal. So that miracles failing, faith also failed.

Again, when the sons of Samuel (1 Sam. viii. 3) being constituted by their father judges in Bersabee, received bribes, and judged unjustly, the people of Israel refused any more to have God to be their king, in other manner than He was king of other people; and therefore cried out to Samuel, to choose them a king after the manner of the nations. So that justice failing, faith also failed: insomuch, as they deposed their God from reigning over them.

And whereas in the planting of Christian religion, the oracles ceased in all parts of the Roman empire, and the number of Christians increased wonderfully every day, and in every place, by the preaching of the Apostles and Evangelists; a great part of that success may reasonably be attributed to the contempt into which the priests of the Gentiles of that time had brought themselves by their uncleanness, avarice, and juggling between princes. Also the religion of the Church of Rome, was partly for the same cause abolished in England, and many other parts of Christendom, insomuch, as the failing of virtue in the pastors, maketh faith fail in the people: and partly from bringing of the philosophy and doctrine of Aristotle into religion, by the schoolmen; from whence there arose so many contradictions and absurdities, as brought the clergy into a reputation both of ignorance and of fraudulent intention; and inclined people to revolt from them, either against the will of their own princes, as in France and Holland; or with their will, as in England.

Lastly, amongst the points by the Church of Rome declared necessary for salvation, there be so many, manifestly to the advantage of the Pope, and of his spiritual subjects, residing in the territories of other Christian princes, that were it not for the mutual emulation of those princes, they might without war or trouble, exclude all foreign authority, as easily as it had been excluded in England. For who is there that does not see to whose benefit it conduceth, to have it believed that a king hath not his authority from Christ, unless a bishop crown him? That a king, if he be a priest, cannot marry? That whether a prince be born in lawful marriage, or not, must be judged by authority from Rome? That subjects may be freed from their allegiance, if by the Court of Rome the king be judged an heretic? That a king, as Chilperic of France, may be deposed by a pope, as Pope Zachary, for no cause; and his kingdom given to one of his subjects? That the clergy and regulars, in what country soever, shall be exempt from the jurisdiction of their king in cases criminal? Or who does not see, to whose profit redound the fees of private masses, and vales of purgatory; with other signs of private interest, enough to mortify the most lively faith, if, as I said, the civil magistrate and custom did not more sustain it, than any opinion they have of the sanctity, wisdom, or probity of their teachers? So that I may attribute all the changes of religion in the world to one and the same cause; and that is, unpleasing priests; and those not only amongst Catholics, but even in that Church that hath presumed most of reformation.

Chapter XIII
Of the Natural Condition of Mankind as Concerning Their Felicity and Misery

Nature hath made men so equal, in the faculties of body and mind; as that though there be found one man sometimes manifestly stronger in body, or of quicker mind than another, yet when all is reckoned together, the difference between man and man, is not so considerable, as that one man can thereupon claim to himself any benefit, to which another may not pretend, as well as he. For as to the strength of body, the weakest has strength enough to kill the strongest, either by secret machination, or by confederacy with others, that are in the same danger with himself.

And as to the faculties of the mind, setting aside the arts grounded upon words, and especially that skill of proceeding upon general and infallible rules, called science; which very few have, and but in few things; as being not a native faculty, born with us; nor attained, as prudence, while we look after somewhat else, I find yet a greater equality amongst men than that of strength. For prudence is but experience; which equal time, equally bestows on all men, in those things they equally apply themselves unto. That which may perhaps make such equality incredible, is but a vain conceit of one's own wisdom, which almost all men think they have in a greater degree than the vulgar; that is, than all men but themselves, and a few

others, whom by fame, or for concurring with themselves, they approve. For such is the nature of men, that howsoever they may acknowledge many others to be more witty, or more eloquent, or more learned; yet they will hardly believe there be many so wise as themselves; for they see their own wit at hand, and other men's at a distance. But this proveth rather that men are in that point equal, than unequal. For there is not ordinarily a greater sign of the equal distribution of anything, than that every man is contented with his share.

From this equality of ability, ariseth equality of hope in the attaining of our ends. And therefore if any two men desire the same thing, which nevertheless they cannot both enjoy, they become enemies; and in the way to their end, which is principally their own conservation, and sometimes their delectation only, endeavour to destroy or subdue one another. And from hence it comes to pass, that where an invader hath no more to fear than another man's single power; if one plant, sow, build, or possess a convenient seat, others may probably be expected to come prepared with forces united, to dispossess and deprive him, not only of the fruit of his labour, but also of his life or liberty. And the invader again is in the like danger of another.

And from this diffidence of one another, there is no way for any man to secure himself, so reasonable, as anticipation; that is, by force, or wiles, to master the persons of all men he can, so long, till he see no other power great enough to endanger him: and this is no more than his own conservation requireth, and is generally allowed. Also because there be some, that taking pleasure in contemplating their own power in the acts of conquest, which they pursue farther than their security requires; if others, that otherwise would be glad to be at ease within modest bounds, should not by invasion increase their power, they would not be able, long time, by standing only on their defence, to subsist. And by consequence, such augmentation of dominion over men being necessary to a man's conservation, it ought to be allowed him.

Again, men have no pleasure, but on the contrary a great deal of grief, in keeping company, where there is no power able to overawe them all. For every man looketh that his companion should value him, at the same rate he sets upon himself: and upon all signs of contempt, or undervaluing, naturally endeavours, as far as he dares, (which amongst them that have no common power to keep them in quiet, is far enough to make them destroy each other,) to extort a greater value from his contemners, by damage; and from others, by the example.

So that in the nature of man, we find three principal causes of quarrel. First, competition; secondly, diffidence; thirdly, glory.

The first, maketh men invade for gain; the second, for safety; and the third, for reputation. The first use violence, to make themselves masters of other men's persons, wives, children, and cattle; the second, to defend them; the third, for trifles, as a word, a smile, a different opinion, and any other sign of undervalue, either direct in their persons, or by reflection in their kindred, their friends, their nation, their profession, or their name.

Hereby it is manifest, that during the time men live without a common power to keep them all in awe, they are in that condition which is called war; and such a war, as is of every man, against every man. For "war" consisteth not in battle only, or the act of fighting, but in a tract of time, wherein the will to contend by battle is sufficiently known: and therefore the notion of "time" is to be considered in the nature of war, as it is in the nature of weather. For as the nature of foul weather lieth not in a shower or two of rain, but in an inclination thereto of many days together; so the nature of war consisteth not in actual fighting, but in the known disposition thereto during all the time there is no assurance to the contrary. All other time is "peace."

Whatsoever therefore is consequent to a time of war, where every man is enemy to every man, the same is consequent to the time wherein men live without other security than what their own strength and their own invention shall furnish them withal. In such condition there is no place for industry, because the fruit thereof is uncertain, and consequently no culture of the earth; no navigation, nor use of the commodities that may be imported by sea; no commodious building; no instruments of moving and removing such things as require much force; no knowledge of the face of the earth; no account of time; no arts; no letters; no society; and, which is worst of all, continual fear and danger of violent death; and the life of man, solitary, poor, nasty, brutish, and short.

It may seem strange to some man, that has not well weighed these things, that Nature should thus dissociate, and render men apt to invade and destroy one another; and he may therefore, not trusting to this inference, made from the passions, desire perhaps to have the same confirmed by experience. Let him therefore consider with himself, when taking a journey, he arms himself, and seeks to go well accompanied; when going to sleep, he locks his doors; when even in his house, he locks his chests; and this when he knows there be laws, and public officers, armed, to revenge all injuries shall be done him; what opinion he has of his fellow-subjects, when he rides armed; of his fellow-citizens, when he locks his doors; and of his children and servants, when he locks his chests. Does he not there as much accuse mankind by his actions as I do by my words? But neither of us accuse man's nature in it. The desires and other passions of man are in themselves no sin. No more are the actions that proceed from those passions, till they know a law that forbids them; which till laws be made they cannot know, nor can any law be made till they have agreed upon the person that shall make it.

It may peradventure be thought there was never such a time nor condition of war as this; and I believe it was never generally so, over all the world, but there are many places where they live so now. For the savage people in many places of America, except the government of small families, the concord whereof dependeth on natural lust, have no government at all, and live at this day in that brutish manner, as I said before. Howsoever, it may be perceived what manner of life there would be, where there were no common power to fear; by the manner of life which men that have formerly lived under a peaceful government, use to degenerate into in a civil war.

But though there had never been any time, wherein particular men were in a condition of war one against another; yet in all times, kings, and persons of sovereign authority, because of their independency, are in continual jealousies, and in the state and posture of gladiators; having their weapons pointing, and their eyes fixed on one another; that is, their forts, garrisons, and guns upon the frontiers of their kingdoms; and continual spies upon their neighbours; which is a posture of war. But because they uphold thereby the industry of their subjects; there does not follow from it that misery which accompanies the liberty of particular men.

To this war of every man, against every man, this also is consequent; that nothing can be unjust. The notions of right and wrong, justice and injustice, have there no place. Where there is no common power, there is no law: where no law, no injustice. Force and fraud, are in war the two cardinal virtues. Justice and injustice are none of the faculties neither of the body nor mind. If they were, they might be in a man that were alone in the world, as well as his senses, and passions. They are qualities that relate to men in society, not in solitude. It is consequent also to the same condition, that there be no propriety, no dominion, no "mine" and "thine" distinct; but only that to be every man's, that he can get; and for so long, as he can keep it. And thus much for the ill condition, which man by mere nature is actually placed in; though with a possibility to come out of it, consisting partly in the passions, partly in his reason.

The passions that incline men to peace, are fear of death; desire of such things as are necessary to commodious living; and a hope by their industry to obtain them. And reason suggesteth convenient articles of peace, upon which men may be drawn to agreement. These articles are they which otherwise are called the Laws of Nature: whereof I shall speak more particularly, in the two following chapters.

Chapter XIV
Of the First and Second Natural Laws,
and of Contracts

"The right of Nature," which writers commonly call *jus naturale*, is the liberty each man hath, to use his own power, as he will himself, for the preservation of his own nature; that is to say, of his own life; and consequently, of doing anything, which in his own judgment and reason he shall conceive to be the aptest means thereunto.

By "liberty," is understood, according to the proper signification of the word, the absence of external impediments: which impediments may oft take away part of a man's power to do what he would; but cannot hinder him from using the power left him, according as his judgment and reason shall dictate to him.

A "law of Nature," *lex naturalis*, is a precept or general rule, found out by reason, by which a man is forbidden to do that which is destructive of his life, or taketh away the means of preserving the same; and to omit that, by which he thinketh it may be best preserved. For though they that speak of this subject, use to confound *jus* and *lex*, "right" and "law": yet they ought to be distinguished; because "right," consisteth in liberty to do, or to forbear; whereas "law," determineth and bindeth to one of them; so that law and

right differ as much as obligation and liberty; which in one and the same matter are inconsistent.

And because the condition of man, as hath been declared in the precedent chapter, is a condition of war of every one against every one; in which case every one is governed by his own reason; and there is nothing he can make use of, that may not be a help unto him, in preserving his life against his enemies; it followeth, that in such a condition, every man has a right to everything; even to one another's body. And therefore, as long as this natural right of every man to everything endureth, there can be no security to any man, how strong or wise soever he be, of living out the time, which Nature ordinarily alloweth men to live. And consequently it is a precept, or general rule of reason, "that every man ought to endeavour peace, as far as he has hope of obtaining it; and when he cannot obtain it, that he may seek, and use, all helps, and advantages of war." The first branch of which rule, containeth the first, and fundamental law of Nature; which is, "to seek peace, and follow it." The second, the sum of the right of Nature: which is, "by all means we can, to defend ourselves."

From this fundamental law of Nature, by which men are commanded to endeavour peace, is derived this second law; "that a man be willing, when others are so too, as far-forth, as for peace, and defence of himself he shall think it necessary, to lay down this right to all things; and be contented with so much liberty against other men, as he would allow other men against himself." For as long as every man holdeth this right, of doing anything he liketh; so long are all men in the condition of war. But if other men will not lay down their right, as well as he; then there is no reason for any one to divest himself of his: for that were to expose himself to prey, which no man is bound to, rather than to dispose himself to peace. This is that law of the Gospel; "whatsoever you require that others should do to you, that do ye to them." And that law of all men, *quod tibi fieri non vis, alteri ne feceris*.

To "lay down" a man's "right" to anything, is to "divest" himself of the "liberty," of hindering another of the benefit of his own right to the same. For he that renounceth, or passeth away his right, giveth not to any other man a right which he had not before; because there is nothing to which every man had not right by Nature: but only standeth out of his way, that he may enjoy his own original right, without hindrance from him; not without hindrance from another. So that the effect which redoundeth to one man, by another man's defect of right, is but so much diminution of impediments to the use of his own right original.

Right is laid aside, either by simply renouncing it; or by transferring it to another. By "simply renouncing"; when he cares not to whom the benefit thereof redoundeth. By "transferring"; when he intendeth the benefit thereof to some certain person or persons. And when a man hath in either manner abandoned, or granted away his right; then is he said to be "obliged," or "bound," not to hinder those, to whom such right is granted, or abandoned, from the benefit of it: and that he "ought," and it is his "duty," not to make void that voluntary act of his own: and that such hindrance is "injustice," and "injury," as being *sine jure;* the right being before renounced, or transferred. So that "injury," or "injustice," in the controversies of the world, is somewhat like to that, which in the disputations of scholars is called "absurdity." For as it is there called an absurdity, to contradict what one maintained in the beginning: so in the world it is called injustice and injury voluntarily to undo that from the beginning he had voluntarily done. The way by which a man either simply renounceth, or transferreth his right, is a declaration, or signification, by some voluntary and sufficient sign, or signs, that he doth so renounce, or transfer; or hath so renounced, or transferred the same, to him that accepteth it. And these signs are either words only, or actions only; or, as it happeneth most often, both words and actions. And the same are the "bonds," by which men are bound, and obliged: bonds, that have their strength, not from their own nature, for nothing is more easily broken than a man's word, but from fear of some evil consequence upon the rupture.

Whensoever a man transferreth his right, or renounceth it, it is either in consideration of some right reciprocally transferred to himself; or for some other good he hopeth for thereby. For it is a voluntary act: and of the voluntary acts of every man, the object is some "good to himself." And therefore there be some rights, which no man can be understood by any words, or other signs, to have abandoned or transferred. As first a man cannot lay down the right of resisting them that assault him by force, to take away his life; because he cannot be understood to aim thereby at any good to himself. The same may be said of wounds, and chains, and imprisonment; both because there is no benefit consequent to such

patience; as there is to the patience of suffering another to be wounded, or imprisoned; as also because a man cannot tell, when he seeth men proceed against him by violence, whether they intend his death or not. And lastly the motive and end for which this renouncing, and transferring of right is introduced, is nothing else but the security of a man's person, in his life, and in the means of so preserving life, as not to be weary of it. And therefore if a man by words, or other signs, seem to despoil himself of the end, for which those signs were intended; he is not to be understood as if he meant it, or that it was his will; but that he was ignorant of how such words and actions were to be interpreted.

The mutual transferring of right, is that which men call "contract."

There is difference between transferring of right to the thing; and transferring, or tradition, that is delivery of the thing itself. For the thing may be delivered together with the translation of the right; as in buying and selling with ready money; or exchange of goods, or lands; and it may be delivered some time after.

Again, one of the contractors may deliver the thing contracted for on his part, and leave the other to perform his part at some determinate time after, and in the meantime be trusted; and then the contract on his part is called "pact," or "covenant": or both parts may contract now, to perform hereafter; in which cases, he that is to perform in time to come, being trusted, his performance is called "keeping of promise," or faith; and the failing of performance, if it be voluntary, "violation of faith."

When the transferring of right, is not mutual: but one of the parties transferreth, in hope to gain thereby friendship, or service from another, or from his friends; or in hope to gain the reputation of charity, or magnanimity, or to deliver his mind from the pain of compassion; or in hope of reward in heaven; this is not contract, but "gift," "free gift," "grace," which words signify one and the same thing.

Signs of contract, are either "express," or "by inference." Express, are words spoken with understanding of what they signify; and such words are either of the time "present," or "past"; as, "I give," "I grant," "I have given," "I have granted," "I will that this be yours"; or of the future, as, "I will give," "I will grant"; which words of the future are called "promise."

Signs by inference are sometimes the consequence of words; sometimes the consequence of silence; sometimes the consequence of actions; sometimes the consequence of forbearing an action: and generally a sign by inference, of any contract, is whatsoever sufficiently argues the will of the contractor.

Words alone, if they be of the time to come, and contain a bare promise, are an insufficient sign of a free gift, and therefore not obligatory. For if they be of the time to come, as "to-morrow I will give," they are a sign I have not given yet, and consequently that my right is not transferred, but remaineth till I transfer it by some other act. But if the words be of the time present, or past, as, "I have given," or, "do give to be delivered to-morrow," then is my to-morrow's right given away to-day; and that by the virtue of the words, though there were no other argument of my will. And there is a great difference in the signification of these words, *volo hoc tuum esse cras*, and *cras dabo;* that is, between "I will that this be thine to-morrow," and, "I will give it thee to-morrow": for the word "I will," in the former manner of speech, signifies an act of the will present; but in the latter, it signifies a promise of an act of the will to come: and therefore the former words, being of the present, transfer a future right; the latter, that be of the future, transfer nothing. But if there be other signs of the will to transfer a right, besides words, then, though the gift be free, yet may the right be understood to pass by words of the future: as if a man propound a prize to him that comes first to the end of a race, the gift is free; and though the words be of the future, yet the right passeth: for if he would not have his words so be understood, he should not have let them run.

In contracts, the right passeth, not only where the words are of the time present, or past, but also where they are of the future: because all contract is mutual translation, or change of right; and therefore he that promiseth only, because he hath already received the benefit for which he promiseth, is to be understood as if he intended the right should pass: for unless he had been content to have his words so understood, the other would not have performed his part first. And for that cause, in buying and selling, and other acts of contracts, a promise is equivalent to a covenant; and therefore obligatory.

He that performeth first in the case of a contract, is said to "merit" that which he is to receive by the performance of the other; and he hath it as "due." Also when a prize is propounded to many, which is to be given to him only that winneth; or money is thrown amongst many, to be enjoyed by them that catch it; though this be a free gift; yet so to win, or so to catch, is to "merit," and to have it as "due." For the right is transferred in the propounding of the prize, and in throwing down the money; though it be not determined to whom, but by the event of the contention. But there is between these two sorts of merit, this difference, that in contract, I merit by virtue of my own power, and the contractor's need; but in this case of free gift, I am enabled to merit only by the benignity of the giver: in contract, I merit at the contractor's hand that he should depart with his right; in this case of gift, I merit not that the giver should part with his right; but that when he has parted with it, it should be mine, rather than another's. And this I think to be the meaning of that distinction of the schools, between *meritum congrui*, and *meritum condigni*. For God Almighty, having promised Paradise to those men, hoodwinked with carnal desires, that can walk through this world according to the precepts and limits prescribed by Him; they say, he that shall so walk, shall merit Paradise *ex congruo*. But because no man can demand a right to it, by his own righteousness, or any other power in himself, but by the free grace of God only; they say, no man can merit Paradise *ex condigno*. This I say, I think is the meaning of that distinction; but because disputers do not agree upon the signification of their own terms of art, longer than it serves their turn; I will not affirm anything of their meaning: only this I say; when a gift is given indefinitely, as a prize to be contended for, he that winneth meriteth, and may claim the prize as due.

If a covenant be made, wherein neither of the parties perform presently, but trust one another; in the condition of mere nature, which is a condition of war of every man against every man, upon any reasonable suspicion, it is void; but if there be a common power set over them both, with right and force sufficient to compel performance, it is not void. For he that performeth first, has no assurance the other will perform after; because the bonds of words are too weak to bridle men's ambition, avarice, anger, and other passions, without the fear of some coercive power; which in the condition of mere nature, where all men are equal, and judges of the justness of their own fears, cannot possibly be supposed. And therefore he which performeth first, does but betray himself to his enemy; contrary to the right, he can never abandon, of defending his life and means of living.

But in a civil estate, where there is a power set up to constrain those that would otherwise violate their faith, that fear is no more reasonable, and for that cause, he which by the covenant is to perform first, is obliged so to do.

The cause of fear, which maketh such a covenant invalid, must be always something arising after the covenant made; as some new fact, or other sign of the will not to perform: else it cannot make the covenant void. For that which could not hinder a man from promising, ought not to be admitted as a hindrance of performing.

He that transferreth any right, transferreth the means of enjoying it, as far as lieth in his power. As he that selleth land, is understood to transfer the herbage, and whatsoever grows upon it: nor can he that sells a mill turn away the stream that drives it. And they that give to a man the right of government in sovereignty, are understood to give him the right of levying money to maintain soldiers; and of appointing magistrates for the administration of justice.

To make covenants with brute beasts, is impossible; because not understanding our speech, they understand not, nor accept of any translation of right; nor can translate any right to another: and without mutual acceptation, there is no covenant.

To make covenant with God, is impossible, but by mediation of such as God speaketh to, either by revelation supernatural, or by His lieutenants that govern under Him, and in His name: for otherwise we know not whether our covenants be accepted, or not. And therefore they that vow anything contrary to any law of Nature, vow in vain; as being a thing unjust to pay such vow. And if it be a thing commanded by the law of Nature, it is not the vow, but the law that binds them.

The matter, or subject of a covenant, is always something that falleth under deliberation; for to covenant is an act of the will; that is to say, an act, and the last act, of deliberation; and is therefore always understood to be something to come; and which is judged possible for him that covenanteth to perform.

And therefore, to promise that which is known to be impossible, is no covenant. But if that prove impossible afterwards, which before was thought possible, the covenant is valid, and bindeth, though not to the thing itself, yet to the value; or, if that also be impossible, to the unfeigned endeavour of performing as much as is possible: for to more no man can be obliged.

Men are freed of their covenants two ways; by performing, or by being forgiven. For performance is the natural end of obligation; and forgiveness the restitution of liberty; as being a retransferring of that right, in which the obligation consisted.

Covenants entered into by fear, in the condition of mere nature, are obligatory. For example, if I covenant to pay a ransom, or service for my life, to an enemy, I am bound by it, for it is a contract, wherein one receiveth the benefit of life; the other is to receive money, or service for it; and consequently, where no other law, as in the condition of mere nature, forbiddeth the performance, the covenant is valid. Therefore prisoners of war, if trusted with the payment of their ransom, are obliged to pay it: and if a weaker prince make a disadvantageous peace with a stronger, for fear, he is bound to keep it; unless, as hath been said before, there ariseth some new and just cause of fear, to renew the war. And even in commonwealths, if I be forced to redeem myself from a thief by promising him money, I am bound to pay it, till the civil law discharge me. For whatsoever I may lawfully do without obligation, the same I may lawfully covenant to do through fear, and what I lawfully covenant, I cannot lawfully break.

A former covenant makes void a later. For a man that hath passed away his right to one man to-day, hath it not to pass to-morrow to another, and therefore the later promise passeth no right, but is null.

A covenant not to defend myself from force, by force, is always void. For, as I have shown before, no man can transfer, or lay down his right to save himself from death, wounds, and imprisonment, the avoiding whereof is the only end of laying down any right; and therefore the promise of not resisting force, in no covenant transferreth any right, nor is obliging. For though a man may covenant thus, "unless I do so, or so, kill me," he cannot covenant thus, "unless I do so, or so, I will not resist you when you come to kill me." For man by nature chooseth the lesser evil, which is danger of death in resisting, rather than the greater, which is certain and present death in not resisting. And this is granted to be true by all men, in that they lead criminals to execution and prison, with armed men, notwithstanding that such criminals have consented to the law by which they are condemned.

A covenant to accuse oneself, without assurance of pardon, is likewise invalid. For in the condition of nature, where every man is judge, there is no place for accusation: and in the civil state, the accusation is followed with punishment; which being force, a man is not obliged not to resist. The same is also true of the accusation of those by whose condemnation a man falls into misery; as of a father, wife, or benefactor. For the testimony of such an accuser, if it be not willingly given, is presumed to be corrupted by nature, and therefore not to be received: and where a man's testimony is not to be credited, he is not bound to give it. Also accusations upon torture, are not to be reputed as testimonies. For torture is to be used but as means of conjecture and light, in the further examination and search of truth: and what is in that case confessed, tendeth to the ease of him that is tortured, not to the informing of the torturers, and therefore ought not to have the credit of a sufficient testimony; for whether he deliver himself by true or false accusation, he does it by the right of preserving his own life.

The force of words being, as I have formerly noted, too weak to hold men to the performance of their covenants; there are in man's nature but two imaginable helps to strengthen it. And those are either a fear of the consequence of breaking their word, or a glory or pride in appearing not to need to break it. This latter is a generosity too rarely found to be presumed on, especially in the pursuers of wealth, command, or sensual pleasure, which are the greatest part of mankind. The passion to be reckoned upon is fear; whereof there be two very general objects: one, the power of spirits invisible; the other, the power of those men they shall therein offend. Of these two, though the former be the greater power, yet the fear of the latter is commonly the greater fear. The fear of the former is in every man his own religion, which hath place in the nature of man before civil society. The latter hath not so, at least not place enough to keep men to their promises; because in the condition of mere nature, the inequality of power is not discerned, but by the event of battle. So that before the time of civil society, or in the interruption thereof by war, there is nothing can strengthen a covenant of peace agreed on, against the temptations of avarice, ambition, lust, or other strong desire, but the fear of that invisible power, which they every one worship as God, and fear as a revenger of their perfidy. All therefore that can be done between two men not subject to civil power, is to put one another to swear by the God he feareth, which "swearing," or "oath," is "a form of speech, added to a promise; by which he that promiseth, signifieth, that unless he perform, he renounceth the mercy of his God, or calleth to Him

for vengeance on himself." Such was the heathen form, "Let Jupiter kill me else, as I kill this beast." So is our form, "I shall do thus, and thus, so help me God." And this, with the rites and ceremonies, which every one useth in his own religion, that the fear of breaking faith might be the greater.

By this it appears, that an oath taken according to any other form, or rite, than his that sweareth, is in vain; and no oath: and that there is no swearing by anything which the swearer thinks not God. For though men have sometimes used to swear by their kings, for fear, or flattery; yet they would have it thereby understood, they attributed to them divine honour. And that swearing unnecessarily by God, is but profaning of His name: and swearing by other things, as men do in common discourse, is not swearing, but an impious custom, gotten by too much vehemence of talking.

It appears also, that the oath adds nothing to the obligation. For a covenant, if lawful, binds in the sight of God, without the oath, as much as with it: if unlawful, bindeth not at all; though it be confirmed with an oath.

Chapter XV
Of Other Laws of Nature

From that law of Nature, by which we are obliged to transfer to another, such rights, as being retained, hinder the peace of mankind, there followeth a third; which is this, "that men perform their covenants made"; without which, covenants are in vain, and but empty words; and the right of all men to all things remaining, we are still in the condition of war.

And in this law of Nature consisteth the fountain and original of "justice." For where no covenant hath preceded, there hath no right been transferred, and every man has right to everything; and consequently, no action can be unjust. But when a covenant is made, then to break it is "unjust": and the definition of "injustice," is no other than "the not performance of covenant." And whatsoever is not unjust, is "just."

But because covenants of mutual trust, where there is a fear of not performance on either part, as hath been said in the former chapter, are invalid; though the original of justice be the making of covenants; yet injustice actually there can be none, till the cause of such fear be taken away; which while men are in the natural condition of war, cannot be done. Therefore before the names of just and unjust can have place, there must be some coercive power, to compel men equally to the performance of their covenants, by the terror of some punishment, greater than the benefit they expect by the breach of their covenant; and to make good that propriety, which by mutual contract men acquire, in recompense of the universal right they abandon: and such power there is none before the erection of a commonwealth. And this is also to be gathered out of the ordinary definition of justice in the schools: for they say, that "justice is the constant will of giving to every man his own." And therefore where there is no "own," that is no propriety, there is no injustice; and where there is no coercive power erected, that is, where there is no commonwealth, there is no propriety; all men having right to all things: therefore where there is no commonwealth, there nothing is unjust. So that the nature of justice, consisteth in keeping of valid covenants: but the validity of covenants begins not but with the constitution of a civil power, sufficient to compel men to keep them; and then it is also that propriety begins.

The fool hath said in his heart, there is no such thing as justice; and sometimes also with his tongue; seriously alleging, that every man's conservation, and contentment, being committed to his own care, there could be no reason why every man might not do what he thought conduced thereunto: and therefore also to make, or not make; keep, or not keep covenants, was not against reason, when it conduced to one's benefit. He does not therein deny, that there be covenants; and that they are sometimes broken, sometimes kept; and that such breach of them may be called injustice, and the observance of them justice; but he questioneth, whether injustice, taking away the fear of God, for the same fool hath said in his heart there is no God, may not sometimes stand with that reason, which dictateth to every man his own good; and particularly then, when it conduceth to such a benefit, as shall put a man in a condition to neglect not only the dispraise, and revilings, but also the power of other men. The kingdom of God is gotten by violence; but what if it could be gotten by unjust violence? were it against reason so to get it, when it is impossible to receive hurt by it? and if it be not against reason, it is not against justice; or else justice is not to be approved for good. From such reasoning as this, successful wickedness hath obtained the name of virtue; and some that in all other things have disallowed the violation of faith; yet have allowed it, when it is for the getting of a kingdom. And the heathen that believed that Saturn was deposed by his son Jupiter, believed nevertheless the same Jupiter to be the avenger of injustice; somewhat like to a piece of law in Coke's "Commentaries on Littleton"; where he says, if the right heir of the crown be attainted of treason; yet the crown shall descend to him, and *eo instante* the attainder be void: from which instances a man will be very prone to infer, that when the heir apparent of a kingdom shall kill him that is in possession, though his father; you may call it injustice, or by what other name you will; yet it can never be against reason, seeing all the voluntary actions of men tend to the benefit of themselves; and those actions are most reasonable, that conduce most to their ends. This specious reasoning is nevertheless false.

For the question is not of promises mutual, where there is no security of performance on either side; as when there is no civil power erected over the parties promising; for such promises are no covenants: but either where one of the parties has performed already; or where there is a power to make him perform; there is the question whether it be against reason, that is, against the benefit of the other to perform, or not. And I say it is not against reason. For the manifestation whereof, we are to consider; first, that when a man doth a thing, which notwithstanding anything can be foreseen and reckoned on, tendeth to his own destruction, howsoever some accident which he could not expect, arriving may turn it to his benefit; yet such events do not make it reasonably or wisely done. Secondly, that in a condition of war, wherein every man to every man, for want of a common power to keep them all in awe, is an enemy, there is no man who can hope by his own strength, or wit, to defend himself from destruction, without the help of confederates; where every one expects the same defence by the confederation, that any one else does: and therefore he which declares he thinks it reason to deceive those that help him, can in reason expect no other means of safety than what can be had from his own single power. He therefore that breaketh his covenant, and consequently declareth that he thinks he may with reason do so, cannot be received into any society, that unite themselves for peace and defence, but by the error of them that receive him; nor when he is received, be retained in it, without seeing the danger of their error; which errors a man cannot reasonably reckon upon as the means of his security; and therefore if he be left, or cast out of society, he perisheth; and if he live in society, it is by the errors of other men, which he could not foresee, nor reckon upon; and consequently against the reason of his preservation; and so, as all men that contribute not to his destruction, forbear him only out of ignorance of what is good for themselves.

As for the instance of gaining the secure and perpetual felicity of heaven, by any way, it is frivolous: there being but one way imaginable; and that is not breaking, but keeping of covenant.

And for the other instance of attaining sovereignty by rebellion; it is manifest, that, though the event follow, yet because it cannot reasonably be expected, but rather the contrary; and because by gaining it so, others are taught to gain the same in like manner, the attempt thereof is against reason. Justice therefore, that is to say, keeping of covenant, is a rule of reason, by which we are forbidden to do anything destructive to our life; and consequently a law of Nature.

There be some that proceed further; and will not have the law of Nature to be those rules which conduce to the preservation of man's life on earth; but to the attaining of an eternal felicity after death; to which they think the breach of government may conduce; and consequently be just and reasonable; such are they that think it a work of merit to kill, or depose, or rebel against the sovereign power constituted over them by their own consent. But because there is no natural knowledge of man's estate after death; much less of the reward that is then to be given to breach of faith; but only a belief grounded upon other men's saying, that they know it supernaturally, or that they know those that knew them, that knew others, that knew it supernaturally; breach of faith cannot be called a precept of reason, or nature.

Others, that allow for a law of Nature the keeping of faith, do nevertheless make exception of certain persons; as heretics, and such as use not to perform their covenant to others: and this also is against reason. For if any fault of a man be sufficient to discharge our covenant made; the same ought in reason to have been sufficient to have hindered the making of it.

The names of just, and unjust, when they are attributed to men, signify one thing; and when they are attributed to actions, another. When they are attributed to men, they signify conformity, or inconformity of manners, to reason. But when they are attributed to actions they signify the conformity or inconformity to reason, not of manners or manner of life, but of particular actions. A just man, therefore, is he that taketh all the care he can that his actions may be all just, and an unjust man is he that neglecteth it. And such men are more often in our language styled by the names of righteous and unrighteous than just and unjust, though the meaning be the same. Therefore, a righteous man does not lose that title by one or a few unjust actions that proceed from sudden passion or mistake of things or persons; nor does an unrighteous man lose his character for such actions as he does, or forbears to do, for fear, because his will is not framed by the justice, but by the apparent benefit of what he is to do. That which gives to human actions the relish of justice is a certain nobleness or gallantness of courage, rarely found, by which a man scorns to be beholden, for the contentment of his life, to fraud or breach of promise. This justice of the manners is that which is meant, where justice is called a virtue, and injustice a vice.

But the justice of actions denominates men, not just, but "guiltless"; and the injustice of the same, which is also called injury, gives them but the name of "guilty."

Again, the injustice of manners is the disposition or aptitude to do injury; and is injustice before it proceeds to act, and without supposing any individual person injured. But the injustice of an action, that is to say injury, supposeth an individual person injured, namely, him to whom the covenant was made; and therefore many times the injury is received by one man when the damage redoundeth to another. As when the master commandeth his servant to give money to a stranger: if it be not done, the injury is done to the master, whom he had before covenanted to obey; but the damage redoundeth to the stranger, to whom he had no obligation, and therefore could not injure him. And so also in commonwealths. Private men may remit to one another their debts, but not robberies or other violences, whereby they are endamaged, because the detaining of debt is an injury to themselves, but robbery and violence are injuries to the person of the commonwealth.

Whatsoever is done to a man, conformable to his own will signified to the doer, is no injury to him. For if he that doeth it, hath not passed away his original right to do what he please, by some antecedent covenant, there is no breach of covenant; and therefore no injury done him. And if he have, then his will to have it done being signified, is a release of that covenant; and so again there is no injury done him.

Justice of actions, is by writers divided into "commutative," and "distributive": and the former they say consisteth in proportion arithmetical; the latter in proportion geometrical. Commutative, therefore, they place in the equality of value of the things contracted for; and distributive, in the distribution of equal benefit, to men of equal merit. As if it were injustice to sell dearer than we buy; or to give more to a man than he merits. The value of all things contracted for, is measured by the appetite of the contractors: and therefore the just value is that which they be contented to give. And merit, besides that which is by covenant, where the performance on one part, meriteth the performance of the other part, and falls under justice commutative, not distributive, is not due by justice; but is rewarded of grace only. And therefore this distinction, in the sense wherein it useth to be expounded, is not right. To speak properly, commutative justice is the justice of a contractor; that is, a performance of covenant, in buying and selling; hiring, and letting to hire; lending, and borrowing; exchanging, bartering, and other acts of contract.

And distributive justice, the justice of an arbitrator; that is to say, the act of defining what is just. Wherein, being trusted by them that make him arbitrator, if he perform his trust, he is said to distribute to every man his own: and this is indeed just distribution, and may be called, though improperly, distributive justice; but more properly equity; which also is a law of Nature, as shall be shown in due place.

As justice dependeth on antecedent covenant; so does "gratitude" depend on antecedent grace; that is to say, antecedent free gift: and is the fourth law of Nature; which may be conceived in this form, "that a man which receiveth benefit from another of mere grace, endeavour that he which giveth it, have no reasonable cause to repent him of his good will." For no man giveth, but with intention of good to himself; because gift is voluntary; and of all voluntary acts, the object is to every man his own good; of which if men see they shall be frustrated, there will be no beginning of benevolence, or trust, nor consequently of mutual help; nor of reconciliation of one man to another; and therefore they are to remain still in the condition of "war," which is contrary to the first and fundamental law of Nature, which commandeth men to "seek peace." The breach of this law, is called "ingratitude," and hath the same relation to grace that injustice hath to obligation by covenant.

A fifth law of Nature is "complaisance": that is to say, "that every man strive to accommodate himself to the rest." For the understanding whereof, we may consider, that there is in men's aptness to society, a diversity of nature, rising from their diversity of affections; not unlike to that we see in stones brought together for building of an edifice. For as that stone which by the asperity, and irregularity of figure, takes more room from others than itself fills; and for the hardness, cannot be easily made plain, and thereby hindereth the building, is by the builders cast away as unprofitable and troublesome: so also, a man that by asperity of nature, will strive to retain those things which to himself are superfluous, and to others necessary; and for the stubbornness of his passions, cannot be corrected, is to be left, or cast out of society, as cumbersome thereunto. For seeing every man, not only by right, but also by necessity of nature, is supposed to endeavour all he can, to obtain that which is necessary for his conservation; he that shall oppose himself against it, for things superfluous, is guilty of the war that thereupon is to follow; and therefore doth that which is contrary to the fundamental law of Nature, which commandeth "to seek peace." The observers of this law, may be called "sociable," the Latins call them *commodi;* the contrary, "stubborn," "insociable," "froward," "intractable."

A sixth law of Nature is this, "that upon caution of the future time, a man ought to pardon the offences past of them that repenting, desire it." For "pardon" is nothing but granting of peace; which though granted to them that persevere in their hostility, be not peace, but fear; yet not granted to them that give caution of the future time, is sign of an aversion to peace; and therefore contrary to the law of Nature.

A seventh is, "that in revenges," that is, retribution of evil for evil, "men look not at the greatness of the evil past, but the greatness of the good to follow." Whereby we are forbidden to inflict punishment with any other design, than for correction of the offender, or direction of others. For this law is consequent to the next before it, that commandeth pardon, upon security of the future time. Besides, revenge, without respect to the example and profit to come, is a triumph or glorying in the hurt of another, tending to no end; for the end is always somewhat to come; and glorying to no end, is vain-glory, and contrary to reason, and to hurt without reason, tendeth to the introduction of war; which is against the law of Nature; and is commonly styled by the name of "cruelty."

And because all signs of hatred, or contempt, provoke to fight; insomuch as most men choose rather to hazard their life than not to be revenged; we may in the eighth place, for a law of Nature, set down this precept, "that no man by deed, word, countenance, or gesture, declare hatred or contempt of another." The breach of which law is commonly called "contumely."

The question who is the better man, has no place in the condition of mere nature; where, as has been shown before, all men are equal. The inequality that now is, has been introduced by the laws civil. I know that Aristotle in the first book of his "Politics," for a foundation of his doctrine, maketh men by nature, some more worthy to command, meaning the wiser sort, such as he thought himself to be for his philosophy; others to serve, meaning those that had strong bodies, but were not philosophers as he; as if master and servant were not introduced by consent of men, but by difference of wit; which is not only against reason, but also against experience. For there are very few so foolish, that had not rather govern themselves than be governed by others: nor when the wise in their own conceit, contend by force with them who distrust their own wisdom, do they always, or often, or almost at any time, get the victory. If Nature therefore have made men equal, that equality is to be acknowledged: or if Nature have made men unequal; yet because men that think themselves equal, will not enter into conditions of peace, but upon equal terms, such equality must be admitted. And therefore for the ninth law of Nature, I put this, "that every man acknowledge another for his equal by nature." The breach of this precept is "pride."

On this law dependeth another, "that at the entrance into conditions of peace, no man require to reserve to himself any right which he is not content should be reserved to every one of the rest." As it is necessary for all men that seek peace to lay down certain rights of nature: that is to say, not to have liberty to do all they list: so is it necessary for man's life to retain some, as right to govern their own bodies; enjoy air, water, motion, ways to go from place to place; and all things else, without which a man cannot live, or not live well. If in this case, at the making of peace, men require for themselves that which they would not have to be granted to others, they do contrary to the precedent law, that commandeth the

acknowledgment of natural equality, and therefore also against the law of Nature. The observers of this law are those we call "modest," and the breakers "arrogant" men. The Greeks call the violation of this law πλεονεξία; that is, a desire of more than their share.

Also if "a man be trusted to judge between man and man," it is a precept of the law of Nature, "that he deal equally between them." For without that, the controversies of men cannot be determined but by war. He therefore that is partial in judgment, doth what in him lies, to deter men from the use of judges and arbitrators; and consequently, against the fundamental law of Nature, is the cause of war.

The observance of this law, from the equal distribution to each man, of that which in reason belongeth to him, is called "equity," and as I have said before, distributive justice: the violation, "acception of persons," προσωποληψία.

And from this followeth another law, "that such things as cannot be divided, be enjoyed in common, if it can be; and if the quantity of the thing permit, without stint; otherwise proportionably to the number of them that have right." For otherwise the distribution is unequal, and contrary to equity.

But some things there be that can neither be divided nor enjoyed in common. Then, the law of Nature, which prescribeth equity, requireth "that the entire right, or else, making the use alternate, the first possession, be determined by lot." For equal distribution is of the law of Nature, and other means of equal distribution cannot be imagined.

Of "lots" there be two sorts, "arbitrary" and "natural." Arbitrary is that which is agreed on by the competitors: natural, is either "primogeniture," which the Greeks calls κληρονομία, which signifies, "given by lot," or "first seizure."

And therefore those things which cannot be enjoyed in common, nor divided, ought to be adjudged to the first possessor; and in some cases to the first born, as acquired by lot.

It is also a law of Nature, "that all men that mediate peace, be allowed safe conduct." For the law that commandeth peace, as the end, commandeth intercession, as the "means"; and to intercession the means is safe conduct.

And because, though men be never so willing to observe these laws, there may nevertheless arise questions concerning a man's action; first, whether it were done, or not done; secondly, if done, whether against the law, or not against the law; the former whereof, is called a question "of fact"; the latter a question "of right," therefore unless the parties to the question covenant mutually to stand to the sentence of another, they are as far from peace as ever. This other to whose sentence they submit, is called an "arbitrator." And therefore it is of the law of Nature, "that they that are at controversy, submit their right to the judgment of an arbitrator."

And seeing every man is presumed to do all things in order to his own benefit, no man is a fit arbitrator in his own cause; and if he were never so fit; yet equity allowing to each party equal benefit, if one be admitted to be judge, the other is to be admitted also; and so the controversy, that is, the cause of war, remains against the law of Nature.

For the same reason no man in any cause ought to be received for arbitrator, to whom greater profit, or honour, or pleasure apparently ariseth out of the victory of one party than of the other: for he hath taken, though an unavoidable bribe, yet a bribe; and no man can be obliged to trust him. And thus also the controversy, and the condition of war remaineth, contrary to the law of Nature.

And in a controversy of "fact," the judge being to give no more credit to one than to the other, if there be no other arguments, must give credit to a third; or to a third and fourth; or more: for else the question is undecided, and left to force, contrary to the law of Nature.

These are the laws of Nature, dictating peace, for a means of the conservation of men in multitudes; and which only concern the doctrine of civil society. There be other things tending to the destruction of particular men; as drunkenness, and all other parts of intemperance; which may therefore also be reckoned amongst those things which the law of Nature hath forbidden; but are not necessary to be mentioned, nor are pertinent enough to this place.

And though this may seem too subtle a deduction of the laws of Nature, to be taken notice of by all men; whereof the most part are too busy in getting food, and the rest too negligent to understand; yet to leave all men inexcusable, they have been contracted into one easy sum, intelligible even to the meanest capacity; and that is, "Do not that to another, which thou wouldst not have done to thyself"; which showeth him that he has no more to do in learning the laws of Nature, but when weighing the actions of other men with his own, they seem too heavy, he put

them into the other part of the balance, and his own into their place, that his own passions and self-love may add nothing to the weight; and then there is none of these laws of Nature that will not appear unto him very reasonable.

The laws of Nature oblige *in foro interno;* that is to say, they bind to a desire they should take place: but *in foro externo;* that is, to the putting them in act, not always. For he that should be modest, and tractable, and perform all he promises, in such time and place where no man else should do so, should but make himself a prey to others, and procure his own certain ruin, contrary to the ground of all laws of Nature, which tend to Nature's preservation. And again, he that having sufficient security, that others shall observe the same laws towards him, observes them not himself, seeketh not peace, but war; and consequently the destruction of his nature by violence.

And whatsoever laws bind *in foro interno,* may be broken, not only by a fact contrary to the law, but also by a fact according to it, in case a man think it contrary. For though his action in this case be according to the law, yet his purpose was against the law; which, where the obligation is *in foro interno,* is a breach.

The laws of Nature are immutable and eternal; for injustice, ingratitude, arrogance, pride, iniquity, acception of persons, and the rest, can never be made lawful. For it can never be that war shall preserve life, and peace destroy it.

The same laws, because they oblige only to a desire and endeavour, I mean an unfeigned and constant endeavour, are easy to be observed. For in that they require nothing but endeavour, he that endeavoureth their performance, fulfilleth them; and he that fulfilleth the law, is just.

And the science of them is the true and only moral philosophy. For moral philosophy is nothing else but the science of what is "good" and "evil," in the conversation and society of mankind. "Good" and "evil" are names that signify our appetites, and aversions; which in different tempers, customs, and doctrines of men, are different: and divers men, differ not only in their judgment, on the senses of what is pleasant and unpleasant to the taste, smell, hearing, touch, and sight; but also of what is conformable or disagreeable to reason, in the actions of common life. Nay, the same man, in divers times, differs from himself; and one time praiseth, that is, calleth good, what another time he dispraiseth, and calleth evil: from whence arise disputes, controversies, and at last war. And therefore so long as a man is in the condition of mere nature, which is a condition of war, as private appetite is the measure of good and evil: and consequently all men agree on this, that peace is good, and therefore also the way or means of peace, which, as I have showed before, are "justice," "gratitude," "modesty," "equity," "mercy," and the rest of the laws of Nature, are good; that is to say, "moral virtues"; and their contrary "vices," evil. Now the science of virtue and vice is moral philosophy; and therefore the true doctrine of the laws of Nature, is the true moral philosophy. But the writers of moral philosophy, though they acknowledge the same virtues and vices; yet not seeing wherein consisted their goodness, nor that they come to be praised, as the means of peaceable, sociable, and comfortable living, place them in a mediocrity of passions: as if not the cause, but the degree of daring, made fortitude; or not the cause, but the quantity of a gift, made liberality.

These dictates of reason, men used to call by the name of laws, but improperly: for they are but conclusions, or theorems concerning what conduceth to the conservation and defence of themselves; whereas law, properly, is the word of him that by right hath command over others. But yet if we consider the same theorems, as delivered in the word of God, that by right commandeth all things; then are they properly called laws.

Chapter XVI
Of Persons, Authors, and Things Personated

A person is he, "whose words or actions are considered, either as his own, or as representing the words or actions of another man, or of any other thing, to whom they are attributed, whether truly or by fiction."

When they are considered as his own, then is he called a "natural person": and when they are considered as representing the words and actions of another, then is he a "feigned" or "artificial person."

The word person is Latin: instead whereof the Greeks have πρόσωπον, which signifies the "face," as persona in Latin signifies the "disguise," or "outward appearance" of a man, counterfeited on the stage; and sometimes more particularly that part of it, which disguiseth the face, as a mask or vizard: and from the stage, hath been translated to any representer of speech and action, as well in tribunals as theatres. So

that a "person," is the same that an "actor" is, both on the stage and in common conversation; and to "personate," is to "act," or "represent" himself or another; and he that acteth another, is said to bear his person, or act in his name; in which sense Cicero useth it where he says, *Unus sustineo tres personas; mei, adversarii, et judicis:* I bear three persons; my own, my adversary's, and the judge's; and is called in divers occasions, diversely; as a "representer," or "representative," a "lieutenant," a "vicar," an "attorney," a "deputy," a "procurator," an "actor," and the like.

Of persons artificial, some have their words and actions "owned" by those whom they represent. And then the person is the "actor"; and he that owneth his words and actions, is the "author": in which case the actor acteth by authority. For that which in speaking of goods and possessions is called an "owner," and in Latin *dominus*, in Greek κύριος, speaking of actions, is called author. And as the right of possession, is called dominion; so the right of doing any action, is called "authority." So that by authority, is always understood a right of doing any act; and "done by authority," done by commission, or license from him whose right it is.

From hence it followeth, that when the actor maketh a covenant by authority, he bindeth thereby the author, no less than if he had made it himself; and no less subjecteth him to all the consequences of the same. And therefore all that hath been said formerly (chap. xiv) of the nature of covenants between man and man in their natural capacity, is true also when they are made by their actors, representers, or procurators, that have authority from them, so far forth as is in their commission, but no further.

And therefore he that maketh a covenant with the actor or representer, not knowing the authority he hath, doth it at his own peril. For no man is obliged by a covenant whereof he is not author; nor consequently by a covenant made against or beside the authority he gave.

When the actor doth anything against the law of Nature by command of the author, if he be obliged by former covenant to obey him, not he but the author breaketh the law of Nature; for though the action be against the law of Nature, yet it is not his: but contrarily, to refuse to do it, is against the law of Nature, that forbiddeth breach of covenant.

And he that maketh a covenant with the author by mediation of the actor, not knowing what authority he hath, but only takes his word, in case such authority be not made manifest unto him upon demand, is no longer obliged, for the covenant made with the author is not valid without his counter-assurance. But if he that so covenanteth knew beforehand he was to expect no other assurance than the actor's word, then is the covenant valid, because the actor in this case maketh himself the author. And therefore, as when the authority is evident, the covenant obligeth the author, not the actor; so when the authority is feigned, it obligeth the actor only, there being no author but himself.

There are few things that are incapable of being represented by fiction. Inanimate things, as a church, an hospital, a bridge, may be personated by a rector, master, or overseer. But things inanimate cannot be authors, nor therefore give authority to their actors; yet the actors may have authority to procure their maintenance, given them by those that are owners or governors of those things. And therefore such things cannot be personated before there be some state of civil government.

Likewise children, fools, and madmen, that have no use of reason, may be personated by guardians or curators; but can be no authors, during that time, of any action done by them longer than, when they shall recover the use of reason, they shall judge the same reasonable. Yet during the folly, he that hath right of governing them may give authority to the guardian. But this again has no place but in a state civil, because before such estate there is no dominion of persons.

An idol, or mere figment of the brain, may be personated, as were the gods of the heathen, which, by such officers as the state appointed, were personated, and held possessions, and other goods and rights, which men from time to time dedicated and consecrated unto them. But idols cannot be authors, for an idol is nothing. The authority proceeded from the state; and therefore, before introduction of civil government, the gods of the heathen could not be personated.

The true God may be personated. As He was, first, Moses; who governed the Israelites, that were not his, but God's people, not in his own name, with *hoc dicit Moses*; but in God's name, with *hoc dicit Dominus*. Secondly, by the Son of man, His own Son, our blessed Saviour Jesus Christ, that came to reduce the Jews, and induce all nations into the kingdom of His Father, not as of Himself, but as sent from His Father. And thirdly, by the Holy Ghost or Comforter, speaking and working in the Apostles; which Holy Ghost was a Comforter that came not of Himself; but was sent, and proceeded from them both.

A multitude of men are made "one" person, when they are by one man or one person represented; so that it be done with the consent of every one of that multitude in particular. For it is the "unity" of the representer, not the "unity" of the represented, that maketh the person "one." And it is the representer that beareth the person, and but one person: and "unity" cannot otherwise be understood in multitude.

And because the multitude naturally is not "one," but "many," they cannot be understood for one; but many authors, of everything their representative saith, or doth in their name; every man giving their common representer authority from himself in particular, and owning all the actions the representer doth, in case they give him authority without stint: otherwise, when they limit him in what and how far he shall represent them, none of them owneth more than they gave him commission to act.

And if the representative consist of many men, the voice of the greater number must be considered as the voice of them all. For if the lesser number pronounce, for example, in the affirmative, and the greater in the negative, there will be negatives more than enough to destroy the affirmatives; and thereby the excess of negatives, standing uncontradicted, are the only voice the representative hath.

And a representative of even number, especially when the number is not great, whereby the contradictory voices are oftentimes equal, is therefore oftentimes mute and incapable of action. Yet in some cases contradictory voices equal in number may determine a question; as in condemning, or absolving, equality of votes, even in that they condemn not, do absolve; but not on the contrary condemn, in that they absolve not. For when a cause is heard, not to condemn is to absolve: but on the contrary, to say that not absolving, is condemning, is not true. The like it is in deliberation of executing presently, or deferring till another time: for when the voices are equal, the not decreeing execution is a decree of dilation.

Or if the number be odd, as three or more, men or assemblies; whereof every one has by a negative voice authority to take away the effect of all the affirmative voices of the rest, this number is no representative; because by the diversity of opinions, and interests of men, it becomes oftentimes, and in cases of the greatest consequence, a mute person, and unapt, as for many things else, so for the government of a multitude, especially in time of war.

Of authors there be two sorts. The first simply so called; which I have before defined to be him, that owneth the action of another simply. The second is he that owneth an action or covenant of another conditionally; that is to say, he undertaketh to do it if the other doth it not at or before a certain time. And these authors conditional, are generally called "sureties," in Latin, *fidejussores*, and *sponsores*; and particularly for debt, *prædes*; and for appearance before a judge, or magistrate, *vades*.

PART II: *OF COMMONWEALTH*

Chapter XVII
Of the Causes, Generation,
and Definition of a Commonwealth

The final cause, end, or design of men, who naturally love liberty, and dominion over others, in the introduction of that restraint upon themselves, in which we see them live in commonwealths, is the foresight of their own preservation, and of a more contented life thereby; that is to say, of getting themselves out from that miserable condition of war, which is necessarily consequent, as hath been shown in chapter xiii, to the natural passions of men, when there is no visible power to keep them in awe, and tie them by fear of punishment to the performance of their covenants, and observation of those laws of Nature set down in the fourteenth and fifteenth chapters.

For the laws of Nature, as "justice," "equity," "modesty," "mercy," and, in sum, "doing to others, as we would be done to," of themselves, without the terror of some power, to cause them to be observed, are contrary to our natural passions, that carry us to partiality, pride, revenge, and the like. And covenants, without the sword, are but words, and of no strength to secure a man at all. Therefore notwithstanding the laws of Nature, which every one hath then kept, when he has the will to keep them, when he can do it safely, if there be no power erected, or not great enough for our security; every man will, and may lawfully rely on his own strength and art, for caution against all other men. And in all places, where men have lived by small families, to rob and spoil one another, has been a trade, and so far from being reputed against the law of Nature, that the greater spoils they gained, the greater was their honour; and men observed no other laws therein, but the laws of honour; that is, to

abstain from cruelty, leaving to men their lives, and instruments of husbandry. And as small families did then; so now do cities and kingdoms, which are but greater families, for their own security, enlarge their dominions, upon all pretences of danger, and fear of invasion, or assistance that may be given to invaders, and endeavour as much as they can, to subdue, or weaken their neighbours, by open force and secret arts, for want of other caution, justly; and are remembered for it in after ages with honour.

Nor is it the joining together of a small number of men, that gives them this security; because in small numbers, small additions on the one side or the other, make the advantage of strength so great, as is sufficient to carry the victory; and therefore gives encouragement to an invasion. The multitude sufficient to confide in for our security, is not determined by any certain number, but by comparison with the enemy we fear; and is then sufficient, when the odds of the enemy is not of so visible and conspicuous moment, to determine the event of war, as to move him to attempt.

And be there never so great a multitude; yet if their actions be directed according to their particular judgments and particular appetites, they can expect thereby no defence, nor protection, neither against a common enemy, nor against the injuries of one another. For being distracted in opinions concerning the best use and application of their strength, they do not help but hinder one another; and reduce their strength by mutual opposition to nothing: whereby they are easily, not only subdued by a very few that agree together; but also when there is no common enemy, they make war upon each other, for their particular interests. For if we could suppose a great multitude of men to consent in the observation of justice, and other laws of Nature, without a common power to keep them all in awe; we might as well suppose all mankind to do the same; and then there neither would be, nor need to be any civil government or commonwealth at all; because there would be peace without subjection.

Nor is it enough for the security, which men desire should last all the time of their life, that they be governed and directed by one judgment, for a limited time: as in one battle, or one war. For though they obtain a victory by their unanimous endeavour against a foreign enemy; yet afterwards, when either they have no common enemy, or he that by one part is held for an enemy, is by another part held for a friend, they must needs by the difference of their interests dissolve, and fall again into a war amongst themselves.

It is true that certain living creatures, as bees and ants, live sociably one with another, which are therefore by Aristotle numbered amongst political creatures; and yet have no other direction, than their particular judgments and appetites; nor speech, whereby one of them can signify to another, what he thinks expedient for the common benefit: and therefore some man may perhaps desire to know, why mankind cannot do the same. To which I answer,

First, that men are continually in competition for honour and dignity, which these creatures are not; and consequently amongst men there ariseth on that ground, envy and hatred, and finally war; but amongst these not so.

Secondly, that amongst these creatures, the common good differeth not from the private; and being by nature inclined to their private, they procure thereby the common benefit. But man, whose joy consisteth in comparing himself with other men, can relish nothing but what is eminent.

Thirdly, that these creatures, having not, as man, the use of reason, do not see, nor think they see any fault, in the administration of their common business; whereas amongst men, there are very many that think themselves wiser, and abler to govern the public, better than the rest; and these strive to reform and innovate, one this way, another that way; and thereby bring it into distraction and civil war.

Fourthly, that these creatures, though they have some use of voice, in making known to one another their desires and other affections; yet they want that art of words, by which some men can represent to others that which is good in the likeness of evil; and evil in the likeness of good; and augment or diminish the apparent greatness of good and evil; discontenting men, and troubling their peace at their pleasure.

Fifthly, irrational creatures cannot distinguish between "injury" and "damage"; and therefore as long as they be at ease, they are not offended with their fellows: whereas man is then most troublesome, when he is most at ease; for then it is that he loves to show his wisdom, and control the actions of them that govern the commonwealth.

Lastly, the agreement of these creatures is natural; that of men is by covenant only, which is artificial: and therefore it is no wonder if there be somewhat else required, besides covenant, to make their agreement constant and lasting; which is a common power, to keep them in awe, and to direct their actions to the common benefit.

The only way to erect such a common power, as may be able to defend them from the invasion of foreigners, and the injuries of one another, and thereby to secure them in such sort, as that by their own industry, and by the fruits of the earth, they may nourish themselves and live contentedly, is, to confer all their power and strength upon one man, or upon one assembly of men, that may reduce all their wills, by plurality of voices, unto one will: which is as much as to say, to appoint one man, or assembly of men, to bear their person; and every one to own, and acknowledge himself to be author of whatsoever he that so beareth their person, shall act, or cause to be acted, in those things which concern the common peace and safety; and therein to submit their wills, every one to his will, and their judgments, to his judgment. This is more than consent, or concord; it is a real unity of them all, in one and the same person, made by covenant of every man with every man, in such manner, as if every man should say to every man, "I authorize and give up my right of governing myself, to this man, or to this assembly of men, on this condition, that thou give up thy right to him, and authorize all his actions in like manner." This done, the multitude so united in one person is called a "commonwealth," in Latin *civitas*. This is the generation of that great "leviathan," or rather, to speak more reverently, of that "mortal god," to which we owe under the "immortal God," our peace and defence. For by this authority, given him by every particular man in the commonwealth, he hath the use of so much power and strength conferred on him, that by terror thereof, he is enabled to perform the wills of them all, to peace at home, and mutual aid against their enemies abroad. And in him consisteth the essence of the commonwealth; which, to define it, is "one person, of whose acts a great multitude, by mutual covenants one with another, have made themselves every one the author, to the end he may use the strength and means of them all, as he shall think expedient, for their peace and common defence."

And he that carrieth this person is called "sovereign," and said to have "sovereign power"; and every one besides, his "subject."

The attaining to this sovereign power is by two ways. One, by natural force; as when a man maketh his children to submit themselves, and their children, to his government, as being able to destroy them if they refuse; or by war subdueth his enemies to his will, giving them their lives on that condition. The other is, when men agree amongst themselves to submit to some man, or assembly of men, voluntarily, on confidence to be protected by him against all others. This latter may be called a political commonwealth, or commonwealth by "institution"; and the former, a commonwealth by "acquisition." And first, I shall speak of a commonwealth by institution.

Chapter XVIII
Of the Rights of Sovereigns by Institution

A "commonwealth" is said to be "instituted," when a "multitude" of men do agree, and "covenant, every one with every one," that to whatsoever "man," or "assembly of men," shall be given by the major part, the "right" to "present" the person of them all, that is to say, to be their "representative"; every one, as well he that "voted for it," as he that "voted against it," shall "authorize" all the actions and judgments, of that man, or assembly of men, in the same manner, as if they were his own, to the end, to live peaceably amongst themselves, and be protected against other men.

From this institution of a commonwealth are derived all the "rights" and "faculties" of him, or them, on whom sovereign power is conferred by the consent of the people assembled.

First, because they covenant, it is to be understood, they are not obliged by former covenant to anything repugnant hereunto. And consequently they that have already instituted a commonwealth, being thereby bound by covenant, to own the actions and judgments of one, cannot lawfully make a new covenant, amongst themselves, to be obedient to any other, in any thing whatsoever, without his permission. And therefore, they that are subjects to a monarch, cannot without his leave cast off monarchy, and return to the confusion of a disunited multitude; nor transfer their person from him that beareth it, to another man, or other assembly of men: for they are bound, every man to every man, to own, and be reputed author of all, that he already is their sovereign, shall do, and judge fit to be done: so that any one man dissenting, all the rest should break their covenant made to that man, which is injustice: and they have also every man given the sovereignty to him

that beareth their person; and therefore if they depose him, they take from him that which is his own, and so again it is injustice. Besides, if he that attempteth to depose his sovereign, be killed, or punished by him for such attempt, he is author of his own punishment, as being by the institution, author of all his sovereign shall do: and because it is injustice for a man to do anything for which he may be punished by his own authority, he is also upon that title unjust. And whereas some men have pretended for their disobedience to their sovereign, a new covenant, made not with men, but with God; this also is unjust: for there is no covenant with God but by mediation of somebody that representeth God's person; which none doth but God's lieutenant, who hath the sovereignty under God. But this pretence of covenant with God, is so evident a lie, even in the pretenders' own consciences, that it is not only an act of an unjust, but also of a vile and unmanly disposition.

Secondly, because the right of bearing the person of them all, is given to him they make sovereign, by covenant only of one to another, and not of him to any of them; there can happen no breach of covenant on the part of the sovereign: and consequently none of his subjects, by any pretence of forfeiture, can be freed from his subjection. That he which is made sovereign maketh no covenant with his subjects beforehand, is manifest; because either he must make it with the whole multitude, as one party to the covenant; or he must make a several covenant with every man. With the whole, as one party, it is impossible; because as yet they are not one person; and if he make so many several covenants as there be men, those covenants after he hath the sovereignty are void; because what act soever can be pretended by any one of them for breach thereof, is the act both of himself and of all the rest, because done in the person and by the right of every one of them in particular. Besides, if any one or more of them, pretend a breach of the covenant made by the sovereign at his institution; and others, or one other of his subjects, or himself alone, pretend there was no such breach, there is in this case no judge to decide the controversy; it returns therefore to the sword again; and every man recovereth the right of protecting himself by his own strength, contrary to the design they had in the institution. It is therefore in vain to grant sovereignty by way of precedent covenant. The opinion that any monarch receiveth his power by covenant, that is to say, on condition, proceedeth from want of understanding this easy truth, that covenants being but words and breath, have no force to oblige, contain, constrain, or protect any man, but what it has from the public sword; that is, from the united hands of that man, or assembly of men that hath the sovereignty, and whose actions are avouched by them all, and performed by the strength of them all, in him united. But when an assembly of men is made sovereign; then no man imagineth any such covenant to have passed in the institution; for no man is so dull as to say, for example, the people of Rome made a covenant with the Romans, to hold the sovereignty on such or such conditions; which not performed, the Romans might lawfully depose the Roman people. That men see not the reason to be alike in a monarchy, and in a popular government, proceedeth from the ambition of some, that are kinder to the government of an assembly, whereof they may hope to participate, than of monarchy, which they despair to enjoy.

Thirdly, because the major part hath by consenting voices declared a sovereign; he that dissented must now consent with the rest; that is, be contented to avow all the actions he shall do, or else justly be destroyed by the rest. For if he voluntarily entered into the congregation of them that were assembled, he sufficiently declared thereby his will, and therefore tacitly covenanted to stand to what the major part should ordain: and therefore if he refuse to stand thereto, or make protestation against any of their decrees, he does contrary to his covenant, and therefore unjustly. And whether he be of the congregation or not; and whether his consent be asked or not, he must either submit to their decrees, or be left in the condition of war he was in before; wherein he might without injustice be destroyed by any man whatsoever.

Fourthly, because every subject is by this institution author of all the actions and judgments of the sovereign instituted, it follows, that whatsoever he doth it can be no injury to any of his subjects, nor ought he to be by any of them accused of injustice. For he that doth anything by authority from another doth therein no injury to him by whose authority he acteth: but by this institution of a commonwealth every particular man is author of all the sovereign doth; and consequently, he that complaineth of injury from his sovereign complaineth of that whereof he himself is author, and therefore ought not to accuse any man but himself; no, nor himself of injury; because to do injury to one's self is impossible. It is true that they that have sovereign power may commit iniquity, but not injustice or injury in the proper signification.

Fifthly, and consequently to that which was said last, no man that hath sovereign power can justly be put to death, or otherwise in any manner by his subjects punished. For seeing every subject is author of the actions of his sovereign, he punisheth another for the actions committed by himself.

And because the end of this institution is the peace and defence of them all; and whosoever has right to the end has right to the means; it belongeth of right to whatsoever man or assembly that hath the sovereignty to be judge both of the means of peace and defence, and also of the hindrances and disturbances of the same, and to do whatsoever he shall think necessary to be done, both beforehand, for the preserving of peace and security, by prevention of discord at home and hostility from abroad; and, when peace and security are lost, for the recovery of the same. And therefore,

Sixthly, it is annexed to the sovereignty to be judge of what opinions and doctrines are averse and what conducing to peace; and consequently, on what occasions, how far, and what men are to be trusted withal, in speaking to multitudes of people, and who shall examine the doctrines of all books before they be published. For the actions of men proceed from their opinions, and in the well governing of opinions consisteth the well governing of men's actions, in order to their peace and concord. And though in matter of doctrine nothing ought to be regarded but the truth; yet this is not repugnant to regulating the same by peace. For doctrine repugnant to peace can be no more true than peace and concord can be against the law of Nature. It is true that in a commonwealth, where, by the negligence or unskilfulness of governors and teachers, false doctrines are by time generally received; the contrary truths may be generally offensive. Yet the most sudden and rough bursting in of a new truth that can be, does never break the peace, but only sometimes awake the war. For those men that are so remissly governed, that they dare take up arms to defend or introduce an opinion, are still in war; and their condition not peace, but only a cessation of arms for fear of one another; and they live, as it were, in the precincts of battle continually. It belongeth therefore to him that hath the sovereign power to be judge, or constitute all judges of opinions and doctrines, as a thing necessary to peace, thereby to prevent discord and civil war.

Seventhly, is annexed to the sovereignty, the whole power of prescribing the rules, whereby every man may know what goods he may enjoy, and what actions he may do, without being molested by any of his fellow-subjects; and this is it men call "propriety." For before constitution of sovereign power, as hath already been shown, all men had right to all things, which necessarily causeth war: and therefore this propriety, being necessary to peace, and depending on sovereign power, is the act of that power, in order to the public peace. These rules of propriety, or *meum* and *tuum*, and of "good," "evil," "lawful," and "unlawful" in the actions of subjects, are the civil laws; that is to say, the laws of each commonwealth in particular; though the name of civil law be now restrained to the ancient civil laws of the city of Rome; which being the head of a great part of the world, her laws at that time were in these parts the civil law.

Eighthly, is annexed to the sovereignty, the right of judicature; that is to say, of hearing and deciding all controversies, which may arise concerning law, either civil or natural, or concerning fact. For without the decision of controversies, there is no protection of one subject against the injuries of another; the laws concerning *meum* and *tuum* are in vain, and to every man remaineth, from the natural and necessary appetite of his own conservation, the right of protecting himself by his private strength, which is the condition of war, and contrary to the end for which every commonwealth is instituted.

Ninthly, is annexed to the sovereignty, the right of making war and peace with other nations and commonwealths; that is to say, of judging when it is for the public good, and how great forces are to be assembled, armed, and paid for that end; and to levy money upon the subjects to defray the expenses thereof. For the power by which the people are to be defended consisteth in their armies, and the strength of an army, in the union of their strength under one command, which command the sovereign instituted, therefore hath; because the command of the "militia," without other institution, maketh him that hath it sovereign. And therefore whosoever is made general of an army, he that hath the sovereign power is always generalissimo.

Tenthly, is annexed to the sovereignty, the choosing of all counsellors, ministers, magistrates, and officers, both in peace and war. For seeing the sovereign is charged with the end, which is the common peace and defence, he is understood to have power to use such means as he shall think most fit for his discharge.

Eleventhly, to the sovereign is committed the power of rewarding with riches or honour, and of punishing with corporal or pecuniary punishment, or with ignominy, every subject according to the law he hath formerly made; or if there be no law made, according as he shall judge most to conduce to the encouraging of men to serve the commonwealth, or deterring of them from doing disservice to the same.

Lastly, considering what value men are naturally apt to set upon themselves; what respect they look for from others; and how little they value other men; from whence continually arise amongst them, emulation, quarrels, factions, and at last war, to the destroying of one another, and diminution of their strength against a common enemy; it is necessary that there be laws of honour, and a public rate of the worth of such men as have deserved, or are able to deserve well of the commonwealth; and that there be force in the hands of some or other, to put those laws in execution. But it hath already been shown, that not only the whole "militia," or forces of the commonwealth; but also the judicature of all controversies, is annexed to the sovereignty. To the sovereign therefore it belongeth also to give titles of honour; and to appoint what order of place and dignity each man shall hold; and what signs of respect, in public or private meetings, they shall give to one another.

These are the rights, which make the essence of sovereignty; and which are the marks whereby a man may discern in what man, or assembly of men, the sovereign power is placed and resideth. For these are incommunicable and inseparable. The power to coin money; to dispose of the estate and persons of infant heirs; to have pre-emption in markets; and all other statute prerogatives, may be transferred by the sovereign; and yet the power to protect his subjects be retained. But if he transfer the "militia," he retains the judicature in vain, for want of execution of the laws: or if he grant away the power of raising money, the "militia" is in vain; or if he give away the government of doctrines, men will be frighted into rebellion with the fear of spirits. And so if we consider any one of the said rights, we shall presently see, that the holding of all the rest will produce no effect, in the conservation of peace and justice, the end for which all commonwealths are instituted. And this division is it, whereof it is said, "a kingdom divided in itself cannot stand": for unless this division precede, division into opposite armies can never happen. If there had not first been an opinion received of the greatest part of England, that these powers were divided between the King, and the Lords, and the House of Commons, the people had never been divided and fallen into this civil war; first between those that disagreed in politics; and after between the dissenters about the liberty of religion; which have so instructed men in this point of sovereign right, that there be few now in England that do not see that these rights are inseparable, and will be so generally acknowledged at the next return of peace; and so continue, till their miseries are forgotten; and no longer, except the vulgar be better taught than they have hitherto been.

And because they are essential and inseparable rights, it follows necessarily, that in whatsoever words any of them seem to be granted away, yet if the sovereign power itself be not in direct terms renounced, and the name of sovereign no more given by the grantees to him that grants them, the grant is void: for when he has granted all he can, if we grant back the sovereignty, all is restored, as inseparably annexed thereunto.

This great authority being indivisible, and inseparably annexed to the sovereignty, there is little ground for the opinion of them that say of sovereign kings, though they be *singulis majores*, of greater power than every one of their subjects, yet they be *universis minores*, of less power than them all together. For if by "all together," they mean not the collective body as one person, then "all together," and "every one," signify the same; and the speech is absurd. But if by "all together," they understand them as one person, which person the sovereign bears, then the power of all together, is the same with the sovereign's power; and so again the speech is absurd: which absurdity they see well enough, when the sovereignty is in an assembly of the people; but in a monarch they see it not; and yet the power of sovereignty is the same in whomsoever it be placed.

And as the power, so also the honour of the sovereign, ought to be greater, than that of any, or all the subjects. For in the sovereignty is the fountain of honour. The dignities of lord, earl, duke, and prince are his creatures. As in the presence of the master, the servants are equal, and without any honour at all; so are the subjects in the presence of the sovereign. And though they shine some more, some less, when they are out of his sight; yet in his presence, they shine no more than the stars in the presence of the sun.

But a man may here object, that the condition of subjects is very miserable; as being obnoxious to the lusts, and other irregular passions of him or them that have so unlimited a power in their hands. And commonly they that live under a monarch, think it the fault of monarchy; and they that live under the government of democracy, or other sovereign assembly, attribute all the inconvenience to that form of commonwealth; whereas the power in all forms, if they be perfect enough to protect them, is the same; not considering that the state of man can never be without some incommodity or other; and that the greatest, that in any form of government can possibly happen to the people in general, is scarce sensible, in respect of the miseries, and horrible calamities, that accompany a civil war, or that dissolute condition of masterless men, without subjection to laws, and a coercive power to tie their hands from rapine and revenge: nor considering that the greatest pressure of sovereign governors proceedeth not from any delight, or profit they can expect in the damage or weakening of their subjects, in whose vigour consisteth their own strength and glory; but in the restiveness of themselves, that unwillingly contributing to their own defence, make it necessary for their governors to draw from them what they can in time of peace, that they may have means on any emergent occasion, or sudden need, to resist, or take advantage on their enemies. For all men are by nature provided of notable multiplying glasses, that is their passions and self-love, through which every little payment appeareth a great grievance; but are destitute of those prospective glasses, namely, moral and civil science, to see afar off the miseries that hang over them, and cannot without such payments be avoided.

Chapter XIX
Of the Several Kinds of Commonwealth by Institution, and of Succession to the Sovereign Power

The difference of commonwealths consisteth in the difference of the sovereign, or the person representative of all and every one of the multitude. And because the sovereignty is either in one man, or in an assembly of more than one; and into that assembly either every man hath right to enter, or not every one, but certain men distinguished from the rest; it is manifest, there can be but three kinds of commonwealth. For the representative must needs be one man, or more: and if more, then it is the assembly of all, or but of a part. When the representative is one man, then is the commonwealth a "monarchy": when an assembly of all that will come together, then it is a "democracy," or popular commonwealth: when an assembly of a part only, then it is called an "aristocracy." Other kind of commonwealth there can be none: for either one or more, or all, must have the sovereign power, which I have shown to be indivisible, entire.

There be other names of government in the histories and books of policy, as "tyranny," and "oligarchy": but they are not the names of other forms of government, but of the same forms misliked. For they that are discontented under "monarchy," call it "tyranny"; and they that are displeased with "aristocracy," call it "oligarchy": so also they which find themselves grieved under a "democracy," call it "anarchy," which signifies want of government; and yet I think no man believes that want of government is any new kind of government: nor by the same reason ought they to believe that the government is of one kind when they like it, and another when they dislike it, or are oppressed by the governors.

It is manifest, that men who are in absolute liberty may, if they please, give authority to one man to represent them every one; as well as give such authority to any assembly of men whatsoever; and consequently may subject themselves, if they think good, to a monarch as absolutely as to other representative. Therefore, where there is already erected a sovereign power, there can be no other representative of the same people, but only to certain particular ends, by the sovereign limited. For that were to erect two sovereigns; and every man to have his person represented by two actors, that by opposing one another, must needs divide that power, which, if men will live in peace, is indivisible, and thereby reduce the multitude into the condition of war, contrary to the end for which all sovereignty is instituted. And therefore as it is absurd to think that a sovereign assembly, inviting the people of their dominion to send up their deputies, with power to make known their advice, or desires, should therefore hold such deputies rather than themselves, for the absolute representatives of

the people: so it is absurd also to think the same in a monarchy. And I know not how this so manifest a truth should of late be so little observed; that in a monarchy, he that had the sovereignty from a descent of six hundred years, was alone called sovereign, had the title of Majesty from every one of his subjects, and was unquestionably taken by them for their king, was notwithstanding never considered as their representative; that name without contradiction passing for the title of those men, which at his command were sent up by the people to carry their petitions, and give him, if he permitted it, their advice. Which may serve as an admonition, for those that are the true and absolute representative of a people, to instruct men in the nature of that office, and to take heed how they admit of any other general representation upon any occasion whatsoever, if they mean to discharge the trust committed to them.

The difference between these three kinds of commonwealth, consisteth not in the difference of power; but in the difference of convenience, or aptitude to produce the peace and security of the people; for which end they were instituted. And to compare monarchy with the other two, we may observe; first, that whosoever beareth the person of the people, or is one of that assembly that bears it, beareth also his own natural person. And though he be careful in his politic person to procure the common interest; yet he is more or no less careful to procure the private good of himself, his family, kindred, and friends; and for the most part, if the public interest chance to cross the private, he prefers the private: for the passions of men are commonly more potent than their reason. From whence it follows, that where the public and private interest are most closely united, there is the public most advanced. Now in monarchy, the private interest is the same with the public. The riches, power, and honour of a monarch, arise only from the riches, strength, and reputation of his subjects. For no king can be rich, nor glorious, nor secure, whose subjects are either poor, or contemptible, or too weak through want or dissension, to maintain a war against their enemies: whereas in a democracy, or aristocracy, the public prosperity confers not so much to the private fortune of one that is corrupt, or ambitious, as doth many times a perfidious advice, a treacherous action, or a civil war.

Secondly, that a monarch receiveth counsel of whom, when, and where he pleaseath; and consequently may hear the opinion of men versed in the matter about which he deliberates, of what rank or quality soever, and as long before the time of action, and with as much secrecy, as he will. But when a sovereign assembly has need of counsel, none are admitted but such as have a right thereto from the beginning; which for the most part are of those who have been versed more in the acquisition of wealth than of knowledge; and are to give their advice in long discourses, which may and do commonly excite men to action, but not govern them in it. For the "understanding" is by the flame of the passions, never enlightened, but dazzled. Nor is there any place, or time, wherein an assembly can receive counsel with secrecy, because of their own multitude.

Thirdly, that the resolutions of a monarch, are subject to no other inconstancy, than that of human nature; but in assemblies, besides that of Nature, there ariseth an inconstancy from the number. For the absence of a few, that would have the resolution once taken, continue firm, which may happen by security, negligence, or private impediments, or the diligent appearance of a few of the contrary opinion, undoes to-day all that was concluded yesterday.

Fourthly, that a monarch cannot disagree with himself, out of envy or interest; but an assembly may; and that to such a height, as may produce a civil war.

Fifthly, that in monarchy there is this inconvenience; that any subject, by the power of one man, for the enriching of a favourite or flatterer, may be deprived of all he possesseth; which I confess is a great and inevitable inconvenience. But the same may as well happen, where the sovereign power is an assembly: for their power is the same; and they are as subject to evil counsel, and to be seduced by orators, as a monarch by flatterers; and becoming one another's flatterers, serve one another's covetousness and ambition by turns. And whereas the favourites of monarchs are few, and they have none else to advance but their own kindred; the favourites of an assembly are many; and the kindred much more numerous than of any monarch. Besides there is no favourite of a monarch, which cannot as well succour his friends as hurt his enemies; but orators, that is to say, favourites of sovereign assemblies, though they have great power to hurt, have little to save. For to accuse, requires less eloquence, such is man's nature, than to excuse; and condemnation, than absolution more resembles justice.

Sixthly, that it is an inconvenience in monarchy, that the sovereignty may descend upon an infant, or one that cannot discern between good and evil: and consisteth in this, that the use of his power, must be in the hand of another man, or of some assembly of men, which are to govern by his right, and in his name; as curators and protectors of his person and authority. But to say there is inconvenience in putting the use of the sovereign power into the hand of a man, or an assembly of men; is to say that all government is more inconvenient than confusion and civil war. And therefore all the danger that can be pretended, must arise from the contention of those, that for an office of so great honour and profit, may become competitors. To make it appear that this inconvenience proceedeth not from that form of government we call monarchy, we are to consider that the precedent monarch hath appointed who shall have the tuition of his infant successor, either expressly by testament, or tacitly, by not controlling the custom in that case received: and then such inconvenience, if it happen, is to be attributed, not to the monarchy, but to the ambition and injustice of the subjects; which in all kinds of government, where the people are not well instructed in their duty and the rights of sovereignty, is the same. Or else the precedent monarch hath not at all taken order for such tuition; and then the law of Nature hath provided this sufficient rule, that the tuition shall be in him that hath, by nature, most interest in the preservation of the authority of the infant, and to whom least benefit can accrue by his death or diminution. For seeing every man by nature seeketh his own benefit, and promotion; to put an infant into the power of those that can promote themselves by his destruction, or damage, is not tuition, but treachery. So that sufficient provision being taken against all just quarrel about the government under a child, if any contention arise to the disturbance of the public peace, it is not to be attributed to the form of monarchy, but to the ambition of subjects, and ignorance of their duty. On the other side, there is no great commonwealth, the sovereignty whereof is in a great assembly, which is not, as to consultations of peace and war, and making of laws, in the same condition as if the government were in a child. For as a child wants the judgment to dissent from counsel given him, and is thereby necessitated to take the advice of them, or him, to whom he is committed: so an assembly wanteth the liberty to dissent from the counsel of the major part, be it good or bad. And as a child has need of a tutor, or protector, to preserve his person and authority: so also, in great commonwealths, the sovereign assembly, in all great dangers and troubles, have need of *custodes libertatis;* that is of dictators, or protectors of their authority; which are as much as temporary monarchs, to whom for a time they may commit the entire exercise of their power; and have, at the end of that time, been oftener deprived thereof than infant kings, by their protectors, regents, or any other tutors.

Though the kinds of sovereignty be, as I have now shown, but three: that is to say, monarchy, where one man has it; or democracy, where the general assembly of subjects hath it; or aristocracy, where it is in an assembly of certain persons nominated, or otherwise distinguished from the rest: yet he that shall consider the particular commonwealths that have been, and are in the world, will not perhaps easily reduce them to three, and may thereby be inclined to think there be other forms, arising from these mingled together. As for example, elective kingdoms; where kings have the sovereign power put into their hands for a time; or kingdoms wherein the king hath a power limited: which governments are nevertheless, by most writers, called monarchy. Likewise if a popular, or aristocratical commonwealth subdue an enemy's country, and govern the same, by a president, procurator, or other magistrate: this may seem perhaps at first sight, to be a democratical, or aristocratical government. But it is not so. For elective kings are not sovereigns, but ministers of the sovereign; nor limited kings, sovereigns, but ministers of them that have the sovereign power: nor are those provinces which are in subjection to a democracy or aristocracy of another commonwealth, democratically or aristocratically governed, but monarchically.

And first, concerning an elective king, whose power is limited to his life, as it is in many places of Christendom at this day; or to certain years or months, as the dictator's power amongst the Romans; if he have right to appoint his successor, he is no more elective but hereditary. But if he have no power to elect his successor, then there is some other man, or assembly known, which after his decease may elect anew; or else the commonwealth dieth and dissolveth with him, and returneth to the condition of war. If it be known who have the power to give the sovereignty after his death, it is known also that the sovereignty was in them before; for none have right to give that which they have not right to possess, and keep to themselves if they think good. But if there be

none that can give the sovereignty after the decease of him that was first elected, then has he power, nay, he is obliged by the law of Nature, to provide, by establishing his successor, to keep those that had trusted him with the government from relapsing into the miserable condition of civil war. And consequently he was, when elected, a sovereign absolute.

Secondly, that king whose power is limited, is not superior to him or them that have the power to limit it; and he that is not superior is not supreme, that is to say, not sovereign. The sovereignty therefore was always in that assembly which had the right to limit him; and by consequence the government not monarchy, but either democracy or aristocracy; as of old time in Sparta, where the kings had a privilege to lead their armies; but the sovereignty was in the Ephori.

Thirdly, whereas heretofore the Roman people governed the land of Judea, for example, by a president; yet was not Judea therefore a democracy; because they were not governed by any assembly into which any of them had right to enter; nor an aristocracy; because they were not governed by any assembly, into which any man could enter by their election: but they were governed by one person, which, though as to the people of Rome, was an assembly of the people, or democracy; yet as to the people of Judea, which had no right at all of participating in the government, was a monarch. For though where the people are governed by an assembly, chosen by themselves out of their own number, the government is called a democracy or aristocracy; yet when they are governed by an assembly not of their own choosing, it is a monarchy; not of "one" man, over another man; but of one people, over another people.

Of all these forms of government, the matter being mortal, so that not only monarchs but also whole assemblies die, it is necessary, for the conservation of the peace of men, that as there was order taken for an artificial man, so there be order also taken for an artificial eternity of life: without which, men that are governed by an assembly should return into the condition of war in every age; and they that are governed by one man, as soon as their governor dieth. This artificial eternity is that which men call the right of "succession."

There is no perfect form of government, where the disposing of the succession is not in the present sovereign. For if it be in any other particular man or private assembly, it is in a person subject, and may be assumed by the sovereign at his pleasure; and consequently the right is in himself. And if it be no particular man, but left to a new choice, then is the commonwealth dissolved, and the right is in him that can get it; contrary to the intention of them that did institute the commonwealth, for their perpetual, and not temporary security.

In a democracy, the whole assembly cannot fail, unless the multitude that are to be governed fail. And therefore questions of the right of succession have in that form of government no place at all.

In an aristocracy, when any of the assembly dieth, the election of another into his room belongeth to the assembly, as the sovereign, to whom belongeth the choosing of all counsellors and officers. For that which the representative doth, as actor, every one of the subjects doth, as author. And though the sovereign assembly may give power to others, to elect new men for supply of their court; yet it is still by their authority that the election is made; and by the same it may, when the public shall require it, be recalled.

The greatest difficulty about the right of succession is in monarchy: and the difficulty ariseth from this, that at first sight, it is not manifest who is to appoint the successor; nor many times, who it is whom he hath appointed. For in both these cases there is required a more exact ratiocination, than every man is accustomed to use. As to the question, who shall appoint the successor, of a monarch that hath the sovereign authority; that is to say, who shall determine of the right of inheritance, (for elective kings and princes have not the sovereign power in propriety, but in use only,) we are to consider that either he that is in possession has right to dispose of the succession, or else that right is again in the dissolved multitude. For the death of him that hath the sovereign power in propriety, leaves the multitude without any sovereign at all; that is, without any representative in whom they should be united, and be capable of doing any one action at all: and therefore they are incapable of election of any new monarch; every man having equal right to submit himself to such as he thinks best able to protect him; or if he can, protect himself by his own sword; which is a return to confusion, and to the condition of a war of every man against every man, contrary to the end for which monarchy had its first institution. Therefore it is manifest, that by the institution of monarchy, the disposing of the successor is always left to the judgment and will of the present possessor.

And for the question which may arise sometimes, who it is that the monarch in possession hath designed to the succession and inheritance of his power; it is determined by his express words and testament, or by other tacit signs sufficient.

By express words, or testament, when it is declared by him in his lifetime, *viva voce*, or by writing, as the first emperors of Rome declared who should be their heirs. For the word *heir* does not of itself imply the children, or nearest kindred of a man; but whomsoever a man shall any way declare he would have to succeed him in his estate. If therefore a monarch declare expressly, that such a man shall be his heir, either by word or writing, then is that man immediately after the decease of his predecessor, invested in the right of being monarch.

But where testament and express words are wanting, other natural signs of the will are to be followed, whereof the one is custom. And therefore where the custom is, that the next of kindred absolutely succeedeth, there also the next of kindred hath right to the succession; for that if the will of him that was in possession had been otherwise, he might easily have declared the same in his lifetime. And likewise where the custom is, that the next of the male kindred succeedeth, there also the right of succession is in the next of the kindred male, for the same reason. And so it is if the custom were to advance the female. For whatsoever custom a man may by a word control, and does not, it is a natural sign he would have that custom stand.

But where neither custom nor testament hath preceded, there it is to be understood, first, that a monarch's will is, that the government remain monarchical; because he hath approved that government in himself. Secondly, that a child of his own, male or female, be preferred before any other; because men are presumed to be more inclined by nature to advance their own children than the children of other men; and of their own, rather a male than a female; because men are naturally fitter than women for actions of labour and danger. Thirdly, where his own issue faileth, rather a brother than a stranger; and so still the nearer in blood, rather than the more remote; because it is always presumed that the nearer of kin is the nearer in affection; and it is evident that a man receives always, by reflection, the most honour from the greatness of his nearest kindred.

But if it be lawful for a monarch to dispose of the succession by words of contract, or testament, men may perhaps object a great inconvenience; for he may sell, or give his right of governing to a stranger; which, because strangers, that is, men not used to live under the same government, nor speaking the same language, do commonly undervalue one another, may turn to the oppression of his subjects; which is indeed a great inconvenience: but it proceedeth not necessarily from the subjection to a stranger's government, but from the unskillfulness of the governors, ignorant of the true rules of politics. And therefore the Romans when they had subdued many nations, to make their government digestible, were wont to take away that grievance, as much as they thought necessary, by giving sometimes to whole nations, and sometimes to principal men of every nation they conquered, not only the privileges, but also the name of Romans; and took many of them into the senate, and offices of charge, even in the Roman city. And this was it our most wise king, King James, aimed at, in endeavouring the union of his two realms of England and Scotland, which if he could have obtained, had in all likelihood prevented the civil wars, which make both those kingdoms, at this present, miserable. It is not therefore any injury to the people for a monarch to dispose of the succession by will; though by the fault of many princes, it hath been sometimes found inconvenient. Of the lawfulness of it, this also is an argument, that whatsoever inconvenience can arrive by giving a kingdom to a stranger, may arrive also by so marrying with strangers, as the right of succession may descend upon them: yet this by all men is accounted lawful.

Chapter XX
Of Dominion Paternal, and Despotical

A commonwealth "by acquisition," is that, where the sovereign power is acquired by force; and it is acquired by force when men singly, or many together by plurality of voices, for fear of death, or bonds, do authorize all the actions of that man, or assembly, that hath their lives and liberty in his power.

And this kind of dominion, or sovereignty, differeth from sovereignty by institution only in this, that men who choose their sovereign do it for fear of one another, and not of him whom they institute: but in this case, they subject themselves to him they are afraid of. In both cases they do it for fear: which is to be noted by them that hold all such covenants, as proceed from fear of death or violence, void: which if it

were true, no man, in any kind of commonwealth, could be obliged to obedience. It is true, that in a commonwealth once instituted, or acquired, promises proceeding from fear of death or violence, are no covenants, nor obliging, when the thing promised is contrary to the laws; but the reason is not because it was made upon fear, but because he that promiseth hath no right in the thing promised. Also, when he may lawfully perform, and doth not, it is not the invalidity of the covenant that absolveth him, but the sentence of the sovereign. Otherwise, whensoever a man lawfully promiseth, he unlawfully breaketh: but when the sovereign, who is the actor, acquitteth him, then he is acquitted by him that extorted the promise, as by the author of such absolution.

But the rights and consequences of sovereignty, are the same in both. His power cannot, without his consent, be transferred to another; he cannot forfeit it: he cannot be accused by any of his subjects of injury: he cannot be punished by them: he is judge of what is necessary for peace; and judge of doctrines: he is sole legislator; and supreme judge of controversies; and of the times, and occasions of war, and peace: to him it belongeth to choose magistrates, counsellors, commanders, and all other officers and ministers; and to determine of rewards and punishments, honour, and order. The reasons whereof, are the same which are alleged in the precedent chapter, for the same rights and consequences of sovereignty by institution.

Dominion is acquired two ways; by generation and by conquest. The right of dominion by generation is that, which the parent hath over his children, and is called "paternal." And is not so derived from the generation, as if therefore the parent had dominion over his child because he begat him; but from the child's consent, either express, or by other sufficient arguments declared. For as to the generation, God hath ordained to man a helper; and there be always two that are equally parents: the dominion therefore over the child should belong equally to both; and he be equally subject to both, which is impossible, for no man can obey two masters. And whereas some have attributed the dominion to the man only, as being of the more excellent sex; they misreckon in it. For there is not always that difference of strength or prudence between the man and the woman, as that the right can be determined without war. In commonwealths, this controversy is decided by the civil law; and for the most part, but not always, the sentence is in favour of the father; because for the most part commonwealths have been erected by the fathers, not by the mothers of families. But the question lieth now in the state of mere nature; where there are supposed no laws of matrimony; no laws for the education of children; but the law of Nature, and the natural inclination of the sexes, one to another, and to their children. In this condition of mere nature, either the parents between themselves dispose of the dominion over the child by contract; or do not dispose thereof at all. If they dispose thereof, the right passeth according to the contract. We find in history that the Amazons contracted with the men of the neighbouring countries, to whom they had recourse for issue, that the issue male should be sent back, but the female remain with themselves: so that the dominion of the females was in the mother.

If there be no contract, the dominion is in the mother. For in the condition of mere nature, where there are no matrimonial laws, it cannot be known who is the father, unless it be declared by the mother: and therefore the right of dominion over the child dependeth on her will, and is consequently hers. Again, seeing the infant is first in the power of the mother, so as she may either nourish or expose it; if she nourish it, it oweth its life to the mother; and is therefore obliged to obey her, rather than any other; and by consequence the dominion over it is hers. But if she expose it, and another find and nourish it, dominion is in him that nourisheth it. For it ought to obey him by whom it is preserved; because preservation of life being the end, for which one man becomes subject to another, every man is supposed to promise obedience to him, in whose power it is to save, or destroy him.

If the mother be the father's subject, the child is in the father's power: and if the father be the mother's subject, as when a sovereign queen marrieth one of her subjects, the child is subject to the mother; because the father also is her subject.

If a man and woman, monarchs of two several kingdoms, have a child, and contract concerning who shall have the dominion of him, the right of the dominion passeth by the contract. If they contract not, the dominion followeth the dominion of the place of his residence. For the sovereign of each country hath dominion over all that reside therein.

He that hath the dominion over the child, hath dominion also over the children of the child; and over their children's children. For he that hath dominion over the person of a man, hath dominion over all that is his; without which, dominion were but a title, without the effect.

The right of succession to paternal dominion, proceedeth in the same manner as doth the right of succession to monarchy; of which I have already sufficiently spoken in the precedent chapter.

Dominion acquired by conquest, or victory in war, is that which some writers call "despotical," from Δεσπότης, which signifieth a "lord," or "master"; and is the dominion of the master over his servant. And this dominion is then acquired to the victor, when the vanquished, to avoid the present stroke of death, covenanteth either in express words, or by other sufficient signs of the will, that so long as his life and the liberty of his body is allowed him, the victor shall have the use thereof, at his pleasure. And after such covenant made, the vanquished is a "servant," and not before: for by the word "servant," whether it be derived from *servire*, to serve, or from *servare*, to save, which I leave to grammarians to dispute, is not meant a captive, which is kept in prison or bonds, till the owner of him that took him, or bought him of one that did, shall consider what to do with him: for such men, commonly called slaves, have no obligation at all; but may break their bonds or the prison; and kill, or carry away captive their master, justly: but one, that being taken, hath corporal liberty allowed him; and upon promise not to run away, nor to do violence to his master, is trusted by him.

It is not therefore the victory that giveth the right of dominion over the vanquished, but his own covenant. Nor is he obliged because he is conquered; that is to say, beaten and taken, or put to flight; but because he cometh in and submitteth to the victor; nor is the victor obliged by an enemy's rendering himself without promise of life, to spare him for this his yielding to discretion, which obliges not the victor longer than in his own discretion he shall think fit.

And that which men do when they demand, as it is now called, "quarter," which the Greeks called Ζωγρία, "taking alive," is to evade the present fury of the victor by submission, and to compound for their life with ransom, or service; and therefore he that hath quarter, hath not his life given, but deferred till further deliberation; for it is not a yielding on condition of life, but to discretion. And then only is his life in security, and his service due, when the victor hath trusted him with his corporal liberty. For slaves that work in prisons, or fetters, do it not of duty, but to avoid the cruelty of their taskmasters.

The master of the servant is master also of all he hath, and may exact the use thereof, that is to say, of his goods, of his labour, of his servants, and of his children, as often as he shall think fit. For he holdeth his life of his master by the covenant of obedience; that is, of owning and authorizing whatsoever the master shall do. And in case the master, if he refuse, kill him, or cast him into bonds, or otherwise punish him for his disobedience, he is himself the author of the same, and cannot accuse him of injury.

In sum, the rights and consequences of both "paternal" and "despotical" dominion, are the very same with those of a sovereign by institution; and for the same reasons: which reasons are set down in the precedent chapter. So that for a man that is monarch of divers nations, whereof he hath in one the sovereignty by institution of the people assembled, and in another by conquest, that is by the submission of each particular, to avoid death or bonds; to demand of one nation more than of the other from the title of conquest, as being a conquered nation, is an act of ignorance of the rights of sovereignty; for the sovereign is absolute over both alike, or else there is no sovereignty at all; and so every man may lawfully protect himself, if he can, with his own sword, which is the condition of war.

By this it appears that a great family, if it be not part of some commonwealth, is of itself, as to the rights of sovereignty, a little monarchy; whether that family consist of a man and his children, or of a man and his servants; or of a man, and his children and servants together, wherein the father or master is the sovereign. But yet a family is not properly a commonwealth, unless it be of that power by its own number, or by other opportunities, as not to be subdued without the hazard of war. For where a number of men are manifestly too weak to defend themselves united, every one may use his own reason in time of danger to save his own life, either by flight or by submission to the enemy, as he shall think best; in the same manner as a very small company of soldiers, surprised by an army, may cast down their arms and demand quarter, or run away, rather than be put to the sword. And thus much shall suffice concerning what I find by speculation, and deduction of sovereign rights, from the nature, need, and designs of men, in erecting of commonwealths, and putting themselves under monarchs, or assemblies entrusted with power enough for their protection.

Let us now consider what the Scripture teacheth in the same point. To Moses, the children of Israel say thus: "Speak thou to us, and we will hear thee; but let not God speak to us, lest we die." (Exod. xx. 19). This is absolute obedience to Moses. Concerning the right of kings, God Himself by the mouth of Samuel, saith, (1 Sam. viii. 11, 12, &c.): "This shall be the right of the king you will have to reign over you. He shall take your sons, and set them to drive his chariots, and to be his horsemen, and to run before his chariots; and gather in his harvest; and to make his engines of war, and instruments of his chariots; and shall take your daughters to make perfumes, to be his cooks, and bakers. He shall take your fields, your vineyards, and your olive yards, and give them to his servants. He shall take the tithe of your corn and wine, and give it to the men of his chamber, and to his other servants. He shall take your manservants and your maidservants, and the choice of your youth, and employ them in his business. He shall take the tithe of your flocks, and you shall be his servants." This is absolute power, and summed up in the last words, "you shall be his servants." Again, when the people heard what power their king was to have, yet they consented thereto, and say thus (verse 10): "We will be as all other nations, and our king shall judge our causes, and go before us, to conduct our wars." Here is confirmed the right that sovereigns have both to the "militia" and to all "judicature"; in which is contained as absolute power as one man can possibly transfer to another. Again, the prayer of King Solomon to God was this (1 Kings iii. 9): "Give to thy servant understanding, to judge thy people, and to discern between good and evil." It belongeth therefore to the sovereign to be "judge," and to prescribe the rules of "discerning good" and "evil"; which rules are laws; and therefore in him is the legislative power. Saul sought the life of David; yet when it was in his power to slay Saul, and his servants would have done it, David forbade them, saying, (1 Sam. xxiv. 6): "God forbid I should do such an act against my lord, the anointed of God." For obedience of servants St. Paul saith (Col. iii. 22): "Servants obey your masters in all things"; and (Col. iii. 20): "Children obey your parents in all things." There is simple obedience in those that are subject to paternal or despotical dominion. Again (Matt. xxiii. 2, 3):

"The Scribes and Pharisees sit in Moses' chair, and therefore all that they shall bid you observe, that observe and do." There again is simple obedience. And St. Paul (Titus iii. 2): "Warn them that they subject themselves to princes, and to those that are in authority, and obey them." This obedience is also simple. Lastly, our Saviour Himself acknowledges, that men ought to pay such taxes as are by kings imposed, where he says, "Give to Cæsar that which is Cæsar's"; and paid such taxes Himself. And that the king's word is sufficient to take anything from any subject, when there is need; and that the king is judge of that need, for He Himself, as king of the Jews, commanded His disciples to take the ass, and ass's colt, to carry Him into Jerusalem, saying (Matt. xxi. 2, 3): "Go into the village over against you, and you shall find a she-ass tied, and her colt with her; untie them, and bring them to me. And if any man ask you what you mean by it, say the Lord hath need of them: and they will let them go." They will not ask whether His necessity be a sufficient title; nor whether He be judge of that necessity; but acquiesce in the will of the Lord.

To these places may be added also that of Genesis (iii. 5): "Ye shall be as gods, knowing good and evil." And (verse 11): "Who told thee that thou wast naked? hast thou eaten of the tree, of which I commanded thee thou shouldest not eat?" For the cognizance or judicature of "good" and "evil," being forbidden by the name of the fruit of the tree of knowledge, as a trial of Adam's obedience; the devil to inflame the ambition of the woman, to whom that fruit already seemed beautiful, told her that by tasting it they should be as gods, knowing "good" and "evil." Whereupon having both eaten, they did indeed take upon them God's office, which is judicature of good and evil; but acquired no new ability to distinguish between them aright. And whereas it is said, that having eaten, they saw they were naked; no man hath so interpreted that place, as if they had been formerly blind, and saw not their own skins: the meaning is plain, that it was then they first judged their nakedness, wherein it was God's will to create them, to be uncomely; and by being ashamed, did tacitly censure God Himself. And thereupon God saith: "Hast thou eaten, &c.," as if He should say, doest thou that owest me obedience, take upon thee to judge of my commandments? Whereby it is clearly, though allegorically, signified that the commands of them that have the right to command, are not by their subjects to be censured nor disputed.

So that it appeareth plainly, to my understanding, both from reason and Scripture, that the sovereign power, whether placed in one man, as in monarchy, or in one assembly of men, as in popular and aristocratical commonwealths, is as great as possibly men can be imagined to make it. And though of so unlimited a power, men may fancy many evil consequences, yet the consequences of the want of it, which is perpetual war of every man against his neighbour, are much worse. The condition of man in this life shall never be without inconveniences; but there happeneth in no commonwealth any great inconvenience but what proceeds from the subject's disobedience, and breach of those covenants, from which the commonwealth has its being. And whosoever thinking sovereign power too great, will seek to make it less, must subject himself to the power that can limit it; that is to say, to a greater.

The greatest objection is, that of the practice; when men ask where and when such power has by subjects been acknowledged. But one may ask them again, when or where has there been a kingdom long free from sedition and civil war. In those nations whose commonwealths have been long-lived, and not being destroyed but by foreign war, the subjects never did dispute of the sovereign power. But howsoever, an argument from the practice of men, that have not sifted to the bottom, and with exact reason weighed the causes and nature of commonwealths, and suffer daily those miseries that proceed from the ignorance thereof, is invalid. For though in all places of the world men should lay the foundation of their houses on the sand, it could not thence be inferred that so it ought to be. The skill of making and maintaining commonwealths, consisteth in certain rules, as doth arithmetic and geometry; not, as tennis-play, on practice only; which rules neither poor men have the leisure, nor men that have had the leisure, have hitherto had the curiosity, or the method to find out.

Chapter XXI
Of the Liberty of Subjects

Liberty, or "freedom," signifieth, properly, the absence of opposition; by opposition, I mean external impediments of motion; and may be applied no less to irrational and inanimate creatures than to rational. For whatsoever is so tied, or environed, as it cannot move but within a certain space, which space is determined by the opposition of some external body, we say it hath not liberty to go further. And so of all living creatures whilst they are imprisoned, or restrained, with walls or chains; and of the water whilst it is kept in by banks or vessels, that otherwise would spread itself into a larger space, we use to say, they are not at liberty to move in such manner, as without those external impediments they would. But when the impediment of motion is in the constitution of the thing itself, we use not to say, it wants the liberty, but the power to move; as when a stone lieth still, or a man is fastened to his bed by sickness.

And according to this proper and generally received meaning of the word, a "freeman, is he, that in those things, which by his strength and wit he is able to do, is not hindered to do what he has a will to." But when the words "free," and "liberty," are applied to anything but "bodies," they are abused; for that which is not subject to motion, is not subject to impediment; and therefore, when it is said for example, the way is free, no liberty of the way is signified, but of those that walk in it without stop. And when we say a gift is free, there is not meant any liberty of the gift, but of the giver, that was not bound by any law or covenant to give it. So when we "speak freely," it is not the liberty of voice, or pronunciation, but of the man, whom no law hath obliged to speak otherwise than he did. Lastly, from the use of the word "free-will," no liberty can be inferred of the will, desire, or inclination, but the liberty of the man; which consisteth in this, that he finds no stop, in doing what he has the will, desire, or inclination to do.

Fear and liberty are consistent; as when a man throweth his goods into the sea for "fear" the ship should sink, he doth it nevertheless very willingly, and may refuse to do it if he will: it is therefore the action of one that was "free"; so a man sometimes pays his debt, only for "fear" of imprisonment, which because nobody hindered him from detaining, was the action of a man at "liberty." And generally all actions which men do in commonwealths, for "fear" of the law, are actions which the doers had "liberty" to omit.

"Liberty" and "necessity" are consistent, as in the water that hath not only "liberty," but a "necessity" of descending by the channel; so likewise in the actions which men voluntarily do: which, because they proceed from their will, proceed from "liberty"; and yet, because every act of man's will, and every desire and inclination proceedeth from some cause, and that

from another cause, in a continual chain, whose first link is in the hand of God the first of all causes, proceed from "necessity." So that to him that could see the connection of those causes, the "necessity" of all men's voluntary actions would appear manifest. And therefore God, that seeth and disposeth all things, seeth also that the "liberty" of man in doing what he will, is accompanied with the "necessity" of doing that which God will, and no more nor less. For though men may do many things which God does not command, nor is therefore author of them; yet they can have no passion, nor appetite to anything, of which appetite God's will is not the cause. And did not His will assure the "necessity" of man's will, and consequently of all that on man's will dependeth, the "liberty" of men would be a contradiction, and impediment to the omnipotence and "liberty" of God. And this shall suffice, as to the matter in hand, of that natural "liberty," which only is properly called "liberty."

But as men, for the attaining of peace, and conservation of themselves thereby, have made an artificial man, which we call a commonwealth; so also have they made artificial chains, called "civil laws," which they themselves, by mutual covenants, have fastened at one end, to the lips of that man, or assembly, to whom they have given the sovereign power; and at the other to their own ears. These bonds, in their own nature but weak, may nevertheless be made to hold, by the danger, though not by the difficulty of breaking them.

In relation to these bonds only it is, that I am to speak now, of the "liberty" of "subjects." For seeing there is no commonwealth in the world, wherein there be rules enough set down for the regulating of all the actions and words of men, as being a thing impossible; it followeth necessarily, that in all kinds of actions by the laws pretermitted, men have the liberty of doing what their own reasons shall suggest, for the most profitable to themselves. For if we take liberty in the proper sense, for corporal liberty; that is to say, freedom from chains and prison; it were very absurd for men to clamour as they do for the liberty they so manifestly enjoy. Again, if we take liberty for an exemption from laws, it is no less absurd for men to demand as they do that liberty by which all other men may be masters of their lives. And yet, as absurd as it is, this is it they demand; not knowing that the laws are of no power to protect them, without a sword in the hands of a man, or men, to cause those laws to be put in execution. The liberty of a subject lieth therefore only in those things which in regulating their actions, the sovereign hath pretermitted: such as is the liberty to buy and sell, and otherwise contract with one another; to choose their own abode, their own diet, their own trade of life, and institute their children as they themselves think fit; and the like.

Nevertheless we are not to understand, that by such liberty, the sovereign power of life and death is either abolished or limited. For it has been already shown, that nothing the sovereign representative can do to a subject, on what pretence soever, can properly be called injustice or injury; because every subject is author of every act the sovereign doth; so that he never wanteth right to anything, otherwise than as he himself is the subject of God, and bound thereby to observe the laws of Nature. And therefore it may, and doth often happen in commonwealths, that a subject may be put to death by the command of the sovereign power; and yet neither do the other wrong: as when Jephtha caused his daughter to be sacrificed; in which, and the like cases, he that so dieth, had liberty to do the action, for which he is nevertheless without injury put to death. And the same holdeth also in a sovereign prince that putteth to death an innocent subject. For though the action be against the law of Nature, as being contrary to equity, as was the killing of Uriah, by David; yet it was not an injury to Uriah, but to God. Not to Uriah, because the right to do what he pleased was given him by Uriah himself: and yet to God, because David was God's subject, and prohibited all iniquity by the law of Nature: which distinction, David himself, when he repented the fact, evidently confirmed, saying, "To thee only have I sinned." In the same manner the people of Athens, when they banished the most potent of their commonwealth for ten years, thought they committed no injustice; and yet they never questioned what crime he had done; but what hurt he would do: nay, they commanded the banishment of they knew not whom; and every citizen bringing his oyster-shell into the market-place, written with the name of him he desired should be banished, without actually accusing him, sometimes banished an Aristides, for his reputation of justice; and sometimes a scurrilous jester, as Hyperbolus, to make a jest of it. And yet a man cannot say, the sovereign people of Athens wanted right to banish them; or an Athenian the liberty to jest or to be just.

The liberty, whereof there is so frequent and honourable mention in the histories and philosophy of the ancient Greeks and Romans, and in the writings and discourse of those that from them have received all their learning in the politics, is not the liberty of particular men; but the liberty of the commonwealth: which is the same with that which every man then should have, if there were no civil laws, nor commonwealth at all. And the effects of it also be the same. For as amongst masterless men there is perpetual war, of every man against his neighbour; no inheritance, to transmit to the son, nor to expect from the father; no propriety of goods, or lands; no security; but a full and absolute liberty in every particular man: so in states and commonwealths not dependent on one another, every commonwealth, not every man, has an absolute liberty to do what it shall judge, that is to say, what that man, or assembly that representeth it, shall judge most conducing to their benefit. But withal, they live in the condition of a perpetual war, and upon the confines of battle, with their frontiers armed, and cannons planted against their neighbours round about. The Athenians and Romans were free; that is, free commonwealths: not that any particular men had the liberty to resist their own representative; but that their representative had the liberty to resist, or invade other people. There is written on the turrets of the city of Lucca, in great characters, at this day, the word "Libertas"; yet no man can thence infer, that a particular man has more liberty, or immunity from the service of the commonwealth there, than in Constantinople. Whether a commonwealth be monarchical, or popular, the freedom is still the same.

But it is an easy thing for men to be deceived by the specious name of liberty; and for want of judgment to distinguish, mistake that for their private inheritance and birthright, which is the right of the public only. And when the same error is confirmed by the authority of men in reputation for their writings on this subject, it is no wonder if it produce sedition, and change of government. In these western parts of the world, we are made to receive our opinions concerning the institution and rights of commonwealths, from Aristotle, Cicero, and other men, Greeks and Romans, that, living under popular states, derived those rights, not from the principles of Nature, but transcribed them into their books, out of the practice of their own commonwealths, which were popular; as the grammarians describe the rules of language out of the practice of the time; or the rules of poetry out of the poems of Homer and Virgil. And because the Athenians were taught to keep them from desire of changing their government, that they were free men, and all that lived under monarchy were slaves; therefore Aristotle put it down in his "Politics" (lib. 6, cap. ii): "In democracy, 'liberty' is to be supposed: for it is commonly held, that no man is 'free' in any other government." And as Aristotle, so Cicero and other writers have grounded their civil doctrine on the opinions of the Romans, who were taught to hate monarchy, at first, by them that having deposed their sovereign, shared amongst them the sovereignty of Rome; and afterwards by their successors. And by reading of these Greek and Latin authors, men from their childhood have gotten a habit, under a false show of liberty, of favouring tumults, and of licentious controlling the actions of their sovereigns, and again of controlling those controllers; with the effusion of so much blood, as I think I may truly say, there was never anything so dearly bought as these western parts have bought the learning of the Greek and Latin tongues.

To come now to the particulars of the true liberty of a subject; that is to say, what are the things, which though commanded by the sovereign, he may nevertheless, without injustice, refuse to do; we are to consider what rights we pass away, when we make a commonwealth; or, which is all one, what liberty we deny ourselves, by owning all the actions, without exception, of the man, or assembly, we make our sovereign. For in the act of our "submission," consisteth both our "obligation," and our "liberty"; which must therefore be inferred by arguments taken from thence; there being no obligation on any man, which ariseth not from some act of his own; for all men equally, are by Nature free. And because such arguments must either be drawn from the express words, I "authorize all his actions," or from the intention of him that submitteth himself to his power, which intention is to be understood by the end for which he so submitteth; the obligation and liberty of the subject, is to be derived, either from those words, or others equivalent; or else from the end of the institution of sovereignty; namely, the peace of the subjects within themselves, and their defence against a common enemy.

First therefore, seeing sovereignty by institution, is by covenant of every one to every one; and sovereignty by acquisition, by covenants of the vanquished to the victor, or child to the parent; it is manifest, that every subject has liberty in all those things, the right whereof cannot by covenant be transferred. I have shown before in the 14th chapter, that covenants, not to defend a man's own body, are void. Therefore,

If the sovereign command a man, though justly condemned, to kill, wound, or maim himself; or not to resist those that assault him; or to abstain from the use of food, air, medicine, or any other thing, without which he cannot live; yet hath that man the liberty to disobey.

If a man be interrogated by the sovereign, or his authority, concerning a crime done by himself, he is not bound, without assurance of pardon, to confess it; because no man, as I have shown in the same chapter, can be obliged by covenant to accuse himself.

Again, the consent of a subject to sovereign power, is contained in these words, "I authorize, or take upon me, all his actions"; in which there is no restriction at all, of his own former natural liberty: for by allowing him to "kill me," I am not bound to kill myself when he commands me. It is one thing to say, "kill me, or my fellow, if you please"; another thing to say, "I will kill myself, or my fellow." It followeth, therefore, that

No man is bound by the words themselves, either to kill himself, or any other man; and consequently, that the obligation a man may sometimes have, upon the command of the sovereign to execute any dangerous or dishonourable office, dependeth not on the words of our submission; but on the intention, which is to be understood by the end thereof. When therefore our refusal to obey, frustrates the end for which the sovereignty was ordained; then there is no liberty to refuse: otherwise, there is.

Upon this ground, a man that is commanded as a soldier to fight against the enemy, though his sovereign have right enough to punish his refusal with death, may nevertheless in many cases refuse, without injustice; as when he substituteth a sufficient soldier in his place: for in this case he deserteth not the service of the commonwealth. And there is allowance to be made for natural timorousness; not only to women, of whom no such dangerous duty is expected, but also to men of feminine courage. When armies fight, there is on one side, or both, a running away; yet when they do it not out of treachery, but fear, they are not esteemed to do it unjustly, but dishonourably. For the same reason, to avoid battle, is not injustice, but cowardice. But he that enrolleth himself a soldier, or taketh impressed money, taketh away the excuse of a timorous nature; and is obliged, not only to go to the battle, but also not to run from it, without his captain's leave. And when the defence of the commonwealth requireth at once the help of all that are able to bear arms, every one is obliged; because otherwise the institution of the commonwealth, which they have not the purpose or courage to preserve, was in vain.

To resist the sword of the commonwealth in defence of another man, guilty or innocent, no man hath liberty; because such liberty takes away from the sovereign the means of protecting us; and is therefore destructive of the very essence of government. But in case a great many men together have already resisted the sovereign power unjustly, or committed some capital crime for which every one of them expecteth death, whether have they not the liberty then to join together, and assist and defend one another? Certainly they have; for they but defend their lives, which the guilty man may as well do as the innocent. There was indeed injustice in the first breach of their duty: their bearing of arms subsequent to it, though it be to maintain what they have done, is no new unjust act. And if it be only to defend their persons, it is not unjust at all. But the offer of pardon taketh from them to whom it is offered the plea of self-defence, and maketh their perseverance in assisting or defending the rest unlawful.

As for other liberties, they depend on the silence of the law. In cases where the sovereign has prescribed no rule, there the subject hath the liberty to do, or forbear, according to his own discretion. And therefore such liberty is in some places more, and in some less; and in some times more, in other times less, according as they that have the sovereignty shall think most convenient. As for example, there was a time when, in England, a man might enter into his own land, and dispossess such as wrongfully possessed it, by force. But in aftertimes, that liberty of forcible entry was taken away by a statute made by the king in parliament. And in some places of the world, men have the liberty of many wives; in other places such liberty is not allowed.

If a subject have a controversy with his sovereign, of debt, or of right of possession of lands or goods, or concerning any service required at his hands, or concerning any penalty, corporal or pecuniary, grounded on a precedent law; he hath the same liberty to sue for his right as if it were against a subject, and before such judges as are appointed by the sovereign. For seeing the sovereign demandeth by force of a former law, and not by virtue of his power; he declareth thereby that he requireth no more than shall appear to be due by that law. The suit therefore is not contrary to the will of the sovereign; and consequently the subject hath the liberty to demand the hearing of his cause; and sentence, according to that law. But if he demand, or take anything by pretence of his power there lieth, in that case, no action of law; for all that is done by him in virtue of his power, is done by the authority of every subject, and consequently he that brings an action against the sovereign, brings it against himself.

If a monarch, or sovereign assembly, grant a liberty to all or any of his subjects, which grant standing, he is disabled to provide for their safety, the grant is void, unless he directly renounce or transfer the sovereignty to another. For in that he might openly, if it had been his will, and in plain terms, have renounced or transferred it, and did not; it is to be understood it was not his will, but that the grant proceeded from ignorance of the repugnancy between such a liberty and the sovereign power, and therefore the sovereignty is still retained; and consequently all those powers, which are necessary to the exercising thereof; such as are the power of war and peace, of judicature, of appointing officers and councillors, of levying money, and the rest named in the 18th chapter.

The obligation of subjects to the sovereign is understood to last as long, and no longer, than the power lasteth by which he is able to protect them. For the right men have by nature to protect themselves, when none else can protect them, can by no covenant be relinquished. The sovereignty is the soul of the commonwealth, which once departed from the body, the members do no more receive their motion from it. The end of obedience is protection, which, wheresoever a man seeth it, either in his own or in another's sword, nature applieth his obedience to it, and his endeavour to maintain it. And though sovereignty, in the intention of them that make it, be immortal, yet is it in its own nature not only subject to violent death by foreign war, but also, through the ignorance and passions of men, it hath in it, from the very institution, many seeds of a natural mortality, by intestine discord.

If a subject be taken prisoner in war, or his person, or his means of life be within the guards of the enemy, and hath his life and corporal liberty given him on condition to be subject to the victor, he hath liberty to accept the condition; and having accepted it, is the subject of him that took him, because he had no other way to preserve himself. The case is the same, if he be detained on the same terms, in a foreign country. But if a man be held in prison, or bonds, or is not trusted with the liberty of his body, he cannot be understood to be bound by covenant to subjection; and therefore may, if he can, make his escape by any means whatsoever.

If a monarch shall relinquish the sovereignty, both for himself and his heirs, his subjects return to the absolute liberty of nature; because, though nature may declare who are his sons, and who are the nearest of his kin, yet it dependeth on his own will, as hath been said in the precedent chapter, who shall be his heir. If therefore he will have no heir, there is no sovereignty, nor subjection. The case is the same if he die without known kindred, and without declaration of his heir. For then there can no heir be known, and consequently no subjection be due.

If the sovereign banish his subject, during the banishment he is not subject. But he that is sent on a message, or hath leave to travel, is still subject; but it is, by contract between sovereigns, not by virtue of the covenant of subjection. For whosoever entereth into another's dominion, is subject to all the laws thereof, unless he have a privilege by the amity of the sovereigns, or by special license.

If a monarch subdued by war render himself subject to the victor, his subjects are delivered from their former obligation, and become obliged to the victor. But if he be held prisoner, or have not the liberty of his own body, he is not understood to have given away the right of sovereignty; and therefore his subjects are obliged to yield obedience to the magistrates formerly placed, governing not in their own name, but in his. For, his right remaining, the question is only of the administration; that is to say, of the magistrates and officers, which, if we have not means to name, he is supposed to approve those which he himself had formerly appointed.

Chapter XXII
Of Systems Subject, Political, and Private

Having spoken of the generation, form, and power of a commonwealth, I am in order to speak next of the parts thereof. And first of systems which resemble the similar parts, or muscles of a body natural. By "systems," I understand any numbers of men joined in one interest, or one business. Of which, some are "regular," and some "irregular." "Regular" are those where one man, or assembly of men, is constituted representative of the whole number. All other are "irregular."

Of regular some are "absolute" and "independent," subject to none but their own representative: such are only commonwealths; of which I have spoken already in the five last precedent chapters. Others are dependent; that is to say, subordinate to some sovereign power, to which every one, as also their representative is "subject."

Of systems subordinate, some are "political," and some "private." "Political," otherwise called "bodies politic," and "persons in law," are those which are made by authority from the sovereign power of the commonwealth. "Private," are those which are constituted by subjects amongst themselves, or by authority from a stranger. For no authority derived from foreign power within the dominion of another, is public there, but private.

And of private systems, some are "lawful": some "unlawful." "Lawful," are those which are allowed by the commonwealth: all other are "unlawful." "Irregular" systems are those which having no representative, consist only in concourse of people: which if not forbidden by the commonwealth, nor made on evil design, such as are conflux of people to markets, or shows, or any other harmless end, are lawful. But when the intention is evil, or (if the number be considerable) unknown, they are unlawful.

In bodies politic, the power of the representative is always limited: and that which prescribeth the limits thereof, is the power sovereign. For power unlimited is absolute sovereignty. And the sovereign, in every commonwealth is the absolute representative of all the subjects; and therefore no other can be representative of any part of them, but so far forth as he shall give leave. And to give leave to a body politic of subjects, to have an absolute representative to all intents and purposes, were to abandon the government of so much of the commonwealth, and to divide the dominion contrary to their peace and defence; which the sovereign cannot be understood to do by any grant that does not plainly and directly discharge them of their subjection. For consequences of words, are not the signs of his will, when other consequences are signs of the contrary; but rather signs of error and misreckoning; to which all mankind is too prone.

The bounds of that power, which is given to the representative of a body politic, are to be taken notice of from two things. One is their writ, or letters from the sovereign: the other is the law of the commonwealth.

For though in the institution or acquisition of a commonwealth, which is independent, there needs no writing, because the power of the representative has there no other bounds, but such as are set out by the unwritten law of Nature; yet in subordinate bodies, there are such diversities of limitation necessary concerning their businesses, times, and places, as can neither be remembered without letters, nor taken notice of, unless such letters be patent, that they may be read to them, and withal sealed, or testified, with the seals, or other permanent signs of the authority sovereign.

And because such limitation is not always easy, or perhaps possible to be described in writing; the ordinary laws, common to all subjects, must determine what the representative may lawfully do in all cases where the letters themselves are silent. And therefore,

In a body politic, if the representative be one man, whatsoever he does in the person of the body which is not warranted in his letters, nor by the laws, is his own act, and not the act of the body, nor of any other member thereof besides himself; because further than his letters, or the law's limit, he representeth no man's person, but his own. But what he does according to these is the act of every one: for the act of the sovereign every one is author, because he is their representative unlimited; and the act him that recedes not from the letters of the sovereign, is the act of the sovereign, and therefore every member of the body is author of it.

But if the representative be an assembly, whatsoever that assembly shall decree, not warranted by their letters or the laws, is the act of the assembly or body politic, and the act of every one by whose vote the decree was made; but not the act of any man that being present voted to the contrary; nor of any man absent, unless he voted it by procuration. It is the act of the assembly, because voted by the major part; and if it be a crime, the assembly may be punished, as far forth as it is capable, as by dissolution or forfeiture of their letters (which is to such artificial and fictitious bodies capital), or, if the assembly have a common stock, wherein none of the innocent members have propriety, by pecuniary mulct. For from corporal penalties Nature hath exempted all bodies politic. But they that gave not their vote are therefore innocent, because the assembly cannot represent any man in

things unwarranted by their letters, and consequently are not involved in their votes.

If the person of the body politic, being in one man, borrow money of a stranger, that is, of one that is not of the same body (for no letters need limit borrowing, seeing it is left to men's own inclinations to limit lending), the debt is the representative's. For if he should have authority from his letters to make the members pay what he borroweth, he should have by consequence the sovereignty of them; and therefore the grant were either void, as proceeding from error, commonly incident to human nature, and an insufficient sign of the will of the granter; or if it be avowed by him, then is the representer sovereign, and falleth not under the present question, which is only of bodies subordinate. No member therefore is obliged to pay the debt so borrowed, but the representative himself; because he that lendeth it, being a stranger to the letters and to the qualification of the body, understandeth those only for his debtors that are engaged; and seeing the representer can engage himself and none else, has him only for debtor, who must therefore pay him out of the common stock, if there be any, or, if there be none, out of his own estate.

If he come into debt by contract or mulct, the case is the same.

But when the representative is an assembly, and the debt to a stranger, all they, and only they, are responsible for the debt that gave their votes to the borrowing of it, or to the contract that made it due, or to the fact for which the mulct was imposed; because every one in voting did engage himself for the payment; for he that is author of the borrowing is obliged to the payment, even of the whole debt, though when paid by any one, he be discharged.

But if the debt be to one of the assembly, the assembly only is obliged to the payment out of their common stock, if they have any: for having liberty of vote, if he vote the money shall be borrowed, he votes it shall be paid; if he vote it shall not be borrowed, or be absent, yet because in lending he voteth the borrowing, he contradicteth his former vote, and is obliged by the latter, and becomes both borrower and lender, and consequently cannot demand payment from any particular man, but from the common treasury only; which failing he hath no remedy nor complaint, but against himself, that being privy to the acts of the assembly, and to their means to pay, and not being enforced, did nevertheless through his own folly lend his money.

It is manifest by this, that in bodies politic subordinate, and subject to a sovereign power, it is sometimes not only lawful, but expedient, for a particular man to make open protestation against the decrees of the representative assembly, and cause their dissent to be registered, or to take witness of it; because otherwise they may be obliged to pay debts contracted, and be responsible for crimes committed by other men. But in a sovereign assembly, that liberty is taken away, both because he that protesteth there denies their sovereignty; and also because whatsoever is commanded by the sovereign power, is as to the subject, though not so always in the sight of God, justified by the command: for of such command every subject is the author.

The variety of bodies politic, is almost infinite: for they are not only distinguished by the several affairs, for which they are constituted, wherein there is an unspeakable diversity; but also by the times, places, and numbers, subject to many limitations. And as to their affairs, some are ordained for government; as first, the government of a province, may be committed to an assembly of men, wherein all resolutions shall depend on the votes of the major part; and then this assembly is a body politic, and their power limited by commission. This word *province* signifies a charge, or care of business, which he whose business it is, committeth to another man, to be administered for, and under him; and therefore when in one commonwealth there be divers countries, that have their laws distinct one from another, or are far distant in place, the administration of the government being committed to divers persons, those countries where the sovereign is not resident, but governs by commission, are called provinces. But of the government of a province, by an assembly residing in the province itself, there be few examples. The Romans, who had the sovereignty of many provinces, yet governed them always by presidents and prætors; and not by assemblies, as they governed the city of Rome, and territories adjacent. In like manner, when there were colonies sent from England, to plant Virginia and Sommer Islands, though the government of them here were committed to assemblies in London, yet did those assemblies never commit the government under them to any assembly there, but did to each plantation send one governor. For though every man, where he can be present by nature, desires to participate of government; yet where they cannot be present, they are by nature also inclined to commit the government of their common interest rather to a monarchical than a popular form of government: which is also evident in those men that have great private estates; who when they are unwilling to take the pains of administering the business that belongs to them, choose rather to trust one servant, than an assembly either of their friends or servants. But howsoever it be in fact, yet we may suppose the government of a province or colony committed to an assembly: and when it is, that which in this place I have to say, is this; that whatsoever debt is by that assembly contracted; or whatsoever unlawful act is decreed, is the act only of those that assented, and not of any that dissented, or were absent, for the reasons before alleged. Also that an assembly residing out of the bounds of that colony whereof they have the government, cannot execute any power over the persons or goods of any of the colony, to seize on them for debt, or other duty, in any place without the colony itself, as having no jurisdiction, nor authority elsewhere, but are left to the remedy which the law of the place alloweth them. And though the assembly have right to impose mulct upon any of their members that shall break the laws they make; yet out of the colony itself, they have no right to execute the same. And that which is said here of the rights of an assembly, for the government of a province or a colony, is applicable also to an assembly for the government of a town, an university, or a college, or a church, or for any other government over the persons of men.

And generally, in all bodies politic, if any particular member conceive himself injured by the body itself, the cognizance of his cause belongeth to the sovereign, and those the sovereign hath ordained for judges in such causes, or shall ordain for that particular cause; and not to the body itself. For the whole body is in this case his fellow-subject, which in a sovereign assembly is otherwise: for there, if the sovereign be not judge, though in his own cause, there can be no judge at all.

In a body politic, for the well ordering of foreign traffic, the most commodious representative is an assembly of all the members; that is to say, such a one, as every one that adventureth his money, may be present at all the deliberations and resolutions of the body, if they will themselves. For proof whereof, we are to consider the end, for which men that are merchants, and may buy and sell, export and import their merchandize, according to their own discretions, do nevertheless bind themselves up in one corporation. It is true, there be few merchants, that with the merchandize they buy at home, can freight a ship, to export it; or with that they buy abroad, to bring it home; and have therefore need to join together in one society; where every man may either participate of the gain, according to the proportion of his adventure; or take his own, and sell what he transports, or imports, at such prices as he thinks fit. But this is no body politic, there being no common representative to oblige them to any other law than that which is common to all other subjects. The end of their incorporating, is to make their gain the greater; which is done two ways; by sole buying and sole selling, both at home and abroad. So that to grant to a company of merchants to be a corporation, or body politic, is to grant them a double monopoly, whereof one is to be sole buyers; another to be sole sellers. For when there is a company incorporate for any particular foreign country, they only export the commodities vendible in that country; which is sole buying at home and sole selling abroad. For at home there is but one buyer and abroad but one that selleth: both which is gainful to the merchant, because thereby they buy at home at lower and sell abroad at higher rates: and abroad there is but one buyer of foreign merchandize and but one that sells them at home; both which again are gainful to the adventurers.

Of this double monopoly one part is disadvantageous to the people at home, the other to foreigners. For at home by their sole exportation they set what price they please on the husbandry and handiworks of the people; and by the sole importation, what price they please on all foreign commodities the people have need of; both which are ill for the people. On the contrary, by the sole selling of the native commodities abroad, and sole buying the foreign commodities upon the place, they raise the price of those, and abate the price of these, to the disadvantage of the foreigner; for where but one selleth, the merchandize is the dearer; and where but one buyeth, the cheaper. Such corporations therefore are no other than monopolies; though they would be very profitable for a commonwealth, if being bound up into one body in foreign markets they were at liberty at home, every man to buy and sell at what price he could.

The end of these bodies of merchants being not a common benefit to the whole body, which have in this case no common stock, but what is deducted out of the particular adventures, for building, buying, vict-ualling, and manning of ships, but the particular gain of every adventurer, it is reason that every one be acquainted with the employment of his own; that is, that every one be of the assembly, that shall have the power to order the same; and be acquainted with their accounts. And therefore the representative of such a body must be an assembly, where every member of the body may be present at the consultations, if he will.

If a body politic of merchants contract a debt to a stranger by the act of their representative assembly, every member is liable by himself for the whole. For a stranger can take no notice of their private laws, but considereth them as so many particular men, obliged every one to the whole payment, till payment made by one dischargeth all the rest: but if the debt be to one of the company, the creditor is debtor for the whole to himself, and cannot therefore demand his debt, but only from the common stock, if there be any.

If the commonwealth impose a tax upon the body, it is understood to be laid upon every member proportionably to his particular adventure in the company. For there is in this case no other common stock, but what is made of their particular adventures.

If a mulct be laid upon the body for some unlawful act, they only are liable by whose votes the act was decreed, or by whose assistance it was executed; for in none of the rest is there any other crime but being of the body; which if a crime, because the body was ordained by the authority of the commonwealth, is not his.

If one of the members be indebted to the body, he may be sued by the body; but his goods cannot be taken, nor his person imprisoned by the authority of the body; but only by authority of the commonwealth: for if they can do it by their own authority, they can by their own authority give judgment that the debt is due; which is as much as to be judge in their own cause.

These bodies made for the government of men, or of traffic, be either perpetual, or for a time prescribed by writing. But there be bodies also whose times are limited, and that only by the nature of their business. For example, if a sovereign monarch, or a sovereign assembly, shall think fit to give command to the towns, and other several parts of their territory, to send to him their deputies, to inform him of the condition and necessities of the subjects, or to advise with him for the making of good laws, or for any other cause, as with one person representing the whole country, such deputies, having a place and time of meeting assigned them, are there, and at that time, a body politic, representing every subject of that dominion; but it is only for such matters as shall be propounded unto them by that man, or assembly, that by the sovereign authority sent for them; and when it shall be declared that nothing more shall be propounded, nor debated by them, the body is dissolved. For if they were the absolute representatives of the people, then were it the sovereign assembly; and so there would be two sovereign assemblies, or two sovereigns, over the same people; which cannot consist with their peace. And therefore where there is once a sovereignty, there can be no absolute representation of the people, but by it. And for the limits of how far such a body shall represent the whole people, they are set forth in the writing by which they were sent for. For the people cannot choose their deputies to other intent than is in the writing directed to them from their sovereign expressed.

Private bodies regular and lawful, are those that are constituted without letters, or other written authority, saving the laws common to all other subjects. And because they be united in one person representative, they are held for regular; such as are all families, in which the father or master ordereth the whole family. For he obligeth his children and servants, as far as the law permitteth, though not further, because none of them are bound to obedience in those actions, which the law hath forbidden to be done. In all other actions, during the time they are under domestic government, they are subject to their fathers and masters, as to their immediate sovereigns. For the father and master, being before the institution of commonwealth, absolute sovereigns in their own families, they lose afterward no more of their authority than the law of the commonwealth taketh from them.

Private bodies regular, but unlawful, are those that unite themselves into one person representative, without any public authority at all: such as are the corporations of beggars, thieves, and gipsies, the better to order their trade of begging and stealing; and the corporations of men, that by authority from any foreign person, unite themselves in another's dominion, for the easier propagation of doctrines, and for making a party against the power of the commonwealth.

Irregular systems, in their nature but leagues, or sometimes mere concourse of people, without union to any particular design, not by obligation of one to another, but proceeding only from a similitude of wills and inclinations, become lawful or unlawful according to the lawfulness or unlawfulness of every particular man's design therein: and his design is to be understood by the occasion.

The leagues of subjects, because leagues are commonly made for mutual defence, are in a commonwealth, which is no more than a league of all the subjects together, for the most part unnecessary, and savour of unlawful design; and are for that cause unlawful, and go commonly by the name of factions, or conspiracies. For a league being a connection of men by covenants, if there be no power given to any one man or assembly, as in the condition of mere nature, to compel them to performance, is so long only valid, as there ariseth no just cause of distrust: and therefore leagues between commonwealths, over whom there is no human power established, to keep them all in awe, are not only lawful, but also profitable for the time they last. But leagues of the subjects of one and the same commonwealth, where every one may obtain his right by means of the sovereign power, are unnecessary to the maintaining of peace and justice, and, in case the design of them be evil or unknown to the commonwealth, unlawful. For all uniting of strength by private men, is, if for evil intent, unjust; if for intent unknown, dangerous to the public, and unjustly concealed.

If the sovereign power be in a great assembly, and a number of men, part of the assembly, without authority consult apart, to contrive the guidance of the rest; this is a faction, or conspiracy unlawful, as being a fraudulent seducing of the assembly for their particular interest. But if he, whose private interest is to be debated and judged in the assembly, make as many friends as he can; in him it is no injustice; because in this case he is no part of the assembly. And though he hire such friends with money, unless there be an express law against it, yet it is not injustice. For sometimes, as men's manners are, justice cannot be had without money; and every man may think his own cause just, till it be heard and judged.

In all commonwealths, if a private man entertain more servants than the government of his estate, and lawful employment he has for them requires, it is faction, and unlawful. For having the protection of the commonwealth, he needeth not the defence of private force. And whereas in nations not thoroughly civilized, several numerous families have lived in continual hostility, and invaded one another with private force; yet it is evident enough that they have done unjustly, or else they had no commonwealth.

And as factions for kindred, so also factions for government of religion, as of Papists, Protestants, &c., or of state, as patricians and plebeians of old time in Rome, and of aristocraticals and democraticals of old time in Greece, are unjust, as being contrary to the peace and safety of the people, and a taking of the sword out of the hand of the sovereign.

Concourse of people is an irregular system, the lawfulness or unlawfulness whereof dependeth on the occasion, and on the number of them that are assembled. If the occasion be lawful and manifest, the concourse is lawful, as the usual meeting of men at church, or at a public show, in usual numbers; for if the numbers be extraordinarily great, the occasion is not evident; and consequently he that cannot render a particular and good account of his being amongst them, is to be judged conscious of an unlawful and tumultuous design. It may be lawful for a thousand men to join to a petition to be delivered to a judge or magistrate, yet if a thousand men come to present it, it is a tumultuous assembly, because there needs but one or two for that purpose. But in such cases as these, it is not a set number that makes the assembly unlawful, but such a number as the present officers are not able to suppress and bring to justice.

When an unusual number of men assemble against a man whom they accuse, the assembly is an unlawful tumult; because they may deliver their accusation to the magistrate by a few, or by one man. Such was the case of St. Paul at Ephesus, where Demetrius, and a great number of other men brought two of Paul's companions before the magistrate, saying with one voice "Great is Diana of the Ephesians," which was their way of demanding justice against them for teaching the people such doctrine as was against their religion and trade. The occasion here, considering the laws of that people, was just, yet was their assembly judged unlawful, and the magistrate reprehended them for it in these words (Acts xix. 38–40): "If Demetrias and the other workmen can accuse any man of anything, there be pleas and deputies, let them accuse one another. And if you have any other thing to demand, your case may be judged in an assembly lawfully called. For we are in danger to be accused for this day's sedition; because there is no cause by which any man can render any reason of this concourse of people." Where he calleth an assembly whereof men can give no just account, a sedition, and

such as they could not answer for. And this is all I shall say concerning "systems" and assemblies of people, which may be compared, as I said, to the similar parts of man's body, such as be lawful, to the muscles; such as are unlawful, to wens, boils, and apostems, engendered by the unnatural conflux of evil humours.

Chapter XXIII
Of the Public Ministers of Sovereign Power

In the last chapter I have spoken of the similar parts of a commonwealth: in this I shall speak of the parts organical, which are public ministers.

A "public minister" is he that by the sovereign, whether a monarch or an assembly, is employed in any affairs, with authority to represent in that employment the person of the commonwealth. And whereas every man or assembly that hath sovereignty, representeth two persons, or, as the more common phrase is, has two capacities, one natural and another politic; as a monarch hath the person not only of the commonwealth, but also of a man, and a sovereign assembly hath the person not only of the commonwealth, but also of the assembly: they that be servants to them in their natural capacity are not public ministers; but those only that serve them in the administration of the public business. And therefore neither ushers, nor sergeants, nor other officers that wait on the assembly for no other purpose but for the commodity of the men assembled in an aristocracy, or democracy; nor stewards, chamberlains, cofferers, or any other officers of the household of a monarch, are public ministers in a monarchy.

Of public ministers, some have charge committed to them of a general administration, either of the whole dominion, or of a part thereof. Of the whole, as to a protector, or regent, may be committed by the predecessor of an infant king, during his minority, the whole administration of his kingdom. In which case every subject is so far obliged to obedience, as the ordinances he shall make and the commands he shall give be in the king's name, and not inconsistent with his sovereign power. Of a part, or province; as when either a monarch, or a sovereign assembly, shall give the general charge thereof to a governor, lieutenant, prefect, or viceroy; and in this case also, every one of that province is obliged to all he shall do in the name of the sovereign, and that not incompatible with the sovereign's right. For such protectors, viceroys, and governors, have no other right, but what depends on the sovereign's will; and no commission that can be given them, can be interpreted for a declaration of the will to transfer the sovereignty, without express and perspicuous words to that purpose. And this kind of public ministers resembleth the nerves and tendons that move the several limbs of a body natural.

Others have special administration; that is to say, charges of some special business, either at home or abroad: as at home, first, for the economy of a commonwealth, they that have authority concerning the "treasure," as tributes, impositions, rents, fines, or whatsoever public revenue, to collect, receive, issue, or take the accounts thereof, are public ministers: ministers, because they serve the person representative, and can do nothing against his command, nor without his authority: public, because they serve him in his political capacity.

Secondly, they that have authority concerning the "militia"; to have the custody of arms, forts, ports; to levy, pay, or conduct soldiers; or to provide for any necessary thing for the use of war, either by land or sea, are public ministers. But a soldier without command, though he fight for the commonwealth, does not therefore represent the person of it; because there is none to represent it to. For every one that hath command, represents it to them only whom he commandeth.

They also that have authority to teach, or to enable others to teach the people their duty to the sovereign power, and instruct them in the knowledge of what is just and unjust, thereby to render them more apt to live in godliness, and in peace amongst themselves, and resist the public enemy, are public ministers: ministers in that they do it not by their own authority, but by another's; and public, because they do it, or should do it, by no authority but that of the sovereign. The monarch, or the sovereign assembly only hath immediate authority from God, to teach and instruct the people; and no man but the sovereign receiveth his power *Dei gratiâ* simply; that is to say, from the favour of none but God: all other receive theirs from the favour and providence of God, and their sovereigns; as in a monarchy *Dei gratiâ et regis;* or *Dei providentiâ et voluntate regis.*

They also to whom jurisdiction is given, are public ministers. For in their seats of justice they represent the person of the sovereign; and their sentence, is his sentence: for, as hath been before declared, all judicature is essentially annexed to the sovereignty; and therefore all other judges are but ministers of him or them that have the sovereign power. And as controversies are of two sorts, namely of "fact" and of "law"; so are judgments, some of fact, some of law: and consequently in the same controversy, there may be two judges, one of fact, another of law.

And in both these controversies, there may arise a controversy between the party judged and the judge; which because they be both subjects to the sovereign, ought in equity to be judged by men agreed on by consent of both; for no man can be judge in his own cause. But the sovereign is already agreed on for judge by them both, and is therefore either to hear the cause and determine it himself, or appoint for judge such as they shall both agree on. And this agreement is then understood to be made between them divers ways; as first, if the defendant be allowed to except against such of his judges whose interest maketh him suspect them (for as to the complainant, he hath already chosen his own judge), those which he excepteth not against are judges he himself agrees on. Secondly, if he appeal to any other judge, he can appeal no further; for his appeal is his choice. Thirdly, if he appeal to the sovereign himself, and he by himself, or by delegates which the parties shall agree on, give sentence, that sentence is final; for the defendant is judged by his own judges, that is to say, by himself.

These properties of just and rational judicature considered, I cannot forbear to observe the excellent constitution of the courts of justice established both for Common and also for Public Pleas in England. By Common Pleas, I mean those where both the complainant and defendant are subject; and by public, which are also called Pleas of the Crown, those where the complainant is the sovereign. For whereas there were two orders of men, whereof one was Lords, the other Commons; the Lords had this privilege, to have for judges in all capital crimes none but Lords; and of them as many as would be present; which being ever acknowledged as a privilege of favour, their judges were none but such as they had themselves desired. And in all controversies, every subject (as also in civil controversies the Lords) had for judges men of the country where the matter in controversy lay; against which he might make his exceptions, till at last twelve men without exception being agreed on, they were judged by those twelve. So that having his own judges, there could be nothing alleged by the party why the sentence should not be final. These public persons, with authority from the sovereign power, either to instruct or judge the people, are such members of the commonwealth as may fitly be compared to the organs of voice in a body natural.

Public ministers are also all those that have authority from the sovereign to procure the execution of judgments given; to publish the sovereign's commands; to suppress tumults; to apprehend and imprison malefactors; and other acts tending to the conservation of the peace. For every act they do by such authority is the act of the commonwealth; and their service, answerable to that of the hands, in a body natural.

Public ministers abroad are those that represent the person of their own sovereign to foreign states. Such are ambassadors, messengers, agents, and heralds, sent by public authority and on public business.

But such as are sent by authority only of some private party of a troubled state, though they be received, are neither public nor private ministers of the commonwealth; because none of their actions have the commonwealth for author. Likewise, an ambassador sent from a prince to congratulate, condole, or to assist at a solemnity; though the authority be public, yet because the business is private, and belonging to him in his natural capacity, is a private person. Also if a man be sent into another country secretly to explore their counsels and strength, though both the authority and the business be public, yet because there is none to take notice of any person in him but his own, he is but a private minister; but yet a minister of the commonwealth, and may be compared to an eye in the body natural. And those that are appointed to receive the petitions or other informations of the people, and are as it were the public ear, are public ministers, and represent their sovereign in that office.

Neither a councillor, nor a council of state, if we consider it with no authority of judicature or command, but only of giving advice to the sovereign when it is required, or of offering it when it is not required, is a public person. For the advice is addressed to the sovereign only, whose person cannot in his own presence be represented to him by another. But a body of councillors are never without some other authority, either of judicature, or of immediate administration: as in a monarchy, they represent the monarch in delivering his commands to the public ministers: in a democracy, the council or senate propounds the result of their deliberations to the people, as a council; but when they appoint judges, or hear causes, or

give audience to ambassadors, it is in the quality of a minister of the people: and in an aristocracy, the council of state is the sovereign assembly itself; and gives counsel to none but themselves.

Chapter XXIV
*Of the Nutrition and Procreation
of a Commonwealth*

The "nutrition" of a commonwealth consisteth in the "plenty" and "distribution" of "materials" conducing to life; in "concoction," or "preparation"; and, when concocted, in the "conveyance" of it, by convenient conduits, to the public use.

As for the plenty of matter, it is a thing limited by Nature to those commodities which from the two breasts of our common mother, land and sea, God usually either freely giveth, or for labour selleth to mankind.

For the matter of this nutriment, consisting in animals, vegetals, and minerals, God hath freely laid them before us, in or near to the face of the earth; so as there needeth no more but the labour and industry of receiving them. Insomuch as plenty dependeth, next to God's favour, merely on the labour and industry of men.

This matter, commonly called commodities, is partly "native," and partly "foreign"; "native," that which is to be had within the territory of the commonwealth; "foreign," that which is imported from without. And because there is no territory under the dominion of one commonwealth, except it be of very vast extent, that produceth all things needful for the maintenance and motion of the whole body; and few that produce not something more than necessary; the superfluous commodities to be had within, become no more superfluous, but supply these wants at home, by importation of that which may be had abroad, either by exchange, or by just war, or by labour. For a man's labour also is a commodity exchangeable for benefit, as well as any other thing; and there have been commonwealths that having no more territory than hath served them for habitation, have nevertheless not only maintained, but also increased their power, partly by the labour of trading from one place to another, and partly by selling the manufactures whereof the materials were brought in from other places.

The distribution of the materials of this nourishment, is the constitution of "mine," and "thine," and "his"; that is to say, in one word "propriety"; and belongeth in all kinds of commonwealth to the sovereign power. For where there is no commonwealth there is, as hath been already shown, a perpetual war of every man against his neighbour; and therefore everything is his that getteth it, and keepeth it by force; which is neither "propriety" nor "community"; but "uncertainty." Which is so evident, that even Cicero, a passionate defender of liberty, in a public pleading, attributeth all propriety to the law civil. "Let the civil law," saith he, "be once abandoned, or but negligently guarded, not to say oppressed, and there is nothing, that any man can be sure to receive from his ancestor, or leave to his children." And again, "Take away the civil law, and no man knows what is his own, and what another man's." Seeing therefore the introduction of "propriety" is an effect of commonwealth, which can do nothing but by the person that represents it, it is the act only of the sovereign; and consisteth in the laws, which none can make that have not the sovereign power. And this they well knew of old, who called that Νόμος, that is to say, "distribution," which we call law; and defined justice, by "distributing" to every man "his own."

In this distribution, the first law is for division of the land itself: wherein the sovereign assigneth to every man a portion, according as he, and not according as any subject, or any number of them, shall judge agreeable to equity, and the common good. The children of Israel were a commonwealth in the wilderness; but wanted the commodities of the earth, till they were masters of the Land of Promise; which afterwards was divided amongst them, not by their own discretion, but by the discretion of Eleazar the Priest and Joshua their General, who, when there were twelve tribes, making them thirteen by subdivision of the tribe of Joseph, made nevertheless but twelve portions of the land; and ordained for the tribe of Levi no land; but assigned them the tenth part of the whole fruits; which division was therefore arbitrary. And though a people coming into possession of a land by war, do not always exterminate the ancient inhabitants, as did the Jews, but leave to many, or most, or all of them their estates; yet it is manifest they hold them afterwards, as of the victors' distribution; as the people of England held all theirs of William the Conqueror.

From whence we may collect, that the propriety which a subject hath in his lands, consisteth in a right to exclude all other subjects from the use of them; and not to exclude their sovereign, be it an assembly or a monarch. For seeing the sovereign, that is to say, the commonwealth, whose person he representeth, is understood to do nothing but in order to the common peace and security, this distribution of lands is to be understood as done in order to the same: and consequently, whatsoever distribution he shall make in prejudice thereof, is contrary to the will of every subject that committed his peace and safety to his discretion and conscience; and therefore by the will of every one of them, it is to be reputed void. It is true that a sovereign monarch, or the greater part of a sovereign assembly, may ordain the doing of many things in pursuit of their passions, contrary to their own consciences, which is a breach of trust and of the law of Nature; but this is not enough to authorize any subject, either to make war upon, or so much as to accuse of injustice, or any way to speak evil of their sovereign; because they have authorized all his actions, and in bestowing the sovereign power, made them their own. But in what cases the commands of sovereigns are contrary to equity and the law of Nature, is to be considered hereafter in another place.

In the distribution of land, the commonwealth itself, may be conceived to have a portion, and possess and improve the same by their representative; and that such portion may be made sufficient to sustain the whole expense to the common peace and defence necessarily required. Which were very true, if there could be any representative conceived free from human passions and infirmities. But the nature of men being as it is, the setting forth of public land, or of any certain revenue for the commonwealth, is in vain; and tendeth to the dissolution of government, and to the condition of mere nature and war, as soon as ever the sovereign power falleth into the hands of a monarch, or of an assembly, that are either too negligent of money, or too hazardous in engaging the public stock into long or costly war. Commonwealths can endure no diet: for seeing their expense is not limited by their own appetite, but by external accidents and the appetites of their neighbours, the public riches cannot be limited by other limits than those which the emergent occasions shall require. And whereas in England, there were by the Conqueror divers lands reserved to his own use, besides forests and chases, either for his recreation, or preservation of woods, and divers services reserved on the land he gave his subjects; yet it seems they were not reserved for his maintenance in his public, but in his natural capacity.

For he and his successors did for all that lay arbitrary taxes on all subjects' land, when they judged it necessary. Or if those public lands and services were ordained as a sufficient maintenance of the commonwealth, it was contrary to the scope of the institution; being, as it appeared by those ensuing taxes, insufficient, and, as it appears by the late small revenue of the crown, subject to alienation and diminution. It is therefore in vain to assign a portion to the commonwealth; which may sell, or give it away; and does sell and give it away, when it is done by their representative.

As the distribution of lands at home; so also to assign in what places, and for what commodities, the subject shall traffic abroad, belongeth to the sovereign. For if it did belong to private persons to use their own discretion therein, some of them would be drawn for gain, both to furnish the enemy with means to hurt the commonwealth and hurt it themselves, by importing such things, as pleasing men's appetites, be nevertheless noxious, or at least unprofitable to them. And therefore it belongeth to the commonwealth, that is, to the sovereign only, to approve or disapprove both of the places and matter of foreign traffic.

Further, seeing it is not enough to the sustentation of a commonwealth, that every man have a propriety in a portion of land, or in some few commodities, or a natural property in some useful art, and there is no art in the world, but is necessary either for the being or well-being almost of every particular man; it is necessary that men distribute that which they can spare, and transfer their propriety therein, mutually one to another by exchange and mutual contract. And therefore it belongeth to the commonwealth, that is to say, to the sovereign, to appoint in what manner all kinds of contract between subjects, as buying, selling, exchanging, borrowing, lending, letting and taking to hire, are to be made; and by what words and signs they shall be understood for valid. And for the matter and distribution of the nourishment, to the several members of the commonwealth, thus much, considering the model of the whole work, is sufficient.

By concoction I understand the reducing of all commodities which are not presently consumed, but reserved for nourishment in time to come, to something of equal value, and withal so portable as not to hinder the motion of men from place to place; to the end a man may have in what place soever such nourishment as the place affordeth. And this is nothing else but gold, and silver, and money. For gold and silver, being, as it happens, almost in all countries of the world highly valued, is a commodious measure of the value of all things else between nations; and money, of what matter soever coined by the sovereign of a commonwealth, is a sufficient measure of the value of all things else between the subjects of that commonwealth. By the means of which measures all commodities, movable and immovable, are made to accompany a man to all places of his resort, within and without the place of his ordinary residence; and the same passeth from man to man within the commonwealth; and goes round about, nourishing as it passeth every part thereof: insomuch as this concoction is as it were the sanguification of the commonwealth; for natural blood is in like manner made of the fruits of the earth, and circulating, nourisheth by the way every member of the body of man.

And because silver and gold have their value from the matter itself, they have first this privilege, that the value of them cannot be altered by the power of one, nor of a few commonwealths, as being a common measure of the commodities of all places. But base money may easily be enhanced or abased. Secondly, they have the privilege to make commonwealths move, and stretch out their arms, when need is, into foreign countries, and supply, not only private subjects that travel, but also whole armies with provision. But that coin, which is not considerable for the matter, but for the stamp of the place, being unable to endure change of air, hath its effect at home only; where also it is subject to the change of laws, and thereby to have the value diminished, to the prejudice many times of those that have it.

The conduits and ways by which it is conveyed to the public use, are of two sorts: one, that conveyeth it to the public coffers; the other, that issueth the same out again for public payments. Of the first sort, are collectors, receivers, and treasurers; of the second are the treasurers again, and the officers appointed for payment of several public or private ministers. And in this also, the artificial man maintains his resemblance with the natural; whose veins receiving the blood from the several parts of the body, carry it to the heart, where being made vital, the heart by the arteries sends it out again, to enliven, and enable for motion all the members of the same.

The procreation or children of a commonwealth are those we call "plantations," or "colonies," which are numbers of men sent out from the commonwealth, under a conductor or governor, to inhabit a foreign country, either formerly void of inhabitants, or made void then by war. And when a colony is settled, they are either a commonwealth of themselves, discharged of their subjection to their sovereign that sent them, as hath been done by many commonwealths of ancient time, in which case the commonwealth from which they went was called their metropolis or mother, and requires no more of them, than fathers require of the children whom they emancipate and make free from their domestic government, which is honour and friendship; or else they remain united to their metropolis, as were the colonies of the people of Rome; and then they are no commonwealths themselves, but provinces, and parts of the commonwealth that sent them. So that the right of colonies, saving honour and league with their metropolis, dependeth wholly on their license or letters, by which their sovereign authorized them to plant.

. . .

Chapter XXIX
*Of Those Things that Weaken, or Tend
to the Dissolution of a Commonwealth*

Though nothing can be immortal which mortals make, yet if men had the use of reason they pretend to, their commonwealths might be secured, at least from perishing by internal diseases. For by the nature of their institution, they are designed to live as long as mankind, or as the laws of Nature or as justice itself, which gives them life. Therefore when they come to be dissolved, not by external violence, but intestine disorder, the fault is not in men, as they are the "matter"; but as they are the "makers," and orderers of them. For men, as they become at last weary of irregular jostling and hewing one another, and desire with all their hearts to conform themselves into one firm and lasting edifice: so for want, both of the art of making fit laws, to square their actions by, and also of humility and patience, to suffer the rude and cumbersome points of their present greatness to be taken off, they cannot without the help of a very able architect, be compiled into any other than a crazy building, such as hardly lasting out their own time, must assuredly fall upon the heads of their posterity.

Amongst the "infirmities" therefore of a commonwealth, I will reckon in the first place, those that arise from an imperfect institution, and resemble the dis-

eases of a natural body, which proceed from a defectuous procreation.

Of which this is one, "that a man to obtain a kingdom, is sometimes content with less power, than to the peace and defence of the commonwealth is necessarily required." From whence it cometh to pass, that when the exercise of the power laid by is for the public safety to be resumed, it hath the resemblance of an unjust act; which disposeth great numbers of men, when occasion is presented, to rebel; in the same manner as the bodies of children, gotten by diseased parents, are subject either to untimely death, or to purge the ill quality, derived from their vicious conception, by breaking out into boils and scabs. And when kings deny themselves some such necessary power, it is not always, though sometimes, out of ignorance of what is necessary to the office they undertake; but many times out of a hope to recover the same again at their pleasure. Wherein they reason not well; because such as will hold them to their promises, shall be maintained against them by foreign commonwealths; who in order to the good of their own subjects let slip few occasions to "weaken" the estate of their neighbours. So was Thomas Becket, Archbishop of Canterbury, supported against Henry the Second, by the Pope; the subjection of ecclesiastics to the commonwealth, having been dispensed with by William the Conqueror at his reception, when he took an oath not to infringe the liberty of the Church. And so were the barons, whose power was by William Rufus, to have their help in transferring the succession from his elder brother to himself, increased to a degree inconsistent with the sovereign power, maintained in their rebellion against King John, by the French.

Nor does this happen in monarchy only. For whereas the style of the ancient Roman commonwealth was "the senate and people of Rome," neither senate nor people pretended to the whole power; which first caused the seditions of Tiberius Gracchus, Caius Gracchus, Lucius Saturninus, and others; and afterwards the wars between the senate and the people, under Marius and Sylla; and again under Pompey and Cæsar, to the extinction of their democracy, and the setting up of monarchy.

The people of Athens bound themselves but from one only action; which was, that no man on pain of death should propound the renewing of the war for the island of Salamis; and yet thereby, if Solon had not caused to be given out he was mad, and afterwards in gesture and habit of a madman, and in verse, propounded it to the people that flocked about him, they had had an enemy perpetually in readiness, even at the gates of their city; such damage or shifts are all commonwealths forced to, that have their power never so little limited.

In the second place, I observe the "diseases" of a commonwealth, that proceed from the poison of seditious doctrines, whereof one is, "That every private man is judge of good and evil actions." This is true in the condition of mere nature, where there are no civil laws; and also under civil government, in such cases as are not determined by the law. But otherwise, it is manifest, that the measure of good and evil actions, is the civil law; and the judge the legislator, who is always representative of the commonwealth. From this false doctrine, men are disposed to debate with themselves and dispute the commands of the commonwealth; and afterwards to obey or disobey them, as in their private judgments they shall think fit; whereby the commonwealth is distracted and "weakened."

Another doctrine repugnant to civil society, is, that "whatsoever a man does against his conscience is sin"; and it dependeth on the presumption of making himself judge of good and evil. For a man's conscience and his judgment is the same thing, and as the judgment, so also the conscience may be erroneous. Therefore, though he that is subject to no civil law, sinneth in all he does against his conscience, because he has no other rule to follow but his own reason; yet it is not so with him that lives in a commonwealth; because the law is the public conscience, by which he hath already undertaken to be guided. Otherwise in such diversity, as there is of private consciences, which are but private opinions, the commonwealth must needs be distracted, and no man dare to obey the sovereign power, further than it shall seem good in his own eyes.

It hath been also commonly taught, "that faith and sanctity, are not to be attained by study and reason, but by supernatural inspiration or infusion." Which granted, I see not why any man should render a reason of his faith; or why every Christian should not be also a prophet; or why any man should take the law of his country rather than his own inspiration for the rule of his action. And thus we fall again into the fault of taking upon us to judge of good and evil; or to make judges of it, such private men as pretend to be supernaturally inspired, to the dissolution of all civil government. Faith comes by hearing, and hearing by those accidents which guide us into the presence of them that speak to us; which accidents are all contrived by God Almighty; and yet are not supernatural, but only, for the great number of them that concur to every effect, unobservable. Faith and sanctity are indeed not very frequent; but yet they are not miracles, but brought to pass by education, discipline, correction, and other natural ways, by which God worketh them in His elect, at such times as He thinketh fit. And these three opinions, pernicious to peace and government, have in this part of the world, proceeded chiefly from the tongues and pens of unlearned divines, who joining the words of Holy Scripture together, otherwise than is agreeable to reason, do what they can to make men think that sanctity and natural reason cannot stand together.

A fourth opinion, repugnant to the nature of a commonwealth, is this, "that he that hath the sovereign power is subject to the civil laws." It is true, that sovereigns are all subject to the laws of Nature; because such laws be divine, and cannot by any man or commonwealth be abrogated. But to those laws which the sovereign himself, that is, which the commonwealth maketh, he is not subject. For to be subject to laws is to be subject to the commonwealth, that is to the sovereign representative, that is to himself; which is not subjection, but freedom from the laws. Which error, because it setteth the laws above the sovereign, setteth also a judge above him and a power to punish him; which is to make a new sovereign; and again for the same reason a third, to punish the second; and so continually without end, to the confusion and dissolution of the commonwealth.

A fifth doctrine that tendeth to the dissolution of a commonwealth is, "that every private man has an absolute propriety in his goods; such as excludeth the right of the sovereign." Every man has indeed a propriety that excludes the right of every other subject: and he has it only from the sovereign power; without the protection whereof every other man should have right to the same. But if the right of the sovereign also be excluded, he cannot perform the office they have put him into; which is, to defend them both from foreign enemies, and from the injuries of one another; and consequently there is no longer a commonwealth.

And if the propriety of subjects exclude not the right of the sovereign representative to their goods; much less to their offices of judicature or execution, in which they represent the sovereign himself.

There is a sixth doctrine plainly and directly against the essence of a commonwealth; and it is this, "that the sovereign power may be divided." For what is it to divide the power of a commonwealth, but to dissolve it; for powers divided mutually destroy each other. And for these doctrines men are chiefly beholding to some of those that making profession of the laws, endeavour to make them depend upon their own learning, and not upon the legislative power.

And as false doctrine, so also oftentimes the example of different government in a neighbouring nation, disposeth men to alteration of the form already settled. So the people of the Jews were stirred up to reject God, and to call upon the prophet Samuel for a king after the manner of the nations: so also the lesser cities of Greece were continually disturbed with seditions of the aristocratical and democratical factions; one part of almost every commonwealth desiring to imitate the Lacedemonians; the other the Athenians. And I doubt not but many men have been contented to see the late troubles in England out of an imitation of the Low Countries; supposing there needed no more to grow rich than to change, as they had done, the form of their government. For the constitution of man's nature is of itself subject to desire novelty. When therefore they are provoked to the same by the neighbourhood also of those that have been enriched by it, it is almost impossible for them not to be content with those that solicit them to change; and love the first beginnings, though they be grieved with the continuance of disorder; like hot bloods, that having gotten the itch, tear themselves with their own nails, till they can endure the smart no longer.

And as to rebellion in particular against monarchy; one of the most frequent causes of it is the reading of the books of policy and histories of the ancient Greeks and Romans; from which young men, and all others that are unprovided of the antidote of solid reason, receiving a strong and delightful impression of the great exploits of war, achieved by the conductors of their armies, receive withal a pleasing idea of all they have done besides; and imagine their great prosperity, not to have proceeded from the emulation of particular men, but from the virtue of their popular form of government: not considering the frequent seditions, and civil wars, produced by the imperfection of their policy. From the reading, I say, of such books, men have undertaken to kill their kings, because the Greek and Latin writers, in their books and discourses of policy, make it lawful and laudable for any man so to do; provided, before he do it, he call him tyrant. For they say not "regicide," that is, killing a king, but "tyrannicide," that is, killing of a tyrant is lawful. From the same books, they that live under a monarch conceive an opinion, that the subjects in a popular commonwealth enjoy liberty; but that in a monarchy they are all slaves. I say, they that live under a monarchy conceive such an opinion; not they that live under a popular government: for they find no such matter. In sum, I cannot imagine how anything can be more prejudicial to a monarchy than the allowing of such books to be publicly read, without present applying such correctives of discreet masters, as are fit to take away their venom: which venom I will not doubt to compare to the biting of a mad dog, which is a disease that physicians call "hydrophobia," or "fear of water." For as he that is so bitten has a continual torment of thirst, and yet abhorreth water; and is in such an estate, as if the poison endeavoured to convert him into a dog: so when a monarchy is once bitten to the quick by those democratical writers, that continually snarl at that estate; it wanteth nothing more than a strong monarch, which nevertheless out of a certain "tyrannophobia," or fear of being strongly governed, when they have him, they abhor.

As there have been doctors that hold there be three souls in a man; so there be also that think there may be more souls, that is, more sovereigns, than one in a commonwealth; and set up a "supremacy" against the "sovereignty"; "canons" against "laws"; and a "ghostly authority" against the "civil"; working on men's minds with words and distinctions, that of themselves signify nothing, but bewray by their obscurity; that there walketh, as some think, invisibly another kingdom, as it were a kingdom of fairies, in the dark. Now seeing it is manifest that the civil power and the power of the commonwealth is the same thing; and that supremacy, and the power of making canons, and granting faculties, implieth a commonwealth; it followeth that where one is sovereign, another supreme; where one can make laws, and another make canons; there must needs be two commonwealths, of one and the same subjects; which is a kingdom divided in itself, and cannot stand. For notwithstanding the insignificant distinction of "temporal" and "ghostly," they are still two kingdoms, and every subject is subject to two masters. For seeing the "ghostly" power challengeth the right to declare what is sin, it challengeth by consequence to declare what is law, sin being nothing but the transgression of the law; and again, the civil power challenging to declare what is law, every subject must obey two masters, who both will have their commands be observed as law; which is impossible. Or, if it be but one kingdom, either the "civil," which is the power of the commonwealth, must be subordinate to the "ghostly," and then there is no sovereignty but the "ghostly"; or the "ghostly" must be subordinate to the "temporal," and then there is no "supremacy" but the "temporal." When therefore these two powers oppose one another, the commonwealth cannot but be in great danger of civil war and dissolution. For the "civil" authority being more visible, and standing in the clearer light of natural reason, cannot choose but draw to it in all times a very considerable part of the people: and the "spiritual," though it stand in the darkness of school distinctions, and hard words, yet because the fear of darkness and ghosts is greater than other fears, cannot want a party sufficient to trouble, and sometimes to destroy a commonwealth. And this is a disease which may not unfitly be compared to the epilepsy, or falling sickness, which the Jews took to be one kind of possession by spirits, in the body natural. For as in this disease, there is an unnatural spirit, or wind in the head that obstructeth the roots of the nerves, and moving them violently, taketh away the motion which naturally they should have from the power of the soul in the brain, and thereby causeth violent and irregular motions which men call convulsions in the parts; insomuch that he that is seized therewith, falleth down sometimes into the water, and sometimes into the fire, as a man deprived of his senses; so also in the body politic, when the spiritual power moveth the members of a commonwealth, by the terror of punishments and hope of rewards, which are the nerves of it, otherwise than by the civil power, which is the soul of the commonwealth, they ought to be moved; and by strange and hard words suffocate their understanding, it must needs thereby distract the people, and either overwhelm the commonwealth with oppression, or cast it into the fire of a civil war.

Sometimes also in the merely civil government, there be more than one soul; as when the power of levying money, which is the nutritive faculty, has depended on a general assembly; the power of conduct and command, which is the motive faculty, on one man; and the power of making laws, which is the rational faculty, on the accidental consent, not only of those two, but also of a third; this endangereth the commonwealth, sometimes for want of consent to good laws, but most often for want of such nourishment as is necessary to life and motion. For although few perceive that such government is not government, but division of the commonwealth into three factions, and call it mixed monarchy; yet the truth is that it is not one independent commonwealth, but three independent factions; nor one representative person, but three. In the kingdom of God, there may be three persons independent, without breach of unity in God that reigneth; but where men reign that be subject to diversity of opinions, it cannot be so. And therefore if the king bear the person of the people, and the general assembly bear also the person of the people, and another assembly bear the person of a part of the people, they are not one person, nor one sovereign, but three persons, and three sovereigns.

To what disease in the natural body of man I may exactly compare this irregularity of a commonwealth, I know not. But I have seen a man, that had another man growing out of his side, with a head, arms, breast, and stomach of his own; if he had had another man growing out of his other side, the comparison might then have been exact.

Hitherto I have named such diseases of a commonwealth as are of the greatest and most present danger. There be other not so great, which nevertheless are not unfit to be observed. As first, the difficulty of raising money for the necessary uses of the commonwealth, especially in the approach of war. This difficulty ariseth from the opinion that every subject hath a propriety in his lands and goods, exclusive of the sovereign's right to the use of the same. From whence it cometh to pass that the sovereign power, which foreseeth the necessities and dangers of the commonwealth, finding the passage of money to the public treasury obstructed by the tenacity of the people, whereas it ought to extend itself to encounter and prevent such dangers in their beginnings, contracteth itself as long as it can, and when it cannot longer, struggles with the people by stratagems of law, to obtain little sums, which not sufficing, he is fain at last violently to open the way for present supply, or perish; and being put often to these extremities, at last reduceth the people to their due temper, or else the commonwealth must perish. Insomuch as we may compare this distemper very aptly to an ague, wherein, the fleshy parts being congealed, or by venomous matter obstructed, the veins which by their natural course empty themselves into the heart, are not, as they ought to be, supplied from the arteries, whereby there succeedeth at first a cold contraction and trembling of the limbs; and afterward a hot and strong endeavour of the heart, to force a passage for the blood; and before it can do that, contenteth itself with the small refreshments of such things as cool for a time, till, if nature be strong enough, it break at last the contumacy of the parts obstructed, and dissipateth the venom into sweat; or, if nature be too weak, the patient dieth.

Again, there is sometimes in a commonwealth, a disease which resembleth the pleurisy; and that is, when the treasure of the commonwealth, flowing out of its due course, is gathered together in too much abundance, in one or a few private men, by monopolies or by farms of the public revenues; in the same manner as the blood in a pleurisy, getting into the membrane of the breast, breedeth there inflammation, accompanied with a fever and painful stitches.

Also the popularity of a potent subject, unless the commonwealth have very good caution of his fidelity, is a dangerous disease; because the people which should receive their motion from the authority of the sovereign, by the flattery and by the reputation of an ambitious man are drawn away from their obedience to the laws, to follow a man, of whose virtues and designs they have no knowledge. And this is commonly of more danger in a popular government than in a monarchy; because an army is of so great force and multitude, as it may easily be made believe they are the people. By this means it was that Julius Cæsar, who was set up by the people against the senate, having won to himself the affections of his army, made himself master both of senate and people. And this proceeding of popular and ambitious men, is plain rebellion; and may be resembled to the effects of witchcraft.

Another infirmity of a commonwealth is the immoderate greatness of a town, when it is able to furnish out of its own circuit the number and expense of a great army: as also the great number of corporations; which are as it were many lesser commonwealths in the bowels of a greater, like worms in the entrails of a natural man. To which may be added the liberty of disputing against absolute power, by pretenders to political prudence; which though bred for the most part in the lees of the people, yet animated by false doctrines, are perpetually meddling with the fundamental laws, to the molestation of the commonwealth; like the little worms, which physicians call *ascarides*.

We may further add, the insatiable appetite, or βουλιμια, of enlarging dominion; with the incurable "wounds" thereby many times received from the enemy; and the "wens" of ununited conquests, which are many times a burthen, and with less danger lost than kept: as also the "lethargy" of ease and "consumption" of riot and vain expense.

Lastly, when in a war, foreign or intestine, the enemies get a final victory; so as, the forces of the commonwealth keeping the field no longer, there is no further protection of subjects in their loyalty; then is the commonwealth "dissolved," and every man at liberty to protect himself by such courses as his own discretion shall suggest unto him. For the sovereign is the public soul, giving life and motion to the commonwealth; which expiring, the members are governed by it no more, than the carcase of a man, by his departed, though immortal soul. For though the right of a sovereign monarch cannot be extinguished by the act of another; yet the obligation of the members may. For he that wants protection may seek it anywhere; and when he hath it, is obliged, without fraudulent pretence of having submitted himself out of fear, to protect his protection as long as he is able. But when the power of an assembly is once suppressed, the right of the same perisheth utterly; because the assembly itself is extinct; and consequently there is no possibility for the sovereignty to re-enter.

John Locke

JOHN LOCKE WAS BORN AUGUST 29, 1632, IN SOMERSET, ENGLAND, INTO A LIBERAL Puritan family; his father was a small landowner who supplemented the income from his holdings (which Locke later inherited) by working as an attorney. Locke senior fought with Cromwell against Charles I in the Civil War, and, though his unit was defeated and disbanded, he became friends with his commander, Alexander Popham, who, as MP for Bath, was important enough to secure fourteen-year-old John a spot at Westminster School, then the most prestigious preparatory school in England. There his studies centered on ancient languages: Latin, Greek, and finally Hebrew. Westminster had an arrangement with Christ Church, Oxford, whereby three of its best young scholars were given studentships, essentially lifetime (though revokable) positions that provided rooms in the college and a small stipend. There Locke went in 1652, where he studied the same Scholastic curriculum that had bored Hobbes fifty years earlier: it had much the same effect on Locke. He must have done well, however, for he was elected to a Senior Studentship in 1658, and taught Latin, Greek, and rhetoric. In 1664 he was appointed Censor of Moral Philosophy.

Apart from his official duties, Locke developed a profound interest in medicine, and it was in a medical capacity that he came to the attention of Lord Ashley, later earl of Shaftesbury, whose service Locke entered in 1666. While at Oxford, Locke grew to know the physicist and chemist Robert Boyle, from whom he learned much about the new sciences and the corpuscularian hypothesis. Locke was elected to the Royal Society in 1668. His writings from this time show him to have been rather conservative in religion and politics. That was soon to change.

In 1667 Locke became the confidential secretary of Shaftesbury, the most prominent political figure of the day, who was named chancellor of England in 1672. Locke entered into all the details of politics, government, and administration. He assisted in framing the constitution of Carolina, and became secretary and treasurer to the Council of Trade and Plantations. Shaftesbury was dismissed from the chancellorship in 1673, but Locke's administrative duties with the government didn't come to an end until 1675. At that point, he took a vacation to France that was to last three and a half years. There, he engaged a tutor in French, began serious study of Descartes and his followers, and also started writing what was to become *An Essay Concerning Human Understanding*, the work that would be his greatest achievement, and that brought him great fame in his own lifetime.

When Locke returned to England in 1679, he found the country in acute crisis. The central issue was the attempt by Shaftesbury and his Whig followers to exclude the Catholic duke of York (later James II) from succeeding to the throne of his childless brother, Charles II. Three attempts to get an Exclusion Act through Parliament failed. Finally, the king had had enough and Shaftesbury was charged with treason. The earl was still powerful enough to get the charges dropped, but he was forced to slip out of England to Holland, where he promptly died. The movement did not die with him, however. They plotted to kidnap or assassinate Charles and James, but the plot was betrayed and the ringleaders arrested. One committed suicide in the Tower, and the other two were executed. A good deal was made at the trials of "seditious manuscripts." Locke was certainly being watched by government spies, and by this time he had in his own possession an extremely seditious manuscript, the work that was to become the *Two Treatises on Government*, which, among other things, argued that even a legitimate ruler could be resisted and overthrown if he abused his power. That doctrine, of course, is only one aspect of this complex work, but it was a red flag to royalists, who suspected that the argument could be used to justify revolution. They were right, as every student of American history knows. Locke slipped away from London a week before the arrests began, and was out of the country in Holland two months later. His caution was well-founded: The government made several attempts to have him extradited, fortunately without success.

In exile in 1683, Locke was past fifty and still had published nothing of real note. The *Two Treatises on Government* was ready, but the moment was hardly right. With time on his hands, he resumed work on the *Essay*, and wrote the *Letter Concerning Toleration*. After the accession of the Protestant William of Orange in 1688, Locke returned to England, though now deprived of his Oxford studentship, which had been terminated by direct order of Charles II. The *Essay* was published in 1690, soon followed by other major works, including the *Two Treatises on Government*. He combined this work with public service, serving as Commissioner of Appeals and of the Council of Trade and Plantations. In 1700, Locke resigned from the Council and retired to the country house of well-to-do friends. On October 28, 1704, Lady Masham was reading Psalms to him when he put his hands to his face to close his eyes and died.

NOTES ON THE TEXT

John Locke's *Second Treatise on Civil Government* presents a view of the justification of political institutions radically different from those of Machiavelli and Hobbes. Indeed, in Locke's view, neither Machiavelli nor Hobbes really describes political institutions at all. They are merely talking about different ways in which some people are able to capture and subdue other people. In effect, Locke sees these arrangements as merely phases in a state of war among men where some have gained the upper hand.

Locke, like Hobbes, thinks that political institutions are justified to the extent that they bring some benefit to people over and above what they would have in a world without political institutions. So Locke starts with a discussion of the state of nature. But while Hobbes sees the state of nature as a war of all against all, where morality has no place because no one can trust anyone else, Locke thinks that in the state of nature men are capable of being guided by the morality of the law of nature. The law of nature, in Locke's account, directs men and women to ensure their own self-preservation and to concern themselves with the preservation of others. Liberty and property are essential prerequisites for self-preservation. So one must respect the lives, liberty, and property of other persons just as one ought to respect them in oneself. The reason the law of nature directs us to concern ourselves with others' lives, liberty, and property is that it shows us that each person's interests are equal in worth to anyone else's. If I demand of another that he not harm me in my interests, then I must heed his demand that I not harm him. Hence, people are free and equal by nature in the sense that no one has a right to subordinate another and that everyone's interests in life, liberty, and property are of equal worth. He thinks that these are dictates of reason and that men and women are generally endowed with and motivated by reason. So Locke not only thinks that men and women have moral rights against each other, he thinks that they are in fact motivated by reason to respect these rights. Hence, there need not be a war of all against all in the state of nature.

Locke's political philosophy is distinctive in that it attempts to justify not only natural rights to life and liberty but also to ownership over external things. A theory of the natural right to property must answer the question, How can a person, independent of social conventions or political institutions or even the consent of others, impose obligations on others to stay away from some external object? Locke's answer is that each person owns his or her self and that a person can come to own an external thing by mixing his or her labor with that thing, thereby fundamentally transforming that object into something that is his or hers.

The trouble comes because some are inclined to act against reason and violate the rights of others in the state of nature. Locke thinks that each person has a right to punish others for their failure to comply with the law of nature. The punishment must be in proportion to the crime, of course. Predictably, a lot of inconvenience arises from everyone having this separate right and exercising it in accordance with their inevitably different conceptions of the law of nature, of when it has been violated, and of how much punishment each person deserves. People of good faith, if they disagree with each other on these matters, are likely to charge each other with having misunderstood the law of nature, or punished the innocent, or caused harm out of proportion to the crime committed, and they may think they have reason to punish others for these violations. In addition, this scheme is likely not to catch and punish criminals very efficiently because it is so disorganized. Hence, Locke thinks that individuals will agree to transfer their rights to a political society that is charged with the tasks of writing clear legislation, executing it, and judging when it has been violated. It can now tell people what to do. It has these powers, however, because individuals have freely consented to its having it and because it protects the life, liberty, and property of citizens. The free consent of individuals is the only basis on which the obligation of individuals to obey a political society can be grounded.

Each person has a basic understanding of the law of nature, and the government of a political society is entrusted with the task of regulating the society in accordance with the law of nature. Hence, Locke thinks that each person has a right to appeal the decisions of the government in terms of the laws of nature. A political society, then, in Locke's view is a community of rational persons joined together by their mutual acknowledgment of the law of nature. Now we can see how far Locke is from Machiavelli or Hobbes. For them, political society is essentially a group of persons dominated by another person. In Locke's view, Hobbes had no more described a political society than a group of persons held at gunpoint by a bandit.

Much of Locke's arguments in the rest of the *Second Treatise* as well as in the *Letter Concerning Toleration* follow from these basic ideas or consist in attempts to shore them up. Persons must consent if the government is to tax them or use their property. This is the basis of Locke's argument for representative government. When the government consistently violates the law of nature and does not allow persons to appeal its decisions, it dissolves political society, and men return to the state of nature, wherein they have a right to set up a new political society. This is the basis for Locke's famous argument for the right to revolution. Locke's *Letter Concerning Toleration* argues that it is irrational for individuals to consent to the government's controlling their beliefs or to consent to obeying the government's demand that they adhere to a particular faith unless, of course, such adherence has implications for the society at large.

The Second Treatise on Civil Government

An Essay Concerning the True Original Extent and End of Civil Government

Chapter I

1. It having been shown in the foregoing discourse:

Firstly. That Adam had not, either by natural right of fatherhood or by positive donation from God, any such authority over his children, nor dominion over the world, as is pretended.

Secondly. That if he had, his heirs yet had no right to it.

Thirdly. That if his heirs had, there being no law of Nature nor positive law of God that determines which is the right heir in all cases that may arise, the right of succession, and consequently of bearing rule, could not have been certainly determined.

Fourthly. That if even that had been determined, yet the knowledge of which is the eldest line of Adam's posterity being so long since utterly lost, that in the races of mankind and families of the world, there remains not to one above another the least pretence to be the eldest house, and to have the right of inheritance.

All these premises having, as I think, been clearly made out, it is impossible that the rulers now on earth should make any benefit, or derive any the least shadow of authority from that which is held to be the fountain of all power, "Adam's private dominion and paternal jurisdiction"; so that he that will not give just occasion to think that all government in the world is the product only of force and violence, and that men live together by no other rules but that of beasts, where the strongest carries it, and so lay a foundation for perpetual disorder and mischief, tumult, sedition, and rebellion (things that the followers of that hypothesis so loudly cry out against), must of necessity find out another rise of government, another original of political power, and another way of designing and knowing the persons that have it than what Sir Robert Filmer hath taught us.[1]

2. To this purpose, I think it may not be amiss to set down what I take to be political power. That the power of a magistrate over a subject may be distinguished from that of a father over his children, a master over his servant, a husband over his wife, and a lord over his slave. All which distinct powers happening sometimes together in the same man, if he be considered under these different relations, it may help us to distinguish these powers one from another, and show the difference betwixt a ruler of a commonwealth, a father of a family, and a captain of a galley.

---

1. Filmer was the author of *Patriarcha* (1680), which supported the divine right of kings.

3. Political power, then, I take to be a right of making laws, with penalties of death, and consequently all less penalties for the regulating and preserving of property, and of employing the force of the community in the execution of such laws, and in the defence of the commonwealth from foreign injury, and all this only for the public good.

Chapter II
Of the State of Nature

4. To understand political power aright, and derive it from its original, we must consider what estate all men are naturally in, and that is, a state of perfect freedom to order their actions, and dispose of their possessions and persons as they think fit, within the bounds of the law of Nature, without asking leave or depending upon the will of any other man.

A state also of equality, wherein all the power and jurisdiction is reciprocal, no one having more than another, there being nothing more evident than that creatures of the same species and rank, promiscuously born to all the same advantages of Nature, and the use of the same faculties, should also be equal one amongst another, without subordination or subjection, unless the lord and master of them all should, by any manifest declaration of his will, set one above another, and confer on him, by an evident and clear appointment, an undoubted right to dominion and sovereignty.

5. This equality of men by Nature, the judicious [theologian Richard] Hooker looks upon as so evident in itself, and beyond all question, that he makes it the foundation of that obligation to mutual love amongst men on which he builds the duties they owe one another, and from whence he derives the great maxims of justice and charity. His words are:

"The like natural inducement hath brought men to know that it is no less their duty to love others than themselves, for seeing those things which are equal, must needs all have one measure; if I cannot but wish to receive good, even as much at every man's hands, as any man can wish unto his own soul, how should I look to have any part of my desire herein satisfied, unless myself be careful to satisfy the like desire, which is undoubtedly in other men weak, being of one and the same nature: to have anything offered them repugnant to this desire must needs, in all respects, grieve them as much as me; so that if I do harm, I must look to suffer, there being no reason that

others should show greater measure of love to me than they have by me showed unto them; my desire, therefore, to be loved of my equals in Nature, as much as possible may be, imposeth upon me a natural duty of bearing to themward fully the like affection. From which relation of equality between ourselves and them that are as ourselves, what several rules and canons natural reason hath drawn for direction of life no man is ignorant." (*Eccl[esiasticall] Pol[itie] i.*)

6. But though this be a state of liberty, yet it is not a state of licence; though man in that state have an uncontrollable liberty to dispose of his person or possessions, yet he has not liberty to destroy himself, or so much as any creature in his possession, but where some nobler use than its bare preservation calls for it. The state of Nature has a law of Nature to govern it, which obliges every one, and reason, which is that law, teaches all mankind who will but consult it, that being all equal and independent, no one ought to harm another in his life, health, liberty or possessions; for men being all the workmanship of one omnipotent and infinitely wise Maker; all the servants of one sovereign Master, sent into the world by His order and about His business; they are His property, whose workmanship they are made to last during His, not one another's pleasure. And, being furnished with like faculties, sharing all in one community of Nature, there cannot be supposed any such subordination among us that may authorise us to destroy one another, as if we were made for one another's uses, as the inferior ranks of creatures are for ours. Every one as he is bound to preserve himself, and not to quit his station wilfully, so by the like reason, when his own preservation comes not in competition, ought he as much as he can to preserve the rest of mankind, and not unless it be to do justice on an offender, take away or impair the life, or what tends to the preservation of the life, the liberty, health, limb, or goods of another.

7. And that all men may be restrained from invading others' rights, and from doing hurt to one another, and the law of Nature be observed, which willeth the peace and preservation of all mankind, the execution of the law of Nature is in that state put into every man's hands, whereby every one has a right to punish the transgressors of that law to such a degree as may hinder its violation. For the law of Nature would, as all other laws that concern men in this world, be in vain if there were nobody that in the state of Nature had a power to execute that law, and thereby pre-

THE SECOND TREATISE ON CIVIL GOVERNMENT | 119

serve the innocent and restrain offenders; and if any one in the state of Nature may punish another for any evil he has done, every one may do so. For in that state of perfect equality, where naturally there is no superiority or jurisdiction of one over another, what any may do in prosecution of that law, every one must needs have a right to do.

8. And thus, in the state of Nature, one man comes by a power over another, but yet no absolute or arbitrary power to use a criminal, when he has got him in his hands, according to the passionate heats or boundless extravagancy of his own will, but only to retribute to him so far as calm reason and conscience dictate, what is proportionate to his transgression, which is so much as may serve for reparation and restraint. For these two are the only reasons why one man may lawfully do harm to another, which is that we call punishment. In transgressing the law of Nature, the offender declares himself to live by another rule than that of reason and common equity, which is that measure God has set to the actions of men for their mutual security, and so he becomes dangerous to mankind; the tie which is to secure them from injury and violence being slighted and broken by him, which being a trespass against the whole species, and the peace and safety of it, provided for by the law of Nature, every man upon this score, by the right he hath to preserve mankind in general, may restrain, or where it is necessary, destroy things noxious to them, and so may bring such evil on any one who hath transgressed that law, as may make him repent the doing of it, and thereby deter him, and, by his example, others from doing the like mischief. And in this case, and upon this ground, every man hath a right to punish the offender, and be executioner of the law of Nature.

9. I doubt not but this will seem a very strange doctrine to some men; but before they condemn it, I desire them to resolve me by what right any prince or state can put to death or punish an alien for any crime he commits in their country? It is certain their laws, by virtue of any sanction they receive from the promulgated will of the legislature, reach not a stranger. They speak not to him, nor, if they did, is he bound to hearken to them. The legislative authority by which they are in force over the subjects of that commonwealth hath no power over him. Those who have the supreme power of making laws in England, France, or Holland are, to an Indian, but like the rest of the world—men without authority. And therefore, if by

the law of Nature every man hath not a power to punish offences against it, as he soberly judges the case to require, I see not how the magistrates of any community can punish an alien of another country, since, in reference to him, they can have no more power than what every man naturally may have over another.

10. Besides the crime which consists in violating the laws, and varying from the right rule of reason, whereby a man so far becomes degenerate, and declares himself to quit the principles of human nature and to be a noxious creature, there is commonly injury done, and some person or other, some other man, receives damage by his transgression; in which case, he who hath received any damage has (besides the right of punishment common to him, with other men) a particular right to seek reparation from him that hath done it. And any other person who finds it just may also join with him that is injured, and assist him in recovering from the offender so much as may make satisfaction for the harm he hath suffered.

11. From these two distinct rights (the one of punishing the crime, for restraint and preventing the like offence, which right of punishing is in everybody, the other of taking reparation, which belongs only to the injured party) comes it to pass that the magistrate, who by being magistrate hath the common right of punishing put into his hands, can often, where the public good demands not the execution of the law, remit the punishment of criminal offences by his own authority, but yet cannot remit the satisfaction due to any private man for the damage he has received. That he who hath suffered the damage has a right to demand in his own name, and he alone can remit. The damnified person has this power of appropriating to himself the goods or service of the offender by right of self-preservation, as every man has a power to punish the crime to prevent its being committed again, by the right he has of preserving all mankind, and doing all reasonable things he can in order to that end. And thus it is that every man in the state of Nature has a power to kill a murderer, both to deter others from doing the like injury (which no reparation can compensate) by the example of the punishment that attends it from everybody, and also to secure men from the attempts of a criminal who, having renounced reason, the common rule and measure God hath given to mankind, hath, by the unjust violence and slaughter he hath committed upon one, declared war against all mankind, and therefore may be destroyed as a lion or a tiger, one of those wild savage

beasts with whom men can have no society nor security. And upon this is grounded that great law of Nature, "Whoso sheddeth man's blood, by man shall his blood be shed." And Cain was so fully convinced that every one had a right to destroy such a criminal, that, after the murder of his brother, he cries out, "Every one that findeth me shall slay me," so plain was it writ in the hearts of all mankind.

12. By the same reason may a man in the state of Nature punish the lesser breaches of that law, it will, perhaps, be demanded, with death? I answer: Each transgression may be punished to that degree, and with so much severity, as will suffice to make it an ill bargain to the offender, give him cause to repent, and terrify others from doing the like. Every offence that can be committed in the state of Nature may, in the state of Nature, be also punished equally, and as far forth, as it may, in a commonwealth. For though it would be beside my present purpose to enter here into the particulars of the law of Nature, or its measures of punishment, yet it is certain there is such a law, and that too as intelligible and plain to a rational creature and a studier of that law as the positive laws of commonwealths, nay, possibly plainer; as much as reason is easier to be understood than the fancies and intricate contrivances of men, following contrary and hidden interests put into words; for truly so are a great part of the municipal laws of countries, which are only so far right as they are founded on the law of Nature, by which they are to be regulated and interpreted.

13. To this strange doctrine—viz., That in the state of Nature every one has the executive power of the law of Nature—I doubt not but it will be objected that it is unreasonable for men to be judges in their own cases, that self-love will make men partial to themselves and their friends; and, on the other side, ill-nature, passion, and revenge will carry them too far in punishing others, and hence nothing but confusion and disorder will follow, and that therefore God hath certainly appointed government to restrain the partiality and violence of men. I easily grant that civil government is the proper remedy for the inconveniences of the state of Nature, which must certainly be great where men may be judges in their own case, since it is easy to be imagined that he who was so unjust as to do his brother an injury will scarce be so just as to condemn himself for it. But I shall desire those who make this objection to remember that absolute monarchs are but men; and if government is to be the remedy of those evils which necessarily follow from men being judges in their own cases, and the state of Nature is therefore not to be endured, I desire to know what kind of government that is, and how much better it is than the state of Nature, where one man commanding a multitude has the liberty to be judge in his own case, and may do to all his subjects whatever he pleases without the least question or control of those who execute his pleasure? and in whatsoever he doth, whether led by reason, mistake, or passion, must be submitted to? which men in the state of Nature are not bound to do one to another. And if he that judges, judges amiss in his own or any other case, he is answerable for it to the rest of mankind.

14. It is often asked as a mighty objection, where are, or ever were, there any men in such a state of Nature? To which it may suffice as an answer at present, that since all princes and rulers of "independent" governments all through the world are in a state of Nature, it is plain the world never was, nor never will be, without numbers of men in that state. I have named all governors of "independent" communities, whether they are, or are not, in league with others; for it is not every compact that puts an end to the state of Nature between men, but only this one of agreeing together mutually to enter into one community, and make one body politic; other promises and compacts men may make one with another, and yet still be in the state of Nature. The promises and bargains for truck, etc., between the two men in Soldania, or between a Swiss and an Indian, in the woods of America, are binding to them, though they are perfectly in a state of Nature in reference to one another for truth, and keeping of faith belongs to men as men, and not as members of society.

15. To those that say there were never any men in the state of Nature, I will not only oppose the authority of the judicious Hooker (*Eccl. Pol.* i. 10), where he says, "the laws which have been hitherto mentioned" —*i.e.*, the laws of Nature—"do bind men absolutely, even as they are men, although they have never any settled fellowship, never any solemn agreement amongst themselves what to do or not to do; but for as much as we are not by ourselves sufficient to furnish ourselves with competent store of things needful for such a life as our Nature doth desire, a life fit for the dignity of man, therefore to supply those defects and imperfections which are in us, as living single and solely by ourselves, we are naturally induced to seek communion and fellowship with others; this was the

cause of men uniting themselves as first in politic societies." But I, moreover, affirm that all men are naturally in that state, and remain so till, by their own consents, they make themselves members of some politic society, and I doubt not, in the sequel of this discourse, to make it very clear.

Chapter III
Of the State of War

16. The state of war is a state of enmity and destruction; and therefore declaring by word or action, not a passionate and hasty, but sedate, settled design upon another man's life puts him in a state of war with him against whom he has declared such an intention, and so has exposed his life to the other's power to be taken away by him, or any one that joins with him in his defence, and espouses his quarrel; it being reasonable and just I should have a right to destroy that which threatens me with destruction; for by the fundamental law of Nature, man being to be preserved as much as possible, when all cannot be preserved, the safety of the innocent is to be preferred, and one may destroy a man who makes war upon him, or has discovered an enmity to his being, for the same reason that he may kill a wolf or a lion, because they are not under the ties of the common law of reason, have no other rule but that of force and violence, and so may be treated as a beast of prey, those dangerous and noxious creatures that will be sure to destroy him whenever he falls into their power.

17. And hence it is that he who attempts to get another man into his absolute power does thereby put himself into a state of war with him; it being to be understood as a declaration of a design upon his life. For I have reason to conclude that he who would get me into his power without my consent would use me as he pleased when he had got me there, and destroy me too when he had a fancy to it; for nobody can desire to have me in his absolute power unless it be to compel me by force to that which is against the right of my freedom—*i.e.* make me a slave. To be free from such force is the only security of my preservation, and reason bids me look on him as an enemy to my preservation who would take away that freedom which is the fence to it; so that he who makes an attempt to enslave me thereby puts himself into a state of war with me. He that in the state of Nature would take away the freedom that belongs to any one

in that state must necessarily be supposed to have a design to take away everything else, that freedom being the foundation of all the rest; as he that in the state of society would take away the freedom belonging to those of that society or commonwealth must be supposed to design to take away from them everything else, and so be looked on as in a state of war.

18. This makes it lawful for a man to kill a thief who has not in the least hurt him, nor declared any design upon his life, any farther than by the use of force, so to get him in his power as to take away his money, or what he pleases, from him; because using force, where he has no right to get me into his power, let his pretence be what it will, I have no reason to suppose that he who would take away my liberty would not, when he had me in his power, take away everything else. And, therefore, it is lawful for me to treat him as one who has put himself into a state of war with me—*i.e.*, kill him if I can; for to that hazard does he justly expose himself whoever introduces a state of war, and is aggressor in it.

19. And here we have the plain difference between the state of Nature and the state of war, which however some men have confounded, are as far distant as a state of peace, goodwill, mutual assistance, and preservation; and a state of enmity, malice, violence, and mutual destruction are one from another. Men living together according to reason without a common superior on earth, with authority to judge between them, is properly the state of Nature. But force, or a declared design of force upon the person of another, where there is no common superior on earth to appeal to for relief, is the state of war; and it is the want of such an appeal gives a man the right of war even against an aggressor, though he be in society and a fellow-subject. Thus, a thief whom I cannot harm, but by appeal to the law, for having stolen all that I am worth, I may kill when he sets on me to rob me but of my horse or coat, because the law, which was made for my preservation, where it cannot interpose to secure my life from present force, which if lost is capable of no reparation, permits me my own defence and the right of war, a liberty to kill the aggressor, because the aggressor allows not time to appeal to our common judge, nor the decision of the law, for remedy in a case where the mischief may be irreparable. Want of a common judge with authority puts all men in a state of Nature; force without right upon a man's person makes a state of war both where there is, and is not, a common judge.

20. But when the actual force is over, the state of war ceases between those that are in society and are equally on both sides subject to the judge; and, therefore, in such controversies, where the question is put, "Who shall be judge?" it cannot be meant who shall decide the controversy; every one knows what Jeptha here tells us, that "the Lord the Judge" shall judge. Where there is no judge on earth the appeal lies to God in Heaven. That question then cannot mean who shall judge, whether another hath put himself in a state of war with me, and whether I may, as Jephtha did, appeal to Heaven in it? Of that I myself can only judge in my own conscience, as I will answer it at the great day to the Supreme Judge of all men.

Chapter IV
Of Slavery

21. The natural liberty of man is to be free from any superior power on earth, and not to be under the will or legislative authority of man, but to have only the law of Nature for his rule. The liberty of man in society is to be under no other legislative power but that established by consent in the commonwealth, nor under the dominion of any will, or restraint of any law, but what that legislative shall enact according to the trust put in it. Freedom, then, is not what Sir Robert Filmer tells us: "A liberty for every one to do what he lists, to live as he pleases, and not to be tied by any laws"; but freedom of men under government is to have a standing rule to live by, common to every one of that society, and made by the legislative power erected in it. A liberty to follow my own will in all things where that rule prescribes not, not to be subject to the inconstant, uncertain, unknown, arbitrary will of another man, as freedom of nature is to be under no other restraint but the law of Nature.

22. This freedom from absolute, arbitrary power is so necessary to, and closely joined with, a man's preservation, that he cannot part with it but by what forfeits his preservation and life together. For a man, not having the power of his own life, cannot by compact or his own consent enslave himself to any one, nor put himself under the absolute, arbitrary power of another to take away his life when he pleases. Nobody can give more power than he has himself, and he that cannot take away his own life cannot give another power over it. Indeed, having by his fault forfeited his own life by some act that deserves death, he to whom he has forfeited it may, when he has him in his power, delay to take it, and make use of him to his own service; and he does him no injury by it. For, whenever he finds the hardship of his slavery outweigh the value of his life, it is in his power, by resisting the will of his master, to draw on himself the death he desires.

23. This is the perfect condition of slavery, which is nothing else but the state of war continued between a lawful conqueror and a captive, for if once compact enter between them, and make an agreement for a limited power on the one side, and obedience on the other, the state of war and slavery ceases as long as the compact endures; for, as has been said, no man can by agreement pass over to another that which he hath not in himself—a power over his own life.

I confess, we find among the Jews, as well as other nations, that men did sell themselves; but it is plain this was only to drudgery, not to slavery; for it is evident the person sold was not under an absolute, arbitrary, despotical power, for the master could not have power to kill him at any time, whom at a certain time he was obliged to let go free out of his service; and the master of such a servant was so far from having an arbitrary power over his life that he could not at pleasure so much as maim him, but the loss of an eye or tooth set him free (Exod. xxi.).

Chapter V
Of Property

24. Whether we consider natural reason, which tells us that men, being once born, have a right to their preservation, and consequently to meat and drink and such other things as Nature affords for their subsistence, or "revelation," which gives us an account of those grants God made of the world to Adam, and to Noah and his sons, it is very clear that God, as King David says (Psalm cxv. 16), "has given the earth to the children of men," given it to mankind in common. But, this being supposed, it seems to some a very great difficulty how any one should ever come to have a property in anything, I will not content myself to answer, that, if it be difficult to make out "property" upon a supposition that God gave the world to Adam and his posterity in common, it is impossible that any man but one universal monarch should have any "property" upon a supposition that God gave the world to Adam and his heirs in succession, exclusive of all the rest of his posterity; but I shall endeavour to show how men might come to have a property in several parts of that which God

gave to mankind in common, and that without any express compact of all the commoners.

25. God, who hath given the world to men in common, hath also given them reason to make use of it to the best advantage of life and convenience. The earth and all that is therein is given to men for the support and comfort of their being. And though all the fruits it naturally produces, and beasts it feeds, belong to mankind in common, as they are produced by the spontaneous hand of Nature, and nobody has originally a private dominion exclusive of the rest of mankind in any of them, as they are thus in their natural state, yet being given for the use of men, there must of necessity be a means to appropriate them some way or other before they can be of any use, or at all beneficial, to any particular men. The fruit or venison which nourishes the wild Indian, who knows no enclosure, and is still a tenant in common, must be his, and so his—*i.e.*, a part of him, that another can no longer have any right to it before it can do him any good for the support of his life.

26. Though the earth and all inferior creatures be common to all men, yet every man has a "property" in his own "person." This nobody has any right to but himself. The "labour" of his body and the "work" of his hands, we may say, are properly his. Whatsoever, then, he removes out of the state that Nature hath provided and left it in, he hath mixed his labour with it, and joined to it something that is his own, and thereby makes it his property. It being by him removed from the common state Nature placed it in, it hath by this labour something annexed to it that excludes the common right of other men. For this "labour" being the unquestionable property of the labourer, no man but he can have a right to what that is once joined to, at least where there is enough, and as good left in common for others.

27. He that is nourished by the acorns he picked up under an oak, or the apples he gathered from the trees in the wood, has certainly appropriated them to himself. Nobody can deny but the nourishment is his. I ask, then, when did they begin to be his? when he digested? or when he ate? or when he boiled? or when he brought them home? or when he picked them up? And it is plain, if the first gathering made them not his, nothing else could. That labour put a distinction between them and common. That added something to them more than Nature, the common mother of all, had done, and so they became his private right. And will any one say he had no right to

those acorns or apples he thus appropriated because he had not the consent of all mankind to make them his? Was it a robbery thus to assume to himself what belonged to all in common? If such a consent as that was necessary, man had starved, notwithstanding the plenty God had given him. We see in commons, which remain so by compact, that it is the taking any part of what is common, and removing it out of the state Nature leaves it in, which begins the property, without which the common is of no use. And the taking of this or that part does not depend on the express consent of all the commoners. Thus, the grass my horse has bit, the turfs my servant has cut, and the ore I have digged in any place, where I have a right to them in common with others, become my property without the assignation or consent of anybody. The labour that was mine, removing them out of that common state they were in, hath fixed my property in them.

28. By making an explicit consent of every commoner necessary to any one's appropriating to himself any part of what is given in common, children or servants could not cut the meat which their father or master had provided for them in common without assigning to every one his peculiar part. Though the water running in the fountain be every one's, yet who can doubt but that in the pitcher is his only who drew it out? His labour hath taken it out of the hands of Nature where it was common, and belonged equally to all her children, and hath thereby appropriated it to himself.

29. Thus this law of reason makes the deer that Indian's who hath killed it; it is allowed to be his goods who hath bestowed his labour upon it, though, before, it was the common right of every one. And amongst those who are counted the civilised part of mankind, who have made and multiplied positive laws to determine property, this original law of Nature for the beginning of property, in what was before common, still takes place, and by virtue thereof, what fish any one catches in the ocean, that great and still remaining common of mankind; or what ambergris any one takes up here is by the labour that removes it out of that common state Nature left it in, made his property who takes that pains about it. And even amongst us, the hare that any one is hunting is thought his who pursues her during the chase. For being a beast that is still looked upon as common, and no man's private possession, whoever has employed so much labour about any of that kind as to find and pursue her has thereby removed her from the state of

Nature wherein she was common, and hath begun a property.

30. It will, perhaps, be objected to this, that if gathering the acorns or other fruits of the earth, etc., makes a right to them, then any one may engross as much as he will. To which I answer, Not so. The same law of Nature that does by this means give us property, does also bound that property too. "God has given us all things richly." Is the voice of reason confirmed by inspiration? But how far has He given it us—"to enjoy"? As much as any one can make use of to any advantage of life before it spoils, so much he may by his labour fix a property in. Whatever is beyond this is more than his share, and belongs to others. Nothing was made by God for man to spoil or destroy. And thus considering the plenty of natural provisions there was a long time in the world, and the few spenders, and to how small a part of that provision the industry of one man could extend itself and engross it to the prejudice of others, especially keeping within the bounds set by reason of what might serve for his use, there could be then little room for quarrels or contentions about property so established.

31. But the chief matter of property being now not the fruits of the earth and the beasts that subsist on it, but the earth itself, as that which takes in and carries with it all the rest, I think it is plain that property in that too is acquired as the former. As much land as a man tills, plants, improves, cultivates, and can use the product of, so much is his property. He by his labour does, as it were, enclose it from the common. Nor will it invalidate his right to say everybody else has an equal title to it, and therefore he cannot appropriate, he cannot enclose, without the consent of all his fellow-commoners, all mankind. God, when He gave the world in common to all mankind, commanded man also to labour, and the penury of his condition required it of him. God and his reason commanded him to subdue the earth—i.e., improve it for the benefit of life and therein lay out something upon it that was his own, his labour. He that, in obedience to this command of God, subdued, tilled, and sowed any part of it, thereby annexed to it something that was his property, which another had no title to, nor could without injury take from him.

32. Nor was this appropriation of any parcel of land, by improving it, any prejudice to any other man, since there was still enough and as good left, and more than the yet unprovided could use. So that, in effect, there was never the less left for others because of his enclosure for himself. For he that leaves as much as another can make use of does as good as take nothing at all. Nobody could think himself injured by the drinking of another man, though he took a good draught, who had a whole river of the same water left him to quench his thirst. And the case of land and water, where there is enough of both, is perfectly the same.

33. God gave the world to men in common, but since He gave it them for their benefit and the greatest conveniencies of life they were capable to draw from it, it cannot be supposed He meant it should always remain common and uncultivated. He gave it to the use of the industrious and rational (and labour was to be his title to it); not to the fancy or covetousness of the quarrelsome and contentious. He that had as good left for his improvement as was already taken up needed not complain, ought not to meddle with what was already improved by another's labour; if he did it is plain he desired the benefit of another's pains, which he had no right to, and not the ground which God had given him, in common with others, to labour on, and whereof there was as good left as that already possessed, and more than he knew what to do with, or his industry could reach to.

34. It is true, in land that is common in England or any other country, where there are plenty of people under government who have money and commerce, no one can enclose or appropriate any part without the consent of all his fellow-commoners; because this is left common by compact—i.e., by the law of the land, which is not to be violated. And, though it be common in respect of some men, it is not so to all mankind, but is the joint propriety of this country, or this parish. Besides, the remainder, after such enclosure, would not be as good to the rest of the commoners as the whole was, when they could all make use of the whole; whereas in the beginning and first peopling of the great common of the world it was quite otherwise. The law man was under was rather for appropriating. God commanded, and his wants forced him to labour. That was his property, which could not be taken from him wherever he had fixed it. And hence subduing or cultivating the earth and having dominion, we see, are joined together. The one gave title to the other. So that God, by commanding to subdue, gave authority so far to appropriate. And the condition of human life, which requires

labour and materials to work on, necessarily introduces private possessions.

35. The measure of property Nature well set, by the extent of men's labour and the conveniency of life. No man's labour could subdue or appropriate all, nor could his enjoyment consume more than a small part; so that it was impossible for any man, this way, to entrench upon the right of another or acquire to himself a property to the prejudice of his neighbour, who would still have room for as good and as large a possession (after the other had taken out his) as before it was appropriated. Which measure did confine every man's possession to a very moderate proportion, and such as he might appropriate to himself without injury to anybody in the first ages of the world, when men were more in danger to be lost, by wandering from their company, in the then vast wilderness of the earth than to be straitened for want of room to plant in.

36. The same measure may be allowed still, without prejudice to anybody, full as the world seems. For, supposing a man or family, in the state they were at first, peopling of the world by the children of Adam or Noah, let him plant in some inland vacant places of America. We shall find that the possessions he could make himself, upon the measures we have given, would not be very large, nor, even to this day, prejudice the rest of mankind or give them reason to complain or think themselves injured by this man's encroachment, though the race of men have now spread themselves to all the corners of the world, and do infinitely exceed the small number [that] was at the beginning. Nay, the extent of ground is of so little value without labour that I have heard it affirmed that in Spain itself a man may be permitted to plough, sow, and reap, without being disturbed, upon land he has no other title to, but only his making use of it. But, on the contrary, the inhabitants think themselves beholden to him who, by his industry on neglected, and consequently waste land, has increased the stock of corn, which they wanted. But be this as it will, which I lay no stress on, this I dare boldly affirm, that the same rule of propriety—viz., that every man should have as much as he could make use of—would hold still in the world, without straitening anybody, since there is land enough in the world to suffice double the inhabitants, had not the invention of money, and the tacit agreement of men to put a value on it, introduced (by consent) larger possessions and a

right to them; which, how it has done, I shall by and by show more at large.

37. This is certain, that in the beginning, before the desire of having more than men needed had altered the intrinsic value of things, which depends only on their usefulness to the life of man, or had agreed that a little piece of yellow metal, which would keep without wasting or decay, should be worth a great piece of flesh or a whole heap of corn, though men had a right to appropriate by their labour, each one to himself, as much of the things of Nature as he could use, yet this could not be much, nor to the prejudice of others, where the same plenty was still left, to those who would use the same industry.

Before the appropriation of land, he who gathered as much of the wild fruit, killed, caught, or tamed as many of the beasts as he could—he that so employed his pains about any of the spontaneous products of Nature as any way to alter them from the state Nature put them in, by placing any of his labour on them, did thereby acquire a propriety in them; but if they perished in his possession without their due use—if the fruits rotted or the venison putrefied before he could spend it, he offended against the common law of Nature, and was liable to be punished: he invaded his neighbour's share, for he had no right farther than his use called for any of them, and they might serve to afford him conveniencies of life.

38. The same measures governed the possession of land, too. Whatsoever he tilled and reaped, laid up and made use of before it spoiled, that was his peculiar right; whatsoever he enclosed, and could feed and make use of, the cattle and product was also his. But if either the grass of his enclosure rotted on the ground, or the fruit of his planting perished without gathering and laying up, this part of the earth, notwithstanding his enclosure, was still to be looked on as waste, and might be the possession of any other. Thus, at the beginning, Cain might take as much ground as he could till and make it his own land, and yet leave enough to Abel's sheep to feed on: a few acres would serve for both their possessions. But as families increased and industry enlarged their stocks, their possessions enlarged with the need of them; but yet it was commonly without any fixed property in the ground they made use of till they incorporated, settled themselves together, and built cities, and then, by consent, they came in time to set out the bounds of their distinct territories and agree

on limits between them and their neighbours, and by laws within themselves settled the properties of those of the same society. For we see that in that part of the world which was first inhabited, and therefore like to be best peopled, even as low down as Abraham's time, they wandered with their flocks and their herds, which was their substance, freely up and down—and this Abraham did in a country where he was a stranger; whence it is plain that, at least, a great part of the land lay in common, that the inhabitants valued it not, nor claimed property in any more than they made use of; but when there was not room enough in the same place for their herds to feed together, they, by consent, as Abraham and Lot did (Gen. xiii. 5), separated and enlarged their pasture where it best liked them. And for the same reason, Esau went from his father and his brother, and planted in Mount Seir (Gen. xxxvi. 6).

39. And thus, without supposing any private dominion and property in Adam over all the world, exclusive of all other men, which can no way be proved, nor any one's property be made out from it, but supposing the world, given as it was to the children of men in common, we see how labour could make men distinct titles to several parcels of it for their private uses, wherein there could be no doubt of right, no room for quarrel.

40. Nor is it so strange as, perhaps, before consideration, it may appear, that the property of labour should be able to overbalance the community of land, for it is labour indeed that puts the difference of value on everything; and let any one consider what the difference is between an acre of land planted with tobacco or sugar, sown with wheat or barley, and an acre of the same land lying in common without any husbandry upon it, and he will find that the improvement of labour makes the far greater part of the value. I think it will be but a very modest computation to say, that of the products of the earth useful to the life of man, nine-tenths are the effects of labour. Nay, if we will rightly estimate things as they come to our use, and cast up the several expenses about them— what in them is purely owing to Nature and what to labour—we shall find that in most of them ninety-nine hundredths are wholly to be put on the account of labour.

41. There cannot be a clearer demonstration of anything than several nations of the Americans are of this, who are rich in land and poor in all the comforts of life; whom Nature, having furnished as liberally as any other people with the materials of plenty—*i.e.*, a fruitful soil, apt to produce in abundance what might serve for food, raiment, and delight; yet, for want of improving it by labour, have not one hundredth part of the conveniencies we enjoy, and a king of a large and fruitful territory there feeds, lodges, and is clad worse than a day labourer in England.

42. To make this a little clearer, let us but trace some of the ordinary provisions of life, through their several progresses, before they come to our use, and see how much they receive of their value from human industry. Bread, wine, and cloth are things of daily use and great plenty; yet notwithstanding acorns, water, and leaves, or skins must be our bread, drink, and clothing, did not labour furnish us with these more useful commodities. For whatever bread is more worth than acorns, wine than water, and cloth or silk than leaves, skins or moss, that is wholly owing to labour and industry. The one of these being the food and raiment which unassisted Nature furnishes us with; the other provisions which our industry and pains prepare for us, which how much they exceed the other in value, when any one hath computed, he will then see how much labour makes the far greatest part of the value of things we enjoy in this world; and the ground which produces the materials is scarce to be reckoned in as any, or at most, but a very small part of it; so little, that even amongst us, land that is left wholly to nature, that hath no improvement of pasturage, tillage, or planting, is called, as indeed it is, waste; and we shall find the benefit of it amount to little more than nothing.

43. An acre of land that bears here twenty bushels of wheat, and another in America, which, with the same husbandry, would do the like, are, without doubt, of the same natural, intrinsic value. But yet the benefit mankind receives from one in a year is worth five pounds, and the other possibly not worth a penny; if all the profit an Indian received from it were to be valued and sold here, at least I may truly say, not one thousandth. It is labour, then, which puts the greatest part of value upon land, without which it would scarcely be worth anything; it is to that we owe the greatest part of all its useful products; for all that the straw, bran, bread, of that acre of wheat, is more worth than the product of an acre of as good land which lies waste is all the effect of labour. For it is not barely the ploughman's pains, the reaper's and thresher's toil, and the baker's sweat, is to be counted into the bread we eat; the labour of those who broke

the oxen, who digged and wrought the iron and stones, who felled and framed the timber employed about the plough, mill, oven, or any other utensils, which are a vast number, requisite to this corn, from its sowing to its being made bread, must all be charged on the account of labour, and received as an effect of that; Nature and the earth furnished only the almost worthless materials as in themselves. It would be a strange catalogue of things that industry provided and made use of about every loaf of bread before it came to our use if we could trace them; iron, wood, leather, bark, timber, stone, bricks, coals, lime, cloth, dyeing-drugs, pitch, tar, masts, ropes, and all the materials made use of in the ship that brought any of the commodities made use of by any of the workmen, to any part of the work, all which it would be almost impossible, at least too long, to reckon up.

44. From all which it is evident, that though the things of Nature are given in common, man (by being master of himself, and proprietor of his own person, and the actions or labour of it) had still in himself the great foundation of property; and that which made up the great part of what he applied to the support or comfort of his being, when invention and arts had improved the conveniencies of life, was perfectly his own, and did not belong in common to others.

45. Thus labour, in the beginning, gave a right of property, wherever any one was pleased to employ it, upon what was common, which remained a long while, the far greater part, and is yet more than mankind makes use of. Men at first, for the most part, contented themselves with what unassisted Nature offered to their necessities; and though afterwards, in some parts of the world, where the increase of people and stock, with the use of money, had made land scarce, and so of some value, the several communities settled the bounds of their distinct territories, and, by laws, within themselves, regulated the properties of the private men of their society, and so, by compact and agreement, settled the property which labour and industry began. And the leagues that have been made between several states and kingdoms, either expressly or tacitly disowning all claim and right to the land in the other's possession, have, by common consent, given up their pretences to their natural common right, which originally they had to those countries; and so have, by positive agreement, settled a property amongst themselves, in distinct parts of the world; yet there are still great tracts of ground to be found, which the inhabitants thereof,

not having joined with the rest of mankind in the consent of the use of their common money, lie waste, and are more than the people who dwell on it, do, or can make use of, and so still lie in common; though this can scarce happen amongst that part of mankind that have consented to the use of money.

46. The greatest part of things really useful to the life of man, and such as the necessity of subsisting made the first commoners of the world look after—as it doth the Americans now—are generally things of short duration, such as—if they are not consumed by use—will decay and perish of themselves. Gold, silver, and diamonds are things that fancy or agreement hath put the value on, more than real use and the necessary support of life. Now of those good things which Nature hath provided in common, every one hath a right (as hath been said) to as much as he could use, and had a property in all he could effect with his labour; all that his industry could extend to, to alter from the state Nature had put it in, was his. He that gathered a hundred bushels of acorns or apples had thereby a property in them; they were his goods as soon as gathered. He was only to look that he used them before they spoiled, else he took more than his share, and robbed others. And, indeed, it was a foolish thing, as well as dishonest, to hoard up more than he could make use of. If he gave away a part to anybody else, so that it perished not uselessly in his possession, these he also made use of. And if he also bartered away plums that would have rotted in a week, for nuts that would last good for his eating a whole year, he did no injury; he wasted not the common stock; destroyed no part of the portion of goods that belonged to others, so long as nothing perished uselessly in his hands. Again, if he would give his nuts for a piece of metal, pleased with its colour, or exchange his sheep for shells, or wool for a sparkling pebble or a diamond, and keep those by him all his life, he invaded not the right of others; he might heap up as much of these durable things as he pleased; the exceeding of the bounds of his just property not lying in the largeness of his possession, but the perishing of anything uselessly in it.

47. And thus came in the use of money; some lasting thing that men might keep without spoiling, and that, by mutual consent, men would take in exchange for the truly useful but perishable supports of life.

48. And as different degrees of industry were apt to give men possessions in different proportions, so this invention of money gave them the opportunity to

continue and enlarge them. For supposing an island, separate from all possible commerce with the rest of the world, wherein there were but a hundred families, but there were sheep, horses, and cows, with other useful animals, wholesome fruits, and land enough for corn for a hundred thousand times as many, but nothing in the island, either because of its commonness or perishableness, fit to supply the place of money. What reason could any one have there to enlarge his possessions beyond the use of his family, and a plentiful supply to its consumption, either in what their own industry produced, or they could barter for like perishable, useful commodities with others? Where there is not something both lasting and scarce, and so valuable to be hoarded up, there men will not be apt to enlarge their possessions of land, were it never so rich, never so free for them to take. For I ask, what would a man value ten thousand or an hundred thousand acres of excellent land, ready cultivated and well stocked, too, with cattle, in the middle of the inland parts of America, where he had no hopes of commerce with other parts of the world, to draw money to him by the sale of the product? It would not be worth the enclosing, and we should see him give up again to the wild common of Nature whatever was more than would supply the conveniencies of life, to be had there for him and his family.

49. Thus, in the beginning, all the world was America, and more so than that is now; for no such thing as money was anywhere known. Find out something that hath the use and value of money amongst his neighbours, you shall see the same man will begin presently to enlarge his possessions.

50. But since gold and silver, being little useful to the life of man, in proportion to food, raiment, and carriage, has its value only from the consent of men—whereof labour yet makes in great part the measure—it is plain that the consent of men have agreed to a disproportionate and unequal possession of the earth—I mean out of the bounds of society and compact; for in governments the laws regulate it; they having, by consent, found out and agreed in a way how a man may, rightfully and without injury, possess more than he himself can make use of by receiving gold and silver, which may continue long in a man's possession without decaying for the overplus, and agreeing those metals should have a value.

51. And thus, I think, it is very easy to conceive, without any difficulty, how labour could at first begin a title of property in the common things of Nature,

and how the spending it upon our uses bounded it; so that there could then be no reason of quarrelling about title, nor any doubt about the largeness of possession it gave. Right and conveniency went together. For as a man had a right to all he could employ his labour upon, so he had no temptation to labour for more than he could make use of. This left no room for controversy about the title, nor for encroachment on the right of others. What portion a man carved to himself was easily seen; and it was useless, as well as dishonest, to carve himself too much, or take more than he needed.

Chapter VI
Of Paternal Power

52. It may perhaps be censured an impertinent criticism in a discourse of this nature to find fault with words and names that have obtained in the world. And yet possibly it may not be amiss to offer new ones when the old are apt to lead men into mistakes, as this of paternal power probably has done, which seems so to place the power of parents over their children wholly in the father, as if the mother had no share in it; whereas if we consult reason or revelation, we shall find she has an equal title, which may give one reason to ask whether this might not be more properly called parental power? For whatever obligation Nature and the right of generation lays on children, it must certainly bind them equal to both the concurrent causes of it. And accordingly we see the positive law of God everywhere joins them together without distinction, when it commands the obedience of children: "Honour thy father and thy mother" (Exod. xx. 12); "Whosoever curseth his father or his mother" (Lev. xx. 9); "Ye shall fear every man his mother and his father" (Lev. xix. 3); "Children, obey your parents" (Eph. vi. 1), etc., is the style of the Old and New Testament.

53. Had but this one thing been well considered without looking any deeper into the matter, it might perhaps have kept men from running into those gross mistakes they have made about this power of parents, which however it might without any great harshness bear the name of absolute dominion and regal authority, when under the title of "paternal" power, it seemed appropriated to the father; would yet have sounded but oddly, and in the very name shown the absurdity, if this supposed absolute power over chil-

dren had been called parental, and thereby discovered that it belonged to the mother too. For it will but very ill serve the turn of those men who contend so much for the absolute power and authority of the fatherhood, as they call it, that the mother should have any share in it. And it would have but ill supported the monarchy they contend for, when by the very name it appeared that that fundamental authority from whence they would derive their government of a single person only was not placed in one, but two persons jointly. But to let this of names pass.

54. Though I have said above (2) "That all men by nature are equal," I cannot be supposed to understand all sorts of "equality." Age or virtue may give men a just precedency. Excellency of parts and merit may place others above the common level. Birth may subject some, and alliance or benefits others, to pay an observance to those to whom Nature, gratitude, or other respects, may have made it due; and yet all this consists with the equality which all men are in in respect of jurisdiction or dominion one over another, which was the equality I there spoke of as proper to the business in hand, being that equal right that every man hath to his natural freedom, without being subjected to the will or authority of any other man.

55. Children, I confess, are not born in this full state of equality, though they are born to it. Their parents have a sort of rule and jurisdiction over them when they come into the world, and for some time after, but it is but a temporary one. The bonds of this subjection are like the swaddling clothes they are wrapt up in and supported by in the weakness of their infancy. Age and reason as they grow up loosen them, till at length they drop quite off, and leave a man at his own free disposal.

56. Adam was created a perfect man, his body and mind in full possession of their strength and reason, and so was capable from the first instance of his being to provide for his own support and preservation, and govern his actions according to the dictates of the law of reason God had implanted in him. From him the world is peopled with his descendants, who are all born infants, weak and helpless, without knowledge or understanding. But to supply the defects of this imperfect state till the improvement of growth and age had removed them, Adam and Eve, and after them all parents were, by the law of Nature, under an obligation to preserve, nourish, and educate the children they had begotten, not as their own workmanship, but the workmanship of their own Maker, the Almighty, to whom they were to be accountable for them.

57. The law that was to govern Adam was the same that was to govern all his posterity, the law of reason. But his offspring having another way of entrance into the world, different from him, by a natural birth, that produced them ignorant, and without the use of reason, they were not presently under that law. For nobody can be under a law that is not promulgated to him; and this law being promulgated or made known by reason only, he that is not come to the use of his reason cannot be said to be under this law; and Adam's children being not presently as soon as born under this law of reason, were not presently free. For law, in its true notion, is not so much the limitation as the direction of a free and intelligent agent to his proper interest, and prescribes no farther than is for the general good of those under that law. Could they be happier without it, the law, as a useless thing, would of itself vanish; and that ill deserves the name of confinement which hedges us in only from bogs and precipices. So that however it may be mistaken, the end of law is not to abolish or restrain, but to preserve and enlarge freedom. For in all the states of created beings, capable of laws, where there is no law there is no freedom. For liberty is to be free from restraint and violence from others, which cannot be where there is no law; and is not, as we are told, "a liberty for every man to do what he lists." For who could be free, when every other man's humour might domineer over him? But a liberty to dispose and order freely as he lists his person, actions, possessions, and his whole property within the allowance of those laws under which he is, and therein not to be subject to the arbitrary will of another, but freely follow his own.

58. The power, then, that parents have over their children arises from that duty which is incumbent on them, to take care of their offspring during the imperfect state of childhood. To inform the mind, and govern the actions of their yet ignorant nonage, till reason shall take its place and ease them of that trouble, is what the children want, and the parents are bound to. For God having given man an understanding to direct his actions, has allowed him a freedom of will and liberty of acting, as properly belonging thereunto within the bounds of that law he is under. But whilst he is in an estate wherein he has no understanding of his own to direct his will, he is not to have any will of his own to follow. He that understands for him must will for him too; he must prescribe to his

will, and regulate his actions, but when he comes to the estate that made his father a free man, the son is a free man too.

59. This holds in all the laws a man is under, whether natural or civil. Is a man under the law of Nature? What made him free of that law? what gave him a free disposing of his property, according to his own will, within the compass of that law? I answer, an estate wherein he might be supposed capable to know that law, that so he might keep his actions within the bounds of it. When he has acquired that state, he is presumed to know how far that law is to be his guide, and how far he may make use of his freedom, and so comes to have it; till then, somebody else must guide him, who is presumed to know how far the law allows a liberty. If such a state of reason, such an age of discretion made him free, the same shall make his son free too. Is a man under the law of England? What made him free of that law—that is, to have the liberty to dispose of his actions and possessions, according to his own will, within the permission of that law? A capacity of knowing that law. Which is supposed, by that law, at the age of twenty-one, and in some cases sooner. If this made the father free, it shall make the son free too. Till then, we see the law allows the son to have no will, but he is to be guided by the will of his father or guardian, who is to understand for him. And if the father die and fail to substitute a deputy in this trust, if he hath not provided a tutor to govern his son during his minority, during his want of understanding, the law takes care to do it: some other must govern him and be a will to him till he hath attained to a state of freedom, and his understanding be fit to take the government of his will. But after that the father and son are equally free, as much as tutor and pupil, after nonage, equally subjects of the same law together, without any dominion left in the father over the life, liberty, or estate of his son, whether they be only in the state and under the law of Nature, or under the positive laws of an established government.

60. But if through defects that may happen out of the ordinary course of Nature, any one comes not to such a degree of reason wherein he might be supposed capable of knowing the law, and so living within the rules of it, he is never capable of being a free man, he is never let loose to the disposure of his own will; because he knows no bounds to it, has not understanding, its proper guide, but is continued under the tuition and government of others all the time his own understanding is incapable of that charge. And so lunatics and idiots are never set free from the government of their parents: "Children who are not as yet come unto those years whereat they may have, and innocents, which are excluded by a natural defect from ever having." Thirdly, "Madmen, which, for the present, cannot possibly have the use of right reason to guide themselves, have, for their guide, the reason that guideth other men which are tutors over them, to seek and procure their good for them," says Hooker (*Eccl. Pol.*, lib. i., s. 7). All which seems no more than that duty which God and Nature has laid on man, as well as other creatures, to preserve their offspring till they can be able to shift for themselves, and will scarce amount to an instance or proof of parents' regal authority.

61. Thus we are born free as we are born rational; not that we have actually the exercise of either: age that brings one, brings with it the other too. And thus we see how natural freedom and subjection to parents may consist together, and are both founded on the same principle. A child is free by his father's title, by his father's understanding, which is to govern him till he hath it of his own. The freedom of a man at years of discretion, and the subjection of a child to his parents, whilst yet short of it, are so consistent and so distinguishable that the most blinded contenders for monarchy, "by right of fatherhood," cannot miss of it; the most obstinate cannot but allow of it. For were their doctrine all true, were the right heir of Adam now known, and, by that title, settled a monarch in his throne, invested with all the absolute unlimited power Sir Robert Filmer talks of, if he should die as soon as his heir were born, must not the child, notwithstanding he were never so free, never so much sovereign, be in subjection to his mother and nurse, to tutors and governors, till age and education brought him reason and ability to govern himself and others? The necessities of his life, the health of his body, and the information of his mind would require him to be directed by the will of others and not his own; and yet will any one think that this restraint and subjection were inconsistent with, or spoiled him of, that liberty or sovereignty he had a right to, or gave away his empire to those who had the government of his nonage? This government over him only prepared him the better and sooner for it. If anybody should ask me when my son is of age to be free, I shall answer, just when his monarch is of age to govern. "But at what time," says the judicious Hooker (*Eccl.*

Pol., lib. i., s. 6), "a man may be said to have attained so far forth the use of reason as sufficeth to make him capable of those laws whereby he is then bound to guide his actions; this is a great deal more easy for sense to discern than for any one, by skill and learning, to determine."

62. Commonwealths themselves take notice of, and allow that there is a time when men are to begin to act like free men, and therefore, till that time, require not oaths of fealty or allegiance, or other public owning of, or submission to, the government of their countries.

63. The freedom then of man, and liberty of acting according to his own will, is grounded on his having reason, which is able to instruct him in that law he is to govern himself by, and make him know how far he is left to the freedom of his own will. To turn him loose to an unrestrained liberty, before he has reason to guide him, is not the allowing him the privilege of his nature to be free, but to thrust him out amongst brutes, and abandon him to a state as wretched and as much beneath that of a man as theirs. This is that which puts the authority into the parents' hands to govern the minority of their children. God hath made it their business to employ this care on their offspring, and hath placed in them suitable inclinations of tenderness and concern to temper this power, to apply it as His wisdom designed it, to the children's good as long as they should need to be under it.

64. But what reason can hence advance this care of the parents due to their offspring into an absolute, arbitrary dominion of the father, whose power reaches no farther than by such a discipline as he finds most effectual to give such strength and health to their bodies, such vigour and rectitude to their minds, as may best fit his children to be most useful to themselves and others, and, if it be necessary to his condition, to make them work when they are able for their own subsistence; but in this power the mother, too, has her share with the father.

65. Nay, this power so little belongs to the father by any peculiar right of Nature, but only as he is guardian of his children, that when he quits his care of them he loses his power over them, which goes along with their nourishment and education, to which it is inseparably annexed, and belongs as much to the foster-father of an exposed child as to the natural father of another. So little power does the bare act of begetting give a man over his issue, if all his care ends

there, and this be all the title he hath to the name and authority of a father. And what will become of this paternal power in that part of the world where one woman hath more than one husband at a time? or in those parts of America where, when the husband and wife part, which happens frequently, the children are all left to the mother, follow her, and are wholly under her care and provision? And if the father die whilst the children are young, do they not naturally everywhere owe the same obedience to their mother, during their minority, as to their father, were he alive? And will any one say that the mother hath a legislative power over her children that she can make standing rules which shall be of perpetual obligation, by which they ought to regulate all the concerns of their property, and bound their liberty all the course of their lives, and enforce the observation of them with capital punishments? For this is the proper power of the magistrate, of which the father hath not so much as the shadow. His command over his children is but temporary, and reaches not their life or property. It is but a help to the weakness and imperfection of their nonage, a discipline necessary to their education. And though a father may dispose of his own possessions as he pleases when his children are out of danger of perishing for want, yet his power extends not to the lives or goods which either their own industry, or another's bounty, has made theirs, nor to their liberty neither, when they are once arrived to the enfranchisement of the years of discretion. The father's empire then ceases, and he can from thenceforward no more dispose of the liberty of his son than that of any other man. And it must be far from an absolute or perpetual jurisdiction from which a man may withdraw himself, having licence from Divine authority to "leave father and mother and cleave to his wife."

66. But though there be a time when a child comes to be as free from subjection to the will and command of his father as he himself is free from subjection to the will of anybody else, and they are both under no other restraint but that which is common to them both, whether it be the law of Nature or municipal law of their country, yet this freedom exempts not a son from that honour which he ought, by the law of God and Nature, to pay his parents, God having made the parents instruments in His great design of continuing the race of mankind and the occasions of life to their children. As He hath laid on them an obligation to nourish, preserve, and bring up their offspring, so He has laid on the children a perpetual obligation of

honouring their parents, which, containing in it an inward esteem and reverence to be shown by all outward expressions, ties up the child from anything that may ever injure or affront, disturb or endanger the happiness or life of those from whom he received his, and engages him in all actions of defence, relief, assistance, and comfort of those by whose means he entered into being and has been made capable of any enjoyments of life. From this obligation no state, no freedom, can absolve children. But this is very far from giving parents a power of command over their children, or an authority to make laws and dispose as they please of their lives or liberties. It is one thing to owe honour, respect, gratitude, and assistance; another to require an absolute obedience and submission. The honour due to parents a monarch on his throne owes his mother, and yet this lessens not his authority nor subjects him to her government.

67. The subjection of a minor places in the father a temporary government which terminates with the minority of the child; and the honour due from a child places in the parents a perpetual right to respect, reverence, support, and compliance, to more or less, as the father's care, cost, and kindness in his education has been more or less, and this ends not with minority, but holds in all parts and conditions of a man's life. The want of distinguishing these two powers which the father hath, in the right of tuition, during minority, and the right of honour all his life, may perhaps have caused a great part of the mistakes about this matter. For, to speak properly of them, the first of these is rather the privilege of children and duty of parents than any prerogative of paternal power. The nourishment and education of their children is a charge so incumbent on parents for their children's good, that nothing can absolve them from taking care of it. And though the power of commanding and chastising them go along with it, yet God hath woven into the principles of human nature such a tenderness for their offspring, that there is little fear that parents should use their power with too much rigour; the excess is seldom on the severe side, the strong bias of nature drawing the other way. And therefore God Almighty, when He would express His gentle dealing with the Israelites, He tells them that though He chastened them, "He chastened them as a man chastens his son" (Deut. viii. 5)—*i.e.*, with tenderness and affection, and kept them under no severer discipline than what was absolutely best for them, and had been less kindness to have slackened. This is that power to

which children are commanded obedience, that the pains and care of their parents may not be increased or ill-rewarded.

68. On the other side, honour and support all that which gratitude requires to return; for the benefits received by and from them is the indispensable duty of the child and the proper privilege of the parents. This is intended for the parents' advantage, as the other is for the child's; though education, the parents' duty, seems to have most power, because the ignorance and infirmities of childhood stand in need of restraint and correction, which is a visible exercise of rule and a kind of dominion. And that duty which is comprehended in the word "honour" requires less obedience, though the obligation be stronger on grown than younger children. For who can think the command, "Children, obey your parents," requires in a man that has children of his own the same submission to his father as it does in his yet young children to him, and that by this precept he were bound to obey all his father's commands, if, out of a conceit of authority, he should have the indiscretion to treat him still as a boy?

69. The first part, then, of paternal power, or rather duty, which is education, belongs so to the father that it terminates at a certain season. When the business of education is over it ceases of itself, and is also alienable before. For a man may put the tuition of his son in other hands; and he that has made his son an apprentice to another has discharged him, during that time, of a great part of his obedience, both to himself and to his mother. But all the duty of honour, the other part, remains nevertheless entire to them; nothing can cancel that. It is so inseparable from them both, that the father's authority cannot dispossess the mother of this right, nor can any man discharge his son from honouring her that bore him. But both these are very far from a power to make laws, and enforcing them with penalties that may reach estate, liberty, limbs, and life. The power of commanding ends with nonage, and though after that honour and respect, support and defence, and whatsoever gratitude can oblige a man to, for the highest benefits he is naturally capable of be always due from a son to his parents, yet all this puts no sceptre into the father's hand, no sovereign power of commanding. He has no dominion over his son's property or actions, nor any right that his will should prescribe to his son's in all things; however, it may become his son

in many things, not very inconvenient to him and his family, to pay a deference to it.

70. A man may owe honour and respect to an ancient or wise man, defence to his child or friend, relief and support to the distressed, and gratitude to a benefactor, to such a degree that all he has, all he can do, cannot sufficiently pay it. But all these give no authority, no right of making laws to any one over him from whom they are owing. And it is plain all this is due, not to the bare title of father, not only because, as has been said, it is owing to the mother too, but because these obligations to parents, and the degrees of what is required of children, may be varied by the different care and kindness, trouble and expense, [that] is often employed upon one child more than another.

71. This shows the reason how it comes to pass that parents in societies, where they themselves are subjects, retain a power over their children and have as much right to their subjection as those who are in the state of Nature, which could not possibly be if all political power were only paternal, and that, in truth, they were one and the same thing; for then, all paternal power being in the prince, the subject could naturally have none of it. But these two powers, political and paternal, are so perfectly distinct and separate, and built upon so different foundations, and given to so different ends, that every subject that is a father has as much a paternal power over his children as the prince has over his. And every prince that has parents owes them as much filial duty and obedience as the meanest of his subjects do to theirs, and can therefore contain not any part or degree of that kind of dominion which a prince or magistrate has over his subject.

72. Though the obligation on the parents to bring up their children, and the obligation on children to honour their parents, contain all the power, on the one hand, and submission on the other, which are proper to this relation, yet there is another power ordinarily in the father, whereby he has a tie on the obedience of his children, which, though it be common to him with other men, yet the occasions of showing it, almost constantly happening to fathers in their private families and in instances of it elsewhere being rare, and less taken notice of, it passes in the world for a part of "paternal jurisdiction." And this is the power men generally have to bestow their estates on those who please them best. The possession of the father being the expectation and inheritance of the children ordinarily, in certain proportions, according to the law and custom of each country, yet it is commonly in the father's power to bestow it with a more sparing or liberal hand, according as the behaviour of this or that child hath comported with his will and humour.

73. This is no small tie to the obedience of children; and there being always annexed to the enjoyment of land a submission to the government of the country of which that land is a part, it has been commonly supposed that a father could oblige his posterity to that government of which he himself was a subject, that his compact held them; whereas, it being only a necessary condition annexed to the land which is under that government, reaches only those who will take it on that condition, and so is no natural tie or engagement, but a voluntary submission; for every man's children being, by Nature, as free as himself or any of his ancestors ever were, may, whilst they are in that freedom, choose what society they will join themselves to, what commonwealth they will put themselves under. But if they will enjoy the inheritance of their ancestors, they must take it on the same terms their ancestors had it, and submit to all the conditions annexed to such a possession. By this power, indeed, fathers oblige their children to obedience to themselves even when they are past minority, and most commonly, too, subject them to this or that political power. But neither of these [is] by any peculiar right of fatherhood, but by the reward they have in their hands to enforce and recompense such a compliance, and is no more power than what a Frenchman has over an Englishman, who, by the hopes of an estate he will leave him, will certainly have a strong tie on his obedience; and if when it is left him, he will enjoy it, he must certainly take it upon the conditions annexed to the possession of land in that country where it lies, whether it be France or England.

74. To conclude, then, though the father's power of commanding extends no farther than the minority of his children, and to a degree only fit for the discipline and government of that age; and though that honour and respect, and all that which the Latins called piety, which they indispensably owe to their parents all their lifetime, and in all estates, with all that support and defence, is due to them, gives the father no power of governing—*i.e.*, making laws and exacting penalties on his children; though by this he has no dominion over the property or actions of his

son, yet it is obvious to conceive how easy it was, in the first ages of the world, and in places still where the thinness of people gives families leave to separate into unpossessed quarters, and they have room to remove and plant themselves in yet vacant habitations, for the father of the family to become the prince of it;[2] he had been a ruler from the beginning of the infancy of his children; and when they were grown up, since without some government it would be hard for them to live together, it was likeliest it should, by the express or tacit consent of the children, be in the father, where it seemed, without any change, barely to continue. And when, indeed, nothing more was required to it than the permitting the father to exercise alone in his family that executive power of the law of Nature which every free man naturally hath, and by that permission resigning up to him a monarchical power whilst they remained in it. But that this was not by any paternal right, but only by the consent of his children, is evident from hence, that nobody doubts but if a stranger, whom chance or business had brought to his family, had there killed any of his children, or committed any other act, he might condemn and put him to death, or otherwise have punished him as well as any of his children, which was impossible he should do by virtue of any paternal authority over one who was not his child, but by virtue of that executive power of the law of Nature which, as a man, he had a right to; and he alone could punish him in his family where the respect of his children had laid by the exercise of such a power, to give way to the dignity and authority they were willing should remain in him above the rest of his family.

---

2. "It is no improbable opinion, therefore, which the arch-philosopher was of, That the chief person in every household was always, as it were, a king; so when numbers of households joined themselves in civil societies together, kings were the first kind of governors among them, which is also, as it seemeth, the reason why the name of fathers continued still in them, who of fathers were made rulers; as also the ancient custom of governors to do as Melchizedec; and being kings, to exercise the office of priests, which fathers did, at the first, grew, perhaps, by the same occasion. Howbeit, this is not the only kind of regimen that has been received in the world. The inconveniencies of one kind have caused sundry others to be devised, so that, in a word, all public regimen, of what kind soever, seemeth evidently to have risen from the deliberate advice, consultation, and composition between men, judging it convenient and behoveful, there being no impossibility in Nature, considered by itself, but that man might have lived without any public regimen."—Hooker (*Eccl. Pol.*, lib. i., s. 10).

75. Thus it was easy and almost natural for children, by a tacit and almost natural consent, to make way for the father's authority and government. They had been accustomed in their childhood to follow his direction, and to refer their little differences to him; and when they were men, who was fitter to rule them? Their little properties and less covetousness seldom afforded greater controversies; and when any should arise, where could they have a fitter umpire than he, by whose care they had every one been sustained and brought up, and who had a tenderness for them all? It is no wonder that they made no distinction betwixt minority and full age, nor looked after one-and-twenty, or any other age, that might make them the free disposers of themselves and fortunes, when they could have no desire to be out of their pupilage. The government they had been under during it continued still to be more their protection than restraint; and they could nowhere find a greater security to their peace, liberties, and fortunes than in the rule of a father.

76. Thus the natural fathers of families, by an insensible change, became the politic monarchs of them too; and as they chanced to live long, and leave able and worthy heirs for several successions or otherwise, so they laid the foundations of hereditary or elective kingdoms under several constitutions and manors, according as chance, contrivance, or occasions happened to mould them. But if princes have their titles in the father's right, and it be a sufficient proof of the natural right of fathers to political authority, because they commonly were those in whose hands we find, *de facto*, the exercise of government, I say, if this argument be good, it will as strongly prove that all princes, nay, princes only, ought to be priests, since it is as certain that in the beginning "the father of the family was priest, as that he was ruler in his own household."

Chapter VII
Of Political or Civil Society

77. God, having made man such a creature that, in His own judgment, it was not good for him to be alone, put him under strong obligations of necessity, convenience, and inclination, to drive him into society, as well as fitted him with understanding and language to continue and enjoy it. The first society was between man and wife, which gave beginning to that between parents and children, to which, in time, that

between master and servant came to be added. And though all these might, and commonly did, meet together, and make up but one family, wherein the master or mistress of it had some sort of rule proper to a family, each of these, or all together, came short of "political society," as we shall see if we consider the different ends, ties, and bounds of each of these.

78. Conjugal society is made by a voluntary compact between man and woman, and though it consist chiefly in such a communion and right in one another's bodies as is necessary to its chief end, procreation, yet it draws with it mutual support and assistance, and a communion of interests too, as necessary not only to unite their care and affection, but also necessary to their common offspring, who have a right to be nourished and maintained by them till they are able to provide for themselves.

79. For the end of conjunction between male and female being not barely procreation, but the continuation of the species, this conjunction betwixt male and female ought to last, even after procreation, so long as is necessary to the nourishment and support of the young ones, who are to be sustained by those that got them till they are able to shift and provide for themselves. This rule, which the infinite wise Maker hath set to the works of His hands, we find the inferior creatures steadily obey. In those vivaporous animals which feed on grass the conjunction between male and female lasts no longer than the very act of copulation, because the teat of the dam being sufficient to nourish the young till it be able to feed on grass, the male only begets, but concerns not himself for the female or young, to whose sustenance he can contribute nothing. But in beasts of prey the conjunction lasts longer, because the dam, not being able well to subsist herself and nourish her numerous offspring by her own prey alone (a more laborious as well as more dangerous way of living than by feeding on grass), the assistance of the male is necessary to the maintenance of their common family, which cannot subsist till they are able to prey for themselves, but by the joint care of male and female. The same is observed in all birds (except some domestic ones, where plenty of food excuses the cock from feeding and taking care of the young brood), whose young, needing food in the nest, the cock and hen continue mates till the young are able to use their wings and provide for themselves.

80. And herein, I think, lies the chief, if not the only reason, why the male and female in mankind are tied to a longer conjunction than other creatures—viz., because the female is capable of conceiving, and, *de facto*, is commonly with child again, and brings forth too a new birth, long before the former is out of a dependency for support on his parents' help and able to shift for himself, and has all the assistance due to him from his parents, whereby the father, who is bound to take care for those he hath begot, is under an obligation to continue in conjugal society with the same woman longer than other creatures, whose young, being able to subsist of themselves before the time of procreation returns again, the conjugal bond dissolves of itself, and they are at liberty till Hymen, at his usual anniversary season, summons them again to choose new mates. Wherein one cannot but admire the wisdom of the great Creator, who, having given to man an ability to lay up for the future as well as supply the present necessity, hath made it necessary that society of man and wife should be more lasting than of male and female amongst other creatures, that so their industry might be encouraged, and their interest better united, to make provision and lay up goods for their common issue, which uncertain mixture, or easy and frequent solutions of conjugal society, would mightily disturb.

81. But though these are ties upon mankind which make the conjugal bonds more firm and lasting in a man than the other species of animals, yet it would give one reason to inquire why this compact, where procreation and education are secured and inheritance taken care for, may not be made determinable, either by consent, or at a certain time, or upon certain conditions, as well as any other voluntary compacts, there being no necessity, in the nature of the thing, nor to the ends of it, that it should always be for life—I mean, to such as are under no restraint of any positive law which ordains all such contracts to be perpetual.

82. But the husband and wife, though they have but one common concern, yet having different understandings, will unavoidably sometimes have different wills too. It therefore being necessary that the last determination (*i.e.*, the rule) should be placed somewhere, it naturally falls to the man's share as the abler and the stronger. But this, reaching but to the things of their common interest and property, leaves the wife in the full and true possession of what by contract is her peculiar right, and at least gives the husband no more power over her than she has over his life; the power of the husband being so far from that

of an absolute monarch that the wife has, in many cases, a liberty to separate from him where natural right or their contract allows it, whether that contract be made by themselves in the state of Nature or by the customs or laws of the country they live in, and the children, upon such separation, fall to the father or mother's lot as such contract does determine.

83. For all the ends of marriage being to be obtained under politic government, as well as in the state of Nature, the civil magistrate doth not abridge the right or power of either, naturally necessary to those ends—viz., procreation and mutual support and assistance whilst they are together, but only decides any controversy that may arise between man and wife about them. If it were otherwise, and that absolute sovereignty and power of life and death naturally belonged to the husband, and were necessary to the society between man and wife, there could be no matrimony in any of these countries where the husband is allowed no such absolute authority. But the ends of matrimony requiring no such power in the husband, it was not at all necessary to it. The condition of conjugal society put it not in him; but whatsoever might consist with procreation and support of the children till they could shift for themselves—mutual assistance, comfort, and maintenance—might be varied and regulated by that contract which first united them in that society, nothing being necessary to any society that is not necessary to the ends for which it is made.

84. The society betwixt parents and children, and the distinct rights and powers belonging respectively to them, I have treated of so largely in the foregoing chapter that I shall not here need to say anything of it; and I think it is plain that it is far different from a politic society.

85. Master and servant are names as old as history, but given to those of far different condition; for a free man makes himself a servant to another by selling him for a certain time the service he undertakes to do in exchange for wages he is to receive; and though this commonly puts him into the family of his master, and under the ordinary discipline thereof, yet it gives the master but a temporary power over him, and no greater than what is contained in the contract between them. But there is another sort of servant which by a peculiar name we call slaves, who being captives taken in a just war are, by the right of Nature, subjected to the absolute dominion and arbitrary power of their masters. These men having, as I say, forfeited their lives and, with it, their liberties, and lost their estates, and being in the state of slavery, not capable of any property, cannot in that state be considered as any part of civil society, the chief end whereof is the preservation of property.

86. Let us therefore consider a master of a family with all these subordinate relations of wife, children, servants, and slaves, united under the domestic rule of a family, with what resemblance soever it may have in its order, offices, and number too, with a little commonwealth, yet is very far from it both in its constitution, power, and end; or if it must be thought a monarchy, and the paterfamilias the absolute monarch in it, absolute monarchy will have but a very shattered and short power, when it is plain by what has been said before, that the master of the family has a very distinct and differently limited power both as to time and extent over those several persons that are in it; for excepting the slave (and the family is as much a family, and his power as paterfamilias as great, whether there be any slaves in his family or no) he has no legislative power of life and death over any of them, and none too but what a mistress of a family may have as well as he. And he certainly can have no absolute power over the whole family who has but a very limited one over every individual in it. But how a family, or any other society of men, differ from that which is properly political society, we shall best see by considering wherein political society itself consists.

87. Man being born, as has been proved, with a title to perfect freedom and an uncontrolled enjoyment of all the rights and privileges of the law of Nature, equally with any other man, or number of men in the world, hath by nature a power not only to preserve his property—that is, his life, liberty, and estate—against the injuries and attempts of other men, but to judge of and punish the breaches of that law in others, as he is persuaded the offence deserves, even with death itself, in crimes where the heinousness of the fact, in his opinion, requires it. But because no political society can be, nor subsist, without having in itself the power to preserve the property, and in order thereunto punish the offences of all those of that society, there, and there only, is political society where every one of the members hath quitted this natural power, resigned it up into the hands of the community in all cases that exclude him not from appealing for protection to the law established by it. And thus all private judgment of every particular

member being excluded, the community comes to be umpire, and by understanding indifferent rules and men authorised by the community for their execution, decides all the differences that may happen between any members of that society concerning any matter of right, and punishes those offences which any member hath committed against the society with such penalties as the law has established; whereby it is easy to discern who are, and are not, in political society together. Those who are united into one body, and have a common established law and judicature to appeal to, with authority to decide controversies between them and punish offenders, are in civil society one with another; but those who have no such common appeal, I mean on earth, are still in the state of Nature, each being where there is no other, judge for himself and executioner; which is, as I have before showed it, the perfect state of Nature.

88. And thus the commonwealth comes by a power to set down what punishment shall belong to the several transgressions they think worthy of it, committed amongst the members of that society (which is the power of making laws), as well as it has the power to punish any injury done unto any of its members by any one that is not of it (which is the power of war and peace); and all this for the preservation of the property of all the members of that society, as far as is possible. But though every man entered into society has quitted his power to punish offences against the law of Nature in prosecution of his own private judgment, yet with the judgment of offences which he has given up to the legislative, in all cases where he can appeal to the magistrate, he has given up a right to the commonwealth to employ his force for the execution of the judgments of the commonwealth whenever he shall be called to it, which, indeed, are his own judgments, they being made by himself or his representative. And herein we have the original of the legislative and executive power of civil society, which is to judge by standing laws how far offences are to be punished when committed within the commonwealth; and also by occasional judgments founded on the present circumstances of the fact, how far injuries from without are to be vindicated, and in both these to employ all the force of all the members when there shall be need.

89. Wherever, therefore, any number of men so unite into one society as to quit every one his executive power of the law of Nature, and to resign it to the public, there and there only is a political or civil society. And this is done wherever any number of men, in the state of Nature, enter into society to make one people one body politic under one supreme government: or else when any one joins himself to, and incorporates with any government already made. For hereby he authorises the society, or which is all one, the legislative thereof, to make laws for him as the public good of the society shall require, to the execution whereof his own assistance (as to his own decrees) is due. And this puts men out of a state of Nature into that of a commonwealth, by setting up a judge on earth with authority to determine all the controversies and redress the injuries that may happen to any member of the commonwealth, which judge is the legislative or magistrates appointed by it. And wherever there are any number of men, however associated, that have no such decisive power to appeal to, there they are still in the state of Nature.

90. And hence it is evident that absolute monarchy, which by some men is counted for the only government in the world, is indeed inconsistent with civil society, and so can be not form of civil government at all. For the end of civil society being to avoid and remedy those inconveniences of the state of Nature which necessarily follow from every man's being judge in his own case, by setting up a known authority to which every one of that society may appeal upon any injury received, or controversy that may arise, and which every one of the society ought to obey.[3] Wherever any persons are who have not such an authority to appeal to, and decide any difference between them there, those persons are still in the state of Nature. And so is every absolute prince in respect of those who are under his dominion.

91. For he being supposed to have all, both legislative and executive, power in himself alone, there is no judge to be found, no appeal lies open to any one, who may fairly and indifferently, and with authority decide, and from whence relief and redress may be

---

3. "The public power of all society is above every soul contained in the same society, and the principal use of that power is to give laws unto all that are under it, which laws in such cases we must obey, unless there be reason showed which may necessarily enforce that the law of reason or of God doth enjoin the contrary."—Hooker (*Eccl. Pol.*, lib. i., s. 16).

expected of any injury or inconveniency that may be suffered from him, or by his order. So that such a man, however entitled, Czar, or Grand Signior, or how you please, is as much in the state of Nature, with all under his dominion, as he is with the rest of mankind. For wherever any two men are, who have no standing rule and common judge to appeal to on earth, for the determination of controversies of right betwixt them, there they are still in the state of Nature, and under all the inconveniencies of it, with only this woeful difference to the subject, or rather slave of an absolute prince.[4] That whereas, in the ordinary state of Nature, he has a liberty to judge of his right, according to the best of his power to maintain it; but whenever his property is invaded by the will and order of his monarch, he has not only no appeal, as those in society ought to have, but, as if he were degraded from the common state of rational creatures, is denied a liberty to judge of, or defend his right, and so is exposed to all the misery and inconveniencies that a man can fear from one, who being in the unrestrained state of Nature, is yet corrupted with flattery and armed with power.

92. For he that thinks absolute power purifies men's blood, and corrects the baseness of human nature, need read but the history of this, or any other age, to be convinced to the contrary. He that would have been insolent and injurious in the woods of America would not probably be much better on a throne, where perhaps learning and religion shall be found out to justify all that he shall do to his subjects, and the sword presently silence all those that dare question it. For what the protection of absolute monarchy is, what kind of fathers of their countries it makes princes to be, and to what a degree of happiness and security it carries civil society, where this sort of government is grown to perfection, he that will look into the late relation of Ceylon may easily see.

93. In absolute monarchies, indeed, as well as other governments of the world, the subjects have an appeal to the law, and judges to decide any controversies, and restrain any violence that may happen betwixt the subjects themselves, one amongst another. This every one thinks necessary, and believes; he deserves to be thought a declared enemy to society and mankind who should go about to take it away. But whether this be from a true love of mankind and society, and such a charity as we owe all one to another, there is reason to doubt. For this is no more than what every man, who loves his own power, profit, or greatness, may, and naturally must do, keep those animals from hurting or destroying one another who labour and drudge only for his pleasure and advantage; and so are taken care of, not out of any love the master has for them, but love of himself, and the profit they bring him. For if it be asked what security, what fence is there in such a state against the violence and oppression of this absolute ruler, the very question can scarce be borne. They are ready to tell you that it deserves death only to ask after safety. Betwixt subject and subject, they will grant, there must be measures, laws, and judges for their mutual peace and security. But as for the ruler, he ought to be absolute, and is above all such circumstances; because he has a power to do more hurt and wrong, it is right when he does it. To ask how you may be guarded from harm or injury on that side, where the strongest hand is to do it, is presently the voice of faction and rebellion. As if when men, quitting the state of Nature, entered into society, they agreed that all of them but one should be under the restraint of laws; but that he should still retain all the liberty of the state of Nature, increased with power, and made licentious by impunity. This is to think that men are so foolish that they take care to avoid what mischiefs may be done them by polecats or foxes, but are content, nay, think it safety, to be devoured by lions.

94. But, whatever flatterers may talk to amuse people's understandings, it never hinders men from feeling; and when they perceive that any man, in what

---

4. "To take away all such mutual grievances, injuries, and wrongs—*i.e.*, such as attend men in the state of Nature, there was no way but only by growing into composition and agreement amongst themselves by ordaining some kind of government public, and by yielding themselves subject thereunto, that unto whom they granted authority to rule and govern, by them the peace, tranquillity, and happy estate of the rest might be procured. Men always knew that where force and injury was offered, they might be defenders of themselves. They knew that, however men may seek their own commodity, yet if this were done with injury unto others, it was not to be suffered, but by all men and all good means to be withstood. Finally, they knew that no man might, in reason, take upon him to determine his own right, and according to his own determination proceed in maintenance thereof, in as much as every man is towards himself, and them whom he greatly affects, partial; and therefore, that strifes and troubles would be endless, except they gave their common consent, all to be ordered by some whom they should agree upon, without which consent there would be no reason that one man should take upon him to be lord or judge over another."—Hooker (*ibid.*, s. 10).

station soever, is out of the bounds of the civil society they are of, and that they have no appeal, on earth, against any harm they may receive from him, they are apt to think themselves in the state of Nature, in respect of him whom they find to be so; and to take care, as soon as they can, to have that safety and security, in civil society, for which it was first instituted, and for which only they entered into it. And therefore, though perhaps at first, as shall be showed more at large hereafter, in the following part of this discourse, some one good and excellent man having got a pre-eminency amongst the rest, had this deference paid to his goodness and virtue, as to a kind of natural authority, that the chief rule, with arbitration of their differences, by a tacit consent devolved into his hands, without any other caution but the assurance they had of his uprightness and wisdom; yet when time giving authority, and, as some men would persuade us, sacredness to customs, which the negligent and unforeseeing innocence of the first ages began, had brought in successors of another stamp, the people finding their properties not secure under the government as then it was[5] (whereas government has no other end but the preservation of property), could never be safe, nor at rest, nor think themselves in civil society, till the legislative was so placed in collective bodies of men, call them senate, parliament, or what you please, by which means every single person became subject equally with other the meanest men, to those laws, which he himself, as part of the legislative, had established; nor could any one, by his own authority, avoid the force of the law, when once made, nor by any pretence of superiority plead exemption, thereby to license his own, or the miscarriages of any of his dependants. No man in civil society can be exempted from the laws of it. For if any man may do what he thinks fit and there be no appeal on earth for redress or security against any harm he shall do, I ask whether he be not perfectly still in the state of Nature, and so can be no part or member of that civil society, unless any one will say the state of Nature and civil society are one and the same thing, which I have never yet found any one so great a patron of anarchy as to affirm.[6]

Chapter VIII
Of the Beginning of Political Societies

95. Men being, as has been said, by nature all free, equal, and independent, no one can be put out of this estate and subjected to the political power of another without his own consent, which is done by agreeing with other men, to join and unite into a community for their comfortable, safe, and peaceable living, one amongst another, in a secure enjoyment of their properties, and a greater security against any that are not of it. This any number of men may do, because it injures not the freedom of the rest; they are left, as they were, in the liberty of the state of Nature. When any number of men have so consented to make one community or government, they are thereby presently incorporated, and make one body politic, wherein the majority have a right to act and conclude the rest.

96. For, when any number of men have, by the consent of every individual, made a community, they have thereby made that community one body, with a power to act as one body, which is only by the will and determination of the majority. For that which acts any community, being only the consent of the individuals of it, and it being one body, must move one way, it is necessary the body should move that way whither the greater force carries it, which is the consent of the majority, or else it is impossible it should act or continue one body, one community, which the consent of every individual that united into it agreed that it should; and so every one is bound by that consent to be concluded by the majority. And therefore we see that in assemblies empowered to act by positive laws where no number is set by that positive law which empowers them, the act of the majority passes for the act of the whole, and of course determines as having, by the law of Nature and reason, the power of the whole.

---

5. "At the first, when some certain kind of regimen was once appointed, it may be that nothing was then further thought upon for the manner of governing, but all permitted unto their wisdom and discretion which were to rule till, by experience, they found this for all parts very inconvenient, so as the thing which they had devised for a remedy did indeed but increase the sore which it should have cured. They saw that to live by one man's will became the cause of all men's misery. This constrained them to come unto laws wherein all men might see their duty beforehand, and know the penalties of transgressing them."—Hooker (*Eccl. Pol.*, lib. i., s. 10).

---

6. "Civil law, being the act of the whole body politic, doth therefore overrule each several part of the same body."—Hooker (*ibid.*).

97. And thus every man, by consenting with others to make one body politic under one government, puts himself under an obligation to every one of that society to submit to the determination of the majority, and to be concluded by it; or else this original compact, whereby he with others incorporates into one society, would signify nothing, and be no compact if he be left free and under no other ties than he was in before in the state of Nature. For what appearance would there be of any compact? What new engagement if he were no farther tied by any decrees of the society than he himself thought fit and did actually consent to? This would be still as great a liberty as he himself had before his compact, or any one else in the state of Nature, who may submit himself and consent to any acts of it if he thinks fit.

98. For if the consent of the majority shall not in reason be received as the act of the whole, and conclude every individual, nothing but the consent of every individual can make anything to be the act of the whole, which, considering the infirmities of health and avocations of business, which in a number though much less than that of a commonwealth, will necessarily keep many away from the public assembly; and the variety of opinions and contrariety of interests which unavoidably happen in all collections of men, it is next impossible ever to be had. And, therefore, if coming into society be upon such terms, it will be only like Cato's coming into the theatre, *tantum ut exiret*. Such a constitution as this would make the mighty leviathan of a shorter duration than the feeblest creatures, and not let it outlast the day it was born in, which cannot be supposed till we can think that rational creatures should desire and constitute societies only to be dissolved. For where the majority cannot conclude the rest, there they cannot act as one body, and consequently will be immediately dissolved again.

99. Whosoever, therefore, out of a state of Nature unite into a community, must be understood to give up all the power necessary to the ends for which they unite into society to the majority of the community, unless they expressly agreed in any number greater than the majority. And this is done by barely agreeing to unite into one political society, which is all the compact that is, or needs be, between the individuals that enter into or make up a commonwealth. And thus, that which begins and actually constitutes any political society is nothing but the consent of any number of freemen capable of majority, to unite and

incorporate into such a society. And this is that, and that only, which did or could give beginning to any lawful government in the world.

100. To this I find two objections made: 1. That there are no instances to be found in story of a company of men, independent and equal one amongst another, that met together, and in this way began and set up a government. 2. It is impossible of right that men should do so, because all men, being born under government, they are to submit to that, and are not at liberty to begin a new one.

101. To the first there is this to answer: That it is not at all to be wondered that history gives us but a very little account of men that lived together in the state of Nature. The inconveniencies of that condition, and the love and want of society, no sooner brought any number of them together, but they presently united and incorporated if they designed to continue together. And if we may not suppose men ever to have been in the state of Nature, because we hear not much of them in such a state, we may as well suppose the armies of Salmanasser or Xerxes were never children, because we hear little of them till they were men and embodied in armies. Government is everywhere antecedent to records, and letters seldom come in amongst a people till a long continuation of civil society has, by other more necessary arts, provided for their safety, ease, and plenty. And then they begin to look after the history of their founders, and search into their original when they have outlived the memory of it. For it is with commonwealths as with particular persons, they are commonly ignorant of their own births and infancies; and if they know anything of it, they are beholding for it to the accidental records that others have kept of it. And those that we have of the beginning of any polities in the world, excepting that of the Jews, where God Himself immediately interposed, and which favours not at all paternal dominion, are all either plain instances of such a beginning as I have mentioned, or at least have manifest footsteps of it.

102. He must show a strange inclination to deny evident matter of fact, when it agrees not with his hypothesis, who will not allow that the beginning of Rome and Venice were by the uniting together of several men, free and independent one of another, amongst whom there was no natural superiority or subjection. And if Josephus Acosta's word may be taken, he tells us that in many parts of America there was no government at all. "There are great and appar-

ent conjectures," says he, "that these men (speaking of those of Peru) for a long time had neither kings nor commonwealths, but lived in troops, as they do this day in Florida—the Cheriquanas, those of Brazil, and many other nations, which have no certain kings, but, as occasion is offered in peace or war, they choose their captains as they please" (lib. i. cap. 25). If it be said, that every man there was born subject to his father, or the head of his family, that the subjection due from a child to a father took not away his freedom of uniting into what political society he thought fit, has been already proved; but be that as it will, these men, it is evident, were actually free; and whatever superiority some politicians now would place in any of them, they themselves claimed it not; but, by consent, were all equal, till, by the same consent, they set rulers over themselves. So that their politic societies all began from a voluntary union, and the mutual agreement of men freely acting in the choice of their governors and forms of government.

103. And I hope those who went away from Sparta, with Palantus, mentioned by Justin, will be allowed to have been freemen independent one of another, and to have set up a government over themselves by their own consent. Thus I have given several examples out of history of people, free and in the state of Nature, that, being met together, incorporated and began a commonwealth. And if the want of such instances be an argument to prove that government were not nor could not be so begun, I suppose the contenders for paternal empire were better let it alone than urge it against natural liberty; for if they can give so many instances out of history of governments began upon paternal right, I think (though at least an argument from what has been to what should of right be of no great force) one might, without any great danger, yield them the cause. But if I might advise them in the case, they would do well not to search too much into the original of governments as they have begun *de facto*, lest they should find at the foundation of most of them something very little favourable to the design they promote, and such a power as they contend for.

104. But, to conclude: reason being plain on our side that men are naturally free; and the examples of history showing that the governments of the world, that were begun in peace, had their beginning laid on that foundation, and were made by the consent of the people; there can be little room for doubt, either where the right is, or what has been the opinion or

practice of mankind about the first erecting of governments.

105. I will not deny that if we look back, as far as history will direct us, towards the original of commonwealths, we shall generally find them under the government and administration of one man. And I am also apt to believe that where a family was numerous enough to subsist by itself, and continued entire together, without mixing with others, as it often happens, where there is much land and few people, the government commonly began in the father. For the father having, by the law of Nature, the same power, with every man else, to punish, as he thought fit, any offences against that law, might thereby punish his transgressing children, even when they were men, and out of their pupilage; and they were very likely to submit to his punishment, and all join with him against the offender in their turns, giving him thereby power to execute his sentence against any transgression, and so, in effect, make him the law-maker and governor over all that remained in conjunction with his family. He was fittest to be trusted; paternal affection secured their property and interest under his care, and the custom of obeying him in their childhood made it easier to submit to him rather than any other. If, therefore, they must have one to rule them, as government is hardly to be avoided amongst men that live together, who so likely to be the man as he that was their common father, unless negligence, cruelty, or any other defect of mind or body, made him unfit for it? But when either the father died, and left his next heir—for want of age, wisdom, courage, or any other qualities—less fit for rule, or where several families met and consented to continue together, there, it is not to be doubted, but they used their natural freedom to set up him whom they judged the ablest and most likely to rule well over them. Conformable hereunto we find the people of America, who—living out of the reach of the conquering swords and spreading domination of the two great empires of Peru and Mexico—enjoyed their own natural freedom, though, *cæteris paribus*, they commonly prefer the heir of their deceased king; yet, if they find him any way weak or incapable, they pass him by, and set up the stoutest and bravest man for their ruler.

106. Thus, though looking back as far as records give us any account of peopling the world, and the history of nations, we commonly find the government to be in one hand, yet it destroys not that which I

affirm—viz., that the beginning of politic society depends upon the consent of the individuals to join into
and make one society, who, when they are thus incorporated, might set up what form of government they
thought fit. But this having given occasion to men to
mistake and think that, by Nature, government was
monarchical, and belonged to the father, it may not be
amiss here to consider why people, in the beginning,
generally pitched upon this form, which, though perhaps the father's pre-eminence might, in the first institution of some commonwealths, give a rise to and
place in the beginning the power in one hand, yet it is
plain that the reason that continued the form of government in a single person was not any regard or
respect to paternal authority, since all petty monarchies—that is, almost all monarchies—near their
original, have been commonly, at least upon occasion,
elective.

107. First, then, in the beginning of things, the
father's government of the childhood of those sprung
from him having accustomed them to the rule of one
man, and taught them that where it was exercised
with care and skill, with affection and love to those
under it, it was sufficient to procure and preserve
men (all the political happiness they sought for in
society), it was no wonder that they should pitch
upon and naturally run into that form of government
which, from their infancy, they had been all accustomed to, and which, by experience, they had found
both easy and safe. To which if we add, that monarchy being simple and most obvious to men, whom
neither experience had instructed in forms of government, nor the ambition or insolence of empire had
taught to beware of the encroachments of prerogative
or the inconveniencies of absolute power, which
monarchy, in succession, was apt to lay claim to and
bring upon them; it was not at all strange that they
should not much trouble themselves to think of methods of restraining any exorbitances of those to whom
they had given the authority over them, and of balancing the power of government by placing several parts
of it in different hands. They had neither felt the
oppression of tyrannical dominion, nor did the fashion of the age, nor their possessions or way of living,
which afforded little matter for covetousness or ambition, give them any reason to apprehend or provide
against it; and, therefore, it is no wonder they put
themselves into such a frame of government as was
not only, as I said, most obvious and simple, but also

best suited to their present state and condition, which
stood more in need of defence against foreign invasions and injuries than of multiplicity of laws where
there was but very little property, and wanted not
variety of rulers and abundance of officers to direct
and look after their execution where there were but
few trespassers and few offenders. Since, then, those
who liked one another so well as to join into society
cannot but be supposed to have some acquaintance
and friendship together, and some trust one in another, they could not but have greater apprehensions
of others than of one another; and, therefore, their
first care and thought cannot but be supposed to be,
how to secure themselves against foreign force. It
was natural for them to put themselves under a frame
of government which might best serve to that end,
and choose the wisest and bravest man to conduct
them in their wars and lead them out against their
enemies, and in this chiefly be their ruler.

108. Thus we see that the kings of the Indians, in
America, which is still a pattern of the first ages in
Asia and Europe, whilst the inhabitants were too few
for the country, and want of people and money gave
men no temptation to enlarge their possessions of
land or contest for wider extent of ground, are little
more than generals of their armies; and though they
command absolutely in war, yet at home, and in time
of peace, they exercise very little dominion, and have
but a very moderate sovereignty, the resolutions of
peace and war being ordinarily either in the people or
in a council, though the war itself, which admits not
of pluralities of governors, naturally evolves the command into the king's sole authority.

109. And thus, in Israel itself, the chief business of
their judges and first kings seems to have been to be
captains in war and leaders of their armies, which
(besides what is signified by "going out and in before
the people," which was, to march forth to war and
home again at the heads of their forces) appears
plainly in the story of Jephtha. The Ammonites making war upon Israel, the Gileadites, in fear, send to
Jephtha, a bastard of their family, whom they had cast
off, and article with him, if he will assist them against
the Ammonites, to make him their ruler, which they
do in these words: "And the people made him head
and captain over them" (Judges xi. 11), which was, as
it seems, all one as to be judge. "And he judged Israel"
(Judges xii. 7)—that is, was their captain-general—
"six years." So when Jotham upbraids the Sheche-

mites with the obligation they had to Gideon, who had been their judge and ruler, he tells them: "He fought for you, and adventured his life for, and delivered you out of the hands of Midian" (Judges ix. 17). Nothing mentioned of him but what he did as a general, and, indeed, that is all is found in his history, or in any of the rest of the judges. And Abimelech particularly is called king, though at most he was but their general. And when, being weary of the ill-conduct of Samuel's sons, the children of Israel desired a king, "like all the nations, to judge them, and to go out before them, and to fight their battles" (1 Sam. viii. 20), God, granting their desire, says to Samuel, "I will send thee a man, and thou shalt anoint him to be captain over my people Israel, that he may save my people out of the hands of the Philistines" (ch. ix. 16). As if the only business of a king had been to lead out their armies and fight in their defence; and, accordingly, at his inauguration, pouring a vial of oil upon him, declares to Saul that "the Lord had anointed him to be captain over his inheritance" (ch. x. 1). And therefore those who, after Saul being solemnly chosen and saluted king by the tribes at Mispah, were unwilling to have him their king, make no other objection but this, "How shall this man save us?" (ch. x. 27), as if they should have said: "This man is unfit to be our king, not having skill and conduct enough in war to be able to defend us." And when God resolved to transfer the government to David, it is in these words: "But now thy kingdom shall not continue: the Lord hath sought Him a man after His own heart, and the Lord hath commanded him to be captain over His people" (ch. xiii. 14). As if the whole kingly authority were nothing else but to be their general; and therefore the tribes who had stuck to Saul's family, and opposed David's reign, when they came to Hebron with terms of submission to him, they tell him, amongst other arguments, they had to submit to him as to their king, that he was, in effect, their king in Saul's time, and therefore they had no reason but to receive him as their king now. "Also," say they, "in time past, when Saul was king over us, thou wast he that leddest out and broughtest in Israel, and the Lord said unto thee, Thou shalt feed my people Israel, and thou shalt be a captain over Israel."

110. Thus, whether a family, by degrees, grew up into a commonwealth, and the fatherly authority being continued on to the elder son, every one in his turn growing up under it tacitly submitted to it, and the easiness and equality of it not offending any one, every one acquiesced till time seemed to have confirmed it and settled a right of succession by prescription; or whether several families, or the descendants of several families, whom chance, neighbourhood, or business brought together, united into society; the need of a general whose conduct might defend them against their enemies in war, and the great confidence the innocence and sincerity of that poor but virtuous age, such as are almost all those which begin governments that ever come to last in the world, gave men one of another, made the first beginners of commonwealths generally put the rule into one man's hand, without any other express limitation or restraint but what the nature of the thing and the end of government required. It was given them for the public good and safety, and to those ends, in the infancies of commonwealths, they commonly used it; and unless they had done so, young societies could not have subsisted. Without such nursing fathers, without this care of the governors, all governments would have sunk under the weakness and infirmities of their infancy, the prince and the people had soon perished together.

111. But the golden age (though before vain ambition, and *amor sceleratus habendi*, evil concupiscence had corrupted men's minds into a mistake of true power and honour) had more virtue, and consequently better governors, as well as less vicious subjects; and there was then no stretching prerogative on the one side to oppress the people, nor, consequently, on the other, any dispute about privilege, to lessen or restrain the power of the magistrate; and so no contest betwixt rulers and people about governors or government.[7] Yet, when ambition and luxury, in future ages, would retain and increase the power, without doing the business for which it was given,

---

[7] "At the first, when some certain kind of regimen was once approved, it may be that nothing was then further thought upon for the manner of governing, but all permitted unto their wisdom and discretion, which were to rule till, by experience, they found this for all parts very inconvenient, so as the thing which they had devised for a remedy did indeed but increase the sore which it should have cured. They saw that to live by one man's will became the cause of all men's misery. This constrained them to come unto laws wherein all men might see their duty beforehand, and know the penalties of transgressing them."—Hooker (*Eccl. Pol.*, lib. 1., s. 10).

and aided by flattery, taught princes to have distinct and separate interests from their people, men found it necessary to examine more carefully the original and rights of government, and to find out ways to restrain the exorbitances and prevent the abuses of that power, which they having entrusted in another's hands, only for their own good, they found was made use of to hurt them.

112. Thus we may see how probable it is that people that were naturally free, and, by their own consent, either submitted to the government of their father, or united together, out of different families, to make a government, should generally put the rule into one man's hands, and choose to be under the conduct of a single person, without so much, as by express conditions, limiting or regulating his power, which they thought safe enough in his honesty and prudence; though they never dreamed of monarchy being *jure Divino*, which we never heard of among mankind till it was revealed to us by the divinity of this last age, nor ever allowed paternal power to have a right to dominion or to be the foundation of all government. And thus much may suffice to show that, as far as we have any light from history, we have reason to conclude that all peaceful beginnings of government have been laid in the consent of the people. I say "peaceful," because I shall have occasion, in another place, to speak of conquest, which some esteem a way of beginning of governments.

The other objection, I find, urged against the beginning of polities, in the way I have mentioned, is this, viz.:

113. "That all men being born under government, some or other, it is impossible any of them should ever be free and at liberty to unite together and begin a new one, or ever be able to erect a lawful government." If this argument be good, I ask, How came so many lawful monarchies into the world? For if anybody, upon this supposition, can show me any one man, in any age of the world, free to begin a lawful monarchy, I will be bound to show him ten other free men at liberty, at the same time, to unite and begin a new government under a regal or any other form. It being demonstration that if any one born under the dominion of another may be so free as to have a right to command others in a new and distinct empire, every one that is born under the dominion of another may be so free too, and may become a ruler or subject of a distinct separate government. And so, by this

their own principle, either all men, however born, are free, or else there is but one lawful prince, one lawful government in the world; and then they have nothing to do but barely to show us which that is, which, when they have done, I doubt not but all mankind will easily agree to pay obedience to him.

114. Though it be a sufficient answer to their objection to show that it involves them in the same difficulties that it doth those they use it against, yet I shall endeavour to discover the weakness of this argument a little farther.

"All men," say they, "are born under government, and therefore they cannot be at liberty to begin a new one. Every one is born a subject to his father or his prince, and is therefore under the perpetual tie of subjection and allegiance." It is plain mankind never owned nor considered any such natural subjection that they were born in, to one or to the other, that tied them, without their own consents, to a subjection to them and their heirs.

115. For there are no examples so frequent in history, both sacred and profane, as those of men withdrawing themselves and their obedience from the jurisdiction they were born under, and the family or community they were bred up in, and setting up new governments in other places, from whence sprang all that number of petty commonwealths in the beginning of ages, and which always multiplied as long as there was room enough, till the stronger or more fortunate swallowed the weaker; and those great ones, again breaking to pieces, dissolved into lesser dominions; all which are so many testimonies against paternal sovereignty, and plainly prove that it was not the natural right of the father descending to his heirs that made governments in the beginning; since it was impossible, upon that ground, there should have been so many little kingdoms but only one universal monarchy if men had not been at liberty to separate themselves from their families and their government, be it what it will that was set up in it, and go and make distinct commonwealths and other governments as they thought fit.

116. This has been the practice of the world from its first beginning to this day; nor is it now any more hindrance to the freedom of mankind, that they are born under constituted and ancient polities that have established laws and set forms of government, than if they were born in the woods amongst the unconfined inhabitants that run loose in them. For those who

would persuade us that by being born under any government we are naturally subjects to it, and have no more any title or pretence to the freedom of the state of Nature, have no other reason (bating that of paternal power, which we have already answered) to produce for it, but only because our fathers or progenitors passed away their natural liberty, and thereby bound up themselves and their posterity to a perpetual subjection to the government which they themselves submitted to. It is true that whatever engagements or promises any one made for himself, he is under the obligation of them, but cannot by any compact whatsoever bind his children or posterity. For his son, when a man, being altogether as free as the father, any act of the father can no more give away the liberty of the son than it can of anybody else. He may, indeed, annex such conditions to the land he enjoyed, as a subject of any commonwealth, as may oblige his son to be of that community, if he will enjoy those possessions which were his father's, because that estate being his father's property, he may dispose or settle it as he pleases.

117. And this has generally given the occasion to the mistake in this matter; because commonwealths not permitting any part of their dominions to be dismembered, nor to be enjoyed by any but those of their community, the son cannot ordinarily enjoy the possessions of his father but under the same terms his father did, by becoming a member of the society, whereby he puts himself presently under the government he finds there established, as much as any other subject of that commonweal. And thus the consent of free men, born under government, which only makes them members of it, being given separately in their turns, as each comes to be of age, and not in a multitude together, people take no notice of it, and thinking it not done at all, or not necessary, conclude they are naturally subjects as they are men.

118. But it is plain governments themselves understand it otherwise; they claim no power over the son because of that they had over the father; nor look on children as being their subjects, by their fathers being so. If a subject of England have a child by an Englishwoman in France, whose subject is he? Not the King of England's; for he must have leave to be admitted to the privileges of it. Nor the King of France's, for how then has his father a liberty to bring him away, and breed him as he pleases; and whoever was judged as a traitor or deserter, if he left, or warred against a coun-

try, for being barely born in it of parents that were aliens there? It is plain, then, by the practice of governments themselves, as well as by the law of right reason, that a child is born a subject of no country nor government. He is under his father's tuition and authority till he come to age of discretion, and then he is a free man, at liberty what government he will put himself under, what body politic he will unite himself to. For if an Englishman's son born in France be at liberty, and may do so, it is evident there is no tie upon him by his father being a subject of that kingdom, nor is he bound up by any compact of his ancestors; and why then hath not his son, by the same reason, the same liberty, though he be born anywhere else? Since the power that a father hath naturally over his children is the same wherever they be born, and the ties of natural obligations are not bounded by the positive limits of kingdoms and commonwealths.

119. Every man being, as has been showed, naturally free, and nothing being able to put him into subjection to any earthly power, but only his own consent, it is to be considered what shall be understood to be a sufficient declaration of a man's consent to make him subject to the laws of any government. There is a common distinction of an express and a tacit consent, which will concern our present case. Nobody doubts but an express consent of any man, entering into any society, makes him a perfect member of that society, a subject of that government. The difficulty is, what ought to be looked upon as a tacit consent, and how far it binds—*i.e.*, how far any one shall be looked on to have consented, and thereby submitted to any government, where he has made no expressions of it at all. And to this I say, that every man that hath any possession or enjoyment of any part of the dominions of any government doth hereby give his tacit consent, and is as far forth obliged to obedience to the laws of that government, during such enjoyment, as any one under it, whether this his possession be of land to him and his heirs for ever, or a lodging only for a week; or whether it be barely travelling freely on the highway; and, in effect, it reaches as far as the very being of any one within the territories of that government.

120. To understand this the better, it is fit to consider that every man when he at first incorporates himself into any commonwealth, he, by his uniting himself thereunto, annexes also, and submits to the community those possessions which he has, or shall

acquire, that do not already belong to any other government. For it would be a direct contradiction for any one to enter into society with others for the securing and regulating of property, and yet to suppose his land, whose property is to be regulated by the laws of the society, should be exempt from the jurisdiction of that government to which he himself, and the property of the land, is a subject. By the same act, therefore, whereby any one unites his person, which was before free, to any commonwealth, by the same he unites his possessions, which were before free, to it also; and they become, both of them, person and possession, subject to the government and dominion of that commonwealth as long as it hath a being. Whoever therefore, from thenceforth, by inheritance, purchases permission, or otherwise enjoys any part of the land so annexed to, and under the government of that commonweal, must take it with the condition it is under—that is, of submitting to the government of the commonwealth, under whose jurisdiction it is, as far forth as any subject of it.

121. But since the government has a direct jurisdiction only over the land and reaches the possessor of it (before he has actually incorporated himself in the society) only as he dwells upon and enjoys that, the obligation any one is under by virtue of such enjoyment to submit to the government begins and ends with the enjoyment; so that whenever the owner, who has given nothing but such a tacit consent to the government will, by donation, sale, or otherwise, quit the said possession, he is at liberty to go and incorporate himself into any other commonwealth, or agree with others to begin a new one *in vacuis locis* [in places that are unoccupied], in any part of the world they can find free and unpossessed; whereas he that has once, by actual agreement and any express declaration, given his consent to be of any commonweal, is perpetually and indispensably obliged to be, and remain unalterably a subject to it, and can never be again in the liberty of the state of Nature, unless by any calamity the government he was under comes to be dissolved.

122. But submitting to the laws of any country, living quietly and enjoying privileges and protection under them, makes not a man a member of that society; it is only a local protection and homage due to and from all those who, not being in a state of war, come within the territories belonging to any government, to all parts whereof the force of its law extends.

But this no more makes a man a member of that society, a perpetual subject of that commonwealth, than it would make a man a subject to another in whose family he found it convenient to abide for some time, though, whilst he continued in it, he were obliged to comply with the laws and submit to the government he found there. And thus we see that foreigners, by living all their lives under another government, and enjoying the privileges and protection of it, though they are bound, even in conscience, to submit to its administration as far forth as any denizen, yet do not thereby come to be subjects or members of that commonwealth. Nothing can make any man so but his actually entering into it by positive engagement and express promise and compact. This is that which, I think, concerning the beginning of political societies, and that consent which makes any one a member of any commonwealth.

Chapter IX
Of the Ends of Political Society and Government

123. If man in the state of Nature be so free as has been said, if he be absolute lord of his own person and possessions, equal to the greatest and subject to nobody, why will he part with his freedom, this empire, and subject himself to the dominion and control of any other power? To which it is obvious to answer, that though in the state of Nature he hath such a right, yet the enjoyment of it is very uncertain and constantly exposed to the invasion of others; for all being kings as much as he, every man his equal, and the greater part no strict observers of equity and justice, the enjoyment of the property he has in this state is very unsafe, very insecure. This makes him willing to quit this condition which, however free, is full of fears and continual dangers; and it is not without reason that he seeks out and is willing to join in society with others who are already united, or have a mind to unite for the mutual preservation of their lives, liberties, and estates, which I call by the general name—property.

124. The great and chief end, therefore, of men uniting into commonwealths, and putting themselves under government, is the preservation of their property; to which in the state of Nature there are many things wanting.

Firstly, there wants an established, settled, known law, received and allowed by common consent to be the standard of right and wrong, and the common measure to decide all controversies between them. For though the law of Nature be plain and intelligible to all rational creatures, yet men, being biased by their interest, as well as ignorant for want of study of it, are not apt to allow of it as a law binding to them in the application of it to their particular cases.

125. Secondly, in the state of Nature there wants a known and indifferent judge, with authority to determine all differences according to the established law. For every one in that state being both judge and executioner of the law of Nature, men being partial to themselves, passion and revenge is very apt to carry them too far, and with too much heat in their own cases, as well as negligence and unconcernedness, make them too remiss in other men's.

126. Thirdly, in the state of Nature there often wants power to back and support the sentence when right, and to give it due execution. They who by any injustice offended will seldom fail where they are able by force to make good their injustice. Such resistance many times makes the punishment dangerous, and frequently destructive to those who attempt it.

127. Thus mankind, notwithstanding all the privileges of the state of Nature, being but in an ill condition while they remain in it are quickly driven into society. Hence it comes to pass, that we seldom find any number of men live any time together in this state. The inconveniencies that they are therein exposed to by the irregular and uncertain exercise of the power every man has of punishing the transgressions of others, make them take sanctuary under the established laws of government, and therein seek the preservation of their property. It is this makes them so willingly give up every one his single power of punishing to be exercised by such alone as shall be appointed to it amongst them, and by such rules as the community, or those authorised by them to that purpose, shall agree on. And in this we have the original right and rise of both the legislative and executive power as well as of the governments and societies themselves.

128. For in the state of Nature to omit the liberty he has of innocent delights, a man has two powers. The first is to do whatsoever he thinks fit for the preservation of himself and others within the permission of the law of Nature; by which law, common to them all, he and all the rest of mankind are one community, make up one society distinct from all other creatures, and were it not for the corruption and viciousness of degenerate men, there would be no need of any other, no necessity that men should separate from this great and natural community, and associate into lesser combinations. The other power a man has in the state of Nature is the power to punish the crimes committed against that law. Both these he gives up when he joins in a private, if I may so call it, or particular political society, and incorporates into any commonwealth separate from the rest of mankind.

129. The first power—viz., of doing whatsoever he thought fit for the preservation of himself and the rest of mankind, he gives up to be regulated by laws made by the society, so far forth as the preservation of himself and the rest of that society shall require; which laws of the society in many things confine the liberty he had by the law of Nature.

130. Secondly, the power of punishing he wholly gives up, and engages his natural force, which he might before employ in the execution of the law of Nature, by his own single authority, as he thought fit, to assist the executive power of the society as the law thereof shall require. For being now in a new state, wherein he is to enjoy many conveniencies from the labour, assistance, and society of others in the same community, as well as protection from its whole strength, he is to part also with as much of his natural liberty, in providing for himself, as the good, prosperity, and safety of the society shall require, which is not only necessary but just, since the other members of the society do the like.

131. But though men when they enter into society give up the equality, liberty, and executive power they had in the state of Nature [into] the hands of the society, to be so far disposed of by the legislative as the good of the society shall require, yet it being only with an intention in every one the better to preserve himself, his liberty and property (for no rational creature can be supposed to change his condition with an intention to be worse), the power of the society or legislative constituted by them can never be supposed to extend farther than the common good, but is obliged to secure every one's property by providing against those three defects above mentioned that made the state of Nature so unsafe and uneasy. And so, whoever has the legislative or supreme power of any commonwealth, is bound to govern by established standing laws, promulgated and known to the

people, and not by extemporary decrees, by indifferent and upright judges, who are to decide controversies by those laws; and to employ the force of the community at home only in the execution of such laws, or abroad to prevent or redress foreign injuries and secure the community from inroads and invasion. And all this to be directed to no other end but the peace, safety, and public good of the people.

Chapter X
Of the Forms of a Commonwealth

132. The majority having, as has been showed, upon men's first uniting into society, the whole power of the community naturally in them, may employ all that power in making laws for the community from time to time, and executing those laws by officers of their own appointing, and then the form of the government is a perfect democracy; or else may put the power of making laws into the hands of a few select men, and their heirs or successors, and then it is an oligarchy; or else into the hands of one man, and then it is a monarchy; if to him and his heirs, it is a hereditary monarchy; if to him only for life, but upon his death the power only of nominating a successor, to return to them, an elective monarchy. And so accordingly of these make compounded and mixed forms of government, as they think good. And if the legislative power be at first given by the majority to one or more persons only for their lives, or any limited time, and then the supreme power to revert to them again, when it is so reverted the community may dispose of it again anew into what hands they please, and so constitute a new form of government; for the form of government depending upon the placing the supreme power, which is the legislative, it being impossible to conceive that an inferior power should prescribe to a superior, or any but the supreme make laws, according as the power of making laws is placed, such is the form of the commonwealth.

133. By "commonwealth" I must be understood all along to mean not a democracy, or any form of government, but any independent community which the Latins signified by the word *civitas*, to which the word which best answers in our language is "commonwealth," and most properly expresses such a society of men which "community" does not (for there may be subordinate communities in a government), and "city" much less. And therefore, to avoid ambiguity, I crave leave to use the word "common-

wealth" in that sense, in which sense I find the word used by King James himself, which I think to be its genuine signification, which, if anybody dislike, I consent with him to change it for a better.

Chapter XI
Of the Extent of the Legislative Power

134. The great end of men's entering into society being the enjoyment of their properties in peace and safety, and the great instrument and means of that being the laws established in that society, the first and fundamental positive law of all commonwealths is the establishing of the legislative power, as the first and fundamental natural law which is to govern even the legislative. Itself is the preservation of the society and (as far as will consist with the public good) of every person in it, this legislative is not only the supreme power of the commonwealth, but sacred and unalterable in the hands where the community have once placed it. Nor can any edict of anybody else, in what form soever conceived, or by what power soever backed, have the force and obligation of a law which has not its sanction from that legislative which the public has chosen and appointed; for without this the law could not have that which is absolutely necessary to its being a law, the consent of the society, over whom nobody can have a power to make laws[8] but by their own consent and by authority received from them; and therefore all the obedience, which by the most solemn ties any one can be obliged to pay, ultimately terminates in this supreme power, and is directed by those laws which it enacts. Nor can any

---

8. "The lawful power of making laws to command whole politic societies of men, belonging so properly unto the same entire societies, that for any prince or potentate, of what kind soever upon earth, to exercise the same of himself, and not by express commission immediately and personally received from God, or else by authority derived at the first from their consent, upon whose persons they impose laws, it is no better than mere tyranny. Laws they are not, therefore, which public approbation hath not made so."—Hooker (*Eccl. Pol.*, lib. i., s.10). "Of this point, therefore, we are to note that such men naturally have no full and perfect power to command whole politic multitudes of men, therefore utterly without our consent we could in such sort be at no man's commandment living. And to be commanded, we do consent when that society, whereof we be a part, hath at any time before consented, without revoking the same after by the like universal agreement."

"Laws therefore human, of what kind soever, are available by consent."—Hooker (*Eccl. Pol.*).

oaths to any foreign power whatsoever, or any domestic subordinate power, discharge any member of the society from his obedience to the legislative, acting pursuant to their trust, nor oblige him to any obedience contrary to the laws so enacted or farther than they do allow, it being ridiculous to imagine one can be tied ultimately to obey any power in the society which is not the supreme.

135. Though the legislative, whether placed in one or more, whether it be always in being or only by intervals, though it be the supreme power in every commonwealth, yet, first, it is not, nor can possibly be, absolutely arbitrary over the lives and fortunes of the people. For it being but the joint power of every member of the society given up to that person or assembly which is legislator, it can be no more than those persons had in a state of Nature before they entered into society, and gave it up to the community. For nobody can transfer to another more power than he has in himself, and nobody has an absolute arbitrary power over himself, or over any other, to destroy his own life, or take away the life or property of another. A man, as has been proved, cannot subject himself to the arbitrary power of another; and having, in the state of Nature, no arbitrary power over the life, liberty, or possession of another, but only so much as the law of Nature gave him for the preservation of himself and the rest of mankind, this is all he doth, or can give up to the commonwealth, and by it to the legislative power, so that the legislative can have no more than this. Their power in the utmost bounds of it is limited to the public good of the society.[9] It is a power that hath no other end but preserva-

tion, and therefore can never have a right to destroy, enslave, or designedly to impoverish the subjects; the obligations of the law of Nature cease not in society, but only in many cases are drawn closer, and have, by human laws, known penalties annexed to them to enforce their observation. Thus the law of Nature stands as an eternal rule to all men, legislators as well as others. The rules that they make for other men's actions must, as well as their own and other men's actions, be conformable to the law of Nature—*i.e.*, to the will of God, of which that is a declaration, and the fundamental law of Nature being the preservation of mankind, no human sanction can be good or valid against it.

136. Secondly, the legislative or supreme authority cannot assume to itself a power to rule by extemporary arbitrary decrees, but is bound to dispense justice and decide the rights of the subject by promulgated standing laws,[10] and known authorised judges. For the law of Nature being unwritten, and so nowhere to be found but in the minds of men, they who, through passion or interest, shall miscite or misapply it, cannot so easily be convinced of their mistake where there is no established judge; and so it serves not as it ought, to determine the rights and fence the properties of those that live under it, especially where every one is judge, interpreter, and executioner of it too, and that in his own case; and he that has right on his side, having ordinarily but his own single strength, hath not force enough to defend himself from injuries or punish delinquents. To avoid these inconveniencies which disorder men's properties in the state of Nature, men unite into societies that they may have the united strength of the whole society to secure and defend their properties, and may have standing rules to bound it by which every one may know what is his. To this end it is that men give up all their natural power to the society they enter into, and the community put the legislative power into such hands as they think fit, with this

---

9. "Two foundations there are which bear up public societies; the one a natural inclination whereby all men desire sociable life and fellowship; the other an order, expressly or secretly agreed upon, touching the manner of their union in living together. The latter is that which we call the law of a commonweal, the very soul of a politic body, the parts whereof are by law animated, held together, and set on work in such actions as the common good requireth. Laws politic, ordained for external order and regimen amongst men, are never framed as they should be, unless presuming the will of man to be inwardly obstinate, rebellious, and averse from all obedience to the sacred laws of his nature; in a word, unless presuming man to be in regard of his depraved mind little better than a wild beast, they do accordingly provide notwithstanding, so to frame his outward actions, that they be no hindrance unto the common good, for which societies are instituted. Unless they do this they are not perfect."—Hooker (*Eccl. Pol.*, lib. i., s. 10).

10. "Human laws are measures in respect of men whose actions they must direct, howbeit such measures they are as have also their higher rules to be measured by, which rules are two—the law of God and the law of Nature; so that laws human must be made according to the general laws of Nature, and without contradiction to any positive law of Scripture, otherwise they are ill made."—Hooker (*Eccl. Pol.*, lib. iii., s. 9).

"To constrain men to anything inconvenient doth seem unreasonable."—(*Ibid.*, i., 10.)

trust, that they shall be governed by declared laws, or else their peace, quiet, and property will still be at the same uncertainty as it was in the state of Nature.

137. Absolute arbitrary power, or governing without settled standing laws, can neither of them consist with the ends of society and government, which men would not quit the freedom of the state of Nature for, and tie themselves up under, were it not to preserve their lives, liberties, and fortunes, and by stated rules of right and property to secure their peace and quiet. It cannot be supposed that they should intend, had they a power so to do, to give any one or more an absolute arbitrary power over their persons and estates, and put a force into the magistrate's hand to execute his unlimited will arbitrarily upon them; this were to put themselves into a worse condition than the state of Nature, wherein they had a liberty to defend their right against the injuries of others, and were upon equal terms of force to maintain it, whether invaded by a single man or many in combination. Whereas by supposing they have given up themselves to the absolute arbitrary power and will of a legislator, they have disarmed themselves, and armed him to make a prey of them when he pleases; he being in a much worse condition that is exposed to the arbitrary power of one man who has the command of a hundred thousand than he that is exposed to the arbitrary power of a hundred thousand single men, nobody being secure, that his will who has such a command is better than that of other men, though his force be a hundred thousand times stronger. And, therefore, whatever form the commonwealth is under, the ruling power ought to govern by declared and received laws, and not by extemporary dictates and undetermined resolutions, for then mankind will be in a far worse condition than in the state of Nature if they shall have armed one or a few men with the joint power of a multitude, to force them to obey at pleasure the exorbitant and unlimited decrees of their sudden thoughts, or unrestrained, and till that moment, unknown wills, without having any measures set down which may guide and justify their actions. For all the power the government has, being only for the good of the society, as it ought not to be arbitrary and at pleasure, so it ought to be exercised by established and promulgated laws, that both the people may know their duty, and be safe and secure within the limits of the law, and the rulers, too, kept within their due bounds, and not be tempted by the power they have in their hands to employ it to purposes, and by such measures as they would not have known, and own not willingly.

138. Thirdly, the supreme power cannot take from any man any part of his property without his own consent. For the preservation of property being the end of government, and that for which men enter into society, it necessarily supposes and requires that the people should have property, without which they must be supposed to lose that by entering into society which was the end for which they entered into it; too gross an absurdity for any man to own. Men, therefore, in society having property, they have such a right to the goods, which by the law of the community are theirs, that nobody hath a right to take them, or any part of them, from them without their own consent; without this they have no property at all. For I have truly no property in that which another can by right take from me when he pleases against my consent. Hence it is a mistake to think that the supreme or legislative power of any commonwealth can do what it will, and dispose of the estates of the subject arbitrarily, or take any part of them at pleasure. This is not much to be feared in governments where the legislative consists wholly or in part in assemblies which are variable, whose members upon the dissolution of the assembly are subjects under the common laws of their country, equally with the rest. But in governments where the legislative is in one lasting assembly, always in being, or in one man as in absolute monarchies, there is danger still, that they will think themselves to have a distinct interest from the rest of the community, and so will be apt to increase their own riches and power by taking what they think fit from the people. For a man's property is not at all secure, though there be good and equitable laws to set the bounds of it between him and his fellow-subjects, if he who commands those subjects have power to take from any private man what part he pleases of his property, and use and dispose of it as he thinks good.

139. But government, into whosesoever hands it is put, being as I have before shown, entrusted with this condition, and for this end, that men might have and secure their properties, the prince or senate, however it may have power to make laws for the regulating of property between the subjects one amongst another, yet can never have a power to take to themselves the whole, or any part of the subjects' property, without their own consent; for this would be in effect to leave

them no property at all. And to let us see that even absolute power, where it is necessary, is not arbitrary by being absolute, but is still limited by that reason, and confined to those ends which required it in some cases to be absolute, we need look no farther than the common practice of martial discipline. For the preservation of the army, and in it of the whole commonwealth, requires an absolute obedience to the command of every superior officer, and it is justly death to disobey or dispute the most dangerous or unreasonable of them; but yet we see that neither the sergeant that could command a soldier to march up to the mouth of a cannon, or stand in a breach where he is almost sure to perish, can command that soldier to give him one penny of his money; nor the general that can condemn him to death for deserting his post, or not obeying the most desperate orders, cannot yet with all his absolute power of life and death dispose of one farthing of that soldier's estate, or seize one jot of his goods; whom yet he can command anything, and hang for the least disobedience. Because such a blind obedience is necessary to that end for which the commander has his power—viz., the preservation of the rest, but the disposing of his goods has nothing to do with it.

140. It is true governments cannot be supported without great charge, and it is fit every one who enjoys his share of the protection should pay out of his estate his proportion for the maintenance of it. But still it must be with his own consent—*i.e.*, the consent of the majority, giving it either by themselves or their representatives chosen by them; for if any one shall claim a power to lay and levy taxes on the people by his own authority, and without such consent of the people, he thereby invades the fundamental law of property, and subverts the end of government. For what property have I in that which another may by right take when he pleases to himself?

141. Fourthly, the legislative cannot transfer the power of making laws to any other hands, for it being but a delegated power from the people, they who have it cannot pass it over to others. The people alone can appoint the form of the commonwealth, which is by constituting the legislative, and appointing in whose hands that shall be. And when the people have said, "We will submit, and be governed by laws made by such men, and in such forms," nobody else can say other men shall make laws for them; nor can they be bound by any laws but such as are enacted by those whom they have chosen and authorised to make laws for them.

142. These are the bounds which the trust that is put in them by the society and the law of God and Nature have set to the legislative power of every commonwealth, in all forms of government. First: They are to govern by promulgated established laws, not to be varied in particular cases, but to have one rule for rich and poor, for the favourite at Court, and the countryman at plough. Secondly: These laws also ought to be designed for no other end ultimately but the good of the people. Thirdly: They must not raise taxes on the property of the people without the consent of the people given by themselves or their deputies. And this properly concerns only such governments where the legislative is always in being, or at least where the people have not reserved any part of the legislative to deputies, to be from time to time chosen by themselves. Fourthly: Legislative neither must nor can transfer the power of making laws to anybody else, or place it anywhere but where the people have.

Chapter XII
The Legislative, Executive, and Federative Power of the Commonwealth

143. The legislative power is that which has a right to direct how the force of the commonwealth shall be employed for preserving the community and the members of it. Because those laws which are constantly to be executed, and whose force is always to continue, may be made in a little time, therefore there is no need that the legislative should be always in being, not having always business to do. And because it may be too great temptation to human frailty, apt to grasp at power, for the same persons who have the power of making laws to have also in their hands the power to execute them, whereby they may exempt themselves from obedience to the laws they make, and suit the law, both in its making and execution, to their own private advantage, and thereby come to have a distinct interest from the rest of the community, contrary to the end of society and government. Therefore in well-ordered commonwealths, where the good of the whole is so considered as it ought, the legislative power is put into the hands of divers persons who, duly assembled, have by themselves, or jointly with others, a power to make laws, which

when they have done, being separated again, they are themselves subject to the laws they have made; which is a new and near tie upon them to take care that they make them for the public good.

144. But because the laws that are at once, and in a short time made, have a constant and lasting force, and need a perpetual execution, or an attendance thereunto, therefore it is necessary there should be a power always in being which should see to the execution of the laws that are made, and remain in force. And thus the legislative and executive power come often to be separated.

145. There is another power in every commonwealth which one may call natural, because it is that which answers to the power every man naturally had before he entered into society. For though in a commonwealth the members of it are distinct persons, still, in reference to one another, and, as such, are governed by the laws of the society, yet, in reference to the rest of mankind, they make one body, which is, as every member of it before was, still in the state of Nature with the rest of mankind, so that the controversies that happen between any man of the society with those that are out of it are managed by the public, and an injury done to a member of their body engages the whole in the reparation of it. So that under this consideration the whole community is one body in the state of Nature in respect of all other states or persons out of its community.

146. This, therefore, contains the power of war and peace, leagues and alliances, and all the transactions with all persons and communities without the commonwealth, and may be called federative if any one pleases. So the thing be understood, I am indifferent as to the name.

147. These two powers, executive and federative, though they be really distinct in themselves, yet one comprehending the execution of the municipal laws of the society within itself upon all that are parts of it, the other the management of the security and interest of the public without with all those that it may receive benefit or damage from, yet they are always almost united. And though this federative power in the well or ill management of it be of great moment to the commonwealth, yet it is much less capable to be directed by antecedent, standing, positive laws than the executive, and so must necessarily be left to the prudence and wisdom of those whose hands it is in,

to be managed for the public good. For the laws that concern subjects one amongst another, being to direct their actions, may well enough precede them. But what is to be done in reference to foreigners depending much upon their actions, and the variation of designs and interests, must be left in great part to the prudence of those who have this power committed to them, to be managed by the best of their skill for the advantage of the commonwealth.

148. Though, as I said, the executive and federative power of every community be really distinct in themselves, yet they are hardly to be separated and placed at the same time in the hands of distinct persons. For both of them requiring the force of the society for their exercise, it is almost impracticable to place the force of the commonwealth in distinct and not subordinate hands, or that the executive and federative power should be placed in persons that might act separately, whereby the force of the public would be under different commands, which would be apt some time or other to cause disorder and ruin.

Chapter XIII
Of the Subordination of the Powers of the Commonwealth

149. Though in a constituted commonwealth standing upon its own basis and acting according to its own nature—that is, acting for the preservation of the community—there can be but one supreme power, which is the legislative, to which all the rest are and must be subordinate, yet the legislative being only a fiduciary power to act for certain ends, there remains still in the people a supreme power to remove or alter the legislative, when they find the legislative act contrary to the trust reposed in them. For all power given with trust for the attaining an end being limited by that end, whenever that end is manifestly neglected or opposed, the trust must necessarily be forfeited, and the power devolve into the hands of those that gave it, who may place it anew where they shall think best for their safety and security. And thus the community perpetually retains a supreme power of saving themselves from the attempts and designs of anybody, even of their legislators, whenever they shall be so foolish or so wicked as to lay and carry on designs against the liberties and properties of the subject. For no man or society of men having a power to deliver up their preservation, or

consequently the means of it, to the absolute will and arbitrary dominion of another, whenever any one shall go about to bring them into such a slavish condition, they will always have a right to preserve what they have not a power to part with, and to rid themselves of those who invade this fundamental, sacred, and unalterable law of self-preservation for which they entered into society. And thus the community may be said in this respect to be always the supreme power, but not as considered under any form of government, because this power of the people can never take place till the government be dissolved.

150. In all cases whilst the government subsists, the legislative is the supreme power. For what can give laws to another must needs be superior to him, and since the legislative is no otherwise legislative of the society but by the right it has to make laws for all the parts, and every member of the society prescribing rules to their actions, and giving power of execution where they are transgressed, the legislative must needs be the supreme, and all other powers in any members or parts of the society derived from and subordinate to it.

151. In some commonwealths where the legislative is not always in being, and the executive is vested in a single person who has also a share in the legislative, there that single person, in a very tolerable sense, may also be called supreme; not that he has in himself all the supreme power, which is that of lawmaking, but because he has in him the supreme execution from whom all inferior magistrates derive all their several subordinate powers, or, at least, the greatest part of them; having also no legislative superior to him, there being no law to be made without his consent, which cannot be expected should ever subject him to the other part of the legislative, he is properly enough in this sense supreme. But yet it is to be observed that though oaths of allegiance and fealty are taken to him, it is not to him as supreme legislator, but as supreme executor of the law made by a joint power of him with others, allegiance being nothing but an obedience according to law, which, when he violates, he has no right to obedience, nor can claim it otherwise than as the public person vested with the power of the law, and so is to be considered as the image, phantom, or representative of the commonwealth, acted by the will of the society declared in its laws, and thus he has no will, no power, but that of the law. But when he quits this representation, this

public will, and acts by his own private will, he degrades himself, and is but a single private person without power and without will; the members owing no obedience but to the public will of the society.

152. The executive power placed anywhere but in a person that has also a share in the legislative is visibly subordinate and accountable to it, and may be at pleasure changed and displaced; so that it is not the supreme executive power that is exempt from subordination, but the supreme executive power vested in one, who having a share in the legislative, has no distinct superior legislative to be subordinate and accountable to, farther than he himself shall join and consent, so that he is no more subordinate than he himself shall think fit, which one may certainly conclude will be but very little. Of other ministerial and subordinate powers in a commonwealth we need not speak, they being so multiplied with infinite variety in the different customs and constitutions of distinct commonwealths, that it is impossible to give a particular account of them all. Only thus much which is necessary to our present purpose we may take notice of concerning them, that they have no manner of authority, any of them, beyond what is by positive grant and commission delegated to them, and are all of them accountable to some other power in the commonwealth.

153. It is not necessary—no, nor so much as convenient—that the legislative should be always in being; but absolutely necessary that the executive power should, because there is not always need of new laws to be made, but always need of execution of the laws that are made. When the legislative hath put the execution of the laws they make into other hands, they have a power still to resume it out of those hands when they find cause, and to punish for any maladministration against the laws. The same holds also in regard of the federative power, that and the executive being both ministerial and subordinate to the legislative, which, as has been shown, in a constituted commonwealth is the supreme, the legislative also in this case being supposed to consist of several persons; for if it be a single person it cannot but be always in being, and so will, as supreme, naturally have the supreme executive power, together with the legislative, may assemble and exercise their legislative at the times that either their original constitution or their own adjournment appoints, or when they please, if neither of these hath appointed any time, or

there be no other way prescribed to convoke them. For the supreme power being placed in them by the people, it is always in them, and they may exercise it when they please, unless by their original constitution they are limited to certain seasons, or by an act of their supreme power they have adjourned to a certain time, and when that time comes they have a right to assemble and act again.

154. If the legislative, or any part of it, be of representatives, chosen for that time by the people, which afterwards return into the ordinary state of subjects, and have no share in the legislative but upon a new choice, this power of choosing must also be exercised by the people, either at certain appointed seasons, or else when they are summoned to it; and, in this latter case, the power of convoking the legislative is ordinarily placed in the executive, and has one of these two limitations in respect of time:—that either the original constitution requires their assembling and acting at certain intervals; and then the executive power does nothing but ministerially issue directions for their electing and assembling according to due forms; or else it is left to his prudence to call them by new elections when the occasions or exigencies of the public require the amendment of old or making of new laws, or the redress or prevention of any inconveniencies that lie on or threaten the people.

155. It may be demanded here, what if the executive power, being possessed of the force of the commonwealth, shall make use of that force to hinder the meeting and acting of the legislative, when the original constitution or the public exigencies require it? I say, using force upon the people, without authority, and contrary to the trust put in him that does so, is a state of war with the people, who have a right to reinstate their legislative in the exercise of their power. For having erected a legislative with an intent they should exercise the power of making laws, either at certain set times, or when there is need of it, when they are hindered by any force from what is so necessary to the society, and wherein the safety and preservation of the people consists, the people have a right to remove it by force. In all states and conditions the true remedy of force without authority is to oppose force to it. The use of force without authority always puts him that uses it into a state of war as the aggressor, and renders him liable to be treated accordingly.

156. The power of assembling and dismissing the legislative, placed in the executive, gives not the executive a superiority over it, but is a fiduciary trust placed in him for the safety of the people in a case where the uncertainty and variableness of human affairs could not bear a steady fixed rule. For it not being possible that the first framers of the government should by any foresight be so much masters of future events as to be able to prefix so just periods of return and duration to the assemblies of the legislative, in all times to come, that might exactly answer all the exigencies of the commonwealth, the best remedy could be found for this defect was to trust this to the prudence of one who was always to be present, and whose business it was to watch over the public good. Constant, frequent meetings of the legislative, and long continuations of their assemblies, without necessary occasion, could not but be burdensome to the people, and must necessarily in time produce more dangerous inconveniencies, and yet the quick turn of affairs might be sometimes such as to need their present help; any delay of their convening might endanger the public; and sometimes, too, their business might be so great that the limited time of their sitting might be too short for their work, and rob the public of that benefit which could be had only from their mature deliberation. What, then, could be done in this case to prevent the community from being exposed some time or other to imminent hazard on one side or the other, by fixed intervals and periods set to the meeting and acting of the legislative, but to entrust it to the prudence of some who, being present and acquainted with the state of public affairs, might make use of this prerogative for the public good? And where else could this be so well placed as in his hands who was entrusted with the execution of the laws for the same end? Thus, supposing the regulation of times for the assembling and sitting of the legislative not settled by the original constitution, it naturally fell into the hands of the executive; not as an arbitrary power depending on his good pleasure, but with this trust always to have it exercised only for the public weal, as the occurrences of times and change of affairs might require. Whether settled periods of their convening, or a liberty left to the prince for convoking the legislative, or perhaps a mixture of both, hath the least inconvenience attending it, it is not my business here to inquire, but only to show that, though the executive power may have the prerogative of convoking and dissolving such conventions of the legislative, yet it is not thereby superior to it.

157. Things of this world are in so constant a flux that nothing remains long in the same state. Thus people, riches, trade, power, change their stations; flourishing mighty cities come to ruin, and prove in time neglected desolate corners, whilst other unfrequented places grow into populous countries filled with wealth and inhabitants. But things not always changing equally, and private interest often keeping up customs and privileges when the reasons of them are ceased, it often comes to pass that in governments where part of the legislative consists of representatives chosen by the people, that in tract of time this representation becomes very unequal and disproportionate to the reasons it was at first established upon. To what gross absurdities the following of custom when reason has left it may lead, we may be satisfied when we see the bare name of a town, of which there remains not so much as the ruins, where scarce so much housing as a sheepcote, or more inhabitants than a shepherd is to be found, send as many representatives to the grand assembly of law-makers as a whole county numerous in people and powerful in riches. This strangers stand amazed at, and every one must confess needs a remedy; though most think it hard to find one, because the constitution of the legislative being the original and supreme act of the society, antecedent to all positive laws in it, and depending wholly on the people, no inferior power can alter it. And, therefore, the people when the legislative is once constituted, having in such a government as we have been speaking of no power to act as long as the government stands, this inconvenience is thought incapable of a remedy.

158. *Salus populi suprema lex* [Let the welfare of the people be the supreme law] is certainly so just and fundamental a rule, that he who sincerely follows it cannot dangerously err. If, therefore, the executive who has the power of convoking the legislative, observing rather the true proportion than fashion of representation, regulates not by old custom, but true reason, the number of members in all places, that have a right to be distinctly represented, which no part of the people, however incorporated, can pretend to, but in proportion to the assistance which it affords to the public, it cannot be judged to have set up a new legislative, but to have restored the old and true one, and to have rectified the disorders which succession of time had insensibly as well as inevitably introduced; for it being the interest as well as intention of the people to have a fair and equal representative, whoever brings it nearest to that is an undoubted friend to and establisher of the government, and cannot miss the consent and approbation of the community; prerogative being nothing but a power in the hands of the prince to provide for the public good in such cases which, depending upon unforeseen and uncertain occurrences, certain and unalterable laws could not safely direct. Whatsoever shall be done manifestly for the good of the people, and establishing the government upon its true foundations is, and always will be, just prerogative. The power of erecting new corporations, and therewith new representatives, carries with it a supposition that in time the measures of representation might vary, and those have a just right to be represented which before had none; and by the same reason, those cease to have a right, and be too inconsiderable for such a privilege, which before had it. It is not a change from the present state which, perhaps, corruption or decay has introduced, that makes an inroad upon the government, but the tendency of it to injure or oppress the people, and to set up one part or party with a distinction from and an unequal subjection of the rest. Whatsoever cannot but be acknowledged to be of advantage to the society and people in general, upon just and lasting measures, will always, when done, justify itself; and whenever the people shall choose their representatives upon just and undeniably equal measures, suitable to the original frame of the government, it cannot be doubted to be the will and act of the society, whoever permitted or proposed to them so to do.

Chapter XIV
Of Prerogative

159. Where the legislative and executive power are in distinct hands, as they are in all moderated monarchies and well-framed governments, there the good of the society requires that several things should be left to the discretion of him that has the executive power. For the legislators not being able to foresee and provide by laws for all that may be useful to the community, the executor of the laws, having the power in his hands, has by the common law of Nature a right to make use of it for the good of the society, in many cases where the municipal law has given no direction, till the legislative can conveniently be assembled to provide for it; nay, many things there are which the law can by no means provide for, and

those must necessarily be left to the discretion of him that has the executive power in his hands, to be ordered by him as the public good and advantage shall require; nay, it is fit that the laws themselves should in some cases give way to the executive power, or rather to this fundamental law of Nature and government—viz., that as much as may be all the members of the society are to be preserved. For since many accidents may happen wherein a strict and rigid observation of the laws may do harm, as not to pull down an innocent man's house to stop the fire when the next to it is burning; and a man may come sometimes within the reach of the law, which makes no distinction of persons, by an action that may deserve reward and pardon; it is fit the ruler should have a power in many cases to mitigate the severity of the law, and pardon some offenders, since the end of government being the preservation of all as much as may be, even the guilty are to be spared where it can prove no prejudice to the innocent.

160. This power to act according to discretion for the public good, without the prescription of the law and sometimes even against it, is that which is called prerogative; for since in some governments the law-making power is not always in being and is usually too numerous, and so too slow for the dispatch requisite to execution, and because, also, it is impossible to foresee and so by laws to provide for all accidents and necessities that may concern the public, or make such laws as will do no harm, if they are executed with an inflexible rigour on all occasions and upon all persons that may come in their way, therefore there is a latitude left to the executive power to do many things of choice which the laws do not prescribe.

161. This power, whilst employed for the benefit of the community and suitably to the trust and ends of the government, is undoubted prerogative, and never is questioned. For the people are very seldom or never scrupulous or nice in the point or questioning of prerogative whilst it is in any tolerable degree employed for the use it was meant—that is, the good of the people, and not manifestly against it. But if there comes to be a question between the executive power and the people about a thing claimed as a prerogative, the tendency of the exercise of such prerogative, to the good or hurt of the people, will easily decide that question.

162. It is easy to conceive that in the infancy of governments, when commonwealths differed little from families in number of people, they differed from them too but little in number of laws; and the governors being as the fathers of them, watching over them for their good, the government was almost all prerogative. A few established laws served the turn, and the discretion and care of the ruler supplied the rest. But when mistake or flattery prevailed with weak princes, to make use of this power for private ends of their own and not for the public good, the people were fain, by express laws, to get prerogative determined in those points wherein they found disadvantage from it, and declared limitations of prerogative in those cases which they and their ancestors had left in the utmost latitude to the wisdom of those princes who made no other but a right use of it—that is, for the good of their people.

163. And therefore they have a very wrong notion of government who say that the people have encroached upon the prerogative when they have got any part of it to be defined by positive laws. For in so doing they have not pulled from the prince anything that of right belonged to him, but only declared that that power which they indefinitely left in his or his ancestors' hands, to be exercised for their good, was not a thing they intended him, when he used it otherwise. For the end of government being the good of the community, whatsoever alterations are made in it tending to that end cannot be an encroachment upon anybody; since nobody in government can have a right tending to any other end; and those only are encroachments which prejudice or hinder the public good. Those who say otherwise speak as if the prince had a distinct and separate interest from the good of the community, and was not made for it; the root and source from which spring almost all those evils and disorders which happen in kingly governments. And, indeed, if that be so, the people under his government are not a society of rational creatures, entered into a community for their mutual good, such as have set rulers over themselves, to guard and promote that good; but are to be looked on as a herd of inferior creatures under the dominion of a master, who keeps them and works them for his own pleasure or profit. If men were so void of reason and brutish as to enter into society upon such terms, prerogative might indeed be, what some men would have it, an arbitrary power to do things hurtful to the people.

164. But since a rational creature cannot be supposed, when free, to put himself into subjection to another for his own harm (though where he finds a good and a wise ruler he may not, perhaps, think it

either necessary or useful to set precise bounds to his power in all things), prerogative can be nothing but the people's permitting their rulers to do several things of their own free choice where the law was silent, and sometimes too against the direct letter of the law, for the public good and their acquiescing in it when so done. For as a good prince, who is mindful of the trust put into his hands and careful of the good of his people, cannot have too much prerogative—that is, power to do good—so a weak and ill prince, who would claim that power his predecessors exercised, without the direction of the law, as a prerogative belonging to him by right of his office, which he may exercise at his pleasure to make or promote an interest distinct from that of the public, gives the people an occasion to claim their right and limit that power, which, whilst it was exercised for their good, they were content should be tacitly allowed.

165. And therefore he that will look into the history of England will find that prerogative was always largest in the hands of our wisest and best princes, because the people observing the whole tendency of their actions to be the public good, or if any human frailty or mistake (for princes are but men, made as others) appeared in some small declinations from that end, yet it was visible the main of their conduct tended to nothing but the care of the public. The people, therefore, finding reason to be satisfied with these princes, whenever they acted without, or contrary to the letter of the law, acquiesced in what they did, and without the least complaint, let them enlarge their prerogative as they pleased, judging rightly that they did nothing herein to the prejudice of their laws, since they acted conformably to the foundation and end of all laws—the public good.

166. Such God-like princes, indeed, had some title to arbitrary power by that argument that would prove absolute monarchy the best government, as that which God Himself governs the universe by, because such kings partake of His wisdom and goodness. Upon this is founded that saying, "That the reigns of good princes have been always most dangerous to the liberties of their people." For when their successors, managing the government with different thoughts, would draw the actions of those good rulers into precedent and make them the standard of their prerogative—as if what had been done only for the good of the people was a right in them to do for the harm of the people, if they so pleased—it has often occasioned contest, and sometimes public disorders, be-

fore the people could recover their original right and get that to be declared not to be prerogative which truly was never so; since it is impossible anybody in the society should ever have a right to do the people harm, though it be very possible and reasonable that the people should not go about to set any bounds to the prerogative of those kings or rulers who themselves transgressed not the bounds of the public good. For "prerogative is nothing but the power of doing public good without a rule."

167. The power of calling parliaments in England, as to precise time, place, and duration, is certainly a prerogative of the king, but still with this trust, that it shall be made use of for the good of the nation as the exigencies of the times and variety of occasion shall require. For it being impossible to foresee which should always be the fittest place for them to assemble in, and what the best season, the choice of these was left with the executive power, as might be best subservient to the public good and best suit the ends of parliament.

168. The old question will be asked in this matter of prerogative, "But who shall be judge when this power is made a right use of?" I answer: Between an executive power in being, with such a prerogative, and a legislative that depends upon his will for their convening, there can be no judge on earth. As there can be none between the legislative and the people, should either the executive or the legislative, when they have got the power in their hands, design, or go about to enslave or destroy them, the people have no other remedy in this, as in all other cases where they have no judge on earth, but to appeal to Heaven; for the rulers in such attempts, exercising a power the people never put into their hands, who can never be supposed to consent that anybody should rule over them for their harm, do that which they have not a right to do. And where the body of the people, or any single man, are deprived of their right, or are under the exercise of a power without right, having no appeal on earth they have a liberty to appeal to Heaven whenever they judge the cause of sufficient moment. And therefore, though the people cannot be judge, so as to have, by the constitution of that society, any superior power to determine and give effective sentence in the case, yet they have reserved that ultimate determination to themselves which belongs to all mankind, where there lies no appeal on earth, by a law antecedent and paramount to all positive laws of men, whether they have just cause to make

their appeal to Heaven. And this judgment they cannot part with, it being out of a man's power so to submit himself to another as to give him a liberty to destroy him; God and Nature never allowing a man so to abandon himself as to neglect his own preservation. And since he cannot take away his own life, neither can he give another power to take it. Nor let any one think this lays a perpetual foundation for disorder; for this operates not till the inconvenience is so great that the majority feel it, and are weary of it, and find a necessity to have it amended. And this the executive power, or wise princes, never need come in the danger of; and it is the thing of all others they have most need to avoid, as, of all others, the most perilous.

Chapter XV
Of Paternal, Political, and Despotical Power, Considered Together

169. Though I have had occasion to speak of these separately before, yet the great mistakes of late about government having, as I suppose, arisen from confounding these distinct powers one with another, it may not perhaps be amiss to consider them here together.

170. First, then, paternal or parental power is nothing but that which parents have over their children to govern them, for the children's good, till they come to the use of reason, or a state of knowledge, wherein they may be supposed capable to understand that rule, whether it be the law of Nature or the municipal law of their country, they are to govern themselves by—capable, I say, to know it, as well as several others, who live as free men under that law. The affection and tenderness God hath planted in the breasts of parents towards their children makes it evident that this is not intended to be a severe arbitrary government, but only for the help, instruction, and preservation of their offspring. But happen as it will, there is, as I have proved, no reason why it should be thought to extend to life and death, at any time, over their children, more than over anybody else, or keep the child in subjection to the will of his parents when grown to a man and the perfect use of reason, any farther than as having received life and education from his parents obliges him to respect, honour, gratitude, assistance, and support, all his life, to both father and mother. And thus, it is true, the paternal is a natural government, but not at all extending itself to the ends and jurisdictions of that which is political. The power of the father doth not reach at all to the property of the child, which is only in his own disposing.

171. Secondly, political power is that power which every man having in the state of Nature has given up into the hands of the society, and therein to the governors whom the society hath set over itself, with this express or tacit trust, that it shall be employed for their good and the preservation of their property. Now this power, which every man has in the state of Nature, and which he parts with to the society in all such cases where the society can secure him, is to use such means for the preserving of his own property as he thinks good and Nature allows him; and to punish the breach of the law of Nature in others so as (according to the best of his reason) may most conduce to the preservation of himself and the rest of mankind; so that the end and measure of this power, when in every man's hands, in the state of Nature, being the preservation of all of his society—that is, all mankind in general—it can have no other end or measure, when in the hands of the magistrate, but to preserve the members of that society in their lives, liberties, and possessions, and so cannot be an absolute, arbitrary power over their lives and fortunes, which are as much as possible to be preserved; but a power to make laws, and annex such penalties to them as may tend to the preservation of the whole, by cutting off those parts, and those only, which are so corrupt that they threaten the sound and healthy, without which no severity is lawful. And this power has its original only from compact and agreement and the mutual consent of those who make up the community.

172. Thirdly, despotical power is an absolute, arbitrary power one man has over another, to take away his life whenever he pleases; and this is a power which neither Nature gives, for it has made no such distinction between one man and another, nor compact can convey. For man, not having such an arbitrary power over his own life, cannot give another man such a power over it, but it is the effect only of forfeiture which the aggressor makes of his own life when he puts himself into the state of war with another. For having quitted reason, which God hath given to be the rule betwixt man and man, and the peaceable ways which that teaches, and made use of

force to compass his unjust ends upon another where he has no right, he renders himself liable to be destroyed by his adversary whenever he can, as any other noxious and brutish creature that is destructive to his being. And thus captives, taken in a just and lawful war, and such only, are subject to a despotical power, which, as it arises not from compact, so neither is it capable of any, but is the state of war continued. For what compact can be made with a man that is not master of his own life? What condition can he perform? And if he be once allowed to be master of his own life, the despotical, arbitrary power of his master ceases. He that is master of himself and his own life has a right, too, to the means of preserving it; so that as soon as compact enters, slavery ceases, and he so far quits his absolute power and puts an end to the state of war who enters into conditions with his captive.

173. Nature gives the first of these—viz., paternal power—to parents for the benefit of their children during their minority, to supply their want of ability and understanding how to manage their property. (By property I must be understood here, as in other places, to mean that property which men have in their persons as well as goods.) Voluntary agreement gives the second—viz., political power—to governors, for the benefit of their subjects, to secure them in the possession and use of their properties. And forfeiture gives the third—despotical power—to lords for their own benefit over those who are stripped of all property.

174. He that shall consider the distinct rise and extent, and the different ends of these several powers, will plainly see that paternal power comes as far short of that of the magistrate as despotical exceeds it; and that absolute dominion, however placed, is so far from being one kind of civil society that it is as inconsistent with it as slavery is with property. Paternal power is only where minority makes the child incapable to manage his property; political where men have property in their own disposal; and despotical over such as have no property at all.

Chapter XVI
Of Conquest

175. Though governments can originally have no other rise than that before mentioned, nor polities be founded on anything but the consent of the people, yet such have been the disorders ambition has filled the world with, that in the noise of war, which makes so great a part of the history of mankind, this consent is little taken notice of; and, therefore, many have mistaken the force of arms for the consent of the people, and reckon conquest as one of the originals of government. But conquest is as far from setting up any government as demolishing a house is from building a new one in the place. Indeed, it often makes way for a new frame of a commonwealth by destroying the former; but, without the consent of the people, can never erect a new one.

176. That the aggressor, who puts himself into the state of war with another, and unjustly invades another man's right, can, by such an unjust war, never come to have a right over the conquered, will be easily agreed by all men, who will not think that robbers and pirates have a right of empire over whomsoever they have force enough to master, or that men are bound by promises which unlawful force extorts from them. Should a robber break into my house, and, with a dagger at my throat, make me seal deeds to convey my estate to him, would this give him any title? Just such a title by his sword has an unjust conqueror who forces me into submission. The injury and the crime is equal, whether committed by the wearer of a crown or some petty villain. The title of the offender and the number of his followers make no difference in the offence, unless it be to aggravate it. The only difference is, great robbers punish little ones to keep them in their obedience; but the great ones are rewarded with laurels and triumphs, because they are too big for the weak hands of justice in this world, and have the power in their own possession which should punish offenders. What is my remedy against a robber that so broke into my house? Appeal to the law for justice. But perhaps justice is denied, or I am crippled and cannot stir; robbed, and have not the means to do it. If God has taken away all means of seeking remedy, there is nothing left but patience. But my son, when able, may seek the relief of the law, which I am denied; he or his son may renew his appeal till he recover his right. But the conquered, or their children, have no court—no arbitrator on earth to appeal to. Then they may appeal, as Jephtha did, to Heaven, and repeat their appeal till they have recovered the native right of their ancestors, which was to have such a legislative over them as the majority should approve and freely acquiesce in. If it be

objected this would cause endless trouble, I answer, no more than justice does, where she lies open to all that appeal to her. He that troubles his neighbour without a cause is punished for it by the justice of the court he appeals to. And he that appeals to Heaven must be sure he has right on his side, and a right, too, that is worth the trouble and cost of the appeal, as he will answer at a tribunal that cannot be deceived, and will be sure to retribute to every one according to the mischiefs he hath created to his fellow-subjects—that is, any part of mankind. From whence it is plain that he that conquers in an unjust war can thereby have no title to the subjection and obedience of the conquered.

177. But supposing victory favours the right side, let us consider a conqueror in a lawful war, and see what power he gets, and over whom.

First, it is plain he gets no power by his conquest over those that conquered with him. They that fought on his side cannot suffer by the conquest, but must, at least, be as much free men as they were before. And most commonly they serve upon terms, and on condition to share with their leader, and enjoy a part of the spoil and other advantages that attend the conquering sword, or, at least, have a part of the subdued country bestowed upon them. And the conquering people are not, I hope, to be slaves by conquest, and wear their laurels only to show they are sacrifices to their leader's triumph. They that found absolute monarchy upon the title of the sword make their heroes, who are the founders of such monarchies, arrant "draw-can-sirs," and forget they had any officers and soldiers that fought on their side in the battles they won, or assisted them in the subduing, or shared in possessing the countries they mastered. We are told by some that the English monarchy is founded in the Norman Conquest, and that our princes have thereby a title to absolute dominion, which, if it were true (as by the history it appears otherwise), and that William had a right to make war on this island, yet his dominion by conquest could reach no farther than to the Saxons and Britons that were then inhabitants of this country. The Normans that came with him and helped to conquer, and all descended from them, are free men and no subjects by conquest, let that give what dominion it will. And if I or anybody else shall claim freedom as derived from them, it will be very hard to prove the contrary; and it is plain, the law that has made no distinction between the one and the other

intends not there should be any difference in their freedom or privileges.

178. But supposing, which seldom happens, that the conquerors and conquered never incorporate into one people under the same laws and freedom; let us see next what power a lawful conqueror has over the subdued, and that I say is purely despotical. He has an absolute power over the lives of those who, by an unjust war, have forfeited them, but not over the lives or fortunes of those who engaged not in the war, nor over the possessions even of those who were actually engaged in it.

179. Secondly, I say, then, the conqueror gets no power but only over those who have actually assisted, concurred, or consented to that unjust force that is used against him. For the people having given to their governors no power to do an unjust thing, such as is to make an unjust war (for they never had such a power in themselves), they ought not to be charged as guilty of the violence and injustice that is committed in an unjust war any farther than they actually abet it, no more than they are to be thought guilty of any violence or oppression their governors should use upon the people themselves or any part of their fellow-subjects, they having empowered them no more to the one than to the other. Conquerors, it is true, seldom trouble themselves to make the distinction, but they willingly permit the confusion of war to sweep all together; but yet this alters not the right; for the conqueror's power over the lives of the conquered being only because they have used force to do or maintain an injustice, he can have that power only over those who have concurred in that force; all the rest are innocent, and he has no more title over the people of that country who have done him no injury, and so have made no forfeiture of their lives, than he has over any other who, without any injuries or provocations, have lived upon fair terms with him.

180. Thirdly, the power a conqueror gets over those he overcomes in a just war is perfectly despotical; he has an absolute power over the lives of those who, by putting themselves in a state of war, have forfeited them, but he has not thereby a right and title to their possessions. This I doubt not but at first sight will seem a strange doctrine, it being so quite contrary to the practice of the world; there being nothing more familiar in speaking of the dominion of countries than to say such an one conquered it, as if con-

quest, without any more ado, conveyed a right of possession. But when we consider that the practice of the strong and powerful, how universal soever it may be, is seldom the rule of right, however it be one part of the subjection of the conquered not to argue against the conditions cut out to them by the conquering swords.

181. Though in all war there be usually a complication of force and damage, and the aggressor seldom fails to harm the estate when he uses force against the persons of those he makes war upon, yet it is the use of force only that puts a man into the state of war. For whether by force he begins the injury, or else having quietly and by fraud done the injury, he refuses to make reparation, and by force maintains it, which is the same thing as at first to have done it by force; it is the unjust use of force that makes the war. For he that breaks open my house and violently turns me out of doors, or having peaceably got in, by force keeps me out, does, in effect, the same thing; supposing we are in such a state that we have no common judge on earth whom I may appeal to, and to whom we are both obliged to submit, for of such I am now speaking. It is the unjust use of force, then, that puts a man into the state of war with another, and thereby he that is guilty of it makes a forfeiture of his life. For quitting reason, which is the rule given between man and man, and using force, the way of beasts, he becomes liable to be destroyed by him he uses force against, as any savage ravenous beast that is dangerous to his being.

182. But because the miscarriages of the father are no faults of the children, who may be rational and peaceable, notwithstanding the brutishness and injustice of the father, the father, by his miscarriages and violence, can forfeit but his own life, and involves not his children in his guilt or destruction. His goods which Nature, that willeth the preservation of all mankind as much as is possible, hath made to belong to the children to keep them from perishing, do still continue to belong to his children. For supposing them not to have joined in the war either through infancy or choice, they have done nothing to forfeit them, nor has the conqueror any right to take them away by the bare right of having subdued him that by force attempted his destruction, though, perhaps, he may have some right to them to repair the damages he has sustained by the war, and the defence of his own right, which how far it reaches to the posses-

sions of the conquered we shall see by-and-by; so that he that by conquest has a right over a man's person, to destroy him if he pleases, has not thereby a right over his estate to possess and enjoy it. For it is the brutal force the aggressor has used that gives his adversary a right to take away his life and destroy him, if he pleases, as a noxious creature; but it is damage sustained that alone gives him title to another man's goods; for though I may kill a thief that sets on me in the highway, yet I may not (which seems less) take away his money and let him go; this would be robbery on my side. His force, and the state of war he put himself in, made him forfeit his life, but gave me no title to his goods. The right, then, of conquest extends only to the lives of those who joined in the war, but not to their estates, but only in order to make reparation for the damages received and the charges of the war, and that, too, with reservation of the right of the innocent wife and children.

183. Let the conqueror have as much justice on his side as could be supposed, he has no right to seize more than the vanquished could forfeit; his life is at the victor's mercy, and his service and goods he may appropriate to make himself reparation; but he cannot take the goods of his wife and children, they too had a title to the goods he enjoyed, and their shares in the estate he possessed. For example, I in the state of Nature (and all commonwealths are in the state of Nature one with another) have injured another man, and refusing to give satisfaction, it is come to a state of war wherein my defending by force what I had gotten unjustly makes me the aggressor. I am conquered; my life, it is true, as forfeit, is at mercy, but not my wife's and children's. They made not the war, nor assisted in it. I could not forfeit their lives, they were not mine to forfeit. My wife had a share in my estate, that neither could I forfeit. And my children also, being born of me, had a right to be maintained out of my labour or substance. Here then is the case: The conqueror has a title to reparation for damages received, and the children have a title to their father's estate for their subsistence. For as to the wife's share, whether her own labour or compact gave her a title to it, it is plain her husband could not forfeit what was hers. What must be done in the case? I answer: The fundamental law of Nature being that all, as much as may be, should be preserved, it follows that if there be not enough fully to satisfy both—viz., for the conqueror's losses and children's maintenance—he that

hath and to spare must remit something of his full satisfaction, and give way to the pressing and preferable title of those who are in danger to perish without it.

184. But supposing the charge and damages of the war are to be made up to the conqueror to the utmost farthing, and that the children of the vanquished, spoiled of all their father's goods, are to be left to starve and perish, yet the satisfying of what shall, on this score, be due to the conqueror will scarce give him a title to any country he shall conquer. For the damages of war can scarce amount to the value of any considerable tract of land in any part of the world, where all the land is possessed, and none lies waste. And if I have not taken away the conqueror's land which, being vanquished, it is impossible I should, scarce any other spoil I have done him can amount to the value of mine, supposing it of an extent any way coming near what I had overrun of his, and equally cultivated too. The destruction of a year's product or two (for it seldom reaches four or five) is the utmost spoil that usually can be done. For as to money, and such riches and treasure taken away, these are none of Nature's goods, they have but a phantastical imaginary value; Nature has put no such upon them. They are of no more account by her standard than the Wampompeke of the Americans to an European prince, or the silver money of Europe would have been formerly to an American. And five years' product is not worth the perpetual inheritance of land, where all is possessed and none remains waste, to be taken up by him that is disseised, which will be easily granted, if one do but take away the imaginary value of money, the disproportion being more than between five and five thousand; though, at the same time, half a year's product is more worth than the inheritance where, there being more land than the inhabitants possess and make use of, any one has liberty to make use of the waste. But their conquerors take little care to possess themselves of the lands of the vanquished. No damage therefore that men in the state of Nature (as all princes and governments are in reference to one another) suffer from one another can give a conqueror power to dispossess the posterity of the vanquished, and turn them out of that inheritance which ought to be the possession of them and their descendants to all generations. The conqueror indeed will be apt to think himself master; and it is the very condition of the subdued not to be able to dispute their right. But, if that be all, it gives no other title than what bare force gives to the stronger over the weaker; and, by this reason, he that is strongest will have a right to whatever he pleases to seize on.

185. Over those, then, that joined with him in the war, and over those of the subdued country that opposed him not, and the posterity even of those that did, the conqueror, even in a just war, hath, by his conquest, no right of dominion. They are free from any subjection to him, and if their former government be dissolved, they are at liberty to begin and erect another to themselves.

186. The conqueror, it is true, usually by the force he has over them, compels them, with a sword at their breasts, to stoop to his conditions, and submit to such a government as he pleases to afford them; but the inquiry is, what right he has to do so? If it be said they submit by their own consent, then this allows their own consent to be necessary to give the conqueror a title to rule over them. It remains only to be considered whether promises, extorted by force, without right, can be thought consent, and how far they bind. To which I shall say, they bind not at all; because whatsoever another gets from me by force, I still retain the right of, and he is obliged presently to restore. He that forces my horse from me ought presently to restore him, and I have still a right to retake him. By the same reason, he that forced a promise from me ought presently to restore it—*i.e.*, quit me of the obligation of it; or I may resume it myself—*i.e.*, choose whether I will perform it. For the law of Nature laying an obligation on me, only by the rules she prescribes, cannot oblige me by the violation of her rules; such is the extorting anything from me by force. Nor does it at all alter the case, to say I gave my promise, no more than it excuses the force, and passes the right, when I put my hand in my pocket and deliver my purse myself to a thief who demands it with a pistol at my breast.

187. From all which it follows that the government of a conqueror, imposed by force on the subdued, against whom he had no right of war, or who joined not in the war against him, where he had right, has no obligation upon them.

188. But let us suppose that all the men of that community being all members of the same body politic, may be taken to have joined in that unjust war, wherein they are subdued, and so their lives are at the mercy of the conqueror.

189. I say this concerns not their children who are in their minority. For since a father hath not, in himself, a power over the life or liberty of his child, no act of his can possibly forfeit it; so that the children, whatever may have happened to the fathers, are free men, and the absolute power of the conqueror reaches no farther than the persons of the men that were subdued by him, and dies with them; and should he govern them as slaves, subjected to his absolute, arbitrary power, he has no such right of dominion over their children. He can have no power over them but by their own consent, whatever he may drive them to say or do, and he has no lawful authority, whilst force, and not choice, compels them to submission.

190. Every man is born with a double right. First, a right of freedom to his person, which no other man has a power over, but the free disposal of it lies in himself. Secondly, a right before any other man, to inherit, with his brethren, his father's goods.

191. By the first of these, a man is naturally free from subjection to any government, though he be born in a place under its jurisdiction. But if he disclaim the lawful government of the country he was born in, he must also quit the right that belonged to him, by the laws of it, and the possessions there descending to him from his ancestors, if it were a government made by their consent.

192. By the second, the inhabitants of any country, who are descended and derive a title to their estates from those who are subdued, and had a government forced upon them, against their free consents, retain a right to the possession of their ancestors, though they consent not freely to the government, whose hard conditions were, by force, imposed on the possessors of that country. For the first conqueror never having had a title to the land of that country, the people, who are the descendants of, or claim under those who were forced to submit to the yoke of a government by constraint, have always a right to shake it off, and free themselves from the usurpation or tyranny the sword hath brought in upon them, till their rulers put them under such a frame of government as they willingly and of choice consent to (which they can never be supposed to do, till either they are put in a full state of liberty to choose their government and governors, or at least till they have such standing laws to which they have, by themselves or their representatives, given their free consent, and also till they are allowed their due property, which is so to be propri-

etors of what they have that nobody can take away any part of it without their own consent, without which, men under any government are not in the state of free men, but are direct slaves under the force of war). And who doubts but the Grecian Christians, descendants of the ancient possessors of that country, may justly cast off the Turkish yoke they have so long groaned under, whenever they have a power to do it?

193. But granting that the conqueror, in a just war, has a right to the estates, as well as power over the persons of the conquered, which, it is plain, he hath not, nothing of absolute power will follow from hence in the continuance of the government. Because the descendants of these being all free men, if he grants them estates and possessions to inhabit his country, without which it would be worth nothing, whatsoever he grants them they have so far as it is granted property in; the nature whereof is, that, without a man's own consent, it cannot be taken from him.

194. Their persons are free by a native right, and their properties, be they more or less, are their own, and at their own dispose, and not at his; or else it is no property. Supposing the conqueror gives to one man a thousand acres, to him and his heirs for ever; to another he lets a thousand acres, for his life, under the rent of £50 or £500 per annum. Has not the one of these a right to his thousand acres for ever, and the other during his life, paying the said rent? And hath not the tenant for life a property in all that he gets over and above his rent, by his labour and industry, during the said term, supposing it be double the rent? Can any one say, the king, or conqueror, after his grant, may, by his power of conqueror, take away all, or part of the land, from the heirs of one, or from the other during his life, he paying the rent? Or, can he take away from either the goods or money they have got upon the said land at his pleasure? If he can, then all free and voluntary contracts cease, and are void in the world; there needs nothing but power enough to dissolve them at any time, and all the grants and promises of men in power are but mockery and collusion. For can there be anything more ridiculous than to say, I give you and yours this for ever, and that in the surest and most solemn way of conveyance can be devised, and yet it is to be understood that I have right, if I please, to take it away from you again tomorrow?

195. I will not dispute now whether princes are exempt from the laws of their country, but this I am sure, they owe subjection to the laws of God and Nature. Nobody, no power can exempt them from the obligations of that eternal law. Those are so great and so strong in the case of promises, that Omnipotency itself can be tied by them. Grants, promises, and oaths are bonds that hold the Almighty, whatever some flatterers say to princes of the world, who, all together, with all their people joined to them, are, in comparison of the great God, but as a drop of the bucket, or a dust on the balance—inconsiderable, nothing!

196. The short of the case in conquest, is this: The conqueror, if he have a just cause, has a despotical right over the persons of all that actually aided and concurred in the war against him, and a right to make up his damage and cost out of their labour and estates, so he injure not the right of any other. Over the rest of the people, if there were any that consented not to the war, and over the children of the captives themselves or the possessions of either he has no power, and so can have, by virtue of conquest, no lawful title himself to dominion over them, or derive it to his posterity; but is an aggressor, and puts himself in a state of war against them, and has no better a right of principality, he, nor any of his successors, than Hingar, or Hubba, the Danes, had here in England, or Spartacus, had he conquered Italy, which is to have their yoke cast off as soon as God shall give those under their subjection courage and opportunity to do it. Thus, notwithstanding whatever title the kings of Assyria had over Judah, by the sword, God assisted Hezekiah to throw off the dominion of that conquering empire. "And the Lord was with Hezekiah, and he prospered; wherefore he went forth, and he rebelled against the king of Assyria, and served him not" (2 Kings xviii. 7). Whence it is plain that shaking off a power which force, and not right, hath set over any one, though it hath the name of rebellion, yet is no offence before God, but that which He allows and countenances, though even promises and covenants, when obtained by force, have intervened. For it is very probable, to any one that reads the story of Ahaz and Hezekiah attentively, that the Assyrians subdued Ahaz, and deposed him, and made Hezekiah king in his father's lifetime, and that Hezekiah, by agreement, had done him homage, and paid him tribute till this time.

Chapter XVII
Of Usurpation

197. As conquest may be called a foreign usurpation, so usurpation is a kind of domestic conquest, with this difference—that an usurper can never have right on his side, it being no usurpation but where one is got into the possession of what another has right to. This, so far as it is usurpation, is a change only of persons, but not of the forms and rules of the government; for if the usurper extend his power beyond what, of right, belonged to the lawful princes or governors of the commonwealth, it is tyranny added to usurpation.

198. In all lawful governments the designation of the persons who are to bear rule being as natural and necessary a part as the form of the government itself, and that which had its establishment originally from the people—the anarchy being much alike, to have no form of government at all, or to agree that it shall be monarchical, yet appoint no way to design the person that shall have the power and be the monarch—all commonwealths, therefore, with the form of government established, have rules also of appointing and conveying the right to those who are to have any share in the public authority; and whoever gets into the exercise of any part of the power by other ways than what the laws of the community have prescribed hath no right to be obeyed, though the form of the commonwealth be still preserved, since he is not the person the laws have appointed, and, consequently, not the person the people have consented to. Nor can such an usurper, or any deriving from him, ever have a title till the people are both at liberty to consent, and have actually consented, to allow and confirm in him the power he hath till then usurped.

Chapter XVIII
Of Tyranny

199. As usurpation is the exercise of power which another hath a right to, so tyranny is the exercise of power beyond right, which nobody can have a right to; and this is making use of the power any one has in his hands, not for the good of those who are under it, but for his own private, separate advantage. When the governor, however entitled, makes not the law, but his will, the rule, and his commands and actions are

not directed to the preservation of the properties of his people, but the satisfaction of his own ambition, revenge, covetousness, or any other irregular passion.

200. If one can doubt this to be truth or reason because it comes from the obscure hand of a subject, I hope the authority of a king will make it pass with him. King James, in his speech to the Parliament, 1603, tells them thus: "I will ever prefer the weal of the public and of the whole commonwealth, in making of good laws and constitutions, to any particular and private ends of mine, thinking ever the wealth and weal of the commonwealth to be my greatest weal and worldly felicity—a point wherein a lawful king doth directly differ from a tyrant; for I do acknowledge that the special and greatest point of difference that is between a rightful king and an usurping tyrant is this—that whereas the proud and ambitious tyrant doth think his kingdom and people are only ordained for satisfaction of his desires and unreasonable appetites, the righteous and just king doth, by the contrary, acknowledge himself to be ordained for the procuring of the wealth and property of his people." And again, in his speech to the Parliament, 1609, he hath these words: "The king binds himself, by a double oath, to the observation of the fundamental laws of his kingdom—tacitly, as by being a king, and so bound to protect, as well the people as the laws of his kingdom; and expressly by his oath at his coronation; so as every just king, in a settled kingdom, is bound to observe that paction made to his people, by his laws, in framing his government agreeable thereunto, according to that paction which God made with Noah after the deluge: 'Hereafter, seedtime, and harvest, and cold, and heat, and summer, and winter, and day, and night, shall not cease while the earth remaineth.' And therefore a king, governing in a settled kingdom, leaves to be a king, and degenerates into a tyrant, as soon as he leaves off to rule according to his laws." And a little after: "Therefore, all kings that are not tyrants, or perjured, will be glad to bound themselves within the limits of their laws, and they that persuade them the contrary are vipers, pests, both against them and the commonwealth." Thus, that learned king, who well understood the notions of things, makes the difference betwixt a king and a tyrant to consist only in this: that one makes the laws the bounds of his power and the good of the public the end of his government; the other makes all give way to his own will and appetite.

201. It is a mistake to think this fault is proper only to monarchies. Other forms of government are liable to it as well as that; for wherever the power that is put in any hands for the government of the people and the preservation of their properties is applied to other ends, and made use of to impoverish, harass, or subdue them to the arbitrary and irregular commands of those that have it, there it presently becomes tyranny, whether those that thus use it are one or many. Thus we read of the thirty tyrants at Athens, as well as one at Syracuse; and the intolerable dominion of the Decemviri at Rome was nothing better.

202. Wherever law ends, tyranny begins, if the law be transgressed to another's harm; and whosoever in authority exceeds the power given him by the law, and makes use of the force he has under his command to compass that upon the subject which the law allows not, ceases in that to be a magistrate, and acting without authority may be opposed, as any other man who by force invades the right of another. This is acknowledged in subordinate magistrates. He that hath authority to seize my person in the street may be opposed as a thief and a robber if he endeavours to break into my house to execute a writ, notwithstanding that I know he has such a warrant and such a legal authority as will empower him to arrest me abroad. And why this should not hold in the highest, as well as in the most inferior magistrate, I would gladly be informed. Is it reasonable that the eldest brother, because he has the greatest part of his father's estate, should thereby have a right to take away any of his younger brothers' portions? Or that a rich man, who possessed a whole country, should from thence have a right to seize, when he pleased, the cottage and garden of his poor neighbour? The being rightfully possessed of great power and riches, exceedingly beyond the greatest part of the sons of Adam, is so far from being an excuse, much less a reason for rapine and oppression, which the endamaging another without authority is, that it is a great aggravation of it. For exceeding the bounds of authority is no more a right in a great than a petty officer, no more justifiable in a king than a constable. But so much the worse in him as that he has more trust put in him, is supposed, from the advantage of education and counsellors, to have better knowledge and less reason to do it, having already a greater share than the rest of his brethren.

203. May the commands, then, of a prince be opposed? May he be resisted, as often as any one shall find himself aggrieved, and but imagine he has not right done him? This will unhinge and overturn all polities, and instead of government and order, leave nothing but anarchy and confusion.

204. To this I answer: That force is to be opposed to nothing but to unjust and unlawful force. Whoever makes any opposition in any other case draws on himself a just condemnation, both from God and man; and so no such danger or confusion will follow, as is often suggested. For—

205. First. As in some countries the person of the prince by the law is sacred, and so whatever he commands or does, his person is still free from all question or violence, not liable to force, or any judicial censure or condemnation. But yet opposition may be made to the illegal acts of any inferior officer or other commissioned by him, unless he will, by actually putting himself into a state of war with his people, dissolve the government, and leave them to that defence, which belongs to every one in the state of Nature. For of such things, who can tell what the end will be? And a neighbour kingdom has showed the world an odd example. In all other cases the sacredness of the person exempts him from all inconveniencies, whereby he is secure, whilst the government stands, from all violence and harm whatsoever, than which there cannot be a wiser constitution. For the harm he can do in his own person not being likely to happen often, nor to extend itself far, nor being able by his single strength to subvert the laws nor oppress the body of the people, should any prince have so much weakness and ill-nature as to be willing to do it. The inconveniency of some particular mischiefs that may happen sometimes when a heady prince comes to the throne are well recompensed by the peace of the public and security of the government in the person of the chief magistrate, thus set out of the reach of danger; it being safer for the body that some few private men should be sometimes in danger to suffer than that the head of the republic should be easily and upon slight occasions exposed.

206. Secondly. But this privilege, belonging only to the king's person, hinders not but they may be questioned, opposed, and resisted, who use unjust force, though they pretend a commission from him which the law authorises not; as is plain in the case of him that has the king's writ to arrest a man which is a full commission from the king, and yet he that has it cannot break open a man's house to do it, nor execute this command of the king upon certain days nor in certain places, though this commission have no such exception in it; but they are the limitations of the law, which, if any one transgress, the king's commission excuses him not. For the king's authority being given him only by the law, he cannot empower any one to act against the law, or justify him by his commission in so doing. The commission or command of any magistrate where he has no authority, being as void and insignificant as that of any private man, the difference between the one and the other being that the magistrate has some authority so far and to such ends, and the private man has none at all; for it is not the commission but the authority that gives the right of acting, and against the laws there can be no authority. But notwithstanding such resistance, the king's person and authority are still both secured, and so no danger to governor or government.

207. Thirdly. Supposing a government wherein the person of the chief magistrate is not thus sacred, yet this doctrine of the lawfulness of resisting all unlawful exercises of his power will not, upon every slight occasion, endanger him or embroil the government; for where the injured party may be relieved and his damages repaired by appeal to the law, there can be no pretence for force, which is only to be used where a man is intercepted from appealing to the law. For nothing is to be accounted hostile force but where it leaves not the remedy of such an appeal. and it is such force alone that puts him that uses it into a state of war, and makes it lawful to resist him. A man with a sword in his hand demands my purse on the highway, when perhaps I have not 12d. in my pocket. This man I may lawfully kill. To another I deliver £100 to hold only whilst I alight, which he refuses to restore me when I am got up again, but draws his sword to defend the possession of it by force. I endeavour to retake it. The mischief this man does me is a hundred, or possibly a thousand times more than the other perhaps intended me (whom I killed before he really did me any); and yet I might lawfully kill the one and cannot so much as hurt the other lawfully. The reason whereof is plain; because the one using force which threatened my life, I could not have time to appeal to the law to secure it, and when it was gone it was too late to appeal. The law could not restore life to my

dead carcass. The loss was irreparable; which to prevent the law of Nature gave me a right to destroy him who had put himself into a state of war with me and threatened my destruction. But in the other case, my life not being in danger, I might have the benefit of appealing to the law, and have reparation for my £100 that way.

208. Fourthly. But if the unlawful acts done by the magistrate be maintained (by the power he has got), and the remedy, which is due by law, be by the same power obstructed, yet the right of resisting, even in such manifest acts of tyranny, will not suddenly, or on slight occasions, disturb the government. For if it reach no farther than some private men's cases, though they have a right to defend themselves, and to recover by force what by unlawful force is taken from them, yet the right to do so will not easily engage them in a contest wherein they are sure to perish; it being as impossible for one or a few oppressed men to disturb the government where the body of the people do not think themselves concerned in it, as for a raving madman or heady malcontent to overturn a well-settled state, the people being as little apt to follow the one as the other.

209. But if either these illegal acts have extended to the majority of the people, or if the mischief and oppression has light only on some few, but in such cases as the precedent and consequences seem to threaten all, and they are persuaded in their consciences that their laws, and with them, their estates, liberties, and lives are in danger, and perhaps their religion too, how they will be hindered from resisting illegal force used against them I cannot tell. This is an inconvenience, I confess, that attends all governments whatsoever, when the governors have brought it to this pass, to be generally suspected of their people, the most dangerous state they can possibly put themselves in; wherein they are the less to be pitied, because it is so easy to be avoided. It being as impossible for a governor, if he really means the good of his people, and the preservation of them and their laws together, not to make them see and feel it, as it is for the father of a family not to let his children see he loves and takes care of them.

210. But if all the world shall observe pretences of one kind, and actions of another, arts used to elude the law, and the trust of prerogative (which is an arbitrary power in some things left in the prince's hand to

do good, not harm, to the people) employed contrary to the end for which it was given; if the people shall find the ministers and subordinate magistrates chosen, suitable to such ends, and favoured or laid by proportionably as they promote or oppose them; if they see several experiments made of arbitrary power, and that religion underhand favoured, though publicly proclaimed against, which is readiest to introduce it, and the operators in it supported as much as may be; and when that cannot be done, yet approved still, and liked the better, and a long train of acting show the counsels all tending that way, how can a man any more hinder himself from being persuaded in his own mind which way things are going; or, from casting about how to save himself, than he could from believing the captain of a ship he was in was carrying him and the rest of the company to Algiers, when he found him always steering that course, though cross winds, leaks in his ship, and want of men and provisions did often force him to turn his course another way for some time, which he steadily returned to again as soon as the wind, weather, and other circumstances would let him?

Chapter XIX
Of the Dissolution of Government

211. He that will, with any clearness, speak of the dissolution of government, ought in the first place to distinguish between the dissolution of the society and the dissolution of the government. That which makes the community, and brings men out of the loose state of Nature into one politic society, is the agreement which every one has with the rest to incorporate and act as one body, and so be one distinct commonwealth. The usual, and almost only way whereby this union is dissolved, is the inroad of foreign force making a conquest upon them. For in that case (not being able to maintain and support themselves as one entire and independent body) the union belonging to that body, which consisted therein, must necessarily cease, and so every one return to the state he was in before, with a liberty to shift for himself and provide for his own safety, as he thinks fit, in some other society. Whenever the society is dissolved, it is certain the government of that society cannot remain. Thus conquerors' swords often cut up governments by the roots, and mangle societies to pieces, separating the

subdued or scattered multitude from the protection of and dependence on that society which ought to have preserved them from violence. The world is too well instructed in, and too forward to allow of this way of dissolving of governments, to need any more to be said of it; and there wants not much argument to prove that where the society is dissolved, the government cannot remain; that being as impossible as for the frame of a house to subsist when the materials of it are scattered and displaced by a whirlwind, or jumbled into a confused heap by an earthquake.

212. Besides this overturning from without, governments are dissolved from within:

First. When the legislative is altered, civil society being a state of peace amongst those who are of it, from whom the state of war is excluded by the umpirage which they have provided in their legislative for the ending all differences that may arise amongst any of them; it is in their legislative that the members of a commonwealth are united and combined together into one coherent living body. This is the soul that gives form, life, and unity to the commonwealth; from hence the several members have their mutual influence, sympathy, and connection; and therefore when the legislative is broken, or dissolved, dissolution and death follows. For the essence and union of the society consisting in having one will, the legislative, when once established by the majority, has the declaring and, as it were, keeping of that will. The constitution of the legislative is the first and fundamental act of society, whereby provision is made for the continuation of their union under the direction of persons and bonds of laws, made by persons authorised thereunto, by the consent and appointment of the people, without which no one man, or number of men, amongst them can have authority of making laws that shall be binding to the rest. When any one, or more, shall take upon them to make laws whom the people have not appointed so to do, they make laws without authority, which the people are not therefore bound to obey; by which means they come again to be out of subjection, and may constitute to themselves a new legislative, as they think best, being in full liberty to resist the force of those who, without authority, would impose anything upon them. Every one is at the disposure of his own will, when those who had, by the delegation of the society, the declaring of the public will, are excluded from it, and others usurp the place who have no such authority or delegation.

213. This being usually brought about by such in the commonwealth, who misuse the power they have, it is hard to consider it aright, and know at whose door to lay it, without knowing the form of government in which it happens. Let us suppose, then, the legislative placed in the concurrence of three distinct persons: First, a single hereditary person having the constant, supreme, executive power, and with it the power of convoking and dissolving the other two within certain periods of time. Secondly, an assembly of hereditary nobility. Thirdly, an assembly of representatives chosen, *pro tempore*, by the people. Such a form of government supposed, it is evident:

214. First, that when such a single person or prince sets up his own arbitrary will in place of the laws which are the will of the society declared by the legislative, then the legislative is changed. For that being, in effect, the legislative whose rules and laws are put in execution, and required to be obeyed, when other laws are set up, and other rules pretended and enforced than what the legislative, constituted by the society, have enacted, it is plain that the legislative is changed. Whoever introduces new laws, not being thereunto authorised, by the fundamental appointment of the society, or subverts the old, disowns and overturns the power by which they were made, and so sets up a new legislative.

215. Secondly, when the prince hinders the legislative from assembling in its due time, or from acting freely, pursuant to those ends for which it was constituted, the legislative is altered. For it is not a certain number of men—no, nor their meeting, unless they have also freedom of debating and leisure of perfecting what is for the good of the society, wherein the legislative consists; when these are taken away, or altered, so as to deprive the society of the due exercise of their power, the legislative is truly altered. For it is not names that constitute governments, but the use and exercise of those powers that were intended to accompany them; so that he who takes away the freedom, or hinders the acting of the legislative in its due seasons, in effect takes away the legislative, and puts an end to the government.

216. Thirdly, when, by the arbitrary power of the prince, the electors or ways of election are altered without the consent and contrary to the common interest of the people, there also the legislative is altered. For if others than those whom the society hath authorised thereunto do choose, or in another

way than what the society hath prescribed, those chosen are not the legislative appointed by the people.

217. Fourthly, the delivery also of the people into the subjection of a foreign power, either by the prince or by the legislative, is certainly a change of the legislative, and so a dissolution of the government. For the end why people entered into society being to be preserved one entire, free, independent society, to be governed by its own laws, this is lost whenever they are given up into the power of another.

218. Why, in such a constitution as this, the dissolution of the government in these cases is to be imputed to the prince is evident, because he, having the force, treasure, and offices of the State to employ, and often persuading himself or being flattered by others, that, as supreme magistrate, he is incapable of control; he alone is in a condition to make great advances towards such changes under pretence of lawful authority, and has it in his hands to terrify or suppress opposers as factious, seditious, and enemies to the government; whereas no other part of the legislative, or people, is capable by themselves to attempt any alteration of the legislative without open and visible rebellion, apt enough to be taken notice of, which, when it prevails, produces effects very little different from foreign conquest. Besides, the prince, in such a form of government, having the power of dissolving the other parts of the legislative, and thereby rendering them private persons, they can never, in opposition to him, or without his concurrence, alter the legislative by a law, his consent being necessary to give any of their decrees that sanction. But yet so far as the other parts of the legislative any way contribute to any attempt upon the government, and do either promote, or not, what lies in them, hinder such designs, they are guilty, and partake in this, which is certainly the greatest crime men can be guilty of one towards another.

219. There is one way more whereby such a government may be dissolved, and that is: When he who has the supreme executive power neglects and abandons that charge, so that the laws already made can no longer be put in execution; this is demonstratively to reduce all to anarchy, and so effectively to dissolve the government. For laws not being made for themselves, but to be, by their execution, the bonds of the society to keep every part of the body politic in its due place and function. When that totally ceases, the government visibly ceases, and the people become a confused multitude without order or connection. Where there is no longer the administration of justice for the securing of men's rights, nor any remaining power within the community to direct the force, or provide for the necessities of the public, there certainly is no government left. Where the laws cannot be executed it is all one as if there were no laws, and a government without laws is, I suppose, a mystery in politics inconceivable to human capacity, and inconsistent with human society.

220. In these, and the like cases, when the government is dissolved, the people are at liberty to provide for themselves by erecting a new legislative differing from the other by the change of persons, or form, or both, as they shall find it most for their safety and good. For the society can never, by the fault of another, lose the native and original right it has to preserve itself, which can only be done by a settled legislative and a fair and impartial execution of the laws made by it. But the state of mankind is not so miserable that they are not capable of using this remedy till it be too late to look for any. To tell people they may provide for themselves by erecting a new legislative, when, by oppression, artifice, or being delivered over to a foreign power, their old one is gone, is only to tell them they may expect relief when it is too late, and the evil is past cure. This is, in effect, no more than to bid them first be slaves, and then to take care of their liberty, and, when their chains are on, tell them they may act like free men. This, if barely so, is rather mockery than relief, and men can never be secure from tyranny if there be no means to escape it till they are perfectly under it; and, therefore, it is that they have not only a right to get out of it, but to prevent it.

221. There is, therefore, secondly, another way whereby governments are dissolved, and that is, when the legislative, or the prince, either of them act contrary to their trust.

For the legislative acts against the trust reposed in them when they endeavour to invade the property of the subject, and to make themselves, or any part of the community, masters or arbitrary disposers of the lives, liberties, or fortunes of the people.

222. The reason why men enter into society is the preservation of their property; and the end while they choose and authorise a legislative is that there may be laws made, and rules set, as guards and fences to the properties of all the society, to limit the power and moderate the dominion of every part and member of

the society. For since it can never be supposed to be the will of the society that the legislative should have a power to destroy that which every one designs to secure by entering into society, and for which the people submitted themselves to legislators of their own making: whenever the legislators endeavour to take away and destroy the property of the people, or to reduce them to slavery under arbitrary power, they put themselves into a state of war with the people, who are thereupon absolved from any farther obedience, and are left to the common refuge which God hath provided for all men against force and violence. Whensoever, therefore, the legislative shall transgress this fundamental rule of society, and either by ambition, fear, folly, or corruption, endeavour to grasp themselves, or put into the hands of any other, an absolute power over the lives, liberties, and estates of the people, by this breach of trust they forfeit the power the people had put into their hands for quite contrary ends, and it devolves to the people, who have a right to resume their original liberty, and by the establishment of a new legislative (such as they shall think fit), provide for their own safety and security, which is the end for which they are in society. What I have said here concerning the legislative in general holds true also concerning the supreme executor, who having a double trust put in him, both to have a part in the legislative and the supreme execution of the law, acts against both, when he goes about to set up his own arbitrary will as the law of the society. He acts also contrary to his trust when he employs the force, treasure, and offices of the society to corrupt the representatives and gain them to his purposes, when he openly pre-engages the electors, and prescribes, to their choice, such whom he has, by solicitation, threats, promises, or otherwise, won to his designs, and employs them to bring in such who have promised beforehand what to vote and what to enact. Thus to regulate candidates and electors, and new model the ways of election, what is it but to cut up the government by the roots, and poison the very fountain of public security? For the people having reserved to themselves the choice of their representatives as the fence to their properties, could do it for no other end but that they might always be freely chosen, and so chosen, freely act and advise as the necessity of the commonwealth and the public good should, upon examination and mature debate, be judged to require. This, those who give their votes before they hear the debate, and have weighed the reasons on all sides, are not capable of doing. To prepare such an assembly as this, and endeavour to set up the declared abettors of his own will, for the true representatives of the people, and the law-makers of the society, is certainly as great a breach of trust, and as perfect a declaration of a design to subvert the government, as is possible to be met with. To which, if one shall add rewards and punishments visibly employed to the same end, and all the arts of perverted law made use of to take off and destroy all that stand in the way of such a design, and will not comply and consent to betray the liberties of their country, it will be past doubt what is doing. What power they ought to have in the society who thus employ it contrary to the trust went along with it in its first institution, is easy to determine; and one cannot but see that he who has once attempted any such thing as this cannot any longer be trusted.

223. To this, perhaps, it will be said that the people being ignorant and always discontented, to lay the foundation of government in the unsteady opinion and uncertain humour of the people, is to expose it to certain ruin; and no government will be able long to subsist if the people may set up a new legislative whenever they take offence at the old one. To this I answer, quite the contrary. People are not so easily got out of their old forms as some are apt to suggest. They are hardly to be prevailed with to amend the acknowledged faults in the frame they have been accustomed to. And if there be any original defects, or adventitious ones introduced by time or corruption, it is not an easy thing to get them changed, even when all the world sees there is an opportunity for it. This slowness and aversion in the people to quit their old constitutions has in the many revolutions [that] have been seen in this kingdom, in this and former ages, still kept us to, or after some interval of fruitless attempts, still brought us back again to our old legislative of king, lords, and commons; and whatever provocations have made the crown be taken from some of our princes' heads, they never carried the people so far as to place it in another line.

224. But it will be said this hypothesis lays a ferment for frequent rebellion. To which I answer:

First: no more than any other hypothesis. For when the people are made miserable, and find themselves exposed to the ill usage of arbitrary power, cry up their governors as much as you will for sons of Jupiter, let them be sacred and divine, descended or authorised from Heaven; give them out for whom or what you please, the same will happen. The people generally ill treated, and contrary to right, will be ready upon any occasion to ease themselves of a burden that sits heavy upon them. They will wish and seek for the opportunity, which in the change, weakness, and accidents of human affairs, seldom delays long to offer itself. He must have lived but a little while in the world, who has not seen examples of this in his time; and he must have read very little who cannot produce examples of it in all sorts of governments in the world.

225. Secondly: I answer, such revolutions happen not upon every little mismanagement in public affairs. Great mistakes in the ruling part, many wrong and inconvenient laws, and all the slips of human frailty will be borne by the people without mutiny or murmur. But if a long train of abuses, prevarications, and artifices, all tending the same way, make the design visible to the people, and they cannot but feel what they lie under, and see whither they are going, it is not to be wondered that they should then rouse themselves, and endeavour to put the rule into such hands which may secure to them the ends for which government was at first erected, and without which, ancient names and specious forms are so far from being better, that they are much worse than the state of Nature or pure anarchy; the inconveniencies being all as great and as near, but the remedy farther off and more difficult.

226. Thirdly: I answer, that this power in the people of providing for their safety anew by a new legislative when their legislators have acted contrary to their trust by invading their property, is the best fence against rebellion, and the probablest means to hinder it. For rebellion being an opposition, not to persons, but authority, which is founded only in the constitutions and laws of the government: those, whoever they be, who, by force, break through, and, by force, justify their violation of them, are truly and properly rebels. For when men, by entering into society and civil government, have excluded force, and introduced laws for the preservation of property, peace, and unity amongst themselves, those who set up force again in opposition to the laws, do *rebellare*—that is, bring back again the state of war, and are properly rebels, which they who are in power, by the pretence they have to authority, the temptation of force they have in their hands, and the flattery of those about them being likeliest to do, the proper way to prevent

the evil is to show them the danger and injustice of it who are under the greatest temptation to run into it.

227. In both the forementioned cases, when either the legislative is changed, or the legislators act contrary to the end for which they were constituted, those who are guilty are guilty of rebellion. For if any one by force takes away the established legislative of any society, and the laws by them made, pursuant to their trust, he thereby takes away the umpirage which every one had consented to for a peaceable decision of all their controversies, and a bar to the state of war amongst them. They who remove or change the legislative take away this decisive power, which nobody can have but by the appointment and consent of the people, and so destroying the authority which the people did, and nobody else can set up, and introducing a power which the people hath not authorised, actually introduce a state of war, which is that of force without authority; and thus by removing the legislative established by the society, in whose decisions the people acquiesced and united as to that of their own will, they untie the knot, and expose the people anew to the state of war. And if those, who by force take away the legislative, are rebels, the legislators themselves, as has been shown, can be no less esteemed so, when they who were set up for the protection and preservation of the people, their liberties and properties shall by force invade and endeavour to take them away; and so they putting themselves into a state of war with those who made them the protectors and guardians of their peace, are properly, and with the greatest aggravation, *rebellantes*, rebels.

228. But if they who say it lays a foundation for rebellion mean that it may occasion civil wars or intestine broils to tell the people they are absolved from obedience when illegal attempts are made upon their liberties or properties, and may oppose the unlawful violence of those who were their magistrates when they invade their properties, contrary to the trust put in them, and that, therefore, this doctrine is not to be allowed, being so destructive to the peace of the world; they may as well say, upon the same ground, that honest men may not oppose robbers or pirates, because this may occasion disorder or bloodshed. If any mischief come in such cases, it is not to be charged upon him who defends his own right, but on him that invades his neighbour's. If the innocent honest man must quietly quit all he has for peace sake to him who will lay violent hands upon it, I desire it may be considered what a kind of a peace there will

be in the world which consists only in violence and rapine, and which is to be maintained only for the benefit of robbers and oppressors. Who would not think it an admirable peace betwixt the mighty and the mean, when the lamb, without resistance, yielded his throat to be torn by the imperious wolf? Polyphemus's den gives us a perfect pattern of such a peace: such a government wherein Ulysses and his companions had nothing to do but quietly to suffer themselves to be devoured. And no doubt Ulysses, who was a prudent man, preached up passive obedience, and exhorted them to a quiet submission by representing to them of what concernment peace was to mankind, and by showing [what] inconveniencies might happen if they should offer to resist Polyphemus, who had now the power over them.

229. The end of government is the good of mankind; and which is best for mankind, that the people should be always exposed to the boundless will of tyranny, or that the rulers should be sometimes liable to be opposed when they grow exorbitant in the use of their power, and employ it for the destruction, and not the preservation, of the properties of their people?

230. Nor let any one say that mischief can arise from hence as often as it shall please a busy head or turbulent spirit to desire the alteration of the government. It is true such men may stir whenever they please, but it will be only to their own just ruin and perdition. For till the mischief be grown general, and the ill designs of the rulers become visible, or their attempts sensible to the greater part, the people, who are more disposed to suffer than right themselves by resistance, are not apt to stir. The examples of particular injustice or oppression of here and there an unfortunate man moves them not. But if they universally have a persuasion grounded upon manifest evidence that designs are carrying on against their liberties, and the general course and tendency of things cannot but give them strong suspicions of the evil intention of their governors, who is to be blamed for it? Who can help it if they, who might avoid it, bring themselves into this suspicion? Are the people to be blamed if they have the sense of rational creatures, and can think of things no otherwise than as they find and feel them? And is it not rather their fault who put things in such a posture that they would not have them thought as they are? I grant that the pride, ambition, and turbulency of private men have sometimes caused great disorders in commonwealths, and factions have been fatal to states and kingdoms. But

whether the mischief hath oftener begun in the people's wantonness, and a desire to cast off the lawful authority of their rulers, or in the rulers' insolence and endeavours to get and exercise an arbitrary power over their people, whether oppression or disobedience gave the first rise to the disorder, I leave it to impartial history to determine. This I am sure, whoever, either ruler or subject, by force goes about to invade the rights of either prince or people, and lays the foundation for overturning the constitution and frame of any just government, he is guilty of the greatest crime I think a man is capable of, being to answer for all those mischiefs of blood, rapine, and desolation, which the breaking to pieces of governments bring on a country; and he who does it is justly to be esteemed the common enemy and pest of mankind, and is to be treated accordingly.

231. That subjects or foreigners attempting by force on the properties of any people may be resisted with force is agreed on all hands; but that magistrates doing the same thing may be resisted, hath of late been denied; as if those who had the greatest privileges and advantages by the law had thereby a power to break those laws by which alone they were set in a better place than their brethren; whereas their offence is thereby the greater, both as being ungrateful for the greater share they have by the law, and breaking also that trust which is put into their hands by their brethren.

232. Whosoever uses force without right—as every one does in society who does it without law— puts himself into a state of war with those against whom he so uses it, and in that state all former ties are cancelled, all other rights cease, and every one has a right to defend himself, and to resist the aggressor. This is so evident that Barclay himself—that great assertor of the power and sacredness of kings— is forced to confess that it is lawful for the people, in some cases, to resist their king, and that, too, in a chapter wherein he pretends to show that the Divine law shuts up the people from all manner of rebellion. Whereby it is evident, even by his own doctrine, that since they may, in some cases, resist, all resisting of princes is not rebellion. His words are these: [. . .]

233. "But if any one should ask: Must the people, then, always lay themselves open to the cruelty and rage of tyranny—must they see their cities pillaged and laid in ashes, their wives and children exposed to the tyrant's lust and fury, and themselves and families reduced by their king to ruin and all the miseries of

want and oppression, and yet sit still—must men alone be debarred the common privilege of opposing force with force, which Nature allows so freely to all other creatures for their preservation from injury? I answer: Self-defence is a part of the law of Nature; nor can it be denied the community, even against the king himself; but to revenge themselves upon him must, by no means, be allowed them, it being not agreeable to that law. Wherefore, if the king shall show an hatred, not only to some particular persons, but sets himself against the body of the commonwealth, whereof he is the head, and shall, with intolerable ill-usage, cruelly tyrannise over the whole, or a considerable part of the people; in this case the people have a right to resist and defend themselves from injury; but it must be with this caution, that they only defend themselves, but do not attack their prince. They may repair the damages received, but must not, for any provocation, exceed the bounds of due reverence and respect. They may repulse the present attempt, but must not revenge past violences. For it is natural for us to defend life and limb, but that an inferior should punish a superior is against nature. The mischief which is designed them the people may prevent before it be done, but, when it is done, they must not revenge it on the king, though author of the villany. This, therefore, is the privilege of the people in general above what any private person hath: That particular men are allowed, by our adversaries themselves (Buchanan only excepted), to have no other remedy but patience; but the body of the people may, with respect, resist intolerable tyranny, for when it is but moderate they ought to endure it."

234. Thus far that great advocate of monarchical power allows of resistance.

235. It is true, he has annexed two limitations to it, to no purpose:

First. He says it must be with reverence.

Secondly. It must be without retribution or punishment; and the reason he gives is, "because an inferior cannot punish a superior."

First. How to resist force without striking again, or how to strike with reverence, will need some skill to make intelligible. He that shall oppose an assault only with a shield to receive the blows, or in any more respectful posture, without a sword in his hand to abate the confidence and force of the assailant, will quickly be at an end of his resistance, and will find such a defence serve only to draw on himself the worse usage. This is as ridiculous a way of resisting

as Juvenal thought it of fighting: ["I writhe with the blows you put upon me."] And the success of the combat will be unavoidably the same he there describes it:

> This is a poor man's freedom; the more he is beaten, the more he implores, and he prostrates himself as he goes down in the struggle, so that he may come back a little with his teeth.

This will always be the event of such an imaginary resistance, where men may not strike again. He, therefore, who may resist must be allowed to strike. And then let our author, or anybody else, join a knock on the head or a cut on the face with as much reverence and respect as he thinks fit. He that can reconcile blows and reverence may, for aught I know, deserve for his pains a civil, respectful cudgelling wherever he can meet with it.

Secondly. As to his second—"An inferior cannot punish a superior"—that is true, generally speaking, whilst he is his superior. But to resist force with force, being the state of war that levels the parties, cancels all former relation of reverence, respect, and superiority; and then the odds that remains is—that he who opposes the unjust aggressor has this superiority over him, that he has a right, when he prevails, to punish the offender, both for the breach of the peace and all the evils that followed upon it. Barclay, therefore, in another place, more coherently to himself, denies it to be lawful to resist a king in any case. But he there assigns two cases whereby a king may unking himself. His words are: [. . .]

237. "What, then, can there no case happen wherein the people may of right, and by their own authority, help themselves, take arms, and set upon their king, imperiously domineering over them? None at all whilst he remains a king. 'Honour the king,' and 'he that resists the power, resists the ordinance of God,' are Divine oracles that will never permit it. The people, therefore, can never come by a power over him unless he does something that makes him cease to be a king; for then he divests himself of his crown and dignity, and returns to the state of a private man, and the people become free and superior; the power which they had in the interregnum, before they crowned him king, devolving to them again. But there are but few miscarriages which bring the matter to this state. After considering it well on all sides, I can find but two. Two cases there are, I say, whereby a king, *ipso facto*, becomes no king, and loses all power

and regal authority over his people, which are also taken notice of by Winzerus. The first is, if he endeavour to overturn the government—that is, if he have a purpose and design to ruin the kingdom and commonwealth, as it is recorded of Nero that he resolved to cut off the senate and people of Rome, lay the city waste with fire and sword, and then remove to some other place; and of Caligula, that he openly declared that he would be no longer a head to the people or senate, and that he had it in his thoughts to cut off the worthiest men of both ranks, and then retire to Alexandria; and he wished that the people had but one neck that he might dispatch them all at a blow. Such designs as these, when any king harbours in his thoughts, and seriously promotes, he immediately gives up all care and thought of the commonwealth, and, consequently, forfeits the power of governing his subjects, as a master does the dominion over his slaves whom he hath abandoned.

238. "The other case is, when a king makes himself the dependent of another, and subjects his kingdom, which his ancestors left him, and the people put free into his hands, to the dominion of another. For however, perhaps, it may not be his intention to prejudice the people, yet he has hereby lost the principal part of regal dignity—viz., to be next and immediately under God, supreme in his kingdom; and also because he betrayed or forced his people, whose liberty he ought to have carefully preserved, into the power and dominion of a foreign nation. By this, as it were, alienation of his kingdom, he himself loses the power he had in it before, without transferring any the least right to those on whom he would have bestowed it; and so by this act sets the people free, and leaves them at their own disposal. One example of this is to be found in the Scotch annals."

239. In these cases Barclay, the great champion of absolute monarchy, is forced to allow that a king may be resisted, and ceases to be a king. That is in short—not to multiply cases—in whatsoever he has no authority, there he is no king, and may be resisted: for wheresoever the authority ceases, the king ceases too, and becomes like other men who have no authority. And these two cases that he instances differ little from those above mentioned, to be destructive to governments, only that he has omitted the principle from which his doctrine flows, and that is the breach of trust in not preserving the form of government agreed on, and in not intending the end of government itself,

which is the public good and preservation of property. When a king has dethroned himself, and put himself in a state of war with his people, what shall hinder them from prosecuting him who is no king, as they would any other man, who has put himself into a state of war with them, Barclay, and those of his opinion, would do well to tell us. Bilson, a bishop of our Church, and a great stickler for the power and prerogative of princes, does, if I mistake not, in his treatise of "Christian Subjection," acknowledge that princes may forfeit their power and their title to the obedience of their subjects; and if there needed authority in a case where reason is so plain, I could send my reader to Bracton, Fortescue, and the author of the "Mirror," and others, writers that cannot be suspected to be ignorant of our government, or enemies to it. But I thought Hooker alone might be enough to satisfy those men who, relying on him for their ecclesiastical polity, are by a strange fate carried to deny those principles upon which he builds it. Whether they are herein made the tools of cunninger workmen, to pull down their own fabric, they were best look. This I am sure, their civil policy is so new, so dangerous, and so destructive to both rulers and people, that as former ages never could bear the broaching of it, so it may be hoped those to come, redeemed from the impositions of these Egyptian under-taskmasters, will abhor the memory of such servile flatterers, who, whilst it seemed to serve their turn, resolved all government into absolute tyranny, and would have all men born to what their mean souls fitted them—slavery.

240. Here it is like[ly] the common question will be made: Who shall be judge whether the prince or legislative act contrary to their trust? This, perhaps, ill-affected and factious men may spread amongst the people, when the prince only makes use of his due prerogative. To this I reply, The people shall be judge; for who shall be judge whether his trustee or deputy acts well and according to the trust reposed in him, but he who deputes him and must, by having deputed him, have still a power to discard him when he fails in his trust? If this be reasonable in particular cases of private men, why should it be otherwise in that of the greatest moment, where the welfare of millions is concerned and also where the evil, if not prevented, is greater, and the redress very difficult, dear, and dangerous?

241. But, farther, this question, Who shall be judge? cannot mean that there is no judge at all. For

where there is no judicature on earth to decide controversies amongst men, God in heaven is judge. He alone, it is true, is judge of the right. But every man is judge for himself, as in all other cases so in this, whether another hath put himself into a state of war with him, and whether he should appeal to the supreme Judge, as Jephtha did.

242. If a controversy arise betwixt a prince and some of the people in a matter where the law is silent or doubtful, and the thing be of great consequence, I should think the proper umpire in such a case should be the body of the people. For in such cases where the prince hath a trust reposed in him, and is dispensed from the common, ordinary rules of the law, there, if any men find themselves aggrieved, and think the prince acts contrary to, or beyond that trust, who so proper to judge as the body of the people (who at first lodged that trust in him) how far they meant it should extend? But if the prince, or whoever they be in the administration, decline that way of determination, the appeal then lies nowhere but to Heaven. Force between either persons who have no known superior on earth, or which permits no appeal to a judge on earth, being properly a state of war, wherein the appeal lies only to Heaven; and in that state the injured party must judge for himself when he will

think fit to make use of that appeal and put himself upon it.

243. To conclude. The power that every individual gave the society when he entered into it can never revert to the individuals again, as long as the society lasts, but will always remain in the community; because without this there can be no community—no commonwealth, which is contrary to the original agreement; so also when the society hath placed the legislative in any assembly of men, to continue in them and their successors, with direction and authority for providing such successors, the legislative can never revert to the people whilst that government lasts: because, having provided a legislative with power to continue for ever, they have given up their political power to the legislative, and cannot resume it. But if they have set limits to the duration of their legislative, and made this supreme power in any person or assembly only temporary; or else when, by the miscarriages of those in authority, it is forfeited; upon the forfeiture of their rulers, or at the determination of the time set, it reverts to the society, and the people have a right to act as supreme, and continue the legislative in themselves or place it in a new form, or new hands, as they think good.

A Letter Concerning Toleration

To the Reader

The Ensuing *Letter concerning Toleration*, first Printed in *Latin* this very Year, in *Holland*, has already been Translated both into *Dutch* and *French*. So general and speedy an Approbation may therefore bespeak its favourable Reception in *England*. I think indeed there is no Nation under Heaven, in which so much has already been said upon that Subject, as Ours. But yet certainly there is no People that stand in more need of having something further both said and done amongst them, in this Point, than We do.

Our Government has not only been partial in Matters of Religion; but those also who have suffered under that Partiality, and have therefore endeavoured by their Writings to vindicate their own Rights and Liberties, have for the most part done it upon narrow

Principles, suited only to the Interests of their own Sects.

This narrowness of Spirit on all sides has undoubtedly been the principal Occasion of our Miseries and Confusions. But whatever have been the Occasion, it is now high time to seek for a thorow Cure. We have need of more generous Remedies than what have yet been made use of in our Distemper. It is neither *Declarations of Indulgence*, nor *Acts of Comprehension*, such as have yet been practised or projected amongst us, that can do the Work. The first will but palliate, the second encrease our Evil.

Absolute Liberty, Just and True Liberty, Equal and Impartial Liberty, is the thing that we stand in need of. Now tho this has indeed been much talked of, I doubt it has not been much understood; I am sure not at all practised, either by our Governours towards the People in general, or by any Dissenting Parties of the People towards one another.

I cannot therefore but hope that this *Discourse*, which treats of that Subject, however briefly, yet more exactly than any we have yet seen, demonstrating both the Equitableness and Practicableness of the thing, will be esteemed highly seasonable, by all Men that have Souls large enough to prefer the true Interest of the Publick before that of a Party.

It is for the use of such as are already so spirited, or to inspire that Spirit into those that are not, that I have Translated it into our Language. But the thing it self is so short, that it will not bear a longer Preface. I leave it therefore to the Consideration of my Countrymen, and heartily wish they make the use of it that it appears to be designed for.

A Letter Concerning Toleration

Honoured Sir,

Since you are pleased to inquire what are my Thoughts about the mutual Toleration of Christians in their different Professions of Religion, I must needs answer you freely, That I esteem that Toleration to be the chief Characteristical Mark of the True Church. For whatsoever some People boast of the Antiquity of Places and Names, or of the Pomp of their Outward Worship; Others, of the Reformation of their Discipline; All, of the Orthodoxy of their Faith; (for every one is Orthodox to himself:) These things, and all others of this nature, are much rather Marks of Men striving for Power and Empire over one another, than of the Church of Christ. Let any one have never so true a Claim to all these things, yet if he be destitute of Charity, Meekness, and Good-will in general towards all Mankind, even to those that are not Christians, he is certainly yet short of being a true Christian himself. *The Kings of the Gentiles exercise Lordship over them*, said our Saviour to his Disciples, *but ye shall not be so.*[1] The Business of True Religion is quite another thing. It is not instituted in order to the erecting of an external Pomp, nor to the obtaining of Ecclesiastical Dominion, nor to the exercising of compulsive Force; but to the regulating of Mens Lives according to the Rules of Vertue and Piety. Whosoever will lift himself under the Banner of Christ, must in the first place, and above all things, make War upon his own Lusts and Vices. It is in vain for any Man to usurp the Name of Christian, without Holiness of Life, Purity of Manners, and Benignity and Meekness of Spirit. *Let every one that nameth the Name of Christ, depart from iniquity.*[2] *Thou, when thou art converted, strengthen thy Brethren,*[3] said our *Lord* to *Peter.* It would indeed be very hard for one that appears careless about his own Salvation, to persuade me that he were extremely concern'd for mine. For it is impossible that those should sincerely and heartily apply themselves to make other People Christians, who have not really embraced the Christian Religion in their own Hearts. If the Gospel and the Apostles may be credited, no Man can be a Christian without *Charity*, and without *that Faith which works*, not by Force, but by *Love.* Now I appeal to the Consciences of those that persecute, torment, destroy, and kill other Men upon pretence of Religion, whether they do it out of Friendship and Kindness towards them, or no: And I shall then indeed, and not till then, believe they do so, when I shall see those fiery Zealots correcting, in the same manner, their Friends and familiar Acquaintance, for the manifest Sins they commit against the Precepts of the Gospel; when I shall see them prosecute with Fire and Sword the Members of their own Communion that are tainted with enormous Vices, and without Amendment are in danger of eternal Perdition; and when I shall see them thus express their Love and Desire of the Salvation of their Souls, by the infliction of Torments, and exercise of all manner of Cruelties. For if

---

1. Luke 22.25.

2. 2 Tim. 2.19.
3. Luke 22.32.

it be out of a Principle of Charity, as they pretend, and Love to Mens Souls, that they deprive them of their estates, maim them with corporal Punishments, starve and torment them in noisom Prisons, and in the end even take away their Lives; I say, if all this be done meerly to make Men Christians, and procure their Salvation, Why then do they suffer *Whoredom, Fraud, Malice,* and *such like enormities,*[4] which (according to the Apostle) manifestly rellish of Heathenish Corruption, to predominate so much and abound amongst their Flocks and People? These, and such like things, are certainly more contrary to the Glory of God, to the Purity of the Church, and to the Salvation of Souls, than any conscientious Dissent from Ecclesiastical Decisions, or Separation from Publick Worship, whilst accompanied with Innocency of Life. Why then does this burning Zeal for God, for the Church, and for the Salvation of Souls; burning, I say, literally, with Fire and Faggot; pass by those moral Vices and Wickednesses, without any Chastisement, which are acknowledged by all Men to be diametrically opposite to the Profession of Christianity; and bend all its Nerves either to the introducing of Ceremonies, or to the establishment of Opinions, which for the most part are about nice and intricate Matters, that exceed the Capacity of ordinary Understandings? Which of the Parties contending about these things is in the right, which of them is guilty of Schism or Heresie, whether those that domineer or those that suffer, will then at last be manifest, when the Cause of their Separation comes to be judged of. He certainly that follows Christ, embraces his Doctrine, and bears his Yoke, tho' he forsake both Father and Mother, separate from the Publick Assemblies and Ceremonies of his Country, or whomsoever, or whatsoever else he relinquishes, will not then be judged an Heretick.

Now, tho' the Divisions that are amongst Sects should be allowed to be never so obstructive of the Salvation of Souls, yet nevertheless *Adultery, Fornication, Uncleanness, Lasciviousness, Idolatry, and such like things, cannot be denied to be Works of the Flesh;* concerning which the Apostle has expressly declared, that *they who do them shall not inherit the Kingdom of God.*[5] Whosoever therefore is sincerely solicitous about the Kingdom of God, and thinks it his Duty to endeavour the Enlargement of it amongst Men, ought to apply himself with no less care and industry to the rooting out of these Immoralities, than to the Extirpation of Sects. But if any one do otherwise, and whilst he is cruel and implacable towards those that differ from him in Opinion, he be indulgent to such Iniquities and Immoralities as are unbecoming the Name of a Christian, let such a one talk never so much of the Church, he plainly demonstrates by his Actions, that 'tis another Kingdom he aims at, and not the Advancement of the Kingdom of God.

That any Man should think fit to cause another Man whose Salvation he heartily desires, to expire in Torment and that even in an unconverted estate, would, I confess, seem very strange to me, and, I think, to any other also. But no body, surely, will ever believe that such a Carriage can proceed from Charity, Love, or Good-will. If any one maintain that Men ought to be compelled by Fire and Sword to profess certain Doctrines, and conform to this or that exteriour Worship, without any regard had unto their Morals; if any one endeavour to convert them that are Erroneous unto the Faith, by forcing them to profess things that they do not believe, and allowing them to practise things that the Gospel does not permit; it can not be doubted indeed but such a one is desirous to have a numerous Assembly joyned in the same Profession with himself; but that he principally intends by those men to compose a truly Christian Church, is altogether incredible. It is not therefore to be wondred at, if those do not really contend for the Advancement of the true Religion, and of the Church of Christ, make use of Arms that do not belong to the Christian Warfare. If, like the Captain of our Salvation, they sincerely desired the Good of Souls, they would tread in the Steps, and follow the perfect Example of that Prince of Peace, who sent out his Soldiers to the subduing of Nations, and gathering them into his Church, not armed with the Sword, or other Instruments of Force, but prepared with the Gospel of Peace, and with the Exemplary Holiness of their Conversation. This was his Method. Tho' if Infidels were to be converted by force, if those that are

---

4. Rom. 1.

5. Gal. 5.

either blind or obstinate were to be drawn off from their Errors by Armed Soldiers, we know very well that it was much more easie for Him to do it with Armies of Heavenly Legions, than for any Son of the Church, how potent soever, with all his Dragoons.

The Toleration of those that differ from others in Matters of Religion, is so agreeable to the Gospel of Jesus Christ, and to the genuine Reason of Mankind, that it seems monstrous for Men to be so blind, as not to perceive the Necessity and Advantage of it, in so clear a Light. I will not here tax the Pride and Ambition of some, the Passion and uncharitable Zeal of others. These are Faults from which Humane Affairs can perhaps scarce ever be perfectly freed; but yet such as no body will bear the plain Imputation of, without covering them with some specious Colour; and so pretend to Commendation, whilst they are carried away by their own irregular Passions. But however, that some may not colour their Spirit of Persecution and unchristian Cruelty with a Pretence of Care of the Publick Weal, and Observation of the Laws; and that others, under pretence of Religion, may not seek Impunity for their Libertinism and Licentiousness; in a word, that none may impose either upon himself or others, by the Pretences of Loyalty and Obedience to the Prince, or of Tenderness and Sincerity in the Worship of God; I esteem it above all things necessary to distinguish exactly the Business of Civil Government from that of Religion, and to settle the just Bounds that lie between the one and the other. If this be not done, there can be no end put to the Controversies that will be always arising, between those that have, or at least pretend to have, on the one side, a Concernment for the Interest of Mens Souls, and on the other side, a Care of the Commonwealth.

The Commonwealth seems to me to be a Society of Men constituted only for the procuring, preserving, and advancing of their own *Civil Interests*.

Civil Interests I call Life, Liberty, Health, and Indolency of Body; and the Possession of outward things, such as Money, Lands, Houses, Furniture, and the like.

It is the Duty of the Civil Magistrate, by the impartial Execution of equal Laws, to secure unto all the People in general, and to every one of his Subjects in particular, the just Possession of these things belonging to this Life. If any one presume to violate the Laws of Publick Justice and Equity, established for the Preservation of those things, his Presumption is to be

check'd by the fear of Punishment, consisting of the Deprivation or Diminution of those Civil Interests, or Goods, which otherwise he might and ought to enjoy. But seeing no Man does willingly suffer himself to be punished by the Deprivation of any part of his Goods, and much less of his Liberty or Life, therefore is the Magistrate armed with the Force and Strength of all his Subjects, in order to the punishment of those that violate any other Man's Rights.

Now that the whole Jurisdiction of the Magistrate reaches only to these Civil Concernments; and that all Civil Power, Right and Dominion, is bounded and confined to the only care of promoting these things; and that it neither can nor ought in any manner to be extended to the Salvation of Souls, these following Considerations seem unto me abundantly to demonstrate.

First. Because the Care of Souls is not committed to the Civil Magistrate, any more than to other Men. It is not committed unto him, I say, by God; because it appears not that God has ever given any such Authority to one Man over another, as to compel any one to his Religion. Nor can any such Power be vested in the Magistrate by the *consent of the People*; because no man can so far abandon the care of his own Salvation, as blindly to leave it to the choice of any other, whether Prince or Subject, to prescribe to him what Faith or Worship he shall embrace. For no Man can, if he would, conform his Faith to the Dictates of another. All the Life and Power of true Religion consists in the inward and full persuasion of the mind; and Faith is not Faith without believing. Whatever Profession we make, to whatever outward Worship we conform, if we are not fully satisfied in our own mind that the one is true, and the other well pleasing unto God, such Profession and such Practice, far from being any furtherance, are indeed great Obstacles to our Salvation. For in this manner, instead of expiating other Sins by the exercise of Religion, I say in offering thus unto God Almighty such a Worship as we esteem to be displeasing unto him, we add unto the number of our other sins, those also of Hypocrisie, and Contempt of his Divine Majesty.

In the second place. The care of Souls cannot belong to the Civil Magistrate, because his Power consists only in outward force; but true and saving Religion consists in the inward persuasion of the Mind, without which nothing can be acceptable to God. And such is the nature of the Understanding, that it cannot be compell'd to the belief of any thing by outward force. Confiscation of Estate, Imprisonment, Torments, nothing of that nature can have any such Efficacy as to make Men change the inward Judgment that they have framed of things.

It may indeed be alleged, that the Magistrate may make use of Arguments, and thereby draw the Heterodox into the way of Truth, and procure their Salvation. I grant it; but this is common to him with other Men. In teaching, instructing, and redressing the Erroneous by Reason, he may certainly do what becomes any good Man to do. Magistracy does not oblige him to put off either Humanity or Christianity. But it is one thing to perswade, another to command; one thing to press with Arguments, another with Penalties. This Civil Power alone has a right to do; to the other Goodwill is Authority enough. Every Man has Commission to admonish, exhort, convince another of Error, and by reasoning to draw him into Truth: but to give Laws, receive Obedience, and compel with the Sword, belongs to none but the Magistrate. And upon this ground I affirm, that the Magistrate's Power extends not to the establishing of any Articles of Faith, or Forms of Worship, by the force of his Laws. For Laws are of no force at all without Penalties, and Penalties in this case are absolutely impertinent; because they are not proper to convince the mind. Neither the Profession of any Articles of Faith, nor the Conformity to any outward Form of Worship (as has already been said) can be available to the Salvation of Souls, unless the truth of the one, and the acceptableness of the other unto God, be thoroughly believed by those that so profess and practise. But Penalties are no ways capable to produce such Belief. It is only Light and Evidence that can work a change in Mens Opinions; which Light can in no manner proceed from corporal Sufferings, or any other outward Penalties.

In the third place. The care of the Salvation of Mens Souls cannot belong to the Magistrate; because, though the rigour of Laws and the force of Penalties were capable to convince and change Mens minds, yet would not that help at all to the Salvation of their Souls. For there being but one Truth, one way to Heaven; what Hopes is there that more Men would be led into it, if they had no Rule but the Religion of the Court, and were put under a necessity to quit the Light of their own Reason, and oppose the Dictates of their own Consciences, and blindly to resign up themselves to the Will of their Governors, and to the Religion, which either Ignorance, Ambition, or Superstition had chanced to establish in the Countries where they were born? In the variety and contradiction of Opinions in Religion, wherein the Princes of the World are as much divided as in their Secular Interests, the narrow way would be much straitned; one Country alone would be in the right, and all the rest of the World put under an obligation of following their Princes in the ways that lead to Destruction; and that which heightens the absurdity, and very ill suits the Notion of a Deity, Men would owe their eternal Happiness or Misery to the places of their Nativity.

These considerations, to omit many others that might have been urged to the same purpose, seem unto me sufficient to conclude that all the Power of Civil Government relates only to Mens Civil Interests, is confined to the care of the things of this World, and hath nothing to do with the World to come.

Let us now consider what a Church is. A Church then I take to be a voluntary Society of Men, joining themselves together of their own accord, in order to the publick worshipping of God, in such a manner as they judge acceptable to him, and effectual to the Salvation of their Souls.

I say it is a free and voluntary Society. No body is born a member of any Church; otherwise the Religion of Parents would descend unto Children, by the same right of Inheritance as their Temporal Estates, and every one would hold his Faith by the same Tenure he does his Lands; than which nothing can be imagined more absurd. Thus therefore that matter stands. No Man by nature is bound unto any particular Church or Sect, but every one joins himself voluntarily to that Society in which he believes he has found that Profession and Worship which is truly acceptable to God. The hopes of Salvation, as it was the only cause of his entrance into that Communion, so it can be the only reason of his stay there. For if afterwards he discover any thing either erroneous in the Doctrine, or incongruous in the Worship of that Society to which he has join'd himself, Why should it not be as free for him to go out as it was to enter? No Member of a Religious Society can be tied with any other Bonds but what proceed from the certain expectation of eternal Life. A Church, then, is a Society of Members voluntarily uniting to this end.

It follows now that we consider what is the Power of this Church, and unto what Laws it is subject.

Forasmuch as no Society, how free soever, or upon whatsoever slight occasion instituted, (whether of Philosophers for Learning, of Merchants for Commerce, or of men of leisure for mutual Conversation and Discourse,) No Church or Company, I say, can in the least subsist and hold together, but will presently dissolve and break to pieces, unless it be regulated by some Laws, and the Members all consent to observe some Order. Place, and time of meeting must be agreed on; Rules for admitting and excluding Members must be establisht; Distinction of Officers, and putting things into a regular Course, and such like, cannot be omitted. But since the joyning together of several Members into this Church-Society, as has already been demonstrated, is absolutely free and spontaneous, it necessarily follows, that the Right of making its Laws can belong to none but the Society it self, or at least (which is the same thing) to those whom the Society by common consent has authorized thereunto.

Some perhaps may object, that no such Society can be said to be a true Church, unless it have in it a Bishop, or Presbyter, with Ruling Authority derived from the very Apostles, and continued down to the present times by an uninterrupted Succession.

To these I answer. *In the first place*, Let them shew me the Edict by which Christ has imposed that Law upon his Church. And let not any man think me impertinent if, in a thing of this consequence, I require that the Terms of that Edict be very express and positive. For the Promise he has made us, that *wheresoever two or three are gathered together in his Name, he will be in the midst of them,*[6] seems to imply the contrary. Whether such an Assembly want any thing necessary to a true Church, pray do you consider. Certain I am, that nothing can be there wanting unto the Salvation of Souls; Which is sufficient to our purpose.

Next, Pray observe how great have always been the Divisions amongst even those who lay so much stress upon the Divine Institution, and continued Succession of a certain Order of Rulers in the Church. Now their very Dissention unavoidably puts us upon a necessity of deliberating, and consequently allows a liberty of choosing that, which upon consideration, we prefer.

And in the last place, I consent that these men have a Ruler of their Church, established by such a long Series of Succession as they judge necessary; provided I may have liberty at the same time to join

my self to that Society, in which I am perswaded those things are to be found which are necessary to the Salvation of my Soul. In this manner Ecclesiastical Liberty will be preserved on all sides, and no man will have a Legislator imposed upon him, but whom himself has chosen.

But since men are so sollicitous about the true Church, I would only ask them, here by the way, if it be not more agreeable to the Church of Christ, to make the Conditions of her Communion consist in such things, and such things only, as the Holy Spirit has in the Holy Scriptures declared, in express Words, to be necessary to Salvation; I ask, I say, whether this be not more agreeable to the Church of Christ, than for men to impose their own Inventions and Interpretations upon others, as if they were of Divine Authority, and to establish by Ecclesiastical Laws, as absolutely necessary to the Profession of Christianity, such things as the Holy Scriptures do either not mention, or at least not expressly command. Whosoever requires those things in order to Ecclesiastical Communion, which Christ does not require in order to Life Eternal, he may perhaps indeed constitute a Society accommodated to his own Opinion and his own Advantage, but how that can be called the Church of Christ, which is established upon Laws that are not his, and which excludes such Persons from its Communion as he will one day receive into the Kingdom of Heaven, I understand not. But this being not a proper place to enquire into the marks of the true Church, I will only mind those that contend so earnestly for the Decrees of their own Society, and that cry out continually the Church, the Church, with as much noise, and perhaps upon the same Principle, as the *Ephesian* Silversmiths did for their *Diana;* this, I say, I desire to mind them of, That the Gospel frequently declares that the true Disciples of Christ must suffer Persecution; but that the Church of Christ should persecute others, and force others by Fire and Sword, to embrace her Faith and Doctrine, I could never yet find in any of the Books of the New Testament.

The End of a Religious Society (as has already been said) is the Publick Worship of God, and by means thereof the acquisition of Eternal Life. All Discipline ought therefore to tend to that End, and all Ecclesiastical Laws to be thereunto confined. Nothing ought, nor can be transacted in this Society, relating to the Possession of Civil and Worldly Goods. No Force is here to be made use of, upon any occasion

---

6. Matth. 18.20.

whatsoever: For Force belongs wholly to the Civil Magistrate, and the Possession of all outward Goods is subject to his Jurisdiction.

But it may be asked, By what means then shall Ecclesiastical Laws be established, if they must be thus destitute of all Compulsive Power? I answer, They must be established by Means suitable to the Nature of such Things, whereof the external Profession and Observation, if not proceeding from a thorow Conviction and Approbation of the Mind, is altogether useless and unprofitable. The Arms by which the Members of this Society are to be kept within their Duty, are Exhortations, Admonitions, and Advices. If by these means the Offenders will not be reclaimed, and the Erroneous convinced, there remains nothing farther to be done, but that such stubborn and obstinate Persons, who give no ground to hope for their Reformation, should be cast out and separated from the Society. This is the last and utmost Force of Ecclesiastical Authority: No other Punishment can thereby be inflicted, than that, the Relation ceasing between the Body and the Member which is cut off, the Person so condemned ceases to be a Part of that Church.

These things being thus determined, let us inquire in the next place, how far the Duty of Toleration extends, and what is required from every one by it.

And first, I hold, That no Church is bound, by the Duty of Toleration to retain any such Person in her Bosom, as, after Admonition, continues obstinately to offend against the Laws of the Society. For these being the Condition of Communion, and the Bond of the Society, if the Breach of them were permitted without any Animadversion, the Society would immediately be thereby dissolved. But nevertheless, in all such Cases care is to be taken that the Sentence of Excommunication, and the Execution thereof, carry with it no rough usage, of Word or Action, whereby the ejected Person may any wise be damnified in Body or Estate. For all Force (as has often been said) belongs only to the Magistrate, nor ought any private Persons, at any time, to use Force; unless it be in self-defence against unjust Violence. Excommunication neither does, nor can, deprive the excommunicated Person of any of those Civil Goods that he formerly possessed. All those things belong to the Civil Government, and are under the Magistrate's Protection. The whole Force of Excommunication consists only in this, that, the Resolution of the Society in that respect being declared, the Union that was between the Body and some Member comes thereby to be dissolved, and that Relation ceasing, the participation of some certain things, which the Society communicated to its Members, and unto which no Man has any Civil Right, comes also to cease. For there is no Civil Injury done unto the excommunicated Person, by the Church-Minister's refusing him that Bread and Wine, in the celebration of the Lord's Supper, which was not bought with his, but other mens Money.

Secondly, No private Person has any Right, in any manner, to prejudice another Person in his Civil Enjoyments, because he is of another Church or Religion. All the Rights and Franchises that belong to him as a Man, or as a Denison, are inviolably to be preserved to him. These are not the Business of Religion. No Violence nor Injury is to be offered him, whether he be Christian or Pagan. Nay, we must not content our selves with the narrow Measures of bare Justice: Charity, Bounty, and Liberality must be added to it. This the Gospel enjoyns, this Reason directs, and this that natural Fellowship we are born into requires of us. If any man err from the right way, it is his own misfortune, no injury to thee: Nor therefore art thou to punish him in the things of this Life, because thou supposest he will be miserable in that which is to come.

What I say concerning the mutual Toleration of private Persons differing from one another in Religion, I understand also of particular Churches; which stand as it were in the same Relation to each other as private Persons among themselves, nor has any one of them any manner of Jurisdiction over any other, no not even when the Civil Magistrate (as it sometimes happens) comes to be of this or the other Communion. For the Civil Government can give no new Right to the Church, nor the Church to the Civil Government. So that whether the Magistrate joyn himself to any Church, or separate from it, the Church remains always as it was before, a free and voluntary Society. It neither acquires the Power of the Sword by the Magistrate's coming to it, nor does it lose the Right of Instruction and Excommunication by his going from it. This is the fundamental and immutable Right of a spontaneous Society, that it has power to remove any of its Members who transgress the Rules of its Institution: But it cannot, by the accession of any new Members, acquire any Right of Jurisdiction over those that are not joined with it. And therefore Peace, Equity, and Friendship, are always mutually to be observed by particular Churches, in the same manner as by private Persons, without any pretence of Superiority or Jurisdiction over one another.

That the thing may be made yet clearer by an Example: Let us suppose two Churches, the one of *Arminians*, the other of *Calvinists*, residing in the City of *Constantinople*. Will any one say, that either of these Churches has Right to deprive the Members of the other of their Estates and Liberty, (as we see practised elsewhere) because of their differing from it in some Doctrines and Ceremonies; whilst the *Turks* in the mean while silently stand by, and laugh to see with what inhumane Cruelty Christians thus rage against Christians? But if one of these Churches hath this Power of treating the other ill, I ask which of them it is to whom that Power belongs, and by what Right? It will be answered, undoubtedly, That it is the Orthodox Church which has the Right of Authority over the Erroneous or Heretical. This is, in great and specious Words, to say just nothing at all. For every Church is Orthodox to it self; to others, Erroneous or Heretical. For whatsoever any Church believes, it believes to be true; and the contrary unto those things, it pronounces to be Error. So that the Controversie between these Churches about the Truth of their Doctrines, and the Purity of their Worship, is on both sides equal; nor is there any Judge, either at *Constantinople*, or elsewhere upon Earth, by whose Sentence it can be determined. The Decision of that Question belongs only to the Supreme Judge of all men, to whom also alone belongs the Punishment of the Erroneous. In the mean while, let those men consider how hainously they sin, Who, adding Injustice, if not to their Error yet certainly to their Pride, do rashly and arrogantly take upon them to misuse the Servants of another Master, who are not at all accountable to them.

Nay, further: If it could be manifest which of these two dissenting Churches were in the right, there would not accrue thereby unto the Orthodox any Right of destroying the other. For Churches have neither any Jurisdiction in Worldly matters, nor are Fire and Sword any proper Instruments wherewith to convince mens minds of Error, and inform them of the Truth. Let us suppose, nevertheless, that the Civil Magistrate inclined to favour one of them, and to put his Sword into their Hands, that (by his Consent) they might chastise the Dissenters as they pleased. Will any man say, that any Right can be derived unto a Christian Church, over its Brethren, from a Turkish Emperor? An Infidel, who has himself no Authority to punish Christians for the Articles of their Faith, cannot confer such an Authority upon any Society of Christians, nor give unto them a Right which he has not himself. This would be the Case at *Constantinople*. And the Reason of the thing is the same in any Christian Kingdom. The Civil Power is the same in every place: nor can that Power, in the Hands of a Christian Prince, confer any greater Authority upon the Church, than in the Hands of a Heathen; which is to say, just none at all.

Nevertheless, it is worthy to be observed, and lamented, that the most violent of these Defenders of the Truth, the Opposers of Errors, the Exclaimers against Schism, do hardly ever let loose this their Zeal for God, with which they are so warmed and inflamed, unless where they have the Civil Magistrate on their side. But so soon as ever Court-favour has given them the better end of the Staff, and they begin to feel themselves the stronger, then presently Peace and Charity are to be laid aside: Otherwise, they are religiously to be observed. Where they have not the Power to carry on Persecution, and to become Masters, there they desire to live upon fair Terms, and preach up Toleration. When they are not strengthened with the Civil Power, then they can bear most patiently, and unmovedly, the Contagion of Idolatry, Superstition, and Heresie, in their Neighbourhood; of which, in other Occasions, the Interest of Religion makes them to be extremely apprehensive. They do not forwardly attack those Errors which are in fashion at Court, or are countenanced by the Government. Here they can be content to spare their Arguments: which yet (with their leave) is the only right Method of propagating Truth, which has no such way of prevailing, as when strong Arguments and good Reason, are joined with the softness of Civility and good Usage.

No body therefore, in fine, neither single Persons, nor Churches, nay, nor even Commonwealths, have any just Title to invade the Civil Rights and Worldly Goods of each other, upon pretence of Religion. Those that are of another Opinion, would do well to consider with themselves how pernicious a Seed of Discord and War, how powerful a provocation to endless Hatreds, Rapines, and Slaughters, they thereby furnish unto Mankind. No Peace and Security, no not so much as Common Friendship, can ever be established or preserved amongst Men, so long as this

Opinion prevails, That *Dominion is founded in Grace*, and that Religion is to be propagated by force of Arms.

In the third place: Let us see what the Duty of Toleration requires from those who are distinguished from the rest of Mankind, (from the Laity, as they please to call us) by some Ecclesiastical Character, and Office; whether they be Bishops, Priests, Presbyters, Ministers, or however else dignified or distinguished. It is not my Business to inquire here into the Original of the Power or Dignity of the Clergy. This only I say, That Whence-soever their Authority be sprung, since it is Ecclesiastical, it ought to be confined within the Bounds of the Church, nor can it in any manner be extended to Civil Affairs; because the Church it self is a thing absolutely separate and distinct from the Commonwealth. The Boundaries on both sides are fixed and immovable. He jumbles Heaven and Earth together, the things most remote and opposite, who mixes these two Societies; which are in their Original, End, Business, and in every thing, perfectly distinct, and infinitely different from each other. No man therefore, with whatsoever Ecclesiastical Office he be dignified, can deprive another man that is not of his Church and Faith, either of Liberty, or of any part of his Worldly Goods, upon the account of that difference between them in Religion. For whatsoever is not lawful to the whole Church, cannot, by any Ecclesiastical Right, become lawful to any of its Members.

But this is not all. It is not enough that Ecclesiastical men abstain from Violence and Rapine, and all manner of Persecution. He that pretends to be a Successor of the Apostles, and takes upon him the Office of Teaching, is obliged also to admonish his Hearers of the Duties of Peace, and Good-will towards all men; as well towards the Erroneous as the Orthodox; towards those that differ from them in Faith and Worship, as well as towards those that agree with them therein: And he ought industriously to exhort all men, whether private Persons or Magistrates, (if any such there be in his Church) to Charity, Meekness, and Toleration; and diligently endeavour to allay and temper all that Heat, and unreasonable averseness of mind, which either any mans fiery Zeal for his own Sect, or the Craft of others, has kindled against Dissenters. I will not undertake to represent how happy and how great would be the Fruit, both in Church and State, if the Pulpits every where founded with this Doctrine of Peace and Toleration; lest I should seem to reflect too severely upon those Men whose Dignity I desire not to detract from, nor would have it diminished either by others or themselves. But this I say, That thus it ought to be. And if any one that professes himself to be a Minister of the Word of God, a Preacher of the Gospel of Peace, teach otherwise, he either understands not, or neglects the Business of his Calling, and shall one day give account thereof unto the Prince of Peace. If Christians are to be admonished that they abstain from all manner of Revenge, even after repeated Provocations and multiplied Injuries, how much more ought they who suffer nothing, who have had no harm done them, forbear Violence, and abstain from all manner of ill usage towards those from whom they have received none. This Caution and Temper they ought certainly to use towards those who mind only their own Business, and are sollicitous for nothing but that (whatever Men think of them) they may worship God in that manner which they are persuaded is acceptable to him, and in which they have the strongest hopes of Eternal Salvation. In private domestick Affairs, in the management of Estates, in the conservation of Bodily Health, every man may consider what suits his own conveniency, and follow what course he likes best. No man complains of the ill management of his Neighbour's Affairs. No man is angry with another for an Error committed in sowing his Land, or in marrying his Daughter. No body corrects a Spendthrift for consuming his Substance in Taverns. Let any man pull down, or build, or make whatsoever Expences he pleases, no body murmurs, no body controuls him; he has his Liberty. But if any man do not frequent the Church, if he do not there conform his Behaviour exactly to the accustomed Ceremonies, or if he brings not his Children to be initiated in the Sacred Mysteries of this or the other Congregation; this immediately causes an Uproar. The Neighbourhood is filled with Noise and Clamour. Every one is ready to be the Avenger of so great a Crime. And the Zealots hardly have the Patience to refrain from Violence and Rapine, so long till the Cause be heard, and the poor man be, according to Form, condemned to the loss of Liberty, Goods, or Life. Oh, that our Ecclesiastical Orators, of every Sect, would apply themselves with all the strength of Arguments that they are able, to the confounding of mens Errors! But let them spare their Persons. Let them not supply their want of Reasons with the

Instruments of Force, which belong to another Jurisdiction, and do ill become a Churchman's Hands. Let them not call in the Magistrate's Authority to the aid of their Eloquence, or Learning; lest, perhaps, whilst they pretend only Love for the Truth, this their intemperate Zeal, breathing nothing but Fire and Sword, betray their Ambition, and shew that what they desire is Temporal Dominion. For it will be very difficult to persuade men of Sense, that he, who with dry Eyes, and satisfaction of mind, can deliver his Brother unto the Executioner, to be burnt alive, does sincerely and heartily concern himself to save that Brother from the Flames of Hell in the World to come.

In the last place. Let us now consider what is the Magistrate's Duty in the Business of Toleration: which certainly is very considerable.

We have already proved, That the Care of Souls does not belong to the Magistrate: Not a Magisterial Care, I mean, (if I may so call it) which consists in prescribing by Laws, and compelling by Punishments. But a charitable Care, which consists in teaching, admonishing, and persuading, cannot be denied unto any man. The Care therefore of every man's Soul belongs unto himself, and is to be left unto himself. But what if he neglect the Care of his Soul? I answer, What if he neglect the Care of his Health, or of his Estate, which things are nearlier related to the Government of the Magistrate than the other? Will the Magistrate provide by an express Law, That such an one shall not become poor or sick? Laws provide, as much as is possible, that the Goods and Health of Subjects be not injured by the Fraud and Violence of others; they do not guard them from the Negligence or Ill-husbandry of the Possessors themselves. No man can be forced to be Rich or Healthful, whether he will or no. Nay, God himself will not save men against their wills. Let us suppose, however, that some Prince were desirous to force his Subjects to accumulate Riches, or to preserve the Health and Strength of their Bodies. Shall it be provided by Law, that they must consult none but *Roman* Physicians, and shall every one be bound to live according to their Prescriptions? What, shall no Potion, no Broth, be taken, but what is prepared either in the *Vatican,* suppose, or in a *Geneva* Shop? Or, to make these Subjects rich, shall they all be obliged by Law to become Merchants, or Musicians? Or, shall every one turn Victualler, or Smith, because there are some that maintain their Families plentifully, and grow rich in those Professions? But it may be said, There are a thousand ways to Wealth, but one only way to Heaven. 'Tis well said indeed, especially by those that plead for compelling men into this or the other Way. For if there were several ways that lead thither, there would not be so much as a pretence left for Compulsion. But now if I be marching on with my utmost Vigour, in that way which, according to the Sacred Geography, leads straight to *Jerusalem;* Why am I beaten and ill used by others, because, perhaps, I wear not Buskins; because my Hair is not of the right Cut; because perhaps I have not been dip't in the right Fashion; because I eat Flesh upon the Road, or some other Food which agrees with my Stomach; because I avoid certain Byways, which seem unto me to lead into Briars or Precipices; because, amongst the several Paths that are in the same Road, I choose that to walk in which seems to be the straightest and cleanest; because I avoid to keep company with some Travellers that are less grave, and others that are more sowre than they ought to be; or in fine, because I follow a Guide that either is, or is not, clothed in White, or crowned with a Miter? Certainly, if we consider right, we shall find that for the most part they are such frivolous things as these, that (without any prejudice to Religion or the Salvation of Souls, if not accompanied with Superstition or Hypocrisie) might either be observed or omitted; I say they are such like things as these, which breed implacable Enmities amongst Christian Brethren, who are all agreed in the Substantial and truly Fundamental part of Religion.

But let us grant unto these Zealots, who condemn all things that are not of their Mode, that from these Circumstances arise different Ends. What shall we conclude from thence? There is only one of these which is the true way to Eternal Happiness. But in this great variety of ways that men follow, it is still doubted which is the right one. Now neither the care of the Commonwealth, nor the right of enacting Laws, does discover this way that leads to Heaven more certainly to the Magistrate, than every private mans Search and Study discovers it unto himself. I have a weak Body, sunk under a languishing Disease, for which (I suppose) there is one only Remedy, but that unknown. Does it therefore belong unto the Magistrate to prescribe me a Remedy, because there is but one, and because it is unknown? Because there is but one way for me to escape Death, will it therefore be safe for me to do whatsoever the Magistrate ordains?

Those things that every man ought sincerely to enquire into himself, and by Meditation, Study, Search, and his own Endeavours, attain the Knowledge of, cannot be looked upon as the Peculiar Possession of any sort of Men. Princes indeed are born Superior unto other men in Power, but in Nature equal. Neither the Right, nor the Art of Ruling, does necessarily carry along with it the certain Knowledge of other things; and least of all of true Religion. For if it were so, how could it come to pass that the Lords of the Earth should differ so vastly as they do in Religious Matters? But let us grant that it is probable the way to Eternal Life may be better known by a Prince than by his Subjects; or at least, that in this incertitude of things, the safest and most commodious way for private Persons is to follow his Dictates. You will say, what then? If he should bid you follow Merchandise for your Livelihood, would you decline that Course for fear it should not succeed? I answer: I would turn Merchant upon the Prince's command, because in case I should have ill Success in Trade, he is abundantly able to make up my Loss some other way. If it be true, as he pretends, that he desires I should thrive and grow rich, he can set me up again when unsuccessful Voyages have broke me. But this is not the Case, in the things that regard the Life to come. If there I take a wrong Course, if in that respect I am once undone, it is not in the Magistrate's Power to repair my Loss, to ease my Suffering, nor to restore me in any measure, much less entirely, to a good Estate. What Security can be given for the Kingdom of Heaven?

Perhaps some will say that they do not suppose this infallible Judgment, that all men are bound to follow in the Affairs of Religion, to be in the Civil Magistrate, but in the Church. What the Church has determined, that the Civil Magistrate orders to be observed; and he provides by his Authority that no body shall either act or believe, in the business of Religion, otherwise than the Church teaches. So that the Judgment of those things is in the Church. The Magistrate himself yields Obedience thereunto, and requires the like Obedience from others. I answer: Who sees not how frequently the Name of the Church, which was so venerable in the time of the Apostles, has been made use of to throw Dust in Peoples Eyes, in the following Ages? But however, in the present case it helps us not. The one only narrow way which leads to Heaven is not better known to the Magistrate

than to private Persons, and therefore I cannot safely take him for my Guide, who may probably be as ignorant of the way as my self, and who certainly is less concerned for my Salvation than I my self am. Amongst so many Kings of the *Jews*, how many of them were there whom any *Israelite*, thus blindly following, had not fall'n into Idolatry, and thereby into Destruction? Yet nevertheless, you bid me be of good Courage, and tell me that all is now safe and secure, because the Magistrate does not now enjoin the observance of his own Decrees in matters of Religion, but only the Decrees of the Church. Of what Church I beseech you? Of that certainly which likes him best. As if he that compells me by Laws and Penalties to enter into this or the other Church, did not interpose his own Judgment in the matter. What difference is there whether he lead me himself, or deliver me over to be led by others? I depend both ways upon his Will, and it is he that determines both ways of my eternal State. Would an *Israelite*, that had worshipped *Baal* upon the Command of his King, have been in any better condition, because some body had told him that the King ordered nothing in Religion upon his own Head, nor commanded any thing to be done by his Subjects in Divine Worship, but what was approved by the Counsel of Priests, and declared to be of Divine Right by the Doctors of their Church? If the Religion of any Church become therefore true and saving, because the Head of that Sect, the Prelates and Priests, and those of that Tribe, do all of them, with all their might, extol and praise it; what Religion can ever be accounted erroneous, false and destructive? I am doubtful concerning the Doctrine of the *Socinians*, I am suspicious of the way of Worship practised by the *Papists*, or *Lutherans;* will it be ever a jot the safer for me to join either unto the one or the other of those Churches, upon the Magistrate's Command, because he commands nothing in Religion but by the Authority and Counsel of the Doctors of that Church?

But to speak the truth, we must acknowledge that the Church (if a Convention of Clergy-men, making Canons, must be called by that Name) is for the most part more apt to be influenced by the Court, than the Court by the Church. How the Church was under the Vicissitude of Orthodox and Arian Emperors is very well known. Or if those things be too remote, our modern *English* History affords us fresh Examples, in the Reigns of *Henry* the *8th, Edward* the *6th, Mary,* and *Elizabeth*, how easily and smoothly the Clergy changed their Decrees, their Articles of Faith, their Form of Worship, everything, according to the inclination of those Kings and Queens. Yet were those Kings and Queens of such different minds, in point of Religion, and enjoined thereupon such different things, that no man in his Wits (I had almost said none but an Atheist) will presume to say that any sincere and upright Worshipper of God could, with a safe Conscience, obey their several Decrees. To conclude. It is the same thing whether a King that prescribes Laws to another mans Religion pretend to do it by his own Judgment, or by the Ecclesiastical Authority and Advice of others. The Decisions of Church-men, whose Differences and Disputes are sufficiently known, cannot be any sounder, or safer than his: Nor can all their Suffrages joined together add a new strength unto the Civil Power. Tho this also must be taken notice of, that Princes seldom have any regard to the Suffrages of Ecclesiasticks that are not Favourers of their own Faith and way of Worship.

But after all, the *principal Consideration*, and which absolutely determines this Controversie, is this. Although the Magistrate's Opinion in Religion be sound, and the way that he appoints be truly Evangelical, yet if I be not thoroughly perswaded thereof in my own mind, there will be no safety for me in following it. No way whatsoever that I shall walk in, against the Dictates of my Conscience, will ever bring me to the Mansions of the Blessed. I may grow rich by an Art that I take not delight in; I may be cured of some Disease by Remedies that I have not Faith in; but I cannot be saved by a Religion that I distrust, and by a Worship that I abhor. It is in vain for an Unbeliever to take up the outward shew of another mans Profession. Faith only, and inward Sincerity, are the things that procure acceptance with God. The most likely and most approved Remedy can have no effect upon the Patient, if his Stomach reject it as soon taken. And you will in vain cram a Medicine down a sick mans Throat, which his particular Constitution will be sure to turn into Poison. In a word. Whatsoever may be doubtful in Religion, yet this at least is certain, that no Religion, which I believe not to be true, can be either true, or profitable unto me. In vain therefore do Princes compel their Subjects to come into their Church-communion, under pretence of saving their Souls. If they believe, they will come of their own accord; if they believe not, their coming will nothing

avail them. How great soever, in fine, may be the pretence of Good-will, and Charity, and concern for the Salvation of mens Souls, men cannot be forced to be saved whether they will or no. And therefore, when all is done, they must be left to their own Consciences.

Having thus at length freed men from all Dominion over one another in matters of Religion, let us now consider what they are to do. All men know and acknowledge that God ought to be publickly worshipped. Why otherwise do they compel one another unto the publick Assemblies? Men therefore constituted in this liberty are to enter into some Religious Society, that they meet together, not only for mutual Edification, but to own to the world that they worship God, and offer unto his divine Majesty such service as they themselves are not ashamed of, and such as they think not unworthy of him, nor unacceptable to him; and finally that by the purity of Doctrine, Holiness of Life, and Decent form of Worship, they may draw others unto the love of the true Religion, and perform such other things in Religion as cannot be done by each private man apart.

These Religious Societies I call Churches: and these I say the Magistrate ought to tolerate. For the business of these Assemblies of the People is nothing but what is lawful for every man in particular to take care of; I mean the Salvation of their Souls: nor in this case is there any difference between the National Church, and other separated Congregations.

But as in every Church there are two things especially to be considered: The outward Form and Rites of Worship, And the Doctrines and Articles of Faith; these things must be handled each distinctly; that so the whole matter of Toleration may the more clearly be understood.

Concerning outward Worship, I say (in the first place) that the Magistrate has no Power to enforce by Law, either in his own Church, or much less in another, the use of any Rites or Ceremonies whatsoever in the Worship of God. And this, not only because these Churches are free Societies, but because whatsoever is practised in the Worship of God, is only so far justifiable as it is believed by those that practise it to be acceptable unto him. Whatsoever is not done with that assurance of Faith, is neither well in it self, nor can it be acceptable to God. To impose such things, therefore upon any People, contrary to their own Judgment, is in effect to command them to offend God; which, considering that the end of all Religion is to please him, and that Liberty is essentially necessary to that End, appears to be absurd beyond expression.

But perhaps it may be concluded from hence, that I deny unto the Magistrate all manner of Power about indifferent things; which if it be not granted, the whole Subject-matter of Law-making is taken away. No, I readily grant that Indifferent Things, and perhaps none but such, are subjected to the Legislative Power. But it does not therefore follow, that the Magistrate may ordain whatsoever he pleases concerning any thing that is indifferent. The Publick Good is the Rule and Measure of all Law-making. If a thing be not useful to the Commonwealth, tho' it be never so indifferent, it may not presently be established by Law.

And further: Things never so indifferent in their own nature, when they are brought into the Church and Worship of God, are removed out of the reach of the Magistrate's Jurisdiction; because in that use they have no connection at all with Civil Affairs. The only business of the Church is the Salvation of Souls: and it no ways concerns the Common-wealth, or any Member of it, that this, or the other Ceremony be there made use of. Neither the Use, nor the Omission of any Ceremonies, in those Religious Assemblies, does either advantage or prejudice the Life, Liberty, or Estate of any man. For Example: Let it be granted, that the washing of an Infant with water is in it self an indifferent thing. Let it be granted also, that if the Magistrate understand such washing to be profitable to the curing or preventing of any Disease that Children are subject unto, and esteem the matter weighty enough to be taken care of by a Law, in that case he may order it to be done. But will any one therefore say, that a Magistrate has the same Right to ordain, by Law, that all Children shall be baptized by Priests, in the sacred Font, in order to the purification of their Souls? The extream difference of these two Cases is visible to every one at first sight. Or let us apply the last Case to the Child of a *Jew,* and the thing speaks it self. For what hinders but a Christian Magistrate may have Subjects that are *Jews?* Now if we acknowledge that such an Inquiry may not be done unto a *Jew,* as to compel him, against his own Opinion, to practise in his Religion a thing that is in its nature indifferent; how can we maintain that any thing of this kind may be done to a Christian?

Again: Things in their own nature indifferent cannot, by any human Authority, be made any part of the Worship of God; for this very reason; because they are indifferent. For since indifferent things are not capable, by any Virtue of their own, to propitiate the Deity; no human Power or Authority can confer on them so much Dignity and Excellency as to enable them to do it. In the common Affairs of Life, that use of indifferent things which God has not forbidden, is free and lawful: and therefore in those things human Authority has place. But it is not so in matters of Religion. Things indifferent are not otherwise lawful in the Worship of God than as they are instituted by God himself; and as he, by some positive command, has ordain'd them to be made a part of that Worship which he will vouchsafe to accept of at the hands of poor sinful men. Nor when an incensed Deity shall ask us, *Who has required these, or such like things at your hands?* will it be enough to answer him, that the Magistrate commanded them. If civil Jurisdiction extended thus far, what might not lawfully be introduced into Religion? What hodge-podge of Ceremonies, what superstitious Inventions, built upon the Magistrate's Authority, might not (against Conscience) be imposed upon the Worshippers of God? For the greatest part of these Ceremonies and Superstitions consists in the Religious Use of such things as are in their own nature indifferent: nor are they sinful upon any other account than because God is not the Author of them. The sprinkling of Water, and the use of Bread and Wine, are both in their own nature, and in the ordinary occasions of Life, altogether indifferent. Will any man therefore say that these things could have been introduced into Religion, and made a part of Divine Worship, if not by Divine Institution? If any Human Authority or Civil Power could have done this, why might it not also injoyn the eating of Fish, the drinking of Ale, in the holy Banquet, as a part of Divine Worship? Why not the sprinkling of the Blood of Beasts in Churches, and Expiations by Water or Fire, and abundance more of this kind? But these things, how indifferent soever they be in common uses, when they come to be annexed unto Divine Worship, without Divine Authority, they are as abominable to God, as the Sacrifice of a Dog. And why a Dog so abominable? What difference is there between a Dog and a Goat, in respect of the Divine Nature, equally and infinitely distant from all Affinity with Matter; unless it be that God required the use of one in his Worship, and not of the other? We see therefore that indifferent things how much soever they be under the Power of the Civil Magistrate, yet cannot upon that pretence be introduced into Religion, and imposed upon Religious Assemblies; because in the Worship of God they wholly cease to be indifferent. He that worships God does it with design to please him and procure his favour. But that cannot be done by him, who, upon the command of another, offers unto God that which he knows will be displeasing to him, because not commanded by himself. This is not to please God, or appease his Wrath, but willingly and knowingly to provoke him, by a manifest Contempt; which is a thing absolutely repugnant to the nature and end of Worship.

But it will here asked: If nothing belonging to Divine Worship be left to human Discretion, how is it then that Churches themselves have the power of ordering any thing about the Time and Place of Worship, and the like? To this I answer: That in Religious Worship we must distinguish between what is part of the Worship it self, and what is but a Circumstance. That is a part of the Worship which is believed to be appointed by God; and to be well-pleasing to him; and therefore that is necessary. Circumstances are such things which, tho' in general they cannot be separated from Worship, yet the particular instances or modifications of them are not determined; and therefore they are indifferent. Of this sort are the Time and Place of Worship, the Habit and Posture of him that worships. These are Circumstances, and perfectly indifferent, where God has not given any express Command about them. For example: Amongst the *Jews*, the Time and Place of their Worship, and the Habits of those that officiated in it, were not mere Circumstances, but a part of the Worship it self; in which if any thing were defective, or different from that Institution, they could not hope that it would be accepted by God. But these, to Christians under the liberty of the Gospel, are meer Circumstances of Worship, which the Prudence of every Church may bring into such use as shall be judged most subservient to the end of Order, Decency, and Edification. But, even under the Gospel, those who believe the First, or the Seventh Day to be set apart by God, and consecrated still to his Worship, to them that Portion of Time is not a simple Circumstance, but a Real Part of Divine Worship, which can neither be changed or neglected.

In the next place: As the Magistrate has no Power to *impose* by his Laws, the use of any Rites and Ceremonies in any Church, so neither has he any Power to *forbid* the use of such Rites and Ceremonies as are already received, approved, and practised by any Church: Because if he did so, he would destroy the Church it self; the end of whose Institution is only to worship God with freedom, after its own manner.

You will say, by this Rule, if some Congregations should have a mind to sacrifice Infants, or (as the Primitive Christians were falsely accused) lustfully pollute themselves in promiscuous Uncleanness, or practise any other such heinous Enormities, is the Magistrate obliged to tolerate them, because they are committed in a Religious Assembly? I answer, No. These things are not lawful in the ordinary course of life, nor in any private house; and therefore neither are they so in the Worship of God, or in any religious Meeting. But indeed if any People congregated upon account of Religion, should be desirous to sacrifice a Calf, I deny that That ought to be prohibited by a Law. *Melibaeus*, whose Calf it is, may lawfully kill his Calf at home and burn any part of it that he thinks fit. For no Injury is thereby done to any one, no prejudice to another mans Goods. And for the same reason he may kill his Calf also in a religious Meeting. Whether the doing so be well-pleasing to God or no, it is their part to consider that do it. The part of the Magistrate is only to take care that the Commonwealth receive no prejudice, and that there be no Injury done to any man, either in Life or Estate. And thus what may be spent on a Feast, may be spent on a Sacrifice. But if peradventure such were the state of things, that the Interest of the Commonwealth required all slaughter of Beasts should be forborn for some while, in order to the increasing of the stock of Cattel, that had been destroyed by some extraordinary Murrain; Who sees not that the Magistrate, in such a case, may forbid all his Subjects to kill any Calves for any use whatsoever? Only 'tis to be observed, that in this case the Law is not made about a Religious, but a Political matter: nor is the Sacrifice, but the Slaughter of Calves thereby prohibited.

By this we see what difference there is between the Church and the Commonwealth. Whatsoever is lawful in the Commonwealth, cannot be prohibited by the Magistrate in the Church. Whatsoever is permitted unto any of his Subjects for their ordinary use, neither can nor ought to be forbidden by him to any Sect of People for their religious Uses. If any man may lawfully take Bread or Wine, either sitting or kneeling, in his own house, the Law ought not to abridge him of the same Liberty in his Religious Worship; tho' in the Church the use of Bread and Wine be very different, and be there applied to the Mysteries of Faith, and Rites of Divine Worship. But those things that are prejudicial to the Commonweal of a People in their ordinary use, and are therefore forbidden by Laws, those things ought not to be permitted to Churches in their sacred Rites. Only the Magistrate ought always to be very careful that he do not misuse his Authority, to the oppression of any Church, under pretence of publick Good.

It may be said: What if a Church be *Idolatrous*, is that also to be tolerated by the Magistrate? I answer. What Power can be given to the Magistrate for the suppression of an Idolatrous Church, which may not, in time and place, be made use of to the ruine of an Orthodox one? For it must be remembered that the Civil Power is the same every where and the Religion of every Prince is Orthodox to himself. If therefore such a Power be granted unto the Civil Magistrate in Spirituals, as that at *Geneva* (for Example) he may extirpate, by Violence and Blood, the Religion which is there reputed Idolatrous; by the same Rule another Magistrate, in some neighbouring Country, may oppress the Reformed Religion; and, in *India*, the Christian. The Civil Power can either change everything in Religion, according to the Prince's pleasure, or it can change nothing. If it be once permitted to introduce any thing into Religion, by the means of Laws and Penalties, there can be no bounds put to it; but it will in the same manner be lawful to alter every thing, according to that Rule of Truth which the Magistrate has framed unto himself. No man whatsoever ought therefore to be deprived of his Terrestrial Enjoyments, upon account of his Religion. Not even *Americans*, subjected unto a Christian Prince, are to be punished either in Body or Goods, for not imbracing our Faith and Worship. If they are perswaded that they please God in observing the Rites of their own Country, and that they shall obtain Happiness by that means, they are to be left unto God and themselves. Let us trace this matter to the bottom. Thus it is. An inconsiderable and weak number of Christians, destitute of every thing, arrive in a Pagan Country: These Foreigners beseech the Inhabitants, by the bowels of Humanity, that they would succour them with the necessaries of life: Those necessaries are given them; Habitations are granted; and they all joyn together, and grow up into one Body of People. The Christian Religion by this means takes root in that Country, and spreads itself; but does not suddenly grow the strongest. While things are in this condition, Peace, Friendship, Faith, and equal Justice, are preserved amongst them. At length the Magistrate becomes a Christian, and by that means their Party becomes the most powerful. Then immediately all Compacts are to be broken, all Civil Rights to be violated, that Idolatry may be extirpated: And unless these innocent Pagans, strict Observers of the Rules of Equity and the Law of Nature, and no ways offending against the Laws of the Society, I say unless they will forsake their ancient Religion, and embrace a new and strange one, they are to be turned out of the Lands and Possessions of their Forefathers, and perhaps deprived of Life it self. Then at last it appears what Zeal for the Church, joyned with the desire of Dominion, is capable to produce; and how easily the pretence of Religion, and of the care of Souls, serves for a Cloak to Covetousness, Rapine, and Ambition.

Now whosoever maintains that Idolatry is to be rooted out of any place by Laws, Punishments, Fire, and Sword, may apply this Story to himself. For the reason of the thing is equal, both in *America* and *Europe*. And neither Pagans there, nor any Dissenting Christians here, can with any right be deprived of their worldly Goods, by the predominating Faction of a Court-Church: nor are any Civil Rights to be either changed or violated upon account of Religion in one place more than another.

But *Idolatry* (say some) is a sin, and therefore not to be tolerated. If they said it were therefore to be avoided, the Inference were good. But it does not follow, that because it is a sin it ought therefore to be punished by the Magistrate. For it does not belong unto the Magistrate to make use of his Sword in punishing every thing, indifferently, that he takes to be a sin against God. Covetousness, Uncharitableness, Idleness, and many other things are sins, by the consent of all men, which yet no man ever said were to be punished by the Magistrate. The reason is, because they are not prejudicial to other mens Rights, nor do they break the publick Peace of Societies. Nay, even the sins of Lying and Perjury, are no where punishable by Laws; unless in certain cases, in which the real Turpitude of the thing, and the offence against God, are not considered, but only the Injury done unto mens Neighbours, and to the Commonwealth. And what if in another Country, to a Mahumetan [Muslim] or a Pagan Prince, the Christian Religion seem false and offensive to God; may not the Christians for the same reason, and after the same manner, be extirpated there?

But it may be urged further, That by the Law of *Moses* Idolaters were to be rooted out. True indeed, by the Law of *Moses*. But that is not obligatory to us Christians. No body pretends that every thing, generally, enjoyed by the Law of *Moses*, ought to be practised by Christians. But there is nothing more frivolous than that common distinction of Moral, Judicial, and Ceremonial Law, which men ordinarily make use of. For no positive Law whatsoever can oblige any People but those to whom it is given. *Hear O Israel;* sufficiently restrains the Obligation of the Law of *Moses* only to that People. And this Consideration alone is Answer enough unto those that urge the Authority of the Law of *Moses;* for the inflicting of Capital Punishments upon Idolaters. But however, I will examine this Argument a little more particularly.

The Case of Idolaters, in respect of the *Jewish* Commonwealth, falls under a double consideration. The first is of those Who, being initiated in the *Mosaical* Rites, and made Citizens of that Commonwealth, did afterwards apostatise from the Worship of the God of *Israel*. These were proceeded against as Traytors and Rebels, guilty of no less than High-treason. For the Commonwealth of the *Jews*, different in that from all others, was an absolute Theocracy: nor was there, or could there be, any difference between that Commonwealth and the Church. The Laws established there concerning the Worship of One Invisible Deity, were the Civil Laws of that People, and a part of their Political Government; in which God himself was the Legislator. Now if any one can shew me where there is a Commonwealth, at this time, constituted upon that Foundation, I will acknowledge that the Ecclesiastical Laws do there unavoidably become a part of the Civil; and that the Subjects of that Government both may, and ought to be kept in strict conformity with that Church, by the Civil Power. But there is absolutely no such thing, under the Gospel, as a Christian Commonwealth. There are, indeed, many Cities and Kingdoms that have embraced the Faith of Christ; but they have retained their ancient Form of Government; with which the Law of Christ hath not at all medled. He, indeed, hath taught men how, by Faith and Good Works, they may attain Eternal Life. But he instituted no Commonwealth; He prescribed unto his Followers no new and peculiar Form of Government; Nor put he the Sword into any Magistrate's Hand, with Commission to make use of it in forcing men to forsake their former Religion, and receive his.

Secondly. Foreigners, and such as were Strangers to the Commonwealth of *Israel*, were not compell'd by force to observe the Rites of the *Mosaical* Law. But, on the contrary, in the very same place where it is ordered that *an Israelite that was an Idolater should be put to death*, there it is provided that *Strangers should not be vexed nor oppressed.*[7] I confess that the Seven Nations that possess the Land which was promised to the *Israelites*, were utterly to be cut off. But this was not singly because they were Idolaters. For, if that had been the Reason, why were the *Moabites* and other Nations to be spared? No; the Reason is this. God being in a peculiar manner the King of the *Jews*, he could not suffer the Adoration of any other Deity (which was properly an Act of High-treason against himself) in the Land of *Canaan*, which was his Kingdom. For such a manifest Revolt could no ways consist with his Dominion, which was perfectly Political, in that Country. All Idolatry was therefore to be rooted out of the Bounds of his Kingdom; because it was an acknowledgment of another God, that is to say, another King; against the Laws of Empire. The Inhabitants were also to be driven out, that the entire possession of the Land might be given to the *Israelites*. And for the like Reason the *Emims* and the *Horims* were driven out of their Countries, by the Children of *Esau* and *Lot*;[8] and their Lands, upon the same grounds, given by God to the Invaders. But tho' all Idolatry was thus rooted out of the Land of *Canaan*, yet every Idolater was not brought to Execution. The whole Family of *Rahab*, the whole Nation of the *Gibeonites*, articled with *Josuah*, and were allowed by Treaty: and there were many Captives amongst the *Jews*, who were Idolaters. *David and Solomon* subdued many Countries without the Confines of the Land of Promise, and carried their Conquests as far as *Euphrates*. Amongst so many Captives taken, so many Nations reduced under their Obedience, we find not one man forced into the Jewish Religion, and the Worship of the True God, and punished for Idolatry, tho' all of them were certainly guilty of it. If any one indeed, becoming a Proselyte, desired to be made a Denison of their Commonwealth, he was obliged to submit unto their Laws; that is, to embrace their Religion. But this he did will-

---

7. Exod. 22.20, 21.
8. Deut. 2.

ingly, on his own accord, not by constraint. He did not unwillingly submit, to shew his Obedience; But he sought and sollicited for it, as a Privilege. And as soon as he was admitted, he became subject to the Laws of the Commonwealth, by which all Idolatry was forbidden within the Borders of the Land of *Canaan*. But that Law (as I have said) did not reach to any of those Regions, however subjected unto the *Jews*, that were situated without those Bounds.

Thus far concerning outward Worship. Let us now consider *Articles of Faith*.

The *Articles* of Religion are some of them *Practical*, and some *Speculative*. Now, tho' both sorts consist in the Knowledge of Truth, yet these terminate simply in the Understanding, Those influence the Will and Manners. Speculative Opinions, therefore, and *Articles of Faith* (as they are called) which are required only to be believed, cannot be imposed on any Church by the Law of the Land. For it is absurd that things should be enjoyned by Laws, which are not in mens power to perform. And to believe this or that to be true, does not depend upon our Will. But of this enough has been said already. But (will some say) let men at least profess that they believe. A sweet Religion indeed, that obliges men to dissemble, and tell Lies both to God and Man, for the Salvation of their Souls! If the Magistrate thinks to save men thus, he seems to understand little of the way of Salvation. And if he does it not in order to save them, why is he so sollicitous about the Articles of Faith as to enact them by a Law?

Further, The Magistrate ought not to forbid the Preaching or Professing of any Speculative Opinions in any Church, because they have no manner of relation to the Civil Rights of the Subjects. If a *Roman Catholick* believe that to be really the Body of Christ, which another man calls Bread, he does no injury thereby to his Neighbour. If a *Jew* do not believe the New Testament to be the Word of God, he does not thereby alter any thing in mens Civil Rights. If a Heathen doubt of both Testaments, he is not therefore to be punished as a pernicious Citizen. The Power of the Magistrate, and the Estates of the People, may be equally secure, whether any man believe these things or no. I readily grant, that these Opinions are false and absurd. But the business of Laws is not to provide for the Truth of Opinions, but for the Safety and Security of the Commonwealth, and of every particular mans Goods and Person. And so it ought to be. For Truth certainly would do well enough, if she were once left to shift for her self. She seldom has received, and I fear never will receive, much Assistance from the Power of Great men, to whom she is but rarely known, and more rarely welcome. She is not taught by Laws, nor has she any need of Force to procure her entrance into the minds of men. Errors indeed prevail by the assistance of foreign and borrowed Succours. But if Truth makes not her way into the Understanding by her own Light she will be but the weaker for any borrowed force Violence can add to her. Thus much for Speculative Opinions. Let us now proceed to *Practical* ones.

A Good Life, in which consists not the least part of Religion and true Piety, concerns also the Civil Government: and in it lies the safety both of Mens Souls, and of the Commonwealth. Moral Actions belong therefore to the Jurisdiction both of the outward and inward Court; both of the Civil and Domestick Governor; I mean, both of the Magistrate and Conscience. Here therefore is great danger, least one of these Jurisdictions intrench upon the other, and Discord arise between the Keeper of the publick Peace and the Overseers of Souls. But if what has been already said concerning the Limits of both these Governments be rightly considered, it will easily remove all difficulty in this matter.

Every man has an Immortal Soul, capable of Eternal Happiness or Misery; whose Happiness depending upon his believing and doing those things in this Life, which are necessary to the obtaining of God's Favour, and are prescribed by God to that end; it follows from thence, *first*, That the observance of these things is the highest Obligation that lies upon Mankind, and that our utmost Care, Application, and Diligence, ought to be exercised in the Search and Performance of them; Because there is nothing in this World that is of any consideration in comparison with Eternity. *Secondly*, That seeing one Man does not violate the Right of another, by his Erroneous Opinions, and undue manner of Worship, nor is his Perdition any prejudice to another Mans Affairs; therefore the care of each Mans Salvation belongs only to himself. But I would not have this understood, as if I meant hereby to condemn all charitable Admonitions, and affectionate Endeavours to reduce Men from Errors; which are indeed the greatest Duty of a Christian. Any one may employ as many Exhortations and Arguments as he pleases, towards the promoting of another man's Salvation. But all Force and Compulsion are to be forborn. Nothing is to be done imperiously. No body is obliged in that matter to yield Obedience unto the Admonitions or Injunctions of another, further than he himself is perswaded. Every man, in that, has the supreme and absolute Authority of judging for himself. And the Reason is, because no body else is concerned in it, nor can receive any prejudice from his Conduct therein.

But besides their Souls, which are Immortal, Men have also their Temporal Lives here upon Earth; the State whereof being frail and fleeting, and the duration uncertain; they have need of several outward Conveniencies to the support thereof, which are to be procured or preserved by Pains and industry. For those things that are necessary to the comfortable support of our Lives are not the spontaneous Products of Nature, nor do offer themselves fit and prepared for our use. This part therefore draws on another care, and necessarily gives another Employment. But the pravity of Mankind being such, that they had rather injuriously prey upon the Fruits of other Mens Labours, than take pains to provide for themselves; the necessity of preserving Men in the Possession of what honest industry has already acquired, and also of preserving their Liberty and strength, whereby they may acquire what they further want; obliges Men to enter into Society with one another; that by mutual Assistance, and joint Force, they may secure unto each other their Properties in the things that contribute to the Comfort and Happiness of this Life; leaving in the mean while to every Man the care of his own Eternal Happiness, the attainment whereof can neither be facilitated by another Mans Industry, nor can the loss of it turn to another Mans Prejudice, nor the hope of it be forced from him by any external Violence. But forasmuch as Men thus entring into Societies, grounded upon their mutual Compacts of Assistance, for the Defence of their Temporal Goods, may nevertheless be deprived of them, either by the Rapine and Fraud of their Fellow-Citizens, or by the hostile Violence of Forreigners; the Remedy of this Evil consists in Arms, Riches, and Multitude of Citizens; the Remedy of the other in Laws; and the Care of all things relating both to the one and the other, is committed by the Society to the Civil Magistrate. This is the Original, this is the Use, and these are the Bounds of the Legislative (which is the Supreme) Power, in every Commonwealth. I mean, that Provision may be made for the security of each Mans private Possessions; for the Peace, Riches, and publick Commodities of the whole People; and, as much as possible, for the Increase of their inward Strength, against Forreign Invasions.

These things being thus explain'd, it is easie to understand to what end the Legislative Power ought to be directed, and by what Measures regulated; and that is the Temporal Good and outward Prosperity of the Society; which is the sole Reason of Mens entring into Society, and the only thing they seek and aim at in it. And it is also evident what Liberty remains to Men in reference to their eternal Salvation, and that is, that every one should do what he in his Conscience is perswaded to be acceptable to the Almighty, on whose good pleasure and acceptance depends their eternal Happiness. For Obedience is due in the first place to God, and afterwards to the Laws.

But some may ask, *What if the Magistrate should enjoyn any thing by his Authority that appears unlawful to the Conscience of a private Person?* I answer, That if Government be faithfully administered, and the Counsels of the Magistrate be indeed directed to the publick Good, this will seldom happen. But if perhaps it do so fall out; I say, that such a private Person is to abstain from the Action that he judges unlawful; and he is to undergo the Punishment, which it is not unlawful for him to bear. For the private judgment of any Person concerning a Law enacted in Political Matters, for the publick Good, does not take away the Obligation of that Law, nor deserve a Dispensation. But if the Law indeed be concerning things that lie not within the Verge of the Magistrate's Authority; (as for Example, that the People, or any Party amongst them, should be compell'd to embrace a strange Religion, and join in the Worship and Ceremonies of another Church,) men are not in these cases obliged by that Law, against their Consciences. For the Political Society is instituted for no other end but only to secure every mans Possession of the things of this life. The care of each mans Soul, and of the things of Heaven, which neither does belong to the Commonwealth, nor can be subjected to it, is left entirely to every mans self. Thus the safeguard of mens lives, and of the things that belong unto this life, is the business of the Commonwealth; and the preserving of those things unto their Owners is the Duty of the Magistrate. And therefore the Magistrate cannot take away these worldly things from this man, or party, and give them to that; nor change Propriety amongst Fellow-Subjects, (no not even by a Law) for a cause that has no relation to the end of Civil Government; I mean, for their Religion; which whether it be true or false, does no prejudice to the worldly concerns of their Fellow-Subjects, which are the things that only belong unto the care of the Commonwealth.

But what if the Magistrate believe such a Law as this to be for the publick Good? I answer: As the private Judgment of any particular Person, if erroneous, does not exempt him from the obligation of Law, so the private Judgment (as I may call it) of the Magistrate does not give him any new Right of imposing Laws upon his subjects, which neither was in the Constitution of the Government granted him, nor ever was in the power of the People to grant: much less, if he make it his business to enrich and advance his Followers and Fellow-sectaries, with the Spoils of others. But what if the Magistrate believe that he has the Right to make such Laws, and that they are for the publick Good; and his Subjects believe the contrary? Who shall be Judge between them? I answer, God alone. For there is no Judge upon earth between the Supreme Magistrate and the People. God, I say, is the only Judge in this case, who will retribute unto every one at the last day according to his Deserts; that is, according to his sincerity and uprightness in endeavouring to promote Piety, and the publick Weal and Peace of Mankind. But what shall be done in the mean while? I answer: The principal and chief care of every one ought to be of his own Soul first, and in the next place of the publick Peace: tho' yet there are very few will think 'tis Peace there, where they see all laid waste.

There are two sorts of Contests amongst men: the one managed by Law, the other by Force: and these are of that nature, that where the one ends, the other always begins. But it is not my business to inquire into the Power of the Magistrate in the different Constitutions of Nations. I only know what usually happens where Controversies arise, without a Judge to determine them. You will say then the Magistrate being the stronger will have his Will, and carry his point. Without doubt. But the Question is not here concerning the doubtfulness of the Event, but the Rule of Right.

But to come to particulars. I say, *First*, No Opinions contrary to human Society, or to those moral Rules which are necessary to the preservation of Civil Society, are to be tolerated by the Magistrate. But of these indeed Examples in any Church are rare. For no Sect can easily arrive to such a degree of madness, as that it should think fit to teach, for Doctrines of Reli-

gion, such things as manifestly undermine the Foundations of Society, and are therefore condemned by the Judgment of all Mankind: because their own Interest, Peace, Reputation, every Thing, would be thereby endangered.

Another more secret Evil, but more dangerous to the Commonwealth, is, when men arrogate to themselves, and to those of their own Sect, some peculiar Prerogative, covered over with a specious shew of deceitful words, but in effect opposite to the Civil Right of the Community. For Example: We cannot find any Sect that teaches expressly, and openly, that men are not obliged to keep their Promise; that Princes may be dethroned by those that differ from them in Religion; or that the Dominion of all things belongs only to themselves. For these things, proposed thus nakedly and plainly, would soon draw on them the Eye and Hand of the Magistrate, and awaken all the care of the Commonwealth to a watchfulness against the spreading of so dangerous an Evil. But nevertheless, we find those that say the same things, in other words. What else do they mean, who teach that *Faith is not to be kept with Hereticks?* Their meaning, forsooth, is that the privilege of breaking Faith belongs unto themselves: For they declare all that are not of their Communion to be Hereticks, or at least may declare them so whensoever they think fit. What can be the meaning of their asserting that *Kings excommunicated forfeit their Crowns and Kingdoms?* It is evident that they thereby arrogate unto themselves the Power of deposing Kings: because they challenge the Power of Excommunication, as the peculiar Right of their Hierarchy. That *Dominion is founded in Grace*, is also an Assertion by which those that maintain it do plainly lay claim to the possession of all things. For they are not so wanting to themselves as not to believe, or at least as not to profess, themselves to be the truly pious and faithful. These therefore, and the like, who attribute unto the Faithful, Religious and Orthodox, that is, in plain terms, unto themselves, any peculiar Privilege of Power above other Mortals, in Civil Concernments; or who, upon pretence of Religion, do challenge any manner of Authority over such, as are not associated with them in the Ecclesiastical Communion; I say these have no right to be tolerated by the Magistrate; as neither those that will not own and teach the Duty of tolerating All men in matters of mere Religion. For what do all these and the like Doctrines signifie, but that they may, and are ready upon any occasion to seise the

Government, and possess themselves of the Estates and Fortunes of their Fellow-Subjects; and that they only ask leave to be tolerated by the Magistrate so long until they find themselves strong enough to effect it?

Again: That Church can have no right to be tolerated by the Magistrate, which is constituted upon such a bottom, that all those who enter into it, do thereby, *ipso facto*, deliver themselves up to the Protection and Service of another Prince. For by this means the Magistrate would give way to the settling of a foreign Jurisdiction in his own Country, and suffer his own People to be listed, as it were, for Souldiers against his own Government. Nor does the frivolous and fallacious distinction between the Court and the Church afford any remedy to this Inconvenience; especially when both the one and the other are equally subject to the absolute Authority of the same person; who has not only power to perswade the Members of his Church to whatsoever he lists, either as purely Religious, or in order thereunto, but can also enjoyn it them on pain of Eternal Fire. It is ridiculous for any one to profess himself to be a *Mahumetan* only in his Religion, but in every thing else a faithful Subject to a Christian Magistrate, whilst at the same time he acknowledges himself bound to yield blind obedience to the *Mufti* of *Constantinople;* who himself is intirely obedient to the *Ottoman* Emperor, and frames the feigned Oracles of that Religion according to his pleasure. But this Mahumetan living among Christians, would yet more apparently renounce their Government, if he acknowledged the same Person to be Head of his Church who is the Supreme Magistrate in the State.

Lastly, Those are not at all to be tolerated who deny the Being of a God. Promises, Covenants, and Oaths, which are the Bonds of Humane Society, can have no hold upon an Atheist. The taking away of God, tho' but even in thought, dissolves all. Besides also, those that by their Atheism undermine and destroy all Religion, can have no pretence of Religion whereupon to challenge the Privilege of a Toleration. As for other Practical Opinions, tho' not absolutely free from all Error, if they do not tend to establish Domination over others, or Civil Impunity to the Church in which they are taught, there can be no Reason why they should not be tolerated.

It remains that I say something concerning those Assemblies, which being vulgarly called, and perhaps having sometimes been *Conventicles,* and Nurseries

of Factions and Seditions, are thought to afford the strongest matter of Objection against this Doctrine of Toleration. But this has not happened by anything peculiar unto the Genius of such Assemblies, but by the unhappy Circumstances of an oppressed or ill-setted Liberty. These Accusations would soon cease, if the Law of Toleration were once so setled, that all Churches were obliged to lay down Toleration as the Foundation of their own Liberty; and teach that Liberty of Conscience is every mans natural Right, equally belonging to Dissenters as to themselves; and that no body ought to be compelled in matters of Religion, either by Law or Force. The Establishment of this one thing would take away all ground of Complaints and Tumults upon account of Conscience. And these Causes of Discontents and Animosities being once removed, there would remain nothing in these Assemblies that were not more peaceable, and less apt to produce Disturbance of State, than in any other Meetings whatsoever. But let us examine particularly the Heads of these Accusations.

You'll say, That *Assemblies and Meetings endanger the Publick Peace, and threaten the Commonwealth.* I answer: If this be so, Why are there daily such numerous Meetings in Markets, and Courts of Judicature? Why are Crowds upon the Exchange, and a Concourse of People in Cities suffered? You'll reply: Those are Civil Assemblies; but These we object against, are Ecclesiastical. I answer: 'Tis a likely thing indeed, that such Assemblies as are altogether remote from Civil Affairs, should be most apt to embroyl them. O, but Civil Assemblies are composed of men that differ from one another in matters of Religion; but these Ecclesiastical Meetings are of Persons that are all of one Opinion. As if an Agreement in matters of Religion, were in effect a Conspiracy against the Commonwealth; or as if men would not be so much the more warmly unanimous in Religion, the less liberty they had of Assembling. But it will be urged still, that Civil Assemblies are open, and free for any one to enter into; whereas Religious Conventicles are more private, and thereby give opportunity to Clandestine Machinations. I answer, That this is not strictly true: For many Civil Assemblies are not open to every one. And if some Religious Meetings be private, Who are they (I beseech you) that are to be blamed for it? those that desire, or those that forbid their being publick? Again: You'll say, That Religious Communion does exceedingly unite mens Minds and Affections to one another, and is therefore the more dangerous.

But if this be so, Why is not the Magistrate afraid of his own Church; and why does he not forbid their Assemblies, as things dangerous to his Government? You'll say, Because he himself is a Part, and even the Head of them. As if he were not also a Part of the Commonwealth, and the Head of the whole People.

Let us therefore deal plainly. The Magistrate is afraid of other Churches, but not of his own; because he is kind and favourable to the one, but severe and cruel to the other. These he treats like Children, and indulges them even to Wantonness. Those he uses as Slaves; and how blamelessly soever they demean themselves, recompenses them no otherwise than by Gallies, Prisons, Confiscations, and Death. These he cherishes and defends: Those he continually scourges and oppresses. Let him turn the Tables: Or let those Dissenters enjoy but the same Privileges in Civils as his other Subjects, and he will quickly find that these Religious Meetings will be no longer dangerous. For if men enter into Seditious Conspiracies, 'tis not Religion that inspires them to it in their Meetings; but their Sufferings and Oppressions that make them willing to ease themselves. Just and moderate Governments are every where quiet, every where safe. But Oppression raises Ferments, and makes men struggle to cast off an uneasie and tyrannical Yoke. I know that Seditions are very frequently raised, upon pretence of Religion. But 'tis as true that, for Religion, Subjects are frequently ill treated, and live miserably. Believe me, the Stirs that are made, proceed not from any peculiar Temper of this or that Church or Religious Society; but from the common Disposition of all Mankind, who when they groan under any heavy Burthen, endeavour naturally to shake off the Yoke that galls their Necks. Suppose this Business of Religion were let alone, and that there were some other Distinction made between men and men, upon account of their different Complexions, Shapes, and Features, so that those who have black Hair (for example) or gray Eyes, should not enjoy the same Privileges as other Citizens; that they should not be permitted either to buy or sell, or live by their Callings; that Parents should not have the Government and Education of their own Children; that all should either be excluded from the Benefit of the Laws, or meet with partial Judges; can it be doubted but these Persons, thus distinguished from others by the Colour of their Hair and Eyes, and united together by one common Persecution, would be as dangerous to the Magistrate, as any others that had associated themselves

meerly upon the account of Religion? Some enter into Company for Trade and Profit: Others, for want of Business, have their Clubs for Clarret. Neighbourhood joyns some, and Religion others. But there is only one thing which gathers People into Seditious Commotions, and that is Oppression.

You'll say: What, will you have People to meet at Divine Service *against the Magistrate's Will?* I answer: Why, I pray, against his Will? Is it not both lawful and necessary that they should meet? Against his Will, do you say? That's what I complain of. That is the very Root of all the Mischief. Why are Assemblies less sufferable in a Church than in a Theater or Market? Those that meet there are not either more vicious, or more turbulent, than those that meet elsewhere. The Business in that is, that they are ill used, and therefore they are not to be suffered. Take away the Partiality that is used towards them in matters of Common Right; change the Laws, take away the Penalties unto which they are subjected, and all things will immediately become safe and peaceable; Nay, those that are averse to the Religion of the Magistrate, will think themselves so much the more bound to maintain the Peace of the Commonwealth, as their Condition is better in that place than elsewhere; And all the several separate Congregations, like so many Guardians of the Publick Peace, will watch one another, that nothing may be innovated or changed in the Form of the Government: Because they can hope for nothing better than what they already enjoy; that is, an equal Condition with their Fellow-Subjects, under a just and moderate Government. Now if that Church, which agrees in Religion with the Prince, be esteemed the chief Support of any Civil Government, and that for no other Reason (as has already been shewn) than because the Prince is kind, and the Laws are favourable to it; how much greater will be the Security of a Government, where all good Subjects, of whatsoever Church they be, without any Distinction upon account of Religion, enjoying the same Favour of the Prince, and the same Benefit of the Laws, shall become the common Support and Guard of it; and where none will have any occasion to fear the Severity of the Laws, but those that do Injuries to their Neighbours, and offend against the Civil Peace?

That we may draw towards a Conclusion. The *Sum of all* we drive at is, *That every Man may enjoy the same Rights that are granted to others.* Is it permitted to worship God in the *Roman* manner? Let it be permitted to do it in the *Geneva* Form also. Is it permitted to speak *Latin* in the Market-place? Let those that have a mind to it, be permitted to do it also in the Church. Is it lawful for any man in his own House, to kneel, stand, sit, or use any other Posture; and to cloath himself in White or Black, in short or in long Garments? Let it not be made unlawful to eat Bread, drink Wine, or wash with Water, in the Church. In a Word: Whatsoever things are left free by Law in the common occasions of Life, let them remain free unto every Church in Divine Worship. Let no Mans Life, or Body, or House, or Estate, suffer any manner of Prejudice upon these Accounts. Can you allow of the *Presbyterian* Discipline? Why should not the *Episcopal* also have what they like? Ecclesiastical Authority, whether it be administered by the Hands of a Single Person, or many, is every where the same; and neither has any Jurisdiction in things Civil, nor any manner of Power of Compulsion, nor any thing at all to do with Riches and Revenues.

Ecclesiastical Assemblies, and Sermons, are justified by daily experience, and publick allowance. These are allowed to People of some one Perswasion: Why not to all? If any thing pass in a Religious Meeting seditiously, and contrary to the publick Peace, it is to be punished in the same manner, and no otherwise, than as if it had happened in a Fair or Market. These Meetings ought not to be Sanctuaries for Factious and Flagitious Fellows: Nor ought it to be less lawful for Men to meet in Churches than in Halls: Nor are one part of the Subjects to be esteemed more blameable, for their meeting together, than others. Every one is to be accountable for his own Actions; and no Man is to be laid under a Suspicion, or Odium, for the Fault of another. Those that are Seditious, Murderers, Thieves, Robbers, Adulterers, Slanderers, etc. of whatsoever Church, whether National or not, ought to be punished and suppressed. But those whose Doctrine is peaceable, and whose Manners are pure and blameless, ought to be upon equal Terms with their Fellow-Subjects. Thus if Solemn Assemblies, Observations of Festivals, publick Worship, be permitted to any one sort of Professors; all these things ought to be permitted to the *Presbyterians, Independents, Anabaptists, Arminians, Quakers*, and others, with the same Liberty. Nay, if we may openly speak the Truth, and as becomes one Man to another, neither *Pagan*, nor *Mahumetan*, nor *Jew*, ought to be excluded from the Civil Rights of the Commonwealth, because of his Religion. The Gospel commands no such thing. The Church, which *judges not those that are without*, wants it not.[9] And the Commonwealth, which embraces indifferently all Men that are honest, peaceable, and industrious, requires it not. Shall we suffer a *Pagan* to deal and trade with us, and shall we not suffer him to pray unto and worship God? If we allow the *Jews* to have private Houses and Dwellings amongst us, Why should we not allow them to have Synagogues? Is their Doctrine more false, their Worship more abominable, or is the Civil Peace more endangered, by their meeting in publick than in their private Houses? But if these things may be granted to *Jews* and *Pagans*, surely the condition of any Christians ought not to be worse than theirs in a Christian Commonwealth.

You'll say, perhaps, Yes, it ought to be: Because they are inclinable to Factions, Tumults, and Civil Wars. I answer: Is this the fault of the Christian Religion? If it be so, truly the Christian Religion is the worst of all Religions, and ought neither to be embraced by any particular Person, nor tolerated by any Commonwealth. For if this be the Genius, this the Nature of the Christian Religion, to be turbulent, and destructive to the Civil Peace, that Church it self which the Magistrate indulges will not always be innocent. But far be it from us to say any such thing of that Religion, which carries the greatest opposition to Covetousness, Ambition, Discord, Contention, and all manner of inordinate Desires; and is the most modest and peaceable Religion that ever was. We must therefore seek another Cause of those Evils that are charged upon Religion. And if we consider right, we shall find it to consist wholly in the Subject that I am treating of. It is not the diversity of Opinions, (which cannot be avoided) but the refusal of Toleration to those that are of different Opinions, (which might have been granted) that has produced all the Bustles and Wars, that have been in the Christian World, upon account of Religion. The Heads and Leaders of the Church, moved by Avarice and insatiable desire of Dominion, making use of the immoderate Ambition of Magistrates, and the credulous Superstition of the giddy Multitude, have incensed and animated them against those that dissent from themselves; by preaching unto them, contrary to the Laws of the Gospel and to the Precepts of Charity, That Schismaticks and Hereticks are to be outed of their Posses-

---

9. 1 Cor. 5.12, 13.

sions, and destroyed. And thus have they mixed together and confounded two things that are in themselves most different, the Church and the Commonwealth. Now as it is very difficult for men patiently to suffer themselves to be stript of the Goods, which they have got by their honest Industry; and contrary to all the Laws of Equity, both Humane and Divine, to be delivered up for a Prey to other mens Violence and Rapine; especially when they are otherwise altogether blameless; and that the Occasion for which they are thus treated does not at all belong to the Jurisdiction of the Magistrate; but intirely to the Conscience of every particular man; for the Conduct of which he is accountable to God only; What else can be expected, but that these men, growing weary of the Evils under which they labour, should in the end think it lawful for them to resist Force with Force, and to defend their natural Rights (which are not forfeitable upon account of Religion) with Arms as well as they can? That this has been hitherto the ordinary Course of things, is abundantly evident in History: And that it will continue to be so hereafter, is but too apparent in Reason. It cannot indeed be otherwise, so long as the Principle of Persecution for Religion shall prevail, as it has done hitherto, with Magistrate and People; and so long as those that ought to be the Preachers of Peace and Concord, shall continue, with all their Art and Strength, to excite men to Arms, and sound the Trumpet of War. But that Magistrates should thus suffer these Incendiaries, and Disturbers of the Publick Peace, might justly be wondred at; if it did not appear that they have been invited by them unto a Participation of the Spoil, and have therefore thought fit to make use of their Covetousness and Pride as means whereby to increase their own Power. For who does not see that *these Good Men* are indeed more Ministers of the Government, than Ministers of the Gospel; and that by flattering the Ambition, and favouring the Dominion of Princes and men in Authority, they endeavour with all their might to promote that Tyranny in the Commonwealth, which otherwise they should not be able to establish in the Church? This is the unhappy Agreement that we see between the Church and State. Whereas if each of them would contain it self within its own Bounds, the one attending to the worldly Welfare of the Commonwealth, the other to the Salvation of Souls, it is impossible that any Discord should ever have hapned between them. *Sed, pudet haec opprobria, etc.* God Almighty grant, I beseech him, that the Gospel of

Peace may at length be preached, and that Civil Magistrates growing more careful to conform their own Consciences to the Law of God, and less sollicitous about the binding of other mens Consciences by Humane Laws, may, like Fathers of their Country, direct all their Counsels and Endeavours to promote universally the Civil Welfare of all their Children; except only of such as are arrogant, ungovernable, and injurious to their Brethren; and that all Ecclesiastical men, who boast themselves to be the Successors of the Apostles, walking peaceably and modestly in the Apostles' steps, without intermedling with State-Affairs, may apply themselves wholly to promote the Salvation of Souls.

Farewell.

Perhaps it may not be amiss to add a few things concerning *Heresy* and *Schism*. A *Turk* is not, nor can be, either Heretick or Schismatick, to a *Christian:* and if any man fall off from the Christian Faith to Mahumetism, he does not thereby become a Heretick or Schismatick, but an Apostate and an Infidel. This no body doubts of. And by this it appears that men of different Religions cannot be Hereticks or Schismaticks to one another.

We are to enquire therefore, what men are of the same Religion. Concerning which, it is manifest that those who have one and the same Rule of Faith and Worship are of the same Religion: and those who have not the same Rule of Faith and Worship are of different Religions. For since all things that belong unto that Religion are contained in that Rule, it follows necessarily that those who agree in one Rule are of one and the same Religion: and *vice versâ.* Thus Turks and Christians are of different Religions: because these take the *Holy Scriptures* to be the Rule of their Religion, and those the *Alcoran* [Koran]. And for the same reason, there may be different Religions also even amongst Christians. The *Papists* and the *Lutherans,* tho' both of them profess Faith in Christ, and are therefore called Christians, yet are not both of the same Religion: because These acknowledge nothing but the Holy Scriptures to be the Rule and Foundation of their Religion; Those take in also Traditions and the Decrees of Popes, and of these together make the Rule of their Religion. And thus the Christians of St. *John* (as they are called) and the Christians of *Geneva* are of different Religions: because

These also take only the Scriptures; and Those I know not what Traditions, for the Rule of their Religion.

This being setled, it follows: *First*, that Heresy is a Separation made in Ecclesiastical Communion between men of the same Religion, for some Opinions no way contained in the Rule it self. And *Secondly*, that amongst those who acknowledge nothing but the Holy Scriptures to be their Rule of Faith, Heresy is a Separation made in their Christian Communion, for Opinions not contained in the express words of Scripture. Now this Separation may be made in a twofold manner.

1. When the greater part, or (by the Magistrate's Patronage) the stronger part, of the Church separates it self from others, by excluding them out of her Communion, because they will not profess their Belief of certain Opinions which are not the express words of the Scripture. For it is not the paucity of those that are separated, nor the Authority of the Magistrate, that can make any man guilty of Heresy. But he only is a Heretick who divides the Church into parts, introduces Names and Marks of Distinction, and voluntarily makes a Separation because of such Opinions.

2. When any one separates himself from the Communion of a Church, because that Church does not publickly profess some certain Opinions which the Holy Scriptures do not expressly teach.

Both these are *Hereticks: because they err in Fundamentals, and they err obstinately against Knowledge.* For when they have determined the Holy Scriptures to be the only Foundation of Faith, they nevertheless lay down certain Propositions as fundamental, which are not in the Scripture; and because others will not acknowledge these additional Opinions of theirs, nor build upon them as if they were necessary and fundamental, they therefore make a Separation in the Church; either by withdrawing themselves from the others, or expelling the others from them. Nor does it signifie any thing for them to say that their Confessions and Symbols are agreeable to Scripture, and to the Analogy of Faith. For if they be conceived in the express words of Scripture, there can be no question about them; because those things are acknowledged by all Christians to be of Divine Inspiration, and therefore fundamental. But if they say that the Articles which they require to be profess'd, are Consequences deduced from the Scripture; it is undoubtedly well done of them who believe and profess such things as seem unto them so agreeable

to the Rule of Faith. But it would be very ill done to obtrude those things upon others, unto whom they do not seem to be the indubitable Doctrines of the Scripture. And to make a Separation for such things as these, which neither are nor can be fundamental, is to become Hereticks. For I do not think there is any man arrived to that degree of madness, as that he dare give out his Consequences and Interpretations of Scripture as Divine Inspirations, and compare the Articles of Faith that he has framed according to his own Fancy with the Authority of Scripture. I know there are some Propositions so evidently agreeable to Scripture, that no body can deny them to be drawn from thence: but about those therefore there can be no difference. This only I say, that however clearly we may think this or the other Doctrine to be deduced from Scripture, we ought not therefore to impose it upon others, as a necessary Article of Faith, because we believe it to be agreeable to the Rule of Faith; unless we would be content also that other Doctrines should be imposed upon us in the same manner; and that we should be compell'd to receive and profess all the different and contradictory Opinions of *Lutherans, Calvinists, Remonstrants, Anabaptists*, and other Sects, which the Contrivers of Symbols, Systems, and Confessions, are accustomed to deliver unto their Followers as genuine and necessary Deductions from the Holy Scripture. I cannot but wonder at the extravagant arrogance of those men who think that they themselves can explain things necessary to Salvation more clearly than the Holy Ghost, the Eternal and Infinite Wisdom of God.

Thus much concerning *Heresy;* which word in common use is applied only to the Doctrinal part of Religion. Let us now consider *Schism*, which is a Crime near a-kin to it. For both those words seem unto me to signifie an *ill-grounded Separation in Ecclesiastical Communion, made about things not necessary.* But since Use, which is the Supream Law in matter of Language, has determined that Heresy relates to Errors in Faith, and Schism to those in Worship or Discipline, we must consider them under that Distinction.

Schism then, for the same reasons that have already been alleged, is nothing else but a Separation made in the Communion of the Church, upon account of something in Divine Worship, or Ecclesiastical Discipline, that is not any necessary part of it. Now nothing in Worship or Discipline can be necessary to

Christian Communion, but what Christ our Legislator, or the Apostles, by Inspiration of the Holy Spirit, have commanded in express words.

In a word: He that denies not any thing that the Holy Scriptures teach in express words, nor makes a Separation upon occasion of any thing that is not manifestly contained in the Sacred Text; however he may be nick-named by any Sect of Christians, and declared by some, or all of them to be utterly void of true Christianity, yet indeed and in truth this man cannot be either a Heretick or Schismatick.

These things might have been explained more largely, and more advantageously: but it is enough to have hinted at them, thus briefly, to a Person of your parts.

FINIS.

David Hume

HUME HIMSELF WROTE A CONVENIENTLY SHORT ACCOUNT OF HIS LIFE, WHICH WE reprint here in lieu of our own short biography. *My Own Life* conveys not only the relevant facts, but a unique glimpse into Hume's character.

It is difficult for a man to speak long of himself without vanity; therefore I shall be short. It may be thought an instance of vanity that I pretend at all to write my life, but this narrative shall contain little more than the history of my writings, as, indeed, almost all my life has been spent in literary pursuits and occupations. The first success of most of my writings was not such as to be an object of vanity.

I was born the 26th of April, 1711, old style, at Edinburgh. I was of a good family, both by father and mother. My father's family is a branch of the Earl of Home's, or Hume's; and my ancestors had been proprietors of the estate, which my brother possesses, for several generations. My mother was daughter of Sir David Falconer, President of the College of Justice; the title of Lord Halkerton came by succession to her brother.

My family, however, was not rich; and being myself a younger brother, my patrimony, according to the mode of my country, was of course very slender. My father, who passed for a man of parts, died when I was an infant, leaving me, with an elder brother and a sister, under the care of our mother, a woman of singular merit, who, though young and handsome, devoted herself entirely to the rearing and educating of her children. I passed through the ordinary course of education with success, and was seized very early with a passion for literature, which has been the ruling passion of my life and the great source of my enjoyments. My studious disposition, my sobriety, and my industry gave my family a notion that the law was a proper profession for me, but I found an unsurmountable aversion to everything but the pursuits of philosophy and general learning; and while they fancied I was poring upon Voet and Vinnius, Cicero and Vergil were the authors which I was secretly devouring.

My very slender fortune, however, being unsuitable to this plan of life, and my health being a little broken by my ardent application, I was tempted, or rather forced, to make a very feeble trial for entering into a more active scene of life. In 1734, I went to Bristol with some recommendations to eminent merchants, but in a few months found that scene totally unsuitable to me. I went over to France with a view of prosecuting my studies in a country retreat; and I there laid that plan of life which I have steadily and successfully pursued. I resolved to make a very rigid frugality supply my deficiency of fortune, to maintain unimpaired my independence, and to regard every object as contemptible except the improvement of my talents in literature.

During my retreat in France, first at Reims, but chiefly at La Flèche, in Anjou, I composed my *Treatise of Human Nature*. After passing three years very agreeably in that country, I came over to London in 1737. In the end of 1738, I published my *Treatise*, and immediately went down to my mother and my brother, who lived at his country house and was employing himself very judiciously and successfully in the improvement of his fortune.

Never literary attempt was more unfortunate than my *Treatise of Human Nature*. It fell *deadborn from the press*, without reaching such distinction as even to excite a murmur among the zealots. But being naturally of a cheerful and sanguine temper, I very soon recovered from the blow and prosecuted with great ardor my studies in the country. In 1742, I printed at Edinburgh the first part of my *Essays;* the work was favorably received, and soon made me entirely forget my former disappointment. I continued with my mother and brother in the country, and in that time recovered the knowledge of the Greek language, which I had too much neglected in my early youth.

In 1745, I received a letter from the Marquis of Annandale, inviting me to come and live with him in England; I found also that the friends and family of that young nobleman were desirous of putting him under my care and direction, for the state of his mind and health required it. I lived with him a twelvemonth. My appointments during that time made a considerable accession to my small fortune. I then received an invitation from General St. Clair to attend him as a secretary to his expedition, which was at first meant against Canada, but ended in an incursion on the coast of France. Next year, to wit, 1747, I received an invitation from the General to attend him in the same station in his military embassy to the courts of Vienna and Turin. I then wore the uniform of an officer, and was introduced at these courts as aide-de-camp to the General, along with Sir Harry Erskine and Captain Grant, now General Grant. These two years were almost the only interruptions which my studies have received during the course of my life. I passed them agreeably and in good company; and my appointments, with my frugality, had made me reach a fortune which I called independent, though most of my friends were inclined to smile when I said so; in short, I was now master of near a thousand pounds.

I had always entertained a notion that my want of success in publishing the *Treatise of Human Nature* had proceeded more from the manner than the matter, and that I had been guilty of a very usual indiscretion in going to the press too early. I therefore cast the first part of that work anew in the *Inquiry concerning Human Understanding*, which was published while I was at Turin. But this piece was at first little more successful than the *Treatise of Human Nature*. On my return from Italy, I had the mortification to find all England in a ferment on account of Dr. Middleton's *Free Inquiry*, while my performance was entirely overlooked and neglected. A new edition, which had been published at London, of my *Essays, Moral and Political* met not with a much better reception.

Such is the force of natural temper that these disappointments made little or no impression on me. I went down in 1749 and lived two years with my brother at his country house, for my mother was now dead. I there composed the second part of my *Essays*, which I called *Political Discourses*, and also my *Inquiry concerning the Principles of Morals*, which is another part of my *Treatise* that I cast anew. Meanwhile, my bookseller, A. Millar, informed me that my former publications (all but the unfortunate *Treatise*) were beginning to be the subject of conversation, that the sale of them was gradually increasing, and that new editions were demanded. Answers by Reverends and Right Reverends came out two or three in a year, and I found, by Dr. Warburton's railing, that the books were beginning to be esteemed in good company. However, I had fixed a resolution which I inflexibly maintained, never to reply to anybody; and not being very irascible in my temper, I have easily kept myself clear of all literary squabbles. These symptoms of a rising reputation gave me encouragement, as I was ever more disposed to see the favorable than unfavorable side of things, a turn of mind which it is more happy to possess than to be born to an estate of ten thousand a year.

In 1751, I removed from the country to the town, the true scene for a man of letters. In 1752 were published at Edinburgh, where I then lived, my *Political Discourses*, the only work of mine that was successful on the first publication. It was well received abroad and at home. In the same year was published at London my *Inquiry concerning the Principles of Morals*, which in my own opinion (who ought not to judge on that subject) is of all my writings, historical, philosophical, or literary, incomparably the best. It came unnoticed and unobserved into the world.

In 1752, the Faculty of Advocates chose me their librarian, an office from which I received little or no emolument, but which gave me the command of a large library. I then formed the plan of writing the *History of England;* but being frightened with the notion of continuing a narrative through a period of 1700 years, I commenced with the accession of the House of Stuart, an epoch when, I thought, the misrepresentations of faction began chiefly to take place. I was, I own, sanguine in my expectations of the success of this work. I thought that I was the only historian that had at once neglected present power, interest, and authority, and the cry of popular prejudices; and as the subject was suited to every capacity, I expected proportional applause. But miserable was my disappointment: I was assailed by one cry of reproach, disapprobation, and even detestation; English, Scotch, and Irish, Whig and Tory, Churchman and Sectary, Freethinker and Religionist, Patriot and Courtier united in their rage against the man who had presumed to shed a generous tear for the fate of Charles I and the Earl of Strafford; and after the first ebullitions of their fury were over, what was still more mortifying, the book seemed to sink into oblivion. Mr. Millar told me that in a twelvemonth he sold only forty-five copies of it. I scarcely, indeed, heard of one man in the three kingdoms, considerable for rank or letters, that could endure the book. I must only except the primate of England, Dr. Herring, and the primate of Ireland, Dr. Stone, which seem two odd exceptions. These dignified prelates separately sent me messages not to be discouraged.

I was, however, I confess, discouraged; and had not the war been at that time breaking out between France and England, I had certainly retired to some provincial town of the former kingdom, have changed my name, and never more have returned to my native country. But as this scheme was not now practicable, and the subsequent volume was considerably advanced, I resolved to pick up courage and to persevere.

In this interval, I published at London my *Natural History of Religion*, along with some other small pieces. Its public entry was rather obscure, except only that Dr. Hurd wrote a pamphlet against it, with all the illiberal petulance, arrogance, and scurrility which distinguish the Warburtonian school. This pamphlet gave me some consolation for the otherwise indifferent reception of my performance.

In 1756, two years after the fall of the first volume, was published the second volume of my *History*, containing the period from the death of Charles I till the Revolution. This performance happened to give less displeasure to the Whigs, and was better received. It not only rose itself, but helped to buoy up its unfortunate brother.

But though I had been taught by experience that the Whig party were in possession of bestowing all places, both in the state and in literature, I was so little inclined to yield to their senseless clamor that in above a hundred alterations, which further study, reading, or reflection engaged me to make in the reigns of the two first Stuarts, I have made all of them invariably to the Tory side. It is ridiculous to consider the English constitution before that period as a regular plan of liberty.

In 1759, I published my *History of the House of Tudor*. The clamor against this performance was almost equal to that against the *History* of the two first Stuarts. The reign of Elizabeth was particularly obnoxious. But I was now callous against the impressions of public folly, and continued very peaceably and contentedly in my retreat at Edinburgh to finish, in two volumes, the more early part of the English *History*, which I gave to the public in 1761, with tolerable, and but tolerable, success.

But, notwithstanding this variety of winds and seasons to which my writings had been exposed, they had still been making such advances that the copy-money given me by the booksellers much exceeded anything formerly known in England; I was become not only independent but opulent. I retired to my native country of Scotland, determined never more to set my foot out of it, and retaining the satisfaction of never having preferred a request to one great man, or even making advances of friendship to any of them. As I was now turned to fifty, I thought of passing all the rest of my life in this philosophical manner, when I received, in 1763, an invitation from the Earl of Hertford, with whom I was not in the least acquainted, to attend him on his embassy to Paris, with a near prospect of being appointed secretary to the embassy, and, in the meanwhile, of performing the functions of that office. This offer, however inviting, I at first declined, both because I was reluctant to begin connections with the great and because I was afraid that the civilities and gay company of Paris would prove disagreeable to a person of my age and humor; but on his Lordship's repeating the invitation, I accepted of it. I have every reason, both of pleasure and interest, to think myself happy in my connections with that nobleman, as well as afterwards with his brother, General Conway.

Those who have not seen the strange effects of modes will never imagine the reception I met with at Paris from men and women of all ranks and stations. The more I resiled from their excessive civilities, the more I was loaded with them. There is, however, a real satisfaction in living at Paris, from the great number of sensible, knowing, and polite company with which that city abounds, above all places in the universe. I thought once of settling there for life.

I was appointed secretary to the embassy; and, in summer 1765, Lord Hertford left me, being appointed Lord Lieutenant of Ireland. I was *chargé d'affaires* till the arrival of the Duke of Richmond, toward the end of the year. In the beginning of 1766, I left Paris, and next summer went to Edinburgh, with the same view as formerly, of burying myself in a philosophical retreat. I returned to that place, not richer, but with much more money and a much larger income, by means of Lord Hertford's friendship, than I left it; and I was desirous of trying what superfluity could produce, as I had formerly made an experiment of a competency. But, in 1767, I received from Mr. Conway an invitation to be Undersecretary; and this invitation both the character of the person and my connections with Lord Hertford prevented me from declining. I returned to Edinburgh in 1769, very opulent (for I possessed a revenue of £1000 a year), healthy, and though somewhat stricken in years, with the prospect of enjoying long my ease and of seeing the increase of my reputation.

In spring 1775, I was struck with a disorder in my bowels, which at first gave me no alarm, but has since, as I apprehend it, become mortal and incurable. I now reckon upon a speedy dissolution. I have suffered very little pain from my disorder, and what is more strange, have, notwithstanding the great decline of my person, never suffered a moment's abatement of my spirits, insomuch that were I to name the period of my life which I should most choose to pass over again, I might be tempted to point to this later period. I possess the same order as ever in study, and the same gaiety in company. I consider, besides, that a man of sixty-five, by dying, cuts off only a few years of infirmities; and though I see many symptoms of my literary reputation's breaking out at last with additional luster, I knew that I could have but few years to enjoy it. It is difficult to be more detached from life than I am at present.

To conclude historically with my own character, I am, or rather was (for that is the style I must now use in speaking of myself, which emboldens me the more to speak my sentiments)—I was, I say, a man of mild dispositions, of command of temper, of an open, social, and cheerful humor, capable of attachment but little susceptible of enmity, and of great moderation in all my passions. Even my love of literary fame, my ruling passion, never soured my temper, notwithstanding my frequent disappointments. My company was not unacceptable to the young and careless, as well as to the studious and literary; and as I took a particular pleasure in the company of modest women, I had no reason to be displeased with the reception I met with from them. In a word, though most men anywise eminent have found reason to complain of calumny, I never was touched or even attacked by her baleful tooth; and though I wantonly exposed myself to the rage of both civil and religious factions, they seemed to be disarmed in my behalf of their wonted fury. My friends never had occasion to vindicate any one circumstance of my character and conduct; not but that the zealots, we may well suppose, would have been glad to invent and propagate any story to my disadvantage, but they could never find any which they thought would wear the face of probability. I cannot say there is no vanity in making this funeral oration of myself, but I hope it is not a misplaced one; and this is a matter of fact which is easily cleared and ascertained.

April 18, 1776.

Hume died August 25, 1776.

NOTES ON THE TEXT

In the *Treatise of Human Nature*, David Hume probes the foundations of morality. In particular, Hume was concerned with defining the role of reason in morality. Hume's views seem to be guided by the twofold aim of showing how morality is essentially based in human beings while at the same time avoiding a thoroughgoing skepticism about the claims of morality on human beings. Machiavelli's views on this subject are not clearly articulated, but one can read him as thinking that morality is essentially an invention of human beings for the purpose of achieving their aims, and that when it gets in the way it ought to be rejected or replaced by another morality. Hobbes, by contrast, does not think of morality as optional and he does not think of it as an invention of human beings. Despite his similarities with Machiavelli, Hobbes believes morality consists in natural law and natural law consists in the rules found out by reason that forbid the pursuit of self-destructive actions. Hobbes thinks natural law is objective and that the ultimate authority of natural law is in the command of God. For Locke, morality also consists in natural law that is objective and discoverable by reason and founded on the will of God. For these thinkers, the principles of morality are very much like the principles of natural science or even mathematics; they concern real and objectively discernible facts in the world.

But there have been many doubters since the early modern period who have suggested that morality is merely the invention of human beings, often for the purpose of advancing the interests of the inventors, or that morality is merely a matter of feeling that may vary from person to person or at least from society to society. This line of skepticism goes back to the ancient world, but the early modern moralists were deeply impressed by the very different moralities of the peoples the Europeans found in their explorations and conquests around the globe. These discoveries led many to adopt the ideas that morality is a matter of convention and not discoverable by reason, and that the validity of moral judgment is entirely relative to culture and not based in objective reality. This kind of skepticism led many to think that they could do whatever they wanted to do to pursue their aims.

We can read Hume as trying to steer a middle course between skepticism and the idea that morality consists in rationally discernible objective principles. Hume's view is that morality is essentially a matter of feeling and not of reason. Moral judgments such as "It is wrong to lie" or "Jane ought not to have murdered John" are essentially feelings that the judger has when he thinks of or observes an action of lying or murder. Negative moral judgments are a certain kind of pain and positive moral judgments such as "She did the right thing" are a certain kind of pleasure. At the same time, Hume thinks that there is a nearly universal mechanism in the minds of human beings that leads them to have at bottom the same moral reactions to actions and events. This mechanism is called sympathy. Here is a crude example of how it works. If you try to imagine a person pressing a hot iron to his skin, you will feel a kind of a shadow of the pain in yourself. Hume thinks that this mechanism is at base what is working when the pains and pleasures called moral judgments arise.

Obviously, feeling, and not reason, is the main component here. What is his argument for this? Essentially, the argument is that moral judgments motivate people to act; that is why we teach morality to children. But reason itself cannot motivate people to act. Reason merely discovers truths about mathematics and the causal relations between things. But these never motivate us to do anything unless we have some prior desire. I don't care about whether what I do causes someone else to be happy unless I care, one way or the other, about that person's happiness. As Hume says, "Reason is and ought to be the slave of the passions." The mainsprings of desire are pleasure and pain. And so if moral judgment motivates us, it must consist in a pleasure or pain. Another argument Hume gives is that if moral judgments can be true or false and therefore are discoverable by reason, they must be about observable matters of fact and not about mathematical or logical relations between ideas. But if judgments are about matters of fact, then they must pick out observable events or things. But when we see one person murdering another, we see only the one person putting the knife in the other, the pain of the other, and the slowing of the heartbeat and breathing. We do not see anything like the wrongness of the action independent of these. Hume concludes that the wrongness of the action is a function of our response to the action and ultimately to the agent.

So far we have seen how Hume thinks that morality is at base a matter of the kinds of feelings all or nearly all human beings have in response to certain kinds of events. But Hume also sees a very important element of convention in morality. Justice, he thinks, is a matter of convention. The rules of justice are invented by primarily self-interested human beings so that they can live with each other in peace and cooperation. But even here, Hume observes that the conventions people invent must solve certain basic problems all human beings have in their relations with others. So the conventions that are elaborated to solve these problems have the same basic features. They consist in systems of property rights that determine what belongs to whom. They include systems of exchange and contract so that people can change their property rights. Of course, societies have different systems, but Hume thinks the basic elements are shared. What the conventions of justice do is advance the public good of the society. As a consequence, human beings will experience pleasure at the thought and observation of just actions and pain at the thought of injustice.

In the *Treatise* and "Of the Original Contract" Hume argues that the government too rests on a set of conventions that are necessary for advancing the good of the members of society. Here, Hume criticizes Locke's social contract view. Our obligation to obey government cannot be based on contract, for contracts are based on the same kind of convention as governments are. Furthermore, virtually all members are born into their society, so they have not agreed to be members; therefore the basis of their relation to government cannot be one of contract. Finally, Hume is quite conservative about government. Unlike Locke, he does not recognize the existence of natural law in terms of which members of a society can criticize the government, and he rejects the idea of consent as a basis for the obligation to obey one's rulers. Hume's view is that Locke's endorsement of revolution is a prescription for disorder and misery for all without being founded on any substance. Of course, Hume is not arguing that one should never change society, he is only saying that all changes in the system of property and government ought to be made in a piecemeal and gradual fashion.

A Treatise of Human Nature

Book III Of Morals

PART I
OF VIRTUE AND VICE IN GENERAL

Section I
Moral Distinctions Not Deriv'd from Reason

There is an inconvenience which attends all abstruse reasoning, that it may silence, without convincing an antagonist, and requires the same intense study to make us sensible of its force, that was at first requisite for its invention. When we leave our closet, and engage in the common affairs of life, its conclusions seem to vanish, like the phantoms of the night on the appearance of the morning; and 'tis difficult for us to retain even that conviction, which we had attain'd with difficulty. This is still more conspicuous in a long chain of reasoning, where we must preserve to the end the evidence of the first propositions, and where we often lose sight of all the most receiv'd maxims, either of philosophy or common life. I am not, however, without hopes, that the present system of philosophy will acquire new force as it advances; and that our reasonings concerning *morals* will corroborate whatever has been said concerning the *understanding* and the *passions*. Morality is a subject that interests us above all others: We fancy the peace of society to be at stake in every decision concerning it; and 'tis evident, that this concern must make our speculations appear more real and solid, than where the subject is, in a great measure, indifferent to us. What affects us, we conclude can never be a chimera; and as our passion is engag'd on the one side or the other, we naturally think that the question lies within human comprehension; which, in other cases of this nature, we are apt to entertain some doubt of. Without this advantage I never should have ventur'd upon a third volume of such abstruse philosophy, in an age, wherein the greatest part of men seem agreed to convert reading into an amusement, and to reject every thing that requires any considerable degree of attention to be comprehended.

It has been observ'd, that nothing is ever present to the mind but its perceptions; and that all the actions of seeing, hearing, judging, loving, hating, and thinking, fall under this denomination. The mind can never exert itself in any action, which we may not comprehend under the term of *perception;* and consequently that term is no less applicable to those judgments, by which we distinguish moral good and evil, than to every other operation of the mind. To approve of one character, to condemn another, are only so many different perceptions.

Now as perceptions resolve themselves into two kinds, viz. *impressions* and *ideas*, this distinction gives rise to a question, with which we shall open up our present enquiry concerning morals, *Whether 'tis by means of our* ideas *or* impressions *we distinguish betwixt vice and virtue, and pronounce an action blameable or praise-worthy?* This will immediately cut off all loose discourses and declamations, and reduce us to something precise and exact on the present subject.

Those who affirm that virtue is nothing but a conformity to reason; that there are eternal fitnesses and unfitnesses of things, which are the same to every rational being that considers them; that the immutable measures of right and wrong impose an obligation, not only on human creatures, but also on the Deity himself: All these systems concur in the opinion, that morality, like truth, is discern'd merely by ideas, and by their juxta-position and comparison. In order, therefore, to judge of these systems, we need only consider, whether it be possible, from reason alone, to distinguish betwixt moral good and evil, or whether there must concur some other principles to enable us to make that distinction.

If morality had naturally no influence on human passions and actions, 'twere in vain to take such pains to inculcate it; and nothing wou'd be more fruitless than that multitude of rules and precepts, with which all moralists abound. Philosophy is commonly divided into *speculative* and *practical;* and as morality is always comprehended under the latter division, 'tis supposed to influence our passions and actions, and to go beyond the calm and indolent judgments of the understanding. And this is confirm'd by common experience, which informs us, that men are often govern'd by their duties, and are deter'd from some actions by the opinion of injustice, and impell'd to others by that of obligation.

Since morals, therefore, have an influence on the actions and affections, it follows, that they cannot be deriv'd from reason; and that because reason alone, as we have already prov'd, can never have any such influence. Morals excite passions, and produce or prevent actions. Reason of itself is utterly impotent in this particular. The rules of morality, therefore, are not conclusions of our reason.

No one, I believe, will deny the justness of this inference; nor is there any other means of evading it, than by denying that principle, on which it is founded. As long as it is allow'd, that reason has no influence on our passions and actions, 'tis in vain to pretend, that morality is discover'd only by a deduction of reason. An active principle can never be founded on an inactive; and if reason be inactive in itself, it must remain so in all its shapes and appearances, whether it exerts itself in natural or moral subjects, whether it considers the powers of external bodies, or the actions of rational beings.

It would be tedious to repeat all the arguments, by which I have prov'd,[1] that reason is perfectly inert, and can never either prevent or produce any action or affection. 'Twill be easy to recollect what has been said upon that subject. I shall only recall on this occasion one of these arguments, which I shall endeavour to render still more conclusive, and more applicable to the present subject.

Reason is the discovery of truth or falshood. Truth or falshood consists in an agreement or disagreement either to the *real* relations of ideas, or to *real* existence and matter of fact. Whatever, therefore, is not susceptible of this agreement or disagreement, is incapable of being true or false, and can never be an object of our reason. Now 'tis evident our passions, volitions, and actions, are not susceptible of any such agreement or disagreement; being original facts and realities, compleat in themselves, and implying no reference to other passions, volitions, and actions. 'Tis impossible, therefore, they can be pronounced either true or false, and be either contrary or conformable to reason.

This argument is of double advantage to our present purpose. For it proves *directly*, that actions do not derive their merit from a conformity to reason, nor their blame from a contrariety to it; and it proves the same truth more *indirectly*, by shewing us, that as reason can never immediately prevent or produce any action by contradicting or approving of it, it cannot be the source of the distinction betwixt moral good and evil, which are found to have that influence. Actions may be laudable or blameable; but they cannot be reasonable or unreasonable: Laudable or blameable, therefore, are not the same with reasonable or unreasonable. The merit and demerit of actions frequently contradict, and sometimes controul our natural propensities. But reason has no such influence. Moral distinctions, therefore, are not the offspring of reason. Reason is wholly inactive, and

---

1. Book II. Part III. sect. 3.

can never be the source of so active a principle as conscience, or a sense of morals.

But perhaps it may be said, that tho' no will or action can be immediately contradictory to reason, yet we may find such a contradiction in some of the attendants of the action, that is, in its causes or effects. The action may cause a judgment, or may be *obliquely* caus'd by one, when the judgment concurs with a passion; and by an abusive way of speaking, which philosophy will scarce allow of, the same contrariety may, upon that account, be ascrib'd to the action. How far this truth or falshood may be the source of morals, 'twill now be proper to consider.

It has been observ'd, that reason, in a strict and philosophical sense, can have an influence on our conduct only after two ways: Either when it excites a passion by informing us of the existence of something which is a proper object of it; or when it discovers the connexion of causes and effects, so as to afford us means of exerting any passion. These are the only kinds of judgment, which can accompany our actions, or can be said to produce them in any manner; and it must be allow'd, that these judgments may often be false and erroneous. A person may be affected with passion, by supposing a pain or pleasure to lie in an object, which has no tendency to produce either of these sensations, or which produces the contrary to what is imagin'd. A person may also take false measures for the attaining his end, and may retard, by his foolish conduct, instead of forwarding the execution of any project. These false judgments may be thought to affect the passions and actions, which are connected with them, and may be said to render them unreasonable, in a figurative and improper way of speaking. But tho' this be acknowledg'd, 'tis easy to observe, that these errors are so far from being the source of all immorality, that they are commonly very innocent, and draw no manner of guilt upon the person who is so unfortunate as to fall into them. They extend not beyond a mistake of *fact*, which moralists have not generally suppos'd criminal, as being perfectly involuntary. I am more to be lamented than blam'd, if I am mistaken with regard to the influence of objects in producing pain or pleasure, or if I know not the proper means of satisfying my desires. No one can ever regard such errors as a defect in my moral character. A fruit, for instance, that is really disagreeable, appears to me at a distance, and thro' mistake I fancy it to be pleasant and delicious. Here is one

error. I choose certain means of reaching this fruit, which are not proper for my end. Here is a second error; nor is there any third one, which can ever possibly enter into our reasonings concerning actions. I ask, therefore, if a man, in this situation, and guilty of these two errors, is to be regarded as vicious and criminal, however unavoidable they might have been? Or if it be possible to imagine, that such errors are the sources of all immorality?

And here it may be proper to observe, that if moral distinctions be deriv'd from the truth or falshood of those judgments, they must take place wherever we form the judgments; nor will there be any difference, whether the question be concerning an apple or a kingdom, or whether the error be avoidable or unavoidable. For as the very essence of morality is suppos'd to consist in an agreement or disagreement to reason, the other circumstances are entirely arbitrary, and can never either bestow on any action the character of virtuous or vicious, or deprive it of that character. To which we may add, that this agreement or disagreement, not admitting of degrees, all virtues and vices wou'd of course be equal.

Shou'd it be pretended, that tho' a mistake of *fact* be not criminal, yet a mistake of *right* often is; and that this may be the source of immorality: I would answer, that 'tis impossible such a mistake can ever be the original source of immorality, since it supposes a real right and wrong; that is, a real distinction in morals, independent of these judgments. A mistake, therefore, of right may become a species of immorality; but 'tis only a secondary one, and is founded on some other, antecedent to it.

As to those judgments which are the *effects* of our actions, and which, when false, give occasion to pronounce the actions contrary to truth and reason; we may observe, that our actions never cause any judgment, either true or false, in ourselves, and that 'tis only on others they have such an influence. 'Tis certain, that an action, on many occasions, may give rise to false conclusions in others; and that a person, who thro' a window sees any lewd behaviour of mine with my neighbour's wife, may be so simple as to imagine she is certainly my own. In this respect my action resembles somewhat a lye or falshood; only with this difference, which is material, that I perform not the action with any intention of giving rise to a false judgment in another, but merely to satisfy my lust and passion. It causes, however, a mistake and false judgment by accident; and the falshood of its effects may be ascribed, by some odd figurative way of speaking, to the action itself. But still I can see no pretext of reason for asserting, that the tendency to cause such an error is the first spring or original source of all immorality.[2]

---

2. One might think it were entirely superfluous to prove this, if a late author [Wollaston], who has had the good fortune to obtain some reputation, had not seriously affirmed, that such a falshood is the foundation of all guilt and moral deformity. That we may discover the fallacy of his hypothesis, we need only consider, that a false conclusion is drawn from an action, only by means of an obscurity of natural principles, which makes a cause be secretly interrupted in its operation, by contrary causes, and renders the connexion betwixt two objects uncertain and variable. Now, as a like uncertainty and variety of causes take place, even in natural objects, and produce a like error in our judgment, if that tendency to produce error were the very essence of vice and immorality, it shou'd follow, that even inanimate objects might be vicious and immoral.

'Tis in vain to urge, that inanimate objects act without liberty and choice. For as liberty and choice are not necessary to make an action produce in us an erroneous conclusion, they can be, in no respect, essential to morality; and I do not readily perceive, upon this system, how they can ever come to be regarded by it. If the tendency to cause error be the origin of immorality, that tendency and immorality wou'd in every case be inseparable.

Add to this, that if I had used the precaution of shutting the windows, while I indulg'd myself in those liberties with my neighbour's wife, I should have been guilty of no immorality; and that because my action, being perfectly conceal'd, wou'd have had no tendency to produce any false conclusion.

For the same reason, a thief, who steals in by a ladder at a window, and takes all imaginable care to cause no disturbance, is in no respect criminal. For either he will not be perceiv'd, or if he be, 'tis impossible he can produce any error, nor will any one, from these circumstances, take him to be other than what he really is.

'Tis well known, that those who are squint-sighted, do very readily cause mistakes in others, and that we imagine they salute or are talking to one person, while they address themselves to another. Are they therefore, upon that account, immoral?

Besides, we may easily observe, that in all those arguments there is an evident reasoning in a circle. A person who takes possession of *another*'s goods, and uses them as his *own*, in a manner declares them to be his own; and this falshood is the source of the immorality of injustice. But is property, or right, or obligation, intelligible, without an antecedent morality?

A man that is ungrateful to his benefactor, in a manner affirms, that he never received any favours from him. But in what manner? Is it because 'tis his duty to be grateful? But this supposes, that there is some antecedent rule of duty and morals. Is it because human nature is generally grateful, and makes us conclude, that a man who does any harm never received any favour from the person he harm'd? But human nature is not so generally grateful, as to justify such a conclusion. Or if it were, is an exception to a general rule in every case criminal, for no other reason than because it is an exception?

Thus upon the whole, 'tis impossible, that the distinction betwixt moral good and evil, can be made by reason; since that distinction has an influence upon our actions, of which reason alone is incapable. Reason and judgment may, indeed, be the mediate cause of an action, by prompting, or by directing a passion: But it is not pretended, that a judgment of this kind, either in its truth or falshood, is attended with virtue or vice. And as to the judgments, which are caused by our judgments, they can still less bestow those moral qualities on the actions, which are their causes.

But to be more particular, and to shew, that those eternal immutable fitnesses and unfitnesses of things cannot be defended by sound philosophy, we may weigh the following considerations.

If the thought and understanding were alone capable of fixing the boundaries of right and wrong, the character of virtuous and vicious either must lie in some relations of objects, or must be a matter of fact, which is discovered by our reasoning. This consequence is evident. As the operations of human understanding divide themselves into two kinds, the comparing of ideas, and the inferring of matter of fact; were virtue discover'd by the understanding; it must be an object of one of these operations, nor is there any third operation of the understanding, which can discover it. There has been an opinion very industriously propagated by certain philosophers, that morality is susceptible of demonstration; and tho' no one has ever been able to advance a single step in those demonstrations; yet 'tis taken for granted, that this science may be brought to an equal certainty with geometry or algebra. Upon this supposition, vice and virtue must consist in some relations; since 'tis allow'd on all hands, that no matter of fact is capable of

---

But what may suffice entirely to destroy this whimsical system is, that it leaves us under the same difficulty to give a reason why truth is virtuous and falshood vicious, as to account for the merit or turpitude of any other action. I shall allow, if you please, that all immorality is derived from this supposed falshood in action, provided you can give me any plausible reason, why such a falshood is immoral. If you consider rightly of the matter, you will find yourself in the same difficulty as at the beginning.

This last argument is very conclusive; because, if there be not an evident merit or turpitude annex'd to this species of truth or falshood, it can never have any influence upon our actions. For, who ever thought of forbearing any action, because others might possibly draw false conclusions from it? Or, who ever perform'd any, that he might give rise to true conclusions?

being demonstrated. Let us, therefore, begin with examining this hypothesis, and endeavour, if possible, to fix those moral qualities, which have been so long the objects of our fruitless researches. Point out distinctly the relations, which constitute morality or obligation, that we may know wherein they consist, and after what manner we must judge of them.

If you assert, that vice and virtue consist in relations susceptible of certainty and demonstration, you must confine yourself to those *four* relations, which alone admit of that degree of evidence; and in that case you run into absurdities, from which you will never be able to extricate yourself. For as you make the very essence of morality to lie in the relations, and as there is no one of these relations but what is applicable, not only to an irrational, but also to an inanimate object; it follows, that even such objects must be susceptible of merit or demerit. *Resemblance, contrariety, degrees in quality*, and *proportions in quantity and number*; all these relations belong as properly to matter, as to our actions, passions, and volitions. 'Tis unquestionable, therefore, that morality lies not in any of these relations, nor the sense of it in their discovery.[3]

Shou'd it be asserted, that the sense of morality consists in the discovery of some relation, distinct from these, and that our enumeration was not compleat, when we comprehended all demonstrable relations under four general heads: To this I know not what to reply, till some one be so good as to point out to me this new relation. 'Tis impossible to refute a system, which has never yet been explain'd. In such a manner of fighting in the dark, a man loses his blows

in the air, and often places them where the enemy is not present.

I must, therefore, on this occasion, rest contented with requiring the two following conditions of any one that wou'd undertake to clear up this system. *First*, As moral good and evil belong only to the actions of the mind, and are deriv'd from our situation with regard to external objects, the relations, from which these moral distinctions arise, must lie only betwixt internal actions, and external objects, and must not be applicable either to internal actions, compared among themselves, or to external objects, when placed in opposition to other external objects. For as morality is supposed to attend certain relations, if these relations cou'd belong to internal actions consider'd singly, it wou'd follow, that we might be guilty of crimes in ourselves, and independent of our situation, with respect to the universe: And in like manner, if these moral relations cou'd be apply'd to external objects, it wou'd follow, that even inanimate beings wou'd be susceptible of moral beauty and deformity. Now it seems difficult to imagine, that any relation can be discover'd betwixt our passions, volitions, and actions, compared to external objects, which relation might not belong either to these passions and volitions, or to these external objects, compar'd among *themselves*.

But it will be still more difficult to fulfil the *second* condition, requisite to justify this system. According to the principles of those who maintain an abstract rational difference betwixt moral good and evil, and a natural fitness and unfitness of things, 'tis not only suppos'd, that these relations, being eternal and immutable, are the same, when consider'd by every rational creature, but their *effects* are also suppos'd to be necessarily the same; and 'tis concluded they have no less, or rather a greater, influence in directing the will of the deity, than in governing the rational and virtuous of our own species. These two particulars are evidently distinct. 'Tis one thing to know virtue, and another to conform the will to it. In order, therefore, to prove, that the measures of right and wrong are eternal laws, *obligatory* on every rational mind, 'tis not sufficient to shew the relations upon which they are founded: We must also point out the connexion betwixt the relation and the will; and must prove that this connexion is so necessary, that in every well-disposed mind, it must take place and have its influence; tho' the difference betwixt these minds be in other respects immense and infinite. Now besides

---

3. As a proof, how confus'd our way of thinking on this subject commonly is, we may observe, that those who assert, that morality is distinguishable, do not say, that morality lies in the relations, and that the relations are distinguishable by reason. They only say, that reason can discover such an action, in such relations, to be virtuous, and such another vicious. It seems they thought it sufficient, if they cou'd bring the word, Relation, into the proposition, without troubling themselves whether it was to the purpose or not. But here, I think, is plain argument. Demonstrative reason discovers only relations. But that reason, according to this hypothesis, discovers also vice and virtue. These moral qualities, therefore, must be relations. When we blame any action, in any situation, the whole complicated object, of action and situation, must form certain relations, wherein the essence of vice consists. This hypothesis is not otherwise intelligible. For what does reason discover, when it pronounces any action vicious? Does it discover a relation or a matter of fact? These questions are decisive, and must not be eluded.

what I have already prov'd, that even in human nature no relation can ever alone produce any action; besides this, I say, it has been shewn, in treating of the understanding, that there is no connexion of cause and effect, such as this is suppos'd to be, which is discoverable otherwise than by experience, and of which we can pretend to have any security by the simple consideration of the objects. All beings in the universe, consider'd in themselves, appear entirely loose and independent of each other. 'Tis only by experience we learn their influence and connexion; and this influence we ought never to extend beyond experience.

Thus it will be impossible to fulfil the *first* condition required to the system of eternal rational measures of right and wrong; because it is impossible to shew those relations, upon which such a distinction may be founded: And 'tis as impossible to fulfil the *second* condition; because we cannot prove, *a priori*, that these relations, if they really existed and were perceiv'd, wou'd be universally forcible and obligatory.

But to make these general reflexions more clear and convincing, we may illustrate them by some particular instances, wherein this character of moral good or evil is the most universally acknowledged. Of all crimes that human creatures are capable of committing, the most horrid and unnatural is ingratitude, especially when it is committed against parents, and appears in the more flagrant instances of wounds and death. This is acknowledg'd by all mankind, philosophers as well as the people; the question only arises among philosophers, whether the guilt or moral deformity of this action be discover'd by demonstrative reasoning, or be felt by an internal sense, and by means of some sentiment, which the reflecting on such an action naturally occasions. This question will soon be decided against the former opinion, if we can shew the same relations in other objects, without the notion of any guilt or iniquity attending them. Reason or science is nothing but the comparing of ideas, and the discovery of their relations; and if the same relations have different characters, it must evidently follow, that those characters are not discover'd merely by reason. To put the affair, therefore, to this trial, let us chuse any inanimate object, such as an oak or elm; and let us suppose, that by the dropping of its seed, it produces a sapling below it, which springing up by degrees, at last overtops and destroys the parent tree: I ask, if in this instance there be wanting any relation,

which is discoverable in parricide or ingratitude? Is not the one tree the cause of the other's existence; and the latter the cause of the destruction of the former, in the same manner as when a child murders his parent? 'Tis not sufficient to reply, that a choice or will is wanting. For in the case of parricide, a will does not give rise to any *different* relations, but is only the cause from which the action is deriv'd; and consequently produces the *same* relations, that in the oak or elm arise from some other principles. 'Tis a will or choice, that determines a man to kill his parent; and they are the laws of matter and motion, that determine a sapling to destroy the oak, from which it sprung. Here then the same relations have different causes; but still the relations are the same: And as their discovery is not in both cases attended with a notion of immorality, it follows, that that notion does not arise from such a discovery.

But to chuse an instance, still more resembling; I would fain ask any one, why incest in the human species is criminal, and why the very same action, and the same relations in animals have not the smallest moral turpitude and deformity? If it be answer'd, that this action is innocent in animals, because they have not reason sufficient to discover its turpitude; but that man, being endow'd with that faculty, which *ought* to restrain him to his duty, the same action instantly becomes criminal to him; should this be said, I would reply, that this is evidently arguing in a circle. For before reason can perceive this turpitude, the turpitude must exist; and consequently is independent of the decisions of our reason, and is their object more properly than their effect. According to this system, then, every animal, that has sense, and appetite, and will; that is, every animal must be susceptible of all the same virtues and vices, for which we ascribe praise and blame to human creatures. All the difference is, that our superior reason may serve to discover the vice or virtue, and by that means may augment the blame or praise : But still this discovery supposes a separate being in these moral distinctions, and a being, which depends only on the will and appetite, and which, both in thought and reality, may be distinguish'd from the reason. Animals are susceptible of the same relations, with respect to each other, as the human species, and therefore wou'd also be susceptible of the same morality, if the essence of morality consisted in these relations. Their want of a sufficient degree of reason may hinder them from perceiving the duties and obligations of morality, but can never hinder these duties from existing; since they must antecedently exist, in order to their being perceiv'd. Reason must find them, and can never produce them. This argument deserves to be weigh'd, as being, in my opinion, entirely decisive.

Nor does this reasoning only prove, that morality consists not in any relations, that are the objects of science; but if examin'd, will prove with equal certainty, that it consists not in any *matter of fact*, which can be discover'd by the understanding. This is the *second* part of our argument; and if it can be made evident, we may conclude, that morality is not an object of reason. But can there be any difficulty in proving, that vice and virtue are not matters of fact, whose existence we can infer by reason? Take any action allow'd to be vicious: Wilful murder, for instance. Examine it in all lights, and see if you can find that matter of fact, or real existence, which you call *vice*. In which-ever way you take it, you find only certain passions, motives, volitions, and thoughts. There is no other matter of fact in the case. The vice entirely escapes you, as long as you consider the object. You never can find it, till you turn your reflexion into your own breast, and find a sentiment of disapprobation, which arises in you, towards this action. Here is a matter of fact; but 'tis the object of feeling, not of reason. It lies in yourself, not in the object. So that when you pronounce any action or character to be vicious, you mean nothing, but that from the constitution of your nature you have a feeling or sentiment of blame from the contemplation of it. Vice and virtue, therefore, may be compar'd to sounds, colours, heat and cold, which, according to modern philosophy, are not qualities in objects, but perceptions in the mind: And this discovery in morals, like that other in physics, is to be regarded as a considerable advancement of the speculative sciences; tho', like that too, it has little or no influence on practice. Nothing can be more real, or concern us more, than our own sentiments of pleasure and uneasiness; and if these be favourable to virtue, and unfavourable to vice, no more can be requisite to the regulation of our conduct and behaviour.

I cannot forbear adding to these reasonings an observation, which may, perhaps, be found of some importance. In every system of morality, which I have hitherto met with, I have always remark'd, that the author proceeds for some time in the ordinary way of reasoning, and establishes the being of a God, or makes observations concerning human affairs; when

of a sudden I am surpriz'd to find, that instead of the usual copulations of propositions, *is*, and *is not*, I meet with no proposition that is not connected with an *ought*, or an *ought not*. This change is imperceptible; but is, however, of the last consequence. For as this *ought*, or *ought not*, expresses some new relation or affirmation, 'tis necessary that it shou'd be observ'd and explain'd; and at the same time that a reason should be given, for what seems altogether inconceivable, how this new relation can be a deduction from others, which are entirely different from it. But as authors do not commonly use this precaution, I shall presume to recommend it to the readers; and am persuaded, that this small attention wou'd subvert all the vulgar systems of morality, and let us see, that the distinction of vice and virtue is not founded merely on the relations of objects, nor is perceiv'd by reason.

Section II
Moral Distinctions Deriv'd from a Moral Sense

Thus the course of the argument leads us to conclude, that since vice and virtue are not discoverable merely by reason, or the comparison of ideas, it must be by means of some impression or sentiment they occasion, that we are able to mark the difference betwixt them. Our decisions concerning moral rectitude and depravity are evidently perceptions; and as all perceptions are either impressions or ideas, the exclusion of the one is a convincing argument for the other. Morality, therefore, is more properly felt than judg'd of; tho' this feeling or sentiment is commonly so soft and gentle, that we are apt to confound it with an idea, according to our common custom of taking all things for the same, which have any near resemblance to each other.

The next question is, Of what nature are these impressions, and after what manner do they operate upon us? Here we cannot remain long in suspense, but must pronounce the impression arising from virtue, to be agreeable, and that proceeding from vice to be uneasy. Every moment's experience must convince us of this. There is no spectacle so fair and beautiful as a noble and generous action; nor any which gives us more abhorrence than one that is cruel and treacherous. No enjoyment equals the satisfaction we receive from the company of those we love and esteem; as the greatest of all punishments is to be oblig'd to pass our lives with those we hate or condemn. A very play or romance may afford us instances of this pleasure, which virtue conveys to us; and pain, which arises from vice.

Now since the distinguishing impressions, by which moral good or evil is known, are nothing but *particular* pains or pleasures; it follows, that in all enquiries concerning these moral distinctions, it will be sufficient to shew the principles, which make us feel a satisfaction or uneasiness from the survey of any character, in order to satisfy us why the character is laudable or blameable. An action, or sentiment, or character is virtuous or vicious; why? because its view causes a pleasure or uneasiness of a particular kind. In giving a reason, therefore, for the pleasure or uneasiness, we sufficiently explain the vice or virtue. To have the sense of virtue, is nothing but to *feel* a satisfaction of a particular kind from the contemplation of a character. The very *feeling* constitutes our praise or admiration. We go no farther; nor do we enquire into the cause of the satisfaction. We do not infer a character to be virtuous, because it pleases: But in feeling that it pleases after such a particular manner, we in effect feel that it is virtuous. The case is the same as in our judgments concerning all kinds of beauty, and tastes, and sensations. Our approbation is imply'd in the immediate pleasure they convey to us.

I have objected to the system, which establishes eternal rational measures of right and wrong, that 'tis impossible to shew, in the actions of reasonable creatures, any relations, which are not found in external objects; and therefore, if morality always attended these relations, 'twere possible for inanimate matter to become virtuous or vicious. Now it may, in like manner, be objected to the present system, that if virtue and vice be determin'd by pleasure and pain, these qualities must, in every case, arise from the sensations; and consequently any object, whether animate or inanimate, rational or irrational, might become morally good or evil, provided it can excite a satisfaction or uneasiness. But tho' this objection seems to be the very same, it has by no means the same force, in the one case as in the other. For, *first*, 'tis evident, that under the term *pleasure*, we comprehend sensations, which are very different from each other, and which have only such a distant resemblance, as is requisite to make them be express'd by the same abstract term. A good composition of music and a bottle of good wine equally produce pleasure; and what is more, their goodness is determin'd merely by the pleasure. But shall we say upon that

account, that the wine is harmonious, or the music of a good flavour? In like manner an inanimate object, and the character or sentiments of any person may, both of them, give satisfaction; but as the satisfaction is different, this keeps our sentiments concerning them from being confounded, and makes us ascribe virtue to the one, and not to the other. Nor is every sentiment of pleasure or pain, which arises from characters and actions, of that *peculiar* kind, which makes us praise or condemn. The good qualities of an enemy are hurtful to us; but may still command our esteem and respect. 'Tis only when a character is considered in general, without reference to our particular interest, that it causes such a feeling or sentiment, as denominates it morally good or evil. 'Tis true, those sentiments, from interest and morals, are apt to be confounded, and naturally run into one another. It seldom happens, that we do not think an enemy vicious, and can distinguish betwixt his opposition to our interest and real villainy or baseness. But this hinders not, but that the sentiments are, in themselves, distinct; and a man of temper and judgment may preserve himself from these illusions. In like manner, tho' 'tis certain a musical voice is nothing but one that naturally gives a *particular* kind of pleasure; yet 'tis difficult for a man to be sensible, that the voice of an enemy is agreeable, or to allow it to be musical. But a person of a fine ear, who has the command of himself, can separate these feelings, and give praise to what deserves it.

Secondly, We may call to remembrance the preceding system of the passions, in order to remark a still more considerable difference among our pains and pleasures. Pride and humility, love and hatred are excited, when there is any thing presented to us, that both bears a relation to the object of the passion, and produces a separate sensation related to the sensation of the passion. Now virtue and vice are attended with these circumstances. They must necessarily be plac'd either in ourselves or others, and excite either pleasure or uneasiness; and therefore must give rise to one of these four passions; which clearly distinguishes them from the pleasure and pain arising from inanimate objects, that often bear no relation to us: And this is, perhaps, the most considerable effect that virtue and vice have upon the human mind.

It may now be ask'd *in general*, concerning this pain or pleasure, that distinguishes moral good and evil, *From what principles is it derived, and whence does it arise in the human mind?* To this I reply, *first*, that 'tis absurd to imagine, that in every particular instance, these sentiments are produc'd by an *original* quality and *primary* constitution. For as the number of our duties is, in a manner, infinite, 'tis impossible that our original instincts should extend to each of them, and from our very first infancy impress on the human mind all that multitude of precepts, which are contain'd in the compleatest system of ethics. Such a method of proceeding is not conformable to the usual maxims, by which nature is conducted, where a few principles produce all that variety we observe in the universe, and every thing is carry'd on in the easiest and most simple manner. 'Tis necessary, therefore, to abridge these primary impulses, and find some more general principles, upon which all our notions of morals are founded.

But in the *second* place, should it be ask'd, Whether we ought to search for these principles in *nature*, or whether we must look for them in some other origin? I wou'd reply, that our answer to this question depends upon the definition of the word, Nature, than which there is none more ambiguous and equivocal. If *nature* be oppos'd to miracles, not only the distinction betwixt vice and virtue is natural, but also every event, which has ever happen'd in the world, *excepting those miracles, on which our religion is founded*. In saying, then, that the sentiments of vice and virtue are natural in this sense, we make no very extraordinary discovery.

But *nature* may also be opposed to rare and unusual; and in this sense of the word, which is the common one, there may often arise disputes concerning what is natural or unnatural; and one may in general affirm, that we are not possess'd of any very precise standard, by which these disputes can be decided. Frequent and rare depend upon the number of examples we have observ'd; and as this number may gradually encrease or diminish, 'twill be impossible to fix any exact boundaries betwixt them. We may only affirm on this head, that if ever there was any thing, which cou'd be call'd natural in this sense, the sentiments of morality certainly may; since there never was any nation of the world, nor any single person in any nation, who was utterly depriv'd of them, and who never, in any instance, shew'd the least approbation or dislike of manners. These sentiments are so rooted in our constitution and temper, that without entirely confounding the human mind by disease or madness, 'tis impossible to extirpate and destroy them.

But *nature* may also be opposed to artifice, as well as to what is rare and unusual; and in this sense it may be disputed, whether the notions of virtue be natural or not. We readily forget, that the designs, and projects, and views of men are principles as necessary in their operation as heat and cold, moist and dry: But taking them to be free and entirely our own, 'tis usual for us to set them in opposition to the other principles of nature. Shou'd it, therefore, be demanded, whether the sense of virtue be natural or artificial, I am of opinion, that 'tis impossible for me at present to give any precise answer to this question. Perhaps it will appear afterwards, that our sense of some virtues is artificial, and that of others natural. The discussion of this question will be more proper, when we enter upon an exact detail of each particular vice and virtue.[1]

Mean while it may not be amiss to observe from these definitions of *natural* and *unnatural*, that nothing can be more unphilosophical than those systems, which assert, that virtue is the same with what is natural, and vice with what is unnatural. For in the first sense of the word, Nature, as opposed to miracles, both vice and virtue are equally natural; and in the second sense, as oppos'd to what is unusual, perhaps virtue will be found to be the most unnatural. At least it must be own'd, that heroic virtue, being as unusual, is as little natural as the most brutal barbarity. As to the third sense of the word, 'tis certain, that both vice and virtue are equally artificial, and out of nature. For however it may be disputed, whether the notion of a merit or demerit in certain actions be natural or artificial, 'tis evident, that the actions themselves are artificial, and are perform'd with a certain design and intention; otherwise they cou'd never be rank'd under any of these denominations. 'Tis impossible, therefore, that the character of natural and unnatural can ever, in any sense, mark the boundaries of vice and virtue.

Thus we are still brought back to our first position, that virtue is distinguished by the pleasure, and vice by the pain, that any action, sentiment, or character gives us by the mere view and contemplation. This decision is very commodious; because it reduces us

---

1. In the following discourse *natural* is also opposed sometimes to *civil*, sometimes to *moral*. The opposition will always discover the sense, in which it is taken.

to this simple question, *Why any action or sentiment upon the general view or survey, gives a certain satisfaction or uneasiness,* in order to shew the origin of its moral rectitude or depravity, without looking for any incomprehensible relations and qualities, which never did exist in nature, nor even in our imagination, by any clear and distinct conception. I flatter myself I have executed a great part of my present design by a state of the question, which appears to me so free from ambiguity and obscurity.

PART II
OF JUSTICE AND INJUSTICE

Section I
Justice, Whether a Natural or Artificial Virtue?

I have already hinted, that our sense of every kind of virtue is not natural; but that there are some virtues, that produce pleasure and approbation by means of an artifice or contrivance, which arises from the circumstances and necessities of mankind. Of this kind I assert *justice* to be; and shall endeavour to defend this opinion by a short, and, I hope, convincing argument, before I examine the nature of the artifice, from which the sense of that virtue is derived.

'Tis evident, that when we praise any actions, we regard only the motives that produced them, and consider the actions as signs or indications of certain principles in the mind and temper. The external performance has no merit. We must look within to find the moral quality. This we cannot do directly; and therefore fix our attention on actions, as on external signs. But these actions are still considered as signs; and the ultimate object of our praise and approbation is the motive, that produc'd them.

After the same manner, when we require any action, or blame a person for not performing it, we always suppose, that one in that situation shou'd be influenc'd by the proper motive of that action, and we esteem it vicious in him to be regardless of it. If we find, upon enquiry, that the virtuous motive was still powerful over his breast, tho' check'd in its operation by some circumstances unknown to us, we retract our blame, and have the same esteem for him, as if he had actually perform'd the action, which we require of him.

It appears, therefore, that all virtuous actions derive their merit only from virtuous motives, and are considered merely as signs of those motives. From

this principle I conclude, that the first virtuous motive, which bestows a merit on any action, can never be a regard to the virtue of that action, but must be some other natural motive or principle. To suppose, that the mere regard to the virtue of the action, may be the first motive, which produc'd the action, and render'd it virtuous, is to reason in a circle. Before we can have such a regard, the action must be really virtuous; and this virtue must be deriv'd from some virtuous motive: And consequently the virtuous motive must be different from the regard to the virtue of the action. A virtuous motive is requisite to render an action virtuous. An action must be virtuous, before we can have a regard to its virtue. Some virtuous motive, therefore, must be antecedent to that regard.

Nor is this merely a metaphysical subtilty; but enters into all our reasonings in common life, tho' perhaps we may not be able to place it in such distinct philosophical terms. We blame a father for neglecting his child. Why? because it shews a want of natural affection, which is the duty of every parent. Were not natural affection a duty, the care of children cou'd not be a duty; and 'twere impossible we cou'd have the duty in our eye in the attention we give to our offspring. In this case, therefore, all men suppose a motive to the action distinct from a sense of duty.

Here is a man, that does many benevolent actions; relieves the distress'd, comforts the afflicted, and extends his bounty even to the greatest strangers. No character can be more amiable and virtuous. We regard these actions as proofs of the greatest humanity. This humanity bestows a merit on the actions. A regard to this merit is, therefore, a secondary consideration, and deriv'd from the antecedent principle of humanity, which is meritorious and laudable.

In short, it may be establish'd as an undoubted maxim, *that no action can be virtuous, or morally good, unless there be in human nature some motive to produce it, distinct from the sense of its morality.*

But may not the sense of morality or duty produce an action, without any other motive? I answer, It may: But this is no objection to the present doctrine. When any virtuous motive or principle is common in human nature, a person, who feels his heart devoid of that principle, may hate himself upon that account, and may perform the action without the motive, from a certain sense of duty, in order to acquire by practice, that virtuous principle, or at least, to disguise to himself, as much as possible, his want of it. A man that really feels no gratitude in his temper, is still pleas'd to perform grateful actions, and thinks he has, by that means, fulfill'd his duty. Actions are at first only consider'd as signs of motives: But 'tis usual, in this case, as in all others, to fix our attention on the signs, and neglect, in some measure, the thing signify'd. But tho', on some occasions, a person may perform an action merely out of regard to its moral obligation, yet still this supposes in human nature some distinct principles, which are capable of producing the action, and whose moral beauty renders the action meritorious.

Now to apply all this to the present case: I suppose a person to have lent me a sum of money, on condition that it be restor'd in a few days; and also suppose, that after the expiration of the term agreed on, he demands the sum: I ask, *What reason or motive have I to restore the money?* It will, perhaps, be said, that my regard to justice, and abhorrence of villainy and knavery, are sufficient reasons for me, if I have the least grain of honesty, or sense of duty and obligation. And this answer, no doubt, is just and satisfactory to man in his civiliz'd state, and when train'd up according to a certain discipline and education. But in his rude and more *natural* condition, if you are pleas'd to call such a condition natural, this answer wou'd be rejected as perfectly unintelligible and sophistical. For one in that situation wou'd immediately ask you, *Wherein consists this honesty and justice, which you find in restoring a loan, and abstaining from the property of others?* It does not surely lie in the external action. It must, therefore, be plac'd in the motive, from which the external action is deriv'd. This motive can never be a regard to the honesty of the action. For 'tis a plain fallacy to say, that a virtuous motive is requisite to render an action honest, and at the same time that a regard to the honesty is the motive of the action. We can never have a regard to the virtue of an action, unless the action be antecedently virtuous. No action can be virtuous, but so far as it proceeds from a virtuous motive. A virtuous motive, therefore, must precede the regard to the virtue; and 'tis impossible, that the virtuous motive and the regard to the virtue can be the same.

'Tis requisite, then, to find some motive to acts of justice and honesty, distinct from our regard to the honesty; and in this lies the great difficulty. For shou'd we say, that a concern for our private interest or reputation is the legitimate motive to all honest actions; it wou'd follow, that wherever that concern ceases, honesty can no longer have place. But 'tis certain, that self-love, when it acts at its liberty, instead of engaging us to honest actions, is the source of all injustice and violence; nor can a man ever correct those vices, without correcting and restraining the *natural* movements of that appetite.

But shou'd it be affirm'd, that the reason or motive of such actions is the *regard to publick interest*, to which nothing is more contrary than examples of injustice and dishonesty; shou'd this be said, I wou'd propose the three following considerations, as worthy of our attention. *First*, public interest is not naturally attach'd to the observation of the rules of justice; but is only connected with it, after an artificial convention for the establishment of these rules, as shall be shewn more at large hereafter. *Secondly*, if we suppose, that the loan was secret, and that it is necessary for the interest of the person, that the money be restor'd in the same manner (as when the lender wou'd conceal his riches) in that case the example ceases, and the public is no longer interested in the actions of the borrower; tho' I suppose there is no moralist, who will affirm, that the duty and obligation ceases. *Thirdly*, experience sufficiently proves, that men, in the ordinary conduct of life, look not so far as the public interest, when they pay their creditors, perform their promises, and abstain from theft, and robbery, and injustice of every kind. That is a motive too remote and too sublime to affect the generality of mankind, and operate with any force in actions so contrary to private interest as are frequently those of justice and common honesty.

In general, it may be affirm'd, that there is no such passion in human minds, as the love of mankind, merely as such, independent of personal qualities, of services, or of relation to ourself. 'Tis true, there is no human, and indeed no sensible, creature, whose happiness or misery does not, in some measure, affect us, when brought near to us, and represented in lively colours: But this proceeds merely from sympathy, and is no proof of such an universal affection to mankind, since this concern extends itself beyond our own species. An affection betwixt the sexes is a passion evidently implanted in human nature; and this passion not only appears in its peculiar symptoms, but also in inflaming every other principle of affection, and raising a stronger love from beauty, wit, kindness, than what wou'd otherwise flow from them. Were there an universal love among all human creatures, it wou'd appear after the same manner. Any degree of a good quality wou'd cause a stronger affection than the same degree of a bad quality wou'd cause hatred;

contrary to what we find by experience. Men's tempers are different, and some have a propensity to the tender, and others to the rougher, affections: But in the main, we may affirm, that man in general, or human nature, is nothing but the object both of love and hatred, and requires some other cause, which by a double relation of impressions and ideas, may excite these passions. In vain wou'd we endeavour to elude this hypothesis. There are no phænomena that point out any such kind affection to men, independent of their merit, and every other circumstance. We love company in general; but 'tis as we love any other amusement. An *Englishman* in *Italy* is a friend: *A European* in *China*; and perhaps a man wou'd be belov'd as such, were we to meet him in the moon. But this proceeds only from the relation to ourselves; which in these cases gathers force by being confined to a few persons.

If public benevolence, therefore, or a regard to the interests of mankind, cannot be the original motive to justice, much less can *private benevolence*, or a *regard to the interests of the party concern'd*, be this motive. For what if he be my enemy, and has given me just cause to hate him? What if he be a vicious man, and deserves the hatred of all mankind? What if he be a miser, and can make no use of what I wou'd deprive him of? What if he be a profligate debauchee, and wou'd rather receive harm than benefit from large possessions? What if I be in necessity, and have urgent motives to acquire something to my family? In all these cases, the original motive to justice wou'd fail; and consequently the justice itself, and along with it all property, right, and obligation.

A rich man lies under a moral obligation to communicate to those in necessity a share of his superfluities. Were private benevolence the original motive to justice, a man wou'd not be oblig'd to leave others in the possession of more than he is oblig'd to give them. At least the difference wou'd be very inconsiderable. Men generally fix their affections more on what they are possess'd of, than on what they never enjoy'd: For this reason, it wou'd be greater cruelty to dispossess a man of any thing, than not to give it him. But who will assert, that this is the only foundation of justice?

Besides, we must consider, that the chief reason, why men attach themselves so much to their possessions is, that they consider them as their property, and as secur'd to them inviolably by the laws of society. But this is a secondary consideration, and dependent on the preceding notions of justice and property.

A man's property is suppos'd to be fenc'd against every mortal, in every possible case. But private benevolence towards the proprietor is, and ought to be, weaker in some persons, than in others: And in many, or indeed in most persons, must absolutely fail. Private benevolence, therefore, is not the original motive of justice.

From all this it follows, that we have naturally no real or universal motive for observing the laws of equity, but the very equity and merit of that observance; and as no action can be equitable or meritorious, where it cannot arise from some separate motive, there is here an evident sophistry and reasoning in a circle. Unless, therefore, we will allow, that nature has establish'd a sophistry, and render'd it necessary and unavoidable, we must allow, that the sense of justice and injustice is not deriv'd from nature, but arises artificially, tho' necessarily from education, and human conventions.

I shall add, as a corollary to this reasoning, that since no action can be laudable or blameable, without some motives or impelling passions, distinct from the sense of morals, these distinct passions must have a great influence on that sense. 'Tis according to their general force in human nature, that we blame or praise. In judging of the beauty of animal bodies, we always carry in our eye the œconomy of a certain species; and where the limbs and features observe that proportion, which is common to the species, we pronounce them handsome and beautiful. In like manner we always consider the *natural* and *usual* force of the passions, when we determine concerning vice and virtue; and if the passions depart very much from the common measures on either side, they are always disapprov'd as vicious. A man naturally loves his children better than his nephews, his nephews better than his cousins, his cousins better than strangers, where every thing else is equal. Hence arise our common measures of duty, in preferring the one to the other. Our sense of duty always follows the common and natural course of our passions.

To avoid giving offence, I must here observe, that when I deny justice to be a natural virtue, I make use of the word, *natural*, only as oppos'd to *artificial*. In another sense of the word; as no principle of the human mind is more natural than a sense of virtue; so no virtue is more natural than justice. Mankind is an inventive species; and where an invention is obvious and absolutely necessary, it may as properly be said to be natural as any thing that proceeds immediately from original principles, without the intervention of thought or reflexion. Tho' the rules of justice be *artificial*, they are not *arbitrary*. Nor is the expression improper to call them *Laws of Nature;* if by natural we understand what is common to any species, or even if we confine it to mean what is inseparable from the species.

Section II
Of the Origin of Justice and Property

We now proceed to examine two questions, viz. *concerning the manner, in which the rules of justice are establish'd by the artifice of men;* and *concerning the reasons, which determine us to attribute to the observance or neglect of these rules a moral beauty and deformity.* These questions will appear afterwards to be distinct. We shall begin with the former.

Of all the animals, with which this globe is peopled, there is none towards whom nature seems, at first sight, to have exercis'd more cruelty than towards man, in the numberless wants and necessities, with which she has loaded him, and in the slender means, which she affords to the relieving these necessities. In other creatures these two particulars generally compensate each other. If we consider the lion as a voracious and carnivorous animal, we shall easily discover him to be very necessitous; but if we turn our eye to his make and temper, his agility, his courage, his arms, and his force, we shall find, that his advantages hold proportion with his wants. The sheep and ox are depriv'd of all these advantages; but their appetites are moderate, and their food is of easy purchase. In man alone, this unnatural conjunction of infirmity, and of necessity, may be observ'd in its greatest perfection. Not only the food, which is requir'd for his sustenance, flies his search and approach, or at least requires his labour to be produc'd, but he must be possess'd of cloaths and lodging, to defend him against the injuries of the weather; tho' to consider him only in himself, he is provided neither with arms, nor force, nor other natural abilities, which are in any degree answerable to so many necessities.

'Tis by society alone he is able to supply his defects, and raise himself up to an equality with his fellow-creatures, and even acquire a superiority above them. By society all his infirmities are compensated; and tho' in that situation his wants multiply every moment upon him, yet his abilities are still more augmented, and leave him in every respect more satisfied and happy, than 'tis possible for him, in his savage and solitary condition, ever to become. When every individual person labours a-part, and only for himself, his force is too small to execute any considerable work; his labour being employ'd in supplying all his different necessities, he never attains a perfection in any particular art; and as his force and success are not at all times equal, the least failure in either of these particulars must be attended with inevitable ruin and misery. Society provides a remedy for these *three* inconveniences. By the conjunction of forces, our power is augmented: By the partition of employments, our ability encreases: And by mutual succour we are less expos'd to fortune and accidents. 'Tis by this additional *force, ability,* and *security,* that society becomes advantageous.

But in order to form society, 'tis requisite not only that it be advantageous, but also that men be sensible of its advantages; and 'tis impossible, in their wild uncultivated state, that by study and reflexion alone, they should ever be able to attain this knowledge. Most fortunately, therefore, there is conjoin'd to those necessities, whose remedies are remote and obscure, another necessity, which having a present and more obvious remedy, may justly be regarded as the first and original principle of human society. This necessity is no other than that natural appetite betwixt the sexes, which unites them together, and preserves their union, till a new tye takes place in their concern for their common offspring. This new concern becomes also a principle of union betwixt the parents and offspring, and forms a more numerous society; where the parents govern by the advantage of their superior strength and wisdom, and at the same time are restrain'd in the exercise of their authority by that natural affection, which they bear their children. In a little time, custom and habit operating on the tender minds of the children, makes them sensible of the advantages, which they may reap from society, as well as fashions them by degrees for it, by rubbing off those rough corners and untoward affections, which prevent their coalition.

For it must be confest, that however the circumstances of human nature may render an union necessary, and however those passions of lust and natural affection may seem to render it unavoidable; yet there are other particulars in our *natural temper*, and in our *outward circumstances*, which are very incommodious, and are even contrary to the requisite conjunction. Among the former, we may justly esteem our *selfishness* to be the most considerable. I am sensible, that, generally speaking, the representations of this quality have been carried much too far; and that the descriptions, which certain philosophers delight so much to form of mankind in this particular, are as wide of nature as any accounts of monsters, which we meet with in fables and romances. So far from thinking, that men have no affection for any thing beyond themselves, I am of opinion, that tho' it be rare to meet with one, who loves any single person better than himself; yet 'tis as rare to meet with one, in whom all the kind affections, taken together, do not over-balance all the selfish. Consult common experience: Do you not see, that tho' the whole expence of the family be generally under the direction of the master of it, yet there are few that do not bestow the largest part of their fortunes on the pleasures of their wives, and the education of their children, reserving the smallest portion for their own proper use and entertainment. This is what we may observe concerning such as have those endearing ties; and may presume, that the case would be the same with others, were they plac'd in a like situation.

But tho' this generosity must be acknowledged to the honour of human nature, we may at the same time remark, that so noble an affection, instead of fitting men for large societies, is almost as contrary to them, as the most narrow selfishness. For while each person loves himself better than any other single person, and in his love to others bears the greatest affection to his relations and acquaintance, this must necessarily produce an opposition of passions, and a consequent opposition of actions; which cannot but be dangerous to the new-establish'd union.

'Tis however worth while to remark, that this contrariety of passions wou'd be attended with but small danger, did it not concur with a peculiarity in our *outward circumstances*, which affords it an opportunity of exerting itself. There are three different species of goods, which we are possess'd of: the internal satisfaction of our mind, the external advantages of our body, and the enjoyment of such possessions as we have acquir'd by our industry and good fortune. We are perfectly secure in the enjoyment of the first. The second may be ravish'd from us, but can be of no advantage to him who deprives us of them. The last only are both expos'd to the violence of others, and may be transferr'd without suffering any loss or alteration; while at the same time, there is not a sufficient quantity of them to supply every one's desires and necessities. As the improvement, therefore, of these goods is the chief advantage of society, so the *instability* of their possession, along with their *scarcity*, is the chief impediment.

In vain shou'd we expect to find, in *uncultivated nature*, a remedy to this inconvenience; or hope for any inartificial principle of the human mind, which might controul those partial affections, and make us overcome the temptations arising from our circumstances. The idea of justice can never serve to this purpose, or be taken for a natural principle, capable of inspiring men with an equitable conduct towards each other. That virtue, as it is now understood, wou'd never have been dream'd of among rude and savage men. For the notion of injury or injustice implies an immorality or vice committed against some other person: And as every immorality is deriv'd from some defect or unsoundness of the passions, and as this defect must be judg'd of, in a great measure, from the ordinary course of nature in the constitution of the mind; 'twill be easy to know, whether we be guilty of any immorality, with regard to others, by considering the natural, and usual force of those several affections, which are directed towards them. Now it appears, that in the original frame of our mind, our strongest attention is confin'd to ourselves; our next is extended to our relations and acquaintance; and 'tis only the weakest which reaches to strangers and indifferent persons. This partiality, then, and unequal affection, must not only have an influence on our behaviour and conduct in society, but even on our ideas of vice and virtue; so as to make us regard any remarkable transgression of such a degree of partiality, either by too great an enlargement, or contraction of the affections, as vicious and immoral. This we may observe in our common judgments concerning actions, where we blame a person, who either centers all his affections in his family, or is so regardless of them, as, in any opposition of interest, to give the preference to a stranger, or mere chance acquaintance. From all which it follows, that our natural un-cultivated ideas of morality, instead of providing a remedy for the partiality of our affections, do rather conform themselves to that partiality, and give it an additional force and influence.

The remedy, then, is not deriv'd from nature, but from *artifice;* or more properly speaking, nature provides a remedy in the judgment and understanding, for what is irregular and incommodious in the affections. For when men, from their early education in society, have become sensible of the infinite advantages that result from it, and have besides acquir'd a new affection to company and conversation; and when they have observ'd, that the principal disturbance in society arises from those goods, which we call external, and from their looseness and easy transition from one person to another; they must seek for a remedy, by putting these goods, as far as possible, on the same footing with the fix'd and constant advantages of the mind and body. This can be done after no other manner, than by a convention enter'd into by all the members of the society to bestow stability on the possession of those external goods, and leave every one in the peaceable enjoyment of what he may acquire by his fortune and industry. By this means, every one knows what he may safely possess; and the passions are restrain'd in their partial and contradictory motions. Nor is such a restraint contrary to these passions; for if so, it cou'd never be enter'd into, nor maintain'd; but it is only contrary to their heedless and impetuous movement. Instead of departing from our own interest, or from that of our nearest friends, by abstaining from the possessions of others, we cannot better consult both these interests, than by such a convention; because it is by that means we maintain society, which is so necessary to their well-being and subsistence, as well as to our own.

This convention is not of the nature of a *promise:* For even promises themselves, as we shall see afterwards, arise from human conventions. It is only a general sense of common interest; which sense all the members of the society express to one another, and which induces them to regulate their conduct by certain rules. I observe, that it will be for my interest to leave another in the possession of his goods, *provided* he will act in the same manner with regard to me. He is sensible of a like interest in the regulation of his conduct. When this common sense of interest is

mutually express'd, and is known to both, it produces a suitable resolution and behaviour. And this may properly enough be call'd a convention or agreement betwixt us, tho' without the interposition of a promise; since the actions of each of us have a reference to those of the other, and are perform'd upon the supposition, that something is to be perform'd on the other part. Two men, who pull the oars of a boat, do it by an agreement or convention, tho' they have never given promises to each other. Nor is the rule concerning the stability of possession the less deriv'd from human conventions, that it arises gradually, and acquires force by a slow progression, and by our repeated experience of the inconveniences of transgressing it. On the contrary, this experience assures us still more, that the sense of interest has become common to all our fellows, and gives us a confidence of the future regularity of their conduct: And 'tis only on the expectation of this, that our moderation and abstinence are founded. In like manner are languages gradually establish'd by human conventions without any promise. In like manner do gold and silver become the common measures of exchange, and are esteem'd sufficient payment for what is of a hundred times their value.

After this convention, concerning abstinence from the possessions of others, is enter'd into, and every one has acquir'd a stability in his possessions, there immediately arise the ideas of justice and injustice; as also those of *property, right,* and *obligation.* The latter are altogether unintelligible without first understanding the former. Our property is nothing but those goods, whose constant possession is establish'd by the laws of society; that is, by the laws of justice. Those, therefore, who make use of the word *property,* or *right,* or *obligation,* before they have explain'd the origin of justice, or even make use of it in that explication, are guilty of a very gross fallacy, and can never reason upon any solid foundation. A man's property is some object related to him. This relation is not natural, but moral, and founded on justice. 'Tis very preposterous, therefore, to imagine, that we can have any idea of property, without fully comprehending the nature of justice, and shewing its origin in the artifice and contrivance of men. The origin of justice explains that of property. The same artifice gives rise to both. As our first and most natural sentiment of morals is founded on the nature of our passions, and gives the preference to ourselves and friends, above strangers; 'tis impossible there can be naturally any such thing as a fix'd right or property, while the opposite passions of men impel them in contrary directions, and are not restrain'd by any convention or agreement.

No one can doubt, that the convention for the distinction of property, and for the stability of possession, is of all circumstances the most necessary to the establishment of human society, and that after the agreement for the fixing and observing of this rule, there remains little or nothing to be done towards settling a perfect harmony and concord. All the other passions, beside this of interest, are either easily restrain'd, or are not of such pernicious consequence, when indulg'd. *Vanity* is rather to be esteem'd a social passion, and a bond of union among men. *Pity* and *love* are to be consider'd in the same light. And as to *envy* and *revenge*, tho' pernicious, they operate only by intervals, and are directed against particular persons, whom we consider as our superiors or enemies. This avidity alone, of acquiring goods and possessions for ourselves and our nearest friends, is insatiable, perpetual, universal, and directly destructive of society. There scarce is any one, who is not actuated by it; and there is no one, who has not reason to fear from it, when it acts without any restraint, and gives way to its first and most natural movements. So that upon the whole, we are to esteem the difficulties in the establishment of society, to be greater or less, according to those we encounter in regulating and restraining this passion.

'Tis certain, that no affection of the human mind has both a sufficient force, and a proper direction to counter-balance the love of gain, and render men fit members of society, by making them abstain from the possessions of others. Benevolence to strangers is too weak for this purpose; and as to the other passions, they rather inflame this avidity, when we observe, that the larger our possessions are, the more ability we have of gratifying all our appetites. There is no passion, therefore, capable of controlling the interested affection, but the very affection itself, by an alteration of its direction. Now this alteration must necessarily take place upon the least reflection ; since 'tis evident, that the passion is much better satisfy'd by its restraint, than by its liberty, and that by preserving society, we make much greater advances in the acquiring possessions, than by running into the solitary and forlorn condition, which must follow upon violence and an universal licence. The question,

therefore, concerning the wickedness or goodness of human nature, enters not in the least into that other question concerning the origin of society; nor is there any thing to be consider'd but the degrees of men's sagacity or folly. For whether the passion of self-interest be esteemed vicious or virtuous, 'tis all a case; since itself alone restrains it: So that if it be virtuous, men become social by their virtue; if vicious, their vice has the same effect.

Now as 'tis by establishing the rule for the stability of possession, that this passion restrains itself; if that rule be very abstruse, and of difficult invention; society must be esteem'd, in a manner, accidental, and the effect of many ages. But if it be found, that nothing can be more simple and obvious than that rule; that every parent, in order to preserve peace among his children, must establish it; and that these first rudiments of justice must every day be improv'd, as the society enlarges: If all this appear evident, as it certainly must, we may conclude, that 'tis utterly impossible for men to remain any considerable time in that savage condition, which precedes society; but that his very first state and situation may justly be esteem'd social. This, however, hinders not, but that philosophers may, if they please, extend their reasoning to the suppos'd *state of nature;* provided they allow it to be a mere philosophical fiction, which never had, and never cou'd have any reality. Human nature being compos'd of two principal parts, which are requisite in all its actions, the affections and understanding; 'tis certain, that the blind motions of the former, without the direction of the latter, incapacitate men for society: And it may be allow'd us to consider separately the effects, that result from the separate operations of these two component parts of the mind. The same liberty may be permitted to moral, which is allow'd to natural philosophers; and 'tis very usual with the latter to consider any motion as compounded and consisting of two parts separate from each other, tho' at the same time they acknowledge it to be in itself uncompounded and inseparable.

This *state of nature,* therefore, is to be regarded as a mere fiction, not unlike that of the *golden age,* which poets have invented; only with this difference, that the former is describ'd as full of war, violence, and injustice; whereas the latter is painted out to us, as the most charming and most peaceable condition, that can possibly be imagin'd. The seasons, in that first age of nature, were so temperate, if we may believe the poets, that there was no necessity for men to provide themselves with cloaths and houses as a security against the violence of heat and cold. The rivers flow'd with wine and milk: The oaks yielded honey; and nature spontaneously produc'd her greatest delicacies. Nor were these the chief advantages of that happy age. The storms and tempests were not alone remov'd from nature; but those more furious tempests were unknown to human breasts, which now cause such uproar, and engender such confusion. Avarice, ambition, cruelty, selfishness, were never heard of: Cordial affection, compassion, sympathy, were the only movements, with which the human mind was yet acquainted. Even the distinction of *mine* and *thine* was banish'd from that happy race of mortals, and carry'd with them the very notions of property and obligation, justice and injustice.

This, no doubt, is to be regarded as an idle fiction; but yet deserves our attention, because nothing can more evidently shew the origin of those virtues, which are the subjects of our present enquiry. I have already observ'd, that justice takes its rise from human conventions; and that these are intended as a remedy to some inconveniences, which proceed from the concurrence of certain *qualities* of the human mind with the *situation* of external objects. The qualities of the mind are *selfishness* and *limited generosity:* And the situation of external objects is their *easy change*, join'd to their *scarcity* in comparison of the wants and desires of men. But however philosophers may have been bewilder'd in those speculations, poets have been guided more infallibly, by a certain taste or common instinct, which in most kinds of reasoning goes farther than any of that art and philosophy, with which we have been yet acquainted. They easily perceiv'd, if every man had a tender regard for another, or if nature supplied abundantly all our wants and desires, that the jealousy of interest, which justice supposes, could no longer have place; nor would there be any occasion for those distinctions and limits of property and possession, which at present are in use among mankind. Encrease to a sufficient degree the benevolence of men, or the bounty of nature, and you render justice useless, by supplying its place with much nobler virtues, and more valuable blessings. The selfishness of men is animated by the few possessions we have, in proportion to our wants; and 'tis to restrain this selfishness, that men have been oblig'd to separate themselves from the community, and to distinguish betwixt their own goods and those of others.

Nor need we have recourse to the fictions of poets to learn this; but beside the reason of the thing, may discover the same truth by common experience and observation. 'Tis easy to remark, that a cordial affection renders all things common among friends; and that married people in particular mutually lose their property, and are unacquainted with the *mine* and *thine*, which are so necessary, and yet cause such disturbance in human society. The same effect arises from any alteration in the circumstances of mankind; as when there is such a plenty of any thing as satisfies all the desires of men: In which case the distinction of property is entirely lost, and every thing remains in common. This we may observe with regard to air and water, tho' the most valuable of all external objects; and may easily conclude, that if men were supplied with every thing in the same abundance, or if *every one* had the same affection and tender regard for *every one* as for himself; justice and injustice would be equally unknown among mankind.

Here then is a proposition, which, I think, may be regarded as certain, *that 'tis only from the selfishness and confin'd generosity of men, along with the scanty provision nature has made for his wants, that justice derives its origin.* If we look backward we shall find, that this proposition bestows an additional force on some of those observations, which we have already made on this subject.

First, we may conclude from it, that a regard to public interest, or a strong extensive benevolence, is not our first and original motive for the observation of the rules of justice; since 'tis allow'd, that if men were endow'd with such a benevolence, these rules would never have been dreamt of.

Secondly, we may conclude from the same principle, that the sense of justice is not founded on reason, or on the discovery of certain connexions and relations of ideas, which are eternal, immutable, and universally obligatory. For since it is confest, that such an alteration as that above-mention'd, in the temper and circumstances of mankind, wou'd entirely alter our duties and obligations, 'tis necessary upon the common system, *that the sense of virtue is deriv'd from reason*, to shew the change which this must produce in the relations and ideas. But 'tis evident, that the only cause, why the extensive generosity of man, and the perfect abundance of every thing, wou'd destroy the very idea of justice, is because they render it useless; and that, on the other hand, his confin'd benevolence, and his necessitous condition, give rise to that virtue, only by making it requisite to the publick interest, and to that of every individual. 'Twas therefore a concern for our own, and the publick interest, which made us establish the laws of justice; and nothing can be more certain, than that it is not any relation of ideas, which gives us this concern, but our impressions and sentiments, without which every thing in nature is perfectly indifferent to us, and can never in the least affect us. The sense of justice, therefore, is not founded on our ideas, but on our impressions.

Thirdly, we may farther confirm the foregoing proposition, *that those impressions, which give rise to this sense of justice, are not natural to the mind of man, but arise from artifice and human conventions.* For since any considerable alteration of temper and circumstances destroys equally justice and injustice; and since such an alteration has an effect only by changing our own and the publick interest; it follows, that the first establishment of the rules of justice depends on these different interests. But if men pursu'd the publick interest naturally, and with a hearty affection, they wou'd never have dream'd of restraining each other by these rules; and if they pursu'd their own interest, without any precaution, they wou'd run head-long into every kind of injustice and violence. These rules, therefore, are artificial, and seek their end in an oblique and indirect manner; nor is the interest, which gives rise to them, of a kind that cou'd be pursu'd by the natural and inartificial passions of men.

To make this more evident, consider, that tho' the rules of justice are establish'd merely by interest, their connexion with interest is somewhat singular, and is different from what may be observ'd on other occasions. A single act of justice is frequently contrary to *public interest;* and were it to stand alone, without being follow'd by other acts, may, in itself, be very prejudicial to society. When a man of merit, of a beneficent disposition, restores a great fortune to a miser, or a seditious bigot, he has acted justly and laudably, but the public is a real sufferer. Nor is every single act of justice, consider'd apart, more conducive to private interest, than to public; and 'tis easily conceiv'd how a man may impoverish himself by a signal instance of integrity, and have reason to wish, that with regard to that single act, the laws of justice were for a moment suspended in the universe. But however single acts of justice may be contrary, either to public or private interest, 'tis certain, that the whole plan or

scheme is highly conducive, or indeed absolutely requisite, both to the support of society, and the well-being of every individual. 'Tis impossible to separate the good from the ill. Property must be stable, and must be fix'd by general rules. Tho' in one instance the public be a sufferer, this momentary ill is amply compensated by the steady prosecution of the rule, and by the peace and order, which it establishes in society. And even every individual person must find himself a gainer, on ballancing the account; since, without justice, society must immediately dissolve, and every one must fall into that savage and solitary condition, which is infinitely worse than the worst situation that can possibly be suppos'd in society. When therefore men have had experience enough to observe, that whatever may be the consequence of any single act of justice, perform'd by a single person, yet the whole system of actions, concurr'd in by the whole society, is infinitely advantageous to the whole, and to every part; it is not long before justice and property take place. Every member of society is sensible of this interest: Every one expresses this sense to his fellows, along with the resolution he has taken of squaring his actions by it, on condition that others will do the same. No more is requisite to induce any one of them to perform an act of justice, who has the first opportunity. This becomes an example to others. And thus justice establishes itself by a kind of convention or agreement; that is, by a sense of interest, suppos'd to be common to all, and where every single act is perform'd in expectation that others are to perform the like. Without such a convention, no one wou'd ever have dream'd, that there was such a virtue as justice, or have been induc'd to conform his actions to it. Taking any single act, my justice may be pernicious in every respect; and 'tis only upon the supposition, that others are to imitate my example, that I can be induc'd to embrace that virtue; since nothing but this combination can render justice advantageous, or afford me any motives to conform my self to its rules.

We come now to the *second* question we propos'd, *viz. Why we annex the idea of virtue to justice, and of vice to injustice.* This question will not detain us long after the principles, which we have already establish'd. All we can say of it at present will be dispatch'd in a few words: And for farther satisfaction, the reader must wait till we come to the *third* part of this book. The *natural* obligation to justice, *viz.* interest, has been fully explain'd; but as to the *moral* obligation, or the sentiment of right and wrong, 'twill first be requisite to examine the natural virtues, before we can give a full and satisfactory account of it.

After men have found by experience, that their selfishness and confin'd generosity, acting at their liberty, totally incapacitate them for society; and at the same time have observ'd, that society is necessary to the satisfaction of those very passions, they are naturally induc'd to lay themselves under the restraint of such rules, as may render their commerce more safe and commodious. To the imposition then, and observance of these rules, both in general, and in every particular instance, they are at first mov'd only by a regard to interest; and this motive, on the first formation of society, is sufficiently strong and forcible. But when society has become numerous, and has encreas'd to a tribe or nation, this interest is more remote; nor do men so readily perceive, that disorder and confusion follow upon every breach of these rules, as in a more narrow and contracted society. But tho' in our own actions we may frequently lose sight of that interest, which we have in maintaining order, and may follow a lesser and more present interest, we never fail to observe the prejudice we receive, either mediately or immediately, from the injustice of others; as not being in that case either blinded by passion, or byass'd [biased] by any contrary temptation. Nay when the injustice is so distant from us, as no way to affect our interest, it still displeases us; because we consider it as prejudicial to human society, and pernicious to every one that approaches the person guilty of it. We partake of their uneasiness by *sympathy;* and as every thing, which gives uneasiness in human actions, upon the general survey, is call'd Vice, and whatever produces satisfaction, in the same manner, is denominated Virtue; this is the reason why the sense of moral good and evil follows upon justice and injustice. And tho' this sense, in the present case, be deriv'd only from contemplating the actions of others, yet we fail not to extend it even to our own actions. The *general rule* reaches beyond those instances, from which it arose; while at the same time we naturally *sympathize* with others in the sentiments they entertain of us. *Thus self-interest is the original motive to the* establishment *of justice: but a* sympathy *with public interest is the source of the* moral approbation, *which attends that virtue.*

Tho' this progress of the sentiments be *natural,* and even necessary, 'tis certain, that it is here for-warded by the artifice of politicians, who, in order to govern men more easily, and preserve peace in human society, have endeavour'd to produce an esteem for justice, and an abhorrence of injustice. This, no doubt, must have its effect; but nothing can be more evident, than that the matter has been carry'd too far by certain writers on morals, who seem to have employ'd their utmost efforts to extirpate all sense of virtue from among mankind. Any artifice of politicians may assist nature in the producing of those sentiments, which she suggests to us, and may even on some occasions, produce alone an approbation or esteem for any particular action; but 'tis impossible it should be the sole cause of the distinction we make betwixt vice and virtue. For if nature did not aid us in this particular, 'twou'd be in vain for politicians to talk of *honourable* or *dishonourable, praiseworthy* or *blameable.* These words wou'd be perfectly unintelligible, and wou'd no more have any idea annex'd to them, than if they were of a tongue perfectly unknown to us. The utmost politicians can perform, is, to extend the natural sentiments beyond their original bounds; but still nature must furnish the materials, and give us some notion of moral distinctions.

As publick praise and blame encrease our esteem for justice; so private education and instruction contribute to the same effect. For as parents easily observe, that a man is the more useful, both to himself and others, the greater degree of probity and honour he is endow'd with; and that those principles have greater force, when custom and education assist interest and reflexion: For these reasons they are induc'd to inculcate on their children, from their earliest infancy, the principles of probity, and teach them to regard the observance of those rules, by which society is maintain'd, as worthy and honourable, and their violation as base and infamous. By this means the sentiments of honour may take root in their tender minds, and acquire such firmness and solidity, that they may fall little short of those principles, which are the most essential to our natures, and the most deeply radicated in our internal constitution.

What farther contributes to encrease their solidity, is the interest of our reputation, after the opinion, *that a merit or demerit attends justice or injustice,* is once firmly establish'd among mankind. There is nothing, which touches us more nearly than our reputation, and nothing on which our reptutation more depends than our conduct, with relation to the property of others. For this reason, every one, who has any regard to his character, or who intends to live on good terms with mankind, must fix an inviolable law to himself, never, by any temptation, to be induc'd to violate those principles, which are essential to a man of probity and honour.

I shall make only one observation before I leave this subject, *viz.* that tho' I assert, that in the *state of nature*, or that imaginary state, which preceded society, there be neither justice nor injustice, yet I assert not, that it was allowable, in such a state, to violate the property of others. I only maintain, that there was no such thing as property; and consequently cou'd be no such thing as justice or injustice. I shall have occasion to make a similar reflexion with regard to *promises*, when I come to treat of them; and I hope this reflexion, when duly weigh'd, will suffice to remove all odium from the foregoing opinions, with regard to justice and injustice.

Section III
Of the Rules, Which Determine Property

Tho' the establishment of the rule, concerning the stability of possession, be not only useful, but even absolutely necessary to human society, it can never serve to any purpose, while it remains in such general terms. Some method must be shewn, by which we may distinguish what particular goods are to be assign'd to each particular person, while the rest of mankind are excluded from their possession and enjoyment. Our next business, then, must be to discover the reasons which modify this general rule, and fit it to the common use and practice of the world.

'Tis obvious, that those reasons are not deriv'd from any utility or advantage, which either the *particular* person or the public may reap from his enjoyment of any *particular* goods, beyond what wou'd result from the possession of them by any other person. 'Twere better, no doubt, that every one were possess'd of what is most suitable to him, and proper for his use: But besides, that this relation of fitness may be common to several at once, 'tis liable to so many controversies, and men are so partial and passionate in judging of these controversies, that such a loose and uncertain rule wou'd be absolutely incompatible with the peace of human society. The convention concerning the stability of possession is enter'd into, in order to cut off all occasions of discord and contention; and this end wou'd never be attain'd, were we allow'd to apply this rule differently in every particular case, according to every particular utility, which might be discover'd in such an application. Justice, in her decisions, never regards the fitness or unfitness of objects to particular persons, but conducts herself by more extensive views. Whether a man be generous, or a miser, he is equally well receiv'd by her, and obtains with the same facility a decision in his favours, even for what is entirely useless to him.

It follows, therefore, that the general rule, *that possession must be stable*, is not apply'd by particular judgments, but by other general rules, which must extend to the whole society, and be inflexible either by spite or favour. To illustrate this, I propose the following instance. I first consider men in their savage and solitary condition; and suppose, that being sensible of the misery of that state, and foreseeing the advantages that wou'd result from society, they seek each other's company, and make an offer of mutual protection and assistance. I also suppose, that they are endow'd with such sagacity as immediately to perceive, that the chief impediment to this project of society and partnership lies in the avidity and selfishness of their natural temper; to remedy which, they enter into a convention for the stability of possession, and for mutual restraint and forbearance. I am sensible, that this method of proceeding is not altogether natural; but besides that I here only suppose those reflexions to be form'd at once, which in fact arise insensibly and by degrees; besides this, I say, 'tis very possible, that several persons, being by different accidents separated from the societies, to which they formerly belong'd, may be oblig'd to form a new society among themselves; in which case they are entirely in the situation above-mention'd.

'Tis evident, then, that their first difficulty, in this situation, after the general convention for the establishment of society, and for the constancy of possession, is, how to separate their possessions, and assign to each his particular portion, which he must for the future inalterably enjoy. This difficulty will not detain them long; but it must immediately occur, as the most natural expedient, that every one continue to enjoy what he is at present master of, and that property or constant possession be conjoin'd to the immediate possession. Such is the effect of custom, that it not only reconciles us to any thing we have long enjoy'd, but even gives us an affection for it, and makes us prefer it to other objects, which may be more valuable, but are less known to us. What has long lain under our eye, and has often been employ'd to our advantage, *that* we are always the most unwilling to part with; but can easily live without possessions, which we never have enjoy'd, and are not accustom'd to. 'Tis evident, therefore, that men wou'd easily acquiesce in this expedient, *that every one continue to enjoy what he is at present possess'd of;* and this is the reason, why they wou'd so naturally agree in preferring it.[1]

---

1. No questions in philosophy are more difficult, than when a number of causes present themselves for the same phænomenon, to determine which is the principal and predominant. There seldom is any very precise argument to fix our choice, and men must be contented to be guided by a kind of taste or fancy, arising from analogy, and a comparison of similar instances. Thus, in the present case, there are, no doubt, motives of public interest for most of the rules, which determine property; but still I suspect, that these rules are principally fix'd by the imagination, or the more frivolous properties of our thought and conception. I shall continue to explain these causes, leaving it to the reader's choice, whether he will prefer those deriv'd from publick utility, or those deriv'd from the imagination. We shall begin with the right of the present possessor.

'Tis a quality, which I have already observ'd in human nature, [*Book* I. *Part* IV. *sect.* 5.], that when two objects appear in a close relation to each other, the mind is apt to ascribe to them any additional relation, in order to compleat the union; and this inclination is so strong, as often to make us run into errors (such as that of the conjunction of thought and matter) if we find that they can serve to that purpose. Many of our impressions are incapable of place or local position; and yet those very impressions we suppose to have a local conjunction with the impressions of sight and touch, merely because they are conjoin'd by causation, and are already united in the imagination. Since, therefore, we can feign a new relation, and even an absurd one, in order to compleat any union, 'twill easily be imagin'd, that if there be any relations, which depend on the mind, 'twill readily conjoin them to any preceding relation, and unite, by a new bond, such objects as have already an union in the fancy. Thus for instance, we never fail, in our arrangement of bodies, to place those which are *resembling* in *contiguity* to each other, or at least in *correspondent* points of view; because we feel a satisfaction in joining the relation of contiguity to that of resemblance, or the resemblance of situation to that of qualities. And this is easily accounted for from the known properties of human nature. When the mind is determin'd to join certain objects, but undetermin'd in its choice of the particular objects, it naturally turns its eye to such as are related together. They are already united in the mind: They present themselves at the same time to the conception; and instead of requiring any new reason for their conjunction, it wou'd require a very powerful reason to make us over-look this natural affinity. This we shall have occasion to explain more fully afterwards, when we come to treat of *beauty*. In the mean time, we may content ourselves with observing, that the same love of order and uniformity, which arranges the books in a library, and the chairs in a parlour, contributes to the forma-

But we may observe, that tho' the rule of the assignment of property to the present possessor be natural, and by that means useful, yet its utility extends not beyond the first formation of society; nor wou'd any thing be more pernicious, than the constant observance of it; by which restitution wou'd be excluded, and every injustice wou'd be authoriz'd and rewarded. We must, therefore, seek for some other circumstance, that may give rise to property after society is once establish'd; and of this kind, I find four most considerable, *viz.* Occupation, Prescription, Accession, and Succession. We shall briefly examine each of these, beginning with *Occupation.*

The possession of all external goods is changeable and uncertain; which is one of the most considerable impediments to the establishment of society, and is the reason why, by universal agreement, express or tactile, men restrain themselves by what we now call the rules of justice and equity. The misery of the condition, which precedes this restraint, is the cause why we submit to that remedy as quickly as possible; and this affords an easy reason, why we annex the idea of property to the first possession, or to *occupation.* Men are unwilling to leave property in suspence, even for the shortest time, or open the least door to violence and disorder. To which we may add, that the first possession always engages the attention most; and did we neglect it, there wou'd be no colour of reason for assigning property to any succeeding possession.[2]

---

tion of society, and to the well-being of mankind, by modifying the general rule concerning the stability of possession. As property forms a relation betwixt a person and an object, 'tis natural to found it on some preceding relation; and as property is nothing but a constant possession, secur'd by the laws of society, 'tis natural to add it to the present possession, which is a relation that resembles it. For this also has its influence. If it be natural to conjoin all sorts of relations, 'tis more so, to conjoin such relations as are resembling, and are related together.

2. Some philosophers account for the right of occupation, by saying, that every one has a property in his own labour; and when he joins that labour to any thing, it gives him the property of the whole: But, 1. There are several kinds of occupation, where we cannot be said to join our labour to the object we acquire: As when we possess a meadow by grazing our cattle upon it. 2. This accounts for the matter by means of *accession;* which is taking a needless circuit. 3. We cannot be said to join our labour to any thing but in a figurative sense. Properly speaking, we only make an alteration on it by our labour. This forms a relation betwixt us and the object; and thence arises the property, according to the preceding principles.

There remains nothing, but to determine exactly, what is meant by possession; and this is not so easy as may at first sight be imagin'd. We are said to be in possession of any thing, not only when we immediately touch it, but also when we are so situated with respect to it, as to have it in our power to use it; and may move, alter, or destroy it, according to our present pleasure or advantage. This relation, then, is a species of cause and effect; and as property is nothing but a stable possession, deriv'd from the rules of justice, or the conventions of men, 'tis to be consider'd as the same species of relation. But here we may observe, that as the power of using any object becomes more or less certain, according as the interruptions we may meet with are more or less probable; and as this probability may increase by insensible degrees; 'tis in many cases impossible to determine when possession begins or ends; nor is there any certain standard, by which we can decide such controversies. A wild boar, that falls into our snares, is deem'd to be in our possession, if it be impossible for him to escape. But what do we mean by impossible? How do we separate this impossibility from an improbability? And how distinguish that exactly from a probability? Mark the precise limits of the one and the other, and shew the standard, by which we may decide all disputes that may arise, and, as we find by experience, frequently do arise upon this subject.[3]

But such disputes may not only arise concerning the real existence of property and possession, but also concerning their extent; and these disputes are often susceptible of no decision, or can be decided by no other faculty than the imagination. A person who lands on the shore of a small island, that is desart and uncultivated, is deem'd its possessor from the very first moment, and acquires the property of the whole; because the object is there bounded and circumscrib'd in the fancy, and at the same time is propor-

---

3. If we seek a solution of these difficulties in reason and public interest, we never shall find satisfaction; and if we look for it in the imagination, 'tis evident, that the qualities, which operate upon that faculty, run so insensibly and gradually into each other, that 'tis impossible to give them any precise bounds or termination. The difficulties on this head must encrease, when we consider, that our judgment alters very sensibly, according to the subject, and that the same power and proximity will be deem'd possession in one case, which is not esteem'd such in another. A person, who has hunted a hare to the last degree of weariness, wou'd look upon it as an injustice for another to rush in before him, and seize his prey. But the same person, advancing to pluck an apple, that hangs within his reach, has no reason to complain, if another, more alert, passes him, and takes possession. What is the reason of this difference, but that immobility, not being natural to the hare, but the effect of industry, forms in that case a strong relation with the hunter, which is wanting in the other?

Here then it appears, that a certain and infallible power of enjoyment, without touch or some other sensible relation, often produces not property: And I farther observe, that a sensible relation, without any present power, is sometimes sufficient to give a title to any object. The sight of a thing is seldom a considerable relation, and is only regarded as such, when the object is hidden, or very obscure; in which case we find, that the view alone conveys a property; according to that maxim, *that even a*

whole continent belongs to the nation, which first discover'd it. 'Tis however remarkable, that both in the case of discovery and that of possession, the discoverer and possessor must join to the relation an intention of rendering himself proprietor, otherwise the relation will not have its effect; and that because the connexion in our fancy betwixt the property and the relation is not so great, but that it requires to be help'd by such an intention.

From all these circumstances, 'tis easy to see how perplex'd many questions may become concerning the acquisition of property by occupation; and the least effort of thought may present us with instances, which are not susceptible of any reasonable decision. If we prefer examples, which are real, to such as are feign'd, we may consider the following one, which is to be met with in almost every writer, that has treated of the laws of nature. Two *Grecian* colonies, leaving their native country, in search of new seats, were inform'd that a city near them was deserted by its inhabitants. To know the truth of this report, they dispatch'd at once two messengers, one from each colony; who finding on their approach, that their information was true, begun a race together with an intention to take possession of the city, each of them for his countrymen. One of these messengers, finding that he was not an equal match for the other, launch'd his spear at the gates of the city, and was so fortunate as to fix it there before the arrival of his companion. This produc'd a dispute betwixt the two colonies, which of them was the proprietor of the empty city; and this dispute still subsists among philosophers. For my part I find the dispute impossible to be decided, and that because the whole question hangs upon the fancy, which in this case is not possess'd of any precise or determinate standard, upon which it can give sentence. To make this evident, let us consider, that if these two persons had been simply members of the colonies, and not messengers or deputies, their actions wou'd not have been of any consequence; since in that case their relation to the colonies wou'd have been but feeble and imperfect. Add to this, that nothing determin'd them to run to the gates rather than the walls, or any other part of the city, but that the gates, being the most obvious and remarkable part, satisfy the fancy best in taking them for the whole; as we find by the poets, who frequently draw their images and metaphors from them. Besides we may consider, that the touch or contact of the one messenger is not properly possession, no more than the piercing the gates with a spear; but only forms a relation; and there is a relation, in the other case, equally obvious, tho' not, perhaps, of equal force. Which of these relations, then, conveys a right and property, or whether any of them be sufficient for that effect, I leave to the decision of such as are wiser than myself.

tion'd to the new possessor. The same person landing on a desert island, as large as *Great Britain*, extends his property no farther than his immediate possession; tho' a numerous colony are esteem'd the proprietors of the whole from the instant of their debarkment.

But it often happens, that the title of first possession becomes obscure thro' time; and that 'tis impossible to determine many controversies, which may arise concerning it. In that case long possession or *prescription* naturally takes place, and gives a person a sufficient property in any thing he enjoys. The nature of human society admits not of any great accuracy; nor can we always remount to the first origin of things, in order to determine their present condition. Any considerable space of time sets objects at such a distance, that they seem, in a manner, to lose their reality, and have as little influence on the mind, as if they never had been in being. A man's title, that is clear and certain at present, will seem obscure and doubtful fifty years hence, even tho' the facts, on which it is founded, shou'd be prov'd with the greatest evidence and certainty. The same facts have not the same influence after so long an interval of time. And this may be receiv'd as a convincing argument for our preceding doctrine with regard to property and justice. Possession during a long tract of time conveys a title to any object. But as 'tis certain, that, however every thing be produc'd in time, there is nothing real, that is produc'd by time; it follows, that property being produc'd by time, is not any thing real in the objects, but is the offspring of the sentiments, on which alone time is found to have any influence.[4]

We acquire the property of objects by *accession*, when they are connected in an intimate manner with objects that are already our property, and at the same time are inferior to them. Thus the fruits of our garden, the offspring of our cattle, and the work of our slaves, are all of them esteem'd our property, even before possession. Where objects are connected together in the imagination, they are apt to be put on the same footing, and are commonly suppos'd to be endow'd with the same qualities. We readily pass from one to the other, and make no difference in our judgments concerning them; especially if the latter be inferior to the former.[5]

---

4. Present possession is plainly a relation betwixt a person and an object; but is not sufficient to counter-ballance the relation of first possession, unless the former be long and uninterrupted: In which case the relation is encreas'd on the side of the present possession, by the extent of time, and diminish'd on that of first possession, by the distance. This change in the relation produces a consequent change in the property.

---

5. This source of property can never be explain'd but from the imaginations; and one may affirm, that the causes are here unmix'd. We shall proceed to explain them more particularly, and illustrate them by examples from common life and experience.

It has been observ'd above, that the mind has a natural propensity to join relations, especially resembling ones, and finds a kind of fitness and uniformity in such an union. From this propensity are deriv'd these laws of nature, *that upon the first formation of society, property always follows the present possession;* and afterwards, *that it arises from first or from long possession.* Now we may easily observe, that relation is not confin'd merely to one degree; but that from an object, that is related to us, we acquire a relation to every other object, which is related to it, and so on, till the thought loses the chain by too long a progress. However the relation may weaken by each remove, 'tis not immediately destroy'd; but frequently connects two objects by means of an intermediate one, which is related to both. And this principle is of such force as to give rise to the right of *accession*, and causes us to acquire the property not only of such objects as we are immediately possess'd of, but also of such as are closely connected with them.

Suppose a *German*, a *Frenchman*, and a *Spaniard* to come into a room, where there are plac'd upon the table three bottles of wine, *Rhenish*, *Burgundy*, and *Port*; and suppose they shou'd fall a quarrelling about the division of them; a person, who was chosen for umpire, wou'd naturally, to shew his impartiality, give every one the product of his own country: And this from a principle, which, in some measure, is the source of those laws of nature, that ascribe property to occupation, prescription and accession.

In all these cases, and particularly that of accession, there is first a *natural* union betwixt the idea of the person and that of the object, and afterwards a new and *moral* union produc'd by that right or property, which we ascribe to the person. But here there occurs a difficulty, which merits our attention, and may afford us an opportunity of putting to tryal that singular method of reasoning, which has been employ'd on the present subject. I have already observ'd, that the imagination passes with greater facility from little to great, than from great to little, and that the transition of ideas is always easier and smoother in the former case than in the latter. Now as the right of accession arises from the easy transition of ideas, by which related objects are connected together, it shou'd naturally be imagin'd, that the right of accession must encrease in strength, in proportion as the transition of ideas is perform'd with greater facility. It may, therefore, be thought, that when we have acquir'd the property of any small object, we shall readily consider any great object related to it as an accession, and as belonging to the proprietor of the small one; since the transition is in that case very easy from the small object to the great one, and shou'd connect them together in the closest manner. But in fact the case is always found to be otherwise. The empire of *Great Britain* seems to draw along with it the dominion of the *Orkneys*, the *Hebrides*, the isle of *Man*, and

The right of *succession* is a very natural one, from the presum'd consent of the parent or near relation, and from the general interest of mankind, which requires, that men's possessions shou'd pass to those, who are dearest to them, in order to render them more industrious and frugal. Perhaps these causes

---

the isle of *Wight;* but the authority over those lesser islands does not naturally imply any title to *Great Britain.* In short, a small object naturally follows a great one as its accession; but a great one is never suppos'd to belong to the proprieter of a small one related to it, merely on account of that property and relation. Yet in this latter case the transition of ideas is smoother from the proprietor to the small object, which is his property, and from the small object to the great one, than in the former case from the proprietor to the great object, and from the great one to the small. It may therefore be thought, that these phænomena are objections to the foregoing hypothesis, *that the ascribing of property to accession is nothing but an [effect] of the relations of ideas, and of the smooth transition of the imagination.*

'Twill be easy to solve this objection, if we consider the agility and unsteadiness of the imagination, with the different views, in which it is continually placing its objects. When we attribute to a person a property in two objects, we do not always pass from the person to one object, and from that to the other related to it. The objects being here to be consider'd as the property of the person, we are apt to join them together, and place them in the same light. Suppose, therefore, a great and a small object to be related together; if a person be strongly related to the great object, he will likewise be strongly related to both the objects, consider'd together, because he is related to the most considerable part. On the contrary, if he be only related to the small object, he will not be strongly related to both, consider'd together, since his relation lies only with the most trivial part, which is not apt to strike us in any great degree, when we consider the whole. And this is the reason, why small objects become accessions to great ones, and not great to small.

'Tis the general opinion of philosophers and civilians, that the sea is incapable of becoming the property of any nation; and that because 'tis impossible to take possession of it, or form any such distinct relation with it, as may be the foundation of property. Where this reason ceases, property immediately takes place. Thus the most strenuous advocates for the liberty of the seas universally allow, that friths and bays naturally belong as an accession to the proprietors of the surrounding continent. These have properly no more bond or union with the land, than the *pacific* ocean wou'd have; but having an union in the fancy, and being at the same time *inferior,* they are of course regarded as an accession.

The property of rivers, by the laws of most nations, and by the natural turn of our thought, is attributed to the proprietors of their banks, excepting such vast rivers as the *Rhine* or the *Danube,* which seem too large to the imagination to follow as an accession the property of the neighbouring fields. Yet even these rivers are consider'd as the property of that nation, thro' whose dominions they run; the idea of a nation being of a suitable bulk to correspond with them, and bear them such a relation in the fancy.

The accessions, which are made to lands bordering upon rivers, follow the land, say the civilians, provided they be made by what they call *alluvion,* that is, insensibly and imperceptibly;

which are circumstances that mightily assist the imagination in the conjunction. Where there is any considerable portion torn at once from one bank, and join'd to another, it becomes not his property, whose land it falls on, till it unite with the land, and till the trees or plants have spread their roots into both. Before that, the imagination does not sufficiently join them.

There are other cases, which somewhat resemble this of accession, but which, at the bottom, are considerably different, and merit our attention. Of this kind is the conjunction of the properties of different persons, after such a manner as not to admit of *separation.* The question is, to whom the united mass must belong.

Where this conjunction is of such a nature as to admit of *division,* but not of *separation,* the decision is natural and easy. The whole mass must be suppos'd to be common betwixt the proprietors of the several parts, and afterwards must be divided according to the proportions of these parts. But here I cannot forbear taking notice of a remarkable subtilty of the *Roman* law, in distinguishing betwixt *confusion* and *commixtion.* Confusion is an union of two bodies, such as different liquors, where the parts become entirely undistinguishable. Commixtion is the blending of two bodies, such as two bushels of corn, where the parts remain separate in an obvious and visible manner. As in the latter case the imagination discovers not so entire an union as in the former, but is able to trace and preserve a distinct idea of each; this is the reason, why the *civil* law, tho' it establish'd an entire community in the case of *confusion,* and after that a proportional division, yet in the case of *commixtion,* supposes each of the proprietors to maintain a distinct right; however necessity may at last force them to submit to the same division.

[But if Titius's grain is mixed with your grain (if in fact this occurs consistently with the consent of you both), it will be joint property because individual bodies, i.e., individual grains, that were the property of each one have been joined consistently with the agreement of you both. But if it is mixed by accident, or if Titius has done it without your consent, it is not consider'd to be joint property because the bodies remain individual in their own essence. But, in these circumstances, the grain would not be joint property any more than a herd is recognized as jointly owned if Titius's cattle were mixed with your cattle. If, however, all the grain should be kept by one or the other of you, a real action is, in fact, appropriate for the amount of each's grain. However, to assess how much grain belonged to each is for the judges to decide—Justinian, *Institutes,* book II, title 1, paragraph 28]

Where the properties of two persons are united after such a manner as neither to admit of *division* nor *separation,* as when one builds a house on another's ground, in that case, the whole must belong to one of the proprietors. And here I assert, that it naturally is conceiv'd to belong to the proprietor of the most considerable part. For however the compound object may have a relation to two different persons, and carry our view at once to are seconded by the influence of *relation*, or the association of ideas, by which we are naturally directed to consider the son after the parent's decease, and ascribe to him a title to his father's possessions. Those goods must become the property of some body: But *of whom* is the question. Here 'tis evident

---

both of them, yet as the most considerable part principally engages our attention, and by the strict union draws the inferior along it; for this reason, the whole bears a relation to the proprietor of that part, and is regarded as his property. The only difficulty is, what we shall be pleas'd to call the most considerable part, and most attractive to the imagination.

This quality depends on several different circumstances, which have little connexion with each other. One part of a compound object may become more considerable than another, either because it is more constant and durable; because it is of greater value; because it is more obvious and remarkable; because it is of greater extent; or because its existence is more separate and independent. 'Twill be easy to conceive, that, as these circumstances may be conjoin'd and oppos'd in all the different ways, and according to all the different degrees, which can be imagin'd, there will result many cases, where the reasons on both sides are so equally ballanc'd, that 'tis impossible for us to give any satisfactory decision. Here then is the proper business of municipal laws, to fix what the principles of human nature have left undetermin'd.

The superficies yields to the soil, says the civil law: The writing to the paper: The canvas to the picture. These decisions do not well agree together, and are a proof of the contrariety of those principles, from which they are deriv'd.

But of all the questions of this kind the most curious is that, which for so many ages divided the disciples of *Proculus* and *Sabinus*. Suppose a person shou'd make a cup from the metal of another, or a ship from his wood, and suppose the proprietor of the metal or wood shou'd demand his goods, the question is, whether he acquires a title to the cup or ship. *Sabinus* maintain'd the affirmative, and asserted that the substance or matter is the foundation of all the qualities; that it is incorruptible and immortal, and therefore superior to the form, which is casual and dependent. On the other hand, *Proculus* observ'd, that the form is the most obvious and remarkable part, and that from it bodies are denominated of this or that particular species. To which he might have added, that the matter or substance is in most bodies so fluctuating and uncertain, that 'tis utterly impossible to trace it in all its changes. For my part, I know not from what principles such a controversy can be certainly determin'd. I shall therefore content my self with observing, that the decision of *Trebonian* seems to me pretty ingenious; that the cup belongs to the proprietor of the metal, because it can be brought back to its first form: But that the ship belongs to the author of its form for a contrary reason. But however ingenious this reason may seem, it plainly depends upon the fancy, which by the possibility of such a reduction, finds a closer connexion and relation betwixt a cup and the proprietor of its metal, than betwixt a ship and the proprietor of its wood, where the substance is more fix'd and unalterable.

the person's children naturally present themselves to the mind; and being already connected to those possessions by means of their deceas'd parent, we are apt to connect them still farther by the relation of property. Of this there are many parallel instances.[6]

Section IV
Of the Transference of Property by Consent

However useful, or even necessary, the stability of possession may be to human society, 'tis attended with very considerable inconveniences. The relation of fitness or suitableness ought never to enter into consideration, in distributing the properties of mankind; but we must govern ourselves by rules, which are more general in their application, and more free from doubt and uncertainty. Of this kind is *present* possession upon the first establishment of society; and afterwards *occupation, prescription, accession,* and *succession.* As these depend very much on chance, they must frequently prove contradictory both to men's wants and desires; and persons and possessions must often be very ill adjusted. This is a grand inconvenience which calls for a remedy. To apply one directly, and allow every man to seize by violence what he judges to be fit for him, wou'd destroy society; and therefore the rules of justice seek some medium betwixt a rigid stability, and this changeable and uncertain adjustment. But there is no medium better than that obvious one, that possession and property shou'd always be stable, except when

---

6. In examining the different titles to authority in government, we shall meet with many reasons to convince us, that the right of succession depends, in a great measure, on the imagination. Mean while I shall rest contented with observing one example, which belongs to the present subject. Suppose that a person die without children, and that a dispute arises among his relations concerning his inheritance; 'tis evident, that if his riches be deriv'd partly from his father, partly from his mother, the most natural way of determining such a dispute, is, to divide his possessions, and assign each part to the family, from whence it is deriv'd. Now as the person is suppos'd to have been once the full and entire proprietor of those goods; I ask, what is it makes us find a certain equity and natural reason in this partition, except it be the imagination? His affection to these families does not depend upon his possessions; for which reason his consent can never be presum'd precisely for such a partition. And as to the public interest, it seems not to be in the least concern'd on the one side or the other.

the proprietor agrees to bestow them on some other person. This rule can have no ill consequence, in occasioning wars and dissentions; since the proprietor's consent, who alone is concern'd, is taken along in the alienation: And it may serve to many good purposes in adjusting property to persons. Different parts of the earth produce different commodities; and not only so, but different men both are by nature fitted for different employments, and attain to greater perfection in any one, when they confine themselves to it alone. All this requires a mutual exchange and commerce; for which reason the translation of property by consent is founded on a law of nature, as well as its stability without such a consent.

So far is determin'd by a plain utility and interest. But perhaps 'tis from more trivial reasons, that *delivery*, or a sensible transference of the object is commonly requir'd by civil laws, and also by the laws of nature, according to most authors, as a requisite circumstance in the translation of property. The property of an object, when taken for something real, without any reference to morality, or the sentiments of the mind, is a quality perfectly insensible, and even inconceivable; nor can we form any distinct notion, either of its stability or translation. This imperfection of our ideas is less sensibly felt with regard to its stability, as it engages less our attention, and is easily past over by the mind, without any scrupulous examination. But as the translation of property from one person to another is a more remarkable event, the defect of our ideas becomes more sensible on that occasion, and obliges us to turn ourselves on every side in search of some remedy. Now as nothing more enlivens any idea than a present impression, and a relation betwixt that impression and the idea; 'tis natural for us to seek some false light from this quarter. In order to aid the imagination in conceiving the transference of property, we take the sensible object, and actually transfer its possession to the person, on whom we wou'd bestow the property. The suppos'd resemblance of the actions, and the presence of this sensible delivery, deceive the mind, and make it fancy, that it conceives the mysterious transition of the property. And that this explication of the matter is just, appears hence, that men have invented a *symbolical* delivery, to satisfy the fancy, where the real one is impracticable. Thus the giving the keys of a granary is understood to be the delivery of the corn contain'd in it: The giving of stone and earth represents the delivery of a mannor. This is a kind of super-stitious practice in civil laws, and in the laws of nature, resembling the *Roman catholic* superstitions in religion. As the *Roman catholics* represent the inconceivable mysteries of the *Christian* religion, and render them more present to the mind, by a taper, or habit, or grimace, which is suppos'd to resemble them; so lawyers and moralists have run into like inventions for the same reason, and have endeavour'd by those means to satisfy themselves concerning the transference of property by consent.

Section V
Of the Obligation of Promises

That the rule of morality, which enjoins the performance of promises, is not *natural*, will sufficiently appear from these two propositions, which I proceed to prove, viz. *that a promise wou'd not be intelligible, before human conventions had establish'd it;* and *that even if it were intelligible, it wou'd not be attended with any moral obligation.*

I say, *first*, that a promise is not intelligible naturally, nor antecedent to human conventions; and that a man, unacquainted with society, could never enter into any engagements with another, even tho' they could perceive each other's thoughts by intuition. If promises be natural and intelligible, there must be some act of the mind attending these words, *I promise;* and on this act of the mind must the obligation depend. Let us, therefore, run over all the faculties of the soul, and see which of them is exerted in our promises.

The act of the mind, exprest by a promise, is not a *resolution* to perform any thing: For that alone never imposes any obligation. Nor is it a *desire* of such a performance: For we may bind ourselves without such a desire, or even with an aversion, declar'd and avow'd. Neither is it the *willing* of that action, which we promise to perform: For a promise always regards some future time, and the will has an influence only on present actions. It follows, therefore, that since the act of the mind, which enters into a promise, and produces its obligation, is neither the resolving, desiring, nor willing any particular performance, it must necessarily be the *willing* of that *obligation,* which arises from the promise. Nor is this only a conclusion of philosophy; but is entirely conformable to our common ways of thinking and of expressing ourselves, when we say that we are bound by our own consent, and that the obligation arises from our mere will and pleasure. The only question, then, is, whether there be not a manifest absurdity in supposing this act of the mind, and such an absurdity as no man cou'd fall into, whose ideas are not confounded by prejudice and the fallacious use of language.

All morality depends upon our sentiments; and when any action, or quality of the mind, pleases us *after a certain manner*, we say it is virtuous; and when the neglect, or non-performance of it, displeases us *after a like manner*, we say that we lie under an obligation to perform it. A change of the obligation supposes a change of the sentiment; and a creation of a new obligation supposes some new sentiment to arise. But 'tis certain we can naturally no more change our own sentiments, than the motions of the heavens; nor by a single act of our will, that is, by a promise, render any action agreeable or disagreeable, moral or immoral; which, without that act, wou'd have produc'd contrary impressions, or have been endow'd with different qualities. It wou'd be absurd, therefore, to will any new obligation, that is, any new sentiment of pain or pleasure; nor is it possible, that men cou'd naturally fall into so gross an absurdity. A promise, therefore, is *naturally* something altogether unintelligible, nor is there any act of the mind belonging to it.[1]

But, *secondly*, if there was any act of the mind belonging to it, it could not *naturally* produce any obligation. This appears evidently from the foregoing reasoning. A promise creates a new obligation. A new obligation supposes new sentiments to arise. The will never creates new sentiments. There could not naturally, therefore, arise any obligation from a promise, even supposing the mind could fall into the absurdity of willing that obligation.

The same truth may be prov'd still more evidently by that reasoning, which prov'd justice in general to be an artificial virtue. No action can be requir'd of us as our duty, unless there be implanted in human nature some actuating passion or motive, capable of producing the action. This motive cannot be the sense of duty. A sense of duty supposes an antecedent obligation: And where an action is not requir'd by any natural passion, it cannot be requir'd by any natural obligation; since it may be omitted without proving any defect or imperfection in the mind and temper, and consequently without any vice. Now 'tis evident we have no motive leading us to the performance of promises, distinct from a sense of duty. If we thought, that promises had no moral obligation, we never shou'd feel any inclination to observe them. This is not the case with the natural virtues. Tho' there was no obligation to relieve the miserable, our humanity wou'd lead us to it; and when we omit that duty, the immorality of the omission arises from its being a proof, that we want the natural sentiments of humanity. A father knows it to be his duty to take care of his children: But he has also a natural inclination to it. And if no human creature had that inclination, no one cou'd lie under any such obligation. But as there is naturally no inclination to observe promises, distinct from a sense of their obligation; it follows, that fidelity is no natural virtue, and that promises have no force, antecedent to human conventions.

If any one dissent from this, he must give a regular proof of these two propositions, viz. *that there is a peculiar act of the mind, annext to promises;* and *that consequent to this act of the mind, there arises an inclination to perform, distinct from a sense of duty.* I presume, that it is impossible to prove either of these two points; and therefore I venture to conclude, that promises are human inventions, founded on the necessities and interests of society.

1. Were morality discoverable by reason, and not by sentiment, 'twou'd be still more evident, that promises cou'd make no alteration upon it. Morality is suppos'd to consist in relation. Every new imposition of morality, therefore, must arise from some new relation of objects; and consequently the will cou'd not produce *immediately* any change in morals, but cou'd have that effect only by producing a change upon the objects. But as the moral obligation of a promise is the pure effect of the will, without the least change in any part of the universe; it follows, that promises have no *natural* obligation.

Shou'd it be said, that this act of the will being in effect a new object, produces new relations and new duties; I wou'd answer, that this is a pure sophism, which may be detected by a very moderate share of accuracy and exactness. To will a new obligation, is to will a new relation of objects; and therefore, if this new relation of objects were form'd by the volition itself, we shou'd in effect will the volition; which is plainly absurd and impossible. The will has here no object to which it cou'd tend; but must return upon itself *in infinitum*. The new obligation depends upon new relations. The new relations depend upon a new volition. The new volition has for object a new obligation, and consequently new relations, and consequently a new volition; which volition again has in view a new obligation, relation, and volition, without any termination. 'Tis impossible, therefore, we cou'd ever will a new obligation; and consequently 'tis impossible the will cou'd ever accompany a promise, or produce a new obligation of morality.

In order to discover these necessities and interests, we must consider the same qualities of human nature, which we have already found to give rise to the preceding laws of society. Men being naturally selfish, or endow'd only with a confin'd generosity, they are not easily induc'd to perform any action for the interest of strangers, except with a view to some reciprocal advantage, which they had no hope of obtaining but by such a performance. Now as it frequently happens, that these mutual performances cannot be finish'd at the same instant, 'tis necessary, that one party be contented to remain in uncertainty, and depend upon the gratitude of the other for a return of kindness. But so much corruption is there among men, that, generally speaking, this becomes but a slender security; and as the benefactor is here suppos'd to bestow his favours with a view to self-interest, this both takes off from the obligation, and sets an example of selfishness, which is the true mother of ingratitude. Were we, therefore, to follow the natural course of our passions and inclinations, we shou'd perform but few actions for the advantage of others, from disinterested views; because we are naturally very limited in our kindness and affection: And we shou'd perform as few of that kind, out of a regard to interest; because we cannot depend upon their gratitude. Here then is the mutual commerce of good offices in a manner lost among mankind, and every one reduc'd to his own skill and industry for his well-being and subsistence. The invention of the law of nature, concerning the *stability* of possession, has already render'd men tolerable to each other; that of the *transference* of property and possession by consent has begun to render them mutually advantageous: But still these laws, however strictly observ'd, are not sufficient to render them so serviceable to each other, as by nature they are fitted to become. Tho' possession be *stable*, men may often reap but small advantage from it, while they are possess'd of a greater quantity of any species of goods than they have occasion for, and at the same time suffer by the want of others. The *transference* of property, which is the proper remedy for this inconvenience, cannot remedy it entirely; because it can only take place with regard to such objects as are *present* and *individual,* but not to such as are *absent* or *general.* One cannot transfer the property of a particular house, twenty leagues distant; because the consent cannot be attended with delivery, which is a requisite circum-

stance. Neither can one transfer the property of ten bushels of corn, or five hogsheads of wine, by the mere expression and consent; because these are only general terms, and have no direct relation to any particular heap of corn, or barrels of wine. Besides, the commerce of mankind is not confin'd to the barter of commodities, but may extend to services and actions, which we may exchange to our mutual interest and advantage. Your corn is ripe to-day; mine will be so to-morrow. 'Tis profitable for us both, that I shou'd labour with you to-day, and that you shou'd aid me to-morrow. I have no kindness for you, and know you have as little for me. I will not, therefore, take any pains upon your account; and should I labour with you upon my own account, in expectation of a return, I know I shou'd be disappointed, and that I shou'd in vain depend upon your gratitude. Here then I leave you to labour alone: You treat me in the same manner. The seasons change; and both of us lose our harvests for want of mutual confidence and security.

All this is the effect of the natural and inherent principles and passions of human nature; and as these passions and principles are inalterable, it may be thought, that our conduct, which depends on them, must be so too, and that 'twou'd be in vain, either for moralists or politicians, to tamper with us, or attempt to change the usual course of our actions, with a view to public interest. And indeed, did the success of their designs depend upon their success in correcting the selfishness and ingratitude of men, they wou'd never make any progress, unless aided by omnipotence, which is alone able to new-mould the human mind, and change its character in such fundamental articles. All they can pretend to, is, to give a new direction to those natural passions, and teach us that we can better satisfy our appetites in an oblique and artificial manner, than by their headlong and impetuous motion. Hence I learn to do a service to another, without bearing him any real kindness; because I forsee, that he will return my service, in expectation of another of the same kind, and in order to maintain the same correspondence of good offices with me or with others. And accordingly, after I have serv'd him, and he is in possession of the advantage arising from my action, he is induc'd to perform his part, as foreseeing the consequences of his refusal.

But tho' this self-interested commerce of men begins to take place, and to predominate in society, it does not entirely abolish the more generous and noble intercourse of friendship and good offices. I may still do services to such persons as I love, and am more particularly acquainted with, without any prospect of advantage; and they may make me a return in the same manner, without any view but that of recompensing my past services. In order, therefore, to distinguish those two different sorts of commerce, the interested and the disinterested, there is a *certain form of words* invented for the former, by which we bind ourselves to the performance of any action. This form of words constitutes what we call a promise, which is the sanction of the interested commerce of mankind. When a man says *he promises any thing*, he in effect expresses a *resolution* of performing it; and along with that, by making use of this *form of words*, subjects himself to the penalty of never being trusted again in case of failure. A resolution is the natural act of the mind, which promises express: But were there no more than a resolution in the case, promises wou'd only declare our former motives, and wou'd not create any new motive or obligation. They are the conventions of men, which create a new motive, when experience has taught us, that human affairs wou'd be conducted much more for mutual advantage, were there certain *symbols* or *signs* instituted, by which we might give each other security of our conduct in any particular incident. After these signs are instituted, whoever uses them is immediately bound by his interest to execute his engagements, and must never expect to be trusted any more, if he refuse to perform what he promis'd.

Nor is that knowledge, which is requisite to make mankind sensible of this interest in the *institution* and *observance* of promises, to be esteem'd superior to the capacity of human nature, however savage and uncultivated. There needs but a very little practice of the world, to make us perceive all these consequences and advantages. The shortest experience of society discovers them to every mortal; and when each individual perceives the same sense of interest in all his fellows, he immediately performs his part of any contract, as being assur'd, that they will not be wanting in theirs. All of them, by concert, enter into a scheme of actions, calculated for common benefit, and agree to be true to their word; nor is there any thing requisite to form this concert or convention, but that every one have a sense of interest in the faithful fulfilling of engagements, and express that sense to other members of the society. This immediately

causes that interest to operate upon them; and interest is the *first* obligation to the performance of promises.

Afterwards a sentiment of morals concurs with interest, and becomes a new obligation upon mankind. This sentiment of morality, in the performance of promises, arises from the same principles as that in the abstinence from the property of others. *Public interest, education*, and *the artifices of politicians*, have the same effect in both cases. The difficulties, that occur to us, in supposing a moral obligation to attend promises, we either surmount or elude. For instance: the expression of a resolution is not commonly suppos'd to be obligatory; and we cannot readily conceive how the making use of a certain form of words shou'd be able to cause any material difference. Here, therefore, we *feign* a new act of the mind, which we call the *willing* an obligation; and on this we suppose the morality to depend. But we have prov'd already, that there is no such act of the mind, and consequently that promises impose no natural obligation.

To confirm this, we may subjoin some other reflexions concerning that will, which is suppos'd to enter into a promise, and to cause its obligation. 'Tis evident, that the will alone is never suppos'd to cause the obligation, but must be express'd by words or signs, in order to impose a tye upon any man. The expression being once brought in as subservient to the will, soon becomes the principal part of the promise; nor will a man be less bound by his word, tho' he secretly give a different direction to his intention, and withhold himself both from a resolution, and from willing an obligation. But tho' the expression makes on most occasions the whole of the promise, yet it does not always so; and one, who shou'd make use of any expression, of which he knows not the meaning, and which he uses without any intention of binding himself, wou'd not certainly be bound by it. Nay, tho' he knows its meaning, yet if he uses it in jest only, and with such signs as shew evidently he has no serious intention of binding himself, he wou'd not lie under any obligation of performance; but 'tis necessary, that the words be a perfect expression of the will, without any contrary signs. Nay, even this we must not carry so far as to imagine, that one, whom, by our quickness of understanding, we conjecture, from certain signs, to have an intention of deceiving us, is not bound by his expression or verbal promise, if we accept of it; but must limit this conclusion to those cases, where the signs are of a different kind from those of deceit. All these contradictions are easily accounted for, if the obligation of promises be merely a human invention for the convenience of society; but will never be explain'd, if it be something *real* and *natural*, arising from any action of the mind or body.

I shall farther observe, that since every new promise imposes a new obligation of morality on the person who promises, and since this new obligation arises from his will, 'tis one of the most mysterious and incomprehensible operations that can possibly be imagin'd, and may even be compar'd to *transubstantiation*, or *holy orders*,[2] where a certain form of words, along with a certain intention, changes entirely the nature of an external object, and even of a human creature. But tho' these mysteries be so far alike, 'tis very remarkable, that they differ widely in other particulars, and that this difference may be regarded as a strong proof of the difference of their origins. As the obligation of promises is an invention for the interest of society, 'tis warp'd into as many different forms as that interest requires, and even runs into direct contradictions, rather than lose sight of its object. But as those other monstrous doctrines are merely priestly inventions, and have no public interest in view, they are less disturb'd in their progress by new obstacles; and it must be own'd, that, after the first absurdity, they follow more directly the current of reason and good sense. Theologians clearly perceiv'd, that the external form of words, being mere sound, require an intention to make them have any efficacy; and that this intention being once consider'd as a requisite circumstance, its absence must equally prevent the effect, whether avow'd or conceal'd, whether sincere or deceitful. Accordingly they have commonly determin'd, that the intention of the priest makes the sacrament, and that when he secretly withdraws his intention, he is highly criminal in himself; but still destroys the baptism, or communion, or holy orders. The terrible consequences of this doctrine were not able to hinder its taking place; as the inconvenience of a similar doctrine, with regard to

promises, have prevented that doctrine from establishing itself. Men are always more concern'd about the present life than the future; and are apt to think the smallest evil, which regards the former, more important than the greatest, which regards the latter.

We may draw the same conclusion, concerning the origin of promises, from the *force*, which is suppos'd to invalidate all contracts, and to free us from their obligation. Such a principle is a proof, that promises have no natural obligation, and are mere artificial contrivances for the convenience and advantage of society. If we consider aright of the matter, force is not essentially different from any other motive of hope or fear, which may induce us to engage our word, and lay ourselves under any obligation. A man, dangerously wounded, who promises a competent sum to a surgeon to cure him, wou'd certainly be bound to performance; tho' the case be not so much different from that of one, who promises a sum to a robber, as to produce so great a difference in our sentiments of morality, if these sentiments were not built entirely on public interest and convenience.

Section VI
Some Farther Reflexions
Concerning Justice and Injustice

We have now run over the three fundamental laws of nature, *that of the stability of possession, of its transference by consent,* and *of the performance of promises.* 'Tis on the strict observance of those three laws, that the peace and security of human society entirely depend; nor is there any possibility of establishing a good correspondence among men, where these are neglected. Society is absolutely necessary for the well-being of men; and these are as necessary to the support of society. Whatever restraint they may impose on the passions of men, they are the real offspring of those passions, and are only a more artful and more refin'd way of satisfying them. Nothing is more vigilant and inventive than our passions; and nothing is more obvious than the convention for the observance of these rules. Nature has, therefore, trusted this affair entirely to the conduct of men, and has not plac'd in the mind any peculiar original principles, to determine us to a set of actions, into which the other principles of our frame and constitution were sufficient to lead us. And to convince us the more fully of this truth we may here stop a moment,

---

2. I mean so far, as holy orders are suppos'd to produce the *indelible character.* In other respects they are only a legal qualification.

and from a review of the preceding reasonings may draw some new arguments, to prove that those laws, however necessary, are entirely artificial, and of human inventions; and consequently that justice is an artificial, and not a natural virtue.

I. The first argument I shall make use of is deriv'd from the vulgar definition of justice. Justice is commonly defin'd to be *a constant and perpetual will of giving every one his due.* In this definition 'tis supposed, that there are such things as right and property, independent of justice, and antecedent to it; and that they wou'd have subsisted, tho' men had never dreamt of practising such a virtue. I have already observ'd, in a cursory manner, the fallacy of this opinion, and shall here continue to open up a little more distinctly my sentiments on that subject.

I shall begin with observing, that this quality, which we call *property,* is like many of the imaginary qualities of the *peripatetic* philosophy, and vanishes upon a more accurate inspection into the subject, when consider'd a-part from our moral sentiments. 'Tis evident property does not consist in any of the sensible qualities of the object. For these may continue invariably the same, while the property changes. Property, therefore, must consist in some relation of the object. But 'tis not in its relation with regard to other external and inanimate objects. For these may also continue invariably the same, while the property changes. This quality, therefore, consists in the relations of objects to intelligent and rational beings. But 'tis not the external and corporeal relation, which forms the essence of property. For that relation may be the same betwixt inanimate objects, or with regard to brute creatures; tho' in those cases it forms no property. 'Tis, therefore, in some internal relation, that the property consists; that is, in some influence, which the external relations of the object have on the mind and actions. Thus the external relation, which we call *occupation* or first possession, is not of itself imagin'd to be the property of the object, but only to cause its property. Now 'tis evident, this external relation causes nothing in external objects, and has only an influence on the mind, by giving us a sense of duty in abstaining from that object, and in restoring it to the first possessor. These actions are properly what we call *justice;* and consequently 'tis on that virtue that the nature of property depends, and not the virtue on the property.

If any one, therefore, wou'd assert, that justice is a natural virtue, and injustice a natural vice, he must assert, that abstracting from the notions of *property,* and *right* and *obligation,* a certain conduct and train of actions, in certain external relations of objects, has naturally a moral beauty or deformity, and causes an original pleasure or uneasiness. Thus the restoring a man's goods to him is consider'd as virtuous, not because nature has annex'd a certain sentiment of pleasure to such a conduct, with regard to the property of others, but because she has annex'd that sentiment to such a conduct, with regard to those external objects, of which others have had the first or long possession, or which they have receiv'd by the consent of those, who have had first or long possession. If nature has given us no such sentiment, there is not, naturally, nor antecedent to human conventions, any such thing as property. Now, tho' it seems sufficiently evident, in this dry and accurate consideration of the present subject, that nature has annex'd no pleasure or sentiment of approbation to such a conduct; yet that I may leave as little room for doubt as possible, I shall subjoin a few more arguments to confirm my opinion.

First, If nature had given us a pleasure of this kind, it wou'd have been as evident and discernible as on every other occasion; nor shou'd we have found any difficulty to perceive, that the consideration of such actions, in such a situation, gives a certain pleasure and a sentiment of approbation. We shou'd not have been oblig'd to have recourse to notions of property in the definition of justice, and at the same time make use of the notions of justice in the definition of property. This deceitful method of reasoning is a plain proof, that there are contain'd in the subject some obscurities and difficulties, which we are not able to surmount, and which we desire to evade by this artifice.

Secondly, Those rules, by which property, right, and obligation are determin'd, have in them no marks of a natural origin, but many of artifice and contrivance. They are too numerous to have proceeded from nature: They are changeable by human laws: And have all of them a direct and evident tendency to public good, and the support of society. This last circumstance is remarkable upon two accounts. *First,* because, tho' the cause of the establishment of these laws had been a *regard* for the public good, as much as the public good is their natural tendency, they wou'd still have been artificial, as being purposely contriv'd and directed to a certain end. *Secondly*, because, if men had been endow'd with such a strong regard for public good, they wou'd never have restrain'd themselves by these rules; so that the laws of justice arise from natural principles in a manner still more oblique and artificial. 'Tis self-love which is their real origin; and as the self-love of one person is naturally contrary to that of another, these several interested passions are oblig'd to adjust themselves after such a manner as to concur in some system of conduct and behaviour. This system, therefore, comprehending the interest of each individual, is of course advantageous to the public; tho' it be not intended for that purpose by the inventors.

II. In the second place we may observe, that all kinds of vice and virtue run insensibly into each other, and may approach by such imperceptible degrees as will make it very difficult, if not absolutely impossible, to determine when the one ends, and the other begins; and from this observation we may derive a new argument for the foregoing principle. For whatever may be the case, with regard to all kinds of vice and virtue, 'tis certain, that rights, and obligations, and property, admit of no such insensible gradation, but that a man either has a full and perfect property, or none at all; and is either entirely oblig'd to perform any action, or lies under no manner of obligation. However civil laws may talk of a perfect *dominion*, and of an imperfect, 'tis easy to observe, that this arises from a fiction, which has no foundation in reason, and can never enter into our notions of natural justice and equity. A man that hires a horse, tho' but for a day, has as full a right to make use of it for that time, as he whom we call its proprietor has to make use of it any other day; and 'tis evident, that however the use may be bounded in time or degree, the right itself is not susceptible of any such gradation, but is absolute and entire, so far as it extends. Accordingly we may observe, that this right both arises and perishes in an instant; and that a man entirely acquires the property of any object by occupation, or the consent of the proprietor; and loses it by his own consent; without any of that insensible gradation, which is remarkable in other qualities and relations. Since, therefore, this is the case with regard to property, and rights, and obligations, I ask, how it stands with regard to justice and injustice? After whatever manner you answer this question, you run into inextricable difficulties. If you reply, that justice and injustice admit of degree, and run insensibly into each other, you expressly contradict the foregoing position, that obligation and property are not susceptible of such a gradation. These depend entirely upon justice and injustice, and follow them in all their variations. Where the justice is entire, the property is also entire: Where the justice is imperfect, the property must also be imperfect. And *vice versa*, if the property admit of no such variations, they must also be incompatible with justice. If you assent, therefore, to this last proposition, and assert, that justice and injustice are not susceptible of degrees, you in effect assert, that they are not *naturally* either vicious or virtuous; since vice and virtue, moral good and evil, and indeed all *natural* qualities, run insensibly into each other, and are, on many occasions, undistinguishable.

And here it may be worth while to observe, that tho' abstract reasoning, and the general maxims of philosophy and law establish this position, *that property, and right, and obligation admit not of degrees*, yet in our common and negligent way of thinking, we find great difficulty to entertain that opinion, and do even *secretly* embrace the contrary principle. An object must either be in the possession of one person or another. An action must either be perform'd or not. The necessity there is of choosing one side in these dilemmas, and the impossibility there often is of finding any just medium, oblige us, when we reflect on the matter, to acknowledge, that all property and obligations are entire. But on the other hand, when we consider the origin of property and obligation, and find that they depend on public utility, and sometimes on the propensities of the imagination, which are seldom entire on any side; we are naturally inclin'd to imagine, that these moral relations admit of an insensible gradation. Hence it is, that in references, where the consent of the parties leave the referees entire masters of the subject, they commonly discover so much equity and justice on both sides, as induces them to strike a medium, and divide the difference betwixt the parties. Civil judges, who have not this liberty, but are oblig'd to give a decisive sentence on some one side, are often at a loss how to determine, and are necessitated to proceed on the most frivolous reasons in the world. Half rights and obligations, which seem so natural in common life, are perfect absurdities in their tribunal; for which reason they are often oblig'd to take half arguments for whole ones, in order to terminate the affair one way or other.

III. The third argument of this kind I shall make use of may be explain'd thus. If we consider the ordinary course of human actions, we shall find, that the mind restrains not itself by any general and universal rules; but acts on most occasions as it is determin'd by its present motives and inclination. As each action is a particular individual event, it must proceed from particular principles, and from our immediate situation within ourselves, and with respect to the rest of the universe. If on some occasions we extend our motives beyond those very circumstances, which gave rise to them, and form something like *general rules* for our conduct, 'tis easy to observe, that these rules are not perfectly inflexible, but allow of many exceptions. Since, therefore, this is the ordinary course of human actions, we may conclude, that the laws of justice, being universal and perfectly inflexible, can never be deriv'd from nature, nor be the immediate offspring of any natural motive or inclination. No action can be either morally good or evil, unless there be some natural passion or motive to impel us to it, or deter us from it; and 'tis evident, that the morality must be susceptible of all the same variations, which are natural to the passion. Here are two persons, who dispute for an estate; of whom one is rich, a fool, and a batchelor; the other poor, a man of sense, and has a numerous family: The first is my enemy: the second my friend. Whether I be actuated in this affair by a view to public or private interest, by friendship or enmity, I must be induc'd to do my utmost to procure the estate to the latter. Nor wou'd any consideration of the right and property of the persons be able to restrain me, were I actuated only by natural motives, without any combination or convention with others. For as all property depends on morality; and as all morality depends on the ordinary course of our passions and actions; and as these again are only directed by particular motives; 'tis evident, such a partial conduct must be suitable to the strictest morality, and cou'd never be a violation of property. Were men, therefore, to take the liberty of acting with regard to the laws of society, as they do in every other affair, they wou'd conduct themselves, on most occasions, by particular judgments, and wou'd take into consideration the characters and circumstances of the persons, as well as the general nature of the question. But 'tis easy to observe, that this

wou'd produce an infinite confusion in human society, and that the avidity and partiality of men wou'd quickly bring disorder into the world, if not restrain'd by some general and inflexible principles. 'Twas, therefore, with a view to this inconvenience, that men have establish'd those principles, and have agreed to restrain themselves by general rules, which are unchangeable by spite and favour, and by particular views of private or public interest. These rules, then, are artificially invented for a certain purpose, and are contrary to the common principles of human nature, which accommodate themselves to circumstances, and have no stated invariable method of operation.

Nor do I perceive how I can easily be mistaken in this matter. I see evidently, that when any man imposes on himself general inflexible rules in his conduct with others, he considers certain objects as their property, which he supposes to be sacred and inviolable. But no proposition can be more evident, than that property is perfectly unintelligible without first supposing justice and injustice; and that these moral qualities are as unintelligible, unless we have motives, independent of the morality, to impel us to just actions, and deter us from unjust ones. Let those motives, therefore, be what they will, they must accommodate themselves to circumstances, and must admit of all the variations, which human affairs, in their incessant revolutions, are susceptible of. They are consequently a very improper foundation for such rigid inflexible rules as the laws of nature; and 'tis evident these laws can only be deriv'd from human conventions, when men have perceiv'd the disorders that result from following their natural and variable principles.

Upon the whole, then, we are to consider this distinction betwixt justice and injustice, as having two different foundations, *viz.* that of *self-interest*, when men observe, that 'tis impossible to live in society without restraining themselves by certain rules; and that of *morality*, when this interest is once observ'd to be common to all mankind, and men receive a pleasure from the view of such actions as tend to the peace of society, and an uneasiness from such as are contrary to it. 'Tis the voluntary convention and artifice of men, which makes the first interest take place; and therefore those laws of justice are so far to be consider'd as *artificial*. After that interest is once establish'd and acknowledg'd, the sense of morality in the observance of these rules follows *naturally*, and of itself; tho' 'tis certain, that it is also augmented by a new *artifice*, and that the public instructions of politicians, and the private education of parents, contribute to the giving us a sense of honour and duty in the strict regulation of our actions with regard to the properties of others.

Section VII
Of the Origin of Government

Nothing is more certain, than that men are, in a great measure, govern'd by interest, and that even when they extend their concern beyond themselves, 'tis not to any great distance; nor is it usual for them, in common life, to look farther than their nearest friends and acquaintance. 'Tis no less certain, that 'tis impossible for men to consult their interest in so effectual a manner, as by an universal and inflexible observance of the rules of justice, by which alone they can preserve society, and keep themselves from falling into that wretched and savage condition, which is commonly represented as the *state of nature*. And as this interest, which all men have in the upholding of society, and the observation of the rules of justice, is great, so is it palpable and evident, even to the most rude and uncultivated of human race; and 'tis almost impossible for any one, who has had experience of society, to be mistaken in this particular. Since, therefore, men are so sincerely attach'd to their interest, and their interest is so much concern'd in the observance of justice, and this interest is so certain and avow'd; it may be ask'd, how any disorder can ever arise in society, and what principle there is in human nature so *powerful* as to overcome so strong a passion, or so *violent* as to obscure so clear a knowledge?

It has been observ'd, in treating of the passions, that men are mightily govern'd by the imagination, and proportion their affections more to the light, under which any object appears to them, than to its real and intrinsic value. What strikes upon them with a strong and lively idea commonly prevails above what lies in a more obscure light; and it must be a great superiority of value, that is able to compensate this advantage. Now as every thing, that is contiguous to us, either in space or time, strikes upon us with such an idea, it has a proportional effect on the will and passions, and commonly operates with more force than any object, that lies in a more distant and obscure light. Tho' we may be fully convinc'd, that the latter object excels the former, we are not able to regulate our actions by this judgment; but yield to the sollicitations of our passions, which always plead in favour of whatever is near and contiguous.

This is the reason why men so often act in contradiction to their known interest; and in particular why they prefer any trivial advantage, that is present, to the maintenance of order in society, which so much depends on the observance of justice. The consequences of every breach of equity seem to lie very remote, and are not able to counterballance any immediate advantage, that may be reap'd from it. They are, however, never the less real for being remote; and as all men are, in some degree, subject to the same weakness, it necessarily happens, that the violations of equity must become very frequent in society, and the commerce of men, by that means, be render'd very dangerous and uncertain. You have the same propension, that I have, in favour of what is contiguous above what is remote. You are, therefore, naturally carried to commit acts of injustice as well as me. Your example both pushes me forward in this way by imitation, and also affords me a new reason for any breach of equity, by shewing me, that I should be the cully of my integrity, if I alone shou'd impose on myself a severe restraint amidst the licentiousness of others.

This quality, therefore, of human nature, not only is very dangerous to society, but also seems, on a cursory view, to be incapable of any remedy. The remedy can only come from the consent of men; and if men be incapable of themselves to prefer remote to contiguous, they will never consent to any thing, which wou'd oblige them to such a choice, and contradict, in so sensible a manner, their natural principles and propensities. Whoever chuses the means, chuses also the end; and if it be impossible for us to prefer what is remote, 'tis equally impossible for us to submit to any necessity, which wou'd oblige us to such a method of acting.

But here 'tis observable, that this infirmity of human nature becomes a remedy to itself, and that the provision we make against our negligence about remote objects, proceeds merely from our natural inclination to that negligence. When we consider any objects at a distance, all their minute distinctions vanish, and we always give the preference to whatever is in itself preferable, without considering its situation and circumstances. This gives rise to what in an improper sense we call *reason*, which is a principle, that is often contradictory to those propensities that display themselves upon the approach of the object. In reflecting on any action, which I am to perform a twelve-month hence, I always resolve to prefer the greater good, whether at that time it will be more contiguous or remote; nor does any difference in that particular make a difference in my present intentions and resolutions. My distance from the final determination makes all those minute differences vanish, nor am I affected by any thing, but the general and more discernable qualities of good and evil. But on my nearer approach, those circumstances, which I at first over-look'd, begin to appear, and have an influence on my conduct and affections. A new inclination to the present good springs up, and makes it difficult for me to adhere inflexibly to my first purpose and resolution. This natural infirmity I may very much regret, and I may endeavour, by all possible means, to free my self from it. I may have recourse to study and reflexion within my self; to the advice of friends; to frequent meditation, and repeated resolution: And having experienc'd how ineffectual all these are, I may embrace with pleasure any other expedient, by which I may impose a restraint upon myself, and guard against this weakness.

The only difficulty, therefore, is to find out this expedient, by which men cure their natural weakness, and lay themselves under the necessity of observing the laws of justice and equity, notwithstanding their violent propension to prefer contiguous to remote. 'Tis evident such a remedy can never be effectual without correcting this propensity; and as 'tis impossible to change or correct any thing material in our nature, the utmost we can do is to change our circumstances and situation, and render the observance of the laws of justice our nearest interest, and their violation our most remote. But this being impracticable with respect to all mankind, it can only take place with respect to a few, whom we thus immediately interest in the execution of justice. These are the persons, whom we call civil magistrates, kings and their ministers, our governors and rulers, who being indifferent persons to the greatest part of the state, have no interest, or but a remote one, in any act of injustice; and being satisfied with their present condition, and with their part in society, have an immediate interest in every execution of justice, which is so necessary to the upholding of society. Here then is the origin of civil government and allegiance. Men are not able radically to cure, either in themselves or others, that narrowness of soul,

which makes them prefer the present to the remote. They cannot change their natures. All they can do is to change their situation, and render the observance of justice the immediate interest of some particular persons, and its violation their more remote. These persons, then, are not only induc'd to observe those rules in their own conduct, but also to constrain others to a like regularity, and inforce the dictates of equity thro' the whole society. And if it be necessary, they may also interest others more immediately in the execution of justice, and create a number of officers, civil and military, to assist them in their government.

But this execution of justice, tho' the principal, is not the only advantage of government. As violent passion hinders men from seeing distinctly the interest they have in an equitable behaviour towards others; so it hinders them from seeing that equity itself, and gives them a remarkable partiality in their own favours. This inconvenience is corrected in the same manner as that above-mention'd. The same persons, who execute the laws of justice, will also decide all controversies concerning them; and being indifferent to the greatest part of the society, will decide them more equitably than every one wou'd in his own case.

By means of these two advantages, in the *execution* and *decision* of justice, men acquire a security against each others' weakness and passion, as well as against their own, and under the shelter of their governors, begin to taste at ease the sweets of society and mutual assistance. But government extends farther its beneficial influence; and not contented to protect men in those conventions they make for their mutual interest, it often obliges them to make such conventions, and forces them to seek their own advantage, by a concurrence in some common end or purpose. There is no quality in human nature, which causes more fatal errors in our conduct, than that which leads us to prefer whatever is present to the distant and remote, and makes us desire objects more according to their situation than their intrinsic value. Two neighbours may agree to drain a meadow, which they possess in common; because 'tis easy for them to know each other's mind; and each must perceive, that the immediate consequence of his failing in his part, is, the abandoning the whole project. But 'tis very difficult, and indeed impossible, that a thousand persons shou'd agree in any such action; it being difficult for them to concert so complicated a design, and still more difficult for them to execute it; while each seeks a pretext to free himself of the trouble and expence, and wou'd lay the whole burden on others. Political society easily remedies both these inconveniences. Magistrates find an immediate interest in the interest of any considerable part of their subjects. They need consult no body but themselves to form any scheme for the promoting of that interest. And as the failure of any one piece in the execution is connected, tho' not immediately, with the failure of the whole, they prevent that failure, because they find no interest in it, either immediate or remote. Thus bridges are built; harbours open'd; ramparts rais'd; canals form'd; fleets equip'd; and armies disciplin'd; every where, by the care of government, which, tho' compos'd of men subject to all human infirmities, becomes, by one of the finest and most subtle inventions imaginable, a composition, that is, in some measure, exempted from all these infirmities.

Section VIII
Of the Source of Allegiance

Though government be an invention very advantageous, and even in some circumstances absolutely necessary to mankind; it is not necessary in all circumstances, nor is it impossible for men to preserve society for some time, without having recourse to such an invention. Men, 'tis true, are always much inclin'd to prefer present interest to distant and remote; nor is it easy for them to resist the temptation of any advantage, that they may immediately enjoy, in apprehension of an evil, that lies at a distance from them: But still this weakness is less conspicuous, where the possessions, and the pleasures of life are few, and of little value, as they always are in the infancy of society. An *Indian* is but little tempted to dispossess another of his hut, or to steal his bow, as being already provided of the same advantages; and as to any superior fortune, which may attend one above another in hunting and fishing, 'tis only casual and temporary, and will have but small tendency to disturb society. And so far am I from thinking with some philosophers, that men are utterly incapable of society without government, that I assert the first rudiments of government to arise from quarrels, not among men of the same society, but among those of different societies. A less degree of riches will suffice to this latter effect, than is requisite for the former. Men fear nothing from public war and violence but the resistance they meet with, which, because they share it in common, seems less terrible; and because it comes from strangers, seems less pernicious in its consequences, than when they are expos'd singly against one whose commerce is advantageous to them, and without whose society 'tis impossible they can subsist. Now foreign war to a society without government necessarily produces civil war. Throw any considerable goods among men, they instantly fall a quarrelling, while each strives to get possession of what pleases him, without regard to the consequences. In a foreign war the most considerable of all goods, life and limbs, are at stake; and as every one shuns dangerous posts, seizes the best arms, seeks excuse for the slightest wounds, the rules of society, which may be well enough observ'd, while men were calm, can now no longer take place, when they are in such commotion.

This we find verified in the *American* tribes, where men live in concord and amity among themselves without any establish'd government; and never pay submission to any of their fellows, except in time of war, when their captain enjoys a shadow of authority, which he loses after their return from the field, and the establishment or peace with the neighbouring tribes. This authority, however, instructs them in the advantages of government, and teaches them to have recourse to it, when either by the pillage of war, by commerce, or by any fortuitous inventions, their riches and possessions have become so considerable as to make them forget, on every emergence, the interest they have in the preservation of peace and justice. Hence we may give a plausible reason, among others, why all governments are at first monarchical, without any mixture and variety; and why republics arise only from the abuses of monarchy and despotic power. Camps are the true mothers of cities; and as war cannot be administred, by reason of the suddenness of every exigency, without some authority in a single person, the same kind of authority naturally takes place in that civil government, which succeeds the military. And this reason I take to be more natural, than the common one deriv'd from patriarchal government, or the authority of a father, which is said first to take place in one family, and to accustom the members of it to the government of a single person. The state of society without government is one of the most natural states of men, and may subsist with the conjunction of many families, and long after the first generation. Nothing but an encrease of riches and possessions cou'd oblige men to quit it; and so barbarous and uninstructed are all societies on their first formation, that many years must elapse before these cou'd encrease to such a degree, as to disturb men in the enjoyment of peace and concord.

But tho' it be possible for men to maintain a small uncultivated society without government, 'tis impossible they shou'd maintain a society of any kind without justice, and the observance of those three fundamental laws concerning the stability of possession, its translation by consent, and the performance of promises. These are, therefore, antecedent to government, and are suppos'd to impose an obligation before the duty of allegiance to civil magistrates has once been thought of. Nay, I shall go farther, and assert, that government, *upon its first establishment,* wou'd naturally be suppos'd to derive its obligation from those laws of nature, and, in particular, from that concerning the performance of promises. When men have once perceiv'd the necessity of government to maintain peace, and execute justice, they wou'd naturally assemble together, wou'd chuse magistrates, determine their power, and *promise* them obedience. As a promise is suppos'd to be a bond or security already in use, and attended with a moral obligation, 'tis to be consider'd as the original sanction of government, and as the source of the first obligation to obedience. This reasoning appears so natural, that it has become the foundation of our fashionable system of politics, and is in a manner the creed of a party amongst us, who value themselves, with reason, on the soundness of their philosophy, and their liberty of thought. *All men,* say they, *are born free and equal: Government and superiority can only be establish'd by consent: The consent of men, in establishing government, imposes on them a new obligation, unknown to the laws of nature. Men, therefore, are bound to obey their magistrates, only because they promise it; and if they had not given their word, either expressly or tacitly, to preserve allegiance, it would never have become a part of their moral duty.* This conclusion, however, when carried so far as to comprehend government in all its ages and situations, is entirely erroneous; and I maintain, that tho' the duty of allegiance be at first grafted on the obligation of promises, and be for some time supported by that obligation, yet it quickly takes root of itself, and has an original obligation and authority, independent of all contracts. This is a principle of moment, which we must examine with care and attention, before we proceed any farther.

'Tis reasonable for those philosophers, who assert justice to be a natural virtue, and antecedent to human conventions, to resolve all civil allegiance into the obligation of a promise, and assert that 'tis our own consent alone, which binds us to any submission to magistracy. For as all government is plainly an invention of men, and the origin of most governments is known in history, 'tis necessary to mount higher, in order to find the source of our political duties, if we wou'd assert them to have any *natural* obligation of morality. These philosophers, therefore, quickly observe, that society is as antient as the human species, and those three fundamental laws of nature as antient as society: So that taking advantage of the antiquity, and obscure origin of these laws, they first deny them to be artificial and voluntary inventions of men, and then seek to ingraft on them those other duties, which are more plainly artificial. But being once undeceiv'd in this particular, and having found that *natural,* as well as *civil* justice, derives its origin from human conventions, we shall quickly perceive, how fruitless it is to resolve the one into the other, and seek, in the laws of nature, a stronger foundation for our political duties than interest, and human conventions; while these laws themselves are built on the very same foundation. On which ever side we turn this subject, we shall find, that these two kinds of duty are exactly on the same footing, and have the same source both of their *first invention* and *moral obligation.* They are contriv'd to remedy like inconveniences, and acquire their moral sanction in the same manner, from their remedying those inconveniences. These are two points, which we shall endeavour to prove as distinctly as possible.

We have already shewn, that men *invented* the three fundamental laws of nature, when they observ'd the necessity of society to their mutual subsistence, and found, that 'twas impossible to maintain any correspondence together, without some restraint on their natural appetites. The same self-love, therefore, which renders men so incommodious to each other, taking a new and more convenient direction, produces the rules of justice, and is the *first* motive of their observance. But when men have observ'd, that tho' the rules of justice be sufficient to maintain any society, yet 'tis impossible for them, of themselves, to observe those rules, in large and polish'd societies; they establish government, as a new invention to attain their ends, and preserve the old, or procure new advantages, by a more strict execution of justice.

So far, therefore, our *civil* duties are connected with our *natural*, that the former are invented chiefly for the sake of the latter; and that the principal object of government is to constrain men to observe the laws of nature. In this respect, however, that law of nature, concerning the performance of promises, is only compriz'd along with the rest; and its exact observance is to be consider'd as an effect of the institution of government, and not the obedience to government as an effect of the obligation of a promise. Tho' the object of our civil duties be the enforcing of our natural, yet the *first*[1] motive of the invention, as well as performance of both, is nothing but self-interest: And since there is a separate interest in the obedience to government, from that in the performance of promises, we must also allow of a separate obligation. To obey the civil magistrate is requisite to preserve order and concord in society. To perform promises is requisite to beget mutual trust and confidence in the common offices of life. The ends, as well as the means, are perfectly distinct; nor is the one subordinate to the other.

To make this more evident, let us consider, that men will often bind themselves by promises to the performance of what it wou'd have been their interest to perform, independent of these promises; as when they wou'd give others a fuller security, by superadding a new obligation of interest to that which they formerly lay under. The interest in the performance of promises, besides its moral obligation, is general, avow'd, and of the last consequence in life. Other interests may be more particular and doubtful; and we are apt to entertain a greater suspicion, that men may indulge their humour, or passion, in acting contrary to them. Here, therefore, promises come naturally in play, and are often requir'd for fuller satisfaction and security. But supposing those other interests to be as general and avow'd as the interest in the performance of a promise, they will be regarded as on the same footing, and men will begin to repose the same confidence in them. Now this is exactly the case with regard to our civil duties, or obedience to the magistrate; without which no government cou'd subsist, nor any peace or order be maintain'd in large societies, where there are so many possessions on the one hand, and so many wants, real or imaginary, on the other. Our civil duties, therefore, must soon

detach themselves from our promises, and acquire a separate force and influence. The interest in both is of the very same kind: 'Tis general, avow'd, and prevails in all times and places. There is, then, no pretext of reason for founding the one upon the other; while each of them has a foundation peculiar to itself. We might as well resolve the obligation to abstain from the possessions of others, into the obligation of a promise, as that of allegiance. The interests are not more distinct in the one case than the other. A regard to property is not more necessary to natural society, than obedience is to civil society or government; nor is the former society more necessary to the being of mankind, than the latter to their well-being and happiness. In short, if the performance of promises be advantageous, so is obedience to government: If the former interest be general, so is the latter: If the one interest be obvious and avow'd, so is the other. And as these two rules are founded on like obligations of interest, each of them must have a peculiar authority, independent of the other.

But 'tis not only the *natural* obligations of interest, which are distinct in promises and allegiance; but also the *moral* obligations of honour and conscience: Nor does the merit or demerit of the one depend in the least upon that of the other. And indeed, if we consider the close connexion there is betwixt the natural and moral obligations, we shall find this conclusion to be entirely unavoidable. Our interest is always engag'd on the side of obedience to magistracy; and there is nothing but a great present advantage, that can lead us to rebellion, by making us over-look the remote interest, which we have in the preserving of peace and order in society. But tho' a present interest may thus blind us with regard to our own actions, it takes not place with regard to those of others; nor hinders them from appearing in their true colours as highly prejudicial to public interest, and to our own in particular. This naturally gives us an uneasiness, in considering such seditious and disloyal actions, and makes us attach to them the idea of vice and moral deformity. 'Tis the same principle, which causes us to disapprove of all kinds of private injustice, and in particular of the breach of promises. We blame all treachery and breach of faith; because we consider, that the freedom and extent of human commerce depend entirely on a fidelity with regard to promises. We blame all disloyalty to magistrates; because we perceive, that the execution of justice, in the stability of possession, its translation by consent, and the perfor-

---

1. First in time, not in dignity or force.

mance of promises, is impossible, without submission to government. As there are here two interests entirely distinct from each other, they must give rise to two moral obligations, equally separate and independent. Tho' there was no such thing as a promise in the world, government wou'd still be necessary in all large and civiliz'd societies; and if promises had only their own proper obligation, without the separate sanction of government, they wou'd have but little efficacy in such societies. This separates the boundaries of our public and private duties, and shews that the latter are more dependant on the former, than the former on the latter. *Education*, and *the artifice of politicians*, concur in bestowing a farther morality on loyalty, and branding all rebellion with a greater degree of guilt and infamy. Nor is it a wonder, that politicians shou'd be very industrious in inculcating such notions, where their interest is so particularly concern'd.

Lest those arguments shou'd not appear entirely conclusive (as I think they are) I shall have recourse to authority, and shall prove, from the universal consent of mankind, that the obligation of submission to government is not deriv'd from any promise of the subjects. Nor need any one wonder, that tho' I have all along endeavour'd to establish my system on pure reason, and have scarce ever cited the judgment even of philosophers or historians on any article, I shou'd now appeal to popular authority, and oppose the sentiments of the rabble to any philosophical reasoning. For it must be observ'd, that the opinions of men, in this case, carry with them a peculiar authority, and are, in a great measure, infallible. The distinction of moral good and evil is founded on the pleasure or pain, which results from the view of any sentiment, or character; and as that pleasure or pain cannot be unknown to the person who feels it, it follows,[2] that there is just so much vice or virtue in any character, as every one places in it, and that 'tis impossible in this particular we can ever be mistaken. And tho' our judgments concerning the *origin* of any vice or

virtue, be not so certain as those concerning their *degrees*; yet, since the question in this case regards not any philosophical origin of an obligation, but a plain matter of fact, 'tis not easily conceiv'd how we can fall into an error. A man, who acknowledges himself to be bound to another, for a certain sum, must certainly know whether it be by his own bond, or that of his father; whether it be of his mere good-will, or for money lent him; and under what conditions, and for what purposes he has bound himself. In like manner, it being certain, that there is a moral obligation to submit to government, because every one thinks so; it must be as certain, that this obligation arises not from a promise; since no one, whose judgment has not been led astray by too strict adherence to a system of philosophy, has ever yet dreamt of ascribing it to that origin. Neither magistrates nor subjects have form'd this idea of our civil duties.

We find, that magistrates are so far from deriving their authority, and the obligation to obedience in their subjects, from the foundation of a promise or original contract, that they conceal, as far as possible, from their people, especially from the vulgar, that they have their origin from thence. Were this the sanction of government, our rulers wou'd never receive it tacitly, which is the utmost that can be pretended; since what is given tacitly and insensibly can never have such influence on mankind, as what is perform'd expressly and openly. A tacit promise is, where the will is signified by other more diffuse signs than those of speech; but a will there must certainly be in the case, and that can never escape the person's notice, who exerted it, however silent or tacit. But were you to ask the far greatest part of the nation, whether they had ever consented to the authority of their rulers, or promis'd to obey them, they wou'd be inclin'd to think very strangely of you; and wou'd certainly reply, that the affair depended not on their consent, but that they were born to such an obedience. In consequence of this opinion, we frequently see them imagine such persons to be their natural rulers, as are at that time depriv'd of all power and authority, and whom no man, however foolish, wou'd voluntarily chuse; and this merely because they are in that line, which rul'd before, and in that degree of it, which us'd to succeed; tho' perhaps in so distant a period, that scarce any man alive cou'd ever have given any promise of obedience. Has a government, then, no authority over such as these, because they never consented to it, and wou'd esteem the very attempt of such a free choice a

---

2. This proposition must hold strictly true, with regard to every quality, that is determin'd merely by sentiment. In what sense we can talk either of a *right* or a *wrong* taste in morals, eloquence, or beauty, shall be consider'd afterwards. In the mean time, it may be observ'd, that there is such an uniformity in the *general* sentiments of mankind, as to render such questions of but small importance.

piece of arrogance and impiety? We find by experience, that it punishes them very freely for what it calls treason and rebellion, which, it seems, according to this system, reduces itself to common injustice. If you say, that by dwelling in its dominions, they in effect consented to the establish'd government; I answer, that this can only be, where they think the affair depends on their choice, which few or none, beside those philosophers, have ever yet imagin'd. It never was pleaded as an excuse for a rebel, that the first act he perform'd, after he came to years of discretion, was to levy war against the sovereign of the state; and that while he was a child he cou'd not bind himself by his own consent, and having become a man, show'd plainly, by the first act he perform'd, that he had no design to impose on himself any obligation to obedience. We find, on the contrary, that civil laws punish this crime at the same age as any other, which is criminal, of itself, without our consent; that is, when the person is come to the full use of reason: Whereas to this crime they ought in justice to allow some intermediate time, in which a tacit consent at least might be suppos'd. To which we may add, that a man living under an absolute government, wou'd owe it no allegiance; since, by its very nature, it depends not on consent. But as that is as *natural* and *common* a government as any, it must certainly occasion some obligation; and 'tis plain from experience, that men, who are subjected to it, do always think so. This is a clear proof, that we do not commonly esteem our allegiance to be deriv'd from our consent or promise; and a farther proof is, that when our promise is upon any account expressly engag'd, we always distinguish exactly betwixt the two obligations, and believe the one to add more force to the other, than in a repetition of the same promise. Where no promise is given, a man looks not on his faith as broken in private matters, upon account of rebellion; but keeps those two duties of honour and allegiance perfectly distinct and separate. As the uniting of them was thought by these philosophers a very subtile invention, this is a convincing proof, that 'tis not a true one; since no man can either give a promise, or be restrain'd by its sanction and obligation unknown to himself.

Section IX
Of the Measures of Allegiance

Those political writers, who have had recourse to a promise, or original contract, as the source of our allegiance to government, intended to establish a principle, which is perfectly just and reasonable; tho' the reasoning, upon which they endeavour'd to establish it, was fallacious and sophistical. They wou'd prove, that our submission to government admits of exceptions, and that an egregious tyranny in the rulers is sufficient to free the subjects from all ties of allegiance. Since men enter into society, say they, and submit themselves to government, by their free and voluntary consent, they must have in view certain advantages, which they propose to reap from it, and for which they are contented to resign their native liberty. There is, therefore, something mutual engag'd on the part of the magistrate, *viz.* protection and security; and 'tis only by the hopes he affords of these advantages, that he can ever persuade men to submit to him. But when instead of protection and security, they meet with tyranny and oppression, they are free'd from their promises, (as happens in all conditional contracts) and return to that state of liberty, which preceded the institution of government. Men wou'd never be so foolish as to enter into such engagements as shou'd turn entirely to the advantage of others, without any view of bettering their own condition. Whoever proposes to draw any profit from our submission, must engage himself, either expressly or tacitly, to make us reap some advantage from his authority; nor ought he to expect, that without the performance of his part we will ever continue in obedience.

I repeat it: This conclusion is just, tho' the principles be erroneous; and I flatter myself, that I can establish the same conclusion on more reasonable principles. I shall not take such a compass, in establishing our political duties, as to assert, that men perceive the advantages of government; that they institute government with a view to those advantages; that this institution requires a promise of obedience; which imposes a moral obligation to a certain degree, but being conditional, ceases to be binding, whenever the other contracting party performs not his part of the engagement. I perceive, that a promise itself arises entirely from human conventions, and is invented with a view to a certain interest. I seek, therefore, some such interest more immediately connected with government, and which may be at once the original motive to its institution, and the source of our obedience to it. This interest I find to consist in the security and protection, which we enjoy in political society, and which we can never attain, when perfectly free and independent. As interest, therefore, is the immediate sanction of government the one can have no longer being than the other; and whenever the civil magistrate carries his oppression so far as to render his authority perfectly intolerable, we are no longer bound to submit to it. The cause ceases; the effect must cease also.

So far the conclusion is immediate and direct, concerning the *natural* obligation which we have to allegiance. As to the *moral* obligation, we may observe, that the maxim wou'd here be false, that *when the cause ceases, the effect must cease also*. For there is a principle of human nature, which we have frequently taken notice of, that men are mightily addicted to *general rules*, and that we often carry our maxims beyond those reasons, which first induc'd us to establish them. Where cases are similar in many circumstances, we are apt to put them on the same footing, without considering, that they differ in the most material circumstances, and that the resemblance is more apparent than real. It may, therefore, be thought, that in the case of allegiance our moral obligation of duty will not cease, even tho' the natural obligation of interest, which is its cause, has ceas'd; and that men may be bound by *conscience* to submit to a tyrannical government against their own and the public interest. And indeed, to the force of this argument I so far submit, as to acknowledge, that general rules commonly extend beyond the principles, on which they are founded; and that we seldom make any exception to them, unless that exception have the qualities of a general rule, and be founded on very numerous and common instances. Now this I assert to be entirely the present case. When men submit to the authority of others, 'tis to procure themselves some security against the wickedness and injustice of men, who are perpetually carried, by their unruly passions, and by their present and immediate interest, to the violation of all the laws of society. But as this imperfection is inherent in human nature, we know that it must attend men in all their states and conditions; and that those, whom we chuse for rulers, do not immediately become of a superior nature to the rest of mankind, upon account of their superior power and authority. What we expect from them depends not on a change of their nature but of their situation, when they acquire a more immediate interest in the preservation of order and the execution of justice. But besides that this interest is only more immediate in the execution of justice among their subjects; besides this, I say, we

may often expect, from the irregularity of human nature, that they will neglect even this immediate interest, and be transported by their passions into all the excesses of cruelty and ambition. Our general knowledge of human nature, our observation of the past history of mankind, our experience of present times; all these causes must induce us to open the door to exceptions, and must make us conclude, that we may resist the more violent effects of supreme power, without any crime or injustice.

Accordingly we may observe, that this is both the general practice and principle of mankind, and that no nation, that cou'd find any remedy, ever yet suffer'd the cruel ravages of a tyrant, or were blam'd for their resistance. Those who took up arms against *Dionysius* or *Nero*, or *Philip the second*, have the favour of every reader in the perusal of their history; and nothing but the most violent perversion of common sense can ever lead us to condemn them. 'Tis certain, therefore, that in all our notions of morals we never entertain such an absurdity as that of passive obedience, but make allowances for resistance in the more flagrant instances of tyranny and oppression. The general opinion of mankind has some authority in all cases; but in this of morals 'tis perfectly infallible. Nor is it less infallible, because men cannot distinctly explain the principles, on which it is founded. Few persons can carry on this train of reasoning: "Government is a mere human invention for the interest of society. Where the tyranny of the governor removes this interest, it also removes the natural obligation to obedience. The moral obligation is founded on the natural, and therefore must cease where *that* ceases; especially where the subject is such as makes us foresee very many occasions wherein the natural obligation may cease, and causes us to form a kind of general rule for the regulation of our conduct in such occurrences." But tho' this train of reasoning be too subtile for the vulgar, 'tis certain, that all men have an implicit notion of it, and are sensible, that they owe obedience to government merely on account of the public interest; and at the same time, that human nature is so subject to frailties and passions, as may easily pervert this institution, and change their governors into tyrants and public enemies. If the sense of interest were not our original motive to obedience, I wou'd fain ask, what other principle is there in human nature capable of subduing the natural ambition of men, and forcing them to such a submission? Imitation and custom are not sufficient. For the question still recurs, what motive first produces those instances of submission, which we imitate, and that train of actions, which produces the custom? There evidently is no other principle than interest; and if interest first produces obedience to government, the obligation to obedience must cease, whenever the interest ceases, in any great degree, and in a considerable number of instances.

Section X
Of the Objects of Allegiance

But tho', on some occasions, it may be justifiable, both in sound politics and morality, to resist supreme power, 'tis certain, that in the ordinary course of human affairs nothing can be more pernicious and criminal; and that besides the convulsions, which always attend revolutions, such a practice tends directly to the subversion of all government, and the causing an universal anarchy and confusion among mankind. As numerous and civiliz'd societies cannot subsist without government, so government is entirely useless without an exact obedience. We ought always to weigh the advantages, which we reap from authority, against the disadvantages; and by this means we shall become more scrupulous of putting in practice the doctrine of resistance. The common rule requires submission; and 'tis only in cases of grievous tyranny and oppression, that the exception can take place.

Since then such a blind submission is commonly due to magistracy, the next question is, *to whom it is due, and whom we are to regard as our lawful magistrates?* In order to answer this question, let us recollect what we have already establish'd concerning the origin of government and political society. When men have once experienc'd the impossibility of preserving any steady order in society, while every one is his own master, and violates or observes the laws of society, according to his present interest or pleasure, they naturally run into the invention of government, and put it out of their own power, as far as possible, to transgress the laws of society. Government, therefore, arises from the voluntary convention of men; and 'tis evident, that the same convention, which establishes government, will also determine the persons who are to govern, and will remove all doubt and ambiguity in this particular. And the voluntary consent of men must here have the greater efficacy, that

the authority of the magistrate does *at first* stand upon the foundation of a promise of the subjects, by which they bind themselves to obedience; as in every other contract or engagement. The same promise, then, which binds them to obedience, ties them down to a particular person, and makes him the object of their allegiance.

But when government has been establish'd on this footing for some considerable time, and the separate interest, which we have in submission, has produc'd a separate sentiment of morality, the case is entirely alter'd, and a promise is no longer able to determine the particular magistrate; since it is no longer consider'd as the foundation of government. We naturally suppose ourselves born to submission; and imagine, that such particular persons have a right to command, as we on our part are bound to obey. These notions of right and obligation are deriv'd from nothing but the *advantage* reapt from government, which gives us a repugnance to practise resistance ourselves, and makes us displeas'd with any instance of it in others. But here 'tis remarkable, that in this new state of affairs, the original sanction of government, which is *interest*, is not admitted to determine the persons, whom we are to obey, as the original sanction did at first, when affairs were on the footing of a *promise*. A *promise* fixes and determines the persons, without any uncertainty: But 'tis evident, that if men were to regulate their conduct in this particular, by the view of a peculiar *interest*, either public or private, they wou'd involve themselves in endless confusion, and wou'd render all government, in a great measure, ineffectual. The private interest of every one is different; and tho' the public interest in itself be always one and the same, yet it becomes the source of as great dissentions, by reason of the different opinions of particular persons concerning it. The same interest, therefore, which causes us to submit to magistracy, makes us renounce itself in the choice of our magistrates, and binds us down to a certain form of government, and to particular persons, without allowing us to aspire to the utmost perfection in either. The case is here the same as in that law of nature concerning the stability of possession. 'Tis highly advantageous, and even absolutely necessary to society, that possession shou'd be stable; and this leads us to the establishment of such a rule: But we find, that were we to follow the same advantage, in assigning particular possessions to particular persons, we shou'd disappoint our end, and perpetuate the confusion, which that rule is intended to prevent. We must, therefore, proceed by general rules, and regulate ourselves by general interests, in modifying the law of nature concerning the stability of possession. Nor need we fear, that our attachment to this law will diminish upon account of the seeming frivolousness of those interests, by which it is determin'd. The impulse of the mind is deriv'd from a very strong interest; and those other more minute interests serve only to direct the motion, without adding any thing to it, or diminishing from it. 'Tis the same case with government. Nothing is more advantageous to society than such an invention; and this interest is sufficient to make us embrace it with ardour and alacrity; tho' we are oblig'd afterwards to regulate and direct our devotion to government by several considerations, which are not of the same importance, and to chuse our magistrates without having in view any particular advantage from the choice.

The *first* of those principles I shall take notice of, as a foundation of the right of magistracy, is that which gives authority to almost all the establish'd governments of the world: I mean, *long possession* in any one form of government, or succession of princes. 'Tis certain, that if we remount to the first origin of every nation, we shall find, that there scarce is any race of kings, or form of a commonwealth, that is not primarily founded on usurpation and rebellion, and whose title is not at first worse than doubtful and uncertain. Time alone gives solidity to their right; and operating gradually on the minds of men, reconciles them to any authority, and makes it seem just and reasonable. Nothing causes any sentiment to have a greater influence upon us than custom, or turns our imagination more strongly to any object. When we have been long accustom'd to obey any set of men, that general instinct or tendency, which we have to suppose a moral obligation attending loyalty, takes easily this direction, and chuses that set of men for its objects. 'Tis interest which gives the general instinct; but 'tis custom which gives the particular direction.

And here 'tis observable, that the same length of time has a different influence on our sentiments of morality, according to its different influence on the mind. We naturally judge of every thing by comparison; and since in considering the fate of kingdoms and republics, we embrace a long extent of time, a small duration has not in this case a like influence on our sentiments, as when we consider any other object. One thinks he acquires a right to a horse, or a

suit of cloaths, in a very short time; but a century is scarce sufficient to establish any new government, or remove all scruples in the minds of the subjects concerning it. Add to this, that a shorter period of time will suffice to give a prince a title to any additional power he may usurp, than will serve to fix his right, where the whole is an usurpation. The kings of *France* have not been possess'd of absolute power for above two reigns; and yet nothing will appear more extravagant to *Frenchmen* than to talk of their liberties. If we consider what has been said concerning *accession*, we shall easily account for this phænomenon.

When there is no form of government establish'd by *long* possession, the *present* possession is sufficient to supply its place, and may be regarded as the *second* source of all public authority. Right to authority is nothing but the constant possession of authority, maintain'd by the laws of society and the interests of mankind; and nothing can be more natural than to join this constant possession to the present one, according to the principles above-mention'd. If the same principles did not take place with regard to the property of private persons, 'twas because these principles were counter-ballanc'd by very strong considerations of interest; when we observ'd, that all restitution wou'd by that means be prevented, and every violence be authoriz'd and protected. And tho' the same motives may seem to have force, with regard to public authority, yet they are oppos'd by a contrary interest; which consists in the preservation of peace, and the avoiding of all changes, which, however they may be easily produc'd in private affairs, are unavoidably attended with bloodshed and confusion, where the public is interested.

Any one, who finding the impossibility of accounting for the right of the present possessor, by any receiv'd system of ethics, shou'd resolve to deny absolutely that right, and assert, that it is not authoriz'd by morality, wou'd be justly thought to maintain a very extravagant paradox, and to shock the common sense and judgment of mankind. No maxim is more conformable, both to prudence and morals, than to submit quietly to the government, which we find establish'd in the country where we happen to live, without enquiring too curiously into its origin and first establishment. Few governments will bear being examin'd so rigorously. How many kingdoms are there at present in the world, and how many more do we find in history, whose governors have no better foundation for their authority than that of present possession? To confine ourselves to the *Roman* and *Grecian* empire; is it not evident, that the long succession of emperors, from the dissolution of the *Roman* liberty, to the final extinction of that empire by the *Turks*, cou'd not so much as pretend to any other title to the empire? The election of the senate was a mere form, which always follow'd the choice of the legions; and these were almost always divided in the different provinces, and nothing but the sword was able to terminate the difference. 'Twas by the sword, therefore, that every emperor acquir'd, as well as defended his right; and we must either say, that all the known world, for so many ages, had no government, and ow'd no allegiance to any one, or must allow, that the right of the stronger, in public affairs, is to be receiv'd as legitimate, and authoriz'd by morality, when not oppos'd by any other title.

The right of *conquest* may be consider'd as a *third* source of the title of sovereigns. This right resembles very much that of present possession; but has rather a superior force, being seconded by the notions of glory and honour, which we ascribe to *conquerors*, instead of the sentiments of hatred and detestation, which attend *usurpers*. Men naturally favour those they love; and therefore are more apt to ascribe a right to successful violence, betwixt one sovereign and another, than to the successful rebellion of a subject against his sovereign.[1]

When neither long possession, nor present possession, nor conquest take place, as when the first sovereign, who founded any monarchy, dies; in that case, the right of *succession* naturally prevails in their stead, and men are commonly induc'd to place the son of their late monarch on the throne, and suppose him to inherit his father's authority. The presum'd consent of the father, the imitation of the succession to private families, the interest, which the state has in chusing the person, who is most powerful, and has the most numerous followers; all these reasons lead men to prefer the son of their late monarch to any other person.[2]

These reasons have some weight; but I am persuaded, that to one, who considers impartially of the matter, 'twill appear, that some principles of the imagination concur with those views of justice and interest. The royal authority seems to be connected with the young prince even in his father's life-time, by the natural transition of the thought; and still more after his death: So that nothing is more natural than to compleat this union by a new relation, and by putting him actually in possession of what seems so naturally to belong to him.

To confirm this we may weigh the following phænomena, which are pretty curious in their kind. In elective monarchies the right of succession has no place by the laws and settled custom; and yet its influence is so natural, that 'tis impossible entirely to exclude it from the imagination, and render the subjects indifferent to the son of their deceas'd monarch. Hence in some governments of this kind, the choice commonly falls on one or other of the royal family; and in some governments they are all excluded. Those contrary phænomena proceed from the same principle. Where the royal family is excluded, 'tis from a refinement in politics, which makes people sensible of their propensity to chuse a sovereign in that family, and gives them a jealousy of their liberty, lest their new monarch, aided by this propensity, shou'd establish his family, and destroy the freedom of elections for the future.

The history of *Artaxerxes*, and the younger *Cyrus*, may furnish us with some reflections to the same purpose. *Cyrus* pretended a right to the throne above his elder brother, because he was born after his father's accession. I do not pretend, that this reason was valid. I wou'd only infer from it, that he wou'd never have made use of such a pretext, were it not for the qualities of the imagination above-mention'd, by which we are naturally inclin'd to unite by a new relation whatever objects we find already united. *Artaxerxes* had an advantage above his brother, as being the eldest son, and the first in succession: But *Cyrus*

---

1. It is not here asserted, that *present possession* or *conquest* are sufficient to give a title against *long possession* and *positive laws*: But only that they have some force, and will be able to cast the ballance where the titles are otherwise equal, and will even be sufficient *sometimes* to sanctify the weaker title. What degree of force they have is difficult to determine. I believe all moderate men will allow, that they have great force in all disputes concerning the rights of princes.

---

2. To prevent mistakes I must observe, that this case of succession is not the same with that of hereditary monarchies, where custom has fix'd the right of succession. These depend upon the principle of long possession above explain'd.

was more closely related to the royal authority, as being begot after his father was invested with it.

Shou'd it here be pretended, that the view of convenience may be the source of all the right of succession, and that men gladly take advantage of any rule, by which they can fix the successor of their late sovereign, and prevent that anarchy and confusion, which attends all new elections: To this I wou'd answer, that perhaps this motive may contribute somewhat to the effect; but that without another principle, 'tis impossible such a motive shou'd take place. The interest of a nation requires, that the succession to the crown shou'd be fix'd one way or other; but 'tis the same thing to its interest in what way it be fix'd: So that if the relation of blood had not an effect independent of public interest, it wou'd never have been regarded, without a positive law; and 'twou'd have been impossible, that so many positive laws of different nations cou'd ever have concur'd precisely in the same views and intentions.

This leads us to consider the *fifth* source of authority, viz. *positive laws;* when the legislature establishes a certain form of government and succession of princes. At first sight it may be thought, that this must resolve into some of the preceding titles of authority. The legislative power, whence the positive law is deriv'd, must either be establish'd by original contract, long possession, present possession, conquest, or succession; and consequently the positive law must derive its force from some of those principles. But here 'tis remarkable, that tho' a positive law can only derive its force from these principles, yet it acquires not all the force of the principle from whence it is deriv'd, but loses considerably in the transition; as it is natural to imagine. For instance; a government is establish'd for many centuries on a certain system of laws, forms, and methods of succession. The legislative power, establish'd by this long succession, changes all on a sudden the whole system of government, and introduces a new constitution in its stead. I believe few of the subjects will think themselves bound to comply with this alteration, unless it have an evident tendency to the public good: But will think themselves still at liberty to return to the antient government. Hence the notion of *fundamental laws;* which are suppos'd to be inalterable by the will of the sovereign: And of this nature the *Salic* law is understood to be in *France.* How far these fundamental laws extend is not determin'd in any government; nor is it possible it ever shou'd. There is such

an insensible gradation from the most material laws to the most trivial, and from the most antient laws to the most modern, that 'twill be impossible to set bounds to the legislative power, and determine how far it may innovate in the principles of government. That is the work more of imagination and passion than of reason.

Whoever considers the history of the several nations of the world; their revolutions, conquests, increase, and diminution; the manner in which their particular governments are establish'd, and the successive right transmitted from one person to another, will soon learn to treat very lightly all disputes concerning the rights of princes, and will be convinc'd, that a strict adherence to any general rules, and the rigid loyalty to particular persons and families, on which some people set so high a value, are virtues that hold less of reason, than of bigotry and superstition. In this particular, the study of history confirms the reasonings of true philosophy; which, shewing us the original qualities of human nature, teaches us to regard the controversies in politics as incapable of any decision in most cases, and as entirely subordinate to the interests of peace and liberty. Where the public good does not evidently demand a change; 'tis certain, that the concurrence of all those titles, *original contract, long possession, present possession, succession,* and *positive laws,* forms the strongest title to sovereignty, and is justly regarded as sacred and inviolable. But when these titles are mingled and oppos'd in different degrees, they often occasion perplexity; and are less capable of solution from the arguments of lawyers and philosophers, than from the swords of the soldiery. Who shall tell me, for instance, whether *Germanicus* or *Drusus,* ought to have succeeded *Tiberius,* had he died while they were both alive, without naming any of them for his successor? Ought the right of adoption to be receiv'd as equivalent to that of blood in a nation, where it had the same effect in private families, and had already, in two instances, taken place in the public? Ought *Germanicus* to be esteem'd the eldest son, because he was born before *Drusus;* or the younger, because he was adopted after the birth of his brother? Ought the right of the elder to be regarded in a nation, where the eldest brother had no advantage in the succession to private families? Ought the *Roman* empire at that time to be esteem'd hereditary, because of two examples; or ought it, even so early, to be regarded as belonging to the stronger, or the present possessor, as being founded on so recent an usurpation? Upon whatever principles we may pretend to answer these and such like questions, I am afraid we shall never be able to satisfy an impartial enquirer, who adopts no party in political controversies, and will be satisfied with nothing but sound reason and philosophy.

But here an *English* reader will be apt to enquire concerning that famous *revolution*, which has had such a happy influence on our constitution, and has been attended with such mighty consequences. We have already remark'd, that in the case of enormous tyranny and oppression, 'tis lawful to take arms even against supreme power; and that as government is a mere human invention for mutual advantage and security, it no longer imposes any obligation, either natural or moral, when once it ceases to have that tendency. But tho' this *general* principle be authoriz'd by common sense, and the practice of all ages, 'tis certainly impossible for the laws, or even for philosophy, to establish any *particular* rules, by which we may know when resistance is lawful; and decide all controversies, which may arise on that subject. This may not only happen with regard to supreme power; but 'tis possible, even in some constitutions, where the legislative authority is not lodg'd in one person, that there may be a magistrate so eminent and powerful, as to oblige the laws to keep silence in this particular. Nor wou'd this silence be an effect only of their *respect*, but also of their *prudence;* since 'tis certain, that in the vast variety of circumstances, which occur in all governments, an exercise of power, in so great a magistrate, may at one time be beneficial to the public, which at another time wou'd be pernicious and tyrannical. But notwithstanding this silence of the laws in limited monarchies, 'tis certain, that the people still retain the right of resistance; since 'tis impossible, even in the most despotic governments, to deprive them of it. The same necessity of self-preservation, and the same motive of public good, give them the same liberty in the one case as in the other. And we may farther observe, that in such mix'd governments, the cases, wherein resistance is lawful, must occur much oftener, and greater indulgence be given to the subjects to defend themselves by force of arms, than in arbitrary governments. Not only where the chief magistrate enters into measures, in themselves, extremely pernicious to the public, but even when he wou'd encroach on the other parts of the constitution, and extend his power beyond the legal bounds, it is allowable to resist and dethrone him; tho' such resistance and violence may, in the general tenor of the laws, be deem'd unlawful and rebellious. For besides that nothing is more essential to public interest, than the preservation of public liberty; 'tis evident, that if such a mix'd government be once suppos'd to be establish'd, every part or member of the constitution must have a right of self-defence, and of maintaining its antient bounds against the encroachment of every other authority. As matter wou'd have been created in vain, were it depriv'd of a power of resistance, without which no part of it cou'd preserve a distinct existence, and the whole might be crowded up into a single point: So 'tis a gross absurdity to suppose, in any government, a right without a remedy, or allow, that the supreme power is shar'd with the people, without allowing, that 'tis lawful for them to defend their share against every invader. Those, therefore, who wou'd seem to respect our free government, and yet deny the right of resistance, have renounc'd all pretensions to common sense, and do not merit a serious answer.

It does not belong to my present purpose to shew, that these general principles are applicable to the late *revolution;* and that all the rights and privileges, which ought to be sacred to a free nation, were at that time threaten'd with the utmost danger. I am better pleas'd to leave this controverted subject, if it really admits of controversy; and to indulge myself in some philosophical reflections, which naturally arise from that important event.

First, We may observe, that shou'd the *lords* and *commons* in our constitution, without any reason from public interest, either depose the king in being, or after his death exclude the prince, who, by laws and settled custom, ought to succeed, no one wou'd esteem their proceedings legal, or think themselves bound to comply with them. But shou'd the king, by his unjust practices, or his attempts for a tyrannical and despotic power, justly forfeit his legal, it then not only becomes morally lawful and suitable to the nature of political society to dethrone him; but what is more, we are apt likewise to think, that the remaining members of the constitution acquire a right of excluding his next heir, and of chusing whom they please for his successor. This is founded on a very singular quality of our thought and imagination. When a king forfeits his authority, his heir ought naturally to remain in the same situation, as if the king were remov'd by death; unless by mixing himself in the tyranny, he forfeit it for himself. But tho' this may seem reasonable, we easily comply with the contrary opinion. The deposition of a king, in such a government as ours, is certainly an act beyond all common authority, and an illegal assuming a power for public good, which, in the ordinary course of government, can belong to no member of the constitution. When the public good is so great and so evident as to justify the action, the commendable use of this licence causes us naturally to attribute to the *parliament* a right of using farther licences; and the antient bounds of the laws being once transgressed with approbation, we are not apt to be so strict in confining ourselves precisely within their limits. The mind naturally runs on with any train of action, which it has begun; nor do we commonly make any scruple concerning our duty, after the first action of any kind, which we perform. Thus at the *revolution*, none who thought the deposition of the father justifiable, esteem'd themselves to be confin'd to his infant son; tho' had that unhappy monarch died innocent at that time, and had his son, by any accident, been convey'd beyond seas, there is no doubt but a regency wou'd have been appointed till he shou'd come to age, and cou'd be restor'd to his dominions. As the slightest properties of the imagination have an effect on the judgments of the people, it shews the wisdom of the laws and of the parliament to take advantage of such properties, and to chuse the magistrates either in or out of a line, according as the vulgar will most naturally attribute authority and right to them.

Secondly, Tho' the accession of the *Prince* of *Orange* to the throne might at first give occasion to many disputes, and his title be contested, it ought not now to appear doubtful, but must have acquir'd a sufficient authority from those three princes, who have succeeded him upon the same title. Nothing is more usual, tho' nothing may, at first sight, appear more unreasonable, than this way of thinking. Princes often *seem* to acquire a right from their successors, as well as from their ancestors; and a king, who during his life-time might justly be deem'd an usurper, will be regarded by posterity as a lawful prince, because he has had the good fortune to settle his family on the throne, and entirely change the antient form of government. *Julius Cæsar* is regarded as the first *Roman* emperor; while *Sylla* and *Marius*, whose titles were really the same as his, are treated as tyrants and usurpers. Time and custom give authority to all forms of government, and all successions of princes; and that power, which at first was founded only on injustice and violence, becomes in time legal and obligatory. Nor does the mind rest there; but returning back upon its footsteps, transfers to their predecessors and ancestors that right, which it naturally ascribes to the posterity, as being related together, and united in the imagination. The present *king* of *France* makes *Hugh Capet* a more lawful prince than *Cromwell*; as the establish'd liberty of the *Dutch* is no inconsiderable apology for their obstinate resistance to *Philip* the second.

Section XI
Of the Laws of Nations

When civil government has been establish'd over the greatest part of mankind, and different societies have been form'd contiguous to each other, there arises a new set of duties among the neighbouring states, suitable to the nature of that commerce, which they carry on with each other. Political writers tell us, that in every kind of intercourse, a body politic is to be consider'd as one person; and indeed this assertion is so far just, that different nations, as well as private persons, require mutual assistance; at the same time that their selfishness and ambition are perpetual sources of war and discord. But tho' nations in this particular resemble individuals, yet as they are very different in other respects, no wonder they regulate themselves by different maxims, and give rise to a new set of rules, which we call *the laws of nations*. Under this head we may comprize the sacredness of the persons of ambassadors, the declaration of war, the abstaining from poison'd arms, with other duties of that kind, which are evidently calculated for the commerce, that is peculiar to different societies.

But tho' these rules be super-added to the laws of nature, the former do not entirely abolish the latter; and one may safely affirm, that the three fundamental rules of justice, the stability of possession, its transference by consent, and the performance of promises, are duties of princes, as well as of subjects. The same interest produces the same effect in both cases. Where possession has no stability, there must be perpetual war. Where property is not transferr'd by consent, there can be no commerce. Where promises are not observ'd, there can be no leagues nor alliances. The advantages, therefore, of peace, commerce, and mutual succour, make us extend to different kingdoms the same notions of justice, which take place among individuals.

There is a maxim very current in the world, which few politicians are willing to avow, but which has been authoriz'd by the practice of all ages, *that there is a system of morals calculated for princes, much more free than that which ought to govern private persons.* 'Tis evident this is not to be understood of the lesser *extent* of public duties and obligations; nor will any one be so extravagant as to assert, that the most solemn treaties ought to have no force among princes. For as princes do actually form treaties among themselves, they must propose some advantage from the execution of them; and the prospect of such advantage for the future must engage them to perform their part, and must establish that law of nature. The meaning, therefore, of this political maxim is, that tho' the morality of princes has the same *extent*, yet it has not the same *force* as that of private persons, and may lawfully be transgress'd from a more trivial motive. However shocking such a proposition may appear to certain philosophers, 'twill be easy to defend it upon those principles, by which we have accounted for the origin of justice and equity.

When men have found by experience, that 'tis impossible to subsist without society, and that 'tis impossible to maintain society, while they give free course to their appetites; so urgent an interest quickly restrains their actions, and imposes an obligation to observe those rules, which we call *the laws of justice.* This obligation of interest rests not here; but by the necessary course of the passions and sentiments, gives rise to the moral obligation of duty; while we approve of such actions as tend to the peace of society, and disapprove of such as tend to its disturbance. The same *natural* obligation of interest takes place among independent kingdoms, and gives rise to the same *morality;* so that no one of ever so corrupt morals will approve of a prince, who voluntarily, and of his own accord, breaks his word, or violates any treaty. But here we may observe, that tho' the intercourse of different states be advantageous, and even sometimes necessary, yet it is not so necessary nor advantageous as that among individuals, without which 'tis utterly impossible for human nature ever to subsist. Since, therefore, the *natural* obligation to justice, among different states, is not so strong as among individuals, the *moral* obligation, which arises from it, must partake of its weakness; and we must

necessarily give a greater indulgence to a prince or minister, who deceives another; than to a private gentleman, who breaks his word of honour.

Shou'd it be ask'd, *what proportion these two species of morality bear to each other?* I wou'd answer, that this is a question, to which we can never give any precise answer; nor is it possible to reduce to numbers the proportion, which we ought to fix betwixt them. One may safely affirm, that this proportion finds itself, without any art or study of men; as we may observe on many other occasions. The practice of the world goes farther in teaching us the degrees of our duty, than the most subtile philosophy, which was ever yet invented. And this may serve as a convincing proof, that all men have an implicit notion of the foundation of those moral rules concerning natural and civil justice, and are sensible, that they arise merely from human conventions, and from the interest, which we have in the preservation of peace and order. For otherwise the diminution of the interest wou'd never produce a relaxation of the morality, and reconcile us more easily to any transgression of justice among princes and republics, than in the private commerce of one subject with another.

Section XII
Of Chastity and Modesty

If any difficulty attend this system concerning the laws of nature and nations, 'twill be with regard to the universal approbation or blame, which follows their observance or transgression, and which some may not think sufficiently explain'd from the general interests of society. To remove, as far as possible, all scruples of this kind, I shall here consider another set of duties, *viz.* the *modesty* and *chastity* which belong to the fair sex: And I doubt not but these virtues will be found to be still more conspicuous instances of the operation of those principles, which I have insisted on.

There are some philosophers, who attack the female virtues with great vehemence, and fancy they have gone very far in detecting popular errors, when they can show, that there is no foundation in nature for all that exterior modesty, which we require in the expressions, and dress, and behaviour of the fair sex. I believe I may spare myself the trouble of insisting on so obvious a subject, and may proceed, without farther preparation, to examine after what manner such notions arise from education, from the voluntary conventions of men, and from the interest of society.

Whoever considers the length and feebleness of human infancy, with the concern which both sexes naturally have for their offspring, will easily perceive, that there must be an union of male and female for the education of the young, and that this union must be of considerable duration. But in order to induce the men to impose on themselves this restraint, and undergo chearfully all the fatigues and expences, to which it subjects them, they must believe, that the children are their own, and that their natural instinct is not directed to a wrong object, when they give a loose to love and tenderness. Now if we examine the structure of the human body, we shall find, that this security is very difficult to be attain'd on our part; and that since, in the copulation of the sexes, the principle of generation goes from the man to the woman, an error may easily take place on the side of the former, tho' it be utterly impossible with regard to the latter. From this trivial and anatomical observation is deriv'd that vast difference betwixt the education and duties of the two sexes.

Were a philosopher to examine the matter *a priori*, he wou'd reason after the following manner. Men are induc'd to labour for the maintenance and education of their children, by the persuasion that they are really their own; and therefore 'tis reasonable, and even necessary, to give them some security in this particular. This security cannot consist entirely in the imposing of severe punishments on any transgressions of conjugal fidelity on the part of the wife; since these public punishments cannot be inflicted without legal proof, which 'tis difficult to meet with in this subject. What restraint, therefore, shall we impose on women, in order to counter-ballance so strong a temptation as they have to infidelity? There seems to be no restraint possible, but in the punishment of bad fame or reputation; a punishment, which has a mighty influence on the human mind, and at the same time is inflicted by the world upon surmizes, and conjectures, and proofs, that wou'd never be receiv'd in any court of judicature. In order, therefore, to impose a due restraint on the female sex, we must attach a peculiar degree of shame to their infidelity, above what arises merely from its injustice, and must bestow proportionable praises on their chastity.

But tho' this be a very strong motive to fidelity, our philosopher wou'd quickly discover, that it wou'd not alone be sufficient to that purpose. All human creatures, especially of the female sex, are apt to overlook remote motives in favour of any present temptation: The temptation is here the strongest imaginable: Its approaches are insensible and seducing: And a woman easily finds, or flatters herself she shall find, certain means of securing her reputation, and preventing all the pernicious consequences of her pleasures. 'Tis necessary, therefore, that, beside the infamy attending such licences, there shou'd be some preceding backwardness or dread, which may prevent their first approaches, and may give the female sex a repugnance to all expressions, and postures, and liberties, that have an immediate relation to that enjoyment.

Such wou'd be the reasonings of our speculative philosopher: But I am persuaded, that if he had not a perfect knowledge of human nature, he wou'd be apt to regard them as mere chimerical speculations, and wou'd consider the infamy attending infidelity, and backwardness to all its approaches, as principles that were rather to be wish'd than hop'd for in the world. For what means, wou'd he say, of persuading mankind, that the transgressions of conjugal duty are more infamous than any other kind of injustice, when 'tis evident they are more excusable, upon account of the greatness of the temptation? And what possibility of giving a backwardness to the approaches of a pleasure, to which nature has inspir'd so strong a propensity; and a propensity that 'tis absolutely necessary in the end to comply with, for the support of the species?

But speculative reasonings, which cost so much pains to philosophers, are often form'd by the world naturally, and without reflection: As difficulties, which seem unsurmountable in theory, are easily got over in practice. Those, who have an interest in the fidelity of women, naturally disapprove of their infidelity, and all the approaches to it. Those, who have no interest, are carried along with the stream. Education takes possession of the ductile minds of the fair sex in their infancy. And when a general rule of this kind is once establish'd, men are apt to extend it beyond those principles, from which it first arose. Thus batchelors, however debauch'd, cannot chuse but be shock'd with any instance of lewdness or impudence in women. And tho' all these maxims have a plain reference to generation, yet women past child-bearing have no more privilege in this respect, than those who are in the flower of their youth and beauty. Men have undoubtedly an implicit notion, that all those ideas of modesty and decency have a regard to generation; since they impose not the same laws, *with the same force*, on the male sex, where that reason takes not place. The exception is there obvious and extensive, and founded on a remarkable difference, which produces a clear separation and disjunction of ideas. But as the case is not the same with regard to the different ages of women, for this reason, tho' men know, that these notions are founded on the public interest, yet the general rule carries us beyond the original principle, and makes us extend the notions of modesty over the whole sex, from their earliest infancy to their extremest old-age and infirmity.

Courage, which is the point of honour among men, derives its merit, in a great measure, from artifice, as well as the chastity of women; tho' it has also some foundation in nature, as we shall see afterwards.

As to the obligations which the male sex lie under, with regard to chastity, we may observe, that according to the general notions of the world, they bear nearly the same proportion to the obligations of women, as the obligations of the law of nations do to those of the law of nature. 'Tis contrary to the interest of civil society, that men shou'd have an *entire* liberty of indulging their appetites in venereal enjoyment: But as this interest is weaker than in the case of the female sex, the moral obligation, arising from it, must be proportionally weaker. And to prove this we need only appeal to the practice and sentiments of all nations and ages.

PART III
OF THE OTHER VIRTUES AND VICES

Section I
Of the Origin of the Natural Virtues and Vices

We come now to the examination of such virtues and vices as are entirely natural, and have no dependence on the artifice and contrivance of men. The examination of these will conclude this system of morals.

The chief spring or actuating principle of the human mind is pleasure or pain; and when these sensations are remov'd, both from our thought and feeling, we are, in a great measure, incapable of passion or action, of desire or volition. The most immediate effects of pleasure and pain are the propense and averse motions of the mind; which are diversified into volition, into desire and aversion, grief and joy, hope and fear, according as the pleasure or pain changes its situation, and becomes probable or improbable, certain or uncertain, or is consider'd as out of our power for the present moment. But when along with this, the objects, that cause pleasure or pain, acquire a relation to ourselves or others; they still continue to excite desire and aversion, grief and joy: But cause, at the same time, the indirect passions of pride or humility, love or hatred, which in this case have a double relation of impressions and ideas to the pain or pleasure.

We have already observ'd, that moral distinctions depend entirely on certain peculiar sentiments of pain and pleasure, and that whatever mental quality in ourselves or others gives us a satisfaction, by the survey or reflexion, is of course virtuous; as every thing of this nature, that gives uneasiness, is vicious. Now since every quality in ourselves or others, which gives pleasure, always causes pride or love; as every one, that produces uneasiness, excites humility or hatred: It follows, that these two particulars are to be consider'd as equivalent, with regard to our mental qualities, *virtue* and the power of producing love or pride, *vice* and the power of producing humility or hatred. In every case, therefore, we must judge of the one by the other; and may pronounce any *quality* of the mind virtuous, which causes love or pride; and any one vicious, which causes hatred or humility.

If any *action* be either virtuous or vicious, 'tis only as a sign of some quality or character. It must depend upon durable principles of the mind, which extend over the whole conduct, and enter into the personal character. Actions themselves, not proceeding from any constant principle, have no influence on love or hatred, pride or humility; and consequently are never consider'd in morality.

This reflexion is self-evident, and deserves to be attended to, as being of the utmost importance in the present subject. We are never to consider any single action in our enquiries concerning the origin of morals; but only the quality or character from which the action proceeded. These alone are *durable* enough to affect our sentiments concerning the person. Actions are, indeed, better indications of a character than words, or even wishes and sentiments; but 'tis only so far as they are such indications, that they are attended with love or hatred, praise or blame.

To discover the true origin of morals, and of that love or hatred, which arises from mental qualities, we must take the matter pretty deep, and compare some principles, which have been already examin'd and explain'd.

We may begin with considering a-new the nature and force of *sympathy*. The minds of all men are similar in their feelings and operations, nor can any one be actuated by any affection, of which all others are not, in some degree, susceptible. As in strings equally wound up, the motion of one communicates itself to the rest; so all the affections readily pass from one person to another, and beget correspondent movements in every human creature. When I see the *effects* of passion in the voice and gesture of any person, my mind immediately passes from these effects to their causes, and forms such a lively idea of the passion, as is presently converted into the passion itself. In like manner, when I perceive the *causes* of any emotion, my mind is convey'd to the effects, and is actuated with a like emotion. Were I present at any of the more terrible operations of surgery, 'tis certain, that even before it begun, the preparation of the instruments, the laying of the bandages in order, the heating of the irons, with all the signs of anxiety and concern in the patient and assistants, wou'd have a great effect upon my mind, and excite the strongest sentiments of pity and terror. No passion of another discovers itself immediately to the mind. We are only sensible of its causes or effects. From *these* we infer the passion: And consequently *these* give rise to our sympathy.

Our sense of beauty depends very much on this principle; and where any object has a tendency to produce pleasure in its possessor, it is always regarded as beautiful; as every object, that has a tendency to produce pain, is disagreeable and deform'd. Thus the conveniency of a house, the fertility of a field, the strength of a horse, the capacity, security, and swift-sailing of a vessel, form the principal beauty of these several objects. Here the object, which is denominated beautiful, pleases only by its tendency to produce a certain effect. That effect is the pleasure or advantage of some other person. Now the pleasure of a stranger, for whom we have no friendship, pleases us only by sympathy. To this principle, therefore, is owing the beauty, which we find in every thing that is useful. How considerable a part this is of beauty will easily appear upon reflexion. Wherever an object has a tendency to produce pleasure in the possessor, or in other words, is the proper *cause* of pleasure, it is sure to please the spectator, by a delicate sympathy with the possessor. Most of the works of art are esteem'd beautiful, in proportion to their fitness for the use of man, and even many of the productions of nature derive their beauty from that source. Hand-some and beautiful, on most occasions, is not an absolute but a relative quality, and pleases us by nothing but its tendency to produce an end that is agreeable.[1]

The same principle produces, in many instances, our sentiments of morals, as well as those of beauty. No virtue is more esteem'd than justice, and no vice more detested than injustice; nor are there any qualities, which go farther to the fixing the character, either as amiable or odious. Now justice is a moral virtue, merely because it has that tendency to the good of mankind; and, indeed, is nothing but an artificial invention to that purpose. The same may be said of allegiance, of the laws of nations, of modesty, and of good-manners. All these are mere human contrivances for the interest of society. And since there is a very strong sentiment of morals, which has always attended them, we must allow, that the reflecting on the tendency of characters and mental qualities, is sufficient to give us the sentiments of approbation and blame. Now as the means to an end can only be agreeable, where the end is agreeable; and as the good of society, where our own interest is not concern'd, or that of our friends, pleases only by sympathy: It follows, that sympathy is the source of the esteem, which we pay to all the artificial virtues.

Thus it appears, *that* sympathy is a very powerful principle in human nature, *that* it has a great influence on our taste of beauty, and *that* it produces our sentiment of morals in all the artificial virtues. From thence we may presume, that it also gives rise to many of the other virtues; and that qualities acquire our approbation, because of their tendency to the good of mankind. This presumption must become a certainty, when we find that most of those qualities, which we *naturally* approve of, have actually that tendency, and render a man a proper member of society: While the qualities, which we *naturally* disapprove of, have a contrary tendency, and render any intercourse with the person dangerous or disagreeable. For having found, that such tendencies have force enough to produce the strongest sentiment of

---

1. Decentior equus cujus astricta sunt ilia; sed idem velocior. Pulcher aspectu sit athleta, cujus lacertos exercitatio expressit; idem certamini paratior. Nunquam vero *species* ab *utilitate* dividitur. Sed hoc quidem discernere, modici judicii est. *Quinct.* lib. 8.

morals, we can never reasonably, in these cases, look for any other cause of approbation or blame; it being an inviolable maxim in philosophy, that where any particular cause is sufficient for an effect, we ought to rest satisfied with it, and ought not to multiply causes without necessity. We have happily attain'd experiments in the artificial virtues, where the tendency of qualities to the good of society, is the *sole* cause of our approbation, without any suspicion of the concurrence of another principle. From thence we learn the force of that principle. And where that principle may take place, and the quality approv'd of is really beneficial to society, a true philosopher will never require any other principle to account for the strongest approbation and esteem.

That many of the natural virtues have this tendency to the good of society, no one can doubt of. Meekness, beneficence, charity, generosity, clemency, moderation, equity, bear the greatest figure among the moral qualities, and are commonly denominated the *social* virtues, to mark their tendency to the good of society. This goes so far, that some philosophers have represented all moral distinctions as the effect of artifice and education, when skilful politicians endeavour'd to restrain the turbulent passions of men, and make them operate to the public good, by the notions of honour and shame. This system, however, is not consistent with experience. For, *first*, there are other virtues and vices beside those which have this tendency to the public advantage and loss. *Secondly*, had not men a natural sentiment of approbation and blame, it cou'd never be excited by politicians; nor wou'd the words *laudable* and *praise-worthy, blameable* and *odious*, be any more intelligible, than if they were a language perfectly unknown to us, as we have already observ'd. But tho' this system be erroneous, it may teach us, that moral distinctions arise, in a great measure, from the tendency of qualities and characters to the interest of society, and that 'tis our concern for that interest, which makes us approve or disapprove of them. Now we have no such extensive concern for society but from sympathy; and consequently 'tis that principle, which takes us so far out of ourselves, as to give us the same pleasure or uneasiness in the characters of others, as if they had a tendency to our own advantage or loss.

The only difference betwixt the natural virtues and justice lies in this, that the good, which results from the former, arises from every single act, and is the object of some natural passion: Whereas a single act of justice, consider'd in itself, may often be contrary to the public good; and 'tis only the concurrence of mankind, in a general scheme or system of action, which is advantageous. When I relieve persons in distress, my natural humanity is my motive; and so far as my succour extends, so far have I promoted the happiness of my fellow-creatures. But if we examine all the questions, that come before any tribunal of justice, we shall find, that, considering each case apart, it wou'd as often be an instance of humanity to decide contrary to the laws of justice as conformable to them. Judges take from a poor man to give to a rich; they bestow on the dissolute the labour of the industrious; and put into the hands of the vicious the means of harming both themselves and others. The whole scheme, however, of law and justice is advantageous to the society; and 'twas with a view to this advantage, that men, by their voluntary conventions, establish'd it. After it is once establish'd by these conventions, it is *naturally* attended with a strong sentiment of morals; which can proceed from nothing but our sympathy with the interests of society. We need no other explication of that esteem, which attends such of the natural virtues, as have a tendency to the public good.

I must farther add, that there are several circumstances, which render this hypothesis much more probable with regard to the natural than the artificial virtues. 'Tis certain, that the imagination is more affected by what is particular, than by what is general; and that the sentiments are always mov'd with difficulty, where their objects are, in any degree, loose and undetermin'd: Now every particular act of justice is not beneficial to society, but the whole scheme or system: And it may not, perhaps, be any individual person, for whom we are concern'd, who receives benefit from justice, but the whole society alike. On the contrary, every particular act of generosity, or relief of the industrious and indigent, is beneficial; and is beneficial to a particular person, who is not undeserving of it. 'Tis more natural, therefore, to think, that the tendencies of the latter virtue will affect our sentiments, and command our approbation, than those of the former; and therefore, since we find, that the approbation of the former arises from their tendencies, we may ascribe, with better reason, the same cause to the approbation of the latter. In any number of similar effects, if a cause can be discover'd for one, we ought to extend that cause to all the other effects, which can be accounted for by it: But much more, if these other effects be attended with peculiar circumstances, which facilitate the operation of that cause.

Before I proceed farther, I must observe two remarkable circumstances in this affair, which may seem objections to the present system. The first may be thus explain'd. When any quality, or character, has a tendency to the good of mankind, we are pleas'd with it, and approve of it; because it presents the lively idea of pleasure; which idea affects us by sympathy, and is itself a kind of pleasure. But as this sympathy is very variable, it may be thought, that our sentiments of morals must admit of all the same variations. We sympathize more with persons contiguous to us, than with persons remote from us: With our acquaintance, than with strangers: With our countrymen, than with foreigners. But notwithstanding this variation of our sympathy, we give the same approbation to the same moral qualities in *China* as in *England*. They appear equally virtuous, and recommend themselves equally to the esteem of a judicious spectator. The sympathy varies without a variation in our esteem. Our esteem, therefore, proceeds not from sympathy.

To this I answer: The approbation of moral qualities most certainly is not deriv'd from reason, or any comparison of ideas; but proceeds entirely from a moral taste, and from certain sentiments of pleasure or disgust, which arise upon the contemplation and view of particular qualities or characters. Now 'tis evident, that those sentiments, whence-ever they are deriv'd, must vary according to the distance or contiguity of the objects; nor can I feel the same lively pleasure from the virtues of a person, who liv'd in *Greece* two thousand years ago, that I feel from the virtues of a familiar friend and acquaintance. Yet I do not say, that I esteem the one more than the other: And therefore, if the variation of the sentiment, without a variation of the esteem, be an objection, it must have equal force against every other system, as against that of sympathy. But to consider the case a-right, it has no force at all; and 'tis the easiest matter in the world to account for it. Our situation, with regard both to persons and things, is in continual fluctuation; and a man, that lies at a distance from us, may, in a little time, become a familiar acquaintance. Besides, every particular man has a peculiar position

with regard to others; and 'tis impossible we cou'd ever converse together on any reasonable terms, were each of us to consider characters and persons, only as they appear from his peculiar point of view. In order, therefore, to prevent those continual *contradictions*, and arrive at a more *stable* judgment of things, we fix on some *steady* and *general* points of view; and always, in our thoughts, place ourselves in them, whatever may be our present situation. In like manner, external beauty is determin'd merely by pleasure; and 'tis evident, a beautiful countenance cannot give so much pleasure, when seen at the distance of twenty paces, as when it is brought nearer us. We say not, however, that it appears to us less beautiful: Because we know what effect it will have in such a position, and by that reflexion we correct its momentary appearance.

In general, all sentiments of blame or praise are variable, according to our situation of nearness or remoteness, with regard to the person blam'd or prais'd, and according to the present disposition of our mind. But these variations we regard not in our general decisions, but still apply the terms expressive of our liking or dislike, in the same manner, as if we remain'd in one point of view. Experience soon teaches us this method of correcting our sentiments, or at least, of correcting our language, where the sentiments are more stubborn and inalterable. Our servant, if diligent and faithful, may excite stronger sentiments of love and kindness than *Marcus Brutus*, as represented in history; but we say not upon that account, that the former character is more laudable than the latter. We know, that were we to approach equally near to that renown'd patriot, he wou'd command a much higher degree of affection and admiration. Such corrections are common with regard to all the senses; and indeed 'twere impossible we cou'd ever make use of language, or communicate our sentiments to one another, did we not correct the momentary appearances of things, and overlook our present situation.

'Tis therefore from the influence of characters and qualities, upon those who have an intercourse with any person, that we blame or praise him. We consider not whether the persons, affected by the qualities, be our acquaintance or strangers, countrymen or foreigners. Nay, we over-look our own interest in those general judgments; and blame not a man for opposing us in any of our pretensions, when his own interest is particularly concern'd. We make allowance for a certain degree of selfishness in men; because we know it to be inseparable from human nature, and inherent in our frame and constitution. By this reflexion we correct those sentiments of blame, which so naturally arise upon any opposition.

But however the general principle of our blame or praise may be corrected by those other principles, 'tis certain, they are not altogether efficacious, nor do our passions often correspond entirely to the present theory. 'Tis seldom men heartily love what lies at a distance from them, and what no way redounds to their particular benefit; as 'tis no less rare to meet with persons, who can pardon another any opposition he makes to their interest, however justifiable that opposition may be by the general rules of morality. Here we are contented with saying, that reason requires such an impartial conduct, but that 'tis seldom we can bring ourselves to it, and that our passions do not readily follow the determination of our judgment. This language will be easily understood, if we consider what we formerly said concerning that *reason*, which is able to oppose our passion; and which we have found to be nothing but a general calm determination of the passions, founded on some distant view or reflexion. When we form our judgments of persons, merely from the tendency of their characters to our own benefit, or to that of our friends, we find so many contradictions to our sentiments in society and conversation, and such an uncertainty from the incessant changes of our situation, that we seek some other standard of merit and demerit, which may not admit of so great variation. Being thus loosen'd from our first station, we cannot afterwards fix ourselves so commodiously by any means as by a sympathy with those, who have any commerce with the person we consider. This is far from being as lively as when our own interest is concern'd, or that of our particular friends; nor has it such an influence on our love and hatred: But being equally conformable to our calm and general principles, 'tis said to have an equal authority over our reason, and to command our judgment and opinion. We blame equally a bad action, which we read of in history, with one perform'd in our neighbourhood t'other day: The meaning of which is, that we know from reflexion, that the former action wou'd excite as strong sentiments of disapprobation as the latter, were it plac'd in the same position.

I now proceed to the *second* remarkable circumstance, which I propos'd to take notice of. Where a

person is possess'd of a character, that in its natural tendency is beneficial to society, we esteem him virtuous, and are delighted with the view of his character, even tho' particular accidents prevent its operation, and incapacitate him from being serviceable to his friends and country. Virtue in rags is still virtue; and the love, which it procures, attends a man into a dungeon or desart, where the virtue can no longer be exerted in action, and is lost to all the world. Now this may be esteem'd an objection to the present system. Sympathy interests us in the good of mankind; and if sympathy were the source of our esteem for virtue, that sentiment of approbation cou'd only take place, where the virtue actually attain'd its end, and was beneficial to mankind. Where it fails of its end, 'tis only an imperfect means; and therefore can never acquire any merit from that end. The goodness of an end can bestow a merit on such means alone as are compleat, and actually produce the end.

To this we may reply, that where any object, in all its parts, is fitted to attain any agreeable end, it naturally gives us pleasure, and is esteem'd beautiful, even tho' some external circumstances be wanting to render it altogether effectual. 'Tis sufficient if every thing be compleat in the object itself. A house, that is contriv'd with great judgment for all the commodities of life, pleases us upon that account; tho' perhaps we are sensible, that no-one will ever dwell in it. A fertile soil, and a happy climate, delight us by a reflexion on the happiness which they wou'd afford the inhabitants, tho' at present the country be desart and uninhabited. A man, whose limbs and shape promise strength and activity, is esteem'd handsome, tho' condemn'd to perpetual imprisonment. The imagination has a set of passions belonging to it, upon which our sentiments of beauty much depend. These passions are mov'd by degrees of liveliness and strength, which are inferior to *belief*, and independant of the real existence of their objects. Where a character is, in every respect, fitted to be beneficial to society, the imagination passes easily from the cause to the effect, without considering that there are still some circumstances wanting to render the cause a compleat one. *General rules* create a species of probability, which sometimes influences the judgment, and always the imagination.

'Tis true, when the cause is compleat, and a good disposition is attended with good fortune, which renders it really beneficial to society, it gives a stronger pleasure to the spectator, and is attended with a more lively sympathy. We are more affected by it; and yet we do not say that it is more virtuous, or that we esteem it more. We know, that an alteration of fortune may render the benevolent disposition entirely impotent; and therefore we separate, as much as possible, the fortune from the disposition. The case is the same, as when we correct the different sentiments of virtue, which proceed from its different distances from ourselves. The passions do not always follow our corrections; but these corrections serve sufficiently to regulate our abstract notions, and are alone regarded, when we pronounce in general concerning the degrees of vice and virtue.

'Tis observ'd by critics, that all words or sentences, which are difficult to the pronunciation, are disagreeable to the ear. There is no difference, whether a man hear them pronounc'd, or read them silently to himself. When I run over a book with my eye, I imagine I hear it all; and also, by the force of imagination, enter into the uneasiness, which the delivery of it wou'd give the speaker. The uneasiness is not real; but as such a composition of words has a natural tendency to produce it, this is sufficient to affect the mind with a painful sentiment, and render the style harsh and disagreeable. 'Tis a similar case, where any real quality is, by accidental circumstances, render'd impotent, and is depriv'd of its natural influence on society.

Upon these principles we may easily remove any contradiction, which may appear to be betwixt the *extensive sympathy*, on which our sentiments of virtue depend, and that *limited generosity* which I have frequently observ'd to be natural to men, and which justice and property suppose, according to the precedent reasoning. My sympathy with another may give me the sentiment of pain and disapprobation, when any object is presented, that has a tendency to give him uneasiness; tho' I may not be willing to sacrifice any thing of my own interest, or cross any of my passions, for his satisfaction. A house may displease me by being ill-contriv'd for the convenience of the owner; and yet I may refuse to give a shilling towards the rebuilding of it. Sentiments must touch the heart, to make them controul our passions: But they need not extend beyond the imagination, to make them influence our taste. When a building seems clumsy and tottering to the eye, it is ugly and disagreeable; tho' we be fully assur'd of the solidity of the workmanship. 'Tis a kind of fear, which causes this sentiment of disapprobation; but the passion is not the same with that which we feel, when oblig'd to stand under a wall, that we really think tottering and insecure. The *seeming tendencies* of objects affect the mind: And the emotions they excite are of a like species with those, which proceed from the *real consequences* of objects, but their feeling is different. Nay, these emotions are so different in their feeling, that they may often be contrary, without destroying each other; as when the fortifications of a city belonging to an enemy are esteem'd beautiful upon account of their strength, tho' we cou'd wish that they were entirely destroy'd. The imagination adheres to the *general* views of things, and distinguishes betwixt the feelings they produce, and those which arise from our particular and momentary situation.

If we examine the panegyrics that are commonly made of great men, we shall find, that most of the qualities, which are attributed to them, may be divided into two kinds, *viz.* such as make them perform their part in society; and such as render them serviceable to themselves, and enable them to promote their own interest. Their *prudence, temperance, frugality, industry, assiduity, enterprize, dexterity,* are celebrated, as well as their *generosity* and *humanity.* If we ever give an indulgence to any quality, that disables a man from making a figure in life, 'tis to that of *indolence,* which is not suppos'd to deprive one of his parts and capacity, but only suspends their exercise; and that without any inconvenience to the person himself, since 'tis, in some measure, from his own choice. Yet indolence is always allow'd to be a fault, and a very great one, if extreme: Nor do a man's friends ever acknowledge him to be subject to it, but in order to save his character in more material articles. He cou'd make a figure, say they, if he pleas'd to give application: His understanding is sound, his conception quick, and his memory tenacious; but he hates business, and is indifferent about his fortune. And this a man sometimes may make even a subject of vanity; tho' with the air of confessing a fault: Because he may think, that this incapacity for business implies much more noble qualities; such as a philosophical spirit, a fine taste, a delicate wit, or a relish for pleasure and society. But take any other case: Suppose a quality, that without being an indication of any other good qualities, incapacitates a man *always* for business, and is destructive to his interest; such as a blundering understanding, and a wrong judgment of every thing in life; inconstancy and irresolution; or a want of address in the management of men and business: These are all allow'd to be imperfections in a character; and many men wou'd rather acknowledge the greatest crimes, than have it suspected, that they are, in any degree, subject to them.

'Tis very happy, in our philosophical researches, when we find the same phænomenon diversified by a variety of circumstances; and by discovering what is common among them, can the better assure ourselves of the truth of any hypothesis we may make use of to explain that phænomenon. Were nothing esteem'd virtue but what were beneficial to society, I am persuaded, that the foregoing explication of the moral sense ought still to be receiv'd, and that upon sufficient evidence: But this evidence must grow upon us, when we find other kinds of virtue, which will not admit of any explication except from that hypothesis. Here is a man, who is not remarkably defective in his social qualities; but what principally recommends him is his dexterity in business, by which he has extricated himself from the greatest difficulties, and conducted the most delicate affairs with a singular address and prudence. I find an esteem for him immediately to arise in me: His company is a satisfaction to me; and before I have any farther acquaintance with him, I wou'd rather do him a service than another, whose character is in every other respect equal, but is deficient in that particular. In this case, the qualities that please me are all consider'd as useful to the person, and as having a tendency to promote his interest and satisfaction. They are only regarded as means to an end, and please me in proportion to their fitness for that end. The end, therefore, must be agreeable to me. But what makes the end agreeable? The person is a stranger: I am no way interested in him, nor lie under any obligation to him: His happiness concerns not me, farther than the happiness of every human, and indeed of every sensible creature: That is, it affects me only by sympathy. From that principle, whenever I discover his happiness and good, whether in its causes or effects, I enter so deeply into it, that it gives me a sensible emotion. The appearance of qualities, that have a *tendency* to promote it, have an agreeable effect upon my imagination, and command my love and esteem.

This theory may serve to explain, why the same qualities, in all cases, produce both pride and love,

humility and hatred; and the same man is always virtuous or vicious, accomplish'd or despicable to others, who is so to himself. A person, in whom we discover any passion or habit, which originally is only incommodious to himself, becomes always disagreeable to us, merely on its account; as on the other hand, one whose character is only dangerous and disagreeable to others, can never be satisfied with himself, as long as he is sensible of that disadvantage. Nor is this observable only with regard to characters and manners, but may be remark'd even in the most minute circumstances. A violent cough in another gives us uneasiness; tho' in itself it does not in the least affect us. A man will be mortified, if you tell him he has a stinking breath; tho' 'tis evidently no annoyance to himself. Our fancy easily changes its situation; and either surveying ourselves as we appear to others, or considering others as they feel themselves, makes us enter, by that means, into sentiments, which no way belong to us, and in which nothing but sympathy is able to interest us. And this sympathy we sometimes carry so far, as even to be displeas'd with a quality commodious to us, merely because it displeases others, and renders us disagreeable in their eyes; tho' perhaps we never can have any interest in rendering ourselves agreeable to them.

There have been many systems of morality advanc'd by philosophers in all ages; but if they are strictly examin'd, they may be reduc'd to two, which alone merit our attention. Moral good and evil are certainly distinguish'd by our *sentiments*, not by *reason:* But these sentiments may arise neither from the mere species or appearance of characters and passions, or from reflexions on their tendency to the happiness of mankind, and of particular persons. My opinion is, that both these causes are intermix'd in our judgments of morals; after the same manner as they are in our decisions concerning most kinds of external beauty: Tho' I am also of opinion, that reflexions on the tendencies of actions have by far the greatest influence, and determine all the great lines of our duty. There are, however, instances, in cases of less moment, wherein this immediate taste or sentiment produces our approbation. Wit, and a certain easy and disengag'd behaviour, are qualities *immediately agreeable* to others, and command their love and esteem. Some of these qualities produce satisfaction in others by particular *original* principles of human nature, which cannot be accounted for: Others may be resolv'd into principles, which are more general. This will best appear upon a particular enquiry.

As some qualities acquire their merit from their being *immediately agreeable* to others, without any tendency to public interest; so some are denominated virtuous from their being *immediately agreeable* to the person himself, who possesses them. Each of the passions and operations of the mind has a particular feeling, which must be either agreeable or disagreeable. The first is virtuous, the second vicious. This particular feeling constitutes the very nature of the passion; and therefore needs not be accounted for.

But however directly the distinction of vice and virtue may seem to flow from the immediate pleasure or uneasiness, which particular qualities cause to ourselves or others; 'tis easy to observe, that it has also a considerable dependance on the principle of *sympathy* so often insisted on. We approve of a person, who is possess'd of qualities *immediately agreeable* to those, with whom he has any commerce; tho' perhaps we ourselves never reap'd any pleasure from them. We also approve of one, who is possess'd of qualities, that are *immediately agreeable* to himself; tho' they be of no service to any mortal. To account for this we must have recourse to the foregoing principles.

Thus, to take a general review of the present hypothesis: Every quality of the mind is denominated virtuous, which gives pleasure by the mere survey; as every quality, which produces pain, is call'd vicious. This pleasure and this pain may arise from four different sources. For we reap a pleasure from the view of a character, which is naturally fitted to be useful to others, or to the person himself, or which is agreeable to others, or to the person himself. One may, perhaps, be surpriz'd, that amidst all these interests and pleasures, we shou'd forget our own, which touch us so nearly on every other occasion. But we shall easily satisfy ourselves on this head, when we consider, that every particular person's pleasure and interest being different, 'tis impossible men cou'd ever agree in their sentiments and judgments, unless they chose some common point of view, from which they might survey their object, and which might cause it to appear the same to all of them. Now, in judging of characters, the only interest or pleasure, which appears the same to every spectator, is that of the person himself, whose character is examin'd; or that of persons, who have a connexion with him. And tho' such interests and pleasures touch us more faintly than our own, yet being

more constant and universal, they counter-ballance the latter even in practice, and are alone admitted in speculation as the standard of virtue and morality. They alone produce that particular feeling or sentiment, on which moral distinctions depend.

As to the good or ill desert of virtue or vice, 'tis an evident consequence of the sentiments of pleasure or uneasiness. These sentiments produce love or hatred; and love or hatred, by the original constitution of human passion, is attended with benevolence or anger; that is, with a desire of making happy the person we love, and miserable the person we hate. We have treated of this more fully on another occasion.

Section II
Of Greatness of Mind

It may now be proper to illustrate this general system of morals, by applying it to particular instances of virtue and vice, and shewing how their merit or demerit arises from the four sources here explain'd. We shall begin with examining the passions of *pride* and *humility,* and shall consider the vice or virtue that lies in their excesses or just proportion. An excessive pride or over-weaning conceit of ourselves is always esteem'd vicious, and is universally hated; as modesty, or a just sense of our weakness, is esteem'd virtuous, and procures the good-will of every one. Of the four sources of moral distinctions, this is to be ascrib'd to the *third; viz.* the immediate agreeableness and disagreeableness of a quality to others, without any reflexions on the tendency of that quality.

In order to prove this, we must have recourse to two principles, which are very conspicuous in human nature. The *first* of these is the *sympathy,* and communication of sentiments and passions abovemention'd. So close and intimate is the correspondence of human souls, that no sooner any person approaches me, than he diffuses on me all his opinions, and draws along my judgment in a greater or lesser degree. And tho', on many occasions, my sympathy with him goes not so far as entirely to change my sentiments, and way of thinking; yet it seldom is so weak as not to disturb the easy course of my thought, and give an authority to that opinion, which is recommended to me by his assent and approbation. Nor is it any way material upon what subject he and I employ our thoughts. Whether we judge of an indifferent person, or of my own character, my sympathy gives equal force to his decision: And even his sentiments of his own merit make me consider him in the same light, in which he regards himself.

This principle of sympathy is of so powerful and insinuating a nature, that it enters into most of our sentiments and passions, and often takes place under the appearance of its contrary. For 'tis remarkable, that when a person opposes me in any sentiment, which I am strongly bent upon, and rouzes up my passion by contradiction, I have always a degree of sympathy with him, nor does my commotion proceed from any other origin. We may here observe an evident conflict or rencounter of opposite principles and passions. On the one side there is that passion or sentiment, which is natural to me; and 'tis observable, that the stronger this passion is, the greater is the commotion. There must also be some passion or sentiment on the other side; and this passion can proceed from nothing but sympathy. The sentiments of others can never affect us, but by becoming, in some measure, our own; in which case they operate upon us, by opposing and encreasing our passions, in the very same manner, as if they had been originally deriv'd from our own temper and disposition. While they remain conceal'd in the minds of others, they can never have any influence upon us: And even when they are known, if they went no farther than the imagination, or conception; that faculty is so accustom'd to objects of every different kind, that a mere idea, tho' contrary to our sentiments and inclinations, wou'd never alone be able to affect us.

The *second* principle I shall take notice of is that of *comparison*, or the variation of our judgments concerning objects, according to the proportion they bear to those with which we compare them. We judge more of objects by comparison, than by their intrinsic worth and value; and regard every thing as mean, when set in opposition to what is superior of the same kind. But no comparison is more obvious than that with ourselves; and hence it is that on all occasions it takes place, and mixes with most of our passions. This kind of comparison is directly contrary to sympathy in its operation, as we have observ'd in treating of *compassion* and *malice*. *In all kinds of comparison an object makes us always receive from another, to which it is compar'd, a sensation contrary to what arises from itself in its direct and immediate survey. The direct survey of another's pleasure naturally gives us pleasure; and therefore produces pain, when compar'd with our own. His pain, consider'd in itself, is painful; but augments the idea of our own happiness, and gives us pleasure.*[1]

Since then those principles of sympathy, and a comparison with ourselves, are directly contrary, it may be worth while to consider, what general rules can be form'd, beside the particular temper of the person, for the prevalence of the one or the other. Suppose I am now in safety at land, and wou'd willingly reap some pleasure from this consideration: I must think on the miserable condition of those who are at sea in a storm, and must endeavour to render this idea as strong and lively as possible, in order to make me more sensible of my own happiness. But whatever pains I may take, the comparison will never have an equal efficacy, as if I were really on the shore,[2] and saw a ship at a distance, tost by a tempest, and in danger every moment of perishing on a rock or sandbank. But suppose this idea to become still more lively. Suppose the ship to be driven so near me, that I can perceive distinctly the horror, painted on the countenance of the seamen and passengers, hear their lamentable cries, see the dearest friends give their last adieu, or embrace with a resolution to perish in each other's arms: No man has so savage a heart as to reap any pleasure from such a spectacle, or withstand the motions of the tenderest compassion and sympathy. 'Tis evident, therefore, there is a medium in this case; and that if the idea be too feint, it has no influence by comparison; and on the other hand, if it be too strong, it operates on us entirely by sympathy, which is the contrary to comparison. Sympathy being the conversion of an idea into an impression, demands a greater force and vivacity in the idea than is requisite to comparison.

All this is easily applied to the present subject. We sink very much in our own eyes, when in the presence of a great man, or one of a superior genius; and this humility makes a considerable ingredient in that

---

1. Book II. Part II. sect. 8.
2. Suave mari magno turbantibus æquora ventis
   E terra magnum alterius spectare laborem;
   Non quia vexari quenquam est jucunda voluptas,
   Sed quibus ipse malis careas quia cernere suav' est.
                Lucret.

respect, which we pay our superiors, according to our foregoing reasonings on that passion.[3] Sometimes even envy and hatred arise from the comparison; but in the greatest part of men, it rests at respect and esteem. As sympathy has such a powerful influence on the human mind, it causes pride to have, in some measure, the same effect as merit; and by making us enter into those elevated sentiments, which the proud man entertains of himself, presents that comparison, which is so mortifying and disagreeable. Our judgment does not entirely accompany him in the flattering conceit, in which he pleases himself; but still is so shaken as to receive the idea it presents, and to give it an influence above the loose conceptions of the imagination. A man, who, in an idle humour, wou'd form a notion of a person of a merit very much superior to his own, wou'd not be mortified by that fiction: But when a man, whom we are really persuaded to be of inferior merit, is presented to us; if we observe in him any extraordinary degree of pride and self-conceit; the firm persuasion he has of his own merit, takes hold of the imagination, and diminishes us in our own eyes, in the same manner, as if he were really possess'd of all the good qualities which he so liberally attributes to himself. Our idea is here precisely in that medium, which is requisite to make it operate on us by comparison. Were it accompanied with belief, and did the person appear to have the same merit, which he assumes to himself, it wou'd have a contrary effect, and wou'd operate on us by sympathy. The influence of that principle wou'd then be superior to that of comparison, contrary to what happens where the person's merit seems below his pretensions.

The necessary consequence of these principles is, that pride, or an over-weaning conceit of ourselves, must be vicious; since it causes uneasiness in all men, and presents them every moment with a disagreeable comparison. 'Tis a trite observation in philosophy, and even in common life and conversation, that 'tis our own pride, which makes us so much displeas'd with the pride of other people; and that vanity becomes insupportable to us merely because we are vain. The gay naturally associate themselves with the gay, and the amorous with the amorous: But the proud never can endure the proud, and rather seek the company of those who are of an opposite disposi-

tion. As we are, all of us, proud in some degree, pride is universally blam'd and condemn'd by all mankind; as having a natural tendency to cause uneasiness in others by means of comparison. And this effect must follow the more naturally, that those, who have an ill-grounded conceit of themselves, are for ever making those comparisons, nor have they any other method of supporting their vanity. A man of sense and merit is pleas'd with himself, independant of all foreign considerations: But a fool must always find some person, that is more foolish, in order to keep himself in good humour with his own parts and understanding.

But tho' an over-weaning conceit of our own merit be vicious and disagreeable, nothing can be more laudable, than to have a value for ourselves, where we really have qualities that are valuable. The utility and advantage of any quality to ourselves is a source of virtue, as well as its agreeableness to others; and 'tis certain, that nothing is more useful to us in the conduct of life, than a due degree of pride, which makes us sensible of our own merit, and gives us a confidence and assurance in all our projects and enterprizes. Whatever capacity any one may be endow'd with, 'tis entirely useless to him, if he be not acquainted with it, and form not designs suitable to it. 'Tis requisite on all occasions to know our own force; and were it allowable to err on either side, 'twou'd be more advantageous to overrate our merit, than to form ideas of it, below its just standard. Fortune commonly favours the bold and enterprising; and nothing inspires us with more boldness than a good opinion of ourselves.

Add to this, that tho' pride, or self-applause, be sometimes disagreeable to others, 'tis always agreeable to ourselves; as on the other hand, modesty, tho' it give pleasure to every one, who observes it, produces often uneasiness in the person endow'd with it. Now it has been observ'd, that our own sensations determine the vice and virtue of any quality, as well as those sensations, which it may excite in others.

Thus self-satisfaction and vanity may not only be allowable, but requisite in a character. 'Tis, however, certain, that good-breeding and decency require that we shou'd avoid all signs and expressions, which tend directly to show that passion. We have, all of us, a wonderful partiality for ourselves, and were we always to give vent to our sentiments in this particular, we shou'd mutually cause the greatest indignation in each other, not only by the immediate presence of so disagreeable a subject of comparison, but also by the contrariety of our judgments. In like manner, therefore, as we establish the *laws of nature*, in order to secure property in society, and prevent the opposition of self-interest; we establish the *rules of good-breeding*, in order to prevent the opposition of men's pride, and render conversation agreeable and inoffensive. Nothing is more disagreeable than a man's overweaning conceit of himself: Every one almost has a strong propensity to this vice: No one can well distinguish *in himself* betwixt the vice and virtue, or be certain, that his esteem of his own merit is well founded: For these reasons, all direct expressions of this passion are condem'd; nor do we make any exception to this rule in favour of men of sense and merit. They are not allow'd to do themselves justice openly, in words, no more than other people; and even if they show a reserve and secret doubt in doing themselves justice in their own thoughts, they will be more applauded. That impertinent, and almost universal propensity of men, to over-value themselves, has given us such a *prejudice* against self-applause, that we are apt to condemn it, by a *general rule*, wherever we meet with it; and 'tis with some difficulty we give a privilege to men of sense, even in their most secret thoughts. At least, it must be own'd, that some disguise in this particular is absolutely requisite; and that if we harbour pride in our breasts, we must carry a fair outside, and have the appearance of modesty and mutual deference in all our conduct and behaviour. We must, on every occasion, be ready to prefer others to ourselves; to treat them with a kind of deference, even tho' they be our equals; to seem always the lowest and least in the company, where we are not very much distinguish'd above them: And if we observe these rules in our conduct, men will have more indulgence for our secret sentiments, when we discover them in an oblique manner.

I believe no one, who has any practice of the world, and can penetrate into the inward sentiments of men, will assert, that the humility, which good-breeding and decency require of us, goes beyond the outside, or that a thorough sincerity in this particular is esteem'd a real part of our duty. On the contrary, we may observe, that a genuine and hearty pride, or self-esteem, if well conceal'd and well founded, is essential to the character of a man of honour, and that there is no quality of the mind, which is more indispensably requisite to procure the esteem and approbation of mankind. There are certain deferences and mutual submissions, which custom requires of the different ranks of men towards each other; and whoever exceeds in this particular, if thro' interest, is accus'd of meanness; if thro' ignorance, of simplicity. 'Tis necessary, therefore, to know our rank and station in the world, whether it be fix'd by our birth, fortune, employments, talents, or reputation. 'Tis necessary to feel the sentiment and passion of pride in conformity to it, and to regulate our actions accordingly. And shou'd it be said, that prudence may suffice to regulate our actions in this particular, without any real pride, I wou'd observe, that here the object of prudence is to conform our actions to the general usage and custom; and that 'tis impossible those tacit airs of superiority shou'd ever have been establish'd and authoriz'd by custom, unless men were generally proud, and unless that passion were generally approv'd, when well grounded.

If we pass from common life and conversation to history, this reasoning acquires new force, when we observe, that all those great actions and sentiments, which have become the admiration of mankind, are founded on nothing but pride and self-esteem. *Go*, says *Alexander* the Great to his soldiers, when they refus'd to follow him to the *Indies, go tell your countrymen, that you left Alexander compleating the conquest of the world.* This passage was always particularly admir'd by the prince of *Conde*, as we learn from *St. Evremond.* "Alexander," said that prince, "abandon'd by his soldiers, among barbarians, not yet fully subdu'd, felt in himself such a dignity and right of empire, that he cou'd not believe it possible any one cou'd refuse to obey him. Whether in *Europe* or in *Asia*, among *Greeks* or *Persians*, all was indifferent to him: Wherever he found men, he fancied he had found subjects."

In general we may observe, that whatever we call *heroic virtue*, and admire under the character of greatness and elevation of mind, is either nothing but a steady and well-establish'd pride and self-esteem, or partakes largely of that passion. Courage, intrepidity, ambition, love of glory, magnanimity, and all the other shining virtues of that kind, have plainly a strong mixture of self-esteem in them, and derive a great part of their merit from that origin. Accordingly we find, that many religious declaimers decry those virtues as purely pagan and natural, and represent to us the excellency of the *Christian* religion, which places humility in the rank of virtues, and corrects the judgment of the world, and even of philosophers, who so generally admire all the efforts of pride and ambition. Whether this virtue of humility has been rightly understood, I shall not pretend to determine. I am content with the concession, that the world naturally esteems a well-regulated pride, which secretly animates our conduct, without breaking out into such indecent expressions of vanity, as may offend the vanity of others.

The merit of pride or self-esteem is deriv'd from two circumstances, *viz.* its utility and its agreeableness to ourselves; by which it capacitates us for business, and, at the same time, gives us an immediate satisfaction. When it goes beyond its just bounds, it loses the first advantage, and even becomes prejudicial; which is the reason why we condemn an extravagant pride and ambition, however regulated by the decorums of good-breeding and politeness. But as such a passion is still agreeable, and conveys an elevated and sublime sensation to the person, who is actuated by it, the sympathy with that satisfaction diminishes considerably the blame, which naturally attends its dangerous influence on his conduct and behaviour. Accordingly we may observe, that an excessive courage and magnanimity, especially when it displays itself under the frowns of fortune, contributes, in a great measure, to the character of a hero, and will render a person the admiration of posterity; at the same time, that it ruins his affairs, and leads him into dangers and difficulties, with which otherwise he wou'd never have been acquainted.

Heroism, or military glory, is much admir'd by the generality of mankind. They consider it as the most sublime kind of merit. Men of cool reflexion are not so sanguine in their praises of it. The infinite confusions and disorder, which it has caus'd in the world, diminish much of its merit in their eyes. When they wou'd oppose the popular notions on this head, they always paint out the evils, which this suppos'd virtue has produc'd in human society; the subversion of empires, the devastation of provinces, the sack of cities. As long as these are present to us, we are more inclin'd to hate than admire the ambition of heroes. But when we fix our view on the person himself, who is the author of all this mischief, there is something so dazzling in his character, the mere contemplation of it so elevates the mind, that we cannot refuse it our admiration. The pain, which we receive from its ten-

dency to the prejudice of society, is over-power'd by a stronger and more immediate sympathy.

Thus our explication of the merit or demerit, which attends the degrees of pride or self-esteem, may serve as a strong argument for the preceding hypothesis, by shewing the effects of those principles above explain'd in all the variations of our judgments concerning that passion. Nor will this reasoning be advantageous to us only by shewing, that the distinction of vice and virtue arises from the *four* principles of the *advantage* and of the *pleasure* of the *person himself,* and of *others:* But may also afford us a strong proof of some under-parts of that hypothesis.

No one, who duly considers of this matter, will make any scruple of allowing, that any piece of ill-breeding, or any expression of pride and haughtiness, is displeasing to us, merely because it shocks our own pride, and leads us by sympathy into a comparison, which causes the disagreeable passion of humility. Now as an insolence of this kind is blam'd even in a person who has always been civil to ourselves in particular; nay, in one, whose name is only known to us in history; it follows, that our disapprobation proceeds from a sympathy with others, and from the reflexion, that such a character is highly displeasing and odious to every one, who converses or has any intercourse with the person possess'd of it. We sympathize with those people in their uneasiness; and as their uneasiness proceeds in part from a sympathy with the person who insults them, we may here observe a double rebound of the sympathy; which is a principle very similar to what we have observ'd on another occasion.[4]

Section III
Of Goodness and Benevolence

Having thus explain'd the origin of that praise and approbation, which attends every thing we call *great* in human affections; we now proceed to give an account of their *goodness,* and shew whence its merit is deriv'd.

When experience has once given us a competent knowledge of human affairs, and has taught us the

___
4. Book II. Part II. sect. 5.

proportion they bear to human passion, we perceive, that the generosity of men is very limited, and that it seldom extends beyond their friends and family, or, at most, beyond their native country. Being thus acquainted with the nature of man, we expect not any impossibilities from him; but confine our view to that narrow circle, in which any person moves, in order to form a judgment of his moral character. When the natural tendency of his passions leads him to be serviceable and useful within his sphere, we approve of his character, and love his person, by a sympathy with the sentiments of those, who have a more particular connexion with him. We are quickly oblig'd to forget our own interest in our judgments of this kind, by reason of the perpetual contradictions, we meet with in society and conversation, from persons that are not plac'd in the same situation, and have not the same interest with ourselves. The only point of view, in which our sentiments concur with those of others, is, when we consider the tendency of any passion to the advantage or harm of those, who have any immediate connexion or intercourse with the person possess'd of it. And tho' this advantage or harm be often very remote from ourselves, yet sometimes 'tis very near us, and interests us strongly by sympathy. This concern we readily extend to other cases, that are resembling; and when these are very remote, our sympathy is proportionably weaker, and our praise or blame fainter and more doubtful. The case is here the same as in our judgments concerning external bodies. All objects seem to diminish by their distance: But tho' the appearance of objects to our senses be the original standard, by which we judge of them, yet we do not say, that they actually diminish by the distance; but correcting the appearance by reflexion, arrive at a more constant and establish'd judgment concerning them. In like manner, tho' sympathy be much fainter than our concern for ourselves, and a sympathy with persons remote from us much fainter than that with persons near and contiguous; yet we neglect all these differences in our calm judgments concerning the characters of men. Besides, that we ourselves often change our situation in this particular, we every day meet with persons, who are in a different situation from ourselves, and who cou'd never converse with us on any reasonable terms, were we to remain constantly in that situation and point of view, which is peculiar to us. The intercourse of sentiments, therefore, in society and conversation, makes us form some general inalterable standard, by which we may approve or disapprove of characters and manners. And tho' the *heart* does not always take part with those general notions, or regulate its love and hatred by them, yet are they sufficient for discourse, and serve all our purposes in company, in the pulpit, on the theatre, and in the schools.

From these principles we may easily account for that merit, which is commonly ascrib'd to *generosity, humanity, compassion, gratitude, friendship, fidelity, zeal, disinterestedness, liberality,* and all those other qualities, which form the character of good and benevolent. A propensity to the tender passions makes a man agreeable and useful in all the parts of life; and gives a just direction to all his other qualities, which otherwise may become prejudicial to society. Courage and ambition, when not regulated by benevolence, are fit only to make a tyrant and public robber. 'Tis the same case with judgment and capacity, and all the qualities of that kind. They are indifferent in themselves to the interests of society, and have a tendency to the good or ill of mankind, according as they are directed by these other passions.

As love is *immediately agreeable* to the person, who is actuated by it, and hatred *immediately disagreeable;* this may also be a considerable reason, why we praise all the passions that partake of the former, and blame all those that have any considerable share of the latter. 'Tis certain we are infinitely touch'd with a tender sentiment, as well as with a great one. The tears naturally start in our eyes at the conception of it; nor can we forbear giving a loose to the same tenderness towards the person who exerts it. All this seems to me a proof, that our approbation has, in those cases, an origin different from the prospect of utility and advantage, either to ourselves or others. To which we may add, that men naturally, without reflexion, approve of that character, which is most like their own. The man of a mild disposition and tender affections, in forming a notion of the most perfect virtue, mixes in it more of benevolence and humanity, than the man of courage and enterprize, who naturally looks upon a certain elevation of mind as the most accomplish'd character. This must evidently proceed from an *immediate* sympathy, which men have with characters similar to their own. They enter with more warmth into such sentiments, and feel more sensibly the pleasure, which arises from them.

'Tis remarkable, that nothing touches a man of humanity more than any instance of extraordinary delicacy in love or friendship, where a person is attentive to the smallest concerns of his friend, and is willing to sacrifice to them the most considerable interest of his own. Such delicacies have little influence on society; because they make us regard the greatest trifles: But they are the more engaging, the more minute the concern is, and are a proof of the highest merit in any one, who is capable of them. The passions are so contagious, that they pass with the greatest facility from one person to another, and produce correspondent movements in all human breasts. Where friendship appears in very signal instances, my heart catches the same passion, and is warm'd by those warm sentiments, that display themselves before me. Such agreeable movements must give me an affection to every one that excites them. This is the case with every thing that is agreeable in any person. The transition from pleasure to love is easy: But the transition must here be still more easy; since the agreeable sentiment, which is excited by sympathy, is love itself; and there is nothing requir'd but to change the object.

Hence the peculiar merit of benevolence in all its shapes and appearances. Hence even its weaknesses are virtuous and amiable; and a person, whose grief upon the loss of a friend were excessive, wou'd be esteem'd upon that account. His tenderness bestows a merit, as it does a pleasure, on his melancholy.

We are not, however, to imagine, that all the angry passions are vicious, tho' they are disagreeable. There is a certain indulgence due to human nature in this respect. Anger and hatred are passions inherent in our very frame and constitution. The want of them, on some occasions, may even be a proof of weakness and imbecillity. And where they appear only in a low degree, we not only excuse them because they are natural; but even bestow our applauses on them, because they are inferior to what appears in the greatest part of mankind.

Where these angry passions rise up to cruelty, they form the most detested of all vices. All the pity and concern which we have for the miserable sufferers by this vice, turns against the person guilty of it, and produces a stronger hatred than we are sensible of on any other occasion.

Even when the vice of inhumanity rises not to this extreme degree, our sentiments concerning it are very much influenc'd by reflexions on the harm that results from it. And we may observe in general, that if we can find any quality in a person, which renders him incommodious to those, who live and converse with him, we always allow it to be a fault or blemish, without any farther examination. On the other hand, when we enumerate the good qualities of any person, we always mention those parts of his character, which render him a safe companion, an easy friend, a gentle master, an agreeable husband, or an indulgent father. We consider him with all his relations in society; and love or hate him, according as he affects those, who have any immediate intercourse with him. And 'tis a most certain rule, that if there be no relation of life, in which I cou'd not wish to stand to a particular person, his character must so far be allow'd to be perfect. If he be as little wanting to himself as to others, his character is entirely perfect. This is the ultimate test of merit and virtue.

Section IV
Of Natural Abilities

No distinction is more usual in all systems of ethics, than that betwixt *natural abilities* and *moral virtues;* where the former are plac'd on the same footing with bodily endowments, and are suppos'd to have no merit or moral worth annex'd to them. Whoever considers the matter accurately, will find, that a dispute upon this head wou'd be merely a dispute of words, and that tho' these qualities are not altogether of the same kind, yet they agree in the most material circumstances. They are both of them equally mental qualities: And both of them equally produce pleasure; and have of course an equal tendency to procure the love and esteem of mankind. There are few, who are not as jealous of their character, with regard to sense and knowledge, as to honour and courage; and much more than with regard to temperance and sobriety. Men are even afraid of passing for good-natur'd; lest *that* shou'd be taken for want of understanding: And often boast of more debauches than they have been really engag'd in, to give themselves airs of fire and spirit. In short, the figure a man makes in the world, the reception he meets with in company, the esteem paid him by his acquaintance; all these advantages depend almost as much upon his good sense and judgment, as upon any other part of his character. Let a man have the best intentions in the world, and be the farthest from all injustice and violence, he will never be able to make himself be much regarded, without a moderate share, at least, of parts and understanding. Since then natural abilities, tho', perhaps, inferior, yet are on the same footing, both as to their causes and effects, with those qualities which we call moral virtues, why shou'd we make any distinction betwixt them?

Tho' we refuse to natural abilities the title of virtues, we must allow, that they procure the love and esteem of mankind; that they give a new lustre to the other virtues; and that a man possess'd of them is much more intitled to our good-will and services, than one entirely void of them. It may, indeed, be pretended, that the sentiment of approbation, which those qualities produce, besides its being *inferior*, is also somewhat *different* from that, which attends the other virtues. But this, in my opinion, is not a sufficient reason for excluding them from the catalogue of virtues. Each of the virtues, even benevolence, justice, gratitude, integrity, excites a different sentiment or feeling in the spectator. The characters of *Cæsar* and *Cato*, as drawn by *Sallust*, are both of them virtuous, in the strictest sense of the word; but in a different way: Nor are the sentiments entirely the same, which arise from them. The one produces love; the other esteem: The one is amiable; the other awful: We cou'd wish to meet with the one character in a friend; the other character we wou'd be ambitious of in ourselves. In like manner, the approbation, which attends natural abilities, may be somewhat different to the feeling from that, which arises from the other virtues, without making them entirely of a different species. And indeed we may observe, that the natural abilities, no more than the other virtues, produce not, all of them, the same kind of approbation. Good sense and genius beget esteem: Wit and humour excite love.[1]

Those, who represent the distinction betwixt natural abilities and moral virtues as very material, may say, that the former are entirely involuntary, and have therefore no merit attending them, as having no dependence on liberty and free-will. But to this I answer, *first*, that many of those qualities, which all moralists, especially the antients, comprehend under

the title of moral virtues, are equally involuntary and necessary, with the qualities of the judgment and imagination. Of this nature are constancy, fortitude, magnanimity; and, in short, all the qualities which form the *great* man. I might say the same, in some degree, of the others; it being almost impossible for the mind to change its character in any considerable article, or cure itself of a passionate or splenetic temper, when they are natural to it. The greater degree there is of these blameable qualities, the more vicious they become, and yet they are the less voluntary. *Secondly*, I wou'd have any one give me a reason, why virtue and vice may not be involuntary, as well as beauty and deformity. These moral distinctions arise from the natural distinctions of pain and pleasure; and when we receive those feelings from the general consideration of any quality or character, we denominate it vicious or virtuous. Now I believe no one will assert, that a quality can never produce pleasure or pain to the person who considers it, unless it be perfectly voluntary in the person who possesses it. *Thirdly*, As to free-will, we have shewn that it has no place with regard to the actions, no more than the qualities of men. It is not a just consequence, that what is voluntary is free. Our actions are more voluntary than our judgments; but we have not more liberty in the one than in the other.

But tho' this distinction betwixt voluntary and involuntary be not sufficient to justify the distinction betwixt natural abilities and moral virtues, yet the former distinction will afford us a plausible reason, why moralists have invented the latter. Men have observ'd, that tho' natural abilities and moral qualities be in the main on the same footing, there is, however, this difference betwixt them, that the former are almost invariable by any art or industry; while the latter, or at least, the actions, that proceed from them, may be chang'd by the motives of reward and punishment, praise and blame. Hence legislators, and divines, and moralists, have principally applied themselves to the regulating of these voluntary actions, and have endeavour'd to produce additional motives for being virtuous in that particular. They knew, that to punish a man for folly, or exhort him to be prudent and sagacious, wou'd have but little effect; tho' the same punishments and exhortations, with regard to justice and injustice, might have a considerable influence. But as men, in common life and conversation, do not carry those ends in view, but naturally praise or blame whatever pleases or displeases them, they do not

---

1. Love and esteem are at the bottom the same passions, and arise from like causes. The qualities, that produce both, are agreeable, and give pleasure. But where this pleasure is severe and serious; or where its object is great, and makes a strong impression; or where it produces any degree of humility and awe: In all these cases, the passion, which arises from the pleasure, is more properly denominated esteem than love. Benevolence attends both: But is connected with love in a more eminent degree.

seem much to regard this distinction, but consider prudence under the character of virtue as well as benevolence, and penetration as well as justice. Nay, we find, that all moralists, whose judgment is not perverted by a strict adherence to a system, enter into the same way of thinking; and that the antient moralists in particular made no scruple of placing prudence at the head of the cardinal virtues. There is a sentiment of esteem and approbation, which may be excited, in some degree, by any faculty of the mind, in its perfect state and condition; and to account for this sentiment is the business of *Philosophers*. It belongs to *Grammarians* to examine what qualities are entitled to the denomination of *virtue*; nor will they find, upon trial, that this is so easy a task, as at first sight they may be apt to imagine.

The principal reason why natural abilities are esteem'd, is because of their tendency to be useful to the person, who is possess'd of them. 'Tis impossible to execute any design with success, where it is not conducted with prudence and discretion; nor will the goodness of our intentions alone suffice to procure us a happy issue to our enterprizes. Men are superior to beasts principally by the superiority of their reason; and they are the degrees of the same faculty, which set such an infinite difference betwixt one man and another. All the advantages of art are owing to human reason; and where fortune is not very capricious, the most considerable part of these advantages must fall to the share of the prudent and sagacious.

When it is ask'd, whether a quick or a slow apprehension be most valuable? whether one, that at first view penetrates into a subject, but can perform nothing upon study; or a contrary character, which must work out every thing by dint of application? whether a clear head, or a copious invention? whether a profound genius, or a sure judgment? in short, what character, or peculiar understanding, is more excellent than another? 'Tis evident we can answer none of these questions, without considering which of those qualities capacitates a man best for the world, and carries him farthest in any of his undertakings.

There are many other qualities of the mind, whose merit is deriv'd from the same origin. *Industry, perseverance, patience, activity, vigilance, application, constancy*, with other virtues of that kind, which 'twill be easy to recollect, are esteem'd valuable upon no other account, than their advantage in the conduct of life. 'Tis the same case with *temperance, frugality, economy, resolution:* As on the other hand, *prodigal-*

ity, luxury, irresolution, uncertainty, are vicious, merely because they draw ruin upon us, and incapacitate us for business and action.

As wisdom and good-sense are valued, because they are *useful* to the person possess'd of them; so *wit* and *eloquence* are valued, because they are *immediately agreeable* to others. On the other hand, *good humour* is lov'd and esteem'd, because it is *immediately agreeable* to the person himself. 'Tis evident, that the conversation of a man of wit is very satisfactory; as a chearful good-humour'd companion diffuses a joy over the whole company, from a sympathy with his gaiety. These qualities, therefore, being agreeable, they naturally beget love and esteem, and answer to all the characters of virtue.

'Tis difficult to tell, on many occasions, what it is that renders one man's conversation so agreeable and entertaining, and another's so insipid and distasteful. As conversation is a transcript of the mind as well as books, the same qualities, which render the one valuable, must give us an esteem for the other. This we shall consider afterwards. In the mean time it may be affirm'd in general, that all the merit a man may derive from his conversation (which, no doubt, may be very considerable) arises from nothing but the pleasure it conveys to those who are present.

In this view, *cleanliness* is also to be regarded as a virtue; since it naturally renders us agreeable to others, and is a very considerable source of love and affection. No one will deny, that a negligence in this particular is a fault; and as faults are nothing but smaller vices, and this fault can have no other origin than the uneasy sensation, which it excites in others, we may in this instance, seemingly so trivial, clearly discover the origin of the moral distinction of vice and virtue in other instances.

Besides all those qualities, which render a person lovely or valuable, there is also a certain *je-ne-sçai[sais]-quoi* of agreeable and handsome, that concurs to the same effect. In this case, as well as in that of wit and eloquence, we must have recourse to a certain sense, which acts without reflexion, and regards not the tendencies of qualities and characters. Some moralists account for all the sentiments of virtue by this sense. Their hypothesis is very plausible. Nothing but a particular enquiry can give the preference to any other hypothesis. When we find, that almost all the virtues have such particular tendencies; and also find, that these tendencies are sufficient alone to give a strong sentiment of approbation: We cannot doubt, after this, that qualities are approv'd of, in proportion to the advantage, which results from them.

The *decorum* or *indecorum* of a quality, with regard to the age, or character, or station, contributes also to its praise or blame. This decorum depends, in a great measure, upon experience. 'Tis usual to see men lose their levity, as they advance in years. Such a degree of gravity, therefore, and such years, are connected together in our thoughts. When we observe them separated in any person's character, this imposes a kind of violence on our imagination, and is disagreeable.

That faculty of the soul, which, of all others, is of the least consequence to the character, and has the least virtue or vice in its several degrees, at the same time, that it admits of a great variety of degrees, is the *memory.* Unless it rise up to that stupendous height as to surprize us, or sink so low as, in some measure, to affect the judgment, we commonly take no notice of its variations, nor ever mention them to the praise or dispraise of any person. 'Tis so far from being a virtue to have a good memory, that men generally affect to complain of a bad one; and endeavouring to persuade the world, that what they say is entirely of their own invention, sacrifice it to the praise of genius and judgment. Yet to consider the matter abstractedly, 'twou'd be difficult to give a reason, why the faculty of recalling past ideas with truth and clearness, shou'd not have as much merit in it, as the faculty of placing our present ideas in such an order, as to form true propositions and opinions. The reason of the difference certainly must be, that the memory is exerted without any sensation of pleasure or pain; and in all its middling degrees serves almost equally well in business and affairs. But the least variations in the judgment are sensibly felt in their consequences; while at the same time that faculty is never exerted in any eminent degree, without an extraordinary delight and satisfaction. The sympathy with this utility and pleasure bestows a merit on the understanding; and the absence of it makes us consider the memory as a faculty very indifferent to blame or praise.

Before I leave this subject of *natural abilities*, I must observe, that, perhaps, one source of the esteem and affection, which attends them, is deriv'd from the *importance* and *weight*, which they bestow on the person possess'd of them. He becomes of greater consequence in life. His resolutions and actions affect a greater number of his fellow-creatures. Both his friendship and enmity are of moment. And 'tis easy to observe, that whoever is elevated, after this manner, above the rest of mankind, must excite in us the sentiments of esteem and approbation. Whatever is important engages our attention, fixes our thought, and is contemplated with satisfaction. The histories of kingdoms are more interesting than domestic stories: The histories of great empires more than those of small cities and principalities: And the histories of wars and revolutions more than those of peace and order. We sympathize with the persons that suffer, in all the various sentiments which belong to their fortunes. The mind is occupied by the multitude of the objects, and by the strong passions, that display themselves. And this occupation or agitation of the mind is commonly agreeable and amusing. The same theory accounts for the esteem and regard we pay to men of extraordinary parts and abilities. The good and ill of multitudes are connected with their actions. Whatever they undertake is important, and challenges our attention. Nothing is to be over-look'd and despis'd, that regards them. And where any person can excite these sentiments, he soon acquires our esteem; unless other circumstances of his character render him odious and disagreeable.

Section V
Some Farther Reflexions Concerning the Natural Virtues

It has been observ'd, in treating of the passions, that pride and humility, love and hatred, are excited by any advantages or disadvantages of the *mind, body,* or *fortune;* and that these advantages or disadvantages have that effect, by producing a separate impression of pain or pleasure. The pain or pleasure, which arises from the general survey or view of any action or quality of the *mind,* constitutes its vice or virtue, and gives rise to our approbation or blame, which is nothing but a fainter and more imperceptible love or hatred. We have assign'd four different sources of this pain and pleasure; and in order to justify more fully that hypothesis, it may here be proper to observe, that the advantages or disadvantages of the *body* and of *fortune,* produce a pain or pleasure from the very same principles. The tendency of any object to be *useful* to the person possess'd of it, or to others; to convey *pleasure* to him or to others; all these circumstances convey an immediate pleasure to the person, who considers the object, and command his love and approbation.

To begin with the advantages of the *body;* we may observe a phænomenon, which might appear somewhat trivial and ludicrous, if any thing cou'd be trivial, which fortified a conclusion of such importance, or ludicrous, which was employ'd in a philosophical reasoning. 'Tis a general remark, that those we call good *women's men,* who have either signaliz'd themselves by their amorous exploits, or whose make of body promises any extraordinary vigour of that kind, are well received by the fair sex, and naturally engage the affections even of those, whose virtue prevents any design of ever giving employment to those talents. Here 'tis evident, that the ability of such a person to give enjoyment, is the real source of that love and esteem he meets with among the females; at the same time that the women, who love and esteem him, have no prospect of receiving that enjoyment themselves, and can only be affected by means of their sympathy with one, that has a commerce of love with him. This instance is singular, and merits our attention.

Another source of the pleasure we receive from considering bodily advantages, is their utility to the person himself, who is possess'd of them. 'Tis certain, that a considerable part of the beauty of men, as well as of other animals, consists in such a conformation of members, as we find by experience to be attended with strength and agility, and to capacitate the creature for any action or exercise. Broad shoulders, a lank belly, firm joints, taper legs; all these are beautiful in our species, because they are signs of force and vigour, which being advantages we naturally sympathize with, they convey to the beholder a share of that satisfaction they produce in the possessor.

So far as to the *utility,* which may attend any quality of the body. As to the immediate *pleasure,* 'tis certain, that an air of health, as well as of strength and agility, makes a considerable part of beauty; and that a sickly air in another is always disagreeable, upon account of that idea of pain and uneasiness, which it conveys to us. On the other hand, we are pleas'd with the regularity of our own features, tho' it be neither useful to ourselves nor others; and 'tis necessary for us, in some measure, to set ourselves at a distance, to make it convey to us any satisfaction. We commonly consider ourselves as we appear in the eyes of others, and sympathize with the advantageous sentiments they entertain with regard to us.

How far the advantages of *fortune* produce esteem and approbation from the same principles, we may satisfy ourselves by reflecting on our precedent reasoning on that subject. We have observ'd, that our approbation of those, who are possess'd of the advantages of fortune, may be ascrib'd to three different causes. *First,* To that immediate pleasure, which a rich man gives us, by the view of the beautiful cloaths, equipage, gardens, or houses, which he possesses. *Secondly,* To the advantage, which we hope to reap from him by his generosity and liberality. *Thirdly,* To the pleasure and advantage, which he himself reaps from his possessions, and which produce an agreeable sympathy in us. Whether we ascribe our esteem of the rich and great to one or all of these causes, we may clearly see the traces of those principles, which give rise to the sense of vice and virtue. I believe most people, at first sight, will be inclin'd to ascribe our esteem of the rich to self-interest, and the prospect of advantage. But as 'tis certain, that our esteem or deference extends beyond any prospect of advantage to ourselves, 'tis evident, that that sentiment must proceed from a sympathy with those, who are dependant on the person we esteem and respect, and who have an immediate connexion with him. We consider him as a person capable of contributing to the happiness or enjoyment of his fellow-creatures, whose sentiments, with regard to him, we naturally embrace. And this consideration will serve to justify my hypothesis in preferring the *third* principle to the other two, and ascribing our esteem of the rich to a sympathy with the pleasure and advantage, which they themselves receive from their possessions. For as even the other two principles cannot operate to a due extent, or account for all the phænomena, without having recourse to a sympathy of one kind or other; 'tis much more natural to chuse that sympathy, which is immediate and direct, than that which is remote and indirect. To which we may add, that where the riches or power are very great, and render the person considerable and important in the world, the esteem attending them, may, in part, be ascrib'd to another source, distinct from these three, *viz.* their interesting the mind by a prospect of the multitude, and importance of their consequences: Tho', in order to account for the operation of this principle, we must also have recourse to *sympathy;* as we have observ'd in the preceding section.

It may not be amiss, on this occasion, to remark the flexibility of our sentiments, and the several changes they so readily receive from the objects, with which they are conjoin'd. All the sentiments of approbation, which attend any particular species of objects, have a great resemblance to each other, tho' deriv'd from different sources; and, on the other hand, those sentiments, when directed to different objects, are different to the feeling, tho' deriv'd from the same source. Thus the beauty of all visible objects causes a pleasure pretty much the same, tho' it be sometimes deriv'd from the mere *species* and appearance of the objects; sometimes from sympathy, and an idea of their utility. In like manner, whenever we survey the actions and characters of men, without any particular interest in them, the pleasure, or pain, which arises from the survey (with some minute differences) is, in the main, of the same kind, tho' perhaps there be a great diversity in the causes, from which it is deriv'd. On the other hand, a convenient house, and a virtuous character, cause not the same feeling of approbation; even tho' the source of our approbation be the same, and flow from sympathy and an idea of their utility. There is something very inexplicable in this variation of our feelings; but 'tis what we have experience of with regard to all our passions and sentiments.

Section VI
Conclusion of This Book

Thus upon the whole I am hopeful, that nothing is wanting to an accurate proof of this system of ethics. We are certain, that sympathy is a very powerful principle in human nature. We are also certain, that it has a great influence on our sense of beauty, when we regard external objects, as well as when we judge of morals. We find, that it has force sufficient to give us the strongest sentiments of approbation, when it operates alone, without the concurrence of any other principle; as in the cases of justice, allegiance, chastity, and good-manners. We may observe, that all the circumstances requisite for its operation are found in most of the virtues; which have, for the most part, a tendency to the good of society, or to that of the person possess'd of them. If we compare all these circumstances, we shall not doubt, that sympathy is the chief source of moral distinctions; especially when we reflect, that no objection can be rais'd against this hypothesis in one case, which will not extend to all cases. Justice is certainly approv'd of for no other reason, than because it has a tendency to the public good: And the public good is indifferent to us, except so far as sympathy interests us in it. We may presume the like with regard to all the other virtues,

which have a like tendency to the public good. They must derive all their merit from our sympathy with those, who reap any advantage from them: As the virtues, which have a tendency to the good of the person possess'd of them, derive their merit from our sympathy with him.

Most people will readily allow, that the useful qualities of the mind are virtuous, because of their utility. This way of thinking is so natural, and occurs on so many occasions, that few will make any scruple of admitting it. Now this being once admitted, the force of sympathy must necessarily be acknowledg'd. Virtue is consider'd as means to an end. Means to an end are only valued so far as the end is valued. But the happiness of strangers affects us by sympathy alone. To that principle, therefore, we are to ascribe the sentiment of approbation, which arises from the survey of all those virtues, that are useful to society, or to the person possess'd of them. These form the most considerable part of morality.

Were it proper in such a subject to bribe the reader's assent, or employ any thing but solid argument, we are here abundantly supplied with topics to engage the affections. All lovers of virtue (and such we all are in speculation, however we may degenerate in practice) must certainly be pleas'd to see moral distinctions deriv'd from so noble a source, which gives us a just notion both of the *generosity* and *capacity* of our nature. It requires but very little knowledge of human affairs to perceive, that a sense of morals is a principle inherent in the soul, and one of the most powerful that enters into the composition. But this sense must certainly acquire new force, when reflecting on itself, it approves of those principles, from whence it is deriv'd, and finds nothing but what is great and good in its rise and origin. Those who resolve the sense of morals into original instincts of the human mind, may defend the cause of virtue with sufficient authority; but want the advantage, which those possess, who account for that sense by an extensive sympathy with mankind. According to the latter system, not only virtue must be approv'd of, but also the sense of virtue: And not only that sense, but also the principles, from whence it is deriv'd. So that nothing is presented on any side, but what is laudable and good.

This observation may be extended to justice, and the other virtues of that kind. Tho' justice be artificial, the sense of its morality is natural. 'Tis the combination of men, in a system of conduct, which renders any act of justice beneficial to society. But when once it has that tendency, we *naturally* approve of it; and if we did not so, 'tis impossible any combination or convention cou'd ever produce that sentiment.

Most of the inventions of men are subject to change. They depend upon humour and caprice. They have a vogue for a time, and then sink into oblivion. It may, perhaps, be apprehended, that if justice were allow'd to be a human invention, it must be plac'd on the same footing. But the cases are widely different. The interest, on which justice is founded, is the greatest imaginable, and extends to all times and places. It cannot possibly be serv'd by any other invention. It is obvious, and discovers itself on the very first formation of society. All these causes render the rules of justice stedfast and immutable; at least, as immutable as human nature. And if they were founded on original instincts, cou'd they have any greater stability?

The same system may help us to form a just notion of the *happiness*, as well as of the *dignity* of virtue, and may interest every principle of our nature in the embracing and cherishing that noble quality. Who indeed does not feel an accession of alacrity in his pursuits of knowledge and ability of every kind, when he considers, that besides the advantages, which immediately result from these acquisitions, they also give him a new lustre in the eyes of mankind, and are universally attended with esteem and approbation? And who can think any advantages of fortune a suffi-

cient compensation for the least breach of the *social* virtues, when he considers, that not only his character with regard to others, but also his peace and inward satisfaction entirely depend upon his strict observance of them; and that a mind will never be able to bear its own survey, that has been wanting in its part to mankind and society? But I forbear insisting on this subject. Such reflexions require a work apart, very different from the genius of the present. The anatomist ought never to emulate the painter: nor in his accurate dissections and portraitures of the smaller parts of the human body, pretend to give his figures any graceful and engaging attitude or expression. There is even something hideous, or at least minute in the views of things, which he presents; and 'tis necessary the objects shou'd be set more at a distance, and be more cover'd up from sight, to make them engaging to the eye and imagination. An anatomist, however, is admirably fitted to give advice to a painter; and 'tis even impracticable to excel in the latter art, without the assistance of the former. We must have an exact knowledge of the parts, their situation and connexion, before we can design with any elegance or correctness. And thus the most abstract speculations concerning human nature, however cold and unentertaining, become subservient to *practical morality;* and may render this latter science more correct in its precepts, and more persuasive in its exhortations.

Of the Original Contract

As no party, in the present age, can well support itself, without a philosophical or speculative system of principles, annexed to its political or practical one; we accordingly find, that each of the factions, into which this nation is divided, has reared up a fabric of the former kind, in order to protect and cover that scheme of actions, which it pursues. The people being commonly very rude builders, especially in this speculative way, and more especially still, when actuated by party-zeal; it is natural to imagine, that their workmanship must be a little unshapely, and discover evident marks of that violence and hurry, in which it was raised. The one party, by tracing up Government to the *Deity*, endeavour to render it so sacred and invio-

late, that it must be little less than sacrilege, however tyrannical it may become, to touch or invade it, in the smallest article. The other party, by founding government altogether on the consent of the *People*, suppose that there is a kind of *original contract*, by which the subjects have tacitly reserved the power of resisting their sovereign, whenever they find themselves aggrieved by that authority, with which they have, for certain purposes, voluntarily entrusted him. These are the speculative principles of the two parties; and these too are the practical consequences deduced from them.

I shall venture to affirm, *That both these* systems *of speculative principles are just; though not in the sense, intended by the parties:* And, *That both the* schemes *of practical consequences are prudent; though not in the extremes, to which each party, in opposition to the other, has commonly endeavoured to carry them.*

That the *Deity* is the ultimate author of all government, will never be denied by any, who admit a general providence, and allow, that all events in the universe are conducted by an uniform plan, and directed to wise purposes. As it is impossible for the human race to subsist, at least in any comfortable or secure state, without the protection of government; this institution must certainly have been intended by that beneficent Being, who means the good of all his creatures: And as it has universally, in fact, taken place, in all countries, and all ages; we may conclude, with still greater certainty, that it was intended by that omniscient Being, who can never be deceived by any event or operation. But since he gave rise to it, not by any particular or miraculous interposition, but by his concealed and universal efficacy; a sovereign cannot, properly speaking, be called his vice-gerent, in any other sense than every power or force, being derived from him, may be said to act by his commission. Whatever actually happens is comprehended in the general plan or intention of providence; nor has the greatest and most lawful prince any more reason, upon that account, to plead a peculiar sacredness or inviolable authority, than an inferior magistrate, or even an usurper, or even a robber and a pyrate. The same divine superintendent, who, for wise purposes, invested a *Titus* or a *Trajan*[1] with authority, did also, for purposes, no doubt, equally wise, though unknown, bestow power on a *Borgia* or an *Angria.* The same causes, which gave rise to the sovereign power in every state, establish'd likewise every petty jurisdiction in it, and every limited authority. A constable, therefore, no less than a king, acts by a divine commission, and possesses an indefeasible right.

When we consider how nearly equal all men are in their bodily force, and even in their mental powers and faculties, till cultivated by education; we must necessarily allow, that nothing but their own consent could, at first, associate them together, and subject them to any authority. The people, if we trace government to its first origin in the woods and desarts, are the source of all power and jurisdiction, and voluntarily, for the sake of peace and order, abandoned their native liberty, and received laws from their equal and companion. The conditions, upon which they were willing to submit, were either expressed, or were so clear and obvious, that it might well be esteemed superfluous to express them. If this, then, be meant by the *original contract,* it cannot be denied, that all government is, at first, founded on a contract, and that the most ancient rude combinations of mankind were formed chiefly by that principle. In vain, are we asked in what records this charter of our liberties is registered. It was not written on parchment, nor yet on leaves or barks of trees. It preceded the use of writing and all the other civilized arts of life. But we trace it plainly in the nature of man, and in the equality, or something approaching equality, which we find in all the individuals of that species. The force, which now prevails, and which is founded on fleets and armies, is plainly political, and derived from authority, the effect of established government. A man's natural force consists only in the vigour of his limbs, and the firmness of his courage; which could never subject multitudes to the command of one. Nothing but their own consent, and their sense of the advantages resulting from peace and order, could have had that influence.

Yet even this consent was long very imperfect, and could not be the basis of a regular administration. The chieftain, who had probably acquired his influence during the continuance of war, ruled more by persuasion than command; and till he could employ force to reduce the refractory and disobedient, the society could scarcely be said to have attained a state of civil government. No compact or agreement, it is evident, was expressly formed for general submission; an idea far beyond the comprehension of savages: Each exertion of authority in the chieftain must have been particular, and called forth by the present exigencies of the case: The sensible utility, resulting from his interposition, made these exertions become daily more frequent; and their frequency gradually produced an habitual, and, if you please to call it so, a voluntary, and therefore precarious, acquiescence in the people.

But philosophers, who have embraced a party (if that be not a contradiction in terms) are not contented with these concessions. They assert, not only that government in its earliest infancy arose from consent or rather the voluntary acquiescence of the

---

1. An Elizabeth or a Henry the IVth of France: in editions before 1770.

people; but also, that, even at present, when it has attained its full maturity, it rests on no other foundation. They affirm, that all men are still born equal, and owe allegiance to no prince or government, unless bound by the obligation and sanction of a *promise.* And as no man, without some equivalent, would forego the advantages of his native liberty, and subject himself to the will of another; this promise is always understood to be conditional, and imposes on him no obligation, unless he meet with justice and protection from his sovereign. These advantages the sovereign promises him in return; and if he fail in the execution, he has broken, on his part, the articles of engagement, and has thereby freed his subject from all obligations to allegiance. Such, according to these philosophers, is the foundation of authority in every government; and such the right of resistance, possessed by every subject.

But would these reasoners look abroad into the world, they would meet with nothing that, in the least, corresponds to their ideas, or can warrant so refined and philosophical a system. On the contrary, we find, every where, princes, who claim their subjects as their property, and assert their independent right of sovereignty, from conquest or succession. We find also, every where, subjects, who acknowledge this right in their prince, and suppose themselves born under obligations of obedience to a certain sovereign, as much as under the ties of reverence and duty to certain parents. These connexions are always conceived to be equally independent of our consent, in *Persia* and *China;* in *France* and *Spain;* and even in *Holland* and *England,* wherever the doctrines abovementioned have not been carefully inculcated. Obedience or subjection becomes so familiar, that most men never make any enquiry about its origin or cause, more than about the principle of gravity, resistance, or the most universal laws of nature. Or if curiosity ever move them; as soon as they learn, that they themselves and their ancestors have, for several ages, or from time immemorial, been subject to such a form of government or such a family; they immediately acquiesce, and acknowledge their obligation to allegiance. Were you to preach, in most parts of the world, that political connexions are founded altogether on voluntary consent or a mutual promise, the magistrate would soon imprison you, as seditious, for loosening the ties of obedience; if your friends did not before shut you up as delirious, for advancing such absurdities. It is strange, that an act of the mind, which every individual is supposed to have formed, and after he came to the use of reason too, otherwise it could have no authority; that this act, I say, should be so much unknown to all of them, that, over the face of the whole earth, there scarcely remain any traces or memory of it.

But the contract, on which government is founded, is said to be the *original contract;* and consequently may be supposed too old to fall under the knowledge of the present generation. If the agreement, by which savage men first associated and conjoined their force, be here meant, this is acknowledged to be real; but being so ancient, and being obliterated by a thousand changes of government and princes, it cannot now be supposed to retain any authority. If we would say any thing to the purpose, we must assert, that every particular government, which is lawful, and which imposes any duty of allegiance on the subject, was, at first, founded on consent and a voluntary compact. But besides that this supposes the consent of the fathers to bind the children, even to the most remote generations, (which republican writers will never allow) besides this, I say, it is not justified by history or experience, in any age or country of the world.

Almost all the governments, which exist at present, or of which there remains any record in story, have been founded originally, either on usurpation or conquest, or both, without any pretence of a fair consent, or voluntary subjection of the people. When an artful and bold man is placed at the head of an army or faction, it is often easy for him, by employing, sometimes violence, sometimes false pretences, to establish his dominion over a people a hundred times more numerous than his partizans. He allows no such open communication, that his enemies can know, with certainty, their number or force. He gives them no leisure to assemble together in a body to oppose him. Even all those, who are the instruments of his usurpation, may wish his fall; but their ignorance of each other's intention keeps them in awe, and is the sole cause of his security. By such arts as these, many governments have been establish'd; and this is all the *original contract,* which they have to boast of.

The face of the earth is continually changing, by the encrease of small kingdoms into great empires, by the dissolution of great empires into smaller kingdoms, by the planting of colonies, by the migration of tribes. Is there any thing discoverable in all these events, but force and violence? Where is the mutual agreement or voluntary association so much talked of?

Even the smoothest way, by which a nation may receive a foreign master, by marriage or a will, is not extremely honourable for the people; but supposes them to be disposed of, like a dowry or a legacy, according to the pleasure or interest of their rulers.

But where no force interposes, and election takes place; what is this election so highly vaunted? It is either the combination of a few great men, who decide for the whole, and will allow of no opposition: Or it is the fury of a multitude, that follow a seditious ringleader, who is not known, perhaps, to a dozen among them, and who owes his advancement merely to his own impudence, or to the momentary caprice of his fellows.

Are these disorderly elections, which are rare too, of such mighty authority, as to be the only lawful foundation of all government and allegiance?

In reality, there is not a more terrible event, than a total dissolution of government, which gives liberty to the multitude, and makes the determination or choice of a new establishment depend upon a number, which nearly approaches to that of the body of the people: For it never comes entirely to the whole body of them. Every wise man, then, wishes to see, at the head of a powerful and obedient army, a general, who may speedily seize the prize, and give to the people a master, which they are so unfit to chuse for themselves. So little correspondent is fact and reality to those philosophical notions.

Let not the establishment at the *Revolution* deceive us, or make us so much in love with a philosophical origin to government, as to imagine all others monstrous and irregular. Even that event was far from corresponding to these refined ideas. It was only the succession, and that only in the regal part of the government, which was then changed: And it was only the majority of seven hundred, who determined that change for near ten millions. I doubt not, indeed, but the bulk of those ten millions acquiesced willingly in the determination: But was the matter left, in the least, to their choice? Was it not justly supposed to be, from that moment, decided, and every man punished, who refused to submit to the new sovereign? How otherwise could the matter have ever been brought to any issue or conclusion?

The republic of *Athens* was, I believe, the most extensive democracy, that we read of in history: Yet if we make the requisite allowances for the women, the slaves, and the strangers, we shall find, that that establishment was not, at first, made, nor any law

ever voted, by a tenth part of those who were bound to pay obedience to it: Not to mention the islands and foreign dominions, which the *Athenians* claimed as theirs by right of conquest. And as it is well known, that popular assemblies in that city were always full of licence and disorder, notwithstanding the institutions and laws by which they were checked: How much more disorderly must they prove, where they form not the established constitution, but meet tumultuously on the dissolution of the ancient government, in order to give rise to a new one? How chimerical must it be to talk of a choice in such circumstances?

The Achæans enjoyed the freest and most perfect democracy of all antiquity; yet they employed force to oblige some cities to enter into their league, as we learn from *Polybius.*[2]

Harry the IVth and *Harry the VIIth* of England, had really no title to the throne but a parliamentary election; yet they never would acknowledge it, lest they should thereby weaken their authority. Strange, if the only real foundation of all authority be consent and promise!

It is in vain to say, that all governments are or should be, at first, founded on popular consent, as much as the necessity of human affairs will admit. This favours entirely my pretension. I maintain, that human affairs will never admit of this consent; seldom of the appearance of it. But that conquest or usurpation, that is, in plain terms, force, by dissolving the ancient governments, is the origin of almost all the new ones, which were ever establish'd in the world. And that in the few cases, where consent may seem to have taken place, it was commonly so irregular, so confined, or so much intermixed either with fraud or violence, that it cannot have any great authority.

My intention here is not to exclude the consent of the people from being one just foundation of government where it has place. It is surely the best and most sacred of any. I only pretend, that it has very seldom had place in any degree, and never almost in its full extent. And that therefore some other foundation of government must also be admitted.

Were all men possessed of so inflexible a regard to justice, that, of themselves, they would totally abstain from the properties of others; they had for ever remained in a state of absolute liberty, without subjec-

2. Lib. ii. cap. 38.

tion to any magistrate or political society: But this is a state of perfection, of which human nature is justly deemed incapable. Again; were all men possessed of so perfect an understanding, as always to know their own interests, no form of government had ever been submitted to, but what was establish'd on consent, and was fully canvassed by every member of the society: But this state of perfection is likewise much superior to human nature. Reason, history, and experience shew us, that all political societies have had an origin much less accurate and regular; and were one to choose a period of time, when the people's consent was the least regarded in public transactions, it would be precisely on the establishment of a new government. In a settled constitution, their inclinations are often consulted; but during the fury of revolutions, conquests, and public convulsions, military force or political craft usually decides the controversy.

When a new government is established, by whatever means, the people are commonly dissatisfied with it, and pay obedience more from fear and necessity, than from any idea of allegiance or of moral obligation. The prince is watchful and jealous, and must carefully guard against every beginning or appearance of insurrection. Time, by degrees, removes all these difficulties, and accustoms the nation to regard, as their lawful or native princes, that family, which, at first, they considered as usurpers or foreign conquerors. In order to found this opinion, they have no recourse to any notion of voluntary consent or promise, which, they know, never was, in this case, either expected or demanded. The original establishment was formed by violence, and submitted to from necessity. The subsequent administration is also supported by power, and acquiesced in by the people, not as a matter of choice, but of obligation. They imagine not that their consent gives their prince a title: but they willingly consent, because they think, that, from long possession, he has acquired a title, independent of their choice or inclination.

Should it be said, that, by living under the dominion of a prince, which one might leave, every individual has given a *tacit* consent to his authority, and promised him obedience; it may be answered, that such an implied consent can only have place, where a man imagines, that the matter depends on his choice. But where he thinks (as all mankind do who are born under established governments) that by his birth he owes allegiance to a certain prince or certain form of government; it would be absurd to infer a consent or

choice, which he expressly, in this case, renounces and disclaims.

Can we seriously say, that a poor peasant or partizan has a free choice to leave his country, when he knows no foreign language or manners, and lives from day to day, by the small wages which he acquires? We may as well assert, that a man, by remaining in a vessel, freely consents to the dominion of the master; though he was carried on board while asleep, and must leap into the ocean, and perish, the moment he leaves her.

What if the prince forbid his subjects to quit his dominions; as in *Tiberius*'s time, it was regarded as a crime in a *Roman* knight that he had attempted to fly to the *Parthians*, in order to escape the tyranny of that emperor?[3] Or as the ancient *Muscovites* prohibited all travelling under pain of death? And did a prince observe, that many of his subjects were seized with the frenzy of migrating to foreign countries, he would doubtless, with great reason and justice, restrain them, in order to prevent the depopulation of his own kingdom. Would he forfeit the allegiance of all his subjects, by so wise and reasonable a law? Yet the freedom of their choice is surely, in that case, ravished from them.

A company of men, who should leave their native country, in order to people some uninhabited region, might dream of recovering their native freedom; but they would soon find, that their prince still laid claim to them, and called them his subjects, even in their new settlement. And in this he would but act conformably to the common ideas of mankind.

The truest *tacit* consent of this kind, that is ever observed, is when a foreigner settles in any country, and is beforehand acquainted with the prince, and government, and laws, to which he must submit: Yet is his allegiance, though more voluntary, much less expected or depended on, than that of a natural born subject. On the contrary, his native prince still asserts a claim to him. And if he punish not the renegade, when he seizes him in war with his new prince's commission; this clemency is not founded on the municipal law, which in all countries condemns the prisoner; but on the consent of princes, who have agreed to this indulgence, in order to prevent reprisals.

Did one generation of men go off the stage at once, and another succeed, as is the case with silk-worms

---

3. *Tacit.* Ann. vi. cap. 14.

and butterflies, the new race, if they had sense enough to choose their government, which surely is never the case with men, might voluntarily, and by general consent, establish their own form of civil polity, without any regard to the laws or precedents, which prevailed among their ancestors. But as human society is in perpetual flux, one man every hour going out of the world, another coming into it, it is necessary, in order to preserve stability in government, that the new brood should conform themselves to the established constitution, and nearly follow the path which their fathers, treading in the footsteps of theirs, had marked out to them. Some innovations must necessarily have place in every human institution, and it is happy where the enlightened genius of the age gives these a direction to the side of reason, liberty, and justice: but violent innovations no individual is entitled to make: they are even dangerous to be attempted by the legislature: more ill than good is ever to be expected from them: and if history affords examples to the contrary, they are not to be drawn into precedent, and are only to be regarded as proofs, that the science of politics affords few rules, which will not admit of some exception, and which may not sometimes be controuled by fortune and accident. The violent innovations in the reign of *Henry VIII* proceeded from an imperious monarch, seconded by the appearance of legislative authority: Those in the reign of *Charles I* were derived from faction and fanaticism, and both of them have proved happy in the issue: But even the former were long the source of many disorders, and still more dangers; and if the measures of allegiance were to be taken from the latter, a total anarchy must have place in human society, and a final period at once be put to every government.

Suppose, that an usurper, after having banished his lawful prince and royal family, should establish his dominion for ten or a dozen years in any country, and should preserve so exact a discipline in his troops, and so regular a disposition in his garrisons, that no insurrection had ever been raised, or even murmur heard, against his administration: Can it be asserted, that the people, who in their hearts abhor his treason, have tacitly consented to his authority, and promised him allegiance, merely because, from necessity, they live under his dominion? Suppose again their native prince restored, by means of an army, which he levies in foreign countries: They receive him with joy and exultation, and shew plainly with what reluctance they had submitted to any other yoke. I may now ask, upon what foundation the prince's title stands? Not on popular consent surely: For though the people willingly acquiesce in his authority, they never imagine, that their consent made him sovereign. They consent; because they apprehend him to be already, by birth, their lawful sovereign. And as to that tacit consent, which may now be inferred from their living under his dominion, this is no more than what they formerly gave to the tyrant and usurper.

When we assert, that all lawful government arises from the consent of the people, we certainly do them a great deal more honour than they deserve, or even expect and desire from us. After the *Roman* dominions became too unwieldly for the republic to govern them, the people, over the whole known world, were extremely grateful to *Augustus* for that authority, which, by violence, he had established over them; and they showed an equal disposition to submit to the successor, whom he left them, by his last will and testament. It was afterwards their misfortune, that there never was, in one family, any long regular succession; but that their line of princes was continually broken, either by private assassinations or public rebellions. The *Prætorian* bands, on the failure of every family, set up one emperor; the legions in the East a second; those in *Germany*, perhaps, a third: And the sword alone could decide the controversy. The condition of the people, in that mighty monarchy, was to be lamented, not because the choice of the emperor was never left to them; for that was impracticable: But because they never fell under any succession of masters, who might regularly follow each other. As to the violence and wars and bloodshed, occasioned by every new settlement; these were not blameable, because they were inevitable.

The house of *Lancaster* ruled in this island about sixty years; yet the partizans of the white rose seemed daily to multiply in *England*. The present establishment has taken place during a still longer period. Have all views of right in another family been utterly extinguished; even though scarce any man now alive had arrived at years of discretion, when it was expelled, or could have consented to its dominion, or have promised it allegiance? A sufficient indication surely of the general sentiment of mankind on this head. For we blame not the partizans of the abdicated family, merely on account of the long time, during which they have preserved their imaginary loyalty. We blame them for adhering to a family, which, we affirm, has been justly expelled, and which, from the moment the new settlement took place, had forfeited all title to authority.

But would we have a more regular, at least a more philosophical, refutation of this principle of an original contract or popular consent; perhaps, the following observations may suffice.

All *moral* duties may be divided into two kinds. The *first* are those, to which men are impelled by a natural instinct or immediate propensity, which operates on them, independent of all ideas of obligation, and of all views, either to public or private utility. Of this nature are, love of children, gratitude to benefactors, pity to the unfortunate. When we reflect on the advantage, which results to society from such humane instincts, we pay them the just tribute of moral approbation and esteem: But the person, actuated by them, feels their power and influence, antecedent to any such reflection.

The *second* kind of moral duties are such as are not supported by any original instinct of nature, but are performed entirely from a sense of obligation, when we consider the necessities of human society, and the impossibility of supporting it, if these duties were neglected. It is thus *justice* or a regard to the property of others, *fidelity* or the observance of promises, become obligatory, and acquire an authority over mankind. For as it is evident, that every man loves himself better than any other person, he is naturally impelled to extend his acquisitions as much as possible; and nothing can restrain him in this propensity, but reflection and experience, by which he learns the pernicious effects of that licence, and the total dissolution of society which must ensue from it. His original inclination, therefore, or instinct, is here checked and restrained by a subsequent judgment or observation.

The case is precisely the same with the political or civil duty of *allegiance*, as with the natural duties of justice and fidelity. Our primary instincts lead us, either to indulge ourselves in unlimited freedom, or to seek dominion over others: And it is reflection only, which engages us to sacrifice such strong passions to the interests of peace and public order. A small degree of experience and observation suffices to teach us, that society cannot possibly be maintained without the authority of magistrates, and that this authority must soon fall into contempt, where exact obedience is not paid to it. The observation of these general and obvious interests is the source of all allegiance, and of that moral obligation, which we attribute to it.

What necessity, therefore, is there to found the duty of *allegiance* or obedience to magistrates on that of *fidelity* or a regard to promises, and to suppose, that it is the consent of each individual, which subjects him to government; when it appears, that both allegiance and fidelity stand precisely on the same foundation, and are both submitted to by mankind, on account of the apparent interests and necessities of human society? We are bound to obey our sovereign, it is said; because we have given a tacit promise to that purpose. But why are we bound to observe our promise? It must here be asserted, that the commerce and intercourse of mankind, which are of such mighty advantage, can have no security where men pay no regard to their engagements. In like manner, may it be said, that men could not live at all in society, at least in a civilized society, without laws and magistrates and judges, to prevent the encroachments of the strong upon the weak, of the violent upon the just and equitable. The obligation to allegiance being of like force and authority with the obligation to fidelity, we gain nothing by resolving the one into the other. The general interests or necessities of society are sufficient to establish both.

If the reason be asked of that obedience, which we are bound to pay to government, I readily answer, *because society could not otherwise subsist:* And this answer is clear and intelligible to all mankind. Your answer is, *because we should keep our word.* But besides, that no body, till trained in a philosophical system, can either comprehend or relish this answer: Besides this, I say, you find yourself embarrassed, when it is asked, *why we are bound to keep our word?* Nor can you give any answer, but what would, immediately, without any circuit, have accounted for our obligation to allegiance.

But *to whom is allegiance due? And who is our lawful sovereign?* This question is often the most difficult of any, and liable to infinite discussions. When people are so happy, that they can answer, *Our present sovereign, who inherits, in a direct line, from ancestors, that have governed us for many ages;* this answer admits of no reply; even though historians, in tracing up to the remotest antiquity, the origin of that royal family, may find, as commonly happens, that its first authority was derived from usurpation and violence. It is confessed, that private justice, or the abstinence from the properties of others, is a most cardinal virtue: Yet reason tells us, that there is no property in durable objects, such as lands or houses, when carefully examined in passing from hand to hand, but must, in some period, have been founded on fraud and injustice. The necessities of human society, neither in private nor public life, will allow of such an accurate enquiry: And there is no virtue or moral duty, but what may, with facility, be refined away, if we indulge a false philosophy, in sifting and scrutinizing it, by every captious rule of logic, in every light or position, in which it may be placed.

The questions with regard to private property have filled infinite volumes of law and philosophy, if in both we add the commentators to the original text; and in the end, we may safely pronounce, that many of the rules, there establish'd, are uncertain, ambiguous, and arbitrary. The like opinion may be formed with regard to the succession and rights of princes and forms of government. Several cases, no doubt, occur, especially in the infancy of any constitution, which admit of no determination from the laws of justice and equity: And our historian *Rapin* pretends,[4] that the controversy between *Edward the IIIrd* and *Philip de Valois* was of this nature, and could be decided only by an appeal to heaven, that is, by war and violence.

Who shall tell me, whether *Germanicus* or *Drusus* ought to have succeeded to *Tiberius*, had he died, while they were both alive, without naming any of them for his successor? Ought the right of adoption to be received as equivalent to that of blood, in a nation, where it had the same effect in private families, and had already, in two instances, taken place in the public? Ought *Germanicus* to be esteemed the elder son because he was born before *Drusus*; or the younger, because he was adopted after the birth of his brother? Ought the right of the elder to be regarded in a nation, where he had no advantage in the succession of private families? Ought the *Roman* empire at that time to be deemed hereditary, because of two examples; or ought it, even so early, to be regarded as belonging to the stronger or to the present possessor, as being founded on so recent an usurpation?

Commodus mounted the throne after a pretty long succession of excellent emperors, who had acquired their title, not by birth, or public election, but by the fictitious rite of adoption. That bloody debauchee being murdered by a conspiracy suddenly formed between his wench and her gallant, who happened at that time to be *Prætorian Præfect;* these immediately deliberated about choosing a master to human kind, to speak in the style of those ages; and they cast their eyes on *Pertinax.* Before the tyrant's death was known, the *Præfect* went secretly to that senator, who, on the appearance of the soldiers, imagined that his execution had been ordered by *Commodus.* He was immediately saluted emperor by the officer and his attendants; cheerfully proclaimed by the populace; unwillingly submitted to by the guards; formally recognized by the senate; and passively received by the provinces and armies of the empire.

The discontent of the *Prætorian* bands broke out in a sudden sedition, which occasioned the murder of that excellent prince: And the world being now without a master and without government, the guards thought proper to set the empire formally to sale. *Julian,* the purchaser, was proclaimed by the soldiers, recognized by the senate, and submitted to by the people; and must also have been submitted to by the provinces, had not the envy of the legions begotten opposition and resistance. *Pescennius Niger* in *Syria* elected himself emperor, gained the tumultuary consent of his army, and was attended with the secret good-will of the senate and people of *Rome. Albinus* in *Britain* found an equal right to set up his claim; but *Severus,* who governed *Pannonia,* prevailed in the end above both of them. That able politician and warrior, finding his own birth and dignity too much inferior to the imperial crown, professed, at first, an intention only of revenging the death of *Pertinax.* He marched as general into *Italy;* defeated *Julian;* and without our being able to fix any precise commencement even of the soldiers' consent, he was from necessity acknowledged emperor by the senate and people; and fully established in his violent authority by subduing *Niger* and *Albinus.*[5]

Inter hæc Gordianus Cæsar (says *Capitolinus,* speaking of another period) *sublatus a militibus,* Imperator *est appellatus, quia non erat alius in præsenti.* It is to be remarked, that *Gordian* was a boy of fourteen years of age.

Frequent instances of a like nature occur in the history of the emperors; in that of *Alexander's* successors; and of many other countries: Nor can any-

---

4. Allows: in editions before 1770.

5. *Herodian,* lib. ii.

thing be more unhappy than a despotic government of this kind; where the succession is disjoined and irregular, and must be determined, on every vacancy, by force or election. In a free government, the matter is often unavoidable, and is also much less dangerous. The interests of liberty may there frequently lead the people, in their own defence, to alter the succession of the crown. And the constitution, being compounded of parts, may still maintain a sufficient stability, by resting on the aristocratical or democratical members, though the monarchical be altered, from time to time, in order to accommodate it to the former.

In an absolute government, when there is no legal prince, who has a title to the throne, it may safely be determined to belong to the first occupant. Instances of this kind are but too frequent, especially in the eastern monarchies. When any race of princes expires, the will or destination of the last sovereign will be regarded as a title. Thus the edict of *Louis the XIVth,* who called the bastard princes to the succession in case of the failure of all the legitimate princes, would, in such an event, have some authority.[6] Thus the will of *Charles the IInd* disposed of the whole *Spanish* monarchy. The cession of the ancient proprietor, especially when joined to conquest, is likewise deemed a good title. The general obligation, which binds us to government, is the interest and necessities of society; and this obligation is very strong. The determination of it to this or that particular prince or form of government is frequently more uncertain and dubious. Present possession has considerable authority in these cases, and greater than in private property; because of the disorders which attend all revolutions and changes of government.

We shall only observe, before we conclude, that, though an appeal to general opinion may justly, in the speculative sciences of metaphysics, natural philosophy, or astronomy, be deemed unfair and inconclusive, yet in all questions with regard to morals, as well as criticism, there is really no other standard, by which any controversy can ever be decided. And nothing is a clearer proof, that a theory of this kind is erroneous, than to find, that it leads to paradoxes, repugnant to the common sentiments of mankind, and to the practice and opinion of all nations and all ages. The doctrine, which founds all lawful government on an *original contract,* or consent of the people, is plainly of this kind; nor has the most noted of its partizans, in prosecution of it, scrupled to affirm, *that absolute monarchy is inconsistent with civil society, and so can be no form of civil government at all; and that the supreme power in a state cannot take from any man, by taxes and impositions, any part of his property, without his own consent or that of his representatives.* What authority any moral reasoning can have, which leads into opinions so wide of the general practice of mankind, in every place but this single kingdom, it is easy to determine.

The only passage I meet with in antiquity, where the obligation of obedience to government is ascribed to a promise, is in *Plato's Crito:* where *Socrates* refuses to escape from prison, because he had tacitly promised to obey the laws. Thus he builds a *tory* consequence of passive obedience, on a *whig* foundation of the original contract.

New discoveries are not to be expected in these matters. If scarce any man, till very lately, ever imagined that government was founded on compact, it is certain that it cannot, in general, have any such foundation.

The crime of rebellion among the ancients was commonly expressed by the terms νεωτερίζειν, *novas res moliri.*

---

6. It is remarkable, that, in the remonstrance of the duke of *Bourbon* and the legitimate princes, against this destination of *Louis the XIVth,* the doctrine of the *original contract* is insisted on, even in that absolute government. The *French* nation, say they, chusing *Hugh Capet* and his posterity to rule over them and their posterity, where the former line fails, there is a tacit right reserved to chuse a new royal family; and this right is invaded by calling the bastard princes to the throne, without the consent of the nation. But the Comte de *Boulainvilliers,* who wrote in defence of the bastard princes, ridicules this notion of an original contract, especially when applied to *Hugh Capet;* who mounted the throne, says he, by the same arts, which have ever been employed by all conquerors and usurpers. He got his title, indeed, recognized by the states after he had put himself in possession: But is this a choice or a contract? The Comte de *Boulainvilliers,* we may observe, was a noted republican; but being a man of learning, and very conversant in history, he knew that the people were never almost consulted in these revolutions and new establishments, and that time alone bestowed right and authority on what was commonly at first founded on force and violence. See *Etat de la France,* Vol. III.

Thomas Reid

REID LED A SUCCESSFUL BUT QUIET AND CONVENTIONAL ACADEMIC LIFE IN SCOT-land. He was born April 26, 1710, about twenty miles from Aberdeen, where he spent the first fifty-four years of his life. At the age of twelve (the usual age at that time), he entered Marischal College of Aberdeen University. The college had recently been purged of suspected Jacobites, and all of the staff Reid encountered except the principal were recent appointees. Marischal offered a four-year bachelor of arts, usually a preparation for specialist training in law or theology, and operated on the regent system: First-year students were taught Latin, Greek, and Hebrew by one specialist professor, and elementary arithmetic and geometry in the first two years by another, but the rest of the curriculum was handled by one professor, the regent, who presided over the same class for three years and was responsible for all other subjects, including logic, history of natural philosophy (science), ethics, metaphysics, and particular sciences. Reid's regent was George Turnbull, who familiarized Reid with the work of Berkeley.

On his graduation at the age of sixteen, Reid turned to theology, a common choice not reflecting any particular religious calling. He completed his courses of theology in 1731 and was admitted to the ministry of the Presbyterian Church of Scotland. After a short appointment as clerk of the presbytery in Aberdeen, he was made librarian at Marischal, a position he retained until 1736, when he took a year off for a tour of England, visiting London, Cambridge, and Oxford. On his return, he was made minister in the town of New Machar. This post was controlled by King's College at Aberdeen University under the patronage system reintroduced by law in 1712. The system was disliked by the populace, who would have preferred to choose their own ministers, and Reid was received with considerable hostility, the traditional story being that he was dunked in a horse pond. Eventually, however, he won his parishioners over, and things went smoothly, especially after his marriage to his cousin Elizabeth in 1740. He remained at New Machar until 1751, during which time he lost a daughter, and nearly lost his wife to illness. (Of Reid's nine children, only one daughter survived him.) At this period, he became familiar with Francis Hutcheson's *Inquiry into the Origins of Our Ideas of Beauty and Virtue* (1725), and Hume's *Treatise of Human Nature*. (Hume, though exactly one year younger than Reid, was philosophically productive at a much earlier age.)

In 1751, Reid became regent at King's College, Aberdeen, a position he initially refused, but later accepted at the urging of his wife. He took over Alexander Rait's class in its third year, and served three and a half additional regencies until he took the chair of moral philosophy in the Old College at Glasgow in 1764. In 1758, he helped to found the Aberdeen Philosophical Society, more generally known as the Wise Club. The group met twice a month to hear and discuss a paper presented by a member or visitor. Reid corresponded with Hume during this period, and completed his *Inquiry into the Human Mind on the Principles of Common Sense*, published in 1764. He was, as one said at the time, a man of many parts, equally at home with philosophy, mathematics, science, farm improvements, trade, and politics. He was a pillar of the establishment elite in Aberdeen society.

The Glasgow chair of moral philosophy had an international reputation through three of its previous four holders, Gershom Carmichael, Francis Hutcheson, and (Reid's immediate predecessor) Adam Smith. Reid himself was quite distinguished by this time. The *Inquiry* was well received and admired, and went through four editions in his lifetime. His appointment was, however, as much a matter of patronage as reputation, the patronage of Lord Deskford and Lord Kames, the latter of whom became a friend and philosophical correspondent. Reid found something of a replacement for his beloved Wise Club in the Glasgow Literary Society, an association that was crucial in turning Reid's attention to issues of political philosophy, jurisprudence, and economic issues. He also used it, as he had the Wise Club, as a place to try out new ideas, in this case the ideas that eventually became the *Essays on the Intellectual Powers of Man*, and the *Essays on the Active Powers of the Human Mind*, both published after his retirement, in 1785 and 1788 respectively.

For sixteen years at Glasgow, Reid gave the two standard courses. From October to June, he taught the "public" class, which met for lecture from 7:30 to 8:30 A.M. and for examination (discussion) at noon Monday through Friday. From November to May, he gave the "private" class, a more advanced series of lectures, which was not part of the prescribed arts curriculum. A professor's income came from class fees. Enrollment was therefore important, and Reid seems to have been a fairly popular and universally respected lecturer. He didn't care for his Irish students, however, who made up about a third of the public class. "I preach to these as St Francis did to the fishes. I don't know what pleasure he had in his audience; but I should have none in mine if there were not in it a mixture of reasonable creatures."

In 1780, at the age of seventy, Reid appointed an assistant, Archibald Arthur, to deliver his lectures (probably because of increasing deafness), and he ceased active teaching, though he still prepared the lectures, and retained his post until his death. He spent the remainder of his time getting the *Essays* ready for publication. His wife died in 1792. In a letter to his most distinguished student, Dugald Stewart, he wrote,

> By the loss of my bosom-friend, with whom I lived fifty-two years, I am brought into a kind of new world, at a time of life when old habits are not easily forgot, or new ones acquired. But every world is God's world, and I am thankful for the comforts He has left me. . . . I have more health than at my time of life I had any reason to expect. I walk about; entertain myself with reading what I soon forget; can converse with one person, if he articulates distinctly, and is within ten inches of my left ear; go to Church, without hearing one word of what is said.

Reid died on October 7, 1796, after a brief illness. He was eighty-six.

NOTES ON THE TEXT

Reid's discussion of moral thought is primarily concerned with the questions about the nature and status of moral judgments and how we can know about them. Reid argues in favor of the objectivity and rationality of moral principles, against Hume, and he argues that we can have clear knowledge of moral principles.

Reid's view is sometimes called a species of intuitionism. He states that moral thinking and reflection are based on first principles that are self-evident to anyone who has carefully considered the matter in a cool and calm hour. The first principles of morality are true judgments about what we might call moral facts. They cannot be deduced from any other kind of judgment, but they are the basis of any sound reasoning concerning morality. Reid compares them to two different kinds of judgment that he thinks are also first principles. He compares moral judgments to the axioms of mathematics and to the deliverances of the senses. Just as I cannot give an argument for the claim that I now see that the cup before me is red or for the claim that $1 + 1 = 2$ (this is not quite an axiom but it is close enough for our purposes), so I cannot give an argument for the claim that "In every case, we ought to act that part towards another, which we would judge to be right in him to act towards us, if we were in his circumstances and he in ours" (a version of the Golden Rule). Though we cannot give an argument from other statements in favor of this judgment, we can grasp that it is true. The only things that would stop us from grasping these truths are lack of a clear understanding of the judgment, or self-deception, or some other obvious distortion in judgment. Now, since one would expect that there be rough agreement on self-evident principles, Reid partly defends his first principles by showing that they are the universal judgments of common sense. But Reid uses this inference in a methodological way as well, rejecting philosophical or metaphysical views if they run counter to the judgments of common sense.

How does Reid defend his views against Hume, who argues that moral judgments are really a species of feeling and that they were not true or false? Reid argues that there is a clear distinction between judgment and feeling that Hume confuses. If moral judgments were really just feelings, then "Jane acted wrongly by stealing bread from the baker to feed her child" would just be a way of saying "Jane's stealing the bread from the baker to feed her child gives me a disagreeable feeling." And someone who believed otherwise would say "Jane's stealing the bread does not give me a disagreeable feeling." But are they really at odds if they merely assert that they have these different feelings? Perhaps the conflict arises because the second person is really saying to the first person, "Jane's stealing the bread does not give you any disagreeable feeling." But this seems merely to be a kind of effrontery, as Reid would put it, and moral argument is not mere rudeness. So to say that moral judgment is a kind of feeling is a confusion. Hume also observes that we don't see the wrongness in the action. Reid responds by saying that we do "see" it, but not through the senses of sight, hearing, or touch. We see the wrongness only through the faculty of what he calls moral sense, or conscience, which is every bit as real as the other.

Are moral judgments rational? Reid says that they are rational both in a theoretical sense and in a practical sense. We can reason correctly from genuinely self-evident premises to true moral judgments. And moral judgments are rational in the practical sense. Reid says two things in this regard. First, moral principles are rational judgments since they involve elements that can be apprehended only through reason. For instance, there is the requirement that we prefer a greater good on the whole for ourselves than a lesser good. The idea of a good on the whole is a rational idea. It is not the object of desire which merely picks out particular things in the near environment to pursue, it is an idea that requires reasoning to put together. Another example is that our idea of duty includes the idea of law or rule of action. But the idea of a law or a rule is not the object of animal desire, as Reid puts it; it is only possible for a being that has reason. Second, it is self-evident that we are motivated by these ideas to pursue our good on the whole and to act in accordance with duty and that these motives often come into conflict with our desires and inclinations or passions.

Reid argues in addition that justice is, contrary to Hume's assertion, not merely conventional. Indeed, Reid's view is that the golden rule is really the basic principle of justice and that it is a natural self-evident principle. For Reid, in addition to the golden rule there are fundamental interests that each person has to be secure in his life, the life of his family, his liberty, and his reputation. As a consequence, each person has a natural right to the protection of these interests. And rights to property are founded on the rights to have what one needs for life and the rights to enjoy the fruits of one's innocent labor. Reid gives a series of vigorous arguments against Hume's contention that justice is a matter of convention as well as against Hume's arguments for this claim. One of Reid's arguments is that if justice is merely a convention established initially by self-interested persons for their mutual advantage, then it would not be unjust if a group of persons were treated like slaves because they happened to be weaker than the others in some way. Hume would have to say that since the unequal treatment was established as a convention, it is just and for the public good to retain it. But, Reid argues, common sense cannot allow that this is a just arrangement.

Essays on the Active Powers of Man

Essay III Of the Principles of Action

PART III
*OF THE RATIONAL PRINCIPLES
OF ACTION*

Chapter I
There Are Rational Principles of Action in Man

Mechanical principles of action produce their effect without any will or intention on our part. We may, by a voluntary effort, hinder the effect; but, if it be not hindered by will and effort, it is produced without them.

Animal principles of action require intention and will in their operation, but not judgment. They are, by ancient moralists, very properly called blind desires.

Having treated of these two classes, I proceed to the third—the *Rational* principles of action in man; which have that name, because they can have no exis-

tence in beings not endowed with reason, and, in all their exertions, require, not only intention and will, but judgment or reason.

That talent which we call *Reason,* by which men that are adult and of a sound mind are distinguished from brutes, idiots, and infants, has, in all ages, among the learned and unlearned, been conceived to have two offices—*to regulate our belief,* and *to regulate our actions and conduct.*

Whatever we believe, we think agreeable to reason, and, on that account, yield our assent to it. Whatever we disbelieve, we think contrary to reason, and, on that account, dissent from it. Reason, therefore, is allowed to be the principle by which our belief and opinions ought to be regulated.

But reason has been no less universally conceived to be a principle by which our actions ought to be regulated.

To act reasonably, is a phrase no less common in all languages, than to judge reasonably. We immediately approve of a man's conduct, when it appears that he had good reason for what he did. And every action we disapprove, we think unreasonable, or contrary to reason.

A way of speaking so universal among men, common to the learned and the unlearned in all nations and in all languages, must have a meaning. To suppose it to be words without meaning, is to treat, with undue contempt, the common sense of mankind.

Supposing this phrase to have a meaning, we may consider in what way reason may serve to regulate human conduct, so the some actions of men are to be denominated reasonable, and others unreasonable.

I take it for granted, that there can be no exercise of Reason without Judgment, nor, on the other hand, any judgment of things, abstract and general, without some degree of reason.

If, therefore, there be any principles of action in the human constitution, which, in their nature, necessarily imply such judgment, they are the principles which we may call rational, to distinguish them from animal principles, which imply desire and will, but not judgment.

Every deliberate human action must be done either as the means, or as an end; as the means to some end, to which it is subservient, or as an end, for its own sake, and without regard to anything beyond it.

That it is a part of the office of reason to determine what are the proper means to any end which we desire, no man ever denied. But some philosophers, particularly Mr Hume, think that it is no part of the office of reason to determine the ends we ought to pursue, or the preference due to one end above another. This, he thinks, is not the office of reason, but of taste or feeling.

If this be so, reason cannot, with any propriety, be called a principle of action. Its office can only be to minister to the principles of action, by discovering the means of their gratification. Accordingly, Mr Hume maintains, that reason is no principle of action; but that it is, and ought to be, the servant of the passions.

I shall endeavour to shew that, among the various ends of human actions, there are some, of which, without reason, we could not even form a conception; and that, as soon as they are conceived, a regard to them is, by our constitution, not only a principle of action, but a leading and governing principle, to which all our animal principles are subordinate, and to which they ought to be subject.

These I shall call *rational* principles; because they can exist only in beings endowed with reason, and because, to act from these principles, is what has always been meant by acting according to reason.

The ends of human actions I have in view, are two—to wit, *What is good for us upon the whole*, and *What appears to be our duty*. They are very strictly connected, lead to the same course of conduct, and cooperate with each other; and, on that account, have commonly been comprehended under one name—that of *reason*. But, as they may be disjoined, and are really distinct principles of action, I shall consider them separately.

Chapter II
Of Regard to Our Good on the Whole

It will not be denied that man, when he comes to years of understanding, is led, by his rational nature, to form the conception of what is good for him upon the whole.

How early in life this general notion of good enters into the mind, I cannot pretend to determine. It is one of the most general and abstract notions we form.

Whatever makes a man more happy or more perfect, is good, and is an object of desire as soon as we are capable of forming the conception of it. The contrary is ill, and is an object of aversion.

In the first part of life, we have many enjoyments of various kinds; but very similar to those of brute-animals.

They consist in the exercise of our senses and powers of motion, the gratification of our appetites, and the exertions of our kind affections. These are chequered with many evils of pain, and fear, and disappointment, and sympathy with the sufferings of others.

But the goods and evils of this period of life are of short duration, and soon forgot. The mind, being regardless of the past, and unconcerned about the future, we have then no other measure of good but the present desire; no other measure of evil but the present aversion.

Every animal desire has some particular and present object, and looks not beyond that object to its consequences, or to the connections it may have with other things.

The present object, which is most attractive, or excites the strongest desire, determines the choice, whatever be its consequences. The present evil that presses most, is avoided, though it should be the road to a greater good to come, or the only way to escape a greater evil. This is the way in which brutes act, and the way in which men must act, till they come to the use of reason.

As we grow up to understanding, we extend our view both forward and backward. We reflect upon what is past, and, by the lamp of experience, discern what will probably happen in time to come. We find that many things which we eagerly desired, were too dearly purchased, and that things grievous for the present, like nauseous medicines, may be salutary in the issue.

We learn to observe the connexions of things, and the consequences of our actions; and, taking an extended view of our existence, past, present, and future, we correct our first notions of good and ill, and form the conception of what is good or ill upon the whole; which must be estimated, not from the present feeling, or from the present animal desire or aversion, but from a due consideration of its consequences, certain or probable, during the whole of our existence.

That which, taken with all its discoverable connections and consequences, brings more good than ill, I call *good upon the whole*.

That brute-animals have any conception of this good, I see no reason to believe. And it is evident that man cannot have the conception of it, till reason is so far advanced that he can seriously reflect upon the past, and take a prospect of the future part of his existence.

It appears, therefore, that the very conception of what is good or ill for us upon the whole, is the offspring of reason, and can be only in beings endowed with reason. And if this conception give rise to any principle of action in man, which he had not before, that principle may very properly be called a rational principle of action.

I pretend not in this to say anything that is new, but what reason suggested to those who first turned their attention to the philosophy of morals. I beg leave to quote one passage from Cicero, in his first book of "Offices"; wherein, with his usual eloquence, he expresses the substance of what I have said. And there is good reason to think that Cicero borrowed it from Panætius, a Greek philosopher whose books of "Offices" are lost.

"But the greatest difference between a human and an animal is this. An animal adapts itself only insofar as it is moved by the senses, and only to what is present and happening now, and scarcely is aware of past or future. A human, however, since he shares in reason, through which he discerns consequences, perceives the causes of things and is not unaware of their advances and, so to speak, antecedents, compares similarities and links and joins future to present events; easily he sees the course of his entire life, and prepares what is requisite for leading it."

I observe, in the *next* place—That as soon as we have the conception of what is good or ill for us upon the whole, we are led, by our constitution, to seek the good and avoid the ill; and this becomes not only a principle of action, but a leading or governing principle, to which all our animal principles ought to be subordinate.

I am very apt to think, with Dr Price, that, in intelligent beings, the desire of what is good, and aversion to what is ill, is necessarily connected with the intelligent nature; and that it is a contradiction to suppose such a being to have the notion of good without the desire of it, or the notice of ill without aversion to it. Perhaps there may be other necessary connections between understanding and the best principles of action, which our faculties are too weak to discern. That they are necessarily connected in him who is perfect in understanding, we have good reason to believe.

To prefer a greater good, though distant, to a less that is present; to choose a present evil, in order to avoid a greater evil, or to obtain a greater good, is, in the judgment of all men, wise and reasonable conduct; and, when a man acts the contrary part, all men will acknowledge that he acts foolishly and unreasonably. Nor will it be denied, that, in innumerable cases in common life, our animal principles draw us one way, while a regard to what is good on the whole, draws us the contrary way. Thus the flesh lusteth against the spirit, and the spirit against the flesh, and these two are contrary. That in every conflict of this kind the rational principle ought to prevail, and the animal to be subordinate, is too evident to need, or to admit of proof.

Thus, I think, it appears, that, to pursue what is good upon the whole, and to avoid what is ill upon the whole, is a rational principle of action grounded upon our constitution as reasonable creatures.

It appears that it is not without just cause, that this principle of action has in all ages been called *reason*, in opposition to our animal principles, which in common language are called by the general name of the *passions*.

The first not only operates in a calm and cool manner, like reason, but implies real judgment in all its operations. The second—to wit, the passions—are blind desires of some particular object, without any judgment or consideration, whether it be good for us upon the whole, or ill.

It appears also, that the fundamental maxim of prudence, and of all good morals—That the passions ought, in all cases, to be under the dominion of reason—is not only self-evident, when rightly understood, but is expressed according to the common use and propriety of language.

The contrary maxim maintained by Mr Hume, can only be defended by a gross and palpable abuse of words. For, in order to defend it, he must include under the *passions* that very principle which has always, in all languages, been called *reason*, and never was, in any language, called a *passion*. And from the meaning of the word *reason* he must exclude the most important part of it, by which we are able to discern and to pursue what appears to be good upon the whole. And thus, including the most important part of reason under passion, and making the least important part of reason to be the whole, he defends his favourite paradox, That reason is, and ought to be, the servant of the passions.

To judge of what is true or false in speculative points, is the office of speculative reason; and to judge of what is good or ill for us upon the whole, is the office of practical reason. Of true and false there are no degrees; but of good and ill there are many degrees, and many kinds; and men are very apt to form erroneous opinions concerning them; misled by their passions, by the authority of the multitude, and by other causes.

Wise men, in all ages, have reckoned it a chief point of wisdom, to make a right estimate of the goods and evils of life. They have laboured to discover the errors of the multitude on this important point, and to warn others against them.

The ancient moralists, though divided into sects, all agreed in this—That opinion has a mighty influence upon what we commonly account the goods and ills of life, to alleviate or to aggravate them.

The Stoics carried this so far, as to conclude that they all depend on opinion. ["All is but supposition"] was a favourite maxim with them.

We see, indeed, that the same station or condition of life, which makes one man happy, makes another miserable, and to a third is perfectly indifferent. We see men miserable through life, from vain fears and anxious desires, grounded solely upon wrong opinions. We see men wear themselves out with toilsome days, and sleepless nights, in pursuit of some object which they never attain; or which, when attained, gives little satisfaction, perhaps real disgust.

The evils of life, which every man must feel, have a very different effect upon different men. What sinks one into despair and absolute misery, rouses the virtue and magnanimity of another, who bears it as the lot of humanity, and as the discipline of a wise and merciful Father in heaven. He rises superior to adversity, and is made wiser and better by it, and, consequently, happier.

It is therefore of the last importance, in the conduct of life, to have just opinions with respect to good and evil; and, surely, it is the province of reason to correct wrong opinions, and to lead us into those that are just and true.

It is true, indeed, that men's passions and appetites too often draw them to act contrary to their cool judgment and opinion of what is best for them. "I see the better and approve, but I go after the worse," is the case in every wilful deviation from our true interest and our duty.

When this is the case, the man is self-condemned; he sees that he acted the part of a brute when he ought to have acted the part of a man. He is convinced that reason ought to have restrained his passion, and not to have given the rein to it.

When he feels the bad effects of his conduct, he imputes them to himself, and would be stung with remorse for his folly, though he had no account to make to a superior Being. He has sinned against himself, and brought upon his own head the punishment which his folly deserved.

From this we may see that this rational principle of a regard to our good upon the whole, gives us the conception of a *right* and a *wrong* in human conduct, at least of a *wise* and a *foolish*. It produces a kind of self-approbation, when the passions and appetites are kept in their due subjection to it; and a kind of remorse and compunction when it yields to them.

In these respects, this principle is so similar to the moral principle, or *Conscience*, and so interwoven with it, that both are commonly comprehended under the name *of Reason*. This similarity led many of the ancient philosophers, and some among the moderns, to resolve conscience, or a sense of duty, entirely into a regard to what is good for us upon the whole.

That they are distinct principles of action, though both lead to the same conduct in life, I shall have occasion to shew when I come to treat of *conscience*.

Chapter III
The Tendency of This Principle

It has been the opinion of the wisest men, in all ages, that this principle, of a regard to our good upon the whole, in a man duly enlightened, leads to the practice of every virtue.

This was acknowledged, even by Epicurus; and the best moralists among the ancients derived all their virtues from this principle. For, among them, the whole of morals was reduced to this question: *What is the greatest good?* or, *What course of conduct is best for us upon the whole?*

In order to resolve this question, they divided goods into *three* classes: the *goods of the body*—the *goods of fortune* or *external goods*—and the *goods of the mind*, meaning, by the last, *wisdom* and *virtue*.

Comparing these different classes of goods, they shewed, with convincing evidence, that the goods of the mind are, in many respects, superior to those of the body and of fortune, not only as they have more dignity, are more durable, and less exposed to the strokes of fortune, but chiefly as they are the only goods in our power, and which depend wholly on our conduct.

Epicurus himself maintained, that the wise man may be happy in the tranquillity of his mind, even when racked with pain and struggling with adversity.

They observed very justly, that the goods of fortune, and even those of the body, depend much on opinion; and that, when our opinion of them is duly corrected by reason, we shall find them of small value in themselves.

How can he be happy who places his happiness in things which it is not in his power to attain, or in things from which, when attained, a fit of sickness, or a strokes of fortune, may tear him asunder?

The value we put upon things, and our uneasiness in the want of them, depend upon the strength of our desires; correct the desire, and the uneasiness ceases.

The fear of the evils of body and of fortune, is often a greater evil than the things we fear. As the wise man moderates his desires by temperance, so, to real or imaginary dangers, he opposes the shield of fortitude and magnanimity, which raises him above himself, and makes him happy and triumphant in those moments wherein others are most miserable.

These oracles of reason led the Stoics so far as to maintain—That all desires and fears, with regard to things not in our power, ought to be totally eradicated; that virtue is the only good; that what we call the goods of the body and of fortune, and really things indifferent, which may, according to circumstances, prove good or ill, and, therefore, have no intrinsic goodness in themselves; that our sole business ought to be, to act our part well, and to do what is right, without the least concern about things, not in our power, which we ought, with perfect acquiescence, to leave to the care of Him who governs the world.

This noble and elevated conception of human wisdom and duty was taught by Socrates, free from the extravagancies which the Stoics afterwards joined with it. We see it in the "Alcibiades" of Plato, from which Juvenal hath taken it in his tenth satire, and adorned it with the graces of poetry.

> In all the lands that stretch from Gades to the Ganges and the Morn, there are but few who can distinguish true blessings from their opposites, putting aside the mists of error. For when does Reason direct our desires or our fears? What project do we form so auspiciously that we do not repent us of our effort and of the granted wish?

> Is there nothing then for which men shall pray? If you ask my counsel, you will leave it to the gods themselves to provide what is good for us, and what will be serviceable for our state; for, in place of what is pleasing, they will give us what is best. Man is dearer to them than he is to himself. Impelled by strong and blind desire in our hearts, we ask for wife and offspring; but the gods know of what sort the sons, of what sort the wife, will be. Still, that you may have something to pray for, and be able to offer to the shrines entrails and presaging sausages from a white porker, you should pray for a sound mind in a sound body; ask for a stout heart that has no fear of death, and deems length of days the least of Nature's gifts; that can endure any kind of toil; that knows neither wrath nor desire, and thinks that the woes and hard labours of Hercules are better than the loves and banquets and the downy cushions of Sardanapalus. What I commend to you, you can give to yourself; for it is assuredly through virtue that lies the one and only path to a life of peace. Thou wouldst have no divinity, O Fortune, if we had but wisdom; it is we that make a goddess of thee, and place thee in the skies.

Even Horace, in his serious moments, falls into this system.

> To admire almost nothing, Numicius, is the one and only principle that can make and keep you happy.

We cannot but admire the Stoical system of morals, even when we think that, in some points, it went beyond the pitch of human nature. The virtue, the temperance, the fortitude, and magnanimity of some who sincerely embraced it, amidst all the flattery of sovereign power and the luxury of a court, will be everlasting monuments to the honour of that system, and to the honour of human nature.

That a due regard to what is best for us upon the whole, in an enlightened mind, leads to the practice of every virtue, may be argued from considering what we think best for those for whom we have the strongest affection, and whose good we tender as our own. In judging for ourselves, our passions and appetites are apt to bias our judgment; but when we judge for others, this bias is removed, and we judge impartially.

What is it, then, that a wise man would wish as the greatest good to a brother, a son, or a friend?

Is it that he may spend his life in a constant round of the pleasures of sense, and fare sumptuously every day?

No, surely; we wish him to be a man of real virtue and worth. We may wish for him an honourable station in life; but only with this condition, that he acquit himself honourably in it, and acquire just reputation, by being useful to his country and to mankind. We would a thousand times rather wish him honourably to undergo the labours of Hercules, than to dissolve in pleasure with Sardanapalus.

Such would be the wish of every man of understanding for the friend whom he loves as his own soul. Such things, therefore, he judges to be best for him upon the whole; and if he judges otherwise for himself, it is only because his judgment is perverted by animal passions and desires.

The sum of what has been said in these three chapters amounts to this:

There is a principle of action in men that are adult and of a sound mind, which, in all ages, has been called *reason*, and set in opposition to the animal principles which we call the *passions*. The ultimate object of this principle is what we judge to be good upon the whole. This is not the object of any of our animal principles; they being all directed to particular objects, without any comparison with others, or any consideration of their being good or ill upon the whole.

What is good upon the whole cannot even be conceived without the exercise of reason, and therefore cannot be an object to beings that have not some degree of reason.

As soon as we have the conception of this object, we are led, by our constitution, to desire and pursue it. It justly claims a preference to all objects of pursuit that can come in competition with it. In preferring it to any gratification that opposes it, or in submitting to any pain or mortification which it requires, we act according to reason; and every such action is accompanied with self-approbation and the approbation of mankind. The contrary actions are accompanied with shame and self-condemnation in the agent, and with contempt in the spectator, as foolish and unreasonable.

The right application of this principle to our conduct requires an extensive prospect of human life, and a correct judgment and estimate of its goods and evils, with respect to their intrinsic worth and dignity, their constancy and duration, and their attainableness. He must be a wise man indeed, if any such man there be, who can perceive, in every instance, or even in every important instance, what is best for him upon the whole, if he have no other rule to direct his conduct.

However, according to the best judgment which wise men have been able to form, this principle leads to the practice of every virtue. It leads directly to the virtues of Prudence, Temperance, and Fortitude. And, when we consider ourselves as social creatures, whose happiness or misery is very much connected with that of our fellow-men; when we consider that there are many benevolent affections planted in our constitution, whose exertions make a capital part of our good and enjoyment: from these considerations, this principle leads us also, though more indirectly, to the practice of justice, humanity, and all the social virtues.

It is true, that a regard to our own good cannot, of itself, produce any benevolent affection. But, if such affections be a part of our constitution, and if the exercise of them make a capital part of our happiness, a regard to our own good ought to lead us to cultivate and exercise them, as every benevolent affection makes the good of others to be our own.

Chapter IV
Defects of This Principle

Having explained the nature of this principle of action, and shewn in general the tenor of conduct to which it leads, I shall conclude what relates to it, by pointing out some of its defects, if it be supposed, as it has been by some philosophers, to be the only regulating principle of human conduct.

Upon that supposition, it would neither be a sufficiently plain rule of conduct, nor would it raise the human character to that degree of perfection of which it is capable, nor would it yield so much real happiness as when it is joined with another rational principle of action—to wit, a disinterested regard to duty.

First, I apprehend the greater part of mankind can never attain such extensive views of human life, and so correct a judgment of good and ill, as the right application of this principle requires.

The authority of the poet before quoted, is of weight in this point. "Few are able to discern true goods, when the fog of error is withdrawn." The ignorance of the bulk of mankind concurs with the strength of their passions to lead them into error in this most important point.

Every man, in his calm moments, wishes to know what is best for him on the whole, and to do it. But the difficulty of discovering it clearly, amidst such variety of opinions and the importunity of present desires, tempt men to give over the search, and to yield to the present inclination.

Though philosophers and moralists have taken much laudable pains to correct the errors of mankind in this great point, their instructions are known to few; they have little influence upon the greater part of those to whom they are known, and sometimes little even upon the philosopher himself.

Speculative discoveries gradually spread from the knowing to the ignorant, and diffuse themselves over all; so that, with regard to them, the world, it may be hoped, will still be growing wiser. But the errors of men, with regard to what is truly good or ill, after being discovered and refuted in every age, are still prevalent.

Men stand in need of a sharper monitor to their duty than a dubious view of distant good. There is reason to believe, that a present sense of duty has, in many cases, a stronger influence than the apprehension of distant good would have of itself. And it cannot be doubted, that a sense of guilt and demerit is a more pungent reprover than the bare apprehension of having mistaken our true interest.

The brave soldier, in exposing himself to danger and death, is animated, not by a cold computation of the good and the ill, but by a noble and elevated sense of military duty.

A philosopher shews, by a copious and just induction, what is our real good, and what our ill. But this kind of reasoning is not easily apprehended by the bulk of men. It has too little force upon their minds to resist the sophistry of the passions. They are apt to think that, if such rules be good in the general, they may admit of particular exceptions, and that what is good for the greater part, may, to some persons, on account of particular circumstances, be ill.

Thus, I apprehend, that, if we had no plainer rule to direct our conduct in life than a regard to our greatest good, the greatest part of mankind would be fatally misled, even by ignorance of the road to it.

Secondly, Though a steady pursuit of our own real good may, in an enlightened mind, produce a kind of virtue which is entitled to some degree of approbation, yet it can never produce the noblest kind of virtue which claims our highest love and esteem.

We account him a wise man who is wise for himself; and, if he prosecutes this end through difficulties and temptations that lie in his way, his character is far superior to that of the man who, having the same end in view, is continually starting out of the road to it from an attachment to his appetites and passions, and doing every day what he knows he shall heartily repent.

Yet, after all, this wise man, whose thoughts and cares are all centred ultimately in himself, who indulges even his social affections only with a view to his own good, is not the man whom we cordially love and esteem.

Like a cunning merchant, he carries his goods to the best market, and watches every opportunity of putting them off to the best account. He does well and wisely. But it is for himself. We owe him nothing upon this account. Even when he does good to others, he means only to serve himself; and, therefore, has no just claim to their gratitude or affection.

This surely, if it be virtue, is not the noblest kind, but a low and mercenary species of it. It can neither give a noble elevation to the mind that possesses it, nor attract the esteem and love of others.

Our cordial love and esteem is due only to the man whose soul is not contracted within itself, but embraces a more extensive object: who loves virtue, not for her dowry only, but for her own sake: whose benevolence is not selfish, but generous and disinterested: who, forgetful of himself, has the common good at heart, not as the means only, but as the end: who abhors what is base, though he were to be a gainer by it; and loves that which is right, although he should suffer by it.

Such a man we esteem the perfect man, compared with whom he who has no other aim but good to himself is a mean and despicable character.

Disinterested goodness and rectitude is the glory of the Divine Nature, without which he might be an object of fear or hope, but not of true devotion. And it is the image of this divine attribute in the human character that is the glory of man.

To serve God and be useful to mankind, without any concern about our own good and happiness, is, I believe, beyond the pitch of human nature. But to serve God and be useful to men, merely to obtain good to ourselves, or to avoid ill, is servility, and not that liberal service which true devotion and real virtue require.

Thirdly, Though one might be apt to think that he has the best chance for happiness who has no other end of his deliberate actions but his own good, yet a little consideration may satisfy us of the contrary.

A concern for our own good is not a principle that, of itself, gives any enjoyment. On the contrary, it is apt to fill the mind with fear, and care, and anxiety. And these concomitants of this principle often give pain and uneasiness, that overbalance the good they have in view.

We may here compare, in point of present happiness, two imaginary characters: The first, of the man who has no other ultimate end of his deliberate actions but his own good; and who has no regard to virtue or duty, but as the means to that end. The second character is that of the man who is not indifferent with regard to his own good, but has another ultimate end perfectly consistent with it—to wit, a disinterested love of virtue, for its own sake, or a regard to duty as an end.

Comparing these two characters in point of happiness, that we may give all possible advantage to the selfish principle, we shall suppose the man who is actuated solely by it, to be so far enlightened as to see it his interest to live soberly, righteously, and godly in the world, and that he follows the same course of conduct from the motive of his own good only, which the other does, in a great measure, or in some measure, from a sense of duty and rectitude.

We put the case so as that the difference between these two persons may be, not in what they do, but in the motive from which they do it; and, I think, there can be no doubt that he who acts from the noblest and most generous motive, will have most happiness in his conduct.

The one labours only for hire, without any love to the work. The other loves the work, and thinks it the noblest and most honourable he can be employed in. To the first, the mortification and self-denial which the course of virtue requires, is a grievous task, which he submits to only through necessity. To the other it is victory and triumph, in the most honourable warfare.

It ought farther to be considered—That although wise men have concluded that virtue is the only road to happiness, this conclusion is founded chiefly upon the natural respect men have for virtue, and the good or happiness that is intrinsic to it and arises from the love of it. If we suppose a man, as we now do, altogether destitute of this principle, who considered virtue only as the means to another end, there is no reason to think that he would ever take it to be the road to happiness, but would wander for ever seeking this object, where it is not to be found.

The road of duty is so plain that the man who seeks it with an upright heart cannot greatly err from it. But the road to happiness, if that be supposed the only end our nature leads us to pursue, would be found dark and intricate, full of snares and dangers, and therefore not to be trodden without fear, and care, and perplexity.

The happy man, therefore, is not he whose happiness is his only care, but he who, with perfect resignation, leaves the care of his happiness to him who made him, while he pursues with ardour the road of his duty.

This gives an elevation to his mind, which is real happiness. Instead of care, and fear, and anxiety, and disappointment, it brings joy and triumph. It gives a relish to every good we enjoy, and brings good out of evil.

And as no man can be indifferent about his happiness, the good man has the consolation to know that he consults his happiness most effectually when, without any painful anxiety about future events, he does his duty.

Thus, I think, it appears—That, although a regard to our good upon the whole, be a rational principle in man, yet if it be supposed the only regulating principle of our conduct, it would be a more uncertain rule, it would give far less perfection to the human character, and far less happiness, than when joined with another rational principle—to wit, a regard to duty.

Chapter V
Of the Notion of Duty, Rectitude, Moral Obligation

A being endowed with the animal principles of action only, may be capable of being trained to certain purposes by discipline, as we see many brute-animals are, but would be altogether incapable of being governed by law.

The subject of law must have the conception of a general rule of conduct, which, without some degree of reason, he cannot have. He must likewise have a sufficient inducement to obey the law, even when his strongest animal desires draw him the contrary way.

This inducement may be a sense of *interest*, or a sense of *duty*, or both concurring.

These are the only principles I am able to conceive, which can reasonably induce a man to regulate all his actions according to a certain general rule or law. They may therefore be justly called the *rational* principles of action, since they can have no place but in a being endowed with reason, and since it is by them only that man is capable either of political or of moral government.

Without them human life would be like a ship at sea without hands, left to be carried by winds and tides as they happen. It belongs to the rational part of our nature to intend a certain port, as the end of the voyage of life; to take the advantage of winds and tides when they are favourable, and to bear up against them when they are unfavourable.

A sense of interest may induce us to do this, when a suitable reward is set before us. But there is a nobler principle in the constitution of man, which, in many cases, gives a clearer and more certain rule of conduct, than a regard merely to interest would give, and a principle, without which man would not be a moral agent.

A man is prudent when he consults his real interest; but he cannot be virtuous, if he has no regard to duty.

I proceed now to consider this *regard to Duty* as a rational principle of action in man, and as that principle alone by which he is capable either of virtue or vice.

I shall first offer some observations with regard to the *general notion of duty, and its contrary, or of right and wrong in human conduct*, and then consider, *how we come to judge and determine certain things in human conduct to be right, and others to be wrong.*

With regard to the *notion* or *conception* of Duty, I take it to be too simple to admit of a logical definition.

We can define it only by synonymous words or phrases, or by its properties and necessary concomitants, as when we say that it is *what we ought to do— what is fair and honest—what is approvable—what every man professes to be the rule of his conduct— what all men praise—and, what is in itself laudable, though no man should praise it.*

I observe, in the *next* place, That the notion of duty cannot be resolved into that of interest, or what is most for our happiness.

Every man may be satisfied of this who attends to his own conceptions, and the language of all mankind shews it. When I say, This is my interest, I mean one thing; when I say, It is my duty, I mean another thing. And, though the same course of action, when rightly understood, may be both my duty and my interest, the conceptions are very different. Both are reasonable motives to action, but quite distinct in their nature.

I presume it will be granted, that, in every man of real worth, there is a principle of honour, a regard to what is honourable or dishonourable, very distinct from a regard to his interest. It is folly in a man to disregard his interest, but to do what is dishonourable, is baseness. The first may move our pity, or, in some cases, our contempt; but the last provokes our indignation.

As these two principles are different in their nature, and not resolvable into one, so the principle of honour is evidently superior in dignity to that of interest.

No man would allow him to be a man of honour who should plead his interest to justify what he acknowledged to be dishonourable; but to sacrifice interest to honour never costs a blush.

It likewise will be allowed by every man of honour, that this principle is not to be resolved into a regard to our reputation among men, otherwise the man of honour would not deserve to be trusted in the dark. He would have no aversion to lie, or cheat, or play the coward, when he had no dread of being discovered.

I take it for granted, therefore, that every man of real honour feels an abhorrence of certain actions, because they are in themselves base, and feels an obligation to certain other actions, because they are in themselves what honour requires, and this independently of any consideration of interest or reputation.

This is an immediate moral obligation. This principle of honour, which is acknowledged by all men who pretend to character, is only another name for what we call a regard to duty, to rectitude, to propriety of conduct. It is a moral obligation which obliges a man to do certain things because they are right, and not to do other things because they are wrong.

Ask the man of honour why he thinks himself obliged to pay a debt of honour? The very question shocks him. To suppose that he needs any other inducement to do it but the principle of honour, is to suppose that he has no honour, no worth, and deserves no esteem.

There is, therefore, a principle in man, which, when he acts according to it, gives him a consciousness of worth, and, when he acts contrary to it, a sense of demerit.

From the varieties of education, of fashion, of prejudices, and of habits, men may differ much in opinion with regard to the extent of this principle, and of what it commands and forbids; but the notion of it, as far as it is carried, is the same in all. It is that which gives a man real worth, and is the object of moral approbation.

Men of rank call it *honour*, and too often confine it to certain virtues that are thought most essential to their rank. The vulgar call it *honesty, probity, virtue, conscience*. Philosophers have given it the names of *the moral sense, the moral faculty, rectitude*.

The universality of this principle in men that are grown up to years of understanding and reflection, is evident. The words that express it, the names of the virtues which it commands, and of the vices which it forbids, the *ought* and *ought not* which express its dictates, make an essential part of every language. The natural affections of respect to worthy characters, of resentment of injuries, of gratitude for favours, of indignation against the worthless, are parts of the human constitution which suppose a right and a wrong in conduct. Many transactions that are found necessary in the rudest societies go upon the same supposition. In all testimony, in all promises, and in all contracts, there is necessarily implied a moral obligation on one party, and a trust in the other, grounded upon this obligation.

The variety of opinions among men in points of morality, is not greater, but, as I apprehend, much less than in speculative points; and this variety is as easily accounted for, from the common causes of error, in the one case as in the other; so that it is not more evident, that there is a real distinction between true and false, in matters of speculation, than that there is a real distinction between right and wrong in human conduct.

Mr Hume's authority, if there were any need of it, is of weight in this matter, because he was not wont to go rashly into vulgar opinions.

"Those," says he, "who have denied the reality of moral distinctions, may be ranked among the disingenuous disputants" (who really do not believe the opinions they defend, but engage in the controversy, from affectation, from a spirit of opposition, or from a desire of shewing wit and ingenuity superior to the rest of mankind); "nor is it conceivable, that any human creature could ever seriously believe that all characters and actions were alike entitled to the regard and affection of every one.

"Let a man's insensibility be ever so great, he must often be touched with the images RIGHT and WRONG; and let his prejudices be ever so obstinate, he must observe that others are susceptible of like impressions. The only way, therefore, of convincing an antagonist of this kind, is to leave him to himself. For, finding that nobody keeps up the controversy with him, it is probable he will at last, of himself, from mere weariness, come over to the side of common sense and reason." [*Principles of Morals*, § I.]

What we call *right* and *honourable* in human conduct, was, by the ancients, called *honestum* τὸ χαλὸν [χαλὸν χαὶ αγαθὸν, and χαλο χαγαθον]; of which Tully says, "Nature is that which we say is truely praiseworthy, even if it be praised by none." [*De Officiis*, L. I. c. ix]

All the ancient sects, except the Epicureans, distinguished the *honestum* from the *utile*, as we distinguish what is a man's duty from what is his interest.

The word *officium*, χαθῆχον, extended both to the *honestum* and the *utile*: so that every reasonable action, proceeding either from a sense of duty or a sense of interest, was called *officium*. It is defined by Cicero to be—"That for which an acceptable account can be given why it is done." We commonly render it by the word *duty*, but it is more extensive; for the word *duty*, in the English language, I think, is commonly applied only to what the ancients called *honestum*. Cicero, and Panætius before him, treating of offices, first point out those that are grounded upon the *honestum*, and next those that are grounded upon the *utile*.

The most ancient philosophical system concerning the principles of action in the human mind, and, I think, the most agreeable to nature, is that which we find in some fragments of the ancient Pythagoreans, and which is adopted by Plato, and explained in some of his dialogues.

According to this system, there is a leading principle in the soul, which, like the supreme power in a commonwealth, has authority and right to govern. This leading principle they called *Reason*. It is that which distinguishes men that are adult from brutes, idiots, and infants. The inferior principles, which are under the authority of the leading principle, are our passions and appetites, which we have in common with the brutes.

Cicero adopts this system, and expresses it well in few words. "For the power of souls and of nature is twofold. One part is situated in the appetite, which hastens a person this way and that; the other is situated in reason, which teaches and sets forth clearly what must be done or avoided. So it is that reason has rule, appetite submits." [*De Officiis*, L. I. c. 28.]

This division of other active principles can hardly, indeed, be accounted a discovery of philosophy, because it has been common to the unlearned in all ages of the world, and seems to be dictated by the common sense of mankind.

What I would now observe concerning this common division of our active powers, is, that the leading principle, which is called *Reason*, comprehends both a regard to what is right and honourable, and a regard to our happiness upon the whole.

Although these be really two distinct principles of action, it is very natural to comprehend them under one name, because both are leading principles, both suppose the use of Reason, and, when rightly understood, both lead to the same course of life. They are like two fountains, whose streams unite and run in the same channel.

When a man, on one occasion, consults his real happiness in things not inconsistent with his duty, though in opposition to the solicitation of appetite or passion; and when, on another occasion, without any selfish consideration, he does what is right and honourable, because it is so—in both these cases, he acts reasonably; every man approves of his conduct, and calls it reasonable, or according to reason.

So that, when we speak of reason as a principle of action in man, it includes a regard both to the *honestum* and to the *utile*. Both are combined under one name; and, accordingly, the dictates of both, in the Latin tongue, were combined under the name *officium*, and in the Greek under χαθῆχον.

If we examine the abstract notion of Duty, or Moral Obligation, it appears to be neither any real quality of the action considered by itself, nor of the agent considered without respect to the action, but a certain relation between the one and the other.

When we say a man ought to do such a thing, the *ought*, which expresses the moral obligation, has a respect, on the one hand, to the person who ought; and, on the other, to the action which he ought to do. Those two correlates are essential to every moral obligation; take away either, and it has no existence. So that, if we seek the place of moral obligation among the categories, it belongs to the category of *relation*.

There are many relations of things, of which we have the most distinct conception, without being able to define them logically. Equality and proportion are relations between quantities, which every man understands, but no man can define.

Moral obligation is a relation of its own kind, which every man understands, but is, perhaps, too simple to admit of logical definition. Like all other relations, it may be changed or annihilated by a change in any of the two related things—I mean the agent or the action.

Perhaps it may not be improper to point out briefly the circumstances, both in the action and in the agent, which are necessary to constitute moral obligation. The universal agreement of men in these, shews that they have one and the same notion of it.

With regard to the action, it must be a voluntary action, or prestation of the person obliged, and not of another. There can be no moral obligation upon a man to be six feet high. Nor can I be under a moral obligation that another person should do such a thing. His actions must be imputed to himself, and mine only to me, either for praise or blame.

I need hardly mention, that a person can be under a moral obligation, only to things within the sphere of his natural power.

As to the party obliged, it is evident there can be no moral obligation upon an inanimate thing. To speak of moral obligation upon a stone or a tree is ridiculous, because it contradicts every man's notion of moral obligation.

The person obliged must have understanding and will, and some degree of active power. He must not only have the natural faculty of understanding, but the means of knowing his obligation. An invincible ignorance of this destroys all moral obligation.

The opinion of the agent in doing the action gives it its moral denomination. If he does a materially good action, without any belief of its being good, but from some other principle, it is no good action in him. And if he does it with the belief of its being ill, it is ill in him.

Thus, if a man should give to his neighbour a potion which he really believes will poison him, but which, in the event, proves salutary, and does much good; in moral estimation, he is a poisoner, and not a benefactor.

These qualifications of the action and of the agent, in moral obligation, are self-evident; and the agreement of all men in them shews that all men have the same notion, and a distinct notion of moral obligation.

Chapter VI
Of the Sense of Duty

We are next to consider, how we learn to judge and determine, that this is right, and that is wrong.

The abstract notion of moral good and ill would be of no use to direct our life, if we had not the power of applying it to particular actions, and determining what is morally good, and what is morally ill.

Some philosophers, with whom I agree, ascribe this to an original power or faculty in man, which they call the *Moral Sense*, the *Moral Faculty, Conscience*. Others think that our moral sentiments may be accounted for without supposing any original sense or faculty appropriated to that purpose, and go into very different systems to account for them.

I am not, at present, to take any notice of those systems, because the opinion first mentioned seems to me to be the truth; to wit, That, by an original power of the mind, when we come to years of understanding and reflection, we not only have the notions of right and wrong in conduct, but perceive certain things to be right, and others to be wrong.

The name of the *Moral Sense*, though more frequently given to Conscience since Lord Shaftesbury and Dr Hutcheson wrote, is not new. The *sensus recti et honesti*, is a phrase not unfrequent among the ancients; neither is the *sense of duty*, among us.

It has got this name of *sense*, no doubt, from some analogy which it is conceived to bear to the external senses. And, if we have just notions of the office of the external senses, the analogy is very evident, and I see no reason to take offence, as some have done, at the name of the *moral sense.*

The offence taken at this name seems to be owing to this, That philosophers have degraded the senses too much, and deprived them of the most important part of their office.

We are taught, that, by the senses, we have only certain ideas which we could not have otherwise. They are represented as powers by which we have sensations and ideas, not as powers by which we judge.

This notion of the senses I take to be very lame, and to contradict what nature and accurate reflection teach concerning them.

A man who has totally lost the sense of seeing, may retain very distinct notions of the various colours; but he cannot judge of colours, because he has lost the sense by which alone he could judge. By my eyes I not only have the ideas of a square and a circle, but I perceive this surface to be a square, that to be a circle.

By my ear, I not only have the idea of sounds, loud and soft, acute and grave, but I immediately perceive and judge this sound to be loud, that to be soft, this to be acute, that to be grave. Two or more synchronous sounds I perceive to be concordant, others to be discordant.

These are judgments of the senses. They have always been called and accounted such, by those whose minds are not tinctured by philosophical theories. They are the immediate testimony of nature by our senses; and we are so constituted by nature, that we must receive their testimony, for no other reason but because it is given by our senses.

In vain do sceptics endeavour to overturn this evidence by metaphysical reasoning. Though we should not be able to answer their arguments, we believe our senses still, and rest our most important concerns upon their testimony.

If this be a just notion of our external senses, as I conceive it is, our moral faculty may, I think, without impropriety, be called the *Moral Sense.*

In its dignity it is, without doubt, far superior to every other power of the mind; but there is this analogy between it and the external senses, That, as by them we have not only the original conceptions of the various qualities of bodies, but the original judgment that this body has such a quality, that such another; so by our moral faculty, we have both the original conceptions of right and wrong in conduct, of merit and demerit, and the original judgments that this conduct is right, that is wrong; that this character has worth, that demerit.

The testimony of our moral faculty, like that of the external senses, is the testimony of nature, and we have the same reason to rely upon it.

The truths immediately testified by the external senses are the first principles from which we reason, with regard to the material world, and from which all our knowledge of it is deduced.

The truths immediately testified by our moral faculty, are the first principles of all moral reasoning, from which all our knowledge of our duty must be deduced.

By moral reasoning, I understand all reasoning that is brought to prove that such conduct is right, and deserving of moral approbation; or that it is wrong; or that it is indifferent, and, in itself, neither morally good nor ill.

I think, all we can properly call moral judgments, are reducible to one or other of these, as all human actions, considered in a moral view, are either good, or bad, or indifferent.

I know the term *moral reasoning* is often used by good writers in a more extensive sense; but, as the reasoning I now speak of is of a peculiar kind, distinct from all others, and, therefore, ought to have a distinct name, I take the liberty to limit the name of *moral reasoning* to this kind.

Let it be understood, therefore, that in the reasoning I call *moral*, the conclusion always is, That something in the conduct of moral agents is good or bad, in a greater or a less degree, or indifferent.

All reasoning must be grounded on first principles. This holds in moral reasoning, as in all other kinds. There must, therefore, be in morals, as in all other sciences, first or self-evident principles, on which all moral reasoning is grounded, and on which it ultimately rests. From such self-evident principles, conclusions may be drawn synthetically with regard to the moral conduct of life; and particular duties or virtues may be traced back to such principles, analytically. But, without such principles, we can no more establish any conclusion in morals, than we can build a castle in the air, without any foundation.

An example or two will serve to illustrate this.

It is a first principle in morals, That we ought not to do to another what we should think wrong to be done to us in like circumstances. If a man is not capa-

ble of perceiving this in his cool moments, when he reflects seriously, he is not a moral agent, nor is he capable of being convinced of it by reasoning.

From what topic can you reason with such a man? You may possibly convince him by reasoning, that it is his interest to observe this rule; but this is not to convince him that it is his duty. To reason about justice with a man who sees nothing to be just or unjust, or about benevolence with a man who sees nothing in benevolence preferable to malice, is like reasoning with a blind man about colour, or with a deaf man about sound.

It is a question in morals that admits of reasoning, Whether, by the law of nature, a man ought to have only one wife?

We reason upon this question, by balancing the advantages and disadvantages to the family, and to society in general, that are naturally consequent both upon monogamy and polygamy. And, if it can be shewn that the advantages are greatly upon the side of monogamy, we think the point is determined.

But, if a man does not perceive that he ought to regard the good of society, and the good of his wife and children, the reasoning can have no effect upon him, because he denies the first principle upon which it is grounded.

Suppose, again, that we reason for monogamy from the intention of nature, discovered by the proportion of males and of females that are born—a proportion which corresponds perfectly with monogamy, but by no means with polygamy—this argument can have no weight with a man who does not perceive that he ought to have a regard to the intention of nature.

Thus we shall find that all moral reasonings rest upon one or more first principles of morals, whose truth is immediately perceived without reasoning, by all men come to years of understanding.

And this indeed is common to every branch of human knowledge that deserves the name of science. There must be first principles proper to that science, by which the whole superstructure is supported.

The first principles of all the sciences, must be the immediate dictates of our natural faculties; nor is it possible that we should have any other evidence of their truth. And in different sciences the faculties which dictate their first principles are very different.

Thus, in astronomy and in optics, in which such wonderful discoveries have been made, that the unlearned can hardly believe them to be within the reach of human capacity, the first principles are phænomena attested solely by that little organ the human eye. If we disbelieve its report, the whole of those two noble fabrics of science, falls to pieces like the visions of the night.

The principles of music all depend upon the testimony of the ear. The principles of natural philosophy, upon the facts attested by the senses. The principles of mathematics, upon the necessary relations of quantities considered abstractly—such as, That equal quantities added to equal quantities make equal sums, and the like; which necessary relations are immediately perceived by the understanding.

The science of politics borrows its principles from what we know by experience of the character and conduct of man. We consider not what he ought to be, but what he is, and thence conclude what part he will act in different situations and circumstances. From such principles we reason concerning the causes and effects of different forms of government, laws, customs, and manners. If man were either a more perfect or a more imperfect, a better or a worse, creature than he is, politics would be a different science from what it is.

The first principles of morals are the immediate dictates of the moral faculty. They shew us, not what man is, but what he ought to be. Whatever is immediately perceived to be just, honest, and honourable, in human conduct, carries moral obligation along with it, and the contrary carries demerit and blame; and, from those moral obligations that are immediately perceived, all other moral obligations must be deduced by reasoning.

He that will judge of the colour of an object, must consult his eyes, in a good light, when there is no medium or contiguous objects that may give it a false tinge. But in vain will he consult every other faculty in this matter.

In like manner, he that will judge of the first principles of morals, must consult his conscience, or moral faculty, when he is calm and dispassionate, unbiassed by interest, affection, or fashion.

As we rely upon the clear and distinct testimony of our eyes, concerning the colours and figures of the bodies about us, we have the same reason to rely with security upon the clear and unbiassed testimony of our conscience, with regard to what we ought and ought not to do. In many cases moral worth and demerit are discerned no less clearly by the last of

those natural faculties, than figure and colour by the first.

The faculties which nature hath given us, are the only engines we can use to find out the truth. We cannot indeed prove that those faculties are not fallacious, unless God should give us new faculties to sit in judgment upon the old. But we are born under a necessity of trusting them.

Every man in his senses believes his eyes, his ears, and his other senses. He believes his consciousness with respect to his own thoughts and purposes; his memory, with regard to what is past; his understanding, with regard to abstract relations of things; and his taste, with regard to what is elegant and beautiful. And he has the same reason, and, indeed, is under the same necessity of believing the clear and unbiassed dictates of his conscience, with regard to what is honourable and what is base.

The sum of what has been said in this chapter is, That, by an original power of the mind, which we call *conscience*, or *the moral faculty*, we have the conceptions of right and wrong in human conduct, of merit and demerit, of duty and moral obligation, and our other moral conceptions; and that, by the same faculty, we perceive some things in human conduct to be right, and others to be wrong; that the first principles of morals are the dictates of this faculty; and that we have the same reason to rely upon those dictates, as upon the determinations of our senses, or of our other natural faculties.

Chapter VII
Of Moral Approbation and Disapprobation

Our moral judgments are not like those we form in speculative matters, dry and unaffecting, but, from their nature, are necessarily accompanied with affections and feelings; which we are now to consider.

It was before observed, that every human action, considered in a moral view, appears to us, good, or bad, or indifferent. When we judge the action to be indifferent, neither good nor bad, though this be a moral judgment, it produces no affection nor feeling, any more than our judgments in speculative matters.

But we approve of good actions, and disapprove of bad; and this approbation and disapprobation, when we analyse it, appears to include, not only a moral judgment of the action, but some affection, favourable or unfavourable, towards the agent, and some feeling in ourselves.

Nothing is more evident than this, That moral worth, even in a stranger, with whom we have not the least connection, never fails to produce some degree of esteem mixed with good will.

The esteem which we have for a man on account of his moral worth, is different from that which is grounded upon his intellectual accomplishments, his birth, fortune, and connection with us.

Moral worth, when it is not set off by eminent abilities and external advantages, is like a diamond in the mine, which is rough and unpolished, and perhaps crusted over with some baser material that takes away its lustre.

But, when it is attended with these advantages, it is like a diamond cut, polished, and set. Then its lustre attracts every eye. Yet these things, which add so much to its appearance, add but little to its real value.

We must farther observe, that esteem and benevolent regard, not only accompany real worth by the constitution of our nature, but are perceived to be really and properly due to it; and that, on the contrary, unworthy conduct really merits dislike and indignation.

There is no judgment of the heart of man more clear, or more irresistible, than this, That esteem and regard are really due to good conduct, and the contrary to base and unworthy conduct. Nor can we conceive a greater depravity in the heart of man, than it would be to see and acknowledge worth without feeling any respect to it; or to see and acknowledge the highest worthlessness without any degree of dislike and indignation.

The esteem that is due to worthy conduct, is not lessened when a man is conscious of it in himself. Nor can he help having some esteem for himself, when he is conscious of those qualities for which he most highly esteems others.

Self-esteem, grounded upon external advantages, or the gifts of fortune, is pride. When it is grounded upon a vain conceit of inward worth which we do not possess, it is arrogance and self-deceit. But when a man, without thinking of himself more highly than he ought to think, is conscious of that integrity of heart and uprightness of conduct which he most highly esteems in others, and values himself duty upon this account, this, perhaps, may be called the pride of virtue; but it is not a vicious pride. It is a noble and

magnanimous disposition, without which there can be no steady virtue.

A man who has a character with himself, which he values, will disdain to act in a manner unworthy of it. The language of his heart will be like that of Job—"My righteousness I hold fast, and will not let it go; my heart shall not reproach me while I live."

A good man owes much to his character with the world, and will be concerned to vindicate it from unjust imputations. But he owes much more to his character with himself. For, if his heart condemns him not, he has confidence towards God; and he can more easily bear the lash of tongues than the reproach of his own mind.

The sense of honour, so much spoken of, and so often misapplied, is nothing else, when rightly understood, but the disdain which a man of worth feels to do a dishonourable action, though it should never be known nor suspected.

A good man will have a much greater abhorrence against doing a bad action, than even against having it unjustly imputed to him. The last may give a wound to his reputation, but the first gives a wound to his conscience, which is more difficult to heal, and more painful to endure.

Let us, on the other hand, consider how we are affected by disapprobation, either of the conduct of others, or of our own.

Everything we disapprove in the conduct of a man lessens him in our esteem. There are, indeed, brilliant faults, which, having a mixture of good and ill in them, may have a very different aspect, according to the side on which we view them.

In such faults of our friends, and much more of ourselves, we are disposed to view them on the best side, and on the contrary side in those to whom we are ill affected.

This partiality, in taking things by the best or by the worst handle, is the chief cause of wrong judgment with regard to the character of others, and of self-deceit with regard to our own.

But when we take complex actions to pieces, and view every part by itself, ill conduct of every kind lessens our esteem of a man, as much as good conduct increases it. It is apt to turn love into indifference, indifference into contempt, and contempt into aversion and abhorrence.

When a man is conscious of immoral conduct in himself, it lessens his self-esteem. It depresses and humbles his spirit, and makes his countenance to fall. He could even punish himself for his misbehaviour, if that could wipe out the stain. There is a sense of dishonour and worthlessness arising from guilt, as well as a sense of honour and worth arising from worthy conduct. And this is the case, even if a man could conceal his guilt from all the world.

We are next to consider the agreeable or uneasy feelings, in the breast of the spectator or judge, which naturally accompany moral approbation and disapprobation.

There is no affection that is not accompanied with some agreeable or uneasy emotion. It has often been observed, that all the benevolent affections give pleasure, and the contrary ones pain, in one degree or another.

When we contemplate a noble character, though but in ancient history, or even in fiction; like a beautiful object, it gives a lively and pleasant emotion to the spirits. It warms the heart, and invigorates the whole frame. Like the beams of the sun, it enlivens the face of nature, and diffuses heat and light all around.

We feel a sympathy with every noble and worthy character that is represented to us. We rejoice in his prosperity, we are afflicted in his distress. We even catch some sparks of that celestial fire that animated his conduct, and feel the glow of his virtue and magnanimity.

This sympathy is the necessary effect of our judgment of his conduct, and of the approbation and esteem due to it; for real sympathy is always the effect of some benevolent affection, such as esteem, love, pity, or humanity.

When the person whom we approve is connected with us by acquaintance, friendship, or blood, the pleasure we derive from his conduct is greatly increased. We claim some property in his worth, and are apt to value ourselves on account of it. This shews a stronger degree of sympathy, which gathers strength from every social tie.

But the highest pleasure of all is, when we are conscious of good conduct in ourselves. This, in sacred scripture, is called the *testimony of a good conscience*; and it is represented, not only in the sacred writings, but in the writings of all moralists, of every age and sect, as the purest, the most noble and valuable of all human enjoyments.

Surely, were we to place the chief happiness of this life (a thing that has been so much sought after) in any one kind of enjoyment, that which arises from the consciousness of integrity, and a uniform endeavour to act the best part in our station, would most justly claim the preference to all other enjoyments the human mind is capable of, on account of its dignity, the intenseness of the happiness it affords, its stability and duration, its being in our power, and its being proof against all accidents of time and fortune.

On the other hand, the view of a vicious character, like that of an ugly and deformed object, is disagreeable. It gives disgust and abhorrence.

If the unworthy person be nearly connected with us, we have a very painful sympathy indeed. We blush even for the smaller faults of those we are connected with, and feel ourselves, as it were, dishonoured by their ill conduct.

But, when there is a high degree of depravity in any person connected with us, we are deeply humbled and depressed by it. The sympathetic feeling has some resemblance to that of guilt, though it be free from all guilt. We are ashamed to see our acquaintance; we would, if possible, disclaim all connection with the guilty person. We wish to tear him from our hearts, and to blot him out of our remembrance.

Time, however, alleviates those sympathetic sorrows which arise from bad behaviour in our friends and connections, if we are conscious that we had no share in their guilt.

The wisdom of God, in the constitution of our nature, hath intended that this sympathetic distress should interest us the more deeply in the good behaviour, as well as in the good fortune of our friends; and that thereby friendship, relation, and every social tie, should be aiding to virtue, and unfavourable to vice.

How common is it, even in vicious parents, to be deeply afflicted when their children go into these courses in which, perhaps, they have gone before them, and, by their example, shew them the way.

If bad conduct in those in whom we are interested be uneasy and painful, it is so much more when we are conscious of it in ourselves. This uneasy feeling has a name in all languages. We call it *remorse*.

It has been described in such frightful colours, by writers sacred and profane, by writers of every age and of every persuasion, even by Epicureans, that I will not attempt the description of it.

It is on account of the uneasiness of this feeling that bad men take so much pains to get rid of it, and to hide, even from their own eyes, as much as possible, the pravity of their conduct. Hence arise all the arts of self-deceit, by which men varnish their crimes, or endeavour to wash out the stain of guilt. Hence the various methods of expiation which superstition has invented, to solace the conscience of the criminal, and give some cooling to his parched breast. Hence also arise, very often, the efforts of men of bad hearts to excel in some amiable quality, which may be a kind of counter-poise to their vices, both in the opinion of others and in their own.

For no man can bear the thought of being absolutely destitute of all worth. The consciousness of this would make him detest himself, hate the light of the sun, and fly, if possible, out of existence.

I have now endeavoured to delineate the natural operations of that principle of action in man which we call the *Moral Sense*, the *Moral Faculty, Conscience*. We know nothing of our natural faculties, but by their operations within us. Of their operations in our own minds we are conscious, and we see the signs of their operations in the minds of others. Of this faculty, the operations appear to be, the judging ultimately of what is right, what is wrong, and what is indifferent in the conduct of moral agents; the approbation of good conduct, and, disapprobation of bad, in consequence of that judgment; and the agreeable emotions which attend obedience, and disagreeable, which attend disobedience to its dictates.

The Supreme Being, who has given us eyes to discern what may be useful and what hurtful to our natural life, hath also given us this light within, to direct our moral conduct.

Moral conduct is the business of every man; and therefore the knowledge of it ought to be within the reach of all.

Epicurus reasoned acutely and justly to shew, that a regard to our present happiness should induce us to the practice of temperance, justice, and humanity. But the bulk of mankind cannot follow long trains of reasoning. The loud voice of the passions drowns the calm and still voice of reasoning.

Conscience commands and forbids with more authority, and in the most common and most important points of conduct, without the labour of reasoning. Its voice is heard by every man, and cannot be disregarded with impunity.

The sense of guilt makes a man at variance with himself. He sees that he is what he ought not to be. He has fallen from the dignity of his nature, and has sold his real worth for a thing of no value. He is conscious of demerit, and cannot avoid the dread of meeting with its reward.

On the other band, he who pays a sacred regard to the dictates of his conscience, cannot fail of a present reward, and a reward proportioned to the exertion required in doing his duty.

The man who, in opposition to strong temptation, by a noble effort, maintains his integrity, is the happiest man on earth. The more severe his conflict has been, the greater is his triumph. The consciousness of inward worth gives strength to his heart, and makes his countenance to shine. Tempests may beat and floods roar, but he stands firm as a rock in the joy of a good conscience, and confidence of divine approbation.

To this I shall only add, what every man's conscience dictates, That he who does his duty from the conviction that it is right and honourable, and what he ought to do, acts from a nobler principle, and with more inward satisfaction, than he who is bribed to do it merely from the consideration of a reward present or future.

Chapter VIII
Observations Concerning Conscience

I shall now conclude this essay with some observations concerning this power of the mind which we call *Conscience*, by which its nature may be better understood.

The *first* is, That, like all our other powers, it comes to maturity by insensible degrees, and may be much aided in its strength and vigour by proper culture.

All the human faculties have their infancy and their state of maturity.

The faculties which we have in common with the brutes, appear first, and have the quickest growth. In the first period of life, children are not capable of distinguishing right from wrong in human conduct; neither are they capable of abstract reasoning in matters of science. Their judgment of moral conduct, as well as their judgment of truth, advances by insensible degrees, like the corn and the grass.

In vegetables, first the blade or the leaf appears, then the flower, and last of all the fruit, the noblest production of the three, and that for which the others were produced. These succeed one another in a regular order. They require moisture, and heat, and air, and shelter to bring them to maturity, and may be much improved by culture. According to the variations of soil, season, and culture, some plants are brought to much greater perfection than others of the same species. But no variation of culture, or season, or soil, can make grapes grow from thorns, or figs from thistles.

We may observe a similar progress in the faculties of the mind: for there is a wonderful analogy among all the works of God, from the least even to the greatest.

The faculties of man unfold themselves in a certain order, appointed by the great Creator. In their gradual progress, they may be greatly assisted or retarded, improved or corrupted, by education, instruction, example, exercise, and by the society and conversation of men, which, like soil and culture in plants, may produce great changes to the better or to the worse.

But these means can never produce any new faculties, nor any other than were originally planted in the mind by the Author of nature. And what is common to the whole species, in all the varieties of instruction and education, of improvement and degeneracy, is the work of God, and not the operation of second causes.

Such we may justly account conscience, or the faculty of distinguishing right conduct from wrong; since it appears, and in all nations and ages, has appeared, in men that are come to maturity.

The seeds, as it were, of moral discernment are planted in the mind by him that made us. They grow up in their proper season, and are at first tender and delicate, and easily warped. Their progress depends very much upon their being duly cultivated and properly exercised.

It is so with the power of reasoning, which all acknowledge to be one of the most eminent natural faculties of man. It appears not in infancy. Its springs up, by insensible degrees, as we grow to maturity. But its strength and vigour depend so much upon its being duly cultivated and exercised, that we see many individuals, nay, many nations, in which it is hardly to be perceived.

Our intellectual discernment is not so strong and vigorous by nature as to secure us from errors in speculation. On the contrary, we see a great part of mankind, in every age, sunk in gross ignorance of things that are obvious to the more enlightened, and fettered by errors and false notions, which the human understanding, duly improved, easily throws off.

It would be extremely absurd, from the errors and ignorance of mankind, to conclude that there is no such thing as truth; or that man has not a natural faculty of discerning it, and distinguishing it from error.

In like manner, our moral discernment of what we ought, and what we ought not to do, is not so strong and vigorous by nature as to secure us from very gross mistakes with regard to our duty.

In matters of conduct, as well as in matters of speculation, we are liable to be misled by prejudices of education, or by wrong instruction. But, in matters of conduct, we are also very liable to have our judgment warped by our appetites and passions, by fashion, and by the contagion of evil example.

We must not therefore think, because man has the natural power of discerning what is right and what is wrong, that he has no need of instruction; that this power has no need of cultivation and improvement; that he may safely rely upon the suggestions of his mind, or upon opinions he has got, he knows not how.

What should we think of a man who, because he has by nature the power of moving all his limbs should therefore conclude that he needs not be taught to dance, or to fence, to ride, or to swim? All these exercises are performed by that power of moving our limbs which we have by nature; but they will be performed very awkwardly and imperfectly by those who have not been trained to them, and practised in them.

What should we think of the man who, because he has the power by nature of distinguishing what is true from what is false, should conclude that he has no need to be taught mathematics, or natural philosophy, or other sciences? It is by the natural power of human understanding that everything in those sciences has been discovered, and that the truths they contain are discerned. But the understanding, left to itself, without the aid of instruction, training, habit, and exercise, would make very small progress, as every one sees, in persons uninstructed in those matters.

Our natural power of discerning between right and wrong, needs the aid of instruction, education, exercise, and habit, as well as our other natural powers.

There are persons who, as the Scripture speaks, have, by reason of use, their senses exercised to discern both good and evil; by that means, they have a much quicker, clearer, and more certain judgment in morals than others.

The man who neglects the means of improvement in the knowledge of his duty, may do very bad things, while he follows the light of his mind. And, though he be not culpable for acting according to his judgment, he may be very culpable for not using the means of having his judgment better informed.

It may be observed, That there are truths, both speculative and moral, which a man left to himself would never discover; yet, when they are fairly laid before him, he owns and adopts them, not barely upon the authority of his teacher, but upon their own intrinsic evidence, and perhaps wonders that he could be so blind as not to see them before.

Like a man whose son has been long abroad, and supposed dead. After many years, the son returns, and is not known by his father. He would never find that this is his son. But, when he discovers himself, the father soon finds, by many circumstances, that this is his son who was lost, and can be no other person.

Truth has an affinity with the human understanding, which error hath not. And right principles of conduct have an affinity with a candid mind, which wrong principles have not. When they are set before it in a just light, a well disposed mind recognises this affinity, feels their authority, and perceives them to be genuine. It was this, I apprehend, that led Plato to conceive that the knowledge we acquire in the present state, is only reminiscence of what, in a former state, we were acquainted with.

A man born and brought up in a savage nation, may be taught to pursue injury with unrelenting malice, to the destruction of his enemy. Perhaps when he does so, his heart does not condemn him.

Yet, if he be fair and candid, and, when the tumult of passion is over, have the virtues of clemency, generosity, and forgiveness laid before him, as they were taught and exemplified by the divine Author of our religion, he will see that it is more noble to overcome himself, and subdue a savage passion, than to destroy his enemy. He will see, that, to make a friend of an enemy, and to overcome evil with good, is the greatest of all victories, and gives a manly and a rational delight, with which the brutish passion of revenge deserves not to be compared. He will see that hitherto he acted like a man to his friends, but like a brute to his enemies; now he knows how to make his whole character consistent, and one part of it to harmonize with another.

He must indeed be a great stranger to his own heart, and to the state of human nature, who does not see that he has need of all the aid which his situation affords him, in order to know how he ought to act in many cases that occur.

A *second* observation is, That Conscience is peculiar to man. We see not a vestige of it in brute animals. It is one of those prerogatives by which we are raised above them.

Brute animals have many faculties in common with us. They see, and hear, and taste, and smell, and feel. They have their pleasure and pains. They have various instincts and appetites. They have an affection for their offspring, and some of them for their herd or flock. Dogs have a wonderful attachment to their masters, and give manifest signs of sympathy with them.

We see, in brute animals, anger and emulation, pride and shame. Some of them are capable of being trained, by habit, and by rewards and punishments, to many things useful to man.

All this must be granted; and, if our perception of what we ought, and what we ought not to do, could be resolved into any of these principles, or into any combination of them, it would follow, that some brutes are moral agents, and accountable for their conduct.

But common sense revolts against this conclusion. A man who seriously charged a brute with a crime, would be laughed at. They may do actions hurtful to themselves, or to man. They may have qualities, or acquire habits, that lead to such actions; and this is all we mean when we call them vicious. But they cannot be immoral; nor can they be virtuous. They are not capable of self-government; and, when they act according to the passion or habit which is strongest at the time, they act according to the nature that God has given them, and no more can be required of them.

They cannot lay down a rule to themselves, which they are not to transgress, though prompted by appetite, or ruffled by passion. We see no reason to think that they can form the conception of a general rule, or of obligation to adhere to it.

They have no conception of a promise or contract; nor can you enter into any treaty with them. They can neither affirm nor deny, nor resolve, nor plight their faith. If nature had made them capable of these operations, we should see the signs of them in their motions and gestures.

The most sagacious brutes never invented a language, nor learned the use of one before invented. They never formed a plan of government, nor transmitted inventions to their posterity.

These things, and many others that are obvious to common observation, shew that there is just reason why mankind have always considered the brute-creation as destitute of the noblest faculties with which God hath endowed man, and particularly of that faculty which makes us moral and accountable beings.

The *next* [*third*] observation is—That Conscience is evidently intended by nature to be the immediate guide and director of our conduct, after we arrive at the years of understanding.

There are many things which, from their nature and structure, shew intuitively the end for which they were made.

A man who knows the structure of a watch or clock, can have no doubt in concluding that it was made to measure time. And he that knows the structure of the eye, and the properties of light, can have as little doubt whether it was made that we might see by it.

In the fabric of the body, the intention of the several parts is, in many instances, so evident as to leave no possibility of doubt. Who can doubt whether the muscles were intended to move the parts in which they are inserted? Whether the bones were intended to give strength and support to the body; and some of them to guard the parts which they inclose?

When we attend to the structure of the mind, the intention of its various original powers is no less evident. Is it not evident that the external senses are given, that we may discern those qualities of bodies which may be useful or hurtful to us?—Memory, that we may retain the knowledge we have acquired—judgment and understanding, that we may distinguish what is true from what is false?

The natural appetites of hunger and thirst; the natural affections of parents to their offspring, and of relations to each other; the natural docility and credulity of children; the affections of pity and sympathy with the distressed; the attachment we feel to neighbours, to acquaintance, and to the laws and constitution of our country—these are parts of our constitution which plainly point out their end, so that he must be blind, or very inattentive, who does not perceive it. Even the passions of anger and resentment appear very plainly to be a kind of defensive armour, given by our Maker to guard us against injuries, and to deter the injurious.

Thus it holds generally with regard both to the intellectual and active powers of man, that the intention for which they are given is written in legible characters upon the face of them.

Nor is this the case of any of them more evidently than of conscience. Its intention is manifestly implied in its office; which is, to shew us what is good, what bad, and what indifferent in human conduct.

It judges of every action before it is done. For we can rarely act so precipitately but we have the consciousness that what we are about to do is right, or wrong, or indifferent. Like the bodily eye, it naturally looks forward, though its attention may be turned back to the past.

To conceive, as some seem to have done, that its office is only to reflect on past actions, and to approve or disapprove, is, as if a man should conceive that the office of his eyes is only to look back upon the road he has travelled, and to see whether it be clean or dirty; a mistake which no man can make who has made the proper use of his eyes.

Conscience prescribes measures to every appetite, affection, and passion, and says to every other principle of action—So far thou mayest go, but no farther.

We may indeed transgress its dictates, but we cannot transgress them with innocence, nor even with impunity.

We condemn ourselves, or, in the language of scripture, *our heart condemns us*, whenever we go beyond the rules of right and wrong which conscience prescribes.

Other principles of action may have more strength, but this only has authority. Its sentence makes us guilty to ourselves, and guilty in the eyes of our Maker, whatever other principle may be set in opposition to it.

It is evident, therefore, that this principle has, from its nature, an authority to direct and determine with regard to our conduct; to judge, to acquit, or to condemn, and even to punish; an authority which belongs to no other principle of the human mind.

It is the candle of the Lord set up within us, to guide our steps. Other principles may urge and impel, but this only authorizes. Other principles ought to be controlled by this; this may be, but never ought to be controlled by any other, and never can be with innocence.

The authority of conscience over the other active principles of the mind, I do not consider as a point that requires proof by argument, but as self-evident. For it implies no more than this—That in all cases a man ought to do his duty. He only who does in all cases what he ought to do, is the perfect man.

Of this perfection in the human nature, the Stoics formed the idea, and held it forth in their writings, as the goal to which the race of life ought to be directed. Their *wise man* was one in whom a regard to the *honestum* swallowed up every other principle of action.

The *wise man* of the Stoics, like the *perfect orator* of the rhetoricians, was an ideal character, and was, in some respects, carried beyond nature; yet it was perhaps the most perfect model of virtue that ever was exhibited to the heathen world; and some of those who copied after it, were ornaments to human nature.

The [*fourth* and] *last* observation is—That the Moral Faculty or Conscience is both an Active and an Intellectual power of the mind.

It is an *active* power, as every truly virtuous action must be more or less influenced by it. Other principles may concur with it, and lead the same way; but no action can be called morally good, in which a regard to what is right, has not some influence. Thus, a man who has no regard to justice, may pay his just debt, from no other motive but that he may not be thrown into prison. In this action there is no virtue at all.

The moral principle, in particular cases, may be opposed by any of our animal principles. Passion or appetite may urge to what we know to be wrong. In every instance of this kind, the moral principle ought to prevail, and the more difficult its conquest is, it is the more glorious.

In some cases, a regard to what is right may be the sole motive, without the concurrence or opposition of any other principle of action; as when a judge or an arbiter determines a plea between two different persons, solely from a regard to justice.

Thus we see that conscience, as an active principle, sometimes concurs with other active principles, sometimes opposes them, and sometimes is the sole principle of action.

I endeavoured before to shew, that a regard to our own good upon the whole is not only a rational principle of action, but a leading principle, to which all our animal principles are subordinate. As these are, therefore, two regulating or leading principles in the constitution of man—a regard to what is best for us upon the whole, and a regard to duty—it may be asked, Which of these ought to yield if they happen to interfere?

Some well-meaning persons have maintained—That all regard to ourselves and to our own happiness ought to be extinguished; that we should love virtue for its own sake only, even though it were to be accompanied with eternal misery.

This seems to have been the extravagance of some Mystics, which perhaps they were led into in opposition to a contrary extreme of the schoolmen of the middle ages, who made the desire of good to ourselves to be the sole motive to action, and virtue to be approvable only on account of its present or future reward.

Juster views of human nature will teach us to avoid both these extremes.

On the one hand, the disinterested love of virtue is undoubtedly the noblest principle in human nature, and ought never to stoop to any other.

On the other hand, there is no active principle which God hath planted in our nature that is vicious in itself, or that ought to be eradicated, even if it were in our power.

They are all useful and necessary in our present state. The perfection of human nature consists, not in extinguishing, but in restraining them within their proper bounds, and keeping them in due subordination to the governing principles.

As to the supposition of an opposition between the two governing principles—that is, between a regard to our happiness upon the whole, and a regard to duty—this supposition is merely imaginary. There can be no such opposition.

While the world is under a wise and benevolent administration, it is impossible that any man should, in the issue, be a loser by doing his duty. Every man, therefore, who believes in God, while he is careful to do his duty, may safely leave the care of his happiness to Him who made him. He is conscious that he consults the last most effectually by attending to the first.

Indeed, if we suppose a man to be an atheist in his belief, and, at the same time, by wrong judgment, to believe that virtue is contrary to his happiness upon the whole, this case, as Lord Shaftesbury justly observes, is without remedy. It will be impossible for the man to act so as not to contradict a leading principle of his nature. He must either sacrifice his happiness to virtue, or virtue to happiness; and is reduced to this miserable dilemma, whether it be best to be a fool or a knave.

This shews the strong connection between morality and the principles of natural religion; as the last only can secure a man from the possibility of an apprehension, that he may play the fool by doing his duty.

Hence, even Lord Shaftesbury, in his gravest work, concludes, *That virtue without piety is incomplete.* Without piety, it loses its brightest example, its noblest object, and its firmest support.

I conclude with observing, That conscience, or the moral faculty, is likewise an *intellectual* power.

By it solely we have the original conceptions or ideas of right and wrong in human conduct. And of right and wrong there are not only many different degrees, but many different species. Justice and injustice, gratitude and ingratitude, benevolence and malice, prudence and folly, magnanimity and meanness, decency and indecency, are various moral forms, all comprehended under the general notion of right and wrong in conduct, all of them objects of moral approbation or disapprobation, in a greater or a less degree.

The conception of these, as moral qualities, we have by our moral faculty; and by the same faculty, when we compare them together, we perceive various moral relations among them. Thus, we perceive that justice is entitled to a small degree of praise, but injustice to a high degree of blame; and the same may be said of gratitude and its contrary. When justice and gratitude interfere, gratitude must give place to justice, and unmerited beneficence must give place to both.

Many such relations between the various moral qualities compared together, are immediately discerned by our moral faculty. A man needs only to consult his own heart to be convinced of them.

All our reasonings in morals, in natural jurisprudence, in the law of nations, as well as our reasonings about the duties of natural religion, and about the moral government of the Deity, must be grounded upon the dictates of our moral faculty, as first principles.

As this faculty, therefore, furnishes the human mind with many of its original conceptions or ideas, as well as with the first principles of many important branches of human knowledge, it may justly be accounted an intellectual as well as an active power of the mind.

• • •

Essay V Of Morals

Chapter I
Of the First Principles of Morals

Morals, like all other sciences, must have *first principles*, on which all moral reasoning is grounded.

In every branch of knowledge where disputes have been raised, it is useful to distinguish the first principles from the super-structure. They are the foundation on which the whole fabric of the science leans; and whatever is not supported by this foundation can have no stability.

In all rational belief, the thing believed is either itself a first principle, or it is by just reasoning deduced from first principles. When men differ about deductions of reasoning, the appeal must be to the rules of reasoning, which have been very unanimously fixed from the days of Aristotle. But when they differ about a first principle, the appeal is made to another tribunal—to that of *Common Sense.*

How the genuine decisions of Common Sense may be distinguished from the counterfeit, has been considered in Essay Sixth, on the *Intellectual Powers of Man*, chapter fourth, to which the reader is referred.

What I would here observe is, That, as first principles differ from deductions of reasoning in the nature of their evidence, and must be tried by a different standard when they are called in question, it is of importance to know to which of these two classes a truth which we would examine, belongs. When they are not distinguished, men are apt to demand proof for everything they think fit to deny. And when we attempt to prove, by direct argument, what is really self-evident, the reasoning will always be inconclusive; for it will either take for granted the thing to be proved, or something not more evident; and so, instead of giving strength to the conclusion, will rather tempt those to doubt of it who never did so before.

I propose, therefore, in this chapter, to point out some of the first principles of morals, without pretending to a complete enumeration.

The principles I am to mention, relate either [A] to *virtue in general*, or [B] to the different *particular branches of virtue*, or [C] to the *comparison of virtues* where they seem to interfere.

[A] 1. *There are some things in human conduct that merit approbation and praise, others that merit blame and punishment; and different degrees either of approbation or of blame, are due to different actions.*

2. *What is in no degree voluntary, can neither deserve moral approbation nor blame.*

3. *What is done from unavoidable necessity may be agreeable or disagreeable, useful or hurtful, but cannot be the object either of blame or of moral approbation.*

4. *Men may be highly culpable in omitting what they ought to have done, as well as in doing what they ought not.*

5. *We ought to use the best means we can to be well informed of our duty*—by serious attention to moral instruction; by observing what we approve, and what we disapprove, in other men, whether our acquaintance, or those whose actions are recorded in history; by reflecting often, in a calm and dispassionate hour, on our own past conduct, that we may discern what was wrong, what was right, and what might have been better; by deliberating coolly and impartially upon our future conduct, as far as we can foresee the opportunities we may have of doing good, or the temptations to do wrong; and by having this principle deeply fixed in our minds, that, as moral excellence is the true worth and glory of a man, so the knowledge of our duty is to every man, in every station of life, the most important of all knowledge.

6. *It ought to be our most serious concern to do our duty as far as we know it, and to fortify our minds against every temptation to deviate from it*—by maintaining a lively sense of the beauty of right conduct, and of its present and future reward, of the turpitude of vice, and of its bad consequences here and hereafter; by having always in our eye the noblest examples; by the habit of subjecting our passions to the government of reason; by firm purposes and resolutions with regard to our conduct; by avoiding occasions of temptation when we can; and by imploring the aid of Him who made us, in every hour of temptation.

These principles concerning virtue and vice *in general*, must appear self-evident to every man who hath a conscience, and who hath taken pains to exercise this natural power of his mind. I proceed to others that are *more particular*.

[B] 1. *We ought to prefer a greater good, though more distant, to a less; and a less evil to a greater.*

A regard to our own good, though we had no conscience, dictates this principle; and we cannot help disapproving the man that acts contrary to it, as deserving to lose the good which he wantonly threw away, and to suffer the evil which he knowingly brought upon his own head.

We observed before, that the ancient moralists, and many among the modern, have deduced the whole of morals from this principle, and that, when we make a right estimate of goods and evils according to their degree, their dignity, their duration, and according as they are more or less in our power, it leads to the practice of every virtue. More directly, indeed, to the virtues of self-government, to prudence, to temperance, and to fortitude; and, though more indirectly, even to justice, humanity, and all the social virtues, when their influence upon our happiness is well understood.

Though it be not the noblest principle of conduct, it has this peculiar advantage, that its force is felt by the most ignorant, and even by the most abandoned.

Let a man's moral judgment be ever so little improved by exercise, or ever so much corrupted by bad habits, he cannot be indifferent to his own happiness or misery. When he is become insensible to every nobler motive to right conduct, he cannot be insensible to this. And though to act from this motive solely may be called *prudence* rather than *virtue*, yet this prudence deserves some regard upon its own account, and much more as it is the friend and ally of virtue, and the enemy of all vice; and as it gives a favourable testimony of virtue to those who are deaf to every other recommendation.

If a man can be induced to do his duty even from a regard to his own happiness, he will soon find reason to love virtue for her own sake, and to act from motives less mercenary.

I cannot therefore approve of those moralists who would banish all persuasives to virtue taken from the consideration of private good. In the present state of human nature these are not useless to the best, and they are the only means left of reclaiming the abandoned.

2. *As far as the intention of nature appears in the constitution of man, we ought to comply with that intention, and to act agreeably to it.*

The Author of our being hath given us not only the power of acting within a limited sphere, but various principles or springs of action, of different nature and dignity, to direct us in the exercise of our active power.

From the constitution of every species of the inferior animals, and especially from the active principles which nature has given them, we easily perceive the manner of life for which nature intended them; and they uniformly act the part to which they are led by their constitution, without any reflection upon it, or intention of obeying its dictates. Man only, of the inhabitants of this world, is made capable of observing his own constitution, what kind of life it is made for, and of acting according to that intention, or contrary to it. He only is capable of yielding an intentional obedience to the dictates of his nature, or of rebelling against them.

In treating of the principles of action in man, if has been shewn, that, as his natural instincts and bodily appetites are well adapted to the preservation of his natural life, and to the continuance of the species; so his natural desires, affections, and passions, when uncorrupted by vicious habits, and under the government of the leading principles of reason and conscience, are excellently fitted for the rational and social life. Every vicious action shews an excess, or defect, or wrong direction of some natural spring of action, and therefore may, very justly, be said to be unnatural. Every virtuous action agrees with the uncorrupted principles of human nature.

The Stoics defined Virtue to be *a life according to nature.* Some of them more accurately, *a life according to the nature of man, in so far as it is superior to that of brutes.* The life of a brute is according to the nature of the brute; but it is neither virtuous nor vicious. The life of a moral agent cannot be according to his nature, unless it be virtuous. That conscience which is in every man's breast, is the law of God written in his heart, which he can not disobey without acting unnaturally, and being self-condemned.

The intention of nature, in the various active principles of man—in the desires of power, of knowledge, and of esteem, in the affection to children, to near relations, and to the communities to which we belong, in gratitude, in compassion, and even in resentment and emulation—is very obvious, and has been pointed out in treating of those principles. Nor is it less evident, that reason and conscience are given us to regulate the inferior principles, so that they may conspire, in a regular and consistent plan of life, in pursuit of some worthy end.

3. *No man is born for himself only.* Every man, therefore, ought to consider himself as a member of the common society of mankind, and of those subordinate societies to which he belongs, such as family, friends, neighbourhood, country, and to do as much

good as he can, and as little hurt to the societies of which he is a part.

This axiom leads directly to the practice of every social virtue, and indirectly to the virtues of self-government, by which only we can be qualified for discharging the duty we owe to society.

4. *In every case, we ought to act that part towards another, which we would judge to be right in him to act toward us, if we were in his circumstances and he in ours;* or, more generally—*What we approve in others, that we ought to practise in like circumstances, and what we condemn in others, we ought not to do.*

If there be any such thing as right and wrong in the conduct of moral agents, it must be the same to all in the same circumstances.

We stand all in the same relation to Him who made us, and will call us to account for our conduct; for with Him there is no respect of persons. We stand in the same relation to one another as members of the great community of mankind. The duties consequent upon the different ranks and offices and relations of men are the same to all in the same circumstances.

It is not want of judgment, but want of candour and impartiality, that hinders men from discerning what they owe to others. They are quicksighted enough in discerning what is due to themselves. When they are injured, or ill-treated, they see it, and feel resentment. It is the want of candour that makes men use one measure for the duty they owe to others, and another measure for the duty that others owe to them in like circumstances. That men ought to judge with candour, as in all other cases, so especially in what concerns their moral conduct, is surely self-evident to every intelligent being. The man who takes offence when he is injured in his person, in his property, in his good name, pronounces judgment against himself if he act so toward his neighbour.

As the equity and obligation of this rule of conduct is self-evident to every man who hath a conscience; so it is, of all the rules of morality, the most comprehensive, and truly deserves the encomium given it by the highest authority, that *"it is the law and the prophets."*

It comprehends every rule of justice without exception. It comprehends all the relative duties, arising either from the more permanent relations of parent and child, of master and servant, of magistrate and subject, of husband and wife, or from the more transient relations of rich and poor, of buyer and seller, of debtor and creditor, of benefactor and bene-ficiary, of friend and enemy. It comprehends every duty of charity and humanity, and even of courtesy and good manners.

Nay, I think, that, without any force or straining, it extends even to the duties of self-government. For, as every man approves in others the virtues of prudence, temperance, self-command, and fortitude, he must perceive that what is right in others must be right in himself in like circumstances.

To sum up all, he who acts invariably by this rule will never deviate from the path of his duty, but from an error of judgment. And, as he feels the obligation that he and all men are under to use the best means in his power to have his judgment well-informed in matters of duty, his errors will only be such as are invincible.

It may be observed, that this axiom supposes a fac-ulty in man by which he can distinguish right conduct from wrong. It supposes also, that, by this faculty, we easily perceive the right and the wrong in other men that are indifferent to us; but are very apt to be blinded by the partiality of selfish passions when the case concerns ourselves. Every claim we have against others is apt to be magnified by self-love, when viewed directly. A change of persons removes this prejudice, and brings the claim to appear in its just magnitude.

5. *To every man who believes the existense, the perfections, and the providence of God, the venera-tion and submission we owe to him is self-evident.* Right sentiments of the Deity and of his works, not only make the duty we owe to him obvious to every intelligent being, but likewise add the authority of a Divine law to every rule of right conduct.

[C] There is another class of axioms in morals, by which, when there seems to be an *opposition* be-tween the actions that different virtues lead to, we determine to which the *preference* is due.

Between the several virtues, as they are disposi-tions of mind, or determinations of will, to act accord-ing to a certain general rule, there can be no opposition. They dwell together most amicably, and give mutual aid and ornament, without the possibility of hostility or opposition, and, taken altogether, make one uniform and consistent rule of conduct. But, between particular external actions, which different virtues would lead to, there may be an opposition. Thus, the same man may be in his heart, generous, grateful, and just. These dispositions strengthen, but

never can weaken one another. Yet it may happen, that an external action which generosity or gratitude solicits, justice may forbid.

That in all such cases, *unmerited generosity should yield to gratitude, and both to justice*, is self-evident. Nor is it less so, that *unmerited beneficence to those who are at ease should yield to compassion to the miserable*, and *external acts of piety to works of mercy*, because God loves mercy more than sacri-fice.

At the same time, we perceive, that those acts of virtue which ought to yield in the case of a competi-tion, have most intrinsic worth when there is no com-petition. Thus, it is evident that there is more worth in pure and unmerited benevolence than in compassion, more in compassion than in gratitude, and more in gratitude than in justice.

I call these *first principles*, because they appear to me to have in themselves an intuitive evidence which I cannot resist. I find I can express them in other words. I can illustrate them by examples and authori-ties, and perhaps can deduce one of them from another; but I am not able to deduce them from other principles that are more evident. And I find the best moral reasonings of authors I am acquainted with, ancient and modern, Heathen and Christian, to be grounded upon one or more of them.

The evidence of mathematical axioms is not dis-cerned till men come to a certain degree of maturity of understanding. A boy must have formed the gen-eral conception of *quantity*, and of *more* and *less* and *equal*, of *sum* and *difference;* and he must have been accustomed to judge of these relations in matters of common life, before he can perceive the evidence of the mathematical axiom—that equal quantities, added to equal quantities, make equal sums.

In like manner, our Moral Judgment or Con-science, grows to maturity from an imperceptible seed, planted by our Creator. When we are capable of contemplating the actions of other men, or of reflect-ing upon our own calmly and dispassionately, we begin to perceive in them the qualities of honest and dishonest, of honourable and base, of right and wrong, and to feel the sentiments of moral approba-tion and disapprobation.

These sentiments are at first feeble, easily warped by passions and prejudices, and apt to yield to author-ity. By use and time, the judgment, in morals, as in other matters, gathers strength, and feels more vigour. We begin to distinguish tile dictates of passion from those of cool reason, and to perceive that it is not always safe to rely upon the judgment of others. By an impulse of nature, we venture to judge for ourselves, as we venture to walk by ourselves.

There is a strong analogy between the progress of the body from infancy to maturity, and the progress of all the powers of the mind. This progression in both is the work of nature, and in both may be greatly aided or hurt by proper education. It is natural to a man to be able to walk, or run, or leap; but, if his limbs had been kept in fetters from his birth, he would have none of those powers. It is no less natural to a man trained in society, and accustomed to judge of his own actions and those of other men, to perceive a right and a wrong, an honourable and a base, in human conduct; and to such a man, I think, the principles of morals I have above mentioned will appear self-evident. Yet there may be individuals of the human species so little accustomed to think or judge of anything but of gratifying their animal appetites, as to have hardly any conception of right or wrong in conduct, or any moral judgment; as there certainly are some who have not the conceptions and the judgment necessary to understand the axioms of geometry.

From the principles above mentioned, the whole system of moral conduct follows so easily, and with so little aid of reasoning, that every man of common understanding, who wishes to know his duty, may know it. The path of duty is a plain path, which the upright in heart can rarely mistake. Such it must be, since every man is bound to walk in it. There are some intricate cases in morals which admit of disputation; but these seldom occur in practice; and, when they do, the learned disputant has no great advantage: for the unlearned man, who uses the best means in his power to know his duty, and acts according to his knowledge, is inculpable in the sight of God and man. He may err, but he is not guilty of immorality.

Chapter II
Of Systems of Morals

If the knowledge of our duty be so level to the apprehension of all men as has been represented in the last chapter, it may seem hardly to deserve the name of a Science. It may seem that there is no need for instruction in morals.

From what cause then has it happened, that we have many large and learned systems of Moral Philos-

ophy, and systems of Natural Jurisprudence, or the Law of Nature and Nations; and that, in modern times, public professions [professorships] have been instituted in most places of education for instructing youth in these branches of knowledge?

This event, I think, may be accounted for, and the utility of such systems and professions justified, without supposing any difficulty or intricacy in the knowledge of our duty.

I am far from thinking instruction in morals unnecessary. Men may, to the end of life, be ignorant of self-evident truths. They may, to the end of life, entertain gross absurdities. Experience shews that this happens often in matters that are indifferent. Much more may it happen in matters where interest, passion, prejudice, and fashion, are so apt to pervert the judgment.

The most obvious truths are not perceived without some ripeness of judgment. For we see that children may be made to believe anything, though ever so absurd. Our judgment of things is ripened, not by time only, but chiefly by being exercised about things of the same or of a similar kind.

Judgment, even in things self-evident, requires a clear, distinct, and steady conception of the things about which we judge. Our conceptions are at first obscure and wavering. The habit of attending to them is necessary to make them distinct and steady; and this habit requires an exertion of mind to which many of our animal principles are unfriendly. The love of truth calls for it; but its still voice is often drowned by the louder call of some passion, or we are hindered from listening to it by laziness and desultoriness. Thus men often remain through life ignorant of things which they needed but to open their eyes to see, and which they would have seen if their attention had been turned to them.

The most knowing derive the greatest part of their knowledge, even in things obvious, from instruction and information, and from being taught to exercise their natural faculties, which, without instruction, would lie dormant.

I am very apt to think, that, if a man could be reared from infancy, without any society of his fellow-creatures, he would hardly ever shew any sign, either of moral judgment, or of the power of reasoning. His own actions would be directed by his animal appetites and passions, without cool reflection, and he would have no access to improve, by observing the conduct of other beings like himself.

The power of vegetation in the seed of a plant, without heat and moisture, would for ever lie dormant. The rational and moral powers of man would perhaps lie dormant without instruction and example. Yet these powers are a part, and the noblest part, of his constitution; as the power of vegetation is of the seed.

Our first moral conceptions are probably got by attending coolly to the conduct of others, and observing what moves our approbation, what our indignation. These sentiments spring from our moral faculty as naturally as the sensations of sweet and bitter from the faculty of taste. They have their natural objects. But most human actions are of a mixed nature, and have various colours, according as they are viewed on different sides. Prejudice against or in favour of the person, is apt to warp our opinion. It requires attention and candour to distinguish the good from the ill, and, without favour or prejudice, to form a clear and impartial judgment. In this we may be greatly aided by instruction.

He must be very ignorant of human nature, who does not perceive that the seed of virtue in the mind of man, like that of a tender plant in an unkindly soil, requires care and culture in the first period of life, as well as our own exertion when we come to maturity.

If the irregularities of passion and appetite be timely checked, and good habits planted; if we be excited by good examples, and bad examples be shewn in their proper colour; if the attention be prudently directed to the precepts of wisdom and virtue, as the mind is capable of receiving them—a man thus trained will rarely be at a loss to distinguish good from ill in his own conduct, without the labour of reasoning.

The bulk of mankind have but little of this culture in the proper season; and what they have is often unskillfully applied; by which means bad habits gather strength, and false notions of pleasure, of honour, and of interest occupy the mind. They give little attention to what is right and honest. Conscience is seldom consulted, and so little exercised that its decisions are weak and wavering. Although, therefore, to a ripe understanding, free from prejudice, and accustomed to judge of the morality of actions, most truths in morals will appear self-evident, it does not follow that moral instruction is unnecessary in the first part of life, or that it may not be very profitable in its more advanced period.

The history of past ages shews that nations, highly civilized and greatly enlightened in many arts and sci-

ences, may, for ages, not only hold the grossest absurdities with regard to the Deity and his worship, but with regard to the duty we owe to our fellow-men, particularly to children, to servants, to strangers, to enemies, and to those who differ from us in religious opinions.

Such corruptions in religion and in morals had spread so wide among mankind, and were so confirmed by custom, as to require a light from heaven to correct them. Revelation was not intended to supersede, but to aid the use of our natural faculties; and I doubt not but the attention given to moral truths, in such systems as we have mentioned, has contributed much to correct the errors and prejudices of former ages, and may continue to have the same good effect in time to come.

It needs not seem strange that systems of morals may swell to great magnitude, if we consider that, although the general principles be few and simple, their application extends to every part of human conduct, in every condition, every relation, and every transaction of life. They are the rule of life to the magistrate and to the subject, to the master and to the servant, to the parent and to the child, to the fellow-citizen and to the alien, to the friend and to the enemy, to the buyer and to the seller, to the borrower and to the lender. Every human creature is subject to their authority in his actions and words, and even in his thoughts. They may, in this respect, be compared to the laws of motion in the natural world, which, though few and simple, serve to regulate an infinite variety of operations throughout the universe.

And as the beauty of the laws of motion is displayed in the most striking manner, when we trace them through all the variety of their effects; so the divine beauty and sanctity of the principles of morals appear most august when we take a comprehensive view of their application to every condition and relation, and to every transaction of human society.

This is, or ought to be, the design of systems of morals. They may be made more or less extensive, having no limits fixed by nature, but the wide circle of human transactions. When the principles are applied to these in detail, the detail is pleasant and profitable. It requires no profound reasoning (excepting, perhaps, in a few disputable points). It admits of the most agreeable illustration from examples and authorities; it serves to exercise, and thereby to strengthen, moral judgment. And one who has given much attention to the duty of man, in all the various related circumstances of life, will probably be more enlightened in his own duty, and more able to enlighten others.

The first writers in morals, we are acquainted with, delivered their moral instructions, not in systems, but in short unconnected sentences, or aphorisms. They saw no need for deductions of reasoning, because the truths they delivered could not but be admitted by the candid and attentive.

Subsequent writers, to improve the way of treating this subject, gave method and arrangement to moral truths, by reducing them under certain divisions and subdivisions, as parts of one whole. By these means the whole is more easily comprehended and remembered, and from this arrangement gets the name of a system and of a science.

A system of morals is not like a system of geometry, where the subsequent parts derive their evidence from the preceding, and one chain of reasoning is carried on from the beginning; so that, if the arrangement is changed, the chain is broken, and the evidence is lost. It resembles more a system of botany, or mineralogy, where the subsequent parts depend not for their evidence upon the preceding, and the arrangement is made to facilitate apprehension and memory, and not to give evidence.

Morals have been methodised in different ways. The ancients commonly arranged them under the four cardinal virtues of Prudence, Temperance, Fortitude, and Justice; Christian writers, I think more properly, under the three heads of the Duty we owe to God—to Ourselves—and to our Neighbour. One division may be more comprehensive, or more natural, than another; but the truths arranged are the same, and their evidence the same in all.

I shall only farther observe, with regard to systems of morals, that they have been made more voluminous and more intricate, partly by mixing political questions with morals, which I think improper, because they belong to a different science, and are grounded on different principles; partly by making what is commonly, but I think improperly, called *the Theory of Morals*, a part of the system.

By the Theory of Morals is meant a just account of the structure of our moral powers—that is, of those powers of mind by which we have our moral conceptions, and distinguish right from wrong in human actions. This, indeed, is an intricate subject, and there have been various theories and much controversy

about it in ancient and in modern times. But it has little connection with the knowledge of our duty; and those who differ most in the theory of our moral powers, agree in the practical rules of morals which they dictate.

As a man may be a good judge of colours, and of the other visible qualities of objects, without any knowledge of the anatomy of the eye, and of the theory of vision; so a man may have a very clear and comprehensive knowledge of what is right and what is wrong in human conduct, who never studied the structure of our moral powers.

A good ear in music may be much improved by attention and practice in that art, but very little by studying the anatomy of the ear, and the theory of sound. In order to acquire a good eye or a good ear in the arts that require them, the theory of vision and the theory of sound are by no means necessary, and indeed of very little use. Of as little necessity or use is what we call the theory of morals, in order to improve our moral judgment.

I mean not to depreciate this branch of knowledge. It is a very important part of the philosophy of the human mind, and ought to be considered as such, but not as any part of morals. By the name we give to it, and by the custom of making it a part of every system of morals, men may be led into this gross mistake, which I wish to obviate, That, in order to understand his duty, a man must needs be a philosopher and a metaphysician.

Chapter III
Of Systems of Natural Jurisprudence

Systems of Natural Jurisprudence, of the Rights of Peace and War, or of the Law of Nature and Nations, are a modern invention, which soon acquired such reputation as gave occasion to many public establishments for teaching it along with the other sciences. It has so close a relation to morals, that it may answer the purpose of a system of morals, and is commonly put in the place of it, as far, at least, as concerns our duty to our fellow-men. They differ in the name and form, but agree in substance. This will appear from a slight attention to the nature of both.

The direct intention of Morals is to teach the duty of men: that of Natural Jurisprudence to teach the rights of men. Right and Duty are things very different, and have even a kind of opposition; yet they are so related that the one cannot even be conceived without the other; and he that understands the one must understand the other.

They have the same relation which credit has to debt. As all credit supposes an equivalent debt, so all right supposes a corresponding duty. There can be no credit in one party without an equivalent debt in another party; and there can be no right in one party, without a corresponding duty in another party. The sum of credit shews the sum of debt; and the sum of men's rights shews, in like manner, the sum of their duty to one another.

The word *Right* has a very different meaning, according as it is applied to actions or to persons. A right action is an action agreeable to our duty. But, when we speak of the *rights of men*, the word has a very different and a more artificial meaning. It is a term of art in law, and signifies all that a man may lawfully do, all that he may lawfully possess and use, and all that he may lawfully claim of any other person.

This comprehensive meaning of the word *right*, and of the Latin word *jus*, which corresponds to it, though long adopted into common language, is too artificial to be the birth of common language. It is a term of art, contrived by Civilians when the Civil Law became a profession.

The whole end and object of Law is to protect the subjects in all that they may lawfully *do*, or *possess*, or *demand*. This threefold object of law, Civilians have comprehended under the word *jus* or *right*, which they define, "*Faeultas aliquid agendi, vel possidendi, vel ab alio consequendi*": "A lawful claim to *do anything*, to *possess anything*, or to *demand some prestation from some other person.*" The first of these may be called the right of *liberty*; the second that of *property*, which is also called a *real right*; the third is called *personal right*, because it respects some particular person or persons of whom the prestation may be demanded.

We can be at no loss to perceive the Duties corresponding to the several kinds of Rights. What I have a right to do, it is the duty of all men not to hinder me from doing. What is my property or real right, no man ought to take from me; or to molest me in the use and enjoyment of it. And what I have a right to demand of any man, it is his duty to perform. Between the right, on the one hand, and the duty, on the other, there is not only a necessary connection, but, in reality, they are only different expressions of the same meaning;

just as it is the same thing to say, I am your debtor, and to say, You are my creditor; or as it is the same thing to say, I am your father, and to say, You are my son.

Thus we see, that there is such a correspondence between the rights of men and the duties of men, that the one points out the other; and a system of the one may be substituted for a system of the other.

But here an objection occurs. It may be said, *That, although every right implies a duty, yet every duty does not imply a right.* Thus, it may be my duty to do a humane or kind office to a man who has no claim of right to it; and therefore a system of the rights of men, though it teach all the duties of strict justice, yet it leaves out all the duties of charity and humanity, without which the system of morals must be very lame.

In answer to this objection, it may be observed, That, as there is a strict notion of justice, in which it is distinguished from humanity and charity, so there is a more extensive signification of it, in which it includes those virtues. The ancient moralists, both Greek and Roman, under the cardinal virtue of justice, included beneficence; and, in this extensive sense, it is often used in common language. The like may be said of right, which, in a sense not uncommon, is extended to every proper claim of humanity and charity, as well as to the claims of strict justice. But, as it is proper to distinguish these two kinds of claims by different names, writers in natural jurisprudence have given the name of *perfect* rights to the claims of strict justice, and that of *imperfect* rights to the claims of charity and humanity. Thus, all the duties of humanity have imperfect rights corresponding to them, as those of strict justice have perfect rights.

Another objection may be, *That there is still a class of duties to which no right, perfect or imperfect, corresponds.*

We are bound in duty to pay due respect, not only to what is truly the right of another, but to what, through ignorance or mistake, we believe to be his right. Thus, if my neighbour is possessed of a horse which he stole, and to which he has no right, while I believe the horse to be really his, and am ignorant of the theft, it is my duty to pay the same respect to this conceived right as if it were real. Here, then, is a moral obligation on one party without any corresponding right on the other.

To supply this defect in the system of rights, so as to make right and duty correspond in every instance, writers in jurisprudence have had recourse to something like what is called a fiction of law. They give the name of *right* to the claim which even the thief hath to the goods he has stolen, while the theft is unknown, and to all similar claims grounded on the ignorance or mistake of the parties concerned. And to distinguish this kind of right from genuine rights, perfect or imperfect, they call it an *external* right.

Thus it appears, That, although a system of the perfect rights of men, or the rights of strict justice, would be a lame substitute for a system of human duty, yet, when we add to it the imperfect and the external rights, it comprehends the whole duty we owe to our fellow-men.

But it may be asked, *Why should men be taught their duty in this indirect way, by reflection, as it were, from the rights of other men?*

Perhaps it may be thought that this indirect way may be more agreeable to the pride of man, as we see that men of rank like better to hear of obligations of honour than of obligations of duty (although the dictates of true honour and of duty be the same); for this reason that honour puts a man in mind of what he owes to himself, whereas duty is a more humiliating idea. For a like reason, men may attend more willingly to their rights which put them in mind of their dignity, than to their duties, which suggest their dependence. And we see that men may give great attention to their rights who give but little to their duty.

Whatever truth there may be in this, I believe better reasons can be given why systems of natural jurisprudence have been contrived and put in the place of systems of morals.

Systems of Civil Law were invented many ages before we had any system of Natural Jurisprudence; and the former seem to have suggested the idea of the latter.

Such is the weakness of human understanding, that no large body of knowledge can be easily apprehended and remembered, unless it be arranged and methodised—that is, reduced into a system. When the laws of the Roman people were multiplied to a great degree, and the study of them became an honourable and lucrative profession, it became necessary that they should be methodised into a system. And the most natural and obvious way of methodising law, was found to be according to the divisions and subdivisions of men's rights, which it is the intention of law to protect.

The study of law produced not only systems of law, but a language proper for expressing them. Every art has its terms of art for expressing the conceptions that belong to it; and the civilian must have terms for expressing accurately the divisions and subdivisions of rights, and the various ways whereby they may be acquired, transferred, or extinguished, in the various transactions of civil society. He must have terms accurately defined, for the various crimes by which men's rights are violated; not to speak of the terms which express the different forms of actions at law, and the various steps of the procedure of judicatories.

Those who have been bred to any profession are very prone to use the terms of their profession in speaking or writing on subjects that have any analogy to it. And they may do so with advantage, as terms of art are commonly more precise in their signification, and better defined, than the words of common language. To such persons, it is also very natural to model and arrange other subjects, as far as their nature admits, into a method similar to that of the system which fills their minds.

It might, therefore, be expected that a civilian, intending to give a detailed system of morals, would use many of the terms of civil law, and mould it, as far as it can be done, into the form of a system of law, or of the rights of mankind.

The necessary and close relation of right to duty, which we before observed, justified this. And Moral Duty had long been considered as a *law of nature*; a law, not wrote on tables of stone or brass, but on the heart of man; a law of greater antiquity and higher authority than the laws of particular states; a law which is binding upon all men of all nations, and, therefore, is called by Cicero *the law of nature and of nations.*

The idea of a system of this law was worthy of the genius of the immortal Hugo Grotius, and he was the first who executed it in such a manner as to draw the attention of the learned in all the European nations; and to give occasion to several princes and states to establish public professions for the teaching of this law.

The multitude of commentators and annotators upon this work of Grotius, and the public establishments to which it gave occasion, are sufficient vouchers of its merit.

It is, indeed, a work so well designed, and so skillfully executed; so free from the scholastic jargon which infected the learned at that time; so much addressed to the common sense and moral judgment of mankind; and so agreeably illustrated by examples from ancient history, and authorities from the sentiments of ancient authors, heathen and Christian, that it must always be esteemed as the capital work of a great genius upon a most important subject.

The utility of a just system of natural jurisprudence appears—1. As it is a system of the moral duty we owe to men, which, by the aid they have taken from the terms and divisions of the civil law, has been given more in detail and more systematically by writers in natural jurisprudence than it was formerly. 2. As it is the best preparation for the study of law, being, as it were, cast in the mould, and using and explaining many of the terms of the civil law, on which the law of most of the European nations is grounded. 3. It is of use to lawgivers, who ought to make their laws as agreeable as possible to the law of nature. And as laws made by men, like all human works, must be imperfect, it points out the errors and imperfections of human laws. 4. To judges and interpreters of the law it is of use, because that interpretation ought to be preferred which is founded in the law of nature. 5. It is of use in civil controversies between states, or between individuals who have no common superior. In such controversies, the appeal must be made to the law of nature; and the standard systems of it, particularly that of Grotius, have great authority. And, 6, To say no more upon this point, it is of great use to sovereigns and states who are above all human laws, to be solemnly admonished of the conduct they are bound to observe to their own subjects, to the subjects of other states, and to one another, in peace and in war. The better and the more generally the law of nature is understood, the greater dishonour, in public estimation, will follow every violation of it.

Some authors have imagined that systems of natural jurisprudence ought to be confined to the perfect rights of men, because the duties which correspond to the imperfect rights, the duties of charity and humanity, cannot be enforced by human laws, but must be left to the judgment and conscience of men, free from compulsion. But the systems which have had the greatest applause of the public, have not followed this plan, and, I conceive, for good reasons. *First*, Because a system of perfect rights could by no means serve the purpose of a system of morals, which surely is an important purpose. *Secondly*, Because, in many cases, it is hardly possible to fix the precise limit between justice and humanity, between perfect and imperfect right. Like the colours in a prismatic image, they run into each other, so that the best eye cannot fix the precise boundary between them.

Thirdly, As wise legislators and magistrates ought to have it as their end to make the citizens good as well as just, we find, in all civilized nations, laws that are intended to encourage the duties of humanity. Where human laws cannot enforce them by punishments, they may encourage them by rewards. Of this the wisest legislators have given examples; and how far this branch of legislation may be carried, no man can foresee.

The substance of the four following chapters was wrote long ago, and read in a literary society, with a view to justify some points of morals from metaphysical objections urged against them in the writings of David Hume, Esq. If they answer that end, and, at the same time, serve to illustrate the account I have given of our moral powers, it is hoped that the reader will not think them improperly placed here; and that he will forgive some repetitions, and perhaps anachronisms, occasioned by their being wrote at different times, and on different occasions.

Chapter IV
Whether an Action Deserving Moral Approbation, Must Be Done with the Belief of Its Being Morally Good

There is no part of philosophy more subtile and intricate than that which is called *The Theory of Morals.* Nor is there any more plain and level to the apprehension of man than the practical part of morals.

In the former, the Epicurean, the Peripatetic, and the Stoic, had each his different system of old; and almost every modern author of reputation has a system of his own. At the same time there is no branch of human knowledge, in which there is so general an agreement among ancients and moderns, learned and unlearned, as in the practical rules of morals.

From this discord in the theory, and harmony in the practical part, we may judge that the rules of morality stand upon another and a firmer foundation than the theory. And of this it is easy to perceive the reason.

For, in order to know what is right and what is wrong in human conduct, we need only listen to the dictates of our conscience when the mind is calm and unruffled, or attend to the judgment we form of others in like circumstances. But, to judge of the various theories of morals, we must be able to analyze and dissect, as it were, the active powers of the human mind, and especially to analyze accurately that conscience or moral power by which we discern right from wrong.

The conscience may be compared to the eye in this as in many other respects. The learned and the unlearned see objects with equal distinctness. The former have no title to dictate to the latter, as far as the eye is judge, nor is there any disagreement about such matters. But, to dissect the eye, and to explain the theory of vision, is a difficult point, wherein the most skilful have differed.

From this remarkable disparity between our decisions in the theory of morals and in the rules of morality, we may, I think, draw this conclusion, That wherever we find any disagreement between the practical rules of morality, which have been received in all ages, and the principles of any of the theories advanced upon this subject, the practical rules ought to be the standard by which the theory is to be corrected, and that it is both unsafe and unphilosophical to warp the practical rules, in order to make them tally with a favourite theory.

The question to be considered in this chapter belongs to the practical part of morals, and therefore is capable of a more easy and more certain determination. And, if it be determined in the affirmative, I conceive that it may serve as a touchstone to try some celebrated theories which are inconsistent with that determination, and which have led the theorists to oppose it by very subtle metaphysical arguments.

Every question about what is or is not the proper object of moral approbation, belongs to practical morals, and such is the question now under consideration:—*Whether actions deserving moral approbation must be done with the belief of their being morally good?* or, *Whether an action, done without any regard to duty or to the dictates of conscience, can be entitled to moral approbation?*

In every action of a moral agent, his conscience is either altogether silent, or it pronounces the action to be *good*, or *bad*, or *indifferent*. This, I think is a complete enumeration. If it be perfectly silent, the action must be very trifling, or appear so. For conscience, in those who have exercised it, is a very pragmatical faculty, and meddles with every part of our conduct, whether we desire its counsel or not. And what a man does in perfect simplicity, without the least suspicion of its being bad, his heart cannot condemn him for, nor will He that knows the heart condemn him. If there was any previous culpable negligence or inat-

tention which led him to a wrong judgment, or hindered his forming a right one, that I do not exculpate. I only consider the action done, and the disposition with which it was done, without its previous circumstances. And in this there appears nothing that merits disapprobation. As little can it merit any degree of moral approbation, because there was neither good nor ill intended. And the same may be said when conscience pronounces the action to be indifferent.

If, in the *second* place, I do what my conscience pronounces to be bad or dubious, I am guilty to myself, and justly deserve the disapprobation of others. Nor am I less guilty in this case, though what I judged to be bad should happen to be good or indifferent. I did it believing it to be bad, and this is an immorality.

Lastly, If I do what my conscience pronounces to be right and my duty, either I have some regard to duty, or I have none. The last is not supposable; for I believe there is no man so abandoned but that he does what he believes to be his duty, with more assurance and alacrity upon that account. The more weight the rectitude of the action has in determining me to do it, the more I approve of my own conduct. And if my worldly interest, my appetites, or inclinations draw me strongly the contrary way, my following the dictates of my conscience, in opposition to these motives, adds to the moral worth of the action.

When a man acts from an erroneous judgment, if his error be invincible, all agree that he is inculpable. But if his error be owing to some previous negligence or inattention, there seems to be some difference among moralists. This difference, however, is only seeming, and not real. For wherein lies the fault in this case? It must be granted by all, that the fault lies in this and solely in this, that he was not at due pains to have his judgment well informed. Those moralists, therefore, who consider the action and the previous conduct that led to it as one whole, find something to blame in the whole; and they do so most justly. But those who take this whole to pieces, and consider what is blameable and what is right in each part, find all that is blameable in what preceded this wrong judgment, and nothing but what is approvable in what followed it.

Let us suppose, for instance, that a man believes that God has indispensably required him to observe a very rigorous fast in Lent; and that, from a regard to this supposed divine command, he fasts in such manner as is not only a great mortification to his appetite, but even hurtful to his health.

His superstitious opinion may be the effect of a culpable negligence, for which he can by no means be justified. Let him, therefore, bear all the blame upon this account that he deserves. But now, having this opinion fixed in his mind, shall he act according to it or against it? Surely we cannot hesitate a moment in this case. It is evident that, in following the light of his judgment, he acts the part of a good and pious man; whereas, in acting contrary to his judgment, he would be guilty of willful disobedience to his Maker.

If my servant, by mistaking my orders, does the contrary of what I commanded, believing, at the same time, that he obeys my orders, there may be some fault in his mistake, but to charge him with the crime of disobedience, would be inhuman and unjust.

These determinations appear to me to have intuitive evidence, no less than that of mathematical axioms. A man who is come to years of understanding, and who has exercised his faculties in judging of right and wrong, sees their truth as he sees daylight. Metaphysical arguments brought against them have the same effect as when brought against the evidence of sense: they may puzzle and confound, but they do not convince. It appears evident, therefore, that those actions only can truly be called virtuous, or deserving of moral approbation, which the agent believed to be right, and to which he was influenced, more or less, by that belief.

If it should be objected, That this principle makes it to be of no consequence to a man's morals, what his opinions may be, providing he acts agreeably to them, the answer is easy.

Morality requires, not only that a man should act according to his judgment, but that he should use the best means in his power that his judgment be according to truth. If he fail in either of these points, he is worthy of blame; but, if he fail in neither, I see not wherein he can be blamed.

When a man must act, and has no longer time to deliberate, he ought to act according to the light of his conscience, even when he is in an error. But, when he has time to deliberate, he ought surely to use all the means in his power to be rightly informed. When he has done so, he may still be in an error; but it is an invincible error, and cannot justly be imputed to him as a fault.

A *second* objection is, That we immediately approve of benevolence, gratitude, and other primary virtues, without inquiring whether they are practised from a persuasion that they are our duty. And the laws of God place the sum of virtue in loving God and our neighbour, without any provision that we do it from a persuasion that we ought to do so.

The answer to this objection is, That the love of God, the love of our neighbour, justice, gratitude, and other primary virtues, are, by the constitution of human nature, necessarily accompanied with a conviction of their being morally good. We may, therefore, safely presume, that these things are never disjoined, and that every man who practises these virtues does it with a good conscience. In judging of men's conduct, we do not suppose things which cannot happen, nor do the laws of God give decisions upon impossible cases, as they must have done if they supposed the case of a man who thought it contrary to his duty to love God or to love mankind.

But if we wish to know how the laws of God determine the point in question, we ought to observe their decision with regard to such actions as may appear good to one man and ill to another. And here the decisions of scripture are clear: "*Let every man be persuaded in his own mind*";—"*He that doubteth is condemned if he eat, because he eateth not of faith, for whatsoever is not of faith is sin*";—"*To him that esteemeth anything to be unclean, it is unclean.*" The Scripture often placeth the sum of virtue in "*living in all good conscience*," in acting so "*that our hearts condemn us not.*"

The last objection I shall mention is a metaphysical one urged by Mr Hume.

It is a favourite point in his system of morals, *That justice is not a natural but an artificial virtue.* To prove this, he has exerted the whole strength of his reason and eloquence. And as the principle we are considering stood in his way, he takes pains to refute it.

"Suppose," says he, "a person to have lent a sum of money, on condition that it be restored in a few days. After the expiration of the term, he demands the sum. I ask, what reason or motive have I to restore the money? It will perhaps be said, That my regard to justice and abhorrence of villainy and knavery are sufficient reasons for me." And this, he acknowledges, would be a satisfactory answer to a man in his civilized state, and when trained up according to a certain discipline and education. "But, in his rude and more natural condition," says he, "if you are pleased to call such a condition natural, this answer would be rejected as perfectly unintelligible and sophistical."

"For wherein consists this honesty and justice? Not surely in the external action. It must, therefore, consist in the motive from which the external action is derived. This motive can never be a regard to the honesty of the action. For it is a plain fallacy to say, That a virtuous motive is requisite to render an action honest, and, at the same time, that a regard to the honesty is the motive to the action. We can never have a regard to the virtue of an action unless the action be antecedently virtuous."

And, in another place—"To suppose that the mere regard to the virtue of the action is that which rendered it virtuous, is to reason in a circle. An action must be virtuous before we can have a regard to its virtue. Some virtuous motive, therefore, must be antecedent to that regard. Nor is this merely a metaphysical subtilty," &c. (*Treatise of Human Nature*, Book III. Part ii. Sect. 1.)

I am not to consider, at this time, how this reasoning is applied to support the author's opinion, That justice is not a natural but an artificial virtue. I consider it only as far as it opposes the principle I have been endeavouring to establish, That, to render an action truly virtuous, the agent must have some regard to its rectitude. And I conceive the whole force of the reasoning amounts to this:

When we judge an action to be good or bad, it must have been so in its own nature antecedent to that judgment, otherwise the judgment is erroneous. If, therefore, the action be good in its nature, the judgment of the agent cannot make it bad, nor can his judgment make it good if, in its nature, it be bad. For this would be to ascribe to our judgment a strange magical power to transform the nature of things, and to say, that my judging a thing to be what it is not, makes it really to be what I erroneously judge it to be. This, I think, is the objection in its full strength. And, in answer to it—

[1] *First*, If we could not loose this metaphysical knot, I think we might fairly and honestly cut it, because it fixes an absurdity upon the clearest and most indisputable principles of morals and of common sense. For I appeal to any man whether there be any principle of morality, or any principle of common sense, more clear and indisputable than that which we just now quoted from the Apostle Paul, That, although a thing be not unclean in itself, yet to him that esteemeth it to be unclean, to him it is unclean. But the metaphysical argument makes this absurd. For, says the metaphysician, If the thing was not unclean in itself, you judged wrong in esteeming it to be unclean; and what can be more absurd than that

your esteeming a thing to be what it is not, should make it what you erroneously esteem it to be?

Let us try the edge of this argument in another instance. Nothing is more evident than that an action does not merit the name of benevolent, unless it be done from a belief that it tends to promote the good of our neighbour. But this is absurd, says the metaphysician. For, if it be not a benevolent action in itself, your belief of its tendency cannot change its nature. It is absurd that your erroneous belief should make the action to be what you believe it to be. Nothing is more evident than that a man who tells the truth, believing it to be a lie, is guilty of falsehood; but the metaphysician would make this to be absurd.

In a word, if there be any strength in this argument, it would follow, That a man might be, in the highest degree, virtuous, without the least regard to virtue; that he might be very benevolent, without ever intending to do a good office; very malicious, without ever intending any hurt; very revengeful, without ever intending to retaliate an injury; very grateful, without ever intending to return a benefit; and a man of strict veracity, with an intention to lie. We might, therefore, reject this reasoning, as repugnant to self-evident truths, though we were not able to point out the fallacy of it.

[2] But let us try, in the *second* place, whether the fallacy of this argument may not be discovered.

We ascribe moral goodness to actions considered abstractly, without any relation to the agent. We likewise ascribe moral goodness to an agent on account of an action he has done; we call it a good action, though, in this case, the goodness is properly in the man, and is only by a figure ascribed to the action. Now, it is to be considered, whether *moral goodness*, when applied to an action considered abstractly, has the same meaning as when we apply it to a man on account of that action; or whether we do not unawares change the meaning of the word, according as we apply it to the one or to the other.

The action considered abstractly, has neither understanding nor will; it is not accountable, nor can it be under any moral obligation. But all these things are essential to that moral goodness which belongs to a man; for, if a man had not understanding and will, he could have no moral goodness. Hence it follows necessarily, that the moral goodness which we ascribe to an action considered abstractly, and that which we ascribe to a person for doing that action, are not the same. The meaning of the word is changed when it is applied to these different subjects.

This will be more evident, when we consider what is meant by the moral goodness which we ascribe to a man for doing an action, and what by the goodness which belongs to the action considered abstractly. A good action in a man is that in which he applied his intellectual powers properly, in order to judge what he ought to do, and acted according to his best judgment. This is all that can be required of a moral agent; and in this his moral goodness, in any good action, consists. But is this the goodness which we ascribe to an action considered abstractly? No, surely. For the action, considered abstractly, is neither endowed with judgment nor with active power; and, therefore, can have none of that goodness which we ascribe to the man for doing it.

But what do we mean by goodness in an action considered abstractly? To me it appears to lie in this, and in this only, That it is an action which ought to be done by those who have the power and opportunity, and the capacity of perceiving their obligation to do it. I would gladly know of any man, what other moral goodness can be in an action considered abstractly. And this goodness is inherent in its nature, and inseparable from it. No opinion or judgment of an agent can in the least alter its nature.

Suppose the action to be that of relieving an innocent person out of great distress. This surely has all the moral goodness that an action, considered abstractly, can have. Yet, it is evident that an agent, in relieving a person in distress, may have no moral goodness, may have great merit, or may have great demerit.

Suppose, *first*, That mice cut the cords which bound the distressed person, and so bring him relief. Is there moral goodness in this act of the mice?

Suppose, *secondly*, That a man maliciously relieves the distressed person, in order to plunge him into greater distress. In this action, there is surely no moral goodness, but much malice and inhumanity.

If, in the *last* place, we suppose a person, from real sympathy and humanity, to bring relief to the distressed person, with considerable expense or danger to himself—here is an action of real worth, which every heart approves and every tongue praises. But wherein lies the worth? Not in the action considered by itself, which was common to all the three, but in the man who, on this occasion, acted the part which became a good man. He did what his heart approved, and therefore he is approved by God and man.

Upon the whole, if we distinguish between that goodness which may be ascribed to an action considered by itself, and that goodness which we ascribe to a man when he puts it in execution, we shall find a key to this metaphysical lock. We admit that the goodness of an action, considered abstractly, can have no dependence upon the opinion or belief of an agent, any more than the truth of a proposition depends upon our believing it to be true. But, when a man exerts his active power well or ill, there is a moral goodness or turpitude which we figuratively impute to the action, but which is truly and properly imputable to the man only; and this goodness or turpitude depends very much upon the intention of the agent, and the opinion he had of his action.

This distinction has been understood in all ages by those who gave any attention to morals, though it has been variously expressed. The Greek moralists gave the name of χαθῆχον to an action good in itself; such an action might be done by the most worthless. But an action done with a right intention, which implies real worth in the agent, they called χατόςθωμα. The distinction is explained by Cicero in his "Offices." He calls the first *officium medium*, and the second *officium perfectum*, or *rectum*. In the scholastic ages, an action good in itself was said to be *materially* good, and an action done with a right intention was called *formally* good. This last way of expressing the distinction is still familiar among Theologians; but Mr Hume seems not to have attended to it, or to have thought it to be words without any meaning.

Mr Hume, in the section already quoted, tells us with great assurance—"In short, it may be established as an undoubted maxim, that no action can be virtuous or morally good, unless there be in human nature some motive to produce it, distinct from the sense of its morality." And upon this maxim he founds many of his reasonings on the subject of morals.

Whether it be consistent with Mr Hume's own system, that an action may be produced merely from the sense of its morality, without any motive of agreeableness or utility, I shall not now inquire. But, if it be true, and I think it evident to every man of common understanding, that a judge or an arbiter acts the most virtuous part when his sentence is produced by no other motive but a regard to justice and a good conscience—nay, when all other motives distinct from this are on the other side:—if this, I say, be true, then that undoubted maxim of Mr Hume must be false, and all the conclusions built upon it must fall to the ground.

From the principle I have endeavoured to establish, I think some consequences may be drawn with regard to the theory of morals.

First, If there be no virtue without the belief that what we do is right, it follows, that a moral faculty—that is, a power of discerning moral goodness and turpitude in human conduct—is essential to every being capable of virtue or vice. A being who has no more conception of moral goodness and baseness, of right and wrong, than a blind man hath of colours, can have no regard to it in his conduct, and therefore can neither be virtuous nor vicious.

He may have qualities that are agreeable or disagreeable, useful or hurtful; so may a plant or a machine. And we sometimes use the word *virtue* in such a latitude as to signify any agreeable or useful quality, as when we speak of the virtues of plants. But we are now speaking of virtue in the strict and proper sense, as it signifies that quality in a man which is the object of moral approbation.

This virtue a man could not have, if he had not a power of discerning a right and a wrong in human conduct, and of being influenced by that discernment. For in so far only he is virtuous as he is guided in his conduct by that part of his constitution. Brutes do not appear to have any such power, and therefore are not moral or accountable agents. They are capable of culture and discipline, but not of virtuous or criminal conduct. Even human creatures, in infancy and nonage, are not moral agents, because their moral faculty is not yet unfolded. These sentiments are supported by the common sense of mankind, which has always determined that neither brutes nor infants can be indicted for crimes.

It is of small consequence what name we give to this moral power of the human mind; but it is so important a part of our constitution as to deserve an appropriated name. The name of *conscience*, as it is the most common, seems to me as proper as any that has been given it. I find no fault with the name *moral sense*, although I conceive this name has given occasion to some mistakes concerning the nature of our moral power. Modern philosophers have conceived of the external senses as having no other office but to give us certain sensations, or simple conceptions, which we could not have without them. And this notion has been applied to the moral sense. But it seems to me a mistaken notion in both. By the sense of seeing, I not only have the conception of the different colours, but I perceive one body to be of this colour, another of that. In like manner, by my moral sense, I not only have the conceptions of right and wrong in conduct, but perceive *this* conduct to be right, *that* to be wrong, and *that* indifferent. All our senses are judging faculties, so also is conscience. Nor is this power only a judge of our own actions and those of others—it is likewise a principle of action in all good men; and so far only can our conduct be denominated virtuous as it is influenced by this principle.

A *second* consequence from the principle laid down in this chapter is, that the formal nature and essence of that virtue which is the object of moral approbation consists neither in a prudent prosecution of our private interest, nor in benevolent affections towards others, nor in qualities useful or agreeable to ourselves or to others, nor in sympathizing with the passions and affections of others, and in attuning our own conduct to the tone of other men's passions; but it consists in living in all good conscience—that is, in using the best means in our power to know our duty, and acting accordingly.

Prudence is a virtue, Benevolence is a virtue, Fortitude is a virtue; but the essence and formal nature of Virtue must lie in something that is common to all these, and to every other virtue. And this I conceive can be nothing else but *the rectitude of such conduct and turpitude of the contrary, which is discerned by a good man*. And so far only he is virtuous as he pursues the former and avoids the latter.

Chapter V
*Whether Justice Be a Natural
or an Artificial Virtue*

Mr Hume's philosophy concerning morals was first presented to the world in the third volume of his "Treatise of Human Nature," in the year 1740; afterwards in his "Inquiry concerning the Principles of Morals," which was first published by itself, and then in several editions of his "Essays and Treatises."

In these two works on morals, the system is the same. A more popular arrangement, great embellishment, and the omission of some metaphysical reasonings, have given a preference in the public esteem to the last; but I find neither any new principles in it, nor any new arguments in support of the system common to both.

In this system, the proper object of Moral Approbation is not actions or any voluntary exertion, but qualities of mind—that is, natural affections or passions, which are involuntary, a part of the constitution of the man, and common to us with many brute animals. When we praise or blame any voluntary action, it is only considered as a sign of the natural affection from which it flows, and from which all its merit or demerit is derived.

Moral Approbation or Disapprobation, is not an *Act of Judgment*, which, like all acts of judgment, must be true or false; it is only a certain *Feeling*, which, from the constitution of human nature, arises upon contemplating certain characters, or qualities of mind, coolly and impartially.

This feeling, when agreeable, is moral approbation; when disagreeable, disapprobation. The qualities of mind which produce this agreeable feeling, are the moral virtues; and those that produce the disagreeable, the vices.

These preliminaries being granted, the question about the foundation of morals is reduced to a simple question of fact—to wit, What are the qualities of mind which produce, in the disinterested observer, the feeling of approbation, or the contrary feeling?

In answer to this question, the author endeavours to prove, by a very copious induction, That all personal merit, all virtue, all that is the object of moral approbation, consists in the qualities of mind which are *agreeable* or *useful* to the person who posesses them, or to others.

The *dulce* and the *utile* is the whole sum of merit in every character, in every quality of mind, and in every action of life. There is no room left for that *honestum* which Cicero thus defines: *Honestum igitur id intelligimus, quod tale est, ut detracta omni utilitate, sine ullis premiis fructibusve, per seipsum jure possit laudari.* (DE FINIBUS, ii. 14.) [By moral worth, therefore, we understand something such that when all utility is removed, it can rightly be praised just for itself, without any rewards or profits.]

Among the ancient moralists, the Epicureans were the only sect who denied that there is any such thing as *honestum,* or moral worth, distinct from pleasure. In this, Mr Hume's system agrees with theirs. For the addition of utility to pleasure, as a foundation of morals, makes only a verbal, but no real difference. What is useful only has no value in itself; but derives all its merit from the end for which it is useful. That end, in this system, is agreeableness, or pleasure; so that, in both systems, pleasure is the only end, the only thing that is good in itself, and desirable for its own sake; and virtue derives all its merit from its tendency to produce pleasure.

Agreeableness and utility are not moral conceptions, nor have they any connection with morality. What a man does, merely because it is agreeable, or useful to procure what is agreeable, is not virtue. Therefore the Epicurean system was justly thought, by Cicero, and the best moralists among the ancients, to subvert morality, and to substitute another principle in its room; and this system is liable to the same censure.

In one thing, however, it differs remarkably from that of Epicurus. It allows that there are disinterested affections in human nature; that the love of children and relations, friendship, gratitude, compassion, and humanity, are not, as Epicurus maintained, different modifications of self-love, but simple and original parts of the human constitution; that, when interest, or envy, or revenge, pervert not our disposition, we are inclined, from natural philanthropy, to desire, and to be pleased with the happiness of the human kind.

All this, in opposition to the Epicurean system, Mr Hume maintains with great strength of reason and eloquence, and, in this respect, his system is more liberal and disinterested than that of the Greek philosopher. According to Epicurus, virtue is whatever is agreeable to ourselves—according to Mr Hume, every quality of mind that is agreeable or useful to ourselves or to others.

This theory of the nature of virtue, it must be acknowledged, enlarges greatly the catalogue of moral virtues, by bringing into that catalogue every quality of mind that is useful or agreeable. Nor does there appear any good reason why the useful and agreeable qualities of body and of fortune, as well as those of the mind, should not have a place among moral virtues in this system. They have the essence of virtue; that is, agreeableness and utility—why then should they not have the name?

But, to compensate this addition to the moral virtues, one class of them seems to be greatly degraded and deprived of all intrinsic merit. The useful virtues, as was above observed, are only ministering servants of the agreeable, and purveyors for them; they must, therefore, be so far inferior in dignity as hardly to deserve the same name.

Mr Hume, however, gives the name of *virtue* to both; and, to distinguish them, calls the agreeable qualities *natural* virtues, and the useful *artificial*.

The natural virtues are those natural affections of the human constitution which give immediate pleasure in their exercise. Such are all the benevolent affections. Nature disposes to them, and from their own nature they are agreeable, both when we exercise them ourselves, and when we contemplate their exercise in others.

The artificial virtues are such as are esteemed solely on account of their utility, either to promote the good of society—as justice, fidelity, honour, veracity, allegiance, chastity; or on account of their utility to the possessor—as industry, discretion, frugality, secrecy, order, perseverance, forethought, judgment, and others, of which, he says, many pages could not contain the catalogue.

This general view of Mr Hume's system concerning the foundation of morals, seemed necessary, in order to understand distinctly the meaning of that principle of his, which is to be the subject of this chapter, and on which he has bestowed much labour—to wit, that justice is not a natural but an artificial virtue.

This system of the foundation of virtue is so contradictory in many of its essential points to the account we have before given of the active powers of human nature, that, if the one be true, the other must be false.

If God has given to man a power which we call *conscience*, the *moral faculty*, the *sense of duty*, by which, when he comes to years of understanding, he perceives certain things that depend on his will to be his duty, and other things to be base and unworthy; if the notion of duty be a simple conception, of its own kind, and of a different nature from the conceptions of utility and agreeableness, of interest or reputation; if this moral faculty be the prerogative of man, and no vestige of it be found in brute animals; if it be given us by God to regulate all our animal affections and passions; if to be governed by it, be the glory of man and the image of God in his soul, and to disregard its dictates be his dishonour and depravity—I say, if these things be so, to seek the foundation of morality in the affections which we have in common with the brutes, is to seek the living among the dead, and to change the glory of man, and the image of God in his soul, into the similitude of an ox that eateth grass.

If virtue and vice be a matter of choice, they must consist in voluntary actions, or in fixed purposes of acting according to a certain rule when there is opportunity, and not in qualities of mind which are involuntary.

It is true that every virtue is both agreeable and useful in the highest degree; that every quality that is agreeable or useful, has a merit upon that account. But virtue has a merit peculiar to itself, a merit which does not arise from its being useful or agreeable, but from its being virtue. This merit is discerned by the same faculty by which we discern it to be virtue, and by no other.

We give the name of *esteem* both to the regard we have for things useful and agreeable, and to the regard we have for virtue; but these are different kinds of esteem. I esteem a man for his ingenuity and learning—I esteem him for his moral worth. The sound of *esteem* in both these speeches is the same, but its meaning is very different.

Good breeding is a very amiable quality; and even if I knew that the man had no motive to it but its pleasure and utility to himself and others, I should like it still; but I would not in that case call it a moral virtue.

A dog has a tender concern for her puppies; so has a man for his children. The natural affection is the same in both, and is amiable in both. But why do we impute moral virtue to the man on account of this concern, and not to the dog? The reason surely is, That, in the man, the natural affection is accompanied with a sense of duty; but in the dog it is not. The same thing may be said of all the kind affections common to us with the brutes. They are amiable qualities; but they are not moral virtues.

What has been said relates to Mr Hume's system in general. We are now to consider his notion of the particular virtue of justice—That its merit consists wholly in its utility to society.

That justice is highly useful and necessary in society, and, on that account, ought to be loved and esteemed by all that love mankind, will readily be granted. And as justice is a social virtue, it is true also, that there could be no exercise of it, and, perhaps, we should have no conception of it, without society. But this is equally true of the natural affections of benevolence, gratitude, friendship, and compassion, which Mr Hume makes to be the natural virtues.

It may be granted to Mr Hume, that men have no conception of the virtue of justice till they have lived some time in society. It is purely a moral conception, and our moral conceptions and moral judgments are not born with us. They grow up by degrees, as our reason does. Nor do I pretend to know how early, or in what order, we acquire the conception of the several virtues. The conception of justice supposes some exercise of the moral faculty, which, being the noblest part of the human constitution, and that to which all its other parts are subservient, appears latest.

It may likewise be granted, that there is no animal affection in human nature that prompts us immediately to acts of justice, as such. We have natural affections of the animal kind, which immediately prompt us to acts of kindness; but none, that I know, that has the same relation to justice. The very conception of justice supposes a moral faculty; but our natural kind affections do not; otherwise we must allow that brutes have this faculty.

What I maintain is, *first*, That when men come to the exercise of their moral faculty, they perceive a turpitude in injustice, as they do in other crimes, and consequently an obligation to justice, abstracting from the consideration of its utility. And, *secondly*, That, as soon as men have any rational conception of a favour, and of an injury, they must have the conception of justice, and perceive its obligation distinct from its utility.

The first of these points hardly admits of any other proof but an appeal to the sentiments of every honest man and every man of honour, Whether his indignation is not immediately inflamed against an atrocious act of villainy, without the cool consideration of its distant consequences upon the good of society?

We might appeal even to robbers and pirates, whether they have not had great struggles with their conscience, when they first resolved to break through all the rules of justice; and whether, in a solitary and serious hour, they have not frequently felt the pangs of guilt. They have very often confessed this at a time when all disguise is laid aside.

The common good of society, though a pleasing object to all men, when presented to their view, hardly ever enters into the thoughts of the far greatest part of mankind; and, if a regard to it were the sole motive to justice, the number of honest men must be small indeed. It would be confined to the higher ranks, who, by their education or by their office, are led to make the public good an object; but that it is so confined, I believe no man will venture to affirm.

The temptations to injustice are strongest in the lowest class of men; and, if nature had provided no motive to oppose those temptations, but a sense of public good, there would not be found an honest man in that class.

To all men that are not greatly corrupted, injustice, as well as cruelty and ingratitude, is an object of dis-

approbation on its own account. There is a voice within us that proclaims it to be base, unworthy, and deserving of punishment.

That there is, in all ingenuous natures, an antipathy to roguery and treachery, a reluctance to the thoughts of villainy and baseness, we have the testimony of Mr Hume himself; who, as I doubt not but he felt it, has expressed it very strongly in the conclusion to his "Enquiry," and acknowledged that, in some cases, without this reluctance and antipathy to dishonesty, a sensible knave would find no sufficient motive from public good to be honest.

I shall give the passage at large from the "Enquiry concerning the Principles of Morals," Section 9, near the end.

"Treating vice with the greatest candour, and making it all possible concessions, we must acknowledge that there is not, in any instance, the smallest pretext for giving it the preference above virtue, with a view to self-interest; except, perhaps, in the case of justice, where a man, taking things in a certain light, may often seem to be a loser by his integrity. And, though it is allowed that, without a regard to property, no society could subsist; yet, according to the imperfect way in which human affairs are conducted, a sensible knave, in particular incidents, may think that an act of iniquity or infidelity will make a considerable addition to his fortune, without causing any considerable breach in the social union and confederacy. That *honesty is the best policy*, may be a good general rule, but it is liable to many exceptions: and he, it may perhaps be thought, conducts himself with most wisdom, who observes the general rule, and takes advantage of all the exceptions.

"I must confess that, if a man think that this reasoning much requires an answer, it will be a little difficult to find any which will to him appear satisfactory and convincing. If his heart rebel not against such pernicious maxims, if he feel no reluctance to the thoughts of villainy and baseness, he has indeed lost a considerable motive to virtue, and we may expect that his practice will be answerable to his speculation. But in all ingenuous natures, the antipathy to treachery and roguery is too strong to be counterbalanced by any views of profit or pecuniary advantage. Inward peace of mind, consciousness of integrity, a satisfactory review of our own conduct—these are circumstances very requisite to happiness, and will be cherished and cultivated by every honest man who feels the importance of them."

The reasoning of the *sensible knave* in this passage, seems to me to be justly founded upon the principles of the "Enquiry" and of the "Treatise of Human Nature," and therefore it is no wonder that the author should find it a little difficult to give any answer which would appear satisfactory and convincing to such a man. To counterbalance this reasoning, he puts in the other scale a reluctance, an antipathy, a rebellion of the heart against such pernicious maxims, which is felt by ingenuous natures.

Let us consider a little the force of Mr Hume's answer to this sensible knave, who reasons upon his own principles. I think it is either an acknowledgment that there is a natural judgment of conscience in man, that injustice and treachery is a base and unworthy practice—which is the point I would establish; or it has no force to convince either the knave or an honest man.

A clear and intuitive judgment, resulting from the constitution of human nature, is sufficient to overbalance a train of subtile reasoning on the other side. Thus the testimony of our senses is sufficient to overbalance all the subtile arguments brought against their testimony. And, if there be a like testimony of conscience in favour of honesty, all the subtile reasoning of the knave against it ought to be rejected without examination, as fallacious and sophistical, because it concludes against a self-evident principle; just as we reject the subtile reasoning of the metaphysician against the evidence of sense.

If, therefore, the *reluctance*, the *antipathy*, the *rebellion of the heart* against injustice, which Mr Hume sets against the reasoning of the knave, include in their meaning a natural intuitive judgment of conscience, that injustice is base and unworthy the reasoning of the knave is convincingly answered; but the principle, *That justice is an artificial virtue, approved solely for its utility*, is given up.

If, on the other hand, the antipathy, reluctance, and rebellion of heart, imply no judgment, but barely an uneasy feeling, and that not natural, but acquired and artificial, the answer is indeed very agreeable to the principles of the "Enquiry," but has no force to convince the knave, or any other man.

The knave is here supposed by Mr Hume to have no such feelings, and therefore the answer does not touch his case in the least, but leaves him in the full possession of his reasoning. And *ingenuous natures*, who have these feelings, are left to deliberate whether they will yield to acquired and artificial feelings, in opposition to rules of conduct, which, to their best judgment, appear wise and prudent.

The *second* thing I proposed to shew was, That, as soon as men have any rational conception of a favour and of an injury, they must have the conception of justice, and perceive its obligation.

The power with which the Author of nature hath endowed us, may be employed either to do good to our fellow-men, or to hurt them. When we employ our power to promote the good and happiness of others, this is a benefit or favour; when we employ it to hurt them, it is an injury. Justice fills up the middle between these two. It is such a conduct as does no injury to others; but it does not imply the doing them any favour.

The notions of a *favour* and of an *injury*, appear as early in the mind of man as any rational notion whatever. They are discovered, not by language only, but by certain affections of mind, of which they are the natural objects. A favour naturally produces gratitude. An injury done to ourselves produces resentment; and even when done to another, it produces indignation.

I take it for granted that gratitude and resentment are no less natural to the human mind than hunger and thirst; and that those affections are no less naturally excited by their proper objects and occasions than these appetites.

It is no less evident, that the proper and formal object of gratitude is a person who has done us a favour, that of resentment, a person who has done us an injury.

Before the use of reason, the distinction between a favour and an agreeable office is not perceived. Every action of another person which gives present pleasure produces love and good will towards the agent. Every action that gives pain or uneasiness produces resentment. This is common to man before the use of reason, and to the more sagacious brutes; and it shews no conception of justice in either.

But, as we grow up to the use of reason, the notion, both of a favour and of an injury, grows more distinct and better defined. It is not enough that a good office be done; it must be done from good will and with a good intention, otherwise it is no favour, nor does it produce gratitude.

I have heard of a physician who gave spiders in a medicine to a dropsical patient, with all intention to poison him, and that this medicine cured the patient, contrary to the intention of the physician. Surely no gratitude, but resentment, was due by the patient, when he knew the real state of the case. It is evident to every man, that a benefit arising from the action of another, either without or against his intention, is not a motive to gratitude; that is, is no favour.

Another thing implied in the nature of a favour is, that it be not due. A man may save my credit by paying what he owes me. In this case, what he does tends to my benefit, and perhaps is done with that intention; but it is not a favour—it is no more than he was bound to do.

If a servant do his work and receive his wages, there is no favour done on either part, nor any object of gratitude; because, though each party has benefited the other, yet neither has done more than he was bound to do.

What I infer from this is, That the conception of a favour in every man come to years of understanding, implies the conception of things not due, and consequently the conception of things that are due.

A negative cannot be conceived by one who has no conception of the correspondent positive. Not to be due is the negative of being due; and he who conceives one of them must conceive both. The conception of things due and not due must therefore be found in every mind which has any rational conception of a favour, or any rational sentiment of gratitude.

If we consider, on the other hand, when an injury is which is the object of the unnatural passion of resentment, every man, capable of reflection, perceives, that an injury implies more than being hurt. If I be hurt by a stone falling out of the wall, or by a flash of lightning, or by a convulsive and involuntary motion of another man's arm, no injury is done, no resentment raised in a man that has reason. In this, as in all moral actions, there must be the will and intention of the agent to do the hurt.

Nor is this sufficient to constitute an injury. The man who breaks my fences, or treads down my corn, when he cannot otherwise preserve himself from destruction, who has no injurious intention, and is willing to indemnify me for the hurt which necessity, and not ill will, led him to do, is not injurious, nor is an object of resentment.

The executioner who does his duty in cutting off the head of a condemned criminal, is not an object of resentment. He does nothing unjust, and therefore nothing injurious.

From this it is evident, that an injury, the object of the natural passion of resentment, implies in it the notion of injustice. And it is no less evident that no man can have a notion of injustice without having the notion of justice.

To sum up what has been said upon this point, a favour, an act of justice, and an injury, are so related to one another that he who conceives one must conceive the other two. They lie, as it were, in one line, and resemble the relations of greater, less, and equal. If one understands what is meant by one line being greater or less than another, he can be at no loss to understand what is meant by its being equal to the other; for, if it be neither greater nor less, it must be equal.

In like manner, of those actions by which we profit or hurt other men, a favour is more than justice, an injury is less; and that which is neither a favour nor an injury is a just action.

As soon, therefore, as men come to have any proper notion of a favour and of an injury; as soon as they have any rational exercise of gratitude and of resentment—so soon they must have the conception of justice and of injustice; and, if gratitude and resentment be natural to man, which Mr Hume allows, the notion of justice must be no less natural.

The notion of justice carries inseparably along with it a perception of its moral obligation. For, to say that such an action is an act of justice, that it is due, that it ought to be done, that we are under a moral obligation to do it, are only different ways of expressing the same thing. It is true, that we perceive no high degree of moral worth in a merely just action, when it is not opposed by interest or passion; but we perceive a high degree of turpitude and demerit in unjust actions, or in the omission of what justice requires.

Indeed, if there were no other argument to prove that the obligation of justice is not solely derived from its utility to procure what is agreeable either to ourselves or to society, this would be sufficient, that the very conception of justice implies its obligation. The morality of justice is included in the very idea of it: nor is it possible that the conception of justice can enter into the human mind, without carrying along with it the conception of duty and moral obligation. Its obligation, therefore, is inseparable from its nature, and is not derived solely from its utility, either to ourselves or to society.

We may farther observe, that, as in all moral estimation, every action takes its denomination from the motive that produces it; so no action can properly be denominated an act of justice, unless it be done from a regard to justice.

If a man pays his debt, only that he may not be cast into prison, he is not a just man, because prudence, and not justice, is his motive. And if a man, from benevolence and charity, gives to another what is really due to him, but what he believes not to be due, this is not an act of justice in him, but of charity or benevolence, because it is not done from a motive of justice. These are self-evident truths; nor is it less evident, that what a man does, merely to procure something agreeable, either to himself or to others, is not an act of justice, nor has the merit of justice.

Good music and good cookery have the merit of utility, in procuring what is agreeable both to ourselves and to society; but they never obtained among mankind the denomination of moral virtues. Indeed, if this author's system be well founded, great injustice has been done them on that account.

I shall now make some observations upon the reasoning of this author, in proof of his favourite principle, That justice is not a natural but an artificial virtue; or, as it is expressed in the "Enquiry," That public utility is the sole origin of justice, and that reflections on the beneficial consequences of this virtue, are the sole foundation of its merit.

1. It must be acknowledged that this principle has a necessary connection with his system concerning the foundation of all virtue; and, therefore, it is no wonder that he hath taken so much pains to support it; for the whole system must stand or fall with it.

If the *dulce* and the *utile*—that is, pleasure, and what is useful to procure pleasure—be the whole merit of virtue, justice can have no merit beyond its utility to procure pleasure. If, on the other hand, an intrinsic worth in justice, and demerit in injustice, be discerned by every man that hath a conscience; if there be a natural principle in the constitution of man by which justice is approved, and injustice disapproved and condemned—then the whole of this laboured system must fall to the ground.

2. We may observe, That, as justice is directly opposed to injury, and as there are various ways in which a man may be injured, so there must be various branches of justice opposed to the different kinds of injury.

A man may be injured, *first*, in his person, by wounding, maiming, or killing him; *secondly*, in his family, by robbing him of his children, or any way injuring those he is bound to protect; *thirdly*, in his liberty, by confinement; *fourthly*, in his reputation;

fifthly, in his goods, or property; and, *lastly*, in the violation of contracts or engagements made with him. This enumeration, whether complete or not, is sufficient for the present purpose.

The different branches of justice, opposed to these different kinds of injury, are commonly expressed by saying, that an innocent man has a right to the safety of his person and family, a right to his liberty and reputation, a right to his goods, and to fidelity to engagements made with him. To say that he has a right to these things, has precisely the same meaning as to say that justice requires that he should be permitted to enjoy them, or that it is unjust to violate them; for injustice is the violation of right, and justice is to yield to every man what is his right.

These things being understood as the simplest and most common ways of expressing the various branches of justice, we are to consider how far Mr Hume's reasoning proves any or all of them to be artificial, or grounded solely upon public utility. The last of them, fidelity to engagements, is to be the subject of the next chapter, and, therefore, I shall say nothing of it in this.

The four first named—to wit, the right of an innocent man to the safety of his person and family, to his liberty and reputation, are, by the writers on jurisprudence, called *natural* rights of man, because they are grounded in the nature of man as a rational and moral agent, and are by his Creator committed to his care and keeping. By being called *natural* or *innate*, they, are distinguished from acquired rights, which suppose some previous act or deed of man by which they are acquired; whereas natural rights suppose nothing of this kind.

When a man's natural rights are violated, he perceives intuitively, and he feels that he is injured. The feeling of his heart arises from the judgment of his understanding; for, if he did not believe that the hurt was intended, and unjustly intended, he would not have that feeling. He perceives that injury is done to himself, and that he has a right to redress. The natural principle of resentment is roused by the view of its proper object, and excites him to defend his right. Even the injurious person is conscious of his doing injury; he dreads a just retaliation; and, if it be in the power of the injured person, he expects it as due and deserved.

That these sentiments spring up in the mind of man as naturally as his body grows to its proper stature; that they are not the birth of instruction, either of parents, priests, philosophers, or politicians, but the pure growth of nature—cannot, I think, without effrontery, be denied. We find them equally strong in the most savage and in the most civilized tribes of mankind; and nothing can weaken them but an inveterate habit of rapine and bloodshed, which benumbs the conscience, and turns men into wild beasts.

The public good is very properly considered by the judge who punishes a private injury, but seldom enters into the thought of the injured person. In all criminal law, the redress due to the private sufferer is distinguished from that which is due to the public; a distinction which could have no foundation, if the demerit of injustice arose solely from its hurting the public. And every man is conscious of a specific difference between the resentment he feels for an injury done to himself, and his indignation against a wrong done to the public.

I think, therefore, it is evident that, of the six branches of justice we mentioned, four are natural, in the strictest sense, being founded upon the constitution of man, and antecedent to all deeds and conventions of society; so that, if there were but two men upon the earth, one might be unjust and injurious, and the other injured.

But does Mr Hume maintain the contrary?

To this question I answer, That his doctrine seems to imply it; but I hope he meant it not.

He affirms, in general, that justice is not a natural virtue; that it derives its origin solely from public utility; and that reflections on the beneficial consequences of this virtue, are the sole foundation of its merit. He mentions no particular branch of justice as an exception to this general rule; yet justice, in common language, and in all the writers on jurisprudence I am acquainted with, comprehends the four branches above mentioned. His doctrine, therefore, according to the common construction of words, extends to these four, as well as to the two other branches of justice.

On the other hand, if we attend to his long and laboured proof of this doctrine, it appears evident that he had in his eye only two particular branches of justice. No part of his reasoning applies to the other four. He seems, I know not why, to have taken up a confined notion of justice, and to have restricted it to a regard to property and fidelity in contracts. As to other branches he is silent. He nowhere says, that it is

not naturally criminal to rob an innocent man of his life, of his children, of his liberty, or of his reputation; and I am apt to think he never meant it.

The only philosopher I know who has had the assurance to maintain this, is Mr Hobbes, who makes the state of nature to be a state of war, of every man against every man; and of such a war in which every man has a right to do and to acquire whatever his power can, by any means, accomplish—that is, a state wherein neither right nor injury, justice nor injustice, can possibly exist.

Mr Hume mentions this system of Hobbes, but without adopting it, though he allows it the authority of Cicero in its favour.

He says, in a note, "This fiction of a state of nature as a state of war was not first started by Mr Hobbes, as is commonly imagined. Plato endeavours to refute an hypothesis very like it, in the 2d, 3d, and 4th books, 'De Republica.' Cicero, on the contrary, supposes it certain and universally acknowledged, in the following passage," &c.—*Pro Sexlio*, § 42.

The passage, which he quotes at large from one of Cicero's orations, seems to me to require some straining to make it tally with the system of Mr Hobbes. Be this as it may, Mr Hume might have added, That Cicero, in his orations, like many other pleaders, sometimes says not what he believed, but what was fit to support the cause of his client. That Cicero's opinion, with regard to the natural obligation of justice, was very different from that of Mr Hobbes, and even from Mr Hume's, is very well known.

3. As Mr Hume, therefore, has said nothing to prove the four branches of justice which relate to the innate rights of men, to be artificial, or to derive their origin solely from public utility, I proceed to the fifth branch, which requires us not to invade another man's property.

The right of property is not innate, but acquired. It is not grounded upon the constitution of man; but upon his actions. Writers on jurisprudence have explained its origin in a manner that may satisfy every man of common understanding.

The earth is given to men in common for the purposes of life, by the bounty of Heaven. But, to divide it, and appropriate one part of its produce to one, another part to another, must be the work of men who have power and understanding given them, by which every man may accommodate himself without hurt to any other.

This common right of every man to what the earth produces, before it be occupied and appropriated by others, was, by ancient moralists, very properly compared to the right which every citizen had to the public theatre, where every man that came might occupy an empty seat, and thereby acquire a right to it while the entertainment lasted, but no man had a right to dispossess another.

The earth is a great theatre, furnished by the Almighty, with perfect wisdom and goodness, for the entertainment and employment of all mankind. Here every man has a right to accommodate himself as a spectator, and to perform his part as an actor, but without hurt to others.

He who does so is a just man, and thereby entitled to some degree of moral approbation; and he who not only does no hurt, but employs his power to do good, is a good man, and is thereby entitled to a higher degree of moral approbation. But he who jostles and molests his neighbour, who deprives him of any accommodation which his industry has provided without hurt to others, is unjust, and a proper object of resentment.

It is true, therefore, that property has a beginning from the actions of men, occupying, and, perhaps, improving by their industry, what was common by nature. It is true, also, that, before property exists, that branch of justice and injustice which regards property cannot exist. But it is also true, that, where there are men, there will very soon be property of one kind or another, and, consequently, there will be that branch of justice which attends property as its guardian.

There are *two kinds of property* which we may distinguish.

The *first* is *what must presently be consumed to sustain life*; the *second*, which is more permanent, is, *what may be laid up and stored for the supply of future wants*.

Some of the gifts of nature must be used and consumed by individuals for the daily support of life; but they cannot be used till they be occupied and appropriated. If another person may, without injustice, rob me of what I have innocently occupied for present subsistence, the necessary consequence must be, that he may, without injustice, take away my life.

A right to life implies a right to the necessary means of life. And that justice which forbids the taking away the life of an innocent man, forbids no less the taking from him the necessary means of life. He

has the same right to defend the one as the other; and nature inspires him with the same just resentment of the one injury as of the other.

The natural right of liberty implies a right to such innocent labour as a man chooses, and to the fruit of that labour. To hinder another man's innocent labour, or to deprive him of the fruit of it, is an injustice of the same kind, and has the same effect, as to put him in fetters or in prison, and is equally a just object of resentment.

Thus it appears, that some kind, or some degree, of property must exist wherever men exist, and that the right to such property is the necessary consequence of the natural right of men to life and liberty.

It has been further observed, that God has made man a sagacious and provident animal, led by his constitution not only to occupy and use what nature has provided for the supply of his present wants and necessities, but to forsee future wants, and to provide for them; and that not only for himself, but for his family, his friends, and connections.

He therefore acts in perfect conformity to his nature, when he stores, of the fruit of his labour, what may afterwards be useful to himself or to others; when he invents and fabricates utensils or machines by which his labour may be facilitated, and its produce increased; and when, by exchanging with his fellow-men commodities or labour, he accommodates both himself and them. These are the natural and innocent exertions of that understanding wherewith his Maker has endowed him. He has therefore a right to exercise them, and to enjoy the fruit of them. Every man who impedes him in making such exertions, or deprives him of the fruit of them, is injurious and unjust, and an object of just resentment.

Many brute animals are led by instinct to provide for futurity, and to defend their store, and their storehouse, against all invaders. There seems to be in man, before the use of reason, an instinct of the same kind. When reason and conscience grow up, they approve and justify this provident care, and condemn, as unjust, every invasion of others, that may frustrate it.

Two instances of this provident sagacity seem to be peculiar to man: I mean the invention of utensils and machines for facilitating labour, and the making exchanges with his fellow-men for mutual benefit. No tribe of men has been found so rude as not to practise these things in some degree. And I know no tribe of brutes that was ever observed to practise them. They neither invent nor use utensils or machines, nor do they traffic by exchanges.

From these observations, I think it evident that man, even in the state of nature, by his powers of body and mind, may acquire permanent property, or what we call *riches*, by which his own and his family's wants are more liberally supplied, and his power enlarged to requite his benefactors, to relieve objects of compassion, to make friends, and to defend his property against unjust invaders. And we know from history, that men, who had no superior on earth, no connection with any public beyond their own family, have acquired property, and had distinct notions of that justice and injustice of which it is the object.

Every man, as a reasonable creature, has a right to gratify his natural and innocent desires, without hurt to others. No desire is more natural, or more reasonable, than that of supplying his wants. When this is done without hurt to any man, to hinder or frustrate his innocent labour, is an unjust violation of his natural liberty. Private utility leads a man to desire property, and to labour for it; and his right to it is only a right to labour for his own benefit.

That public utility is the sole origin, even of that branch of justice which regards property, is so far from being true, that, when men confederate and constitute a public, under laws and government, the right of each individual to his property is, by that confederation, abridged and limited. In the state of nature every man's property was solely at his own disposal, because he had no superior. In civil society it must be subject to the laws of the society. He gives up to the public part of that right which he had in the state of nature, as the price of that protection and security which he receives from civil society. In the state of nature, he was sole judge in his own cause, and had right to defend his property, his liberty, and life, as far as his power reached. In the state of civil society, he must submit to the judgment of the society, and acquiesce in its sentence, though he should conceive it to be unjust.

What was said above, of the natural right every man has to acquire permanent property, and to dispose of it, must be understood with this condition, That no other man be thereby deprived of the necessary means of life. The right of an innocent man to the necessaries of life, is, in its nature, superior to that which the rich man has to his riches, even though they be honestly acquired. The use of riches, or permanent property, is to supply future and casual wants, which ought to yield to present and certain necessity.

As, in a family, justice requires that the children who are unable to labour, and those who, by sickness, are disabled, should have their necessities supplied out of the common stock, so, in the great family of God, of which all mankind are the children, justice, I think, as well as charity, requires, that the necessities of those who, by the providence of God, are disabled from supplying themselves, should be supplied from what might otherwise be stored for future wants.

From this it appears, That the right of acquiring and that of disposing of property, may be subject to limitations and restrictions, even in the state of nature, and much more in the state of civil society, in which the public has what writers in jurisprudence call an *eminent dominion* over the property, as well as over the lives of the subjects, as far as the public good requires.

If these principles be well founded, Mr Hume's arguments to prove that justice is an artificial virtue, or that its public utility is the sole foundation of its merit, may be easily answered.

He supposes, first, a state in which nature has bestowed on the human race, such abundance of external goods, that every man, without care or industry, finds himself provided of whatever he can wish or desire. It is evident, says he, that, in such a state, the cautious, jealous virtue of justice would never once have been dreamed of.

It may be observed, *first*, That this argument applies only to one of the six branches of justice before mentioned. The other five are not in the least affected by it; and the reader will easily perceive that this observation applies to almost all his arguments, so that it needs not be repeated.

Secondly, All that this argument proves is, That a state of the human race may be conceived wherein no property exists, and where, of consequence, there can be no exercise of that branch of justice which respects property. But does it follow from this, that where property exists, and must exist, that no regard ought to be had to it?

He next supposes that the necessities of the human race continuing the same as at present, the mind is so enlarged with friendship and generosity, that every man feels as much tenderness and concern for the interest of every man, as for his own. It seems evident, he says, that the use of justice would be suspended by such an extensive benevolence, nor would the divisions and barriers of property and obligation have ever been thought of.

I answer, The conduct which this extensive benevolence leads to, is either perfectly consistent with justice, or it is not. *First*, If there be any case where this benevolence would lead us to do injustice, the use of justice is not suspended. Its obligation is superior to that of benevolence; and, to shew benevolence to one, at the expense of injustice to another, is immoral. *Secondly*, Supposing no such case could happen, the use of justice would not be suspended, because by it we must distinguish good offices to which we had a right, from those to which he had no right, and which therefore require a return of gratitude. *Thirdly*, Supposing the use or justice to be suspended, as it must be in every case where it cannot be exercised, Will it follow, that its obligation is suspended, where there is access to exercise it?

A *third* supposition is, the reverse of the first, That a society falls into extreme want of the necessaries of life: The question is put, Whether, in such a case, an equal partition of bread, without regard to private property, though effected by power, and even by violence, would be regarded as criminal and injurious? And the author conceives that this would be a suspension of the strict laws of justice.

I answer, That such an equal partition as Mr Hume mentions, is so far from being criminal or injurious, that justice requires it; and surely that cannot be a suspension of the laws of justice which is an act of justice. All that the strictest justice requires in such a case, is, That the man whose life is preserved at the expense of another, and without his consent, should indemnify him when he is able. His case is similar to that of a debtor who is insolvent, without any fault on his part. Justice requires that he should be forborne till he is able to pay. It is strange that Mr Hume should think that an action, neither criminal nor injurious, should be a suspension of the laws of justice. This seems to me a contradiction; for *justice* and *injury* are contradictory terms.

The next argument is thus expressed: "When any man, even in political society, renders himself, by crimes, obnoxious to the public, he is punished in his goods and person—that is, the ordinary rules of justice are, with regard to him, suspended for a moment, and it becomes equitable to inflict on him what otherwise he could not suffer without wrong or injury."

This argument, like the former, refutes itself. For that an action should be a suspension of the rules of justice, and at the same time equitable, seems to me a contradiction. It is possible that equity may interfere with the letter of human laws, because all the cases that may fall under them, cannot be foreseen; but that equity should interfere with justice is impossible. It is strange that Mr Hume should think that justice requires that a criminal should be treated in the same way as an innocent man.

Another argument is taken from public war. What is it, says he, but a suspension of justice among the warring parties? The laws of war, which then succeed to those of equity and justice, are rules calculated for the advantage and utility of that particular state in which men are now placed.

I answer, when war is undertaken for self-defence, or for reparation of intolerable injuries, justice authorizes it. The laws of war, which have been described by many judicious moralists, are all drawn from the fountain of justice and equity; and everything contrary to justice, is contrary to the laws of war. That justice which prescribes one rule of conduct to a master, another to a servant; one to a parent, another to a child—prescribes also one rule of conduct towards a friend, another towards an enemy. I do not understand what Mr Hume means by the *advantage* and *utility* of a state of war, for which he says the laws of war are calculated, and succeed to those of justice and equity. I know no laws of war that are not calculated for justice and equity.

The next argument is this—Were there a species of creatures intermingled with men, which, though rational, were possessed of such inferior strength, both of body and mind, that they were incapable of all resistance, and could never, upon the highest provocation, make us feel the effects of their resentment; the necessary consequence, I think, is, that we should be bound, by the laws of humanity, to give gentle usage to these creatures, but should not, properly speaking, lie under any restraint of justice with regard to them, nor could they possess any right or property, exclusive of such arbitrary lords.

If Mr Hume had not owned this sentiment as a consequence of his Theory of Morals, I should have thought it very uncharitable to impute it to him. However, we may judge of the Theory by its avowed consequence. For there cannot be better evidence that a theory of morals, or of any particular virtue, is false, than when it subverts the practical rules of morals. This defenceless species of rational creatures, is doomed by Mr Hume to have no rights. Why? Because they have no power to defend themselves. Is not this to say—That right has its origin from power; which, indeed, was the doctrine of Mr Hobbes. And to illustrate this doctrine, Mr Hume adds—That, as no inconvenience ever results from the exercise of a power so firmly established in nature, the restraints of justice and property being totally useless, could never have place in so unequal a confederacy; and, to the same purpose, he says, that the female part of our own species owe the share they have in the rights of society, to the power which their address and their charms give them. If this be sound morals, Mr Hume's Theory of Justice may be true.

We may here observe, that, though, in other places, Mr Hume founds the obligation of justice upon its utility to *ourselves* or to *others*, it is here founded solely upon utility to *ourselves*. For surely to be treated with justice would be highly useful to the defenceless species he here supposes to exist. But, as no inconvenience to ourselves can ever result from our treatment of them, he concludes, that justice would be useless, and therefore can have no place. Mr Hobbes could have said no more.

He supposes, in the *last* place, a state of human nature wherein all society and intercourse is cut off between man and man. It is evident, he says, that so solitary a being would be as much incapable of justice as of social discourse and conversation.

And would not so solitary a being be as incapable of friendship, generosity, and compassion, as of justice? If this argument prove justice to be an artificial virtue, it will, with equal force, prove every social virtue to be artificial.

These are the arguments which Mr Hume has advanced in his "Enquiry," in the first part of a long section upon justice.

In the *second* part, the arguments are not so clearly distinguished, nor can they be easily collected. I shall offer some remarks upon what seems most specious in this second part.

He begins with observing—"That, if we examine the particular laws by which justice is directed and property determined, they present us with the same conclusion. The good of mankind is the only object of all those laws and regulations."

It is not easy to perceive where the stress of this argument lies. *The good of mankind is the object of all the laws and regulations by which justice is directed and property determined; therefore, justice is not a natural virtue, but has its origin solely from*

public utility, and its beneficial consequences are the sole foundation of its merit.

Some step seems to be wanting to connect the antecedent proposition with the conclusion, which, I think, must be one or other of these two propositions—first, *All the rules of justice tend to public utility;* or, secondly, *Public utility is the only standard of justice, from which alone all it rules must be deduced.*

If the argument be, That justice must have its origin solely from public utility, because all its rules tend to public utility, I cannot admit the consequence; nor can Mr Hume admit it without overturning his own system; for the rules of benevolence and humanity do all tend to the public utility; and yet, in his system, they have another foundation in human nature; so likewise may the rules of justice.

I am apt to think, therefore, that the argument is to be taken in the last sense, That public utility is the only standard of justice, from which all its rules must be deduced; and therefore justice has its origin solely from public utility.

This seems to be Mr Hume's meaning, because, in what follows, be observes, That, in order to establish laws for the regulation of property, we must be acquainted with the nature and situation of man; must reject appearances which may be false though specious; and must search for those rules which are, on the whole, most useful and beneficial; and endeavours to shew, that the established rules which regard property are more for the public good than the system, either of those religious fanatics of the last age who held that saints only should inherit the earth, or of those political fanatics who claimed an equal division of property.

We see here, as before, that, though Mr Hume's conclusion respects justice in general, his argument is confined to one branch of justice—to wit, the right of property; and it is well known that, to conclude from a part to the whole is not good reasoning.

Besides, the proposition from which his conclusion is drawn cannot be granted, either with regard to property, or with regard to the other branches of justice.

We endeavoured before to shew that property, though not an innate but an acquired right, may be acquired in the state of nature, and agreeably to the laws of nature; and that this right has not its origin from human laws, made for the public good, though, when men enter into political society, it may and ought to be regulated by those laws.

If there were but two men upon the face of the earth, of ripe faculties, each might have his own property, and might know his right to defend it, and his obligation not to invade the property of the other. He would have no need to have recourse to reasoning from public good, in order to know when he was injured, either in his property or in any of his natural rights, or to know what rules of justice he ought to observe towards his neighbour.

The simple rule, of not doing to his neighbour what he would think wrong to be done to himself, would lead him to the knowledge of every branch of justice, without the consideration of public good, or of laws and statutes made to promote it.

It is not true, therefore, that public utility is the only standard of justice, and that the rules of justice can be deduced only from their public utility.

Aristides, and the people of Athens, had surely another notion of justice, when he pronounced the counsel of Themistocles, which was communicated to him only, to be highly useful, but unjust; and the assembly, upon this authority, rejected the proposal unheard. These honest citizens, though subject to no laws but of their own making, far from making utility the standard of justice, made justice to be the standard of utility.

"What is a man's property? Anything which it is lawful for him, and for him alone, to use. *But what rule have we by which we can distinguish these objects?* Here we must have recourse to statutes, customs, precedents, analogies, &c."

Does not this imply that, in the state of nature, there can be no distinction of property? If so, Mr Hume's state of nature is the same with that of Mr Hobbes.

It is true that, when men become members of a political society, they subject their property, as well as themselves, to the laws, and must either acquiesce in what the laws determine, or leave the society. But justice, and even that particular branch of it which our author always supposes to be the whole, is antecedent to political societies and to their laws; and the intention of these laws is, to be the guardians of justice, and to redress injuries.

As all the works of men are imperfect, human laws may be unjust; which could never be, if justice had its origin from law, as the author seems here to insinuate.

Justice requires that a member of a state should submit to the laws of the state, when they require nothing unjust or impious. There may, therefore, be statutory rights and statutory crimes. A statute may create a right which did not before exist, or make that to be criminal which was not so before. But this could never be, if there were not an antecedent obligation upon the subjects to obey the statutes. In like manner, the command of a master may make that to be the servant's duty which, before, was not his duty, and the servant may be chargeable with injustice if he disobeys, because he was under an antecedent obligation to obey his master in lawful things.

We grant, therefore, that particular laws may direct justice and determine property, and sometimes even upon very slight reasons and analogies, or even for no other reason but that it is better that such a point should be determined by law than that it should be left a dubious subject of contention. But this, far from presenting us with the conclusion which the author would establish, presents us with a contrary conclusion. For all these particular laws and statutes derive their whole obligation and force from a general rule of justice antecedent to them—to wit, That subjects ought to obey the laws of their country.

The author compares the rules of justice with the most frivolous superstitions, and can find no foundation for moral sentiment in the one more than in the other, excepting that justice is requisite to the well-being and existence of society.

It is very true that, if we examine *mine* and *thine* by the senses of *sight, smell,* or *touch,* or scrutinize them by the sciences of *medicine, chemistry,* or *physics,* we perceive no difference. But the reason is, that none of these senses or sciences are the judge of right or wrong, or can give any conception of them any more than the ear of colour, or the eye of sound. Every man of common understanding, and every savage, when he applies his moral faculty to those objects, perceives a difference as clearly as he perceives day-light. When that sense or faculty is not consulted, in vain do we consult every other, in a question of right and wrong.

To perceive that justice tends to the good of mankind, would lay no moral obligation upon us to be just, unless we be conscious of a moral obligation to do what tends to the good of mankind. If such a moral obligation be admitted, why may we not admit a stronger obligation to do injury to no man? The last obligation is as easily conceived as the first, and there is as clear evidence of its existence in human nature.

The last argument is a dilemma, and is thus expressed: "The dilemma seems obvious. As justice evidently tends to promote public utility, and to support civil society, the sentiment of justice is either derived from our reflecting on that tendency, or, like hunger, thirst, and other appetites, resentment, love of life, attachment to offspring, and other passions, arises from a simple original instinct in the human breast, which nature has implanted for like salutary purposes. If the latter be the case, it follows, That property, which is the object of justice, is also distinguished by a simple original instinct, and is not ascertained by any argument or reflection. But who is there that ever heard of such an instinct," & c.

I doubt not but Mr Hume has heard of a principle called *conscience*, which nature has implanted in the human breast. Whether he will call it a simple original instinct I know not, as he gives that name to all our appetites, and to all our passions. From this principle, I think, we derive the sentiment of justice.

As the eye not only gives us the conception of colours, but makes us perceive one body to have one colour, and another body another; and as our reason not only gives us the conception of true and false, but makes us perceive one proposition to be true and another to be false; so our conscience, or moral faculty, not only gives us the conception of honest and dishonest, but makes us perceive one kind of conduct to be honest, another to be dishonest. By this faculty we perceive a merit in honest conduct, and a demerit in dishonest, without regard to public utility.

That these sentiments are not the effect of education or of acquired habits, we have the same reason to conclude as that our perception of what is true and what false, is not the effect of education or of acquired habits. There have been men who professed to believe that there is no ground to assent to any one proposition rather than its contrary; but I never yet heard of a man who had the effrontery to profess himself to be under no obligation of honour or honesty, of truth or justice, in his dealings with men.

Nor does this faculty of conscience *require innate ideas of property, and of the various ways of acquiring and transferring it, or innate ideas of kings and senators, of prætors, and chancellors, and juries,* any more than the faculty of seeing requires innate ideas of colours, or than the faculty of reasoning requires innate ideas of cones, cylinders, and spheres.

Chapter VI
Of the Nature and Obligation of a Contract

The obligation of *Contracts* and *Promises* is a matter so sacred, and of such consequence to human society,

that speculations which have a tendency to weaken that obligation, and to perplex men's notions on a subject so plain and so important, ought to kneel with the disapprobation of all honest men.

Some such speculations, I think, we have in the third volume of Mr Hume's "Treatise of Human Nature," and in his "Enquiry into the Principles of Morals"; and my design in this chapter is, to offer some observations on the nature of a contract or promise, and on two passages of that author on this subject.

I am far from saying or thinking that Mr Hume meant to weaken men's obligations to honesty and fair dealing, or that he had not a sense of these obligations himself. It is not the man I impeach, but his writings. Let us think of the first as charitably as we can, while we freely examine the import and tendency of the last.

Although the nature of a contract and of a promise is perfectly understood by all men of common understanding; yet, by attention to the operations of mind signified by these words, we shall be better enabled to judge of the metaphysical subtilties which have been raised about them. A promise and a contract differ so little in what concerns the present disquisition, that the same reasoning (as Mr Hume justly observes) extends to both. In a promise, one party only comes under the obligation, the other acquires a right to the prestation promised. But we give the name of a contract to a transaction in which each party comes under an obligation to the other, and each reciprocally acquires a right to what is promised by the other.

The Latin word *Pactum* seems to extend to both; and the definition given of it in the Civil Law, and borrowed from Ulpian, is, *Duorum pluriumve in idem placitum consensus.* Titius, a modern Civilian, has endeavoured to make this definition more complete, by adding the words, *obligationis licitè constituendæ vel tollendæ causa datus.* With this addition, the definition is, that *a Contract is the consent of two or more persons in the same thing, given with the intention of constituting or dissolving lawfully some obligation.*

This definition is, perhaps, as good as any other that can be given; yet, I believe, every man will acknowledge that it gives him no clearer or more distinct notion of a contract than he had before. If it is considered as a strictly logical definition, I believe some objections might be made to it; but I forbear to mention them, because I believe that similar objections might be made to any definition of a contract that can be given.

Nor can it be inferred from this, that the notion of a contract is not perfectly clear in every man come to years of understanding. For this is common to many operations of the mind, that, although we understand them perfectly, and are in no danger of confounding them with anything else; yet we cannot define them according to the rules of logic, by a genus and a specific difference. And when we attempt it, we rather darken than give light to them.

Is there anything more distinctly understood by all men, than what it is to see, to hear, to remember, to judge? Yet it is the most difficult thing in the world to define these operations according to the rules of logical definition. But it is not more difficult than it is useless.

Sometimes philosophers attempt to define them; but, if we examine their definitions, we shall find that they amount to no more than giving one synonymous word for another, and commonly a worse for a better. So, when we define a contract, by calling it a consent, a convention, an agreement, what is this but giving a synonymous word for it, and a word that is neither more expressive nor better understood?

One boy has a top, another a scourge; says the first to the other, If you will lend me your scourge as long as I can keep up my top with it, you shall next have the top as long as you can keep it up. Agreed, says the other. This is a contract perfectly understood by both parties, though they never heard of the definition given by Ulpian or by Titius. And each of them knows that he is injured if the other breaks the bargain, and that he does wrong if he breaks it himself.

The operations of the human mind may be divided into *two* classes, the *Solitary* and the *Social*. As promises and contracts belong to the last class, it may be proper to explain this division.

I call those operations *solitary* which may be performed by a man in solitude, without intercourse with any other intelligent being.

I call those operations *social* which necessarily imply social intercourse with some other intelligent being who bears a part in them.

A man may see, and hear, and remember, and judge, and reason; he may deliberate and form purposes, and execute them, without the intervention of any other intelligent being. They are solitary acts. But, when he asks a question for information, when he tes-

tifies a fact, when he gives a command to his servant, when he makes a promise, or enters into a contract, these are social acts of mind, and can have no existence without the intervention of some other intelligent being, who acts a part in them. Between the operations of the mind, which, for want of a more proper name, I have called *solitary*, and those I have called *social*, there is this very remarkable distinction, that, in the solitary, the expression of them by words, or any other sensible sign, is accidental. They may exist, and be complete, without being expressed, without being known to any other person. But, in the social operations, the expression is essential. They cannot exist without being expressed by words or signs, and known to the other party.

If nature had not made man capable of such social operations of mind, and furnished him with a language to express them, he might think, and reason, and deliberate, and will; he might have desires and aversions, joy and sorrow; in a word, he might exert all those operations of mind which the writers in logic and pneumatology have so copiously described; but, at the same time, he would still be a solitary being, even when in a crowd; it would be impossible for him to put a question, or give a command, to ask a favour, or testify a fact, to make a promise, or a bargain.

I take it to be the common opinion of philosophers, That the social operations of the human mind are not specifically different from the solitary, and that they are only various modifications or compositions of our solitary operations, and may be resolved into them.

It is for this reason, probably, that, in enumerating the operations of the mind, the solitary only are mentioned, and no notice at all taken of the social, though they are familiar to every man, and have names in all languages.

I apprehend, however, it will be found extremely difficult, if not impossible, to resolve our social operations into any modification or composition of the solitary; and that an attempt to do this would prove as ineffectual as the attempts that have been made to resolve all our social affections into the selfish. The social operations appear to be as simple in their nature as the solitary. They are found in every individual of the species, even before the use of reason.

The power which man has of holding social intercourse with his kind, by asking and refusing, threatening and supplicating, commanding and obeying, testifying and promising, must either be a distinct faculty given by our Maker, and a part of our constitution, like the powers of seeing and hearing, or it must be a human invention. If men have invented this art of social intercourse, it must follow, that every individual of the species must have invented it for himself. It cannot be taught; for, though, when once carried to a certain pitch, it may be improved by teaching; yet it is impossible it can begin in that way, because all teaching supposes a social intercourse and language already established between the teacher and the learner. This intercourse must, from the very first, be carried on by sensible signs; for the thoughts of other men can be discovered in no other way. I think it is likewise evident, that this intercourse, in its beginning at least, must be carried on by natural signs, whose meaning is understood by both parties, previous to all compact or agreement. For there can be no compact without signs, nor without social intercourse.

I apprehend, therefore, that the social intercourse of mankind, consisting of those social operations which I have mentioned, is the exercise of a faculty appropriated to that purpose, which is the gift of God, no less than the powers of seeing and hearing. And that, in order to carry on this intercourse, God has given to man a natural language, by which his social operations are expressed, and without which, the artificial languages of articulate sounds, and of writing, could never have been invented by human art.

The signs in this natural language are looks, changes of the features, modulations of the voice, and gestures of the body. All men understand this language without instruction, and all men can use it in some degree. But they are most expert in it who use it most. It makes a great part of the language of savages, and therefore they are more expert in the use of natural signs than the civilized.

The language of dumb persons is mostly formed of natural signs; and they are all great adepts in this language of nature. All that we call action and pronunciation, in the most perfect orator, and the most admired actor, is nothing else but superadding the language of nature to the language of articulate sounds. The pantomimes among the Romans carried it to the highest pitch of perfection. For they could act parts of comedies and tragedies in dumb-show, so as to be understood, not only by those who were accustomed to this entertainment, but by all the strangers that came to Rome, from all the corners of the earth.

For it may be observed of this natural language (and nothing more clearly demonstrates it to be a part of the human constitution), that, although it require practice and study to enable a man to express his sentiments by it in the most perfect manner; yet it requires neither study nor practice in the spectator to understand it. The knowledge of it was before latent in the mind, and we no sooner see it than we immediately recognise it, as we do an acquaintance whom we had long forgot, and could not have described; but no sooner do we see him, than we know for certain that he is the very man.

This knowledge, in all mankind, of the natural signs of men's thoughts and sentiments, is indeed so like to reminiscence that it seems to have led Plato to conceive all human knowledge to be of that kind.

It is not by reasoning that all mankind know that an open countenance and a placid eye is a sign of amity; that a contracted brow and a fierce look is the sign of anger. It is not from reason that we learn to know the natural signs of consenting and refusing, of affirming and denying, of threatening and supplicating.

No man can perceive any necessary connection between the signs of such operations, and the things signified by them. But we are so formed by the Author of our nature, that the operations themselves become visible, as it were, by their natural signs. This knowledge resembles reminiscence, in this respect, that it is immediate. We form the conclusion with great assurance, without knowing any premises from which it may be drawn by reasoning.

It would lead us too far from the intention of the present inquiry, to consider, more particularly, in what degree the social intercourse is natural, and a part of our constitution; how far it is of human invention.

It is sufficient to observe, that this intercourse of human minds, by which their thoughts and sentiments are exchanged, and their souls mingle together, as it were, is common to the whole species from infancy.

Like our other powers, its first beginnings are weak, and scarcely perceptible. But it is a certain fact, that we can perceive some communication of sentiments between the nurse and her nursling, before it is a month old. And I doubt not but that, if both had grown out of the earth, and had never seen another human face, they would be able in a few years to converse together.

There appears, indeed, to be some degree of social intercourse among brute animals, and between some of them and man. A dog exults in the caresses of his master, and is humbled at his displeasure. But there are two operations of the social kind, of which the brute animals seem to be altogether incapable. They can neither plight their veracity by testimony, nor their fidelity by any engagement or promise. If nature had made them capable of these operations, they would have had a language to express them by, as man has: But of this we see no appearance.

A fox is said to use stratagems, but he cannot lie; because be cannot give his testimony, or plight his veracity. A dog is said to be faithful to his master; but no more is meant but that he is affectionate, for he never came under any engagement. I see no evidence that any brute animal is capable of either giving testimony, or making a promise.

A dumb man cannot speak any more than a fox or a dog; but he can give his testimony by signs as early in life as other men can do by words. He knows what a lie is as early as other men, and hates it as much. He can plight his faith, and is sensible of the obligation of a promise or contract.

It is therefore a prerogative of man, that he can communicate his knowledge of facts by testimony, and enter into engagements by promise or contract. God has given him these powers by a part of his constitution, which distinguishes him from all brute animals. And whether they are original powers, or resolvable into other original powers, it is evident that they spring up in the human mind at an early period of life, and are found in every individual of the species, whether savage or civilized.

These prerogative powers of man, like all his other powers, must be given for some end, and for a good end. And if we consider a little farther the economy of nature, in relation to this part of the human constitution, we shall perceive the wisdom of nature in the structure of it, and discover clearly our duty in consequence of it.

It is evident, in the *first* place, that, if no credit was given to testimony, if there was no reliance upon promises, they would answer no end at all, not even that of deceiving.

Secondly, Supposing men disposed by some principle in their nature to rely on declarations and promises; yet, if men found in experience that there was no fidelity on the other part in making and in keeping them, no man of common understanding would trust to them, and so they would become useless.

Hence it appears, *thirdly,* That this power of giving testimony, and of promising, can answer no end in society, unless there be a considerable degree, both of fidelity on the one part, and of trust on the other. These two must stand or fall together, and one of them cannot possibly subsist without the other.

Fourthly, It may be observed that fidelity in declarations and promises, and its counterpart, trust and reliance upon them, form a system of social intercourse, the most amiable, the most useful, that can be among men. Without fidelity and trust, there can be no human society. There never was a society, even of savages—nay, even of robbers or pirates—in which there was not a great degree of veracity and of fidelity among themselves. Without it man would be the most dissocial animal that God has made. His state would be in reality what Hobbes conceived the state of nature to be—a state of war of every man against every man; nor could this war ever terminate in peace.

It may be observed in the *fifth* place, that man is evidently made for living in society. His social affections shew this as evidently as that the eye was made for seeing. His social operations, particularly those of testifying and promising, make it no less evident.

From these observations it follows, that, if no provision were made by nature, to engage men to fidelity in declarations and promises, human nature would be a contradiction to itself, made for an end, yet without the necessary means of attaining it. As if the species had been furnished with good eyes, but without the power of opening their eyelids. There are no blunders of this kind in the works of God. Wherever there is an end intended, the means are admirably fitted for the attainment of it; and so we find it to be in the case before us.

For we see that children, as soon as they are capable of understanding declarations and promises, are led by their constitution to rely upon them. They are no less led by constitution to veracity and candour, on their own part. Nor do they ever deviate from this road of truth and sincerity, until corrupted by bad example and bad company. This disposition to sincerity in themselves, and to give credit to others, whether we call it *instinct*, or whatever name we give it, must be considered as the effect of their constitution.

So that the things essential to human society—I mean good faith on the one part, and trust on the other—are formed by nature in the minds of children, before they are capable of knowing their utility, or being influenced by considerations either of duty or interest.

When we grow up so far as to have the conception of a right and a wrong in conduct, the turpitude of lying, falsehood, and dishonesty, is discerned, not by any train of reasoning, but by an immediate perception. For we see that every man disapproves it in others, even those who are conscious of it in themselves.

Every man thinks himself injured and ill used, and feels resentment, when he is imposed upon by it. Every man takes it as a reproach when falsehood is imputed to him. These are the clearest evidences, that all men disapprove of falsehood, when their judgment is not biassed.

I know of no evidence that has been given of any nation so rude as not to have these sentiments. It is certain that dumb people have them, and discover them about the same period of life in which they appear in those who speak. And it may reasonably be thought, that dumb persons, at that time of life, have had as little advantage, with regard to morals, from their education, as the greatest savages.

Every man, come to years of reflection, when he pledges his veracity or fidelity, thinks he has a right to be credited, and is affronted if he is not. But there cannot be a shadow of right to be credited, unless there be an obligation to good faith. For right on one hand, necessarily implies obligation on the other.

When we see that, in the most savage state that ever was known of the human race, men have always lived in societies greater or less, this of itself is a proof from fact, that they have had that sense of their obligation to fidelity without which no human society can subsist.

From these observations, I think, it appears very evident, that, as fidelity on one part, and trust on the other, are essential to that intercourse of men which we call human society; so the Author of our nature has made wise provision for perpetuating them among men, in that degree that is necessary to human society, in all the different periods of human life, and in all the stages of human improvement and degeneracy.

In early years, we have an innate disposition to them. In riper years, we feel our obligation to fidelity as much as to any moral duty whatsoever.

Nor is it necessary to mention the collateral inducements to this virtue, from considerations of prudence, which are obvious to every man that reflects. Such as, that it creates trust, the most effectual engine of human power; that it requires no artifice or concealment; dreads no detection; that it inspires courage and magnanimity, and is the natural ally of every virtue; so that there is no virtue whatsoever, to which our natural obligation appears more strong or more apparent.

An observation or two, with regard to the nature of a contract, will be sufficient for the present purpose.

It is obvious that the prestation promised must be understood by both parties. One party engages to do such a thing, another accepts of this engagement. An engagement to do, one does not know what, can neither be made nor accepted. It is no less obvious, that a contract is a voluntary transaction.

But it ought to be observed, that the will, which is essential to a contract, is only a will to engage, or to become bound. We must beware of confounding this will with a will to perform what we have engaged. The last can signify nothing else than an intention and fixed purpose to do what we have engaged to do. The will to become bound, and to confer a right upon the other party, is indeed the very essence of a contract; but the purpose of fulfilling our engagement, is no part of the contract at all.

A purpose is a solitary act of mind, which lays no obligation on the person, nor confers any right on another. A fraudulent person may contract with a fixed purpose of not performing his engagement. But this purpose makes no change with regard to his obligation. He is as much bound as the honest man, who contracts with a fixed purpose of performing.

As the contract is binding without any regard to the purpose, so there may be a purpose without any contract. A purpose is no contract, even when it is declared to the person for whose benefit it is intended. I may say to a man, I intend to do such a thing for your benefit, but I come under no engagement. Every man understands the meaning of this speech, and sees no contradiction in it: whereas, if a purpose declared were the same thing with a contract, such a speech would be a contradiction, and would be the same as if one should say, I promise to do such a thing, but I do not promise.

All this is so plain to every man of common sense, that it would have been unnecessary to be mentioned, had not so acute a man as Mr Hume grounded some of the contradictions he finds in a contract, upon confounding a will to engage in a contract with a will or purpose to perform the engagement.

I come now to consider the speculations of that author with regard to contracts.

In order to support a favourite notion of his own, That justice is not a natural but an artificial virtue, and that it derives its whole merit from its utility, he has laid down some principles which, I think, have a tendency to subvert all faith and fair-dealing among mankind.

In the third volume of the "Treatise of Human Nature," p. 40, he lays it down as an undoubted maxim, That no action can be virtuous or morally good, unless there be in human nature, some motive to produce it, distinct from its morality. Let us apply this undoubted maxim in an instance or two. If a man keeps his word, from this sole motive, that he ought to do so, this is no virtuous or morally good action. If a man pays his debt from this motive, that justice requires this of him, this is no virtuous or morally good action. If a judge or an arbiter gives a sentence in a cause, from no other motive but regard to justice, this is no virtuous or morally good action. These appear to me to be shocking absurdities, which no metaphysical subtilty can ever justify.

Nothing is more evident than that every human action takes its denomination and its moral nature from the motive from which it is performed. That is a benevolent action which is done from benevolence. That is an act of gratitude which is done from a sentiment of gratitude. That is an act of obedience to God, which is done from a regard to his command. And, in general, that is an act of virtue which is done from a regard to virtue.

Virtuous actions are so far from needing other motives, besides their being virtuous, to give them merit, that their merit is then greatest and most conspicuous, when every motive that can be put in the opposite scale is outweighed by the sole consideration of their being our duty.

This maxim, therefore, of Mr Hume, That no action can be virtuous or morally good, unless there be some motive to produce it distinct from its morality, is so far from being undoubtedly true, that it is undoubtedly false. It was never, so far as I know, maintained by any moralist, but by the Epicureans; and it savours of the very dregs of that sect. It agrees well with the principles of those who maintained, that virtue is an empty name, and that it is entitled to no regard but in as far as it ministers to pleasure or profit.

I believe the author of this maxim acted upon better moral principles than he wrote; and that what Cicero says of Epicurus, may be applied to him: "He is refuted by himself, and his writings are defeated by his own integrity and character; and as others are thought to speak better than they act, so he acts. I think, better than he speaks."

But let us see how he applies this maxim to contracts. I give you his words from the place formerly cited: "I suppose," says he, "a person to have lent me a sum of money, on condition that it be restored in a few days; and, after the expiration of the term agreed on, he demands the sum. I ask, what reason or motive have I to restore the money? It will, perhaps, be said, that my regard to justice, and abhorrence of villainy and knavery, are sufficient reasons for me, if I have the least grain of honesty, or sense of duty and obligation. And this answer, no doubt, is just and satisfactory to man in his civilized state, and when trained up according to a certain discipline and education. But, in his rude and more natural condition, if you are pleased to call such a condition natural, this answer would be rejected as perfectly unintelligible and sophistical."

The doctrine we are taught in this passage is this, That, though a man, in a civilized state, and when trained up according to a certain discipline and education, may have a regard to justice and an abhorrence of villainy and knavery, and some sense of duty and obligation; yet, to a man in his rude and more natural condition, the considerations of honesty, justice, duty, and obligation, will be perfectly unintelligible and sophistical. And this is brought as an argument to shew that justice is not a natural but an artificial virtue.

I shall offer some observations on this argument.

1. Although it may be true that what is unintelligible to man in his rude state may be intelligible to him in his civilized state, I cannot conceive that what is sophistical in the rude state should change its nature, and become just reasoning when man is more improved. What is a sophism, will always be so; nor can any change in the state of the person who judges make that to be just reasoning which before was sophistical. Mr Hume's argument requires that to man, in his rude state, the motives to justice and honesty should not only appear to be sophistical, but should really be so. If the motives were just in themselves, then justice would be a natural virtue, although the rude man, by an error of his judgment, thought otherwise. But if justice be not a natural virtue, which is the point Mr Hume intends to prove, then every argument, by which man in his natural state may be urged to it, must be a sophism in reality, and not in appearance only; and the effect of discipline and education in the civilized state can only be

to make those motives to justice appear just and satisfactory, which, in their own nature, are sophistical.

2. It were to be wished that this ingenious author had shewn us why that state of man, in which the obligation to honesty, and an abhorrence of villainy, appear perfectly unintelligible and sophistical, should be his *more natural state.*

It is the nature of human society to be progressive, as much as it is the nature of the individual. In the individual, the state of infancy leads to that of childhood, childhood to youth, youth to manhood, manhood to old age. If one should say that the state of infancy is a more natural state than that of manhood or of old age, I am apt to think that this would be words without any meaning. In like manner, in human society, there is a natural progress from rudeness to civilization, from ignorance to knowledge. What period of this progress shall we call man's natural state? To me they appear all equally natural. Every state of society is equally natural, wherein men have access to exert their natural powers about their proper objects, and to improve those powers by the means which their situation affords.

Mr Hume, indeed, shews some timidity in affirming the rude state to be the more natural state of man; and, therefore, adds this qualifying parenthesis, If you are pleased to call such a condition natural.

But it ought to be observed, That, if the premises of his argument be weakened by this clause, the same weakness must be communicated to the conclusion; and the conclusion, according to the rules of good reasoning, ought to be, That justice is an artificial virtue, if you be pleased to call it artificial.

3. It were likewise to be wished, that Mr Hume had shewn, from fact, that there ever did exist such a state of man as that which he calls his more natural state. It is a state wherein a man borrows a sum of money, on the condition that he is to restore it in a few days; yet, when the time of payment comes, his obligation to repay what he borrowed is perfectly unintelligible and sophistical. It would have been proper to have given, at least, a single instance of some tribe of the human race that was found to be in this natural state. If no such instance can be given, it is, probably, a state merely imaginary; like that state, which some have imagined, wherein men were *ouran outangs*, or wherein they were fishes with tails.

Indeed, such a state seems impossible. That a man should lend without any conception of his having a right to be repaid; or that a man should borrow on the condition of paying in a few days, and yet have no conception of his obligation—seems to me to involve a contradiction.

I grant that a humane man may lend without any expectation of being repaid; but that he should lend without any conception of a right to be repaid, is a contradiction. In like manner, a fraudulent man may borrow without an intention of paying back; but that he could borrow, while an obligation to repay is perfectly unintelligible to him, this is a contradiction.

The same author, in his "Enquiry into the Principles of Morals," § 3, treating of the same subject, has the following note:

"'Tis evident that the will or consent alone, never transfers property, nor causes the obligation of a promise (for the same reasoning extends to both); but the will must be expressed by words or signs, in order to impose a tie upon any man. The expression being once brought in as subservient to the will, soon becomes the principal part of the promise; nor will a man be less bound by his word, though he secretly give a different direction to his intention, and withhold the assent of his mind. But, though the expression makes, on most occasions, the whole of the promise; yet it does not always so; and one who should make use of any expression of which he knows not the meaning, and which be uses without any sense of the consequences, would not certainly be bound by it. Nay, though he know its meaning, yet, if he uses it in jest only, and with such signs as shew evidently he has no serious intention of binding himself, he would not be under any obligation of performance; but it is necessary that the words be a perfect expression of the will, without any contrary signs; nay, even this we must not carry so far as to imagine that one whom, from our quickness of understanding, we conjectured to have an intention of deceiving us, is not bound by his expression or verbal promise, if we accept of it; but must limit this conclusion to those cases where the signs are of a different nature from those of deceit. All these contradictions are easily accounted for, if justice arises entirely from its usefulness to society, but will never be explained on any other hypothesis."

Here we have the opinion of this grave moralist and acute metaphysician, that the principles of honesty and fidelity are at bottom a bundle of contradictions. This is one part of his moral system which, I cannot help thinking, borders upon licentiousness. It surely tends to give a very unfavourable notion of that cardinal virtue without which no man has a title to be called an honest man. What regard can a man pay to the virtue of fidelity, who believes that its essential rules contradict each other? Can a man be bound by contradictory rules of conduct? No more, surely, than he can be bound to believe contradictory principles.

He tells us, "that all these contradictions are easily accounted for, if justice arises entirely from its usefulness to society, but will never be explained upon any other hypothesis."

I know not, indeed, what is meant by accounting for contradictions, or explaining them. I apprehend that no hypothesis can make that which is a contradiction to be no contradiction. However, without attempting to account for these contradictions upon his own hypothesis, he pronounces, in a decisive tone, that they will never be explained upon any other hypothesis.

What if it shall appear that the contradictions mentioned in this paragraph do all take their rise from two capital mistakes the author has made with regard to the nature of promises and contracts; and if, when these are corrected, there shall not appear a shadow of contradiction in the cases put by him?

The first mistake is, That a promise is some kind of will, consent, or intention, which may be expressed, or may not be expressed. This is to mistake the nature of a promise. For no will, no consent, or intention, that is not expressed, is a promise. A promise, being a social transaction between two parties, without being expressed can have no existence.

Another capital mistake that runs through the passage cited is, That this will, consent, or intention, which makes a promise, is a will or intention to perform what we promise. Every man knows that there may be a fraudulent promise, made without intention of performing. But the intention to perform the promise, or not to perform it, whether the intention be known to the other party or not, makes no part of the promise—it is a solitary act of the mind, and can neither constitute nor dissolve an obligation. What makes a promise is, that it be expressed to the other party with understanding, and with an intention to become bound, and that it be accepted by him.

Carrying these remarks along with us, let us review the passage cited.

First, He observes, that the will or consent alone does not cause the obligation of a promise, but it must be expressed.

I answer, The will not expressed is not a promise; and is it a contradiction that that which is not a promise should not cause the obligation of a promise? He goes on, The expression being once brought in as subservient to the will, soon *becomes* a principal part of the promise. Here it is supposed, that the expression was not originally a constituent part of the promise, but it soon *becomes* such. It is brought in to aid and be subservient to the promise which was made before by the will. If Mr Hume had considered that it is the expression accompanied with understanding and will to become bound, that constitutes a promise, he would never have said, that the expression soon becomes a part, and is brought in as subservient.

He adds, Nor will a man be less bound by his word, though he secretly gives a different direction to his intention, and withholds the assent of his mind.

The case here put needs some explication. Either it means, that the man knowingly and voluntarily gives his word, without any intention of giving his word; or that he gives it without the intention of keeping it, and performing what he promises. The last of these is indeed a possible case, and is, I apprehend, what Mr Hume means. But the intention of keeping his promise is no part of the promise, nor does it in the least affect the obligation of it, as we have often observed.

If the author meant that the man may knowingly and voluntarily give his word, without the intention of giving his word, this is impossible: For such is the nature of all social acts of the mind, that, as they cannot be without being expressed, so they cannot be expressed knowingly and willingly, but they must be. If a man puts a question knowingly and willingly, it is impossible that he should at the same time will not to put it. If he gives a command knowingly and willingly, it is impossible that he should at the same time will not to give it. We cannot have contrary wills at the same time. And, in like manner, if a man knowingly and willingly becomes bound by a promise, it is impossible that he should at the same time will not to be bound.

To suppose, therefore, that, when a man knowingly and willingly gives his word, he withholds that will and intention which makes a promise, is indeed a contradiction; but the contradiction is not in the nature of the promise, but in the case supposed by Mr Hume.

He adds, though the expression, for the most part, makes the whole of the promise, it does not always so.

I answer, That the expression, if it is not accompanied with understanding and will to engage, never makes a promise. The author here assumes a postulate, which nobody ever granted, and which can only be grounded on the impossible supposition made in the former sentence. And as there can be no promise without knowledge and will to engage, is it marvellous that words which are not understood, or words spoken in jest, and without any intention to become bound, should not have the effect of a promise?

The last case put by Mr Hume, is that of a man who promises fraudulently with an intention not to perform, and whose fraudulent intention is discovered by the other party, who, notwithstanding, accepts the promise. He is bound, says Mr Hume, by his verbal promise. Undoubtedly he is bound, because an intention not to perform the promise, whether known to the other party or not, makes no part of the promise, nor affects its obligation, as has been repeatedly observed.

From what has been said, I think it evident, that to one who attends to the nature of a promise or contract, there is not the least appearance of contradiction in the principles of morality relating to contracts.

It would, indeed, appear wonderful that such a man as Mr Hume should have imposed upon himself in so plain a matter, if we did not see frequent instances of ingenious men, whose zeal in supporting a favourite hypothesis darkens their understanding, and hinders them from seeing what is before their eyes.

Chapter VII
That Moral Approbation Implies a Real Judgment

The approbation of good actions, and disapprobation of bad, are so familiar to every man come to years of understanding, that it seems strange there should be any dispute about their nature.

Whether we reflect upon our own conduct, or attend to the conduct of others with whom we live, or of whom we hear or read, we cannot help approving of some things, disapproving of others, and regarding many with perfect indifference.

These operations of our minds we are conscious of every day and almost every hour we live. Men of ripe understanding are capable of reflecting upon them, and of attending to what passes in their own thoughts on such occasions; yet, for half a century, it has been a serious dispute among philosophers, what this approbation and disapprobation is, *Whether there be a real judgment included in it, which, like all other judgments, must be true or false; or, Whether it include no more but some agreeable or uneasy feeling, in the person who approves or disapproves.*

Mr Hume observes very justly, that this is a controversy *started of late.* Before the modern system of Ideas and Impressions was introduced, nothing would have appeared more absurd than to say, that when I condemn a man for what he has done, I pass no judgment at all about the man, but only express some uneasy feeling in myself.

Nor did the new system produce this discovery at once, but gradually, by several steps, according as its consequences were more accurately traced, and its spirit more thoroughly imbibed by successive philosophers.

Des Cartes and Mr Locke went no farther than to maintain that the Secondary Qualities of body—Heat and Cold, Sound, Colour, Taste, and Smell—which we perceive and judge to be in the external object, are mere feelings or sensations in our minds, there being nothing in bodies themselves to which these names can be applied; and that the office of the external senses is not to judge of external things, but only to give us ideas of sensations, from which we are by reasoning to deduce the existence of a material world without us, as well as we can.

Arthur Collier and Bishop Berkeley discovered, from the same principles, that the Primary, as well as the Secondary, Qualities of bodies, such as Extension, Figure, Solidity, Motion, are only sensations in our minds; and, therefore, that there is no material world without us at all.

The same philosophy, when it came to be applied to matters of taste, discovered that beauty and deformity are not anything in the objects, to which men, from the beginning of the world, ascribed them, but certain feelings in the mind of the spectator.

The next step was an easy consequence from all the preceding, that Moral Approbation and Disapprobation are not Judgments, which must be true or false, but barely agreeable and uneasy Feelings or Sensations.

Mr Hume made the last step in this progress, and crowned the system by what he calls his *hypothesis*—to wit, That Belief is more properly an act of the Sensitive than of the Cogitative part of our nature.

Beyond this I think no man can go in this track; sensation or feeling is all, and what is left to the cogitative part of our nature, I am not able to comprehend.

I have had occasion to consider each of these paradoxes, excepting that which relates to morals, in "Essays on the Intellectual Powers of Man"; and though they be strictly connected with each other, and with the system which has produced them, I have attempted to shew that they are inconsistent with just notions of our intellectual powers, no less than they are with the common sense and common language of mankind. And this, I think, will likewise appear with regard to the conclusion relating to morals—to wit, That moral approbation is only an agreeable feeling, and not a real judgment.

To prevent ambiguity as much as possible, let us attend to the meaning of *Feeling* and of *Judgment*. These operations of the mind, perhaps, cannot be logically defined; but they are well understood, and easily distinguished, by their properties and adjuncts.

Feeling, or sensation, seems to be the lowest degree of animation we can conceive. We give the name of *animal* to every being that feels pain and pleasure; and this seems to be the boundary between the inanimate and animal creation.

We know no being of so low a rank in the creation of God as to possess this animal power only without any other.

We commonly distinguish *Feeling* from *Thinking*, because it hardly deserves the name; and though it be, in a more general sense, a species of thought, is least removed from the passive and inert state of things inanimate.

A feeling must be agreeable, or uneasy, or indifferent. It may be weak or strong. It is expressed in language either by a single word, or by such a contexture of words as may be the subject or predicate of a proposition, but such as cannot by themselves make a proposition. For it implies neither affirmation nor negation; and therefore cannot have the qualities of true or false, which distinguish propositions from all other forms of speech, and judgments from all other acts of the mind.

That I have such a feeling, is indeed an affirmative proposition, and expresses testimony grounded upon an intuitive judgment. But the feeling is only one term of this proposition; and it can only make a proposition when joined with another term, by a verb affirming or denying.

As feeling distinguishes the animal nature from the inanimate; so judging seems to distinguish the rational nature from the merely animal.

Though judgment in general is expressed by one word in language, as the most complex operations of the mind may be; yet a particular judgment can only be expressed by a sentence, and by that kind of sentence which logicians call a *proposition*, in which there must necessarily be a verb in the indicative mood, either expressed or understood.

Every judgment must necessarily be true or false, and the same may be said of the proposition which expresses it. It is a determination of the understanding, with regard to what is true, or false, or dubious.

In judgment, we can distinguish the object about which we judge, from the act of the mind in judging of that object. In mere feeling there is no such distinction. The object of judgment must be expressed by a proposition; and belief, disbelief, or doubt, always accompanies the judgment we form. If we judge the proposition to be true, we must believe it; if we judge it to be false, we must disbelieve it; and if we be uncertain whether it be true or false, we must doubt.

The *toothache*, the *headache*, are words which express uneasy feelings; but to say that they express a judgment would be ridiculous.

That the sun is greater than the earth, is a proposition, and therefore the object of judgment; and, when affirmed or denied, believed or disbelieved, or doubted, it expresses judgment; but to say that it expresses only a feeling in the mind of him that believes it, would be ridiculous.

These two operations of mind, when we consider them separately, are very different, and easily distinguished. When we feel without judging, or judge without feeling, it is impossible, without very gross inattention, to mistake the one for the other.

But in many operations of the mind, both are inseparably conjoined under one name; and when we are not aware that the operation is complex, we may take one ingredient to be the whole, and overlook the other.

In former ages, that moral power by which human actions ought to be regulated, was called *Reason*, and considered, both by philosophers and by the vulgar, as the power of judging what we ought and what we ought not to do.

This is very fully expressed by Mr Hume, in his "Treatise of Human Nature," Book II. Part iii. § 3. "Nothing is more usual in philosophy, and even in common life, than to talk of the combat of passion and reason, to give the preference to reason, and assert that men are only so far virtuous as they conform themselves to its dictates. Every rational creature, 'tis said, is obliged to regulate his actions by reason; and, if any other motive or principle challenge the direction of his conduct, he ought to oppose it, till it be entirely subdued, or, at least, brought to a conformity to that superior principle. On this method of thinking, the greatest part of moral philosophy, ancient and modern, seems to be founded."

That those philosophers attended chiefly to the judging power of our moral faculty, appears from the names they gave to its operations, and from the whole of their language concerning it.

The modern philosophy has led men to attend chiefly to their sensations and feelings, and thereby to resolve into mere feeling, complex acts of the mind, of which feeling is only one ingredient.

I had occasion, in the preceding Essays, to observe, that several operations of the mind, to which we give one name, and consider as one act, are compounded of more simple acts inseparably united in our constitution, and that, in these, sensation or feeling often makes one ingredient.

Thus, the appetites of hunger and thirst are compounded of an uneasy sensation, and the desire of food or drink. In our benevolent affections, there is both an agreeable feeling, and a desire of happiness to the object of our affection; and malevolent affections have ingredients of a contrary nature.

In these instances, sensation or feeling is inseparably conjoined with desire. In other instances, we find sensation inseparably conjoined with judgment or belief, and that in two different ways. In some instances, the judgment or belief seems to be the consequence of the sensation, and to be regulated by it. In other instances, the sensation is the consequence of the judgment.

When we perceive an external object by our senses, we have a sensation conjoined with a firm belief of the existence and sensible qualities of the external object. Nor has all the subtilty of metaphysics been able to disjoin what nature has conjoined in our constitution. Des Cartes and Locke endeavoured, by reasoning, to deduce the existence of external objects from our sensations, but in vain. Subsequent philosophers, finding no reason for this connection, endeavoured to throw off the belief of external objects as being unreasonable; but this attempt is no less vain. Nature has doomed us to believe the testimony of our senses, whether we can give a good reason for doing so or not.

In this instance, the belief or judgment is the consequence of the sensation, as the sensation is the consequence of the impression made on the organ of sense.

But in most of the operations of mind in which judgment or belief is combined with feeling, the feeling is the consequence of the judgment, and is regulated by it.

Thus, an account of the good conduct of a friend at a distance gives me a very agreeable feeling, and a contrary account would give me a very uneasy feeling; but these feelings depend entirely upon my belief of the report.

In hope, there is an agreeable feeling, depending upon the belief or expectation of good to come: fear is made up of contrary ingredients; in both, the feeling is regulated by the degree of belief.

In the respect we bear to the worthy, and in our contempt of the worthless, there is both judgment and feeling, and the last depends entirely upon the first.

The same may be said of gratitude for good offices and resentment of injuries.

Let me now consider how I am affected when I see a man exerting himself nobly in a good cause. I am conscious that the effect of his conduct on my mind is complex, though it may be called by one name. I look up to his virtue, I approve, I admire it. In doing so, I have pleasure indeed, or an agreeable feeling; this is granted. But I find myself interested in his success and in his fame. This is affection; it is love and esteem, which is more than mere feeling. The man is the object of this esteem; but in mere feeling there is no object.

I am likewise conscious that this agreeable feeling in me, and this esteem of him, depend entirely upon the judgment I form of his conduct. I judge that this conduct merits esteem; and, while I thus judge, I cannot but esteem him, and contemplate his conduct with pleasure. Persuade me that he was bribed, or that he acted from some mercenary or bad motive, immediately my esteem and my agreeable feeling vanish.

In the approbation of a good action, therefore, there is feeling indeed, but there is also esteem of the agent; and both the feeling and the esteem depend upon the judgment we form of his conduct.

When I exercise my moral faculty about my own actions or those of other men, I am conscious that I judge as well as feel. I accuse and excuse, I acquit and condemn, I assent and dissent, I believe and disbelieve, and doubt. These are sets of judgment, and not feelings.

Every determination of the understanding, with regard to what is true or false, is judgment. That I ought not to steal, or to kill, or to bear false witness, are propositions, of the truth of which I am as well convinced as of any proposition in Euclid. I am conscious that I judge them to be true propositions; and my consciousness makes all other arguments unnecessary, with regard to the operations of my own mind.

That other men judge, as well as feel, in such cases, I am convinced, because they understand me when I express my moral judgment, and express theirs by the same terms and phrases.

Suppose that, in a case well known to both, my friend says—*Such a man did well and worthily, his conduct is highly approvable.* This speech, according to all rules of interpretation, expresses my friend's judgment of the man's conduct. This judgment may be true or false, and I may agree in opinion with him, or I may dissent from him without offence, as we may differ in other matters of judgment.

Suppose, again, that, in relation to the same case, my friend says—*The man's conduct gave me a very agreeable feeling.*

This speech, if approbation be nothing but an agreeable feeling, must have the very same meaning with the first, and express neither more nor less. But this cannot be, for two reasons.

First, Because there is no rule in grammar or rhetoric, nor any usage in language, by which these two speeches can be construed so as to have the same meaning.

The *first* expresses plainly an opinion or judgment of the conduct of the man, but says nothing of the speaker. The *second* only testifies a fact concerning the speaker—to wit, that he had such a feeling.

Another reason why these two speeches cannot mean the same thing is, that the first may be contradicted without any ground of offence, such contradiction being only a difference of opinion, which, to a reasonable man, gives no offence. But the second speech cannot be contradicted without an affront: for, as every man must know his own feelings, to deny that a man had a feeling which he affirms he had, is to charge him with falsehood.

If moral approbation be a real judgment, which produces an agreeable feeling in the mind of him who judges, both speeches are perfectly intelligible, in the most obvious and literal sense. Their meaning is different, but they are related, so that the one may be inferred from the other, as we infer the effect from the cause, or the cause from the effect. I know, that what a man judges to be a very worthy action, he contemplates with pleasure; and what he contemplates with pleasure must, in his judgment, have worth. But the judgment and the feeling are different acts of his mind, though connected as cause and effect. He can express either the one or the other with perfect propriety; but the speech, which expresses his feeling, is altogether improper and inept to express his judgment, for this evident reason, that judgment and feeling, though in some cases connected, are things in their nature different.

If we suppose, on the other hand, that moral approbation is nothing more than an agreeable feeling, occasioned by the contemplation of an action, the second speech, above mentioned, has a distinct meaning, and expresses all that is meant by moral approbation. But the first speech either means the very same thing, (which cannot be, for the reasons already mentioned), or it has no meaning.

Now, we may appeal to the reader, whether, in conversation upon human characters, such speeches as the first are not as frequent, as familiar, and as well understood, as anything in language; and whether they have not been common in all ages that we can trace, and in all languages?

This doctrine, therefore, That moral approbation is merely a feeling without judgment, necessarily carries along with it this consequence, that a form of speech, upon one of the most common topics of discourse, which either has no meaning, or a meaning irreconcilable to all rules of grammar or rhetoric, is found to be common and familiar in all languages and in all ages of the world, while every man knows how to express the meaning, if it have any, in plain and proper language.

Such a consequence I think sufficient to sink any philosophical opinion on which it hangs.

A particular language may have some oddity, or even absurdity, introduced by some man of eminence, from caprice or wrong judgment, and followed by servile imitators, for a time, till it be detected, and, of consequence, discountenanced and dropt; but that the same absurdity should pervade all languages, through all ages, and that, after being detected and exposed, it should still keep its countenance and its place in language as much as before, this can never be while men have understanding.

It may be observed, by the way, that the same argument may be applied, with equal force, against those other paradoxical opinions of modern philosophy, which we before mentioned as connected with this; such as, that beauty and deformity are not at all in the objects to which language universally ascribes them, but are merely feelings in the mind of the spectator; that the secondary qualities are not in external objects, but are merely feelings or sensations in him that perceives them; and, in general, that our external and internal senses are faculties by which we have sensations or feelings only, but by which we do not judge.

That every form of speech which language affords to express our judgment, should, in all ages and in all languages, be used to express what is no judgment; and that feelings which are easily expressed in proper language, should as universally be expressed by language altogether improper and absurd, I cannot believe; and, therefore, must conclude, that, if language be the expression of thought, men judge of the primary and secondary qualities of body by their external senses, of beauty and deformity by their taste, and of virtue and vice by their moral faculty.

A truth so evident as this is, can hardly be obscured and brought into doubt, but by the abuse of words. And much abuse of words there has been upon this subject. To avoid this as much as possible, I have used the word *judgment* on one side, and *sensation* or *feeling* upon the other; because these words have been least liable to abuse or ambiguity. But it may be proper to make some observations upon other words that have been used in this controversy.

Mr Hume, in his "Treatise of Human Nature," has employed two sections upon it, the titles of which are, "*Moral Distinctions not derived from Reason*," and "*Moral Distinctions derived from a Moral Sense.*"

When he is not, by custom, led unawares to speak of Reason like other men, he limits that word to signify only the power of judging in matters merely speculative. Hence he concludes, "That reason of itself is inactive and perfectly inert"; that "actions may be laudable or blamable, but cannot be reasonable or unreasonable"; that "it is not contrary to reason to prefer the destruction of the whole world to the scratching of my finger"; that "it is not contrary to reason for me to chuse my total ruin to prevent the least uneasiness of an Indian, or of a person wholly unknown to me"; that "reason is, and ought only to be, the slave of the passions, and can never pretend to any other office than to serve and obey them."

If we take the word *reason* to mean what common use, both of philosophers and of the vulgar, hath made it to mean, these maxims are not only false, but licentious. It is only his abuse of the words *reason* and *passion* that can justify them from this censure.

The meaning of a common word is not to be ascertained by philosophical theory, but by common usage; and, if a man will take the liberty of limiting or extending the meaning of common words at his pleasure, he may, like Mandeville, insinuate the most licentious paradoxes with the appearance of plausibility. I have before made some observations upon the meaning of this word (Essay II., chap. 2, and Essay III., part iii. chap. 1), to which the reader is referred.

When Mr Hume derives moral distinctions from a Moral Sense, I agree with him in words, but we differ about the meaning of the word *sense*. Every power to which the name of a Sense has been given, is a power of judging of the objects of that Sense, and has been accounted such in all ages; the moral sense, therefore, is the power of judging in morals. But Mr Hume will have the Moral Sense to be only a power of feeling without judging—this I take to be an abuse of a word.

Authors who place moral approbation in feeling only, very often use the word *Sentiment*, to express feeling without judgment. This I take likewise to be an abuse of a word. Our moral determinations may, with propriety, be called *moral sentiments*. For the word *sentiment*, in the English language, never, as I conceive, signifies mere feeling, but *judgment accompanied with feeling*. It was wont to signify opinion or judgment of any kind, but, of late, is appropriated to signify an opinion or judgment, that strikes, and produces some agreeable or uneasy emotion. So we speak of sentiments of respect, of esteem, of gratitude; but I never heard the pain of the gout, or any other mere feeling, called a sentiment.

Even the word *judgment* has been used by Mr Hume to express what he maintains to be only a feeling. "Treatise of Human Nature," part iii., page 3: "The term *perception* is no less applicable to those *judgments* by which we distinguish moral good and evil than to every other operation of the mind." Perhaps he used this word inadvertently; for I think there cannot be a greater abuse of words than to put judgment for what he held to be mere feeling.

All the words most commonly used, both by philosophers and by the vulgar, to express the operations of our moral faculty—such as, *decision, determination, sentence, approbation, disapprobation, applause, censure, praise, blame*—necessarily imply judgment in their meaning. When, therefore, they are used by Mr Hume, and others who hold his opinion, to signify feelings only, this is an abuse of words. If these philosophers wish to speak plainly and properly, they must, in discoursing of morals, discard these words altogether, because their established signification in the language is contrary to what they would express by them.

They must likewise discard from morals the words *ought* and *ought not*, which very properly express judgment, but cannot be applied to mere feelings. Upon these words Mr Hume has made a particular observation in the conclusion of his first section above mentioned. I shall give it in his own words, and make some remarks upon it.

"I cannot forbear adding to these reasonings an observation which may, perhaps, be found of some importance. In every system of morality which I have hitherto met with, I have always remarked that the author proceeds for some time in the ordinary way of reasoning, and establishes the being of a God, or makes observations concerning human affairs; when, of a sudden, I am surprised to find that, instead of the usual copulations of propositions, *is*, and *is not*, I meet with no proposition that is not connected with an *ought* or an *ought not*. This chance is imperceptible, but is, however, of the last consequence. For, as this *ought* or *ought not* expresses some new relation or affirmation, 'tis necessary that it should be observed and explained; and, at the same time, that a reason should be given for what seems altogether inconceivable—how this new relation can be a deduction from others which are entirely different from it. But, as authors do not commonly use this precaution, I shall presume to recommend it to the readers; and am persuaded that this small attention would subvert all the vulgar systems of morality, and let us see that the distinction of vice and virtue is not founded merely on the relations of objects, nor is perceived by reason."

We may here observe, that it is acknowledged that the words *ought* and *ought not* express some relation or affirmation; but a relation or affirmation which Mr Hume thought inexplicable, or, at least, inconsistent with his system of morals. He must, therefore, have thought that they ought not to be used in treating of that subject.

He likewise makes two demands, and, taking it for granted that they cannot be satisfied, is persuaded that an attention to this is sufficient to subvert all the vulgar systems of morals.

The *first* demand is, that *ought* and *ought not* be explained.

To a man that understands English, there are surely no words that require explanation less. Are not all men taught, from their early years, that they ought not to lie, nor steal, nor swear falsely? But Mr Hume thinks, that men never understood what these precepts mean, or rather that they are unintelligible. If this be so, I think indeed it will follow, that all the vulgar systems of morals are subverted.

Dr Johnson, in his Dictionary, explains the word *ought* to signify, *being obliged by duty;* and I know no better explication that can be given of it. The reader will see what I thought necessary to say concerning the moral relation expressed by this word in Essay III., part iii, chap. 5.

The *second* demand is, That a reason should be given why this relation should be a deduction from others which are entirely different from it.

This is to demand a reason for what does not exist. The first principles of morals are not deductions. They are self-evident; and their truth, like that of other axioms, is perceived without reasoning or deduction. And moral truths that are not self-evident are deduced, not from relations quite different from them, but from the first principles of morals.

In a matter so interesting to mankind, and so frequently the subject of conversation among the learned and the unlearned as morals is, it may surely be expected that men will express both their judgments and their feelings with propriety, and consistently with the rules of language. An opinion, therefore, which makes the language of all ages and nations, upon this subject, to be improper, contrary to all rules of language, and fit to be discarded, needs no other refutation.

As mankind have, in all ages, understood *reason* to mean the power by which not only our speculative opinions, but our actions ought to be regulated, we may say, with perfect propriety, that all vice is contrary to reason; that, by reason, we are to judge of what we ought to do, as well as of what we ought to believe.

But, though all vice be contrary to reason, I conceive that it would not be a proper definition of vice to say that it is a conduct contrary to reason, because this definition would apply equally to folly, which all men distinguish from vice.

There are other phrases which have been used on the same side of the question, which I see no reason for adopting, such as—*acting contrary to the relations of things—contrary to the reason of things—to the fitness of things—to the truth of things—to absolute fitness*. These phrases have not the authority of common use, which, in matters of language, is great. They seem to have been invented by some authors, with a view to explain the nature of vice; but I do not think they answer that end. If intended as definitions of vice, they are improper; because, in the most favourable sense they can bear, they extend to every kind of foolish and absurd conduct, as well as to that which is vicious.

I shall conclude this chapter with some observations upon the five arguments which Mr Hume has offered upon his point in his "Enquiry."

The *first* is, That it is impossible that the hypothesis he opposes, can, in any particular instance, be so much as rendered intelligible, whatever specious figure it may make in general discourse. "Examine," says he, "the crime of *ingratitude*, anatomize all its circumstances, and examine, by your reason alone, in what consists the demerit or blame, you will never come to any issue or conclusion."

I think it unnecessary to follow him through all the accounts of ingratitude which he conceives may be given by those whom he opposes, because I agree with him in that which he himself adopts—to wit, "That this crime arises from a complication of circumstances, which, being presented to the spectator, excites the sentiment of blame by the particular structure and fabric of his mind."

This he thought a true and intelligible account of the criminality of ingratitude. So do I. And therefore I think the hypothesis he opposes is intelligible, when applied to a particular instance.

Mr Hume, no doubt, thought that the account he gives of ingratitude is inconsistent with the hypothesis he opposes, and could not be adopted by those who hold that hypothesis. He could be led to think so, only by taking for granted one of these two things. Either, *first*, That the *sentiment of blame* is a feeling only, without judgment; or, *secondly*, That whatever is excited by the particular fabric and structure of the mind must be feeling only, and not judgment. But I cannot grant either the one or the other.

For, as to the *first*, it seems evident to me, that both *sentiment* and *blame* imply judgment; and, therefore, that the *sentiment of blame* is a judgment accompanied with feeling, and not mere feeling without judgment.

The *second* can as little be granted; for no operation of mind, whether judgment or feeling, can be excited but by that particular structure and fabric of the mind which makes us capable of that operation.

By that part of our fabric which we call *the faculty of seeing*, we judge of visible objects; by *taste*, another part of our fabric, we judge of beauty and deformity; by that part of our fabric which enables us to form abstract conceptions, to compare them, and perceive their relations, we judge of abstract truths; and by that part of our fabric which we call the *moral faculty*, we judge of virtue and vice. If we suppose a being without any moral faculty in his fabric, I grant that he could not have the sentiments of blame and moral approbation.

There are, therefore, judgments, as well as feelings, that are excited by the particular structure and fabric of the mind. But there is this remarkable difference between them, That every judgment is, in its own nature, true or false; and, though it depends upon the fabric of a mind, whether it have such a judgment or not, it depends not upon that fabric whether the judgment be true or not. A true judgment will be true, whatever be the fabric of the mind; but a particular structure and fabric is necessary, in order to our perceiving that truth. Nothing like this can be said of mere feelings, because the attributes of true or false do not belong to them.

Thus I think it appears, that the hypothesis which Mr Hume opposes is not unintelligible, when applied to the particular instance of ingratitude; because the account of ingratitude which he himself thinks true and intelligible, is perfectly agreeable to it.

The *second* argument amounts to this: That, in moral deliberation, we must be acquainted beforehand with all the objects and all their relations. After these things are known, the understanding has no farther room to operate. Nothing remains but to feel, on our part, some sentiment of blame or approbation.

Let us apply this reasoning to the office of a judge. In a cause that comes before him, he must, be made acquainted with all the objects, and all their relations. After this, his understanding has no farther room to operate. Nothing remains, on his part, but to feel the right or the wrong: and mankind have, very absurdly, called him a *judge*—he ought to be called a *feeler*.

To answer this argument more directly: The man who deliberates, after all the objects and relations mentioned by Mr Hume are known to him, has a point to determine; and that is, whether the action under his deliberation ought to be done or ought not. In most cases, this point will appear self-evident to a man who has been accustomed to exercise his moral judgment; in some cases it may require reasoning.

In like manner, the judge, after all the circumstances of the cause are known, has to judge whether the plaintiff has a just plea or not.

The *third* argument is taken from the analogy between moral beauty and natural, between moral sentiment and taste. As beauty is not a quality of the object, but a certain feeling of the spectator, so virtue and vice are not qualities in the persons to whom language ascribes them, but feelings of the spectator.

But is it certain that beauty is not any quality of the object? This is indeed a paradox of modern philosophy, built upon a philosophical theory; but a paradox so contrary to the common language and common sense of mankind, that it ought rather to overturn the theory on which it stands, than receive any support from it. And if beauty be really a quality of the object, and not merely a feeling of the spectator, the whole force of this argument goes over to the other side of the question.

"Euclid," he says, "has fully explained all the qualities of the circle, but has not, in any proposition, said a word of its beauty. The reason is evident. The beauty is not a quality of the circle."

By the *qualities of the circle*, he must mean its properties; and there are here two mistakes.

First, Euclid has not fully explained all the properties of the circle. Many have been discovered and demonstrated which he never dreamt of.

Secondly, The reason why Euclid has not said a word of the beauty of the circle, is not, *that beauty is not a quality of the circle;* the reason is, that Euclid never digresses from his subject. His purpose was to demonstrate the mathematical properties of the circle. Beauty is a quality of the circle, not demonstrable by mathematical reasoning, but immediately perceived by a good taste. To speak of it would have been a digression from his subject; and that is a fault he is never guilty of.

The *fourth* argument is, That inanimate objects may bear to each other all the same relations which we observe in moral agents.

If this were true, it would be very much to the purpose; but it seems to be thrown out rashly, without any attention to its evidence. Had Mr Hume reflected but a very little upon this dogmatical assertion, a thousand instances would have occurred to him in direct contradiction to it.

May not one animal be more tame, or more docile, or more cunning, or more fierce, or more ravenous, than another? Are these relations to be found in inanimate objects? May not one man be a better painter, or sculptor, or ship-builder, or tailor, or shoemaker, than another? Are these relations to be found in inanimate objects, or even in brute animals? May not one moral agent be more just, more pious, more attentive to any moral duty, or more eminent in any moral virtue, than another? Are not these relations peculiar to moral agents? But to come to the relations most essential to morality.

When I say that *I ought to do such an action*, that *it is my duty,* do not these words express a relation between me and a certain action in my power; a relation which cannot be between inanimate objects, or between any other objects but a moral agent and his moral actions; a relation which is well understood by all men come to years of understanding, and expressed in all languages?

Again, when in deliberating about two actions in my power, which cannot both be done, I say *this* ought to be preferred to the other—that justice, for instance, ought to be preferred to generosity—I express a moral relation between two actions of a moral agent, which is well understood, and which cannot exist between objects of any other kind.

There are, therefore, moral relations which can have no existence but between moral agents and their voluntary actions. To determine these relations is the object of morals; and to determine relations is the province of judgment, not of mere feeling.

The *last* argument is a chain of several propositions, which deserve distinct consideration. They may, I think, be summed up in these four: 1. There must be ultimate ends of action, beyond which it is absurd to ask a reason of acting. 2. The ultimate ends of human actions can never be accounted for by reason; 3. but recommend themselves entirely to the sentiments and affections of mankind, without any dependence on the intellectual faculties. 4. As virtue is an end, and is desirable on its own account, without fee or reward, merely for the immediate satisfaction it conveys; it is requisite that there should be some sentiment which it touches, some internal taste or feeling, or whatever you please to call it, which distinguishes moral good and evil, and which embraces the one and rejects the other.

To the *first* of these propositions I entirely agree. The ultimate ends of action are what I have called *the principles of action*, which I have endeavoured, in the third Essay, to enumerate, and to class under three heads of mechanical, animal, and rational.

The *second* proposition needs some explication. I take its meaning to be, That there cannot be another end, for the sake of which an ultimate end is pursued. For the reason of an action means nothing but the end for which the action is done; and the reason of an end of action can mean nothing but another end, for the sake of which that end is pursued, and to which it is the means.

That this is the author's meaning is evident from his reasoning in confirmation of it. "Ask a man, *why he uses exercise?* he will answer, *because he desires to keep his health.* If you then inquire, *why he desires health?* He will readily reply, *because sickness is painful.* If you push your inquiries further, and desire a reason why he hates pain, it is impossible he can ever give any. This is an ultimate end, and is never referred to any other object." To account by reason for an end, therefore, is to shew another end, for the sake of which that end is desired and pursued. And that, in this sense, an ultimate end can never be accounted for by reason, is certain, because that can-

not be an ultimate end which is pursued only for the sake of another end.

I agree therefore with Mr Hume in this second proposition, which indeed is implied in the first.

The *third* proposition is, That ultimate ends recommend themselves entirely to the sentiments and affections of mankind, without any dependence on the intellectual faculties.

By *sentiments* he must here mean feelings without judgment, and by *affections*, such affections as imply no judgment. For surely any operation that implies judgment, cannot be independent of the intellectual faculties.

This being understood, I cannot assent to this proposition.

The author seems to think it implied in the preceding, or a necessary consequence from it, that because an ultimate end cannot be accounted for by reason—that is, cannot be pursued merely for the sake of another end—therefore it can have no dependence on the intellectual faculties. I deny this consequence, and can see no force in it.

I think it not only does not follow from the preceding proposition, but that it is contrary to truth.

A man may act from gratitude as an ultimate end; but gratitude implies a judgment and belief of favours received, and therefore is dependent on the intellectual faculties. A man may act from respect to a worthy character as an ultimate end; but this respect necessarily implies a judgment of worth in the person, and therefore is dependent on the intellectual faculties.

I have endeavoured, in the third Essay before mentioned, to shew that, beside the animal principles of our nature, which require will and intention, but not judgment, there are also in human nature rational principles of action, or ultimate ends, which have, in all ages, been called rational, and have a just title to that name, not only from the authority of language, but because they can have no existence but in beings endowed with reason, and because, in all their exertions, they require not only intention and will, but judgment or reason.

Therefore, until it can be proved that an ultimate end cannot be dependent on the intellectual faculties, this third proposition, and all that hangs upon it, must fall to the ground.

The *last* proposition assumes, with very good reason, That virtue is an ultimate end, and desirable on its own account. From which, if the third proposition were true, the conclusion would undoubtedly follow, That virtue has no dependence on the intellectual faculties. But, as that proposition is not granted, nor proved, this conclusion is left without any support from the whole of the argument.

I should not have thought it worth while to insist so long upon this controversy, if I did not conceive that the consequences which the contrary opinions draw after them are important.

If what we call *moral judgment* be no real judgment, but merely a feeling, it follows that the principles of morals which we have been taught to consider as an immutable law to all intelligent beings, have no other foundation but an arbitrary structure and fabric in the constitution of the human mind. So that, by a change in our structure, what is immoral might become moral, virtue might be turned into vice, and vice into virtue. And beings of a different structure, according to the variety of their feelings, may have different, nay opposite measures of moral good and evil.

It follows that, from our notions of morals, we can conclude nothing concerning a moral character in the Deity, which is the foundation of all religion, and the strongest support of virtue.

Nay, this opinion seems to conclude strongly against a moral character in the Deity, since nothing arbitrary or mutable can be conceived to enter into the description of a nature eternal, immutable, and necessarily existent. Mr Hume seems perfectly consistent with himself, in allowing of no evidence for the moral attributes of the Supreme Being, whatever there may be for his natural attributes.

On the other hand, if moral judgment be a true and real judgment, the principles of morals stand upon the immutable foundation of truth, and can undergo no change by any difference of fabric, or structure of those who judge of them. There may be, and there are, beings, who have not the faculty of conceiving moral truths, or perceiving the excellence of moral worth, as there are beings incapable of perceiving mathematical truths; but no defect, no error of understanding, can make what is true be false.

If it be true that piety, justice, benevolence, wisdom, temperance, fortitude, are, in their own nature, the most excellent and most amiable qualities of a human creature; that vice has an inherent turpitude, which merits disapprobation and dislike; these truths cannot be hid from Him whose understanding is infinite, whose judgment is always according to truth, and who must esteem everything according to its real value.

The Judge of all the earth, we are sure, will do right. He has given to men the faculty of perceiving the right and the wrong in conduct, as far as is necessary to our present state, and of perceiving the dignity of the one, and the demerit of the other; and surely there can be no real knowledge or real excellence in man, which is not in his Maker.

We may therefore justly conclude, That what we know in part, and see in part, of right and wrong, He sees perfectly; that the moral excellence, which we see and admire in some of our fellow-creatures is a faint but true copy of that moral excellence which is essential to His nature; and that to tread the path of virtue, is the true dignity of our nature, an imitation of God, and the way to obtain His favour.

Jean-Jacques Rousseau

ROUSSEAU WAS BORN IN GENEVA ON JUNE 28, 1712, TO A SENTIMENTAL BUT INAT-tentive watchmaker and his wife, who died in childbirth, a tragedy for which Isaac Rousseau apparently blamed his son. The young Rousseau was cared for mostly by his aunts, his father often being absent abroad to ply his trade. Rousseau was a precocious child, whose education seems to have consisted mainly in reading—most notably Plutarch (in French translation)—his father's limited library. When he was twelve, he was sent to a Calvinist pastor named Lambercier to be educated. In the following years Rousseau was apprenticed to various trades, including engraving, which he deserted to escape brutality. When nearly seventeen, he was sent by a Catholic priest to the house of a recently converted Catholic, the Baronne de Warens, a young widow who lived in Annecy. Rousseau converted (though he never took his religion very seriously), and, by the age of twenty, was sharing the Baronne's bed in a relationship that he later compared to incest.

For the next ten years, Rousseau studied and wrote, accepting several casual posts that periodically separated him from Mme. De Warens. His first publication of any note, *Project for the Education of M. de Sainte-Marie*, appeared in 1741. In 1742, he went to live in Paris, and, at the age of thirty, began a new career. He managed to connect himself well, one influential patron leading to another. He met Voltaire and Diderot, and read his *Project for a New Musical Notation* to the Academy of Science. In 1743, he became secretary to the ambassador in Venice, and wrote *A Dissertation on Modern Music*. A year later, however, he had a falling out with the ambassador and returned to Paris. There he met Thérèse Levasseur, who became his mistress and bore him five children in rapid succession, all of whom they turned over to foundling homes. He did eventually marry her, but not until twenty-four years later. The same year, 1745, he completed his first opera, *Les Muses galantes*, and, in the following four years, a play and the articles on music for Diderot's *Encyclopedia*.

Rousseau's breakthrough as a public figure came in 1750. On the way to visit Diderot in prison, Rousseau saw an announcement for a prize essay offered by the Academy of Dijon on the topic "Has the reestablishment of the arts and sciences contributed to the purification or the corruption of morals?" Rousseau took the negative side of the question, and won the prize with *A Discourse on the Arts and Sciences* (The First Discourse). In the following year, he engaged in some highly visible polemical exchanges over this essay. Though the establishment dubbed him a subversive, the whole incident made him a major figure, bearing out the adage that there is no such thing as bad publicity. The following year, 1752, saw the successful presentation at Fontainebleau of his opera *Le Devin du village*, and the year after that, we have the *Letter on French Music*.

By 1754, Rousseau was estranged from Catholicism, and he returned to Geneva and the Calvinist church. In 1755, he published the Second Discourse, *A Discourse on the Origins of Inequality*, and *Discourse on Political Economy* (a chapter in Diderot's *Encyclopedia*).

In 1756, he went to live at the Hermitage, a cottage near Montmorency, with his mistress and her mother, where he continued writing, and began work on *La Nouvelle Héloïse (ou Julie)*, published in 1761 with huge success. At this time also, he wrote a reply to d'Alembert's article on Geneva, which opposed the introduction of a (gasp!) theater to Calvinist Geneva. By 1760, he was hard at work on his two greatest essays, *Émile* and *The Social Contract*, which were published in 1762. In the same year, *The Social Contract* was condemned by the Genevan Council of Twenty-Five as seditious, an opinion in which Voltaire, then living in Geneva and active in politics, concurred. Outrage was not limited to Geneva; the following year, 1763, found Rousseau replying to an attack on *Émile* written by the archbishop of Paris, as well as preparing the *Dictionary of Music*.

At the age of fifty-two, Rousseau was beginning to work on the first part of the *Confessions*, and the following year he began the *Project for a Constitution of Corsica*, a work he never finished. In 1766, he went to England in the company of David Hume. Quarreling with Hume, he returned to Paris in 1767. Though gratified to find the *Dictionary of Music* on sale, he seems to have suffered serious mental distress and depression at this time. In 1768, he finally married Thérèse. Three years later, he finished the second part of the *Confessions*, and *Considerations on the Government of Poland*, and began work on *Rousseau juge de Jean-Jacques*. In 1774, he wrote a *Dictionary of Botanical Terms*. In 1776, he began his last substantial work, *Reveries of a Solitary Walker*. He died July 2, 1778.

NOTES ON THE TEXT

Jean-Jacques Rousseau departs from Locke and Hobbes in that he rejects the idea of natural law as a foundation for moral and political theory. Indeed, he seems to reject the idea of all external sources of value. For Rousseau, the source of value is in ourselves, not God or nature. Despite this, Rousseau has the most ambitious and demanding moral and political theory of all. Rousseau does posit a central value around which all his thought revolves: the value of liberty. To be a free person entails not being subordinate to the will of another person. This is not an external value; rather, it is one to which human beings are committed by virtue of being human. In arguing against the possibility of selling oneself into slavery, in *The Social Contract* Rousseau says, "To renounce your liberty is to renounce your very quality of manhood . . . such a renunciation is incompatible with the nature of man" (book I, chapter 4). Thus starts a long tradition from Rousseau to Kant, to Hegel and to Marx, and into the twentieth century through innumerable variants of these four thinkers. It is around this idea of the fundamental value of liberty that the *Discourse on Inequality* and *The Social Contract* must be understood. The first is basically about humanity's loss of liberty and the second is about the kind of social and political organization that can restore it.

Rousseau's *Discourse on Inequality* is an early anthropological essay that seeks to elaborate a model of social development to answer the question of how men have become unequal in wealth, power, and status in civilization and thus why some have become subordinated to others. The discourse relates the long and sad tale of the change from natural liberty in savage man to civilized enslavement among men. Rousseau's image of the initial state of nature in which human beings find themselves is nearly the reverse of what Locke or Hobbes thought. There is little or no conflict in this state of nature, and social relations are few. The reason for this is that human beings are essentially stupid and unimaginative. As a consequence, they have few desires; all they seek is to satisfy basic needs. Since this doesn't take much effort, men and women work for only a few hours a day and do not need each other's cooperation. Nor do they enter into competition as Hobbes had thought, since they do not have the imagination to think about the future. They live merely from day to day. They do not come into conflict over sexual partners because they do not make distinctions. Here humanity is happy because its simple and limited desires are all geared to the natural environment around them and so are rarely frustrated.

But this is not a stable situation. For human beings have another feature that Rousseau calls perfectibility. Though humans are unimaginative at first, there is a mechanism in them that expands the imagination. The more one sees and has, the more one can imagine seeing and having. And the more objects one can imagine, the more objects one desires. Savage man is happy because he doesn't know what he is missing, but that can't remain the case. Each person's horizon expands over time and over different objects. And over generations, this imagination expands even more. Hence at the end of the road, humans' desires far outstrip anything they can possibly have. In order to satisfy their increasing desires, humans must eventually enter into communities to cooperate with others. But this simply produces more grist for the imagination, and they must have more. They eventually develop a division of labor. Then they develop technologies that enable them to farm and then to mine metals. Eventually an institution develops for dividing up the land: property. And this institution brings about the distinction between those who own property and those who do not and who must thereby work for others: the first great inequality. Since it is hard to be happy working all the time for others, political institutions develop that make sure the poor stay in their place. But these institutions bring about a new form of inequality: that between the politically powerful and the powerless. Initially, political institutions are elective, but this form of government brings about so much conflict as a result of the overreaching ambition of politicians that eventually the only way to achieve stability is to place all power in the hands of omnipotent despots. And so, as Rousseau puts it in the beginning of *The Social Contract*, "Man is born free, and everywhere he is in chains."

It is the goal of *The Social Contract* to show how liberty can be regained and how political institutions can be made legitimate. Human beings are so fundamentally transformed by the development of civilization that there is no possibility for them to return to the state of natural liberty from which they came. But Rousseau thinks they can regain a liberty of even greater importance: moral liberty, which lets them become masters of themselves. The question Rousseau poses is how "to find a form of association which defends and protects the person and property of each member with the whole force of the community, and where each, while joining with all the rest, still obeys no one but himself and remains as free as before" (book I, chapter 6). Rousseau's answer to this is to find a form of political organization wherein each puts his person and powers under the direction of the general will. What is this general will? Essentially, the idea is that there is a way of organizing society that everyone can willingly agree to. Everyone shares a concern that the society be structured in that way, as long as each takes into account the fact that everyone else wants to be free as much as he or she does. Hence, they share a will about how to organize society. To the extent that they submit to the direction of this will, each is only following his or her own will. Thus each person is subjected to rules that he or she willingly agrees to. So each person lives only under a rule that he or she imposes on himself or herself. Rousseau calls the people, which has the general will, the sovereign. The basic aim of the general will is the common good. And the only method by which the general will can be achieved is by means of general laws. Laws that are chosen in accordance with the general will cannot discriminate in favor of or against any particular persons or group of persons in the society. Otherwise, they would merely be the will of the group that was favored.

Rousseau's view is complicated by the fact that individuals do not always know what the general will is. It isn't just what everyone happens to think or want at a particular point in time. The reason for this is that what people think is conditioned by their social and political environment. And some social environments can corrupt people and make them think only of their individual self-interest or only of their short-term interests, while other environments can encourage serious and careful thought about the common good. Even under these circumstances, individuals will not always understand what the general will is in their society. Hence, people will probably end up disagreeing on what the general will is even after the most thoughtful and careful reflection. What Rousseau says here is quite illuminating: Individuals ought to come together to vote on what they think ought to be done. Each person ought to vote only on the basis of what he or she judges to be the general will. Rousseau thinks that under favorable circumstances of reflection, the majority is more likely to be right than the minority and so majority rule is the way to decide most political questions. Those in the minority, knowing that the majority is most likely to be right and that they are in the minority, have reason to adopt the position of the majority. Hence even though they lost out in the vote, they have reason to think that the outcome is in accordance with the general will. This is Rousseau's justification of majority rule and his attempt to demonstrate that it is consistent with each person obeying himself or herself alone.

The other aspects of Rousseau's discussion elaborate the kinds of institutions that are favorable to the understanding of the general will among the people. Hence Rousseau argues, as Locke did, that the executive branch of the association (which he calls the government) ought to be separate from the legislative branch (which is the sovereign). He also articulates principles for how to design the government. One other recommendation that Rousseau makes is his rejection of unlimited religious toleration. He thinks that those whose religious beliefs commit them to thinking that others are damned must be suppressed. Rousseau argues that "it is impossible to live in peace with people whom you consider damned; to love them would be to hate the God who punishes them; you are either to save them or to torment them." He advocates a civil religion that everyone accepts in public and that teaches people to be sociable and just.

The Social Contract

Foreword

This little treatise is part of a larger work which I undertook many years ago without thinking of the limitations of my powers, and have long since abandoned. Of the various fragments that might have been taken from what I wrote, this is the most considerable, and the one I think the least unworthy of being offered to the public. The rest no longer exists.

Book I

My purpose is to consider if, in political society, there can be any legitimate and sure principle of government, taking men as they are and laws as they might be. In this inquiry I shall try always to bring together what right permits with what interest prescribes so that justice and utility are in no way divided.

I start without seeking to prove the importance of my subject. I may be asked whether I am a prince or a legislator that I should be writing about politics. I answer no: and indeed that that is my reason for doing so. If I were a prince or a legislator I should not waste my time saying what ought to be done; I should do it or keep silent.

Born as I was the citizen of a free state and a member of its sovereign body, the very right to vote imposes on me the duty to instruct myself in public affairs, however little influence my voice may have in them. And whenever I reflect upon governments, I am happy to find that my studies always give me fresh reasons for admiring that of my own country.

Chapter 1
The Subject of Book I

Man was born free, and he is everywhere in chains. Those who think themselves the masters of others are indeed greater slaves than they. How did this transformation come about? I do not know. How can it be made legitimate? That question I believe I can answer.

If I were to consider only force and the effects of force, I should say: "So long as a people is constrained to obey, and obeys, it does well; but as soon as it can shake off the yoke, and shakes it off, it does better; for since it regains its freedom by the same right as that which removed it, a people is either justified in taking back its freedom, or there is no justifying those who took it away." But the social order is a sacred right which serves as a basis for all other rights. And as it is not a natural right, it must be one founded on covenants. The problem is to determine what those covenants are. But before we pass on to that question, I must substantiate what I have so far said.

Chapter 2
The First Societies

The oldest of all societies, and the only natural one, is that of the family; yet children remain tied to their father by nature only so long as they need him for their preservation. As soon as this need ends, the natural bond is dissolved. Once the children are freed from the obedience they owe their father, and the father is freed from his responsibilities towards them, both parties equally regain their independence. If they continue to remain united, it is no longer nature, but their own choice, which unites them; and the family as such is kept in being only by agreement.

This common liberty is a consequence of man's nature. Man's first law is to watch over his own preservation; his first care he owes to himself; and as soon as he reaches the age of reason, he becomes the only judge of the best means to preserve himself; he becomes his own master.

The family may therefore perhaps be seen as the first model of political societies: the head of the state bears the image of the father, the people the image of his children, and all, being born free and equal, surrender their freedom only when they see advantage in doing so. The only difference is that in the family, a father's love for his children repays him for the care he bestows on them, while in the state, where the ruler can have no such feeling for his people, the pleasure of commanding must take the place of love.

Grotius denies that all human government is established for the benefit of the governed, and he cites the example of slavery. His characteristic method of reasoning is always to offer fact as a proof of right.[1] It is possible to imagine a more logical method, but not one more favourable to tyrants.

According to Grotius, therefore, it is doubtful whether humanity belongs to a hundred men, or whether these hundred men belong to humanity, though he seems throughout his book to lean to the first of these views, which is also that of Hobbes. These authors show us the human race divided into herds of cattle, each with a master who preserves it only in order to devour its members.

Just as a shepherd possesses a nature superior to that of his flock, so do those shepherds of men, their rulers, have a nature superior to that of their people. Or so, we are told by Philo, the Emperor Caligula argued, concluding, reasonably enough on this same analogy, that kings were gods or alternatively that the people were animals.

The reasoning of Caligula coincides with that of Hobbes and Grotius. Indeed Aristotle, before any of them, said that men were not at all equal by nature, since some were born for slavery and others born to be masters.

Aristotle was right; but he mistook the effect for the cause. Anyone born in slavery is born for slavery —nothing is more certain. Slaves, in their bondage, lose everything, even the desire to be free. They love their servitude even as the companions of Ulysses loved their life as brutes.[2] But if there are slaves by nature, it is only because there has been slavery against nature. Force made the first slaves; and their cowardice perpetuates their slavery.

I have said nothing of the King Adam or of the Emperor Noah, father of the three great monarchs who shared out the universe among them, like the children of Saturn, with whom some authors have identified them. I hope my readers will be grateful for this moderation, for since I am directly descended from one of those princes, and perhaps in the eldest line, how do I know that if the deeds were checked, I might not find myself the legitimate king of the human race? However that may be, there is no gainsaying that Adam was the king of the world, as was Robinson Crusoe of his island, precisely because he was the sole inhabitant; and the great advantage of such an empire was that the monarch, secure upon his throne, had no occasion to fear rebellions, wars, or conspirators.

Chapter 3
The Right of the Strongest

The strongest man is never strong enough to be master all the time, unless he transforms force into right and obedience into duty. Hence "the right of the strongest"—a "right" that sounds like something intended ironically, but is actually laid down as a principle. But shall we never have this phrase explained? Force is a physical power; I do not see how its effects could produce morality. To yield to force is an act of necessity, not of will; it is at best an act of prudence. In what sense can it be a moral duty?

Let us grant, for a moment, that this so-called right exists. I suggest it can only produce a tissue of bewildering nonsense; for once might is made to be right, cause and effect are reversed, and every force which overcomes another force inherits the right which belonged to the vanquished. As soon as man can disobey with impunity, his disobedience becomes legitimate; and as the strongest is always right, the only problem is how to become the strongest. But what can be the validity of a right which perishes with the

---

1. "Learned researches on public law are often only the history of ancient abuses, and one is misled when one gives oneself the trouble of studying them too closely." *Traité manuscrit des intérêts de la France avec ses voisins* par M. L. M. d'A. This is exactly what Grotius does. [Rousseau's quotation is from the Marquis d'Argenson. *Trans.*]

2. See a short treatise of Plutarch entitled: *That Animals use Reason*.

force on which it rests? If force compels obedience, there is no need to invoke a duty to obey, and if force ceases to compel obedience, there is no longer any obligation. Thus the word "right" adds nothing to what is said by "force"; it is meaningless.

"Obey those in power." If this means "yield to force" the precept is sound, but superfluous; it has never, I suggest, been violated. All power comes from God, I agree; but so does every disease, and no one forbids us to summon a physician. If I am held up by a robber at the edge of a wood, force compels me to hand over my purse. But if I could somehow contrive to keep the purse from him, would I still be obliged in conscience to surrender it? After all, the pistol in the robber's hand is undoubtedly a *power.*

Surely it must be admitted, then, that might does not make right, and that the duty of obedience is owed only to legitimate powers. Thus we are constantly led back to my original question.

Chapter 4
Slavery

Since no man has any natural authority over his fellows, and since force alone bestows no right, all legitimate authority among men must be based on covenants.

Grotius says: "If an individual can alienate his freedom and become the slave of a master, why may not a whole people alienate its freedom and become the subject of a king?" In this remark there are several ambiguous words which call for explanation; but let us confine ourselves to one—to "alienate." To alienate is to give or sell. A man who becomes the slave of another does not give himself, he sells himself in return for at least a subsistence. But in return for what could a whole people be said to sell itself? A king, far from nourishing his subjects, draws his nourishment from them; and kings, according to Rabelais, need more than a little nourishment. Do subjects, then, give their persons to the king on condition that he will accept their property as well? If so, I fail to see what they have left to preserve.

It will be said that a despot gives his subjects the assurance of civil tranquillity. Very well, but what does it profit them, if those wars against other powers which result from a despot's ambition, if his insatiable greed, and the oppressive demands of his administration, cause more desolation than civil strife would cause? What do the people gain if their very condition

of civil tranquillity is one of their hardships? There is peace in dungeons, but is that enough to make dungeons desirable? The Greeks lived in peace in the cave of Cyclops awaiting their turn to be devoured.

To speak of a man giving himself in return for nothing is to speak of what is absurd, unthinkable; such an action would be illegitimate, void, if only because no one who did it could be in his right mind. To say the same of a whole people is to conjure up a nation of lunatics; and right cannot rest on madness.

Even if each individual could alienate himself, he cannot alienate his children. For they are born men; they are born free; their liberty belongs to them; no one but they themselves has the right to dispose of it. Before they reach the years of discretion, their father may, in their name, make certain rules for their protection and their welfare, but he cannot give away their liberty irrevocably and unconditionally, for such a gift would be contrary to the natural order and an abuse of paternal right. Hence, an arbitrary government would be legitimate only if every new generation were free to accept or reject it, and in that case the government would cease to be arbitrary.

To renounce freedom is to renounce one's humanity, one's rights as a man and equally one's duties. There is no possible *quid pro quo* for one who renounces everything; indeed such renunciation is contrary to man's very nature; for if you take away all freedom of the will, you strip a man's actions of all moral significance. Finally, any covenant which stipulated absolute dominion for one party and absolute obedience for the other would be illogical and nugatory. Is it not evident that he who is entitled to demand everything owes nothing? And does not the single fact of there being no reciprocity, no mutual obligation, nullify the act? For what right can my slave have against me? If everything he has belongs to me, his right is *my* right, and it would be nonsense to speak of my having a right *against* myself.

Grotius and the rest claim to find in war another justification for the so-called right of slavery. They argue that the victor's having the right to kill the vanquished implies that the vanquished has the right to purchase his life at the expense of his liberty—a bargain thought to be the more legitimate because it is advantageous to both parties.

But it is clear that this so-called right to kill the vanquished cannot be derived from the state of war. For this reason alone, that men living in their primitive condition of independence have no intercourse regular enough to constitute either a state of peace or a state of war; and men are not naturally enemies. It is conflicts over things, not quarrels between men which constitute war, and the state of war cannot arise from mere personal relations, but only from property relations. Private wars between one man and another can exist neither in a state of nature, where there is no fixed property, nor in society, where everything is under the authority of law.

Private fights, duels, encounters, do not constitute any kind of state; and as for the private wars that were permitted by the ordinances of Louis IX, King of France, and suspended by the Peace of God, these were no more than an abuse of feudal government, an irrational system if there ever was one, and contrary both to natural justice and to all sound polity.

War, then, is not a relation between men, but between states; in war individuals are enemies wholly by chance, not as men, not even as citizens,[1] but only as soldiers; not as members of their country, but only as its defenders. In a word, a state can have as an enemy only another state, not men, because there can be no real relation between things possessing different intrinsic natures.

This principle conforms to the established rules of all times and to the constant practice of every political society. Declarations of war are warnings not so much to governments as to their subjects. The foreigner—whether he is a king, a private person or a whole people—who robs, kills, or detains the subjects of another prince without first declaring war against that prince, is not an enemy but a brigand. Even in the midst of war, a just prince, seizing what

he can of public property in the enemy's territory, nevertheless respects the persons and possessions of private individuals; he respects the principles on which his own rights are based. Since the aim of war is to subdue a hostile state, a combatant has the right to kill the defenders of that state while they are armed; but as soon as they lay down their arms and surrender, they cease to be either enemies or instruments of the enemy; they become simply men once more, and no one has any longer the right to take their lives. It is sometimes possible to destroy a state without killing a single one of its members, and war gives no right to inflict any more destruction than is necessary for victory. These principles were not invented by Grotius, nor are they founded on the authority of the poets; they are derived from the nature of things; they are based on reason.

The right of conquest has no other foundation than the law of the strongest. And if war gives the conqueror no right to massacre a conquered people, no such right can be invoked to justify their enslavement. Men have the right to kill their enemies only when they cannot enslave them, so the right of enslaving cannot be derived from the right to kill. It would therefore be an iniquitous barter to make the vanquished purchase with their liberty the lives over which the victor has no legitimate claim. An argument basing the right over life and death on the right to enslave, and the right to enslave on the right over life and death, is an argument trapped in a vicious circle.

Even if we assumed that this terrible right of massacre did exist, then slaves of war, or a conquered people, would be under no obligation to obey their master any further than they were forced to do so. By taking an equivalent of his victim's life, the victor shows him no favour; instead of destroying him unprofitably, he destroys him by exploiting him. Hence, far from the victor having acquired some further authority beside that of force over the vanquished, the state of war between them continues; their mutual relation is the effect of war, and the continuation of the rights of war implies that there has been no treaty of peace. An agreement has assuredly been made, but that agreement, far from ending the state of war, presupposes its continuation.

Thus, however we look at the question, the "right" of slavery is seen to be void; void, not only because it cannot be justified, but also because it is nonsensical, because it has no meaning. The words "slavery" and "right" are contradictory, they cancel each other out.

---

1. The Romans, who understood and respected the rights of war better than any other nation, carried their scruples on this subject so far that a citizen was forbidden to volunteer without engaging himself expressly against the enemy and against an enemy specifically named. When the legion in which the younger Cato fought his first campaign under Popilius was re-formed, the elder Cato wrote to Popilius saying that if he wished his son to continue to serve under him, he should administer a fresh military oath, on the grounds that his son's first oath was annulled, and that he could no longer bear arms against the enemy. Cato also wrote to his son warning him not to go into battle without first taking the oath.

I realize that the siege of Clusium and other incidents from Roman history may be quoted against me, but I am citing laws and customs. No nation has broken its own laws less frequently than the Romans, and no nation has ever had such excellent laws. [Footnote added in the Edition of 1782.]

Whether as between one man and another, or between one man and a whole people, it would always be absurd to say: "I hereby make a covenant with you which is wholly at your expense and wholly to my advantage; I will respect it so long as I please and you shall respect it so long as I wish."

Chapter 5
That We Must Always Go Back to an Original Covenant

Even if I were to concede all that I have so far refuted, the champions of despotism would be no better off. There will always be a great difference between subduing a multitude and ruling a society. If one man successively enslaved many separate individuals, no matter how numerous, he and they would never bear the aspect of anything but a master and his slaves, not at all that of a people and their ruler; an aggregation, perhaps, but certainly not an association, for they would neither have a common good nor be a body politic. Even if such a man were to enslave half the world, he would remain a private individual, and his interest, always at variance with that of the others, would never be more than a personal interest. When he died, the empire he left would be scattered for lack of any bond of union, even as an oak crumbles and falls into a heap of ashes when fire has consumed it.

"A people," says Grotius, "may give itself to a king." Therefore, according to Grotius a people is *a people* even before the gift to the king is made. The gift itself is a civil act; it presupposes public deliberation. Hence, before considering the act by which a people submits to a king, we ought to scrutinize the act by which people become *a* people, for that act, being necessarily antecedent to the other, is the real foundation of society.

Indeed, if there were no earlier agreement, then how, unless the election were unanimous, could there be any obligation on the minority to accept the decision of the majority? What right have the hundred who want to have a master to vote on behalf of the ten who do not? The law of majority-voting itself rests on a covenant, and implies that there has been on at least one occasion unanimity.

Chapter 6
The Social Pact

I assume that men reach a point where the obstacles to their preservation in a state of nature prove greater than the strength that each man has to preserve himself in that state. Beyond this point, the primitive condition cannot endure, for then the human race will perish if it does not change its mode of existence.

Since men cannot create new forces, but merely combine and control those which already exist, the only way in which they can preserve themselves is by uniting their separate powers in a combination strong enough to overcome any resistance, uniting them so that their powers are directed by a single motive and act in concert.

Such a sum of forces can be produced only by the union of separate men, but as each man's own strength and liberty are the chief instruments of his preservation, how can he merge his with others' without putting himself in peril and neglecting the care he owes to himself? This difficulty, which brings me back to my present subject, may be expressed in these words:

"How to find a form of association which will defend the person and goods of each member with the collective force of all, and under which each individual, while uniting himself with the others, obeys no one but himself, and remains as free as before." This is the fundamental problem to which the social contract holds the solution.

The articles of this contract are so precisely determined by the nature of the act, that the slightest modification must render them null and void; they are such that, though perhaps never formally stated, they are everywhere the same, everywhere tacitly admitted and recognized; and if ever the social pact is violated, every man regains his original rights and, recovering his natural freedom, loses that social freedom for which he exchanged it.

These articles of association, rightly understood, are reducible to a single one, namely the total alienation by each associate of himself and all his rights to the whole community. Thus, in the first place, as every individual gives himself absolutely, the conditions are the same for all, and precisely because they are the same for all, it is in no one's interest to make the conditions onerous for others.

Secondly, since the alienation is unconditional, the union is as perfect as it could be, and no individual associate has any longer any rights to claim; for if rights were left to individuals, in the absence of any higher authority to judge between them and the public, each individual, being his own judge in some causes, would soon demand to be his own judge in all; and in this way the state of nature would be kept in being, and the association inevitably become either tyrannical or void.

Finally, since each man gives himself to all, he gives himself to no one; and since there is no associate over whom he does not gain the same rights as others gain over him, each man recovers the equivalent of everything he loses, and in the bargain he acquires more power to preserve what he has.

If, then, we eliminate from the social pact everything that is not essential to it, we find it comes down to this: "Each one of us puts into the community his person and all his powers under the supreme direction of the general will; and as a body, we incorporate every member as an indivisible part of the whole."

Immediately, in place of the individual person of each contracting party, this act of association creates an artificial and collective body composed of as many members as there are voters in the assembly, and by this same act that body acquires its unity, its common *ego*, its life and its will. The public person thus formed by the union of all other persons was once called the *city*,[1] and is now known as the *republic* or the *body politic*. In its passive role it is called the *state*, when it plays an active role it is the *sovereign*; and when it is compared to others of its own kind, it is a *power*. Those who are associated in it take collectively the name of *a people*, and call themselves individually *citizens*, in so far as they share in the sovereign power, and *subjects*, in so far as they put themselves under the laws of the state. However, these words are often confused, each being mistaken for another; but the essential thing is to know how to recognize them when they are used in their precise sense.

Chapter 7
The Sovereign

This formula shows that the act of association consists of a reciprocal commitment between society and the individual, so that each person, in making a contract, as it were, with himself, finds himself doubly committed, first, as a member of the sovereign body in relation to individuals, and secondly as a member of the state in relation to the sovereign. Here there can be no invoking the principle of civil law which says that no man is bound by a contract with himself, for there is a great difference between having an obligation to oneself and having an obligation to something of which one is a member.

We must add that a public decision can impose an obligation on all the subjects towards the sovereign, by reason of the two aspects under which each can be seen, while, contrariwise, such decisions cannot impose an obligation on the sovereign towards itself; and hence it would be against the very nature of a political body for the sovereign to set over itself a law which it could not infringe. The sovereign, bearing only one single and identical aspect, is in the position of a private person making a contract with himself, which shows that there neither is, nor can be, any kind of fundamental law binding on the people as a body, not even the social contract itself. This does not mean that the whole body cannot incur obligations to other nations, so long as those obligations do not infringe the contract; for in relation to foreign powers, the body politic is a simple entity, an individual.

However, since the body politic, or sovereign, owes its being to the sanctity of the contract alone, it cannot commit itself, even in treaties with foreign powers, to anything that would derogate from the original act of association; it could not, for example, alienate a part of itself or submit to another sovereign. To violate the act which has given it existence would be to annihilate itself; and what is nothing can produce nothing.

As soon as the multitude is united thus in a single body, no one can injure any one of the members without attacking the whole, still less injure the whole without each member feeling it. Duty and self-interest

---

1. The real meaning of this word has been almost entirely lost in the modern world, when a town and a city are thought to be identical, and a citizen the same as a burgess. People forget that houses may make a town, while only citizens can make a city. The Carthaginians once paid dearly for this mistake. I have never read of the title *cives* being given to the subject of any prince, not even to the Macedonians in ancient times or the English today, in spite of their being closer to liberty than any other people. The French alone apply the name "Citizen" freely to everyone, and that is because they do not know what it means, as their Dictionaries prove; if they did know, they would be guilty, in usurping it, of *lèse-majesté*; as it is, they use the word to designate social status and not legal right. When Bodin wanted to speak of citizens and burgesses, he made the gross error of mistaking the one for the other. Monsieur d'Alembert avoids this mistake; and in his article on "Geneva" he correctly distinguishes between the four orders of men (five, if aliens are included) which are found in our town, and of which only two compose the republic. No other French author to my knowledge has understood the real meaning of the word "citizen."

thus equally oblige the two contracting parties to give each other mutual aid; and the same men should seek to bring together in this dual relationship, all the advantages that flow from it.

Now, as the sovereign is formed entirely of the individuals who compose it, it has not, nor could it have, any interest contrary to theirs; and so the sovereign has no need to give guarantees to the subjects, because it is impossible for a body to wish to hurt all of its members, and, as we shall see, it cannot hurt any particular member. The sovereign by the mere fact that it is, is always all that it ought to be.

But this is not true of the relation of subject to sovereign. Despite their common interest, subjects will not be bound by their commitment unless means are found to guarantee their fidelity.

For every individual as a man may have a private will contrary to, or different from, the general will that he has as a citizen. His private interest may speak with a very different voice from that of the public interest; his absolute and naturally independent existence may make him regard what he owes to the common cause as a gratuitous contribution, the loss of which would be less painful for others than the payment is onerous for him; and fancying that the artificial person which constitutes the state is a mere rational entity (since it is not a man), he might seek to enjoy the rights of a citizen without doing the duties of a subject. The growth of this kind of injustice would bring about the ruin of the body politic.

Hence, in order that the social pact shall not be an empty formula, it is tacitly implied in that commitment—which alone can give force to all others—that whoever refuses to obey the general will shall be constrained to do so by the whole body, which means nothing other than that he shall be forced to be free; for this is the condition which, by giving each citizen to the nation, secures him against all personal dependence, it is the condition which shapes both the design and the working of the political machine, and which alone bestows justice on civil contracts—without it, such contracts would be absurd, tyrannical, and liable to the grossest abuse.

Chapter 8
Civil Society

The passing from the state of nature to the civil society produces a remarkable change in man; it puts justice as a rule of conduct in the place of instinct, and gives his actions the moral quality they previously lacked. It is only then, when the voice of duty has taken the place of physical impulse, and right that of desire, that man, who has hitherto thought only of himself, finds himself compelled to act on other principles, and to consult his reason rather than study his inclinations. And although in civil society man surrenders some of the advantages that belong to the state of nature, he gains in return far greater ones; his faculties are so exercised and developed, his mind is so enlarged, his sentiments so ennobled, and his whole spirit so elevated that, if the abuse of his new condition did not in many cases lower him to something worse than what he had left, he should constantly bless the happy hour that lifted him for ever from the state of nature and from a narrow, stupid animal made a creature of intelligence and a man.

Suppose we draw up a balance sheet, so that the losses and gains may be readily compared. What man loses by the social contract is his natural liberty and the absolute right to anything that tempts him and that he can take; what he gains by the social contract is civil liberty and the legal right of property in what he possesses. If we are to avoid mistakes in weighing the one side against the other, we must clearly distinguish between *natural* liberty, which has no limit but the physical power of the individual concerned, and *civil* liberty, which is limited by the general will; and we must distinguish also between *possession*, which is based only on force or "the right of the first occupant," and *property*, which must rest on a legal title.

We might also add that man acquires with civil society, moral freedom, which alone makes man the master of himself; for to be governed by appetite alone is slavery, while obedience to a law one prescribes to oneself is freedom. However, I have already said more than enough on this subject, and the philosophical meaning of the word "freedom" is no part of my subject here.

Chapter 9
Of Estate

Every member of the community gives himself to it at the moment it is brought into being just as he is—he himself, with all his resources, including all his goods. This is not to say that possession by this act changes its nature in changing hands and becomes property in the grasp of the sovereign; but rather, that as the resources of the nation are incomparably greater than those of an individual, public possession is in simple fact more secure and more irrevocable than private possession, without being any more legitimate—at any rate, in the eyes of foreigners; for the state, *vis-à-vis* its own members, becomes master of all their goods by virtue of the social contract, which serves, within the state, as the basis of all other rights; while *vis-à-vis* other nations, the state has only the "right of the first occupant," which it derives from individuals.

The "right of the first occupant," although more real than the "right of the strongest," does not become a true right until the institution of property. Every man has a natural right to what he needs; but the positive act which makes a man the proprietor of any estate excludes him from everything else. His share having once been settled, he must confine himself to it, and he has no further right against the community. Thus, we see how "the right of the first occupant," weak as it is in the state of nature, compels in political society the respect of all men. What this right makes one aware of is less what belongs to others than what does *not* belong to oneself.

As a general rule, to justify the right of the first occupant to any piece of land whatever, the following conditions must obtain: first, that the land shall not already be inhabited by anyone else; secondly, that the claimant occupies no more than he needs for subsistence; thirdly, that he takes possession, not by an idle ceremony, but by actually working and cultivating the soil—the only sign of ownership which need be respected by other people in the absence of a legal title.

It can, indeed, be said that tying "the right of the first occupant" to need and work is stretching it as far as it will go. Can one really avoid setting limits on the right? Is it enough to put one's feet on a piece of common land in order to claim it at once as one's own? Is it enough to have the power to keep other men off for one moment in order to deprive them of the right ever to return? How could a man or a people seize a vast territory and keep out the rest of the human race except by a criminal usurpation—since the action would rob the rest of mankind of the shelter and the food that nature has given them all in common? When Nunez Balboa stood on the shore and took possession of the southern seas and of South America in the name of the crown of Castille, was that enough to dis-

possess all the inhabitants and to exclude all the other princes of the world? If so, such idle ceremonies would have had no end; and the Catholic king might without leaving his royal chamber have taken possession of the whole universe, only excepting afterwards those parts of his empire already belonging to other princes.

We can see how the lands of private persons, when they are united and contiguous, become public territory; and how the right of sovereignty, extending from the subjects to the soil they occupy, covers both property and persons; it makes the owners all the more dependent, and turns their own strength into the guarantee of their fidelity. This advantage seems to have eluded the ancient monarchs, who, in calling themselves simply the King of the Persians or the Scythians or the Macedonians, appear to have regarded themselves rather as rulers of men than as masters of their countries. Monarchs of the present day call themselves more shrewdly the King of France, or of Spain, or of England and so on; in holding thus the land, they are very sure of holding the inhabitants.

What is unique about the alienation entailed by the social contract is that the community in accepting the goods of an individual is far from depriving him of them; on the contrary it simply assures him of their lawful possession; it changes usurpation into valid right and mere enjoyment into legal ownership. Since every owner is regarded as a trustee of the public property, his rights are respected by every other member of the state, and protected with its collective force against foreigners; men have, by a surrender which is advantageous to the public and still more to themselves, acquired, so to speak, all that they have given up—a paradox which is easily explained by the distinction between the rights which the sovereign has and which the owner has over the same property, as will be seen later.

It may also happen that men begin to unite before they possess anything, and spreading over a territory large enough for them all, proceed to enjoy it in common, or, alternatively, divide it among themselves either equally or in shares determined by the sovereign. In whatever manner this acquisition is made, the right of any individual over his own estate is always subordinate to the right of the community over everything; for without this there would be neither strength in the social bond nor effective force in the exercise of sovereignty.

I shall end this chapter—and Book I—with an observation which might serve as a basis for the whole social system: namely, that the social pact, far from destroying natural equality, substitutes, on the contrary, a moral and lawful equality for whatever physical inequality that nature may have imposed on mankind; so that however unequal in strength and intelligence, men become equal by covenant and by right.[1]

Book II

Chapter 1
That Sovereignty Is Inalienable

The first and most important consequence of the principles so far established is that the general will alone can direct the forces of the state in accordance with that end which the state has been established to achieve—the common good; for if conflict between private interests has made the setting up of civil societies necessary, harmony between those same interests has made it possible. It is what is common to those different interests which yields the social bond; if there were no point on which separate interests coincided, then society could not conceivably exist. And it is precisely on the basis of this common interest that society must be governed.

My argument, then, is that sovereignty, being nothing other than the exercise of the general will, can never be alienated; and that the sovereign, which is simply a collective being, cannot be represented by anyone but itself—power may be delegated, but the will cannot be.

For indeed while it is not impossible for a private will to coincide with the general will on some point or other, it is impossible for such a coincidence to be regular and enduring; for the private will inclines by its very nature towards partiality, and the general will towards equality. It is even more inconceivable that there should be a guarantee of harmony between the private and the general will, even if it were to continue always, for such lasting harmony would be the result of chance and not of design. The sovereign could say: "What I want at present is precisely what this man wants, or at least what he says he wants"; but no sovereign could say: "What this man is going to want tomorrow I too shall want," for it is absurd that anyone should wish to bind himself for the future, and it is a contradiction in terms to say that any human being should wish to consent to something that is the reverse of his own good. If a people promises simply and solely to obey, it dissolves itself by that very pledge; it ceases to be a people; for once there is a master, there is no longer a sovereign, and the body politic is therefore annihilated.

This is not to say that the commands of leaders may not pass for the general will if the sovereign, being free to oppose them, does not do so. In such a case the silence of the people permits the assumption that the people consents. This will be explained more fully in a later chapter.

Chapter 2
That Sovereignty Is Indivisible

Just as sovereignty is inalienable, it is for the same reason indivisible; for either the will is general[1] or it is not; either it is the will of the body of the people, or merely that of a part. In the first case, a declaration of will is an act of sovereignty and constitutes law; in the second case, it is only a declaration of a particular will or an act of administration, it is at best a mere decree.

Nevertheless, our political theorists, unable to divide the principle of sovereignty, divide it in its purpose; they divide it into power and will, divide it, that is, into executive and legislative, into the rights of levying taxation, administering justice, and making war, into domestic jurisdiction and the power to deal with foreign governments. Sometimes our theorists confuse all the parts and sometimes they separate

---

1. Under a bad government, this equality is only an appearance and an illusion; it serves only to keep the poor in their wretchedness and sustain the rich in their usurpation. In truth, laws are always useful to those with possessions and harmful to those who have nothing; from which it follows that the social state is advantageous to men only when all possess something and none has too much.
1. For the will to be general, it does not always have to be unanimous; but all the votes must be counted. Any formal exclusion destroys its universality.

them. They make the sovereign a creature of fantasy, a patchwork of separate pieces, rather as if they were to construct a man of several bodies—one with eyes, one with legs, the other with feet and nothing else. It is said that Japanese mountebanks can cut up a child under the eyes of spectators, throw the different parts into the air, and then make the child come down, alive and all of a piece. This is more or less the trick that our political theorists perform—after dismembering the social body with a sleight of hand worthy of the fairground, they put the pieces together again anyhow.

The mistake comes from having no precise notion of what sovereign authority is, and from taking mere manifestations of authority for parts of the authority itself. For instance, the acts of declaring war and making peace have been regarded as acts of sovereignty, which they are not; for neither of these acts constitutes a *law*, but only an application of law, a particular act which determines how the law shall be interpreted—and all this will be obvious as soon as I have defined the idea which attaches to the word "law."

If we were to scrutinize in the same way the other supposed divisions of sovereignty, we should find that whenever we thought that sovereignty was divided, we had been mistaken, for the rights which are taken to be part of that sovereignty prove in fact to be subordinate to it, and presuppose the existence of a supreme will which they merely serve to put into effect.

This want of precision has obfuscated immeasurably the conclusions of our legal theorists when they have come to apply their own principles to determine the respective rights of kings and of peoples. Every reader of the third and fourth chapters of the first Book of Grotius can see how that learned man and his translator, Barbeyrac, are trapped in their own sophisms, frightened of saying either too much or alternatively too little (according to their prejudices) and so offending the interests they wish to flatter. Grotius, a refugee in France, discontented with his own country and out to pay court to Louis XIII, to whom his book is dedicated, spares no pains to rob peoples of all their rights and to invest those rights, by every conceivable artifice, in kings. This would have been very much to the taste of Barbeyrac, who dedicated his translation of Grotius to the King of England, George I. But unfortunately the expulsion of James II—which Barbeyrac calls an "abdication"—obliged him to speak with a marked reserve, to hesitate and equivocate, so as not to suggest that William III was a usurper. If these two writers had adopted sound principles, all their difficulties would have vanished, and their arguments would have been logical; but then they would, alas for them, have told the truth and paid court only to the people. The truth brings no man a fortune; and it is not the people who hand out embassies, professorships, and pensions.

Chapter 3
Whether the General Will Can Err

It follows from what I have argued that the general will is always rightful and always tends to the public good; but it does not follow that the decisions of the people are always equally right. We always want what is advantageous but we do not always discern it. The people is never corrupted, but it is often misled; and only then does it seem to will what is bad.

There is often a great difference between the will of all [what all individuals want] and the general will; the general will studies only the common interest while the will of all studies private interest, and is indeed no more than the sum of individual desires. But if we take away from these same wills, the pluses and minuses which cancel each other out, the sum of the difference is the general will.[1]

From the deliberations of a people properly informed, and provided its members do not have any communication among themselves, the great number of small differences will always produce a general will and the decision will always be good. But if groups, sectional associations are formed at the expense of the larger association, the will of each of these groups will become general in relation to its own members and private in relation to the state; we might then say that there are no longer as many votes as there are men but only as many votes as there are groups. The differences become less numerous and

---

1. "Every interest," says the Marquis d'Argenson, "has its different principles. Harmony between two interests is created by opposition to that of a third." He might have added that the harmony of all interests is created by opposition to those of each. If there were no different interests, we should hardly be conscious of a common interest, as there would be no resistance to it; everything would run easily of its own accord, and politics would cease to be an art.

yield a result less general. Finally, when one of these groups becomes so large that it can dominate the rest, the result is no longer the sum of many small differences, but one great divisive difference; then there ceases to be a general will, and the opinion which prevails is no more than a private opinion.

Thus if the general will is to be clearly expressed, it is imperative that there should be no sectional associations in the state, and that every citizen should make up his own mind for himself[2]—such was the unique and sublime invention of the great Lycurgus. But if there are sectional associations, it is wise to multiply their number and to prevent inequality among them, as Solon, Numa, and Servius did. These are the only precautions which can ensure that the general will is always enlightened and the people protected from error.

Chapter 4
The Limits of Sovereign Power

If the state, or the nation, is nothing other than a legal person, the life of which consists in the union of its members, and if the most important of its cares is its own preservation, it must have a universal and compelling power to move and dispose of each part in whatever manner is beneficial to the whole. Just as nature gives each man an absolute power over all his own limbs, the social pact gives the body politic an absolute power over all its members; and it is this same power which, directed by the general will, bears, as I have said, the name of sovereignty.

However, we have to consider beside the public person those private persons who compose it, and whose life and liberty is naturally independent of it. Here we have to distinguish clearly the respective rights of the citizen and of the sovereign,[1] and distinguish those duties which the citizens have as subjects from the natural rights which they ought to enjoy as men.

We have agreed that each man alienates by the social pact only that part of his power, his goods and his liberty which is the concern of the community; but it must also be admitted that the sovereign alone is judge of what is of such concern.

Whatever services the citizen can render the state, he owes whenever the sovereign demands them; but the sovereign, on its side, may not impose on the subjects any burden which is not necessary to the community; the sovereign cannot, indeed, even will such a thing, since according to the law of reason no less than to the law of nature nothing is without a cause.

The commitments which bind us to the social body are obligatory only because they are mutual; and their nature is such that in fulfilling them a man cannot work for others without at the same time working for himself. How should it be that the general will is always rightful and that all men constantly wish the happiness of each but for the fact that there is no one who does not take that word "each" to pertain to himself and in voting for all think of himself? This proves that the equality of rights and the notion of justice which it produces derive from the predilection which each man has for himself and hence from human nature as such. It also proves that the general will, to be truly what it is, must be general in its purpose as well as in its nature; that it should spring from all and apply to all; and that it loses its natural rectitude when it is directed towards any particular and circumscribed object—for in judging what is foreign to us, we have no sound principle of equity to guide us.

For, indeed, whenever we are dealing with a particular fact or right, on a matter which has not been settled by an earlier and general agreement, that question becomes contentious. It is a conflict in which private interests are ranged on one side and the public interest on the other; and I can see neither the law which is to be followed nor the judge who is to arbitrate. It would be absurd in such a dispute to seek an express decision of the general will; for a decision could only be a conclusion in favour of one of the contending parties, and it would be regarded by the other party as an alien, partial will, a will prone to error and liable in such circumstances to fall into injustice. So we see that even as a private will cannot represent the general will, so too the general will

---

2. "Divisions," says Machiavelli, "sometimes injure and sometimes aid a republic. The injury is done by cabals and factions; the service is rendered by a party which maintains itself without cabals and factions. Since, therefore, it is impossible for the founder of a republic to provide against enmities, he must make the best provision he can against factions." *History of Florence*, Book VII [Original in Italian. *Trans.*]

1. Please, attentive reader, do not hasten to accuse me of contradiction. I cannot avoid a contradiction of words, because of the poverty of language, but wait.

changes its nature if it seeks to deal with an individual case; it cannot as a *general* will give a ruling concerning any one man or any one fact. When the people of Athens, for example, appointed or dismissed its leaders, awarding honours to one, inflicting penalties on another, and by a multitude of particular decrees indiscriminately exercised all the functions of an administration, then the people of Athens no longer had what is correctly understood as a general will and ceased to act as sovereign and acted instead as magistrate. All this may seem at variance with commonly accepted notions; but I must be given time to expound my own.

It should nevertheless be clear from what I have so far said that the general will derives its generality less from the number of voices than from the common interest which unites them, for the general will is an institution in which each necessarily submits himself to the same conditions which he imposes on others; this admirable harmony of interest and justice gives to social deliberations a quality of equity which disappears at once from the discussion of any individual dispute precisely because in these latter cases there is no common interest to unite and identify the decision of the judge with that of the contending parties.

Whichever way we look at it, we always return to the same conclusion: namely that the social pact establishes equality among the citizens in that they all pledge themselves under the same conditions and must all enjoy the same rights. Hence, by the nature of the compact, every act of sovereignty, that is every authentic act of the general will, binds or favours all the citizens equally, so that the sovereign recognizes only the whole body of the nation and makes no distinction between any of the members who compose it. What then is correctly to be called an act of sovereignty? It is not a covenant between a superior and an inferior, but a covenant of the body with each of its members. It is a legitimate covenant, because its basis is the social contract; an equitable one, because it is common to all; a useful one, because it can have no end but the common good; and it is a durable covenant because it is guaranteed by the armed forces and the supreme power. So long as the subjects submit to such covenants alone, they obey nobody but their own will; and to ask how far the respective rights of the sovereign and the citizen extend is to ask how far these two can pledge themselves together, each to all and all to each.

From this it is clear that the sovereign power, wholly absolute, wholly sacred, wholly inviolable as it is, does not go beyond and cannot go beyond the limits of the general covenants; and thus that every man can do what he pleases with such goods and such freedom as is left to him by these covenants; and from this it follows that the sovereign has never any right to impose greater burdens on one subject than on another, for whenever that happens a private grievance is created and the sovereign's power is no longer competent.

Granted these distinctions, it becomes manifestly false to assert that individuals make any real renunciation by the social contract; indeed, as a result of the contract they find themselves in a situation preferable in real terms to that which prevailed before; instead of an alienation, they have profitably exchanged an uncertain and precarious life for a better and more secure one; they have exchanged natural independence for freedom, the power to destroy others for the enjoyment of their own security; they have exchanged their own strength which others might overcome for a right which the social union makes invincible. Their very lives, which they have pledged to the state, are always protected by it; and even when they risk their lives to defend the state, what more are they doing but giving back what they have received from the state? What are they doing that they would not do more often, and at greater peril, in the state of nature, where every man is inevitably at war and at the risk of his life, [and] defends whatever serves him to maintain life? Assuredly, all must now fight in case of need for their country, but at least no one has any longer to fight for himself. And is there not something to be gained by running, for the sake of the guarantee of safety, a few of those risks we should each have to face alone if we were deprived of that assurance?

Chapter 5
The Right of Life and Death

It will be asked how individuals, who have no right whatever to take their own lives, can transfer to the sovereign a right they do not possess. This question looks difficult to answer only because it is badly formulated. Every man has the right to risk his own life in order to preserve it. Has it ever been said that a man who leaps out of a window to escape from a fire is guilty of suicide? Would the same crime be imputed to a man who perishes in a storm on the grounds that he knew of the danger when he embarked?

The purpose of the social treaty is the preservation of contracting parties. Whoever wills the end wills also the means, and certain risks, even certain casualties are inseparable from these means. Whoever wishes to preserve his own life at the expense of others must give his life for them when it is necessary. Now, as citizen, no man is judge any longer of the danger to which the law requires him to expose himself, and when the prince says to him: "It is expedient for the state that you should die," then he should die, because it is only on such terms that he has lived in security as long as he has and also because his life is no longer the bounty of nature but a gift he has received conditionally from the state.

The death-penalty inflicted on criminals may be seen in much the same way: it is in order to avoid becoming the victim of a murderer that one consents to die if one becomes a murderer oneself. Far from taking one's life under the social treaty, one thinks only of assuring it, and we shall hardly suppose that any of the contracting parties contemplates being hanged.

Moreover, since every wrongdoer attacks the society's law, he becomes by his deed a rebel and a traitor to the country; by violating its law, he ceases to be a member of it; indeed, he makes war against it. And in this case, the preservation of the state is incompatible with *his* preservation; one or the other must perish; and when the guilty man is put to death, it is less as a citizen than as an enemy. Trial and judgement are the proof and declaration that he has broken the social treaty, and is in consequence no longer a member of the state. And since he has accepted such membership, if only by his residence, he must either be banished into exile as a violator of the social pact or be put to death as a public enemy: such an enemy is not a fictitious person, but a man, and therefore the right of war makes it legitimate to kill him.

But, it will be said, the condemnation of a criminal is an individual act. Agreed; and it follows that such duties do not pertain to the sovereign; condemnation of criminals is a right the sovereign can confer but not exercise himself. All my ideas hold together, but I cannot elaborate them all at once.

In any case, frequent punishments are a sign of weakness or slackness in the government. There is no man so bad that he cannot be made good for something. No man should be put to death, even as an example, if he can be left to live without danger to society.

As for the right of pardon, or of exempting a guilty man from the penalty prescribed by law and imposed by a judge, this belongs only to that entity which is superior to both the judge and the law, namely the sovereign; but even this right is not entirely clear and it must be exercised very seldom. In a well-governed state there are few penalties, not because there are many pardons but because there are few criminals. In a decaying state the very multiplicity of crimes assures impunity. Under the Roman Republic neither the senate nor the consuls ever attempted to pardon criminals; nor did the people do so, though they sometimes revoked their own sentences. Frequent pardons signalize that crimes will soon need no pardon; and anyone can see what that must lead to. However, I can feel my heart whispering and restraining my pen; let us leave the discussion of these questions to the just man who has never erred and has therefore had no need of pardons.

Chapter 6
On Law

We have given life and existence to the body politic by the social pact; now it is a matter of giving it movement and will by legislation. For the primitive act by which the body politic is formed and united does not determine what it shall do to preserve itself.

What is good and in conformity with order is such by the very nature of things and independently of human agreements. All justice comes from God, who alone is its source; and if only we knew how to receive it from that exalted fountain, we should need neither governments nor laws. There is undoubtedly a universal justice which springs from reason alone, but if that justice is to be admitted among men it must be reciprocal. Humanly speaking, the laws of natural justice, lacking any natural sanction, are unavailing among men. In fact, such laws merely benefit the wicked and injure the just, since the just respect them while others do not do so in return. So there must be covenants and positive laws to unite rights with duties and to direct justice to its object. In the state of nature, where everything is common, I owe nothing to those to whom I have promised nothing, and I recognize as belonging to others only those things that are of no use to me. But this is no longer the case in civil society, where all rights are determined by law.

Yet what, in the last analysis, is law? If we simply try to define it in terms of metaphysical ideas, we shall go on talking without reaching any understanding; and when we have said what natural law is, we shall still not know what the law of the state is.

I have already said that the general will cannot relate to any particular object. For such a particular object is either within the state or outside the state. If it is outside, then a will which is alien to it is not general with regard to it: if the object is within the state, it forms a part of the state. Then there comes into being a relationship between the whole and the part which involves two separate entities, the part being one, and the whole, less that particular part, being the other. But a whole less a particular part is no longer a whole; and so as long as this relationship exists there is no whole but only two unequal parts, from which it follows that the will of the one is no longer general with respect to the other.

But when the people as a whole makes rules for the people as a whole, it is dealing only with itself; and if any relationship emerges, it is between the entire body seen from one perspective and the same entire body seen from another, without any division whatever. Here the matter concerning which a rule is made is as general as the will which makes it. And *this* is the kind of act which I call a law.

When I say that the province of the law is always general, I mean that the law considers all subjects collectively and all actions in the abstract; it does not consider any individual man or any specific action. Thus the law may well lay down that there shall be privileges, but it may not nominate the persons who shall have those privileges; the law may establish several classes of citizen, and even specify the qualifications which shall give access to those several classes, but it may not say that this man or that shall be admitted; the law may set up a royal government and an hereditary succession, but it may not elect a king or choose a royal family—in a word, no function which deals with the individual falls within the province of the legislative power.

On this analysis, it is immediately clear that we no longer ask *who* is to make laws, because laws are acts of the general will; no longer ask if the prince is above the law, because he is a part of the state; no longer

ask if the law can be unjust, because no one is unjust to himself; and no longer ask how we can be both free and subject to laws, for the laws are but registers of what we ourselves desire.

It is also clear that since the law unites universality of will with universality of the field of legislation, anything that any man, no matter who, commands on his own authority is not a law; even what the sovereign itself commands with respect to a particular object is not a law but a decree, not an act of sovereignty but an act of government.

Any state which is ruled by law I call a "republic," whatever the form of its constitution; for then, and then alone, does the public interest govern and then alone is the "public thing"—the *res publica*—a reality. All legitimate government is "republican,"[1] I shall explain later what government is.

Laws are really nothing other than the conditions on which civil society exists. A people, since it is subject to laws, ought to be the author of them. The right of laying down the rules of society belongs only to those who form the society; but how can they exercise it? Is it to be by common agreement, by a sudden inspiration? Has the body politic an organ to declare its will? Who is to give it the foresight necessary to formulate enactments and proclaim them in advance, and how is it to announce them in the hour of need? How can a blind multitude, which often does not know what it wants, because it seldom knows what is good for it, undertake by itself an enterprise as vast and difficult as a system of legislation? By themselves the people always will what is good, but by themselves they do not always discern it. The general will is always rightful, but the judgement which guides it is not always enlightened. It must be made to see things as they are, and sometimes as they should be seen; it must be shown the good path which it is seeking, and secured against seduction by the desires of individuals; it must be given a sense of situation and season, so as to weigh immediate and tangible advantages against distant and hidden evils. Individuals see the good and reject it; the public desires the good but

---

1. By this word I understand not only an aristocracy or democracy, but generally any government directed by the general will, which is law. If it is to be legitimate, the government must not be united with the sovereign, but must serve it as its ministry. So even a monarchy can be a republic. This will be clarified in Book III.

does not see it. Both equally need guidance. Individuals must be obliged to subordinate their will to their reason; the public must be taught to recognize what it desires. Such public enlightenment would produce a union of understanding and will in the social body, bring the parts into perfect harmony, and lift the whole to its fullest strength. Hence the necessity of a lawgiver.

Chapter 7
The Lawgiver

To discover the rules of society that are best suited to nations, there would need to exist a superior intelligence, who could understand the passions of men without feeling any of them, who had no affinity with our nature but knew it to the full, whose happiness was independent of ours, but who would nevertheless make our happiness his concern, who would be content to wait in the fullness of time for a distant glory, and to labour in one age to enjoy the fruits in another.[1] Gods would be needed to give men laws.

The same reasoning which Caligula used empirically, Plato used philosophically in his dialogue *The Statesman* to reach a definition of civil or kingly man. But if it is true that great princes seldom appear, how much more rare must a great lawgiver be? A prince has only to follow a model which the lawgiver provides. The lawgiver is the engineer who invents the machine; the prince is merely the mechanic who sets it up and operates it. Montesquieu says that at the birth of political societies, it is the leaders of the republic who shape the institutions but that afterwards it is the institutions which shape the leaders of the republic.

Whoever ventures on the enterprise of setting up a people must be ready, shall we say, to change human nature, to transform each individual, who by himself is entirely complete and solitary, into a part of a much greater whole, from which that same individual will then receive, in a sense, his life and his being. The founder of nations must weaken the structure of man in order to fortify it, to replace the physical and independent existence we have all received from nature

with a moral and communal existence. In a word, each man must be stripped of his own powers, and given powers which are external to him, and which he cannot use without the help of others. The nearer men's natural powers are to extinction or annihilation, and the stronger and more lasting their acquired powers, the stronger and more perfect is the social institution. So much so, that if each citizen can do nothing whatever except through cooperation with others, and if the acquired power of the whole is equal to, or greater than, the sum of the natural powers of each of the individuals, then we can say that lawmaking has reached the highest point of perfection.

The lawgiver is, in every respect, an extraordinary man in the state. Extraordinary not only because of his genius, but equally because of his office, which is neither that of the government nor that of the sovereign. This office which gives the republic its constitution has no place in that constitution. It is a special and superior function which has nothing to do with empire over men; for just as he who has command over men must not have command over laws, neither must he who has command over laws have command over men; otherwise, the laws, in ministering to the legislator's passions, would often merely perpetuate his injustices, and partial judgements would inevitably vitiate the sanctity of his works.

When Lycurgus gave laws to his country, he began by abdicating his monarchical functions. It was the habit of most Greek cities to confer on foreigners the task of framing their laws. The modern republics of Italy have often copied this custom; the republic of Geneva did so, and found that it worked well.[2] Rome in its happiest age saw all the crimes of the Tyranny revived within its borders, and came near to perishing simply because it had put both the legislative authority and the sovereign power in the same hands.

And yet even the decemvirs themselves never arrogated the right to make any law on their own authority alone. "Nothing we propose to you," they said to the people, "can become law without your

1. A people does not become famous until its constitution begins to decline. We do not know for how many centuries the constitution of Lycurgus gave happiness to the Spartans before there was talk about them in the rest of Greece.

2. Those who think of Calvin merely as a theologian do not realize the extent of his genius. The codification of our wise edicts, in which he had a large share, does him as much credit as his *Institutes*. Whatever revolutions may take place in our church, the memory of that great man will not cease to be honoured among the adepts of that religion while the love of country and of liberty still lives among us.

consent. Romans, be yourselves the authors of the laws which are to ensure your happiness."

Thus the man who frames the laws ought not to have any legislative right, and the people itself cannot, even should it wish, strip itself of this untransferable right; for, according to the fundamental compact, it is only the general will which compels individuals and there can be no assurance that an individual will is in conformity with the general will until it has submitted to the free suffrage of the people—I have said this already, but it is worth repeating.

And so we find in the work of the lawgiver two things which look contradictory—a task which is beyond human powers and a non-existant authority for its execution.

There is another difficulty which deserves mention. Those sages who insist on speaking in their own language to the vulgar instead of in the vulgar language will not be understood. For there are thousands of ideas which cannot be translated into the popular idiom. Perspectives which are general and goals remote are alike beyond the range of the common herd; it is difficult for the individual, who has no taste for any scheme of government but that which serves his private interest, to appreciate the advantages to be derived from the lasting austerities which good laws impose. For a newly formed people to understand wise principles of politics and to follow the basic rules of statecraft, the effect would have to become the cause; the social spirit which must be the product of social institutions would have to preside over the setting up of those institutions; men would have to have already become before the advent of law that which they become as a result of law. And as the lawgiver can for these reasons employ neither force nor argument, he must have recourse to an authority of another order, one which can compel without violence and persuade without convincing.

It is this which has obliged the founders of nations throughout history to appeal to divine intervention and to attribute their own wisdom to the Gods; for then the people, feeling subject to the laws of the state as they are to those of nature, and detecting the same hand in the creation of both man and the nation, obey freely and bear with docility the yoke of the public welfare.

A sublime reason, which soars above the heads of the common people, produces those rules which the lawgiver puts into the mouth of the immortals, thus compelling by divine authority persons who cannot be moved by human prudence.[3] But it is not for every man to make the Gods speak, or to gain credence if he pretends to be an interpreter of the divine word. The lawgiver's great soul is the true miracle which must vindicate his mission. Any man can carve tablets of stone, or bribe an oracle, claim a secret intercourse with some divinity, train a bird to whisper in his ear, or discover some other vulgar means of imposing himself on the people. A man who can do such things may conceivably bring together a company of fools, but he will never establish an empire, and his bizarre creation will perish with him. Worthless authority may set up transitory bonds, but only wisdom makes lasting ones. The Law of the Hebrews, which still lives, and that of the child of Ishmael which has ruled half the world for ten centuries, still proclaim today the greatness of the men who first enunciated them; and even though proud philosophy and the blind spirit of faction may regard them as nothing but lucky impostors, the true statesman sees, and admires in their institutions, the hand of that great and powerful genius which lies behind all lasting things.

Even so, we must not conclude from this, with Warburton, that religion and politics have the same purpose among men; it is simply that at the birth of nations, the one serves as the instrument of the other.

Chapter 8
The People

Just as an architect who puts up a large building first surveys and tests the ground to see if it can bear the weight, so the wise lawgiver begins not by laying down laws good in themselves, but by finding out whether the people for whom the laws are intended is able to support them. Such reasoning led Plato to refuse to provide laws for the Arcadians or the Cyreneans, because he well knew that those peoples, being rich, would not tolerate equality. Crete, too, provides an example of good laws and bad men, for the people Milos tried to discipline were dominated by their vices.

---

3. "The truth is," writes Machiavelli, "that there has never been in any country an extraordinary legislator who has not invoked the deity; for otherwise his laws would not have been accepted. A wise man knows many useful truths which cannot be demonstrated in such a way as to convince other people." (*Discourses on Livy*, Book V, Chapter xi.) [In Italian in original. *Trans.*]

The world has seen a thousand splendid nations that could not have accepted good laws, and even those that might have accepted them could have done so only for short periods of their long history. Nations,[1] like men, are teachable only in their youth; with age they become incorrigible. Once customs are established and prejudices rooted, reform is a dangerous and fruitless enterprise; a people cannot bear to see its evils touched, even if only to be eradicated; it is like a stupid, pusillanimous invalid who trembles at the sight of a physician.

I am not denying that just as certain afflictions unhinge men's minds and banish their memory of the past, so there are certain violent epochs and revolutions in states which have the same effect on peoples that psychological shocks may have on individuals; only instead of forgetting the past, they look back on it in horror, and then the state, after being consumed by civil war, is born again, so to speak, from its own ashes, and leaps from the arms of death to regain the vigour of youth. Such was the experience of Sparta at the time of Lycurgus, of Rome after the Tarquins, and, in the modern world, of Holland and Switzerland after the expulsion of the tyrants.

But such events are unusual; they are exceptional cases to be explained by the special constitution of the states concerned. It could not even happen twice to the same people; because although a people can make itself free while it is still uncivilized, it cannot do so when its civil energies are worn out. Disturbances may well destroy a civil society without a revolution being able to restore it, so that as soon as the chains are broken, the state falls apart and exists no longer; then what is needed is a master, not a liberator. Free peoples, remember this maxim: liberty can be gained, but never *regained.*

For nations, as for men, there is a time of maturity which they must reach before they are made subject to law; but the maturity of a people is not always easily recognized; and something done too soon will prove abortive.[2] Peoples differ; one is amenable to discipline from the beginning; another is not, even after ten centuries. The Russians have never been effectively governed because the attempt to govern them was made too early. Peter the Great had the talent of a copyist; he had no true genius, which is creative and makes everything from nothing. Some of the things he did were sound; most were misguided. He saw that his people was uncivilized, but he did not see that it was unready for government; he sought to civilize his subjects when he ought rather to have drilled them. He tried to turn them into Germans or Englishmen instead of making them Russians. He urged his subjects to be what they were not and so prevented them from becoming what they might have been. This is just how a French tutor trains his pupil to shine for a brief moment in his childhood and then grow up into a nonentity. The Russian Empire would like to subjugate Europe and will find itself subjugated. The Tartars, its subjects or neighbours, will become its masters—and ours. Such a revolution seems to me inevitable. All the kings of Europe are labouring in concert to hasten its coming.

Chapter 9
The People: Continued

Just as nature has set bounds to the stature of a well-formed man, outside which he is either a giant or a dwarf, so, in what concerns the best constitution for a state, there are limits to the size it can have if it is to be neither too large to be well-governed nor too small to maintain itself. In the body politic there is a maximum of strength which must not be exceeded, and which is often fallen short of as a result of expansion. The more the social bond is stretched, the slacker it becomes, and in general a small state is relatively stronger for its size than a large one.

A thousand considerations bear witness to the truth of this. First, administration becomes more difficult over great distances, just as a weight becomes heavier at the end of a long lever. Government becomes more burdensome as the area is enlarged, for each town has its own administration, which the people pays for, and each region has its administration, which the people also pays for, then each province has one, and so on up to the greater governments, the satrapies, the vice-royalties, each costing more the higher they rise and always paid for by the unfortunate populace; and then on top of all comes the supreme administration, bearing down on everyone. Such a great number of charges added to charges continually exhausts the subjects; and far from being

---

1. [Altered in Edition of 1782 to "Most nations . . ." *Trans.*]
2. [In the Edition of 1782, this sentence is revised as follows: "Youth is not childhood. For nations, as for men, there is a time of youth or, if you prefer, of maturity which they must reach before they are made subject to law . . ." *Trans.*]

better governed by this hierarchy of orders, they are much worse off than they would be if they had only one administration over them. As it is, there is hardly any public revenue available for emergencies, and when the state is faced with such a need, it trembles on the verge of ruin.

Nor is this all. Not only is the government less vigorous and swift in enforcing respect for the law, in preventing nuisances, correcting abuses and thwarting any seditious movements that may arise in distant quarters, but at the same time the people has less feeling for governors whom it never sees, for a homeland that seems as vast as the world, and for fellow-citizens who are mostly strangers. The same laws will not suit so many various provinces, which, with their different customs and contrasting climates, cannot tolerate the same form of government. Having different laws only creates misunderstanding and confusion among peoples who live under the same governors and are in continuous communication with one another; they intermingle and intermarry, but if different sets of rules prevail, they will not even know if what they call their patrimony is really their own. Talents are hidden, virtues are ignored, and vices remain unpunished when such a multitude of men, who do not know one another, is brought together in the same place by one single seat of supreme administration. The governors have too much to do to see everything for themselves; their clerks rule the state. And the measures needed to maintain a general authority, which so many scattered officials try to evade or exploit, absorb all political attention, so none is left to study the people's happiness, and hardly any left for its defence in case of need. This body which is too big for its constitution collapses and perishes, crushed by its own weight.

On the other hand, a state if it is to have strength must give itself some solid foundation, so that it can resist the shocks that it is bound to experience and sustain the exertions that it must make to preserve itself; for all peoples generate a kind of centrifugal force, by which they brush continuously against one another, and they all attempt to expand at the expense of their neighbours, like the vortices of Descartes. Thus the weak are always in danger of being swallowed up, and indeed no people can well preserve itself except by achieving a kind of equilibrium with all the others which makes the pressure everywhere the same for all.

This shows us that there are reasons for expansion and reasons for contraction; and indeed it is not the least part of political wisdom to judge, as between the one and the other, the precise balance which is most conducive to the preservation of the state. In general one might say that any reasons for expansion, which are exterior and relative, ought to be less compelling than the reasons for contraction, which are internal and absolute. A strong and healthy constitution is the first thing to look for because the strength which comes from good government is more reliable than the resources which large territories yield.

One may add that there have been states whose political structure was such that the necessity of conquest was part of their very constitution, states which, in order to maintain themselves at all, were obliged to enlarge themselves unceasingly. Possibly they have congratulated themselves on this, as a fortunate necessity; but reflection on the same necessity must also have shown them that at the end of their greatness lay the inevitable moment of their fall.

Chapter 10
The People: Continued

There are two ways of measuring a body politic, by the extent of its territory and by the number of its people; and there must be a certain balance between these two dimensions if the state is to achieve its best size. Men make the state and the soil nourishes men; thus the right balance requires that there be land enough to feed the inhabitants and as many inhabitants as the land can feed. It is in this proportion that the maximum strength of a given number of persons is brought forth; for if there is too much territory, defence is burdensome, cultivation inadequate and produce excessive; and this soon becomes the cause of defensive wars; while if, on the other hand, there is too little land, the state must live on what it can import at the discretion of its neighbours, and this soon becomes the cause of offensive wars. Any people which has to choose between commerce and war is essentially weak; it depends on its neighbours; it depends on contingencies; it will never have more than a short, uncertain existence; either it conquers and ends its predicament, or it is conquered and exists no more. It can safeguard itself in freedom only by means of littleness or bigness.

One cannot specify the exact mathematical proportion there should be between the area of the land and the number of inhabitants, because of the different characteristics of different places, differences in degrees of fertility, in the nature of the produce, in the effects of climate; and also because of the differences there are between the temperaments of men who inhabit the different territories, some consuming little in a fertile country and others living well off a frugal soil. Again we should have to consider the greater or lesser fecundity of the women, the distinctive features of the land, whether more or less favourable to population; the number of immigrants that the lawgiver might hope to attract by his institutions. From this it follows that he must make his decisions in the light not of what he sees, but of what he foresees, calculating not so much the number of the existing population as the number which the population must naturally reach. Finally, there are a thousand occasions when some particular accident of situation demands or allows the assimilation of more land than appears necessary. In a mountainous country, where the type of cultivation—woodland and pastures—requires less work, where the women are shown by experience to be more fecund than in the plains, and where the steep slopes of hills leave only a marginal degree of that flat land which alone can be relied on for vegetation, men will spread out more widely. The contrary is the case on the edge of the sea, where men will draw together in a small area, even among rocks and sands that are almost barren; for fishing can make up for much of the deficiency of agricultural produce; and being close together enables such men the better to resist pirates; and they can easily rid themselves by overseas settlement of any surplus population.

There is yet another condition for the institution of a people, one condition which no other can replace and without which all the rest are unavailing: a plenitude of peace must be enjoyed; for the period of the formation of a state, like that of the lining up of a regiment, is the time when it is least capable of resistance and most open to destruction. A state can defend itself more effectively amid total chaos than during the time of fermentation, when everyone is thinking about his own position and not about the common danger. If there is a war, famine, or sedition during this critical period, the state will inevitably be overthrown.

It is true that many governments have been set up during such disturbances, but then it is the governments themselves which destroy the state. Usurpers always choose troubled times to enact, in the atmosphere of general panic, laws which the public would never adopt when passions were cool. One of the surest ways of distinguishing the work of a lawgiver from that of a tyrant is to note the moment he chooses to give a people its constitution.

Which people, then, is fit to receive laws? I answer: a people which, finding itself already bound together by some original association, interest, or agreement, has not yet borne the yoke of law; a people without deep-rooted customs or superstitions; one which does not fear sudden invasion, and which, without intervening in the quarrels of its neighbours, can stand up to any of them, or secure the help of one to resist another; a people in which every member may be known to all; where there is no need to burden any man with more than he can bear; a people which can do without other peoples and which other peoples can do without;[1] one which is neither rich nor poor, but has enough to keep itself; and lastly one which combines the cohesion of an ancient people with the malleability of a new one. What makes the task of the lawgiver so difficult is less what has to be established than what has to be destroyed; and what makes success so rare is the impossibility of finding the simplicity of nature together with the needs that society creates. It is difficult to combine all these conditions; and that is why so few well-constituted states exist.

There is still one country in Europe which is fit to receive laws, and that is the island of Corsica. The valour and fidelity with which this brave people has recovered and defended its freedom entitle it to be taught by some wise man how to preserve that freedom. I have a presentiment that this little island will one day astonish Europe.

Chapter 11
Various Systems of Law

If we enquire wherein lies precisely the greatest good of all, which ought to be the goal of every system of law, we shall find that it comes down to two main

---

1. If two neighbouring peoples cannot do without one another the situation is hard for the one and dangerous for the other. Any wise nation, in such a case, will hasten to deliver the other from its dependence. The republic of Thlascala, an enclave within the Mexican Empire, preferred to do without salt rather than buy it from the Mexicans, rather even than take it from them when it was offered as a gift. The wise Thlascalians saw the trap concealed in the Mexican generosity. They kept their freedom; and their little state, locked within the territory of a great Empire, was in the end the instrument of that Empire's ruin.

objects, *freedom* and *equality:* freedom because any individual dependence means that much strength withdrawn from the body of the state, and equality because freedom cannot survive without it. I have already explained what civil freedom is; as for equality, this word must not be taken to imply that degrees of power and wealth should be absolutely the same for all, but rather that power shall stop short of violence and never be exercised except by virtue of authority and law, and, where wealth is concerned, that no citizen shall be rich enough to buy another and none so poor as to be forced to sell himself; this in turn implies that the more exalted persons need moderation in goods and influence and the humbler persons moderation in avarice and covetousness.[1]

Such equality, we shall be told, is a chimera of theory and could not exist in reality. But if abuse is inevitable, ought we not then at least to control it? Precisely because the force of circumstance tends always to destroy equality, the force of legislation ought always to tend to preserve it.

However, these general objectives of all institutions must be modified in each country to meet local conditions and suit the character of the people concerned. It is in the light of such factors that one must assign to each people the particular form of constitution which is best, not perhaps in itself, but for that state for which it is destined. For example, is your soil meagre and barren or the territory too narrow for its inhabitants? Then look to industry and crafts, so that manufactured goods may be exchanged for the natural resources that are lacking. Suppose, on the other hand, you have rich plains and fertile slopes, good land too little inhabited. Then concentrate on agriculture, to increase the population, and eschew artisanry, which invariably depopulates the countryside and brings the few inhabitants there are together in certain urban centres.[2] Have you a long and conve-

nient coastline? Then fill the sea with ships, develop trade and navigation, and you will have a brilliant if short existence. Does the sea, along your shores, wash against almost inaccessible rocks? Then remain ichthyphagous barbarians; you will live more peacefully, better perhaps, and certainly more happily. In short, apart from those principles which are common to all, each people has its own special reasons for ordering itself in a certain way and for having laws that are fitted to itself alone. Thus it was, in the past, that the Hebrews, and more recently the Arabs, took religion as their chief object, while the Athenians had literature, Carthage and Tyre trade, Rhodes seafaring, Sparta war, and Rome civic virtue. The author of *L'Esprit des lois* has shown with scores of examples how the art of the lawgiver directs the constitution towards each of its ends.

What makes the constitution of a state really strong and durable is such a close observance of conventions that natural relations and laws come to be in harmony on all points, so that the law, shall we say, seems only to ensure, accompany, and correct what is natural. But if the lawgiver mistakes his object and builds on principles that differ from what is demanded by the circumstances; if his principle tends towards servitude while circumstances tend towards liberty, the one towards wealth and the other towards increased population, the one towards peace and the other towards conquest, then the laws will be weakened imperceptibly, the constitution will deteriorate, and the state will continue to be disturbed until it is finally destroyed or transformed, and invincible Nature regains her empire.

Chapter 12
Classification of Laws

For everything to be well ordered and the best possible form given to the republic, there are various relations to be considered. First, there is the action of the whole body politic on itself, that is to say, the relation of all with all, or of the sovereign with the state, and this relation, as we shall see, is made up of relations between intermediate terms.

The laws which regulate this relation bear the name of Political Laws, and are also called Fundamental Laws—not unreasonably, if the laws are wise ones. For if in each state there is only one good way of regulating it, the people which has found that way ought to keep to it. But if the established order is bad, why should the laws which prevent its being good be

---

1. Do you want coherence in the state? Then bring the two extremes as close together as possible; have neither very rich men nor beggars, for these two estates, naturally inseparable, are equally fatal to the common good; from the one class come friends of tyranny, from the other, tyrants. It is always these two classes which make commerce of the public freedom: the one buys, the other sells.
2. Any branch of foreign trade, says the Marquis d'Argenson, brings only an illusory advantage to the kingdom in general; it may enrich a few individuals, even a few big towns, but the nation as a whole gains nothing and the people is none the better for it.

regarded as fundamental? Besides, a people is in any case entirely at liberty to alter its laws, even its best laws; and if it chooses to do itself an injury, who has the right to prevent it from doing so?

The second relation is that of the members of the body politic among themselves, or of each with the entire body: their relations among themselves should be as limited, and relations with the entire body as extensive, as possible, in order that each citizen shall be at the same time perfectly independent of all his fellow citizens and excessively dependent on the republic—this result is always achieved by the same means, since it is the power of the state alone which makes the freedom of its members. It is from this second relationship that Civil Laws are born.

We may consider a third kind of relation between the person and the law, namely that of disobedience and its penalty. It is this which gives rises to the establishment of Criminal Laws, though at bottom these are less a specific kind of law than the sanction behind all laws.

To these three sorts of law must be added a fourth, the most important of all, which is inscribed neither on marble nor brass, but in the hearts of the citizens, a law which forms the true constitution of the state, a law which gathers new strength every day and which, when other laws age or wither away, reanimates or replaces them; a law which sustains a nation in the spirit of its institution and imperceptibly substitutes the force of habit for the force of authority. I refer to morals, customs, and, above all, belief: this feature, unknown to our political theorists, is the one on which the success of all the other laws depends; it is the feature on which the great lawgiver bestows his secret care, for though he seems to confine himself to detailed legal enactments, which are really only the arching of the vault, he knows that morals, which develop more slowly, ultimately become its immovable keystone.

Among these various classes of law, it is only Political Laws, which constitute the form of government, that are relevant to my subject.

Book III

Before speaking of the various forms of government, let us try to fix the precise meaning of this word, which has not hitherto been very well explained.

Chapter 1
Of Government in General

I must warn the reader that this chapter should be read with care, for I have not the skill to make myself clear to those who do not wish to concentrate their attention.

Every free action has two causes which concur to produce it, one moral—the will which determines the act, the other physical—the strength which executes it. When I walk towards an object, it is necessary first that I should resolve to go that way and secondly that my feet should carry me. When a paralytic resolves to run and when a fit man resolves not to move, both stay where they are. The body politic has the same two motive powers—and we can make the same distinction between will and strength, the former is *legislative power* and the latter *executive power*. Nothing can be, or should be, done in the body politic without the concurrence of both.

We have seen that the legislative power belongs, and can only belong, to the people. On the other hand, it is easy to see from principles established above [Book II, Chapters 4 and 6] that executive power cannot belong to the generality of the people as legislative or sovereign, since executive power is exercised only in particular acts which are outside the province of law and therefore outside the province of the sovereign which can act only to make laws.

The public force thus needs its own agent to call it together and put it into action in accordance with the instructions of the general will, to serve also as a means of communication between the state and the sovereign, and in a sense to do for the public person what is done for the individual by the union of soul and body. This is the reason why the state needs a government, something often unhappily confused with the sovereign, but of which it is really only the minister.

What, then, is the government? An intermediary body established between the subjects and the sovereign for their mutual communication, a body charged with the execution of the laws and the maintenance of freedom, both civil and political.

The members of this body are called magistrates or *kings*, that is to say *governors*, and the whole body bears the name of the *prince*.[1] Thus, those theorists who deny that the act by which a people submits itself to leaders is a contract are wholly correct. For that act is nothing other than a commission, a form of employment in which the governors, as simple officers of the sovereign, exercise in its name the power it has placed in their hands, a power which the sovereign can limit, modify, and resume at pleasure, since the alienation of such a right would be incompatible with the nature of the social body and contrary to the purpose of the social union.

I therefore call "government" or "supreme administration" the legitimate exercise of the executive power, and I call "prince" or "magistrate" the man or the body charged with that administration.

It is in the government that we may discern those intermediary forces whose relations constitute those of all with all, or of the sovereign with the state. This last relation can be depicted as one between the extremes of a continuous proportion, of which the geometrical mean is the government. The government receives from the sovereign the orders which it gives to the people; and if the state is to be well balanced, it is necessary, all things being weighed, that the product and power of the government considered in itself should equal the product and power of the citizens who are sovereign in one sense and subjects in another.

Furthermore, no one of these three factors can be changed without destroying the balance. If the sovereign seeks to govern, or if the magistrate seeks to legislate, or if the subjects refuse to obey, then order gives way to chaos, power and will cease to act in concert, and the state, disintegrating, will lapse either into despotism or into anarchy. Lastly, as there is only one geometrical mean between two extremes, there is only one good government possible for any state; but as a thousand events may change the relations within a nation, different governments may not only be good for different peoples, but good for the same people at different times.

To try to give some idea of the various relations which may exist between the two extremes, I shall take as an example the number of the people, as this is a relation easily expressed.

Suppose the state is made up of ten thousand citizens. The sovereign can only be considered collectively and as a body, but every member as a subject has to be considered as an individual. Thus the sovereign is to the subject as ten thousand is to one, that is to say, each single member of the state has for his own share only a ten-thousandth part of the sovereign authority, although he submits himself entirely to it. Now if the people is increased to a hundred thousand men, the position of the subject is unaltered, for each bears equally with the rest the whole empire of the laws, while as sovereign his share of the suffrage is reduced to one hundred-thousandth, so that he has ten times less influence in the formulation of the laws. Hence, as the subject remains always one single individual, the ratio of sovereign to subject increases according to the number of citizens. Whence it follows that the more the state is enlarged, the more freedom is diminished.

When I say that the ratio increases, I mean that it is farther removed from parity. So the greater the ratio in the geometrical sense, the smaller the ratio in the popular sense; for in the former, the ratio, considered according to quantity, is measured by the quotient, whereas in the latter, the ratio, considered according to identity, is judged by similarity.

The smaller the ratio between the particular wills and the general will, that is, between the people's morals and the law, the more will repressive force have to be employed. Hence, for the government to be good, its strength must be increased to the extent that the people is more numerous.

In proportion as the enlargement of the state means offering the holders of public authority more temptations and more opportunities to abuse their power, it follows that the more power the government needs to control the people, the more power the sovereign needs, in its turn, to control the government. I am speaking here not of an absolute power, but of the relative power of the different elements in the state.

It follows from this double ratio that the continuous proportion between sovereign, prince, and people is by no means an arbitrary idea, but a necessary consequence of the nature of the body politic. It follows further that since one of the extremes, namely the people as subject, is represented by unity, every time the double ratio is increased or diminished, the simple ratio increases or diminishes in the same way,

---

1. Thus in Venice the ruling college is called the Most Serene Prince even when the Doge is not present.

and the middle term is in consequence changed. This shows that there is no one unique and absolute constitution of government, but that there may be as many different kinds of government as there are states of different sizes.

If anyone, wishing to ridicule this system, suggested that in order to find the geometrical mean and construct the body of the government one need only on my view take the square root of the number of the people, I should reply that I am here using that number only as an example; and the ratios of which I speak are not measured merely by the number of men but more generally by the amount of activity, which results from the concurrence of innumerable causes; I should add that although I have borrowed momentarily for the sake of expressing myself in fewer words, the language of geometry, I am still well aware that geometrical precision has no place in moral calculations.

The government is in small what the body politic (which includes it) is in large. It is a fictitious person endowed with certain faculties, active like the sovereign, passive like the state; and it can be broken down into similar relations; in consequence these relations yield a new ratio; and within each we can continue the process of analysis according to the order of the magistracies until we reach a single indivisible middle term, that is, a single chief or supreme magistrate, who may be shown at the centre of this pattern, as the unity between the series of fractions and the series of whole numbers.

Without burdening ourselves with such a multiplication of terms, let us simply consider the government as a new body within the state, distinct from both people and sovereign and intermediary between the two.

There is this essential difference between the two bodies—the state exists in itself while the government exists only through the sovereign. Thus the dominant will of the prince is, or ought to be, only the general will or the law, and his force nothing other than the public force concentrated in his hands; as soon as he resolves to perform on his own authority some absolute and independent act, the union of all begins to slacken. And if in the end it comes about that the prince has a particular will more active than that of the sovereign, and if, to enforce obedience to this particular will, he uses the public force which is in his hands, with the result that there are, so to speak, two sovereigns, one *de jure* and the other *de facto*, then the social bond vanishes at once and the body politic is dissolved.

Even so, for the body of the government to have an existence, a real life distinct from the body of the state, and for all its members to be able to act in concert and serve the purpose for which the government has been set up, it must have a particular *ego*, a consciousness common to its members, a force, a will of its own tending to its preservation. Such a particular existence implies assemblies, councils, a power to deliberate and determine rights, titles, and privileges which belongs exclusively to the prince, and which should make the position of the magistrate the more honourable in proportion to the extent to which it is the more arduous. The difficulty is to find a method of ordering this subordinate whole within the greater whole, so that it does not weaken the general constitution while strengthening its own, and so that its private force, designed for its own preservation, shall always be distinct from the public force, designed for the preservation of the state; in short, so that it will always be ready to sacrifice the government to the people and not the people to the government.

Moreover, even though the artificial body of the government is the work of another equally artificial body, and even though it has only a kind of borrowed and subordinate life, this does not prevent its being able to act with greater or less vigour and speed, and enjoying, so to speak, a health that may be more robust or less. Lastly, without departing directly from the purposes for which it has been set up, it may deviate from them in varying degrees according to the manner in which it has been constituted.

It is all these differences which give rise to the various relations that ought to exist between the government and the body of the state, in accordance with the fortuitous and particular relations by which this same state is changed. For often the government which is in itself the best becomes the most evil unless its relations with the state are modified to meet the defects of the body politic to which it belongs.

Chapter 2
The Constitutive Principle of the Different Forms of Government

To explain the general reason for these differences, it is necessary to distinguish here between the prince and the government, as I have already distinguished between the state and the sovereign.

The body of the magistrates may be composed of a greater or lesser number of members. We have already observed that the ratio of sovereign to subjects is greater to the extent that the people are more numerous, and by an obvious analogy we can say the same of the government in relation to the magistrates.

As the total power of the government is at all times that of the state, it never varies; and from this it follows that the more force the government exerts over its own members, the less there remains for it to use over the whole people.

Hence the more numerous the magistrates, the weaker the government. As this principle is fundamental, let us try to make it clearer.

We may distinguish in the person of the magistrate three essentially different wills. First, there is the will which belongs to the individual, and tends only to his personal advantage. Secondly, there is the collective will of the magistrates; this is concerned only with the advantage of the prince, and might be called the corporate will, since it is general *vis-à-vis* the government and particular *vis-à-vis* the state of which the government is a part. Thirdly, there is the will of the people or the sovereign will, which is general both with regard to the state considered as a whole and with regard to the government considered as part of the whole.

In a perfect system of legislation, the individual or particular will would be nonexistent, the government's own corporate will very subordinate, and the general or sovereign will therefore always dominant and always the sole regulator of all the others.

In the order of nature, on the contrary, these different wills become the more active as they are the more concentrated. Hence, the general will is always the weakest, the corporate will takes second place, and the particular will comes first of all; so much so, that within the government, each member is primarily a private self, secondly a magistrate, and thirdly a citizen. This sequence is exactly the reverse of what the social order demands.

That being so, let us suppose that the government is in the hands of a single individual. Then the particular will and this corporate will will be perfectly united, and the corporate will accordingly raised to its highest possible degree of intensity. Now, since the exercise of power depends on the degree of will, and since the absolute power of the government is invari-able, it follows that the most active government is that of one man.

If, on the other hand, we combine the government and the legislative authority, make the prince the sovereign, and each citizen a magistrate—then the corporate will, being merged in the general will, will be no more active than the general will, and so leave the particular will to command the totality of power. Thus the government, having always the same absolute power, will be left with a minimum of relative strength and activity.

These relations are indisputable, and other considerations add further confirmation. It is clear, for example, that each magistrate is more active within the body of the government than is each citizen within the body of the state, and hence that the particular will has more influence over the acts of the government than it has over those of the sovereign, for every magistrate is nearly always entrusted with some distinct function of government, while no citizen, taken singly, has any distinct function of sovereignty. Besides, the more the state expands, the more its real strength is increased, though not in proportion to its expansion; but while the state remains the same size, the magistrates can be multiplied without the government gaining thereby any real strength, since its strength is that of the state, which is always the same. In this way the relative strength or activity of the government diminishes without there being any possibility of its absolute or real power increasing.

Again, there is no doubt that the dispatch of public business becomes slower in proportion as there are more persons responsible for it; attaching too much importance to prudence, large bodies attach too little to luck; they miss opportunities, and they deliberate so long that they lose the profits of deliberation.

I have just shown that the government slackens to the extent that the magistrates are multiplied, and I showed earlier that the more numerous the people, the more the repressive force must increase. From this it follows that the ratio of magistrates to government should be the inverse of the ratio of subjects to sovereign; that is to say, the more the state is enlarged, the more the government must reduce its ranks, so that the number of magistrates diminishes in proportion to the increase of the people.

I should add that I am speaking here of the relative strength of the government and not the quality of its behaviour; for, on the contrary, the more numerous the magistrates, the closer their corporate will approaches the general will, while under a single magistrate that same corporate will is, as I have said, only a particular will. Thus there is lost on the one side what could be gained on the other; and the art of the lawgiver is to know how to settle the point at which the strength and the will of the government, which always stand in inverse ratio, can be combined in the proportion most beneficial to the state.

Chapter 3
Classification of Governments

In the preceding chapter we saw why the different types or forms of government are distinguished according to the number of members who compose them; it remains to be seen in the present chapter how this classification is made.

First, the sovereign may put the government in the hands of the whole people, or of the greater part of the people, so that there are more citizen-magistrates than there are ordinary private citizens. This form of government is known as *democracy.*

Alternatively, the sovereign may confine the government to the hands of a few, so that there are more ordinary citizens than there are magistrates: this form of government is called *aristocracy.*

Yet again, the sovereign may concentrate the entire government in the hands of one single magistrate, from whom all the others will derive their power. This third form of government is the most common, and is called *monarchy* or royal government.

It should be noticed that all these forms, or at any rate the first two, can be had in greater or lesser degrees; they have a fairly marked elasticity. Democracy may include all the people or it may be limited so as to include only half. Aristocracy in its turn may extend to half the people or be limited to the smallest possible number. Even royal government can to some extent be shared. Sparta had always two kings according to its constitution, and the Roman Empire is known to have had as many as eight Emperors at once without it being true to say that the Empire was divided. Thus there is always a point at which each form of government overlaps the next form; and it is clear that although government has only three names, it is actually open to as many variations of form as the state has citizens.

Moreover, since a government is able in certain respects to divide itself into separate parts, one administered in one way and the other in another way, the three forms of government may be combined to yield a multitude of mixed forms, each of which it can multiply by the three simple forms.

Throughout the ages men have debated the question "What is government?", and yet they have failed to see that each of the possible forms is the best in some cases and the worst in others.

If in each particular state the number of supreme magistrates should be in inverse ratio to the number of citizens, it follows that, in general, democratic government suits small states, aristocratic government suits states of intermediate size, and monarchy suits large states. This rule follows directly from our axiom; but how are we to calculate the multitude of particular circumstances which may offer exceptions to the rule?

Chapter 4
Democracy

He who makes the law knows better than anyone how it should be executed and interpreted. So it might seem that there could be no better constitution than one which united the executive power with the legislative; in fact, this very union makes that form of government deficient in certain respects, for things which ought to be kept apart are not, and the prince and the sovereign being the same person constitute, so to speak, a government without government.

It is not good that he who makes the law should execute it or that the body of the people should turn its attention away from general perspectives and give it to particular objects. Nothing is more dangerous in public affairs than the influence of private interests, and the abuse of the law by the government is a lesser evil than that corruption of the legislator which inevitably results from the pursuit of private interests. When this happens, the state is corrupted in its very substance and no reform is possible. A people which never misused the powers of government would never misuse independence, and a people which always governed itself well would not need to be governed.

In the strict sense of the term, there has never been a true democracy, and there never will be. It is contrary to the natural order that the greater number should govern and the smaller number be governed. One can hardly imagine that all the people would sit permanently in an assembly to deal with public affairs; and one can easily see that they could not appoint commissions for that purpose without the form of administration changing.

I believe indeed that one can lay down as an axiom that when the functions of government are divided between several commissions, those with the fewest members acquire sooner or later the greatest authority, if only because the facility of dispatching business leads naturally in that direction.

Besides, how many things that are difficult to have at the same time does the democratic form of government not presuppose? First, a very small state, where the people may be readily assembled and where each citizen may easily know all the others. Secondly, a great simplicity of manners and morals, to prevent excessive business and thorny discussions. Thirdly, a large measure of equality in social rank and fortune, without which equality in rights and authority will not last long. Finally, little or no luxury; for luxury is either the effect of riches or it makes riches necessary; it corrupts both the rich and the poor; it sells the country to effeminacy and vanity; it deprives the state of all its citizens by making some the slaves of others and all the slaves of opinion.

This is why a celebrated author has made virtue the cardinal principle of a republic; for all the conditions that I have named cannot prevail without virtue. But this same great genius, having failed to make the necessary distinctions, was often wrong and sometimes obscure, and failed to see that since the sovereign authority is everywhere the same, the same principles should have a place in every well-constituted state, though to a greater or lesser extent, assuredly, according to the form of the government.

We may add that there is no government so liable to civil war and internecine strife as is democracy or popular government, for there is none which has so powerful and constant a tendency to change to another form or which demands so much vigilance and courage to maintain it unchanged. It is under this constitution, before all others, that the citizen must be armed with strength and fidelity, and repeat from the bottom of his heart every day of his life the words a virtuous Palatine[1] once spoke in the Diet of Poland: "*Malo periculosam libertatem quam quietum servitium.*"[2]

If there were a nation of Gods, it would govern itself democratically. A government so perfect is not suited to men.

Chapter 5
Aristocracy

We have here two distinct artificial persons, namely the government and the sovereign, and therefore two general wills, one belonging to all the citizens, and the other to members of the administration only. Thus, although the government may regulate its interior discipline as it pleases, it can never speak to the people except in the name of the sovereign, that is, in the name of the people itself—something that must never be forgotten.

The first societies were governed aristocratically. The heads of families deliberated on public business among themselves; the young people yielded willingly to the authority of experience. Hence the names of *priests, elders, the senate, gerontes.* The savages of North America still retain today this method of government, and they are very well governed.

But to the extent that artificial inequality came to prevail over natural inequality, riches and power[1] came to be preferred to age, and aristocracy became elective. Lastly, the bequeathing of power together with goods by fathers to their children made families patrician and so made government hereditary; and then there appeared senators aged twenty.

There are thus three types of aristocracy, natural, elective, and hereditary. The first is suited only to primitive peoples; the third is the worst of all governments; the second is the best, and this is aristocracy in the true sense of the word.

Aristocracy has not only the advantage of distinguishing between the sovereign and the government, it has also the advantage of selecting its magistrates. Under popular government all the citizens are born magistrates, while this other system limits itself to a small number of magistrates, every one of whom is elected,[2] a method which makes honesty, sagacity,

---

1. The Palatine of Posen, father of the King of Poland and Duke of Lorraine.
2. "Better freedom with danger than peace with slavery." [*Trans.*]

---

1. It is clear that the word *Optimates*, for the ancients, did not mean the best but the strongest.
2. It is of the utmost importance that the law should regulate the procedure of election of magistrates, for if this is left to the will of the prince, there will be no avoiding a decline into hereditary aristocracy, as happened in the Republics of Venice and Berne.

experience, and all the other grounds of popular preference and esteem further guarantees of wise government.

Besides, assemblies can be more easily arranged, business can be better discussed and be dispatched with more order and diligence; the credit of the state is better upheld in the eyes of foreigners by venerable senators than it is by an unknown and despised multitude.

In a word, it is the best and most natural arrangement for the wisest to govern the multitude, if we are sure that they will govern it for its advantage and not for their own. One ought never to multiply devices uselessly, or employ twenty thousand men to do what a hundred picked men could do much better. But it must be noted that the corporate interest begins at this point to direct the national energies less strictly in accordance with the general will, and that a further inevitable tendency is for a part of the executive power to escape the domain of law.

As for the circumstances which suit this form of government, it is not necessary to have the state so small or the people so simple and upright that the execution of the law follows directly from the public will, as is the case in a good democracy. Nor must the nation be so large that the magistrates, being widely scattered, have to take upon themselves some of the powers of the sovereign, each in his own region; and so begin by making themselves independent and end by becoming masters.

But if aristocracy calls for rather fewer virtues than does popular government, it still calls for virtues of its own, such as moderation among the rich and contentment among the poor; for it seems that strict equality would be out of place; it was not observed even in Sparta.

Moreover, if this form of government involves a certain inequality of wealth, that is simply so that the administration of public affairs may be entrusted to those who can best give all their time to it, and not, as Aristotle asserted, so that the rich should always be chosen. On the contrary, it is necessary that an opposite choice should occasionally teach people that

merit is a more important qualification than riches for preference.

Chapter 6
Monarchy

So far we have considered the prince as a collective and artificial person, unified by the force of the law and acting as trustee of executive power in the state. We have now to consider that power being held in the hands of a natural person, a real man, one having the sole right to exercise it according to the law. Such a man is known as a monarch or king.

Contrary to the other administrations, where a collective being represents an individual, in this one an individual represents a collective being; so that the moral unity which constitutes the prince is at the same time a physical unity, naturally bringing together those faculties which the law brings together with such difficulty in the other forms of administration.

Thus the will of the people and the will of the prince, the public force of the state and the individual power of the government, all respond to the same mover; all the levers of the machine are in the same hands; all act towards the same end; there are no conflicting movements to counteract one another, and we cannot imagine any constitution where more action would be produced by less effort. Archimedes sitting quietly on the shore and effortlessly launching a large ship is the model of a skilful monarch governing his vast kingdom from his chamber and making everything move while he himself seems motionless.

But if there is no government more vigorous than monarchy, there is also none where the particular will has more command, and more easily dominates the other wills. Everything moves towards the same end, it is true, but that end is not the public happiness; and the very strength of the administration operates continuously to the disadvantage of the state.

Kings want to be absolute, and from afar men cry out to them that the best way of becoming absolute is to make themselves loved by their people. This is a fine precept; and even in some respects a very true one. Unfortunately, it will always be laughed at in courts. The power which rests on the love of the people is undoubtedly the greatest, but is precarious and contingent; and princes will never be satisfied with it. The best kings want to be able to be bad if they feel like it without ceasing to be masters; a political sermonizer may well tell kings that since the people's

---

The first of these two states has long since fallen into decay, while the other preserves itself only by the extreme wisdom of its senate—a very honourable and very dangerous exception to the rule.

force is the king's force, a king's best interest is to have the people flourishing, numerous and formidable; but kings know very well that this is not true. Their personal interest is primarily that the people should be weak, wretched and never able to resist them. I admit that if the subjects were always perfectly submissive, then it would be to the interest of the prince for the people to be strong, so that the people's strength, being also the prince's strength, should make him feared by his neighbours; but since this is only a secondary and subordinate advantage, and since strength is incompatible with submissiveness, it is natural that princes always prefer the doctrine that is more immediately useful to them. This is what Samuel put forcefully to the Hebrews, and what Machiavelli has proved very clearly—under the pretence of instructing kings, he has taught important lessons to the people. Machiavelli's *Prince* is a handbook for republicans.[1]

We have seen from the discussion of general proportions that monarchy is suited only to large states, and we find this again when we examine monarchy in itself. The more numerous the public administrators, the more the ratio between prince and subjects diminishes and approaches parity, coming to a point where the ratio is one to one, or equality itself, in democracy. This same ratio is greater to the extent that the government contracts, and reaches its maximum when the government is in the hands of a single man. Then there is too great a distance between the prince and the people and the state lacks bonds of union. For such bonds to be formed, there must be intermediary ranks, with princelings, grandees, and a nobility to fill them. But all this is unsuited to a small state, which would be ruined by so many social orders.

---

1. Machiavelli was a gentleman and a good citizen; but being attached to the house of Medici, he was forced during the oppression of his country to disguise his love of liberty. The very choice of an execrable hero reveals his secret intention, and the antithesis between his principles in his book *The Prince* and those in his *Discourses on Livy* and *The History of Florence* proves that this profound political thinker has so far had only superficial or corrupted readers. The Pope's court strictly prohibited his book, which I can well believe, since that was the Court he depicts most plainly. [Note added to the Edition of 1782.]

But if it is difficult for a large state to be well governed, it is still more difficult for it to be well governed by a single man; and everyone knows what happens when a king rules through deputies.

An essential and inevitable defect, which will always make monarchical government inferior to republican government, is that whereas in republics the popular choice almost always elevates to the highest places only intelligent and capable men, who fill their office with honour, those who rise under monarchies are nearly always muddled little minds, petty knaves and intriguers with small talents which enable them to rise to high places in courts, but which betray their ineptitude to the public as soon as they are appointed. The people is much less often mistaken in such choices than is a prince, and a man of real merit is almost as rare in a royal ministry as a fool at the head of a republican government. Thus, when by some happy chance a born ruler takes the helm of affairs in a monarchy that is almost wrecked by swarms of egregious administrators, then everyone is amazed at the resources he discovers, and his reign marks an epoch in the history of the country.

For a monarchy to be well governed, its size and extent ought to be proportionate to the talents of those who govern. It is easier to conquer than to administer. With enough leverage, a finger could overturn the world; but to support the world, one must have the shoulders of Hercules. However small the state may be, princes are almost always inadequate. When, on the other hand, it happens that the state is too small for its ruler, a very rare thing, then it is even worse governed, because such a ruler, in following his own broad vision, forgets the people's interest; and he makes them no less miserable by the misuse of his superabundant abilities than a mediocre ruler would make them through the defects of an insufficient talent. It is as if kingdoms ought, so to speak, to expand or contract with each successive reign, according to the capacity of the prince. In a republic, on the other hand, where the talents of the senate are of a more settled measure, the state can have fixed boundaries without the administration working any less well.

The most perceptible disadvantage of government by one man is the lack of that continuity of succession which provides an uninterrupted bond of union in the other two systems. When a king dies, another is needed; elections leave a dangerous interval; they are stormy; and unless the citizens have more disinterestedness and integrity than is usual under such governments, there will be bribery and corruption. It is difficult for one to whom the state has been sold not to sell it in his turn, and recover from the weak the gold which the strong have extorted from him. Sooner or later, under such an administration everything becomes venal; and the peace which is enjoyed under kings is worse than the disturbances of interregnums.

What has been done to prevent this evil? Thrones have been made hereditary in certain families, and an order of succession thus set up to prevent any dispute on the death of the king—that is to say, by substituting for the disadvantages of elections, the disadvantages of regencies, apparent peace has been preferred to wise administration, and the risk of having children or monsters or imbeciles for rulers preferred to having to dispute the choice of a good king. People do not realize that in exposing themselves to the hazards of these alternatives, they are gambling against all the odds. It was a very shrewd remark that the young Dionysus made to his father, when his father, reproaching him for a dishonourable action, said: "Did I set you such an example?" "Ah," replied the son, "your father was not a king."

When someone is brought up to command others, everything conspires to rob him of justice and reason. Great pains are taken, we are told, to teach young princes the art of ruling; but it does not appear that this education does them any good. It would be better to begin by teaching them the art of obeying. The greatest kings known to history were not among those brought up to rule, for ruling is a science that is least well mastered by too much practice; it is one a man learns better in obeying than in commanding. *Nam utilissimus idem ac brevissimus bonarum malarumque rerum delectus, cogitare quid aut nolueris sub alio Principe aut volueris.*[2]

One consequence of this lack of coherence is the instability of royal government, which, being some-

times directed according to one plan and sometimes according to another, depending on the personality of the king who rules, or of those who rule for him, cannot long have a fixed objective or a consistent policy; this unsettledness makes the state drift from principle to principle, and from project to project, a defect not found in those forms of government where the prince is always the same. Thus we see that, in general, if there is more cunning in a royal court, there is more wisdom in a republican senate, and that republics have a more stable and effective guidance—something which cannot obtain where every revolution in the administration means a revolution in the state—for it is the universal rule of all ministers and nearly all kings to reverse the policy of their predecessors.

This same lack of cohesion gives the lie to a sophism which is very common among royalist political thinkers, that is, not only of comparing civil government to household government and the prince to the father of a family—a fallacy I have already refuted —but also of generously attributing to a royal ruler all the virtues he has need of, and always assuming that the prince is everything he should be. With the help of these assumptions, royal government becomes manifestly preferable to all other kinds, because it is incontestably the strongest, and needs only a corporate will more in harmony with the general will to be also the best form of government.

But if, according to Plato, a born king is a very rare being—how often do Nature and Fortune combine to enthrone such a man? And if a royal education necessarily corrupts those who receive it, what must be expected of a succession of men brought up to rule?

It is deliberate self-deception to confuse royal government with the government of a good king. To understand what this form of government is inherently, one must consider it as it is under mediocre or evil princes, for either princes will be such when they accede to the throne or such is what occupying the throne will make them.

Although these difficulties do not escape our authors, they have never been in the least embarrassed by them. The remedy, they say, is to obey without a murmur. God in his wrath inflicts bad kings on us, so they must be endured as a divine punishment. This argument is undoubtedly edifying, but I fancy it is more suited to the pulpit than to a book on political theory. What would be said about a physician who

---

2. "The best as well as the shortest way to find out what is good and what is bad is to consider what you would have wished to happen if someone other than yourself had been Prince." (Tacitus, *History*, Book I.) [*Trans.*]

promised miracles, and whose whole art was to teach the sick to practise patience?

We all know that we have to put up with a bad government when it is bad; the problem is to find a good government.

Chapter 7
Mixed Forms of Government

Strictly speaking, no government of a simple form exists. A single head of state has to have subordinate magistrates; a people's government must have a head. Thus in the division of executive power there is always a gradation from the larger number to the smaller—with this difference, that sometimes the many depend on the few, and sometimes the few depend on the many.

Sometimes there is an equal division, either when the constitutive parts are mutually dependent, as in the government of England, or when the authority of each part is independent but imperfect, as in the case of Poland. This latter form is bad, because there is no unity in the government, and the state lacks bonds of union. Which is better: a simple form of government or a mixed one? This is a question much debated by political theorists, and one to which I myself must give the answer I gave earlier about all forms of government.

In itself, the simple form of government is the best, precisely because it is simple. But when the executive power is not sufficiently subordinate to the legislative—that is to say, when the ratio of prince to sovereign is greater than that of people to prince—this lack of proportion has to be remedied by dividing the government, for then all the diverse elements of the government will have no less authority over the subjects, but their separation will make them less powerful against the sovereign.

The same disadvantage can also be prevented by establishing intermediate magistrates who, separated from the government altogether, serve only to balance the two powers, and uphold their respective rights. Then the government is not mixed, it is tempered.

The opposite disadvantage can be remedied by similar means; and when the government is too slack, commissions can be set up to give it concentration. In the first case, the government is divided in order to weaken it; in the second, in order to strengthen it. This is the practice of all democracies. The maximum of strength and of weakness are equally found in the simple forms of government, whereas the mixed forms provide a moderate degree of strength.

Chapter 8
*That All Forms of Government
Do Not Suit All Countries*

Freedom is not a fruit of every climate, and it is not therefore within the capacity of every people. The more one reflects on this doctrine of Montesquieu, the more one is conscious of its truth. And the more often it is challenged, the more opportunities are given to establish it with new evidence.

In every government in the world, the public person consumes but does not produce anything. Whence does it obtain the substance it consumes? From the labour of its members. It is the surplus of private production which furnishes public subsistence. From this it follows that the civil state can subsist only if men's work yields more than they themselves need.

But this surplus is not the same in every country of the world. In some it is substantial, in others middling, in some nil, in others a deficit. The proportion depends on the fertility of the climate, on the kind of labour which the soil requires, on the nature of its products, on the strength of the inhabitants, and on the degree of consumption that is necessary for them, and on various other factors which go to make up the whole proportion.

In addition, all governments do not have the same nature; some are more voracious than others; and their differences are based on this next principle— that the further public contributions are from their source, the more burdensome they are. This burden should not be measured by the quantity of the contributions exacted, but by the distance they have to go to return to the hands from which they come; when this circulation is rapid and well established, it does not matter whether much or little is paid; the people will always be rich and finances will flourish. Correspondingly, however little the people gives, when that little does not return to it, it soon exhausts itself in continuous payments; the state is never rich and the people is always penurious.

This demonstrates that the greater the distance between the people and the government, the more onerous the taxes become; so that in a democracy the people is least burdened, in an aristocracy more burdened, and in a monarchy it bears the greatest weight of all. Monarchy is thus suited only to opulent nations, aristocracy to those of moderate wealth and size, and democracy to small and poor countries.

Indeed, the more one reflects, the more one recognizes that in this matter there are differences between free states and monarchies: in the former everything is used for the common advantage, while in the latter, private power and public power are competitive, and the one is increased only by weakening the other. As for despotism, instead of governing the subjects in order to make them happy, it makes them miserable in order to govern them.

Thus in every climate there are natural factors on the basis of which one can determine the form of government which that climate necessitates; and we can even say what sort of inhabitants each must have.

Mean and sterile places, where the product does not repay the labour, must remain uncultivated and deserted, or peopled only by savages. Places which yield only the bare necessities of men's lives must be inhabited by barbarous peoples, since no political society is possible. Places where the surplus of product over labour is moderate are suited to free peoples. Places where an abundant and fertile soil gives a lavish return for little labour will want monarchical government, so that the luxury of the prince may consume the surplus of the product of the subjects— for it is better that this surplus should be absorbed by the government than dissipated by private persons. There are exceptions, I know, but these exceptions themselves confirm the rule, in that sooner or later they produce revolutions which put things back into the order of nature.

We must always distinguish general laws from particular causes which can modify their effect. If all the South were covered with republics and all the North with despotic states, it would still be true that, in terms of climate, despotism suits hot countries, barbarism cold countries, and that a good polity suits temperate regions. I realize that this general rule may be admitted and its application disputed; it could be argued that there are very fertile cold countries and very barren southern ones. But this is a difficulty only for those who fail to see the thing in all its ramifications. One must, as I have already said, consider the factors of production, strength, consumption, and so on.

Suppose there are two equal territories, one yielding five units, the other ten. If the inhabitants of the former consume four and those of the latter nine, the surplus of the one will be one-fifth and of the other one-tenth. The ratio of these surpluses will then be the inverse of that of their products, so that the territory yielding five units will show a surplus double that of the territory yielding ten.

But there is no question of a double product, and I do not believe anyone could venture to equate the fertility of a cold country with that of a hot country. But let us assume such equality; let us, for example, equate England and Sicily, Poland and Egypt. Farther south there will be Africa and India; farther north, there will be nothing. What differences in agricultural technique will be needed to achieve this equality of product? In Sicily, it is enough simply to scratch the soil, while in England, how much effort is needed to work it! But where more hands are required to obtain the same product, the surplus is necessarily less.

Note a further point, that the same number of men consume much less in hot countries. The climate requires a man to be abstemious to keep fit—and Europeans who try to live in hot countries as they live at home die of dysentery and stomach disorders. "We," says Chardin, "are carnivorous beasts, wolves, compared to the Asians. Some attribute the abstemiousness of the Persians to the fact that their country is less cultivated; but I, on the contrary, believe that their country is less rich in commodities because the inhabitants need less. If their frugality [he continues] were the effect of the poverty of the soil, it would be the poor alone who ate little; in fact everybody does; and instead of finding people eating less or more in each province according to the fertility of the land, one finds the same frugality throughout the kingdom. They are very proud of their way of life, and say that one has only to look at their complexions to see how superior their way is to that of other nations. And indeed, the complexion of the Persians is clear, their skin is fair, delicate and smooth, while that of the Armenians, their subjects who live in the European manner, is rough and blotchy, and their bodies are fat and heavy."

The closer men are to the equator, the more frugally they live. They eat hardly any meat; rice, maize, couscous, millet, and cassava are their daily food. In India there are millions of men whose food costs less than a penny a day. In Europe itself we notice a marked difference of appetite between the peoples of the north and those of the south. A Spaniard could live eight days on the dinner of a German. In countries where men are more gluttonous, luxury is turned towards the things men consume. In England, it shows itself in tables loaded with meats; in Italy one is regaled on sugar and flowers.

Luxury in clothing reveals similar differences. In countries where the changes of season are swift and violent, people have better and simpler clothes; in countries where they dress only for appearance, people care more for show than utility, and clothes themselves are a luxury. In Naples you will see men strolling daily along the Posillipo in gold-embroidered jackets and no hose. It is the same thing with buildings; people attach importance to magnificence when they have nothing to fear from the climate. In Paris or London people want to be housed warmly and comfortably. In Madrid, they have superb reception rooms, but no windows that close and their bedrooms are like rat holes.

Foodstuffs are more substantial and richer in hot countries—this is a third difference and it does not fail to influence the second. Why does one eat so many vegetables in Italy? Because they are good, nourishing and of excellent flavour. In France, where they get nothing but water, they are not at all nourishing, and count for nothing at the table; but even so they take up no less ground and cost just as much to cultivate. Experiment has shown that the wheats of Barbary, otherwise inferior to those of France, yield much more flour; and that the French wheats in turn, yield more than those of the North. From this one can deduce that a similar gradation may be observed along a line from the equator to the pole. Now is it not a tangible disadvantage to have a smaller amount of nourishment in an equal quantity of produce?

To all these various considerations, I may add another which is drawn from, and which reinforces them, that is, that hot countries need fewer inhabitants than cold countries, and can feed more—which provides a double surplus to the advantage of despotism. The wider the area that is occupied by the same number of people, the more difficult revolts become, for the inhabitants cannot get together quickly and secretly, while it is always easy for the government to discover plots and to cut communications. On the other hand, the more a numerous people is packed together, the less easily can the government infringe on the sovereign; popular leaders deliberate as securely in their private rooms as the prince in his council, and the crowd gathers as swiftly in the public squares as the troops in their barracks. It is thus to the advantage of tyrannical government to act over great distances. With the aid of strongpoints to serve as fulcra, its strength increases with distance, on the principle of leverage.[1]

The strength of the people, on the contrary, is effective only if it is concentrated; it evaporates and is lost when it is dispersed, just as gunpowder scattered on the ground ignites only grain by grain. The least populous countries are thus the most fitted to tyranny; wild beasts reign only in deserts.

Chapter 9
The Signs of a Good Government

When, therefore, one asks what in absolute terms is the best government, one is asking a question which is unanswerable because it is indeterminate; or alternatively one might say that there are as many good answers as there are possible combinations in the absolute and relative positions of peoples.

But if it is asked by what signs one can tell whether a given people is well or badly governed, that is another matter; and the question of fact can be answered.

Even so, it is not really answered, because everyone will want to answer it in his own way. Subjects prize public tranquillity; citizens the freedom of the individual—the former prefer security of possessions, the latter security of person; subjects think the best government is the most severe, citizens that it is the mildest; the former want crimes to be punished, the latter want them prevented; subjects think it is a good thing to be feared by their neighbours, citizens prefer to be ignored by them; the former are satisfied so long as money circulates, the latter demand that the people shall have bread. But even if there were agreement on these and suchlike points, should we be any

---

1. This does not contradict what I said in Book II, Chapter 9, about the disadvantages of a large state, for there I was dealing with the authority of the government over its members, and here it is a question of the government's strength over the subjects. Its scattered members serve it as so many fulcra to exert pressure on the people from a distance, but it has no such fulcrum to exert pressure on its own members. Thus in the one case the length of the lever is its weakness; in the other, its strength.

more advanced? Moral dimensions have no precise standard of measurement; even if we could agree about signs, how should we agree in appraisal?

For myself, I am always astonished that people should fail to recognize so simple a sign, or be so insincere as not to agree about it. What is the object of any political association? It is the protection and the prosperity of its members. And what is the surest evidence that they are so protected and prosperous? The numbers of their population. Then do not look beyond this much debated evidence. All other things being equal, the government under which, without external aids like naturalization and immigration, the citizens increase and multiply most, is infallibly the best government. That under which the people diminishes and wastes away is the worst. Statisticians, this is your problem: count, measure, compare.[1]

---

1. One must judge on the same principle the centuries that merit preference in respect of the prosperity of the human race. People have too much admired those that have witnessed a flourishing of crafts and letters without penetrating the secret purpose of their culture, and without considering its fatal consequences, *idque apud imperitos humanitas vocabatur, cum pars servitutis esset.* Shall we never see behind the precepts of books the crude self-interest which prompts the authors to speak? No, whatever they may say, when, notwithstanding its brilliance, a country is depopulated, it is simply not true that all is going well; and it is not enough for a poet to have an income of 100,000 livres for his century to be the best of all. It is less important to consider the apparent repose and tranquillity of rulers than the wellbeing of whole nations and above all of the most populous states. A hailstorm may devastate a few cantons, but it rarely causes famine. Riots and civil wars may greatly alarm rulers, but they are not the true misfortunes of peoples, who can at least have a few months' respite during the quarrels as to who is to be the next tyrant. Their calamities and their happiness both arise from their permanent condition. When all remain supine under the yoke, it is then that everything decays, it is then that the rulers can destroy them at their ease, *ubi solitudinem faciunt pacem appellant.* When the quarrels of the state disturbed the kingdom of France, and the Coadjutor of Paris attended the *Parlement* with a dagger in his pocket, this did not prevent the French people living happily and multiplying in a free and decent ease. In ancient times, Greece flourished at the height of the cruellest wars; blood flowed in torrents, but the whole country was thickly populated. "It appeared," says Machiavelli, "that in the midst of murder, proscription, and civil wars, our republic became stronger than ever; the civil virtue of the citizens, their morals, and their independence, served more effectively to strengthen it than all their dissensions may have done to weaken it." A little disturbance gives vigour to the soul, and what really makes the species prosper is not peace but freedom.

Chapter 10
The Abuse of Government and Its Tendency to Degenerate

Just as the particular will acts unceasingly against the general will, so does the government continually exert itself against the sovereign. And the more this exertion increases, the more the constitution becomes corrupt, and, as in this case there is no distinct corporate will to resist the will of the prince and so to balance it, sooner or later it is inevitable that the prince will oppress the sovereign and break the social treaty. This is the inherent and inescapable defect which, from the birth of the political body, tends relentlessly to destroy it, just as old age and death destroy the body of a man.

There are two common ways by which a government degenerates—when it itself contracts and when the state dissolves.

The government contracts when its members pass from a greater to a smaller number, that is, from democracy to aristocracy, or from aristocracy to royal government. This is its natural tendency.[1] If

---

1. The slow formation and progress of the Republic of Venice in its lagoons provides a notable example of this progression; and it is really astonishing that after more than twelve hundred years, the Venetians seem still to be at the second stage, which began with the Serrar di Consiglio in 1198. As for the ancient Doges, for whom the Venetians are reproached, whatever may be said by the *squittinio della libertà veneta*, there is proof that the Doges were not their sovereigns.

People will not fail to quote against me the case of the Roman Republic, which is said to have followed a reverse sequence, from monarchy to aristocracy and from aristocracy to democracy. But I am very far from sharing this opinion.

The first constitution of Romulus was a mixed government, which promptly degenerated into a despotism. For special reasons, the state perished before its time, just as one sometimes sees an infant die before reaching the age of maturity. The expulsion of the Tarquins was the real moment of the birth of the Republic. But it did not at first assume a fixed form, because the failure to abolish the patriciate left the task half-finished. For the hereditary aristocracy, which is the worst of all legitimate administrations, remained in conflict with democracy, and the form of government, continuously uncertain and wavering, was not fixed (as Machiavelli has proved) until the establishment of the tribunes; only then was there a true government and a true democracy. For indeed the people then was not only sovereign, but also magistrate and judge; and the senate was no more than a subordinate commission to temper and concentrate the government, while the consuls themselves—in spite of their being patricians, chief magistrates, and absolute commanders in war—were never more in Rome than presidents of the people.

it were to move in the other direction from a smaller number to a greater, the government might be said to slacken; but such an inverse progression is impossible.

For indeed, a government never changes its form unless its exhausted energies are too feeble to maintain its original form. If it slackened while expanding, its strength would be absolutely null, and it would be even less likely to survive. It must therefore wind up and tighten the mechanism as it begins to slacken, for otherwise the state which depends on it will fall into ruin.

The dissolution of the state may take place in two ways.

First it takes place when the prince ceases to administer the state according to the law and usurps the sovereign power. Then a remarkable change occurs; for it is not the government but the state which contracts—by which I mean that the state as a whole is dissolved and another is formed inside it, one composed only of members of the government and having no significance for the rest of the people except that of a master and a tyrant. Now, at the moment the government usurps sovereignty, the social pact is broken, and all the ordinary citizens, recovering by right their natural freedom, are compelled by force, but not morally obliged, to obey.

The same situation occurs when the members of the government separately usurp the power which they ought only to exercise as a body; for this is no less an infraction of the law, and it produces an even greater disorder. For then there are, so to speak, as many princes as there are magistrates, and the state being no less divided than the government, perishes or changes its form.

When the state is dissolved, the abuse of government, whatever it may be, takes the general name of *anarchy*. More precisely democracy degenerates into *ochlocracy*, aristocracy into *oligarchy*, and I would add that royal government degenerates into *tyranny*, except that this last word is ambiguous and requires explanation.

In the commonly understood sense, a tyrant is a king who governs violently and without regard to justice and the law. In the exact sense, a tyrant is an individual who arrogates to himself royal authority without having any right to it. It is thus that the Greeks understood the word "tyrant." They applied it indiscriminately to good and bad princes whenever their authority was not legitimate.[2] Thus *tyrant* and *usurper* are perfectly synonymous words. To give different names to different things, I call a usurper of royal authority a "tyrant" and the usurper of the sovereign power a "despot." The tyrant is one who intrudes, contrary to law, to govern according to the law; the despot is one who puts himself above the law. Thus the tyrant need not be a despot, but a despot is always a tyrant.

Chapter 11
The Death of the Body Politic

Such is the natural and inevitable inclination of the best constituted governments. If Sparta and Rome perished, what state can hope to last for ever? If we wish, then, to set up a lasting constitution, let us not dream of making it eternal. We can succeed only if we avoid attempting the impossible and flattering ourselves that we can give to the work of man a durability that does not belong to human things.

The body politic, no less than the body of a man, begins to die as soon as it is born, and bears within

---

From that time, the government was seen to follow its natural inclination, and tend strongly towards aristocracy. The patriciate having as it were abolished itself, the aristocracy was no longer seated in the body of the patricians, as in Venice and Genoa, but in the body of the senate composed of patricians and plebeians, even in the body of the tribunes, when they began to usurp the active power. For words do not alter things, and when the people have chiefs who govern on their behalf, this is still an aristocracy no matter what name those persons bear.

The abuse of aristocracy gave birth to civil war and the triumvirate. Sulla, Julius Caesar, and Augustus became in fact as good as monarchs, and finally under the despotism of Tiberius the state was dissolved. Roman history, then, does not belie my principle: it confirms it.

---

2. "*Omnes enim et habentur et dicuntur Tyranni qui potestate utuntur perpetua, in ea Civitate quae libertate usa est.*" ("For all are thought and called tyrants who exercise perpetual power in a city accustomed to freedom." Cornelius Nepos, *Life of Miltiades*.) It is true that Aristotle (*Nicomachean Ethics*, VIII, 10) distinguishes between a tyrant and a king, saying the former governs for his own advantage while the latter governs only for the advantage of his subjects; but in addition to the fact that in general all the Greek authors use the word "tyrant" in another sense, as we see above all in the *Hiero* of Xenophon, it would follow from Aristotle's criterion, that there had never yet been a single king since the beginning of the world.

itself the causes of its own destruction. Either kind of body may have a constitution of greater or less robustness, fitted to preserve it for a longer or shorter time. The constitution of a man is the work of nature; that of the state is the work of artifice. It is not within the capacity of men to prolong their own lives, but it is within the capacity of men to prolong the life of the state as far as possible by giving it the best constitution it can have. And although even the best constitution will come to an end, it will do so later than any other, unless some unforeseen hazard fells it before its time.

The principle of political life dwells in the sovereign authority. The legislative power is the heart of the state, the executive power is the brain, which sets all the parts in motion. The brain may become paralysed and the individual still live. A man can be an imbecile and survive, but as soon as his heart stops functioning, the creature is dead.

It is not only through the law that the state keeps alive; it is through the legislative power. Yesterday's law is not binding today, but for the fact that silence gives a presumption of tacit consent and the sovereign is taken to confirm perpetually the laws it does not abrogate while it has power to abrogate them. Everything which it has once declared to be its will, it wills always—at least until it issues a revocation.

Why then do ancient laws command so much respect? Precisely because they are ancient. We must believe that it is only the excellence of such laws that has enabled them to last so long; if the sovereign had not continually recognized them as salutary, they would have been revoked a thousand times. This is why the laws, far from growing weaker, constantly gain new strength in every well-constituted state; the prejudice in favour of antiquity makes them every day more venerable; in those cases, on the other hand, where the laws become weaker with age, this shows that there is no longer any legislative power and that the state is dead.

Chapter 12
How the Sovereign Authority Maintains Itself

The sovereign, having no other force than the legislative power, acts only through the laws, and since the laws are nothing other than authentic acts of the general will, the sovereign can act only when the people is assembled. The people assembled, it will be said—what an illusion! It is indeed an illusion today; but two thousand years ago it was not. Has human nature so much changed?

The boundaries of the possible in the moral realm are less narrow than we think; it is our own weaknesses, our vices and our prejudices that limit them. Base minds do not believe in great men; low slaves smile in mockery at the word "freedom." In the light of what has been done, let us consider what can be done. I shall not speak of the ancient republics of Greece; but the Roman Republic was, it seems to me, a large state and the town of Rome a large town: the last census gave four hundred thousand men in Rome carrying arms, and the last census calculation under the Empire more than four million citizens without counting subjects, foreigners, women, children, or slaves.

One would suppose that it must have been difficult to bring together frequently the numerous people of the capital and its surroundings. In fact, very few weeks passed without the Roman people being assembled, even several times in one week. This people not only exercised the rights of sovereignty, but also a part of the government. It dealt with certain business; it tried certain cases; and the entire people in the public assemblies enacted the role of magistrate almost as often as that of citizen.

Looking back to the earliest history of nations, we notice that the majority of ancient governments, even monarchical ones like those of the Macedonians and the Franks, had similar assemblies. In any case, the one indisputable fact I have cited answers our question; it seems to me good logic to reason from the actual to the possible.

Chapter 13
The Same—Continued

It is not enough that the assembled people should have once determined the constitution of the state by giving sanction to a body of laws; it is not enough that it should set up a perpetual government, or that it should have provided once and for all for the election of magistrates. In addition to the extraordinary assemblies that unforeseen events may necessitate, there must be fixed and periodic assemblies which nothing can abolish or prorogue, so that on the appointed day the people is rightfully summoned by the law itself without any further formal convocation being needed.

But apart from these assemblies which are lawful by their date alone, any assembly of the people which has not been summoned by the magistrate appointed for that duty and according to the prescribed form must be held to be unlawful, and everything it does must be void, for the order to assemble should itself emanate from the law.

As to whether legitimate assemblies should be more or less frequent, this depends on so many circumstances that one cannot lay down in advance any precise rules. One can only say that in general the more strength the government has, the more frequently the sovereign should reveal itself.

This, I shall be told, may be good for one single town, but what is to be done if the state consists of several towns? Is the sovereign authority to be divided? Or should it be concentrated in one single town holding the others as subject? I answer that neither the one thing nor the other should be done. In the first place, the sovereign authority is simple and single; it cannot be divided without being destroyed. In the second place, a town cannot legitimately be subject to another any more than a nation may be, because the essence of the political body lies in the union of freedom and obedience so that the "subject" and "sovereign" are identical correlatives, the meaning of which is brought together in the single word "citizen."

I should answer further that it is always an evil to unite several towns in one nation, and whoever wishes to form such a union should not flatter himself that the natural disadvantages can be avoided. It is no use complaining about the evils of a large state to someone who wants only small ones. But how are small states to be given enough strength to resist large states, as the Greek cities once resisted a great king and as, more recently, Holland and Switzerland resisted the House of Austria?

Nevertheless, if the state cannot be limited to reasonable boundaries, there remains one remedy, and that is to have no fixed capital, but to move the seat of government from one place to another and to assemble the estates of the country in each in turn.

People the territory evenly, extend the same rights to everyone, carry the same abundance and life into every quarter—it is by these means that the state will become at once the strongest and the best governed that is possible. Remember that the walls of towns are made only from the debris of rural houses. Every time I see a mansion being built in the capital I fancy I can see the whole countryside covered with hovels.

Chapter 14
The Same—Continued

The moment the people is lawfully assembled as a sovereign body all jurisdiction of the government ceases; the executive power is suspended, and the person of the humblest citizen is as sacred and inviolable as that of the highest magistrate, for in the presence of the represented there is no longer any representation. Most of the disturbances which took place in the Roman assemblies were the result of this rule being either unknown or neglected. The consuls were no more than the presidents of the people; the tribunes were mere speakers;[1] the senate was nothing at all.

These intervals of suspension, when the prince recognizes—or ought to recognize—a real superior, are always alarming for princes; and the assemblies of the people, which are the shield of the body politic and the brake on the government, have always been the nightmare of magistrates; hence the latter spare no effort in raising objections, problems, promises to turn the citizens against assemblies. When the citizens are avaricious, cowardly, pusillanimous, and love repose more than freedom, they do not hold out against the redoubled efforts of the government. It is then that, as the opposing force increases continuously, the sovereign authority atrophies in the end and the majority of republics fall and perish before their time.

But between the sovereign authority and arbitrary government there sometimes appears an intermediate power of which we must now speak.

Chapter 15
Deputies or Representatives

As soon as public service ceases to be the main concern of the citizens and they come to prefer to serve the state with their purse rather than their person, the state is already close to ruin. Are troops needed to march to war? They pay mercenaries and stay at

---

1. The word is used here somewhat in the sense it has in the English parliament. The resemblance between these functions would have caused conflict between the Consuls and the Tribunes, even if all jurisdiction had been suspended.

home. Is it time to go to an assembly? They pay deputies and stay at home. Thanks to laziness and money, they end up with soldiers to enslave the country and deputies to sell it.

It is the bustle of commerce and the crafts, it is the avid thirst for profit, it is effeminacy and the love of comfort that commute personal service for money. Men give up a part of their profits so as to increase the rest at their ease. Use money thus, and you will soon have chains. The word "finance" is the word of a slave; it is unknown in the true republic. In a genuinely free state, the citizens do everything with their own hands and nothing by means of money; far from paying for exemption from their duties, they would pay to discharge them in person. I am very far from sharing received ideas: I believe that compulsory service is less contrary to liberty than is taxation.

The better the state is constituted, the more does public business take precedence over private in the minds of the citizens. There is indeed much less private business, because the sum of the public happiness furnishes a larger proportion of each individual's happiness, so there remains less for him to seek on his own. In a well-regulated nation, every man hastens to the assemblies; under a bad government, no one wants to take a step to go to them, because no one feels the least interest in what is done there, since it is predictable that the general will will not be dominant, and, in short, because domestic concerns absorb all the individual's attention. Good laws lead men to make better ones; bad laws lead to worse. As soon as someone says of the business of the state—"What does it matter to me,"—then the state must be reckoned lost.

The cooling-off of patriotism, the activity of private interest, the vastness of states, conquests, the abuse of government—all these have suggested the expedient of having deputies or representatives of the people in the assemblies of the nation. This is what in certain countries they dare to call the third estate—the private interest of two classes being there given first and second place, and the public interest only third place.

Sovereignty cannot be represented, for the same reason that it cannot be alienated; its essence is the general will, and will cannot be represented—either it is the general will or it is something else; there is no intermediate possibility. Thus the people's deputies are not, and could not be, its representatives; they are merely its agents; and they cannot decide anything finally. Any law which the people has not ratified in

person is void; it is not law at all. The English people believes itself to be free; it is gravely mistaken; it is free only during the election of Members of Parliament; as soon as the Members are elected, the people is enslaved; it is nothing. In the brief moments of its freedom, the English people makes such a use of that freedom that it deserves to lose it.

The idea of representation is a modern one. It comes to us from feudal government, from that iniquitous and absurd system under which the human race is degraded and which dishonours the name of man. In the republics and even in the monarchies of the ancient world, the people never had representatives; the very word was unknown. It is remarkable in the case of Rome, where the tribunes were so sacred, that no one ever imagined that they might usurp the functions of the people; and in the midst of such a great multitude, they never attempted to pass on their own authority a single *plebiscitium*. One can judge, however, the embarrassment the crowd sometimes caused from what happened at the time of the Gracchi, when a great part of the citizens voted from the rooftops.

Where rights and freedom are everything, inconveniences are nothing. Among these wise people, everything was given its just measure; the lictors were allowed to do what the tribunes would not have dared to do; the people were not afraid that their lictors would wish to represent them.

To explain how, even so, the tribunes did represent the people, it is enough to consider how the government represents the sovereign. Since the law is nothing other than a declaration of the general will, it is clear that there cannot be representation of the people in the legislative power; but there may and should be such representation in the executive power, which is only the instrument for applying the law. This indicates that if we look carefully, we shall find that very few nations have laws. However that may be, it is certain that the tribunes, having no part of the executive power, could never represent the Roman people by the rights of their own office, but only by usurping those of the senate.

Among the Greeks, all that the people had to do, it did itself; it was continuously assembled in the market place. The Greek people lived in a mild climate; it was not at all avaricious; slaves did the work; its chief concern was its freedom. Without the same advantages, how can the same rights be preserved? Your harsher climate creates more necessities;[1] six months of the year the public places are uninhabitable; your muted tongues cannot make themselves heard in the open air; you care more for your profits than your freedom; and you fear slavery less than you fear poverty.

What? Is freedom to be maintained only with the support of slavery? Perhaps. The two extremes meet. Everything outside nature has its disadvantages, civil society more than all the rest. There are some situations so unfortunate that one can preserve one's freedom only at the expense of the freedom of someone else; and the citizen can be perfectly free only if the slave is absolutely a slave. Such was the situation of Sparta. You peoples of the modern world, you have no slaves, but you are slaves yourselves; you pay for their liberty with your own. It is in vain that you boast of this preference; I see more cowardice than humanity in it.

I do not mean by all this to suggest that slaves are necessary or that the right of slavery is legitimate, for I have proved the contrary. I simply state the reasons why peoples of the modern world, believing themselves to be free, have representatives, and why peoples of the ancient world did not. However that may be, the moment a people adopts representatives it is no longer free; it no longer exists.

All things carefully considered, I do not see how it will be possible henceforth among people like us for the sovereign to maintain the exercise of its rights unless the republic is very small. But if it is very small, will it not be subjugated? No. I shall show later[2] how the external strength of a large people can be combined with the free government and good order of a small state.

Chapter 16
That the Institution of the Government Is Not a Contract

Once the legislative power is well established, it remains to establish similarly the executive power; for the latter, which operates only by particular acts, is essentially different from the former, and is naturally separate from it. If it were possible for the sovereign, considered as such, to have the executive power, then the *de jure* and the *de facto* would be so confused that people would no longer know what was law and what was not; and the body politic, thus perverted, would soon fall prey to that very violence it was instituted to prevent.

The citizens being all equal by the social contract, all may prescribe what all must do, instead of nobody having a right to demand that another shall do what he does not do himself. For it is precisely this right, indispensable for giving life and movement to the body politic, that the sovereign gives to the prince in instituting the government.

Several theorists have claimed that this act of institution is a contract between the people and the magistrates it sets over itself, a contract which stipulates between the two parties the conditions under which the one undertakes to command and the other to obey. It will be admitted, I am sure, that this is a strange way of contracting. But let us see if the theory is tenable.

First, the supreme authority can no more be modified than it can be alienated; to limit it is to destroy it. It is absurd and self-contradictory that the sovereign should give itself a superior; to undertake to obey a master would be to return to absolute freedom.

Furthermore, it is clear that this contract of the people with such or such persons would be a particular act. From this it follows that this contract could not be a law, or an act of sovereignty, and hence that it would be illegitimate.

We see further that the contracting parties would, between themselves, be subject only to natural law, and so without any guarantee of their reciprocal commitments—and this is wholly repugnant to the civil state. Since the man who has force in his hand is always the master of what shall be done, this is like giving the name of "contract" to the act of a man who says to another: "I give you all my property on condition that you give me back what you please."

There is only one contract in the state: that of the association itself, and this excludes all others. One cannot imagine any public contract that would not be a violation of the original contract.

---

1. To adopt in cold countries the luxury and softness of the orientals is to ask to have their chains, to make submission even more inevitable than theirs.

2. This is what I intended to do in the remaining part of this work, when, in dealing with foreign relations, I should have come to the subject of confederations. This subject is entirely new, and its principles have yet to be established.

Chapter 17
The Institution of the Government

In what conceptual terms then should we think of the act by which the government is instituted? I shall explain first that this act is complex, or composed of two others, namely the establishment of the law and the execution of the law.

By the first, the sovereign enacts that there shall be a body of government established with such or such form; and it is clear that this act is a law.

By the second, the people names the magistrates who are to be invested with the government thus established. Since this nomination is a particular act, it is not a second law, but simply a sequel to the first and a function of government.

The difficulty is to understand how there can be an act of government before the government exists, and how the people, which is only sovereign or subject, can in certain circumstances become prince or magistrate.

Now it is here once more that the body politic reveals one of those astonishing properties by which it reconciles operations that seem to be contradictory. For this operation is accomplished by the sudden transformation of the sovereignty into democracy in such a way that without undergoing any visible change, and simply through a new relation of all to all, the citizens become magistrates and pass from general acts to particular acts, and from the law to its execution.

This change of relation is not a refinement of speculative theory without example in practice; it happens every day in the English parliament, where the lower House on certain occasions transforms itself into a committee of the whole House the better to discuss affairs, and so becomes a simple committee of that sovereign court which it was itself a moment before; then later it reports to itself, in its capacity of House of Commons, on what it has just settled as a committee of the whole House, and again debates under one name what it has already decided under another.

It is the advantage peculiar to democratic government that it can be established in fact by a simple act of the general will. After this, the provisional government remains in office if such is the form adopted, or there is established in the name of the sovereign whatever government is prescribed by the law; and everything is then in order. It is not possible to institute the government in any other legitimate manner, without abandoning the principles established in earlier chapters.

Chapter 18
Means of Preventing the Usurpation of Government

From these explanations, it follows, in confirmation of Chapter 16, that the act which institutes the government is not a contract but a law, and that the holders of the executive power are not the people's masters but its officers; and that the people can appoint them and dismiss them as it pleases; and that there is no question of their contracting, but of obeying; and that in discharging the functions which the state imposes on them, they are only doing their duty as citizens, without having any sort of right to argue terms.

Thus when it happens that the people institutes a hereditary government, whether monarchical in one family, or aristocratic in a class of citizens, it does not enter into any undertaking; hereditary government is simply a provisional form that it gives to the administration until such time as it pleases to arrange it differently.

It is true that such changes are always dangerous, and that one should never touch an established government unless it has become incompatible with the public welfare; but such circumspection is a precept of politics and not a rule of law; and the state is no more bound to leave civil authority to its magistrates than military authority to its generals.

It is true again that in such cases one cannot observe with too great care all the formalities required to distinguish a regular and legitimate act from a seditious tumult, and the will of a whole people from the clamour of a faction. It is here above all that one must avoid yielding to socially harmful claims any more than is required by the strict application of the law; and it is from this obligation too that the prince derives a great opportunity of holding his power in defiance of the people, without it being possible to say that he has usurped it. For while appearing to exercise only his rights it is very easy for him to enlarge those rights and to prevent, on the pretext of public tranquillity, assemblies designed to re-establish good government; thus he exploits the silence which he prevents men breaking, and the irregularities which he makes them commit, to assume in his own favour the tacit consent of those whose mouths are closed by fear and to punish those who dare to speak. It was thus that the decemvirs, having been first elected for one year, and then continued for another, tried to retain their power in perpetuity, by no longer allowing the *comitia* to assemble. And it is by this simple means that all the governments of the world, once armed with the public force, sooner or later usurp the public authority.

The periodic assemblies of which I have already spoken are the right means to prevent or postpone this evil, above all those assemblies where no formal convocation is needed; for then the prince cannot prevent their meeting without openly proclaiming himself a violator of the laws and an enemy of the state.

At the opening of these assemblies, of which the only purpose is the maintenance of the social treaty, two motions should be put, motions which may never be annulled and which must be voted separately:

The first: "Does it please the sovereign to maintain the present form of government?"

The second: "Does it please the people to leave the administration to those at present charged with it?"

I assume here what I believe I have demonstrated, namely, that there is not in the state any fundamental law which may not be revoked, not even the social pact; for if all the citizens assemble to end this pact by a common accord, one cannot doubt that it is very legitimately ended. Grotius indeed thinks that each citizen may renounce his membership of the state, and recover his natural liberty and his goods on withdrawing from the country.[1] And it would be absurd if all the citizens united could not do what each of them separately can do.

Book IV

Chapter 1
That the General Will Is Indestructible

So long as several men joined together consider themselves a single body, they have only one will, which is directed towards their common preservation and general well-being. Then all the animating forces of the state are vigorous and simple; its principles are clear and luminous; it has no incompatible or conflicting interests; the common good makes itself so manifestly evident that only common sense is needed to discern it. Peace, unity, equality are enemies of political sophistication. Upright and simple men are difficult to deceive precisely because of their simplicity; stratagems and clever arguments do not prevail upon them; they are not indeed subtle enough to be dupes. When we see among the happiest people in the world bands of peasants regulating the affairs of state under an oak tree, and always acting wisely, can we help feeling a certain contempt for the refinements of other nations, which employ so much skill and mystery to make themselves at once illustrious and wretched?

A state thus governed needs very few laws, and whenever there is a need to promulgate new ones, that need is universally seen. The first man to propose such a law is only giving voice to what everyone already feels, and there is no question either of intrigues or of eloquence to secure the enactment of what each has already resolved to do as soon as he is sure that all the others will do likewise.

What misleads theorists is that, as a result of looking only at states which are badly constituted from the beginning, they are struck by the impossibility of maintaining such a régime there. They laugh at the thought of all the follies that a clever knave or a sly orator could persuade the people of Paris or London to commit. They do not realize that Cromwell would have been put to forced labour by the people of Berne,[1] and the Duc de Beaufort imprisoned by the Genevese.[2]

However, when the social tie begins to slacken and the state to weaken, when particular interests begin to make themselves felt and sectional societies begin to exert an influence over the greater society, the common interest becomes corrupted and meets

---

1. It being understood that none may leave the country to evade his duty, or avoid saving his country when it needs him. In such a case, flight would be criminal and punishable; it would not be withdrawal but desertion.

1. Literally "belled." It was the custom in Berne to hang bells round the necks of prisoners employed as forced labour on public works. [*Trans.*]

2. Literally "disciplined." In Geneva *la discipline* was a prison for the intractable rogues of the town. See Pléiade. *Œuvres complètes de Jean-Jacques Rousseau*, vol. 3 p. 1491. [*Trans.*]

opponents; voting is no longer unanimous; the general will is no longer the will of all; contradictions and disputes arise; and even the best opinion is not allowed to prevail unchallenged.

In the end, when the state, on the brink of ruin, can maintain itself only in an empty and illusory form, when the social bond is broken in every heart, when the meanest interest impudently flaunts the sacred name of the public good, then the general will is silenced: everyone, animated by secret motives, ceases to speak as a citizen any more than as if the state had never existed; and the people enacts in the guise of laws iniquitous decrees which have private interests as their only end.

Does it follow from this that the general will is annihilated or corrupted? No, that is always unchanging, incorruptible and pure, but it is subordinated to other wills which prevail over it. Each man, in detaching his interest from the common interest, sees clearly that he cannot separate it entirely, but his share of the public good seems to him to be nothing compared to the exclusive good he seeks to make his own. Where his private good is not concerned, he wills the general good in his own interest as eagerly as anyone else. Even in selling his vote for money, he does not extinguish the general will in himself; he evades it. The fault he commits is to change the form of the question, and to answer something different from what is asked him; so that instead of saying, with his vote, "It is advantageous to the state," he says, "It is advantageous to this man or to that party that such or such a proposal should be adopted." For this reason the sensible rule for regulating public assemblies is one intended not so much to uphold the general will there as to ensure that it is always questioned and always responds.

I might say a great deal here about the simple right of voting in every act of sovereignty, a right of which nothing can deprive citizens, and also about the right of speaking, proposing, dividing, and debating—a right which the government always takes great care to assign only to its own members—but this important subject would require a separate treatise, and I cannot put everything in this one.

Chapter 2
The Suffrage

It will be evident from what has been said in the preceding chapter that the manner in which public affairs are conducted gives a sufficiently accurate indication of the moral character and the state of health of the body politic. The greater harmony that reigns in the public assemblies, the more, in other words, that public opinion approaches unanimity, the more the general will is dominant; whereas long debates, dissensions and disturbances bespeak the ascendance of particular interests and the decline of the state.

This will seem less evident when two or several orders enter into the constitution, as in Rome with its patricians and plebeians, whose quarrels often disturbed the *comitia* even in the finest days of the Republic; but this exception to the rule is more apparent than real, for in Rome, as a result of an inherent defect in the body politic, there were, in a manner of speaking, two states in one, and what is not true of both together is true of each separately. And, indeed, even in the most tumultuous times, the plebiscites of the people always proceeded peacefully when the senate did not interfere, and votes were given with large majorities. The citizens having only one interest, the people had only one will.

At the other extreme of the cycle, unanimity reappears. This is when the citizens, lapsed into servitude, have no longer either freedom or will. Then fear and flattery change voting into acclamation; people no longer deliberate, they worship or they curse. Such was the shameful manner in which the senate gave voice to its opinions under the emperors. Sometimes it did so with absurd precautions. Tacitus mentions that under Otho, the senators covered Vitellius with execrations, but took care at the same time to make a deafening noise, so that Vitellius would not be able to distinguish what each one of them had said, lest he should ever by any chance become master.

These various considerations suggest the principles by which the counting of votes and the comparing of opinions should be arranged, depending on whether the general will is more or less easy to recognize, and on whether the state is more or less in decline.

There is only one law which by its nature requires unanimous assent. This is the social pact: for the civil association is the most voluntary act in the world; every man having been born free and master of himself, no one else may under any pretext whatever subject him without his consent. To assert that the son of

398 | JEAN-JACQUES ROUSSEAU

a slave is born a slave is to assert that he is not born a man.

If, then, there are opposing voices at the time when the social pact is made, this opposition does not invalidate the contract; it merely excludes the dissentients; they are foreigners among the citizens. After the state is instituted, residence implies consent: to inhabit the territory is to submit to the sovereign.[1]

Apart from this original contract, the votes of the greatest number always bind the rest; and this is a consequence of the contract itself. Yet it may be asked how a man can be at once free and forced to conform to wills which are not his own. How can the opposing minority be both free and subject to laws to which they have not consented?

I answer that the question is badly formulated. The citizen consents to all the laws, even to those that are passed against his will, and even to those which punish him when he dares to break any one of them. The constant will of all the members of the state is the general will; it is through it that they are citizens and free.[2] When a law is proposed in the people's assembly, what is asked of them is not precisely whether they approve of the proposition or reject it, but whether it is in conformity with the general will which is theirs; each by giving his vote gives his opinion on this question, and the counting of votes yields a declaration of the general will. When, therefore, the opinion contrary to my own prevails, this proves only that I have made a mistake, and that what I believed to be the general will was not so. If my particular opinion had prevailed against the general will, I should have done something other than what I had willed, and then I should not have been free.

This presupposes, it is true, that all the characteristics of the general will are still to be found in the majority; when these cease to be there, no matter what position men adopt, there is no longer any freedom.

When I showed earlier in this essay how particular wills come to take the place of the general will in public deliberations, I made sufficiently clear what practical means may prevent that abuse, and I shall return to this subject later. As for the proportional number of votes required to declare the general will, I have also set forth the principles by which that number can be determined. A difference of a single vote destroys an equal division; a single opposing voice destroys unanimity; but between unanimity and an equal division there are numerous unequal divisions, and the desired proportion can be fixed at any of these points in accordance with the condition and on the needs of the body politic.

Two general maxims may serve to determine these ratios: the first, that the more important and serious the matter to be decided, the closer should the opinion which is to prevail approach unanimity; the second, the swifter the decision the question demands, the smaller the prescribed majority may be allowed to become; and in decisions which have to be given immediately, a majority of one must suffice. The first of these maxims might seem to be more suited to the enactment of laws, the second to the dispatch of administrative business. At all events, it is by a combination of the two maxims that we can determine the right size for the majority that is to decide on any question.

Chapter 3
Elections

Elections of the prince and magistrates, which are, as I have said, complex acts, can be arranged in two ways, by choice or by lot. Both means have been employed in different republics, and a very complicated mixture of the two can still be seen in the election of the Doge of Venice. "Election by lot," says Montesquieu, "is natural to democracy." I agree. But why is this so? "Drawing lots," he continues, "is a method of election that wounds no one and gives every citizen a reasonable hope of serving his country." But these are not good reasons.

If we remember that the election of chiefs is a function of government and not of sovereignty, we

---

1. This should always be understood to refer only to free states, for elsewhere family, property, lack of asylum, necessity, or violence may keep an inhabitant in the country unwillingly, and then his mere residence no longer implies consent either to the contract or to the violation of the contract.

2. In Genoa the word *Libertas* may be seen on the doors of all the prisons and on the fetters of the galleys. This use of the motto is excellent and just. In fact, it is only the malefactors of all states who prevent the citizens from being free. In a country where all such people were in the galleys, the most perfect liberty would be enjoyed.

shall see why the method of lot is natural to democracy, where the administration is all the better in proportion as its acts are fewer.

In every true democracy, magistrature is not a privilege but a heavy responsibility, so that it cannot justly be imposed on one man rather than another. The law alone can impose this burden on the man to whom the lot falls. For in this case, since the conditions are equal for all and the choice does not depend on any human will, the universality of the law is not distorted by any particular application.

In an aristocracy the prince chooses the prince, the government perpetuates itself by its own actions; and then election by choice is appropriate.

The example of the election of the Doge of Venice, far from undermining this distinction, confirms it: such a mixed form suits a mixed government. It is a mistake to regard the government of Venice as a genuine aristocracy. For while the Venetian people has no part in the government, the Venetian nobility is itself a people. A multitude of poor Barnabites never comes near any magistrature, and its nobility rests on the empty title of Excellency and the right to attend the Great Council. And since this Great Council is as numerous as our General Council in Geneva, its illustrious members have no more privileges than our plain citizens. Hence there is no doubt that, apart from the extreme disparity between the two republics, the bourgeoisie of Geneva corresponds precisely to the patriciate of Venice; our natives and inhabitants correspond to the townsmen and the people of Venice, and our peasants to their subjects on the mainland; to sum up, from whatever point of view the Venetian Republic is considered, apart from its size, its government is no more aristocratic than our own. The whole difference lies in the fact that we have no head of state who holds office for life, and so we have not the same need for the method of election by lot.

Election by lot would have few disadvantages in a true democracy, for where all men were equal in character and talent as well as in principles and fortune, it would hardly matter who was chosen. But as I have already said, no true democracy exists.

When election by choice and election by lot are both employed, choice should be used to fill places that call for special skills, such as military commands, and lot for those where common sense, justice, and integrity are enough, as in the case of political offices,

for in a well constituted state, such qualities are found among all the citizens.

Under monarchical government, neither election by lot nor election by choice has any place. Since the monarch is by right the sole prince and only magistrate, the choice of his lieutenants belongs to him alone. When the Abbé de St. Pierre proposed to increase the Councils of the King of France and have their members elected by ballot, he did not realize that he was proposing to change the form of government!

I have yet to speak of the method of voting and collecting votes in the people's assembly, but perhaps the history of the Roman system would serve to demonstrate more forcefully all the principles that I might myself set forth. It will not be beneath the dignity of a thoughtful reader to consider in some detail how public and private business was conducted in an assembly of two hundred thousand men.

Chapter 4
The Roman Comitia

We have no trustworthy records of the early history of Rome, and there is every likelihood that most of the tales we are told are fables;[1] indeed, in general, that most instructive part of the annals of peoples, which is the history of their institution, is the part we most lack. Experience teaches us daily the causes of revolutions in empires, but as peoples are no longer instituted, we have nothing better than conjecture to explain how they were once instituted.

The customs that we find established show at least that such customs must have had an origin. Traditions that recall these origins, that are supported by the best authorities, and confirmed by the best reasons, should pass for the most certain. Such are the principles I have tried to follow in enquiring how the freest and strongest people of the world exercised its supreme power.

After the foundation of Rome, the new-born Republic—that is, the founder's army, made up of

---

1. The name "Rome," which is said to derive from *Romulus*, is really Greek, and it means *force*; the name "Numa" is also Greek, and it means *law*. Is it very probable that the first two kings of that city should have borne before they reigned names so clearly related to what they did?

Albans, Sabines, and foreigners—was divided into three classes, which acquired by this division the name of *tribes*. Each of these tribes was further divided into ten *curiae*, and each *curia* subdivided into *decuriae*, with chiefs named *curiones* and *decuriones* placed at their head.

In addition to this, there was drawn from each tribe a body of a hundred equites or knights, called a *century*, which indicates that these divisions, hardly necessary in a city, were in the first place purely military. But it seems that an instinct for greatness led this little town of Rome to provide itself from the outset with a system well suited to the capital of the world.

However, this original division soon had one disadvantageous consequence. The tribes of Albans[2] and Sabines[3] remained constant, while the tribe of foreigners[4] grew continuously as more foreigners were recruited, and it soon contained more members than the other two tribes combined. The remedy that Servius found for this dangerous fault was to alter the basis of the division, and in place of the racial distinction, which he abolished, he introduced one based on the district of the town occupied by each of the tribes. Instead of three tribes, he set up four, each occupying one of the hills of Rome and bearing its name. Thus he both corrected an existing inequality and forestalled any future inequality; and to ensure that the division should be one of men and not of places, he forbade the inhabitants of one district to move to another, and so prevented the races from merging together.

He also doubled the three original centuries of equites and added twelve new ones, but he let them keep their former names—a shrewd and simple means by which he succeeded in distinguishing the body of knights from that of the people without making the latter complain.

To these four urban tribes, Servius added fifteen others which were called rustic tribes, because they were formed of inhabitants of the country, arranged in so many cantons. Afterwards as many new tribes were formed, and the Roman people found itself divided into thirty-five tribes, a number which remained unchanged until the end of the Republic.

This distinction between tribes of the town and tribes of the country had one consequence worth noting since there is no other instance of it, and since Rome was indebted to it both for the preservation of her morals and for the growth of her empire. It might have been thought that the urban tribes would have soon monopolized the power and the honours and have been quick to diminish the standing of the rustic tribes. What happened was the contrary. The taste of the early Romans for a country life is well known. This taste came from their wise founder, who made freedom go together with rural labour and military service and, in a manner of speaking, relegated crafts, trades, intrigue, wealth, and slavery to the city.

Since all the illustrious men in Rome thus lived in the country and cultivated the land, it became customary to look to the country for the mainstays of the Republic. And as this way of life was that of the most noble patricians, it was honoured by everyone; the simple and laborious life of villagers was preferred to the loose and idle life of the Roman bourgeois, and a man who would have been nothing but a miserable proletarian in the town became as a tiller of the soil a respected citizen. It was not without reason, says Varro, that our magnanimous ancestors established in the village the nursery of those robust and valiant men who defended them in time of war and nourished them in time of peace. Pliny states positively that the rustic tribes were honoured because of the men who belonged to them, and that whenever it was intended to degrade a coward, he was transferred in disgrace to one of the urban tribes. When Appius Claudius, the Sabine, came to set himself up in Rome, he was loaded with honours and inscribed as a member of a rustic tribe which afterwards took the name of his family. Finally, all the freed men joined the urban and never the rustic tribes, and throughout the Republic there was not a single example of any one of these freed men acceding to any magistrature, even though he had become a citizen.

This principle was excellent; but it was pushed so far that it finally produced an alteration, and certainly an abuse in the political system.

First, the censors, having long arrogated to themselves the right arbitrarily to transfer citizens from one tribe to another, allowed most men to enrol in the tribe of their choice, a concession which certainly did no good and which deprived the censorship of one of its great advantages. Moreover, the exalted and powerful men all had themselves enrolled in the rustic

---

2. Ramnenses.
3. Tatientes.
4. Luceres.

tribes, and the freed men remained with the common people in the urban tribes, so that the tribes generally ceased to have any local or territorial bases, and all were so muddled together that it was no longer possible to identify anyone without consulting the register; and this is why the word *tribe* came to have a personal instead of a territorial meaning, or rather came to be virtually fictitious.

It also came about that the urban tribes, being closer to the centre, often found themselves the strongest group in the *comitia*, and sold the state to such as deigned to buy the votes of the rabble who composed that assembly.

As for the *curiae*, since the founder had created ten in each tribe, the whole of the Roman people, at that time enclosed within the walls of the city, was composed of thirty *curiae*, each with its own temples, its Gods, its officials, its priests, and its festivals called *compitalia*, which resembled the *Paganalia* later held by the rustic tribes.

When Servius introduced his new division, this number of thirty could not be divided equally between his four tribes, and he did not wish to alter it; in consequence, the *curiae*, becoming independent of the tribes, formed another category of inhabitants of Rome. But there was no question of *curiae* in the rustic tribes or among the people who belonged to them; for after the tribes had become a purely civil institution, and another system introduced for the levying of troops, the military divisions of Romulus proved superfluous. Thus, although each citizen was enrolled in a tribe, there were many who were not members of a *curia*.

Servius made yet a third division, which had nothing to do with the first two, and which became by reason of its consequences the most important of all. He distributed the whole Roman people into six classes, arranged neither on a personal nor on a residential basis, but according to wealth; so that the first classes were filled with the rich, the last with the poor, and the intermediate classes with men of moderate fortunes. These six classes were subdivided into 193 other bodies called *centuries*, and these bodies were so distributed that the first class accounted for more than half of them, and the last class for a single one only. Thus it came about that the class with the fewest number of men had the greatest number of centuries, while the last whole class counted only as one single subdivision, although it contained more than half the inhabitants of Rome.

In order that the people should less well perceive the consequences of this division, Servius disguised it in a military uniform; he put into the second class two centuries of armourers and into the fourth class two centuries of weapon-makers. In each class, except the last, he differentiated between young and old, that is to say, between those liable to bear arms and those legally exempt on grounds of age; and this distinction, more than that of wealth, made it necessary to hold frequent censuses. Finally he prescribed that the assembly should be held in the Campus Martius, and that all those of military age should attend bearing arms.

The reason he did not make the same differentiation between young and old in the last class is simply that the common people who belonged to it did not have the honour of bearing arms in the service of their country; only those who owned hearths had the right to defend them. Among the countless hordes of beggars who ornament the armies of kings today there is perhaps none who would not have been expelled with disdain from a Roman cohort in the days when soldiers were the defenders of liberty.

In the last class, however, a distinction was made between *proletarians* and those who were called *capite censi*. The former, not wholly reduced to nothing, at least gave citizens to the state, even sometimes soldiers in times of pressing need. But those who possessed nothing whatever, and could be reckoned only by the counting of heads, were considered altogether null, and Marius was the first who condescended to enrol them.

Without deciding here whether this third classification was good or bad in itself, one can, I think, safely say that it was practicable only because of the simple habits of the early Romans, their taste for agriculture, and their contempt alike for commerce and for the pursuit of profit. Where is the modern people, whose devouring greed, unsettled hearts, intrigue, continual movement, and constant reversals of fortune would have allowed such a system to last for twenty-two years without overturning the whole state? It should also be remembered that the morals of the Roman people and the office of censorship had the strength to correct the evils of this system, and that a rich man could find himself relegated to the class of the poor for making too ostentatious a display of his wealth.

From all this it is easy to understand why more than five Roman classes are hardly ever mentioned, even though there were actually six. The sixth, which provided neither soldiers for the army nor voters for the Campus Martius[5] and had therefore virtually no function in the Republic, was seldom given any thought.

Such were the different divisions of the Roman people. Let us now consider the effect the divisions had in the assemblies. The assemblies which were lawfully convened were called *comitia*, and generally met in the Roman forum or in the Campus Martius; they were distinguished as *comitia curiata*, *comitia centuriata*, and *comitia tributa*, according to which form was employed. The *comitia curiata* was founded by Romulus, the *comitia centuriata* by Servius, and the *comitia tributa* originated in the tribunes of the people. No law was sanctioned and no magistrate elected except in the *comitia*, and as there was no citizen who was not enrolled in a *curia*, century, or tribe, it follows that no citizen was excluded from the right to vote, and that the Roman people was truly sovereign, both in law and in fact.

For the *comitia* to be legally convened and for its decisions to have the force of law, three conditions had to be observed: first, the body or the magistrate convening the assembly had to be vested with the necessary authority; secondly, the assembly had to be held on one of the days permitted by law; thirdly, the auguries had to be favourable.

The reason for the first of these rules needs no explanation. The second was a matter of policy; the assembly was not allowed to meet on holidays or market days, because the country people, who came to Rome to do business, did not have time to spend the day in the forum. The third rule enabled the Senate to keep a restraining hand on a proud and restless people and temper the ardour of seditious tribunes—although the latter found more than one way of evading this check.

Laws and the election of chiefs were not the only matters submitted to the judgement of the *comitia*. Since the Roman people had usurped the most important functions of government, one could say that the fate of Europe was determined in those assemblies.

The variety of public business explains the several forms which the *comitia* took, according to the matters which had to be decided.

To judge these various forms it is necessary only to compare them. Romulus, in establishing the *curiae*, aimed to balance the Senate against the people and balance the people against the Senate, while himself dominating both alike. Under this arrangement he gave the people all the authority of numbers to balance the authority of power and wealth which he left to the patricians. But true to the spirit of monarchy, he nevertheless gave the great advantage to the patricians, in that they could buy clients to influence numerical majorities. This admirable institution of patrons and clients was a masterpiece of politics and humanity, without which the patriciate, so contrary to the spirit of the Republic, could not have survived. To Rome alone belongs the honour of giving the world this noble example, from which no abuse has ever come, but which has never been followed elsewhere.

This same form of *curiae* continued under the kings up to Servius, and as the reign of the last of the Tarquins was not held to be legitimate, the royal laws were generally known by the name of *leges curiatae*.

Under the Republic, the *curiae*, which were still limited to the four urban tribes, and still included only the population of Rome, pleased neither the Senate, which led the patricians, nor the tribunes who, in spite of being plebeian, led the more moneyed citizens. Thus the *curiae* fell into discredit, fell so low indeed that their thirty lictors met to do what the *comitia curiae* should have done.

The division into centuries was so favourable to the aristocracy that it is not at first easy to see why the Senate did not always carry the day in the *comitia* which bore that name, and by which the consuls, censors, and other cural magistrates were elected. For indeed, of the 193 centuries which formed the six classes of the entire Roman people, the first class contained 98, and since votes were counted by centuries only, this first class had a majority over all the others. When all these centuries were in agreement, the rest of the votes were not even counted; and what had been decided by a minority passed for a decision of the multitude; so it can be said that in the centuriate assemblies matters were decided by majorities of money rather than of votes.

But this excessive power was tempered in two ways. First, the tribunes ordinarily, and a large number of plebeians always, were in a class with the rich,

---

5. I say "Campus Martius" because this was where the *comitia centuriata* met. In the other two forms of assembly, the people met in the forum or elsewhere, and then the *capite censi* had as much influence and authority as the leading citizens.

and balanced the influence of the patricians in the first class.

Secondly, the centuries were not always summoned to vote in their order or rank, which would have meant beginning with the first class; instead, a century was chosen by lot[6] and that century alone went on to elect, after which the other centuries were convened on a different day by order of rank to repeat the election, and generally they confirmed it. Thus the authority of example was taken away from rank and given to chance, according to the principle of democracy.

This custom had yet another advantage; it meant that the citizens from the country had time between the elections to inform themselves of the merits of the candidates provisionally nominated, and therefore did not vote in ignorance. But under the pretext of speeding up procedure this custom was finally abolished, and both elections were held on the same day.

The *comitia tributa* was, strictly speaking, the council of the Roman people. It could be convened only by the tribunes; it was the assembly where the tribunes were elected and it was there that they passed their plebiscites. Not only had the Senate no status in the assembly, but no senator had even the right to attend, and being thus forced to submit to laws in the enactment of which they had no voice, the senators were to that extent less free than the humblest citizen. This injustice was altogether ill conceived, and alone sufficed to invalidate the decrees of a body to which all its members were not admitted. Had all the patricians attended the *comitia*, according to their rights as citizens, they would not, as simple individuals, have had any great influence on a vote taken by enumerating heads, and in which the humblest proletarian would count for as much as the prince of the Senate.

Thus, it will be seen that besides the order which emerged from the various systems of collecting the votes of so vast a people, these several methods were not in themselves insignificant, but that each had effects connected with the opinions that led to its being chosen.

Without going further into long details, it emerges from the explanation already given, that the *comitia tributa* was the assembly most favourable to popular government and the *comitia centuriata* to aristocracy. In the case of the *comitia curiata*, where the populace of Rome alone formed the majority, their tendency to favour tyranny and evil designs led them to fall into disrepute, so that even the seditious elements avoided these assemblies lest their presence should arouse suspicion concerning their conspiracies. There is no doubt that the whole majesty of the Roman people was to be seen only in the *comitia centuriata;* this alone was a full assembly, for the *comitia curiata* excluded the rustic tribes and the *comitia tributa* excluded the Senate and patricians.

The system of voting used by the Romans was as simple as were their manners and morals, if less simple than that of Sparta. Each man gave his vote by word of mouth, and a clerk recorded it; the majority of individual votes in each tribe determined the decision of that tribe, the majority of tribal votes the decision of the people; and the same thing was done in the *curiae* and *centuriae*. This was a good method so long as honesty prevailed among the citizens and everyone was ashamed to give his vote to an unjust cause or an unworthy candidate. But when the people grew corrupt and votes were bought, it became expedient for the ballot to be cast in secret, so that the buyers of votes might be restrained by mistrust of the sellers, and scoundrels given the chance of not being traitors also.

I am aware that Cicero condemns this change of method, and holds it partly responsible for the ruin of the Republic. But while I am mindful of the weight which the authority of Cicero ought to bear, I do not agree with him. On the contrary, I think that it was by having too few such changes that the ruin of the state was accelerated. For just as the diet of healthy people is unsuited to the sick, so one should not try to give to a corrupt people the same laws as those which suit a virtuous people. Nothing does more to bear out this principle than the long life of the Republic of Venice, which still retains a simulacrum of existence solely because its laws are uniquely suited to wicked men.

Now the Roman citizens had tablets distributed among them, so that each might cast his vote without anyone's knowing his opinion. New arrangements were also devised for the collection of tablets, the counting of votes, the comparison of numbers, and so

---

6. The century thus drawn was called *praerogativa* because it was the first required to cast its vote; and this is the origin of our word "prerogative."

forth. This did not prevent the officers[7] entrusted with these functions from being suspected of dishonesty. Finally, edicts designed to prevent intrigue and the buying and selling of votes were passed in such numbers that their very multiplicity proclaims their ineffectiveness.

Towards the last years of the Republic, the Romans were often forced to resort to extraordinary expedients to make up for the inadequacy of the law. Sometimes miracles were invoked, but this device, if it could impose on the people, did not impose on those who ruled them. Sometimes assemblies were hurriedly convened, before candidates had time to pay out their bribes; sometimes a whole session was taken up with filibustering, when it was seen that the people had been seduced and was about to make a wrong decision. But ambition in the end overcame all obstacles; and the most incredible fact of all is that so numerous a people, in the midst of so many abuses, still continued, thanks to its ancient rules of order, to elect magistrates, to enact laws, to judge cases, and to conduct private and public business with almost as much facility as the Senate itself might have commanded.

Chapter 5
The Tribunate

When it is impossible to settle an exact balance between the constitutive parts of the state, or when causes beyond control go on altering the relations between them, then a special magistrate is established, as a body separate from the other magistrates, to put every element in its right balance and to serve as a link or middle term, either between the prince and the people or between the prince and the sovereign, or alternatively, between both at the same time if that is necessary.

This body, which I shall call the *tribunate*, is the guardian of the laws and of the legislative power. It serves sometimes to protect the sovereign against the government, as did the tribunes of the people in Rome, sometimes to uphold the government against the people, as does the Council of Ten today in Venice, and sometimes to keep a balance between the two, as did the Ephors of Sparta.

The tribunate is not a constitutive part of the republic, and it ought to have no share of either the legislative or executive power, but for this very reason its own power is all the greater, for although it can do nothing, it can prevent anything from being done. As the defender of the laws, it is more sacred and more venerated than the prince who executes laws or the sovereign which legislates. This is very clearly shown in the case of Rome, where the proud patricians, who always despised the people as a whole, were forced to bow before an ordinary officer of the people who wielded neither sacred nor legal authority.

A wisely tempered tribunate is the strongest buttress of a good constitution, but if it has the least degree of power beyond what is necessary, it will overthrow everything. It is not by its nature prone to weakness, and if it is anything at all, it will never be less than it ought to be.

It degenerates into tyranny when it usurps the executive power of which it is only the moderator, and when it tries to make the laws it ought only to protect. The enormous power of the Ephors, which represented no danger so long as Sparta preserved its morale, sped corruption once corruption began. The blood of Agis shed by the tyrants was avenged by his successor; the crimes and the punishments of the Ephors equally hastened the collapse of the Republic, and after Cleomenes, Sparta was nothing. Rome perished in the same way, and the excessive power which the tribunes usurped by degrees finally served, with the aid of laws made to defend liberty, to protect the very emperors who destroyed liberty. As for the Council of Ten in Venice, it is a tribunal of blood, which is baneful as much to the patricians as to the people, and which, far from giving supreme protection to the law, serves only, now that the law has been debased, for the striking of stealthy blows that none dare look upon.

A tribunate, like a government, is weakened by the multiplication of its members. When the tribunes of the Roman people, originally two, then five, sought to double their number, the Senate gave its consent, confident of using one part to check the others; and this it did not fail to effect.

The best method of preventing the usurpations of such a formidable body—though it is a method which no government has ever yet employed—would be not to make the tribunate permanent but to prescribe the intervals during which it should remain suspended.

---

7. *Custodes, Diribitores, Rogatores suffragiorum.*

These intervals, which should not be so great as to give abuses time to take root, could be specified by law in such a manner that in case of need they might be shortened by an extraordinary commission.

This method appears to me to have no disadvantages, for since, as I have said, the tribunate is in no sense a part of the constitution, it can be removed without detriment to it; this also seems to me an efficacious method, since a newly established magistrate would not enter office with the power that his predecessors had, but only with that given him by law.

Chapter 6
Dictatorship

The inflexibility of the laws, which prevents them from bending to circumstances, may in certain cases make them injurious, and bring about in a time of crisis the ruin of the state. The ordered and slow procedures of legal formalities require a measure of time that circumstances do not always afford. There may be a thousand eventualities which the lawgiver has not foreseen, and it is a very necessary part of foresight to know that one cannot foresee everything.

For this reason, one should not seek to make political situations so rigid that one is deprived of the power to suspend their operation. Even Sparta allowed its laws at times to lie dormant.

But it is only the greatest emergency that can counterweigh the dangers of tampering with the public order; and the sacred power of the laws should never be suspended except when the safety of the fatherland is at stake. In these rare and obvious cases, the public security is provided for by a special act making that security the responsibility of the person who is most worthy. This responsibility may be assigned in two ways, according to the nature of the emergency.

If increasing the activity of the government is adequate to counteract the danger, then this activity should be concentrated in the hands of one or two members of the government. In this case, it is not the authority of the laws which is being diminished, but only the form of the administration. But if the danger is such that the apparatus of law is itself an obstacle to safety, then a supreme head must be nominated with power to silence all the laws and temporarily suspend the sovereign authority. In such a case the general will is indubitable; for it is clear that the prime concern of the people is that the state shall not perish. Thus the suspension of the legislative authority does not abolish it; the magistrate who silences it cannot make it speak; he dominates it, without having the power to represent it; he can do everything, except make laws.

The first of these two methods was used by the Roman Senate when, according to a hallowed formula, it entrusted the consuls with the safety of the Republic; the second was used when one of the two consuls nominated a dictator[1]—a device that Rome had learned from Alba.

At the beginning of the Republic, the Romans often resorted to dictatorship, because conditions were not yet sufficiently settled for the state to maintain itself by the strength of its constitution. The people's moral character made unnecessary at that time many of the precautions which might have been needed at other times, so men did not fear that a dictator would abuse his position or that he would attempt to prolong his office beyond its term. It seemed, on the contrary, that so much power was a burden to those who wielded it; for they hastened to divest themselves of it, as if standing in the place of the laws made it altogether too onerous and perilous an office.

So it is not because there was a danger of its being abused, but because there was a danger of its being degraded that one condemns the imprudent employment of this supreme magistrature in the early days of the Republic. For while it was wasted on elections, dedications, and purely formal things, there was reason to fear that it would become less forceful when it was really needed, and that the people would come to regard dictatorship as an empty title used only to give dignity to idle ceremonies.

Towards the end of the Republic, the Romans, becoming more circumspect, were as sparing in their use of dictatorship as they had once been prodigal, and with as little reason. It was easy to see that their fears were ill founded, and that the weakness of the capital was at that time its protection against the magistrates it had in its midst, that a dictator could in certain cases defend the public freedom without ever being able to invade it, and that the fetters of Rome were not forged in Rome itself, but in the Roman

---

1. This nomination took place by night and in secret, as if they were ashamed to put a man above the law.

armies; the weak resistance that Marius offered Sulla, and Pompey Caesar, showed plainly what could be expected of internal authority faced with external force.

This mistake led the Romans to commit great wrongs. There was, for example, their failure to nominate a dictator in the Catilina affair; for since this was a matter which concerned only the city itself, or at most a few Italian provinces, the unlimited authority which the law gave a dictator would have facilitated the ready crushing of that conspiracy, which was in fact suppressed only by a concurrence of lucky accidents, such as human prudence could never have expected.

Instead of naming a dictator, the Senate was content to transmit all its powers to the consuls, as a result of which Cicero, in order to act effectively, was obliged to exceed his powers on a crucial point; and though, in a first transport of joy, the Romans approved of his conduct, it was not without justice that he was afterwards asked to account for the blood of citizens shed in violation of the laws—a reproach which could not have been addressed to a dictator. But the consul's eloquence carried everything before him, and he himself, though a Roman, loved his own glory better than his country; and instead of seeking a lawful and certain means of serving the state, he sought all the honour of the affair for himself.[2] Thus he was justly honoured as the liberator of Rome, and no less justly punished as the violator of Roman laws. However splendid his recall from exile may have been, it was undoubtedly an act of pardon.

For the rest, in whatever manner this important commission of dictatorship is conferred, it is imperative to limit its duration to one short term that can never be prolonged; in the emergencies which call for its institution, the state is soon lost or saved, and once the urgent need is over, dictatorship becomes either tyrannical or useless. In Rome, where the term was of six months, most of the dictators abdicated before that time had expired. If the term had been longer, they might have been tempted to prolong it still further, like the decemvirs, who held office for a year. The dictator, having only the time to meet the need which had prompted his appointment, had none in which to meditate on further projects.

Chapter 7
The Censorial Tribunal

Just as the general will is declared by the law, so is the public judgement declared by the censorial office; public opinion is that form of law of which the censor is the minister, and which he, on the model of the prince, merely applies to particular cases.

Far, then, from the censorial tribunal being the arbiter of the people's opinion, it is only the spokesman; and as soon as it departs from this, its decisions are void and without effect. It is useless to separate the morals of a nation from the objects of its esteem; for both spring from the same principle and both necessarily merge together. Among all the peoples of the world, it is not nature but opinion which governs the choice of their pleasures. Reform the opinions of men, and their morals will be purified of themselves. Men always love what is good or what they think is good, but it is in their judgement that they err; hence it is their judgement that has to be regulated. To judge morals is to judge what is honoured; to judge what is honoured is to look to opinion as law.

The opinions of a people spring from its constitution; although the law does not regulate morals, it is legislation that gives birth to morals; when legislation weakens, morals degenerate; and then the rulings of the censors will not accomplish what the law has failed to achieve.

From this it follows that the censorial office may be useful in preserving morals, but never in restoring morals. Set up censors while the laws are still vigorous; for as soon as the vigour is lost, everything is hopeless; nothing legitimate has any force once the laws have force no longer.

The censorial office sustains morals by preventing opinions from being corrupted, by preserving their integrity with wise rulings, and sometimes even by settling points on which opinion is uncertain. The use of seconds in duels, carried to an impassioned extreme in the kingdom of France, was abolished by a single edict of the king: "as for those who are cowardly enough to name seconds." This judgement anticipated that of the public, and settled it with one stroke. But when the same edicts sought to declare that it was cowardice also to fight duels—which is very true, but at variance with popular opinion—the

---

2. He could not have been sure of this if he had proposed appointing a dictator, for he did not dare to name himself, and he could not be sure that his colleagues would name him.

public scoffed at this decision on a matter about which its mind was made up.

I have said elsewhere[1] that since public opinion is not subject to constraint, there should be no vestige of constraint in the tribunal established to represent it. We cannot too greatly admire the skill with which this device, entirely alien to the moderns, was put into effect by the Romans and even by the Lacedaemonians.

Once when a man of bad character put forward a good idea in the council of Sparta, the Ephors, ignoring him, had the same thing proposed by a virtuous citizen. What an honour for the one, what a disgrace for the other; yet neither praise nor blame was given to either. Certain drunkards from Samos[2] once defiled the tribunal of the Ephors; the following day the Samians were given permission by public edict to be filthy. An actual punishment would have been less severe than such a form of impunity. When Sparta has pronounced on what is and what is not decent, Greece does not dispute its judgements.

Chapter 8
The Civil Religion

At first men had no kings but the Gods, and their only government was theocratic. They reasoned like Caligula, and in the circumstances they reasoned rightly. A prolonged debasement of feelings and ideas was needed before man could make up his mind to accept one of his own kind as master, and to persuade himself that in doing so he had done well.

From this single fact, that a God was placed at the head of every political society, it follows that there were as many Gods as peoples. Two peoples alien to one another, and nearly always enemies, could not long recognize the same master: two armies going into battle could not obey the same commander. Thus national divisions produced polytheism, and this in turn produced religious and civil intolerance, which are naturally the same, as I shall explain later.

The fanciful idea of the Greeks that they had rediscovered their own Gods being worshipped by barbarian peoples originated in the Greek habit of regarding themselves as the natural sovereigns of those same peoples. But in our own times, it is a ludicrous parody of learning which studies the identity of the Gods of different nations, as if Moloch, Saturn, and Chronos could be the same God; as if the Baal of their Phoenicians, the Zeus of the Greeks, and the Jupiter of the Romans could be identical; as if there could be anything in common between chimerical beings with different names!

But if it is asked why under paganism, when each state had its own religious cult and its own Gods, there were no wars of religion, I answer that it was due to this very fact that each state, having its own faith as well as its own government, did not distinguish between its Gods and its laws. Political war was just as much theological war; the provinces of the Gods were determined, so to speak, by the frontiers of nations. The God of one people had no rights over other peoples. The Gods of the Pagans were in no sense jealous Gods; they divided the empire of the world between them; even Moses and the Hebrew people sometimes countenanced this idea by speaking of the God of Israel. It is true that they did not recognize the Gods of the Canaanites, a proscribed people who were doomed to destruction, and whose country they were to occupy; but consider how they spoke of the divinities of neighbouring peoples, whom they were forbidden to attack: "Is not the possession of that which belongs to Chamos your God lawfully your due?" says Jephthah to the Ammonites. "By the same title, we possess the lands which our conquering God has taken."[1]

But when the Jews, subject to the Kings of Babylon, and afterwards to the Kings of Syria, stubbornly sought to recognize no other God but their own, this

---

1. In this chapter I have only indicated what I have already discussed at great length in my *Lettre à d'Alembert*.
2. They were actually from another island, but delicacy of language forbids me to name it here. [Note added in Edition of 1782. In a manuscript note, Rousseau explained "They were of Chios, and not of Samos, but in view of the subject matter I did not dare use that word in the text." In French the word *Chio*, the Greek root of the modern French verb *chier* (to shit), was "not in decent use." *Trans.*]

---

1. *Nonne ea quae possidet Chamos deus tuus, tibi jure debentur?* Such is the text of the Vulgate. Father de Carrières translates it thus: "Do you not believe that you have a right to possess that which belongs to your God Chamos?" I do not know the bearing of the Hebrew text, but I notice that in the Vulgate, Jephthah positively recognizes the rights of the God Chamos, and that the French translation weakens this recognition by adding an "according to you" which is not in the Latin.

refusal was regarded as a rebellion against their con-querors, and it brought on the Jews those persecu-tions of which we read in their history, and of which we find no other example before the coming of Chris-tianity.[2]

Since each religion was thus attached exclusively to the laws of the state which prescribed it, and since there was no means of converting people except by subduing them, the only missionaries were con-querors; and since the obligation to change faith was part of the law of conquest, it was necessary to con-quer before preaching conversion. Far from men fighting for the Gods, it was, as in Homer, the Gods who fought for men; each people asked its own God for victory, and paid for it with new altars. The Romans, before taking a town, called upon its Gods to abandon it; when they allowed the Tarentines to keep their angry Gods, it was in the belief that those Gods were subject to their own and obliged to pay them homage. They let the vanquished keep their own Gods just as they let them keep their own laws. A crown dedicated to Jupiter of the Capitol was often the only tribute they exacted.

In the end, when the Romans had spread their faith and their Gods with their empire, and often themselves adopted those of the vanquished in giving one or the other the rights of citizenship, the peoples of this vast empire gradually found themselves with a multitude of Gods and faiths, which were everywhere almost the same; and this is how paganism became one and the same religion throughout the known world.

It was in these circumstances that Jesus came to establish a spiritual kingdom on earth; this kingdom, by separating the theological system from the politi-cal, meant that the state ceased to be a unity, and it caused those intestine divisions which have never ceased to disturb Christian peoples. Now as this new idea of a kingdom of another world could never have entered the minds of pagans, they always regarded the Christians as true rebels who, under the cloak of hypocritical submission, only awaited the moment to make themselves independent and supreme, and cun-ningly to usurp that authority which they made a show of respecting while they were weak. Such was the cause of the persecutions.

What the pagans feared did indeed happen; then everything altered its countenance; the humble Chris-tians changed their tune and soon the so-called king-dom of the other world was seen to become, under a visible ruler, the most violent despotism of this world.

However, since princes and civil laws have always existed, the consequence of this dual power has been an endless conflict of jurisdiction, which has made any kind of good polity impossible in Christian states, where men have never known whether they ought to obey the civil ruler or the priest.

Many peoples, even in Europe or nearby, have tried to preserve or re-establish the ancient system, but without success: the spirit of Christianity has won completely. The religious cult has always kept, or recovered, its independence of the sovereign, and has lacked its necessary connexion with the state. Mahomet had very sound opinions, taking care to give unity to his political system, and for as long as the form of his government endured under the caliphs who succeeded him, the government was undivided and, to that extent, good. But the Arabs, in becoming prosperous, cultured, polished, effeminate, and soft, were subjugated by the barbarians; then the division between the two powers was started afresh, and even though the division is less apparent among the Moslems than among the Christians, it nevertheless exists, above all in the sect of Ali and in states like Persia where it has never ceased to make itself felt.

Among us, the Kings of England have established themselves as heads of the church and the Czars have done the same. But with this title they have made themselves not so much masters as ministers, and have acquired not so much the right to change the church as the power to preserve it; they are not legis-lators, they are only princes. Wherever the clergy con-stitutes a body,[3] it is master and legislator in its own

---

2. It is clear beyond dispute that the Phocian war, called the Holy War, was not a war of religion. Its object was to punish sacrilege, and not to make unbelievers submit.

3. It should be noted that it is not so much the formal assemblies, like those of France, which bind the clergy together in a body, but rather the communion of churches. Communion and excom-munication are the social compact of the clergy, one through which they will always be masters of both peoples and kings. All

house. Thus there are two powers, two sovereigns, in England and in Russia, just as there are elsewhere.

Of all Christian authors, the philosopher Hobbes is the only one who saw clearly both the evil and the remedy, and who dared to propose reuniting the two heads of the eagle and fully restoring that political unity without which neither the state nor the government will ever be well constituted. But he should have seen that the dominant spirit of Christianity was incompatible with his system, and that the interest of the prince will always be stronger than that of the state. It is not so much the horrible and false parts of Hobbes's system that have made it hated, but the parts which are just and true.[4]

I believe that if the historical facts were analysed from this point of view, we could easily refute the opposing beliefs of both Bayle and Warburton, the one holding that no religion is useful to the body politic, the other that Christianity is its best support. We could refute the first by showing that no state has ever been founded without religion as its base; and we could refute the second by showing that the Christian law is at bottom more injurious than serviceable to a robust constitution of the state. For this to be clearly understood, I think I have only to give a little more precision to the exceedingly vague idea of religion, as it bears upon my subject.

Religion, considered in connexion with societies, whether general or particular, can be divided into two categories, the religion of the man and the religion of the citizen. The first, without temples, altars, or rituals, and limited to inward devotion to the supreme God and the eternal obligations of morality, is the pure and simple religion of the Gospel, the true theism, and might be called the divine natural law. The religion of the citizen is the religion established in a single country; it gives that country its Gods and its special tutelary deities; it has its dogmas, its rituals, its external forms of worship laid down by law; and to the one nation which practises this religion, everything outside is infidel, alien, barbarous; and it extends the rights and duties of man only so far as it extends its altars. Such were the religions of all the early peoples; and we might give it the name of civil or positive divine law.

There is a third and more curious kind of religion, which gives men two legislative orders, two rulers, two homelands, puts them under two contradictory obligations, and prevents their being at the same time both churchmen and citizens. Such is the religion of the Lamas, such is that of the Japanese, and such is Catholic Christianity. One might call this the religion of the priest. It produces a kind of mixed and antisocial system of law which has no name.

From the political point of view, each of these three kinds of religion has its defects. The third kind is so manifestly bad that the pleasure of demonstrating its badness would be a waste of time. Everything that destroys social unity is worthless; and all institutions that set man at odds with himself are worthless.

The second kind of religion is good in that it joins divine worship to a love of the law, and that in making the homeland the object of the citizens' adoration, it teaches them that the service of the state is the service of the tutelary God. This is a kind of theocracy, in which there can be no pontiff other than the prince, and no priests except the magistrates. Then to die for one's country is to become a martyr, to break the law to be impious, and to subject a guilty man to public execration is to hand him over to the wrath of God: *sacer esto*.

But this kind of religion is also bad; since it is based on error and lies, it deceives men, and makes them credulous and superstitious; it buries the true worship of God in empty ceremonials. It is bad, again, when it becomes exclusive and tyrannical, and makes a people bloodthirsty and intolerant, so that men breathe only murder and massacre, and believe they are doing a holy deed in killing those who do not accept their Gods. This puts the people concerned into a natural state of war with all others, and this is something destructive of its own security.

There remains the religion of the private person, or Christianity, not the Christianity of today, but that of the Gospel, which is altogether different. Under this holy, sublime and true religion, men, as children of the same God, look on all others as brothers, and

---

the priests who communicate together are fellow citizens, even though they are at opposite ends of the earth. This invention is a masterpiece of politics. There was nothing like it among the pagan priests; hence they never constituted a body of clergy.

4. See, among other things, in a letter of Grotius to his brother dated 11 April 1643, what that learned man approved of and what he disapproved of in Hobbes's *De Cive*. It is true that, being inclined to indulgence, he forgives that author the bad for the sake of the good, but not everyone is so merciful.

the society which unites them is not even dissolved by death.

But this religion, having no specific connexion with the body politic, leaves the law with only the force the law itself possesses, adding nothing to it; and hence one of the chief bonds necessary for holding any particular society together is lacking. Nor is this all: for far from attaching the hearts of the citizens to the state, this religion detaches them from it as from all other things of this world; and I know of nothing more contrary to the social spirit.

It is said that a people of true Christians would form the most perfect society imaginable. I see but one great flaw in this hypothesis, namely that a society of true Christians would not be a society of men.

I would say, too, that this imagined society, for all its perfection, would be neither the strongest nor the most durable. Being perfect, it would be without bonds of union; its ruinous defect would lie in its very perfection.

Everyone would do his duty; the people would obey the law; the rulers would be just and moderate; the magistrates would be honest and incorruptible; the soldiers would scorn death; there would be neither vanity nor luxury. But let us look further.

Christianity is a wholly spiritual religion, concerned solely with the things of heaven; the Christian's homeland is not of this world. The Christian does his duty, it is true, but he does it with profound indifference towards the good or ill success of his deeds. Provided that he has nothing to reproach himself for, it does not matter to him whether all goes well or badly here on earth. If the state prospers, he hardly dares to enjoy the public happiness; he fears lest he become proud of his country's glory; if the state perishes, he blesses the hand of God that weighs heavily on His people.

For such a society to be peaceful and for harmony to prevail, every citizen without exception would have to be an equally good Christian. If, unhappily, there should appear one ambitious man, one hypocrite, one Catilina, for example, or one Cromwell among them, that man would readily trample over his pious compatriots. Christian charity does not allow us readily to think ill of our neighbours. When a man is cunning enough to master the art of imposing on others, and gains a part of the public authority, there, behold, is a man of established dignity; and God wills that he be respected; soon, we see a man of power, and God wills that he be obeyed. Suppose he abuses the power of which he is the depositary? Then he is the scourge with which God chastises his children. Christians would have scruples about expelling the usurper; for that would mean disturbing the public peace, using violence, shedding blood, and all this accords ill with Christian mildness. And after all, what does it matter whether one is free or a slave in this vale of tears? The essential thing is to go to paradise, and resignation is but one more means to that end.

Suppose a foreign war breaks out. The citizens will march without reluctance to war; no one among them will think of flight; all will do their duty—but they will do it without passion for victory; they know better how to die than to conquer. It does not matter to them whether they are victors or vanquished. Does not providence know better than they what is needful? One can imagine what advantage a proud, impetuous, and passionate enemy would draw from their stoicism. Set them at war against a generous people whose hearts are devoured by an ardent love of glory and their country; imagine your Christian republic confronted by Sparta or Rome, and your pious Christians will be beaten, crushed, destroyed before they have time to collect their wits, or they will owe their salvation only to the contempt which their enemy feels for them.

I myself think it was an excellent oath that was taken by the soldiers of Fabius; they did not swear to conquer or die, but to return as conquerors, and they kept their word. Christians would never have dared to do this; they would have felt that it was tempting God.

But I err in speaking of a Christian republic; for each of these terms contradicts the other. Christianity preaches only servitude and submission. Its spirit is too favourable to tyranny for tyranny not to take advantage of it. True Christians are made to be slaves; they know it and they hardly care; this short life has too little value in their eyes.

It is said that Christian troops are excellent. I deny it. Show me these Christian troops. Personally I know of none. You may mention the crusades. But without disputing the valour of the crusaders, I shall say that they were far from being Christians. They were soldiers of the priests. They were citizens of the Church; they were fighting for its spiritual homeland, which it had in some strange way made temporal. Strictly speaking, this comes under the heading of paganism; for since the Gospel never sets up any national religion, holy war is impossible among Christians.

Under the pagan Emperors, Christian soldiers were brave. All the Christian authors tell us this, and I believe them; but those soldiers were competing for honour against pagan troops. Once the Emperors became Christian, this emulation ceased; and once the cross had driven out the eagle, all Roman valour disappeared.

But leaving aside considerations of politics, let us return to those of right; and settle the principles which govern this important question. The right which the social pact gives the sovereign over the subjects does not, as I have said, go beyond the boundaries of public utility.[5] Subjects have no duty to account to the sovereign for their beliefs except when those beliefs are important to the community. Now it is very important to the state that each citizen should have a religion which makes him love his duty, but the dogmas of that religion are of interest neither to the state nor its members, except in so far as those dogmas concern morals and the duties which everyone who professes that religion is bound to perform towards others. Moreover, everyone may hold whatever opinions he pleases, without the sovereign having any business to take cognizance of them. For the sovereign has no competence in the other world; whatever may be the fate of the subjects in the life to come, it is nothing to do with the sovereign, so long as they are good citizens in this life.

There is thus a profession of faith which is purely civil and of which it is the sovereign's function to determine the articles, not strictly as religious dogmas, but as sentiments of sociability, without which it is impossible to be either a good citizen or a loyal subject.[6] Without being able to oblige anyone to believe these articles, the sovereign can banish from the state anyone who does not believe them; banish him not for impiety but as an anti-social being, as one unable

sincerely to love law and justice, or to sacrifice, if need be, his life to his duty. If anyone, after having publicly acknowledged these same dogmas, behaves as if he did not believe in them, then let him be put to death, for he has committed the greatest crime, that of lying before the law.

The dogmas of the civil religion must be simple and few in number, expressed precisely and without explanations or commentaries. The existence of an omnipotent, intelligent, benevolent divinity that foresees and provides; the life to come; the happiness of the just; the punishment of sinners; the sanctity of the social contract and the law—these are the positive dogmas. As for the negative dogmas, I would limit them to a single one: no intolerance. Intolerance is something which belongs to the religions we have rejected.

In my opinion, those who distinguish between civil and theological intolerance are mistaken. These two forms of intolerance are inseparable. It is impossible to live in peace with people one believes to be damned; to love them would be to hate the God who punishes them; it is an absolute duty either to redeem or to torture them. Wherever theological intolerance is admitted, it is bound to have some civil consequences,[7] and when it does so, the sovereign is no longer sovereign, even in the temporal sphere; at this stage the priests become the real masters, and kings are only their officers.

---

5. "In the republic," says the M(arquis) d'A(rgenson), "everyone is perfectly free to do what does not injure others." Here is the invariable boundary; one could not express it more exactly. I have not been able to deny myself the pleasure of quoting sometimes from this manuscript, although it is not known to the public, in order to pay homage to the memory of an illustrious and honourable man, who, even as a Minister of State, kept the heart of a true citizen, together with just and sound opinions on the government of his country.
6. Caesar pleading for Catilina tried to establish the dogma of the mortality of the soul. Cato and Cicero, to refute it, did not waste time with philosophy; they were content to show that Caesar was speaking like a bad citizen and advancing a doctrine that was injurious to the state. And this was what the Senate had to give judgement on, not any question of theology.

---

7. Marriage, for example, being a civil contract, has civil consequences without which it would be impossible for society itself to subsist. Let us suppose that in a given country the clergy reached the point of gaining the sole right of permitting marriage, a right which it is bound to usurp under any intolerant religion. Is it not then clear that in making the authority of the church supreme in this matter, it will nullify that of the prince, who will then have no subjects other than those the clergy allow him to have? Enable priests to decide whether to marry people according to their assent to this or that doctrine, their assent to this or that formula, or according to their being more or less devout, then is it not clear that if the clergy acts shrewdly and holds firm, it will in time alone dispose of inheritances, offices, the citizens, and the state itself, since the latter could not endure if composed only of bastards? But, you may say, men will call upon the temporal power, issue summonses and warrants, seize church properties. What a sorry sight! If the clergy has even a little, I do not say courage, but common sense, it will allow everything to go its own way; it will quietly let the summonses, the warrants and seizures take place and still end up as master. It is no great sacrifice, I feel, to give up a part when you are sure of securing the whole.

Now that there is not, and can no longer be, an exclusive national religion, all religions which themselves tolerate others must be tolerated, provided only that their dogmas contain nothing contrary to the duties of the citizen. But anyone who dares to say "Outside the church there is no salvation" should be expelled from the state, unless the state is the church and the prince the pontiff. Such a dogma is good only in a theocratic government; in any other, it is pernicious. The reason for which Henri IV is said to have embraced the Catholic religion is one which should make all honest men abandon it, above all any prince who knows how to reason.

Chapter 9
Conclusion

After setting out the true principles of political right, and trying to establish the state on the basis of those principles, I should complete my study by considering the foreign relations of the state, including the law of nations, commerce, the rights of war and conquest, international law, leagues, negotiations, treaties, and so forth. But all this would represent a new subject too vast for my weak vision; and I would have had to keep my eyes fixed on matters within my range.

A Discourse on the Origin and the Foundations of the Inequality of Mankind

It is of man that I have to speak; and the question I am investigating shows me that it is to men that I must address myself: for questions of this sort are not asked by those who are afraid to honour truth. I shall then confidently uphold the cause of humanity before the wise men who invite me to do so, and shall not be dissatisfied if I acquit myself in a manner worthy of my subject and of my judges.

I conceive that there are two kinds of inequality among the human species; one, which I call natural or physical, because it is established by nature, and consists in a difference of age, health, bodily strength, and the qualities of the mind or of the soul: and another, which may be called moral or political inequality, because it depends on a kind of convention, and is established, or at least authorized, by the consent of men. This latter consists of the different privileges which some men enjoy to the prejudice of others; such as that of being more rich, more honoured, more powerful, or even in a position to exact obedience.

It is useless to ask what is the source of natural inequality, because that question is answered by the simple definition of the word. Again, it is still more useless to inquire whether there is any essential connection between the two inequalities; for this would be only asking, in other words, whether those who command are necessarily better than those who obey, and if strength of body or of mind, wisdom, or virtue are always found in particular individuals, in proportion to their power or wealth: a question fit perhaps to be discussed by slaves in the hearing of their masters, but highly unbecoming to reasonable and free men in search of the truth.

The subject of the present discourse, therefore, is more precisely this. To mark, in the progress of things, the moment at which right took the place of violence and nature became subject to law, and to explain by what sequence of miracles the strong came to submit to serve the weak, and the people to purchase imaginary repose at the expense of real felicity.

The philosophers, who have inquired into the foundations of society, have all felt the necessity of going back to a state of nature; but not one of them has got there. Some of them have not hesitated to ascribe to man, in such a state, the idea of just and unjust, without troubling themselves to show that he must be possessed of such an idea, or that it could be of any use to him. Others have spoken of the natural right of every man to keep what belongs to him, without explaining what they meant by "belongs." Others again, beginning by giving the strong authority over the weak, proceeded directly to the birth of government, without regard to the time that must have elapsed before the meaning of the words "authority" and "government" could have existed among men. Every one of them, in short, constantly dwelling on wants, avidity, oppression, desires, and pride, has transferred to the state of nature ideas which were acquired in society; so that, in speaking of the savage, they described the social man. It has not even entered into the heads of most of our writers to doubt whether the state of nature ever existed; but it is clear from the Holy Scriptures that the first man, having received his understanding and commandments immediately from God, was not himself in such a state; and that, if we give such credit to the writings of Moses as every Christian philosopher ought to give, we must deny that, even before the deluge, men were ever in the pure state of nature; unless, indeed, they fell back into it from some very extraordinary circumstance; a paradox which it would be very embarrassing to defend, and quite impossible to prove.

Let us begin then by laying all facts aside, as they do not affect the question. The investigations we may enter into, in treating this subject, must not be considered as historical truths, but only as mere conditional and hypothetical reasonings, rather calculated to explain the nature of things, than to ascertain their actual origin; just like the hypotheses which our physicists daily form respecting the formation of the world. Religion commands us to believe that God Himself having taken men out of a state of nature immediately after the creation, they are unequal only because it is His will they should be so: but it does not forbid us to form conjectures based solely on the nature of man, and the beings around him, concerning what might have become of the human race, if it had been left to itself. This then is the question asked me, and that which I propose to discuss in the following discourse. As my subject interests mankind in general, I shall endeavour to make use of a style adapted to all nations, or rather, forgetting time and place, to attend only to men to whom I am speaking. I shall suppose myself in the Lyceum of Athens, repeating the lessons of my masters, with Plato and Xenocrates for judges, and the whole human race for audience.

O man, of whatever country you are, and whatever your opinions may be, behold your history, such as I have thought to read it, not in books written by your fellow-creatures, who are liars, but in nature, which never lies. All that comes from her will be true; nor will you meet with anything false, unless I have involuntarily put in something of my own. The times of which I am going to speak are very remote: how much

are you changed from what you once were! It is, so to speak, the life of your species which I am going to write, after the qualities which you have received, which your education and habits may have depraved, but cannot have entirely destroyed. There is, I feel, an age at which the individual man would wish to stop: you are about to inquire about the age at which you would have liked your whole species to stand still. Discontented with your present state, for reasons which threaten your unfortunate descendants with still greater discontent, you will perhaps wish it were in your power to go back; and this feeling should be a panegyric on your first ancestors, a criticism of your contemporaries, and a terror to the unfortunates who will come after you.

The First Part

Important as it may be, in order to judge rightly of the natural state of man, to consider him from his origin, and to examine him, as it were, in the embryo of his species, I shall not follow his organization through its successive developments, nor shall I stay to inquire what his animal system must have been at the beginning, in order to become at length what it actually is. I shall not ask whether his long nails were at first, as Aristotle supposes, only crooked talons; whether his whole body, like that of a bear, was not covered with hair; or whether the fact that he walked upon all fours, with his looks directed toward the earth, confined to a horizon of a few paces, did not at once point out the nature and limits of his ideas. On this subject I could form none but vague and almost imaginary conjectures. Comparative anatomy has as yet made too little progress, and the observations of naturalists are too uncertain, to afford an adequate basis for any solid reasoning. So that, without having recourse to the supernatural information given us on this head, or paying any regard to the changes which must have taken place in the internal, as well as the external, conformation of man, as he applied his limbs to new uses, and fed himself on new kinds of food, I shall suppose his conformation to have been at all times what it appears to us at this day; that he always walked on two legs, made use of his hands as we do, directed his looks over all nature, and measured with his eyes the vast expanse of the heavens.

If we strip this being, thus constituted, of all the supernatural gifts he may have received, and all the artificial faculties he can have acquired only by a long process; if we consider him, in a word, just as he must have come from the hands of nature, we behold in him an animal weaker than some, and less agile than others; but, taking him all round, the most advantageously organized of any. I see him satisfying his hunger at the first oak, and slaking his thirst at the first brook: finding his bed at the foot of the tree which afforded him a repast; and, with that, all his wants supplied.

While the earth was left to its natural fertility and covered with immense forests, whose trees were never mutilated by the axe, it would present on every side both sustenance and shelter for every species of animal. Men, dispersed up and down among the rest, would observe and imitate their industry, and thus attain even to the instinct of the beasts, with the advantage that, whereas every species of brutes was confined to one particular instinct, man, who perhaps has not any one peculiar to himself, would appropriate them all, and live upon most of those different foods, which other animals shared among themselves; and thus would find his subsistence much more easily than any of the rest.

Accustomed from their infancy to the inclemencies of the weather and the rigour of the seasons, inured to fatigue, and forced, naked and unarmed, to defend themselves and their prey from other ferocious animals, or to escape them by flight, men would acquire a robust and almost unalterable constitution. The children, bringing with them into the world the excellent constitution of their parents, and fortifying it by the very exercises which first produced it, would thus acquire all the vigour of which the human frame is capable. Nature in this case treats them exactly as Sparta treated the children of her citizens: those who come well formed into the world she renders strong and robust, and all the rest she destroys; differing in this respect from our modern communities, in which the State, by making children a burden to their parents, kills them indiscriminately before they are born.

The body of a savage man being the only instrument he understands, he uses it for various purposes, of which ours, for want of practice, are incapable: for our industry deprives us of that force and agility which necessity obliges him to acquire. If he had had an axe, would he have been able with his naked arm to break so large a branch from a tree? If he had had a sling, would he have been able to throw a stone with so great velocity? If he had had a ladder, would he have been so nimble in climbing a tree? If he had had

a horse, would he have been himself so swift of foot? Give civilized man time to gather all his machines about him, and he will no doubt easily beat the savage; but if you would see a still more unequal contest, set them together naked and unarmed, and you will soon see the advantage of having all our forces constantly at our disposal, of being always prepared for every event, and of carrying one's self, as it were, perpetually whole and entire about one.

Hobbes contends that man is naturally intrepid, and is intent only upon attacking and fighting. Another illustrious philosopher holds the opposite, and Cumberland and Pufendorf also affirm that nothing is more timid and fearful than man in the state of nature; that he is always in a tremble, and ready to fly at the least noise or the slightest movement. This may be true of things he does not know; and I do not doubt his being terrified by every novelty that presents itself, when he neither knows the physical good or evil he may expect from it, nor can make a comparison between his own strength and the dangers he is about to encounter. Such circumstances, however, rarely occur in a state of nature, in which all things proceed in a uniform manner, and the face of the earth is not subject to those sudden and continual changes which arise from the passions and caprices of bodies of men living together. But savage man, living dispersed among other animals, and finding himself betimes in a situation to measure his strength with theirs, soon comes to compare himself with them; and, perceiving that he surpasses them more in adroitness than they surpass him in strength, learns to be no longer afraid of them. Set a bear, or a wolf, against a robust, agile, and resolute savage, as they all are, armed with stones and a good cudgel, and you will see that the danger will be at least on both sides, and that, after a few trials of this kind, wild beasts, which are not fond of attacking each other, will not be at all ready to attack man, whom they will have found to be as wild and ferocious as themselves. With regard to such animals as have really more strength than man has adroitness, he is in the same situation as all weaker animals, which notwithstanding are still able to subsist; except indeed that he has the advantage that, being equally swift of foot, and finding an almost certain place of refuge in every tree, he is at liberty to take or leave it at every encounter, and thus to fight or fly, as he chooses. Add to this that it does not appear that any animal naturally makes war on man, except in case of self-defence or excessive hunger, or betrays any of those violent antipathies, which seem to indicate that one species is intended by nature for the food of another.

This is doubtless why negroes and savages are so little afraid of the wild beasts they may meet in the woods. The Caribs of Venezuela among others live in this respect in absolute security and without the smallest inconvenience. Though they are almost naked, Francis Corréal tells us, they expose themselves freely in the woods, armed only with bows and arrows; but no one has ever heard of one of them being devoured by wild beasts.

But man has other enemies more formidable, against which he is not provided with such means of defence: these are the natural affirmities of infancy, old age, and illness of every kind, melancholy proofs of our weakness, of which the two first are common to all animals, and the last belongs chiefly to man in a state of society. With regard to infancy, it is observable that the mother, carrying her child always with her, can nurse it with much greater ease than the females of many other animals, which are forced to be perpetually going and coming, with great fatigue, one way to find subsistence, and another to suckle or feed their young. It is true that if the woman happens to perish, the infant is in great danger of perishing with her; but this risk is common to so many other species of animals, whose young take a long time before they are able to provide for themselves. And if our infancy is longer than theirs, our lives are longer in proportion; so that all things are in this respect fairly equal; though there are other rules to be considered regarding the duration of the first period of life, and the number of young, which do not affect the present subject. In old age, when men are less active and perspire little, the need for food diminishes with the ability to provide it. As the savage state also protects them from gout and rheumatism, and old age is, of all ills, that which human aid can least alleviate, they cease to be, without others perceiving that they are no more, and almost without perceiving it themselves.

With respect to sickness, I shall not repeat the vain and false declamations which most healthy people pronounce against medicine; but I shall ask if any solid observations have been made from which it may be justly concluded that, in the countries where the art of medicine is most neglected, the mean duration of man's life is less than in those where it is most cultivated. How indeed can this be the case, if we bring on ourselves more diseases than medicine can furnish remedies? The great inequality in manner of living, the extreme idleness of some, and the excessive labour of others, the easiness of exciting and gratifying our sensual appetites, the too exquisite foods of the wealthy which over-heat and fill them with indigestion, and, on the other hand, the unwholesome food of the poor, often, bad as it is, insufficient for their needs, which induces them, when opportunity offers, to eat voraciously and overcharge their stomachs; all these, together with sitting up late, and excesses of every kind, immoderate transports of every passion, fatigue, mental exhaustion, the innumerable pains and anxieties inseparable from every condition of life, by which the mind of man is incessantly tormented; these are too fatal proofs that the greater part of our ills are of our own making, and that we might have avoided them nearly all by adhering to that simple, uniform, and solitary manner of life which nature prescribed. If she destined man to be healthy, I venture to say that a state of reflection is one contrary to nature and that the man who meditates is a depraved animal. When we think of the good constitution of the savages, at least of those whom we have not ruined with our spirituous liquors, and reflect that they are troubled with hardly any disorders, save wounds and old age, we are tempted to believe that, in following the history of civil society, we shall be telling also that of human sickness. Such, at least, was the opinion of Plato, who inferred from certain remedies prescribed, or approved, by Podalirius and Machaon at the siege of Troy, that several sicknesses which these remedies gave rise to in his time, were not then known to mankind; and Celsus tells us that diet, which is now so necessary, was first invented by Hippocrates.

Being subject therefore to so few causes of sickness, man, in the state of nature, can have no need of remedies, and still less of physicians: nor is the human race in this respect worse off than other animals, and it is easy to learn from hunters whether they meet with many infirm animals in the course of the chase. It is certain they frequently meet with such as carry the marks of having been considerably wounded, with many that have had bones or even limbs broken, yet have been healed without any other surgical assistance than that of time, or any other regimen than that of their ordinary life. At the same time their cures seem not to have been less perfect, for their not having been tortured by incisions, poisoned with drugs, or wasted by fasting. In short, however useful medicine, properly administered, may be among us, it is certain that, if the savage, when he is sick and left to himself, has nothing to hope but from nature, he has, on the other hand, nothing to fear but from his disease; which renders his situation often preferable to our own.

We should beware, therefore, of confounding the savage man with the men we have daily before our eyes. Nature treats all the animals left to her care with a predilection that seems to show how jealous she is of that right. The horse, the cat, the bull, and even the ass are generally of greater stature, and always more robust, and have more vigour, strength, and courage, when they run wild in the forests than when bred in the stall. By becoming domesticated, they lose half these advantages; and it seems as if all our care to feed and treat them well serves only to deprave them. It is thus with man also: as he becomes sociable and a slave, he grows weak, timid, and servile; his effeminate way of life totally enervates his strength and courage. To this it may be added that there is still a greater difference between savage and civilized man than between wild and tame beasts; for men and brutes having been treated alike by nature, the several conveniences in which men indulge themselves still more than they do their beasts, are so many additional causes of their deeper degeneracy.

It is not therefore so great a misfortune to these primitive men, nor so great an obstacle to their preservation, that they go naked, have no dwellings, and lack all the superfluities which we think so necessary. If their skins are not covered with hair, they have no need of such covering in warm climates; and, in cold countries, they soon learn to appropriate the skins of the beasts they have overcome. If they have but two legs to run with, they have two arms to defend themselves with, and provide for their wants. Their children are slowly and with difficulty taught to walk; but their mothers are able to carry them with ease; an advantage which other animals lack, as the mother, if pursued, is forced either to abandon her young, or to regulate her pace by theirs. Unless, in short, we suppose a singular and fortuitous concurrence of circumstances of which I shall speak later, and which could well never come about, it is plain in every state of the case, that the man who first made himself clothes or a dwelling was furnishing himself with things not at all necessary; for he had till then done without them, and

there is no reason why he should not have been able to put up in manhood with the same kind of life as had been his in infancy.

Solitary, indolent, and perpetually accompanied by danger, the savage cannot be fond of sleep; his sleep too must be light, like that of the animals, which think but little and may be said to slumber all the time they do not think. Self-preservation being his chief and almost sole concern, he must exercise most those faculties which are most concerned with attack or defence, either for overcoming his prey, or for preventing him from becoming the prey of other animals. On the other hand, those organs which are perfected only by softness and sensuality will remain in a gross and imperfect state, incompatible with any sort of delicacy; so that, his senses being divided on this head, his touch and taste will be extremely coarse, his sight, hearing, and smell exceedingly fine and subtle. Such in general is the animal condition, and such, according to the narratives of travellers, is that of most savage nations. It is therefore no matter for surprise that the Hottentots of the Cape of Good Hope distinguish ships at sea, with the naked eye, at as great a distance as the Dutch can do with their telescopes; or that the savages of America should trace the Spaniards, by their smell, as well as the best dogs could have done; or that these barbarous peoples feel no pain in going naked, or that they use large quantities of pimento with their food, and drink the strongest European liquors like water.

Hitherto I have considered merely the physical man; let us now take a view of him on his metaphysical and moral side.

I see nothing in any animal but an ingenious machine, to which nature hath given senses to wind itself up, and to guard itself, to a certain degree, against anything that might tend to disorder or destroy it. I perceive exactly the same things in the human machine, with this difference, that in the operations of the brute, nature is the sole agent, whereas man has some share in his own operations, in his character as a free agent. The one chooses and refuses by instinct, the other from an act of free will: hence the brute cannot deviate from the rule prescribed to it, even when it would be advantageous for it to do so; and, on the contrary, man frequently deviates from such rules to his own prejudice. Thus a pigeon would be starved to death by the side of a dish of the choicest meats, and a cat on a heap of fruit or grain; though it is certain that either might find nourishment in the foods which it thus rejects with disdain, did it think of trying them. Hence it is that dissolute men run into excesses which bring on fevers and death; because the mind depraves the senses, and the will continues to speak when nature is silent.

Every animal has ideas, since it has senses; it even combines those ideas in a certain degree; and it is only in degree that man differs, in this respect, from the brute. Some philosophers have even maintained that there is a greater difference between one man and another than between some men and some beasts. It is not, therefore, so much the understanding that constitutes the specific difference between the man and the brute, as the human quality of free agency. Nature lays her commands on every animal, and the brute obeys her voice. Man receives the same impulsion, but at the same time knows himself at liberty to acquiesce or resist: and it is particularly in his consciousness of this liberty that the spirituality of his soul is displayed. For physics may explain, in some measure, the mechanism of the senses and the formation of ideas; but in the power of willing or rather of choosing, and in the feeling of this power, nothing is to be found but acts which are purely spiritual and wholly inexplicable by the laws of mechanism.

Yet, if the difficulties attending all these questions should still leave room for dispute about this difference between men and brutes, there is another very specific quality which distinguishes them, and which will admit of no dispute. This is the faculty of self-improvement, which, by the help of circumstances, gradually develops all the rest of our faculties, and is inherent in the species as in the individual: whereas a brute is, at the end of a few months, all he will ever be during his whole life, and his species, at the end of a thousand years, exactly what it was the first year of that thousand. Why is man alone liable to grow into a dotard? Is it not because he returns, in this, to his primitive state; and that, while the brute, which has acquired nothing and has therefore nothing to lose, still retains the force of instinct, man, who loses, by age or accident, all that his *perfectibility* had enabled him to gain, falls by this means lower than the brutes themselves? It would be melancholy, were we forced to admit that this distinctive and almost unlimited faculty is the source of all human misfortunes; that it is this which, in time, draws man out of his original state, in which he would have spent his days insensibly in peace and innocence; that it is this faculty, which, successively producing in different ages his

discoveries and his errors, his vices and his virtues, makes him at length a tyrant both over himself and over nature.[1] It would be shocking to be obliged to regard as a benefactor the man who first suggested to the Oroonoko Indians the use of the boards they apply to the temples of their children, which secure to them some part at least of their imbecility and original happiness.

Savage man, left by nature solely to the direction of instinct, or rather indemnified for what he may lack by faculties capable at first of supplying its place, and afterwards of raising him much above it, must accordingly begin with purely animal functions: thus seeing and feeling must be his first condition, which would be common to him and all other animals. To will, and not to will, to desire and to fear, must be the first, and almost the only operations of his soul, till new circumstances occasion new developments of his faculties.

Whatever moralists may hold, the human understanding is greatly indebted to the passions, which, it is universally allowed, are also much indebted to the understanding. It is by the activity of the passions that our reason is improved; for we desire knowledge only because we wish to enjoy; and it is impossible to conceive any reason why a person who has neither fears nor desires should give himself the trouble of reasoning. The passions, again, originate in our wants, and their progress depends on that of our knowledge; for we cannot desire or fear anything, except from the idea we have of it, or from the simple impulse of nature. Now savage man, being destitute of every species of enlightenment, can have no passions save those of the latter kind: his desires never go beyond his physical wants. The only goods he recognizes in the universe are food, a female, and sleep: the only evils he fears are pain and hunger. I say pain, and not death: for no animal can know what it is to die; the knowledge of death and its terrors being one of the first acquisitions made by man in departing from an animal state.

It would be easy, were it necessary, to support this opinion by facts, and to show that, in all the nations of the world, the progress of the understanding has been exactly proportionate to the wants which the peoples had received from nature, or been subjected

---

1. See Appendix.

to by circumstances, and in consequence to the passions that induced them to provide for those necessities. I might instance the arts, rising up in Egypt and expanding with the inundation of the Nile. I might follow their progress into Greece, where they took root afresh, grew up and towered to the skies, among the rocks and sands of Attica, without being able to germinate on the fertile banks of the Eurotas: I might observe that in general, the people of the North are more industrious than those of the South, because they cannot get on so well without being so: as if nature wanted to equalize matters by giving their understandings the fertility she had refused to their soil.

But who does not see, without recurring to the uncertain testimony of history, that everything seems to remove from savage man both the temptation and the means of changing his condition? His imagination paints no pictures; his heart makes no demands on him. His few wants are so readily supplied, and he is so far from having the knowledge which is needful to make him want more, that he can have neither foresight nor curiosity. The face of nature becomes indifferent to him as it grows familiar. He sees in it always the same order, the same successions: he has not understanding enough to wonder at the greatest miracles; nor is it in his mind that we can expect to find that philosophy man needs, if he is to know how to notice for once what he sees every day. His soul, which nothing disturbs, is wholly wrapped up in the feeling of its present existence, without any idea of the future, however near at hand; while his projects, as limited as his views, hardly extend to the close of day. Such, even at present, is the extent of the native Caribbean's foresight: he will improvidently sell you his cotton-bed in the morning, and come crying in the evening to buy it again, not having foreseen he would want it again the next night.

The more we reflect on this subject, the greater appears the distance between pure sensation and the most simple knowledge: it is impossible indeed to conceive how a man, by his own powers alone, without the aid of communication and the spur of necessity, could have bridged so great a gap. How many ages may have elapsed before mankind were in a position to behold any other fire than that of the heavens! What a multiplicity of chances must have happened to teach them the commonest uses of that element! How often must they have let it out before they acquired the art of reproducing it! and how often

may not such a secret have died with him who had discovered it! What shall we say of agriculture, an art which requires so much labour and foresight, which is so dependent on others that it is plain it could only be practised in a society which had at least begun, and which does not serve so much to draw the means of subsistence from the earth—for these it would produce of itself—but to compel it to produce what is most to our taste? But let us suppose that men had so multiplied that the natural produce of the earth was no longer sufficient for their support; a supposition, by the way, which would prove such a life to be very advantageous for the human race; let us suppose that, without forges or workshops, the instruments of husbandry had dropped from the sky into the hands of savages; that they had overcome their natural aversion to continual labour; that they had learnt so much foresight for their needs; that they had divined how to cultivate the earth, to sow grain and plant trees; that they had discovered the arts of grinding corn, and of setting the grape to ferment—all being things that must have been taught them by the gods, since it is not to be conceived how they could discover them for themselves—yet after all this, what man among them would be so absurd as to take the trouble of cultivating a field, which might be stripped of its crop by the first comer, man or beast, that might take a liking to it; and how should each of them resolve to pass his life in wearisome labour, when, the more necessary to him the reward of his labour might be, the surer he would be of not getting it? In a word, how could such a situation induce men to cultivate the earth, till it was regularly parcelled out among them; that is to say, till the state of nature had been abolished?

Were we to suppose savage man as trained in the art of thinking as philosophers make him; were we, like them, to suppose him a very philosopher capable of investigating the sublimest truths, and of forming, by highly abstract chains of reasoning, maxims of reason and justice, deduced from the love of order in general, or the known will of his Creator; in a word, were we to suppose him as intelligent and enlightened, as he must have been, and is in fact found to have been, dull and stupid, what advantage would accrue to the species, from all such metaphysics, which could not be communicated by one to another, but must end with him who made them? What progress could be made by mankind, while dispersed in the woods among other animals? and how far could men improve or mutually enlighten one another, when, having no fixed habitation, and no need of one another's assistance, the same persons hardly met twice in their lives, and perhaps then, without knowing one another or speaking together?

Let it be considered how many ideas we owe to the use of speech; how far grammar exercises the understanding and facilitates its operations. Let us reflect on the inconceivable pains and the infinite space of time that the first invention of languages must have cost. To these reflections add what preceded, and then judge how many thousand ages must have elapsed in the successive development in the human mind of those operations of which it is capable.

I shall here take the liberty for a moment, of considering the difficulties of the origin of languages, on which subject I might content myself with a simple repetition of the Abbé Condillac's investigations, as they fully confirm my system, and perhaps even first suggested it. But it is plain, from the manner in which this philosopher solves the difficulties he himself raises, concerning the origin of arbitrary signs, that he assumes what I question, viz. that a kind of society must already have existed among the first inventors of language. While I refer, therefore, to his observations on this head, I think it right to give my own, in order to exhibit the same difficulties in a light adapted to my subject. The first which presents itself is to conceive how language can have become necessary; for as there was no communication among men and no need for any, we can neither conceive the necessity of this invention, nor the possibility of it, if it was not somehow indispensable. I might affirm, with many others, that languages arose in the domestic intercourse between parents and their children. But this expedient would not obviate the difficulty, and would besides involve the blunder made by those who, in reasoning on the state of nature, always import into it ideas gathered in a state of society. Thus they constantly consider families as living together under one roof, and the individuals of each as observing among themselves a union as intimate and permanent as that which exists among us, where so many common interests unite them: whereas, in this primitive state, men had neither houses, nor huts, nor any kind of property whatever; every one lived where he could, seldom for more than a single night; the sexes united without design, as accident, opportunity, or inclination brought them together, nor had they any great needs of words to communicate their designs to each other; and they parted with the same indifference. The mother gave suck to her children at first for her own sake; and afterwards, when habit had made them dear, for theirs: but as soon as they were strong enough to go in search of their own food, they forsook her of their own accord; and, as they had hardly any other method of not losing one another than that of remaining continually within sight, they soon became quite incapable of recognizing one another when they happened to meet again. It is further to be observed that the child, having all his wants to explain, and of course more to say to his mother than the mother could have to say to him, must have borne the brunt of the task of invention, and the language he used would be of his own device, so that the number of languages would be equal to that of the individuals speaking them, and the variety would be increased by the vagabond and roving life they led, which would not give time for any idiom to become constant. For to say that the mother dictated to her child the words he was to use in asking her for one thing or another, is an explanation of how languages already formed are taught, but by no means explains how languages were originally formed.

We will suppose, however, that this first difficulty is obviated. Let us for a moment then take ourselves as being on this side of the vast space which must lie between a pure state of nature and that in which languages had become necessary, and, admitting their necessity, let us inquire how they could first be established. Here we have a new and worse difficulty to grapple with; for if men need speech to learn to think, they must have stood in much greater need of the art of thinking, to be able to invent that of speaking. And though we might conceive how the articulate sounds of the voice came to be taken as the conventional interpreters of our ideas, it would still remain for us to inquire what could have been the interpreters of this convention for those ideas, which, answering to no sensible objects, could not be indicated either by gesture or voice; so that we can hardly form any tolerable conjectures about the origin of this art of communicating our thoughts and establishing a correspondence between minds: an art so sublime, that far distant as it is from its origin, philosophers still behold it at such an immeasurable distance from perfection, that there is none rash enough to affirm it will ever reach it, even though the revolutions time necessarily produces were suspended in its favour, though prejudice should be banished from our academies or condemned to silence, and those learned societies should devote themselves uninterruptedly for whole ages to this thorny question.

The first language of mankind, the most universal and vivid, in a word the only language man needed, before he had occasion to exert his eloquence to persuade assembled multitudes, was the simple cry of nature. But as this was excited only by a sort of instinct on urgent occasions, to implore assistance in case of danger, or relief in case of suffering, it could be of little use in the ordinary course of life, in which more moderate feelings prevail. When the ideas of men began to expand and multiply, and closer communication took place among them, they strove to invent more numerous signs and a more copious language. They multiplied the inflexions of the voice, and added gestures, which are in their own nature more expressive, and depend less for their meaning on a prior determination. Visible and movable objects were therefore expressed by gestures, and audible ones by imitative sounds: but, as hardly anything can be indicated by gestures, except objects actually present or easily described, and visible actions; as they are not universally useful—for darkness or the interposition of a material object destroys their efficacy—and as besides they rather request than secure our attention; men at length bethought themselves of substituting for them the articulate sounds of the voice, which, without bearing the same relation to any particular ideas, are better calculated to express them all, as conventional signs. Such an institution could only be made by common consent, and must have been effected in a manner not very easy for men whose gross organs had not been accustomed to any such exercise. It is also in itself still more difficult to conceive, since such a common agreement must have had motives, and it seems that speech must needs have existed before its use could be established.

It is reasonable to suppose that the first words which men used had for them a much wider meaning than the ones we use in languages which have already developed, and that, ignorant as they were of the division of discourse into its constituent parts, they at first gave every single word the sense of a whole proposition. When they began to distinguish subject and attribute, and noun and verb, which was itself no common effort of genius, substantives were at first only so many proper names; the present infinitive was the only tense of verbs; and the very idea of adjectives must have been developed with great difficulty; for every adjective is an abstract idea, and abstractions are painful and unnatural operations.

Every object at first received a particular name without regard to genus or species, which these primitive originators were not in a position to distinguish; every individual presented itself to their minds in isolation, as they are in the picture of nature. If one oak was called A, another was called B; for the primitive idea of two things is that they are not the same, and it often takes a long time for what they have in common to be seen: so that, the narrower the limits of their knowledge of things, the more copious their dictionary must have been. The difficulty of using such a vocabulary could not be easily removed; for, to arrange beings under common and generic denominations, it became necessary to know their distinguishing properties: the need arose for observation and definition, that is to say, for natural history and metaphysics of a far more developed kind than men can at that time have possessed.

Add to this, that general ideas cannot be introduced into the mind without the assistance of words, nor can the understanding seize them except by means of propositions. This is one of the reasons why animals cannot form such ideas, or ever acquire that capacity for self-improvement which depends on them. When a monkey goes from one nut to another, are we to conceive that he entertains any general idea of that kind of fruit, and compares its archetype with the two individual nuts? Assuredly he does not; but the sight of one of these nuts recalls to his memory the sensations which he received from the other, and his eyes, being modified after a certain manner, give information to the palate of the modification it is about to receive. Every general idea is purely intellectual; if the imagination meddles with it ever so little, the idea immediately becomes particular. If you endeavour to trace in your mind the image of a tree in general, you never attain to your end. In spite of all you can do, you will have to see it as great or little, bare or leafy, light or dark, and were you capable of seeing nothing in it but what is common to all trees, it would no longer be like a tree at all. Purely abstract beings are perceivable in the same manner, or are only conceivable by the help of language. The definition of a triangle alone gives you a true idea of it: the moment you imagine a triangle in your mind, it is some particular triangle and not another, and you cannot avoid giving it sensible lines on a coloured area. We must then make use of propositions and of language in order to form general ideas. For no sooner does the imagination cease to operate than the understanding proceeds only by the help of words. If then the first inventors of speech could give names only to ideas they already had, it follows that the first substantives could be nothing more than proper names.

But when our new grammarians, by means of which I have no conception, began to extend their ideas and generalize their terms, the ignorance of the inventors must have confined this method within very narrow limits; and, as they had at first gone too far in multiplying the names of individuals, from ignorance of their genus and species, they made afterwards too few of these, from not having considered beings in all their specific differences. It would indeed have needed more knowledge and experience than they could have, and more pains and inquiry than they would have bestowed, to carry these distinctions to their proper length. If, even today, we are continually discovering new species, which have hitherto escaped observation, let us reflect how many of them must have escaped men who judged things merely from their first appearance! It is superfluous to add that the primitive classes and the most general notions must necessarily have escaped their notice also. How, for instance, could they have understood or thought of the words *matter, spirit, substance, mode, figure, motion,* when even our philosophers, who have so long been making use of them, have themselves the greatest difficulty in understanding them; and when, the ideas attached to them being purely metaphysical, there are no models of them to be found in nature?

But I stop at this point, and ask my judges to suspend their reading a while, to consider, after the invention of physical substantives, which is the easiest part of language to invent, that there is still a great way to go, before the thoughts of men will have found perfect expression and constant form, such as would answer the purposes of public speaking, and produce their effect on society. I beg of them to consider how much time must have been spent, and how much knowledge needed, to find out numbers, abstract terms, aorists, and all the tenses of verbs, particles, syntax, the method of connecting propositions, the forms of reasoning, and all the logic of speech. For myself, I am so aghast at the increasing difficulties which present themselves, and so well convinced of the almost demonstrable impossibility that languages should owe their original institution to merely human means, that I leave, to any one who will undertake it, the discussion of the difficult problem: which was the more necessary, the existence of society to the invention of language, or the invention of language to the establishment of society. But be the origins of language and society what they may, it may be at least inferred, from the little care which nature has taken to unite mankind by mutual wants, and to facilitate the use of speech, that she has contributed little to make them sociable, and has put little of her own into all they have done to create such bonds of union. It is in fact impossible to conceive why, in a state of nature, one man should stand more in need of the assistance of another, than a monkey or a wolf of the assistance of another of its kind: or, granting that he did, what motives could induce that other to assist him; or, even then, by what means they could agree about the conditions. I know it is incessantly repeated that man would in such a state have been the most miserable of creatures; and indeed, if it be true, as I think I have proved, that he must have lived many ages, before he could have either desire or an opportunity of emerging from it, this would only be an accusation against nature, and not against the being which she had thus unhappily constituted. But as I understand the word "miserable," it either has no meaning at all, or else signifies only a painful privation of something, or a state of suffering either in body or soul. I should be glad to have explained to me, what kind of misery a free being, whose heart is at ease and whose body is in health, can possibly suffer. I would like to know which is the more likely to become insupportable to those who take part in it: the life of society or the life of nature. We hardly see anyone around us except people who are complaining of their existence; many even deprive themselves of it if they can and all divine and human laws put together can hardly put a stop to this disorder. I would like to know if anyone has heard of a savage who took it into his head, when he was free, to complain of life and to kill himself. Let us be less arrogant, then, when we judge on which side real misery is found. Nothing, on the other hand, could be more miserable than a savage exposed to the dazzling light of our "civilization," tormented by our passions and reasoning about a state different from his own. It appears that providence most wisely determined that the faculties, which he potentially possessed, should develop themselves only as occasion offered to exercise them, in order that they might not be superfluous or perplexing to him, by appearing before their time, nor slow and useless when the need for them arose. In instinct alone, he had all he required for living in the state of nature; and with a developed understanding he has only just enough to support life in society.

It appears, at first view, that men in a state of nature, having no moral relations or determinate obligations one with another, could not be either good or bad, virtuous or vicious; unless we take these terms in a physical sense, and call, in an individual, those qualities vices which may be injurious to his preservation, and those virtues which contribute to it; in which case, he would have to be accounted most virtuous, who put least check on the pure impulses of nature. But without deviating from the ordinary sense of the words, it will be proper to suspend the judgment we might be led to form on such a state, and be on our guard against our prejudices, till we have weighed the matter in the scales of impartiality, and seen whether virtues or vices preponderate among civilized men: and whether their virtues do them more good than their vices do harm; till we have discovered whether the progress of the sciences sufficiently indemnifies them for the mischiefs they do one another, in proportion as they are better informed of the good they ought to do; or whether they would not be, on the whole, in a much happier condition if they had nothing to fear or to hope from any one, than as they are, subjected to universal dependence, and obliged to take everything from those who engage to give them nothing in return.

Above all, let us not conclude, with Hobbes, that because man has no idea of goodness, he must be naturally wicked; that he is vicious because he does not know virtue; that he always refuses to do his fellow-creatures services which he does not think they have a right to demand; or that by virtue of the right he justly claims to all he needs, he foolishly imagines himself the sole proprietor of the whole universe. Hobbes had seen clearly the defects of all the modern definitions of natural right: but the consequences which he deduces from his own show that he understands it in an equally false sense. In reasoning on the principles he lays down, he ought to have said that the state of nature, being that in which the care for our own preservation is the least prejudicial to that of others, was consequently the best calculated to pro-

mote peace, and the most suitable for mankind. He does say the exact opposite, in consequence of having improperly admitted, as a part of savage man's care for self-preservation, the gratification of a multitude of passions which are the work of society, and have made laws necessary. A bad man, he says, is a robust child. But it remains to be proved whether man in a state of nature is this robust child: and, should we grant that he is, what would he infer? Why truly, that if this man, when robust and strong, were dependent on others as he is when feeble, there is no extravagance he would not be guilty of; that he would beat his mother when she was too slow in giving him her breast; that he would strangle one of his younger brothers, if he should be troublesome to him, or bite the leg of another, if he put him to any inconvenience. But that man in the state of nature is both strong and dependent involves two contrary suppositions. Man is weak when he is dependent, and is his own master before he comes to be strong. Hobbes did not reflect that the same cause, which prevents a savage from making use of his reason, as our jurists hold, prevents him also from abusing his faculties, as Hobbes himself allows: so that it may be justly said that savages are not bad merely because they do not know what it is to be good: for it is neither the development of the understanding nor the restraint of law that hinders them from doing ill; but the peacefulness of their passions, and their ignorance of vice: *tanto plus in illis proficit vitiorum ignoratio, quam in his cognitio virtutis.*[2] There is another principle which has escaped Hobbes; which, having been bestowed on mankind, to moderate, on certain occasions, the impetuosity of *amour-propre*, or, before its birth, the desire of self-preservation, tempers the ardour with which he pursues his own welfare, by an innate repugnance at seeing a fellow-creature suffer.[3] I think

---

2. [Justin, *Hist.* ii, 2. So much more does the ignorance of vice profit the one sort than the knowledge of virtue the other.]

3. *Amour-propre* must not be confused with love of self: for they differ both in themselves and in their effects. Love of self is a natural feeling which leads every animal to look to its own preservation, and which, guided in man by reason and modified by compassion, creates humanity and virtue. *Amour-propre* is a purely relative and factitious feeling, which arises in the state of society, leads each individual to make more of himself than of any other, causes all the mutual damage men inflict one on another, and is the real source of the "sense of honour." This being understood, I maintain that, in our primitive condition, in the true state of nature, *amour-propre* did not exist; for as each

I need not fear contradiction in holding man to be possessed of the only natural virtue, which could not be denied him by the most violent detractor of human virtue. I am speaking of compassion, which is a disposition suitable to creatures so weak and subject to so many evils as we certainly are: by so much the more universal and useful to mankind, as it comes before any kind of reflection; and at the same time so natural, that the very brutes themselves sometimes give evident proofs of it. Not to mention the tenderness of mothers for their offspring and the perils they encounter to save them from danger, it is well known that horses show a reluctance to trample on living bodies. One animal never passes by the dead body of another of its species without disquiet: some even give their fellows a sort of burial; while the mournful lowings of the cattle when they enter the slaughter-house show the impressions made on them by the horrible spectacle which meets them. We find, with pleasure, the author of *The Fable of the Bees* obliged to own that man is a compassionate and sensible being, and laying aside his cold subtlety of style, in the example he gives, to present us with the pathetic description of a man who, from a place of confinement, is compelled to behold a wild beast tear a child from the arms of its mother, grinding its tender limbs with its murderous teeth, and tearing its palpitating entrails with its claws. What horrid agitation must not the eye-witness of such a scene experience, although he would not be personally concerned! What anguish would he not suffer at not being able to give any assistance to the fainting mother and the dying infant!

Such is the pure emotion of nature, prior to all kinds of reflection! Such is the force of natural com-

passion, which the greatest depravity of morals has as yet hardly been able to destroy! for we daily find at our theatres men affected, nay, shedding tears at the sufferings of a wretch who, were he in the tyrant's place, would probably even add to the torments of his enemies; like the bloodthirsty Sulla, who was so sensitive to ills he had not caused, or that Alexander of Pheros who did not dare to go and see any tragedy acted, for fear of being seen weeping with Andromache and Priam, though he could listen without emotion to the cries of all the citizens who were daily strangled at his command.

Mollissima corda
Humano generi dare se natura fatetur
Quae lacrimas dedit.
Juvenal, *Satires*, XV. 131[4]

Mandeville well knew that, in spite of all their morality, men would have never been better than monsters, had not nature bestowed on them a sense of compassion, to aid their reason: but he did not see that from this quality alone flow all those social virtues, of which he denied man the possession. But what is generosity, clemency, or humanity but compassion applied to the weak, to the guilty, or to mankind in general? Even benevolence and friendship are, if we judge rightly, only the effects of compassion, constantly set upon a particular object: for how is it different to wish that another person may not suffer pain and uneasiness and to wish him happy? Were it even true that pity is no more than a feeling, which puts us in the place of the sufferer, a feeling obscure yet lively in a savage, developed yet feeble in civilized man; this truth would have no other consequence than to confirm my argument. Compassion must, in fact, be the stronger, the more the animal beholding any kind of distress identifies himself with the animal that suffers. Now, it is plain that such identification must have been much more perfect in a state of nature than it is in a state of reason. It is reason that engenders *amour-propre*, and reflection that confirms it: it is reason which turns man's mind back upon itself, and divides him from everything that could disturb or afflict him. It is philosophy that isolates him, and bids him say, at sight of the misfortunes of others: "Perish if you will, I am secure." Nothing

---

man regarded himself as the only observer of his actions, the only being in the universe who took any interest in him, and the sole judge of his deserts, no feeling arising from comparisons he could not be led to make could take root in his soul; and for the same reason, he could know neither hatred nor the desire for revenge, since these passions can spring only from a sense of injury: and as it is the contempt or the intention to hurt, and not the harm done, which constitutes the injury, men who neither valued nor compared themselves could do one another much violence, when it suited them, without feeling any sense of injury. In a word, each man, regarding his fellows almost as he regarded animals of different species, might seize the prey of a weaker or yield up his own to a stronger, and yet consider these acts of violence as mere natural occurrences, without the slightest emotion of insolence or despite, or any other feeling than the joy or grief of success or failure.

---

4. [Nature avows she gave the human race the softest hearts, who gave them tears.]

but such general evils as threaten the whole community can disturb the tranquil sleep of the philosopher, or tear him from his bed. A murder may with impunity be committed under his window; he has only to put his hands to his ears and argue a little with himself, to prevent nature, which is shocked within him, from identifying itself with the unfortunate sufferer. Uncivilized man has not this admirable talent; and for want of reason and wisdom, is always foolishly ready to obey the first promptings of humanity. It is the populace that flocks together at riots and street brawls, while the wise man prudently makes off. It is the mob and the market-women who part the combatants, and stop decent people from cutting one another's throats.

It is then certain that compassion is a natural feeling, which, by moderating the activity of love of self in each individual, contributes to the preservation of the whole species. It is this compassion that hurries us without reflection to the relief of those who are in distress: it is this which in a state of nature supplies the place of laws, morals, and virtues, with the advantage that none are tempted to disobey its gentle voice: it is this which will always prevent a sturdy savage from robbing a weak child or a feeble old man of the sustenance they may have with pain and difficulty acquired, if he sees a possibility of providing for himself by other means: it is this which, instead of inculcating that sublime maxim of rational justice, *Do to others as you would have them do unto you*, inspires all men with that other maxim of natural goodness, much less perfect indeed, but perhaps more useful; *Do good to yourself with as little evil as possible to others*. In a word, it is rather in this natural feeling than in any subtle arguments that we must look for the cause of that repugnance, which every man would experience in doing evil, even independently of the maxims of education. Although it might belong to Socrates and other minds of the like craft to acquire virtue by reason, the human race would long since have ceased to be, had its preservation depended only on the reasonings of the individuals composing it.

With passions so little active, and so good a curb, men, being rather wild than wicked, and more intent to guard themselves against the mischief that might be done them, than to do mischief to others, were by no means subject to very perilous dissensions. They maintained no kind of intercourse with one another, and were consequently strangers to vanity, deference, esteem, and contempt; they had not the least idea of

"mine" and "thine," and no true conception of justice; they looked upon every violence to which they were subjected, rather as an injury that might easily be repaired than as a crime that ought to be punished; and they never thought of taking revenge, unless perhaps mechanically and on the spot, as a dog will sometimes bite the stone which is thrown at him. Their quarrels therefore would seldom have very bloody consequences; for the subject of them would be merely the question of subsistence. But I am aware of one greater danger, which remains to be noticed.

Of the passions that stir the heart of man, there is one which makes the sexes necessary to each other, and is extremely ardent and impetuous; a terrible passion that braves danger, surmounts all obstacles, and in its transports seems calculated to bring destruction on the human race which it is really destined to preserve. What must become of men who are left to this brutal and boundless rage, without modesty, without shame, and daily upholding their amours at the price of their blood?

It must, in the first place, be allowed that, the more violent the passions are, the more are laws necessary to keep them under restraint. But, setting aside the inadequacy of laws to effect this purpose, which is evident from the crimes and disorders to which these passions daily give rise among us, we should do well to inquire if these evils did not spring up with the laws themselves; for in this case, even if the laws were capable of repressing such evils, it is the least that could be expected from them, that they should check a mischief which would not have arisen without them.

Let us begin by distinguishing between the physical and moral ingredients in the feeling of love. The physical part of love is that general desire which urges the sexes to union with each other. The moral part is that which determines and fixes this desire exclusively upon one particular object; or at least gives it a greater degree of energy toward the object thus preferred. It is easy to see that the moral part of love is a factitious feeling, born of social usage, and enhanced by the women with much care and cleverness, to establish their empire, and put in power the sex which ought to obey. This feeling, being founded on certain ideas of beauty and merit which a savage is not in a position to acquire, and on comparisons which he is incapable of making, must be for him almost non-existent; for, as his mind cannot form abstract ideas of proportion and regularity, so his heart is not susceptible of the feelings of love and admiration, which are even insensibly produced by the application of these ideas. He follows solely the character nature has implanted in him, and not tastes which he could never have acquired; so that every woman equally answers his purpose.

Men in a state of nature being confined merely to what is physical in love, and fortunate enough to be ignorant of those excellences, which whet the appetite while they increase the difficulty of gratifying it, must be subject to fewer and less violent fits of passion, and consequently fall into fewer and less violent disputes. The imagination, which causes such ravages among us, never speaks to the heart of savages, who quietly await the impulses of nature, yield to them involuntarily, with more pleasure than ardour, and, their wants once satisfied, lose the desire. It is therefore incontestable that love, as well as all other passions, must have acquired in society that glowing impetuosity, which makes it so often fatal to mankind. And it is the more absurd to represent savages as continually cutting one another's throats to indulge their brutality, because this opinion is directly contrary to experience; the Caribbeans, who have as yet least of all deviated from the state of nature, being in fact the most peaceable of people in their amours, and the least subject to jealousy, though they live in a hot climate which seems always to inflame the passions.

With regard to the inferences that might be drawn, in the case of several species of animals, the males of which fill our poultry-yards with blood and slaughter, or in spring make the forests resound with their quarrels over their females; we must begin by excluding all those species, in which nature has plainly established, in the comparative power of the sexes, relations different from those which exist among us: thus we can base no conclusion about men on the habits of fighting cocks. In those species where the proportion is better observed, these battles must be entirely due to the scarcity of females in comparison with males; or, what amounts to the same thing, to the intervals during which the female constantly refuses the advances of the male: for if each female admits the male but during two months in the year, it is the same as if the number of females were five-sixths less. Now, neither of these two cases is applicable to the human species, in which the number of females usually exceeds that of males, and among whom it has never been observed, even among savages, that the females

have, like those of other animals, their stated times of passion and indifference. Moreover, in several of these species, the individuals all take fire at once, and there comes a fearful moment of universal passion, tumult, and disorder among them; a scene which is never beheld in the human species, whose love is not thus seasonal. We must not then conclude from the combats of such animals for the enjoyment of the females, that the case would be the same with mankind in a state of nature: and, even if we drew such a conclusion, we see that such contests do not exterminate other kinds of animals, and we have no reason to think they would be more fatal to ours. It is indeed clear that they would do still less mischief than is the case in a state of society; especially in those countries in which, morals being still held in some repute, the jealousy of lovers and the vengeance of husbands are the daily cause of duels, murders, and even worse crimes; where the obligation of eternal fidelity only occasions adultery, and the very laws of honour and continence necessarily increase debauchery and lead to the multiplication of abortions.

Let us conclude then that man in a state of nature, wandering up and down the forests, without industry, without speech, and without home, an equal stranger to war and to all ties, neither standing in need of his fellow-creatures nor having any desire to hurt them, and perhaps even not distinguishing them one from another; let us conclude that, being self-sufficient and subject to so few passions, he could have no feelings or knowledge but such as befitted his situation; that he felt only his actual necessities, and disregarded everything he did not think himself immediately concerned to notice, and that his understanding made no greater progress than his vanity. If by accident he made any discovery, he was the less able to communicate it to others, as he did not know even his own children. Every art would necessarily perish with its inventor, where there was no kind of education among men, and generations succeeded generations without the least advance; when, all setting out from the same point, centuries must have elapsed in the barbarism of the first ages; when the race was already old, and man remained a child.

If I have expatiated at such length on this supposed primitive state, it is because I had so many ancient errors and inveterate prejudices to eradicate, and therefore thought it incumbent on me to dig down to their very root, and show, by means of a true picture of the state of nature, how far even the natural inequalities of mankind are from having that reality and influence which modern writers suppose.

It is in fact easy to see that many of the differences between men which are ascribed to nature stem rather from habit and the diverse modes of life of men in society. Thus a robust or delicate constitution, and the strength or weakness attaching to it, are more frequently the effects of a hardy or effeminate method of education than of the original endowment of the body. It is the same with the powers of the mind; for education not only makes a difference between such as are cultured and such as are not, but even increases the differences which exist among the former, in proportion to their respective degrees of culture: as the distance between a giant and a dwarf on the same road increases with every step they take. If we compare the prodigious diversity, which obtains in the education and manner of life of the various orders of men in the state of society, with the uniformity and simplicity of animal and savage life, in which every one lives on the same kind of food and in exactly the same manner, and does exactly the same things, it is easy to conceive how much less the difference between man and man must be in a state of nature than in a state of society, and how greatly the natural inequality of mankind must be increased by the inequalities of social institutions.

But even if nature really affected, in the distribution of her gifts, that partiality which is imputed to her, what advantage would the greatest of her favourites derive from it, to the detriment of others, in a state that admits of hardly any kind of relation between them? Where there is no love, of what advantage is beauty? Of what use is wit to those who do not converse, or cunning to those who have no business with others? I hear it constantly repeated that, in such a state, the strong would oppress the weak; but what is here meant by oppression? Some, it is said, would violently domineer over others, who would groan under a servile submission to their caprices. This indeed is exactly what I observe to be the case among us; but I do not see how it can be inferred of men in a state of nature, who could not easily be brought to conceive what we mean by dominion and servitude. One man, it is true, might seize the fruits which another had gathered, the game he had killed, or the cave he had chosen for shelter; but how would he ever be able to exact obedience, and what ties of dependence could there be among men without possessions? If, for instance, I am driven from one tree, I

can go to the next; if I am disturbed in one place, what hinders me from going to another? Again, should I happen to meet with a man so much stronger than myself, and at the same time so depraved, so indolent, and so barbarous, as to compel me to provide for his sustenance while he himself remains idle; he must take care not to have his eyes off me for a single moment; he must bind me fast before he goes to sleep, or I shall certainly either knock him on the head or make my escape. That is to say, he must in such a case voluntarily expose himself to much greater trouble than he seeks to avoid, or can give me. After all this, let him be off his guard ever so little; let him but turn his head aside at any sudden noise, and I shall be instantly twenty paces off, lost in the forest, and, my fetters burst asunder, he would never see me again.

Without my expatiating thus uselessly on these details, every one must see that as the bonds of servitude are formed merely by the mutual dependence of men on one another and the reciprocal needs that unite them, it is impossible to make any man a slave, unless he be first reduced to a situation in which he cannot do without the help of others: and, since such a situation does not exist in a state of nature, every one is there his own master, and the law of the strongest is of no effect.

Having proved that the inequality of mankind is hardly felt, and that its influence is next to nothing in a state of nature, I must next show its origin and trace its progress in the successive developments of the human mind. Having shown that human *perfectibility*, the social virtues, and the other faculties which natural man potentially possessed, could never develop of themselves, but must require the fortuitous concurrence of many foreign causes that might never arise, and without which he would have remained for ever in his primitive conditions, I must now collect and consider the different accidents which may have improved the human understanding while depraving the species, and made man wicked while making him sociable; so as to bring him and the world from that distant period to the point at which we now behold them.

I confess that, as the events I am going to describe might have happened in various ways, I have nothing to determine my choice but conjectures: but such conjectures become reasons when they are the most probable that can be drawn from the nature of things, and the only means of discovering the truth. The consequences, however, which I mean to deduce will not be barely conjectural; as, on the principles just laid down, it would be impossible to form any other theory that would not furnish the same results, and from which I could not draw the same conclusions.

This will be a sufficient apology for my not dwelling on the manner in which the lapse of time compensates for the little probability in the events; on the surprising power of trivial causes, when their action is constant; on the impossibility, on the one hand, of destroying certain hypotheses, though on the other we cannot give them the certainty of known matters of fact; on its being within the province of history, when two facts are given as real, and have to be connected by a series of intermediate facts, which are unknown or supposed to be so, to supply such facts as may connect them; and on its being in the province of philosophy when history is silent, to determine similar facts to serve the same end; and lastly, on the influence of similarity, which, in the case of events, reduces the facts to a much smaller number of different classes than is commonly imagined. It is enough for me to offer these hints to the consideration of my judges, and to have so arranged that the general reader has no need to consider them at all.

The Second Part

The first man who, having enclosed a piece of ground, bethought himself of saying "This is mine," and found people simple enough to believe him, was the real founder of civil society. From how many crimes, wars, and murders, from how many horrors and misfortunes might not any one have saved mankind, by pulling up the stakes, or filling up the ditch, and crying to his fellows: "Beware of listening to this impostor; you are undone if you once forget that the fruits of the earth belong to us all, and the earth itself to nobody." But there is great probability that things had then already come to such a pitch, that they could no longer continue as they were; for the idea of property depends on many prior ideas, which could only be acquired successively, and cannot have been formed all at once in the human mind. Mankind must have made very considerable progress, and acquired considerable knowledge and industry which they must also have transmitted and increased from age to age, before they arrived at this last point of the state of nature. Let us then go farther back, and endeavour to unify under a single point of view that slow succession of events and discoveries in the most natural order.

Man's first feeling was that of his own existence, and his first care that of self-preservation. The produce of the earth furnished him with all he needed, and instinct told him how to use it. Hunger and other appetites made him at various times experience various modes of existence; and among these was one which urged him to propagate his species—a blind propensity that, having nothing to do with the heart, produced a merely animal act. The want once gratified, the two sexes knew each other no more; and even the offspring was nothing to its mother, as soon as it could do without her.

Such was the condition of infant man; the life of an animal limited at first to mere sensations, and hardly profiting by the gifts nature bestowed on him, much less capable of entertaining a thought of forcing anything from her. But difficulties soon presented themselves, and it became necessary to learn how to surmount them: the height of the trees, which prevented him from gathering their fruits, the competition of other animals desirous of the same fruits, and the ferocity of those who sought to deprive man himself of life, all obliged him to apply himself to bodily exercises. He had to be active, swift of foot, and vigorous in fight. Natural weapons, stones, and sticks, were easily found: he learnt to surmount the obstacles of nature, to contend in case of necessity with other animals, and to dispute for the means of subsistence even with other men, or to indemnify himself for what he was forced to give up to a stronger.

In proportion as the human race grew more numerous, men's cares increased. The difference of soils, climates, and seasons, must have introduced some differences into their manner of living. Barren years, long and sharp winters, scorching summers which parched the fruits of the earth, must have demanded a new industry. On the seashore and the banks of rivers, they invented the hook and line, and became fishermen and eaters of fish. In the forests they made bows and arrows, and became huntsmen and warriors. In cold countries they clothed themselves with the skins of the beasts they had slain. The lightning, a volcano, or some lucky chance acquainted them with fire, a new resource against the rigours of winter: they next learned how to preserve this element, then how to reproduce it, and finally how to prepare with it the flesh of animals which before they had eaten raw.

The way these different beings and phenomena impinged on him and on each other must naturally have engendered in man's mind the awareness of certain relationships. Thus the relationships which we denote by the terms *great, small, strong, weak, swift, slow, fearful, bold,* and the like, almost insensibly compared at need, must have at length produced in him a kind of reflection, or rather a mechanical prudence, which would indicate to him the precautions most necessary to his security.

The new intelligence which resulted from this development increased his superiority over other animals, by making him sensible of it. He would now endeavour, therefore, to ensnare them, would play them a thousand tricks, and though many of them might surpass him in swiftness or in strength, would in time become the master of some and the scourge of others. Thus, the first time he looked into himself, he felt the first emotion of pride; and, at a time when he scarce knew how to distinguish the different orders of beings, by looking upon his species as of the highest order, he prepared the way for assuming preeminence as an individual.

Other men, it is true, were not then to him what they now are to us, and he had no greater intercourse with them than with other animals; yet they were not neglected in his observations. The conformities, which he would in time discover between them, and between himself and his female, led him to judge of others which were not then perceptible; and finding that they all behaved as he himself would have done in like circumstances, he naturally inferred that their manner of thinking and acting was altogether in conformity with his own. This important truth, once deeply impressed on his mind, must have induced him, from an intuitive feeling more certain and much more rapid than any kind of reasoning, to pursue the rules of conduct, which he had best observe towards them, for his own security and advantage.

Taught by experience that the love of well-being is the sole motive of human actions, he found himself in a position to distinguish the few cases, in which mutual interest might justify him in relying upon the assistance of his fellows; and also the still fewer cases in which a conflict of interests might give cause to suspect them. In the former case, he joined in the same herd with them, or at most in some kind of loose association, that laid no restraint on its members, and lasted no longer than the transitory occasion that formed it. In the latter case, every one sought his own private advantage, either by open force, if he thought himself strong enough, or by address and cunning, if he felt himself the weaker.

In this manner, men may have insensibly acquired some gross ideas of mutual undertakings, and of the advantages of fulfilling them: that is, just so far as their present and apparent interest was concerned: for they were perfect strangers to foresight, and were so far from troubling themselves about the distant future, that they hardly thought of the morrow. If a deer was to be taken, every one saw that, in order to succeed, he must abide faithfully by his post: but if a hare happened to come within the reach of any one of them, it is not to be doubted that he pursued it without scruple, and, having seized his prey, cared very little, if by so doing he caused his companions to miss theirs.

It is easy to understand that such intercourse would not require a language much more refined than that of rooks or monkeys, who associate together for much the same purpose. Inarticulate cries, plenty of gestures, and some imitative sounds, must have been for a long time the universal language; and by the addition, in every country, of some conventional articulate sounds (of which, as I have already intimated, the first institution is not too easy to explain) particular languages were produced; but these were rude and imperfect, and nearly such as are now to be found among some savage nations.

Hurried on by the rapidity of time, by the abundance of things I have to say, and by the almost insensible progress of things in their beginnings, I pass over in an instant a multitude of ages; for the slower the events were in their succession, the more rapidly may they be described.

These first advances enabled men to make others with greater rapidity. In proportion as they grew enlightened, they grew industrious. They ceased to fall asleep under the first tree, or in the first cave that afforded them shelter; they invented several kinds of implements of hard and sharp stones, which they used to dig up the earth, and to cut wood; then they made huts out of branches, and afterwards learnt to plaster them over with mud and clay. This was the epoch of a first revolution, which established and distinguished families, and introduced a kind of property, in itself the source of a thousand quarrels and conflicts. As, however, the strongest were probably the first to build themselves huts which they felt themselves able to defend, it may be concluded that the weak found it much easier and safer to imitate, than to attempt to dislodge them: and of those who were once provided with huts, none could have any inducement to appropriate that of his neighbour; not indeed so much because it did not belong to him, as because it could be of no use, and he could not make himself master of it without exposing himself to a desperate battle with the family which occupied it.

The first expansions of the human heart were the effects of a novel situation, which united husbands and wives, fathers and children, under one roof. The habit of living together soon gave rise to the finest feelings known to humanity, conjugal love and paternal affection. Every family became a little society, the more united because liberty and reciprocal attachment were the only bonds of its union. The sexes, whose manner of life had been hitherto the same, began now to adopt different ways of living. The women became more sedentary, and accustomed themselves to mind the hut and their children, while the men went abroad in search of their common subsistence. From living a softer life, both sexes also began to lose something of their strength and ferocity: but, if individuals became to some extent less able to encounter wild beasts separately, they found it, on the other hand, easier to assemble and resist in common.

The simplicity and solitude of man's life in this new condition, the paucity of his wants, and the implements he had invented to satisfy them, left him a great deal of leisure, which he employed to furnish himself with many conveniences unknown to his fathers: and this was the first yoke he inadvertently imposed on himself, and the first source of the evils he prepared for his descendants. For, besides continuing thus to enervate both body and mind, these conveniences lost with use almost all their power to please, and even degenerated into real needs, till the want of them became far more disagreeable than the possession of them had been pleasant. Men would have been unhappy at the loss of them, though the possession did not make them happy.

We can here see a little better how the use of speech became established, and insensibly improved in each family, and we may form a conjecture also concerning the manner in which various causes may have extended and accelerated the progress of language, by making it more and more necessary. Floods or earthquakes surrounded inhabited districts with precipices or waters: revolutions of the globe tore off portions from the continent, and made them islands.

It is readily seen that among men thus collected and compelled to live together, a common idiom must have arisen much more easily than among those who still wandered through the forests of the continent. Thus it is very possible that after their first essays in navigation the islanders brought over the use of speech to the continent: and it is at least very probable that communities and languages were first established in islands, and even came to perfection there before they were known on the mainland.

Everything now begins to change its aspect. Men, who have up to now been roving in the woods, by taking to a more settled manner of life, come gradually together, form separate bodies, and at length in every country arises a distinct nation, united in character and manners, not by regulations or laws, but by uniformity of life and food, and the common influence of climate. Permanent neighbourhood could not fail to produce, in time, some connection between different families. Young people of opposite sexes lived in neighbouring huts and the casual unions between them which resulted from the call of nature soon led, as they came to know each other better, to another kind which was no less pleasant and more permanent. They became accustomed to looking more closely at the different objects of their desires and to making comparisons; imperceptibly they acquired ideas of beauty and merit which led to feelings of preference. In consequence of seeing each other often, they could not do without seeing each other constantly. A tender and pleasant feeling insinuated itself into their souls, and the least opposition turned it into an impetuous fury: with love arose jealousy; discord triumphed, and human blood was sacrificed to the gentlest of all passions.

As ideas and feelings succeeded one another, and heart and head were brought into play, men continued to lay aside their original wildness; their private connections became every day more intimate as their limits extended. They accustomed themselves to assemble before their huts round a large tree; singing and dancing, the true offspring of love and leisure, became the amusement, or rather the occupation, of men and women thus assembled together with nothing else to do. Each one began to consider the rest, and to wish to be considered in turn; and thus a value came to be attached to public esteem. Whoever sang or danced best, whoever was the handsomest, the strongest, the most dexterous, or the most eloquent, came to be of most consideration; and this was the first step towards inequality, and at the same time towards vice. From these first distinctions arose on the one side vanity and contempt and on the other shame and envy: and the fermentation caused by these new leavens ended by producing combinations fatal to innocence and happiness.

As soon as men began to value one another, and the idea of consideration had got a footing in the mind, every one put in his claim to it, and it became impossible to refuse it to any with impunity. Hence arose the first obligations of civility even among savages; and every intended injury became an affront; because, besides the hurt which might result from it, the party injured was certain to find in it a contempt for his person, which was often more insupportable than the hurt itself.

Thus, as every man punished the contempt shown him by others, in proportion to his opinion of himself, revenge became terrible, and men bloody and cruel. This is precisely the state reached by most of the savage nations known to us: and it is for want of having made a proper distinction in our ideas, and seen how very far they already are from the state of nature, that so many writers have hastily concluded that man is naturally cruel, and requires civil institutions to make him more mild; whereas nothing is more gentle than man in his primitive state, as he is placed by nature at an equal distance from the stupidity of brutes, and the fatal ingenuity of civilized man. Equally confined by instinct and reason to the sole care of guarding himself against the mischiefs which threaten him, he is restrained by natural compassion from doing any injury to others, and is not led to do such a thing even in return for injuries received. For, according to the axiom of the wise Locke, "There can be no injury, where there is no property."

But it must be remarked that the society thus formed, and the relations thus established among men, required of them qualities different from those which they possessed from their primitive constitution. Morality began to appear in human actions, and every one, before the institution of law, was the only judge and avenger of the injuries done him, so that the goodness which was suitable in the pure state of nature was no longer proper in the new-born state of society. Punishments had to be made more severe, as opportunities of offending became more frequent, and the dread of vengeance had to take the place of the rigour of the law. Thus, though men had become less patient, and their natural compassion had already

suffered some diminution, this period of expansion of the human faculties, keeping a just mean between the indolence of the primitive state and the petulant activity of our *amour-propre*, must have been the happiest and most stable of epochs. The more we reflect on it, the more we shall find that this state was the least subject to revolutions, and altogether the very best man could experience; so that he can have departed from it only through some fatal accident, which, for the public good, should never have happened. The example of savages, most of whom have been found in this state, seems to prove that men were meant to remain in it, that it is the real youth of the world, and that all subsequent advances have been apparently so many steps towards the perfection of the individual, but in reality towards the decrepitude of the species.

So long as men remained content with their rustic huts, so long as they were satisfied with clothes made of the skins of animals and sewn together with thorns and fish-bones, adorned themselves only with feathers and shells, and continued to paint their bodies different colours, to improve and beautify their bows and arrows, and to make with sharp-edged stones fishing boats or clumsy musical instruments; in a word, so long as they undertook only what a single person could accomplish, and confined themselves to such arts as did not require the joint labour of several hands, they lived free, healthy, honest, and happy lives, in so far as their nature allowed, and they continued to enjoy the pleasures of mutual and independent intercourse. But from the moment one man began to stand in need of the help of another; from the moment it appeared advantageous to any one man to have enough provisions for two, equality disappeared, property was introduced, work became indispensable, and vast forests became smiling fields, which man had to water with the sweat of his brow, and where slavery and misery were soon seen to germinate and grow up with the crops.

Metallurgy and agriculture were the two arts which produced this great revolution. The poets tell us it was gold and silver, but, for the philosophers, it was iron and corn, which first civilized men, and ruined humanity. Thus both were unknown to the savages of America, who for that reason are still savage: the other nations also seem to have continued in a state of barbarism while they practised only one of these arts. One of the best reasons, perhaps, why Europe has been, if not longer, at least more constantly and highly civilized than the rest of the world, is that it is at once the most abundant in iron and the most fertile in corn.

It is difficult to conjecture how men first came to know and use iron; for it is impossible to suppose they would of themselves think of digging the ore out of the mine, and preparing it for smelting, before they knew what would be the result. On the other hand, we have the less reason to suppose this discovery the effect of any accidental fire, as mines are only formed in barren places, bare of trees and plants; so that it looks as if nature had taken pains to keep the fatal secret from us. There remains, therefore, only the extraordinary accident of some volcano which, by ejecting metallic substances already in fusion, suggested to the spectators the idea of imitating the natural operation. And we must further conceive them as possessed of uncommon courage and foresight, to undertake so laborious a work, with so distant a prospect of drawing advantage from it; yet these qualities are united only in minds more advanced than we can suppose those of these first discoverers to have been.

With regard to agriculture, the principles of it were known long before they were put in practice; and it is indeed hardly possible that men, constantly employed in drawing their subsistence from plants and trees, should not readily acquire a knowledge of the means made use of by nature for the propagation of plant life. It was in all probability very long, however, before their industry took that turn, either because trees, which together with hunting and fishing afforded them food, did not require their attention; or because they were ignorant of the use of corn, or without instruments to cultivate it; or because they lacked foresight to future needs; or lastly, because they were without means of preventing others from robbing them of the fruit of their labour.

When they grew more industrious, it is natural to believe that they began, with the help of sharp stones and pointed sticks, to cultivate a few vegetables or roots around their huts; though it was long before they knew how to prepare corn, or were provided with the implements necessary for raising it in any large quantity; not to mention how essential it is, for husbandry, to consent to immediate loss, in order to reap a future gain—a precaution very foreign to the turn of a savage's mind; for, as I have said, he hardly foresees in the morning what he will need at night.

The invention of the other arts must therefore have been necessary to compel mankind to apply themselves to agriculture. No sooner were artificers wanted to smelt and forge iron, than others were required to maintain them; the more hands that were employed in manufactures, the fewer were left to provide for the common subsistence, though the number of mouths to be furnished with food remained the same: and as some required commodities in exchange for their iron, the rest at length discovered the method of making iron serve for the multiplication of commodities. By this means the arts of husbandry and agriculture were established on the one hand, and the art of working metals and multiplying their uses on the other.

The cultivation of the earth necessarily brought about its distribution; and property, once recognized, gave rise to the first rules of justice; for, to secure each man his own, it had to be possible for each to have something. Besides, as men began to look forward to the future, and all had something to lose, every one had reason to apprehend that reprisals would follow any injury he might do to another. This origin is so much the more natural, as it is impossible to conceive how property can come from anything but manual labour: for what else can a man add to things which he does not originally create, so as to make them his own property? It is the husbandman's labour alone that, giving him a title to the produce of the ground he has tilled, gives him a claim also to the land itself, at least till harvest; and so, from year to year, a constant possession which is easily transformed into property. When the ancients, says Grotius, gave to Ceres the title of Legislatrix, and to a festival celebrated in her honour the name of Thesmophoria, they meant by that that the distribution of lands had produced a new kind of right: that is to say, the right of property, which is different from the right deducible from the law of nature.

In this state of affairs, equality might have been sustained, had the talents of individuals been equal, and had, for example, the use of iron and the consumption of commodities always exactly balanced each other; but, as there was nothing to preserve this balance, it was soon distributed; the strongest did most work; the most skilful turned his labour to best account; the most ingenious devised methods of diminishing his labour: the husbandman wanted more iron, or the smith more corn, and, while both laboured equally, the one gained a great deal by his work, while the other could hardly support himself. Thus natural inequality unfolds itself insensibly with that of combination, and the difference between men, developed by their different circumstances, becomes more sensible and permanent in its effects, and begins to have an influence, in the same proportion, over the lot of individuals.

Matters once at this pitch, it is easy to imagine the rest. I shall not detain the reader with a description of the successive invention of other arts, the development of language, the trial and utilization of talents, the inequality of fortunes, the use and abuse of riches, and all the details connected with them which the reader can supply for himself. I shall confine myself to a glance at mankind in this new situation.

Behold then all human faculties developed, memory and imagination in full play, *amour-propre* interested, reason active, and the mind almost at the highest point of its perfection. Behold all the natural qualities in action, the rank and condition of every man assigned him; not merely his share of property and his power to serve or injure others, but also his wit, beauty, strength or skill, merit or talents: and these being the only qualities capable of commanding respect, it soon became necessary to possess or to affect them.

It now became the interest of men to appear what they really were not. To be and to seem became two totally different things; and from this distinction sprang insolent pomp and cheating trickery, with all the numerous vices that go in their train. On the other hand, free and independent as men were before, they were now, in consequence of a multiplicity of new wants, brought into subjection, as it were, to all nature, and particularly to one another; and each became in some degree a slave even in becoming the master of other men: if rich, they stood in need of the services of others; if poor, of their assistance; and even a middle condition did not enable them to do without one another. Man must now, therefore, have been perpetually employed in getting others to interest themselves in his lot, and in making them, apparently at least, if not really, find their advantage in promoting his own. Thus he must have been sly and artful in his behaviour to some, and imperious and cruel to others; being under a kind of necessity to ill-use all the persons of whom he stood in need, when he could not frighten them into compliance, and did not judge it his interest to be useful to them. Insatiable ambition, the thirst of raising their respective fortunes, not so much from real want as from the desire to surpass others, inspired all men with a vile propensity to injure one another, and with a secret jealousy, which is the more dangerous, as it puts on the mask of benevolence, to carry its point with greater security. In a word, there arose rivalry and competition on the one hand, and conflicting interests on the other, together with a secret desire on both of profiting at the expense of others. All these evils were the first effects of property, and the inseparable attendants of growing inequality.

Before the invention of signs to represent riches, wealth could hardly consist in anything but lands and cattle, the only real possessions men can have. But, when inheritances so increased in number and extent as to occupy the whole of the land, and to border on one another, one man could aggrandize himself only at the expense of another; at the same time the supernumeraries, who had been too weak or too indolent to make such acquisitions, and had grown poor without sustaining any loss, because, while they saw everything change around them, they remained still the same, were obliged to receive their subsistence, or steal it, from the rich; and this soon bred, according to their different characters, dominion and slavery, or violence and rapine. The wealthy, on their part, had no sooner begun to taste the pleasure of command, than they disdained all others, and, using their old slaves to acquire new, thought of nothing but subduing and enslaving their neighbours; like ravenous wolves, which, having once tasted human flesh, despise every other food and thenceforth seek only men to devour.

Thus, as the most powerful or the most miserable considered their might or misery as a kind of right to the possessions of others, equivalent, in their opinion, to that of property, the destruction of equality was attended by the most terrible disorders. Usurpations by the rich, robbery by the poor, and the unbridled passions of both, suppressed the cries of natural compassion and the still feeble voice of justice, and filled men with avarice, ambition, and vice. Between the title of the strongest and that of the first occupier, there arose perpetual conflicts, which never ended but in battles and bloodshed. The new-born state of society thus gave rise to a horrible state of war; men thus harassed and depraved were no longer capable of retracing their steps or renouncing the fatal acquisitions they had made, but, labouring by the abuse of the faculties which do them honour, merely to their own confusion, brought themselves to the brink of ruin.

Attonitus novitate mali, divesque miserque,
Effugere optat opes; et quae modo voverat odit.[5]

It is impossible that men should not at length have reflected on so wretched a situation, and on the calamities that overwhelmed them. The rich, in particular, must have felt how much they suffered by a constant state of war, of which they bore all the expense; and in which, though all risked their lives, they alone risked their property. Besides, however speciously they might disguise their usurpations, they knew that they were founded on precarious and false titles; so that, if others took from them by force what they themselves had gained by force, they would have no reason to complain. Even those who had been enriched by their own industry, could hardly base their proprietorship on better claims. It was in vain to repeat: "I built this well; I gained this spot by my industry." Who gave you your standing, it might be answered, and what right have you to demand payment of us for doing what we never asked you to do? Do you not know that numbers of your fellow-creatures are starving, for want of what you have too much of? You ought to have had the express and universal consent of mankind, before appropriating more of the common subsistence than you needed for your own maintenance. Destitute of valid reasons to justify and sufficient strength to defend himself, able to crush individuals with ease, but easily crushed himself by a troop of bandits, one against all, and incapable, on account of mutual jealousy, of joining with his equals against numerous enemies united by the common hope of plunder, the rich man, thus urged by necessity, conceived at length the profoundest plan that ever entered the mind of man: this was to employ in his favour the forces of those who attacked him, to make allies of his adversaries, to inspire them with different maxims, and to give them other institutions as favourable to himself as the law of nature was unfavourable.

With this view, after having represented to his neighbours the horror of a situation which armed every man against the rest, and made their posses-

sions as burdensome to them as their wants, and in which no safety could be expected either in riches or in poverty, he readily devised plausible arguments to make them close with his design. "Let us join," said he, "to guard the weak from oppression, to restrain the ambitious, and secure to every man the possession of what belongs to him: let us institute rules of justice and peace, to which all without exception may be obliged to conform; rules that may in some measure make amends for the caprices of fortune, by subjecting equally the powerful and the weak to the observance of reciprocal obligations. Let us, in a word, instead of turning our forces against ourselves, collect them in a supreme power which may govern us by wise laws, protect and defend all the members of the association, repulse their common enemies, and maintain eternal harmony among us."

Far fewer words to this purpose would have been enough to impose on men so barbarous and easily seduced; especially as they had too many disputes among themselves to do without arbitrators, and too much ambition and avarice to go long without masters. All ran headlong to their chains, in hopes of securing their liberty; for they had just wit enough to perceive the advantages of political institutions, without experience enough to enable them to foresee the dangers. The most capable of foreseeing the dangers were the very persons who expected to benefit by them; and even the most prudent judged it not inexpedient to sacrifice one part of their freedom to ensure the rest; as a wounded man has his arm cut off to save the rest of his body.

Such was, or may well have been, the origin of society and law, which bound new fetters on the poor, and gave new powers to the rich; which irretrievably destroyed natural liberty, eternally fixed the law of property and inequality, converted clever usurpation into unalterable right, and, for the advantage of a few ambitious individuals, subjected all mankind to perpetual labour, slavery, and wretchedness. It is easy to see how the establishment of one community made that of all the rest necessary, and how, in order to make head against united forces, the rest of mankind had to unite in turn. Societies soon multiplied and spread over the face of the earth, till hardly a corner of the world was left in which a man could escape the yoke, and withdraw his head from beneath the sword which he saw perpetually hanging over him by a thread. Civil right having thus become the common rule among the members of each community, the law

---

5. [Ovid, *Metamorphoses*, xi, 127.
   Both rich and poor, shocked at their new-found ills,
   Would fly from wealth, and lose what they had sought.]

of nature maintained its place only between different communities, where, under the name of the right of nations, it was qualified by certain tacit conventions, in order to make commerce practicable, and serve as a substitute for natural compassion, which lost, when applied to societies, almost all the influence it had over individuals, and survived no longer except in some great cosmopolitan spirits, who, breaking down the imaginary barriers that separate different peoples, follow the example of our Sovereign Creator, and include the whole human race in their benevolence.

But bodies politic, remaining thus in a state of nature among themselves, presently experienced the inconveniences which had obliged individuals to forsake it; for this state became still more fatal to these great bodies than it had been to the individuals of whom they were composed. Hence arose national wars, battles, murders, and reprisals, which shock nature and outrage reason; together with all those horrible prejudices which class among the virtues the honour of shedding human blood. The most distinguished men hence learned to consider cutting each other's throats a duty; at length men massacred their fellow-creatures by thousands without so much as knowing why, and committed more murders in a single day's fighting, and more violent outrages in the sack of a single town, than were committed in the state of nature during whole ages over the whole earth. Such were the first effects which we can see to have followed the division of mankind into different communities. But let us return to their institution.

I know that some writers have given other explanations of the origin of political societies, such as the conquest of the powerful, or the association of the weak. It is, indeed, indifferent to my argument which of these causes we choose. That which I have just laid down, however, appears to me the most natural for the following reasons. First: because, in the first case, the right of conquest, being no right in itself, could not serve as a foundation on which to build any other; the victor and the vanquished people still remained with respect to each other in the state of war, unless the vanquished, restored to the full possession of their liberty, voluntarily made choice of the victor for their chief. For till then, whatever capitulation may have been made being founded on violence, and therefore *ipso facto* void, there could not have been on this hypothesis either a real society or body politic, or any law other than that of the strongest.

Secondly: because the words "strong" and "weak" are, in the second case, ambiguous; for during the interval between the establishment of a right of property, or prior occupancy, and that of political government, the meaning of these words is better expressed by the terms "rich" and "poor"; because, in fact, before the institution of laws, men had no other way of reducing their equals to submission, than by attacking their goods, or making some of their own over to them. Thirdly: because, as the poor had nothing but their freedom to lose, it would have been in the highest degree absurd for them to resign voluntarily the only good they still enjoyed, without getting anything in exchange: whereas the rich having feelings, if I may so express myself, in every part of their possessions, it was much easier to harm them, and therefore more necessary for them to take precautions against it; and, in short, because it is more reasonable to suppose a thing to have been invented by those to whom it would be of service, than by those whom it must have harmed.

Government had, in its infancy, no regular and constant form. The want of experience and philosophy prevented men from seeing any but present inconveniences, and they thought of providing against others only as they presented themselves. In spite of the endeavours of the wisest legislators, the political state remained imperfect, because it was little more than the work of chance; and, as it had begun ill, though time revealed its defects and suggested remedies, the original faults were never repaired. It was continually being patched up, when the first task should have been to get the site cleared and all the old materials removed, as was done by Lycurgus at Sparta, if a stable and lasting edifice was to be erected. Society consisted at first merely of a few general conventions, which every member bound himself to observe; and for the performance of covenants the whole body went security to each individual. Experience only could show the weakness of such a constitution, and how easily it might be infringed with impunity, from the difficulty of convicting men of faults, where the public alone was to be witness and judge: the laws could not but be eluded in many ways; disorders and inconveniences could not but multiply continually, till it became necessary to commit the dangerous trust of public authority to private persons, and the care of enforcing obedience to the deliberations of the people to the magistrate. For to say that chiefs were chosen before the confederacy was formed, and that the administrators of the laws were there before the laws themselves, is too absurd a supposition to consider seriously.

It would be as unreasonable to suppose that men at first threw themselves irretrievably and unconditionally into the arms of an absolute master, and that the first expedient which proud and unsubdued men hit upon for their common security was to run headlong into slavery. For what reason, in fact, did they take to themselves superiors, if it was not in order that they might be defended from oppression, and, have protection for their lives, liberties, and properties, which are, so to speak, the constituent elements of their being? Now, in the relations between man and man, the worst that can happen is for one to find himself at the mercy of another, and it would have been inconsistent with common sense to begin by bestowing on a chief the only things they wanted his help to preserve. What equivalent could he offer them for so great a right? And if he had presumed to exact it under pretext of defending them, would he not have received the answer recorded in the fable: "What more can the enemy do to us?" It is therefore beyond dispute, and indeed the fundamental maxim of all political right, that people have set up chiefs to protect their liberty, and not to enslave them. "If we have a prince," said Pliny to Trajan, "it is to save ourselves from having a master."

Politicians indulge in the same sophistry about the love of liberty as philosophers about the state of nature. They judge, by what they see, of very different things, which they have not seen; they attribute to man a natural propensity to servitude, because the slaves within their observation are seen to bear the yoke with patience; they fail to reflect that it is with liberty as with innocence and virtue; the value is known only to those who possess them, and the taste for them is forfeited when they are forfeited themselves. "I know the charms of your country," said Brasidas to a Satrap, who was comparing the life at Sparta with that at Persepolis, "but you cannot know the pleasures of mine."

An unbroken horse erects his mane, paws the ground, and starts back impetuously at the sight of the bridle; while one which is property trained suffers patiently even whip and spur: so savage man will not bend his neck to the yoke to which civilized man submits without a murmur, but prefers the most turbu-

lent state of liberty to the most peaceful slavery. We cannot therefore, from the servility of nations already enslaved, judge of the natural disposition of mankind for or against slavery; we should go by the prodigious efforts of every free people to save itself from oppression. I know that the former are for ever holding forth in praise of the tranquillity they enjoy in their chains, and that they call a state of wretched servitude a state of peace: *miserrimam servitutem pacem appellant.*[6] But when I observe the latter sacrificing pleasure, peace, wealth, power, and life itself to the preservation of that one treasure, which is so disdained by those who have lost it; when I see free-born animals dash their brains out against the bars of their cage, from an innate impatience of captivity; when I behold numbers of naked savages, that despise European pleasures, braving hunger, fire, the sword, and death, to preserve nothing but their independence, I feel that it is not for slaves to argue about liberty.

With regard to paternal authority, from which some writers have derived absolute government and all society, it is enough, without going back to the contrary arguments of Locke and Sidney, to remark that nothing on earth can be farther from the ferocious spirit of despotism than the mildness of that authority which looks more to the advantage of him who obeys than to that of him who commands; that, by the law of nature, the father is the child's master no longer than his help is necessary; that from that time they are both equal, the son being perfectly independent of the father, and owing him only respect, and not obedience. For gratitude is a duty which ought to be paid, but not a right to be exacted: instead of saying that civil society is derived from paternal authority, we ought to say rather that the latter derives its principal force from the former. No individual was ever acknowledged as the father of many, till his sons and daughters remained settled around him. The goods of the father, of which he is really the master, are the ties which keep his children in dependence, and he may bestow on them, if he pleases, no share of his property, unless they merit it by constant deference to his will. But the subjects of an arbitrary despot are so far from having the like favour to

6. [Tacitus, *Hist.* iv. 17. The most wretched slavery they call peace.]

expect from their chief, that they themselves and everything they possess are his property, or at least are considered by him as such; so that they are forced to receive, as a favour, the little of their own he is pleased to leave them. When he despoils them, he does but justice, and mercy in that he permits them to live.

By proceeding thus to test fact by right, we should discover as little reason as truth in the voluntary establishment of tyranny. It would also be no easy matter to prove the validity of a contract binding on only one of the parties, where all the risk is on one side, and none on the other; so that no one could suffer but he who bound himself. This hateful system is indeed, even in modern times, very far from being that of wise and good monarchs, and especially of the kings of France; as may be seen from several passages in their edicts; particularly from the following passage in a celebrated edict published in 1667 in the name and by order of Louis XIV.

"Let it not, therefore, be said that the Sovereign is not subject to the laws of his State; since the contrary is a true proposition of the right of nations, which flattery has sometimes attacked but good princes have always defended as the tutelary divinity of their dominions. How much more legitimate is it to say with the wise Plato, that the perfect felicity of a kingdom consists in the obedience of subjects to their prince, and of the prince to the laws, and in the laws being just and constantly directed to the public good!"[7]

I shall not stay here to inquire whether, as liberty is the noblest faculty of man, it is not degrading our very nature, reducing ourselves to the level of the brutes, which are mere slaves of instinct, and even an affront to the Author of our being, to renounce without reserve the most precious of all His gifts, and to bow to the necessity of committing all the crimes He has forbidden, merely to gratify a mad or a cruel master; or if this sublime craftsman ought not to be less angered at seeing His workmanship entirely destroyed than thus dishonoured. I will waive (if my opponents please) the authority of Barbeyrac, who, following Locke, roundly declares that no man can so far sell his liberty as to submit to an arbitrary power

which may use him as it likes. *For*, he adds, *this would be to sell his own life, of which he is not master.* I shall ask only what right those who were not afraid thus to debase themselves could have to subject their posterity to the same ignominy, and to renounce for them those blessings which they do not owe to the liberality of their progenitors, and without which life itself must be a burden to all who are worthy of it.

Pufendorf says that we may divest ourselves of our liberty in favour of other men, just as we transfer our property from one to another by contracts and agreements. But this seems a very weak argument. For in the first place, the property I alienate becomes quite foreign to me, nor can I suffer from the abuse of it; but it very nearly concerns me that my liberty should not be abused, and I cannot without incurring the guilt of the crimes I may be compelled to commit, expose myself to become an instrument of crime. Besides, the right of property being only a convention of human institution, men may dispose of what they possess as they please: but this is not the case with the essential gifts of nature, such as life and liberty, which every man is permitted to enjoy, and of which it is at least doubtful whether any have a right to divest themselves. By giving up the one, we degrade our being; by giving up the other, we do our best to annul it; and, as no temporal good can indemnify us for the loss of either, it would be an offence against both reason and nature to renounce them at any price whatsoever. But, even if we could transfer our liberty, as we do our property, there would be a great difference with regard to the children, who enjoy the father's substance only by the transmission of his right; whereas, liberty being a gift which they hold from nature as being men, their parents have no right whatever to deprive them of it. As then, to establish slavery, it was necessary to do violence to nature, so, in order to perpetuate such a right, nature would have to be changed. Jurists who have gravely determined that the child of a slave comes into the world a slave, have decided, in other words, that a man shall come into the world not a man.

I regard it then as certain, that government did not begin with arbitrary power, but that this is the depravation, the extreme term, of government, and brings it back, finally, to just the law of the strongest, which it was originally designed to remedy. Supposing, however, it had begun in this manner, such power, being in itself illegitimate, could not have served as a basis

---

7. *Of the Rights of the Most Christian Queen over various States of the Monarchy of Spain,* 1667.

for the laws of society, nor, consequently, for the inequality they instituted.

Without entering at present upon the investigations which still remain to be made into the nature of the fundamental compact underlying all government, I content myself with adopting the common opinion concerning it, and regard the establishment of the political body as a real contract between the people and the chiefs chosen by them: a contract by which both parties bind themselves to observe the laws therein expressed, which form the ties of their union. The people having in respect of their social relations concentrated all their wills in one, the several articles, concerning which this will is explained, become so many fundamental laws, obligatory on all the members of the State without exception, and one of these articles regulates the choice and power of the magistrates appointed to watch over the execution of the rest. This power extends to everything which may maintain the constitution, without going so far as to alter it. It is accompanied by honours, in order to bring the laws and their administrators into respect. The ministers are also distinguished by personal prerogatives, in order to recompense them for the cares and labour which good administration involves. The magistrate, on his side, binds himself to use the power he is entrusted with only in conformity with the intention of his constituents, to maintain them all in the peaceable possession of what belongs to them, and to prefer on every occasion the public interest to his own.

Before experience had shown, or knowledge of the human heart enabled men to foresee, the unavoidable abuses of such a constitution, it must have appeared so much the more excellent, as those who were charged with the care of its preservation had themselves most interest in it; for magistracy and the rights attaching to it being based solely on the fundamental laws, the magistrates would cease to be legitimate as soon as these ceased to exist; the people would no longer owe them obedience; and as not the magistrates, but the laws, are essential to the being of a State, the members of it would regain the right to their natural liberty.

If we reflect with ever so little attention on this subject, we shall find new arguments to confirm this truth, and be convinced from the very nature of the contract that it cannot be irrevocable; for, if there were no superior power capable of ensuring the fidelity of the contracting parties, or compelling them to perform their reciprocal engagements, the parties would be sole judges in their own cause, and each would always have a right to renounce the contract, as soon as he found that the other had violated its terms, or that they no longer suited his convenience. It is upon this principle that the right of abdication may possibly be founded. Now, if, as here, we consider only what is human in this institution, it is certain that, if the magistrate, who has all the power in his own hands, and appropriates to himself all the advantages of the contract, has none the less a right to renounce his authority, the people, who suffer for all the faults of their chief, must have a much better right to renounce their dependence. But the terrible and innumerable quarrels and disorders that would necessarily arise from so dangerous a privilege, show, more than anything else, how much human governments stood in need of a more solid basis than mere reason, and how expedient it was for the public tranquillity that the divine will should interpose to invest the sovereign authority with a sacred and inviolable character, which might deprive subjects of the fatal right of disposing of it. If the world had received no other advantages from religion, this would be enough to impose on men the duty of adopting and cultivating it, abuses and all, since it has been the means of saving more blood than fanaticism has ever split. But let us follow the thread of our hypothesis.

The different forms of government owe their origin to the differing degrees of inequality which existed between individuals at the time of their institution. If there happened to be any one man among them pre-eminent in power, virtue, riches, or personal influence, he became sole magistrate, and the State assumed the form of monarchy. If several, nearly equal in point of eminence, stood above the rest, they were elected jointly, and formed an aristocracy. Again, among a people who had deviated less from a state of nature, and between whose fortune or talents there was less disproportion, the supreme administration was retained in common, and a democracy was formed. It was discovered in process of time which of these forms suited men the best. Some peoples continued to be ruled solely by their laws; others soon came to obey masters. Citizens wished to preserve their liberty; subjects, however, irritated at seeing others enjoying a blessing they had lost, thought only of making slaves of their neighbours. In a word, on the one side arose riches and conquests, and on the other happiness and virtue.

In these different governments, all the offices were at first elective; and when the influence of wealth did not carry the day, the preference was given to merit, which gives a natural ascendancy, and to age, which is experienced in business and deliberate in council. The Elders of the Hebrews, the Gerontes at Sparta, the Senate at Rome, and the very etymology of our word Seigneur, show how old age was once held in veneration. But the more often the choice fell upon old men, the more often elections had to be repeated, and the more they became a nuisance; intrigues set in, factions were formed, party feeling grew bitter, civil wars broke out; the lives of individuals were sacrificed to the pretended happiness of the State; and at length men were on the point of relapsing into their primitive anarchy. Ambitious chiefs profited by these circumstances to perpetuate their offices in their own families: at the same time the people, already used to dependence, ease, and the conveniences of life, and already incapable of breaking its fetters, agreed to an increase of its slavery, in order to secure its tranquillity. Thus magistrates, having become hereditary, contracted the habit of considering their offices as a family estate, and themselves as proprietors of the communities of which they were at first only the officers, of regarding their fellow-citizens as their slaves, and numbering them, like cattle, among their belongings, and of calling themselves the equals of the gods and kings of kings.

If we follow the progress of inequality in these various revolutions, we shall find that the establishment of laws and of the right of property was its first term, the institution of magistracy the second, and the conversion of legitimate into arbitrary power the third and last; so that the condition of rich and poor was authorized by the first period; that of powerful and weak by the second; and only by the third that of master and slave, which is the last degree of inequality, and the term at which all the rest remain, when they have got so far, till the government is either entirely dissolved by new revolutions, or brought back again to legitimacy.

To understand this progress as necessary we must consider not so much the motives for the establishment of the body politic, as the forms it assumes in actuality, and the faults that necessarily attend it: for the flaws which make social institutions necessary are the same as make the abuse of them unavoidable. If we except Sparta, where the laws were mainly concerned with the education of children, and where Lycurgus established such morality as practically made laws needless—for laws as a rule, being weaker than the passions, restrain men without altering them —it would not be difficult to prove that every government, which scrupulously complied with the ends for which it was instituted, and guarded carefully against change and corruption, was set up unnecessarily. For a country in which no one evaded the laws and no one made a bad use of the powers of a magistrate would require neither laws nor magistrates.

Political distinctions necessarily produce civil distinctions. The growing inequality between the people and its leaders is soon felt by individuals and among them it takes a thousand different forms according to their passions, their talents, and their circumstances. The magistrate could not usurp illegitimate power without the help of creatures to whom he is forced to give a share of that power. Besides, individuals only allow themselves to be oppressed so far as they are hurried on by blind ambition, and, looking rather below than above them, come to love authority more than independence, and submit to slavery, that they may in turn enslave others. It is no easy matter to reduce to obedience a man who has no ambition to command; nor would the most adroit politician find it possible to enslave a people whose only desire was to be independent. But inequality easily makes its way among cowardly and ambitious minds, which are ever ready to run the risks of fortune, and almost indifferent whether they command or obey, as it is favourable or adverse. Thus, there must have been a time, when the eyes of the people were so fascinated, that their rulers had only to say to the least of men, "Be great, you and all your posterity," to make him immediately appear great in the eyes of every one as well as in his own. His descendants took still more upon them, in proportion to their distance from him; the more obscure and uncertain the cause, the greater the effect: the greater the number of idlers one could count in a family, the more illustrious it was held to be.

If this were the place to go into details, I could readily explain how, even without the intervention of government, inequality of credit and authority became unavoidable among private persons, as soon as their union in a single society made them compare themselves one with another, and take into account the differences which they found out from the continual intercourse every man had to have with his neighbours.[8] These differences are of several kinds; but riches, nobility or rank, power, and personal merit being the principal distinctions by which men form an estimate of each other in society, I could prove that the harmony or conflict of these different forces is the surest indication of the good or bad constitution of a State. I could show that among these four kinds of inequality, personal qualities being the origin of all the others, wealth is the one to which they are all reduced in the end; for, as riches tend most immediately to the prosperity of individuals, and are easiest to communicate, they are used to purchase every other distinction. By this observation we are enabled to judge pretty exactly how far a people has departed from its primitive constitution, and of its progress towards the extreme term of corruption. I could explain how

---

8. Distributive justice would oppose this rigorous equality of the state of nature, even were it practicable in civil society; as all the members of the State owe it their services in proportion to their talents and abilities, they ought, on their side, to be distinguished and favoured in proportion to the services they have actually rendered. It is in this sense we must understand that passage of Isocrates, in which he extols the primitive Athenians, for having determined which of the two kinds of equality was the most useful, viz. that which consists in dividing the same advantages indiscriminately among all the citizens, or that which consists in distributing them to each according to his deserts. These able politicians, adds the orator, banishing that unjust inequality which makes no distinction between good and bad men, adhered inviolably to that which rewards and punishes every man according to his deserts.

But in the first place, there never existed a society, however corrupt some may have become, where no difference was made between the good and the bad; and with regard to morality, where no measures can be prescribed by law exact enough to serve as a practical rule for a magistrate, it is with great prudence that, in order not to leave the fortune or quality of the citizens to his discretion, it prohibits him from passing judgment on persons and confines his judgment to actions. Only morals such as those of the ancient Romans can bear censors, and such a tribunal among us would throw everything into confusion. The difference between good and bad men is determined by public esteem; the magistrate being strictly a judge of right alone; whereas the public is the truest judge of morals, and is of such integrity and penetration on this head, that although it may be sometimes deceived, it can never be corrupted. The rank of citizens ought, therefore, to be regulated, not according to their personal merit—for this would put it in the power of the magistrate to apply the law almost arbitrarily—but according to the actual services done to the State, which are capable of being more exactly estimated.

much this universal desire for reputation, honours, and advancement, which inflames us all, exercises and holds up to comparison our faculties and powers; how it excites and multiplies our passions, and, by creating universal competition and rivalry, or rather enmity, among men, occasions numberless failures, successes, and disturbances of all kinds by making so many aspirants run the same course. I could show that it is to this desire of being talked about, and this unremitting rage of distinguishing ourselves, that we owe the best and the worst things we possess, both our virtues and our vices, our science and our errors, our conquerors and our philosophers; that is to say, a great many bad things, and a very few good ones. In a word, I could prove that, if we have a few rich and powerful men on the pinnacle of fortune and grandeur, while the crowd grovels in want and obscurity, it is because the former prize what they enjoy only in so far as others are destitute of it; and because, without changing their condition, they would cease to be happy the moment the people ceased to be wretched.

These details alone, however, would furnish matter for a considerable work, in which the advantages and disadvantages of every kind of government might be weighed, as they are related to man in the state of nature, and at the same time all the different aspects, under which inequality has up to the present appeared, or may appear in ages yet to come, according to the nature of the several governments, and the alterations which time must unavoidably occasion in them, might be demonstrated. We should then see the multitude oppressed from within, in consequence of the very precautions it had taken to guard against foreign tyranny. We should see oppression continually gain ground without its being possible for the oppressed to know where it would stop, or what legitimate means was left them of checking its progress. We should see the rights of citizens and the freedom of nations slowly extinguished, and the complaints, protests, and appeals of the weak treated as seditious murmurings. We should see the honour of defending the common cause confined by statecraft to a mercenary part of the people. We should see taxes made necessary by such means, and the disheartened husbandman deserting his fields even in the midst of peace, and leaving the plough to gird on the sword. We should see fatal and capricious codes of honour established; and the champions of their country sooner or later becoming its enemies, and for ever holding their daggers to the breasts of their fellow-citizens. The time would come when they would be heard saying to the oppressor of their country:

Pectore si fratris gladium juguloque parentis
Condere me jubeas, gravidaeque in viscera partu
Conjugis, invita peragam tamen omnia dextra.
Lucan, 1. 376.[9]

From great inequality of fortunes and conditions, from the vast variety of passions and of talents, of useless and pernicious arts, of vain sciences, would arise a multitude of prejudices equally contrary to reason, happiness, and virtue. We should see the magistrates fomenting everything that might weaken men united in society, by promoting dissension among them; everything that might sow in it the seeds of actual division, while it gave society the air of harmony; everything that might inspire the different ranks of people with mutual hatred and distrust, by setting the rights and interests of one against those of another, and so strengthen the power which comprehended them all.

It is from the midst of this disorder and these revolutions, that despotism, gradually raising up its hideous head and devouring everything that remained sound and untainted in any part of the State, would at length trample on both the laws and the people, and establish itself on the ruins of the republic. The times which immediately preceded this last change would be times of trouble and calamity; but at length the monster would swallow up everything, and the people would no longer have either chiefs or laws, but only tyrants. From this moment there would be no question of virtue or morality; for despotism (*cui ex honesto nulla est spes*), wherever it prevails, admits no other master; it no sooner speaks than probity and duty lose their weight and blind obedience is the only virtue which slaves can still practise.

This is the last term of inequality, the extreme point that closes the circle, and meets that from which we set out. Here all private persons return to their first equality, because they are nothing; and, subjects having no law but the will of their master, and

their master no restraint but his passions, all notions of good and all principles of equity again vanish. There is here a complete return to the law of the strongest, and so to a new state of nature, differing from that we set out from; for the one was a state of nature in its first purity, while this is the consequence of excessive corruption. There is so little difference between the two states in other respects, and the contract of government is so completely dissolved by despotism, that the despot is master only so long as he remains the strongest; as soon as he can be expelled, he has no right to complain of violence. The popular insurrection that ends in the death or deposition of a Sultan is as lawful an act as those by which he disposed, the day before, of the lives and fortunes of his subjects. As he was maintained by force alone, it is force alone that overthrows him. Thus everything takes place according to the natural order; and, whatever may be the result of such frequent and precipitate revolutions, no one man has reason to complain of the injustice of another, but only of his own ill-fortune or indiscretion.

If the reader thus discovers and retraces the lost and forgotten road, by which man must have passed from the state of nature to the state of society; if he carefully restores, along with the intermediate situations which I have just described, those which want of time has compelled me to suppress, or my imagination has failed to suggest, he cannot fail to be struck by the vast distance which separates the two states. It is in tracing this slow succession that he will find the solution of a number of problems of politics and morals, which philosophers cannot settle. He will feel that, men being different in different ages, the reason why Diogenes could not find a man was that he sought among his contemporaries a man of an earlier period. He will see that Cato died with Rome and liberty, because he did not fit the age in which he lived; the greatest of men served only to astonish a world which he would certainly have ruled, had he lived five hundred years sooner. In a word, he will explain how the soul and the passions of men insensibly change their very nature; why our wants and pleasures in the end seek new objects; and why, the original man having vanished by degrees, society offers to us only an assembly of artificial men and factitious passions, which are the work of all these new relations, and without any real foundation in nature. We are taught nothing on this subject, by reflection, that is not entirely confirmed by observation. The savage and

---

9. [If you order me to thrust my sword into my brother's breast or my father's throat or the bowels of my pregnant wife, I will do all this though with an unwilling right arm.]

the civilized man differ so much in the bottom of their hearts and in their inclinations, that what constitutes the supreme happiness of one would reduce the other to despair. The former breathes only peace and liberty; he desires only to live and be free from labour; even the *ataraxia* of the Stoic falls far short of his profound indifference to every other object. Civilized man, on the other hand, is always moving, sweating, toiling, and racking his brains to find still more laborious occupations: he goes on in drudgery to his last moment, and even seeks death to put himself in a position to live, or renounces life to acquire immortality. He pays his court to men in power, whom he hates, and to the wealthy, whom he despises; he stops at nothing to have the honour of serving them; he is not ashamed to value himself on his own meanness and their protection; and, proud of his slavery, he speaks with disdain of those, who have not the honour of sharing it. What a sight would the perplexing and envied labours of a European minister of State present to the eyes of a Caribbean! How many cruel deaths would not this indolent savage prefer to the horrors of such a life, which is seldom even sweetened by the pleasure of doing good! But, for him to see into the motives of all this solicitude the words "power" and "reputation" would have to bear some meaning in his mind; he would have to know that there are men who set a value on the opinion of the rest of the world; who can be made happy and satisfied with themselves rather on the testimony of other people than on their own. In reality, the source of all these differences is, that the savage lives within himself, while social man lives constantly outside himself, and only knows how to live in the opinion of others, so that he seems to receive the consciousness of his own existence merely from the judgment of others concerning him. It is not to my present purpose to insist on the indifference to good and evil which arises from this disposition, in spite of our many fine works on morality, or to show how, everything being reduced to appearances, there is but art and mummery in even honour, friendship, virtue, and often vice itself, of which we at length learn the secret of boasting; to show, in short, how, always asking others what we are, and never daring to ask ourselves, in the midst of so much philosophy, humanity, and civilization, and of such sublime codes of morality, we have nothing to show for ourselves but a frivolous and deceitful appearance, honour without virtue, reason without wisdom, and pleasure without happiness.

It is sufficient that I have proved that this is not by any means the original state of man, but that it is merely the spirit of society, and the inequality which society produces, that thus transform and alter all our natural inclinations.

I have endeavoured to trace the origin and progress of inequality, and the institution and abuse of political societies, as far as these are capable of being deduced from the nature of man merely by the light of reason, and independently of those sacred dogmas which give the sanction of divine right to sovereign authority. It follows from this survey that, as there is hardly any inequality in the state of nature, all the inequality which now prevails owes its strength and growth to the development of our faculties and the advance of the human mind, and becomes at last permanent and legitimate by the establishment of property and laws. Secondly, it follows that moral inequality, authorized by positive right alone, clashes with natural right, whenever it is not proportionate to physical inequality—a distinction which sufficiently determines what we ought to think of that species of inequality which prevails in all civilized countries; since it is plainly contrary to the law of nature, however defined, that children should command old men, fools wise men, and that the privileged few should gorge themselves with superfluities, while the starving multitude are in want of the bare necessities of life.

Appendix

A famous author, reckoning up the good and evil of human life, and comparing the aggregates, finds that our pains greatly exceed our pleasures: so that, all things considered, human life is not at all a valuable gift. This conclusion does not surprise me; for the writer drew all his arguments from man in civilization. Had he gone back to the state of nature, his inquiries would clearly have had a different result, and man would have been seen to be subject to very few evils not of his own creation. It has indeed cost us not a little trouble to make ourselves as wretched as we are. When we consider, on the one hand, the immense labours of mankind, the many sciences brought to perfection, the arts invented, the powers employed, the deeps filled up, the mountains levelled, the rocks shattered, the rivers made navigable, the tracts of land cleared, the lakes emptied, the marshes drained, the enormous structures erected on land, and the teeming vessels that cover the sea; and, on the other hand, estimate with ever so little thought, the real advantages that have accrued from all these works to mankind, we cannot help being amazed at the vast disproportion there is between these things, and deploring the infatuation of man, which, to gratify his silly pride and vain self-admiration, induces him eagerly to pursue all the miseries he is capable of feeling, though beneficent nature had kindly placed them out of his way.

That men are actually wicked, a sad and continual experience of them proves beyond doubt: but, all the same I think I have shown that man is naturally good. What then can have depraved him to such an extent, except the changes that have happened in his constitution, the advances he has made, and the knowledge he has acquired? We may admire human society as much as we please; it will be none the less true that it necessarily leads men to hate each other in proportion as their interests clash, and to do one another apparent services, while they are really doing every imaginable mischief. What can be thought of a relation, in which the interest of every individual dictates rules directly opposite to those the public reason dictates to the community in general—in which every man finds his profit in the misfortunes of his neighbour? There is not perhaps any man in a comfortable position who has not greedy heirs, and perhaps even children, secretly wishing for his death; not a ship at sea, of which the loss would not be good news to some merchant or other; not a house, which some debtor of bad faith would not be glad to see reduced to ashes with all the papers it contains; not a nation which does not rejoice at the disasters that befall its neighbours. Thus it is that we find our advantage in the misfortunes of our fellow-creatures, and that the loss of one man almost always constitutes the prosperity of another. But it is still more pernicious that public calamities are the objects of the hopes and expectations of innumerable individuals. Some desire sickness, some mortality, some war, and some famine. I have seen men wicked enough to weep for sorrow at the prospect of a plentiful season; and the great and fatal fire of London, which cost so many unhappy persons their lives or their fortunes, made the fortunes of perhaps ten thousand others. I know that Montaigne censures Demades the Athenian for having caused to be punished a workman who, by selling his coffins very dear, was a great gainer by the deaths of his fellow-citizens; but, the reason alleged by Montaigne being that everybody ought to be pun-

ished, my point is clearly confirmed by it. Let us penetrate, therefore, the superficial appearances of benevolence, and survey what passes in the inmost recesses of the heart. Let us reflect what must be the state of things, when men are forced to caress and destroy one another at the same time; when they are born enemies by duty, and knaves by interest. It will perhaps be said that society is so formed that every man gains by serving the rest. That would be all very well, if he did not gain still more by injuring them. There is no legitimate profit so great, that it cannot be greatly exceeded by what may be made illegitimately; we always gain more by hurting our neighbours than by doing them good. Nothing is required but to know how to act with impunity; and to this end the powerful employ all their strength, and the weak all their cunning.

Savage man, when he has dined, is at peace with all nature, and the friend of all his fellow-creatures. If a dispute arises about a meal, he rarely comes to blows, without having first compared the difficulty of conquering his antagonist with the trouble of finding subsistence elsewhere: and, as pride does not come in, it all ends in a few blows; the victor eats, and the vanquished seeks provision somewhere else, and all is at peace. The case is quite different with man in the state of society, for whom first necessaries have to be provided, and then superfluities; delicacies follow next, then immense wealth, then subjects, and then slaves. He enjoys not a moment's relaxation; and what is yet stranger, the less natural and pressing his wants, the more headstrong are his passions, and, still worse, the more he has it in his power to gratify them; so that after a long course of prosperity, after having swallowed up treasures and ruined multitudes, the hero ends up by cutting every throat till he finds himself, at last, sole master of the world. Such is in miniature the moral picture, if not of human life, at least of the secret pretensions of the heart of civilized man.

Compare without partiality the state of the citizen with that of the savage, and trace out, if you can, how many inlets the former has opened to pain and death, besides those of his vices, his wants, and his misfortunes. If you reflect on the mental afflictions that prey on us, the violent passions that waste and exhaust us, the excessive labour with which the poor are burdened, the still more dangerous indolence to which the wealthy give themselves up, so that the poor perish of want, and the rich of surfeit; if you reflect but a moment on the heterogeneous mixtures and pernicious seasonings of foods; the corrupt state in which they are frequently eaten; on the adulteration of medicines, the wiles of those who sell them, the mistakes of those who administer them, and the poisonous vessels in which they are prepared; on the epidemics bred by foul air in consequence of great numbers of men being crowed together, or those which are caused by our delicate way of living, by our passing from our houses into the open air and back again, by the putting on or throwing off our clothes with too little care, and by all the precautions which sensuality has converted into necessary habits, and the neglect of which sometimes costs us our life or health; if you take into account the conflagrations and earthquakes, which, devouring or overwhelming whole cities, destroy the inhabitants by thousands; in a word, if you add together all the dangers with which these causes are always threatening us, you will see how dearly nature makes us pay for the contempt with which we have treated her lessons.

I shall not here repeat, what I have elsewhere said of the calamities of war; but wish that those, who have sufficient knowledge, were willing or bold enough to make public the details of the villainies committed in armies by the contractors for commissariat and hospitals: we should see plainly that their monstrous frauds, already none too well concealed, which cripple the finest armies in less than no time, occasion greater destruction among the soldiers than the swords of the enemy.

The number of people who perish annually at sea, by famine, the scurvy, pirates, fire, and shipwrecks, affords matter for another shocking calculation. We must also place to the credit of the establishment of property, and consequently to the institution of society, assassinations, poisonings, highway robberies, and even the punishments inflicted on the wretches guilty of these crimes; which, though expedient to prevent greater evils, yet by making the murder of one man cost the lives of two or more, double the loss to the human race.

What shameful methods are sometimes practised to prevent the birth of men, and cheat nature; either by brutal and depraved appetites which insult her beautiful work—appetites unknown to savages or mere animals, which can spring only from the corrupt imagination of mankind in civilized countries; or by secret abortions, the fitting effects of debauchery and vitiated notions of honour; or by the exposure or murder of multitudes of infants, who fall victims to the

poverty of their parents, or the cruel shame of their mothers; or, finally, by the mutilation of unhappy wretches, part of whose life, with their hope of posterity, is given up to vain singing, or, still worse, the brutal jealousy of other men: a mutilation which, in the last case, becomes a double outrage against nature from the treatment of those who suffer it, and from the use to which they are destined. But is it not a thousand times more common and more dangerous for paternal rights openly to offend against humanity? How many talents have not been thrown away, and inclinations forced, by the unwise constraint of fathers? How many men, who would have distinguished themselves in a fitting estate, have died dishonoured and wretched in another for which they had no taste! How many happy, but unequal, marriages have been broken or disturbed, and how many chaste wives have been dishonoured, by an order of things continually in contradiction with that of nature! How many good and virtuous husbands and wives are reciprocally punished for having been ill-assorted! How many young and unhappy victims of their parents' avarice plunge into vice, or pass their melancholy days in tears, groaning in the indissoluble bonds which their hearts repudiate and gold alone has formed! Fortunate sometimes are those whose courage and virtue remove them from life before inhuman violence makes them spend it in crime or in despair. Forgive me, fathers and mothers, who are ever to be pitied: I regret having to increase your pain; I only hope it may serve as an eternal and terrible example to anyone who dares, in the very name of nature, to violate the most sacred of natural rights.

If I have spoken only of those ill-starred unions which are the result of our system, is it to be thought that those over which love and sympathy preside are free from disadvantages? What if I should undertake to show humanity attacked in its very source, and even in the most sacred of all ties, in which fortune is consulted before nature, and, the disorders of society confounding all virtue and vice, continence becomes a criminal precaution, and a refusal to give life to a fellow-creature, an act of humanity? But, without drawing aside the veil which hides all these horrors, let us content ourselves with pointing out the evil which others will have to remedy.

To all this add the multiplicity of unhealthy trades, which shorten men's lives or destroy their bodies, such as working in the mines, and the preparing of metals and minerals, particularly lead, copper, mercury, cobalt, and arsenic: add those other dangerous trades which are daily fatal to many tilers, carpenters, masons, and miners; put all these together and we can see, in the establishment and perfection of societies, the reasons for that diminution of our species, which has been noticed by many philosophers.

Luxury, which cannot be avoided among men greedy for their own comfort and for the respect of others, soon completes the evil which society had begun and, under the pretence of giving bread to the poor whom it should never have made such, impoverishes all the rest, and sooner or later depopulates the State. Luxury is a remedy much worse than the disease it sets up to cure; or rather it is in itself the greatest of all evils, for every State, great or small: for, in order to maintain all the servants and vagabonds it creates, it brings oppression and ruin on the citizen and the labourer; it is like those scorching winds, which, covering the trees and plants with devouring insects, deprive useful animals of their subsistence and spread famine and death wherever they blow.

From society and the luxury to which it gives birth arise the liberal and mechanical arts, commerce, letters, and all those superfluities which make industry flourish, and enrich and ruin nations. The reason for such destruction is plain. It is easy to see, from the very nature of agriculture, that it must be the least lucrative of all the arts; for, its produce being the most universally necessary, the price must be proportionate to the abilities of the very poorest of mankind.

From the same principle may be deduced this rule, that the arts in general are more lucrative in proportion as they are less useful; and that, in the end, the most useful becomes the most neglected. From this we may learn what to think of the real advantages of industry and the actual effects of its progress.

Such are the sensible causes of all the miseries, into which opulence at length plunges the most celebrated nations. In proportion as arts and industry flourish, the despised husbandman, burdened with the taxes necessary for the support of luxury, and condemned to pass his days between labour and hunger, forsakes his native field, to seek in towns the bread he ought to carry thither. The more our capital cities strike the vulgar eye with admiration, the greater reason is there to lament the sight of the abandoned countryside, the large tracts of land that lie uncultivated, the roads crowded with unfortunate citizens turned beggars or highwaymen, and doomed to end their wretched lives either on a dunghill or on the gallows. Thus the State grows rich on the one hand, and feeble and depopulated on the other; the mightiest monarchies, after having taken immense pains to enrich and depopulate themselves, fall at last a prey to some poor nation, which has yielded to the fatal temptation of invading them, and then, growing opulent and weak in its turn, is itself invaded and ruined by some other.

Would someone be so kind as to explain to us what produced the hordes of barbarians who overran Europe, Asia, and Africa for so many centuries? Was their prodigious increase due to their industry and arts, to the wisdom of their laws, or to the excellence of their political system? Let the learned tell us why, instead of multiplying to such a degree, these fierce and brutal men, without sense or science, without education, without restraint, did not destroy each other hourly in quarrelling over the productions of their fields and woods. Let them tell us how these wretches could have the presumption to oppose such clever people as we were, so well trained in military discipline, and possessed of such excellent laws and institutions: and why, since society has been brought to perfection in northern countries, and so much pains taken to instruct their inhabitants in their social duties and in the art of living happily and peaceably together, we see them no longer produce such numberless hosts as they used once to send forth to be the plague and terror of other nations. I fear someone may at last answer me by saying, that all these fine things, arts, sciences, and laws, were wisely invented by men, as a salutary plague, to prevent the too great multiplication of mankind, lest the world, which was given us for a habitation, should in time be too small for its inhabitants.

What, then, is to be done? Must we destroy society, abolish *mine* and *yours* and go back to living in the forests with the bears? This is the sort of conclusion my adversaries would come to and I would sooner forestall it than leave to them the shame of drawing it. O you, who have never heard the voice of heaven, who think man destined only to live this little life and die in peace; you, who can resign in the midst of populous cities your fatal acquisitions, your restless spirits, your corrupt hearts and endless desires; resume, since it depends entirely on yourselves, your ancient and primitive innocence: retire to the woods, there to lose the sight and remembrance of the crimes of your contemporaries, and be not apprehensive of degrading your species, by renouncing its advances in order to renounce its vices. As for men like me, whose passions have destroyed their original simplicity, who can no longer subsist on plants or acorns, or live without laws and magistrates; those who were honoured in their first father with supernatural instructions; those who discover, in the design of giving human actions at the start a morality which they must otherwise have been so long in acquiring, the reason for a precept in itself indifferent and inexplicable on every other system; those, in short, who are persuaded that the Divine Being has called all mankind to be partakers in the happiness and perfection of celestial intelligences, all these will endeavour to merit the eternal prize they are to expect from the practice of those virtues, which they make themselves follow in learning to know them. They will respect the sacred bonds of their respective communities; they will love their fellow-citizens, and serve them with all their might: they will scrupulously obey the laws, and all those who make or administer them; they will particularly honour those wise and good princes, who find means of preventing, curing, or even palliating all these evils and abuses, by which we are constantly threatened; they will animate the zeal of their deserving rulers, by showing them, without flattery or fear, the importance of their office and the severity of their duty. But they will not therefore have less contempt for a constitution that cannot support itself without the aid of so many splendid characters, much oftener wished for than found; and from which, notwithstanding all their pains and solicitude, there always arise more real calamities than even apparent advantages.

Immanuel Kant

COMPARED TO THE OTHER AUTHORS REPRESENTED IN THIS VOLUME (WITH THE possible exception of Reid), Kant led what can only be described as a boring life. Königsberg (later Kaliningrad), on the south shore of the Baltic Sea , where he was born April 22, 1724, was an important cosmopolitan port. It was the capital of East Prussia, and became a kingdom in 1701. In Kant's time, it was a city of fifty thousand, larger than Berlin, with its own major university, the Albertus University, founded in 1544. Kant was the fourth of many children (of whom five survived to adulthood) born to a harness maker, a grandson of a Scottish emigrant. A family friend, the Lutheran minister Franz Schultz, recommended that Immanuel, then thirteen, be sent from grammar school to the Lutheran Collegium Fredericianum, a strict Latin school that stressed rote learning, but had the necessary prestige to secure Kant a place at the university in 1740. It is difficult to know how much influence Schultz had on Kant, but Schultz was a student of Christian Wolff, a Leibnizian and the leading philosopher in Germany at the time.

Kant remained at the university until 1746, supported by his uncle, by tutoring, and by playing cards and billiards for money. He studied mathematics, natural science (including Newton, whose work he admired greatly), and philosophy, which he had from Martin Knutzen, another student of Wolff's. In his final year at the university Kant wrote *True Estimation of Living Forces*, a paper in mechanics concerning a dispute between Leibniz and Descartes.

Kant graduated with a Habilitation, licensing him as a private lecturer at the university, meaning that, like Reid, he was paid directly by the students. In these early years, he was a popular lecturer in logic, mathematics, morals, metaphysics, physics, and geography. His teaching load was heavy, between twenty and thirty hours a week, involving as many as six courses at a time. In spite of this, Kant was also a productive scholar, publishing articles in several of these fields. As his reputation grew, he received several offers of appointments in other German cities, but he was determined on a professorship at Königsberg, which he finally received in 1770 at the age of forty-five. This reduced his teaching load to around fifteen hours a week. Although he was professor of logic and metaphysics, he continued to offer courses in all the areas mentioned above, and added anthropology, education, natural theology, and natural law during the next decade. Perhaps not surprisingly, he published next to nothing during this decade.

During this time, however, he seems to have been working out the ideas for his most important work, the *Critique of Pure Reason*, which was actually written in only a few months. The *Critique* was eagerly anticipated by Kant's colleagues, but when it at last appeared in 1781, the general reaction to this difficult work was bewilderment, prompting a revised edition in 1787. Nevertheless, by the 1790s Kant enjoyed a tremendous reputation in Germany, and was beginning to be read abroad. In his final years, however, he was horrified to find young German philosophers such as Fichte and Schelling revamping his system on the grounds that Kant had not properly understood his own philosophical insights!

Kant's only brush with "the real world" came in 1794 when, in response to *Religion within the Bounds of Mere Reason*, the Prussian king asked him to desist writing on a topic on which his theories were causing alarm to the orthodox. Kant obeyed, and that was the end of it. Kant admired Rousseau and the French Revolution from afar, but never traveled himself, though he is said to have conversed eagerly with travelers who came to Königsberg from abroad. He dined out with friends most days, or had guests to dinner in his own home (with a half bottle of wine for each). Aside from the social meal, he lived the life of the stereotypical German academic, adhering to a rigid schedule of the same activities (including an evening walk, which, the story goes, was so regular the neighbors set their watches by his appearance) every day of the week. Toward the end of his life he suffered a steady deterioration of mental and physical powers of the sort we would today associate with Alzheimer's disease. He died February 12, 1804. His funeral was attended by everyone of consequence in Königsberg, and by many others from all over Germany. In 1881, his body was moved to a monument created to mark the centenary of the publication of the *Critique of Pure Reason*. In 1950, his grave was robbed by unknown persons for unknown reasons.

NOTES ON THE TEXT

Kant's moral and political philosophy ought to be understood against the background of the other thinkers we have looked at. In the area of moral philosophy, Kant argued vehemently against Hume's attempt to show that moral judgment is a species of feeling and that justice is a matter of convention. For Kant, morality and justice are founded in reason, which is universal and the foundation of all justified action. But contrary to Locke, Hobbes, and Reid, Kant shares with Hume the idea that reason does not discover moral truths. Here Kant distinguishes between theoretical reason, which aims at discerning truths about the world, and practical reason, which determines what rational beings ought to do. Morality is not external to human beings; it lies within them. For Kant, practical reason is not the discoverer of moral truths, it is the source of the claims of morality that binds us. But since reason is what makes human beings the kind of beings they are, it is universal, its dictates are always and everywhere the same, and it consists in necessary requirements on action. In addition, Kant takes a page from Rousseau's conception of morality. Like Rousseau, Kant thinks that the central value of morality and of justice is liberty. And Kant's first principle of morality and his most famous contribution to moral thought, the categorical imperative, is a descendant of Rousseau's idea of the general will, though clearer and more distinct and applicable to all actions.

How does Kant defend these ideas? His argument for the rationality of morality and the idea of the categorical imperative as well as the idea of the centrality of freedom to morality comes in two quite distinct parts. First, in parts one and two of the *Foundations of the Metaphysics of Morals*, Kant argues that our commonsense morality must be interpreted as grounded in these principles. Second, Kant argues in part three of the *Foundations* that we do and must conceive of ourselves as free and rational beings when we are in the process of making decisions, and he argues that this conception can be defended as at least possible from the point of view of theoretical reason.

Kant's first line of argument is essentially an analysis of our commonsense way of thinking about morality. He states that the only unconditionally good thing in the world is a good will. It is unconditionally good because no matter what accompanies the good will, we still approve of it. A person may make a mess of things as a consequence of his action, but if he has acted from a good will, we still approve of the good will (though we are unhappy about the mess). Intelligence is not unconditionally good, because when it serves an evil purpose, it itself is bad. Or if a person gets pleasure from torturing someone, we do not in any way approve of that person's having the pleasure.

Now, to act from a good will is to act from a sense of duty or a sense of the moral rightness of one's action. Kant says that one can do the right thing—for example, not cheat another person—but if the motive for doing the right thing is merely self-interest, then it is not done from a motive of duty and therefore not from a good will. Only if I desist from cheating others because I take it to be right not to cheat others do I act from a good will. So Kant argues that an action done from a good will is one that is not motivated by one's self-interest or one's inclinations; it is motivated by one's sense of duty. This separates the motive of duty quite strongly from inclination or desire or self-interest.

What could this motive consist in? Kant argues that rational beings act in accordance with general rules or principles of action that are contained in what he calls a maxim of action. The maxim is just the way I am conceiving of my action as I plan it. It consists of the features of my action which make it an action to be pursued. Acting from a motive of duty is acting from a rule or principle or law of action. But it is independent of any inclination or desire that I might have. Hence, acting from a motive of duty must consist in acting out of respect for law itself, because any particular law of action must be a particular means for satisfying a particular inclination or desire. Kant says that the way we act out of respect for law itself without being motivated by inclination is by acting in accordance with what he calls the categorial imperative. It says "Act only on that maxim which you can at the same time will to be a universal law."

Kant argues that practical reason is essentially none other than acting from imperatives of action. This is what it means to say "I ought to do" something. There are two kinds of imperatives: a hypothetical imperative that instructs us to act in a certain way if we want to satisfy a certain desire, and a categorical imperative that tells us to act in a certain way regardless of what we desire. There are many hypothetical imperatives for all the different desires we have and the different means to achieve them, but there is only one categorical imperative that always binds us regardless of the particular circumstances we are in or the desires we have. Kant argues that there are three versions of this categorical imperative. The first and most important is the one stated above. The second one, which follows from the first, states that one ought to act so as to treat humanity in oneself or in others always as an end in itself and never merely as a means. The moral imperative instructs us here not to use others as if they were mere objects but to treat them with respect. The third version of the imperative states that one must act on that maxim which one can will to be a universal law for a possible kingdom of ends.

For Kant, these three versions of the imperative point to one main idea, that of the autonomy of the will. The moral will imposes a law on itself independent of any outside forces. Hence, autonomy or freedom is the basic idea behind morality. Kant states in the second line of argument that human beings must conceive of themselves as free. If we did not think of ourselves that way, there would be no more reason for us to think about how we ought to act than to think about how the mountains ought to act. When we act, we think of the future as essentially open to our determination and choice. Is this merely a massive illusion? Ordinarily we look at the world as if everything were caused by something else in accordance with laws of nature. So the future is determined on this way of looking at things. But Kant argues that we look at the world from two different standpoints: the phenomenal standpoint, from which the world appears as an integrated causal system where everything is causally determined; and the noumenal standpoint, which sees that our phenomenal standpoint is merely a function of our way of interpreting the world. It can ask the question, What is the world like independent of the way we perceive it and think about it? Causality and determinism are features of the world as we interpret it through our lenses, so to speak. But we know that the world is independent of the way we see it and we know that we are part of that world in itself. Kant argues that it is insofar as we see ourselves this way that we can see ourselves as independent of the causal order of things. Or at least, he says, it is not incoherent to see ourselves this way. Hence, we can see ourselves as free.

Justice, for Kant, is based on the idea of freedom. His basic principle is that we have a right to that liberty which is compatible with giving the same liberty to everyone else. Hence, for Kant, the foundations of our treatment of each other, of property, and of the state lie in the principle of freedom. But Kant derives a number of principles from this idea that are quite different from Locke's. He argues that the right to property, which implies that others have duties to respect my property, cannot come about merely through my labor, since then I would be giving duties to other people without their consent. He argues that not only do people have reason to agree to become members of a state, they have a duty to join a state, because only when a state is formed can the liberty and property of individuals be properly respected. He argues for the idea that the state ought to provide for the needs of its members who cannot help themselves. Finally and quite remarkably, Kant argues that each member of a state has an absolute obligation to obey the sovereign authority of that state.

Foundations of the Metaphysics of Morals

Preface

Ancient Greek philosophy was divided into three sciences: physics, ethics, and logic. This division conforms perfectly to the nature of the subject, and one can improve on it perhaps only by supplying its principle in order both to insure its exhaustiveness and to define correctly the necessary subdivisions.

All rational knowledge is either material, and concerns some object, or formal, and is occupied merely with the form of understanding and reason itself and with the universal rules of thinking without regard to distinctions between objects. Formal philosophy is called logic. Material philosophy, however, which has to do with definite objects and the laws to which they are subject, is itself divided into two parts. This is because these laws are either laws of nature or laws of freedom. The science of the former is called physics and that of the latter ethics. The former is also called theory of nature and the latter theory of morals.

Logic can have no empirical part—a part in which universal and necessary laws of thinking would rest upon grounds taken from experience. For in that case it would not be logic, i.e., a canon for understanding or reason which is valid for all thinking and which must be demonstrated. But, on the other hand, natural and moral philosophy can each have its empirical part. The former must do so, for it must determine the laws of nature as an object of experience, and the latter because it must determine the human will so far as it is affected by nature. The laws of the former are laws according to which everything happens; those of the latter are laws according to which everything should happen, but allow for conditions under which what should happen often does not.

All philosophy, so far as it is based on experience, may be called empirical; but, so far as it presents its doctrines solely on the basis of a priori principles, it may be called pure philosophy. The latter, when merely formal, is logic; when limited to definite objects of understanding, it is metaphysics.

In this way there arises the idea of a twofold metaphysics—a metaphysics of nature and a metaphysics of morals. Physics, therefore, will have an empirical and also a rational part, and ethics likewise. In ethics, however, the empirical part may be called more specifically practical anthropology; the rational part, morals proper.

All crafts, handiworks, and arts have gained by the division of labor, for when one person does not do everything, but each limits himself to a particular job which is distinguished from all the others by the treatment it requires, he can do it with greater perfection and with more facility. Where work is not thus differentiated and divided, where everyone is a jack-of-all-trades, the crafts remain at a barbaric level. It might be worth considering whether pure philosophy in each of its parts does not require a man particularly devoted to it, and whether it would not be better for the learned profession as a whole to warn those who are in the habit of catering to the taste of the public by mixing up the empirical with the rational in all sorts of proportions which they do not themselves know and who call themselves independent thinkers (giving the name of speculator to those who apply themselves to the merely rational part). This warning would be that they should not at one and the same time carry on two employments which differ widely in the treatment they require, and for each of which perhaps a special talent is needed since the combination of these talents in one person produces only bunglers. I ask only whether the nature of the science does not require that a careful separation of the empirical from the rational part be made, with a metaphysics of nature put before real (empirical) physics and a metaphysics of morals before practical anthropology. These prior sciences must be carefully purified of everything empirical so that we can know how much pure reason can accomplish in each case and from what sources it creates its a priori teaching, whether the latter inquiry be conducted by all moralists (whose name is legion) or only by some who feel a calling to it.

Since my purpose here is directed to moral philosophy, I narrow the proposed question to this: Is it not of the utmost necessity to construct a pure moral philosophy which is completely freed from everything which may be only empirical and thus belong to anthropology? That there must be such a philosophy is self-evident from the common idea of duty and moral laws. Everyone must admit that a law, if it is to hold morally, i.e., as a ground of obligation, must imply absolute necessity; he must admit that the command, "Thou shalt not lie," does not apply to men only, as if other rational beings had no need to observe it. The same is true for all other moral laws properly so called. He must concede that the ground of obligation here must not be sought in the nature of man or in the circumstances in which he is placed, but sought a priori solely in the concepts of pure reason, and that every other precept which rests on principles of mere experience, even a precept which is in certain respects universal, so far as it leans in the least on empirical grounds (perhaps only in regard to the motive involved), may be called a practical rule but never a moral law.

Thus not only are moral laws together with their principles essentially different from all practical knowledge in which there is anything empirical, but all moral philosophy rests solely on its pure part. Applied to man, it borrows nothing from knowledge of him (anthropology) but gives him, as a rational being, a priori laws. No doubt these laws require a power of judgment sharpened by experience, partly in order to decide in what cases they apply and partly to procure for them an access to man's will and an impetus to their practice. For man is affected by so many inclinations that, though he is capable of the idea of a practical pure reason, he is not so easily able to make it concretely effective in the conduct of his life.

A metaphysics of morals is therefore indispensable, not merely because of motives to speculate on the source of the a priori practical principles which lie in our reason, but also because morals themselves remain subject to all kinds of corruption so long as the guide and supreme norm for their correct estimation is lacking. For it is not sufficient to that which should be morally good that it conform to the law; it must be done for the sake of the law. Otherwise the conformity is merely contingent and spurious, because, though the unmoral ground may indeed now and then produce lawful actions, more often it brings forth unlawful ones. But the moral law can be found in its purity and genuineness (which is the central concern in the practical) nowhere else than in a pure philosophy; therefore, this (i.e., metaphysics) must lead the way, and without it there can be no moral philosophy. Philosophy which mixes pure principles with empirical ones does not deserve the name, for what distinguishes philosophy from common rational knowledge is its treatment in separate sciences of what is confusedly comprehended in such knowledge. Much less does it deserve the name of moral philosophy, since by this confusion it spoils the purity of morals themselves and works contrary to its own end.

It should not be thought that what is here required is already present in the celebrated Wolff's propaedeutic to his moral philosophy, i.e., in what he calls universal practical philosophy, and that it is not an entirely new field that is to be opened. Precisely because his work was to be universal practical philosophy, it deduced no will of any particular kind, such as one determined without any empirical motives but completely by a priori principles; in a word, it had nothing which could be called a pure will, since it considered only volition in general with all the actions and conditions which pertain to it in this general sense. Thus his propaedeutic differs from a metaphysics of morals in the same way that general logic is distinguished from transcendental philosophy, the former expounding the actions and rules of thinking in general, and the latter presenting the particular

actions and rules of pure thinking, i.e., of thinking by which objects are known completely a priori. For the metaphysics of morals is meant to investigate the idea and principles of a possible pure will and not the actions and conditions of the human volition as such, which are for the most part drawn from psychology.

That in general practical philosophy laws and duty are discussed (though improperly) is no objection to my assertion. For the authors of this science remain even here true to their idea of it. They do not distinguish the motives which are presented completely a priori by reason alone, and which are thus moral in the proper sense of the word, from the empirical motives which the understanding, by comparing experiences, elevates to universal concepts. Rather, they consider motives without regard to the difference in their source but only with reference to their greater or smaller number (as they are considered to be all of the same kind); they thus formulate their concept of obligation, which is anything but moral, but which is all that can be desired in a philosophy that does not decide whether the origin of all possible practical concepts is a priori or only a posteriori.

As a preliminary to a metaphysics of morals which I intend some day to publish, I issue these *Foundations*. There is, to be sure, no other foundation for such a metaphysics than a critical examination of a pure practical reason, just as there is no other foundation for metaphysics than the already published critical examination of the pure speculative reason. But, in the first place, a critical examination of pure practical reason is not of such extreme importance as that of speculative reason, because human reason, even in the commonest mind, can easily be brought to a high degree of correctness and completeness in moral matters, while, on the other hand, in its theoretical but pure use it is entirely dialectical. In the second place, I require of a critical examination of a pure practical reason, if it is to be complete, that its unity with the speculative be subject to presentation under a common principle, because in the final analysis there can be but one and the same reason which must be differentiated only in application. But I could not bring this to such a completeness without bringing in observations of an altogether different kind and without thereby confusing the reader. For these reasons I leave employed the title, *Foundations of the Metaphysics of Morals*, instead of *Critique of Pure Practical Reason*.

Because, in the third place, a metaphysics of morals, in spite of its forbidding title, is capable of a high degree of popularity and adaptation to common understanding, I find it useful to separate this preliminary work of laying the foundation in order not to have to introduce unavoidable subtleties into the later, more comprehensive, work.

The present foundations, however, are nothing more than the search for and establishment of the supreme principle of morality. This constitutes a task altogether complete in its intention and one which should be kept separate from all other moral inquiry.

My conclusions concerning this important question, which has not yet been discussed nearly enough, would, of course, be clarified by application of the principle to the whole system of morality, and it would receive much confirmation by the adequacy which it would everywhere show. But I must forgo this advantage, which would in the final analysis be more privately gratifying than commonly useful, because ease of use and apparent adequacy of a principle are not any sure proof of its correctness, but rather awaken a certain partiality which prevents a rigorous investigation and evaluation of it for itself without regard to consequences.

I have adopted in this writing the method which is, I think, most suitable if one wishes to proceed analytically from common knowledge to the determination of its supreme principle, and then synthetically from the examination of this principle and its sources back to common knowledge where it finds its application. The division is therefore as follows:

1. First Section. Transition from the Common Rational Knowledge of Morals to the Philosophical

2. Second Section. Transition from the Popular Moral Philosophy to the Metaphysics of Morals

3. Third Section. Final Step from the Metaphysics of Morals to the Critical Examination of Pure Practical Reason.

First Section Transition from the Common Rational Knowledge of Morals to the Philosophical

Nothing in the world—indeed nothing even beyond the world—can possibly be conceived which could be called good without qualification except a *good will*. Intelligence, wit, judgment, and the other talents of the mind, however they may be named, or courage, resoluteness, and perseverance as qualities of temperament, are doubtless in many respects good and desirable. But they can become extremely bad and harmful if the will, which is to make use of these gifts of nature and which in its special constitution is called character, is not good. It is the same with the gifts of fortune. Power, riches, honor, even health, general well-being, and the contentment with one's condition which is called happiness, make for pride and even arrogance if there is not a good will to correct their influence on the mind and on its principles of action so as to make it universally conformable to its end. It need hardly be mentioned that the sight of a being adorned with no feature of a pure and good will, yet enjoying uninterrupted prosperity, can never give pleasure to a rational impartial observer. Thus the good will seems to constitute the indispensable condition even of worthiness to be happy.

Some qualities seem to be conducive to this good will and can facilitate its action, but, in spite of that, they have no intrinsic unconditional worth. They rather presuppose a good will, which limits the high esteem which one otherwise rightly has for them and prevents their being held to be absolutely good. Moderation in emotions and passions, self-control, and calm deliberation not only are good in many respects but even seem to constitute a part of the inner worth of the person. But however unconditionally they were esteemed by the ancients, they are far from being good without qualification. For without the principle of a good will they can be come extremely bad, and the coolness of a villain makes him not only far more dangerous but also more directly abominable in our eyes than he would have seemed without it.

The good will is not good because of what it effects or accomplishes or because of its adequacy to achieve some proposed end; it is good only because of its willing, i.e., it is good of itself. And, regarded for itself, it is to be esteemed incomparably higher than anything which could be brought about by it in favor of any inclination or even of the sum total of all inclinations. Even if it should happen that, by a particularly unfortunate fate or by the niggardly provision of a stepmotherly nature, this will should be wholly lacking in power to accomplish its purpose, and if even the greatest effort should not avail it to achieve anything of its end, and if there remained only the good will (not as a mere wish but as the summoning of all the means in our power), it would sparkle like a jewel in its own right, as something that had its full worth in itself. Usefulness or fruitlessness can neither diminish nor augment this worth. Its usefulness would be only its setting, as it were, so as to enable us to handle it more conveniently in commerce or to attract the attention of those who are not yet connoisseurs, but not to recommend it to those who are experts or to determine its worth.

But there is something so strange in this idea of the absolute worth of the will alone, in which no account is taken of any use, that, notwithstanding the agreement even of common sense, the suspicion must arise that perhaps only high-flown fancy is its hidden basis, and that we may have misunderstood the purpose of nature in its appointment of reason as the ruler of our will. We shall therefore examine this idea from this point of view.

In the natural constitution of an organized being, i.e., one suitably adapted to life, we assume as an axiom that no organ will be found for any purpose which is not the fittest and best adapted to that purpose. Now if its preservation, its welfare—in a word, its happiness—were the real end of nature in a being having reason and will, then nature would have hit upon a very poor arrangement in appointing the reason of the creature to be the executor of this purpose. For all the actions which the creature has to perform with this intention, and the entire rule of its conduct, would be dictated much more exactly by instinct, and that end would be far more certainly attained by instinct than it ever could be by reason. And if, over and above this, reason should have been granted to the favored creature, it would have served only to let it contemplate the happy constitution of its nature, to admire it, to rejoice in it, and to be grateful for it to its beneficent cause. But reason would not have been given in order that the being should subject its faculty of desire to that weak and delusive guidance and to meddle with the purpose of nature. In a word, nature would have taken care that reason did not break forth into practical use nor have the presumption, with its weak insight, to think out for itself the plan of happiness and the means of attaining it. Nature would have taken over not only the choice of ends but also that of the means, and with wise foresight she would have entrusted both to instinct alone.

And, in fact, we find that the more a cultivated reason deliberately devotes itself to the enjoyment of life and happiness, the more the man falls short of true contentment. From this fact there arises in many persons, if only they are candid enough to admit it, a certain degree of misology, hatred of reason. This is particularly the case with those who are most experienced in its use. After counting all the advantages which they draw—I will not say from the invention of the arts of common luxury—from the sciences (which in the end seem to them to be also a luxury of the understanding), they nevertheless find that they have actually brought more trouble on their shoulders instead of gaining in happiness; they finally envy, rather than despise, the common run of men who are better guided by mere natural instinct and who do not permit their reason much influence on their conduct. And we must at least admit that a morose attitude or ingratitude to the goodness with which the world is governed is by no means found always among those who temper or refute the boasting eulogies which are given of the advantages of happiness and contentment with which reason is supposed to supply us. Rather their judgment is based on the idea of another and far more worthy purpose of their existence for which, instead of happiness, their reason is properly intended, this purpose, therefore, being the supreme condition to which the private purposes of men must for the most part defer.

Reason is not, however, competent to guide the will safely with regard to its objects and the satisfaction of all our needs (which it in part multiplies), and to this end an innate instinct would have led with far more certainty. But reason is given to us as a practical faculty, i.e., one which is meant to have an influence on the will. As nature has elsewhere distributed capacities suitable to the functions they are to perform, reason's proper function must be to produce a will good in itself and not one good merely as a means, for to the former reason is absolutely essential. This will must indeed not be the sole and complete good but the highest good and the condition of all others, even of the desire for happiness. In this case it is entirely compatible with the wisdom of nature that the cultivation of reason, which is required for the former unconditional purpose, at least in this life restricts in many ways—indeed can reduce to less than nothing—the achievement of the latter conditional purpose, happiness. For one perceives that nature here does not proceed unsuitably to its purpose, because reason which recognizes its highest practical vocation in the establishment of a good will, is capable only of a contentment of its own kind, i.e., one that springs from the attainment of a purpose which is determined by reason, even though this injures the ends of inclination.

We have, then, to develop the concept of a will which is to be esteemed as good of itself without regard to anything else. It dwells already in the natural sound understanding and does not need so much to be taught as only to be brought to light. In the estimation of the total worth of our actions it always takes first place and is the condition of everything else. In order to show this, we shall take the concept of duty. It contains that of a good will, though with certain subjective restrictions and hindrances; but these are far from concealing it and making it unrecognizable, for they rather bring it out by contrast and make it shine forth all the brighter.

I here omit all actions which are recognized as opposed to duty, even though they may be useful in one respect or another, for with these the question does not arise at all as to whether they may be carried out *from* duty, since they conflict with it. I also pass over the actions which are really in accordance with duty and to which one has no direct inclination, rather executing them because impelled to do so by another inclination. For it is easily decided whether an action in accord with duty is performed from duty or for some selfish purpose. It is far more difficult to note this difference when the action is in accordance with duty and, in addition, the subject has a direct inclination to do it. For example, it is in fact in accordance with duty that a dealer should not overcharge an inexperienced customer, and wherever there is much business the prudent merchant does not do so, having a fixed price for everyone, so that a child may buy of him as cheaply as any other. Thus the customer is honestly served. But this is far from sufficient to justify the belief that the merchant has behaved in this way from duty and principles of honesty. His own advantage required this behavior; but it cannot be assumed that over and above he had a direct inclination to the purchaser and that, out of love, as it were, he gave none an advantage in price over another. Therefore the action was done neither from duty nor from direct inclination but only for a selfish purpose.

On the other hand, it is a duty to preserve one's life, and moreover everyone has a direct inclination to do so. But for that reason the often anxious care which most men take of it has no intrinsic worth, and the maxim of doing so has no moral import. They preserve their lives according to duty, but not from duty. But if adversities and hopeless sorrow completely take away the relish for life, if an unfortunate man, strong in soul, is indignant rather than despondent or dejected over his fate and wishes for death, and yet preserves his life without loving it and from neither inclination nor fear but from duty—then his maxim has a moral import.

To be kind where one can is duty, and there are, moreover, many persons so sympathetically constituted that without any motive of vanity or selfishness they find an inner satisfaction in spreading joy, and rejoice in the contentment of others which they have made possible. But I say that, however dutiful and amiable it may be, that kind of action has no true moral worth. It is on a level with [actions arising from] other inclinations, such as the inclination to honor, which, if fortunately directed to what in fact accords with duty and is generally useful and thus honorable, deserve praise and encouragement but no esteem. For the maxim lacks the moral import of an action done not from inclination but from duty. But assume that the mind of that friend to mankind was clouded by a sorrow of his own which extinguished all sympathy with the lot of others and that he still had the power to benefit others in distress, but that their need left him untouched because he was preoccupied with his own need. And now suppose him to tear himself, unsolicited by inclination, out of this dead insensibility and to perform this action only from duty and without any inclination—then for the first time his action has genuine moral worth. Furthermore, if nature has put little sympathy in the heart of a man, and if he, though an honest man, is by temperament cold and indifferent to the sufferings of others, perhaps because he is provided with special gifts of patience and fortitude and expects or even requires that others should have the same—and such a man would certainly not be the meanest product of nature—would not he find in himself a source from which to give himself a far higher worth than he could have got by having a good-natured temperament? This is unquestionably true even though nature did not make him philanthropic, for it is just here that the worth of the character is brought out, which is morally and incomparably the highest of all: he is beneficent not from inclination but from duty.

To secure one's own happiness is at least indirectly a duty, for discontent with one's condition under pressure from many cares and amid unsatisfied wants could easily become a great temptation to transgress duties. But without any view to duty all men have the strongest and deepest inclination to happiness, because in this idea all inclinations are summed up. But the precept of happiness is often so formulated that it definitely thwarts some inclinations, and men can make no definite and certain concept of the sum of satisfaction of all inclinations which goes under the name of happiness. It is not to be wondered at, therefore, that a single inclination, definite as to what it promises and as to the time at which it can be satisfied, can outweigh a fluctuating idea, and that, for example, a man with the gout can choose to enjoy what he likes and to suffer what he may, because according to his calculations at least on this occasion he has not sacrificed the enjoyment of the present moment to a perhaps groundless expectation of a happiness supposed to lie in health. But even in this case, if the universal inclination to happiness did not determine his will, and if health were not at least for him a necessary factor in these calculations, there yet would remain, as in all other cases, a law that he ought to promote his happiness, not from inclination but from duty. Only from this law would his conduct have true moral worth.

It is in this way, undoubtedly, that we should understand those passages of Scripture which command us to love our neighbor and even our enemy, for love as an inclination cannot be commanded. But beneficence from duty, when no inclination impels it and even when it is opposed by a natural and unconquerable aversion, is practical love, not pathological love; it resides in the will and not in the propensities of feeling, in principles of action and not in tender sympathy; and it alone call be commanded.

[Thus the first proposition of morality is that to have moral worth an action must be done from duty.] The second proposition is: An action performed from duty does not have its moral worth in the purpose which is to be achieved through it but in the maxim by which it is determined. Its moral value, therefore, does not depend on the realization of the object of the action but merely on the principle of volition by which the action is done, without any regard to the objects of the faculty of desire. From the preceding discussion it is clear that the purposes we may have

for our actions and their effects as ends and incentives of the will cannot give the actions any unconditional and moral worth. Wherein, then, can this worth lie, if it is not in the will in relation to its hoped-for effect? It can lie nowhere else than in the principle of the will, irrespective of the ends which can be realized by such action. For the will stands, as it were, at the crossroads halfway between its a priori principle which is formal and its a posteriori incentive which is material. Since it must be determined by something, if it is done from duty it must be determined by the formal principle of volition as such since every material principle has been withdrawn from it.

The third principle, as a consequence of the two preceding, I would express as follows: Duty is the necessity of an action executed from respect for law. I can certainly have an inclination to the object as an effect of the proposed action, but I can never have respect for it precisely because it is a mere effect and not an activity of a will. Similarly, I can have no respect for any inclination whatsoever, whether my own or that of another; in the former case I can at most approve of it and in the latter I can even love it, i.e., see it as favorable to my own advantage. But that which is connected with my will merely as ground and not as consequence, that which does not serve my inclination but overpowers it or at least excludes it from being considered in making a choice—in a word, law itself—can be an object of respect and thus a command. Now as an act from duty wholly excludes the influence of inclination and therewith every object of the will, nothing remains which can determine the will objectively except the law, and nothing subjectively except pure respect for this practical law. This subjective element is the maxim[1] that I ought to follow such a law even if it thwarts all my inclinations.

Thus the moral worth of an action does not lie in the effect which is expected from it or in any principle of action which has to borrow its motive from this expected effect. For all these effects (agreeableness of my own condition, indeed even the promotion of the happiness of others) could be brought about through other causes and would not require the will

---

1. A maxim is the subjective principle of volition. The objective principle (i.e., that which would serve all rational beings also subjectively as a practical principle if reason had full power over the faculty of desire) is the practical law.

of a rational being, while the highest and unconditional good can be found only in such a will. Therefore, the pre-eminent good can consist only in the conception of the law in itself (which can be present only in a rational being) so far as this conception and not the hoped-for effect is the determining ground of the will. This pre-eminent good, which we call moral, is already present in the person who acts according to this conception, and we do not have to look for it first in the result.[2]

But what kind of a law can that be, the conception of which must determine the will without reference to the expected result? Under this condition alone the will can be called absolutely good without qualification. Since I have robbed the will of all impulses which could come to it from obedience to any law, nothing remains to serve as a principle of the will except universal conformity of its action to law as such. That is, I should never act in such a way that I could not also will that my maxim should be a universal law. Mere conformity to law as such (without assuming any particular law applicable to certain actions) serves as the principle of the will, and it must

serve as such a principle if duty is not to be a vain delusion and chimerical concept. The common reason of mankind in its practical judgments is in perfect agreement with this and has this principle constantly in view.

Let the question, for example, be: May I, when in distress, make a promise with the intention not to keep it? I easily distinguish the two meanings which the question can have, viz., whether it is prudent to make a false promise, or whether it conforms to my duty. Undoubtedly the former can often be the case, though I do see clearly that it is not sufficient merely to escape from the present difficulty by this expedient, but that I must consider whether inconveniences much greater than the present one may not later spring from this lie. Even with all my supposed cunning, the consequences cannot be so easily foreseen. Loss of credit might be far more disadvantageous than the misfortune I now seek to avoid, and it is hard to tell whether it might not be more prudent to act according to a universal maxim and to make it a habit not to promise anything without intending to fulfill it. But it is soon clear to me that such a maxim is based only on an apprehensive concern with consequences.

To be truthful from duty, however, is an entirely different thing from being truthful out of fear of disadvantageous consequences, for in the former case the concept of the action itself contains a law for me, while in the latter I must first look about to see what results for me may be connected with it. For to deviate from the principle of duty is certainly bad, but to be unfaithful to my maxim of prudence can sometimes be very advantageous to me, though it is certainly safer to abide by it. The shortest but most infallible way to find the answer to the question as to whether a deceitful promise is consistent with duty is to ask myself: Would I be content that my maxim (of extricating myself from difficulty by a false promise) should hold as a universal law for myself as well as for others? And could I say to myself that everyone may make a false promise when he is in a difficulty from which he otherwise cannot escape? I immediately see that I could will the lie but not a universal law to lie. For with such a law there would be no promises at all, inasmuch as it would be futile to make a pretense of my intention in regard to future actions to those who would not believe this pretense or—if they overhastily did so—who would pay me back in my own coin. Thus my maxim would

---

2. It might be objected that I seek to take refuge in an obscure feeling behind the word "respect," instead of clearly resolving the question with a concept of reason. But though respect is a feeling, it is not one received through any [outer] influence but is self-wrought by a rational concept; thus it differs specifically from all feelings of the former kind which may be referred to inclination or fear. What I recognize directly as a law for myself I recognize with respect, which means merely the consciousness of the submission of my will to a law without the intervention of other influences on my mind. The direct determination of the will by the law and the consciousness of this determination is respect; thus respect can be regarded as the effect of the law on the subject and not as the cause of the law. Respect is properly the conception of a worth which thwarts my self-love. Thus it is regarded as an object neither of inclination nor of fear, though it has something analogous to both. The only object of respect is the law, and indeed only the law which we impose on ourselves and yet recognize as necessary in itself. As a law, we are subject to it without consulting self-love; as imposed on us by ourselves, it is a consequence of our will. In the former respect it is analogous to fear and in the latter to inclination. All respect for a person is only respect for the law (of righteousness, etc.) of which the person provides an example. Because we see the improvement of our talents as a duty, we think of a person of talents as the example of a law, as it were (the law that we should by practice become like him in his talents), and that constitutes our respect. All so-called moral interest consists solely in respect for the law.

necessarily destroy itself as soon as it was made a universal law.

I do not, therefore, need any penetrating acuteness in order to discern what I have to do in order that my volition may be morally good. Inexperienced in the course of the world, incapable of being prepared for all its contingencies, I ask myself only: Can I will that my maxim become a universal law? If not, it must be rejected, not because of any disadvantage accruing to myself or even to others, but because it cannot enter as a principle into a possible universal legislation, and reason extorts from me an immediate respect for such legislation. I do not as yet discern on what it is grounded (a question the philosopher may investigate), but I at least understand that it is an estimation of the worth which far outweighs all the worth of whatever is recommended by the inclinations, and that the necessity of my actions from pure respect for the practical law constitutes duty. To duty every other motive must give place, because duty is the condition of a will good in itself, whose worth transcends everything.

Thus within the moral knowledge of common human reason we have attained its principle. To be sure, common human reason does not think of it abstractly in such a universal form, but it always has it in view and uses it as the standard of its judgments. It would be easy to show how common human reason, with this compass, knows well how to distinguish what is good, what is bad, and what is consistent or inconsistent with duty. Without in the least teaching common reason anything new, we need only to draw its attention to its own principle, in the manner of Socrates, thus showing that neither science nor philosophy is needed in order to know what one has to do in order to be honest and good, and even wise and virtuous. We might have conjectured beforehand that the knowledge of what everyone is obliged to do and thus also to know would be within the reach of everyone, even the most ordinary man. Here we cannot but admire the great advantages which the practical faculty of judgment has over the theoretical in ordinary human understanding. In the theoretical, if ordinary reason ventures to go beyond the laws of experience and perceptions of the senses, it falls into sheer inconceivabilities and self-contradictions, or at least into a chaos of uncertainty, obscurity, and instability. In the practical, on the other hand, the power of judgment first shows itself to advantage when common understanding excludes all sensuous incentives from practical laws. It then becomes even subtle, quibbling with its own conscience or with other claims to what should be called right, or wishing to determine correctly for its own instruction the worth of certain actions. But the most remarkable thing about ordinary reason in its practical concern is that it may have as much hope as any philosopher of hitting the mark. In fact, it is almost more certain to do so than the philosopher, because he has no principle which the common understanding lacks, while his judgment is easily confused by a mass of irrelevant considerations, so that it easily turns aside from the correct way. Would it not, therefore, be wiser in moral matters to acquiesce in the common rational judgment, or at most to call in philosophy in order to make the system of morals more complete and comprehensible and its rules more convenient for use (especially in disputation) than to steer the common understanding from its happy simplicity in practical matters and to lead it through philosophy into a new path of inquiry and instruction?

Innocence is indeed a glorious thing, but, on the other hand, it is very sad that it cannot well maintain itself, being easily led astray. For this reason, even wisdom—which consists more in acting than in knowing—needs science, not to learn from it but to secure admission and permanence to its precepts. Man feels in himself a powerful counterpoise against all commands of duty which reason presents to him as so deserving of respect; this counterpoise is his needs and inclinations, the complete satisfaction of which he sums up under the name of happiness. Now reason issues inexorable commands without promising anything to the inclinations. It disregards, as it were, and holds in contempt those claims which are so impetuous and yet so plausible, and which will not allow themselves to be abolished by any command. From this a natural dialectic arises, i.e., a propensity to argue against the stern laws of duty and their validity, or at least to place their purity and strictness in doubt and, where possible, to make them more accordant with our wishes and inclinations. This is equivalent to corrupting them in their very foundations and destroying their dignity—a thing which even common practical reason cannot ultimately call good.

In this way common human reason is impelled to go outside its sphere and to take a step into the field of practical philosophy. But it is forced to do so not by any speculative need, which never occurs to it so long as it is satisfied to remain merely healthy reason;

rather, it is so impelled on practical grounds in order to obtain information and clear instruction respecting the source of its principle and the correct determination of this principle in its opposition to the maxims which are based on need and inclination. It seeks this information in order to escape from the perplexity of opposing claims and to avoid the danger of losing all genuine moral principles through the equivocation in which it is easily involved. Thus, when practical common reason cultivates itself, a dialectic surreptitiously ensues which forces it to seek aid in philosophy, just as the same thing happens in the theoretical use of reason. In this case, as in the theoretical, it will find rest only in a thorough critical examination of our reason.

Second Section Transition from the Popular Moral Philosophy to the Metaphysics of Morals

If we have derived our earlier concept of duty from the common use of our practical reason, it is by no means to be inferred that we have treated it as an empirical concept. On the contrary, if we attend to our experience of the way men act, we meet frequent and, as we ourselves confess, justified complaints that we cannot cite a single sure example of the disposition to act from pure duty. There are also justified complaints that, though much may be done that accords with what duty commands, it is nevertheless always doubtful whether it is done from duty, and thus whether it has moral worth. There have always been philosophers who for this reason have absolutely denied the reality of this disposition in human actions, attributing everything to more or less refined self-love. They have done so without questioning the correctness of the concept of morality. Rather they have spoken with sincere regret of the frailty and corruption of human nature, which is noble enough to take as its precept an idea so worthy of respect but which at the same time is too weak to follow it, employing reason, which should legislate for human nature, only to provide for the interest of the inclinations either singly or, at best, in their greatest possible harmony with one another.

It is in fact absolutely impossible by experience to discern with complete certainty a single case in which the maxim of an action, however much it may conform to duty, rested solely on moral grounds and on the conception of one's duty. It sometimes happens that in the most searching self-examination we can find nothing except the moral ground of duty which could have been powerful enough to move us to this or that good action and to such great sacrifice. But from this we cannot by any means conclude with certainty that a secret impulse of self-love, falsely appearing as the idea of duty, was not actually the true determining cause of the will. For we like to flatter ourselves with a pretended nobler motive, while in fact even the strictest examination can never lead us entirely behind the secret incentives, for, when moral worth is in question, it is not a matter of actions which one sees but of their inner principles which one does not see.

Moreover, one cannot better serve the wishes of those who ridicule all morality as a mere phantom of human imagination overreaching itself through self-conceit than by conceding to them that the concepts of duty must be derived only from experience (for they are ready to believe from indolence that this is true of all other concepts too). For, by this concession, a sure triumph is prepared for them. Out of love for humanity I am willing to admit that most of our actions are in accordance with duty; but, if we look more closely at our thoughts and aspirations, we everywhere come upon the dear self, which is always there, and it is this instead of the stern command of duty (which would often require self-denial) which supports our plans. One need not be an enemy of virtue, but only a cool observer who does not confuse even the liveliest aspiration for the good with its reality, to be doubtful sometimes whether true virtue can really be found anywhere in the world. This is especially true as one's years increase and one's power of judgment is made wiser by experience and more acute in observation. This being so, nothing can secure us against the complete abandonment of our ideas of duty and preserve in us a well-founded respect for its law except the clear conviction that, even if there never were actions springing from such pure sources, our concern is not whether this or that was done but that reason of itself and independently of all appearances commands what ought to be done. Our concern is with actions of which perhaps the world has never had an example, with actions whose feasibility might be seriously doubted by those who base everything on experience, and yet with actions inexorably commanded by reason. For example, pure sincerity in friendship can be demanded of every man, and this demand is not in the least diminished if a sincere friend has never existed, because this duty, as duty in general, prior to all experience, lies in the idea of a reason which determines the will by a priori grounds.

It is clear that no experience can give occasion for inferring the possibility of such apodictic laws. This is especially clear when we add that, unless we wish to deny all truth to the concept of morality and renounce its application to any possible object, we cannot refuse to admit that the law of this concept is of such broad significance that it holds not merely for men but for all rational beings as such; we must grant that it must be valid with absolute necessity and not merely under contingent conditions and with exceptions. For with what right could we bring into unlimited respect something that might be valid only under contingent human conditions? And how could laws of the determination of our will be held to be laws of the determination of the will of a rational being in general and of ourselves in so far as we are rational beings, if they were merely empirical and did not have their origin completely a priori in pure, but practical, reason?

Nor could one give poorer counsel to morality than to attempt to derive it from examples. For each example of morality which is exhibited to me must itself have been previously judged according to principles of morality to see whether it is worthy to serve as an original example, i.e., as a model. By no means could it authoritatively furnish the concept of morality. Even the Holy One of the Gospel must be compared with our ideal of moral perfection before He is recognized as such; even He says of Himself, "Why call ye Me (whom you see) good? None is good (the archetype of the good) except God only (whom you do not see)." But whence do we have the concept of God as the highest good? Solely from the idea of moral perfection which reason formulates a priori and which it inseparably connects with the concept of a free will. Imitation has no place in moral matters, and examples serve only for encouragement. That is, they put beyond question the practicability of what the law commands, and they make visible that which the practical rule expresses more generally. But they can never justify our guiding ourselves by examples and our setting aside their true original which lies in reason.

If there is thus no genuine supreme principle of morality which does not rest merely on pure reason independently of all experience, I do not believe it is necessary even to ask whether it is well to exhibit these concepts generally (*in abstracto*), which, together with the principles belonging to them, are established a priori. At any rate, this question need not be asked if knowledge which establishes this is to be distinguished from ordinary knowledge and called philosophical. But in our times this question may perhaps be necessary. For if we collected votes as to whether pure rational knowledge separated from all experience, i.e., metaphysics of morals, or popular practical philosophy is to be preferred, it is easily guessed on which side the majority would stand.

This condescension to popular notions is certainly very commendable once the ascent to the principles of pure reason has been satisfactorily accomplished. That would mean the prior establishment of the doctrine of morals on metaphysics and then, when it is established, to procure a hearing for it through popularization. But it is extremely absurd to want to achieve popularity in the first investigation, where everything depends on the correctness of the fundamental principles. Not only can this procedure never make claim to that rarest merit of true philosophical popularity, since there is really no art in being generally comprehensible if one thereby renounces all basic insight, but it produces a disgusting jumble of patched-up observations and half-reasoned principles. Shallowpates enjoy this, for it is very useful in everyday chitchat, while the more sensible feel confused and dissatisfied without being able to help themselves. They turn their eyes away, even though philosophers, who see very well through the delusion, find little audience when they call men away for a time from this pretended popularization in order that they may rightly appear popular after they have attained a definite insight.

One need only look at the essays on morality which that popular taste favors. One will sometimes meet with the particular vocation of human nature (but occasionally also the idea of a rational nature in general), sometimes perfection, and sometimes happiness, here moral feeling, there fear of God, a little of this and a little of that in a marvelous mixture. However, it never occurs to the authors to ask whether the principles of morality are, after all, to be sought anywhere in knowledge of human nature (which we can derive only from experience). And if this is not the case, if the principles are completely a priori, free from everything empirical, and found exclusively in pure rational concepts and not at all in any other place, they never ask whether they should undertake this investigation as a separate inquiry, i.e., as pure practical philosophy or (if one may use a name so decried) a metaphysics[1] of morals. They never think of dealing with it alone and bringing it by itself to completeness, and of requiring the public, which desires popularization, to await the outcome of this undertaking.

But a completely isolated metaphysics of morals, mixed with no anthropology, no theology, no physics or hyperphysics, and even less with occult qualities (which might be called hypo-physical), is not only an indispensable substrate of all theoretically sound and definite knowledge of duties; it is also a desideratum of the highest importance to the actual fulfillment of its precepts. For the pure conception of duty and of the moral law generally, with no admixture of empirical inducements, has an influence on the human heart so much more powerful than all other incentives[2] which may be derived from the empirical field that

reason, in the consciousness of its dignity, despises them and gradually becomes master over them. It has this influence only through reason, which thereby first realizes that it can of itself be practical. A mixed theory of morals which is put together both from incentives of feelings and inclinations and from rational concepts must, on the other hand, make the mind vacillate between motives which cannot be brought under any principle and which can lead only accidentally to the good and often to the bad.

From what has been said it is clear that all moral concepts have their seat and origin entirely a priori in reason. This is just as much the case in the most ordinary reason as in reason which is speculative to the highest degree. It is obvious that they cannot be abstracted from any empirical and hence merely contingent cognitions. In the purity of their origin lies their worthiness to serve us as supreme practical principles, and to the extent that something empirical is added to them just this much is subtracted from their genuine influence and from the unqualified worth of actions. Furthermore, it is evident that it is not only of the greatest necessity in a theoretical point of view when it is a question of speculation but also of the utmost practical importance to derive the concepts and laws of morals from pure reason and to present them pure and unmixed, and to determine the scope of this entire practical but pure rational knowledge (the entire faculty of pure practical reason) without making the principles depend upon the particular nature of human reason as speculative philosophy may permit and even sometimes find necessary. But since moral laws should hold for every rational being as such, the principles must be derived from the universal concept of a rational being generally. In this manner all morals, which need anthropology for their application to men, must be completely developed first as pure philosophy, i.e., metaphysics, independently of anthropology (a thing which is easily done in such distinct fields of knowledge). For we know well that if we are not in possession of such a metaphysics, it is not merely futile to define accurately for the purposes of speculative judgment the moral element of duty in all actions which accord with duty, but impossible to base morals on legitimate principles for merely ordinary and practical use, especially in moral instruction; and it is only in this manner that pure moral dispositions can be produced and engrafted on men's minds for the purpose of the highest good in the world.

---

1. If one wishes, the pure philosophy of morals (metaphysics) can be distinguished from the applied (i.e., applied to human nature), just as pure mathematics and pure logic are distinguished from applied mathematics and applied logic. By this designation one is immediately reminded that moral principles are not founded on the peculiarities of human nature but must stand of themselves a priori, and that from such principles practical rules for every rational nature, and accordingly for man, must be derivable.

2. I have a letter from the late excellent Sulzer [Johann Georg Sulzer (1720–79), an important figure at the court and in literary circles in Berlin; cf. Allgemeine deutsche Biographie, XXXVII, 144–47] in which he asks me why the theories of virtue accomplish so little even though they contain so much that is convincing to reason. My answer was delayed in order that I might make it complete. The answer is only that the teachers themselves have not completely clarified their concepts, and when they wish to make up for this by hunting in every quarter for motives to the morally good so as to make their physic right strong, they spoil it. For the commonest observation shows that if we imagine an act of honesty performed with a steadfast soul and sundered from all view to any advantage in this or another world and even under the greatest temptations of need or allurement, it far surpasses and eclipses any similar action which was affected in the least by any foreign incentive; it elevates the soul and arouses the wish to be able to act in this way. Even moderately young children feel this impression, and one should never represent duties to them in any other way.

In this study we do not advance merely from the common moral judgment (which here is very worthy of respect) to the philosophical, as this has already been done, but we advance by natural stages from a popular philosophy (which goes no further than it can grope by means of examples) to metaphysics (which is not held back by anything empirical and which, as it must measure out the entire scope of rational knowledge of this kind, reaches even Ideas, where examples fail us). In order to make this advance, we must follow and clearly present the practical faculty of reason from its universal rules of determination to the point where the concept of duty arises from it.

Everything in nature works according to laws. Only a rational being has the capacity of acting according to the conception of laws, i.e., according to principles. This capacity is will. Since reason is required for the derivation of actions from laws, will is nothing else than practical reason. If reason infallibly determines the will, the actions which such a being recognizes as objectively necessary are also subjectively necessary. That is, the will is a faculty of choosing only that which reason, independently of inclination, recognizes as practically necessary, i.e., as good. But if reason of itself does not sufficiently determine the will, and if the will is subjugated to subjective conditions (certain incentives) which do not always agree with objective conditions; in a word, if the will is not of itself in complete accord with reason (the actual case of men), then the actions which are recognized as objectively necessary are subjectively contingent, and the determination of such a will according to objective laws is constraint. That is, the relation of objective laws to a will which is not completely good is conceived as the determination of the will of a rational being by principles of reason to which this will is not by nature necessarily obedient.

The conception of an objective principle, so far as it constrains a will, is a command (of reason), and the formula of this command is called an *imperative.*

All imperatives are expressed by an "ought" and thereby indicate the relation of an objective law of reason to a will which is not in its subjective constitution necessarily determined by this law. This relation is that of constraint. Imperatives say that it would be good to do or to refrain from doing something, but they say it to a will which does not always do something simply because it is presented as a good thing to do. Practical good is what determines the will by means of the conception of reason and hence not by

subjective causes but, rather, objectively, i.e., on grounds which are valid for every rational being as such. It is distinguished from the pleasant as that which has an influence on the will only by means of a sensation from merely subjective causes, which hold only for the senses of this or that person and not as a principle of reason which holds for everyone.[3]

A perfectly good will, therefore, would be equally subject to objective laws (of the good), but it could not be conceived as constrained by them to act in accord with them, because, according to its own subjective constitution, it can be determined to act only through the conception of the good. Thus no imperatives hold for the divine will or, more generally, for a holy will. The "ought" is here out of place, for the volition of itself is necessarily in unison with the law. Therefore imperatives are only formulas expressing the relation of objective laws of volition in general to the subjective imperfection of the will of this or that rational being, e.g., the human will.

All imperatives command either hypothetically or categorically. The former present the practical necessity of a possible action as a means to achieving something else which one desires (or which one may possibly desire). The categorical imperative would be one which presented an action as of itself objectively necessary, without regard to any other end.

Since every practical law presents a possible action as good and thus as necessary for a subject practically determinable by reason, all imperatives are formulas of the determination of action which is necessary by the principle of a will which is in any

---

3. The dependence of the faculty of desire on sensations is called inclination, and inclination always indicates a need. The dependence of a contingently determinable will on principles of reason, however, is called interest. An interest is present only in a dependent will which is not of itself always in accord with reason; in the divine will we cannot conceive of an interest. But even the human will can take an interest in something without thereby acting from interest. The former means the practical interest in the action; the latter, the pathological interest in the object of the action. The former indicates only the dependence of the will on principles of reason in themselves, while the latter indicates dependence on the principles of reason for the purpose of inclination, since reason gives only the practical rule by which the needs of inclination are to be aided. In the former case the action interests me, and in the latter the object of the action (so far as it is pleasant for me) interests me. In the first section we have seen that, in the case of an action performed from duty, no regard must be given to the interest in the object, but merely in the action itself and its principle in reason (i.e., the law).

way good. If the action is good only as a means to something else, the imperative is hypothetical; but if it is thought of as good in itself, and hence as necessary in a will which of itself conforms to reason as the principle of this will, the imperative is categorical.

The imperative thus says what action possible to me would be good, and it presents the practical rule in relation to a will which does not forthwith perform an action simply because it is good, in part because the subject does not always know that the action is good and in part (when he does know it) because his maxims can still be opposed to the objective principles of practical reason.

The hypothetical imperative, therefore, says only that the action is good to some purpose, possible or actual. In the former case it is a problematical, in the latter an assertorical, practical principle. The categorical imperative, which declares the action to be of itself objectively necessary without making any reference to a purpose, i.e., without having any other end, holds as an apodictical (practical) principle.

We can think of that which is possible through the mere powers of some rational being as a possible purpose of any will. As a consequence, the principles of action, in so far as they are thought of as necessary to attain a possible purpose which can be achieved by them, are in reality infinitely numerous. All sciences have some practical part which consists of problems of some end which is possible for us and of imperatives as to how it can be reached. These can therefore generally be called imperatives of skill. Whether the end is reasonable and good is not in question at all, for the question is only of what must be done in order to attain it. The precepts to be followed by a physician in order to cure his patient and by a poisoner in order to bring about certain death are of equal value in so far as each does that which will perfectly accomplish his purpose. Since in early youth we do not know what ends may occur to us in the course of life, parents seek to let their children learn a great many things and provide for skill in the use of means to all sorts of arbitrary ends among which they cannot determine whether any one of them may later become an actual purpose of their pupil, though it is possible that he may some day have it as his actual purpose. And this anxiety is so great that they commonly neglect to form and correct their judgment on the worth of things which they may make their ends.

There is one end, however, which we may presuppose as actual in all rational beings so far as imperatives apply to them, i.e., so far as they are dependent beings; there is one purpose not only which they *can* have but which we can presuppose that they all *do* have by a necessity of nature. This purpose is happiness. The hypothetical imperative which represents the practical necessity of action as means to the promotion of happiness is an assertorical imperative. We may not expound it as merely necessary to an uncertain and a merely possible purpose, but as necessary to a purpose which we can a priori and with assurance assume for everyone because it belongs to his essence. Skill in the choice of means to one's own highest welfare can be called prudence[4] in the narrowest sense. Thus the imperative which refers to the choice of means to one's own happiness, i.e., the precept of prudence, is still only hypothetical; the action is not absolutely commanded but commanded only as a means to another end.

Finally, there is one imperative which directly commands a certain conduct without making its condition some purpose to be reached by it. This imperative is categorical. It concerns not the material of the action and its intended result but the form and the principle from which it results. What is essentially good in it consists in the intention, the result being what it may. This imperative may be called the imperative of morality.

Volition according to these three principles is plainly distinguished by dissimilarity in the constraint to which they subject the will. In order to clarify this dissimilarity, I believe that they are most suitably named if one says that they are either rules of skill, counsels of prudence, or commands (laws) of morality, respectively. For law alone implies the concept of an unconditional and objective and hence universally valid necessity, and commands are laws which must

---

4. The word "prudence" may be taken in two senses, and it may bear the name of prudence with reference to things of the world and private prudence. The former sense means the skill of a man in having an influence on others so as to use them for his own purposes. The latter is the ability to unite all these purposes to his own lasting advantage. The worth of the first is finally reduced to the latter, and of one who is prudent in the former sense but not in the latter we might better say that he is clever and cunning yet, on the whole, imprudent.

be obeyed, even against inclination. Counsels do indeed involve necessity, but a necessity that can hold only under a subjectively contingent condition, i.e., whether this or that man counts this or that as part of his happiness; but the categorical imperative, on the other hand, is restricted by no condition. As absolutely, though practically, necessary it can be called a command in the strict sense. We could also call the first imperative technical (belonging to art), the second pragmatic[5] (belonging to welfare), and the third moral (belonging to free conduct as such, i.e., to morals).

The question now arises: how are all these imperatives possible? This question does not require an answer as to how the action which the imperative commands can be performed but merely as to how the constraint of the will, which the imperative expresses in the problem, can be conceived. How an imperative of skill is possible requires no particular discussion. Whoever wills the end, so far as reason has decisive influence on his action, wills also the indispensably necessary means to it that lie in his power. This proposition, in what concerns the will, is analytical; for, in willing an object as my effect, my causality as an acting cause, i.e., the use of the means, is already thought, and the imperative derives the concept of necessary actions to this end from the concept of willing this end. Synthetical propositions undoubtedly are necessary in determining the means to a proposed end, but they do not concern the ground, the act of the will, but only the way to make the object real. Mathematics teaches, by synthetical propositions only, that in order to bisect a line according to an infallible principle I must make two intersecting arcs from each of its extremities; but if I know the proposed result can be obtained only by such an action, then it is an analytical proposition that, if I fully will the effect, I must also will the action necessary to produce it. For it is one and the same

thing to conceive of something as an effect which is in a certain way possible through me and to conceive of myself as acting in this way.

If it were only easy to give a definite concept of happiness, the imperatives of prudence would completely correspond to those of skill and would be likewise analytical. For it could be said in this case as well as in the former that whoever wills the end wills also (necessarily according to reason) the only means to it which are in his power. But it is a misfortune that the concept of happiness is so indefinite that, although each person wishes to attain it, he can never definitely and self-consistently state what it is he really wishes and wills. The reason for this is that all elements which belong to the concept of happiness are empirical, i.e., they must be taken from experience, while for the idea of happiness an absolute whole, a maximum, of well-being is needed in my present and in every future condition. Now it is impossible even for a most clear-sighted and most capable but finite being to form here a definite concept of that which he really wills. If he wills riches, how much anxiety, envy, and intrigue might he not thereby draw upon his shoulders! If he wills much knowledge and vision, perhaps it might become only an eye that much sharper to show him as more dreadful the evils which are now hidden from him and which are yet unavoidable, or to burden his desires—which already sufficiently engage him—with even more needs! If he wills a long life, who guarantees that it will not be long misery? If he wills at least health, how often has not the discomfort of the body restrained him from excesses into which perfect health would have led him? In short, he is not capable, on any principle and with complete certainty, of ascertaining what would make him truly happy; omniscience would be needed for this. He cannot, therefore, act according to definite principles so as to be happy, but only according to empirical counsels, e.g., those of diet, economy, courtesy, restraint, etc., which are shown by experience best to promote welfare on the average. Hence the imperatives of prudence cannot, in the strict sense, command, i.e., present actions objectively as practically necessary; thus they are to be taken as counsels (*consilia*) rather than as commands (*praecepta*) of reason, and the task of determining infallibly and universally what action will promote the happiness of a rational being is completely unsolvable. There can be no

5. It seems to me that the proper meaning of the word "pragmatic" could be most accurately defined in this way. For sanctions which properly flow not from the law of states as necessary statutes but from provision for the general welfare are called pragmatic. A history is pragmatically composed when it teaches prudence, i.e., instructs the world how it could provide for its interest better than, or at least as well as, has been done in the past.

imperative which would, in the strict sense, command us to do what makes for happiness, because happiness is an ideal not of reason but of imagination, depending only on empirical grounds which one would expect in vain to determine an action through which the totality of consequences—which is in fact infinite—could be achieved. Assuming that the means to happiness could be infallibly stated, this imperative of prudence would be an analytical proposition, for it differs from the imperative of skill only in that its end is given while in the latter case it is merely possible. Since both, however, only command the means to that which one presupposes, the imperative which commands the willing of the means to him who wills the end is in both cases analytical. There is, consequently, no difficulty in seeing the possibility of such an imperative.

To see how the imperative of morality is possible is, then, without doubt the only question needing an answer. It is not hypothetical, and thus the objectively conceived necessity cannot be supported by any presupposition, as was the case with the hypothetical imperatives. But it must not be overlooked that it cannot be shown by any example (i.e., it cannot be empirically shown) whether or not there is such an imperative; it is rather to be suspected that all imperatives which appear to be categorical may yet be hypothetical, but in a hidden way. For instance, when it is said, "Thou shalt not make a false promise," we assume that the necessity of this avoidance is not a mere counsel for the sake of escaping some other evil, so that it would read, "Thou shalt not make a false promise so that, if it comes to light, thou ruinest thy credit"; we assume rather that an action of this kind must be regarded as of itself bad and that the imperative of the prohibition is categorical. But we cannot show with certainty by any example that the will is here determined by the law alone without any other incentives, even though this appears to be the case. For it is always possible that secret fear of disgrace, and perhaps also obscure apprehension of other dangers, may have had an influence on the will. Who can prove by experience the non-existence of a cause when experience shows us only that we do not perceive the cause? But in such a case the so-called moral imperative, which as such appears to be categorical and unconditional, would be actually only a pragmatic precept which makes us attentive to our own advantage and teaches us to consider it.

Thus we shall have to investigate purely a priori the possibility of a categorical imperative, for we do not have the advantage that experience would give us the reality of this imperative, so that the [demonstration of its] possibility would be necessary only for its explanation and not for its establishment. In the meantime, this much may at least be seen: the categorical imperative alone can be taken as a practical *law*, while all the others may be called principles of the will but not laws. This is because what is necessary merely for the attainment of an arbitrary purpose can be regarded as itself contingent, and we get rid of the precept once we give up the purpose, whereas the unconditional command leaves the will no freedom to choose the opposite. Thus it alone implies the necessity which we require of a law.

Secondly, in the case of the categorical imperative or law of morality, the cause of difficulty in discerning its possibility is very weighty. This imperative is an a priori synthetical practical proposition,[6] and, since to discern the possibility of propositions of this sort is so difficult in theoretical knowledge, it may well be gathered that it will be no less difficult in the practical.

In attacking this problem, we will first inquire whether the mere concept of a categorical imperative does not also furnish the formula containing the proposition which alone can be a categorical imperative. For even when we know the formula of the imperative, to learn how such an absolute law is possible will require difficult and special labors which we shall postpone to the last section.

If I think of a hypothetical imperative as such, I do not know what it will contain until the condition is stated [under which it is an imperative]. But if I think of a categorical imperative, I know immediately what it contains. For since the imperative contains besides the law only the necessity that the maxim[7] should

---

6. I connect a priori, and hence necessarily, the action with the will without supposing as a condition that there is any inclination [to the action] (though I do so only objectively, i.e., under the idea of a reason which would have complete power over all subjective motives). This is, therefore, a practical proposition which does not analytically derive the willing of an action from some other volition already presupposed (for we do not have such a perfect will); it rather connects it directly with the concept of the will of a rational being as something which is not contained within it.

7. A maxim is the subjective principle of acting and must be distinguished from the objective principle, i.e., the practical law.

accord with this law, while the law contains no condition to which it is restricted, there is nothing remaining in it except the universality of law as such to which the maxim of the action should conform; and in effect this conformity alone is represented as necessary by the imperative.

There is, therefore, only one categorical imperative. It is: Act only according to that maxim by which you can at the same time will that it should become a universal law.

Now if all imperatives of duty can be derived from this one imperative as a principle, we can at least show what we understand by the concept of duty and what it means, even though it remain undecided whether that which is called duty is an empty concept or not.

The universality of law according to which effects are produced constitutes what is properly called nature in the most general sense (as to form), i.e., the existence of things so far as it is determined by universal laws. [By analogy], then, the universal imperative of duty can be expressed as follows: Act as though the maxim of your action were by your will to become a universal law of nature.

We shall now enumerate some duties, adopting the usual division of them into duties to ourselves and to others and into perfect and imperfect duties.[8]

1. A man who is reduced to despair by a series of evils feels a weariness with life but is still in possession of his reason sufficiently to ask whether it would not be contrary to his duty to himself to take his own life. Now he asks whether the maxim of his action could become a universal law of nature. His maxim, however, is: For love of myself, I make it my principle to shorten my life when by a longer duration it threatens more evil than satisfaction. But it is questionable whether this principle of self-love could become a universal law of nature. One immediately sees a contradiction in a system of nature whose law would be to destroy life by the feeling whose special office is to impel the improvement of life. In this case it would not exist as nature; hence that maxim cannot obtain as a law of nature, and thus it wholly contradicts the supreme principle of all duty.

2. Another man finds himself forced by need to borrow money. He well knows that he will not be able to repay it, but he also sees that nothing will be loaned him if he does not firmly promise to repay it at a certain time. He desires to make such a promise, but he has enough conscience to ask himself whether it is not improper and opposed to duty to relieve his distress in such a way. Now, assuming he does decide to do so, the maxim of his action would be as follows: When I believe myself to be in need of money, I will borrow money and promise to repay it, although I know I shall never do so. Now this principle of self-love or of his own benefit may very well be compatible with his whole future welfare, but the question is whether it is right. He changes the pretension of self-love into a universal law and then puts the question: How would it be if my maxim became a universal law? He immediately sees that it could never hold as a universal law of nature and be consistent with itself; rather it must necessarily contradict itself. For the universality of a law which says that anyone who believes himself to be in need could promise what he pleased with the intention of not fulfilling it would make the promise itself and the end to be accomplished by it impossible; no one would believe what was promised to him but would only laugh at any such assertion as vain pretense.

3. A third finds in himself a talent which could, by means of some cultivation, make him in many respects a useful man. But he finds himself in comfortable circumstances and prefers indulgence in pleasure to troubling himself with broadening and improving his fortunate natural gifts. Now, however, let him ask whether his maxim of neglecting his gifts, besides agreeing with his propensity to idle amusement, agrees also with what is called duty. He sees that a system of nature could indeed exist in accordance with such a law, even though man (like the inhabitants of the South Sea Islands) should let his

<hr/>

The former contains the practical rule which reason determines according to the conditions of the subject (often its ignorance or inclinations) and is thus the principle according to which the subject acts. The law, on the other hand, is the objective principle valid for every rational being, and the principle by which it ought to act, i.e., an imperative.

8. It must be noted here that I reserve the division of duties for a future *Metaphysics of Morals* and that the division here stands as only an arbitrary one (chosen in order to arrange my examples). For the rest, by a perfect duty I here understand a duty which permits no exception in the interest of inclination; thus I have not merely outer but also inner perfect duties. This runs contrary to the usage adopted in the schools, but I am not disposed to defend it here because it is all one to my purpose whether this is conceded or not.

talents rust and resolve to devote his life merely to idleness, indulgence, and propagation—in a word, to pleasure. But he cannot possibly will that this should become a universal law of nature or that it should be implanted in us by a natural instinct. For, as a rational being, he necessarily wills that all his faculties should be developed, inasmuch as they are given to him for all sorts of possible purposes.

4. A fourth man, for whom things are going well, sees that others (whom he could help) have to struggle with great hardships, and he asks, "What concern of mine is it? Let each one be as happy as heaven wills, or as he can make himself; I will not take anything from him or even envy him; but to his welfare or to his assistance in time of need I have no desire to contribute." If such a way of thinking were a universal law of nature, certainly the human race could exist, and without doubt even better than in a state where everyone talks of sympathy and good will, or even exerts himself occasionally to practice them while, on the other hand, he cheats when he can and betrays or otherwise violates the rights of man. Now although it is possible that a universal law of nature according to that maxim could exist, it is nevertheless impossible to will that such a principle should hold everywhere as a law of nature. For a will which resolved this would conflict with itself, since instances can often arise in which he would need the love and sympathy of others, and in which he would have robbed himself, by such a law of nature springing from his own will, of all hope of the aid he desires.

The foregoing are a few of the many actual duties, or at least of duties we hold to be actual, whose derivation from the one stated principle is clear. We must be able to will that a maxim of our action become a universal law; this is the canon of the moral estimation of our action generally. Some actions are of such a nature that their maxim cannot even be *thought* as a universal law of nature without contradiction, far from it being possible that one could will that it should be such. In others this internal impossibility is not found, though it is still impossible to *will* that their maxim should be raised to the universality of a law of nature, because such a will would contradict itself. We easily see that the former maxim conflicts with the stricter or narrower (imprescriptible) duty, the latter with broader (meritorious) duty. Thus all duties, so far as the kind of obligation (not the object of their action) is concerned, have been completely exhibited by these examples in their dependence on the one principle.

When we observe ourselves in any transgression of a duty, we find that we do not actually will that our maxim should become a universal law. That is impossible for us; rather, the contrary of this maxim should remain as a law generally, and we only take the liberty of making an exception to it for ourselves or for the sake of our inclination, and for this one occasion. Consequently, if we weighed everything from one and the same standpoint, namely, reason, we would come upon a contradiction in our own will, viz., that a certain principle is objectively necessary as a universal law and yet subjectively does not hold universally but rather admits exceptions. However, since we regard our action at one time from the point of view of a will wholly conformable to reason and then from that of a will affected by inclinations, there is actually no contradiction, but rather an opposition of inclination to the precept of reason (*antagonismus*). In this the universality of the principle (*universalitas*) is changed into mere generality (*generalitas*), whereby the practical principle of reason meets the maxim halfway. Although this cannot be justified in our own impartial judgment, it does show that we actually acknowledge the validity of the categorical imperative and allow ourselves (with all respect to it) only a few exceptions which seem to us to be unimportant and forced upon us.

We have thus at least established that if duty is a concept which is to have significance and actual legislation for our actions, it can be expressed only in categorical imperatives and not at all in hypothetical ones. For every application of it we have also clearly exhibited the content of the categorical imperative which must contain the principle of all duty (if there is such). This is itself very much. But we are not yet advanced far enough to prove a priori that that kind of imperative really exists, that there is a practical law which of itself commands absolutely and without any incentives, and that obedience to this law is duty.

With a view to attaining this, it is extremely important to remember that we must not let ourselves think that the reality of this principle can be derived from the particular constitution of human nature. For duty is practical unconditional necessity of action; it must, therefore, hold for all rational beings (to which alone an imperative can apply), and only for that reason can it be a law for all human wills. Whatever is derived from the particular natural situation of man as such, or from certain feelings and propensities, or even from a particular tendency of the human reason which might not hold necessarily for the will of every rational being (if such a tendency is possible), can give a maxim valid for us but not a law; that is, it can give a subjective principle by which we might act only if we have the propensity and inclination, but not an objective principle by which we would be directed to act even if all our propensity, inclination, and natural tendency were opposed to it. This is so far the case that the sublimity and intrinsic worth of the command is the better shown in a duty the fewer subjective causes there are for it and the more there are against it; the latter do not weaken the constraint of the law or diminish its validity.

Here we see philosophy brought to what is, in fact, a precarious position, which should be made fast even though it is supported by nothing in either heaven or earth. Here philosophy must show its purity as the absolute sustainer of its laws, and not as the herald of those which an implanted sense or who knows what tutelary nature whispers to it. Those may be better than no laws at all, but they can never afford fundamental principles, which reason alone dictates. These fundamental principles must originate entirely a priori and thereby obtain their commanding authority; they can expect nothing from the inclination of men but everything from the supremacy of the law and due respect for it. Otherwise they condemn man to self-contempt and inner abhorrence.

Thus everything empirical is not only wholly unworthy to be an ingredient in the principle of morality but is even highly prejudicial to the purity of moral practices themselves. For, in morals, the proper and inestimable worth of an absolutely good will consists precisely in the freedom of the principle of action from all influences from contingent grounds which only experience can furnish. We cannot too much or too often warn against the lax or even base manner of thought which seeks principles among empirical motives and laws, for human reason in its weariness is glad to rest on this pillow. In a dream of sweet illusions (in which it embraces not Juno but a cloud), it substitutes for morality a bastard patched up from limbs of very different parentage, which looks like anything one wishes to see in it, but not like virtue to anyone who has ever beheld her in her true form.[9]

The question then is: Is it a necessary law for all rational beings that they should always judge their actions by such maxims as they themselves could will to serve as universal laws? If it is such a law, it must be connected (wholly a priori) with the concept of the will of a rational being as such. But in order to discover this connection we must, however reluctantly, take a step into metaphysics, although into a region of it different from speculative philosophy, i.e., into metaphysics of morals. In a practical philosophy it is not a question of assuming grounds for what happens but of assuming laws of what ought to happen even though it may never happen—that is to say, objective, practical laws. Hence in practical philosophy we need not inquire into the reasons why something pleases or displeases, how the pleasure of mere feeling differs from taste, and whether this is distinct from a general satisfaction of reason. Nor need we ask on what the feeling of pleasure or displeasure rests, how desires and inclinations arise, and how, finally, maxims arise from desires and inclination under the co-operation of reason. For all these matters belong to an empirical psychology, which would be the second part of physics if we consider it as philosophy of nature so far as it rests on empirical laws. But here it is a question of objectively practical laws and thus of the relation of a will to itself so far as it determines itself only by reason; for everything which has a relation to the empirical automatically falls away, because if reason of itself alone determines conduct it must necessarily do so a priori. The possibility of reason thus determining conduct must now be investigated.

The will is thought of as a faculty of determining itself to action in accordance with the conception of certain laws. Such a faculty can be found only in rational beings. That which serves the will as the objective ground of its self-determination is an end, and, if it is given by reason alone, it must hold alike for all rational beings. On the other hand, that which contains the ground of the possibility of the action, whose result is an end, is called the means. The subjective ground of desire is the incentive, while the objective ground of volition is the motive. Thus arises the distinction between subjective ends, which rest

_____
9. To behold virtue in her proper form is nothing else than to exhibit morality stripped of all admixture of sensuous things and of every spurious adornment of reward or self-love. How much she then eclipses everything which appears charming to the senses can easily be seen by everyone with the least effort of his reason, if it be not spoiled for all abstraction.

on incentives, and objective ends, which depend on motives valid for every rational being. Practical principles are formal when they disregard all subjective ends; they are material when they have subjective ends, and thus certain incentives, as their basis. The ends which a rational being arbitrarily proposes to himself as consequences of his action are material ends and are without exception only relative, for only their relation to a particularly constituted faculty of desire in the subject gives them their worth. And this worth cannot, therefore, afford any universal principles for all rational beings or valid and necessary principles for every volition. That is, they cannot give rise to any practical laws. All these relative ends, therefore, are grounds for hypothetical imperatives only.

But suppose that there were something the existence of which in itself had absolute worth, something which, as an end in itself, could be a ground of definite laws. In it and only in it could lie the ground of a possible categorical imperative, i.e., of a practical law.

Now, I say, man and, in general, every rational being exists as an end in himself and not merely as a means to be arbitrarily used by this or that will. In all his actions, whether they are directed to himself or to other rational beings, he must always be regarded at the same time as an end. All objects of inclinations have only a conditional worth, for if the inclinations and the needs founded on them did not exist, their object would be without worth. The inclinations themselves as the sources of needs, however, are so lacking in absolute worth that the universal wish of every rational being must be indeed to free himself completely from them. Therefore, the worth of any objects to be obtained by our actions is at all times conditional. Beings whose existence does not depend on our will but on nature, if they are not rational beings, have only a relative worth as means and are therefore called "things"; on the other hand, rational beings are designated "persons" because their nature indicates that they are ends in themselves, i.e., things which may not be used merely as means. Such a being is thus an object of respect and, so far, restricts all [arbitrary] choice. Such beings are not merely subjective ends whose existence as a result of our action has a worth for us, but are objective ends, i.e., beings whose existence in itself is an end. Such an end is one for which no other end can be substituted, to which these beings should serve merely as means. For, with-out them, nothing of absolute worth could be found, and if all worth is conditional and thus contingent, no supreme practical principle for reason could be found anywhere.

Thus if there is to be a supreme practical principle and a categorical imperative for the human will, it must be one that forms an objective principle of the will from the conception of that which is necessarily an end for everyone because it is an end in itself. Hence this objective principle can serve as a universal practical law. The ground of this principle is: rational nature exists as an end in itself. Man necessarily thinks of his own existence in this way; thus far it is a subjective principle of human actions. Also every other rational being thinks of his existence by means of the same rational ground which holds also for myself;[10] thus it is at the same time an objective principle from which, as a supreme practical ground, it must be possible to derive all laws of the will. The practical imperative, therefore, is the following: Act so that you treat humanity, whether in your own person or in that of another, always as an end and never as a means only. Let us now see whether this can be achieved.

To return to our previous examples:

First, according to the concept of necessary duty to one's self, he who contemplates suicide will ask himself whether his action can be consistent with the idea of humanity as an end in itself. If, in order to escape from burdensome circumstances, he destroys himself, he uses a person merely as a means to maintain a tolerable condition up to the end of life. Man, however, is not a thing, and thus not something to be used merely as a means; he must always be regarded in all his actions as an end in himself. Therefore, I cannot dispose of man in my own person so as to mutilate, corrupt, or kill him. (It belongs to ethics proper to define more accurately this basic principle so as to avoid all misunderstanding, e.g., as to the amputation of limbs in order to preserve myself, or to exposing my life to danger in order to save it; I must, therefore, omit them here.)

Second, as concerns necessary or obligatory duties to others, he who intends a deceitful promise to others sees immediately that he intends to use

---

10. Here I present this proposition as a postulate, but in the last section grounds for it will be found.

another man merely as a means, without the latter containing the end in himself at the same time. For he whom I want to use for my own purposes by means of such a promise cannot possibly assent to my mode of acting against him and cannot contain the end of this action in himself. This conflict against the principle of other men is even clearer if we cite examples of attacks on their freedom and property. For then it is clear that he who transgresses the rights of men intends to make use of the persons of others merely as a means, without considering that, as rational beings, they must always be esteemed at the same time as ends, i.e., only as beings who must be able to contain in themselves the end of the very same action.[11]

Third, with regard to contingent (meritorious) duty to one's self, it is not sufficient that the action not conflict with humanity in our person as an end in itself; it must also harmonize with it. Now in humanity there are capacities for greater perfection which belong to the end of nature with respect to humanity in our own person; to neglect these might perhaps be consistent with the preservation of humanity as an end in itself but not with the furtherance of that end.

Fourth, with regard to meritorious duty to others, the natural end which all men have is their own happiness. Humanity might indeed exist if no one contributed to the happiness of others, provided he did not intentionally detract from it; but this harmony with humanity as an end in itself is only negative rather than positive if everyone does not also endeavor, so far as he can, to further the ends of others. For the ends of any person, who is an end in himself, must as far as possible also be my end, if that conception of an end in itself is to have its full effect on me.

This principle of humanity and of every rational creature as an end in itself is the supreme limiting condition on freedom of the actions of each man. It is not borrowed from experience, first, because of its

11. Let it not be thought that the banal "*quod tibi non vis fieri, etc.,*" could here serve as guide or principle, for it is only derived from the principle and is restricted by various limitations. It cannot be a universal law, because it contains the ground neither of duties to one's self nor of the benevolent duties to others (for many a man would gladly consent that others should not benefit him, provided only that he might be excused from showing benevolence to them). Nor does it contain the ground of obligatory duties to another, for the criminal would argue on this ground against the judge who sentences him. And so on.

universality, since it applies to all rational beings generally and experience does not suffice to determine anything about them; and, secondly, because in experience humanity is not thought of (subjectively) as the end of men, i.e., as an object which we of ourselves really make our end. Rather it is thought of as the objective end which should constitute the supreme limiting condition of all subjective ends, whatever they may be. Thus this principle must arise from pure reason. Objectively the ground of all practical legislation lies (according to the first principle) in the rule and in the form of universality, which makes it capable of being a law (at most a natural law); subjectively, it lies in the end. But the subject of all ends is every rational being as an end in itself (by the second principle); from this there follows the third practical principle of the will as the supreme condition of its harmony with universal practical reason, viz., the idea of the will of every rational being as making universal law.

By this principle all maxims are rejected which are not consistent with the universal lawgiving of will. The will is thus not only subject to the law but subject in such a way that it must be regarded also as self-legislative and only for this reason as being subject to the law (of which it can regard itself as the author).

In the foregoing mode of conception, in which imperatives are conceived universally either as conformity to law by actions—a conformity which is similar to a natural order—or as the prerogative of rational beings as such, the imperatives exclude from their legislative authority all admixture of any interest as an incentive. They do so because they were conceived as categorical. They were only assumed to be categorical, however, because we had to make such an assumption if we wished to explain the concept of duty. But that there were practical propositions which commanded categorically could not here be proved independently, just as little as it can be proved anywhere in this section. One thing, however, might have been done: to indicate in the imperative itself, by some determination which it contained, that in volition from duty the renunciation of all interest is the specific mark of the categorical imperative, distinguishing it from the hypothetical. And this is now being done in the third formulation of the principle, i.e., in the idea of the will of every rational being as a will giving universal law. A will which stands under laws can be bound to this law by an interest. But if we think of a will giving universal laws, we find that a supreme legislating will cannot possibly depend on any interest, for such a dependent will would itself need still another law which would restrict the interest of its self-love to the condition that [the maxims of this will] should be valid as universal law.

Thus the principle of every human will as a will giving universal laws in all its maxims[12] is very well adapted to being a categorical imperative, provided it is otherwise correct. Because of the idea of universal lawgiving, it is based on no interest, and, thus of all possible imperatives, it alone can be unconditional. Or, better, converting the proposition: if there is a categorical imperative (a law for the will of every rational being), it can only command that everything be done from the maxim of its will as one which could have as its object only itself considered as giving universal laws. For only in this case are the practical principle and the imperative which the will obeys unconditional, because the will can have no interest as its foundation.

If we now look back upon all previous attempts which have ever been undertaken to discover the principle of morality, it is not to be wondered at that they all had to fail. Man was seen to be bound to laws by his duty, but it was not seen that he is subject only to his own, yet universal, legislation, and that he is only bound to act in accordance with his own will, which is, however, designed by nature to be a will giving universal laws. For if one thought of him as subject only to a law (whatever it may be), this necessarily implied some interest as a stimulus or compulsion to obedience because the law did not arise from his will. Rather, his will was constrained by something else according to a law to act in a certain way. By this strictly necessary consequence, however, all the labor of finding a supreme ground for duty was irrevocably lost, and one never arrived at duty but only at the necessity of action from a certain interest. This might be his own interest or that of another, but in either case the imperative always had to be conditional and could not at all serve as a moral command. This principle I will call the principle of *autonomy* of the will in contrast to all other principles which I accordingly count under *heteronomy*.

---

12. I may be excused from citing examples to elucidate this principle, for those which have already illustrated the categorical imperative and its formula can here serve the same purpose.

The concept of each rational being as a being that must regard itself as giving universal law through all the maxims of its will, so that it may judge itself and its actions from this standpoint, leads to a very fruitful concept, namely, that of a *realm of ends*.

By "realm" I understand the systematic union of different rational beings through common laws. Because laws determine ends with regard to their universal validity, if we abstract from the personal difference of rational beings and thus from all content of their private ends, we can think of a whole of all ends in systematic connection, a whole of rational beings as ends in themselves as well as of the particular ends which each may set for himself. This is a realm of ends, which is possible on the aforesaid principles. For all rational beings stand under the law that each of them should treat himself and all others never merely as means but in every case also as an end in himself. Thus there arises a systematic union of rational beings through common objective laws. This is a realm which may be called a realm of ends (certainly only an ideal), because what these laws have in view is just the relation of these beings to each other as ends and means.

A rational being belongs to the realm of ends as a member when he gives universal laws in it while also himself subject to these laws. He belongs to it as sovereign when he, as legislating, is subject to the will of no other. The rational being must regard himself always as legislative in a realm of ends possible through the freedom of the will, whether he belongs to it as member or as sovereign. He cannot maintain the latter position merely through the maxims of his will but only when he is a completely independent being without need and with power adequate to his will.

Morality, therefore, consists in the relation of every action to that legislation through which alone a realm of ends is possible. This legislation, however, must be found in every rational being. It must be able to arise from his will, whose principle then is to take no action according to any maxim which would be inconsistent with its being a universal law and thus to act only so that the will through its maxims could regard itself at the same time as universally lawgiving. If now the maxims do not by their nature already necessarily conform to this objective principle of rational beings as universally lawgiving, the necessity of acting according to that principle is called practical constraint, i.e., duty. Duty pertains not to the sovereign in the realm of ends, but rather to each member, and to each in the same degree.

The practical necessity of acting according to this principle, i.e., duty, does not rest at all on feelings, impulses, and inclinations; it rests merely on the relation of rational beings to one another, in which the will of a rational being must always be regarded as legislative, for otherwise it could not be thought of as an end in itself. Reason, therefore, relates every maxim of the will as giving universal laws to every other will and also to every action toward itself; it does so not for the sake of any other practical motive or future advantage but rather from the idea of the dignity of a rational being who obeys no law except that which he himself also gives.

In the realm of ends everything has either a *price* or a *dignity*. Whatever has a price can be replaced by something else as its equivalent; on the other hand, whatever is above all price, and therefore admits of no equivalent, has a dignity.

That which is related to general human inclinations and needs has a *market price*. That which, without presupposing any need, accords with a certain taste, i.e., with pleasure in the mere purposeless play of our faculties, has an *affective price*. But that which constitutes the condition under which alone something can be an end in itself does not have mere relative worth, i.e., a price, but an intrinsic worth, i.e., *dignity*.

Now morality is the condition under which alone a rational being can be an end in itself, because only through it is it possible to be a legislative member in the realm of ends. Thus morality and humanity, so far as it is capable of morality, alone have dignity. Skill and diligence in work have a market value; wit, lively imagination, and humor have an affective price; but fidelity in promises and benevolence on principle (not from instinct) have intrinsic worth. Nature and likewise art contain nothing which could replace their lack, for their worth consists not in effects which flow from them, nor in advantage and utility which they procure; it consists only in intentions, i.e., maxims of the will which are ready to reveal themselves in this manner through actions even though success does not favor them. These actions need no recommendation from any subjective disposition or taste in order that they may be looked upon with immediate favor and satisfaction, nor do they have need of any immediate propensity or feeling directed to them. They exhibit the will which performs them as the object of an immediate respect, since nothing but reason is required in order to impose them on the will. The will is not to be cajoled into them, for this, in the case of

duties, would be a contradiction. This esteem lets the worth of such a turn of mind be recognized as dignity and puts it infinitely beyond any price, with which it cannot in the least be brought into competition or comparison without, as it were, violating its holiness.

And what is it that justifies the morally good disposition or virtue in making such lofty claims? It is nothing less than the participation it affords the rational being in giving universal laws. He is thus fitted to be a member in a possible realm of ends to which his own nature already destined him. For, as an end in himself, he is destined to be legislative in the realm of ends, free from all laws of nature and obedient only to those which he himself gives. Accordingly, his maxims can belong to a universal legislation to which he is at the same time also subject. A thing has no worth other than that determined for it by the law. The legislation which determines all worth must therefore have a dignity, i.e., unconditional and incomparable worth. For the esteem which a rational being must have for it, only the word "respect" is a suitable expression. Autonomy is thus the basis of the dignity of both human nature and every rational nature.

The three aforementioned ways of presenting the principle of morality are fundamentally only so many formulas of the very same law, and each of them unites the others in itself. There is, nevertheless, a difference in them, but the difference is more subjectively than objectively practical, for it is intended to bring an idea of reason closer to intuition (by means of a certain analogy) and thus nearer to feeling. All maxims have:

1. A form, which consists in universality; and in this respect the formula of the moral imperative requires that the maxims be chosen as though they should hold as universal laws of nature.

2. A material, i.e., an end; in this respect the formula says that the rational being, as by its nature an end and thus as an end in itself, must serve in every maxim as the condition restricting all merely relative and arbitrary ends.

3. A complete determination of all maxims by the formula that all maxims which stem from autonomous legislation ought to harmonize with a possible realm of ends as with a realm of nature.[13]

---

13. Teleology considers nature as a realm of ends; morals regards a possible realm of ends as a realm of nature. In the former the

There is a progression here like that through the categories of the unity of the form of the will (its universality), the plurality of material (the objects, i.e., the ends), and the all-comprehensiveness or totality of the system of ends. But it is better in moral evaluation to follow the rigorous method and to make the universal formula of the categorical imperative the basis: Act according to the maxim which can at the same time make itself a universal law. But if one wishes to gain a hearing for the moral law, it is very useful to bring one and the same action under the three stated principles and thus, so far as possible, to bring it nearer to intuition.

We can now end where we started, with the concept of an unconditionally good will. That will is absolutely good which cannot be bad, and thus it is a will whose maxim, when made a universal law, can never conflict with itself. Thus this principle is also its supreme law: Always act according to that maxim whose universality as a law you can at the same time will. This is the only condition under which a will can never come into conflict with itself, and such an imperative is categorical. Because the validity of the will, as a universal law for possible actions, has an analogy with the universal connection of the existence of things under universal laws, which is the formal element of nature in general, the categorical imperative can also be expressed as follows: Act according to maxims which can at the same time have themselves as universal laws of nature as their object. Such, then, is the formula of an absolutely good will.

Rational nature is distinguished from others in that it proposes an end to itself. This end would be the material of every good will. Since, however, in the idea of an absolutely good will without any limiting condition of the attainment of this or that end, every end to be effected must be completely abstracted (as any particular end would make each will only relatively good), the end here is not conceived as one to be effected but as an independent end, and thus merely negatively. It is that which must never be acted against, and which must consequently never be valued as merely a means but in every volition also as

an end. Now this end can never be other than the subject of all possible ends themselves, because this is at the same time the subject of a possible will which is absolutely good; for the latter cannot be made secondary to any other object without contradiction. The principle: Act with reference to every rational being (whether yourself or another) so that it is an end in itself in your maxim, is thus basically identical with the principle: Act by a maxim which involves its own universal validity for every rational being.

That in the use of means to every end I should restrict my maxim to the condition of its universal validity as a law for every subject is tantamount to saying that the subject of ends, i.e., the rational being itself, must be made the basis of all maxims of actions and must thus be treated never as a mere means but as the supreme limiting condition in the use of all means, i.e., as an end at the same time.

It follows incontestably that every rational being must be able to regard himself as an end in himself with reference to all laws to which he may be subject, whatever they may be, and thus as giving universal laws. For it is just the fitness of his maxims to a universal legislation that indicates that he is an end in himself. It also follows that his dignity (his prerogative) over all merely natural beings entails that he must take his maxims from the point of view which regards himself, and hence also every other rational being, as legislative. (The rational beings are, on this account, called persons.) In this way, a world of rational beings (*mundus intelligibilis*) is possible as a realm of ends, because of the legislation belonging to all persons as members. Consequently, every rational being must act as if he, by his maxims, were at all times a legislative member in the universal realm of ends. The formal principle of these maxims is: So act as if your maxims should serve at the same time as the universal law (of all rational beings). A realm of ends is thus possible only by analogy with a realm of nature. The former, however, is possible only by maxims, i.e., self-imposed rules, while the latter is possible by laws of efficient causes of things externally necessitated. Regardless of this difference, by analogy we call the natural whole a realm of nature so far as it is related to rational beings as its end; we do so even though the natural whole is looked at as a machine. Such a realm of ends would actually be realized through maxims whose rule is prescribed to all rational beings by the categorical imperative, if they were universally obeyed. But a rational being, though

---

realm of ends is a theoretical idea for the explanation of what actually is. In the latter it is a practical idea for bringing about that which is not actually real but which can become real through our conduct, and which is in accordance with this idea.

he scrupulously follow this maxim, cannot for that reason expect every other rational being to be true to it; nor can he expect the realm of nature and its orderly design to harmonize with him as a fitting member of a realm of ends which is possible through himself. That is, he cannot count on its favoring his expectation of happiness. Still the law: Act according to the maxims of a universally legislative member of a merely potential realm of ends, remains in full force, because it commands categorically. And just in this lies the paradox that merely the dignity of humanity as rational nature without any end or advantage to be gained by it, and thus respect for a mere idea, should serve as the inflexible precept of the will. There is the further paradox that the sublimity of the maxims and the worthiness of every rational subject to be a legislative member in the realm of ends consist precisely in independence of the maxims from all such incentives. Otherwise he would have to be viewed as subject only to the natural law of his needs. Although the realm of nature as well as that of ends would be thought of as united under a sovereign so that the latter would no longer remain a mere idea but would receive true reality, the realm of ends would undoubtedly gain a strong urge in its favor, but its intrinsic worth would not be augmented. Regardless of this, even the one and only absolute legislator would still have to be conceived as judging the worth of rational beings only by the disinterested conduct which they prescribe to themselves merely from the idea [of dignity]. The essence of things is not changed by their external relations, and without reference to these relations a man must be judged only by what constitutes his absolute worth; and this is true whoever his judge is, even if it be the Supreme Being. Morality is thus the relation of actions to the autonomy of the will, i.e., to possible universal lawgiving by maxims of the will. The action which can be compatible with the autonomy of the will is permitted; that which does not agree with it is prohibited. The will whose maxims necessarily are in harmony with the laws of autonomy is a holy will or an absolutely good will. The dependence of a will not absolutely good on the principle of autonomy (moral constraint) is *obligation*. Hence obligation cannot be applied to a holy will. The objective necessity of an action from obligation is called *duty*.

From what has just been said, it can easily be explained how it happens that, although in the concept of duty we think of subjection to law, we do nev-

ertheless ascribe a certain sublimity and dignity to the person who fulfills all his duties. For though there is no sublimity in him in so far as he is subject to the moral law, yet he is sublime in so far as he is legislative with reference to the law and subject to it only for this reason. We have also shown above how neither fear of nor inclination to the law is the incentive which can give a moral worth to action; only respect for it can do so. Our own will, so far as it would act only under the condition of a universal legislation rendered possible by its maxims—this will, ideally possible for us, is the proper object of respect, and the dignity of humanity consists just in its capacity of giving universal laws, although with the condition that it is itself subject to the same legislation.

The Autonomy of the Will as the Supreme Principle of Morality

Autonomy of the will is that property of it by which it is a law to itself independently of any property of objects of volition. Hence the principle of autonomy is: Never choose except in such a way that the maxims of the choice are comprehended in the same volition as a universal law. That this practical rule is an imperative, that is, that the will of every rational being is necessarily bound to it as a condition, cannot be proved by a mere analysis of the concepts occurring in it, because it is a synthetical proposition. To prove it, we would have to go beyond the knowledge of objects to a critical examination of the subject, i.e., of the pure practical reason, for this synthetical proposition which commands apodictically must be susceptible of being known completely a priori. This matter, however, does not belong in the present section. But that the principle of autonomy, which is now in question, is the sole principle of morals can be readily shown by mere analysis of concepts of morality; for by this analysis we find that its principle must be a categorical imperative and that the imperative commands neither more nor less than this very autonomy.

The Heteronomy of the Will as the Source of All Spurious Principles of Morality

If the will seeks the law which is to determine it anywhere else than in the fitness of its maxims to its own universal legislation, and if it thus goes outside itself and seeks this law in the property of any of its objects, heteronomy always results. For then the will does not give itself the law, but the object through its relation to the will gives the law to it. This relation, whether it rests on inclination or on conceptions of reason, only admits of hypothetical imperatives: I should do something for the reason that I will something else. The moral, and therewith categorical, imperative, on the other hand, says I should act this or that way even though I will nothing else. For example, the former says I should not lie if I wish to keep my reputation. The latter says I should not lie even though it would not cause me the least injury. The latter, therefore, must disregard every object to such an extent that it has absolutely no influence on the will, so that practical reason (will) may not merely minister to an interest not its own but rather may show its commanding authority as the supreme legislation. Thus, for instance, I should seek to further the happiness of others, not as though its realization was any concern of mine (whether because of direct inclination or of some satisfaction related to it indirectly through reason); I should do so merely because the maxim which excludes it from my duty cannot be comprehended as a universal law in one and the same volition.

Classification of All Possible Principles of Morality Following from the Assumed Principle of Heteronomy

Here as everywhere in the pure use of reason, so long as a critical examination of it is lacking, human reason at first tries all possible wrong ways before it succeeds in finding the one true way.

All principles which can be taken in this point of view are either empirical or rational. The former, drawn from the principle of happiness, are based on physical or moral feeling; the latter, drawn from the principle of perfection, are based either on the rational concept of perfection as a possible result or on the concept of an independent perfection (the will of God) as the determining cause of our will.

Empirical principles are not at all suited to serve as the basis of moral laws. For if the basis of the universality by which they should be valid for all rational beings without distinction (the unconditional practical necessity which is thereby imposed upon them) is derived from a particular tendency of human nature or the accidental circumstance in which it is found,

that universality is lost. But the principle of one's own happiness is the most objectionable of all. This is not merely because it is false and because experience contradicts the supposition that well-being is always proportional to good conduct, nor yet because this principle contributes nothing to the establishment of morality, inasmuch as it is a very different thing to make a man happy from making him good, and to make him prudent and farsighted for his own advantage is far from making him virtuous. Rather, it is because this principle supports morality with incentives which undermine it and destroy all its sublimity, for it puts the motives to virtue and those to vice in the same class, teaching us only to make a better calculation while obliterating the specific difference between them. On the other hand, there is the alleged special sense,[14] the moral feeling. The appeal to it is superficial, since those who cannot think expect help from feeling, even with respect to that which concerns universal laws; they do so even though feelings naturally differ so infinitely in degree that they are incapable of furnishing a uniform standard of the good and bad, and also in spite of the fact that one cannot validly judge for others by means of his own feeling. Nevertheless, the moral feeling is nearer to morality and its dignity, inasmuch as it pays virtue the honor of ascribing the satisfaction and esteem for her directly to morality, and does not, as it were, say to her face that it is not her beauty but only our advantage which attaches us to her.

Among the rational principles of morality, there is the ontological concept of perfection. It is empty, indefinite, and consequently useless for finding in the immeasurable field of possible reality the greatest possible sum which is suitable to us; and, in specifically distinguishing the reality which is here in question from all other reality, it inevitably tends to move in a circle and cannot avoid tacitly presupposing the morality which it ought to explain. Nevertheless, it is better than the theological concept, which derives morality from a most perfect divine will. It is better

---

14. I count the principle of moral feeling under that of happiness, because every empirical interest promises to contribute to our well-being by the agreeableness that a thing affords, either directly and without a view to future advantage or with a view to it. We must likewise, with Hutcheson, count the principle of sympathy with the happiness of others under the moral sense which he assumed.

not merely because we cannot intuit its perfection, having rather to derive it only from our own concepts of which morality itself is foremost, but also because if we do not so derive it (and to do so would involve a most flagrant circle in explanation), the only remaining concept of the divine will is made up of the attributes of desire for glory and dominion combined with the awful conceptions of might and vengeance, and any system of ethics based on them would be directly opposed to morality.

But if I had to choose between the concept of the moral sense and that of perfection in general (neither of which at any rate weakens morality, although they are not capable of serving as its foundations), I would decide for the latter, because it preserves the indefinite idea (of a will good in itself) free from corruption until it can be more narrowly defined. It at least withdraws the decision of the question from sensibility and brings it to the court of pure reason, although it does not even here decide the question.

For the rest, I think that I may be excused from a lengthy refutation of all these doctrines. It is so easy, and presumably so well understood even by those whose office requires them to decide for one of these theories (since the hearers would not tolerate suspension of judgment), that such a refutation would be only superfluous work. What interests us more, however, is to know that all these principles set up nothing other than the heteronomy of the will as the first ground of morality and thus necessarily miss their aim.

In every case in which an object of the will must be assumed as prescribing the rule which is to determine the will, the rule is nothing else but heteronomy. The imperative in this case is conditional, stating that if or because one wills this object, one should act thus or so. Therefore the imperative can never command morally, that is, categorically. The object may determine the will by means of inclination, as in the principle of one's own happiness, or by means of reason directed to objects of our possible volition in general, as in the principle of perfection; but the will in these cases never determines itself directly by the conception of the action itself but only by the incentive which the foreseen result of the action incites in the will—that is, "I ought to do something because I will something else." And here still another law must be assumed in my person as the basis of this imperative; it would be a law by which I would necessarily will that other thing; but this law

would again require an imperative to restrict this maxim. Since the conception of an object commensurate to our power incites in the will an impulse according to the natural characteristic of our person, this impulse belongs to the nature of the subject (either to the sensibility, i.e., inclination and taste, or to understanding and reason, which faculties, according to the particular constitution of their nature, take pleasure in exercising themselves on an object). It follows that it would be really nature that would give the law. As a law of nature, known and proved by experience, it would be contingent and therefore unfit to be an apodictical practical rule such as the moral rule must be. Such a law always represents heteronomy of the will; the will does not give itself the law, but an external impulse gives it to the will according to the nature of the subject which is adapted to receive it.

The absolutely good will, the principle of which must be a categorical imperative, is thus undetermined with reference to any objects. It contains only the form of volition in general, and this form is autonomy. That is, the capability of the maxims of every good will to make themselves universal laws is itself the sole law which the will of every rational being imposes on itself, and it does not need to support this on any incentive or interest.

How such a synthetical practical a priori proposition is possible and why it is necessary is a problem whose solution does not lie within the boundaries of the metaphysics of morals. Moreover, we have not here affirmed its truth, and even less professed to command a proof of it. We showed only through the development of the universally received concept of morals that autonomy of the will is unavoidably connected with it, or rather that it is its foundation. Whoever, therefore, holds morality to be something real and not a chimerical idea without truth must also concede its principle which has been adduced here. Consequently, this section was merely analytical, like the first. To prove that morality is not a mere phantom of the mind—and if the categorical imperative, and with it the autonomy of the will, is true and absolutely necessary as an a priori principle, it follows that it is no phantom—requires that a synthetical use of pure practical reason is possible. But we must not venture on this use without first making a critical examination of this faculty of reason. In the last section we shall give the principal features of such an examination that will be sufficient for our purpose.

Third Section Transition from the Metaphysics of Morals to the Critical Examination of Pure Practical Reason

The Concept of Freedom is the Key
to the Explanation of the Autonomy of the Will

As will is a kind of causality of living beings so far as they are rational, freedom would be that property of this causality by which it can be effective independently of foreign causes determining it, just as natural necessity is the property of the causality of all irrational beings by which they are determined in their activity by the influence of foreign causes.

The preceding definition of freedom is negative and therefore affords no insight into its essence. But a positive concept of freedom flows from it which is so much the richer and more fruitful. Since the concept of a causality entails that of laws according to which something, i.e., the effect, must be established through something else which we call cause, it follows that freedom is by no means lawless even though it is not a property of the will according to laws of nature. Rather, it must be a causality according to immutable laws, but of a peculiar kind. Otherwise a free will would be an absurdity. Natural necessity is, as we have seen, a heteronomy of efficient causes, for every effect is possible only according to the law that something else determines the efficient cause to its causality. What else, then, can the freedom of the will be but autonomy, i.e., the property of the will to be a law to itself? The proposition that the will is a law to itself in all its actions, however, only expresses the principle that we should act according to no other maxim than that which can also have itself as a universal law for its object. And this is just the formula of the categorical imperative and the principle of morality. Therefore a free will and a will under moral laws are identical.

Thus if freedom of the will is presupposed, morality together with its principle follows from it by the mere analysis of its concept. But the principle is nevertheless a synthetical proposition: an absolutely good will is one whose maxim can always include itself as a universal law. It is synthetical because by analysis of the concept of an absolutely good will that property of the maxim cannot be found. Such synthetical propositions, however, are possible only by the fact that both cognitions are connected through their union with a third in which both of them are to be found. The positive concept of freedom furnishes this third cognition, which cannot be, as in the case of physical causes, the nature of the sensuous world, in the concept of which we find conjoined the concepts of something as cause in relation to something else as effect. We cannot yet show directly what this third cognition is to which freedom directs us and of which we have an a priori idea, nor can we explain the deduction of the concept of freedom from pure practical reason and therewith the possibility of a categorical imperative. For this some further preparation is needed.

Freedom Must Be Presupposed
as the Property of the Will of All Rational Beings

It is not enough to ascribe freedom to our will, on any grounds whatever, if we do not also have sufficient grounds for attributing it to all rational beings. For since morality serves as a law for us only as rational beings, morality must hold valid for all rational beings, and since it must be derived exclusively from the property of freedom, freedom as the property of the will of all rational beings must be demonstrated. And it does not suffice to prove it from certain alleged experiences of human nature (which is indeed impossible, as it can be proved only a priori), but we must prove it as belonging generally to the activity of rational beings endowed with a will. Now I say that every being which cannot act otherwise than under the idea of freedom is thereby really free in a practical respect. That is to say, all laws which are inseparably bound up with freedom hold for it just as if its will were proved free in itself by theoretical philosophy.[1] Now I affirm that we must necessarily grant that every rational being who has a will also has the idea

---

1. I follow this method, assuming that it is sufficient for our purpose that rational beings take merely the idea of [*in der Idee*] freedom as basic to their actions, in order to avoid having also to prove freedom in its theoretical aspect. For if the latter is left unproved, the laws which would obligate a being who was really free would hold for a being who cannot act except under the idea of his own freedom. Thus we can escape here from the onus which presses on the theory.

of freedom and that it acts only under this idea. For in such a being we think of a reason which is practical, i.e., a reason which has causality with respect to its objects. Now, we cannot conceive of a reason which consciously responds to a bidding from the outside with respect to its judgments, for then the subject would attribute the determination of its power of judgment not to reason but to an impulse. Reason must regard itself as the author of its principles, independently of foreign influences; consequently, as practical reason or as the will of a rational being, it must regard itself as free. That is to say, the will of a rational being can be a will of its own only under the idea of freedom, and therefore in a practical point of view such a will must be ascribed to all rational beings.

Of the Interest Attaching to the Ideas of Morality

We have finally reduced the definite concept of morality to the idea of freedom, but we could not prove freedom to be real in ourselves and in human nature. We saw only that we must presuppose it if we would think of a being as rational and conscious of his causality with respect to actions, that is, as endowed with a will; and so we find that on the very same grounds we must ascribe to each being endowed with reason and will the property of determining himself to action under the idea of freedom.

From presupposing this idea [of freedom] there followed also consciousness of a law of action: that the subjective principles of actions, i.e., maxims, in every instance must be so chosen that they can hold also as objective, i.e., universal, principles, and thus can serve as principles for the universal laws we give. But why should I subject myself as a rational being, and thereby all other beings endowed with reason, to this law? I will admit that no interest impels me to do so, for that would then give no categorical imperative. But I must nevertheless take an interest in it and see how it comes about, for this "ought" is properly a "would" that is valid for every rational being provided reason is practical for him without hindrance [i.e., exclusively determines his action]. For beings who like ourselves are affected by the senses as incentives different from reason and who do not always do that which reason for itself alone would have done, that necessity of action is expressed only as an "ought." The subjective necessity is thus distinguished from the objective.

It therefore seems that the moral law, i.e., the principle of the autonomy of the will, is, properly speaking, only presupposed in the idea of freedom, as if we could not prove its reality and objective necessity by itself. Even if that were so, we would still have gained something because we would at least have defined the genuine principle more accurately than had been done before. But with regard to its validity and to the practical necessity of subjection to it, we would not have advanced a single step, for we could give no satisfactory answer to anyone who asked us why the universal validity of our maxim as of a law had to be the restricting condition of our action. We could not tell on what is based the worth we ascribe to actions of this kind—a worth so great that there can be no higher interest, nor could we tell how it happens that man believes it is only through this that he feels his own personal worth, in contrast to which the worth of a pleasant or unpleasant condition is to be regarded as nothing.

We do find sometimes that we can take an interest in a personal quality which involves no [personal] interest in any [external] condition, provided only that [possession of] this quality makes us capable of participating in the [desired] condition in case reason were to effect the allotment of it. That is, mere worthiness to be happy even without the motive of participating in it can interest us of itself. But this judgment is in fact only the effect of the already assumed importance of moral laws (if by the idea of freedom we detach ourselves from every empirical interest). But that we ought to detach ourselves, i.e., regard ourselves as free in acting and yet as subject to certain laws, in order to find a worth merely in our person which would compensate for the loss of everything which makes our situation desirable— how this is possible and hence on what grounds the moral law obligates us we still cannot see in this way.

We must openly confess that there is a kind of circle here from which it seems that there is no escape. We assume that we are free in the order of efficient causes so that we can conceive of ourselves as subject to moral laws in the order of ends. And then we think of ourselves as subject to these laws because we have ascribed freedom of the will to ourselves. This is circular because freedom and self-legislation of the will are both autonomy and thus are reciprocal concepts, and for that reason one of them cannot be used to explain the other and to furnish a ground for it. At most they can be used for the logical purpose of bringing apparently different conceptions of the same object under a single concept (as we reduce different fractions of the same value to the lowest common terms).

One recourse, however, remains open to us, namely, to inquire whether we do not assume a different standpoint when we think of ourselves as causes a priori efficient through freedom from that which we occupy when we conceive of ourselves in the light of our actions as effects which we see before our eyes.

The following remark requires no subtle reflection, and we may suppose that even the commonest understanding can make it, though it does so, after its fashion, by an obscure discernment of judgment which it calls feeling: all conceptions, like those of the senses, which come to us without our choice enable us to know the objects only as they affect us, while what they are in themselves remains unknown to us; therefore, as regards this kind of conception, even with the closest attention and clearness which understanding may ever bring to them we can attain only to knowledge of appearances and never to knowledge of things in themselves. As soon as this distinction is made (perhaps merely because of a difference noticed between conceptions which are given to us from somewhere else and to which we are passive and those which we produce only from ourselves and in which we show our own activity), it follows of itself that we must admit and assume behind the appearances something else which is not appearance, namely, things in themselves; we do so although we must admit that we cannot approach them more closely and can never know what they are in themselves, since they can never be known by us except as they affect us. This must furnish a distinction, though a crude one, between a world of sense and a world of understanding. The former, by differences in the sensuous faculties, can be very different among various observers, while the latter, which is its foundation, remains always the same. A man may not presume to know even himself as he really is by knowing himself through inner sensation. For since he does not, as it were, produce himself or derive his concept of himself a priori but only empirically, it is natural that he obtains his knowledge of himself through inner sense and consequently only through the appearance of his nature and the way in which his consciousness is affected. But beyond the characteristic of his own subject which is compounded of these mere appear-ances, he necessarily assumes something else as its basis, namely, his ego as it is in itself. Thus in respect to mere perception and receptivity to sensations he must count himself as belonging to the world of sense; but in respect to that which may be pure activity in himself (i.e., in respect to that which reaches consciousness directly and not by affecting the senses) he must reckon himself as belonging to the intellectual world. But he has no further knowledge of that world.

To such a conclusion the thinking man must come with respect to all things which may present themselves to him. Presumably it is to be met with in the commonest understanding which, as is well known, is very much inclined to expect behind the objects of the senses something else invisible and acting of itself. But such an understanding soon spoils it by trying to make the invisible again sensuous, i.e., to make it an object of intuition. Thus common understanding becomes not in the least wiser.

Now man really finds in himself a faculty by which he distinguishes himself from all other things, even from himself so far as he is affected by objects. This faculty is reason. As pure spontaneous activity it is elevated even above understanding. For though the latter is also a spontaneous activity and does not, like sense, merely contain conceptions which arise only when one is affected by things, being passive, it nevertheless cannot produce by its activity any other concepts than those which serve to bring the sensuous conceptions under rules, and thereby to unite them in one consciousness. Without this use of sensibility it would not think at all, while, on the other hand, reason shows such a pure spontaneity in the case of ideas that it far transcends everything that sensibility can give to consciousness and shows its chief occupation in distinguishing the world of sense from the world of understanding, thereby prescribing limits to the understanding itself.

For this reason a rational being must regard himself as intelligence (and not from the side of his lower powers), as belonging to the world of understanding and not to that of the senses. Thus he has two standpoints from which he can consider himself and recognize the laws of the employment of his powers and consequently of all his actions: first, as belonging to the world of sense under laws of nature (heteronomy), and, second, as belonging to the intelligible world under laws which, independent of nature, are not empirical but founded only on reason.

As a rational being and thus as belonging to the intelligible world, man cannot think of the causality of his own will except under the idea of freedom, for independence from the determining causes of the world of sense (an independence which reason must always ascribe to itself) is freedom. The concept of autonomy is inseparably connected with the idea of freedom, and with the former there is inseparably bound the universal principle of morality, which ideally is the ground of all actions of rational beings, just as natural law is the ground of all appearances.

Now we have removed the suspicion which we raised that there might be a hidden circle in our reasoning from freedom to autonomy and from the latter to the moral law. This suspicion was that we laid down the idea of freedom for the sake of the moral law in order later to derive the latter from freedom, and that we were thus unable to give any ground for the law, presenting it only as a *petitio principii* that well-disposed minds would gladly allow us but which we could never advance as a demonstrable proposition. But we now see that, if we think of ourselves as free, we transport ourselves into the intelligible world as members of it and know the autonomy of the will together with its consequence, morality; while, if we think of ourselves as obligated, we consider ourselves as belonging both to the world of sense and at the same time to the intelligible world.

How Is a Categorical Imperative Possible?

The rational being counts himself, qua intelligence, as belonging to the intelligible world, and only as an efficient cause belonging to it does he call his causality a will. On the other side, however, he is conscious of himself as a part of the world of sense in which his actions are found as mere appearances of that causality. But we do not discern how they are possible on the basis of that causality which we do not know; rather, those actions must be regarded as determined by other appearances, namely, desires and inclinations, belonging to the world of sense. As a mere member of the intelligible world, all my actions would completely accord with the principle of the autonomy of the pure will, and as a part only of the world of sense would they have to be assumed to conform wholly to the natural law of desires and inclinations and thus to the heteronomy of nature. (The former actions would rest on the supreme principle of moral-

ity, and the latter on that of happiness.) But since the intelligible world contains the ground of the world of sense and hence of its laws, the intelligible world is (and must be conceived as) directly legislative for my will, which belongs wholly to the intelligible world. Therefore I recognize myself qua intelligence as subject to the law of the world of understanding and to the autonomy of the will. That is, I recognize myself as subject to the law of reason which contains in the idea of freedom the law of the intelligible world, while at the same time I must acknowledge that I am a being which belongs to the world of sense. Therefore I must regard the laws of the intelligible world as imperatives for me, and actions in accord with this principle as duties.

Thus categorical imperatives are possible because the idea of freedom makes me a member of an intelligible world. Consequently, if I were a member of only that world, all my actions *would* always be in accordance with the autonomy of the will. But since I intuit myself at the same time as a member of the world of sense, my actions *ought* to conform to it, and this categorical ought presents a synthetic a priori proposition, since besides my will affected by my sensuous desires there is added the idea of exactly the same will as pure, practical of itself, and belonging to the intelligible world, which according to reason contains the supreme condition of the former [sensuously affected] will. It is similar to the manner in which concepts of the understanding, which of themselves mean nothing but lawful form in general, are added to the intuitions of the sensuous world, thus rendering possible a priori synthetic propositions on which all knowledge of a system of nature rests.

The practical use of common human reason confirms the correctness of this deduction. When we present examples of honesty of purpose, of steadfastness in following good maxims, and of sympathy and general benevolence even with great sacrifice of advantages and comfort, there is no man, not even the most malicious villain (provided he is otherwise accustomed to using his reason), who does not wish that he also might have these qualities. But because of his inclinations and impulses he cannot bring this about, yet at the same time he wishes to be free from such inclinations which are burdensome even to himself. He thus proves that, with a will free from all impulses of sensibility, he in thought transfers himself into an order of things altogether different from that of his desires in the field of sensibility. He cannot expect to obtain by that wish any gratification of desires or any condition which would satisfy his real or even imagined inclinations, for the idea itself, which elicits this wish from him, would lose its preeminence if he had any such expectation. He can expect only a greater inner worth of his person. He imagines himself to be this better person when he transfers himself to the standpoint of a member of the intelligible world to which he is involuntarily impelled by the idea of freedom, i.e., independence from the determining causes of the world of sense; and from this standpoint he is conscious of a good will, which on his own confession constitutes the law for his bad will as a member of the world of sense. He acknowledges the authority of this law even while transgressing it. The moral ought is therefore his own volition as a member of the intelligible world, and it is conceived by him as an ought only in so far as he regards himself at the same time as a member of the world of sense.

On the Extreme Limit of All Practical Philosophy

In respect to their will, all men think of themselves as free. Hence arise all judgments of actions as being such as ought to have been done, although they were not done. But this freedom is not an empirical concept and cannot be such, for it still remains even though experience shows the contrary of the demands which are necessarily conceived as consequences of the supposition of freedom. On the other hand, it is equally necessary that everything which happens should be inexorably determined by natural laws, and this natural necessity is likewise no empirical concept, because it implies the concept of necessity and thus of a priori knowledge. But this concept of a system of nature is confirmed by experience, and it is inevitably presupposed if experience, which is knowledge of the objects of the senses interconnected by universal laws, is to be possible. Therefore freedom is only an idea of reason whose objective reality in itself is doubtful, while nature is a concept of the understanding which shows and necessarily must show its reality by examples in experience.

There now arises a dialectic of reason, since the freedom ascribed to the will seems to stand in contradiction to natural necessity. At this parting of the ways reason in its speculative purpose finds the way

of natural necessity more well-beaten and usable than that of freedom; but in its practical purpose the footpath of freedom is the only one on which it is possible to make use of reason in our conduct. Hence it is as impossible for the subtlest philosophy as for the commonest reasoning to argue freedom away. Philosophy must therefore assume that no true contradiction will be found between freedom and natural necessity in the same human actions, for it cannot give up the concept of nature any more than that of freedom.

Hence even if we should never be able to conceive how freedom is possible, at least this apparent contradiction must be convincingly eradicated. For if even the thought of freedom contradicts itself or nature, which is equally necessary, it would have to be surrendered in competition with natural necessity.

But it would be impossible to escape this contradiction if the subject, who seems to himself free, thought of himself in the same sense or in the same relationship when he calls himself free as when he assumes that in the same action he is subject to natural law. Therefore it is an inescapable task of speculative philosophy to show at least that its illusion about the contradiction rests in the fact that we [do not] think of man in a different sense and relationship when we call him free from that in which we consider him as a part of nature and subject to its laws. It must show not only that they can very well coexist but also that they must be thought of as necessarily united in one and the same subject; for otherwise no ground could be given why we should burden reason with an idea which, though it may without contradiction be united with another that is sufficiently established, nevertheless involves us in a perplexity which sorely embarrasses reason in its speculative use. This duty is imposed only on speculative philosophy, so that it may clear the way for practical philosophy. Thus the philosopher has no choice as to whether he will remove the apparent contradiction or leave it untouched, for in the latter case the theory of it would be *bonum vacans*, into the possession of which the fatalist can rightly enter and drive all morality from its alleged property as occupying it without title.

Yet we cannot say here that we have reached the beginnings of practical philosophy. For the settlement of the controversy does not belong to practical philosophy, as the latter demands from speculative reason only that it put an end to the discord in which it entangles itself in theoretical questions, so that practical reason may have rest and security from outer attacks which could dispute with it the ground on which it desires to erect its edifice.

The title to freedom of the will claimed by common reason is based on the consciousness and the conceded presupposition of the independence of reason from merely subjectively determining causes which together constitute what belongs only to sensation, being comprehended under the general name of sensibility. Man, who in this way regards himself as intelligence, puts himself in a different order of things and in a relationship to determining grounds of an altogether different kind when he thinks of himself as intelligence with a will and thus as endowed with causality, compared with that other order of things and that other set of determining grounds which become relevant when he perceives himself as a phenomenon in the world of sense (as he really also is) and submits his causality to external determination according to natural laws. Now he soon realizes that both can subsist together—indeed, that they must. For there is not the least contradiction between a thing in appearance (as belonging to the world of sense) being subject to certain laws of which it is independent as a thing or a being in itself. That it must think of itself in this twofold manner rests, with regard to the first, on the consciousness of itself as an object affected through the senses, and, with regard to what is required by the second, on the consciousness of itself as intelligence, i.e., as independent of sensuous impressions in the use of reason and thus as belonging to the intelligible world.

This is why man claims to possess a will which does not let him become accountable for what belongs merely to his desires and inclinations, but thinks of actions which can be performed only by disregarding all desires and sensuous attractions, as possible and indeed necessary for him. The causality of these actions lies in him as an intelligence and in effects and actions in accordance with principles of an intelligible world, of which he knows only that reason alone and indeed pure reason independent of sensibility gives the law in it. Moreover, since it is only as intelligence that he is his proper self (being as man only appearance of himself), he knows that those laws apply to him directly and categorically, so that that to which inclinations and impulses and hence the entire nature of the world of sense incite him cannot in the least impair the laws of his volition as an intelligence. He does not even hold himself responsible for these inclinations and impulses or attribute them to his proper self, i.e., his will, though he does ascribe to his will the indulgence which he may grant to them when he permits them an influence on his maxims to the detriment of the rational laws of his will.

When practical reason thinks itself into an intelligible world, it does in no way transcend its limits. It would do so, however, if it tried to intuit or feel itself into it. The intelligible world is only a negative thought with respect to the world of sense, which does not give reason any laws for determining the will. It is positive only in the single point that freedom as negative determination is at the same time connected with a positive faculty and even a causality of reason. This causality we call a will to act so that the principle of actions will accord with the essential characteristic of a rational cause, i.e., with the condition of the universal validity of a maxim as a law. But if it were to borrow an object of the will, i.e., a motive, from the intelligible world, it would overstep its boundaries and pretend to be acquainted with something of which it knows nothing. The concept of a world of understanding is therefore only a standpoint which reason sees itself forced to take outside of appearances, in order to think of itself as practical. If the influences of sensibility were determining for man, this would not be possible; but it is necessary unless he is to be denied the consciousness of himself as an intelligence, and thus as a rational and rationally active cause, i.e., a cause acting in freedom. This thought certainly implies the idea of an order and legislation different from that of natural mechanism which applies to the world of sense; and it makes necessary the concept of an intelligible world, the whole of rational beings as things in themselves. But it does not give us the least occasion to think of it otherwise than according to its formal condition only, i.e., the universality of the maxim of the will as law and thus the autonomy of the will, which alone is consistent with freedom. All laws, on the other hand, which are directed to an object make for heteronomy, which belongs only to natural laws and which can apply only to the world of sense.

But reason would overstep all its bounds if it undertook to explain how pure reason can be practical, which is the same problem as explaining how freedom is possible.

For we can explain nothing but what we can reduce to laws whose object can be given in some possible experience. But freedom is a mere idea, the objective reality of which can in no way be shown according to natural laws or in any possible experience. Since no example in accordance with any analogy can support it, it can never be comprehended or even imagined. It holds only as the necessary presupposition of reason in a being that believes itself conscious of a will, i.e., of a faculty different from the mere faculty of desire, or a faculty of determining itself to act as intelligence and thus according to laws of reason independently of natural instincts. But where determination according to natural laws comes to an end, there too all explanation ceases and nothing remains but defense, i.e., refutation of the objections of those who pretend to have seen more deeply into the essence of things and therefore boldly declare freedom to be impossible. We can only show them that the supposed contradiction they have discovered lies nowhere else than in their necessarily regarding man as appearance in order to make natural law valid with respect to human actions. And now when we require them to think of him qua intelligence as a thing in itself, they still persist in considering him as appearance. Obviously, then, the separation of his causality (his will) from all natural laws of the world of sense in one and the same subject is a contradiction, but this disappears when they reconsider and confess, as is reasonable, that behind the appearances things in themselves must stand as their hidden ground and that we cannot expect the laws of the activity of these grounds to be the same as those under which their appearances stand.

The subjective impossibility of explaining the freedom of the will is the same as the impossibility of discovering and explaining an interest[2] which man can

take in moral laws. Nevertheless, he does actually take an interest in them, and the foundation in us of this interest we call the moral feeling. This moral feeling has been erroneously construed by some as the standard for our moral judgment, whereas it must rather be regarded as the subjective effect which the law has upon the will to which reason alone gives objective grounds.

In order to will that which reason alone prescribes to the sensuously affected rational being as that which he ought to will, certainly there is required a power of reason to instill a feeling of pleasure or satisfaction in the fulfillment of duty, and hence there must be a causality of reason to determine the sensibility in accordance with its own principles. But it is wholly impossible to discern, i.e., to make a priori conceivable, how a mere thought containing nothing sensuous is to produce a sensation of pleasure or displeasure. For that is a particular kind of causality of which, as of all causality, we cannot determine anything a priori but must consult experience only. But since experience can exemplify the relation of cause to effect only as subsisting between two objects of experience, while here pure reason by mere Ideas (which furnish no object for experience) is to be the cause of an effect which does lie in experience, an explanation of how and why the universality of the maxim as law (and hence morality) interests us is completely impossible for us men. Only this much is certain: that it is valid for us not because it interests us (for that is heteronomy and dependence of practical reason on sensibility, i.e., on a basic feeling, and thus it could never be morally legislative), but that it interests us because it is valid for us as men, inasmuch as it has arisen from our will as intelligence and hence from our proper self; but what belongs to mere appearance is necessarily subordinated by reason to the nature of the thing in itself.

Thus the question, "How is a categorical imperative possible?" can be answered to this extent: We can cite the only presupposition under which it is alone possible. This is the Idea of freedom, and we can discern the necessity of this presupposition which is sufficient to the practical use of reason, i.e., to the conviction of the validity of this imperative and hence also of the moral law. But how this presupposition itself is possible can never be discerned by any human reason. However, on the presupposition of freedom of the will of an intelligence, its autonomy as

---

2. Interest is that by which reason becomes practical, i.e., a cause determining the will. We therefore say only of a rational being that he takes an interest in something; irrational creatures feel only sensuous impulses. A direct interest in the action is taken by reason only if the universal validity of its maxim is a sufficient determining ground of the will. Only such an interest is pure. But if reason can determine the will only by means of another object of desire or under the presupposition of a particular feeling of the subject, reason takes merely an indirect interest in the action, and since reason by itself alone without experience can discover neither objects of the will nor a particular feeling which lies at its root, that indirect interest would be only empirical and not a pure interest of reason. The logical interest of reason in advancing its insights is never direct but rather presupposes purposes for which they are to be used.

the formal condition under which alone it can be determined is a necessary consequence. To presuppose the freedom of the will is not only quite possible, as speculative philosophy itself can prove, for it does not involve itself in a contradiction with the principle of natural necessity in the interconnection of appearances in the world of sense. But it is also unconditionally necessary that a rational being conscious of his causality through reason and thus conscious of a will different from desires should practically presuppose it, i.e., presuppose it in the idea as the fundamental condition of all his voluntary actions. Yet how pure reason, without any other incentives, wherever they may be derived, can by itself be practical, i.e., how the mere principle of the universal validity of all its maxims as laws (which would certainly be the form of a pure practical reason), without any material (object) of the will in which we might in advance take some interest, can itself furnish an incentive and produce an interest which would be called purely moral; or, in other words, how pure reason can be practical—to explain this, all human reason is wholly incompetent, and all the pains and work of seeking an explanation of it are wasted.

It is just the same as if I sought to find out how freedom itself as causality of a will is possible; for, in so doing, I would leave the philosophical basis of explanation behind, and I have no other. Certainly I could revel in the intelligible world, the world of intelligences, which still remains to me; but although I have a well-founded idea of it, still I do not have the least knowledge of it, nor can I ever attain to it by all the exertions of my natural capacity of reason. This intelligible world signifies only a something which remains when I have excluded from the determining grounds of my will everything belonging to the world of sense in order to withhold the principle of motives from the field of sensibility. I do so by limiting it and showing that it does not contain absolutely everything in itself but that outside it there is still more; but this more I do not further know. After banishing all material, i.e., knowledge of objects, from pure reason which formulates this ideal, there remain to me only the form, the practical law of universal validity of maxims, and, in conformity with this, reason in relation to a pure intelligible world as a possible effective cause, i.e., as determining the will. An incentive must here be wholly absent unless this idea of an intelligible world itself be the incentive or that in which reason primarily takes an interest. But to make this conceivable is precisely the problem we cannot solve.

Here is, then, the supreme limit of all moral inquiry. To define it is very important, both in order that reason may not seek around, on the one hand, in the world of sense, in a way harmful to morals, for the supreme motive and for a comprehensible but empirical interest; and so that it will not, on the other hand, impotently flap its wings in the space (for it, an empty space) of transcendent concepts which we call the intelligible world, without being able to move from its starting point, or lose itself amid phantoms. Furthermore, the idea of a pure intelligible world as a whole of all intelligences to which we ourselves belong as rational beings (though on the other side we are at the same time members of the world of sense) is always a useful and permissible idea for the purpose of a rational faith. This is so even though all knowledge terminates at its boundary, for through the glorious ideal of a universal realm of ends-in-themselves (rational beings) a lively interest in the moral law can be awakened in us. To that realm we can belong as members only when we carefully conduct ourselves according to maxims of freedom as if they were laws of nature.

Concluding Remark

The speculative use of reason with respect to nature leads to the absolute necessity of some supreme cause of the world. The practical use of reason with respect to freedom leads also to an absolute necessity, but to the necessity only of laws of actions of a rational being as such. Now it is an essential principle of all use of reason to push its knowledge to a consciousness of its necessity, for otherwise it would not be rational knowledge. But it is also an equally essential restriction of this very same reason that it cannot discern the necessity of what is or what occurs or what ought to be done, unless a condition under which it is or occurs or ought to be done is presupposed. In this way, however, the satisfaction of reason is only further and further postponed by the constant inquiry after the condition. Therefore, reason restlessly seeks the unconditionally necessary and sees itself compelled to assume it, though it has no means by which to make it comprehensible and is happy enough if it can only discover the concept which is consistent with this presupposition. It is therefore no objection to our deduction of the supreme principle of morality, but a reproach which we must make to human reason generally, that it cannot render comprehensible the absolute necessity of an unconditional practical law (such as the categorical imperative must be). Reason cannot be blamed for being unwilling to explain it by a condition, i.e., by making some interest its basis, for the law would then cease to be moral, i.e., a supreme law of freedom. And so we do not indeed comprehend the practical unconditional necessity of the moral imperative; yet we do comprehend its incomprehensibility, which is all that can be fairly demanded of a philosophy which in its principles strives to reach the limit of human reason.

The Metaphysics of Morals

Preface

The critique of *practical* reason was to be followed by a system, the metaphysics of morals, which falls into metaphysical first principles of the *doctrine of Right* and metaphysical first principles of the *doctrine of virtue.* (This is the counterpart of the metaphysical first principles of *natural science,* already published.) The Introduction that follows presents and to some degree makes intuitive the form which the system will take in both these parts.

For the doctrine of Right, the first part of the doctrine of morals, there is required a system derived from reason which could be called the *metaphysics of Right.* But since the concept of Right is a pure concept which still looks to practice (application to cases that come up in experience), a *metaphysical system* of Right would also have to take account, in its divisions, of the empirical variety of such cases, in order to make its division complete (as is essential in constructing a system of reason). But *what is empirical* cannot be divided completely, and if this is attempted (at least to approximate to it), empirical concepts cannot be brought into the system as integral parts of it but can be used only as examples in remarks. So the only appropriate title for the first part of *The Metaphysics of Morals* will be *Metaphysical First Principles of the Doctrine of Right;* for in the application of these principles to cases the system itself cannot be expected, but only approximation to it. Accordingly, it will be dealt with as in the (earlier) *Metaphysical First Principles of Natural Science:* namely, that Right which belongs to the system outlined a priori will go into the text, while rights taken from particular cases of experience will be put into remarks, which will sometimes be extensive; for otherwise it would be hard to distinguish what is metaphysics here from what is empirical application of rights.

Philosophic treatises are often charged with being obscure, indeed deliberately unclear, in order to affect an illusion of deep insight. I cannot better anticipate or forestall this charge than by readily complying with a duty that Garve, a philosopher in the true sense of the word, lays down for all writers, but especially for philosophic writers. My only reservation is imposed by the nature of the science that is to be corrected and extended.

This wise man rightly requires (in his work entitled *Vermischte Aufsätze,* pages 352 ff.) that every philosophic teaching be capable of being made *popular* (that is, of being made sufficiently clear to the senses to be communicated to everyone) if the teacher is not to be suspected of being muddled in his own concepts. I gladly admit this with the exception only of the systematic critique of the capacity for reason itself, along with all that can be established only by means of it; for this has to do with the distinction of the sensible in our knowledge from that which is supersensible but yet belongs to reason. This can never become popular—no formal metaphysics can —although its results can be made quite illuminating for the healthy reason (of an unwitting metaphysician). Popularity (common language) is out of the question here; on the contrary, scholastic *precision* must be insisted upon, even if this is censured as hair-splitting (since it is the *language of the schools*); for only by this means can precipitate reason be brought to understand itself, before making its dogmatic assertions.

But if *pedants* presume to address the public (from pulpits or in popular writings) in technical terms that belong only in the schools, the critical philosopher is no more responsible for that than the grammarian is for the folly of those who quibble over words (*logodaedalus*). Here ridicule can touch only the man, not the science.

It sounds arrogant, conceited, and belittling of those who have not yet renounced their old system to assert that before the coming of the critical philosophy there was as yet no philosophy at all. In order to decide about this apparent presumption, it need but be asked *whether there could really be more than one philosophy.* Not only have there been different ways of philosophizing and of going back to the first principles of reason in order to base a system, more or less successfully, upon them, but there had to be many experiments of this kind, each of which made its contribution to present-day philosophy. Yet since, considered objectively, there can be only one human reason, there cannot be many philosophies; in other words, there can be only one true system of philosophy from principles, in however many different and even conflicting ways men have philosophized about one and the same proposition. So the *moralist* rightly says that there is only one virtue and one doctrine of virtue, that is, a single system that connects all duties of virtue by one principle; the *chemist*, that there is only one chemistry (Lavoisier's); the *teacher of medicine*, that there is only one principle for systematically classifying diseases (Brown's). Although the *new system* excludes all the others, it does not detract from the merits of earlier moralists, chemists, and teachers of medicine, since without their discoveries and even their unsuccessful attempts we should not have attained that unity of the true principle which unifies the whole of philosophy into one system. So anyone who announces a system of philosophy as his own work says in effect that before this philosophy there was none at all. For if he were willing to admit that there had been another (and a true) one, there would then be two different and true philosophies on the same subject, which is self-contradictory. If, therefore, the critical philosophy calls itself a philosophy before which there had as yet been no philosophy at all, it does no more than has

been done, will be done, and indeed must be done by anyone who draws up a philosophy on his own plan.

The charge that one thing which essentially distinguishes the critical philosophy is not original to it but was perhaps borrowed from another philosophy (or from mathematics) would be *less* important but not altogether negligible. A reviewer in Tübingen claims to have discovered that the definition of philosophy which the author of the *Critique of Pure Reason* gives out as his own, not inconsiderable, discovery had been put forth many years earlier by someone else in almost the same words.[1] I leave it to anyone to judge whether the words *intellectualis quaedam constructio* could have yielded the thought of *the presentation of a given concept in an a priori intuition,* which at once completely distinguishes philosophy from mathematics. I am sure that Hausen himself would not have allowed his words to be interpreted in this way; for the possibility of an a priori intuition, and that space is an a priori intuition and not (as Wolff explains it) a juxtaposition of a variety of items outside one another given merely to empirical intuition (perception), would already have frightened him off, since he would have felt that this was getting him entangled in far-reaching philosophic investigations. To this acute mathematician the presentation *made as it were by means of the understanding* meant nothing more than an (empirical) *drawing* of a *line* corresponding to a concept, in which attention is paid only to the rule and abstraction is made from unavoidable deviations in carrying it out, as can also be perceived in equalities constructed in geometry.

As far as the spirit of the critical philosophy is concerned, the *least*-important consideration is the mischief that certain imitators of it have made by using some of its terms, which in the *Critique of Pure Reason* itself cannot well be replaced by more customary words, outside the *Critique* in public exchange of

---

1. *Porro de actuali constructione hic non quaeritur, cum ne possint quidem sensibiles figurae ad rigorem definitionem effingi; sed requiritur cognitio eorum, quibus absolvitur formatio, quae intellectualis quaedam constructio est.* C. A. Hausen, *Elem. Mathes, Pars* I, p. 86A (1734). [Moreover, what is in question here is not an actual construction, since sensible figures cannot be devised in accordance with the strictness of a definition; what is required is, rather, knowledge of what goes to make up the figure, and this is, as it were, a construction made by the intellect.]

thoughts. This certainly deserves to be condemned, although in condemning it Nicolai reserves judgment as to whether such terms can be entirely dispensed with in their own proper field, as though they were used everywhere merely to hide poverty of thought. Meanwhile it is more amusing to laugh at an *unpopular pendant* than at an *uncritical ignoramus* (for, in fact, a metaphysician who clings obstinately to his own system, heedless of any critique, can be classed as an uncritical ignoramus, even though he willfully *ignores* what he does not want to let spread since it does not belong to his older school of thought). But if it is true, as Shaftesbury asserts, that a doctrine's ability to withstand *ridicule* is not a bad touchstone of its truth (especially in the case of a practical doctrine), then the critical philosophy's turn must finally come to laugh *last* and so laugh *best* when it sees the systems of those who have talked big for such a long time collapse like houses of cards one after another and their adherents scatter, a fate they cannot avoid.

Toward the end of the book I have worked less thoroughly over certain sections than might be expected in comparison with the earlier ones, partly because it seems to me that they can be easily inferred from the earlier ones and partly, too, because the later sections (dealing with public Right) are currently subject to so much discussion, and still so important, that they can well justify postponing a decisive judgment for some time.

I hope to have the *Metaphysical First Principles of the Doctrine of Virtue* ready shortly.

Introduction to the Metaphysics of Morals

I
On the Relation of the Capacities of the Human Mind to Moral Laws

The *capacity for desire* is the capacity to be by means of one's representations the cause of the objects of these representations. The capacity of a being to act in accordance with its representations is called *life*.

First, pleasure or *displeasure*, susceptibility to which is called *feeling*, is always connected with desire or aversion; but the converse does not always hold, since there can be a pleasure that is not connected with any desire for an object but is already connected with a mere representation that one forms of an object (regardless of whether the object of the representation exists or not). *Second*, pleasure or dis-

pleasure in an object of desire does not always precede the desire and need not always be regarded as the cause of the desire but can also be regarded as the effect of it.

The capacity for taking pleasure or displeasure in a representation is called *feeling* because both of these involve what is *merely subjective* in the relation of our representation and contain no relation at all to an object for possible knowledge of it[1] (or even

---

1. One can characterize sensibility as the subjective aspect of our representations in general; for it is the understanding that first refers representations to an object, i.e., only it *thinks* something by means of them. What is subjective in our representations may be such that it can also be referred to an object for knowledge of it (either in terms of its form, in which case it is

knowledge of our own condition). While even sensations, apart from the quality (of, e.g., red, sweet, and so forth) they have because of the nature of the subject, are still referred to an object as elements in our knowledge of it, pleasure or displeasure (in what is red or sweet) expresses nothing at all in the object but simply a relation to the subject. For this very reason pleasure and displeasure cannot be explained more clearly in themselves; instead, one can only specify what results they have in certain circumstances, so as to make them recognizable in practice.

That pleasure which is necessarily connected with desire (for an object whose representation affects feeling in this way) can be called *practical pleasure*, whether it is the cause or the effect of the desire. On the other hand, that pleasure which is not necessarily connected with desire for an object, and so is not at bottom a pleasure in the existence of the object of a representation but is attached only to the representation by itself, can be called merely contemplative pleasure or *inactive delight*. We call feeling of the latter kind of pleasure *taste*. Practical philosophy, accordingly, speaks of contemplative pleasure only *in passing*, not as if the concept *belonged within* it. As for practical pleasure, that determination of the capacity for desire which is caused and therefore necessarily *preceded* by such pleasure is called *desire* in the narrow sense; habitual desire in this narrow sense is called *inclination;* and a connection of pleasure with the capacity for desire that the understanding judges to hold as a general rule (though only for the subject) is called an *interest*. So if a pleasure necessarily precedes a desire, the practical pleasure must be called an interest of inclination. But if a pleasure can only follow upon an antecedent determination of the capacity for desire it is an intellectual pleasure, and the interest in the object must be called an interest of reason; for if the interest were based on the senses and not on pure rational principles alone, sensation would then have to have pleasure connected with it and in this way be able to determine the capacity for desire. Although where a merely pure interest of reason must be assumed no interest of inclination can be substituted for it, yet in order to conform to ordinary speech we can speak of an inclination for what can be an object only of an intellectual pleasure as a habitual desire from a pure interest of reason; but an inclination of this sort would not be the cause but rather the effect of this pure interest of reason, and we could call it a *sense-free inclination (propensio intellectualis)*.

Concupiscence (lusting after something) must also be distinguished from desire itself, as a stimulus to determining desire. Concupiscence is always a sensible modification of the mind but one that has not yet become an act of the capacity for desire.

The capacity for desiring in accordance with concepts, insofar as the ground determining it to action lies within itself and not in its object, is called the capacity for *doing or refraining from doing as one pleases*. Insofar as it is joined with one's consciousness of the capacity to bring about its object by one's action it is called the *capacity for choice;* if it is not joined with this consciousness its act is called a *wish*. The capacity for desire whose inner determining ground, hence even what pleases it, lies within the subject's reason is called the *will*. The will is therefore the capacity for desire considered not so much in relation to action (as the capacity for choice is) but rather in relation to the ground determining choice to action. The will itself, strictly speaking, has no determining ground; insofar as it can determine the capacity for choice, it is instead practical reason itself.

Insofar as reason can determine the capacity for desire in general, not only *choice* but also mere *wish* can be included under the will. That choice which can be determined by *pure reason* is called free choice. That which can be determined only by *inclination* (sensible impulse, *stimulus*) would be animal choice (*arbitrium brutum*). Human choice, however, is a capacity for choice that can indeed be *affected* but not *determined* by impulses, and is therefore of itself (apart from an acquired aptitude of reason) not pure but can still be determined to actions by pure will. *Freedom* of choice is this independence from being *determined* by sensible

---

called pure intuition, or in terms of its matter, in which case it is called sensation); in this case sensibility, as susceptibility to such a representation, is *sense*. Or else what is subjective in our representations cannot become *an element in our knowledge* because it involves *only* a relation of the representation to the *subject* and nothing that can be used for knowledge of an object; and then susceptibility to the representation is called *feeling*, which is the effect of a representation (that may be either sensible or intellectual) upon a subject and belongs to sensibility, even though the representation itself may belong to the understanding or to reason.

impulses; this is the negative concept of freedom. The positive concept of freedom is that of the capacity of pure reason to be of itself practical. But this is not possible except by the subjection of the maxim of every action to the condition of its qualifying as universal law. For as pure reason applied to the capacity for choice irrespective of its objects, it does not have within it the matter of the law; so, as a capacity for principles (here practical principles, hence a lawgiving capacity), there is nothing it can make the supreme law and determining ground of choice except the form, the fitness of maxims of choice to be universal law. And since men's maxims, being based on subjective causes, do not of themselves conform with those objective principles, reason can prescribe this law only as an imperative that commands or prohibits absolutely.

In contrast to laws of nature, these laws of freedom are called *moral* laws. As directed merely to external actions and their conformity to law they are called *juridical* laws; but if they also require that they (the laws) themselves be the determining grounds of actions, they are *ethical* laws, and then one says that conformity with juridical laws is the *legality* of an action and conformity with ethical laws is its *morality*. The freedom to which the former laws refer can be only freedom in the *external* use of choice, but the freedom to which the latter refer is freedom in both the external and the internal use of choice, insofar as it is determined by laws of reason. In theoretical philosophy it is said that only objects of outer sense are in space, whereas objects of outer as well as of inner sense are in time, since the representations of both are still representations, and as such belong together to inner sense. So too, whether freedom in the external or in the internal use of choice is considered, its laws, as pure practical laws of reason for free choice generally, must also be internal determining grounds of choice, although they should not always be considered in this respect.

II

On the Idea of and the Necessity for a Metaphysics of Morals

It has been shown elsewhere that for natural science, which has to do with objects of outer sense, one must

have a priori principles, and that it is possible, indeed necessary, to prefix a system of these principles, called a metaphysical science of nature, to natural science applied to particular experiences, that is, to physics. Such principles must be derived from a priori grounds if they are to hold as universal in the strict sense. But physics (at least when it is a question of keeping its propositions free from error) can accept many principles as universal on the evidence of experience. So Newton assumed on the basis of experience the principle of the equality of action and reaction in the action of bodies upon one another, yet extended it to all material nature. Chemists go still further and base their most universal laws of the combination and separation of substances by their own forces entirely on experience, and yet so trust to the universality and necessity of those laws that they have no fear of discovering an error in experiments made with them.

But it is different with moral laws. They hold as laws only insofar as they can be *seen* to have an a priori basis and to be necessary. Indeed, concepts and judgments about ourselves and our deeds and omissions signify nothing moral if what they contain can be learned merely from experience. And should anyone let himself be led astray into making something from that source into a moral principle, he would run the risk of the grossest and most pernicious errors.

If the doctrine of morals were merely the doctrine of happiness it would be absurd to seek a priori principles for it. For however plausible it may sound to say that reason, even before experience, could see the means for achieving a lasting enjoyment of the true joys of life, yet everything that is taught a priori on this subject is either tautological or assumed without any basis. Only experience can teach what brings us joy. Only the natural drives for food, sex, rest, and movement, and (as our natural predispositions develop) for honor, for enlarging our knowledge and so forth, can tell each of us, and each only in his particular way, in what he will *find* those joys; and, in the same way, only experience can teach him the means by which to *seek* them. All apparently a priori reasoning about this comes down to nothing but experience raised by induction to generality, a generality (*secundum principia generalis, non universalis*) still so tenuous that everyone must be allowed countless exceptions in order to adapt his choice of a way of life to his particular inclinations and his susceptibility to satisfaction and still, in the end, to become prudent only from his own or others' misfortunes.

But it is different with the teachings of morality. They command for everyone, without taking account of his inclinations, merely because and insofar as he is free and has practical reason. He does not derive instruction in its laws from observing himself and his animal nature or from perceiving the ways of the world, what happens and how men behave (although the German word *Sitten*, like the Latin *mores*, means only manners and customs). Instead, reason commands how men are to act even though no example of this could be found, and it takes no account of the advantages we can thereby gain, which only experience could teach us. For although reason allows us to seek our advantage in every way possible to us and can even promise us, on the testimony of experience, that it will probably be more to our advantage on the whole to obey its commands than to transgress them, especially if obedience is accompanied with prudence, still the authority of its precepts *as commands* is not based on these considerations. Instead it uses them (as counsels) only as a counterweight against inducements to the contrary, to offset in advance the error of biased scales in practical appraisal, and only then to ensure that the weight of a pure practical reason's a priori grounds will turn the scales in favor of the authority of its precepts.

If, therefore, a system of a priori knowledge from concepts alone is called *metaphysics*, a practical philosophy, which has not nature but freedom of choice for its object, will presuppose and require a metaphysics of morals, that is, it is itself a *duty* to *have* such a metaphysics, and every man also has it within himself, though as a rule only in an obscure way; for without a priori principles how could he believe that he has a giving of universal law within himself? But just as there must be principles in a metaphysics of nature for applying those highest universal principles of a nature in general to objects of experience, a metaphysics of morals cannot dispense with principles of application, and we shall often have to take as our object the particular *nature* of man, which is known only by experience, in order to *show* in it what can be inferred from universal moral principles. But this will in no way detract from the purity of these principles or cast doubt on their a priori source. This is to say, in effect, that a metaphysics of morals can-

not be based upon anthropology but can still be applied to it.

The counterpart of a metaphysics of morals, the other member of the division of practical philosophy as a whole, would be moral anthropology, which, however, would deal only with the subjective conditions in human nature that hinder men or help them in *fulfilling* the laws of a metaphysics of morals. It would deal with the development, spreading, and strengthening of moral principles (in education in schools and in popular instruction), and with other similar teachings and precepts based on experience. It cannot be dispensed with, but it must not precede a metaphysics of morals or be mixed with it; for one would then run the risk of bringing forth false or at least indulgent moral laws, which would misrepresent as unattainable what has only not been attained just because the law has not been seen and presented in its purity (in which its strength consists) or because spurious or impure incentives were used for what is itself in conformity with duty and good. This would leave no certain moral principles, either to guide judgment or to discipline the mind in observance of duty, the precepts of which must be given a priori by pure reason alone.

As for the higher division under which the division just mentioned falls, namely that of philosophy into theoretical and practical philosophy, I have already explained myself elsewhere (in the *Critique of Judgment*) and explained that practical philosophy can be none other than moral wisdom. Anything that is practical and possible in accordance with laws of nature (the distinctive concern of art) depends for its precepts entirely upon the theory of nature: Only what is practical in accordance with laws of freedom can have principles that are independent of any theory; for there is no theory of what goes beyond the properties of nature. Hence, philosophy can understand by its practical part (as compared with its theoretical part) no *technically practical* doctrine but only a *morally practical* doctrine; and if the proficiency of choice in accordance with laws of freedom, in contrast to laws of nature, is also to be called *art* here, by this would have to be understood a kind of art that makes possible a system of freedom like a system of nature, truly a divine art were we in a position also to carry out fully, by means of it, what reason prescribes and to put the Idea of it into effect.

III

On the Division of a Metaphysics of Morals[2]

In all lawgiving (whether it prescribes internal or external actions, and whether it prescribes them a priori by reason alone or by the choice of another) there are two elements: first, a *law*, which represents an action that is to be done as *objectively* necessary, that is, which makes the action a duty; and second, an *incentive*, which connects a ground for determining choice to this action *subjectively* with the representation of the law. Hence, the second element is this: that the law makes duty the incentive. By the first the action is represented as a duty, and this is a merely theoretical cognition of a possible determination of choice, that is, of practical rules. By the second the obligation so to act is connected in the subject with a ground for determining choice generally.

All lawgiving can therefore be distinguished with respect to the incentive (even if it agrees with another kind with respect to the action that it makes a duty, e.g., these actions might in all cases be external). That lawgiving which makes an action a duty and also makes this duty the incentive is *ethical*. But that lawgiving which does not include the incentive of duty in the law and so admits an incentive other than the Idea of duty itself is *juridical*. It is clear that in the latter case this incentive that is something other than the Idea of duty must be drawn from *sensibly dependent* determining grounds of choice, inclinations and aversions, and among these, from aversions; for it is a lawgiving, which constrains, not an allurement, which invites.

The mere conformity or nonconformity of an action with law, irrespective of the incentive to it, is called its *legality* (lawfulness); but that conformity in which the Idea of duty arising from the law is also the incentive to the action is called its *morality*.

Duties in accordance with rightful lawgiving can be only external duties, since this lawgiving does not require that the Idea of this duty, which is internal, itself be the determining ground of the agent's choice; and since it still needs an incentive suited to the law, it can connect only external incentives with it. On the other hand, ethical lawgiving, while it also makes internal actions duties, does not exclude external actions but applies to everything that is a duty in general. But just because ethical lawgiving includes within its law the internal incentive to action (the Idea of duty), and this feature must not be present in external lawgiving, ethical lawgiving cannot be external (not even the external lawgiving of a divine will), although it does take up duties that rest on another, namely an external, lawgiving by making them, *as duties*, incentives in its lawgiving.

It can be seen from this that all duties, just because they are duties, belong to ethics; but it does not follow that the *lawgiving* for them is always contained in ethics: For many of them it is outside ethics. Thus, ethics commands that I still fulfill a contract I have entered into, even though the other party could not coerce me to do so; but it takes the law (*pacta sunt servanda*) and the duty corresponding to it from the doctrine of Right, as already given there. Accordingly the giving of the law that promises agreed to must be kept lies not in ethics but in *Ius*. All that ethics teaches is that if the incentive which juridical lawgiving connects with that duty, namely external constraint, were absent, the Idea of duty by itself would be sufficient as an incentive. For if this were not the case, and if the lawgiving itself were not juridical so that the duty arising from it was not really a duty of Right (as distinguished from a duty of virtue), then faithful performance (in keeping with promises made in a contract) would be put in the same class with actions of benevolence and the obligation to them, and this must not happen. It is no duty of virtue to keep one's promises but a duty of Right, to the performance of which one can be coerced. But it is still a virtuous action (a proof of virtue) to do it even where no coercion may be *applied*. The doctrine of Right and the doctrine of virtue are therefore distinguished not so much by their different duties as by the difference in their lawgiving, which connects one incentive or the other with the law.

---

2. A *deduction* of the division of a system, i.e. a proof that it is both complete and *continuous*—that is, that a transition from the concept divided to the members of the division takes place without a leap (*divisio per saltum*) in the entire series of subdivisions—is one of the most difficult conditions which the architect of a system has to fulfill. Even what the *highest divided concept* would be, the divisions of which are *right* and *wrong* (*aut fas aut nefas*), calls for reflection. This concept is the *act of free choice* in general. Teachers of ontology similarly begin with the concepts of *something* and *nothing*, without being aware that these are already members of a division for which the concept divided is missing. This concept can be only that of an *object* in general.

Ethical lawgiving (even if the duties might be external) is that which *cannot* be external; juridical lawgiving is that which can also be external. So it is an external duty to keep a promise made in a contract; but the command to do this merely because it is a duty, without regard for any other incentive, belongs to *internal* lawgiving alone. So the obligation is assigned to ethics not because the duty is of a particular kind (a particular kind of action to which one is bound)—for there are external duties in ethics as well as in Right—but rather because the lawgiving in this case is an internal one and can have no external lawgiver. For the same reason duties of benevolence, even though they are external duties (obligations to external actions), are still assigned to ethics because their lawgiving can be only internal. Ethics has its special duties as well (e.g., duties to oneself), but it also has duties in common with Right; what it does not have in common with Right is only the kind of *obligation*. For what is distinctive of ethical lawgiving is that one is to perform actions just because they are duties and to make the principle of duty itself, wherever the duty comes from, the sufficient incentive for choice. So while there are many *directly ethical* duties, internal lawgiving makes the rest of them, one and all, indirectly ethical.

IV

Preliminary Concepts of the Metaphysics of Morals (Philosophia practica universalis)

The concept of *freedom* is a pure rational concept, which for this very reason is transcendent for theoretical philosophy, that is, it is a concept such that no instance corresponding to it can be given in any possible experience, and of an object of which we cannot obtain any theoretical knowledge: The concept of freedom cannot hold as a constitutive but solely as a regulative and, indeed, merely negative principle of speculative reason. But in reason's practical use the concept of freedom proves its reality by practical principles, which are laws of a causality of pure reason for determining choice independently of any empirical conditions (of sensibility generally) and prove a pure will in us, in which moral concepts and laws have their source.

On this concept of freedom, which is positive (from a practical point of view), are based unconditional practical laws, which are called *moral*. For us, whose choice is sensibly affected and so does not of itself conform to the pure will but often opposes it, moral laws are *imperatives* (commands or prohibitions) and indeed categorical (unconditional) imperatives. As such they are distinguished from technical imperatives (precepts of art), which always command only conditionally. By categorical imperatives certain actions are *permitted* or *forbidden*, that is, morally possible or impossible, while some of them or their opposites are morally necessary, that is, obligatory. For those actions, then, there arises the concept of a duty, observance or transgression of which is indeed connected with a pleasure or pain of a distinctive kind (moral *feeling*), although in practical laws of reason we take no account of the feelings (since they have nothing to do with the *basis* of practical laws but only with the subjective *effect* in the mind when our choice is determined by them, which can differ from one subject to another [without objectively, i.e., in the judgment of reason, at all adding to or detracting from the validity or influence of these laws]).

The following concepts are common to both parts of *The Metaphysics of Morals*.

Obligation is the necessity of a free action under a categorical imperative of reason.

An imperative is a practical rule by which an action in itself contingent is *made* necessary. An imperative differs from a practical law in that a law indeed represents an action as necessary but takes no account of whether this action already inheres by an *inner* necessity in the acting subject (as in a holy being) or whether it is contingent (as in man); for where the former is the case there is no imperative. Hence an imperative is a rule the representation of which *makes* necessary an action that is subjectively contingent and thus represents the subject as one that must be *constrained* (necessitated) to conform with the rule. A categorical (unconditional) imperative is one that represents an action as objectively necessary and makes it necessary not indirectly, through the representation of some *end* that can be attained by the action, but through the mere representation of this action itself (its form), and hence directly. No other practical doctrine can furnish instances of such imperatives than that which prescribes obligation (the doctrine of morals). All other imperatives are *technical* and are, one and all, conditional. The ground of the possibility of categorical imperatives is this: that they refer to no other property of choice (by which some purpose can be ascribed to it) than simply to its *freedom*.

That action is *permitted* (*licitum*) which is not contrary to obligation; and this freedom, which is not limited by any opposing imperative, is called an authorization (*facultas moralis*). Hence it is obvious what is meant by *forbidden* (*illicitum*).

Duty is that action to which someone is bound. It is therefore the matter of obligation, and there can be one and the same duty (as to the action) although we can be bound to it in different ways.

> A categorical imperative, because it asserts an obligation with respect to certain actions, is a morally practical *law*. But since obligation involves not merely practical necessity (such as a law in general asserts) but also *necessitation*, a categorical imperative is a law which either commands or prohibits, depending on whether it represents as a duty the commission or omission of an action. An action that is neither commanded nor prohibited is merely *permitted*, since there is no law limiting one's freedom (one's authorization) with regard to it and so too no duty. Such an action is called morally indifferent (*indifferens, adiaphoron, res merae facultatis*). The question can be raised whether there are such actions and, if there are, whether there must be permissive laws (*lex permissiva*), in addition to laws that command and prohibit (*lex praeceptiva, lex mandati* and *lex prohibitiva, lex vetiti*), in order to account for someone's being free to do or not to do something as he pleases. If so, the authorization would not always have to do with an indifferent action (*adiaphoron*); for, considering the action in terms of moral laws, no special law would be required for it.

An action is called a *deed* insofar as it comes under obligatory laws and hence insofar as the subject, in doing it, is considered in terms of the freedom of his choice. By such an action the agent is regarded as the *author* of its effect, and this, together with the action itself, can be *imputed* to him, if one is previously acquainted with the law by virtue of which an obligation rests on these.

A *person* is a subject whose actions can be *imputed* to him. *Moral* personality is therefore nothing other than the freedom of a rational being under moral laws (whereas psychological personality is merely the capacity for being conscious of one's identity in different conditions of one's existence). From this it follows that a person is subject to no other laws than those he gives to himself (either alone or at least along with others).

A *thing* is that to which nothing can be imputed. Any object of free choice which itself lacks freedom is therefore called a thing (*res corporalis*).

A deed is *right* or *wrong* (*rectum aut minus rectum*) in general insofar as it conforms with duty or is contrary to it (*factum licitum aut illicitum*); the duty itself, in terms of its content or origin, may be of any kind. A deed contrary to duty is called a *transgression* (*reatus*).

An *unintentional* transgression which can still be imputed to the agent is called a mere *fault* (*culpa*). An *intentional* transgression (i.e., one accompanied by consciousness of its being a transgression) is called a *crime* (*dolus*). What is right in accordance with external laws is called *just* (*iustum*); what is not, *unjust* (*iniustum*).

A *conflict of duties* (*collisio officiorum s. obligationum*) would be a relation between them in which one would cancel the other (wholly or in part). But since duty and obligation are concepts that express the objective practical *necessity* of certain actions and two rules opposed to each other cannot be necessary at the same time, if it is a duty to act in accordance with one rule, to act in accordance with the opposite rule is not a duty but even contrary to duty; so a *collision of duties* and obligations is inconceivable (*obligationes non colliduntur*). However, a subject may have, in a rule he prescribes to himself, two *grounds* of obligation (*rationes obligandi*), one or the other of which is not sufficient to put him under obligation (*rationes obligandi non obligantes*), so that one of them is not a duty. When two such grounds conflict with each other, practical philosophy says, not that the stronger obligation takes precedence (*fortior obligatio vincit*), but that the stronger *ground of obligation* prevails (*fortior obligandi ratio vincit*).

Obligatory laws for which there can be an external lawgiving are called *external* laws (*leges externae*) in general. Those among them that can be recognized as obligatory a priori by reason even without external lawgiving are indeed external but *natural* laws, whereas those that do not bind without actual external lawgiving (and so without it would not be laws) are called *positive* laws. One can therefore conceive of external lawgiving that would contain only positive laws; but then a natural law would still have to precede it, which would establish the authority of the lawgiver (i.e., his authorization to bind others by his mere *choice*).

A principle that makes certain actions duties is a practical law. A rule that the agent himself makes his principle on subjective grounds is called his *maxim*; hence different agents can have very different maxims with regard to the same law.

The categorical imperative, which as such only affirms what obligation is, is: Act upon a maxim that can also hold as a universal law. You must therefore first consider your actions in terms of their subjective principles; but you can know whether this principle also holds objectively only in this way: That when your reason subjects it to the test of conceiving yourself as also giving universal law through it, it qualifies for such a giving of universal law.

The simplicity of this law in comparison with the great and various consequences that can be drawn from it must seem astonishing at first, as must also its authority to command without appearing to carry any incentive with it. But in wondering at a capacity of our reason to determine choice by the mere Idea that a maxim qualifies for the *universality* of a practical law, one learns that just these practical (moral) laws first make known a property of choice, namely its freedom, which speculative reason would never have arrived at, either on a priori grounds or through any experience whatever, and which, once reason has arrived at it, could in no way be shown theoretically to be possible, although these practical laws show incontestably that our choice has this property. It then seems less strange to find that these laws, like mathematical postulates, are *incapable of being proved* and yet *apodictic*, but at the same time to see a whole field of practical knowledge open up before one, where reason in its theoretical use, with the same Idea of freedom or with any other of its Ideas of the supersensible, must find everything closed tight against it. The conformity of an action with the law of duty is its *legality* (*legalitas*); the conformity of the maxim of an action with a law is the *morality* (*moralitas*) of the action. A *maxim* is a *subjective* principle of action, a principle which the subject himself makes his rule (how he wills to act). A principle of duty, on the other hand, is a principle that reason prescribes to him absolutely and so objectively (how he *ought to* act).

The supreme principle of the doctrine of morals is, therefore: Act on a maxim that can also hold as a universal law. Any maxim that does not so qualify is contrary to morals.

Laws proceed from the will, *maxims* from choice. In man the latter is a capacity for free choice; the will, which is directed to nothing beyond the law itself, cannot be called either free or unfree, since it is not directed to actions but immediately to giving laws for the maxims of actions (and is, therefore, practical reason itself).

Hence the will directs with absolute necessity and is itself *subject to* no necessitation. Only *choice* can therefore be called *free*.

But freedom of choice cannot be defined—as some have tried to define it—as the capacity to make a choice for or against the law (*libertas indifferentiae*) even though choice as a *phenomenon* provides frequent examples of this in experience. For we know freedom (as it first becomes manifest to us through the moral law) only as a *negative* property in us, namely that of not being *necessitated* to act through any sensible determining grounds. But we cannot present *theoretically* freedom as a *noumenon*, that is, freedom regarded as the capacity of man merely as an intelligence, and show how it can *exercise constraint* upon his sensible choice; we cannot therefore present freedom as a positive property. But we can indeed see that, although experience shows that man as a *sensible being* has the capacity to choose *in opposition to* as well as *in conformity with* the law, his freedom as an *intelligible being* cannot be *defined* by this, since appearances cannot make any supersensible object (such as free choice) understandable. We can also see that freedom can never be located in a rational subject's being able to make a choice in opposition to his (lawgiving) reason, even though experience proves often enough that this happens (though we still cannot conceive how this is possible). For it is one thing to accept a proposition (on the basis of experience) and another thing to make it the *expository principle* (of the concept of free choice) and the universal feature for distinguishing it (from *arbitrio bruto s. servo*); for the first does not maintain that the feature belongs *necessarily* to the concept, but the second requires this. Only freedom in relation to the internal lawgiving of reason is really a capacity; the possibility of deviating from it is an incapacity. How can that capacity be defined by this incapacity? It would be a definition that added to the practical concept the *exercise* of it, as this is taught by experience, a *hybrid definition* (*definitio hybrida*) that puts the concept in a false light.

A (morally practical) *law* is a proposition that contains a categorical imperative (a command). One who commands (*imperans*) through a law is the *lawgiver* (*legislator*). He is the author (*autor*) of the obligation in accordance with the law, but not always the author of the law. In the latter case the law would be a positive (contingent) and chosen law. A law that binds us a priori and unconditionally by our own reason can also be expressed as proceeding from the will of a supreme lawgiver, that is, one who has only rights and no duties (hence from the divine will); but this signifies only the Idea of a moral being whose will is a law for everyone, without his being thought as the author of the law.

Imputation (*imputatio*) in the moral sense is the *judgment* by which someone is regarded as the author (*causa libera*) of an action, which is then called a *deed* (*factum*) and stands under laws. If the judgment also carries with it the rightful consequences of this deed, it is an imputation having rightful force (*imputatio iudiciaria s. valida*); otherwise it is merely an imputation *appraising* the deed (*imputatio diiudicatoria*). The (natural or moral) person that is authorized to impute with rightful force is called a *judge* or a court (*iudex s. forum*).

If someone does *more* in the way of duty than he can be coerced by law to do, what he does is *meritorious* (*meritum*); if what he does is just exactly what the law *requires*, he does *what is owed* (*debitum*); finally, if what he does is *less* than the law requires, it is morally *culpable* (*demeritum*). The *rightful* effect of what is culpable is *punishment* (*poena*); that of a meritorious deed is *reward* (*praemium*) (assuming that the reward, promised in the law, was the inducement to it); conduct in keeping with what is owed has no rightful effect at all. Charitable *recompense* (*re-muneratio s. respensio*) stands in no *relation of Right* to a deed.

The good or bad results of an action that is owed, like the results of omitting a meritorious action, cannot be imputed to the subject (*modus imputationis tollens*).

The good results of a meritorious action, like the bad results of a wrongful action, can be imputed to the subject (*modus imputationis ponens*).

Subjectively, the degree to which an action *can be imputed* (*imputabilitas*) has to be assessed by the magnitude of the obstacles that had to be overcome. The greater the natural obstacles (of sensibility) and the less the moral obstacle (of duty), so much the more merit is to be accounted for a *good deed*, as when, for example, at considerable self-sacrifice I rescue a complete stranger from great distress.

On the other hand, the less the natural obstacles and the greater the obstacle from grounds of duty, so much the more is a transgression to be imputed (as culpable). Hence, the state of mind of the subject, whether he committed the deed in a state of agitation or with cool deliberation, makes a difference in imputation, which has results.

Introduction to the Doctrine of Right

§A.
What the Doctrine of Right Is

The sum of those laws for which an external lawgiving is possible is called the *Doctrine of Right* (*Ius*). If there has actually been such lawgiving, it is the doctrine of *positive Right*, and one versed in this, a jurist (*Iurisconsultus*), is said to be *experienced in the law* (*Iurisperitus*) when he not only knows external laws but also knows them externally, that is, in their application to cases that come up in experience. Such knowledge can also be called *legal expertise* (*Iurisprudentia*), but without both together it remains mere *juridical science* (*Iurisscientia*). The last title belongs to *sytematic* knowledge of the doctrine of natural Right (*Ius naturae*), although one versed in this must supply the immutable principles for any giving of positive law.

§B.
What Is Right?

Like the much-cited query "what is truth?" put to the logician, the question "what is Right?" might well embarrass the *jurist* if he does not want to lapse into a tautology or, instead of giving a universal solution, refer to what the laws in some country at some time prescribe. He can indeed state what is laid down as right (*quid sit iuris*), that is, what the laws in a certain place and at a certain time say or have said. But whether what these laws prescribed is also right, and what the universal criterion is by which one could recognize right as well as wrong (*iustum et iniustum*)—this would remain hidden from him unless he leaves those empirical principles behind for a while and seeks the sources of such judgments in reason alone, so as to establish the basis for any possible giving of positive laws (although positive laws can serve as excellent guides to this). Like the wooden head in Phaedrus' fable, a merely empirical doctrine of Right is a head that may be beautiful but unfortunately it has no brain.

The concept of Right, insofar as it is related to an obligation corresponding to it (i.e., the moral concept of Right), has to do, *first*, only with the external and indeed practical relation of one person to another, insofar as their actions, as facts, can have (direct or indirect) influence on each other. But, *second*, it does not signify the relation of one's choice to the mere wish (hence also to the mere need) of the other, as in actions of beneficence or callousness, but only a relation to the other's *choice*. *Third,* in this reciprocal relation of choice no account at all is taken of the *matter* of choice, that is, of the end each has in mind with the object he wants; it is not asked, for example, whether someone who buys goods from me for his own commercial use will gain by the transaction or not. All that is in question is the *form* in the relation of choice on the part of both, insofar as choice is regarded merely as *free*, and whether the action of one can be united with the freedom of the other in accordance with a universal law.

Right is therefore the sum of the conditions under which the choice of one can be united with the choice of another in accordance with a universal law of freedom.

§C.
The Universal Principle of Right

"Any action is *right* if it can coexist with everyone's freedom in accordance with a universal law, or if on its maxim the freedom of choice of each can coexist with everyone's freedom in accordance with a universal law."

If then my action or my condition generally can coexist with the freedom of everyone in accordance with a universal law, whoever hinders me in it does me *wrong;* for this hindrance (resistance) cannot coexist with freedom in accordance with a universal law.

It also follows from this that it cannot be required that this principle of all maxims be itself in turn my maxim, that is, it cannot be required that *I make it the maxim* of my action; for anyone can be free as long as I do not impair his freedom by my *external action,* even though I am quite indifferent to his freedom or would like in my heart to infringe upon it. That I make it my maxim to act rightly is a demand that ethics makes on me.

Thus the universal law of Right, so act externally that the free use of your choice can coexist with the freedom of everyone in accordance with a universal law, is indeed a law, which lays an obligation on me, but it does not at all expect, far less demand, that I *myself should* limit my freedom to those conditions just for the sake of this obligation; instead, reason says only that freedom *is* limited to those conditions in conformity with the Idea of it and that it may also be actively limited by others; and it says this as a postulate that it is incapable of further proof. When one's

aim is not to teach virtue but only to set forth what is *right*, one may not and should not represent that law of Right as itself the incentive to action.

§D.
Right Is Connected with an Authorization to Use Coercion

Resistance that counteracts the hindering of an effect promotes this effect and is consistent with it. Now whatever is wrong is a hindrance to freedom in accordance with universal laws. But coercion is a hindrance or resistance to freedom. Therefore, if a certain use of freedom is itself a hindrance to freedom in accordance with universal laws (i.e., wrong), coercion that is opposed to this (as a *hindering of a hindrance to freedom*) is consistent with freedom in accordance with universal laws, that is, it is right. Hence there is connected with Right by the principle of contradiction an authorization to coerce someone who infringes upon it.

§E.
A Strict Right Can Also Be Represented as the Possibility of a Fully Reciprocal Use of Coercion That Is Consistent with Everyone's Freedom in Accordance with Universal Laws

This proposition says, in effect, that Right should not be conceived as made up of two elements, namely an obligation in accordance with a law and an authorization of him who by his choice puts another under obligation to coerce him to fulfill it. Instead one can locate the concept of Right directly in the possibility of connecting universal reciprocal coercion with the freedom of everyone. That is to say, just as Right generally has as its object only what is external in actions, so strict Right, namely that which is not mingled with anything ethical, requires only external grounds for determining choice; for only then is it pure and not mixed with any precepts of virtue. Only a completely external Right can therefore be called *strict* (Right in the narrow sense). This is indeed based on everyone's consciousness of obligation in accordance with a law; but if it is to remain pure, this consciousness may not and cannot be appealed to as an incentive to determine his choice in accordance with this law. Strict Right rests instead on the principle of its being possible to use external constraint that can coexist with the freedom of everyone in accordance with universal laws. Thus, when it is said that a creditor has a right to require his debtor to pay his debt, this does not mean that he can remind the debtor that his reason itself puts him under obligation to perform this; it means instead that coercion which constrains everyone to pay his debts can coexist with the freedom of everyone, including that of debtors, in accordance with a universal external law. Right and authorization to use coercion therefore mean one and the same thing.

The law of a reciprocal coercion necessarily in accord with the freedom of everyone under the principle of universal freedom is, as it were, the *construction* of that concept, that is, the presentation of it in pure intuition a priori, by analogy with presenting the possibility of bodies moving freely under the law of the *equality of action and reaction*. In pure mathematics we cannot derive the properties of its objects immediately from concepts but can discover them only by constructing concepts. Similarly, it is not so much the *concept* of Right as rather a fully reciprocal and equal coercion brought under a universal law and consistent with it, that makes the presentation of that concept possible. Moreover, just as a purely formal concept of pure mathematics (e.g., of geometry) underlies the dynamical concept [of the equality of action and reaction], reason has taken care to furnish the understanding as far as possible with a priori intuitions for constructing the concept of Right. A right line (*rectum*), one that is straight, is opposed to one that is *curved* on the one hand and to one that is *oblique* on the other hand. As opposed to one that is curved, straightness is that *inner property* of a line such that there is only one line between two given points. As opposed to one that is oblique, straightness is that *position* of a *line* toward another intersecting or touching it such that there can be only *one* line (the perpendicular) that does not incline more to one side than to the other and that divides the space on both sides equally. Analogously to this, the doctrine of Right wants to be sure that *what belongs* to each has been determined (with mathematical exactitude). Such exactitude cannot be expected in the doctrine of virtue, which cannot refuse some room for exceptions (*latitudinem*). But without making incursions into the province of ethics, one finds two cases that lay claim to a decision about rights, although no one can be found to decide them, and that belong as it were within the *intermundia* of Epicurus. We must first separate these two cases from the doctrine of Right proper, to which we are about to proceed, so that their wavering principles will not affect the firm basic principles of the doctrine of Right.

Appendix to the Introduction to the Doctrine of Right

*On Equivocal Rights (*Ius aequivocum*)*

An authorization to use coercion is connected with any right in the *narrow* sense (*ius strictum*). But people also think of a right in a *wider* sense (*ius latium*), in which there is no law by which an authorization to use coercion can be determined. There are two such true or alleged rights, *equity* and the *right of necessity*. The first admits a right without coercion, the second, coercion without a right. It can easily be seen that this equivocation really arises from the fact that there are cases in which a right is in question but for which no judge can be appointed to render a decision.

I.
*Equity (*Aequitas*)*

Equity (considered objectively) is in no way a basis for merely calling upon another to fulfill an ethical duty (to be benevolent and kind). One who demands something on this basis stands instead upon his *right*, except that he does not have the conditions that a judge needs in order to determine by how much or in what way his claim could be satisfied. Suppose that the terms on which a trading company was formed were that the partners should share equally in the profits, but that one partner nevertheless *did* more than the others and so *lost* more when the company met with reverses. By *equity* he can demand more from the company than merely an equal share with the others. In accordance with proper (strict) Right, however, his demand would be refused; for if one thinks of a judge in this case, he would have no definite particulars (*data*) to enable him to decide how much is due by the contract. Or suppose that a domestic servant is paid his wages at the end of a year in money that has depreciated in the interval, so that he cannot buy with it what he could have bought with it when he concluded the contract. The servant cannot appeal to his right to be compensated when he gets the same amount of money but it is of unequal value. He can appeal only on grounds of equity (a mute divinity who cannot be heard); for nothing was specified about this in the contract, and a judge cannot pronounce in accordance with indefinite conditions.

It also follows from this that a *court of equity* (in a conflict with others about their rights) involves a contradiction. Only where the judge's own rights are concerned, and he can dispose of the case for his own person, may and should he listen to equity, as, for example, when the crown itself bears the damages that others have incurred in its service and for which they petition it to indemnify them, even though it could reject their claim by strict Right on the pretext that they undertook this service at their own risk.

The *motto* (*dictum*) of *equity* is, "the strictest Right is the greatest wrong" (*summum ius summa iniuria*). But this evil cannot be remedied by way of what is laid down as right, even though it concerns a claim to a right; for this claim belongs only to the *court of conscience* (*forum poli*), whereas every question of what is laid down as right must be brought before *civil Right* (*forum soli*).

II.

The Right of Necessity (Ius Necessitatis)

This alleged right is supposed to be an authorization to take the life of another who is doing nothing to harm me, when I am in danger of losing my own life. It is evident that were there such a right the doctrine of Right would have to be in contradiction with itself. For the issue here is not that of a *wrongful* assailant upon my life whom I forestall by depriving him of his life (*ius inculpatae tutelae*), in which case a recommendation to show moderation (*moderamen*) belongs not to Right but only to ethics. It is instead a matter of violence being permitted against someone who has used no violence against me.

It is clear that this assertion is not to be understood objectively, in terms of what a law prescribes, but only subjectively, as the verdict that would be given by a court. In other words, there can be no *penal law* that would assign the death penalty to someone in a shipwreck who, in order to save his own life, shoves another, whose life is equally in danger, off a plank on which he had saved himself. For the punishment threatened by the law could not be greater than the loss of his own life. A penal law of this sort could not have the effect intended, since a threat of an evil that is still *uncertain* (death by a judicial verdict) cannot outweigh the fear of an evil that is certain (drowning). Hence the deed of saving one's life by violence is not to be judged *inculpable* (*inculpabile*) but only *unpunishable* (*impunibile*), and by a strange confusion jurists take this *subjective* impunity to be *objective* impunity (conformity with law).

The motto of the right of necessity says: "Necessity has no law" (*necessitas non habet legem*). Yet there could be no necessity that would make what is wrong conform with law.

One sees that in both appraisals of what is right (in terms of a right of equity and a right of necessity) the *equivocation* (*aequivocatio*) arises from confusing the objective with the subjective basis of exercising the right (before reason and before a court). What someone by himself recognizes on good grounds as right will not be confirmed by a court, and what he must judge to be of itself wrong is treated with indulgence by a court; for the concept of Right, in these two cases, is not taken in the same sense.

Division of the Doctrine of Right

A.

General Division of Duties of Right

One can follow Ulpian in making this division if a sense is ascribed to his formulas which he may not have thought distinctly in them but which can be explicated from them or put into them. They are the following:

1) *Be an honorable man* (*honeste vive*). *Rightful honor* (*honestas iuridica*) consists in asserting one's worth as a man in relation to others, a duty

expressed by the saying, "Do not make yourself a mere means for others but be at the same time an end for them." This duty will be explained later as obligation from the *Right* of humanity in our own person (*Lex iusti*).

2) *Do not wrong anyone* (*neminem laede*) even if, to avoid doing so, you should have to stop associating with others and shun all society (*Lex iuridica*).

3) (If you cannot help associating with others), *enter into a society with them in which each can keep

what is his (*suum cuique tribue*). If this last formula were translated "Give to each what is *his*," what it says would be absurd, since one cannot give anyone something he already has. In order to make sense it would have to read: "*Enter* a condition in which what belongs to each can be secured to him against everyone else" (*Lex iustitiae*).

So the above three classical formulas serve also as principles for dividing the system of duties of Right into *internal* duties, *external* duties, and duties that involve the derivation of the latter from the principle of the former by subsumption.

B.
General Division of Rights

1) As systematic *doctrines*, Rights are divided into *natural Right*, which rests only on a priori principles, and *positive* (statutory) Right, which proceeds from the will of a legislator.

2) The highest division of rights, as (moral) *capacities* for putting others under obligations (i.e., as a lawful basis, *titulum*, for doing so), is the division into *innate* and *acquired* right. An innate right is that which belongs to everyone by nature, independently of any act that would establish a right; an acquired right is that for which such an act is required.

What is innately mine or yours can also be called what is *internally* mine or yours (*meum vel tuum internum*); for what is externally mine or yours must always be acquired.

There Is Only One Innate Right

Freedom (independence from being constrained by another's choice), insofar as it can coexist with the freedom of every other in accordance with a universal law, is the only original right belonging to every man by virtue of his humanity. This principle of innate freedom already involves the following authorizations, which are not really distinct from it (as if they were members of the division of some higher concept of a right): innate *equality*, that is, independence from being bound by others to more than one can in turn bind them; hence a man's quality of being *his own master* (*sui iuris*), as well as being a man

beyond reproach (*iusti*), since before he performs any act affecting rights he has done no wrong to anyone; and finally, his being authorized to do to others anything that does not in itself diminish what is theirs, so long as they do not want to accept it—such things as merely communicating his thoughts to them, telling or promising them something, whether what he says is true and sincere or untrue and insincere (*veriloquium aut falsiloquium*); for it is entirely up to them whether they want to believe him or not.[1]

The aim in introducing such a division within the system of natural Right (so far as it is concerned with innate right) is that when a dispute arises about an acquired right and the question comes up, on whom does the burden of proof (*onus probandi*) fall, either about a controversial fact or, if this is settled, about a controversial right, someone who refuses to accept this obligation can appeal methodically to his innate right to freedom (which is now specified in its various relations), as if he were appealing to various bases for rights.

With regard to what is innately, hence internally, mine or yours, there are not several *rights;* there is only *one* right. Since this highest division consists of two members very unequal in content, it can be put in the prolegomena and the division of the doctrine of Right can refer only to what is externally mine or yours.

Division of the Metaphysics of Morals as a Whole
I.

All duties are either *duites of Right* (*officia iuris*), that is, duties for which external lawgiving is possi-

---

1. Telling an untruth intentionally, even though merely frivolously, is usually called a *lie* (*mendacium*), because it can also harm someone, at least to the extent that if he ingenuously repeats it others ridicule him as gullible. The only kind of untruth we want to call a lie, in the sense *bearing upon rights*, is one that directly infringes upon another's right, e.g., the false allegation that a contract has been concluded with someone, made in order to deprive him of what is his (*falsiloquium dolosum*). And this distinction between closely related concepts is not without basis; for when someone merely says what he thinks, another always remains free to take it as he pleases. But a rumor, having some basis, that this is a man whose talk cannot be believed comes so close to the reproach of calling him a liar that the borderline separating what belongs to *Ius* from what must be assigned to ethics can only be drawn in just this way.

ble, or *duties of virtue (officia virtutis s. ethica)*, for which external lawgiving is not possible. Duties of virtue cannot be subject to external lawgiving simply because they have to do with an end which (or the having of which) is also a duty. No external lawgiving can bring about someone's setting an end for himself (because this is an internal act of the mind), although it may prescribe external actions that lead to an end without the subject making it his end.

> But why is the doctrine of morals usually called (especially by Cicero) a doctrine of *duties* and not also a doctrine of *rights*, even though rights have reference to duties? The reason is that we know our own freedom (from which all moral laws, and so all rights as well as duties proceed) only through the *moral imperative*, which is a proposition commanding duty, from which the capacity for putting others under obligation, that is, the concept of a right, can afterward be explicated.

II.

In the doctrine of duties man can and should be represented in terms of the property of his capacity for freedom, which is wholly supersensible, and so too merely in terms of his *humanity*, his personality independent of physical attributes (*homo noumenon*), as distinguished from the same subject represented as affected by physical attributes, *man (homo phaenomenon)*. Accordingly Right and end, related in turn to duty in this twofold property, yield the following division:

DIVISION
in Accordance with the
Objective Relation of Law to Duty

Perfect Duty

Imperfect Duty

III.

The subjects between whom a relation of right to duty can be thought of (whether admissibly or not) can stand related to each other in different ways, and so a division can also be made from this point of view.

DIVISION
in Accordance with the Relation of the Subject Imposing Obligation to the Subject Put Under Obligation.

1.
The relation in terms of rights of men toward beings that have neither rights nor duties.

Vacat[2]
For these are beings lacking reason, which can neither bind us nor by which we can be bound.

2.
The relation in terms of rights of men toward beings that have rights as well as duties.

Adest
For this is a relation of men to men.

3.
The relation in terms of rights of men toward beings that have only duties but no rights.

Vacat
For these would be men without personality (serfs, slaves).

4.
The relation in terms of rights of men toward a being that has only rights but no duties (God).

Vacat
At least in philosophy, since such a being is not an object of possible experience.

So only in Number 2 is there found a *real* relation between right and duty. The reason that it is not to be found in Number 4 is that this would be a *transcendent* duty, that is, a duty for which no corresponding external subject imposing the obligation can *be given*, so that the relation here is only *ideal* from a theoretical point of view, that is, a relation to a thought-entity. We ourselves *make* the concept of this being, but this concept is not altogether *empty;* instead it is fruitful

---

2. *Vacat* might be rendered "has no members," *Adest* "has members."

in reference to ourselves and to maxims of internal morality, and so for an internal practical purpose, inasmuch as our entire *immanent duty* (that which can be fulfilled) lies only in this relation that can merely be thought of.

On the Division of Morals as a System of Duties in General

Doctrine of Elements   Doctrine of Method

Duties of Right   Duties of Virtue   Didactic   Ascetic

Private Right   Public Right
                    and so on, everything

that involves not only the contents of a scientific doctrine of morals but also its architectonic form, once its metaphysical first principles have traced out completely the universal principles for it.

The highest division of natural Right cannot be the division (sometimes made) into *natural* and *social* Right; it must instead be the division into natural and *civil* Right, the former of which is called *private Right* and the latter *public Right*. For a *state of nature* is not opposed to a social but to a civil condition, since there can certainly be society in a state of nature, but not *civil* society (which secures what is mine or yours by public laws). This is why Right in a state of nature is called private Right.

PRIVATE RIGHT
CONCERNING WHAT IS EXTERNALLY MINE OR YOURS IN GENERAL
Chapter I. How to Have Something External as One's Own

§1.

That is *rightfully mine (meum iuris)* with which I am so connected that another's use of it without my consent would wrong me. The subjective condition of any possible use is *possession*.

But something *external* would be mine only if I may assume that I could be wronged by another's use of a thing even *though I am not in possession of it*. So it would be self-contradictory to say that I have something external as my own if the concept of possession could not have different meanings, namely *sensible* possession and *intelligible* possession, and by the former could be understood *physical* possession but by the latter a *merely rightful* possession of the same object.

But the expression "an object is *external to me*" can mean either that it is an object merely *distinct* from me (the subject) or else that it is also to be found in *another location (positus)* in space or time. Only if it is taken in the first sense can possession be thought of as rational possession; if taken in the second sense it would have to be called empirical possession. *Intelligible* possession (if this is possible) is possession of an object *without holding it (detentio)*.

§2.
Postulate of Practical Reason with Regard to Rights

It is possible for me to have any external object of my choice as mine, that is, a maxim by which, if it were to become a law, an object of choice would *in itself* (objectively) have to *belong to no one (res nullius)* is contrary to rights.

For an object of my choice is something that I have the *physical* power to use. If it were nevertheless absolutely not within my *rightful* power to make use of it, that is, if the use of it could not coexist with the freedom of everyone in accordance with a universal law (would be wrong), then freedom would be depriving itself of the use of its choice with regard to an object of choice, by putting *usable* objects beyond any possibility of being *used;* in other words, it would annihilate them in a practical respect and make them into *res nullius*, even though in the use of things choice was formally consistent with everyone's outer freedom in accordance with universal laws. But since pure practical reason lays down only formal laws as the basis for using choice and thus abstracts from its matter, that is, from other properties of the object *provided only that it is an object of choice*, it can contain no absolute prohibition against using such an object, since this would be a contradiction of outer freedom with itself. But an object of my *choice* is that which I have the physical capacity to use as I please, that whose use lies within my *power* (*potentia*). This must be distinguished from having the same object under my control (*in potestatem meam redactum*), which presupposes not merely [such] a *capacity* but also an *act* of choice. But in order to *think of* something simply as an object of my choice it is sufficient for me to be conscious of having it within my power. It is therefore an a priori presupposition of practical reason to regard and treat any object of my choice as something that could objectively be mine or yours.

This postulate can be called a permissive principle (*lex permissiva*) of practical reason, which gives us an authorization that could not be got from mere concepts of Right as such, namely to put all others under an obligation, which they would not otherwise have, to refrain from using certain objects of our choice because we have been the first to take them into our possession. Reason wills that this hold as a principle, and it does this as *practical* reason, which extends itself a priori by this postulate of reason.

§3.

Whoever wants to assert that he has a thing as his own must be in possession of an object, since otherwise he could not be wronged by another's use of it without his consent. For if something outside this object which is not connected with it by rights affects it, it would not be able to affect himself (the subject) and do him any wrong.

§4.
Exposition of the Concept of External Objects That Are Mine or Yours

There can be only *three* external objects of my choice: (1) a (corporeal) *thing* external to me; (2) another's *choice* to perform a specific deed (*praestatio*); (3) another's *status* in relation to me. These are objects of my choice in terms of the categories of *substance*, *causality*, and *community* between myself and external objects in accordance with laws of freedom.

a) I cannot call an object in *space* (a corporeal thing) mine unless, *even though I am not in physical possession of it*, I can still assert that I am actually in some other (hence not physical) possession of it. So I shall not call an apple mine because I have it in my hand (possess it physically), but only if I can say that I possess it even though I have put it down, no matter where. In the same way, I shall not be able to say that the land on which I have lain down is mine because I am on it, but only if I can assert that it still remains in my possession even though I have left the place. For someone who tried in the first case (of empirical possession) to wrest the apple from my hand or to drag me away from my resting place would indeed wrong me with regard to what is *internally* mine (freedom); but he would not wrong me with regard to what is externally mine unless I could assert that I am in possession of the object even without holding it. I could not then call these objects (the apple and the resting place) mine.

b) I cannot call the *performance* of something by another's choice mine if all I can say is that it came into my possession *at the same time* that he promised it (*pactum re initum*) but only if I can assert that I am in possession of the other's choice (to determine him to perform it) even though the time for his performing it is still to come. The other's promise is therefore included in my belongings and goods (*obligatio activa*), and I can count it as mine not merely if (as in the first case) I already have *what was promised* in my possession, but even though I do not possess it yet. So I must be able to think that I am in possession of this object independently of being limited by temporal conditions, and so independently of empirical possession.

c) I cannot call a *wife*, a *child*, a *servant*, or, in general, another person mine because I am now in charge of them as members of my household or have them within my restraining walls and in my control and possession, but only if, although they have withdrawn from such constraint and I do not possess them (empirically), I can still say that I possess them merely by my will, hence *merely rightfully*, as long as they exist somewhere or at some time. Only if and insofar as I can assert this are they included in my belongings.

§5.

Definition of the Concept of External Objects That Are Mine or Yours

The *nominal definition* of what is externally mine—that which suffices only to *distinguish* the object from all others and arises from a complete and determinate *exposition* of the concept—would be: That outside me is externally mine which it would be a wrong (an infringement upon my freedom that can coexist with the freedom of everyone in accordance with a universal law) to prevent me from using as I please. But the *real definition* of this concept—that which also suffices for the *deduction* of it (for knowledge of the possibility of the object)—goes like this: Something external is mine if I would be wronged by being disturbed in my use of it *even though I am not in possession of it* (not holding the object). I must be in some sort of possession of an external object if it is to be called *mine*, for otherwise someone who affected this object against my will would not also affect me and so would not wrong me. So, in consequence of §4, *intelligible possession (possessio noumenon)* must be assumed to be possible if something external is to be mine or yours. Empirical possession (holding) is then only possession in *appearance (possessio phaenomenon)*, although the *object* itself that I possess is not here treated, as it was in the Transcendental Analytic, as an appearance but as a thing in itself; for there reason was concerned with theoretical knowledge of the nature of things and how far it could extend, but here it is concerned with the practical determination of choice in accordance with laws of *freedom*, whether the object can be known through the senses or through the pure understanding alone, and *Right* is a pure practical *rational concept* of choice under laws of freedom.

For the same reason it is not appropriate to speak of possessing a right to this or that object but rather of possessing it *merely rightfully*; for a right is already an intellectual possession of an object and it would make no sense to speak of possessing a possession.

§6.

Deduction of the Concept of Merely Rightful Possession of an External Object (possessio noumenon)

The question, How is it possible for *something external to be mine or yours?* resolves itself into the question, How is *merely rightful* (intelligible) *possession* possible? and this, in turn, into the third question, How is a *synthetic* a priori proposition of Right possible?

All propositions of Right are a priori propositions, since they are principles of reason (*dictamina rationis*). An a priori proposition of Right with regard to *empirical possession* is *analytic*, for it says nothing more than what follows from empirical possession in accordance with the principle of contradiction, namely that if I am holding a thing (and so physically connected with it), someone who affects it without my consent (e.g., snatches an apple from my hand) affects and diminishes what is internally mine (my freedom), so that his maxim is in direct contradiction with the axiom of Right. So the proposition about empirical possession in conformity with rights does not go beyond the right of a person with regard to himself.

On the other hand, a proposition about the possibility of possessing a thing *external to myself*, which puts aside any conditions of empirical possession in space and time (and hence presupposes the possibility of *possessio noumenon*), goes beyond those limiting conditions; and since it affirms possession of something even without holding it, as necessary for the concept of something external that is mine or yours, *it is synthetic*. Reason has then the task of showing how such a proposition, which goes beyond the concept of empirical possession, is possible a priori.

[In this way, for example, taking possession of a separate piece of land is an act of private choice, without being *unsanctioned*. The possessor bases his act on an innate *possession in common* of the surface of the earth and on a general will corresponding a priori to it, which permits *private possession* on it (otherwise, unoccupied things would in themselves and in accordance with a law be made things that belong to no one). By being the first to take possession he originally acquires a definite piece of land and resists with right (*iure*) anyone else who would prevent him from making private use of it. Yet since he is in a state of nature, he cannot do so by legal proceedings (*de iure*) because there does not exist any public law in this state.

Even if a piece of land were considered or declared to be *free*, that is, open to anyone's use, one could still not say that it is free by nature or *originally* free, prior to any act establishing a right; for that would again be a relation to things, namely to the land, which would refuse possession of itself to anyone; instead one would say that this land is free because of a prohibition on everyone to make use of it, and for this, possession of it in common is required, which cannot take place without a contract. But land that can be free only in this way must really be in the possession of all those (joined together) who forbid or suspend one another's use of it.

This *original* community of land, and with it of things upon it (*communio fundi originaria*), is an Idea that has objective (rightfully practical) reality. This kind of community must be sharply distinguished from a *primitive community* (*communio primaeva*), which is a fiction; for a primitive community would have to be one that was *instituted* and arose from a contract by which everyone gave up private possessions and, by uniting his possessions with those of everyone else, transformed them into a collective possession; and history would have to give us proof of such a contract. But it is contradictory to claim that such a procedure is an *original* taking possession and that each man could and should have based his separate possession upon it.

Residing on land (*sedes*) is to be distinguished from being in possession (*possessio*) of it, and *settling* or making a settlement (*incolatus*), which is a lasting private possession of a place dependent upon the presence of the subject on it, is to be distinguished from taking possession of land with the intention of some day acquiring it. I am not talking here about settling as a second act to establish a right, which can either follow upon taking possession or not take place at all; for settling of this kind would not be original possession but would be possession derived from others' consent.

Merely physical possession of land (holding it) is already a right to a thing, though certainly not of itself sufficient for regarding it as mine. Relative to others, since (as far as one knows) it is first possession, it is consistent with the principle of outer freedom and is also implied in original possession in common, which provides a priori the basis on which any private possession is possible. Accordingly, to interfere with the use of a piece of land by the first occupant of it is to wrong him. Taking first possession has therefore a rightful basis (*titulus possessionis*), which is original possession in common; and the saying "Happy are those who are in possession" (*beati possidentes*), because none is bound to certify his possession, is a basic principle of natural Right, which lays down taking first possession as a rightful basis for acquisition on which every first possessor can rely.]

In an a priori *theoretical* principle, namely, an a priori intuition would have to underlie the given concept (as was established in the *Critique of Pure Reason*); and so something would have to be *added to* the concept of possession of an object. But with this practical principle the opposite procedure is followed and all conditions of intuition that establish empirical possession must be *removed* (disregarded), in order to *extend* the concept of possession beyond empirical possession and to be able to say: It is possible for any external object of my choice to be reckoned as rightfully mine if I have control of it (and only insofar as I have control of it) without being in possession of it.

The possibility of this kind of possession, and so the deduction of the concept of nonempirical possession, is based on the postulate of practical reason with regard to rights: "that it is a duty of Right to act toward others so that what is external (usable) could also become someone's," together with the exposition of the concept of an external object that belongs to someone, since that concept rests simply on that of *nonphysical* possession. There is, however, no way of proving of itself the possibility of nonphysical possession or of having any insight into it (just because it is a rational concept for which no corresponding intuition can be given); its possibility is instead an immediate consequence of the postulate referred to. For if it is necessary to act in accordance with that principle of Right, its intelligible condition (a merely rightful possession) must then also be possible. No one need be surprised that *theoretical* principles about external objects that are mine or yours get lost in the intelligible and represent no extension of knowledge, since no theoretical deduction can be given for the possibility of the concept of freedom on which they are based. It can only be inferred from the practical law of reason (the categorical imperative), as a fact of reason.

§7.
*Application to Objects of Experience
of the Principle That It Is Possible
for Something External to Be Mine or Yours*

The concept of merely rightful possession is not an empirical concept (dependent upon conditions of space and time) and yet it has practical reality, that is, it must be applicable to objects of experience, knowledge of which is dependent upon those conditions. The way to proceed with the concept of a right with respect to such objects, so that they can be external objects that are mine or yours, is the following. Since the concept of a right is simply a rational concept, it cannot be applied *directly* to objects of experience and to the concept of empirical *possession*, but must first be applied to the understanding's pure concept of *possession* in general. So the concept to which the concept of a right is directly applied is not that of *holding* (*detentio*), which is an empirical way of thinking of possession, but rather the concept of *having*, in which abstraction is made from all spatial and temporal conditions and the object is thought of only as *under my control* (*in potestate mea positum esse*). So too the expression *external* does not mean existing in a *place other* than where I am, or that my decision and acceptance are occurring at a different time from the making of the offer; it means only an object *distinct* from me. Now practical reason requires me, by its principle of Right, to apply mine or yours to objects not in accordance with sensible conditions but in abstraction from them, since it has to do with a determination of choice in accordance with laws of freedom, and it also requires me to think of possession of them in this way, since only a *concept of the understanding* can be subsumed under concepts of Right. I shall therefore say that I possess a field even though it is in a place quite different from where I actually am. For here we are speaking only of an intellectual relation to an object, insofar as I have it *under my control* (the understanding's concept of possession independent of spatial determinations), and the object is *mine* because my will to use it as I please does not conflict with the law of outer freedom. Here practical reason requires us to think of possession *apart from* possession of this object of my choice in appearance (holding it), to think of it not in terms of empirical concepts but of concepts of the understanding, those that can contain a priori conditions of empirical concepts. Upon this is based the validity of such a concept of possession (*possessio noumenon*), as a *giving of law* that holds for everyone; for such lawgiving is involved in the expression "this external object is *mine*," since by it an obligation is laid upon all others, which they would not otherwise have, to refrain from using the object.

So the way to have something external as what is mine consists in a merely rightful connection of the subject's will with that object in accordance with the concept of intelligible possession, independently of any relation to it in space and time. It is not because I occupy a place on the earth with my body that this place is something external that is mine (for that concerns only my outer *freedom*, hence only possession

of myself, not a thing external to me, so that it is only an internal right). It is mine if I still possess it even though I have left it for another place; only then is my external right involved. And anyone who wants to make my continuous occupation of this place by my person the condition of my having it as mine must either assert that it is not at all possible to have something external as mine (and this conflicts with the Postulate §2) or else require that in order to have it as mine I be in two places at once. Since this amounts to saying that I am to be in a place and also not be in it, he contradicts himself.

This can also be applied to the case of my having accepted a promise. For my having and possession in what was promised is not annulled by the promisor's saying at one time "this thing is to be yours" and then at a later time saying of the same thing "I now will that it not be yours." For in such intellectual relations it is as if the promisor had said, without any time between the two declarations of his will, "this is to be yours" and also "this is not to be yours," which is self-contradictory.

The same holds of the concept of rightful possession of a person, as included in the subject's belongings (his wife, child, servant). This domestic community and the possession of their respective status vis-à-vis one another by all its members is not annulled by their being authorized to separate from one another and go to different *places;* for what connects them is a relation *in terms of rights*, and what is externally mine or yours here is based, as in the preceding cases, entirely on the assumption that purely rational possession without holding each other is possible.

> Rightfully practical reason is forced into a critique of itself in the concept of something external that is mine or yours, and this by an antinomy of propositions concerning the possibility of such a concept; that is, only by an unavoidable dialectic in which both thesis and antithesis make equal claims to the validity of two conditions that are inconsistent with each other is reason forced, even in its practical use (having to do with rights), to make a distinction between possession as appearance and possession that is thinkable merely by the understanding.
>
> The *thesis* says: *It is possible* to have something external as mine even though I am not in possession of it.
>
> The *antithesis* says: *It is not possible* to have something external as mine unless I am in possession of it.
>
> *Solution:* Both propositions are true, the first if I understand, by the word possession, empirical possession (*possessio phaenomenon*), the second if I understand by it purely intelligible possession (*possessio*

noumenon). But we cannot see how intelligible possession is possible and so how it is possible for something external to be mine or yours, but must infer it from the postulate of practical reason. With regard to this postulate it is particularly noteworthy that practical reason *extends* itself without intuitions and without even needing any that are a priori, merely by *leaving out* empirical conditions, as it is justified in doing by the law of freedom. In this way it can lay down *synthetic* a priori propositions about Right, the proof of which (as will soon be shown) can afterwards be adduced, in a practical respect, in an analytic way.

§8.
It Is Possible to Have Something External as One's Own Only in a Rightful Condition, Under an Authority Giving Laws Publicly, That Is, in a Civil Condition

When I declare (by word or deed), I will that something external is to be mine, I thereby declare that everyone else is under obligation to refrain from using that object of my choice, an obligation no one would have were it not for this act of mine to establish a right. This claim involves, however, acknowledging that I in turn am under obligation to every other to refrain from using what is externally his; for the obligation here arises from a universal rule having to do with external rightful relations. I am therefore not under obligation to leave external objects belonging to others untouched unless everyone else provides me assurance that he will behave in accordance with the same principle with regard to what is mine. This assurance does not require a special act to establish a right, but is already contained in the concept of an obligation corresponding to an external right, since the universality, and with it the reciprocity, of obligation arises from a universal rule. Now a unilateral will cannot serve as a coercive law for everyone with regard to possession that is external and therefore contingent, since that would infringe upon freedom in accordance with universal laws. So it is only a will putting everyone under obligation, hence only a collective general (common) and powerful will, that can provide everyone this assurance. But the condition of being under a general external (i.e., public) lawgiving accompanied with power is the civil condition. So only in a civil condition can something external be mine or yours.

Corollary: If it must be possible, in terms of rights, to have an external object as one's own, the subject must also be permitted to constrain everyone else with whom he comes into conflict about whether an external object is his or another's to enter along with him into a civil constitution.

§9.
In a State of Nature Something External Can Actually Be Mine or Yours but Only Provisionally

When people are under a civil constitution, the statutory laws obtaining in this condition cannot infringe upon *natural Right* (i.e., that Right which can be derived from a priori principles for a civil constitution); and so the rightful principle "whoever acts on a maxim by which it becomes impossible to have an object of my choice as mine wrongs me," remains in force. For a civil constitution is just the rightful condition, by which what belongs to each is only secured, but not actually settled and determined. Any guarantee, then, already presupposes what belongs to someone (to whom it secures it). Prior to a civil constitution (or in *abstraction* from it) external objects that are mine or yours must therefore be assumed to be possible, and with them a right to constrain everyone with whom we could have any dealings to enter with us into a constitution in which external objects can be secured as mine or yours. Possession in anticipation of and preparation for the civil condition, which can be based only on a law of a common will, possession which therefore accords with the *possibility* of such a condition, is *provisionally rightful* possession, whereas possession found in an *actual* civil condition would be *conclusive* possession. Prior to entering such a condition, a subject who is ready for it resists with right those who are not willing to submit to it and who want to interfere with his present possession; for the will of all others except for himself, which proposes to put him under obligation to give up a certain possession, is merely *unilateral*, and hence has as little lawful force in denying him possession as he has in asserting it (since this can be found only in a general will), whereas he at least has the advantage of being compatible with the introduction and establishment of a civil condition. In summary, the way to have something external as one's own *in a state of nature* is physical possession that has in its favor the rightful *presumption* that it will be made into rightful possession through being united with the will of all in a public lawgiving, and in anticipation of this holds *comparatively* as rightful possession.

> In accordance with the formula *Happy is he who is in possession (beati possedentes)*, this prerogative of Right arising from empirical possession does not consist in its being unnecessary for the possessor, since he is presumed to be an *honest man*, to furnish proof that his possession is in conformity with right (for this holds only in disputes about rights). This prerogative arises instead from the capacity anyone has, by the postulate of practical reason, to have an external object of his choice as his own. Consequently, any holding of an external object is a condition whose conformity with right is based on that postulate by a previous act of will; and so long as this condition does not conflict with another's earlier possession of the same object he is provisionally justified, in accordance with the law of outer freedom, in preventing anyone who does not want to enter with him into a condition of public lawful freedom from usurping the use of that object, in order to put to his own use, in conformity with the postulate of reason, a thing that would otherwise be annihilated practically.

Chapter II How to Acquire Something External

§10.
General Principle of External Acquisition

I acquire something when I bring it about (*efficio*) that it becomes *mine*. Something external is originally mine which is mine without any act that establishes a right to it. But that *acquisition* is original which is not derived from what is another's.

Nothing external is originally mine, but it can indeed be *acquired* originally, that is, without being derived from what is another's. A condition of community (*communio*) of what is mine and yours can never be thought to be original but must be acquired (by an act that establishes an external right), although possession of an external object can originally be only possession in common. Even if one thinks (problematically) of an *original* community (*communio mei et tui originaria*), it must still be distinguished from a *primitive* community (*communio primaeva*), which is supposed to have been instituted in the earliest *time* of relations of rights among men and cannot be based, like the former, on principles but only on history. Although primitive, it would always have to be thought to be acquired and derived (*communio derivata*).

The principle of external acquisition is as follows: That is mine which I bring under my *control* (in accordance with the law of outer *freedom*); which, as an object of my choice, is something that I have the capacity to use (in accordance with the postulate of practical reason); and which, finally, I *will* to be mine (in conformity with the Idea of a possible united *will*).

The aspects (*attendenda*) of *original* acquisition are therefore: (1) *Apprehension* of an object that belongs to no one; otherwise it would conflict with another's freedom in accordance with universal laws. This *apprehension* is taking possession of an object of choice in space and time, so that the possession in which I put myself is *possessio phaenomenon*. (2) *Giving a sign* (*declaratio*) of my possession of this object and of my act of choice to exclude everyone else from it. (3) *Appropriation* (*appropriatio*), as the act of a general will (in Idea) giving an external law through which everyone is bound to agree with my choice. The validity of this last aspect of acquisition, on which rests the conclusion "this external object is *mine*," that is, the conclusion that my possession holds as possession *merely by right* (*possessio noumenon*), is based on this: Since all these acts *have to do with a right* and so proceed from practical reason, in the question of what is laid down as right abstraction can be made from the empirical conditions of possession, so that the conclusion, "the external object is mine," is correctly drawn from sensible to intelligible possession.

Original acquisition of an external object of choice is called *taking control* of it (*occupatio*), and only corporeal things (substances) can be acquired originally. When it takes place, what it requires as the condition of empirical possession is priority in time to anyone else who wants to take control of the object (*qui prior tempore potior iure*). As original, it is only the result of a *unilateral* choice, for if it required a bilateral choice the acquisition would be derived from the contract of two (or more) persons and so from what is another's. It is not easy to see how an act of choice of that kind could establish what belongs to someone. However, if an acquisition is *first* it is not therefore *original*. For the acquisition of a public rightful condition by the union of the will of all for giving universal law would be an acquisition such that none could precede it, yet it would be derived from the particular wills of each and would be *omnilateral*, whereas original acquisition can proceed only from a unilateral will.

Division of the Acquisition of Something External That Is Mine or Yours

1) In terms of the *matter* (the object), I acquire either a corporeal *thing* (substance), or another's *performance* (causality), or another *person* himself, that is, the status of that person, insofar as I get a right to make arrangements about him (deal with him).

2) In terms of the *form* (the kind of acquisition), it is either a *right to a thing* (*ius reale*), or a *right against a person (ius personale)*, or a *right to a person akin to a right to a thing (ius realiter personale)*, that is, possession (though not use) of another person as a thing.

3) In terms of the *basis* of the acquisition *in Right* (*titulus*), something external is acquired through the act of a *unilateral, bilateral,* or *omnilateral* choice (*facto, pacto, lege*). Although this is not, strictly speaking, a special member of the division of rights, it is still an aspect of the way acquisition is carried out.

SECTION I
ON PROPERTY RIGHT

§11.
What Is a Right to a Thing?

The usual exposition of a *right to a thing (ius reale, ius in re)*, that "it is a right *against every possessor of it*," is a correct nominal definition. But what is it that enables me to recover an external object from anyone who is holding it and to constrain him (*per vindicationem*) to put me in possession of it again? Could this external rightful relation of my choice be a *direct* relation to a corporeal thing? Someone who thinks that his right is a direct relation to things rather than to persons would have to think (though only obscurely) that since there corresponds to a right on one side a duty on the other, an external thing always remains *under obligation* to the first possessor even though it has left his hands; that, because it is already under obligation to him, it rejects anyone else who

pretends to be the possessor of it. So he would think of my right as if it were a *guardian spirit* accompanying the thing, always pointing me out to whoever else wanted to take possession of it and protecting it against any incursions by them. It is therefore absurd to think of an obligation of a person to things or the reverse, even though it may be permissible, if need be, to make this rightful relation perceptible by picturing it and expressing it in this way.

So the real definition would have to go like this: *A right to a thing* is a right to the private use of a thing of which I am in (original or instituted) possession in common with all others. For this possession in common is the only condition under which it is possible for me to exclude every other possessor from the private use of a thing (*ius contra quemlibet huius rei possessorem*) since, unless such a possession in common is assumed, it is inconceivable how I, who am not in possession of the thing, could still be wronged by others who are in possession of it and are using it. By my unilateral choice I cannot bind another to refrain from using a thing, an obligation he would not otherwise have; hence I can do this only through the united choice of all who possess it in common. Otherwise I would have to think of a right to a thing as if the thing had an obligation to me, from which my right against every other possessor of it is then derived; and this is an absurd way of representing it.

By the term Property Right (*ius reale*) should be understood not only a right to a thing (*ius in re*) but also the *sum* of all the principles having to do with things being mine or yours. But it is clear that a man who was all alone on the earth could really neither have nor acquire any external thing as his own, since there is no relation whatever of obligation between him, as a person, and any other external object, as a thing. Hence, speaking strictly and literally, there is also no (direct) right to a thing. What is called a right to a thing is only that right someone has against a person who is in possession of it in common with all others (in the civil condition).

§12.
First Acquisition of a Thing Can Be Only Acquisition of Land

Land (understood as all habitable ground) is to be regarded as the *substance* with respect to whatever is movable upon it, whereas the existence of the latter is to be regarded only as *inherence*. Just as in a theoretical sense accidents cannot exist apart from a substance, so in a practical sense no one can have what is movable on a piece of land as his own unless he is assumed to be already in rightful possession of the land.

For suppose that the land belonged to no one: I could then remove every movable thing on it from its place and take it for myself until they were all gone, without thereby infringing upon the freedom of anyone else who is not now holding it; but whatever can be destroyed, a tree, a house, and so forth, is movable (at least in terms of its matter), and if a thing that cannot be moved without destroying its form is called *immovable*, then by what is mine or yours with regard to that is understood not its substance but what adheres to it, which is not the thing itself.

§13.
Any Piece of Land Can Be Acquired Originally, and the Possibility of Such Acquisition Is Based on the Original Community of Land in General

The first proposition rests on the postulate of practical reason (§2). The proof of the second proposition is as follows.

All men are originally (i.e., prior to any act of choice that establishes a right) in a possession of land that is in conformity with right, that is, they have a right to be wherever nature or chance (apart from their will) has placed them. This kind of possession (*possessio*)—which is to be distinguished from residence (*sedes*), a chosen and therefore an acquired *lasting* possession—is possession *in common* because the spherical surface of the earth unites all the places on its surface; for if its surface were an unbounded plane, men could be so dispersed on it that they would not come into any community with one another, and community would not then be a necessary result of their existence on the earth. The possession by all men on the earth that precedes any acts of theirs which would establish rights (that is constituted by nature itself) is an *original possession in common* (*communio possessionis originaria*), the concept of which is not empirical and dependent upon temporal conditions, like that of a supposed *primitive possession in common* (*communio primaeva*), which can never be proved. Original possession in common is, rather, a practical rational concept which contains a priori the principle in accordance

with which alone men can use a place on the earth in accordance with principles of Right.

§14.
In Original Acquisition, the Act Required to Establish a Right Is Taking Control (occupatio)

The only condition under which *taking possession* (*apprehensio*), beginning to hold (*possessionis physicae*) a corporeal thing in space, conforms with the law of everyone's outer freedom (hence a priori) is that of *priority* in time, that is, only insofar as it is the *first* taking possession (*prior apprehensio*), which is an act of choice. But the will that a thing (and so too a specific, separate place on the earth) is to be mine, that is, appropriation of it (*appropriatio*), in original acquisition can be only *unilateral* (*voluntas unilateralis s. propria*). Acquisition of an external object of choice by a unilateral will is *taking control* of it. So original acquisition of an external object, and hence too of a specific and separate piece of land, can take place only through taking control of it (*occupatio*).

No insight can be had into the possibility of acquiring in this way, nor can it be demonstrated by reasons; its possibility is instead an immediate consequence of the postulate of practical reason. But the aforesaid will can justify an external acquisition only insofar as it is included in a will that is united a priori (i.e., only through the union of the choice of all who can come into practical relations with one another) and that commands absolutely. For a unilateral will (and a bilateral but still *particular* will is also unilateral) cannot put everyone under an obligation that is in itself contingent; this requires a will that is *omnilateral*, that is united not contingently but a priori and therefore necessarily, and because of this is the only will that is lawgiving. For only in accordance with this principle of the will is it possible for the free choice of each to accord with the freedom of all, and therefore possible for there to be any right, and so too possible for any external object to be mine or yours.

§15.
Something Can Be Acquired Conclusively Only in a Civil Constitution; in a State of Nature It Can Also Be Acquired, but Only Provisionally

A civil constitution, though its realization is subjectively contingent, is still objectively necessary, that is, necessary as a duty. With regard to such a constitution and its establishment there is therefore a real principle of natural Right to which any external acquisition is subject.

The *empirical title* of acquisition was taking physical possession (*apprehensio physica*), based on the original community of land. Since there is only possession in *appearance* to put under possession in accordance with rational concepts of Right, a title to take intellectual possession (setting aside all empirical conditions of space and time) must correspond to this empirical title of acquisition. This intellectual title is the basis of the proposition: "What I bring under my control in accordance with laws of outer freedom and will to become mine becomes mine."

But the *rational title* of acquisition can lie only in the Idea of a will of all united a priori (necessarily to be united), which is here tacitly assumed as a necessary condition (*conditio sine qua non*); for a unilateral will cannot put others under an obligation they would not otherwise have. But the condition in which the will of all is actually united for giving law is the civil condition. Therefore something external can be *originally* acquired only in conformity with the Idea of a civil condition, that is, with a view to it and to its being brought about, but prior to its realization (for otherwise acquisition would be derived). Hence *original* acquisition can be only *provisional*. *Conclusive* acquisition takes place only in the civil condition.

Still, that provisional acquisition is true acquisition; for, by the postulate of practical reason with regard to rights, the possibility of acquiring something external in whatever condition men may live together (and so also in a state of nature) is a principle of private Right, in accordance with which each is justified in using that coercion which is necessary if men are to leave the state of nature and enter the civil condition, which can alone make any acquisition conclusive.

The question arises, how far does authorization to take possession of a piece of land extend? As far as the capacity for controlling it extends, that is, as far as whoever wants to appropriate it can defend it—as if the land were to say, if you cannot protect me you cannot command me. This is how the dispute over whether the sea is *free* or *closed* also has to be decided; for example, as far as a cannon shot can reach no one may fish, haul up amber from the ocean floor, and so forth, along the coast of a territory that already belongs to a certain state. Moreover, in order to acquire land is it necessary to develop it (build on it, cultivate it, drain it, and so on)? No. For since these forms (of specification) are only accidents, they make no object of direct possession and can belong to what the subject possesses only insofar as the substance is already recognized as his. When first acquisition is in question, developing land is nothing more than an external sign of taking possession, for which many other signs that cost less effort can be substituted. Furthermore, may one party interfere with another in its *act* of taking possession, so that neither enjoys the right of priority and the land remains always free, belonging to no one? Not *entirely*; since one party can prevent another from taking possession only by being on adjacent land, where it itself can be prevented from being, *absolute* hindrance would be a contradiction. But *with respect to* a certain piece of land (lying between the two), leaving it unused, as *neutral* territory to separate the two parties, would still be consistent with the right of taking control. In that case, however, this land really belongs to both in common and is not something *belonging to no one* (*res nullius*), just because it is *used* by both to keep them apart. Again, can anyone have a thing as his own on land no part of which belongs to someone? Yes, as in Mongolia where, since all the land belongs to the people, the use of it belongs to each individual, so that anyone can leave his pack lying on it or recover possession of his horse if it runs away, since it is his. However, it is only by means of a *contract* that anyone can have a movable thing as his on land that belongs to another. Finally, can two neighboring peoples (or families) resist each other in adopting a certain use of land, for example, can a hunting people resist a pasturing people or a farming people, or the latter resist a people that wants to plant orchards, and so forth? Certainly, since as long as they keep within their boundaries the way they want to *live* on their land is up to their own discretion (*res merae facultatis*).

Lastly, it can still be asked whether, when neither nature nor chance but just our own will brings us into the neighborhood of a people that holds out no prospect of a civil union with it, we should not be authorized to found colonies, by force if need be, in order to establish a civil union with them and bring these men (savages) into a rightful condition (as with the American Indians, the Hottentots, and the inhabitants of New Holland); or (which is not much better), to found colonies by fraudulent purchase of their land, and so become owners of their land, making use of our superiority without regard for their first possession. Should we not be authorized to do this, especially since nature itself (which abhors a vacuum) seems to demand it, and great expanses of land in other parts of the world, which are now splendidly populated, would have otherwise remained uninhabited by civilized people or, indeed, would have to remain forever uninhabited, so that the end of creation would have been frustrated? But it is easy to see through this veil of injustice (Jesuitism), which would sanction any means to good ends. Such a way of acquiring land is therefore to be repudiated.

The indeterminacy, with respect to quantity as well as quality, of the external object that can be acquired makes this problem (of the sole, original external acquisition) the hardest of all to solve. Still, there must be some original acquisition or other of what is external, since not all acquisition can be derived. So this problem cannot be abandoned as insoluble and intrinsically impossible. But even if it is solved through the original contract, such acquisition will always remain only provisional unless this contract extends to the entire human race.

§16.
Exposition of the Concept of Original Acquisition of Land

All men are originally in *common possession* of the land of the entire earth (*communio fundi originaria*) and each has by nature the *will* to use it (*lex iusti*), which, because the choice of one is unavoidably opposed by nature to that of another, would do away with any use of it if this will did not also contain the principle for choice by which a *particular possession* for each on the common land could be determined (*lex iuridica*). But the law that is to determine for each what land is mine or yours will be in accordance with the axiom of outer freedom only if it proceeds from a will that is united *originally* and a priori (that presupposes no rightful act for its union). Hence it proceeds only from a will in the civil condition (*lex iustitiae distributivae*), which alone determines what is *right*, what is *rightful*, and what is *laid down as right*. But in the former condition, that is, before the establishment of the civil condition but with a view to it, that is, *provisionally*, it is a *duty* to proceed in accordance with the principle of external acquisition. Accordingly, there is also a rightful *capacity* of the will to bind everyone to recognize the act of taking possession and of appropriation as valid, even though it is only unilateral. Therefore provisional acquisition of land, together with all its rightful consequences, is possible.

Provisional acquisition, however, needs and gains the favor of a principle (*lex permissiva*) for determining the limits of possible rightful possession. Since this acquisition precedes a rightful condition and, as only leading to it, is not yet conclusive, this favor does not extend beyond the point at which *others* (participants) consent to its establishment. But if they are opposed to entering it (the civil condition), and as long as their opposition lasts, this favor carries with it all the effects of acquisition in conformity with right, since leaving the state of nature is based upon duty.

§ 17.
Deduction of the Concept of Original Acquisition

We have found the *title* of acquisition in an original community of land, and therefore of external possession subject to spatial conditions. We have found the *manner of acquisition* in the empirical conditions of taking possession (*apprehensio*), joined with the will to have the external object as one's own. Now we still need to explicate from principles of pure practical reason with regard to rights *acquisition* itself, that is, the external mine or yours, which follows from the two elements given; that is, we need to explicate intelligible possession (*possessio noumenon*) of an object from what is contained in the concept of it.

The *concept belonging to Right* of what is *externally* mine or yours, so far as this is a *substance*, cannot mean, as far as the term *external to me* is concerned, in another *place* than where I am, for it is a rational concept; instead, since only a pure concept of the understanding can be subsumed under a rational concept, the term can mean merely something *distinct* from me. And [as far as the term *mine* is concerned] this rational concept cannot signify the concept of empirical possession (a continual taking possession, as it were), but only that of *having an external object under my control* (the connection of the object with me insofar as this is the subjective condition of its being possible for me to use it), which is a pure concept of the understanding. Now if these sensible conditions of possession, as a relation of a person to *objects* that have no obligation, are left out or disregarded (abstracted from), possession is nothing other than a relation of a person to persons, all of whom are *bound*, with regard to the use of the thing, by the *will* of the first person, insofar as his will conforms with the axiom of outer freedom, with the *postulate* of his capacity to use external objects of choice, and with the *lawgiving* of the will of all thought as united a priori. This, then, is *intelligible possession* of a thing, that is, possession by mere right, even though the object (the thing I possess) is a sensible object.

The first working, enclosing, or, in general, *transforming* of a piece of land can furnish no title of acquisition to it; that is, possession of an accident can provide no basis for rightful possession of the substance. What is mine or yours must instead be derived from ownership of the substance in accordance with this rule (*accessorium sequitur suum principale*), and whoever expends his labor on land that was not already his has lost his pains and toil to who was first. This is so clear of itself that it is hard to assign any other cause for that opinion, which is so old and still so widespread, than the tacit prevalent deception of personifying things and of thinking of a right to things as being a right *directly* against them, as if someone could, by the work he expends upon them, put things under an obligation to serve him and no one else; for otherwise people would probably not have passed so lightly over the question that naturally arises (already noted above), "How is a right to a thing possible?" For a right against every possessor of a thing means only an authorization on the part of someone's particular choice to use an object, insofar as this authorization can be thought as contained in a synthetic general will and as in accord with the law of this will.

As for corporeal things on land that is already mine, if they do not otherwise belong to another they belong *to me* without my needing a particular act establishing a right in order to make them mine (not *facto* but *lege*), for they can be regarded as accidents inhering in the substance (*iure rei meae*). Anything else that is so connected with a thing of mine that another cannot separate it from what is mine without changing this also belongs to me (e.g., gold plating, mixing some stuff belonging to me with other materials, alluvium, or also, a change in a riverbed adjoining my land and the resulting extension of my land, and so forth). Whether land that extends beyond dry land can be acquired—that is, whether a tract of the ocean floor can be acquired (the right to fish off my shore, to bring up amber, and so forth)—must be decided in accordance with the same principles. My *possession* extends as far as I have the mechanical ability, from where I *reside*, to secure my land against encroachment by others (e.g., as far as cannon reach from the shore), and up to this limit the sea is closed (*mare clausum*). But since it is not possible to *reside* on the high seas themselves, possession also cannot extend to them and the open seas are free (*mare liberum*). But the owner of a shore cannot include, in his right to acquire, what is unintentionally *washed up on shore*, whether men or things belonging to them, since this is not wronging him (not a deed at all), and though a thing has been cast up on land which belongs to someone, it cannot be treated as a *res nullius*. On the other hand, a river can be originally acquired by someone who is in possession of both banks, as far as his possession of the banks

extends; he can acquire the river just as he can acquire any dry land subject to the conditions mentioned above.

An external object that in terms of its substance belongs to someone is his *property (dominium)*, in which all rights in this thing inhere (as accidents of a substance) and which the owner (*dominus*) can, accordingly, dispose of as he pleases (*ius disponendi de re sua*). But from this it follows that an object of this sort can be only a corporeal thing (to which one has no obligation). So a man can be his own master (*sui iuris*) but cannot be the owner *of himself* (*sui dominus*) (cannot dispose of himself as he pleases) —still less can he dispose of other men as he pleases—since he is accountable to the humanity in his own person. This is not, however, the proper place to discuss this point, which has to do with the Right of humanity, not that of men. It is mentioned only incidentally, for a better understanding of what was discussed a little earlier. Furthermore, there can be two complete owners of one and the same thing, without its being both mine and yours in common; they may only be possessors in common of what *belongs to only one of them as his*. This happens when one of the so-called joint owners (*condomini*) has only full possession without use, while the other has all the use of the thing along with possession of it. So the one who has full possession without use (*dominus directus*) only restricts the other (*dominos utilis*) to some continual performance without thereby limiting his use of the thing.

SECTION II
ON CONTRACT RIGHT

§18.

My possession of another's choice, in the sense of my capacity to determine it by my own choice to a certain deed in accordance with laws of freedom (what is externally mine or yours with respect to the causality of another), is *a* right (of which I can have several against the same person or against others); but there is only a single sum (system) of principles, *contract Right*, in accordance with which I can be in this sort of possession.

A right against a person can never be acquired originally and on one's own initiative (for then it would not conform to the principle of the consistency of my choice with the freedom of everyone, and would therefore be wrong). So too, I cannot acquire a right against another through a deed of his that is *contrary to right* (*facto iniusto alterius*); for even if he has wronged me and I have a right to demand compensation from him, by this I will still only preserve what is mine undiminished but will not acquire more than what I previously had.

Acquisition through another's deed to which I determine him in accordance with principles of Right is, accordingly, always derived from what is his; and this derivation, as an act that establishes a right, cannot take place through a *negative* act of the other, namely his *abandoning* or *renouncing* what is his (*per derelictionem aut renunciationem*); for by such an act this would only cease to belong to one or the other, but nothing would be acquired. This derivation can take place only by *transferring* (*translatio*), which is possible only through a common will by means of which the object is always under the control of one or the other, since as one gives up his share in this common undertaking the object becomes the other's through his acceptance of it (and so by a positive act of choice). Transfer of the *property* of one to another is *alienation*. An act of the united choice of two persons by which anything at all that belongs to one passes to the other is a *contract*.

§19.

For every contract there are two *preparatory* and two *constitutive* rightful acts of choice. The first two (of *negotiating*) are *offering* (*oblatio*) and *assent* (*approbatio*) to it; the two others (of *concluding*) are *promise* (*promissum*) and *acceptance* (*acceptatio*). For an offering cannot be called a promise apart from a preliminary judgment that what is offered (*oblatum*) would be *acceptable* to the promisee. This is indicated by the first two declarations, but by them alone nothing is as yet acquired.

But what belongs to the promisor does not pass to the promisee (as acceptant) by the *separate* will of either but only by the *united will* of both, and consequently only insofar as both wills are declared *simultaneously*. But this cannot take place by empirical acts of declaration, which must necessarily *follow* each other in time and are never simultaneous. For if I have promised and the other now wants to accept, I

can still during the interval (however short it may be) regret having promised, since I am still free before he accepts; and because of this the one who accepts it, for his part, can consider himself as not bound to his counterdeclaration after the promise. The external formalities (*solemnia*) in concluding a contract (shaking hands, or breaking a straw, *stipula*, held by both persons), and all the confirmations back and forth of the declarations they have made, manifest the perplexity of the contracting parties as to how and in what way they are going to represent their declarations as existing *simultaneously*, at the same moment, although they can only be successive. They still do not succeed in this, since their acts can only follow each other in time, so that when one act *is* the other is either *not yet* or is *no longer*.

Only a transcendental deduction of the concept of acquisition by contract can remove all these difficulties. It is true that in an external relation of *rights* my taking possession of another's choice (and his taking possession of mine in turn), as the basis for determining it to a deed, is first thought of empirically, by means of a declaration and counterdeclaration of the choice of each in time; this is the sensible condition of taking possession, in which both acts required for establishing the right can only follow one upon another. Since, however, that relation (as a rightful relation) is purely intellectual, that possession is represented through the will, which is a rational capacity for giving laws, as intelligible possession (*possessio noumenon*) in abstraction from those empirical conditions, as what is mine or yours. Here both acts, promise and acceptance, are represented not as following one upon another but (as if it were *pactum re initum*) as proceeding from a single *common* will (this is expressed by the word *simultaneously*); and the object (*promissum*) is represented, by omitting empirical conditions, as acquired in accordance with a principle of pure practical reason.

That this is the true and the only possible deduction of the concept of acquisition by contract is sufficiently confirmed by the painstaking but always futile efforts of those who investigate rights (e.g., Moses Mendelssohn in his *Jerusalem*) to produce a proof of its possibility. The question was, *why ought* I to keep my promise? for *that I ought* to keep it everyone readily grasps. But it is absolutely impossible to furnish a proof of this categorical imperative, just as it is impossible for a geometer to prove by means of inferences based on reason alone that in order to make a triangle he must take three lines (an analytic proposition), two of which together must be greater than the third (a synthetic proposition, but both propositions are a priori). That I ought to keep my promise is a postulate of pure reason (pure as abstracting from all sensible conditions of space and time in what concerns the concept of Right). The doctrine that it is possible to abstract from those conditions without giving up possession of the promise is itself the deduction of the concept of acquisition by contract, just as was the case in the preceding heading for the doctrine of acquisition of external things taking control of them.

§20.

By a contract I acquire something external. But what is it that I acquire? Since it is only the causality of another's choice with respect to a performance he has promised me, what I acquire directly by a contract is not an external thing but rather his deed, by which that thing is brought under my control so that I make it mine. By a contract I therefore acquire another's promise (not what he promised), and yet something is added to my external belongings; I have become *enriched* (*locupletior*) by acquiring an active obligation on the freedom and the means of the other. The *right* of mine is, however, only a right *against a person*, namely a right against a *specific* physical person, and indeed a right to act upon his causality (his choice) to *perform* something for me; it is not a *right to a thing*, a right against that *moral person* which is nothing other than the Idea of the *choice of all united a priori*, by which alone I can acquire *a right against every possessor of the thing*, which is what constitutes any right to a thing.

Transfer by contract of what is mine takes place in accordance with the law of continuity (*lex continui*), that is, possession of the object is not interrupted for a moment during this act; for otherwise I would acquire, in this condition, an object as something that has no possessor (*res vacua*), hence would acquire it originally, and this contradicts the concept of contract. Because of this continuity, however, that which transfers what is mine to the other is not one of the two separate wills (*promittentis et acceptantis*), but their united will. So the transfer does not take place in such a way that the promisor first abandons (*derelinquit*) his possession for the other's advantage, or renounces (*renunciat*) his right, and the other immediately takes it up, or the reverse. Transfer is therefore an act in which an object belongs, for a moment, to both together, just as when a stone that has been thrown

reaches the apex of its parabolic path it can be regarded as, for just a moment, simultaneously rising and falling, and so first passing from its rising motion to its falling.

§21.

In a contract by which a thing is acquired, it is not acquired by *acceptance* (*acceptatio*) of the promise, but only by *delivery* (*traditio*) of what was promised. For any promise has to do with a *performance*, and if what is promised is a thing, the performance can be discharged only by an act in which the promisor puts the promisee in possession of the thing, that is, delivers it to him. So before the thing is delivered and received, the performance has not yet taken place; the thing has not yet passed from one to the other and so has not been acquired by the promisee. Hence the right that arises from a contract is only a right against a person, and becomes a right to a *thing* only by delivery of the thing.

A contract that is immediately followed by delivery (*pactum re initum*) excludes any interval between its being concluded and its being discharged and requires no further separate act by which what belongs to one is transferred to the other. But if a (definite or indefinite) time for delivering the thing is allowed between the conclusion and the discharge of the contract, the question arises whether the thing already belongs to the acceptor by the contract, prior to its being delivered, and his right is a right to the thing, or whether a separate contract having to do only with its being delivered must be added, so that the right acquired by mere acceptance is only a right against a person and becomes a right to a thing only by its being delivered. That the latter is really the case is clear from the following.

If I conclude a contract about a thing that I want to acquire, for example, a horse, and at the same time put it in my stable or otherwise in my physical possession, it is then mine (*vi pacti re initi*), and my right is a *right to a thing*. But if I leave it in the seller's hands, without making any separate arrangements with him as to who is to be in physical possession of the thing (*holding* it) before I take possession of it (*apprehensio*), and so before the change of possession, then this horse is not yet mine, and what I have acquired is only a right against a specific person, namely the seller, *to put me in possession* (*poscendi traditionem*), which is the subjective condition of its being possible for me to use it as I please. My right is only a right against a person, to require of the seller *performance* (*praestatio*) of his promise to put me in possession of the thing. Now if a contract does not include delivery *at the same time* (as *pactum re initum*), so that some time elapses between its being concluded and my taking possession of what I am acquiring, during this time I cannot gain possession without exercising a separate act to establish that right, namely a *possessory act* (*actum possessorium*), which constitutes a separate contract. This contract consists in my saying that I shall send for the thing (the horse) and the seller's agreeing to it. For it is not a matter of course that the seller will take charge, at his own risk, of something for another's use; this instead requires a separate contract, by which the one who is alienating a thing still remains its owner *for a specified time* (and must bear any risk that might affect it). Only if the one who is acquiring the thing delays beyond this time can the seller regard him as its owner and the thing as delivered to him. Before this possessory act all that has been acquired through the contract is therefore a right against a person, and the promisee can acquire an external thing only by its being delivered.

SECTION III
ON RIGHTS TO PERSONS AKIN TO RIGHTS TO THINGS

§22.

This Right is that of possession of an external object *as a thing* and use of it *as a person*. What is mine or yours in terms of this Right is what is mine or yours *domestically*, and the relation of persons in the domestic condition is that of a community of free beings who form a society of members of a whole called a *household* (of persons standing in *community* with one another) by their affecting one another in accordance with the principle of outer freedom (*causality*). Acquisition of this status, and within it, therefore takes place neither by a deed on one's own initiative (*facto*) nor by a contract (*pacto*) alone but by principle (*lege*); for, since this kind of right is neither a right to a thing nor merely a right against a person but also possession of a person, it must be a right lying beyond any rights to things and any rights against persons. That is to say, it must be the Right of humanity in our own person, from which there follows a natural permissive principle, by the favor of which this sort of acquisition is possible for us.

§23.

In terms of the object, acquisition in accordance with this principle is of three kinds: A *man* acquires a *wife;*

a *couple* acquires *children;* and a *family* acquires *servants*. Whatever is acquired in this way is also inalienable and the right of possessors of these objects is the *most personal* of all rights.

On the Right of Domestic Society
Title I:
Marriage Right
§24.

Sexual union (*commercium sexuale*) is the reciprocal use that one human being makes of the sexual organs and capacities of another (*usus membrorum et facultatum sexualium alterius*). This is either a *natural* use (by which procreation of a being of the same kind is possible) or an *unnatural* use, and unnatural use takes place either with a person of the same sex or with an animal of a nonhuman species. Since such transgressions of principle, called unnatural (*crimina carnis contra naturam*) or also unmentionable vices, do wrong to humanity in our own person, there are no limitations or exceptions whatsoever that can save them from being repudiated completely.

Natural sexual union takes place either in accordance with mere animal *nature* (*vaga libido, venus volgivaga, fornicatio*) or in accordance with *principle*. Sexual union in accordance with principle is *marriage* (*matrimonium*), that is, the union of two persons of different sexes for lifelong possession of each other's sexual attributes. The end of begetting and bringing up children may be an end of nature, for which it implanted the inclinations of the sexes for each other; but it is not *requisite* for human beings who marry to make this their end in order for their union to be compatible with rights, for otherwise marriage would be dissolved when procreation ceases.

Even if it is supposed that their end is the pleasure of using each other's sexual attributes, the marriage contract is not up to their discretion but is a contract that is necessary by the principle of humanity, that is, if a man and a woman want to enjoy each other's sexual attributes they *must* necessarily marry, and this is necessary in accordance with pure reason's principles of Right.

§25.

For the natural use that one sex makes of the other's sexual organs is *enjoyment*, for which one gives itself up to the other. In this act a human being makes himself into a thing, which conflicts with the Right of humanity in his own person. There is only one condition under which this is possible: that while one person is acquired by the other *as if it were a thing*, the one who is acquired acquires the other in turn; for in this way each reclaims itself and restores its personality. But acquiring a member of a human being is at the same time acquiring the whole person, since a person is an absolute unity. Hence it is not only admissible for the sexes to surrender to and accept each other for enjoyment under the condition of marriage, but it is possible for them to do so *only* under this condition. That this *right against a person* is also *akin to a right to a thing* rests on the fact that if one of the partners in a marriage has left or given itself into someone else's possession, the other partner is justified, always and without question, in bringing its partner back under its control, just as it is justified in retrieving a thing.

§26.

For the same reasons, the relation of the partners in a marriage is a relation of *equality* of possession, equality both in their possession of each other as persons (hence only in *monogamy*, since in polygamy the person who surrenders herself gains only a part of the man who gets her completely, and therefore makes herself into a mere thing), and also equality in their possession of material goods. As for these, the partners are still authorized to forgo the use of a part, though only by a separate contract.

> For this reason it follows that neither concubinage nor hiring a person for enjoyment on one occasion (*pactum fornicationis*) is a contract that could hold in Right. As for the latter, everyone will admit that a person who has concluded such a contract could not rightfully be held to the fulfillment of her promise if she regrets it. So, with regard to the former, a contract to be a *concubine* (as *pactum turpe*) also comes to nothing; for this would be a contract to *let* and *hire* (*locatio–conductio*) a member for another's use, in which, because of the inseparable unity of members in a person, she would be surrendering herself as a thing to the other's choice. Accordingly, either party can cancel the contract with the other as soon as it pleases without the other having grounds for complaining about any infringement of its rights. The same considerations also hold for a morganatic marriage, which takes advantage of the inequality of Estate of the two parties to give one of them domination over

the other; for in fact morganatic marriage is not different, in terms of natural Right only, from concubinage and is no true marriage. If the question is therefore posed, whether it is also in conflict with the equality of the partners for the law to say of the husband's relation to the wife, he is to be your master (he is the party to direct, she to obey): This cannot be regarded as conflicting with the natural equality of a couple if this dominance is based only on the natural superiority of the husband to the wife in his capacity to promote the common interest of the household, and the right to direct that is based on this can be derived from the very duty of unity and equality with respect to the *end*.

§27.

A marriage contract is *consummated* only *by conjugal sexual intercourse* (*copula carnalis*). A contract made between two persons of opposite sex, either with a tacit understanding to refrain from sexual intercourse or with awareness that one or both are incapable of it, is a *simulated contract*, which institutes no marriage and can also be dissolved by either of them who pleases. But if incapacity appears only afterwards, that right cannot be forfeited through this accident for which no one is at fault.

Acquisition of a wife or of a husband therefore takes place neither *facto* (by intercourse) without a contract preceding it nor *pacto* (by a mere marriage contract without intercourse following it) but only *lege*, that is, as the rightful consequence of the obligation not to engage in sexual union except through *possession* of each other's person, which is realized only through the use of their sexual attributes by each other.

Title II:
Parental Right
§28.

Just as there arose from one's duty to oneself, that is, to the humanity in one's own person, a right (*ius personale*) of both sexes to acquire each other as persons *in the manner of things* by marriage, so there follows from *procreation* in this community a duty to preserve and care for its *offspring*; that is, children, as persons, have by their procreation an original innate (not acquired) right to the care of their parents until they are able to look after themselves, and they have this right directly on the basis of principle (*lege*), that is, without any special act being required to establish this right.

For the offspring is a *person*, and it is impossible to form a concept of the production of a being endowed with freedom through a physical operation.[1] So from a *practical* point of view it is a quite correct and even necessary Idea to regard the act of procreation as one by which we have brought a person into the world without his consent and on our own initiative, for which deed the parents incur an obligation to make the child content with his condition so far as they can. They cannot destroy their child as if he were something they had *made* (since a being endowed with freedom cannot be a product of this kind) or as if he were their property, nor can they even just abandon him to chance, since they have brought not merely a worldly being but a citizen of the world into a condition which cannot now be indifferent to them even just according to concepts of Right.

§29.

From this duty there must necessarily also arise the right of parents to *manage* and develop the child, as long as he has not yet mastered the use of his members or of his understanding: the right not only to feed and care for him but to educate him, to develop him both *pragmatically*, so that in the future he can look after himself and make his way in life, and *morally*, since otherwise the fault for having neglected him would fall on the parents. They have the right to do all this until the time of his emancipation (*emancipatio*), when they renounce their parental right to direct him as well as any claim to be compensated for their support and pains up till now. After they have completed his education, the only obligation (to his parents) with which they can charge him is a mere duty of virtue, namely the duty of gratitude.

From a child's personality it also follows that the right of parents is not just a right to a thing, since a child can never be considered as the property of his parents, so that their right is not alienable (*ius personalissimum*). But this right is also not just a right against a person, since a child still belongs to his parents as what is theirs (is still in their *possession* like a thing and can be brought back even against his will into his parents' possession from another's possession). It is, instead, a right to a person *akin to a right to a thing*.

From this it is evident that, in the doctrine of Right, there must necessarily be added to the headings rights to things and rights against persons the heading *rights to persons akin to rights to things;* the division made up till now has not been complete. For when we speak of the rights of parents to children as part of their household, we are referring not merely to the children's duty to return when they have run away but to the parents' being justified in taking control of them and impounding them as things (like domestic animals that have gone astray).

Title III:
Right of a Head of the Household
§30.

The children of a household, who together with their parents formed a *family*, reach their *majority* (*maiorennes*) without any contract to withdraw from their former dependence, merely by attaining the ability to support themselves (which happens partly as a natural coming of age in the general course of nature, partly in keeping with their particular natural qualities). In other words, they become their own masters (*sui iuris*) and acquire this right without any special act to establish it and so merely by principle (*lege*).

---

1. No concept can be formed of how it is possible for *God to create* free beings, for it seems as if all their future actions would have to be predetermined by that first act, included in the chain of natural necessity and therefore not free. But that such beings (we men) are still free the categorical imperative proves for morally practical purposes, as through an authoritative decision of reason without its being able to make this relation of cause to effect comprehensible for theoretical purposes, since both are supersensible. All that one can require of reason here would be merely to prove that there is no contradiction in the concept of a *creation of free beings*, and it can do this if it shows that the contradiction arises only if, along with the category of causality, the *temporal condition*, which cannot be avoided in relation to sensible objects (namely, that the ground of an effect precedes it), is also introduced in the relation of supersensible beings. As for the supersensible, if the causal concept is to obtain objective reality for theoretical purposes, the temporal condition would have to be introduced here too. But the contradiction vanishes if the pure category (without a schema put under it) is used in the concept of creation with a morally practical and therefore nonsensible intent.

If the philosophic jurist reflects on the difficulty of the problem to be resolved and the necessity of solving it to satisfy principles of Right in this matter, he will not hold this investigation, all the way back to the first elements of transcendental philosophy in a metaphysics of morals, to be unnecessary pondering that gets lost in pointless obscurity.

Just as they are not in debt to their parents for their education, so the parents are released in the same way from their obligation to their children, and both children and parents acquire or reacquire their natural freedom. The domestic society that was necessary on principle is now dissolved.

Both parties can now maintain what is actually the same household but with a different form of obligation, namely, as the connection of the head of the household with servants (male or female servants of the house). What they maintain is the same domestic society but it is now a society *under the head of the household* (*societas herelis*), formed by a contract through which the head of the household establishes a domestic society with the children who have now attained their majority or, if the family has no children, with other free persons (members of the household). This would be a society of unequals (one party *being in command* or being its head, the other *obeying*, i.e., serving) (*imperantis et subiecti domestici*).

Servants are included in what belongs to the head of a household and, as far as the form (the *way of his being in possession*) is concerned, they are his by a right that is like a right to a thing; for if they run away from him he can bring them back in his control by his unilateral choice. But as far as the matter is concerned, that is, what *use* he can make of these members of his household, he can never behave as if he owned them (*dominus servi*); for it is only by a contract that he has brought them under his control, and a contract by which one party would completely renounce its freedom for the other's advantage would be self-contradictory, that is, null and void, since by it one party would cease to be a person and so would have no duty to keep the contract but would recognize only force. (The right of ownership with regard to someone who has forfeited his personality by a crime is not under consideration here.)

The contract of the head of a household with servants can therefore not be such that his *use* of them would amount to *using them up;* and it is not for him alone to judge about this, but also for the servants (who, accordingly, can never be serfs); so the contract cannot be concluded for life but at most only for an unspecified time, within which one party may give the other notice. But children (even those of someone who has become a slave through his crime) are at all times free. For every man is born free, since he has not yet committed a crime; and the cost of educating him until he comes of age cannot be accounted

against him as a debt that he has to pay off. For the slave would have to educate his children if he could, without charging them with the cost of their education, and if he cannot the obligation devolves on his possessor.

So we see here again, as in the two preceding headings, that there is a right to persons akin to a right to things (of the head of the house over servants); for he can fetch servants back and demand them from anyone in possession of them, as what is externally his, even before the reasons that may have led them to run away and their rights have been investigated.

Dogmatic Division of All Rights
That Can Be Acquired by Contract
§31.

A metaphysical doctrine of Right can be required to enumerate *a priori* the members of a division (*divisio logica*) in a complete and definite way, and to establish thereby a true *system* of them. Instead of providing a system, any *empirical division* is merely *fragmentary* (*partitio*), and leaves it uncertain whether there are not additional members that would be needed to fill out the entire sphere of the concept divided. A division in accordance with an a priori principle (in contrast with empirical divisions) can be called *dogmatic.*

Every contract consists in itself, that is, considered *objectively*, of two acts that establish a right: a promise, and its acceptance. Acquisition through acceptance is not a *part* of a contract (unless the contract is a *pactum re initum*, which requires delivery) but the rightfully necessary *result* of it. But considered *subjectively*—that is, as to whether this rationally necessary result (the *acquisition* which *ought* to occur) will actually *result* (be the *natural* result)—accepting the promise still gives me no *guarantee* that it will actually result. Since this guarantee belongs externally to the modality of a contract, namely *certainty* of acquisition by means of a contract, it is an additional factor serving to complete the means for achieving the acquisition that is the purpose of a contract. For this, three persons are involved: a *promisor*, an *acceptor*, and a *guarantor.* The acceptor, indeed, gains nothing more with regard to the object by means of the guarantor and his separate contract with the promisor, but he still gains the means of coercion for obtaining what is his.

In accordance with these principles of logical (rational) division there are, strictly speaking, only three simple and *pure* kinds of contract. There are innumerable mixed and empirical kinds of contract, which add statutory and conventional laws to the principles of what is mine or yours in accordance with pure laws of reason; but they lie beyond the sphere of the metaphysical doctrine of Right, which is all that should be considered here.

Every contract has for its purpose either A, *unilateral* acquisition (a gratuitous contract) or B, acquisition *by both parties* (an onerous contract), or no acquisition but only C, *guaranteeing what belongs to someone* (this contract can be gratuitous on one side but can still be onerous on the other side).

A. A *gratuitous* contract (*pactum gratuitum*) is:
   a) *Keeping* goods on trust (*depositum*),
   b) *Lending* a thing (*commodatum*),
   c) *Making a gift* (*donatio*).

B. Onerous contracts.
  I. A contract to *alienate* something (*permutatio late sic dicta*).
    a) *Barter* (*permutatio stricte sic dicta*). Goods for goods.
    b) *Buying and selling* (*emtio venditio*). Goods for money.
    c) *Loan for Consumption* (*mutuum*). Lending a thing on the condition of its being returned only in kind (e.g., grain for grain, or money for money).
  II. A contract to *let* and *hire* (*locatio conductio*).
    a) *Lending a thing of mine* to another for his use (*locatio rei*). Insofar as the contract is onerous, a *payment of interest* may also be added (*pactum usurarium*) if repayment can be made only in kind.
    b) A contract of *letting of work* on hire, that is, granting another the use of my powers for a specified price (*merces*). By this contract the worker is hired help (*mercennarius*).
    c) A *contract empowering an agent.* Carrying on another's affairs in his place and *in his name.* If someone carries on another's affairs in place of him but not also in his name, this is called *carrying on his affairs* without being *commissioned* to do so (*gestio negotii*); but when this is done in the other's name we speak of a *mandate.* As a contract

of hiring this is an onerous contract (*mandatum onerosum*).
C. *Contracts providing security* (*cautio*).
   a) A joint *giving and taking of a pledge* (*pignus*).
   b) *Assuming liability* for another's promise (*fideiussio*).
   c) *Personally vouching for a person's performance* of something (*praestatio obsidis*).

In this table of all the ways of *transferring* (*translatio*) what belongs to one to another are to be found concepts of objects or instruments of transfer that [seem to be] entirely empirical and that, even in terms of their possibility, have no proper place in a *metaphysical* doctrine of Right, in which division must be made in accordance with a priori principles, abstracting from the matter that is exchanged (which could be conventional) and considering only the form. Such, for example, is the concept of *money*, in contrast to all other alienable things, namely *goods*, under the heading of *buying and selling*, as well as the concept of a *book*. But it will be shown that the concept of money, as the greatest and most useful means men have for *exchange* of things, called *buying and selling* (commerce), and so too the concept of a book, as the greatest means for exchanging thoughts, can still be resolved into pure intellectual relations. So the table of pure contracts need not be made impure by anything empirical mixed into it.

I.
What Is Money?

Money is a thing that can be *used* only by being *alienated.* This is a good *nominal definition* of it (as given by Achenwall); that is to say, it is sufficient for distinguishing this kind of object of choice from any other, though it tells us nothing about the possibility of such a thing. Still, from the nominal definition one can see this much: *first,* that the alienation of money in exchange is intended not as a gift but for *reciprocal* acquisition (by a *pactum onerosum*); and *second,* that money *represents* all goods, since it is conceived as a universally accepted mere *means* of commerce (within a nation), as opposed to things which are *goods,* which have value in themselves and are related to the particular needs of one or another in the nation.

A bushel of grain has the greatest direct value as a means for satisfying human needs. It can be used as fodder for animals, which nourish us, transport us, and work in place of us; by means of it, furthermore, the human population is increased and preserved, and in turn not only raises these natural products again but also helps to satisfy our needs with the products of art, by building houses, making clothes, providing the enjoyments we seek and, in general, all the conveniences that form the goods of industry. By contrast, the value of money is only indirect. One cannot enjoy money itself or make immediate use of it in any way. Yet it is still a means that, among all things, has the greatest usefulness.

On this basis a preliminary *real definition* of money can be given: it is the universal *means by which men exchange their industriousness* [or industry] *with one another*. Thus a nation's wealth, insofar as it is acquired by means of money, is really only the sum of the industry with which men pay one another and which is represented by the money in circulation within it.

The thing to be called money must, therefore, have cost as much *industry* to produce or to obtain from other men as the *industry* by which those goods (natural or artificial products) are acquired for which that industry is exchanged. For if it were easier to procure the stuff called money than goods, more money would then come into the market than goods for sale; and since the seller would have to have expended more industry for his goods than the buyer, who got the money more readily, industry in producing goods, and therefore trade in general, would diminish and be curtailed, along with the productive industry that results in the nation's wealth. Hence bank notes and promissory notes cannot be regarded as money, though they can substitute for it temporarily; for they cost almost no industry to produce and their value is based solely on the opinion that they will continue as before to be convertible into *hard cash;* but if it is eventually discovered that there is not enough hard cash for which they can be readily and securely exchanged, this opinion suddenly collapses and makes failure of payment inevitable. So the productive industry of those who work the gold and silver mines in Peru or New Mexico, especially in view of the industry vainly expended in searches for deposits that are so often unsuccessful, is apparently still greater than that expended on the manufacture of goods in Europe; and this excess of industry would be discontinued from not being paid, letting those countries soon sink into poverty, if the Europeans did not increase their industry proportionately through being stimulated by those very materials, so that the luxu-

ries they offer constantly stimulate in others a desire for mining. In this way industry [in one country] always rivals industry [in another].

But how is it possible that what were originally only goods finally became money? This would happen if a powerful, opulent *ruler* who originally used a material for the adornment and splendor of his attendants (his court) came to levy taxes on his subjects in this material (as goods) (e.g., gold, silver, copper, or a kind of beautiful seashell, *cowries;* or as in the Congo a kind of matting called *makutes*, in Senegal iron ingots, or on the coast of Guinea even black slaves), and in turn paid with this same material those his demand moved to industry in procuring it, in accordance with exchange regulations with them and among them (on a market or exchange). In this way only (so it seems to me) could a certain merchandise have become a lawful means of exchange of the industry of subjects with one another, and thereby also become the wealth of the nation, that is, *money.*

The intellectual concept under which the empirical concept of money falls is therefore the concept of a thing that, in the circulation of possessions (*permutatio publica*), determines the *price* of all other things (goods), among which even the sciences belong, insofar as they would not otherwise be taught to others. The amount of money in a nation therefore constitutes its wealth (*opulentia*). For the price (*pretium*) of a thing is the judgment of the public about its *value* (*valor*) in proportion to that which serves as the universal means to represent reciprocal exchange of *industry* (its circulation). Accordingly, where there is a great deal of trade, neither *gold* nor copper is regarded as strictly money but only as merchandise, since there is too little gold and too much copper for them to be easily put into circulation and yet available in sufficiently small parts, as is necessary for the exchange of merchandise, or a mass of it, in the smallest purchase. *Silver* (more or less alloyed with copper) is, accordingly, taken as the proper material for money and the measure for reckoning prices in the great trade of the world; other metals (even more so, nonmetallic materials) can be found as money only in a nation where there is little trade. But when the first two metals are not only weighed but also stamped, that is, provided with a sign indicating how much they are to be worth, they are lawful money, that is, *coinage.*

"Money is therefore" (according to Adam Smith) "that material thing the alienation of which is the means and at the same time the measure of the industry by which men and nations carry on trade with one another." This definition brings the empirical concept of money to an intellectual concept by looking only to the *form* of what each party provides in return for the other in onerous contracts (and abstracting from their matter), thereby bringing it to the concept of Right in the exchange of what is mine or yours generally (*commutatio late sic dicta*), so as to present the table above as a dogmatic division a priori, which is appropriate to the metaphysics of Right as a system.

II.
What Is a Book?

A book is a writing (it does not matter, here, whether it is written in hand or set in type, whether it has few or many pages), which represents a discourse that someone delivers to the public by visible linguistic signs. One who *speaks* to the public in his own name is called the *author* (*autor*). One who, through a writing, discourses publicly in another's (the author's) name is a *publisher*. When a publisher does this with the author's permission, he is the legitimate publisher; but if he does it without the author's permission, he is an illegitimate publisher, that is, an *unauthorized publisher*. The sum of all the reproductions of the original writing (the copies) is an *edition*.

Unauthorized Publishing of Books Is Forbidden as a Matter of Right

A *writing* is not an immediate sign of a *concept* (as is, for example, an etching that represents a certain person in a *portrait*, or a work in plaster that is a *bust*). It is rather a *discourse* to the public; that is, the author *speaks* publicly through the publisher. But the *publisher* speaks (through his foreman, *operarius*, the printer), not in his own name (for he would then pass himself off as the author), but in the name of the author; and so he is entitled to do this only when the author *gives him a mandate* (*mandatum*). Now it is true that an unauthorized publisher also speaks, by an edition on his own initiative, in the name of the author, but he does so without having been given a mandate by the author (*gerit se mandatarium absque mandata*). He therefore commits the crime of stealing the profits from the publisher who was appointed by the author (who is therefore the only legitimate one), profits the legitimate publisher could and would have derived from the use of his right (*fur-*

tum usus). So *unauthorized publishing of books is forbidden as a matter of Right.*

Why does unauthorized publishing, which strikes one even at first glance as unjust, still have an appearance of being rightful? Because *on the one hand* a book is a corporeal *artifact* (*opus mechanicum*) that can be reproduced (by someone in legitimate possession of a copy of it), so that there is a *right to a thing* with regard to it. *On the other hand* a book is also a mere *discourse* of the publisher to the public, which the publisher may not repeat publicly without having a mandate from the author to do so (*praestatio operae*), and this is a *right against a person*. The error consists in mistaking one of these rights for the other.

There is another case, under contracts to let and hire (B,II,a), in which the confusion of a right against a person with a right to a thing is material for disputes, that of *renting to a tenant* (*ius incolatus*). The question arises whether an owner who has leased his house (or land) to someone and sells it to someone else before the lease expires is bound to attach to the contract of sale the condition that the lease is to continue, or whether one can say that purchase breaks a lease (though notice is to be given the lessee, the time being determined by custom). On the first alternative the house actually had an *encumbrance* (*onus*) on it, a right to this thing that the lessee had acquired in it (the house). This can indeed take place (by entering this encumbrance in the land register, as included in the contract to lease); but then this would not be a mere contract to lease, but one to which another contract had had to be added (one to which few landlords would agree). So the saying "Purchase breaks a lease" is valid, that is, a full right to a thing (property) outweighs any right against a person that cannot exist together with it. But it is still left open for the lessee to complain, on the basis of his right against a person, that he is to be compensated for any damages arising from the breaking of the contract.

EPISODIC SECTION.
ON IDEAL ACQUISITION OF AN EXTERNAL OBJECT OF CHOICE

§32.

I call acquisition *ideal* if it involves no causality in time and is therefore based on a mere *Idea* of pure reason. It is nonetheless *true*, not imaginary, acquisition, and the only reason I do not call it real is that the act of acquiring is not empirical, since the subject acquires from another who either *does not yet* exist (only the possibility that he may exist is admitted) or who has *ceased to exist*, or when the subject *no longer exists*, so that coming into possession is merely a practical Idea of reason. There are three kinds of such acquisition: (1) by *prolonged possession*, (2) by *inheritance*, and (3) by *merit surviving death* (*meritum immortale*), that is, the claim to a good reputation after death. All three can, indeed, take effect only in a public rightful condition, but they are not *based* only on its constitution and the chosen statutes in it: they are also conceivable a priori in the state of nature and must be conceived as prior to such statutes, in order that laws in the civil constitution may afterwards be adapted to them (*sunt iuris naturae*).

I.

Acquisition by Prolonged Possession
§33.

I acquire another's property merely by *long possession of it (usucapio)*, not because I may legitimately *presume* that he consents to my acquiring it (*per consensum praesumtum*), nor because I can assume that, since he does not contradict me, he *has given it up* (*rem derelictam*), but because, even if there should be someone who was the true owner and as such laid claim to it (a claimant) I may still *exclude* him merely by virtue of my long possession, ignore his existence up to now, and carry on as if he existed up to the time of my possession only as a thought-entity, even if I should later learn of his reality as well as that of his claim. Although this way of acquiring is called acquisition by superannuation of claims (*per praescriptionem*), this is not altogether correct, since exclusion of claims is to be regarded only as a result of acquisition: Acquisition must have come first. It has now to be proved that it is possible to acquire something in this way.

Someone who does not exercise a continuous *possessory act* (*actus possessorius*) with regard to an external thing, as something that is his, is rightly regarded as someone who does not exist at all (as its possessor). For he cannot complain of being wronged as long as he does nothing to justify his title of possessor; and even if later on, when another has already taken possession of it, he declares himself its possessor, all he is saying is that he was once its owner, not that he still is and that his possession has remained

uninterrupted without a continuous rightful act. Hence if someone does not use a thing for a long time, only a rightful possessory act, and indeed one that is continuously maintained and documented, can guarantee that it is his.

For suppose that failure to perform this possessory act did not result in another's being able to base a firm right (*possessio irrefragabilis*) on his lawful possession in good faith (*possessio bonae fidei*) and regard himself as having acquired the thing that is in his possession. Then no acquisition at all would be conclusive (guaranteed); all acquisition would be only provisional (up to the present), since investigation of the past cannot reach all the way back to the first possessor and his act of acquisition. The presumption on which prolonged possession (*usucapio*) is based is therefore not merely in *conformity with right* (permitted, *iusta*) as a *conjecture* but is also in accord with rights (*praesumtio iuris et de iure*) as an assumption in terms of coercive laws (*suppositio legalis*). Whoever fails to document his possessory act has lost his claim to the present possessor, and the length of time during which he failed to do it (which cannot and need not be specified) is put forward only to support the certainty of his omission. That a hitherto unknown possessor could always get something back (recover it) when his possessory act has been interrupted (even through no fault of his own) contradicts the above postulate of practical reason with regard to rights (*dominia rerum incerta facere*).

If he is a member of a commonwealth, that is, lives in the civil condition, the state (representing him) can indeed preserve his possession for him, although it was interrupted as private possession, and a present possessor need not prove his title of acquisition by tracing it back to the first possessor or basing it on prolonged possession. In the state of nature, however, prolonged possession is in conformity with right not, strictly speaking, for acquiring a thing but for maintaining possession of it without an act establishing the right; and this immunity from claims is also usually called acquisition. Prescription of an earlier possessor therefore belongs to natural Right (*est iuris naturae*).

II.

Inheritance
(Acquisitio haereditatis)
§34.

Inheritance is transfer (*translatio*) of the belongings and goods of someone who is dying to a survivor by agreement of the wills of both. Acquisition by the *heir* (*haeredis instituti*) and leaving by the *testator* (*testatoris*), that is, this change of belongings, takes place in one moment, namely the moment at which the testator ceases to exist (*articulo mortis*). It is therefore not, strictly speaking, a transfer (*translatio*) in the empirical sense, since this assumes two acts following each other, namely the acts by which one person first leaves his possessions and the other then comes into them. Instead it is an ideal acquisition. Now, inheritance in the state of nature cannot be conceived of without a *last will* (*dispositio ultimae voluntatis*). Whether this is a *contract of inheritance* (*pactum successorium*) or a *unilateral disposition to the heir* (*testamentum*) amounts to the question, whether and how it is possible for belongings to pass from one to the other precisely at the moment at which the subject ceases to exist. The question of how it is possible to acquire by inheritance must accordingly be investigated apart from the many ways in which it can be carried out (which are found only in a commonwealth).

"It is possible to acquire something through disposition to the heir." For the testator, Caius, promises and in his last will declares to Titius, who knows nothing of this promise, that upon his death his belongings are to pass to Titius. As long as he lives, Caius therefore remains sole owner of his belongings. Now it is true that by a unilateral will alone nothing can pass to the other person; for this there is required, besides the promise, acceptance (*acceptatio*) by the other party and a simultaneous will (*voluntas simultanea*), which is still lacking here; for as long as Caius is alive, Titius cannot explicitly accept, so as to acquire by his acceptance, since Caius has promised only on the occasion of his death (otherwise the property would for a moment be common property, and this is not the testator's will). Titius, however, still tacitly acquires a proprietary right to the legacy as a right to a thing: Namely, he has the exclusive right to accept it (*ius in re iacente*), so that the legacy at the moment of death is called *haereditas iacens*. Now, since every man would necessarily accept such a right (since he can always gain but never lose by it), and so accepts tacitly, and since Titius, after Caius' death, is in this situation, he can acquire the bequest by acceptance of the promise, and the bequest has not become altogether ownerless (*res nullius*) in the meantime but only *vacant* (*res vacua*). For Titius alone has the right to make the

choice as to whether or not he wants to make the belongings left to him his own.

> Accordingly, testaments are also valid in accordance with mere natural Right (*sunt iuris naturae*). This assertion, however, is to be taken as meaning that testaments are fit for and worth being introduced and sanctioned in the civil condition (if this makes its appearance some day). For only the civil condition (the general will in it) confirms possession of a legacy while it hovers between acceptance and rejection and strictly speaking belongs to no one.

III.
Leaving Behind a Good Reputation After One's Death
(Bona fama defuncti)
§35.

It would be absurd to think that someone who has died can still possess something after his death (and so when he no longer exists), if what he left behind were a thing. But a *good reputation* is an innate external belonging, though an ideal one only, that clings to the subject as a person, a being of such a nature that I can and must abstract from whether he ceases to be entirely at his death or whether he survives as a person; for in the context of his rights in relation to others, I actually regard every person simply in terms of his humanity, hence as *homo noumenon*. So any attempt to stain someone's reputation by falsehood after his death is suspect, because it is at least ungenerous to spread reproaches against one who is absent and cannot defend himself, unless one is quite certain of them. Nevertheless, a well-founded accusation against him is still in order (so that the principle *de mortuis nihil nisi bene*[2] is incorrect).

For a man to acquire by an irreproachable life and the death that ends it a (negatively) good name, which continues to be his when he no longer exists as *homo phaenomenon;* for those who survive him (relatives or strangers) to be also authorized by right to defend him (for unproved charges are dangerous to them as well, since they could get similar treatment when they die); for a man to be able to acquire such a right, is, I say, a phenomenon as strange as it is undeniable, a phenomenon of reason giving law a priori that extends its commands and prohibitions even beyond the limits of life. If anyone spreads it abroad that someone who has died committed a crime which

---

2. "Speak nothing but good about the dead."

in his lifetime would have made him dishonorable or only contemptible, whoever can produce proof that this charge is an intentional untruth and a lie can then publicly declare the one who spread the evil gossip a calumniator and so take away his honor. He could not do this unless he could rightly assume that the dead man was wronged by it, even though he is dead, and that this defense brings him satisfaction even though he no longer exists.[3] An apologist need not prove his authorization to play the role of apologist for the

dead, for every man inevitably arrogates this to himself as belonging not merely to duty of virtue (duty regarded ethically) but to the right of humanity as such; and the stain on the dead person need not have been prejudicial to any particular person, such as his friends and relatives, to justify such censure. It is therefore indisputable that there is a basis for such an ideal acquisition and for a man's right after his death against those who survive him, even though no deduction of its possibility can be given.

CHAPTER III
On Acquisition That Is Dependent Subjectively upon the Decision of a Public Court of Justice

§36.

If by natural Right is understood only nonstatutory Right, hence simply Right that can be known a priori by everyone's reason, natural Right will include not only the *justice* that holds among persons in their exchanges with one another (*iustitia commutativa*) but also distributive justice (*iustitia distributiva*), insofar as it can be known a priori in accordance with the principle of distributive justice how its decisions (*sententia*) would have to be reached.

The moral person that administers justice is a *court* (*forum*) and its administration of justice is a

judgment (*iudicium*). All this is here thought out a priori only in accordance with conditions of Right, without taking account of how such a constitution is to be actually set up and organized (*statutes*, hence empirical principles, belong to an actual constitution).

So the question here is not merely what is *right in itself*, that is, how every man has to judge about it on his own, but what is right before a court, that is, what is laid down as right. And here there are *four* cases in which two different and opposing judgments can result and persist side by side, because they are made from two different points of view, both of which are true: one in accordance with private Right, the other in accordance with the Idea of public Right. These cases are: (1) a *contract to make a gift* (*pactum donationis*): (2) a *contract to lend a thing* (*commodatum*); (3) *recovering* something (*vindicatio*); (4) *taking an oath* (*iuramentum*).

> It is a common fault (*vitium subreptionis*) of experts on Right to *misrepresent*, as if it were also the objective principle of what is right in itself, that rightful principle which a court is authorized and indeed bound to adopt for its own use (hence for a subjective purpose) in order to pronounce and judge what belongs to each as his right, although the latter is very different from the former. It is therefore of no slight importance to recognize this specific distinction and to draw attention to it.

A.
On a Contract to Make a Gift
§37.

In accordance with *private Right*, this contract (*donatio*), by which I *alienate without remuneration*

---

3. But one is not to draw from this any visionary conclusions about presentiments of a future life or about unseen relations to disembodied souls. For what is under discussion here does not go beyond the purely moral and rightful relations to be found among men during life as well. These are relations in which men stand as intelligible beings, insofar as one *logically puts aside*, that is, *abstracts from*, everything physical (i.e., everything belonging to their existence in space and time); but one does not remove men from this nature of theirs and let them become spirits, in which condition they would feel the injury of those who slander them. Someone who, a hundred years from now, falsely repeats something evil about me injures me right now; for in a relation purely of rights, which is entirely intellectual, abstraction is made from any physical conditions (of time), and whoever robs me of my honor (a slanderer) is just as punishable as if he had done it during my lifetime—punishable, however, not by a criminal court but only by public opinion, which, in accordance with the right of retribution, inflicts on him the same loss of the honor he diminished in another. Even a *plagiarism* that a writer perpetrates on a dead person, though it does not indeed stain the dead person's honor but only steals a part of it from him, is still avenged with right, as having wronged him (robbed the man).

(*gratis*) what is mine, a thing of mine (or my right), involves a relation of myself, the donor (*donans*), to another, the recipient (*donatorius*), by which what is mine passes to the recipient by his acceptance of it (*donum*). But it is not to be presumed that I intend by this contract to be coerced to keep my promise and so also to give up my *freedom* gratuitously and, as it were, to throw myself away (*nemo suum iactare praesumitur*). Yet this is what would happen in accordance with Right in the civil condition, where the one who is to receive my gift can *coerce* me to carry out my promise. So, if the matter were to come before a court, that is, in accordance with public Right, it would either have to be presumed that the donor consented to this coercion, which is absurd, or else the court in its judgment (verdict) simply takes no account of whether the donor did or did not want to reserve his freedom to go back on his promise, but takes account only of what is certain, namely, the promise and the promisee's acceptance of it. So even if, as can well be supposed, the promisor thought that he could not be bound to keep his promise should he regret having made it before it is time to fulfill it, the court assumes that he would have had to make this reservation expressly, and that if he did not he could be coerced to fulfill his promise. The court adopts this principle because otherwise its verdict on rights would be made infinitely more difficult or even impossible.

B.
On a Contract to Lend a Thing
§38.

In this contract (*commodatum*) by which I permit someone to use without compensation something of mine, if the parties to the contract agree that *this very same thing* is to be brought under my control again, the borrower (*commodatarius*) cannot presume that the thing's owner (*commodans*) also assumes risk (*casus*) of possible loss of the thing, or of what makes it useful, that might arise from its having been put into the borrower's possession. For it is not a matter of course that the owner, in addition to granting the borrower the use of his thing (such loss to himself as is inseparable from parting with it), has also issued the borrower a *guarantee* against any damage that could arise from his having let it out of his custody. A separate contract would have to be made about that. So the question can only be, on which of the two, the lender or the borrower, is it incumbent to attach expressly to a contract to lend the condition about assuming the risk for possible damage to the thing? Or, if no such condition is attached, who can be *presumed* to have *agreed* to guarantee the lender's property (by the return of it, or its equivalent, to him)? Not the lender, for it cannot be presumed that he has gratuitously agreed to more than the mere use of the thing (namely, that he has also undertaken to guarantee the property). It is, rather, the borrower, because in taking on this guarantee he performs nothing more than is already contained in the contract.

Suppose, for example, that having been caught in the rain I go into a house and ask to borrow a coat, which is then perhaps permanently stained when someone carelessly pours discoloring material from a window, or is stolen from me when I go into another house and take it off. Everyone would find it absurd to say that I need do nothing more than return the coat as it is, or that I have only to report that the theft occurred and that it was at most a matter of courtesy for me to commiserate with the owner over his loss, since he could demand nothing on the basis of his right. But no one would think it absurd if, in requesting to use something, I also ask its owner beforehand to take on himself the risk of any mischance that might happen to it while it is in my hands, because I am poor and unable to compensate him for the loss. No one will find this superfluous and ridiculous, except, perhaps, when the lender is known to be a rich and considerate man, since it would then be almost insulting him not to presume that he would generously remit my debt in this case.

Now if (as the nature of a contract to lend involves) nothing is stipulated in it about a possible mischance (*casus*) that might affect the thing, so that agreement about this can only be presumed, a contract to lend is an uncertain contract (*pactum incertum*) with regard to what is mine and what is yours by it. Consequently, the judgment about this, that is, the decision as to who must bear the misfortune, cannot be made from the conditions of the contract itself, it can be decided only as it would be decided *before a court*, which always considers only what is certain in the case (which is here the possession of the thing as property). So the judgment in the *state of nature*, that is, in terms of the intrinsic character of the matter, will go like this: The damage resulting from mischance to a thing loaned falls on the *borrower* (*casum sentit commodatarius*). But in the *civil condition*, and so before a court, the verdict will come out: The damage falls on the *lender* (*casum sentit dominus*). This verdict will indeed be given on different grounds from the decree of sound reason alone, since a public judge cannot get involved in presumptions as to what the one party or the other may have thought. He can consider only that whoever has not attached a separate contract stipulating that he is free from any damages to the thing lent must himself bear them. Hence the difference between the judgment that a court must make and that which each is justified in making for himself by his private reason is a point that is by no means to be overlooked in amending judgments about rights.

C.
On Recovery (Repossession) of Something Lost (vindicatio)
§39.

It is clear from the foregoing that something of mine that continues to exist remains mine even though I am not continuously holding it; that it does not of itself cease to be mine apart from some act by which I give up my right to it (*derelictionis vel alienationis*); and that I have a right to this thing (*ius reale* and therefore a right against *whoever* holds it, not merely a right against a specific person (*ius personale*). But the question now is whether this right must also be regarded *by everyone else* as ownership that continues of itself, *if I have only not renounced* it, when the thing is in another's possession.

Suppose that someone has lost a thing (*res amissa*) and that someone else takes it *in good faith* (*bona fide*), as a supposed find. Or suppose that I get a thing by its being formally alienated by someone possessing it who represents himself as its owner although he is not. Since I cannot acquire a thing from someone who *is not its owner* (*a non domino*), the question arises whether I am excluded by the real owner from any right to this thing and left with only a personal right against the illegitimate possessor. This is obviously the case if acquisition is judged merely in accordance with the intrinsic grounds that justify it (in the state of nature), not in accordance with what is appropriate for a court.

It must be possible for whatever can be alienated to be acquired by someone or other. The legitimacy of

acquisition, however, rests entirely on the form in accordance with which what is possessed by another is transferred to me and accepted by me, that is, on the formalities of the act of exchange (*commutatio*) between the possessor of the thing and the one acquiring it, by which a right is established; I may not ask how the possessor obtained possession of it, since this would already be an offense (*quilibet praesumitur bonus, donec etc.*). Suppose, now, that it later turns out that the possessor was not the owner but that someone else was. I cannot then say that the owner could straightway take the thing from me (as he could from anyone else who might be holding it). For I have stolen nothing from him, but have, for example, bought a horse offered for sale in the public market in conformity with the law (*titulo emti venditi*). The title of acquisition on my part is indisputable since I (as buyer) am not bound or even authorized to search the other's (the seller's) title of possession—this investigation would go on to infinity in an ascending series. If the purchase is formally correct, I become not just the *putative* but the *true* owner of the horse.

But against this, the following argument arises with regard to rights. Any acquisition from one who is not the owner of a thing (*a non domino*) is null and void. I can derive no more from another than what he legitimately has. Even though, in buying a stolen horse for sale in the market, I proceed quite correctly as far as the form of acquisition (*modus acquierendi*) is concerned, my title of acquisition is still defective, since the horse did not belong to the one who actually sold it. I may well be its possessor *in good faith* (*possessor bona fidei*), but I am still only its putative owner (*dominus putativus*) and the true owner has a right to *recover* it (*rem suam vindicandi*).

If one asks what is to be laid down as right *in itself* (in the state of nature) in the acquisition of external things in accordance with principles of justice in men's exchanges with one another (*iustitia commutativa*), then one must answer as follows. If someone intends to acquire an external thing in this way it is in fact necessary for him to investigate whether the thing he wants to acquire does not already belong to someone else; that is to say, even if he has strictly observed the formal conditions for deriving the thing from what belongs to another (has bought the horse in the market in the proper way), as long as he remains ignorant as to whether someone else (other than the seller) is the true owner of it, the most he could have acquired is only a *right against a person* with regard to the thing (*ius ad rem*), so that if someone comes forth who can document his previous ownership of it, nothing is left to the alleged new owner but to have legitimately enjoyed the use of it up to this moment as its possessor in good faith. Since it is largely impossible to discover who was absolutely first (the original owner) in the series of putative owners deriving their right from each other, no trade in external things, no matter how well it may agree with the formal conditions of this kind of justice (*iustitia commutativa*), can guarantee a secure acquisition.

Here again reason giving laws with regard to rights comes forth with a principle of *distributive justice*, of adopting as its guiding rule for the legitimacy of possession, not the way it would be judged *in itself* by the private will of each (in the state of nature), but the way it would be judged before a court in a condition brought about by the united will of all (in a civil condition). In a civil condition, conformity with the formal conditions of acquisition, which of themselves establish only a right against a person, is postulated as an adequate substitute for the material grounds (which establish derivation from what belonged to a previous alleged owner); and what is *in itself* a right against a person, *when brought before a court*, holds as a right to a thing. A horse, for example, that someone puts up for sale in a public market regulated by police ordinances becomes my property if all the rules of buying and selling are strictly observed (but in such a way that the true owner retains the right to put forward a claim against the seller on the ground of his earlier, unforfeited possession of it); and what would otherwise be my right against a person is converted into a right to a thing, in accordance with which I can take (recover) it as mine wherever I find it, without having to get involved in how the seller obtained it.

So it is only for the sake of a court's verdict (*in favorem iustitiae distributivae*) that a right to a thing is taken and treated not *as it is in itself* (as a right against a person) but as it can be *most readily and surely judged* (as a right to a thing), and yet in accordance with a pure a priori principle. On this principle various statutory laws (ordinances) are subsequently based, the primary purpose of which is to set up conditions under which alone a way of acquiring is to have rightful force, conditions *such that a*

judge can assign to each what is his *most readily and with least hesitation.* For example, in the saying "Purchase breaks a lease," what is a right to a thing (the lease) in accordance with the nature of the contract, that is, in itself, holds as a mere right against a person; and conversely, as in the case discussed above, what is in itself only a right against a person holds as a right to a thing. In such cases the question is what principles a court in the civil condition should rely on in order to proceed most surely in its verdicts about the rights belonging to each.

D.
On Acquiring Guarantees by Oath
(Cautio iuratoria)
§40.

No other reason could be given that could bind men as a matter of Right to *believe* and acknowledge that there are gods than that they could thereby swear an oath and be constrained to be truthful in what they say and faithful in keeping their promises by their fear of an all-seeing, almighty power whose vengeance they would have solemnly called down upon themselves in case their declarations were false. That in requiring oaths one does not count on men's morality in these two respects but only on their blind superstition is clear from this: that one does not expect any guarantee *merely* from their *solemn* declarations before a court in matters of rights, even though everyone clearly sees the duty to be truthful in a case having to do with what is most sacred of all among men (the Right of men). So mere fairy tales are the incentive in taking oaths, as, for example, according to Marsden's testimony, the Rajangs, a pagan people of Sumatra, swear by the bones of their dead ancestors even though they do not believe that there is a life after death; or as the Negroes of Guinea take an oath on their *fetish*, such as a bird's feather, calling upon it to break their neck, and so forth. They believe that an invisible power, whether it has understanding or not, already has by its nature this magical power that will come into play by their invocations. This sort of belief is called religion but should strictly be called superstition. It is, however, indispensable for the administration of justice since, without counting on it, a *court* would not be sufficiently in a position to ascertain facts kept secret and give the right verdict. A law binding a people to take oaths is therefore obviously laid down only on behalf of the judicial authority.

But now the question is, what basis is there for the obligation that someone before a court is supposed to have, to accept another's oath as a proof, valid for Right, of the truth of his testimony, which puts an end to all dispute? That is to say, what binds me as a matter of Right to believe that another (who swears an oath) has any religion, so as to make my rights dependent upon his oath? So too, can I be bound to take an oath? Both are wrong in themselves.

Yet with reference to a court, and so in the civil condition, if one admits that there is no other means than an oath for getting at the truth in certain cases, one must assume that everyone has a religion, so that it can be used as an expedient (*in casu necessitatis*) for the purpose of proceedings about rights *before a court*, which regards this spiritual coercion (*tortura spiritualis*) as a handy means, in keeping with men's propensity to superstition, for uncovering secrets and considers itself authorized to use it because of this. But the legislative authority acts in a way that is fundamentally wrong in conferring authorization to do this on the judicial authority, since even in the civil condition coercion to take oaths is contrary to human freedom, which must not be lost.

An oath of office is usually *promissory*, an oath, namely, that the official earnestly *resolves* to fulfill his post in conformity with his duties. If it were changed into an *assertoric* oath—if, that is, the official was bound, perhaps at the end of a year (or more), to swear that he had faithfully fulfilled his office during that time—this would arouse his conscience more than an oath he takes as a promise; for having taken a promissory oath, he can always make the excuse to himself later on that with the best of intentions he did not foresee the difficulties which he experienced only later, during the administration of his office. Moreover, he would be more concerned about being accused of failing in his duty if an observer were going to look at the sum of his offenses than if they were merely censured one after the other (and the earlier ones have been forgotten). But a court can certainly not demand swearing to a *belief* (*de credulitate*). For in the first place it involves a self-contradiction; this thing intermediate between opinion and knowledge is the sort of thing that one can dare to bet on but certainly not to swear to. Second, a judge who requires swearing to a belief from a party in order to find out something relevant to his purpose, even if this purpose is the common

good, commits a grave offense against the conscientiousness of the person taking the oath, partly by the thoughtlessness to which the oath misleads him and by which the judge defeats his own purpose, partly by the pangs of conscience a man must feel, when he can find a certain matter very likely today, considered from a certain point of view, but quite unlikely tomorrow, when he considers it from a different point of view. A judge therefore wrongs one whom he constrains to take such an oath.

Transition from What Is Mine or Yours in a State of Nature to What Is Mine or Yours in a Rightful Condition Generally
§41.

A rightful condition is that relation of men among one another that contains the conditions under which alone everyone is able to *enjoy* his rights, and the formal condition under which this is possible in accordance with the Idea of a will giving laws for everyone is called public justice. With reference to either the possibility or the actuality or the necessity of possession of objects (the matter of choice) in accordance with laws, public justice can be divided into *protective justice* (*iustitia tutatrix*), *justice in men's acquiring from one another* (*iustitia commutativa*) and *distributive justice* (*iustitia distributiva*). In these the law says, *first*, merely what conduct is intrinsically *right* in terms of its form (*lex iusti*); *second*, what [objects] are capable of being covered externally by law, in terms of their matter, that is, what way of being in possession is *rightful* (*lex iuridica*); *third*, what is the decision of a court in a particular case in accordance with the given law under which it falls, that it what is *laid down as right* (*lex iustitiae*). Because of this a court is itself called the *justice* of a country, and whether such a thing exists or does not exist is the most important question that can be asked about any arrangements having to do with rights.

A condition that is not rightful, that is, a condition in which there is no distributive justice, is called a state of nature (*status naturalis*). What is opposed to a state of nature is not (as Achenwall thinks) a condition that is *social* and that could be called an artificial condition (*status artificialis*), but rather the *civil* condition (*status civilis*), that of a society subject to distributive justice. For in the state of nature, too, there can be societies compatible with rights (e.g., conjugal, paternal, domestic societies in general, as well as many others); but no law, "You ought to enter this condition," holds a priori for these societies, whereas it can be said of a *rightful* condition that all men who could (even involuntarily) come into relations of rights with one another *ought* to enter this condition.

The first and second of these conditions can be called the condition of *private Right*, whereas the third and last can be called the condition of *public Right*. The latter contains no further or other duties of men among themselves than can be conceived in the former state; the matter of private Right is the same in both. The laws of the condition of public Right, accordingly, have to do only with the rightful form of men's association (constitution), in view of which these laws must necessarily be conceived as public.

The *civil union* (*unio civilis*) cannot itself be called a *society*, for between the *commander* (*imperans*) and the *subject* (*subditus*) there is no partnership. They are not fellow-members: One is *subordinated to*, not *coordinated with*, the other; and those who are coordinate with one another must for this very reason consider themselves equals since they are subject to common laws. The civil union *is* not so much a society but rather *makes* one.

§42.

From private Right in the state of nature there proceeds the postulate of public Right: When you cannot avoid living side by side with all others, you ought to leave the state of nature and proceed with them into a rightful condition, that is, a condition of distributive justice. The ground of this postulate can be explicated analytically from the concept of *Right* in external relations, in contrast with *violence* (*violentia*).

No one is bound to refrain from encroaching on what another possesses if the other gives him no equal assurance that he will observe the same restraint toward him. No one, therefore, need wait until he has learned by bitter experience of the other's contrary disposition; for what should bind him to wait till he has suffered a loss before he becomes prudent, when he can quite well perceive within himself the inclination of men generally to lord it over others as their master (not to respect the superiority of the rights of others when they feel superior to them in strength or cunning)? And it is not necessary to wait for actual hostility; one is authorized to use coercion against someone who already, by his nature, threatens him with coercion. (*Quilibet praesumitur malus, donec securitatem dederit oppositi.*)

Given the intention to be and to remain in this state of externally lawless freedom, men do *one another* no wrong at all when they feud among themselves; for what holds for one holds also in turn for the other, as if by mutual consent (*uti partes de iure suo disponunt, ita ius est*). But in general they do wrong in the highest degree[1] by wanting to be and to remain in a condition that is not rightful, that is, in which no one is assured of what is his against violence.

PUBLIC RIGHT

SECTION I.
THE RIGHT OF A STATE

§43.

The sum of the laws that need to be promulgated generally in order to bring about a rightful condition is *public Right*. Public Right is therefore a system of laws for a people, that is, a multitude of men, or for a multitude of peoples, that, because they affect one another, need a rightful condition under a will uniting them, a *constitution* (*constitutio*), so that they may enjoy what is laid down as right. This condition of the

---

1. This distinction between what is merely formally wrong and what is also materially wrong has many applications in the doctrine of Right. An enemy who, instead of honorably carrying out his surrender agreement with the garrison of a besieged fortress, mistreats them as they march out or otherwise breaks the agreement, cannot complain of being wronged if his opponent plays the same trick on him when he can. But in general they do wrong in the highest degree, because they take away any validity from the concept of Right itself and hand everything over to savage violence, as if by law, and so subvert the Right of men as such.

individuals within a people in relation to one another is called a *civil* condition (*status civilis*), and the whole of individuals in a rightful condition in relation to its own members is called a *state* (*civitas*). Because of its form, by which all are united through their common interest in being in a rightful condition, a state is called a *commonwealth* (*res publica latius sic dicta*). In relation to other peoples, however, a state is called simply a *power potentia*) (hence the word *potentate*). Because the union of the members is (presumed to be) one they inherited, a state is also called a *nation* (*gens*). Hence, under the general concept of public Right we are led to think not only of the Right of a state but also of a *Right of nations* (*ius gentium*). Since the earth's surface is not unlimited but closed, the concepts of the Right of a state and of a Right of nations lead inevitably to the Idea of a *Right for all nations* (*ius gentium*) or *cosmopolitan Right* (*ius cosmopoliticum*). So if the principle of outer freedom limited by law is lacking in any one of these three possible forms of rightful condition, the framework of all the others is unavoidably undermined and must finally collapse.

§44.

It is not experience from which we learn of men's maxim of violence and of their malevolent tendency to attack one another before external legislation endowed with power appears. It is therefore not some fact that makes coercion through public law necessary. On the contrary, however well disposed and law-abiding men might be, it still lies a priori in the rational Idea of such a condition (one that is not rightful) that before a public lawful condition is established, individual men, peoples, and states can never be secure against violence from one another, since each has its own right to do *what seems right and good to it* and not to be dependent upon another's opinion about this. So, unless it wants to renounce any concepts of Right, the first thing it has to resolve upon is the principle that it must leave the state of nature, in which each follows its own judgment, unite itself with all others (with which it cannot avoid interacting), subject itself to a public lawful external coercion, and so enter into a condition in which what is to be recognized as belonging to it is determined *by law* and is allotted to it by adequate

power (not its own but an external power); that is to say, it ought above all else to enter a civil condition.

It is true that the state of nature need not, just because it is natural, be a state of *injustice* (*iniustus*), of dealing with one another only in terms of the degree of force each has. But it would still be a state *devoid of justice* (*status iustitia vacuus*), in which, when rights are *in dispute* (*ius controversum*), there would be no judge competent to render a verdict having rightful force. Hence each may impel the other by force to leave this state and enter into a rightful condition; for although each can acquire something external by taking control of it or by contract in accordance with its *concepts of Right*, this acquisition is still only *provisional* as long as it does not yet have the sanction of public law, since it is not determined by public (distributive) justice and secured by an authority putting this right into effect.

> If no acquisition were recognized as rightful even in a provisional way prior to entering the civil condition, the civil condition itself would be impossible. For in terms of their form, laws concerning what is mine or yours in the state of nature contain the same thing that they prescribe in the civil condition, insofar as the civil condition is thought of by pure rational concepts alone. The difference is only that the civil condition provides the conditions under which these laws are put into effect (in keeping with distributive justice). So if external objects were not even *provisionally* mine or yours in the state of nature, there would also be no duties of Right with regard to them and therefore no command to leave the state of nature.

§45.

A *state* (*civitas*) is a union of a multitude of men under laws of Right. Insofar as these are a priori necessary as laws, that is, insofar as they follow of themselves from concepts of external Right as such (are not statutory), its form is the form of a state as such, that is, of *the state as Idea*, as it ought to be in accordance with pure principles of Right. This Idea serves as a norm (*norma*) for every actual union into a commonwealth (hence serves as a norm for its internal constitution).

Every state contains three *authorities* within it, that is, the general united will consists of three persons (*trias politica*): the (*sovereign authority* (sovereignty) in the person of the legislator; the *executive authority* in the person of the ruler (in conformity to law); and the *judicial authority* (to award to each what is his in accordance with the law) in the person of the judge (*potestas legislatoria, rectoria et iudiciaria*). These are like the three propositions in a practical syllogism: the major premise, which contains the *law* of that will; the minor premise, which contains the *command* to behave in accordance with the law, i.e. the principle of subsumption under the law; and the conclusion, which contains the *verdict* (sentence), what is laid down as right in the case at hand.

§46.

The legislative authority can belong only to the united will of the people. For since all Right is to proceed from it, it *cannot* do anyone wrong by its law. Now, when someone makes arrangements about *another*, it is always possible for him to do the other wrong; but he can never do wrong in what he decides upon with regard to himself (for *volenti non fit iniuria*).[2] Therefore only the concurring and united will of all, insofar as each decides the same thing for all and all for each, and so only the general united will of the people, can be legislative.

The members of such a society who are united for giving law (*societas civilis*), that is, the members of a state, are called *citizens of a state* (*cives*). In terms of rights, the attributes of a citizen, inseparable from his essence (as a citizen), are: lawful *freedom*, the attribute of obeying no other law than that to which he has given his consent; civil *equality*, that of not recognizing among the *people* any superior with the moral capacity to bind him as a matter of Right in a way that he could not in turn bind the other; and third, the attribute of civil *independence*, of owing his existence and preservation to his own rights and powers as a member of the commonwealth, not to the choice of another among the people. From his independence follows his civil personality, his attribute of not needing to be represented by another where rights are concerned.

The only qualification for being a citizen is being fit to vote. But being fit to vote presupposes the independence of someone who, as one of the people, wants to be not just a part of the commonwealth but also a member of it, that is, a part of the commonwealth acting from his own choice in community with others. This quality of being independent, however, requires a distinction between *active* and *passive* citizens, though the concept of a passive citizen seems to contradict the concept of a citizen as such. The following examples can serve to remove this difficulty: an apprentice in the service of a merchant or artisan; a domestic servant (as distinguished from a civil servant); a minor (*naturaliter vel civiliter*); all women and, in general, anyone whose preservation in existence (his being fed and protected) depends not on his management of his own business but on arrangements made by another (except the state). All these people lack civil personality and their existence is, as it were, only inherence. The woodcutter I hire to work in my yard; the blacksmith in India, who goes into people's houses to work on iron with his hammer, anvil, and bellows, as compared with the European carpenter or blacksmith who can put the products of his work up as goods for sale to the public; the private tutor, as compared with the schoolteacher; the tenant farmer as compared with the leasehold farmer, and so forth; these are mere underlings of the commonwealth because they have to be under the direction or protection of other individuals, and so do not possess civil independence.

This dependence upon the will of others and this inequality is, however, in no way opposed to their freedom and equality *as men*, who together make up a people; on the contrary, it is only in conformity with the conditions of freedom and equality that this people can become a state and enter into a civil constitution. But not all persons qualify with equal right to vote within this constitution, that is, to be citizens and not mere associates in the state. For from their capacity to demand that all others treat them in accordance with the laws of natural freedom and equality as *passive* parts of the state it does not follow that they also have the right to manage the state itself as *active* members of it, the right to organize it or to cooperate for introducing certain laws. It follows only that, whatever sort of positive laws the citizens might vote for, these laws must still not be contrary to the natural laws of freedom and of the equality of everyone in the people corresponding to this freedom, namely that anyone can work his way up from this passive condition to an active one.

§47.

All those three authorities in a state are dignities, and since they arise necessarily from the Idea of a state as such, as essential for the establishment (constitution) of it, they are *civic dignities*. They comprise the relation of a *superior* over all (which, from the viewpoint

2. "No wrong is done to someone who consents."

of laws of freedom, can be none other than the united people itself) to the multitude of that people severally as *subjects*, that is, the relation of a *commander* (*imperans*) to *those who obey* (*subditus*). The act by which a people forms itself into a state is the *original contract*. Properly speaking, the original contract is only the Idea of this act, in terms of which alone we can think of the legitimacy of a state. In accordance with the original contract, everyone (*omnes et singuli*) within a *people* gives up his external freedom in order to take it up again immediately as a member of a commonwealth, that is, of a people considered as a state (*universi*). And one cannot say: A state, man in a state has sacrificed a *part* of his innate outer freedom for the sake of an end, but rather, he has relinquished entirely his wild, lawless freedom in order to find his freedom as such undiminished, in a dependence upon laws, that is, in a rightful condition, since this dependence arises from his own lawgiving will.

§48.

Accordingly, the three authorities in a state are, *first*, coordinate with one another (*potestates coordinatae*) as so many moral persons, that is, each complements the others to complete the constitution of a state (*complementum ad sufficientiam*). But, *second*, they are also subordinate (*subordinatae*) to one another, so that one of them, in assisting another, cannot also usurp its function; instead, each has its own principle, that is, it indeed commands in its capacity as a particular person, but still under the condition of the will of a superior. *Third*, through the union of both each subject is apportioned his rights.

It can be said of these authorities, regarded in their dignity, that the will of the *legislator* (*legislatoris*) with regard to what is externally mine or yours is *irreproachable* (*irreprehensible*); that the executive power of the *supreme ruler* (*summi rectoris*) is *irresistible*; and that the verdict of the highest *judge* (*supremi iudicis*) is *irreversible* (cannot be appealed).

§49.

The *ruler* of a state (*rex, princeps*) is that (moral or natural) person to whom the executive authority (*postestas executoria*) belongs. He is the *agent* of the state, who appoints the magistrates and prescribes to the people rules in accordance with which each of them can acquire something or preserve what is his in conformity with the law (through subsumption of a case under it). Regarded as a moral person, he is called the *directorate*, the government. His *directives* to the people, and to the magistrates and their superior (the minister) whom he charges with *administering the state* (*gubernatio*), are ordinances or *decrees* (not laws); for they are directed to decisions in particular cases and are given as subject to being changed. A *government* that was also legislative would have to be called a *despotic* as opposed to a *patriotic* government; but by a patriotic government is understood not a *paternalistic* one (*regimen paternale*), which is the most despotic of all (since it treats citizens as children), but one *serving the native land* (*regimen civitatis et patriae*). In it the state (*civitas*) does treat its subjects as members of one family but it also treats them as citizens of the state, that is, in accordance with laws of their own independence: Each is in possession of himself and is not dependent upon the absolute will of another alongside him or above him.

So a people's head of state (legislator) cannot also be its *ruler*, since the ruler is subject to the law and so is put under obligation through the law by *another*, namely the sovereign. The sovereign can also take the ruler's authority away from him, depose him, or reform his administration. But it cannot *punish* him (and the saying common in England, that the king, that is, the supreme executive authority, can do no wrong, means no more than this); for punishment is, again, an act of the executive authority, which has the supreme capacity to *exercise coercion* in conformity with the law, and it would be self-contradictory for him to be subject to coercion.

Finally, neither the head of state nor its ruler can *judge*, but can only appoint judges as magistrates. A people judges itself through those of its fellow citizens whom it designates as its representatives for this by a free choice and, indeed, designates especially for each act. For a verdict (a sentence) is an individual act of public justice (*iustitiae distributivae*) performed by an administrator of the state (a judge or court) upon a subject, that is, upon someone belonging to the people; and so this act is invested with no authority to assign (allot) to a subject what is his. Since each individual among a people is only passive in this relationship (to the authorities), if either the legislative or the executive authority were to decide in a controversial case what belongs to him, it might do him a wrong, since it would not be the people itself doing this and pronouncing a verdict of *guilty* or *not guilty* upon a fellow citizen. But once the facts in a lawsuit have been established, the court has judicial authority to apply the law, and to render to each what is his with the help of the executive authority. Hence only the *people* can give a judgment upon one of its members, although only indirectly, by means of representatives (the jury) whom it has delegated. It would also be beneath the dignity of the head of state to play the judge, that is, to put himself in a position where he could do wrong and so have his decision appealed (*a rege male informato ad regem melius informandum*).[3]

There are thus three distinct authorities (*potestas legislatoria, executoria, iudiciaria*) by which a state (*civitas*) has its autonomy, that is, by which it forms and preserves itself in accordance with laws of freedom. A state's *well-being* consists in their being united (*salus rei publicae suprema lex est*).[4] By the well-being of a state must not be understood the *welfare* of its citizens and their *happiness;* for happiness can perhaps come to them more easily and as they would like it to in a state of nature (as Rousseau asserts) or even under a despotic government. By the well-being of a state is understood, instead, that condition in which its constitution conforms most fully to principles of Right; it is that condition which reason, *by a categorical imperative*, makes it obligatory for us to strive after.

General Remark
On the Effects with Regard to Rights That Follow
from the Nature of the Civil Union
A.

A people should not *inquire* with any practical aim in view into the origin of the supreme authority to which it is subject, that is, a subject *ought not to rationalize* for the sake of action about the origin of this authority, as a right that can still be called into question (*ius controversum*) with regard to the obedience he owes it. For, since a people must be regarded as already united under a general legislative will in order to

judge with rightful force about the supreme authority (*summum imperium*), it cannot and may not judge otherwise than as the present head of state (*summus imperans*) wills it to. Whether a state began with an actual contract of submission (*pactum subiectionis civilis*) as a fact, or whether power came first and law arrived only afterward, or even whether they should have followed in this order: For a people already subject to civil law these rationalizations are altogether pointless and, moreover, threaten a state with danger. If a subject, having pondered over the ultimate origin of the authority now ruling, wanted to resist this authority, he would be punished, got rid of, or expelled (as an outlaw, *exlex*) in accordance with the laws of this authority, that is, with every right. A law that is so holy (inviolable) that it is already a crime even to call it in doubt *in a practical way*, and so to suspend its effect for a moment, is thought as if it must have arisen not from men but from some highest, flawless lawgiver; and that is what the saying "All authority is from God" means. This saying is not an assertion about the *historical basis* of the civil constitution; it instead sets forth an Idea as a practical principle of reason: the principle that the presently existing legislative authority ought to be obeyed, whatever its origin.

Now from this principle follows the proposition: The head of a state has only rights against his subjects and no duties (that he can be coerced to fulfill). Moreover, even if the organ of the head of a state, the *ruler*, proceeds contrary to law, for example, if he goes against the law of equality in assigning the burdens of the state in matters of taxation, recruiting, and so forth, subjects may indeed oppose this injustice by *complaints* (*gravamina*) but not by resistance.

Indeed, even the constitution cannot contain any article that would make it possible for there to be some authority in a state to resist the supreme commander in case he should violate the law of the constitution, and so to limit him. For someone who is to limit the authority in a state must have even more power than he whom he limits, or at least as much power as he has; and, as a legitimate commander who directs the subjects to resist, he must also be able to *protect* them and to render a judgment having rightful force in any case that comes up; consequently he has to be able to command resistance publicly. In that case, however, the supreme commander in a state is not the supreme commander; instead it is the one who can resist him, and this is self-contradictory. In

---

3. "from a king badly instructed to a king to be better instructed"
4. "The well-being of the commonwealth is the supreme law." The saying seems to stem from Cicero, *De Legibus* 3, 8: *"Salus populi suprema lex esto."*

that case the sovereign behaves through its minister as also the ruler and so as a despot; and the illusion that allows us to think of the people, through its deputies, as the limiting authority (though it has, properly speaking, only legislative authority) cannot conceal the despotism, so that it does not come to light from the measures the minister takes. The people, in being represented by its deputies (in parliament), has, in these guardians of its freedom and rights, men who have a lively interest in positions for themselves and their families, in the army, the navy, and the civil service, that depend on the minister, and who are always ready to play into the government's hands (instead of resisting its encroachments; besides, a public declaration of resistance requires unanimity in a people which has been prepared in advance, and this cannot be permitted in time of peace). Hence a so-called moderate constitution, as a constitution for the inner rights of a state, is an absurdity. Instead of belonging to Right it is only a principle of prudence, not so much to make it more difficult for a powerful transgressor of the people's rights to exercise at will his influence upon the government as to disguise his influence under the illusion of an opposition permitted to the people.

Therefore a people cannot offer any resistance to the legislative head of a state that would be consistent with right, since a rightful condition is possible only by submission to its general legislative will. There is, therefore, no right to *sedition* (*seditio*), still less to *rebellion* (*rebellio*), and least of all is there a right against the head of a state as an individual person (the monarch), *to attack his person* or even his life (*monarchomachismus sub specie tyrannicidii*) on the pretext that he has abused his authority (*tyrannis*). Any attempt whatsoever at this is *high treason* (*proditio eminens*), and whoever commits such treason must be punished by nothing less than death for attempting *to destroy his fatherland* (*parricida*). The reason a people has a duty to put up with even what is held to be an unbearable abuse of supreme authority is that its resistance to the highest legislation can never be regarded as other than contrary to law, and indeed as abolishing the entire legal constitution. For a people to be authorized to resist, there would have to be a public law permitting it to resist, that is, the highest legislation would have to contain a provision that it is not the highest and that makes the people, as subject, by one and the same judgment sovereign over him to whom it is subject.

This is self-contradictory, and the contradiction is evident as soon as one asks who is to be the judge in this dispute between people and sovereign (for, considered in terms of rights, these are always two distinct moral persons). For it is then apparent that the people wants to be the judge in its own suit.[5]

---

5. The *dethronement* of a monarch can still be thought of as if he had *voluntarily* laid aside the crown and abdicated his authority, giving it back to the people, or as if, without any attack on the highest person, he had relinquished his authority and been reduced to the rank of a private person. Because of this the people who extorted this from him has at least the pretext of a *right of necessity* (*casus necessitatis*) in favor of its crime. But it never has the least right to punish him, the head of state, because of his previous administration, since everything he did, in his capacity as head of state, must be regarded as having been done in external conformity with rights, and he himself, as the source of the law, can do no wrong. Of all the atrocities involved in overthrowing a state by rebellion, the *assassination* of the monarch is not itself the worst, for we can still think of the people as doing it from fear that if he remained alive he could marshal his forces and inflict on them the punishment they deserve, so that their killing him would not be an enactment of punitive justice but merely a dictate of self-preservation. It is the formal *execution* of a monarch that strikes horror in a soul filled with the Idea of men's rights, a horror that one feels repeatedly as soon as and as often as one thinks of such scenes as the fate of Charles I or Louis XVI. But how are we to explain this feeling, which is not aesthetic feeling (sympathy, an effect of imagination by which we put ourselves in the place of the sufferer) but moral feeling resulting from the complete overturning of all concepts of Right? It is regarded as a crime that remains forever and can never be expiated (*crimen immortale, inexpiabile*), and it seems to be like what theologians call the sin that cannot be forgiven either in this world or the next. The explanation of this phenomenon in the human mind seems to arise from the following reflections upon itself, which throw light on the principles of political rights themselves.

Any transgression of the law can and must be explained only as arising from a maxim of the criminal (to make such a crime his rule); for if we were to derive it from a sensible impulse, he would not be committing it as a *free* being and it could not be imputed to him. But how it is possible for the subject to form such a maxim contrary to the clear prohibition of lawgiving reason absolutely cannot be explained, since only what happens in accordance with the mechanism of nature is capable of being explained. Now the criminal can commit his misdeed either on a maxim he has taken as an objective rule (as holding universally) or only as an exception to the rule (exempting himself from it occasionally). In the *latter* case he only *deviates* from the law (though intentionally); he can at the same time detest his transgression and, without formally renouncing obedience to the law, only want to evade it. In the *first* case, however, he rejects the authority of the law itself, whose validity he still cannot deny before his own reason, and makes it his rule to act contrary to the law. His maxim is therefore opposed to the law not by way of

A change in a (defective) constitution, which may certainly be necessary at times, can therefore be carried out only through *reform* by the sovereign itself, but not by the people, and therefore not by *revolution;* and when such a change takes place this reform can affect only the *executive authority,* not the legislative. In what is called a limited constitution, the constitution contains a provision that the people can legally *resist* the executive authority and its representative (the minister) by means of its representatives (in parliament). Nevertheless, no active resistance (by the people combining at will to coerce the government to take a certain course of action, and so itself performing an act of executive authority) is permitted, but only *negative* resistance, that is, a *refusal* of the people (in parliament) to accede to every demand the government puts forth as necessary for administering the state. Indeed, if these demands were always complied with, this would be a sure sign that the people is corrupt, that its representatives can be bought, that the head of the government is ruling despotically through his minister, and that the minister himself is betraying the people.

---

default only (*negative*) but by *rejecting* it (*contrarie*) or, as we put it, his maxim is *diametrically* opposed to the law, as contradictory to it (hostile to it, so to speak). As far as we can see, it is impossible for a man to commit a crime of this kind, a formally evil (wholly pointless) crime; and yet it is not to be ignored in a system of morals (although it is only the Idea of the most extreme evil).

The reason for horror at the thought of the formal execution of a monarch *by his people* is therefore this: that while his *murder* is regarded as only an *exception* to the rule that the people makes its maxim, his *execution* must be regarded as a complete *overturning* of the principles of the relation between a sovereign and his people (in which the people, which owes its existence only to the sovereign's legislation, makes itself his master), so that violence is elevated above the most sacred rights brazenly and in accordance with principle. Like a chasm that irretrievably swallows everything, the execution of a monarch seems to be a crime from which the people cannot be absolved, for it is as if the state commits suicide. There is, accordingly, reason for assuming that the agreement to execute the monarch actually originates not from what is supposed to be a rightful principle but from fear of the state's vengeance upon the people if it revives at some future time, and that these formalities are undertaken only to give that deed the appearance of punishment, and so of a *rightful procedure* (such as murder would not be). But this disguising of the deed miscarries; such a presumption on the people's part is still worse than murder, since it involves a principle that would have to make it impossible to generate again a state that has been overthrown.

Moreover, once a revolution has succeeded and a new constitution has been established, the lack of legitimacy with which it began and has been implemented cannot release the subjects from the obligation to comply with the new order of things as good citizens, and they cannot refuse honest obedience to the authority that now has the power. A dethroned monarch (who survives the upheaval) cannot be held to account, still less be punished, for what he previously carried out, provided he returns to the Estate [*Stand*] of a citizen and prefers peace for himself and the state to the risk of running away in order to engage in the adventure of trying, as a claimant [or pretender], to get his throne back, whether by covertly inciting a counterrevolution or by the assistance of other powers. But if he prefers the latter course, his right to do so cannot be challenged since the insurrection that dispossessed him was unjust. But do other powers have the right to band together in an alliance on behalf of this deposed monarch, merely so as not to let that crime perpetrated by the people go unavenged and persist as a scandal for all states? Are they therefore authorized and called upon to restore by force the old constitution in any other state where the presently existing constitution has come about *by revolution?* These questions belong to the Right of Nations.

B.

Can the head of state be regarded as the supreme proprietor (of the land) or must he be regarded only as the one who has supreme command over the people by law? Since the land is the ultimate condition that alone makes it possible to have external things as one's own, and the first right that can be acquired is to possession and use of such things, all such rights must be derived from the sovereign as *lord of the land,* or better, as the supreme proprietor of it (*dominus territorii*). The people, the multitude of subjects, also belong to him (they are his people). But they belong to him not as if he owned them (by a right to things); they instead belong to him as their supreme commander (by a right against persons). This supreme proprietorship is, however, only an Idea of the civil union that serves to represent in accordance with concepts of Right the necessary union of the private property of everyone within the people under a general public possessor, so that determination of the particular property of each is in accordance with the necessary formal principle of *division* (division of land), instead of with principles of *aggregation* (which proceeds empirically from the parts to the whole). In accordance with concepts of Right, the supreme proprietor cannot have any land at all as his private property (for otherwise he would make himself a private person). All land belongs only to the people (and indeed to the people taken distributively, not collectively), except in the case of a nomadic people under a head of state, with whom there is no private ownership of land. The supreme commander can therefore have no *domains*, that is, no estates for his private use (for maintaining his court). For if he did, it would then be up to his own discretion how far they should be extended, so that the state would run the risk of seeing all ownership of land in the hands of the government and all subjects as serfs (*gelbae adscripti*), possessors only of what is the property of another, and therefore deprived of all freedom (*servi*). One can say of the lord of the land that *he possesses nothing* (of his own) except himself; for if he had something of his own alongside others in the state, a dispute could arise between them and there would be no judge to settle it. But one can also say that *he possesses everything*, since he has the right of command over the people, to whom all external things belong (*divisim*) (the right to assign to each what is his).

From this it follows that there can also be no corporation, Estate, or order in the state that, as owner of land, can pass it on in accordance with certain statutes to succeeding generations for their exclusive use (in perpetuity). The state can repeal such statutes at any time, provided it compensates those who are left. A *knightly order* (whether a corporation or merely a rank of individual persons who enjoy special honors) or a *clerical order*, called the church, can never acquire from those privileges with which they are favored ownership in land to pass on to their successors; they can acquire only use of it up to the present. The estates of a knightly order can be revoked without scruple (though under the condition mentioned above) if public opinion has ceased to favor *military honors* as a means for safeguarding the state against indifference in defending it. The holdings of the church can be similarly revoked if public opinion has ceased to want masses for souls, prayers, and a multitude of clerics appointed for this as the means for saving the people from eternal fire. Those affected by such reforms cannot complain of their property

being taken from them, since the reason for their possession hitherto lay only in the *people's opinion* and also had to hold as long as that lasted. But as soon as this opinion lapses, and even lapses only in the judgment of those who by their merit have the strongest claim to guide judgment, the supposed property has to cease, as if by an appeal of the people to the state (*a rege male informato ad regem melius informandum*).

On this originally acquired ownership of land rests, again, the right of the supreme commander, as supreme proprietor (lord of the land), to *tax* private owners of land, that is, to require payment of taxes on land, excise taxes, and import duties, or to require the performance of services (such as providing troops for military service). This must, however, be done in such a way that the people taxes itself, since the only way of proceeding in accordance with principles of Right in this matter is for taxes to be levied by those deputized by the people, even in case of forced loans (deviating from previously existing law), which it is permissible to exact by the right of majesty in case the state is in danger of dissolution.

On this supreme proprietorship also rests the right to administer the state's economy, finances, and police. Police provide for public *security, convenience*, and *decency;* for the government's business of guiding the people by laws is made easier when the feeling for decency (*sensus decori*), as negative taste, is not deadened by what offends the moral sense, such as begging, uproar on the streets, stenches, and public prostitution (*venus volgivaga*).

A third right also belongs to the state for its preservation, that of *inspection* (*ius inspectionis*), so that no association (of political or religious fanatics) that could affect the *public* well-being of society (*publicum*) remains concealed. Instead, no association can refuse to disclose its constitution when the police demand it. But the police are not authorized to search anyone's private residence except in a case of necessity, and in every particular case they must be warranted to do so by a higher authority.

C.

To the supreme commander there belongs *indirectly*, that is, insofar as he has taken over the duty of the people, the right to impose taxes on the people for its own preservation, such as taxes to support organizations providing for the *poor, foundling homes*, and *church organizations,* usually called charitable or pious institutions.

The general will of the people has united itself into a society that is to maintain itself perpetually; and for this end it has submitted itself to the internal authority of the state in order to maintain those members of the society who are unable to maintain themselves. For reasons of state the government is therefore authorized to constrain the wealthy to provide the means of sustenance to those who are unable to provide for even their most necessary natural needs. The wealthy have acquired an obligation to the commonwealth, since they owe their existence to an act of submitting to its protection and care, which they need in order to live; on this obligation the state now bases its right to contribute what is theirs to maintaining their fellow citizens. This can be done either by imposing a tax on the property or commerce of citizens, or by establishing funds and using the interest from them, not for the needs of the state (for it is rich), but for the needs of the people. (Since we are speaking here only of the right of the state against the people) it will do this by way of coercion, by public taxation, not merely by *voluntary* contributions, some of which are made for gain (such as lotteries, which produce more poor people and more danger to public property than there would otherwise be, and which should therefore not be permitted). The question arises whether the care of the poor should be provided for by *current contributions*—collected not by begging, which is closely akin to robbery, but by legal levies—so that each generation supports its own poor, or instead by *assets* gradually accumulated and by *pious* institutions generally (such as widows' homes, hospitals, and the like). Only the first arrangement, which no one who has to live can withdraw from, can be considered in keeping with the Right of a state; for even if current contributions increase with the number of the poor, this arrangement does not make poverty a means of acquisition for the lazy (as is to be feared of religious institutions) and so does not become an *unjust* burdening of the people by government.

As for maintaining those children abandoned because of poverty or shame, or indeed murdered because of this, the state has a right to charge the people with the duty of not knowingly letting them die, even though they are an unwelcome addition to the resources of the state. Whether this should be done by taxing elderly unmarried people of both sexes generally (by which I mean *wealthy* unmarried people), since they are in part to blame for there being abandoned children, in order to establish foundling homes, or whether it can be done rightly in another way (it would be hard to find another means for preventing this) is a problem which has not yet been solved in such a way that the solution offends against neither rights nor morality.

As for *churches,* they must be carefully distinguished from religion, which is an inner disposition lying wholly beyond the civil power's sphere of influence. (As institutions for public *divine worship* on the part of the people, to whose opinion or conviction they owe their origin) churches become a true need of a state, the need for a people to regard themselves as subjects of a supreme *invisible* power to which they must pay homage and which can often come into very unequal conflict with the civil power. So a state does have a right with regard to churches. It does not have the right to legislate the internal constitutions of churches or to organize them in accordance with its own views, in ways it deems advantageous to itself, that is, to prescribe to the people or command beliefs and forms of divine worship (*ritus*) (for this must be left entirely to the teachers and directors the people itself has chosen). A state has only a *negative* right to prevent public teachers from exercising an influence on the *visible* political commonwealth that might be prejudicial to public peace. Its right is therefore that of policing, of not letting a dispute arising within a church or among different churches endanger civil harmony. For the supreme authority to say that a church should have a certain belief, or to say which it should have or that it must maintain it unalterably and may not reform itself, are interferences by it that are *beneath its dignity;* for in doing this, as in meddling in the quarrels of the schools, it puts itself on a level of equality with its subjects (the monarch makes himself a priest), and they can straightway tell him that he understands nothing about it. The supreme authority especially has no right to prohibit internal reform of churches, for what the whole people cannot decide upon for itself the legislator also cannot decide for the people. But no people can decide never to make further progress in its insight (enlightenment) regarding beliefs, and so never to reform its churches, since this would be opposed to the humanity in their own persons and so to the highest Right of the people. So no supreme authority can decide on this for the people. But as for the expenses of maintaining churches: For the very same reason these cannot be charged to the state but must rather be charged to the part of the people who profess one or another belief, that is, only to the congregation.

D.

The rights of the supreme commander of a state also include (1) the distribution of *offices*, which are salaried administrative positions; (2) the distribution of *dignities*, which are eminent Estates without pay, based on honor alone, that is, a division of rank into the higher (destined to command) and the lower (which, though free and bound only by public law, is still destined to obey the former); and (3) besides these (relatively beneficent) rights, the *right to punish* as well.

With regard to civil offices, the question arises whether the sovereign, once having given someone an office, has a right to take it away as he pleases (if the official has not committed a crime). I say, no. For the head of state can never make a decision about a civil official which the united will of the people would not make. Now the people (which has to bear the costs incurred from appointing an official) undoubtedly wants him to be competent for the position he is assigned to; and this he can be only after he has spent sufficiently long time in preparation and training, time he could have spent in training for another position that would have supported him. If the head of state had this right, offices would be filled as a rule by people who had not acquired the skill requisite for them and the mature judgment achieved by practice, and this would be contrary to the intention of the state, which also requires that everyone be able to rise from lower to higher offices (which would otherwise fall into the hands of sheer incompetence). Hence civil officials must be able to count on lifelong support.

Among *dignities*, not just those attached to an office but also that which makes its possessors members of a higher Estate even without any special services on their part, is that of the *nobility*, which is distinct from the civil Estate of the people and is transmitted to male descendants and by them to a wife born as a commoner, though if a woman born into the nobility marries a commoner she does not

pass this rank on to her husband but herself reverts to the mere civil rank (of the people). Now the question is whether the sovereign is entitled to establish a nobility, insofar as it is an Estate intermediate between himself and the rest of the citizens that *can be inherited*. What this question comes down to is not whether it would be prudent for the sovereign to do this, with a view to his own or the people's advantage, but only whether it would be in accord with the rights of the people for it to have an Estate of persons above it who, while themselves subjects, are still *born* rulers (or at least privileged) with respect to the people. The answer to this question comes from the same principle as the reply to the preceding one: "What a people (the entire mass of subjects) cannot decide with regard to itself and its fellows, the sovereign can also not decide with regard to it." Now a *hereditary* nobility is a rank that precedes merit and also provides no basis to hope for merit, and is thus a thought-entity without any reality. For if an ancestor had merit he could still not bequeath it to his descendants: They must acquire it for themselves, since nature does not arrange things in such a way that talent and will, which make meritorious service to the state possible, are also *hereditary*. Since we cannot admit that any man would throw away his freedom, it is impossible for the general will of the people to assent to such a groundless prerogative, and therefore for the sovereign to validate it. The anomaly of subjects who want to be more than citizens of the state, namely born officials (a born professor, perhaps) may have crept into the machinery of government from older times (feudalism, which was organized almost entirely for war). The only way the state can then gradually correct this mistake it has made, of conferring hereditary privileges contrary to right, is by letting them lapse and not filling vacancies in these positions. So it has a provisional right to let these titled positions of dignity continue until even in public opinion the division into sovereign, nobility, and commoners has been replaced by the only natural division into sovereign and people.

Certainly no man in a state can be without any dignity, since he at least has the dignity of a citizen. The exception is someone who has lost it by his own *crime*, because of which, though he is kept alive, he is made a mere tool of another's choice (either of the state or of another citizen). Whoever is another's tool (which he can become only by judgment and Right) is a *bondsman* (*servus in sensu stricto*) and is the *property* (*dominium*) of another, who is accordingly not merely his *master* (*herus*) but also his *owner* (*dominus*) and can therefore alienate him as a thing, use him as he pleases (only not for shameful purposes) and *dispose of his powers*, though not of his life and members. No one can bind himself to this kind of dependence, by which he ceases to be a person, by a contract, since it is only as a person that he can make a contract. Now it might seem that a man could put himself under obligation to another person, by a contract to let and hire (*locatio conductio*), to perform services (in return for wages, board, or protection) that are permissible in terms of their quality but *indeterminate* in terms of their quantity, and that he thereby becomes just a subject (*subiectus*), not a bondsman (*servus*). But this is only a deceptive appearance. For if the master is authorized to use the powers of his subject as he pleases, he can also exhaust them until his subject dies or is driven to despair (as with the Negroes on the Sugar Islands); his subject will in fact have given himself away, as property, to his master, which is impossible. Someone can therefore hire himself out only for work that is determined as to its kind and its amount, either as a day laborer or as a subject living on his master's property. In the latter case he can make a contract, for a time or indefinitely, to perform services by working on his master's land in exchange for the use of it instead of receiving wages as a day laborer, or to pay rent (a tax) specified by a lease in return for his own use of it, without thereby making himself a *serf* (*gelbae adscriptus*), by which he would forfeit his personality. Even if he has become a *personal* subject by his crime, his subjection cannot be *inherited*, because he has incurred it only by his own guilt. Nor can a bondsman's offspring be claimed as a bondsman because he has given rise to the expense of being educated; for parents have an absolute natural duty to educate their children and, in case the parents are in bondage, their masters take over this duty along with possession of their subjects.

E.
On the Right to Punish and to Grant Clemency

I.

The *right to punish* is the right a ruler has against a subject to inflict pain upon him because of his having committed a crime. The head of a state can therefore not be punished; one can only withdraw from his dominion. A transgression of public law that makes someone who commits it unfit to be a citizen is called a *crime* simply (*crimen*) but is also called a public crime (*crimen publicum*); so the first (private crime) is brought before a civil court, the latter before a criminal court. *Embezzlement*, that is, misappropriation of money or goods entrusted for commerce, and fraud in buying and selling, when committed in such a way that the other could detect it, are private crimes. On the other hand, counterfeiting money or bills of exchange, theft and robbery, and the like are public crimes, because they endanger the commonwealth and not just an individual person. They can be divided into crimes arising from a *mean* character (*indolis abiectae*) and crimes arising from a *violent* character (*indolis violentae*).

Punishment by a court (*poena forensis*)—this is distinct from *natural punishment* (*poena naturalis*), in which vice punishes itself and which the legislator does not take into account—can never be inflicted merely as a means to promote some other good for the criminal himself or for civil society. It must always be inflicted upon him only *because he has committed a crime*. For a man can never be treated merely as a means to the purposes of another or be put among the objects of rights to things: His innate personality protects him from this, even though he can be condemned to lose his civil personality. He must previously have been found *punishable* before any thought can be given to drawing from his punishment something of use for himself or his fellow citizens. The principle of punishment is a categorical imperative, and woe to him who crawls through the windings of eudaemonism in order to discover something that releases the criminal from punishment or even reduces its amount by the advantage it promises, in accordance with the Pharisaical saying, "It is better for *one* man to die than for an entire people to perish." For if justice goes, there is no longer any value in men's living on the earth. What, therefore, should one think of the proposal to preserve the life of a criminal sentenced to death if he agrees to let dangerous experiments be made on him and is lucky enough to survive them, so that in this way physicians learn something new of benefit to the commonwealth? A court would reject with contempt such a proposal from a medical college, for justice ceases to be justice if it can be bought for any price whatsoever.

But what kind and what amount of punishment is it that public justice makes its principle and measure? None other than the principle of equality (in the position of the needle on the scale of justice), to incline no more to one side than to the other. Accordingly, whatever undeserved evil you inflict upon another within the people, that you inflict upon yourself. If you insult him, you insult yourself; if you steal from him, you steal from yourself; if you strike him, you strike yourself; if you kill him, you kill yourself. But only the *law of retribution* (*ius talionis*)—it being understood, of course, that this is applied by a court (not by your private judgment)—can specify definitely the quality and the quantity of punishment; all other principles are fluctuating and unsuited for a sentence of pure and strict justice because extraneous considerations are mixed into them. Now it would indeed seem that differences in social rank would not allow the principle of retribution, of like for like; but even when this is not possible in terms of the letter, the principle can always remain valid in terms of its effect if account is taken of the sensibilities of the upper classes. A fine, for example, imposed for a verbal injury has no relation to the offense, for someone wealthy might indeed allow himself to indulge in a verbal injury on some occasion; yet the outrage he has done to someone's love of honor can still be quite similar to the hurt done to his pride if he is constrained by judgment and Right not only to apologize publicly to the one he has insulted but also to kiss his hand, for instance, even though he is of a lower class. Similarly, someone of high standing given to violence could be condemned not only to apologize for striking an innocent citizen socially inferior to himself but also to undergo a solitary confinement involving hardship; in addition to the discomfort he undergoes, the offender's vanity would be painfully affected, so that through his shame like would be fittingly repaid with like. But what does it mean to say, "If you steal from someone, you steal from yourself"? Whoever steals makes the property of everyone else insecure and therefore deprives himself (by the principle of retribution) of security in any possible property. He has nothing and can also acquire nothing; but he still wants to live, and this is now possible only if others provide for him. But since the state will not provide for him free of charge, he must let it have his powers for any kind of work it pleases (in convict or prison labor) and is reduced to the status of a slave for a certain time, or permanently if the state sees fit.

If, however, he has committed murder he must *die*. Here there is no substitute that will satisfy justice. There is no *similarity* between life, however wretched it may be, and death, hence no likeness between the crime and the retribution unless death is judicially carried out upon the wrongdoer, although it must still be freed from any mistreatment that could make the humanity in the person suffering it into something abominable. Even if a civil society were to be dissolved by the consent of all its members (e.g., if a people inhabiting an island decided to separate and disperse throughout the world), the last murderer remaining in prison would first have to be executed, so that each has done to him what his deeds deserve and blood guilt does not cling to the people for not having insisted upon this punishment; for otherwise the people can be regarded as collaborators in this public violation of justice.

This fitting of punishment to the crime, which can occur only by a judge imposing the death sentence in accordance with the strict law of retribution, is shown by the fact that only by this is a sentence of death pronounced on every criminal in proportion to his *inner wickedness* (even when the crime is not murder but another crime against the state that can be paid for only by death). Suppose that some (such as Balmerino and others) who took part in the recent Scottish rebellion believed that by their uprising they were only performing a duty they owed the House of Stuart, while others on the contrary were out for their private interests; and suppose that the judgment pronounced by the highest court had been that each is free to make the choice between death and convict labor. I say that in this case the man of honor would choose death, and the scoundrel convict labor. This comes along with the nature of the human mind; for the man of honor is acquainted with something that he values even more highly than life, namely *honor*, while the scoundrel considers it better to live in shame than not to live at all (*animam praeferre pudori;* Juvenal [Satires III, 8, 83]). Since the man of honor is undeniably less deserving of punishment than the other, both would be punished quite proportionately if all alike were sentenced to death; the man of honor would be punished mildly in terms of his sensibilities and the scoundrel severely in terms of his. On the other hand, if both were sentenced to convict labor the man of honor would be punished too severely and the other too mildly for his vile action. And so here too, when sentence is pronounced on a number of criminals united in a plot, the best equalizer before public justice is *death*. Moreover, one has never heard of anyone who was sentenced to death for murder complaining that he was dealt with too severely and therefore wronged; everyone would laugh in his face if he said this. If his complaint were justified it would have to be assumed that even though no wrong is done to the criminal in accordance with the law, the legislative authority of the state is still not authorized to inflict this kind of punishment and that, if it does so, it would be in contradiction with itself.

Accordingly, every murderer—anyone who commits murder, orders it, or is an accomplice in it—must suffer death; this is what justice, as the Idea of judicial authority, wills in accordance with universal laws that are grounded a priori. If, however, the number of accomplices (*correi*) to such a deed is so great that the state, in order to have no such criminals in it, could soon find itself without subjects; and if the state still does not want to dissolve, that is, to pass over into the state of nature, which is far worse because there is no external justice at all in it (and if it especially does not want to dull the people's feeling by the spectacle of a slaughterhouse), then the sovereign must also have it in his power, in this case of necessity (*casus necessitatis*), to assume the role of judge (to represent him) and pronounce a judgement that decrees for the criminals a sentence other than capital punishment, such as deportation, which still preserves the population. This cannot be done in accordance with public law, but it can be done by an executive decree, that is, by an act of the right of majesty which, as clemency, can always be exercised only in individual cases.

In opposition to this the Marchese Beccaria, moved by overly compassionate feelings of an affected humanity (*compassibilitas*), has put forward his assertion that any capital punishment is wrongful because it could not be contained in the original civil contract; for if it were, everyone in a people would have to have consented to lose his life in case he murdered someone else (in the people), whereas it is impossible for anyone to consent to this because no one can dispose of his own life. This is all sophistry and juristic trickery.

No one suffers punishment because he has willed *it* but because he has willed a *punishable action;* for it is no punishment if what is done to someone is what he wills, and it is impossible *to will* to be punished. Saying that I will to be punished if I murder someone is saying nothing more than that I subject myself together with everyone else to the laws, which will naturally also be penal laws if there are any criminals among the people. As a colegislator in dictating the *penal law*, I cannot possibly be the same person who, as a subject, is punished in accordance with the law; for as one who is punished, namely as a criminal, I cannot possibly have a voice in legislation (the legislator is holy). Consequently, when I draw up a penal law against myself as a criminal, it is pure reason in me (*homo noumenon*), legislating with regard to rights, which subjects me, as someone capable of crime and so as another person (*homo phaenomenon*), to the penal law, together with all others in a civil union. In other words, it is not the people (each individual in it) that dictates capital punishment but rather the court (public justice), and so another than the criminal; and the social contract contains no promise to let oneself be punished and so to dispose of oneself and one's life. For if the authorization to punish had to be based on the offender's *promise*, on his *willing* to let himself be punished, it would also have to be left to him to find himself punishable and the criminal would be his own judge. The chief point of error (πρῶτον ψεῦδος) in this sophistry consists in its confusing the criminal's own judgment (which must necessarily be ascribed to his *reason*) that he has to forfeit his life with a resolve on the part of his *will* take his own life, and so in representing as united in one and the same person the judgment upon a right and the realization of that right.

There are, however, two crimes deserving of death, with regard to which it still remains doubtful whether *legislation* is also authorized to impose the death penalty. The feeling of honor leads to both, in one case the *honor of one's sex*, in the other *military honor,* and indeed true honor, which is incumbent as duty on each of these two classes of people. The one crime is a mother's *murder of her child (infanticidium maternale);* the other is *murdering a fellow soldier (commilitonicidium)* in a *duel.* Legislation cannot remove the disgrace of an illegitimate birth any more than it can wipe away the stain of suspicion of cowardice from a subordinate officer who fails to respond to a humiliating affront with a force of his own rising above fear of death. So it seems that in these two cases people find themselves in the state of nature, and that these acts of *killing* (*homocidium*), which would then not even have to be called murder (*homocidium dolosum*), are certainly punishable but cannot be punished with death by the supreme power. A child that comes into the world apart from marriage is born outside the law (for the law is marriage) and therefore outside the protection of the law. It has, as it were, stolen into the commonwealth (like contraband merchandise), so that the commonwealth can ignore its existence (since it rightly should not have come to exist in this way), and can therefore also ignore its annihilation; and no decree can remove the mother's shame when it becomes known that she gave birth without being married. So too, when a junior officer is insulted he sees himself constrained by the public opinion of the other members of his Estate to obtain satisfaction for himself and, as in the state of nature, *punishment* of the offender not by law, taking him before a court, but by a *duel*, in which he exposes himself to death in order to prove his military courage, upon which the honor of his Estate essentially rests. Even if the duel should involve *killing* his opponent, the killing that occurs in this fight which takes place in public and with the consent of both parties, though reluctantly, cannot strictly be called *murder* (*homocidium dolosum*). What, now, is to be laid down as right in both cases (coming under criminal justice)? Here penal justice finds itself very much in a quandary. Either it must declare by law that the concept of honor (which is here no illusion) counts for nothing and so punish with death, or else it must remove from the crime the capital punishment appropriate to it, and so be either cruel or indulgent. The knot can be undone in the following way: The categorical imperative of penal justice remains (unlawful killing of another must be punished by death); but the legislation itself (and consequently also the civil constitution), as long as it remains barbarous and undeveloped, is responsible for the discrepancy between the incentives of honor in the people (subjectively) and the measures that are (objectively) suitable for its purpose. So the public justice arising from the state becomes an *injustice* from the perspective of the justice arising from the people.

II.

Of all the rights of a sovereign, the *right to grant clemency* to a criminal (*ius aggratiandi*), either by

lessening or entirely remitting punishment, is the slipperiest one for him to exercise; for it must be exercised in such a way as to show the splendor of his majesty although he is thereby doing injustice in the highest degree. With regard to crimes of *subjects* against one another it is absolutely not for him to exercise it; for here failure to punish (*impunitas criminis*) is the greatest wrong against his subjects. He can make use of it, therefore, only in case of a wrong done *to himself* (*crimen laesae maiestatis*). But he cannot make use of it even then if his failure to punish could endanger the people's security. This right is the only one that deserves to be called the right of majesty.

On the Relation with Regard to Rights of a Citizen to His Native Land and to Foreign Countries
§50.

A *country* (*territorium*) whose inhabitants are citizens of it simply by its constitution, without their having to perform any special act to establish the right (and so are citizens by birth), is called their *native land*. A country of which they are not citizens apart from this condition is called a *foreign country*. If a foreign country forms part of a larger realm it is called a *province* (in the sense in which the Romans used this word), which must respect the land of the state that rules it as the *mother country* (*regio domina*); for a province is not an integral part of the realm (*imperii*), a place of *residence* for fellow-citizens, but only a possession of it, a *secondary house* for them.

1) A *subject* (regarded also as a citizen) has the right to emigrate, for the state could not hold him back as its property. But he can take out of it with him only his movable belongings, not his fixed belongings, as he would be doing if he were authorized to sell the land he previously possessed and take with him the money he got for it.

2) The *lord of the land* has the right to encourage *immigration* and settling by foreigners (colonists), even though his native subjects might look askance at this, provided that their private ownership of land is not curtailed by it.

3) He also has the right to *banish* a subject to a province outside the country, where he will not

enjoy any of the rights of a citizen, that is, to *deport* him, if he has committed a crime that makes it harmful to the state for his fellow citizens to associate with him.

4) He also has the right to *exile* him altogether (*ius exilii*), to send him out into the wide world, that is, entirely outside his country (in Old German, this is called *Elend* [*misery*]). Since the lord of the land then withdraws all protection from him, this amounts to making him an outlaw within his boundaries.

§51.

The three authorities in a state, which arise from the concept of a *commonwealth* as such (*res publica latius dicta*), are only the three relations of united will of the people, which is derived a priori from reason. They are a pure Idea of a head of state, which has objective practical reality. But this head of state (the sovereign) is only a *thought-entity* (to represent the entire people) as long as there is no physical person to represent the supreme authority in the state and to make this Idea effective on the people's will. Now the relation of this physical person to the people's will can be thought of in three different ways: either that *one* in the state has command over all; or that *several*, equal among themselves, are united in command over all the others; or that *all* together have command over each and so over themselves as well. In other words, the *form of a state* is either *autocratic, aristocratic,* or *democratic.* (The expression *monarchical,* in place of *autocratic,* is not suitable for the concept intended here; for a *monarch* is one who has the *highest* authority, whereas an *autocrat,* who *rules by himself,* has *all* the authority. The autocrat is the sovereign, whereas the monarch merely represents the sovereign.) It is easy to see that the autocratic form of state is the *simplest,* namely the relation of one (the king) to the people, so that only one is legislator. The aristocratic form of state is already *composed* of two relations: the relation of the nobility (as legislator) to one another, to constitute the sovereign, and then the relation of this sovereign to the people. But the democratic form of state is the most composite of all, since it involves the following relations: First, it unites the will of all to form a people; then it unites the will of the citizens to form a commonwealth; then it sets this *sovereign,* which is itself the united will of the citi-

zens, over the commonwealth.[6] It is true that, with regard to the administration of Right within a state, the simplest form is also the best. With regard to Right itself, however, this form of state is the most dangerous for a people, in view of how conducive it is to despotism. It is indeed the most reasonable maxim to simplify the mechanism of unifying a nation by coercive laws, that is, when all the members of the nation are passive and obey *one* who is over them; but in that case none who are subjects are also *citizens of the state.* As for the consolation with which the people is supposed to be content—that monarchy (strictly speaking here, autocracy) is the best constitution *when the monarch is good* (i.e., when he not only intends what is good but also has insight into it)—this is one of those wise remarks that are tautologous. It says nothing more than that the best constitution is the one by which the administrator of the state is made into the best ruler, that is, that the best constitution is that which is best.

§52.

It is *futile* to inquire into the *historical warrant* of the mechanism of government, that is, one cannot reach back to the time at which civil society began (for savages draw up no record of their submission to law; besides, we can already gather from the nature of uncivilized men that they were originally subjected to it by force). But it is *punishable* to undertake this inquiry with a view to possibly changing by force the constitution that now exists. For this transformation would have to take place by the people acting as a mob, not by legislation; but insurrection in a constitution that already exists overthrows all civil rightful relations and therefore all Right; that is, it is not change in the civil constitution but dissolution of it. The transition to a better constitution is not then a metamorphosis but a palingenesis, which requires a new social contract on which the previous one (now annulled) has no effect. But it must still be possible, if the existing constitution cannot well be reconciled with the Idea of the original contract, for the sovereign to change it, so as to allow to continue in exis-

---

6. I shall not mention the adulterations of these forms that arise from invasion by powerful unauthorized people (*oligarchy* and *ochlocracy*), or the so-called mixed constitutions, since this would take us too far afield.

tence that form which is essentially required for a people to constitute a state. Now this change cannot consist in a state's reorganizing itself from one of the three forms into another, as, for example, aristocrats agreeing to submit to autocracy or deciding to merge into a democracy, or the reverse, as if it rested on the sovereign's free choice and discretion which kind of constitution it would subject the people to. For even if the sovereign decided to transform itself into a democracy, it could still do the people a wrong, since the people itself could abhor such a constitution and find one of the other forms more to its advantage.

The different forms of states are only the *letter* (*littera*) of the original legislation in the civil state, and they may therefore remain as long as they are taken, by old and long-standing custom (and so only subjectively), to belong necessarily to the machinery of the constitution. But the *spirit* of the original contract (*anima pacti originarii*) involves an obligation on the part of the constituting authority to make the *kind of government* suited to the Idea of the original contract. Accordingly, even if this cannot be done all at once, it is under obligation to change the kind of government gradually and continually so that it harmonizes *in its effect* with the only constitution that accords with right, that of a pure republic, in such a way that the old (empirical) statutory forms, which served merely to bring about the *submission* of the people, are replaced by the original (rational) form, the only form that makes *freedom* the principle and indeed the condition for any exercise of *coercion*, as is required by a rightful constitution of a state in the strict sense of the word. Only it will finally lead to what is literally a state. This is the only constitution of a state that lasts, the constitution in which *law* itself rules and depends on no particular person. It is the final end of all public Right, the only condition in which each can be assigned *conclusively* what is his; on the other hand, so long as those other forms of state are supposed to represent literally just so many different moral persons invested with supreme authority, no absolutely rightful condition of civil society can be acknowledged, but only *provisional* Right within it.

Any true republic is and can only be a *system representing* the people, in order to protect its rights in its name, by all citizens united and acting through their delegates (deputies). But as soon as a person who is head of state (whether it be a king, nobility, or the whole of the population, the democratic union)

also lets itself be represented, then the united people does not merely *represent* the sovereign: It *is* the sovereign itself. For in it (the people) is originally found the supreme authority from which all rights of individuals as mere subjects (and in any event as officials of the state) must be derived; and a republic, once established, no longer has to let the reins of government out of its hands and give them over again to those who previously held them and could again nullify all new institutions by their absolute choice.

A powerful ruler in our time therefore made a very serious error in judgment when, to extricate himself from the embarrassment of large state debts, he left it to the people to take this burden on itself and distribute it as it saw fit; for then the legislative authority naturally came into the people's hands, not only with regard to the taxation of subjects but also with regard to the government, namely to prevent it from incurring new debts by extravagance or war. The consequence was that the monarch's sovereignty wholly disappeared (it was not merely suspended) and passed to the people, to whose legislative will the belongings of every subject became subjected. Nor can it be said that in this case one must assume a tacit but still contractual promise of the National Assembly not to make itself the sovereign but only to administer this business of the sovereign and, having attended to it, return the reins of government into the monarch's hands; for such a contract is in itself null and void. The right of supreme legislation in a commonwealth is not an alienable right but the most personal of all rights. Whoever has it can control the people only through the collective will of the people; he cannot control the collective will itself, which is the ultimate basis of any public contract. A contract that would impose obligation on the people to give back its authority would not be incumbent upon the people as the legislative power, yet would still be binding upon it; and this is a contradiction, in accordance with the saying "No man can serve two masters."

SECTION II
THE RIGHT OF NATIONS

§53.

As natives of a country, those who constitute a nation can be looked upon analogously to descendants of the same *ancestors* (*congeniti*) even though they are not. Yet in an intellectual sense and from the perspective of rights, since they are born of the same mother (the republic) they constitute as it were one family (*gens, natio*), whose members (citizens of the state) are of equally high birth and do not mix with those who may live near them in a state of nature, whom they regard as inferior; the latter (savages), however, for their own part consider themselves superior because of the lawless freedom they have chosen, even though they do not constitute states but only tribes. The Right of *states* in relation to one another (which in German is called, not quite correctly, the *Right of Nations*, but should instead be called the Right of States, *ius publicum civitatum*) is what we have to consider under the title the Right of Nations. Here a state, as a moral person, is considered as living in relation to another state in the condition of natural freedom and therefore in a condition of constant war. The rights of states consist, therefore, partly of their right *to go to* war, partly of their right *in* war, and partly of their right to constrain each other to leave this condition of war and so form a constitution that will establish lasting peace, that is, its right *after* war. In this problem the only difference between the state of nature of individual men and of families (in relation to one another) and that of nations is that in the Right of Nations we have to take into consideration not only the relation of one state toward another as a whole, but also the relation of individual persons of one state toward the individuals of another, as well as toward another state as a whole. But this difference from the rights of individuals in a state of nature makes it necessary to consider only such features as can be readily inferred from the concept of a state of nature.

§54.

The elements of the Right of Nations are these: (1) States, considered in external relation to one another, are (like lawless savages) by nature in a nonrightful condition. (2) This nonrightful condition is a *condition* of war (of the right of the stronger), even if it is not a condition of actual war and actual attacks being constantly made (hostilities). Although no state is wronged by another in this condition (insofar as neither wants anything better), this condition is in itself still wrong in the highest degree, and states neighboring upon one another are under obligation to leave it. (3) A league of nations in accordance with the Idea of an original social contract is necessary, not in order to meddle in one another's internal dissensions but to protect against attacks from without. (4) This alliance must, however, involve no sovereign authority (as in a civil constitution), but only an *association* (federa-

tion); it must be an alliance that can be renounced at any time and so must be renewed from time to time. This is a right *in subsidium* of another and original right, to avoid getting involved in a state of actual war among the other members (*foedus Amphictyonum*).

§55.

As regards the original right that free states in a state of nature have to go to war with one another (in order, perhaps, to establish a condition more closely approaching a rightful condition), the first question that arises is: What right has a state *against its own subjects* to use them for war against other states, to expend their goods and even their lives in it, or to put them at risk, in such a way that whether they shall go to war does not depend on their own judgment but they may be sent into it by the supreme command of the sovereign?

It might seem that this right can be easily proved, namely from the right to do what one wants with what belongs to one (one's property). Anyone has an incontestable property in anything the substance of which he has himself *made*. What follows, then, is the deduction, as a mere jurist would draw it up.

There are various *natural products* in a country that must still be considered *artifacts* (*artefacta*) of the state as far as the *abundance* of natural products of a certain kind is concerned, since the country would not have yielded them in such abundance had there not been a state and an orderly, powerful government, but the inhabitants had been in a state of nature. Whether from lack of food or from the presence of predatory animals in the country where I live, hens (the most useful kind of fowl), sheep, swine, cattle, and so forth would either not exist at all or at best would be scarce unless there were a government in this country, which secures the inhabitants in what they acquire and possess. This holds true of the human population as well, which can only be small, as it is in the American wilderness, even if we attribute to these people the greatest industry (which they do not have). The inhabitants would be very scarce since they could not take their attendants and spread out on a land that is always in danger of being laid waste by men or by wild and predatory beasts. There would therefore not be adequate sustenance for such a great abundance of men as now live in a country. Now just as we say that since vegetables (e.g., potatoes) and domestic animals are, as regards their abundance, a *product* of man, which he can use, wear out or destroy (kill), it seems we can also say that since most of his subjects are his own product, the supreme authority in a state, the sovereign, has the right to lead them into war as he would take them on a hunt, and into battles as on a pleasure trip.

Although such an argument for this right (which may well be present obscurely in the monarch's mind) holds with regard to animals, which can be a man's *property*, it simply cannot be applied to men, especially as citizens of a state. For they must always be regarded as colegislating members of a state (not merely as means, but also as ends in themselves), and must therefore give their free assent, through their representatives, not only to waging war in general but also to each particular declaration of war. Only under this limiting condition can a state direct them to serve in a way full of danger to them.

We shall therefore have to derive this right from the *duty* of the sovereign to the people (not the reverse); and for this to be the case the people will have to be regarded as having given its vote to go to war. In this capacity it is, although passive (letting itself be disposed of), also active and represents the sovereign itself.

§56.

In the state of nature among states, the *right to go to war* (to engage in hostilities) is the way in which a state is permitted to prosecute its right against another state, namely by its own *force*, when it believes it has been wronged by the other state; for this cannot be done in the state of nature by a lawsuit (the only means by which disputes are settled in a rightful condition). In addition to active violations [of its rights] (first aggression, which is not the same as first hostility) it may be *threatened*. This includes another state's being the first to undertake *preparations*, upon which is based the right of *prevention (ius praeventionis)*, or even just the *menacing* increase in another state's *power* (by its acquisition of territory) (*potentia tremenda*). This is a wrong to the lesser power merely by the *condition* of the *superior power*, before any deed on its part, and in the state of nature an attack by the lesser power is indeed legitimate. Accordingly, this is also the basis of the right to a balance of power among all states that are contiguous and could act on one another.

As for *active violations* that give a *right to go to war*, these include *acts of retaliation (retorsio)*, a state's taking it upon itself to obtain satisfaction for an offense committed against its people by the people of another state, instead of seeking compensation (by peaceful methods) from the other state. In terms of formalities, this resembles starting a war without first renouncing peace (without a *declaration of war*); for if one wants to find a right in a condition of war, something analogous to a contract must be assumed, namely, *acceptance* of the declaration of the other party that both want to seek their right in this way.

§57.

The greatest difficulty in the Right of Nations has to do precisely with Right during a war; it is difficult even to form a concept of this or to think of law in this lawless state without contradicting oneself (*inter arma silent leges*).[7] Right during a war would, then, have to be the waging of war in accordance with principles that always leave open the possibility of leaving the state of nature among states (in external relation to one another) and entering a rightful condition.

No war of independent states against each other can be a *punitive war (bellum punitivum)*. For punishment occurs only in the relation of a superior (*imperantis*) to those subject to him (*subditum*), and states do not stand in that relation to each other. Nor, again, can any war be either a *war of extermination (bellum internecinum)* or of subjugation (*bellum subiugatorium*), which would be the moral annihilation of a state (the people of which would either become merged in one mass with that of the conqueror or reduced to servitude). The reason there cannot be a war of subjugation is not that this extreme measure a state might use to achieve a condition of peace would in itself contradict the right of a state; it is rather that the Idea of the Right of Nations involves only the concept of an antagonism in accordance with principles of outer freedom by which each can preserve what belongs to it, but not a way of acquiring, by which one state's increase of power could threaten others.

A state against which war is being waged is permitted to use any means of defense except those that would make its subjects unfit to be citizens; for it would then also make itself unfit to qualify, in accordance with the Right of Nations, as a person in the

---

7. "In time of war the laws are silent." Cicero, *Pro Milone*, 4, 10.

relation of states (as one who would enjoy the same rights as others). Means of defense that are not permitted include using its own subjects as spies; using them or even foreigners as assassins or poisoners (among whom so-called snipers, who lie in wait to ambush individuals, might well be classed); or using them merely for spreading false reports—in a word, using such underhanded means as would destroy the trust requisite to establishing a lasting peace in the future.

In war it is permissible to exact supplies and contributions from a defeated enemy, but not to plunder the people, that is, not to force individual persons to give up their belongings (for that would be robbery, since it was not the conquered people that waged the war; rather, the state under whose rule they lived waged the war *through the people*). Instead, receipts should be issued for everything requisitioned, so that in the peace that follows the burden imposed on the country or province can be divided proportionately.

§58.

The right of a state *after a war*, that is, at the time of the peace treaty and with a view to its consequences, consists in this: The victor lays down the conditions on which it will come to an agreement with the vanquished and hold *negotiations* for concluding peace. The victor does not do this from any right he pretends to have because of the wrong his opponent is supposed to have done him; instead, he lets this question drop and relies on his own force. The victor can therefore not propose compensation for the costs of the war, since he would then have to admit that his opponent had fought an unjust war. While he may well think of this argument he still cannot use it, since he would then be saying that he had been waging a punitive war and so, for his own part, committing an offense against the vanquished. Rights after a war also include a right to an exchange of prisoners (without ransom), without regard for their being equal in number.

A defeated state or its subjects do not lose their civil freedom through the conquest of their country, so that the state would be degraded to a colony and its subjects to bondage; for if they did the war would have been a *punitive war*, which is self-contradictory. A *colony* or province is a people that indeed has its own constitution, its own legislation, and its own land, on which those who belong to another state are only foreigners even though this other state has supreme *executive* authority over the colony or province. The state having that executive authority is called the *mother state*, and the daughter state, though ruled by it, still governs itself (by its own parliament, possibly with a viceroy presiding over it) (*civitas hybrida*). This was the relation Athens had with respect to various islands and that Great Britain now has with regard to Ireland.

Still less can *bondage* and its legitimacy be derived from a people's being overcome in war, since for this one would have to admit that a war could be punitive. Least of all can hereditary bondage be derived from it; hereditary bondage as such is absurd since guilt from someone's crime cannot be inherited.

The concept of a peace treaty already contains the provision that an *amnesty* goes along with it.

§59.

The right to peace is (1) the right to be at peace when there is a war in the vicinity, or the right to *neutrality*; (2) the right to be assured of the continuance of a peace that has been concluded, that is, the right to a *guarantee*; (3) the right to an *alliance* (confederation) of several states for their common *defense* against any external or internal attacks, but not a league for attacking others and adding to their own territory.

§60.

There are no limits to the rights of a state against an *unjust enemy* (no limits with respect to quantity or degree, though there are limits with respect to quality); that is to say, an injured state may not use *any* means *whatever* but may use those means that are allowable to any degree that it is able to, in order to maintain what belongs to it. But what is an *unjust enemy* in terms of the concepts of the Right of Nations, in which—as is the case in a state of nature generally—each state is judge in its own case? It is an enemy whose publicly expressed will (whether by word or deed) reveals a maxim by which, if it were made a universal rule, any condition of peace among nations would be impossible and, instead, a state of nature would be perpetuated. Violation of public contracts is an expression of this sort. Since this can be assumed to be a matter of concern to all nations whose freedom is threatened by it, they are called upon to unite against such misconduct in order to deprive the state of its power to do it. But they are not called upon *to divide its territory among themselves* and to make the state, as it were, disappear from the earth, since that would be an injustice against its people, which cannot lose its original right to unite itself into a commonwealth, though it can be made to adopt a new constitution that by its nature will be unfavorable to the inclination for war.

It is *redundant*, however, to speak of an unjust enemy in a state of nature; for a state of nature is itself a condition of injustice. A just enemy would be one that I would be doing wrong by resisting; but then he would also not be my enemy.

§61.

Since a state of nature among nations, like a state of nature among individual men, is a condition that one ought to leave in order to enter a lawful condition, before this happens any rights of nations, and anything external that is mine or yours that states can acquire or retain by war, are merely *provisional*. Only in a universal *association of states* (analogous to that by which a people becomes a state) can rights come to hold *conclusively* and a true *condition of peace* come about. But if such a state made up of nations were to extend too far over vast regions, governing it and so too protecting each of its members would finally have to become impossible, while several such corporations would again bring on a state of war. So *perpetual peace*, the ultimate goal of the whole Right of Nations, is indeed an unachievable Idea. Still, the political principles directed toward perpetual peace, of entering into such alliances of states, which serve for continual *approximation* to it, are not unachievable. Instead, since continual approximation to it is a task based on duty and therefore on the Right of men and of states, this can certainly be achieved.

Such an *association* of several *states* to preserve peace can be called a *permanent congress of states*, which each neighboring state is at liberty to join. Something of this kind took place (at least as regards the formalities of the Right of Nations for the sake of keeping the peace) in the first half of the present century, in the assembly of the States General at the Hague. The ministers of most of the courts of Europe and even of the smallest republics lodged with it their complaints about attacks being made on one of them by another. In this way they thought of the whole of Europe as a single confederated state that they ac-

cepted as arbiter, so to speak, in their public disputes. But later, instead of this, the Right of Nations survived only in books; it disappeared from cabinets or else, after force had already been used, was relegated in the form of a deduction to the obscurity of archives.

By a *congress* is here understood only a voluntary coalition of different states that can be *dissolved* at any time, not a federation (like that of the American states) which is based on a constitution and can therefore not be dissolved. Only by such a congress can the Idea of a public Right of Nations be realized, one to be established for deciding their disputes in a civil way, as if by a lawsuit, rather than in a barbaric way (the way of savages), namely by war.

SECTION III
COSMOPOLITAN RIGHT

§62.

This rational Idea of a *peaceful*, even if not friendly, thoroughgoing community of all nations on the earth that can come into relations affecting one another is not a philanthropic (ethical) principle but a principle *having to do with rights*. Nature has enclosed them all together within determinate limits (by the spherical shape of the place they live in, a *globus terraqueus*). And since possession of the land, on which an inhabitant of the earth can live, can be thought only as possession of a part of a determinate whole, and so as possession of that to which each of them originally has a right, it follows that all nations stand *originally* in a community of land, though not of *rightful* community of possession (*communio*) and so of use of it, or of property in it; instead they stand in a community of possible physical *interaction* (*commercium*), that is, in a thoroughgoing relation of each to all the others of *offering to engage in commerce* with any other, and each has a right to make this attempt without the other being authorized to behave toward it as an enemy because it has made this attempt. This right, since it has to do with the possible union of all nations with a view to certain universal laws for their possible commerce, can be called *cosmopolitan Right* (*ius cosmopoliticum*).

Although the seas might seem to remove nations from any community with one another, they are the arrangements of nature most favoring their commerce by means of navigation; and the more *coastlines* these nations have in the vicinity of one another (as in the Mediterranean), the more lively their commerce can be. However, visiting these coasts, and still more settling there to connect them with the mother country, provide the occasion for evils and acts of violence in one place on our globe to be felt all over it. Yet this possible abuse cannot annul the right of citizens of the world *to try to* establish community with all and, to this end, to *visit* all regions of the earth. This is not, however, a right to *make a settlement* on the land of another nation (*ius incolatus*); for this, a specific contract is required.

The question arises, however: In newly discovered lands, may a nation undertake to *settle* (*accolatus*) and take possession in the neighborhood of a people that has already settled in the region, even without its consent?

If the settlement is made so far from where that people resides that there is no encroachment on anyone's use of his land, the right to settle is not open to doubt. But if these peoples are shepherds or hunters (like the Hottentots, the Tungusi, or most of the American Indian nations) who depend for their sustenance on great open regions, this settlement may not take place by force but only by contract, and indeed by a contract that does not take advantage of the ignorance of those inhabitants with respect to ceding their lands. This is true despite the fact that sufficient specious reasons to justify the use of force are available: that it is to the world's advantage, partly because these crude peoples will become civilized (this is like the pretext by which even Büsching tries to excuse the bloody introduction of Christianity into Germany), and partly because one's own country will be cleaned of corrupt men, and they or their descendants will, it is hoped, become better in another part of the world (such as New Holland). But all these supposedly good intentions cannot wash away the stain of injustice in the means used for them. Someone may reply that such scruples about using force in the beginning, in order to establish a lawful condition, might well mean that the whole earth would still be in a lawless condition; but this consideration can no more annul that condition of Right than can the pretext of revolutionaries within a state, that when constitutions are bad it is up to the people to reshape them by force and to be unjust once and for all so that afterward they can establish justice all the more securely and make it flourish.

Conclusion

If someone cannot prove that a thing is, he can try to prove that it is not. If (as often happens) he cannot succeed in either, he can still ask whether he has any *interest* in assuming one or the other (as a hypothesis), either from a theoretical or from a practical point of view. An assumption is adopted from a theoretical point of view in order merely to explain a certain phenomenon (such as, for astronomers, the retrograde motion and stationary state of the planets). An assumption is adopted from a practical point of view in order to achieve a certain end, which may be either a *pragmatic* (merely technical end) or a *moral* end, that is, an end such that the maxim of adopting it is itself a duty. Now it is evident that what would be made our duty in this case is not the *assumption* (*suppositio*) that this end can be realized, which would be a judgment about it that is merely theoretical and, moreover, problematic; for there can be no obligation to do this (to believe something). What is incumbent on us as a duty is rather to act in conformity with the Idea of that end, even if there is not the slightest theoretical likelihood that it can be realized, as long as its impossibility cannot be demonstrated either.

Now, morally practical reason pronounces in us its irresistible *veto: There is to be no war*, neither war between you and me in the state of nature nor war between us as states, which, although they are internally in a lawful condition, are still externally (in relation to one another) in a lawless condition; for war is not the way in which everyone should seek his rights. So the question is no longer whether perpetual peace is something real or a fiction, and whether we are not deceiving ourselves in our theoretical judgment when we assume that it is real. Instead, we must act as if it is something real, though perhaps it is not; we must work toward establishing perpetual peace and the kind of constitution that seems to us most conducive to it (perhaps a republicanism of all states, together and separately) in order to bring about perpetual peace and put an end to the heinous waging of war, to which as their chief aim all states without exception have hitherto directed their internal arrangements. And even if the complete realization of this objective always remains a pious wish, still we are certainly not deceiving ourselves in adopting the maxim of working incessantly toward it. For this is our duty, and to admit that the moral law within us is itself deceptive would call forth in us the wish, which arouses our abhorrence, rather to be rid of all reason and to regard ourselves as thrown by one's principles into the same mechanism of nature as all the other species of animals.

It can be said that establishing universal and lasting peace constitutes not merely a part of the doctrine of Right but rather the entire final end of the doctrine of Right within the limits of reason alone; for the condition of peace is the only condition in which what is mine and what is yours are secured under *laws* for a multitude of men living in proximity to one another, and therefore under a constitution. But the rule for this constitution, as a norm for others, cannot

be derived from the experience of those who have hitherto found it most to their advantage; it must, rather, be derived a priori by reason from the ideal of a rightful association of men under public laws as such. For all examples (which only illustrate but cannot prove anything) are treacherous, so that they certainly require a metaphysics. Even those who ridicule metaphysics admit its necessity, though carelessly, when they say, for example, as they often do, "the best constitution is that in which power belongs not to men but to the laws." For what can be more metaphysically sublimated than this very Idea, which even according to their own assertion has the most confirmed objective reality, as can also be easily shown in actually occurring cases? The attempt to realize this Idea should not be made by way of revolution, by a leap, that is, by violent overthrow of an already existing defective constitution (for there would then be an intervening moment in which any rightful condition would be annihilated). But if it is attempted and carried out by gradual reform in accordance with firm principles, it can lead to continual approximation to the highest political good, perpetual peace.

APPENDIX
Explanatory Remarks on
The Metaphysical First Principles of the Doctrine of Right

I take the occasion for these remarks chiefly from the review of this book in the *Göttingen Journal* (No. 28, 18 Feb. 1797). In this review the book was examined with insight and rigor, but also with appreciation and "the hope that those first principles will be a lasting gain for the science." I shall use this review as a guide for my criticism as well as for some elaboration of this system.

My astute critic takes exception to a definition at the very beginning of the *Introduction* to the *Doctrine of Right*. What is meant by the capacity for desire? It is, the text says, the capacity to be by means of one's representations the cause of the objects of these representations. To this exposition he objects "that it comes to nothing as soon as one abstracts from the

external conditions of the result of desire. But the capacity for desire is something even for an idealist, even though the external world is nothing for him." *I reply:* But are there not also intense but still consciously futile longings (e.g., Would to God that man were still alive!), which are *devoid of any deed* but not *devoid of any result*, since they still work powerfully within the subject himself (make him ill), though not on external things? A desire, as a *striving (nisus)* to be a *cause* by means of one's representations, is still always causality, at least within the subject, even when he sees the inadequacy of his representations for the effect he envisages. The misunderstanding here amounts to this: that since consciousness of one's capacity *in general* is (in the case mentioned) also consciousness of one's *incapacity* with respect to the external world, the definition is not applicable to an idealist. Since, however, all that is in question here is the relation of a cause (a representation) to an effect (a feeling) in general, the causality of a representation (whether the causality is external or internal) with regard to its object must unavoidably be thought in the concept of the capacity for desire.

1.
Logical Preparation for a Recently Proposed Concept of a Right

If philosophers versed in Right want to rise or venture all the way to metaphysical first principles of the doctrine of Right (without which all their juridical science would be merely statutory), they cannot be indifferent to assurance of the completeness of their *division* of concepts of rights, since otherwise that science would not be a *rational system* but merely an aggregate hastily collected. For the sake of the form of the system, the *Topic* of principles must be complete, that is, the *place* for a concept (*locus communis*) must be indicated, the place that is left open for this concept by the synthetic form of the division. Afterward one may also show that one or another concept that might be put in this place would be self-contradictory and falls from this place.

Up to now jurists have admitted two common places: that of a right to *things* and that of a right against *persons*. By the mere form of joining these two concepts together into one, two more places are opened up for concepts, as members of an a priori division: that of a right to a thing akin to a right against a person and that of a right to a person akin to a thing. It is therefore natural to ask whether we have to add some such new concept and whether we must come across it in the complete table of division, even if it is only problematic. There can be no doubt that this is the case. For a merely logical division (which abstracts from the content of knowledge, from the object) is always a *dichotomy*—for example, any right is either a right to a thing or not a right to a thing. But the division in question here, namely the metaphysical division, might also be a fourfold division; for besides the two simple members of the division, two further relations might have to be added, namely those of the conditions limiting a right, under which one right enters into combination with the other. This possibility requires further investigation. The concept of a *right to a thing akin to a right against a person* drops out

without further ado, since no right of a *thing* against a *person* is conceivable. Now the question is whether the reverse of this relation is just as inconceivable or whether this concept, namely that of a *right to a person akin to a right to a thing*, is a concept that not only contains no self-contradiction but also belongs necessarily (as given a priori in reason) to the concept of what is externally mine or yours, of not *treating* persons in a similar way to *things* in all respects, but still of *possessing* them as things and dealing with them as things in many relations.

2.
Justification of the Concept of a Right to a Person Akin to a Right to a Thing

Put briefly and well, the definition of a right to a person akin to a right to a thing is this: "It is the right of a human being to have a *person* other than himself as *his own.*"[1] I take care to say "a *person*"; for while it is true that someone can have as his own another *human being* who by his crime has forfeited his personality (become a bondsman), this right to a thing is not what is in question here.

We must now examine whether this concept, this "new phenomenon in the juristic sky," is a *stella mirabilis* (a phenomenon never seen before, growing into a star of the first magnitude but gradually disappearing again, perhaps to return at some time) or merely a *shooting star.*

3.
Examples

To have something external as one's own means to possess it rightfully; but possessing something is the condition of its being possible to use it. If this condi-

---

1. I do not say here "to have a person as mine" (using the adjective), but "to have a person as *what is mine*, το '*meum*," (using the substantive). For I can say "this is *my father*," and that signifies only my physical relation (of connection) to him in a general way, e.g., I *have* a father; but I cannot say "I have him as *what is mine.*" However, if I say "my wife" this signifies a special, namely a rightful, relation of the possessor to an object as a *thing* (even though the object is also a person). Possession (*physical* possession), however, is the condition of being able to *manage* (*manipulatio*) something as a thing, even if this must, in another respect, be treated at the same time as a person.

tion is thought as merely physical, possession is called *holding*. That I am legitimately holding something is not of itself sufficient for saying that the object is mine or for making it mine. But if I am authorized, for whatever reason, to insist upon holding an object that has escaped from my control or been torn from it, this concept of a right is a *sign* (as an effect is a sign of its cause) that I consider myself authorized to treat this object and to use it as *what is mine*, and consider myself as also in intelligible possession of it.

What is one's own here does not, indeed, mean what is one's own in the sense of property in the person of another (for a human being cannot have property in himself, much less in another person), but means what is one's own in the sense of usufruct (*ius utendi fruendi*), to make direct use of a person *as of* a thing, as a means to my end, but still without infringing upon his personality.

But this end, as the condition under which such use is legitimate, must be morally necessary. A man cannot desire a woman in order to *enjoy* her as a thing, that is, in order to take immediate satisfaction in merely animal intercourse with her, nor can a woman give herself to him for this without both renouncing their personalities (in carnal or bestial cohabitation), that is, this can be done only under the condition of *marriage*. Since marriage is a reciprocal giving of one's very person into the possession of the other, it must *first* be concluded, so that neither is dehumanized through the bodily use that one makes of the other.

Apart from this condition carnal enjoyment is *cannibalistic* in principle (even if not always in its effect). Whether something is *consumed* by mouth and teeth, or whether the woman is consumed by pregnancy and the perhaps fatal delivery resulting from it, or the man by exhaustion of his sexual capacity from the woman's frequent demands upon it, the difference is merely in the manner of enjoyment. In this sort of use by each of the sexual organs of the other, each is actually a *consumable* thing (*res fungibilis*) with respect to the other, so that if one were to make oneself such a thing by *contract*, the contract would be contrary to law (*pactum turpe*).

Similarly, a man and a woman cannot beget a child as their joint *work* (*res artificialis*) and without both of them incurring an obligation toward the child and toward each other to maintain it. This is, again, acquisition of a human being *as of* a thing, but only formally so (as befits a right to a person that is only akin

to a right to a thing). Parents[2] have a right against every possessor (*ius in re*) of their child who has been removed from their control. Since they also have a right to constrain it to carry out and comply with any of their directions that are not contrary to a possible lawful freedom (*ius ad rem*), they also have a right against a person against the child.

Finally, when their duty to provide for their children comes to an end as they reach maturity, parents still have a right to use them as members of the household subject to their direction, for maintaining the household, until they leave. This is a duty of parents toward them which follows from the natural limitation of the parents' right. Up until this time children are indeed members of the household and belong to the *family;* but from now on they belong to the *service* of the family (*famulatus*), so that the head of the house cannot add them to what is his (as his domestics) except by contract. In the same way, the head of a house can also make the service of those *outside the family* his own in terms of a right to them akin to a right to a thing and acquire them as domestics (*famulatus domesticus*) by a contract. Such a contract is not just a contract to *let and hire* (*locatio conductio operae*), but a giving up of their persons into the possession of the head of the house, a lease (*locatio conductio personae*). What distinguishes such a contract from letting and hiring is that the servant agrees *to do whatever is permissible* for the welfare of the household, instead of being commissioned for a specifically determined job, whereas someone who is hired for a specific job (an artisan or day laborer) does not give himself up as part of the other's belongings and so is not a member of the household. Since he is not in the rightful possession of another who puts him under obligation to perform certain services, even if he lives in the other's house (*inquilinus*) the head of the house cannot *take possession* of him as a thing (*via facti*); he must instead insist upon the laborer's doing what he promised in terms of a right against a person, as something he can command by rightful proceedings (*via iuris*). So much for the clarification and defense of a strange type of right which has recently been added to the doctrine of natural law, although it has always been tacitly in use.

---

2. In written German *Aeltern* means *Seniores* and *Eltern* means *Parentes*. Although the two words cannot be distinguished in speech, they are very different in meaning.

4.
On Confusing a Right to a Thing
With a Right Against a Person

I have also been censured for heterodoxy in natural private Right for the proposition that *sale breaks a lease*. (*The Doctrine of Right*, §31. [last paragraph]).

It does seem at first glance to conflict with all rights arising from a contract that someone could give notice to someone leasing his house before the period of residence agreed upon is up and, so it seems, break his promise to the lessee, provided he grants him the time for vacating it that is customary by the civil laws where they live. But if it can be proved that the lessee knew or must have known, when he contracted to lease it, that the promise made to him by the *lessor*, the owner, naturally (without its needing to be stated expressly in the contract) and therefore tacitly included the condition, *as long as the owner does not sell the house during this time* (or does not have to turn it over to his creditors if he should become bankrupt), then the lessor has not broken his promise, which was already a conditional one in terms of reason, and the lessee's right was not encroached upon if he was given notice before the lease expired.

For the right a lessee has by a contract to lease is a right *against a person*, to something a certain person has to perform for another (*ius ad rem*); it is not a right against *every* possessor of a thing (*ius in re*), not a right to a *thing*.

A lessee could, indeed, secure himself in his *contract to lease* and procure a right to a thing as regards the house; he could, namely, have this right only to the lessor's house *registered* (entered in the land registry), as attached to the land. Then he could not be turned out of his lease, before the time settled upon had expired, by the owner's giving notice or even by his death (his natural death or also his civil death, bankruptcy). If he does not do this, perhaps because he wanted to be free to conclude a lease on better terms elsewhere or because the owner did not want to encumber his house with such an *onus*, it may be concluded that, as regards the time for giving notice, each of the parties was aware that he had made a contract subject to the tacit condition that it could be dissolved if this became convenient (except for the period of grace for vacating, as determined by civil law). Certain rightful consequences of a *bare* contract to lease give further confirmation of one's authorization to break a lease by sale; for if a lessor dies, no

obligation to continue the lease is ascribed to his heir, since this is an obligation only on the part of a certain person and ceases with his death (though the legal time for giving notice must still be taken into account in this case). Neither can the right of a lessee, as such, pass to his heir without a separate contract; nor, as long as both parties are alive, is a lessee authorized to sublet to anyone without an explicit agreement.

5.
Further Discussion of the Concept
of the Right to Punish

The mere Idea of a civil constitution among *men* carries with it the concept of punitive justice belonging to the supreme authority. The only question is whether it is a matter of indifference to the legislator what kinds of punishment are adopted, as long as they are effective measures for eradicating crime (which violates the security a state gives each in his possession of what is his), or whether the legislator must also take into account respect for the humanity in the person of the wrongdoer (i.e., respect for the species) simply on grounds of Right. I said that the *ius talionis* is by its form always the principle for the right to punish since it alone is the principle determining this Idea a priori (not derived from experience of which measures would be most effective for eradicating crime).[3] But what is to be done in the case of crimes that cannot be punished by a return for them because this would be either impossible or itself a punishable crime against *humanity* as such, for example, rape as well as pederasty or bestiality? The punishment for rape and pederasty is castration (like that of a white or black eunuch in a Seraglio), that for

---

3. In every punishment there is something that (rightly) offends the accused's feeling of honor, since it involves coercion that is unilateral only, so that his dignity as a citizen is suspended, at least in this particular case; for he is subjected to an external duty to which he, for his own part, may offer no resistance. A man of nobility or wealth who has to pay a fine feels the loss of his money less than the humiliation of having to submit to the will of an inferior. *Punitive justice* (*iustitia punitiva*) must be distinguished from *punitive prudence*, since the argument for the former is *moral*, in terms of being *punishable* (*quia peccatum est*) while that for the latter is *merely pragmatic* (*ne peccetur*) and based on experience of what is most effective in eradicating crime; and punitive justice has an entirely different *place* in the Topic of concepts of Right, *locus iusti*; its place is not that of the *conducibilis*, of what is *useful* for a certain purpose, nor that of the mere *honesti*, which must be sought in ethics.

bestiality, permanent expulsion from civil society, since the criminal has made himself unworthy of human society. *Per quod quis peccat, per idem punitur et idem.*[4] The crimes mentioned are called unnatural because they are perpetrated against humanity itself. To inflict *whatever* punishments *one chooses* for these crimes would be literally contrary to the concept of *punitive justice.* For the only time a criminal cannot complain that a wrong is done to him is when he brings his evil deed back upon himself, and what is done to him in accordance with penal law is what he has perpetrated on others, if not in terms of its letter at least in terms of its spirit.

6.
On a Right from Prolonged Possession

"A right based on *prolonged possession (usucapio)* should, according to §33, be established by natural Right. For unless one admits that an *ideal acquisition,* as it is here called, is established by possession in good faith, no acquisition at all would be conclusively secured. (Yet Kant himself admits only provisional acquisition in the state of nature, and because of this insists on the juristic necessity of a civil constitution. I assert that I am the *possessor* of something *in good faith,* however, only against someone who cannot prove that he was *possessor* of the same thing *in good faith* before me and has not ceased by his will to be its possessor.)"

This is not the question here. The question is whether I can also *assert* that I am the owner even if someone should come forward claiming to be the *earlier* true owner of the thing, but where it was *absolutely* impossible to learn of his existence as its possessor and of his being in possession as its owner. This occurs if the claimant has not (whether by his own fault or not) given any publicly valid sign of his uninterrupted possession, for example, by recording it in the registry or by voting as undisputed owner in civil assemblies.

For the question here is, who ought to prove his legitimate acquisition? This obligation (*onus probandi*) cannot be imposed on the possessor since he has been in possession of it as far back as his confirmed history reaches. In accordance with principles of Right, the one who claims to be the earlier owner of the thing is cut completely out of the series of successive possessors by the interval during which he

has given no civilly valid sign of his ownership. This failure to perform any public possessory act makes him a claimant without a title. (Against his claim it can be said here, as in theology, *conservatio est continua creatio.*)[5] Even if a claimant who had not previously appeared should later come forward supplied with documents he found, there would be room for doubt, in his case again, whether a still earlier claimant could appear at some future time and base his claim on earlier possession. Finally acquiring something by *prolonged possession* of it (*acquirere per usucaptionem*) does not depend at all on the *length of time* one has possessed it. For it is absurd to suppose that a wrong becomes a right because it has continued for a long time. Far from a right in a thing being based on use of it, *use* of it (however long) presupposes a right in it. Therefore *prolonged possession (usucapio),* regarded as acquisition of a thing by long use of it, is a self-contradictory concept. Superannuation of claims as a means of conserving possession (*conservatio possessionis per praescriptionem*) is no less self-contradictory, although it is a distinct concept as far as the argument for appropriation is concerned. That is to say, a negative basis, that is, the entire *non-use* of one's right, not even that which is necessary to show oneself as possessor, is taken to be an *abandonment* of this right (*derelictio*), [which supposed abandonment would be] a rightful act, that is, the use of one's right against another, so as to acquire the object of the earlier possessor by excluding it (*per praescriptionem*) from his claim; and this involves a contradiction.

I therefore acquire without giving proof and without any act establishing my right. I have no need for proof; instead I acquire by principle (*lege*). What follows? *Public* immunity from claims, that is, *security in my possession* by law, since I do not need to produce proof, and take my stand on my uninterrupted possession. But that any *acquisition* in a state of nature is only provisional has no bearing on the question of the security of *possession* of what is acquired, which must precede acquisition.

7.
On Inheritance

As for the right of inheritance, this time the acuteness of the reviewer has failed to find him the nerve

---

4. "One who commits a sin is punished through it and in the same way."

5. "Conservation is continuous creation."

of the proof of my assertion. I did not say (§34) that every man necessarily accepts any *thing offered* him which he can only gain and not lose by accepting (for there are indeed no such things). I said, rather, that everyone always in fact accepts, unavoidably and tacitly but still validly, the *right to accept the offer* at the same moment, namely when the nature of the matter involves the absolute impossibility of the offer being retracted, the moment of the testator's death; for then the promisor cannot withdraw it and the promisee, without needing to do any act to establish the right, is at the same moment the acceptor, not of the legacy promised but of the right to accept or refuse it. When the will is opened he sees that he had already at that moment, before accepting the legacy, become richer than he was before, since he had acquired the exclusive *authorization to accept* and this is already an enriching circumstance. Although a civil condition is presupposed in order for someone who no longer exists to make *something belong to another*, this transfer of possession by one who is dead does not alter the possibility of acquiring in accordance with universal principles of natural Right, even though a civil constitution is the necessary basis for applying these principles to the case at hand. That is to say, something left unconditionally to my free choice to accept or refuse is called a *res iacens*. If the owner of something offers it to me gratuitously (promises that it will be mine), for example, when he offers me a piece of furniture of the house I am about to move from, I have the exclusive right to accept his offer (*ius in re iacente*) so long as he does not withdraw it (and if he dies in the meantime this is impossible), that is, I alone can accept it or refuse it as I please; and I do not get this exclusive right to make the choice through any special rightful act of declaring that I will to have this right. I acquire it without any such act (*lege*). So I can indeed declare that I will *not to have the thing* (because accepting it might involve me in unpleasantness with others), but I cannot will to have the exclusive choice of *whether it is to belong to me or not*; for I have this right (to accept or refuse) immediately from the offer, without my declaring my acceptance of it, since if I could refuse even to have this choice I would be choosing not to choose, which is a contradiction. Now this right to choose passes to me at the moment of the testator's death, and by his testament (*institutio haeredis*) I acquire, not yet his belongings and goods, but nevertheless *merely rightful* (intelligible) possession of his belongings or a part

of them, which I can now refuse to accept to the advantage of others. Consequently this possession is not interrupted for a moment; succession passes instead in a continuous series from the dying man to his appointed heirs by their acceptance. The proposition *testamenta sunt iuris naturae* is thus established beyond any doubt.

8.
On the Right of a State with Regard to Perpetual Foundations for Its Subjects

A *foundation* (*sanctio testamentaria beneficii perpetui*) is an institution that has been voluntarily established, and confirmed by a state, for the benefit of certain members of it who succeed one another until they have all died out. It is called *perpetual* if the statute for maintaining it is bound up with the constitution of the state itself (for a state must be regarded as perpetual). Those who are to benefit from a foundation are either the *people* generally, or a part of them united by certain special principles, or a certain *Estate*, or a *family* and its descendants continuing in perpetuity. An example of the first kind is a *hospital*; of the second, a *church*; of the third, an *order* (spiritual or secular); and of the fourth, an estate that is *entailed*.

It is said that such corporations and their *right* of succession cannot be annulled, since it became by a *bequest* the property of the heirs appointed, so that annulling such a constitution (*corpus mysticum*) would amount to depriving someone of his belongings.

A.

Those institutions for the benefit of the poor, invalids, and the sick that have been set up at the expense of the state (foundations and hospitals) can certainly not be done away with. But if the intention of the testator's will rather than its letter is to have priority, circumstances can arise in time that make it advisable to nullify such a foundation at least in terms of its form. So it has been found that the poor and the sick (except for patients in mental hospitals) are cared for better and more economically when they are helped with certain sums of money (proportioned to the needs of the time), with which they can board where they want, with relatives or acquaintances, than when—as in the hospital at Greenwich—they are provided with splendid institutions, serviced by expensive personnel, which severely limit their freedom. It cannot be said then that the state is depriving the people, which is entitled to the benefits of this foundation, of what is theirs; the state is instead promoting this by choosing wiser means for preserving it.

B.

The clergy that does not propagate itself carnally (the Catholic clergy) possesses, with the favor of the state, estates and the subjects attached to them. These belong to a spiritual state (called a church), to which the laity, for the salvation of their souls, have given themselves by their bequests as its property. And so the clergy, as a special Estate, has possessions that can be bequeathed by law from one generation to the next and that are adequately documented by papal bulls. But may one assume that this relation to the laity can be directly taken from the clergy by the absolute power of the secular state? Would this not amount to depriving someone by force of what is his, as the unbelievers of the French republic are attempting to do?

The question here is whether the church can belong to the state or the state belong to the church; for two supreme authorities cannot without contradiction be subordinate one to the other. It is evident that only the *first constitution (politico-hierarchica)* could subsist by itself, since every civil constitution is of *this* world because it is an earthly authority (of men) that, along with its results, can be confirmed in experience. Even if we concede to believers, whose *kingdom* is in heaven and the *other world*, a constitution relating to that world (*hierarchico-politica*), they must submit to the sufferings of this era under the higher authority of men of this world. Hence only the first constitution is to be found.

Religion (in appearance), as belief in the dogmas of a church and in the power of priests, who are the aristocrats of such a constitution though it can also be monarchical (papal), can neither be imposed upon a people nor taken away from them by any civil authority; nor can a citizen be excluded from the service of the state and the advantages this brings him because his religion is different from that of the court (as Great Britain has done with the Irish nation).

In order to partake of the grace a church promises to show believers even after their death, certain devout and believing souls establish foundations in perpetuity, by which certain estates of theirs are to become the property of a church after their death; and the state may pledge itself to fealty to a church

regarding this or that foundation, or indeed all of them, so that these people may have the prayers, indulgences, and penances by which the servants of the church appointed for this (clergy) promise that they will fare well in the other world. But such a foundation, supposedly instituted in perpetuity, is not at all established in perpetuity; the state can cast off this burden a church has laid upon it when it wants to. For a church itself is an institution built merely upon belief, so that when the illusion arising from this opinion disappears through popular enlightenment, the fearful authority of the clergy based on it also falls away and the state, with full right, takes control of the property the church has arrogated to itself, namely the land bestowed on it through bequests. However, the feudal tenants of the institution that hitherto existed have the right to demand compensation as long as they live.

Even perpetual foundations for the poor, and educational institutions, cannot be founded in perpetuity and be a perpetual encumbrance on the land because they have a certain character specified by the founder in accordance with his ideas; instead the state must be free to adapt them to the needs of the time. No one need be surprised that it becomes more and more difficult for this idea to be carried out in all its details (e.g., that poor students must supplement by singing for alms an inadequate educational fund beneficently established); for if the one who sets up the foundation is somewhat ambitious as well as good-natured, he does not want someone else to alter it in accordance with his concepts; he wants to be immortalized in it. That, however, does not change the nature of the matter itself and the right, indeed the duty, of a state to alter any foundation if it is opposed to the preservation of the state and its progress to the better. Such a foundation, therefore, can never be regarded as established in perpetuity.

C.

The nobility of a country that is not under an aristocratic but a monarchical constitution is an institution that may be permitted for a certain period of time and may even be necessary by circumstances. But it cannot be asserted that this Estate can be established in perpetuity, and that the head of a state should not be authorized to annul this preeminence of Estate entirely, or that if he does this he has deprived his (noble) subjects of what was *theirs*, of what belonged to them by inheritance. A nobility is a temporary fraternity authorized by the state, which must go along with the circumstances of the time and not infringe upon the universal Right of men, which has been suspended for so long. For the rank of nobleman in a state is not only dependent upon the constitution itself; it is only an accident of the constitution, which can exist only by inherence in a state (a nobleman as such is conceivable only in a state, not in the state of nature). Accordingly, when a state alters its constitution, someone who thereby loses his title and precedence cannot say that he is being deprived of what is his, since he could call it his only under the condition that this form of state continued; but a state has the right to alter its form (e.g., to reform itself into a republic). Orders and the privilege of bearing certain signs of them, therefore, give no *perpetual* right of possession.

D.

Finally, as regards the *foundation of entailed estates*, in which someone possessed of goods arranges his inheritance so that the next of kin in the series of successive heirs should always be lord of the estate (by analogy with a state having a hereditary monarchy, where the *lord of the land* is determined in this way): not only can such a foundation be annulled at any time with the consent of all male relatives and need not last in perpetuity—as if the right of inheritance were attached to the land—and it cannot be said that letting an entailment terminate violates the foundation and the will of the original lord who established it, its founder; but a state also has a right and indeed a duty in this matter: as reasons for reforming itself gradually become apparent, not to let such a federative system of its subjects, as if they were viceroys (analogous to dynasties and satrapies), revive when it has once become extinct.

Conclusion

Finally, the reviewer has made the following remark about the ideas I presented under the heading of Public Right, with regard to which, as he says, space does not permit him to express himself:

> "So far as we know, no philosopher has yet admitted that most paradoxical of all paradoxical propositions: the proposition that the mere *Idea* of sovereignty should constrain me to obey as my lord whoever has set himself up as my lord, without my asking who has given him the right to command me. Is there to be no difference

between saying that one ought to recognize sovereignty and supreme authority and saying that one ought to hold a priori as his lord this or that person, whose existence is not even given a priori?"

Now, granting the *paradox* here, I at least hope that, once the matter is considered more closely, I cannot be convicted of *heterodoxy*. I hope, rather, that my astute and careful reviewer, who criticizes with moderation (and who, despite the offense he takes, "regards these metaphysical first principles of a doctrine of Right on the whole as a gain for the science") will not regret having taken them under his protection against the obstinate and superficial condemnation of others, at least as an attempt not unworthy of a second examination.

That one who finds himself in possession of supreme executive and legislative authority over a people must be obeyed; that obedience to him is so rightfully unconditional that even to *investigate* publicly the title by which he acquired his authority, and so to cast doubt upon it with a view to resisting him should this title be found deficient, is already punishable; that there is a categorical imperative, *Obey the authority who has power over you* (in whatever does not conflict with inner morality)—this is the offensive proposition called in question. But what seems to shock the reviewer's reason is not only this principle, which makes an actual deed (taking control) the condition and the basis for a right, but also that the *mere Idea* of sovereignty over a people constrains me, as belonging to that people, to obey without previously investigating the right that is claimed (*The Doctrine of Right* §49).

Every actual deed (fact) is an object in *appearance* (to the senses). On the other hand, what can be represented only by pure reason and must be counted among *Ideas*, to which no object given in experience can be adequate—and a perfectly *rightful constitution* among men is of this sort—is the thing in itself.

If then a people united by laws under an authority exists, it is given as an object of experience in conformity with the Idea of the unity of a people *as such* under a powerful supreme will, though it is indeed given only in appearance, that is, a rightful constitution in the general sense of the term exists. And even though this constitution may be afflicted with great defects and gross faults and be in need eventually of important improvements, it is still absolutely unpermitted and punishable to resist it. For if the people should hold that it is justified in opposing force to this constitution, however faulty, and to the supreme authority, it would think that it had the right to put force in place of the supreme legislation that prescribes all rights, which would result in a supreme will that destroys itself.

The *Idea* of a civil constitution as such, which is also an absolute command that practical reason, judging according to concepts of Right, gives to every people, is *sacred* and irresistible. And even if the organization of a state should be faulty by itself, no subordinate authority in it may actively resist its legislative supreme authority; the defects attached to it must instead be gradually removed by reforms the state itself carries out. For otherwise, if a subject acts on the contrary maxim (of proceeding by unsanctioned choice), a good constitution can come into being only by blind chance. The command "Obey the authority that has power over you" does not inquire how it came to have this power (in order perhaps to undermine it); for the authority which already exists, under which you live, is already in possession of legislative authority, and though you can indeed reason publicly about its legislation, you cannot set yourself up as an opposing legislator.

Unconditional submission of the people's will (which in itself is not united and is therefore without law) to a *sovereign* will (uniting all by means of *one* law) is a *fact* that can begin only by [someone's] seizing supreme power and so first establishing public Right. To permit any resistance to this absolute power (resistance that would limit that supreme power) would be self-contradictory; for then this supreme power (which may be resisted) would not be the lawful supreme power which first determines what is to be publicly right or not. This principle is already present a priori in the *Idea* of a civil constitution as such, that is, in a concept of practical reason; and although no example in experience is *adequate* to be put under this concept, still none must contradict it as a norm.

Credits

Page 175 "A Letter Concerning Toleration," by John Locke, reprinted by permission from *A Letter Concerning Toleration*, edited by James H. Tully, 1983, Hackett Publishing Company. All rights reserved.

Page 357 *The Social Contract* by Jean-Jacques Rousseau, Penguin Books, Ltd., 1968. Reprinted by permission of The Peters Fraser and Dunlop Group Limited on behalf of: The Estate of Maurice Cranston. Copyright © 1968 Maurice Cranston.

Page 412 *A Discourse on the Origin and the Foundations of the Inequality of Mankind* by Jean-Jacques Rousseau, translation by G. D. H. Cole, Everyman's Library, 1913. Reprinted by permission of Everyman's Library, David Campbell Publishers, Ltd.

Page 449 *Foundations of the Metaphysics of Morals* by Immanuel Kant, translation by Lewis White Beck, 1990. Copyright © 1990 Prentice-Hall, Inc. Reprinted by permission of Prentice-Hall, Inc., Upper Saddle River, N.J.

Page 484 Immanuel Kant, *The Metaphysics of Morals*, Mary J. Gregor, editor and translator, Cambridge University Press, 1991. Reprinted with the permission of Cambridge University Press.